Rev. Albert H. Cason

The Fisherman's Encyclopedia

EDITORIAL STAFF

DR. IRA N. GABRIELSON, *Editor*

Associate Editors

FRANCESCA LAMONTE

CHARLES K. FOX

CONTRIBUTORS

Allen, George W.—Alabama
Allen, James S.—Illinois
Atz, James—Predation
Barrett, Pete—Photography
Bartells, Ernest—West Virginia
Bates, Joseph D.—Spinning, Streamer Flies, Limnology
Bode, I. T.—Float Fishing
Bradnor, Enos—Strip Fishing
Brooks, Don—Rocky Mountain States, Rainbow Trout, Cutthroat, Brown Trout
Brooks, Joseph—Introduction, Largemouth Bass
Brown, W. L.—Trophies
Butler, George E.—Manitoba
Cahalane, Victor—National Parks
Caine, Lou S.—Fresh Water Game Fishes
Carhart, Arthur—Fishing Tackle, Fishing Techniques
Chamberlain Bev—Missouri
Circle, Homer E.—Trolling
Clark, Minor—Kentucky
Clarke, C. H. D.—Smallmouth Bass
Cook, A. B.—Michigan
Corson, Allen—Florida
Craig, Vernon—Montana
Davis, J. Charles, II—Pacific Fishing
Day, Albert M.—Fish and Wildlife Service
Dean, Dr. Roy B.—Mexico
Denmead, Talbott—Atlantic Fishing
Dufresne, Frank—Alaska, Sheefish
East, Ben—Panfish, Midwest Ice Fishing
Elliot, Bob—Maine
Finlay, Eddie—South Carolina
Ford, Corey—Foreword
Fredin, Reynold—North Carolina
Freeman, Barry O.—Mississippi
Galligan, James P.—Connecticut
Godfrey, Joe, Jr.—Lake States, Muskellunge, Lake Trout
Gregory, W. K.—Introduction
Gutermuth, C. R.—Photographs, Editorial
Gwathmey, John H.—Virginia
Hampton, Harry—South Carolina
Hewston, John—North Dakota
Heinhold, George—Shad
Jenkins, Robert M.—Reservoirs
Kalman, Paul—Gulf Fishing
Keen, James—Spearfishing and Skindiving
Knight, John Alden—Solunar Theory
Lambuth, Letcher—Rod Making
LaMonte, Francesca—Salt Water Game Fishes
Lerner, Michael—International Game Fish Association
Lincoln, Robert Page—Northern Pike, Carp, Walleye
Lodge, William T.—Illinois
Lucas, Jason—Sunfish
McLeod, Ken—Washington, Steelhead, Pacific Salmon
MacDonald, A. H.—Saskatchewan
MacNamara, Lester—New Jersey
Meehean, Lloyd—Fish Culture
Middleton, G. Barton—Georgia
Miller, R. B.—Alberta
Needham, Paul—California, Golden Trout
Newell, David M.—Tarpon
Orr, Russell—Pennsylvania
Pritchett, Jay H.—Utah
Rhode, Clarence—Grayling
Richard, L. A.—Quebec
Rodman, O. H. P.—Surf Casting, Bait Fishing, New England Ice Fishing, Channel Bass, Bluefish, Striped Bass
Roman, Erl—Marine Fishing Techniques
Ryder, R. A.—Ontario
Seaman, Wayne R.—Colorado
Shiner, Don—Fly Tying
Steel, Frank R.—Temperature Fishing
Stiles, Bruce F.—Iowa
Strohm, G. Robert—Ohio
Stroud, Richard H.—Fish Conservation
Swift, Lloyd—National Forests
Tapply, H. G.—New England, Landlocked Salmon, Brook Trout
Tomkins, William A.—Massachusetts
Trefethen, James B.—Fishing Craft, Sportsmanship, Bowfishing
Valyer, George—Kansas
Vaughn, Ernest A.—Maryland
Wall, Roy—Plains States, Catfish, Crappies, White Bass, Care and Preservation of Fish
Wallace, Earl—Lower Mississippi Valley
Wells, Robert A.—New York
Westman, James R.—Fish Predators
Wilder, Norman G.—Delaware
Wire, Frank S.—Oregon
Wright, Thomas J.—Rhode Island
Wulff, Lee—Newfoundland and Maritimes, Altantic Salmon

The *New* FISHERMAN'S ENCYCLOPEDIA

IRA N. GABRIELSON, EDITOR

FRANCESCA LAMONTE, ASSOCIATE EDITOR

THE STACKPOLE COMPANY

HARRISBURG, PENNSYLVANIA

FIRST EDITION
First Printing, 1950
Second Printing, 1954
Third Printing, 1958

SECOND EDITION
First (Revised) Printing, 1963
Second Printing, 1964

Library of Congress Catalog Card Number: 63-22468

Printed and bound in the United States of America
By THE TELEGRAPH PRESS, *Established 1831*
Harrisburg, Pennsylvania

ACKNOWLEDGMENTS

The preparation of this volume would have been an impossible task without the wholehearted cooperation of a long list of anglers and writers who have contributed their knowledge and work to it.

In addition to those specifically listed, every state fish and game organization has furnished information or photographs, or both, either directly to the editors or to the writers assigned to develop certain subject matter. The conservation organizations of the Canadian Provinces did likewise. The U. S. Fish and Wildlife Service, the National Park Service, the U. S. Forest Service, the American Museum of Natural History, the International Game Fish Association, the Smithsonian Institution, the New York Zoological Society, and a host of organizations other than those mentioned have been helpful in many ways.

The fishing tackle industry and the boat building groups have likewise been generous with their help and information.

Every effort has been made to give suitable acknowledgment for drawings, diagrams, and photographs, and it is hoped that no mistakes or omissions have occurred.

The individuals who have contributed material, together with the subjects covered by them are listed in the Editorial Staff which appears opposite the title page.

The color plates of flies, plugs, spinners, spoons and odd lures are from original Kodachromes by Wagstaff and from art and photos by William F. Blades.

The fly patterns shown are based on original designs of Orvis and other pioneer fly dressers, as tied by Lucille Oliver.

The color plates of the panfishes, the Bass, the Walleye Pike, the Pickerel, and the Muskellunge are from original paintings by Fred Everett.

The color plates of the Salmon and Trout are from original paintings by Campbell Grant.

James B. Trefethen, Jr., in addition to subject matter credited to him, has been most helpful in various editorial tasks.

A large share of the burden of checking, editing, and proofreading has, however, been the responsibility of Peggy Wagner, to whom special credit and thanks are due.

The mechanical production of the book was under the direction of George F. Miley of The Telegraph Press, Harrisburg, Pennsylvania.

The editors wish to express their profound gratitude to these individuals listed above and to all others who have helped in this undertaking. They hope that the resulting book will be useful enough to North American anglers to justify such effort.

IRA N. GABRIELSON, *Editor*
FRANCESCA LAMONTE, *Associate Editor*

TABLE OF CONTENTS

SECTION II—FISHING EQUIPMENT AND FISHING METHODS

SECTION III—CRAFT FOR FISHING

SECTION IV—FISH CONSERVATION

SECTION V—WHERE TO FISH

SUPPLEMENT

AN EXPERT SPEAKS

In this age of ever-increasing appreciation of the importance of water in our daily lives, especially with regard to its recreational value, there is a corresponding increase in interest in the creatures that swell in the water. Following right along with this, in logical sequence, comes a tremendous increase in interest in fishing. And every fisherman, whether he be a veteran of many years astream, or a tyro trying out his first rod, wants to know more about his favorite sport: what fish he will find, where, when, and how to catch them.

The new, revised Fisherman's Encyclopedia has the answers. This very complete compilation of practically everything to do with fishing is crammed with authentic information. It is a fine volume, a tome, in fact, covering all phases of angling from A: the beginnings of fish and fishing, to Z: the latest in tackle and technique and boating innovations. It provides all the pertinent data about many species of fish, both fresh and salt water dwellers, including their habitat, their habits, their food, the best time to go for them, the best methods; and it encompasses the complete range of interest to anglers, from tiny bream to giant oceanic swimmers which inhabit waters far out of sight of land.

If the beginner would take this encyclopedia, pick out a single fish he would like to catch, go through the information about it, step by step, the where, when, and how, he would be able to go astream with this new-found information, and catch fish.

Aside from the technical data regarding the species of fish, the angler will find many more items of interest and education, including up-to-date world record charts on many species of both lake and stream as well as ocean.

From the pages of the Fisherman's Encyclopedia you may discover how to fashion a fly, construct a rod, tie the many intricate knots that are so important to the angler. You may pick up a hundred other tips that give the reader a head start towards better fishing and greater enjoyment of the wonderful sport of fishing. Nothing is left out of this great book, in a text that covers many sidelines to fishing as well as the sport itself. You can find the kind of fishing craft you should use, and the motors. There is detailed information about camping, a chapter full of suggestions and points for more safety and greater comfort out of doors, informative matter about insect repellents, pack trips, what to do when lost in the woods—name it, look for it, and almost certainly you will find it here, in a truly great encyclopedia welded together from the contributions of a fine group of men each one of whom is an expert in his field.

The color plates add the finishing touch. These are excellent illustrations of flies and lures, as well as many species of fish, adding greatly to the beauty of a volume which should be in every fisherman's library.

JOE BROOKS

PREFACE

Man, having always been an omnivorous animal, undoubtedly has caught and eaten fish along with other aquatic foods from earliest times. It is entirely probable that when the human ancestors first commenced to walk upright, they fished much as do the most primitive tribes known today by catching stranded fish in shallow pools with the hands, knocking shellfish from the rocks of the ocean beach with stones or prying them loose by means of sticks, even perhaps taking advantage of of fish already dead and washed up on the shores. Numerous tribes still fish with primitive traps made of sticks which are placed upright across the stream to form a blockade against which fish are driven by men wading up or down the stream. Long before historical records began, men had learned to make and use more efficient devices for catching fish. Some obscure early genius had developed a fish spear made of a stick, perhaps only sharpened at first, but later tipped with a stone or bone point; primitive lines were made of vegetable fiber and gorges which are the earliest known ancestors of the modern hook of wood or bone were in use. Some remote Eskimo tribes have fished with these gorges until recent times and perhaps some still do.

The point at which man first began to fish for fun as well as for food is likewise unknown. Earliest historical paintings and records from Assyria, Egypt, China, and the cave dwellers of Europe, all depict fishing scenes. In the earliest of these, the spear, the net, the rod and the line, were known and pictured. Obviously the rod and line were used as a device for sport, as well as for getting food.

Since these written records cover but a fraction of the period that man has lived on the earth, there has undoubtedly been a close, and for man a fortunate, association since his earliest days.

Zoologists are generally agreed that fish or fishlike creatures were the first to develop a backbone and are therefore the presumed forerunners of all vertebrate life. Fossil remains of fish have been found back into the Cambrian period of the Paleozoic era—that is almost as far back into the Paleontological record as any remains of living forms have been discovered.

While modern fishes have developed into forms far different from these earlier forms, primitive fish much like them still exist along side their more modern relatives.

Fish were an abundant and ancient group when ancestral forms of man first appeared. They are still an abundant and successful group that has furnished food and later both food and recreation to man throughout his entire existence.

Man has always used fish as a source of food and still utilizes a great many species for food. Fish provides the main source of protein foods in many lands and many more species are thus utilized than are considered sport fish.

Man undoubtedly had crude fishing implements many thousands of years before the historical record began. Since that time, changes in implements have been slow. For example, it required a period from about 2000 years B. C. to the 16th or 17th century to make the change from the Egyptian method of fastening the line to the end of the rod to a running line. This revolutionary new running line passed through a series of guides on the pole and was drawn in by hand and later stored on the first crude reels.

The first reel, according to Dr. Turrell was mentioned by T. Barker in a book entitled *The Art of Angling* printed in 1651. Dr. Turrell pays Mr. Barker the doubtful compliment of saying that in addition to writing about the first reel, he was also the father of poachers. Up to that time the running line was not used for salmon and big pike, and before the reel was developed, the anglers only hope of handling an exceptionally large fish was to throw rod, line, and all into the water, and hope to recover it later when the fish had worn himself out fighting the rod.

While progress was slow, development of modern tackle, which began in comparatively recent time, has greatly expanded the number of devices used successfully in fishing, as well as the number of people enjoying the sport.

Bone, stone, horns, and even wood were used successfully in forming the first crude hooks which were developed from the gorge, a straight piece of bone or stick of wood with a line about the middle. Naturally, artificial baits, such as spinners and flies, were among the last to appear, but there are now thousands of pattern variations of the few basic forms of artificial lures.

Many fishermen enthusiastically debate the merits of the various types of angling. Advocates of each form regard it as pleasurable above all others. In truth, the frame of mind of the angler and ability to enjoy the time out-of-doors is perhaps more important than the type of fishing. A growing number of people get their greatest enjoyment in using very light tackle in angling, but the old cane pole, bobber, and worm still have devotees by the hundreds of thousands. To these the bullhead and catfish furnish as much recreation and relaxation as the finest fly fishing for trout gives to the confirmed flyrod enthusiast.

This is the important element of fishing. Fishing has grown into the greatest single avocation pursued by those interested in the out-of-doors. There is no way to estimate the total number, but annual state fishing licenses in the United States are close to 20 million and growing each year. When those who can and do fish on their own lands without licenses, women who are still exempt from licensing provisions in many states, children under the minimum license age, and the other categories of persons who for one reason or another are not required to buy a license are included, it all adds up to a huge army fishing for recreation and relaxation. Angling, in one form or another, occupies the attention of more people than any other participation sport or recreation. Hunting undoubtedly comes next, and the total number of people who enjoy these forms of outdoor recreation exceed that of all other participation sports combined.

This, then, is the justification for this volume. It is an attempt to gather within the covers of one book useful and pertinent information for this great army of people who are interested in fishing in North American waters.

In preparing this volume, the "Standard Check List of Common Names for Principal American Sport Fishes," compiled by the Outdoor Writers Association of America, has been generally followed. In a few cases, particularly for Pacific Coast species and those found in Mexican waters, names are not included in this list. In such cases Miss Francesca LaMonte's *North American Game Fishes* or Special Publication No. 1 of American Fisheries Society entitled "A List of Common and Scientific Names of the Better Known Fishes of the United States and Canada" have been used. The first-named publication has been widely circulated among outdoor writers and anglers in a praiseworthy effort to reduce the confusion in common names for common game fish. It seems fitting that the *Fisherman's Encyclopedia* designed to aid anglers follow the same pattern. Some local names remain partly because of an effort to tie these names to those selected for general use. Some lapses have inevitably occurred despite every care to follow an established pattern.

IRA N. GABRIELSON, *Editor*

FOREWORD

Here it all is: everything that every fisherman ever needs to know about fishing. Here are the game-fish themselves, equipment and methods of angling, fishery management, places to go—the what, the where, the when and the how. Everything, in fact, but the why.

Why do people fish? The FISHERMAN'S ENCYCLOPEDIA doesn't say. Nary a word is to be found, amid all these voluminous contents, to explain what perverse impulse, what freakish strain, what incomprehensible urge causes an otherwise normal and sane citizen to don a pair of uncomfortable rubber waders, lace a dozen pounds of hobnailed boots onto his aching feet, truss himself helplessly in canvas-vest and landing net and creel, and hike upstream ten miles in a pouring rain, fighting midges and black flies, scratching his face on brambles, wincing whenever the elastic strap of his landing net catches on a twig and then lets go like a slingshot, smacking him smartly between the shoulder blades. Why does he undergo all this, in order to stand patiently all day in icy water up to his hubs, casting his rod back and forth till his arm aches, wet and sore and blistered and mosquito-bitten and hungry. And, in all probability, fishless.

Why, indeed? Is it because he wants the fish to eat? I doubt it. For a few cents, and one-tenth the amount of time and trouble, he could walk down to the market and buy a pound of halibut. Moreover, I've seen too many fishermen work an hour to bring a trout to the net, reach down and grab him firmly behind the gills, release the fly—and then turn him loose again, to disappear under a rock with a final grateful wag of his square tail.

Is it for the sport of casting, then? Maybe, a little. There is no thrill like that of presenting a fly accurately, watching it ride well-cocked down a riffle, and suddenly seeing the water explode around it in a shower of iridescent drops, feeling the heavy weight on the line, hearing the skirl of the reel as the captive trout races for white water. I still remember the expression of profound pleasure on the face of Ted Townsend, who initiated me into the mysteries of dry-fly fishing several decades ago on the Beaverkill. Ted had paused on the bank and tied an exquisite copy of the fly that was on the water, a Female Beaverkill, and had cast it across the pool, setting it down as lightly as thistledown on the water. As we watched, a live male fly, with love-light shining in his eye, spotted the artificial female and settled down amorously beside her. A trout rose just then, but it didn't choose the real fly. It grabbed Ted's. You can't ask a nicer tribute to an angler than that.

But I think there is another and deeper reason why people fish. It is an age-old desire that moves all of us—whether the dry-fly purist, the spinner-fisherman, the salt water angler, or the kid with the willow pole and catawba worm. It is something that cannot be defined, even in an encyclopedia; but the urge is there whenever an angler wades into a new pool, or looks down from a bridge at the water below, or starts in his canoe across a silent lake at dusk. It has something to do with peace, and contentment, and soul-satisfaction, and the realization that for a moment, at least, nothing else in the world really matters.

So, if you are an angler, that is why you fish; and, if you fish, this book will tell you how and where and when, as described by the leading experts in their fields, gathered together and edited with loving care by one of the country's outstanding authorities on wildlife and the out-doors, Dr. Ira N. Gabrielson. Read it, study it in camp at night, take it along with you in your canoe.

But don't drop it overboard, I warn you. If a fish should happen to swallow this Encyclopedia, and digest all the information contained in its pages, there'd be no more taking him on a hook and line. He'd know as much as the fisherman.

—COREY FORD.

INTRODUCTION

Fish Biology and Evolution*

DEFINITION OF FISH

A lone fisherman on the end of a city dock was asked—

1) To define a fish: "A fish has scales and fins with sharp spines in them."

2) Why does a fish die so soon after it is caught? "Its gills dry up and it can't breathe."

3) Why can't it breathe? Isn't there lots of air? "Yes, but it can only breathe in the water."

4) Is an eel a fish? "Yes." Has it got gills? "Yes." Scales? "No."

5) Is a shark a fish? "No. What good is it?" Has it gills? "Maybe." Or scales? "No only little sharp points on the tough skin."

6) Is a whale a fish? "Yes." Has it scales? "No."

7) What is an animal? "Cats, dogs, cows." Is a fish an animal? "No. A fish is a fish." Is a bird an animal? "No. A bird is a bird—with wings."

8) Does a fish have a backbone? "Yes." How about an eel? "An eel is like a snake or a worm; no backbone."

9) Can you name any others with a backbone? "Cows, sheep, dogs."

10) What is a vertebrae? "Part of the backbone."

11) Does a fish suffer much when it is caught? "Not much. Their nerves ain't sensitive like ours."

Fishermen with a wider experience will note that the "lone fisherman's" answers are a mixture of truth and error. For example, not all fish have sharp spines on the fins. Many, such as Salmon, Trout, Bonefish and Pickerel have soft-rayed fins. It is, alas, much easier to *describe* a "typical" fish, such as a Striped Bass, than it is to give a brief comprehensive *definition* that will include all of the thousands of known species of fish and at the same time exclude all other known kinds of animals. Scales, for example, while characteristic of most fish are very small in Eels and entirely wanting in most Eels and Morays, as well as in Seahorses, Trunkfish, and others.

A relatively simple definition of fish is as follows: *A cold blooded, aquatic vertebrate animal with internal gills, which are supported in a segmental skeletal frame.*

This definition covers all known living and fossil fishes, which are comprised in the following super classes and classes, or main divisions:

1) Agnatha ("jawless") including fossil Ostracoderms and the living Lampreys and Hagfishes.

2) Chondrichthyes (cartilage fishes): Sharks, Rays, Chimaeroids.

3) Placodermi (plate skins): armored Devonian fishes with peculiar jaws.

4) Osteichthyes (bony fishes): fossil and recent Ganoids and Heleosts.

5) Choanichthyes (fishes with internal nares); fossil and recent Lobefins (Crossopterygii) and Lungfishes (Dipnoi).

THE PYRAMID OF OCEAN LIFE

The pyramid of fish life is based upon the billions of marine algae and other plants, including the microscopic diatoms. These contain chlorophyll or similar pigment, which under the influence of sunlight builds up carbohydrates and other food material. These minute plants with their food products are taken in by myriads of copepods or shrimplike crustaceans. The great schools of Herrings consume both diatoms and copepods, and are, in turn, pursued and devoured by many swift oceanic fishes, including Bonitos, Marlins and Swordfishes, as well as by flocks of sea birds. Even the greatest of the whalebone whales fill their vast mouth-cavities with the copepods and Herrings.

JAWS AND TEETH OF THE BONY FISHES

Most fish have sharp teeth and jaws for killing and cutting up smaller fish. The highly protrusile lip-jaws of some spiny finned fishes will be noted below.

In the Parrot-Wrasses, the front teeth are fused into a solid, parrotlike beak. These fish also have a crushing and grinding mechanism in the throat, for cracking and grinding the shells of crustaceans and mollusks. The Porgy and the Sheepshead have short, very strong jaws with cutting incisors and pebblelike molar teeth. Similar adaptations are found in the Drum *(Pogonias)*. The Marlins and Swordfish have the rostrum or front part of the skull prolonged into a great spear, cylindrical in the Marlins, flattened in the Swordfish, with which they can pierce or strike other fish. Swordfish, on account of their great weight and speed, develop a great momentum and piercing force, and there are authentic cases of Swordfish piercing the copper-sheathed sides of wooden ships. In the Spoonbill, a highly specialized Sturgeon, the huge rostrum forms a flat bill not unlike that of an ibis. It is probably used for probing in the mud for small creatures and is covered with sensory nerves. In the Seahorses and Tubefishes the very minute jaws are at the end of a long tubular structure, and only very small food bits can be taken into the tube.

Some fish with toothless jaws, including the Carp, have toothlike structures in the muscular pharynx

* By William K. Gregory, Curator Emeritus of Fishes and Comparative Anatomy, American Museum of National History. Da Costa Professor Emeritus of Vertebrate Paleontology, Columbia University.

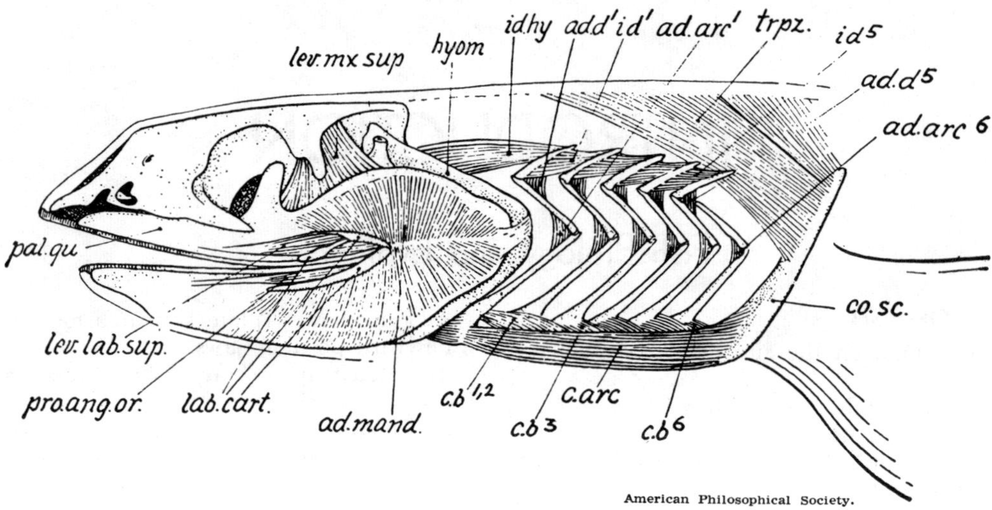

A skull and branchial arches of frilled shark.

or throat. In most fish the inner surfaces of the gill-arches are studded with sharp, horny spines usually directed backward and serving to push the prey down the throat. In the Whale Shark these structures are organized into an enormous, complex sieve which permits the water to escape but retains the small creatures which form most of the food.

JAWS AND TEETH OF THE CARTILAGE FISHES

The cartilage fishes have also a very wide variety of jaws and dental apparatus. The teeth of Sharks correspond with the minute prickly denticles on the surface of their skins and are likewise formed in pockets on the embryonic skin. In typical Sharks the teeth have sharp points and/or jagged cutting edges, but in the Port Jackson or Heterodont Sharks the teeth are flattened down and arranged in transverse whorls around the margins of the upper and lower jaws. Such pavement teeth are used in breaking and crushing the shells of crabs and molluscs, and in some of the larger Eagle Rays they give rise to a powerful dental mill. In the giant Manta or Devil Ray, however, the teeth are reduced to a narrow strip of minute denticles running around the inner border of the jaws, and the huge mouth is used for engulfing small creatures.

The typical fish has the same *general* arrangement of the parts of the digestive tract as in higher animals, including man. That is, its digestive tract includes the mouth cavity, jaws, pharynx (containing the gills and gill arches), esophagus or gullet, stomach, intestine. The latter, however, in bony fishes usually has many fingerlike outgrowths or pyloric caeca. In Sharks and Rays there is a large "spiral" valve in the intestine which greatly increases the surface for absorption of the nutritive contents.

THE "JAWLESS" LAMPREYS AND HAGFISHES

The Lampreys and Hagfishes, although eel-like in external appearance, are not at all closely related to the Eels, but seem to be the sole existing representatives of a long extinct class, the Ostracoderms (see below). These voracious fish prey upon other fishes by fastening themselves to them with their suctorial lips and by rasping the flesh of their victims with their flexible filelike "tongue." Their dental apparatus consists of two main parts: 1) the circular sucker formed by the large lips which are studded with concentric rows of thornlike, horny teeth. Within these lips are three curved, smooth cartilaginous plates, one within the other, the first two sliding over each other and the third attached to the fore part of the skull which is braced to support them. 2) The long, narrow tongue bears a long strip of small, sharp horny teeth and it can be protruded and pressed against the victim and held there by the suction of the lips. Unless the rasplike "tongue" is really a much changed lower jaw, the Lampreys and Hagfishes have no internal jaws, and partly on this account they have been classified as a separate grand division, subphylum or superclass, Agnatha (jawless), whereas the subphylum or superclass Gnathostomata (jaw mouths) includes all the "normal" fishes, as well as the classes of Amphibia (frogs, toads, salamanders, etc.), Reptilia, Aves (birds), and Mammalia (mammals).

SOUNDS MADE BY FISHES

Many kinds of fish make sounds under water, some by grinding their molar teeth, as in the Drum, others by rubbing the strong front ray of the pectoral fin against part of the shoulder girdle. Malay fishermen, by submerging their heads, can hear these sounds and can distinguish the direction and type of fish that is making them.

FISH AS COLD-BLOODED ANIMALS

Fish are "cold-blooded" animals. The body temperatures of fishes vary with that of the environment. Some, including the Icefish *(Salanx)* of the far north, can even be frozen in ice and yet remain capable of resuscitation whenever the temperature of the water rises. At the other extreme, a few fishes live in the hot springs of volcanic regions. But in between are the multitudes which live in tropical and temperate waters while some thrive in arctic and antarctic waters. Even in the great ocean depths, where the temperature is barely above the freezing point, many kinds of deep sea fishes pass their lives in this chilly environment. Thus in fishes from cold climates or considerable depths, the temperature of the body is barely above that of the medium. This has the advantage that very little food has to be used in maintaining a high body temperature, while a relatively greater amount may be spent in searching for more food. However, in the Bonitos and Albacores which are swift and untiring in their pursuit of the Herring schools, the breast is partly insulated by a network of fine blood vessels beneath the corselet which comprises the scales of the pectoral region. This no doubt facilitates the greater oxidation in the gills and conserves part of the heat which is always generated by muscular action.

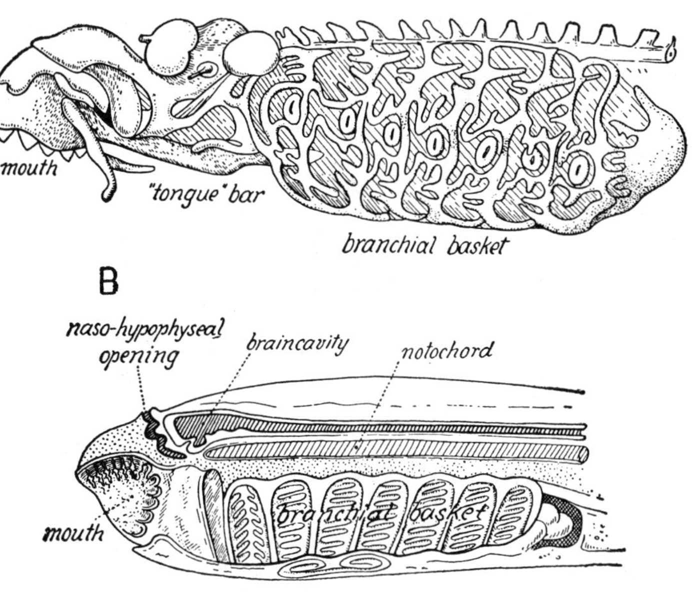

American Philosophical Society.

Cartilaginous skull of lamprey adult (A) and larval (B) stages.

REPRODUCTION

The methods of reproduction also vary widely among fishes. Among the cartilage fishes (Sharks and Rays), the rear parts of the ventral fins of the males are rolled up into large grooved or tubular rods called claspers. In breeding, these are inserted into the cloaca of the female and serve for the passage of the sperms. Thus the ova in Sharks are fertilized *internally,* whereas in *typical* bony fishes they are fertilized *externally,* that is by the union of the eggs and sperm outside the body of the mother, namely in the water. A few highly specialized bony fishes have however become "live bearers," especially the Guppies and Swordtails (*Xiphophorus*) in which the males have developed copulatory tubes and fertilization is *internal.*

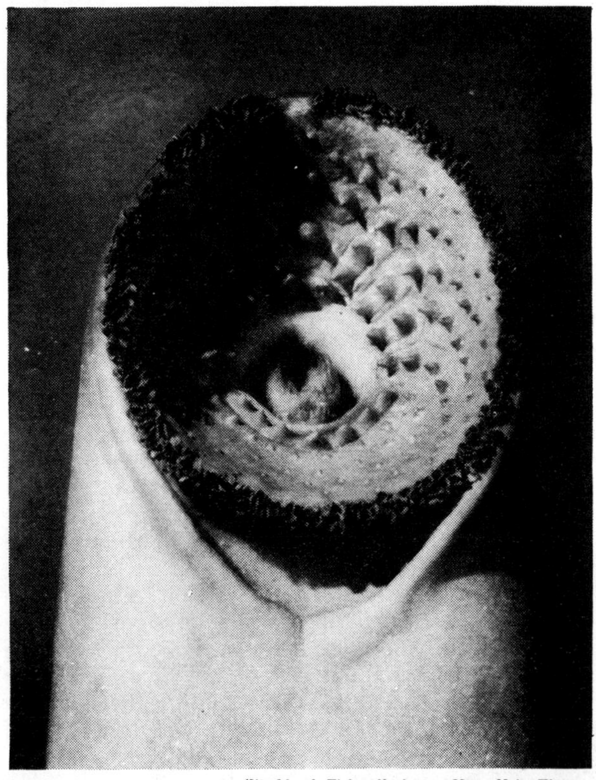

'World of Fishes," Amer. Mus. Nat. History.

The lamprey's suctorial, rasping mouth.

In the cartilage fishes the yolk or nutritive material for the young (which is secreted in the uterus) is usually very voluminous and the egg when extruded is already covered with a tough fibrous horny shell. The shell is usually four cornered with spiral threads at each corner. The embryo slowly develops in the shell into a little Shark or Ray. In some Sharks and Rays, however, the egg shell is very thin and the young are long retained in the uterus, where they may even get additional nourishment by diffusion from the walls of the uterus through their yolk sac.

In the typical bony fishes the fertilized eggs floating in the water develop rapidly into minute actively swimming larvae. These feed on very small food until they grow large enough to change into young fishes that can seize, take in and digest the same kind of food that sustains their parents. Although Sharks and Rays richly endow their young with nutritive material they care little for the young after the latter are hatched or born. A few of the bony fishes, on the contrary, make nests (*e.g.* Bowfins, Sticklebacks) in which the female lays the eggs. The Gouramis make "bubble nests," the female Seahorse (*Hippocampus*) deposits her eggs in a broad pouch on the ventral surface of the male where they develop into miniature Seahorses. Certain male Catfishes and Cichlids hold the eggs in their mouths until the young are large enough to be hatched. On the whole, however, the bony fishes have, as it were, chosen to produce very large numbers of small yoked eggs, running up to over 400,000 (as in the case of the Codfish). Most of them are lost or devoured, but a very few live to go through the larval and young stages and grow up to reproduce their kind.

FISH MIGRATION

Some fishes make long migrations from the place where they are hatched to the distant breeding grounds. The Common Eels, for example, spawn in the sea south of Bermuda. The larvae and young to the westward part of the area gradually drift toward America; those in the eastern part drift toward Europe. The former enter the rivers of North America and work up the streams into the interior. The latter reach the shores of Europe and enter the rivers there.

As the spawning instinct comes on, the adults descend the rivers and eventually find their way to the breeding grounds but not without enormous losses from marauding fishes, storms, etc. Possibly they are guided in part by some sort of preference, *e.g.* on the way up for lower temperatures and less and less salt; on the way down for the opposite conditions.

HOW FISH SWIM

The normal fish body may be roughly described as consisting of two cones, flattened transversely and placed base to base, the head forming the smaller front cone and the body forming the rear one. The greatest cross section is a little behind the head, through the shoulder-girdle and bases of the pectoral fins. In high backed, deep bellied forms such as the Angelfish, this section is a high narrow oval; in wide low-headed forms it is more transversely oval as in certain Cottids (*Myoxocephalus*). Nearer the tail the cross-section narrows and the ovals become higher, ending in the vertically placed tail fan.

The height and width of the cross-section behind the head are determined by the dimensions of the muscles of the back, back and flanks and in the lower part by 1) the amount of food in the digestive tract, 2) the quantity of eggs in the oviduct, and especially by 3) the position of the ventral fins. If the latter are attached beneath the pectoral fins, the belly is usually deep; if they are far behind the pectoral fins, the depth is usually slight, as in many long-bodied fishes. Sometimes the dorsal fin becomes very high and its right and left muscles extend on to the top of the skull. Meanwhile the skull-roof has grown upward to form a supraoccipital crest which braces the skull-roof and affords anchorage for the dorsal fin muscles.

In side view, the two cones with a common base are adjusted to each other and enclosed in a flowing streamlined skin, the "entering angle" being greater than the "run" or slope of the back.

The head, including the jaws, cranium, gill arches and gill covers, being swung a little to one side by the muscles of the same side, then serve as the fulcrum for starting a wave along the side of the body toward which it is turning; at the next instant the head is pulled toward the opposite side to start a wave along that side of the body. The body itself is not limp or inert but possesses more or less elasticity, spring or recoil, due in part to the resistance of the dice-boxlike vertebral centra, to the relative incompressibility of the interarticular discs, and to the tensions and compressions that are set up in the ligaments that tie one centrum to the next. In Marlins the strength of the recoil is greatly increased by the overlapping of long vertical bladelike processes called zygapophyses which pass on either side from the base of the neural arch of one vertebra to the next.

It is often thought that the fanlike caudal fin of typical bony fishes is the chief organ of propulsion, but the fact is that the principal thrusts come from the sides of the body. These are pressed against the water by the muscle segments which bend the body now on one side and then on the other, much as a skater thrusts alternately with the right or left leg. The caudal fin may deliver part of these thrusts which pass like waves down the body to the tail, but its chief service is that of a flexible rudder.

In the side view the myomeres or muscle-segments reveal a zigzag arrangement, each one being separated from the next by connective tissue sheets or septa. In cross-section the myomeres on either side of the mid plane appear as concentric series of circles, for they are like conical foolscaps, one within the other, each extending forward several vertebrae beyond the one to which each myomere is mainly tied. The myomeres of opposite sides do not act simultaneously, like the rowers in an eight-oared shell, but in succession and alternately. In general the muscles of locomotion and those of the jaws and gill-bars are arranged in opposing pairs, like flexors and extensors of the human arm. Thus one muscle can act as a brake on its opponent, permitting fast action or slowing down and preventing jerkiness, or dislocation at the joints.

The rib-like processes springing from the sides of the vertebrae are formed in the spaces between the septa surrounding the myomeres and serve both to protect the abdominal cavity and to transmit the tensions from the myomeres to the vertebral centra. The slender neural arches perform a similar service for the spinal nerve cord and its lateral branches, the spinal nerves.

The core of the vertebral column is the notochord, which is formed in the embryo as a cylinder of connective tissue filled with vacuolated cells. As growth proceeds, the vertebral centra form around in notochord which contracts in the middle of each centrum to a thread and expands between the centra to form the intervertebral discs or buffers.

PRINCIPAL BODY-FORMS

Among the more ancient and primitive types of bony fishes the body was fairly elongate or spindle-shaped, not eel-shaped, and already provided with single median dorsal and anal fins, a pair of long based rather short pectoral fins with their muscles mostly inside the body, and a pair of long-based rather low pelvic fins. The fins were supported by rows of little scales united into dermal rays. The muscles that moved the median fins including the tail fins were numerous and small. There were little or no webs on the fins which were not very flexible and served as rudders rather than as prime movers. The caudal fin was of the heterocercal or low sharklike type, in contrast with the strongly muscled fantail fin of modernized bony fishes which can be bent, twisted or cupped in various ways. From this primitive type arose the following, along different branches.

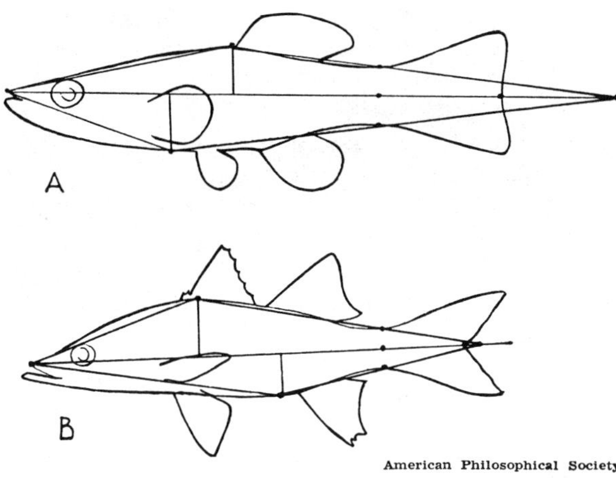

American Philosophical Society.

Body forms of fishes.

1) Many short, highbacked, quick-dodging forms, with wide fantails and long-based vigorously waved dorsal and anal fins, on the steep rear slopes of the back and anal regions.

2) Heavy, long-bodied, sinous eel-like forms, with all fins reduced.

3) Short and deep bodied forms, with the abdominal fins moved forward and tied by the rod-like pelvic bones to the lower arch of the pectoral girdle. These are the spiny finned bony fishes which in turn gave rise to very many kinds of body-form from short and high to very long and eel-like.

4) Short bodied, plump or boxlike forms covered with prickles (Porcupine Fish) or enclosed in a mosaic of bony plaques (Trunkfish). In these the greater part of the backbone is immobilized and the pectoral fins have become the principal motors, the caudal section serving chiefly as a rudder, but partly for sculling.

5) The Ocean Sunfish *(Mola)* type, in which the body became extremely short, the backbone nearly immobilized and the dorsal and anal fins, becoming enormously high, took over the chief locomotor function. Extensions of these fins meeting behind the stump of the original caudal fin fused to form a large new or false caudal fin.

6) Some originally compressed deep-bodied forms of the Scorpaenoids of Bonefish family, became secondarily elongate while their heads were widened and enclosed in a bony helmet or shield. Here belong the bottom-feeding members of this family, including the Gurnards and some of the Cottids and related families.

There are many other strange body-forms, such as those of the Tubefish and Seahorses already noted, but the more central types from which they seem to have been derived are in numerous cases still existing.

Among the cartilage fishes, the relatively large pectoral and pelvic fins suggest that the most primitive forms lived in shallow water and rested on the bottom. Some of them, however, developing a more spindle shaped body and a large crescentic tail, took to ranging on the open seas, as in the Tiger Sharks, Mackerel Sharks, and others.

The tail in primitive Sharks is *heterocercal,* that is, long and rather slender, turned up more or less, the end with a long web on the lower border, and a very small fin on the tip. The tail-fin like all the other fins is supported by blocks, rods, or rays of cartilage, not by scales fused into dermal rays.

At the other extreme, the ancestral Skates specialized in searching for shellfish on the bottom. In them the pectoral fins became enormously large and finally acted somewhat like wings, thrusting against the water both on the upstroke and down-stroke and culminating in *Pteroplatea,* the "Butterfly" Ray, with very wide pectorals, reduced pelvics and a vestigial tail.

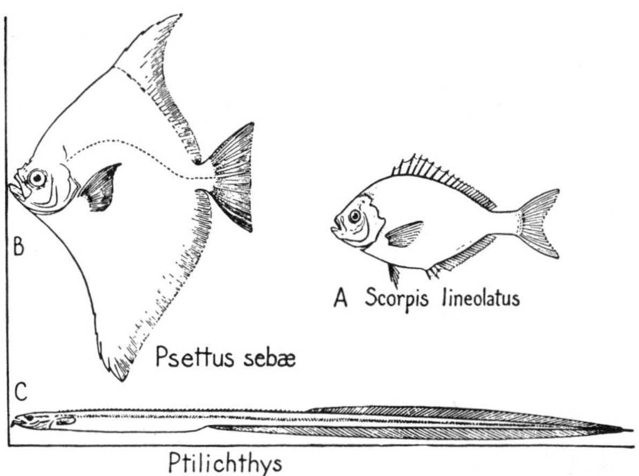

American Philosophical Society.

Body forms of fishes.

THE SKELETAL FRAME

There is a close correlation between the outer body-form and its skeletal frame. As noted above, in fish with a small entering angle the skull is low, and usually the back and its neural spines are also low. In the Opah or Moonfish the back is only

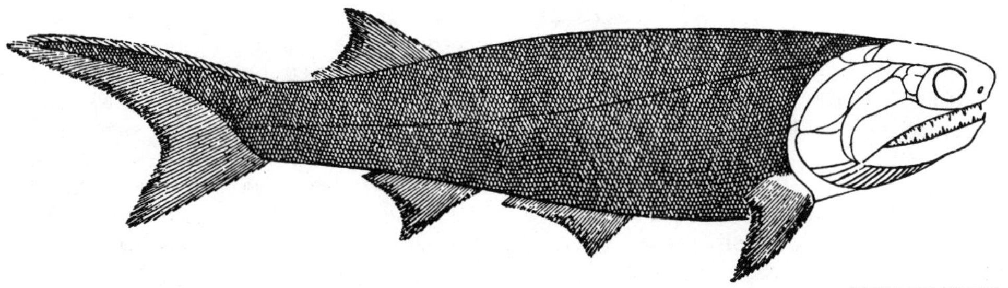

Parker and Haswell.

Primitive Devonian Ganoid.

Mounted by Mr. Theo. Schneider, Amer. Mus. Nat. History.

Skeleton of striped bass.

moderately high, but the belly is extremely deep, and with it the lower part of the shoulder girdle is enlarged and produced far downward. Again both the dorsal and the anal fin of the short-bodied *Psettus sebae* are exceedingly high, so that the upward slope of the forehead and the downward slope of the throat and belly are very steep, and the skeletal frame closely follows these contours.

The skull, as a whole, forms the prow or entering wedge, but experience shows that this wedge is usually rounded in front and that the greatest transverse diameter of the body is across the shoulder girdle just behind the skull and the skull and the gill covers. A long bill, flattened from above downward, as in the Swordfish, must have a considerable effect as a bow rudder, and in swift swimming it must tend to keep the fish from pitching up and down. The upwardly sloping skullroof consists mainly of the right and left frontal bones fused in the midline and usually strengthened by oblique ridges. The frontal rests in front on two stout tranversely wedgelike bones, the parethmoids; these in turn rest on the long keel bone (parasphenoid) in the midline of the skull floor. The lower front part of the wedge is formed by the median vomer and behind this by the ethmoid bone containing the smelling organs and braced against the frontals and parethmoids. The latter also form the front part of the great orbital depression or socket for the eyes. The nasals are small surface bones lying above the nostrils. They rest in the rear on the frontals and in front on the ethmoid. They are usually tunneled by the forepart of the lateral line canals which are continued backward along the roof of the skull, over the shoulder girdle and along the sides of the body. The lateral-line organs which they enclose are said to respond to vibrations of low frequency, such as those reflected from other objects. Thus, they may be useful either in pursuit or avoidance.

The core of the upper and lower jaws of bony fishes, and the entire upper and lower jaws of Sharks, have essential structural features in common with the hyoid and branchial arches behind them, and are believed to be parts of two much modified gill arches which have lost their gills. In the Acanthodians (ancient fossil fishes of the late Paleozoic era, estimated age 250 million years) there were rows of little gill-covers attached to the rear of the upper and lower jaw-bones as well as others on the upper and lower segments of the hyoid arch, and on all the branchial arches. This arrangement further supports the view that the inner jaws and hyoid arches were once part of the "oralo-branchial" (mouthgill) apparatus.

The front part of the upper jaw in such typical spiny-finned fishes as the Perch and Bass consists of two bones, the "premaxilla" and "maxilla," on each side. These bones are sometimes called "lip-jaws" but they are not fleshy lips. When such a fish gets near its prey the sudden lowering of the jaws and protrusion of the lip-jaws creates a partial vacuum in the water and the prey is sucked into the mouth-cavity where further movements of the hyoid and branchial arches tend to pull and push it down the throat. This sucking adaptation is much less developed in the less progressive, more old fashioned types of surviving fishes, such as the Garpike and the Bowfin *(Amia),* where the upper lip-jaws are firmly attached to the cheeks.

The front upper "lip-jaws" (premaxillae) rest on top of the vomer and against the ethmoid. They are movably tied by ligaments to the neighboring bones. The rear upper lip-jaws (maxillae) were originally fastened to the surface bones of the cheek below the eye, but in the typical spiny-finned fishes they have become separated from the cheek bones at their rear ends and remodelled into levers for protruding the front upper lip-jaws (premaxillae). Their rear ends are tied by ligament both to the rear part of the premaxillae and to the upper part of the lower jaw. Their front or upper end bears two knobs: the front inner one on each side slides and rolls upon the upper surface of the vomer, and has an upper roller bearing surface for the premaxilla. The rear outer knob rolls chiefly on the ethmoid and is held in place by an overlapping fork coming up from the palatine. When the lower jay is lowered in front, the rear ends of the maxillae are depressed and the premaxillae are automatically rolled and pushed forward and downward by the maxillae.

Protrusile premaxillae of a somewhat different type have been evolved convergently among the Carps. In these fishes the lower jaw is both thrust forward and lowered and its large ascending processes on each side push forward the maxillae and premaxillae.

The inner upper jaws of bony fishes form the bony palate or roof of the mouth and are divided on each side into paired bony plates named palatines, pterygoids, entopterygoids, and metapterygoids. They converge in front, the palatines fitting behind the median vomer, while the entopterygoids spread out toward the sides and the rear, and attach themselves above to the metapterygoids and below to the quadrates. The metapterygoid of each side extends upward to the upper front border of the hyomandibular, and the quadrate extends to the lower front border of that bone. Consequently when the hyomandibulars are swung outward like elbows by their muscles, they spread the rear parts of the palate outward and, through the quadrate bones, they widen the space between the rear sides of the lower jaw. Meanwhile the muscular floor of the jaws may be contracting or relaxing. Thus the whole walls and floor of the mouth chamber can be expanded or contracted in dealing with the food and in breathing.

The rear lower part of the inner upper jaw consists in part of the large quadrate bones on either side; these are braced in front by the heavy plates of the palate and in the rear by the large hyoid arch; the main part of the latter is called the hyomandibular. This important bone of the skull fits above into two sockets on the under surface of the skull roof, and by means of these knuckle-like joints and appropriate muscles the opposite hyomandibulars can be bowed out away from the skull at their lower ends, spreading apart the opposite sockets in the quadrates for the lower jaw and thus adding to the pumping, sucking, and swallowing effects of the branchial apparatus and jaws as noted below.

In the embryo bony fish, the core of the lower jaw on either side is a bar of cartridge, called Meckel's cartilage, which corresponds with the cartilaginous lower jaw in the Sharks, Skates, and Rays. The rear part of the Meckel's cartilage on either side is replaced by bone cells and that part is called the articular bone. The articular bone on either side bears on its rear end a paired groove into which fit the knuckle-like condyles of the quadrate bones. The front parts of the Meckel's cartilage become enclosed on each side in a sheath of dermal bones bearing teeth on their upper surfaces and called dentary bones.

Thus the jaws of bony fishes are complex mechanisms including the outer upper lip-jaws, the inner or palato-pterygoid plates, the quadrates with which the lower jaws articulate; while parts of the hyoid arch (hyomandibular and symplectic) impart lateral swallowing movements to the jaws.

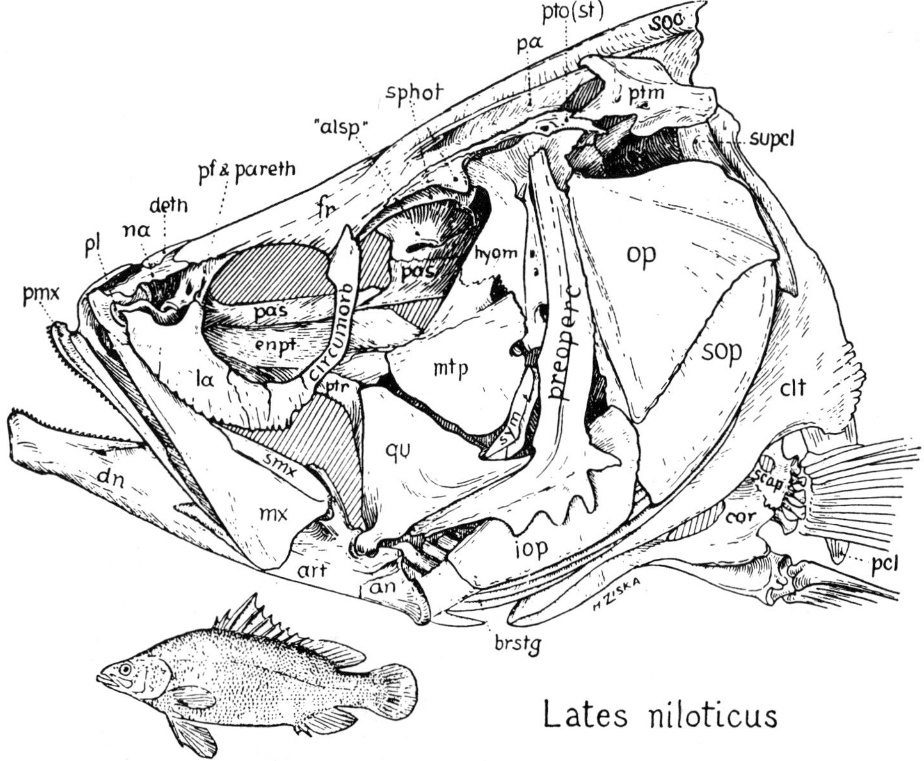

American Philosophical Society

Skull of Lates niloticus.

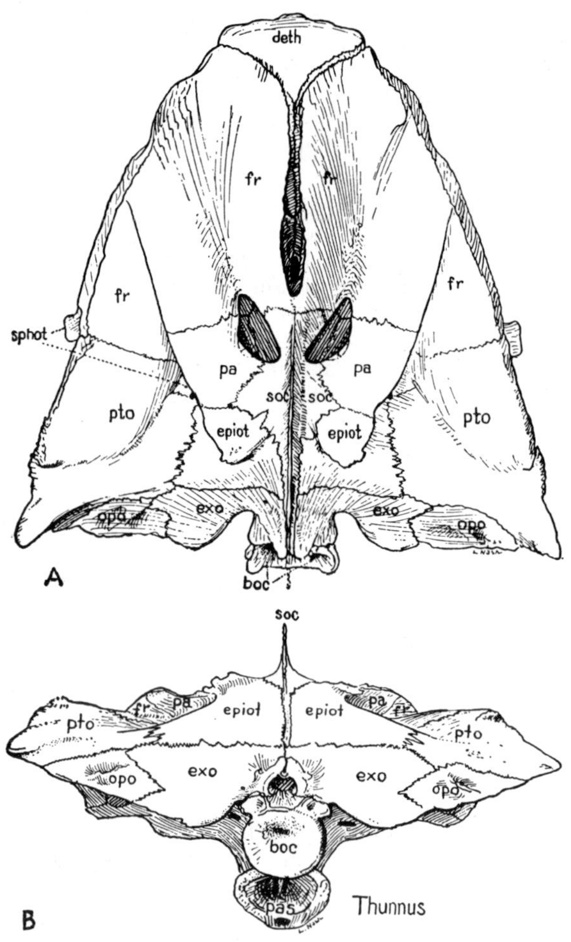

American Philosophical Society.

Skull of Thunnus.

The cranial vault or rear part of the skull houses the brain in the middle and, on each side, the very large chambers of the "inner ear." The entire "inner ear" of each side is formed in the embryo from a pouch of ectoderm or outer embryonic skin, which sinks into the lower layer of the skin and later divides itself into an upper division, containing the semi-circular canals, and a lower sac containing the end-branches of the acoustic or hearing nerves. These are partly imbedded in a limey or eventually stony mass, called the otoliths. When the dried fish skull is moved or shaken, these otoliths rattle about like dice in a dice box. In life, if the head is inclined toward one side or the other, the otoliths will tend to shift their weight in the same direction and no doubt stimulate parts of the nerve mass which are attached to them. Moreover, the otoliths may respond to vibrations coming through the water from ships or other fishes.

The chief organs of equilibrium are the semicircular canals which are arranged on the base and two sides of a pyramid. When the head is inclined in any direction the liquid in the canals runs over their sensitive nerves, which send the record of their reactions to the central receiving stations in the brain. There, in turn, nerves running to the motor system start its complex adjustments.

The eyes in most fishes seem to be the dominant directive organs, and doubtless play an an important part in the capture of a dodging fish. By keeping one or both his eyes on the target, the fish may, as it were, automatically make the right adjustments as he dashes at the prey.

Near the upper end of the hyomandibular on each side on the rear border of that bone is a prominent ball-like eminence upon which fits the socket on the inside of the large curved operculum or lid; the operculum, sub and inter-operculum together with the branchiostegals below, cover the branchial apparatus and the operculum projects backward so as to overlap the outer curved margin of the main bone of the shoulder girdle, which is called the cleithrum. This cleithrum is a crescent-shaped bone with a long lower horn directed forward under the throat and tied to its fellow on the opposite side. The cleithrum of either side is overlapped on top by a lathlike bone and this in turn leads to a rodlike bone, the post temporal, which ends above in three forks each of which is attached by ligaments to different points of the occiput or rear wall of the skull. Thus the entire complex shoulder girdle in the typical fish is tied to the skull above; below it is embedded in the muscles of the floor of the throat. The shoulder girdle not only forms the bony frame for the body wall but also protects the heart and gives anchorage to the coracoid and scapular plates. These in turn are the bases for the muscles that raise and lower the pectoral fins and at the same time they furnish the row of sockets for the several small bones at the base of the fin.

The pelvic fins usually form a horizontally placed double fan on either side of the vent and are based upon a pair of forward and inwardly directed rods, the pelvic bones which are imbedded in the ventral muscles.

The paired fins of bony fishes are usually webbed, with thin supporting rays, except for the large stiff front ray. In the Australian Lungfish, however, the paired fins form large muscular fleshy paddles with a well developed jointed inner skeleton. These represent the fore-and-hind limbs of land living animals, but although they can be turned downward, like limbs, they are not able to support the weight of the body on land; moreover, they lack hands and feet. However, in the Mud Skipping Goby of the Far East, the large pectoral fins can be curved outward and downward like elbows and their fanlike ends look like hands. In the Sea Bats also the large pectoral and pelvic fins serve as limbs for shuffling around on sandy or rocky bottoms.

The pelvic fins of the lobefinned (Crossopterygian) fishes, were likewise equipped with strong muscles for turning and twisting the fin and may have been used to some extent as limbs.

The base of the occiput is connected with the vertebral column by a three-part joint; one median ventral joint is cup-shaped and is bound by ligaments to the checkerlike centrum of the first vertebra, the other two condyles are on either side just above the exit of the spinal cord from the skull to the vertebral column. These lateral condyles are tied by ligaments on either side to the centrum of the first vertebra and they prevent both vertical and oblique dislocation of the spinal column, while permitting enough sliding movements for turning the head and undulating the column.

Below the tail end of the vertebral column are attached two triangular bony plates, called urohyal bones and several rodlike bones (hypurals); from these arise the complex muscles that move the tail fan. This is composed chiefly of strong dermal rays forking at the lower ends where they are fastened to the tail-bones. The tail-fan is provided with several strong straight or oblique muscles at the base on the urohyal bones, which can elevate or depress or twist the fan. There are also smaller stringlike muscles running radially outward to the individual fin-rays. These undulate the outer border of the fin, somewhat as the human fingers can run up and down along five white keys of a piano.

Thus the skeleton of a typical fish is very complex and composed of a great many pieces; but it is full of meaning and interest if studied as part of a living mechanism. But it should not be overlooked that most of the individual bones resist bending or compression, while the tendons and ligaments transmit to the bones the tensional forces generated by the muscles. Hence a dried skeleton without the ligaments, tendons, and muscles presents a very imperfect picture of the entire machine.

FOSSIL HISTORY, EVOLUTION, AND MAIN DIVISIONS

The oldest known fossil fish-remains consists of minute scales and part of a small head shield, found in sandstones of the Ordovician period near Boulder, Colorado. Physicists and geologists estimate that these sandstones were deposited about 380 million years ago, long before the Rocky Mountains were uplifted.

More and better preserved fossil material of the same class is found in rocks of the succeeding Silurian and Devonian ages, especially in Russia, Great Britain, and North America.

These earliest fishes are called Ostracoderms (literally, shard skins) because their fossilized scales and head shields now look like small fragments of pottery. In the family Cephalaspidae (head shield) true bone cells, secreting concentric layers, may be seen under the miscoscope in thin sections of the head shields. The base of the head shield consisted of horizontally deposited layers; the middle parts were perforated by numerous larger canals and smaller blood vessels; the outer layer comprised rows of tiny blocks, each with a bushlike system of fine canals in the middle and a thin layer of glassy enamel on the surface. This very complex many-layered, hard crust was less fully developed in the Coelolepids (hollow scales) and Thelodonts. Here the front part of the body was somewhat skatelike and the surface was covered not with continuous armor, but with small thorny or flattened denticles resembling those on the skin of Sharks.

The heavily armored Cephalaspid Ostracoderms were probably slow moving bottom-living fishes, grubbing in the muddy sands for small creatures. The Anaspid Ostracoderms on the other hand had small heads and thinner scales and were gracefully formed, not unlike small Herring, but with downturn tails and apparently lacking a bony inner skeleton. Another group of Ostracoderms included the Pteraspids, which had a many layered shield around the head and thorax but were lacking in bone cells. In some of them the shield was

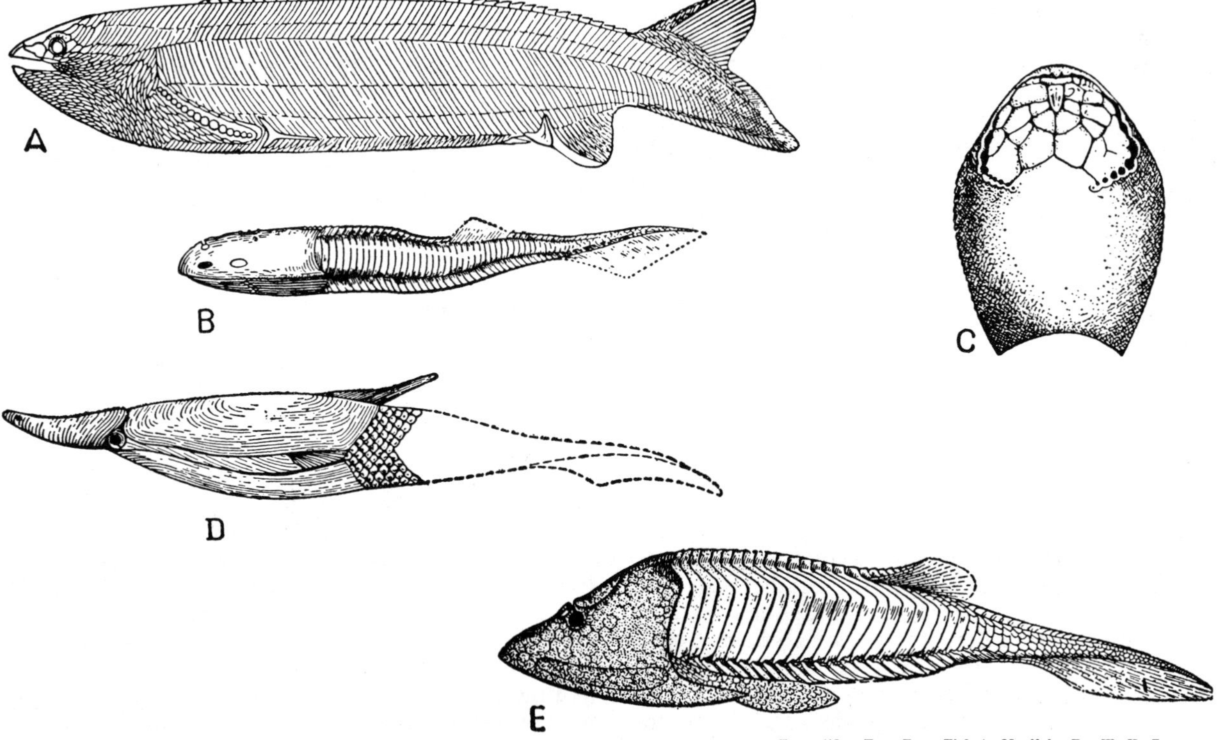

Ostracoderms.

subdivided into small units which seem to be comparable to those of the Coelolepids and Thelodonts.

The Ostracoderms already possessed a notochord which is a thin flexible tube covered with tough connective tissue and serving as the core and forerunner of the backbone or vertebral column of later fish. They also were well equipped with myomeres or muscle flakes along either side of the body. These muscles, as in later fish, were the prime movers or locomotor units; the fins were folds of skin, usually strengthened externally by small overlapping scale rows; they acted chiefly as rudders.

A remarkably primitive looking fish, named Jaymoytius by Dr. Errol I. White of the British Museum of Natural History, was found in the Silurian beds of Lanarkshire, Scotland. It was a long spindle shaped fish with a small head and a long lateral fin-fold on either side, ending in an elongate tail-fin. The scales and head covering were thin and the skeleton cartilaginous.

The modern Lamprey "eels" (see page xx) are not true Eels but are believed to be highly specialized descendants of the Ostracoderms.

The Sharks and Skates, or cartilage fishes, are probably not direct descendants of the Ostracoderms but seem to have arisen from certain members (e.g. *Pseudopetalichthys)* of another Silurian and Devonian group, the Placoderms, which had complex outer and inner jaws basically like those of bony fishes.

The modernized bony fishes, including most of the fish sought by fishermen, are the descendants of still another ancient fish group, the Devonian "Ganoids," so named from the shiny enamel on their scales.

The most ancient and primitive Ganoids belonged to the order Chondrostei or Palaenoiscoidei, and of these the oldest was the Devonian *Cheirolepis.* Its fairly long streamlined body was covered with very small scales of complex structure and with shiny surface. It had a wide-based single dorsal fin, above the similar anal fin. The tail was heterocercal, sharklike, but with long dermal scale-rays on its lower border. The skull was covered with many dermal bones the arrangement of which was basically that of the typical bony fishes already described.

The modern diverse descendants of the Devonian Ganoid stock are 1) the Sturgeons, 2) the African *Polypterus,* 3) the intermediate Ganoids (includin the Garpike and the Bowfin, *Amia),* and 4) all the thronging hosts of the Teleosts (completely bony) or modernized bony fishes.

1) The Sturgeons are in some respect retrogressive or degenerate derivatives of the Palaeoniscoids: a) they have delayed the process of ossifying the internal skeleton and the adults retain its cartilaginous unossified conditions; b) they have acquired a new specialized skin skeleton consisting of small and large bony scutes, which have largely replaced the original scales. The Spoonbill or Paddlefish of the Lower Mississippi region has emphasized the cartilaginous conditions of the skeleton and lost nearly all scales and bony scutes, the skin being naked. Its flattened bill seems to have sensory functions and it engulfs small creatures in its large mouth cavity. The Sturgeons have very small downturned mouths and suck in small animals and plants from the muddy river-bottoms.

2) The *Polypterus,* or Bichir, from the rivers of tropical Africa has in some ways preserved more of the primitive Ganoid characters: a) its skull and skeleton generally are well ossified not cartilaginous; b) its bony lip-jaws retain teeth, and the outer upper jaw has not yet become wholly free from the cheek bones. Large paired gular bones protect the flattened throat; c) its scales are rhomboid in outline and retain a bony base and the enamel of the surface; d) its shoulder girdle retains the ventral plates called clavicles which are lost in typical bony fishes. Among its specialized features are: a) the extension of the muscles of the pectoral fins to form fleshy lobes outside the body wall; b) the transformation of the slender Ganoid heterocercal tail into a spreading tail with strong radiating dermal rays; c) the transformation of the dorsal fin into a long series of finlets which are continuous at the rear end with the rays of the dorsal fin; d) the emphasis of the large enamel fulcral scales which serve as masts for the row of dorsal finlets.

3a) The bony Garpikes of North America seem to be derived from the Triassic-Jurassic Protospondyli *(Dapedius, Lepidotus,* et al.) with which they agree in: a) the circular arrangement of the bones around the eye; 2) the forward position of the lower jaw; c) the thick rhombic ganoid scales. But they have become specialized especially in: a) the forward elongation of the snout and jaws to form a bill; 2) the breaking up of the postorbital cheek plate into many platelets; 3) the marked elongation of the body, with lowering of the forehead and the assumption of a somewhat pipelike form; 4) the thorough ossification of the vertebrae which have evolved bony ball and socket joints.

3b) The Bowfin *(Amia)* of the rivers of the middle United States is a lone survivor of a once diversified group, the Amioidei of the Triassic, Jurassic, and Cretaceous periods. These were swift-swimming, pikelike fishes retaining ganoid scales but with tails shortened and extremely symmetrical. *Amia* itself is a fairly long-bodied fish with a low entering angle, very long dorsal fin and round tail. The scales have lost the ganoin and become cycloid. It retains a few ganoid characters such as a jugal plate under the lower jaw and the unexpanded hypural rods at the base of the tail, but on the whole it is much nearer to the soft-rayed bony fishes than are any of the other surviving Ganoids.

Another Triassic family (Pholidophoridae) while retaining ganoid scales was near, or actually ancestral, to the Leptolepidae (Jurassic and Cretaceous) which, in turn, stood at the very base of the Teleosts (completely bony) or modernized bony fishes. The Leptolepids are nearly represented today by the Ten Pounders *(Elops)* which are small relatives of the Tarpons, as well as by the less specialized members of the Herring family (Clupeidae). These are the more primitive families of the Order Isospondyli (which means "equal vertebrae") because, in contrast with the Ostariophysi (Characins, Carps, Catfishes), the first four

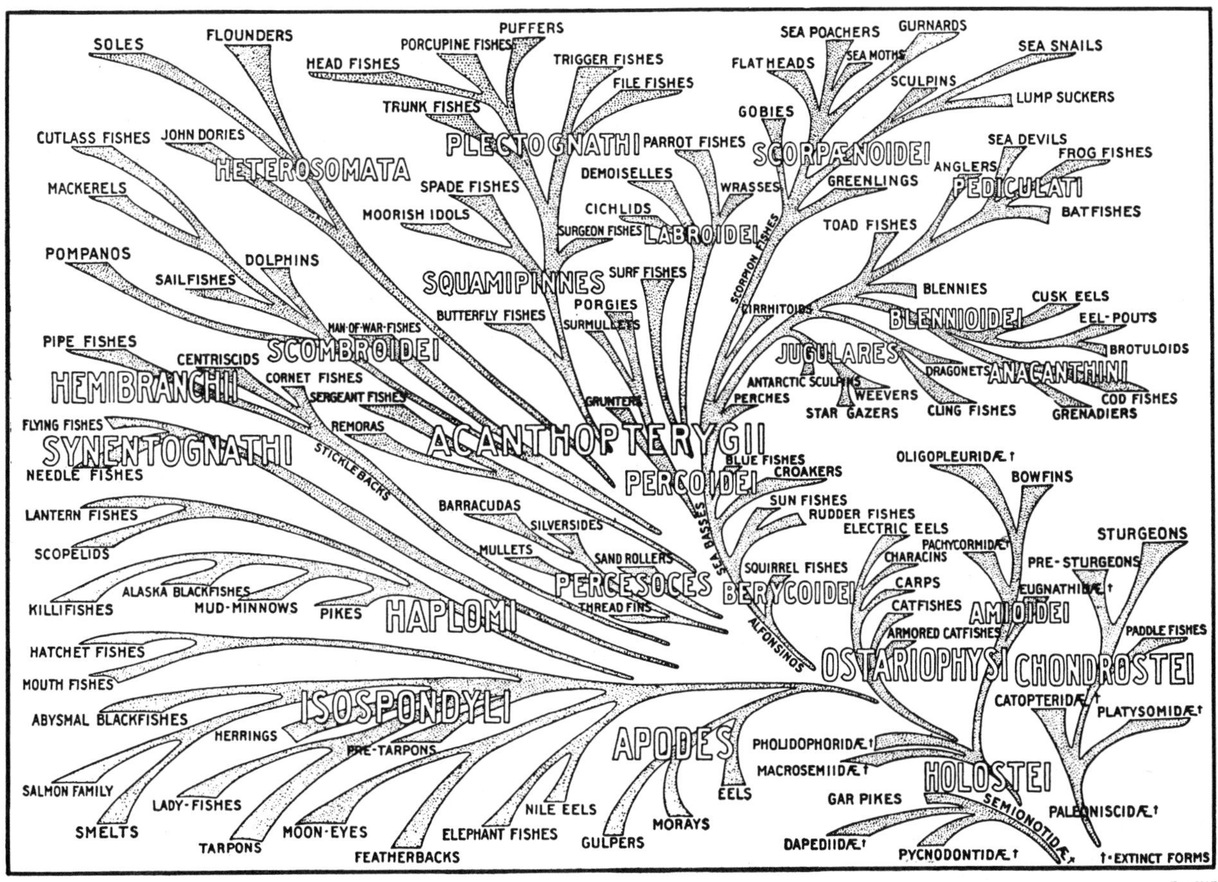

Credit7

Family Tree of fishes.

vertebrae behind the skull were *not* greatly modified. The Isospondyli have completely lost the banoin surface and bony base of the scales which are now horny and cycloid. The Salmon, Smelt, Trout, and related families also belong to the Isospondyli. Their internal skeleton, however, has become more or less cartilaginous merely by retaining the larval condition and reducing the adult process of bone formation. Among the more specialized families of the Isospondyli are the Osteoglossidae or bony-tongued family including the giant Arapaima of Brazil and related genera in Africa and Australia. Still more specialized are the strange Elephant Fishes (Normyrids) of the Nile and the ferocious Stomiatidae or Deep Sea Boa Fishes. By Upper Certaceous times almost all the modern orders and many of the modern families were already in existence.

Next comes the order Ostariophysi, including the Characins, Carps and Catfishes, in all of which there is a chain of small bones, representing modified parts of the first four vertebrae behind the head, extending forward from the swim bladder to the auditory capsule of the skull. This apparatus is found through this great order, which includes many thousands of species mostly living in rivers and other fresh waters, except the Gaff-Topsail Catfishes, the only sea-faring members of the order.

The Eels and Morays form a more compact order, called Apodes, from their lack of "feet" (fins). Their upper Cretaceous ancestors however retained distinct traces of the pelvic fins which have been completely lost in the modern Eels.

The Deep Sea Lizard Fishes (Order Iniomi), the Gulpers (Lyomeri), the Pikes (Haplomi), the Top Minnows (Microcyprini), Needlefishes, Gars, and Flying Fish (Synentognathi), and the Sticklebacks, Tube Mouths, Seahorses, etc. (Thoracostei) have but little in common, except that they have all evolved beyond the grade of the soft rayed Teleosts (Isospondyli) without having attained the features which are so characteristic of the spiny finned Teleosts (Acanthopterygli). This is another vast assemblage including thousands of species and according to some classifications, several hundred families. They have been the dominant and most diversified of all marine orders since Upper Cretaceous times, perhaps for the last 70 million years or more, and it is small wonder that they include most of the prizes of the salt-water fisherman which are noted in the present work (see Bass, Snappers, Barracudas, Mackerel, Tunas, Marlins, etc.)

Transitional characters from the Isospondyli to the spiny-finned fishes are indicated in the Upper Cretaceous genus *Ctenothrissa* in which the ventral fins are displayed forward, underneath the pectorals and there are unbranched rays in the dorsal fin in front of the soft rayed fins, as in the spiny finned fishes. There are also two supramaxillary bones as in both Herrings and some Berycoids (primitive spiny fins).

National Park Service

Fishing at Chain Lakes in Yosemite National Park. Gale Peak rises in the distance.

SECTION I

GAME FISHES

Part 1. Introduction

Many well known food fishes are also fine game fishes; the small bullhead caught after much concentrated effort by a boy with cane pole and line is a game fish to him; in sections of the world where better species are absent, fishes looked down upon by anglers elsewhere are game fishes. Then, too, there is the slight margin between a fish which is caught for food and one caught for sport but later eaten. Some divide fishes into game fishes, and big game fishes (those usually running over one hundred pounds). To some anglers, game fish mean only the very large ones—the speared fishes and the tunas; to others, the only fish worth going after are trout and salmon. Sharks are game to some anglers and taboo to others.

The truth of the matter seems to be that, unless the angling is competitive, any fish caught on rod and line, putting up any fight, and not thrown back in disgust by the angler is a game fish. In addition, there is an enormous variety of methods within the sport: fly fishing, plug casting, spinning, surf casting, still fishing, trolling, fishing from the shore, from skiffs, from party boats, from fishing launches. Furthermore, anyone can be an angler—man, woman, or child. There are game fish records made by fifteen-year olds, and in 1949 a 1006-pound Black Marlin was caught by a young man with only one arm and one leg.

Narrowly speaking, a game fish should put up a fight when hooked. The fish has more advantage in this matter than many people realize, inasmuch as it is very largely supported by the water and is not carrying anything like its own weight. Still more narrowly speaking, tackle and method should comply with certain generally accepted angling rules, but this also is a matter of taste. In competitive angling, rules are rigidly followed. Many anglers also follow them because they believe that in so doing they will ultimately achieve more skill and better catches. However, all ways of angling are fun, and anglers who go in for the very strict observance of rules and form may also be seen happily dangling handlines off tropical docks!

This informality and leeway within the sport is one of its most appealing traits and probably the reason why there is such a friendly feeling among anglers all over the world. It is primarily an independent and lone-hand sport and cannot be compared to a sport like tennis. A person on a tennis court hitting balls hither and yon with no regard to rules or form, is not playing tennis. But anyone with rod and line catching fish for the fun of it is definitely angling. Angling is more comparable to ice skating—a sport in which rules are applied for competition or exhibition or by those who wish to do so, but which remains skating as long as the participant is upright on the skates and the skates are on ice.

Considering the nature of the sport, it is understandable that it has not developed in an orderly way. To trace the origin and development of some of the existing rules is possible, although inconclusive and complicated at best. The development of tackle can, however, be outlined to some extent. Line has developed from the tight lines of horsehair, fibres of plants, linen, or silk to modern running lines of linen, Nylon and other synthetics. The present rod and reel developed from the simple rod and line and the much later developed fishing "wheel." The hook was a natural offshoot of the barbed hook of the hunting spear.

There is no way of knowing how long ago or where people first fished for pleasure, nor do we know where or when they first fished for food, which occupation was the natural predecessor of fishing for pleasure.

Accounts of fishing with rod and line (whether for food or amusement) go back as far as 2000 B.C. in Egypt. At an uncertain date early in the 15th Century, the *Book of St. Albans* mentions the use of the artificial fly. Such are the scattered, and very likely inaccurate, bits and pieces upon which any genealogy of fishing would have to rest. Tackle has developed in various ways and in various parts of the world. There are many expert fly tiers who are continually developing new lures. Lines, of recent years, have been the most discussed part of tackle because of the new synthetics, and because of the International Game Fish Association's decision a decade ago to change its record classes from "thread" to wet tensile strength in pounds.

Fishing in North America has followed the settling of our country, and while there are still unfished waters, in all probability there are no new game fish. New trout are quite often publicized, but these so far have proven to be local varieties of some well known species, for color and even shape of a fish can vary to a surprising degree

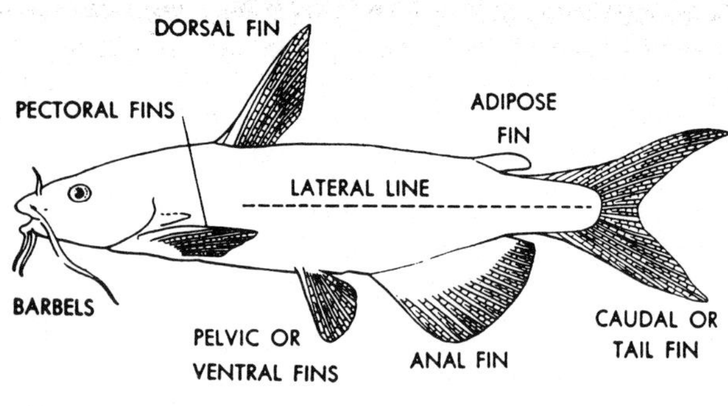

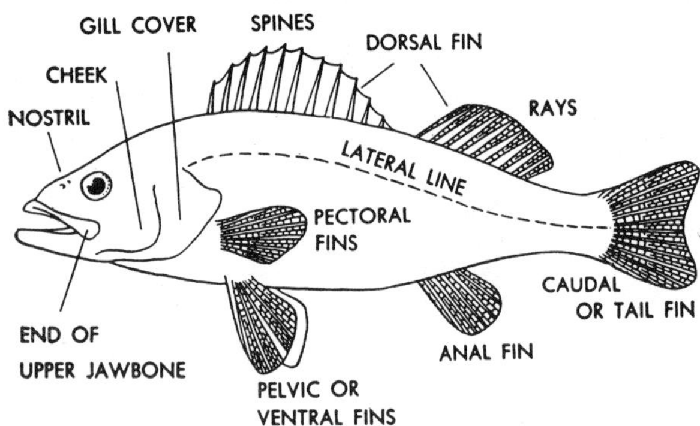

From: "North American Game Fishes" by Francesca LaMonte. Copyright 1945 by Francesca LaMonte, reprinted by permission of Doubleday & Co.

Identification characteristics of the fish.

with habitat. Game fishing has increased greatly with increased travel facilities and with the discovery that sport fishing is a very material source of income to a community.

Fishing for the larger marine game fishes, many of which have been taken commercially for years, has followed the development of travel facilities with an intermediate step—a pioneering angling job by some outstanding big-game anglers. Publications of all kinds have done their bit, and tournaments, gathering their competitors from a wider and wider range, have given a great boost to the sport.

Trout and salmon fishing, modeled originally on that in Great Britain, goes its serious but enthusiastic way. Rules for both fresh and salt water fishing are based on those of some of the famous angling clubs throughout the world, and after modification by local clubs to suit particular conditions, are amicably adopted by tournament committees. It seems obvious from this résumé that a game fish is simply a fish that is fun to catch on a rod and line; that game fishing is a natural result of the utilization of natural resources for food, and that its spread as a sport follows the development of travel facilities of any section of the country.

Although well known to scientific workers, some facts about fishes should be explained to the average angler.

First of all, just what is a fish? Although much lower in the scale of life as man has worked it out, man and fish belong in the same category—vertebrate animals. The fish has a backbone; lobsters crabs, shrimps, oysters, etc. are therefore not fish. A fish does not suckle its young; therefore whales, manatees, porpoises, etc. are not fishes. Fish live in water, breathe through gills, and have backbones and fins.

The fins, are composed of either spiny or soft rays usually connected by fragile membranes. The shape and position of the fins varies greatly in the different kinds of fishes, and the number of rays and spines may differ in individuals of the same species. There may be one, two, or three dorsal fins; pelvics or ventrals may be present or absent; there may be one anal or two anals; and there may also be a small fin back of the dorsal known as the adipose fin.

Scales vary greatly in shape, number, and size, and there are some scaleless fishes. In some species the scales are very large and in others so small and imbedded as to be almost invisible. In some fishes the scales of the young vary greatly from those of the adult; in the swordfish the young are scaled but the adults are entirely scaleless.

The lateral line is usually clearly visible from the back of the gill cover to the base of the tail fin and is present although not so clearly visible, on other parts of the body. It appears as a line of small pores. This serves, as far as known, to receive vibrations, and to aid in adjustment to sudden temperature changes.

Teeth of fishes vary even more than scales. Some are toothless; others have teeth only in one jaw; some have teeth not only in the jaws but also on the roof of the mouth and in the throat; some have replacement rows behind the front row; in some the front teeth have fused into a beak. The dentition of larval and very young fishes is apt to be entirely different from adults. In the same way, the jaws differ: some are prognathous, or under hung while some are over hung, and in some the mouth is vertical.

With such a variety of teeth goes an equal variety in food. Forms with paved throat teeth can crush small crustaceans; some scrape for their food; others must suck it up; the huge whale shark has small teeth and such a small throat that it subsists on minute marine organisms strained by its gill rakers. Most marine fishes eat other fishes and crustaceans although some are scavengers like the cod and some of the sharks. Most fresh water fishes eat insects and algae.

Anglers realize that it is important to know the food of fishes in order to plan bait for their capture, but fish do not always respond to such bait—they may be plentifully fed already or they may be spawning—and sometimes do respond to substances unlike natural foods, such as doughballs.

The internal structure of fishes is also varied but this is of more concern to the scientific worker than the angler, and it is sufficient to state here that the digestive system, to put it very simply, consists of stomach, intestines, and a vent which may be situated anywhere from under the head to near the tail. The reproductive organs vary in size and shape and should not be mistaken for "roe." It is usually difficult to determine the sex of a fish by examination with the naked eye, unless the fish is a ripe female or one of the fishes in which there is a contant difference in shape, form or color between the sexes.

The greatest variation in fishes is color, which is therefore one of the most unreliable identification characteristics. Many fishes have various color phases, one differing from the other even from black to white; many take on, when fighting or dying, bright colors never seen in other circumstances. Many assume not only different shapes but different colors during the breeding season. Young and adult are seldom the same in color, and there is variation in individuals within a species. Fishes change and lose color immediately after leaving the water and often assume quite different markings. Gradually all color and nearly all markings fade. Red, which becomes yellow before disappearing, and any metallic sheen, are the last to go. This is the reason why mounted fish must be painted. As a fish in life is not only in water, but usually also coated with slime, the preparation of fish for exhibit is the most difficult of the taxidermist's tasks.

It should be repeated that the color of a fish is a poor way to identify a species except as a minor check in combination with the other more stable characteristics such as proportion of body parts to each other and the nature of teeth, fins, and scales. It seems desirable to mention the technical "keys" without which the majority of fishes cannot be definitely identified. Even with these keys, which are not always simple to use, some fishes cannot be identified without prolonged external and internal examination and comparison with known material in the same group. Fortunately for anglers, most game fishes are well known, and there are, particularly in North America, few that are not simple to identify.

In measuring fishes, most ichthyologists take three lengths: "Total," which is taken from snout tip to center of a perpendicular dropped between the tail lobes; "fork" (if the tail is forked or lunate), from snout tip to center of tail margin; and "standard," from snout tip to tail base. Standard measurement is the one on which ichthyologists base proportional measurements. It should also be noted that "depth" and "girth" are not the same measurement. Depth is taken by dropping a perpendicular from the line of the back to the line of the belly; girth is an all-around measurement at the thickest part of the fish. The head is usually measured from the tip of the snout to the hind margin of the gill cover.

Various formulae have been used for computing the weight of fish from its length and girth. Quite often these work for species for which they have been devised but not for other fish. Very often, however, they fail to be correct by a number of pounds, and for this reason record-keepers will not accept estimated weights.

In identifying fishes a vast amount of confusion has been caused by local names. Some fishes have as many as fifty common names. A few have no common name, but the majority have at least five. Scientific names are given under international rules and can only apply to one fish, and the best informed anglers know and use the scientific names of many fishes. Standardized lists of common names of fishes both for anglers and for commercial fishermen have been developed, and their general adoption and use would be of value to angler and scientific worker alike.

It may be added that no ichthyologist can remember the names and descriptions and ranges of the twenty to thirty thousand kinds of fishes, but such trained individuals can direct anyone who is interested to literature in which most of the known answers are to be found.

Anglers want to know as much as possible about fishes, if for no other reason than to find the best fishing grounds in the best season. Among the most important and the most interesting aspects of fish life to the angler are their migrations and breeding habits.

Most large or long migrations of fishes take place for one of two reasons: search for food or for the purpose of spawning. Many fishes go deeper or farther off shore at various times. There are fishes, like the tunas, which appear with regularity in certain areas at definite seasons and disappear as regularly. Whence they come and where they go and when and where they breed is still unknown. Some fishes, like the eels go from fresh water to the sea to spawn; others like the salmons and shad go from the sea to fresh water for the same purpose. Some fishes, like the swordfish and marlins, swim inshore in pairs at the spawning season, whereas otherwise they appear to be solitary fishes; some feed deep but spend much time near the surface; as living organisms, they are affected by food, temperature, currents, salinity, over populations, and many other factors. The young of many fishes drift considerable distances. Because of this and because of the small size of the young and the fact that very often they bear no resemblance to the adult, the entire life cycle of a number of fishes is not yet known.

Although the reproduction of fishes has little immediate bearing on game fishing, it is a matter of great interest to most anglers. There are three general patterns by which reproduction is accomplished. The female may deposit the eggs in the water and the male then deposits the sperm over them. The union of egg and sperm takes place in the water entirely outside the female's body. In

J. F. Louden

Jaw of Mako Shark showing functional and replacement teeth.

other fishes, the male introduces the sperm into the female's body. After the eggs are fertilized they are released by the female into the water where they develop and hatch. In still others, the male introduces sperm into the female's body and the eggs develop inside the female and the young are born alive.

Some fishes congregate in large numbers for spawning; some obviously pair. Some deposit enormous numbers of eggs; some just a few; some do not deposit them all at once, but at intervals, moving around at the same time and thus making it more difficult to learn where they have spawned.

Some fishes show a marked degree of parental care, building nests, or hollows in the lakes, or stream floor and protecting the eggs and young.

Fresh water fishes are, of course, easier to locate and study, but the breeding habits and spawning grounds of marine species are far harder to observe. Hunting for young and eggs often requires special boats and crews and apparatus beyond the financial ability of most scientific institutions to supply. To keep a well equipped boat out for months or even years searching for minute specimens is a dream of many ichthyologists which is seldom realized. Until such intensive work can be done over wide areas, the breeding habits and ranges of marine fishes will be imperfectly known.

Angling centers are more than places where fish may be found in quantity. There must also be areas where facilities for the angler exist or can be developed. All of North America itself, except the desert areas, presents unusual opportunities for angling. It has an endless variety of fish off its huge coastlines and in its innumerable lakes, ponds, rivers, and brooks. Comparatively few streams are closed to the public, and one can fish anywhere on the coast. However, before going fishing anywhere, it would be well to inquire about permits, size limits, and seasons.

Fishing is a varied sport which can be shown poorly by statistics. As an example, even the tabulations of license sales fail to furnish a true record of the number of fishermen, since an enormous number of men, women, and children who are not required for various reasons to buy licenses, fish regularly.

This country offers any kind of fishing an angler wants, and in some places, such as North Carolina, fresh and salt water fishing is available in the same area and almost from the same spot! North Carolina, New Jersey, Long Island, Florida, and California; and many other states offer fishing from piers, causeways, bridges, roadsides, casting from beaches, skiff fishing, or charter boat fishing, either on party boats, or on more exclusive and expensive boats fully equipped with outriggers, guide, captain, mates, and provisions. Any one who has seen the fishing train from New York City to Montauk, Long Island, discharge its anglers who race to the docks to get a good place on the party boats, will have little doubt of the popularity of this sport. In contrast to this type of fishing was that off Wedgeport, Nova Scotia, whose recent history is of particular interest. Wedgeport, in 1935, was a small French Canadian village subsisting on a small commercial tuna and lobster fishery. In that year Michael Lerner went to see the tuna run off the now famous Rip, and against the advice of the local commercial fishermen, tried his luck in a make-shift boat with such startling success that the town was not only converted to the possibilities of sports fishing, but made an extraordinary effort to exploit it. Other big game anglers followed to Wedgeport, and Mr. Roy Cann, of the Yarmouth division of the Nova Scotia Bureau of Information, bent every effort to serve these anglers and to publicize Wedgeport. In 1935, there were no hotels or inns and no boats and tackle at Wedgeport. In 1937, it became the scene of the International Cup Matches, and by 1948 the local income from anglers was one hundred thousand dollars. In 1949 teams from the United States, Great Britain, Cuba, Argentina, and Brazil competed in the Cup Matches. Then, in the late 1950's, the Wedgeport tuna made a typically erratic fish move and in part deserted the grounds. Those remaining were not interested in bait. The last Wedgeport Tuna match was held in 1958.

Every year there are more fishing tournaments such as those at Cat Cay, Bimini, Wedgeport, Miami, Bailey Island, Ipswich Bay, Acapulo, and a score of others. They range from those devoted to one special fish (like the Bailey's Island (Maine) Tuna Tournament, Ipswich Bay Tuna Tournament, the Tampico Tarpon Tournament, the International Light Tackle Sailfish Tournaments, the Wellfleet Striped Bass Derby), to those which include all game fishes. New grounds are constantly being developed and each year a new crop of anglers enter the angling game.

North America is lucky in having so many fishing spots, but this is a truly international sport, carried on with the same enthusiasm, if not by the same large numbers, from Malaya to Alaska.

Part 2. Salt Water Species

SHARKS

Although not among the most popular game fishes, there is so much general curiosity about sharks and their ways that it seems appropriate to refer to a few authoritative books on various aspects of the subject.

The most comprehensive of all, although geographically limited to the western North Atlantic, is the explicit monograph by H. B. Bigelow and W. C. Schroeder: "Sharks", published in 1948, as No. 1, Part 1, of "Fishes of the Western North Atlantic", a series of monographs on fishes published by the Sears Foundation for Marine Research.

A very interesting pamphlet by Stewart Springer is "Sharks and their Behavior," with particular reference to eight genera implicated in reports of attacks on man. This was published in 1943 by the Coordinator of Research and Development, USN Emergency Rescue Equipment Section, Washington.

Collectors of fossil sharks' teeth usually find most useful the plates and descriptions in Dr. Henry W. Fowler's "A description of the fossil fish remains of the Cretaceous, Eocene and Miocene formations of New Jersey", published in the Bulletin of the Geological Survey of New Jersey, 1911, Number 4.

Most of the sharks cannot properly be called game fishes, although many of them occasionally take the hook and may or may not put up a good fight. Such are the Manta (a ray) and sharks like the Dusky, Blue, Southern Ground, Leopard, Black-Tip, Soup-fin, and others. Neither of the two largest, the Basking Shark and the world's largest fish the Whale Shark, are game fish. On the other hand, a few sharks are consistently good fighters and much sought by anglers.

Shark fishing on rod and reel is, however, not as popular on American coasts as it is off the Durban section of Africa where sharks are fished constantly and excitingly from piers or from high cliffs, or as off Australia and New Zealand where a Mako weighing 1000 pounds, a Man-Eater of 2664 pounds, and a Tiger of 1422 pounds hold World Records.

There is much commercial fishing for sharks all over the world, profitable both from the skins and the vitamin content of the liver oil.

The ancestors of present-day sharks lived millions of years ago, and the cartilaginous skeleton,

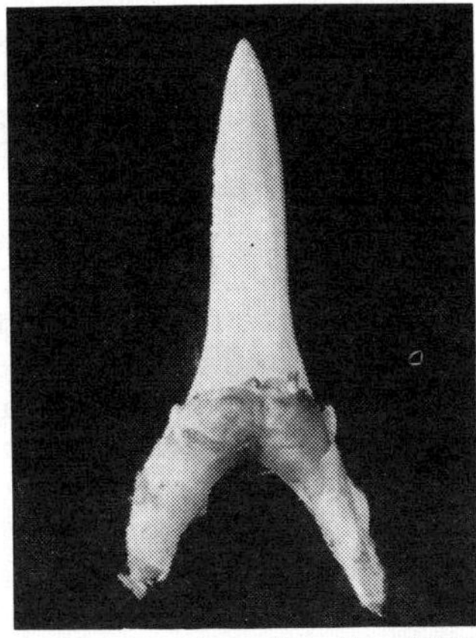

Amer. Mus. Nat. History

Porbeagle Shark Tooth.

Amer. Mus. Nat. History

Mackerel Shark Tooth.

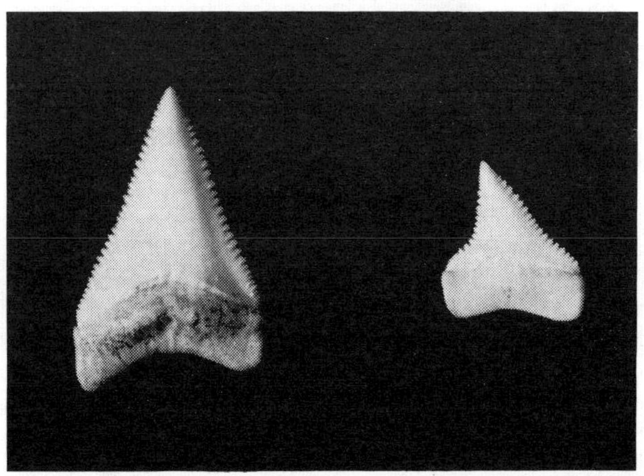

Amer. Mus. Nat. History

Teeth of the Man-eater Shark.

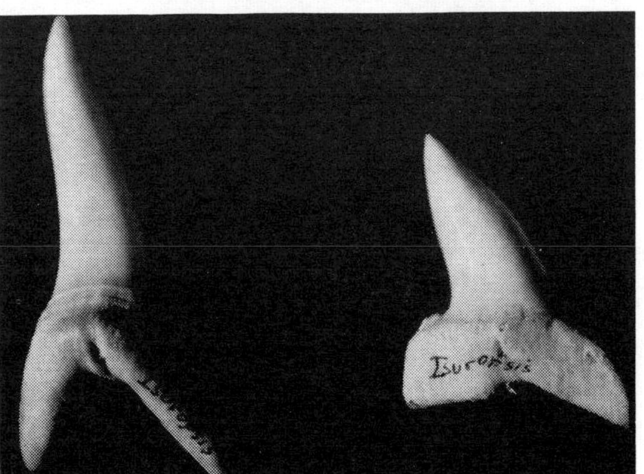

Amer. Mus. Nat. History

Teeth of the Mako Shark.

brain, blood, and digestive systems of the living descendants are still primitive or generalized structures and organs. Fossil teeth of some ancient sharks are found in large quantities, particularly in the marls of North Carolina and New Jersey, where the teeth of Mackerel Sharks are very common and easily identified.

There is a tremendous variety of size within this group; some deep sea forms are only a few inches long, while the Whale Shark, reaches a length of 40 to 60 feet and a weight of some 26,000 pounds. This giant creature, despite its size, is sluggish and harmless, it is easily recognized by its large flat head and color pattern of black crossed by narrow white lines enclosing white dots, the general effect being that of a checkerboard.

J. F. Louden

A world's record rod-and-reel Mako Shark. Weighing 1000 pounds, this Shark was taken March 14, 1943 off Mayor Island by Squadron leader B. D. H. Ross.

While in general the form of sharks' bodies is somewhat similar, they vary greatly, particularly in the shape and size of the head and tail. Some have very broad rounded snouts; others very triangular and pointed ones. Some have widely lunate tails; on others the tail lobes are completely unlike in length and shape. A distinctive feature shared by all sharks is the gill openings on the sides of the body, which consist of five or more narrow slits. The body covering of small, rough denticles is also typical.

Sharks are remarkable in having series of reserve teeth lying behind the functional teeth. The teeth are set in the gums, not embedded in the jawbones as in most fishes. Contrary to popular belief, in most sharks the functional row or rows of teeth do not drop out simultaneously, but gradually, single teeth often remaining lower down on the jaw; this makes the whole dental arrangement seem haphazard, as these displaced teeth often stick out at different angles. The teeth differ widely in form and size and are often the easiest way of distinguishing one shark from another.

There is a conspicuous absence of the greens, yellows, and silver of many other fishes, and a tendency toward brown, gray, black, and grayish-blue above, and dirty white below. Young sharks closely resemble the adults, but any blotches or other color markings are apt to be much more conspicuous in the young.

Fertilization in sharks is internal and the males have claspers which are to be seen as appendages of the pelvic fins. These are the organs through which the seminal fluid is introduced into the oviducts of the female fish. The horny, squarish egg capsules with the long corner trailers are familiar to everyone who has wandered about the beaches. This represents one method of reproduction in sharks. However, others liberate the young from the egg inside the female's body and they are then born as young fish, while still others are viviparous, that is, the young are developed in the oviducts and born as young fish.

The number in a brood is small when compared to that of other fishes, the highest number observed in a female being slightly over 80. It is usually less.

Sharks customarily eat fishes, but some of them are scavengers and, like a goat, eat anything within reach. There are authentic accounts of attacks on humans. The Man-Eater Shark on the rare occasions when it comes inshore is known to attack living human beings; whether from a fear of being cornered or for some other reason. In Australia, the Mako is feared by bathers, and many also fear the Hammerhead.

The sharks most often sought by sports fishermen are the Tiger Shark, the Hammerhead Shark, the Thresher Shark, the Porbeagle, Mako, and Man-Eater or White Sharks. Other sharks, such as the Leopard, Dusky, Blue, Soup-fin, Black-tip, etc., are occasionally taken on rod and reel, but not sufficiently valued by anglers to be generally considered game fishes.

The Tiger, Black-Tip, Blue, Ground, Yellow,

and Smooth Dogfish are in the same group of Sharks, characterized by the fact that the tail fin is not lunate but has an upper lobe at least twice as long as the lower. There are no keels on the caudal peduncle; the last gill opening is over the base of the pectoral fin, and the spiracles (small openings behind the eyes, connected with the respiratory chamber) are either very small or absent.

The Hammerheads, in which group the Bonnetheads also belong, are characterized by their strange, hammer-shaped heads.

The Thresher, alone in its family, is recognizable instantly by its long, lashlike upper tail lobe which is about half the total length of the body.

The Porbeagle, Mako, and Man-Eater belong in the Mackerel Shark Group, and are recognized by a combination of pointed nose, lunate tail fins, keels on either side of the tail stem, and large sharp teeth. They are easily distinguished from each other by their teeth. These are the fastest of all sharks.

THE MACKEREL SHARKS

(MAKO, PORBEAGLE, MAN-EATER)

These sharks have lunate tail fins with equal or nearly equal lobes, there is a keel on either side of the tail stem; the teeth are conspicuous, and the three game species of this family are easily distinguished by the teeth.

The teeth of the Mako Shark are narrowly triangular and high, without small cusps at the base of any teeth. Those of the Porbeagle Shark are similar in shape, but some of them have very tiny cusps, like small teeth, at the base and on either side of the main triangle. The teeth of the Man-Eater Shark are massive, broad triangles, with serrated edges.

MAKO SHARK

Atlantic: *Isurus oxyrinchus* Rafinesque
Pacific: *Isurus glaucus* (Gill)

There are probably several closely related Pacific species, but for anglers they are all "Mako".

RANGE: Both of the above species occur around the Cape of Good Hope. The Atlantic form is found from Cape Cod to Brazil and from Norway to the Cape of Good Hope. The Pacific form is found from Catalina south for an unknown distance. This, or a very similar fish, is the famous Mako of New Zealand and Australia, also reported from other spots in the south Pacific. Occurrence and frequency are highly irregular.

COLOR: Varies from slate blue or dark slate above, whitish below, to all slate gray.

DISTINGUISHING CHARACTERISTICS: The teeth.

SIZE: The rod and reel record, taken off New Zealand in 1943 by a young Squadron Leader on his first fishing trip, weighed 1000 pounds. The fish has not been taken in sufficient numbers to establish an accurate average size, but American specimens are somewhat smaller; one weighing 745 pounds was taken in Shinnecock Inlet, New York.

Drawing by Fowler in "The Fish Culturist"

White Shark (Man-eater Shark).

FOOD: Fishes.

HABITS: This is one of the hardest fighters and swiftest of fishes. It is reputed to leap as high as a masthead, both when hooked and when free. The fish is often sighted "finning" near the surface, the tips of the first dorsal and the upper tail fin lobe showing above the water. The Mako is believed to spend most of its time near the surface. But little is known of its life history, and nothing, of its breeding habits.

PORBEAGLE SHARK *Lamna nasus* (Bonnaterre)

This is frequently confused with the Mako Shark, but can be distinguished easily by its teeth, some of which always have a small cusp on either side of the base of the main narrow high triangular tooth. It is reported to be less gamey than either the Man-Eater or the Mako.

RANGE: Newfoundland to New Jersey and probably farther south. Iceland to northwestern Africa, and in the Mediterranean. San Diego, California to Alaska, Japan, Australia, and New Zealand. Usual in the Gulf of Maine in summer, but irregular in numbers.

COLOR: The usual gray or brownish gray above; lighter below; sometimes entirely gray or gray with bluish tinge.

SIZE: The fish usually taken weigh less than specimens of the Mako, although the lengths are similar.

FOOD: Fishes, especially schooling fish.

HABITS: Often sighted on the surface, but has also been taken on set lines near the bottom. It apparently ranges from the surface to the bottom, but is most often seen near the surface.

Very young Porbeagles are reported from northern New England in August, October, November, and January, and it is possible that the fish remain in restricted geographical ranges but go to deeper water in winter. The litter is small—from one to four.

MAN-EATER or WHITE SHARK

Carcharodon carcharias (Linnaeus)

RANGE: A warm water fish, widely distributed but not abundant anywhere. Most frequent in Australia. It has been recorded in various places between Nova Scotia and Brazil, and from Spain

Fish & Wildlife Service

Thresher Shark.

to the Cape of Good Hope. Because of the size of the Basking Shark, casual observers sometimes report Man-Eaters when they have really seen a Basking Shark.

COLOR: Larger specimens may be entirely dull whitish or beige, or they may be black above and dirty white below. Specimens up to 12 feet are generally brownish or grayish blue above, and whitish below.

DISTINGUISHING CHARACTERISTICS: The teeth.

SIZE: The fish may reach a length of 40 feet, and a 21-foot specimen weighing 7,100 pounds has been reported from Havana. The present rod and reel record weighed 2664 pounds and was taken off Senuda, South Australia. It measured 16 feet, 10 inches. A previous record disqualified on a technicality, taken off the Cape Province, South Africa, weighed 2176 pounds.

FOOD: Fishes, sea turtles, squid. The Man-Eater is a scavenger and is also known to have attacked human beings.

HABITS: The Man-Eater is infrequently and irregularly reported. It is said to have been hooked off Cuba at 700 fathoms, but is generally taken on the surface. Its breeding habits are not known.

This shark puts up a savage fight when hooked, but does not leap.

THRESHER SHARK

Alopias vulpinus (Bonnaterre)

RANGE: Northern Argentina to Nova Scotia, North Sea to Cape of Good Hope, Oregon to Chile, Hawaiian Islands, Japan to Australia and New Zealand, Red Sea, Natal. Most abundant off Great Britain, and, in America, off southern New England in summer; never in winter.

COLOR: Gray, gray-blue, or brown. Sometimes very dark above. White below. The lower part of the snout is sometimes very dark.

DISTINGUISHING CHARACTERISTICS: The Thresher Shark is easily distinguished by its exceedingly long upper tail lobe which comprises about one-half the total length of the fish.

SIZE: Specimens of 13 to 16 feet are fairly common. The fish is not mature much under 14 feet at which length a female was found to contain an embryo of 5 feet 1 inch. A Thresher Shark of 922 pounds was taken on rod and reel in New Zealand.

FOOD: Fishes and squid. The lash-like tail is used in rounding up schools of smaller fish.

HABITS: The female bears few young at a time, but these are quite large when born. Little is known about its breeding habits. Small ones have been taken off Florida and off New England.

This is an offshore fish, but may often be seen pursuing food inshore. Off England, where it is common, it is considered a nuisance by commercial fishermen in whose nets it gets entangled.

TIGER SHARK

Galeocerdo cuvier (Lesueur)

RANGE: Uruguay to Woods Hole; Canary Islands; Senegambia; South Africa on the western side; Iceland. Most common in the Caribbean and the tropics.

COLOR: Gray or brown above; lighter below. Sometimes marked with bars or broken bars, but these are more conspicuous in the young.

DISTINGUISHING CHARACTERISTICS: Its teeth are large in front and alike in both jaws. The outer margin is convex and the inner deeply notched.

Mrs. Zane Grey

A former world's record Tiger Shark. Weight 1036 pounds.

Fish & Wildlife Service

Hammerhead Shark.

The eggs are serrated. The snout is very short. The pointed upper lobe of the tail is much longer than the lower and notched near the tip.

SIZE: Averages less than 12 feet long. The present world rod and reel record weighed 1382 pounds and measured 13 feet, 10 inches. This was taken off Sydney Heads, Australia.

FOOD: Fishes, squid, turtles.

HABITS: The Tiger Shark runs both in and offshore and has been seen coming into extremely shallow water in pursuit of other fishes.

This fish has large litters and has been reported with as many as 50 embryos. Bigelow and Schroeder state that the young may be born at any time of year.

HAMMERHEAD SHARK

Sphyrna zygaena (Linnaeus)

The peculiar genus, *Sphyrna,* is widely distributed in tropical and warm temperate zones. There have probably been many mistakes in identifying the species, as there is more than one Hammerhead, and a related species, the Bonnethead, has also been mistaken for a Hammerhead.

RANGE: Massachusetts to Uruguay and reported to run off Argentina. England to South Africa. It, or similar fishes, are found in the Pacific from Point Conception, California, to Peru; off Japan, and in other localities in the Indo-Pacific. It is a migratory fish, fairly common in summer from Massachusetts to South Carolina. Many very small specimens of Hammerhead Shark have been taken off New York in August. After October, they are seldom found in the northern part of their range.

COLOR: Brown, gray, or greenish above; white below. Pectorals sometimes tipped with black.

DISTINGUISHING CHARACTERISTICS: The head is hammer shaped, with the eyes on each end of the hammer. The nostrils are long slits occupying the front edge of the hammer. The upper lobe of the tail is much longer than the lower and is notched near the tip. The caudal peduncle is not keeled.

SIZE: Averages 7 to 9 feet and runs to 17 feet and a weight of about 1500 pounds.

FOOD: Fishes and squid.

HABITS: A rapid, strong fish, often sighted by the tips of dorsal and caudal fins above the surface of the water. It occurs both in and offshore and sometimes schools. It moves north in the summer.

Females have been taken which contained from 29 to 37 embryos.

SAWFISH *Pristis*

There are about six species of sawfish, at least two of which do not occur in American waters. The most commonly caught are *Pristis pectinatus* Lathem, and a southern species, *Pristis perrotteti* Valenciennes. The chief difference between species is in the number of teeth on the saw; otherwise they are similar in appearance.

The Sawfish does not belong in the same group as Saw Shark *(Pristiophorus)* which is a shark,

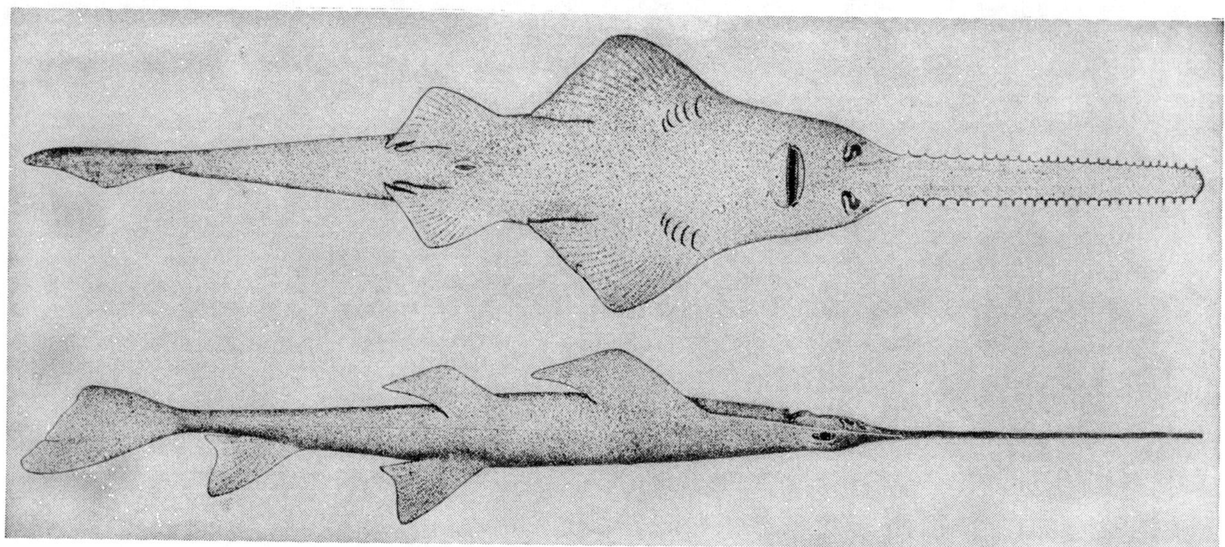

Fish & Wildlife Service

Sawfish—side and ventral views.

whereas the Sawfish properly belongs with the skates and rays. The Saw Shark has a prolonged snout with teeth on either side, but in addition has two long tentacles coming from the saw, which are not present in the Sawfish. The gill slits of the Saw Shark are on the side, whereas the gill slits on the Sawfish are on the under surface of the body.

RANGE: The Sawfish has a wide range, in some parts of which it is found almost entirely in tidal streams and rivers. It is a warm sea fish. It is found in the Philippine Islands; India; Thailand; Malaya; East Indies; Australia; tidal streams on the Pacific coast of Panama north to Mazatlán, Mexico, the Amazon and tributaries; Gulf of Mexico off Mexico, Texas and Florida; and up the Lower Mississippi River; West Indies; Cuba; Florida and straggling north to New Jersey; Mediterranean; Red Sea; West Africa south to the Cape of Good Hope; Natal; Mozambique; Madagascar; and Mauritius.

They are abundant in the Gulf of Mexico.

COLOR: Upper part of body brown or grayish-brown; lighter below.

DISTINGUISHING CHARACTERISTICS: The long, flat, heavy saw, running forward from the upper jaw and equipped on either side with peg like teeth. Nostrils, mouth, and gill slits on under side of body. Teeth in mouth paved.

SIZE: The present rod and reel record, caught off Fort Amador, Canal Zone, weighed 890 pounds, 8 ounces and was 16′ 1″ long. The fish is reported to reach a weight of over 1000 pounds.

FOOD: Chiefly marine animals living on or near the bottom.

HABITS: The Sawfish is not generally considered a game fish, but the International Game Fish Association has placed it on their record charts of rod and reel catches, and it occasionally puts up a hard fight.

This fish frequents warm water over sand or mud, some of the species ascending fresh-water streams for a considerable distance. It bears as many as fifteen living young at a time.

The flesh is reputed to be good eating.

Irvine, in "Fishes and Fisheries of the Gold Coast" writes that "in the Keta district, the 'saw' is removed and used for fetish purposes being specially coloured alternately with red, white and blue colors. It is then set up and worshipped." He adds that a saw bought in Accra, Gold Coast, was three feet, eleven inches long, thirteen inches wide at the base; and eight inches at the tip.

TARPON

Tarpon atlanticus (Cuvier & Valenciennes)

RANGE: The Tarpon is undoubtedly present in many waters which have not been fished. In the southern part of its range, it is present all year round.

Panama: The 1948 International Game Fish Association Yearbook reports that a number of Tarpon have been caught in the Gatun Lake, undoubtedly reaching it through the Canal from the Atlantic.

Atlantic: Mexico (Gulf Coast), Central America, Canal Zone. In the Gulf of Mexico off Mexico, Texas, Louisiana, Alabama, and Florida. Nova

N. Y. Zoological Society

Young Tarpon in New York Aquarium Tank.

J. F. Cicero

A 154-pound Tarpon caught on 9-thread line.

Scotia (two recorded some years ago) to Argentina, including the West Indies, Cuba, and the lesser Antilles. Senegambia, Gold Coast, Nigeria, and Cameroons.

Numerous in the famous Pánuco River, near Tampico, Mexico (February, to the rains of July or August and sometimes later), and other points along the Gulf coast. Former and present records were taken in the Pánuco River in March and April. Said to be numerous in the rivers of British Honduras in March, April, and May. In Costa Rica, thousands are reported at Laguna de Moin, a fresh-water lagoon about fourteen miles from Puerto Limon. They are especially numerous around Aransas Pass in Texas. Tarpon are abundant on the west coast of Florida from March to May, and in west coast rivers in June. They are also abundant off the Florida keys. On the Florida east coast they are present in June and in east coast rivers in May, but in far lesser numbers than on the west. In Cuba they are numerous in all the coastal rivers (March-April), especially in the well-known Rio Encantado which cuts the southern coast. In Brazil, they occur in numbers in almost every coastal river (November-January). In the lagoon, off Lagos, Nigeria, they are numerous from January to March.

COLOR: Heavy silver; irridescent and silvery on head. Often bluish on upper sides.

DISTINGUISHING CHARACTERISTICS: Very large, thick scales. Dorsal fin with last ray prolonged into a long filament. Narrow bony plate on throat between the branches of the lower jaw.

SIZE: The rod and reel record weighed 247 pounds. There is no favorite size for anglers, as both the young and adult of this fish are eagerly sought by them. Tarpon of over 100 pounds are not at all uncommon.

FOOD: Fishes, particularly mullet, crabs.

HABITS: This very popular game fish is characterized by its spectacular leaps while fighting—leaps which have been known to land it in the angler's boat. C. M. Breder, in his *Field Book of Marine Fishes,* says that the "produced last dorsal ray functions in the tremendous leaps . . . It is concave below and adheres to the side of the fish, bending and securing the dorsal to the right or left, so determining the direction of the fall." These leaps are often as high as 12 feet.

The Tarpon is usually found inshore, most frequently in inlets or rivers. Along the coast, the sizes run from 3 feet up. Under that size, the fish is most often found in small bodies of water in which, probably through heavy blows and subsequently receding water, it often becomes landlocked.

The fish is generally assumed to spawn somewhere around the Florida Gulf coast in summer,

Amer. Mus. Nat. History

Tarpon jumping, Broad River, Florida.

Dimoch—Amer. Mus. Nat. History

Tarpon jumping, Florida.

in blue water, and a 142-pound fish has been estimated to contain twelve million eggs. Other spawning areas have not been determined. The fish is mature when it reaches its sixth or seventh winter, at which time it is about four feet long. The earliest stages of its development, before it is recognizable because of external resemblance to its adult, are unknown. It is possible that the fish at this time is either offshore or deep in the water.

The Tarpon is a schooling fish which congregates in huge numbers in some parts of its range. There is a northward drift in spring, and a movement in and out of streams; otherwise no known migration.

Whether or not its soft pinkish flesh is good eating is a matter of individual opinion, although many anglers do not consider it valuable for food.

BONEFISH, TENPOUNDER, MILKFISH

Any range outlined for the Bonefish, Tenpounder, and Milkfish is subject to error, due to the constant confusion and misidentification of these fishes, and to the use of the same common names for at least two of the trio.

All these fishes are spindle-shaped, with a short, spineless dorsal fin situated approximately in the middle of the back. The Bonefish and Tenpounder have teeth on the jaws, back of tongue and roof of mouth while the Milkfish lacks teeth. The Bonefish has an elongate, bony plate beneath the throat between the branches of the lower jaw, and a peculiar, pig-like snout, overlapping the small mouth. The lower jaw of the Tenpounder is slightly longer than the upper and the mouth is large. The upper jaw of the Milkfish slightly overlaps the lower.

Another fish, *Dixonina,* for which there is no common name, is found in the West Indies, the Gulf of California, and Costa Rica. It is seldom if ever taken by anglers but because of danger of confusion with these fishes, it will be discussed.

These are all warm water fishes and may be found in the same waters.

BONEFISH *Albula vulpes* (Linnaeus)

RANGE: Warm and tropical seas of the world. West Indies, Cuba, Gulf of Mexico, straggling as far north as Cape Cod, Massachusetts. At least as far south as Panama, north to Monterey Bay, California; Hawaiian Islands to Tahiti, Malaya and the Dutch East Indies; Japan; Durban; Mauritius; Red Sea; West Africa.

Abundant off southern Florida, the Bahama Islands and the north coast of Cuba; apparently plentiful in Bermuda and the Hawaiian Islands. In all these places, the fish appears to be present all year.

Present and former record fish were taken off Hawaiian Islands, Durban, Florida, Bermuda, the Bahama Islands. Islamorada, Florida; Bimini, and the west coast of Andros Island are known concentration centers.

COLOR: Varies considerably; may be almost entirely gleaming silver, or silver with green or dark blue above; or a silver background almost covered by darker greenish with indications of dark stripes.

DISTINGUISHING CHARACTERISTICS: Pig-like snout overhanging the small mouth. Teeth. Short, stubby gill-rakers. Bony plate between branches of lower jaw on throat.

SIZE: Averages 2 to 5 pounds, reaches 20″. The rod and reel record, taken off Mana, Kauai, Hawaii, on October 14, 1954, weighed 18 pounds, 2 ounces. The previous record, taken off West Molokai, Hawaii, on November 30, 1948, weighed 16 pounds. Such large individuals are seldom taken, a statement verified by the fact that a record fish of 13¾ pounds, taken at Bimini, was not exceeded for twenty-nine years.

FOOD: Chiefly crabs, mollusks, sandfleas, worms. A bottom feeder.

HABITS: The Bonefish is most frequently encountered in very shallow water on the incoming tide, flooded mud flats, sand bars and inlets. Its purpose in coming into the shallows is primarily to feed. At other times it retreats into deep holes or channels. It is usually seen in small schools, but larger individuals may be solitary or in pairs.

One lot of Bonefish is believed to spawn off Bermuda in deep water. Other spawning areas have not been discovered. The larval fishes, flat, transparent, and ribbon-like, and much like the larvae of the eel, have been taken at night on the surface in the West Indies.

When hooked, the Bonefish is reputed to be about the fastest of all fish.

TENPOUNDER also called LADYFISH

Elops saurus Linnaeus and *Elops affinis* Regan

There are several species of *Elops,* some of which are not surely distinct. There appears to be a definite West African species, an American Atlantic coast species *(E. saurus),* and an Amer-

Al Johns, San Pedro

Bonefish.

Todd-Fish & Wildlife Service

Ten Pounder or Big-eyed Herring.

ican Pacific coast species *(E. affinis)*. Other forms have been named from West Africa, the Indian Ocean, Australia, and the Hawaiian Islands. The range here given includes all species, as for angling purposes, they are the same fish.

RANGE: Almost all warm seas of the world. West Indies and Gulf of Mexico north to Long Island, occurs in the Salton Sea and lower Colorado River, Gulf of California and north in the Pacific to southern California; Coast of West Africa; Cape of Good Hope; Natal, Red Sea; Japan; China; East Indies; Samoa; and Australia.

Abundant off Bimini and southern Florida and doubtless also in other localities where such abundance has not yet been noted. Seems to be most plentiful in the warmer months.

COLOR: Sometimes completely silvery; sometimes dark blue above, silver tinted with blue on the sides. Frequently shows a few widely scattered dark spots on the sides.

DISTINGUISHING CHARACTERISTICS: Lower jaw projects slightly beyond upper. No gular plate (on throat between branches of lower jaw). Ventral fins begin on a perpendicular line directly beneath the beginning of the dorsal fin.

SIZE: Averages 1 to 3 pounds; seldom over 10.

FOOD: Squid, crustaceans, fishes.

HABITS: The Tenpounder is a coastwise fish, often found in lagoons and estuaries. It moves in schools. In Bimini, large scattering schools of this fish come into one location just at sunset, preceded by Google-eyes on which they feed.

The spawning grounds are not known but the young are known to be transparent and ribbon like.

On the hook, the Tenpounder is very fast and makes spectacular six to eight foot leaps. It also frequently rushes the boat.

MILKFISH *Chanos chanos* (Forskål)

There are probably at least two species or geographical races of the Milkfish. Much less is known of this fish than of the Bonefish or Tenpounder, with both of which it is often confused.

RANGE: In outlining its range, it should be emphasized that some data is based on uncertain identifications. The fish has been authoritatively identified from San Francisco Bay to Panama; in the Hawaiian Islands, the western Pacific, and the Indian Ocean. It is reported from the Riu Kiu Islands, Formosa, Australia and New Zealand, Fiji Islands, Seychelles Islands, Mauritius, and off Arabia.

COLOR: Greyish green above; pale silvery below; the fins dusky on their tips.

DISTINGUISHING CHARACTERISTICS: No teeth. Very fine gill-rakers. Mouth normal.

SIZE: Reported to reach a length of 5 feet. Several of these fish weighing around 30 pounds have been taken off the Marianas Islands.

Dixonina *(No common name)*

This genus, of which there are both Atlantic and Pacific species, has been reported from the West Indies, the Gulf of California, Acapulco, Mexico and Costa Rica.

COLOR: Silvery, with dark greenish above, and traces of darker markings. There are two rows of dark spots on the young.

DISTINGUISHING CHARACTERISTICS: Last ray of both dorsal and anal fins is elongated. The mouth is underslung and looks much like that of a Bonefish. The jaws, roof of mouth and back of tongue are toothed.

FOOD: Crustaceans, fishes.

HABITS: On the Zaca Expedition, William Beebe collected several of these fish off Costa Rica on January 24th and reports them as numerous on mud or sand bottom in shallow water. One measuring about 14 inches to the base of the tail, proved to be a "full grown female with ovaries well developed and eggs almost ready for deposition." A careful estimate of the eggs in the ovaries put the number at 70,000.

THE MULLETS *Mugil*

There are many species of mullet in the warm and temperate waters of the world. They are much better known as food or bait than as game fish.

RANGE: World-wide in warm and temperate waters.

COLOR: The general color is silvery, darker on the back. In some species there are horizontal dark stripes running the length of the body along the scale rows.

DISTINGUISHING CHARACTERISTICS: Cylindrical body, broad back. Small mouth with very small teeth in the jaws and none on the roof of the mouth. No lateral line. The first dorsal fin consists of four slender spines connected by membrane and is separated from the second, soft-rayed dorsal. There are three spines in the anal fin in the adult; two in the very young.

SIZE: Varies with the species. (See following page.)

FOOD: Small organisms from the mud. Bottom feeders.

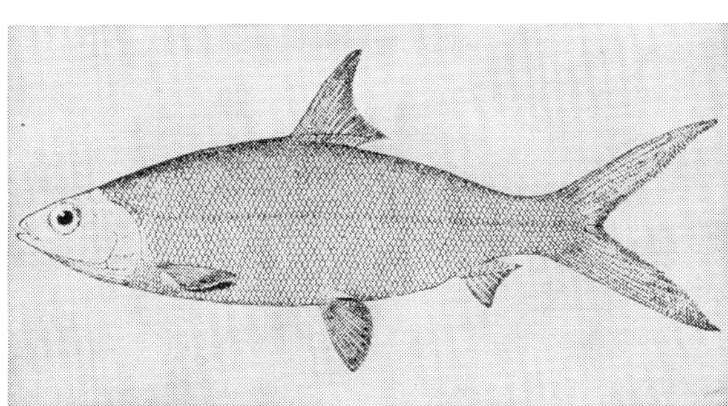

Fish & Wildlife Service

Milkfish.

HABITS: The Mullets are inshore, shallow-water fish, apparently present all year on their grounds. In the north, they go deeper in winter and often hibernate. Fishermen spearing for eels through the ice frequently catch mullet. The fish moves in huge schools and in some localities ascends fresh waters for considerable distances. The breeding grounds are not known, but the Striped Mullet appears to spawn in autumn or early winter and the White Mullet is breeding in May and June.

Some of the mullets when free swimming have been seen to leap out of the water to a height of several feet.

The three species taken by anglers in our waters are the Striped Mullet, the White Mullet, and probably the Brazilian Mullet.

They differ from each other in range and in external characteristics as follows:

STRIPED MULLET *Mugil cephalus* Linnaeus

RANGE: Atlantic: Maine (straggler) to Brazil. Not abundant north of New York. Pacific: Monterey, California; south to Chile. Also found around the Hawaiian Islands and in the Salton Sea. Not abundant north of Los Angeles County.

COLOR AND DISTINGUISHING CHARACTERISTICS: Silvery with dark horizontal stripes on the scale rows. No scales on soft dorsal and anal fins. The mouth cleft only slightly wider than deep. 37 to 41 scales in a lengthwise row from hind margin of gill cover to tail base.

SIZE: Reaches a length of about one foot in the northern part of its range although very frequently smaller; reaches 2 feet in the southern part of its range.

WHITE MULLET

Mugil curema Cuvier & Valenciennes

RANGE: Cape Cod to Brazil; plentiful in the southern part of its range. Gulf of California to Chile.

COLOR AND DISTINGUISHING CHARACTERISTICS: Soft rayed dorsal and anal fins closely scaled. No stripes

SIZE: Reaches a length of 3 feet.

BRAZILIAN MULLET *Mugil braziliensis* Agassiz

RANGE: Cuba to Argentina; probably straggling north to Florida. Common off Cuba and Puerto Rico.

COLOR AND DISTINGUISHING CHARACTERISTICS: Horizontal dark stripes. No scales on soft dorsal and anal fins. Cleft of mouth much wider than deep. 31 to 36 scales in a lengthwise row.

SIZE: Reaches a length of 18 inches.

THE BARRACUDAS

GREAT BARRACUDA

Sphyraena barracuda (Walbaum)

GUAGUANCHE

S. guachancho Cuvier & Valenciennes

NORTHERN BARRACUDA *S. borealis* DeKay

EUROPEAN BARRACUDA *S. sphyraena* (Linnaeus)

PACIFIC BARRACUDA *S. argentea* Girard

MEXICAN BARRACUDA *S. ensis* Jordan & Gilbert

This genus should not be confused with the Barracouta, *Thyrsites atun* (Euphrasen) of the Cape Province, South Africa, a fish of the mackerel group, or with one of the kingfishes sometimes called Barracuda or Kuda in East Africa.

Barracudas have a world-wide distribution in warm waters and consist of a number of species, all looking very much alike on casual inspection. Their most noticeable difference is that some forms are consistently smaller than others. This has sometimes led to reports of the presence of young fish, when in reality adults of one of the smaller species were observed.

The Barracudas of interest to North American anglers are listed above. They may be distinguished by the following characteristics. Such distinction is important because their ranges overlap.

Atlantic species: The Great Barracuda has from 75 to 85 scales in a row from the back of the gill cover to base of the tail. There is a fleshy tip on its lower jaw. The European Barracuda, possibly present on our North Atlantic coast, also has this fleshy flap, but the scales number about 150. The Guaguanche is a small fish with a maximum length of two feet. Its lower jaw has no fleshy tip. The scale count is about 120. The pectoral fins extend as far as the front of the dorsal fin.

Longley-Fish & Wildlife Service

One of the first under-water photographs ever taken of a Barracuda.

The Northern Barracuda has no fleshy tip on the lower jaw; the scale count is about 135, and the pectoral fins do not extend as far as the front of the dorsal.

Pacific species: The Pacific Barracuda usually has no bars or stripes. Its ventral fins begin some distance behind a perpendicular dropped from the tip of the pectoral.

The Mexican Barracuda shows more or less distinct dark bars, especially on the front half of its body. The ventral fins begin on a perpendicular dropped from the tip of the pectoral fins.

RANGE: Great Barracuda: Brazil to South Carolina, straggling north to Massachusetts in summer. Numerous off Florida, the West Indies, and in the Gulf of Mexico. It is present all year and is abundant. Most of the records and catches of large fish have been made between April and August off Florida and the northern Bahamas.

Guachancho: West Indies north to Florida and straggling to Massachusetts. Abundant in the tropics.

Northern Barracuda: Cape Fear to Cape Cod, much more abundant in the southern part of its range. Young and adults are present as far north as Massachusetts in summer and into the fall. The young are fairly common.

European Barracuda: Probably present on the north Atlantic coast.

Pacific Barracuda: Pudget Sound to Cape San Lucas, and in the Gulf of California. Plentiful from Point Conception to Cape San Lucas. The season of greatest abundance is March to October.

Mexican Barracuda: Gulf of California to Panama. Most plentiful October to March.

COLOR: The basic colors of all barracudas are silver, with a green or blue back. The tail fin is very dark; the other fins dusky, greenish, or yellowish. The fish is usually green or blue for a short distance down the side. The Pacific Barracuda is usually silvery with traces of lightish blue or green on the upper parts of the body, and without spots or bars. The Mexican Barracuda has a general bluish-green tone, with more or less distinct dark bars crossing the sides. The Great Barracuda is a bright silver, with green or blue for a short distance below the ridge of the back, and with a few rather large black spots, usually below the lateral line, on the sides. The Northern Barracuda is also marked with dark blotches, more common in the young than in the adult. The Guaguanche usually has dark spots both on the upper part of its sides and on the spinous dorsal fin.

There is great variation in color, depending somewhat on the nature of the bottom and the proximity of the fish to it.

DISTINGUISHING CHARACTERISTICS: The barracudas are all pike-like in build, with strong, unequal, very large and sharp teeth in their long pointed jaws. They have no gill rakers. The two short dorsal fins are widely separated. The characteristics distinguishing one species from the other have been stated above.

SIZE: The Great Barracuda reaches a length of 10 feet, but is seldom over 5 feet. Its average weight is between five and ten pounds but it grows to over one hundred. The Northern Barracuda seldom exceeds 1 foot in length. The Guaguanche reaches a length of 2 feet. The Mexican Barracuda is said to reach a weight of 75 pounds, but its average weight is between 3 and 4 pounds; the Pacific Barracuda is large at 10 pounds but has been known to weigh 16. A Barracuda weighing 103¼ pounds was taken at Bimini, B.W.I., in August, 1932. This fish was less than six feet long; others over sixty pounds have been taken on rod and reel off Bimini and Florida.

FOOD: Fishes, squid.

HABITS: The barracuda has been studied more intensively in the Pacific than in the Atlantic. It is said to spawn off Tortugas in the Spring, and young in considerable numbers are present in the north in summer and fall. Dr. Walford showed that the Pacific Barracuda may spawn more than once in a season. The number of mature eggs produced for one spawning of the Pacific Barracuda were carefully estimated at from 51,000 to 484,000, the number depending on the size of the fish. The 51,000 figure was taken from a two-year-old fish about 19½ inches long, in which the ovary weighed 28 grams; the 484,000 estimate was for a six-year-old fish, about 4 feet long, in which the ovary from which the eggs were taken weighed 340 grams. The spawning season is known to be from May to September, with the height of activity in May, June and July. The Pacific Barracuda appears in Spring off the California coast in schools, and stays until winter, at which time it moves into deeper water. The greatest numbers are usually taken about three miles off shore fishing at a depth of about one fathom, but they have been taken down as far as five fathoms.

Barracudas are found wherever there is an abundance of food. This is usually around reefs; schools of the younger and smaller fishes frequent the shallower reefs and inland bays, and the older fish forage alone in deeper water.

The Barracuda has been known to attain an age of eleven years.

Much very real damage to bathers has been done by this swift, voracious, and well-armed fish, and many well acquainted with it feel that the potential danger it offers cannot be exaggerated. On the hook the larger Atlantic barracuda fights savagely, leaping and making long runs. The Pacific forms are not such fighters.

All barracudas are edible.

THE MACKEREL AND TUNA GROUP

The mackerel group is distinguished by the presence of small, detached finlets behind the dorsal and anal fins.

These fish are streamlined, pelagic inhabitants of temperate and tropical oceans; rapid swimmers and good fighters. Some of the most famous sport and food fishes of the world are found in this family, notably, the mackerels, albacores, tunas, bonitos, king mackerels, and the wahoo, and all their innumerable geographical varieties.

KEY TO IDENTIFICATION OF THE MACKEREL AND TUNA GROUP

No median keel on the caudal peduncle. Teeth on the vomer (roof of mouth).

Body fully scaled.

Air Bladder present.

Chub Mackerel. *Scomber colias*
Pacific Mackerel. *Scomber japonicus*

No air bladder.

Common Mackerel. *Scomber scombrus*

Median keel and a smaller keel on either side of it on caudal peduncle.

Body only partially scaled.

Teeth on vomer

A long space between the two dorsal fins

Frigate Mackerel. *Auxis thazard*

No teeth on the vomer

The two dorsal fins almost touching

Four stripes below the lateral line which is sharply curved downward.

Oceanic Bonito. *Euthynnus pelamis*

No stripes below the lateral line which is not sharply decurved.

False Albacore. *Euthynnus alletteratus*

Body entirely scaled

Teeth on the vomer

Jaw teeth slender

Pectorals short

Eyes small, vent round, dorsal and anal lobes not produced in adult, finlets predominantly yellow.

Bluefin Tuna. *Thunnus thynnus*

Eyes large, vent oval, dorsal and anal lobes produced in adult, finlets not predominantly yellow.

Atlantic Big-eyed Tuna. *Thunnus obesus*

Pectorals long

Eyes small, vent oval, dorsal and anal lobes greatly produced in adult, finlets bright yellow, black edged.

Yellowfin Tuna. *Thunnus albacares*

Eyes large, vent oval, dorsal and anal lobes not produced in adult, finlets yellow.

Pacific Big-eyed Tuna. *Thunnus mebachi*

Eyes large, vent oval, dorsal and anal lobes not produced in adult, finlets brown or gray.

Blackfin Tuna. *Thunnus atlanticus*

Eyes large, vent round, dorsal and anal lobes not produced in adult, finlets yellow.

Long-finned Albacore. *Thunnus alalunga*

Jaw teeth strong

Lateral line not abruptly curved downward; fins not closely scaled; beginning of soft dorsal in front of that of the anal; body usually has spots.

Spanish Mackerel. *Scomberomorus maculatus*

Lateral line abruptly curved downward; fins closely scaled; beginning of soft dorsal directly over that of the anal; body usually without spots.

Painted Mackerel. *Scomberomorus regalis*
Kingfish or Cero. *Scomberomorus cavalla*

No teeth on the vomer

Mouth very large; conspicuous horizontal black stripes above the lateral line.

Striped Bonito. *Sarda velox*

Mouth not very large; inconspicuous oblique stripes; end of upper jaw bone reaching beyond the hind margin of the eye.

Atlantic Bonito. *Sarda sarda*

Mouth not very large. Oblique stripes which cross the lateral line; end of upper jaw bone not reaching beyond the eye.

Pacific Bonito. *Sarda chiliensis*

Dorsal fin long, low, even in height. Jaws extended forward into a short beak.

Wahoo. *Acanthocybium solandri*

There is some uncertainty in the classification of these fishes, chiefly because they range so widely and are still insufficiently known in some stages of growth. For example, much time and effort has been spent on tuna, especially to determine whether or not the Atlantic and Pacific Bluefin Tuna are the same or distinct forms, and whether or not the Yellowfin Tuna and the Allison Tuna are different. As with the speared fishes, a large number of specimens of both adult and young and of both sexes are needed to insure correct answers to such problems.

Much confusion in distribution data is also caused by the practice of frequently lumping all forms of tuna in any locality under the one word "tuna."

Due to the commercial fisheries, more Pacific material is available than from the Atlantic. Before the war, the Japanese carried on large tuna fishing operations and used all marketable fish of this group. They fished from their own coast, over the Mandated Territory, around Borneo, and the Philippines, off Australia and into the Indian Ocean. The American center for commercial tuna fishing extends from southern California south far into South American waters. W. McC. Chapman, who has made an extensive survey of the Pacific tuna fisheries, states that the vessels go far offshore, sometimes for from six to seven hundred miles.

Fish & Wildlife Service

Spanish Mackerel.

Most of the young collected in this group have been secured at night, by means of lights.

Distributions outlined must remain rather general in this group as its members are so widely distributed in the open ocean.

Anglers will find the key on the opposite page the easiest method of identification for members of this group.

COMMON MACKEREL

Scomber scombrus Linnaeus

Range: Labrador to Hatteras; Norway to the Gold Coast. Everywhere abundant.

Color: Upper part of body silvery-blue or green-blue with dark, wavy marks regularly arranged and just crossing the lateral line. Sides below the lateral line silvery and without dark marks. Fins dusky or brownish grey.

Distinguishing characteristics: Lack of marks below the lateral line. Two small, but no median, keels on the caudal peduncle. Fully scaled body. Teeth on roof of mouth. No air bladder.

Size: Average weight about one pound, but individuals run several pounds larger.

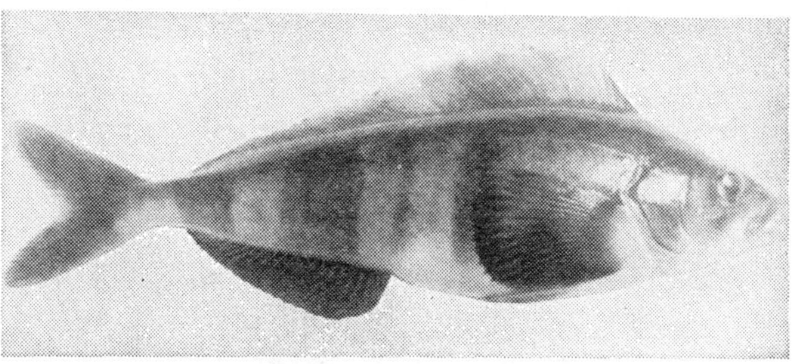

Fish & Wildlife Service

Atka Mackerel.

Food: Fishes, crustaceans.

Habits: The Mackerels, travelling in huge schools, move inshore in spring and offshore and into deeper water in the fall. They spawn from May to July. This fish is off Hatteras in March and April and off New England in May. It is a very important commercial fish and the basis of large fisheries, but a minor game fish.

CHUB MACKEREL

Scomber colias Gmelin

The Chub Mackerel, which ranges from Virginia to the Gulf of St. Lawrence, is often mixed with schools of the Common Mackerel and is somewhat similarly marked. The dark markings, however, are finer and less regular, and some dark marks often occur below the lateral line. The fish has an air bladder. The Chub Mackerel takes the hook, but is of minor interest as a game fish.

PACIFIC MACKEREL

Scomber japonicus (Houttuyn)

This fish ranges from Alaska to Cape San Lucas, Lower California, and is abundant along the coast of southern California from July to November. It is extensively fished commercially, and although a good sport fish, it is not the object of competitive fishing and is much better known as a food than as a game fish.

It has ten oblique dark bars on the upper sides and occasionally there are spots on the lower sides. The body is fully scaled and the air bladder present. It is known to spawn in open bays, and its growth rate is also known: a four-year-old fish measures about 15 inches. The fish, like other mackerels, eats fish, squid, shrimp, copepods, etc., and, according to Walford, is also a scavenger.

Sierra Mackerel.

FRIGATE MACKEREL *Auxis thazard* (Lacépède)

RANGE: Cape Cod to Puerto Rico and probably farther south; Madeira to the Gold Coast and south to the Cape; Mediterranean; San Pedro, California to Costa Rica and probably farther south; Japan; New Guinea, Australia; Oceania; Cape to Natal.

COLOR: Blue or blue-green above, silvery below. Usually, but not always, has oblique dark stripes from the lateral line to the ridge of the back.

DISTINGUISHING CHARACTERISTICS: Median keel and small one on each side on caudal peduncle. Body only scaled around the lateral line and on an anterior "corselet" in the pectoral region. These scales are somewhat larger than the others. Teeth on the roof of the mouth. A long space between the two dorsal fins.

SIZE: A small fish; seldom over five pounds; said to reach 10.

FOOD: As of other mackerels.

HABITS: This pelagic, tropical and temperate water fish is erratic in its appearance. When and where is does appear, it runs in large schools.

Juveniles, taken with dip nets and night lights, have been found off Costa Rica, northern Panama, and in the Mediterranean.

OCEANIC BONITO

Euthynnus pelamis (Linnaeus)

RANGE: Abundant in the trade wind belts. Cape Cod to the Leeward Islands; Madeira to Senegambia; The Channel Islands (California); Hawaiian Islands; Japan; Philippine Islands; Australia; South Africa; Kenya; Chapman reported it plentiful on Midway in September and October, and Canton Island in late October. He also saw schools of young off the New Hebrides and the Solomons in late October.

The Oceanic Bonito occurs most frequently in the southern part of its range.

COLOR: Body blue-green above; silvery below. Four lengthwise stripes on the body *below* the lateral line.

DISTINGUISHING CHARACTERISTICS: The stripes below the lateral line; lateral line curving sharply downward below the second dorsal fin; almost no space between the two dorsals; the median and the two smaller lateral keels present on caudal peduncle. The fish is only scaled along the lateral line and on the corselet around the pectoral region. There are no teeth on the roof of the mouth.

SIZE: Usually not over 20 pounds. The present rod and reel world record, caught off Walker Cay, Bahamas, weighed 39 pounds, 15 ounces.

FOOD: Fishes, squid, flying fish where available. Feeds mainly on the surface.

HABITS: Usually found offshore in large schools. Very plentiful and the object of a large sampan fishing fleet (before the war) in the Hawaiian Islands. In Hawaiian waters, the Oceanic Bonito comes close inshore in the summer months.

FALSE ALBACORE

Euthynnus alletteratus (Rafinesque)

BLACK SKIPJACK *Euthynnus lineatus* Kishinouye

SKIPJACK (western Pacific)

Euthynnus yaito Kishinouye

Confusion occurs in reports of the presence of these fish because in many cases the species has been undetermined. There appear to be at least three distinct species, looking very much alike, and, for angling purposes, the same fish in different geographical ranges.

RANGE: The False Albacore occurs from Cape Cod, south at least to the Leeward Islands and also off Texas. In the eastern Atlantic, it has been found in the Mediterranean, and from St. Helena to Senegal. It is reported by J. L. B. Smith as off the east coast of Africa, from East London north to Delagoa Bay. The Black Skipjack's distribution is given by Walford as "off the west coast of Lower California as far north as Cape San Lázaro, at Los Frailes, along both coasts of the Gulf of California, and off the coasts of Mexico and Central America to Cocos Island." In Hawaii it is common in the markets, particularly in summer when it is running inshore.

Euthynnus yaito is found around the Hawaiian Islands, and from Formosa south to the Dutch East Indies, in the Philippine Islands, and around Australia and the mandated islands.

Longley reports young of the False Albacore, up to 5¾ inches, quite common off Tortugas. Ripe and running fish and juveniles of the Black Skipjack have been observed off Costa Rica. Hiatt and Brock (1948) report an interesting observation made while on the Bikini Scientific Resurvey in

False Albacore.

the northern Marshall Islands in the summer of 1947: "three medium sized black skipjack *(Euthynnus yaito)* herding a closely packed school of several hundred scads over a large coral head in Rongerik lagoon . . . the three tuna usually followed the school of scads rather closely with one tuna at each rear flank of the school and the third lagging behind them." These authors continue that the skipjack "made no attempt to prey upon the scads during our period of observation . . . the food habits of thirty-three black skipjack caught outside of the lagoons failed to show any scads in the diet of this species." They add that Scads were most frequently encountered in the stomachs of the Dog-tooth Tuna *(Gymnosarda nuda,* a fish outside our range).

COLOR: The three species do not differ materially in appearance. There are dark wavy bands on the upper and back part of the sides, beginning below the middle of the dorsal fin. The lower part of the sides is usually plain silver with a few dark spots below the pectoral fin. The Black Skipjack is said to show dark stripes on the lower sides, but this marking disappears very shortly after the fish is removed from water.

DISTINGUISHING CHARACTERISTICS: The color pattern. Median and side keels present on the caudal peduncle. The body is only scaled along the lateral line and on the pectoral corselet. No teeth on the roof of the mouth. The lateral line does not curve abruptly downward. The two dorsal fins almost touch.

SIZE: Averages about 10-15 pounds, but grows slightly larger.

FOOD: Fishes.

HABITS: Travels in large schools. Dr. Herre reports that *E. yaito* in the Philippine Islands is a "hard fighter caught in tide rips and boiling surf around rocky isles."

BLUEFIN TUNA *Thunnus thynnus* (Linnaeus)

Also known as *Thunnus secundodorsalis* (Storer) by authors who distinguish eastern from western Atlantic Bluefin Tuna.

There is some evidence that the North American east coast and west coast Bluefin Tuna, and the European Tuna (Tunny) are one species, but not all authorities are agreed on this point. Some experienced western anglers insist that the Bluefins of the east and west coasts are different. This opinion is based on the fact that the flesh of the Pacific coast fish tends to be gray instead of red, and that the behavior of the two fishes when hooked is entirely different.

It should be noted that the expression "school tuna," used in most parts of the world to indicate Bluefin Tuna weighing less than 60 pounds, is used in North Carolina in reference to the genus *Euthynnus.*

RANGE: Labrador to Bimini, Cuba (?), and probably farther south; Norway to the Cape of Good Hope; Mediterranean and Black Seas; Hokkaido, Japan to Australia; California north to Oregon.

Amer. Mus. Nat. History

Photo of an exhibit of Blue Fin Tuna in American Museum.

Concentrations in our area are: Bimini-Cat Cay (a migratory way station, May 15 to June 15). New Jersey-Long Island (August to September is the height of commercial and sports season). Off the southern New Jersey coast, school tuna are close inshore in the latter part of June and farther off the shore to the north. Gulf of Maine (July-September). The tuna arrive off Maine at the end of June. The tournaments begin in August. Before the tuna left Wedgeport, the Cup Matches, which were international, were held there every September. None has been held since 1958. Off California the run seems to be very irregular from year to year, with the height in good years in June, July and August. Fishing centers off Europe, are Scarborough and Whitby, England, and the Hälsingborg area, Sweden, where there is both commercial and sports fishing. There is a commercial Tuna fishery off the coast of Brittany, but little sports fishing has been done there, as is also true off Italy and the west African coast.

COLOR: This varies considerably, but it is usually dark greenish-blue on the upper part of the sides, growing lighter toward the center, below that the body is silvery shading into white on the belly. Fins dark; finlets yellow or yellowish. Sometimes there is a broad yellowish band running down the body from the back of the gill cover to near the tail.

DISTINGUISHING CHARACTERISTICS: A bulky body; middle and side keels on the caudal stem; body covered with small scales which are slightly larger around the lateral line and on the anterior corselet; teeth on roof of mouth. The pectoral fin is shorter than the head; no dark marks on the body; soft dorsal and anal fins are short.

SIZE: The average varies with locality from 60 to over 200 pounds. In some northern localities, such as Nova Scotia, Tuna are caught fairly frequently weighing over 800 pounds. The record rod and reel fish was taken in St. Ann Bay, Nova Scotia, and weighed 977 pounds. The fish is said to reach 1600 pounds.

FOOD: Fishes, squid, crustaceans.

HABITS: This fish and its relatives are the objects of enormous commercial fisheries wherever it runs regularly and in sufficient quantity to warrent such undertakings. The livers are sold for their oil content. The Tuna is caught by various commercial methods varying from stationary nets to flag lines, and harpoons.

Mrs. B. D. Crowninshield, Gov. Bur. of Info., Halifax, N.S.

Woman's all-tackle world-record Tuna weighing 882 pounds. Taken off Wedgeport, Nova Scotia, September 1, 1947 by Mrs. Anne Crowninshield.

Big boats like this lapstrake Barbour runabout need big motors. The 75-h.p. Evinrude provides adequate speed for safety and will throttle down for slow trolling.

This is a migratory fish, although its migrations may be exaggerated. Its populations could consist of localized units, rather than the same group of fish migrating between widely distant points.

Knowledge of Tuna migration routes and spawning grounds is still fragmentary. Small specimens have been taken on the New Jersey and Long Island coasts (weighing just over a pound). Scale readings have determined the approximate growth rate, and we know the developmental stage of the fish at certain sizes. By the second summer, Bluefin Tuna are about 20 to 24 inches long; all of both sexes in the five year group (42 to 46 inches long) were adults in the Long Island tuna fishery survey which was conducted in 1941. (See Westmen and Neville, 1942). The investigators came to the conclusion that the Atlantic Bluefin spawns in winter or early spring but spawning grounds were not located.

In certain spots, such as Bimini-Cat Cay, the appearance of the Tuna on migration is very regular; in the Mediterranean, off Sicily, and on the northwest African coast, commercial fishermen can count on its appearance and set their nets accordingly.

A world-wide study of the Tuna has been made by the Commission Internationale pour L'Exploration Scientifique de la Mer, which has published authoritative articles on its findings.

BLACK-FINNED TUNA

Thunnus atlanticus (Lesson)

An Atlantic fish running from Brazil to Cape Cod, and plentiful off Cuba and southern Florida. The distinguishing characterists are mainly osteological, and therefore the fish is sometimes diffcult for anglers to identify. The body is blue-black above and silvery gray below. The dorsal surface of the pectoral fin is black, bordered with bright blue. There are light vertical bars and rows of light spots on the lower sides. The finlets are dusky with faint traces of yellow.

(For osteological characteristcs, see deSylva, Donald P. Bull. Marine Science, Gulf and Caribbean, 1955, vol. 5, no. 1)

ALLISON TUNA *Thunnus albacares* (Bonnaterre) and

YELLOWFIN TUNA

Neothunnus macropterus (Temminck & Schlegel)

Most ichthyologists think that these two famous sports fish are the same fish, and the tendency is to call it the Yellowfin Tuna. Apparently there is a wide margin of individual variation in the length of the fins, a characteristic which was previously considered sufficient to distinguish between the two fish.

Further studies on the tunas are needed to secure more definite information on this subject and also to determine whether or not the North American, Hawaiian, Japanese, and Peruvian fishes are the same or are geographical races of one fish.

RANGE: Maryland to Miami, Bermuda, Cuba and the Barbados; Hawaiian Islands; California, Mexico, Costa Rica, Peru, Japan, and the Philippine Islands; New Guinea, and Borneo to Australia. Reported by Chapman as plentiful off the mandated islands, but none present off Canton Island when the observers were there in October, November or September, or in the New Hebrides or Solomons when they were there in December, and again in April to July. The fish is known to be very abundant off Ascension Island, and is plentiful off the Hawaiian Islands and southern California.

COLOR: Dark blue on back and upper sides; sometimes a golden band from back of the eye to the tail region. Lower part of sides silvery. Fins yellowish or dusky; finlets yellow margined with black.

DISTINGUISHING CHARACTERISTICS: Median and side keels present; body completely scaled; teeth on roof of mouth; dorsal fins very close together, no dark lengthwise stripes; pectoral fins may be as long as the head or longer.

SIZE: The rod and reel record fish, taken off Hawaii, June 22, 1959, weighed 266 pounds, 8 ounces, but the species is said to average between 150 and 200 pounds.

FOOD: Fishes, squid.

HABITS: In the Hawaiian Islands, this fish is called "ahi", meaning ball of fire, and the name is said to be very descriptive of its sudden, hard, sustained runs when it is hooked. It appears to be plentiful in many localities, but particularly off Hawaii (August and September). It moves in schools and either off or in shore, in tropical and temperate regions but is rare north of 35° N. Latitude.

The Yellowfin Tuna is reported by Schaefer and Mar (1948) as ready to spawn somewhere in the vicinity of Costa Rica in the early spring months. Otherwise, very little is yet known of its life history. It is the object of extensive commercial fishing by California fleets between southern California and the Equator.

Mrs. Zane Grey

Allison Tuna caught by the late Captain Laurie Mitchell.

ALBACORE or LONG-FINNED ALBACORE

Thunnus Alalunga (Bonnaterre)

RANGE: Kirkneys to Cape of Good Hope; Mediterranean. Not common on our coast north of Florida; reported as far north on the Pacific side as British Columbia; substantiated from Puget Sound to California and south to Chile; Hawaiian Islands; Philippine Islands; East Indies; Cape Town to Lourenço Marques.

COLOR: Dark on the upper part of the sides, shading into an intense blue, a broad yellow area in center of side from behind the gill cover to the tail; lower sides and belly silvery or whitish; fins bluish or dusky.

DISTINGUISHING CHARCTERISTICS: Body covered with small scales; median and the smaller lateral keels present on the caudal peduncle; pectorals usually very long, reaching past the anal fin; smaller than many of the other tunas.

SIZE: The rod and reel record is 69 pounds, a fish taken off St. Helena in 1956. The average size is from 15 to 30 pounds. All the other records, both men's and women's, were made off Catalina, California.

FOOD: Fishes, shrimp, squid, crustacea.

HABITS: The fish feeds on or near the surface. It is apparently migratory, but is very irregular in its appearances both as to seasons and localities. It schools offshore near the surface and is more common in warm months.

STRIPED BONITO *Sarda velox* Meek & Hildebrand

The fish is not very well known, and its range is very incompletely known. It is reported off Block Island, Rhode Island, and has been found in Lower California, Panama Bay, the Galapagos Islands and northern Peru. It is dark blue above, silvery below, with horizontal black stripes on the upper part of the sides. The fins are dusky. The horizontal stripes distinguish it from related species in which the stripes are oblique. Otherwise, it is characterized by having the median and the two side keels on the caudal peduncle, a wholly scaled body, no teeth on the roof of the mouth, a wavy lateral line and a very large mouth.

It is recorded as weighing as much as 7 pounds, but averages less.

Its food is like that of other bonitos.

ALTANTIC BONITO *Sarda sarda* (Bloch)

RANGE: Maine to Rio de Janeiro and probably farther south; Gulf of Mexico off Texas; Norway to the English Channel; Madeira to the Cape; Mediterranean.

COLOR: Back gray-blue; sides silvery; narrow dark stripes run obliquely from slightly below the lateral line back to the base of the dorsal fin and the finlets; fins dusky.

DISTINGUISHING CHARACTERISTICS: Median and side keels present; body completely scaled; twenty-one dorsal spines; No teeth on roof of mouth; Mouth not unusually large, but with conspicuous large teeth on the front of the lower jaw.

SIZE: Averages well under 15 pounds, which seems to be near the maximum weight.

FOOD: Fishes, squid.

HABITS: An open sea fish which comes inshore occasionally to feed. In summer there are large schools from Cape Cod to Cape Hatteras.

PACIFIC BONITO

Sarda chilensis (Cuvier & Valenciennes)

CALIFORNIA BONITO *Sarda lineolata* (Girard)

The distinction between these fish is not definitely established and probably they are the same. The fish has been taken from Oregon to Mexico. It is abundant from Santa Barbara to Magdalena Bay and spawns during Spring and Summer. If the same as *chilensis,* it is also present off Peru and Chile. It is caught all year, but is most abundant in summer.

SPANISH MACKEREL

Scomberomorus maculatus (Mitchill)

SIERRA MACKEREL

Scomberomorus sierra Jordan & Starks

These two are almost certainly the same species.

RANGE: Maine to Brazil; Gulf of Mexico; West coast of Africa from Cape Blanco to the Gaboon; Southern California to northern Peru. Not listed for South Africa where one would expect to find it.

Abundant in the Gulf of Mexico, and north to North Carolina. Reported to be uncommon in Bermuda, and rare or unknown in Cuba.

COLOR: Dark brown above, shading into grayish silver along the middle of the sides; silvery below. There are irregular rows of bronze spots in some individuals, but these are not present in many of the smaller specimens, and they vary in number with size and age. The spinous dorsal is black; the ventrals greyish and the other fins dusky.

DISTINGUISHING CHARACTERISTICS: 'Median and side keels present; body wholly scaled; teeth on the roof of the mouth; lateral line not abruptly curved downward; fins not closely scaled as are those of the Painted Mackerel. The easiest recognizable characteristic is that the soft dorsal fin of this fish begins well ahead of the anal fin.

SIZE: Reaches 20 pounds, but usually nearer 2.

FOOD: Feeds at the surface on fishes and squid.

HABITS: This is an important food fish in some localities. In the Gulf of Mexico and along the coasts of the Carolinas, where it is very abundant, it runs in large schools, spawning offshore in spring and summer. Each female deposits about 20,000 eggs. The fish is in the northern part of its range in summer and fall.

CERO

Scomberomorus regalis (Bloch)

RANGE: Cape Cod to Brazil; Gulf of Mexico: Fairly abundant around the Florida keys; and abundant off Cuba.

COLOR: Much like that of the Spanish Mackerel —silvery, with darker spots, and sometimes a narrow dark stripe from the region of the pectoral fin to near the tail.

DISTINGUISHING CHARACTERISTICS: The most outstanding difference between this fish and the Spanish Mackerel is that in this fish the soft dorsal fin begins directly above the anal.

SIZE: Said to reach 20 pounds, but usually much smaller.

FOOD: Fishes.

KINGFISH

Scomberomorus cavalla (Cuvier & Valenciennes)

RANGE: Cape Cod to Brazil; Gulf of Mexico; very abundant off Florida and South Carolina, where it appears from November to April.

COLOR: Bright greenish blue on the upper part of the body, silvery below. The young show spots below the lateral line, but the adult has none.

DISTINGUISHING CHARACTERISTICS: Lack of spots in the adult (however, this is not entirely reliable); Median and side keels on caudal peduncle; teeth on the roof of the mouth; lateral line abruptly down-curved; soft dorsal beginning at anal fin.

SIZE: Averages from 10 to 50 pounds. The rod and reel record is an 81 pound fish taken off Karachi, Pakistan in 1960. The previous record was held by a fish weighing 76 pounds, 8 ounces, caught off Bimini, B.W.I., May 22, 1952. All other records except the previous record were taken off Miami Beach. The fish has been recorded up to 100 pounds in weight.

FOOD: Fishes, shrimp, squid.

HABITS: A strong fish, putting up a hard fight when hooked. It is said to school at spawning

From: "North American Game Fishes" by Francesca LaMonte. Copyright 1945 by Francesca LaMonte, reprinted by permission of Doubleday & Co.

Wahoo.

time. Frequents offshore reefs, seldom going into shallow water and moving farther out in winter. It frequently feeds near the surface but may also be deep down. Spawning is reported off Puerto Rico in late winter.

This fish is taken in large numbers for the market.

WAHOO

Acanthocybium solandri (Cuvier & Valenciennes)

RANGE: North Carolina to the West Indies; Gulf of Mexico off Texas; Sicily; Lower California to Cocos Island; Hawaiian Islands; Japan; Philippine Islands; Oceania; off Africa it is recorded (although very rare) from Delagoa Bay and Durban.

The fish appears to be solitary and infrequent in most places from which is has been reported. However, it is fairly common off Panama; reported as present all year, with the height of the season from April to November, and schooling off Bermuda; also plentiful and schooling in the vicinity of Midway Island in September and October. A number of records have been taken in the northern Bahamas in late March and early April, and off Miami in December and in May.

COLOR: This varies from pale silvery and greenish to the more usual color of dark greenish on the upper body, shading into paler and then into silver. The fins are dark. Occasionally gray or yellowish vertical bars run across the body almost to the belly. These are more distinct in the young and in a fighting or struggling fish.

DISTINGUISHING CHARACTERISTICS: Long cigar-shaped body; Median and side keels on the caudal peduncle; teeth on the roof of the mouth; dorsal fin long, low and even in height throughout its length, with from 24 to 26 spines; the teeth large, and irregular; snout is drawn out into a beak.

SIZE: The fish averages 15 to 20 pounds, but often runs much larger. The present rod and reel record, taken off Marathon, Florida, on May 18, 1960, weighed 139 pounds.

FOOD: Fishes.

HABITS: This is a swift, strong fish of tropical and subtropical waters. It is usually found in clear open water or around reefs, generally in the upper levels of the water. It is reported to leap out of water like the marlin when not on the hook.

THE SPEARED FISHES

(Marlin, Sailfish, Spearfish, Swordfish)

The speared fishes have a world-wide distribution, but the exact concentration and distribution points are by no means all established, due to lack of facilities for the capture of these very large fishes which appear both quite close inshore and many miles offshore where they are not often spotted by either commercial or sports fishermen.

These fishes all have a similar body form, grow to a large size and have the spear or sword which extends from their upper jaw. Many are often found together on the same grounds, for example Blue Marlin, White Marlin, and Swordfish; Silver, Striped and Black Marlins and Sailfish; Spearfish, Striped, Silver and Pacific Blue Marlins. There are probably other combinations.

The chief external differences are that Marlin, Sailfish, and Spearfish have pelvic fins and two keels on the caudal peduncle (tail stem), long, thorn-shaped scales and cylindrical spears; whereas the Swordfish has no pelvics, the adult is scaleless, there is only one keel on the caudal peduncle, and the sword is heavy and flat beneath.

These fishes are said to use their spears to kill smaller fishes for food. There are also well authenticated cases of both Swordfish and Marlin piercing the oak planking of boats with their spears. The International Game Fish Association's 1948 Yearbook reported an interesting item from Cuba, supplied by Mr. Emilio de Mesa of Havana. He wrote that "during the war, near the port of Nuevitas, a German submarine sank a boat load of crude rubber. Bundles of the stuff were picked up by fishermen and sold to dealers for repairing automobile tires. In a number of bundles of this extremely hard material marlin spears were found. The spears had penetrated into the hard rubber from three to five inches; the fish had then been unable to extricate itself, and finally the spear had broken off. One bundle contained three such spears."

Speared fishes have been reported from many sections of the globe, but it has not always been possible to determine which species was represented. Marlin have been seen leaping above the surface in various waters, but, while it was possible to distinguish them as marlin, the species could not be determined.

Fish & Wildlife Service

Releasing a Tagged Marlin.

The Spearfish, *Tetrapturus,* of which there are at least two species, is not plentiful anywhere. United States ichthyologists have only recently secured specimens for study, but these are now available in various sizes and from both the Atlantic and Pacific. Considerable mystery surrounds this fish of two oceans.

The Sailfish is widely distributed and easily recognizable because of its huge sail-like dorsal fin. It cannot be confused with any other fish but there is some difference of opinion regarding the number of species.

The migration routes of Swordfish, Sailfish, Marlin, and Spearfish are only partially known. The breeding habits of Swordfish, their eggs and larval stages up to the thirteenth day of extra-embryonic life have been scientifically and thoroughly studied by Professors Sanzo and Sella of Messina. The Sicilian and southern Italian run has a convenient habit of swimming into the stationary tuna nets when coming inshore to spawn.

The early stages—(two to four feet) of Swordfish are known from various localities; and a few small Marlin have been secured as well as a number of larval and young Sailfish.

It is obvious, however, that knowledge of runs of these fishes is scanty. Furthermore, nothing is known of the migrations, life habits, or growth stages of the Spearfish, and very little of those of the Marlins.

One method of acquiring some of this missing information is tagging. The only difficulty is that eggs, young and larval stages are not secured by this method. To collect such specimens, equipment unsuited to anglers' launches must be used, and this requires more time and expense than is generally available for such a purpose. The best hope of collecting such stages, is in general collections made by oceanographic vessels working on other problems. Naturally this would be a slow process. Tagging, however, could yield valuable migration data. Tagging experiments on the west coast of Mexico, where Sailfish are very abundant, have been in progress for three years, but there has not been one return. Experiments of the same kind have also been initiated at Palm Beach, Florida, but no returns have been received. Various attempts made off the United States, Mexico, and Australia to tag marlin and Swordfish, have produced no results. There is little possibility that the tags now used can dissolve or loosen and it is more probable that the fish do not survive even the small amount of handling necessary to tag them.

THE MARLINS *Makaira*

Both common and scientific names for the marlins are confusing to anyone not working with these fishes constantly. This is primarily due to the fact that specific distinctions are as yet uncertain. The names are tentative until sufficient material upon which to base definite scientific conclusions becomes available. The task of collecting data on the marlin grounds is very slow and almost entirely dependent on anglers' catches. Without sufficient data many of these problems cannot be solved.

The Blue and the White Marlins are the only Atlantic forms. The Black, Striped and Pacific Blue are found in the Pacific, as is also a Marlin called Silver Marlin, which is possibly a subspecies or an albino form of the Black.

Anglers should realize that it is not always easy or possible to make an immediate identification of the species of Pacific marlins. In fact it is easy, in certain stages, to confuse Silver, Black, Pacific Blue and Striped. Some experienced anglers in Pacific waters are almost always correct in their identifications, but without experience and without careful scientific examination it is unsafe to announce the species of a marlin too quickly.

It is not possible to mistake a marlin for any other fish if one is close enough to see it clearly. At a distance, it might possibly be mistaken for a Swordfish. In the Pacific, where sailfish run very large, it could be mistaken for a sailfish with folded sail, although the sailfish body is much more slender than that of any Pacific marlin.

All marlins have both pectoral and pelvic fins. The pectorals are normal looking fins which lie behind the gill cover on the sides of the body. The pelvics lie almost on the ventral ridge and consist of two flat, dark blades which vary considerably in length. They are often wholly or partially broken, and are sometimes folded close to the body and hard to see at a distance.

The marlins have two definite keels on the stem of the tail, cylindrical spears which vary in length according to the species, and long, thorn-like scales rather unevenly arranged on the body.

Marlin, questionably identified as to species, have been reported off the Gold Coast (Africa), Guam, Brazil, Fiji Islands, and Colombia.

WHITE MARLIN *Makaira albida* (Poey)

One who has seen this slender fish with its long narrow spear, is not apt to confuse it with the only other Atlantic marlin, the Blue.

RANGE: The original White Marlin was described from Cuba. It is found from the British West Indies and Cuba, north along the Atlantic coast to Brown's Banks off Nova Scotia.

Its presence is reported but unconfirmed off Texas, the Windward Islands, and various other parts of the world.

Most numerous: Cuba (April-June, straggling to September), Bimini (February-May, straggling into July), Florida (December-June), Ocean City, Maryland (June-September).

COLOR: This marlin is consistently more vividly colored than others. Its most usual phase is bright blue-green on upper body and sides; silvery on lower sides and belly. From the back, running vertically across the body and ending slightly below the middle of the sides, there are usually light, lavender-grey bands. The dorsal fin is vivid blue with dark spots, the pelvics black, and the other fins dark greyish-green.

DISTINGUISHING CHARACTERISTICS: The fish is small and delicate in build. Its body is not as bulky or deep as that of the other marlins, and its spear is more slender and runs to a finer point. The dorsal fin lobe is less sharply pointed and less sickle-shaped than that of the Blue Marlin.

SIZE: The record rod and reel White Marlin weighed 161 pounds and the women's record weighed 152 pounds, but the fish seldom reaches one hundred pounds and averages between that and fifty.

FOOD: The White Marlin's diet consists of other fishes and squid.

HABITS: This fish occurs in congregations more frequently than other marlins which are inclined to be solitary, but it is also found singly. White Marlin are sometimes taken within a mile of shore, and usually not more than twenty-five miles offshore.

The smallest recorded specimen recognizable as a White Marlin was caught off Bimini, B.W.I. in 1941. It weighed 4¼ pounds. Another, weighing about 6¾ pounds was taken off Cat Cay. Other juvenile specimens reported were one of 5 pounds and one of 10¾ pounds. From the data available it is not possible to definitely identify these individuals as either White or Blue Marlin. All of these specimens had the very long dorsal fin characteristic of the young of speared fishes. Al Pflueger, of Miami, who has seen hundreds of marlin, writes that by the time the fish weighs 20 pounds it is like the adult form.

Ernest Hemingway, whose belief that the Blue Marlin were breeding near the north coast of Cuba was later confirmed, believes that the White Marlin also breed there. He says they head inshore in pairs in May and that females are ripe at that time. White Marlin have also been reported heading inshore in pairs (typical spawning behavior) off Montauk, Long Island.

BLACK MARLIN *Makaira nigricans* Lacépède

The original "Black" Marlin was called in French Makaira Noirâtre (blackish), and was named from a crudely sketched drawing, with a few dimensions jotted at its side, of a specimen washed ashore at La Rochelle, France. This, according to present knowledge, would probably have been a Blue Marlin, but the sketch is not accurate enough to permit a definite decision. However, according to the rules of zoological nomenclature, this scientific name must be retained. It is unfortunate that the fish now known in the Pacific as the Black Marlin was not given some other popular name, and equally unfortunate that the Blue Marlin is often called the Cuban Black Marlin.

As far as anglers are concerned, it would be wise to ignore the fish to which this original name was given.

PACIFIC BLACK MARLIN

Makaira nigricans marlina (Jordan & Hill)

RANGE: Its presence has been authenticated in Australia, New Zealand, Tahiti, Peru, Canal Zone, and the west coast of Mexico.

Reported: Ecuador and Chile. Although this species continues to be reported off Chile, the "Black Marlin" brought into Tocopilla for study in 1940 were all Striped Marlin.

Most numerous: Australia (December to April, especially off Bermagui); New Zealand (December to March, straggling into June, especially off

Mrs. Eastham Guild

Black Marlin weighing 823 pounds, the women's former all-tackle rod and reel record. The present women's record weighed 1,525 pounds.

Whangaroa, the Cavalli Islands, Bay of Islands, and near Tauranga); Canal Zone (Panama Bay, June to October); west coast of Mexico (Guaymas, April to June; Acapulco, most plentiful January to March).

COLOR: This fish varies from entirely dark to dark on the back, head, upper sides and fins, with dirty silver or whitish below. Occasionally there are traces of lighter vertical bars which are more apt to be noticeable when the fish is fighting, gaffed, or dying.

DISTINGUISHING CHARACTERISTICS: The Black Marlin is easily recognizable by its rigid pectoral fins, great bulk at the shoulder and its comparatively short spear. This thickness at the shoulder is greater in proportion to the body length than that of its close relative, the Silver Marlin.

SIZE: This is a heavy marlin. The famous Boydtown Ben, a Black Marlin stranded near Eden, New South Wales, in April, 1938, weighed 1226 pounds, and a Black Marlin caught on rod and reel in the Canal Zone by Louis Schmidt, Jr. weighed 1006 pounds. The fact that Mr. Schmidt, who had lost his left arm and leg, finally had to have help in landing this fish, prevented it being accepted as a record. The present recognized record, however, is a 1560 pound fish caught off Cabo Blanco, Peru, in 1953.

FOOD: Fishes, squid.

Eastham Guild

Marlin from which the Silver Marlin was named.

HABITS: Both males and females were present in a small number examined off New Zealand. The females were adult and sexually inactive. Australians suspect a breeding ground for either Black or Striped Marlin, or both, off their east coast. A small marlin weighing 4 lbs., 5½ ounces was taken off Mooloolabah, Australia, on January 13, 1944 and identified there as a Black. Further information is lacking. No exact information is available about their movements but they are caught both inshore and offshore.

SILVER MARLIN

Makaira nigricans tahitiensis Nichols & LaMonte

RANGE: Tahiti, Hawaiian Islands, west coast of Mexico. Specimens taken off the Hawaiian Islands have only been checked by photographs and angler's measurements. The Tahitian specimen was named from measurements of photographs, a method no longer used by ichthyologists. Specimens of Silver Marlin have been taken in Acapulco, Mexico.

No information regarding abundance is available as only a small number of this fish have been taken. Tahiti has little sports fishing, and off Acapulco most anglers are seeking Sailfish with light tackle unsuited to taking these heavy fish. The record fish weighed 911 pounds and was taken off Kuna, Hawaii; the specimen from which the Silver Marlin was named weighed 504 pounds. A fish taken off Acapulco and weighing 465 pounds would be the women's rod and reel record had it not been harpooned instead of properly gaffed.

This fish is heavy through the shoulder, but the body is longer in comparison with the girth at the shoulder than is that of the Black Marlin. The scales are reported to be frequently bifid. The color varies slightly from dark on the upper part of the sides and silvery below, to an entirely light colored fish, which seems to be the more usual color phase. The head and fins are darker than the body. Very few specimens of the Silver Marlin have been taken and a general belief is developing that this is a case of albinism in the Black Marlin; not a subspecies of that fish. It has also been found that several specimens previously identified as Silver Marlins were, in all probability, Pacific Blues.

Both males and adult sexually inactive females were present off Acapulco.

All the Silver Marlin examined had been feeding on smaller fishes.

STRIPED MARLIN

Makaira audax (Philippi)

RANGE: California, west coast of Mexico, Japan, Philippine Islands, Australia, New Zealand, Hawaiian Islands, Canal Zone, Ecuador, Peru, Chile (south to Calderá).

Most numerous: New Zealand (December to March), Australia (January to April), Chile (February to October, most abundant March to June); vicinity of Cape San Lucas, Lower California to Guaymas, Mexico (March to October).

COLOR: The color varies considerably. In some New Zealand specimens the stripes are so prominent as to be zebra-like. Other individuals are not infrequently a general darkish tone, or dark above and whitish or silvery below, with about fourteen light blue or lavendar stripes all, or part way, across the sides. All the fins are dark except the dorsal which is deep blue. In fighting or in leaping or in death, the colors become intensified, the upper sides showing dark greenish-blue tones, the lower becoming bright silver with the stripes very prominent.

DISTINGUISHING CHARACTERISTICS: This fish is much more slender for its length than the Black and the Silver, and has a longer and more slender spear.

SIZE: The record rod and reel Striped Marlin, weighing 692 pounds, was taken off Balboa, California. However, the fish is known to grow much larger. The Striped Marlin taken by Zane Grey off Tahiti weighed 1040 pounds even after the sharks had torn off much of the flesh thereby preventing it from becoming a record. These, however, are extraordinary sizes and the majority of individuals taken are between 250 and 350 pounds.

Off Acapulco, a small marlin known as the Aguja de Paladar is popularly thought to differ from either Black, Silver, or Striped. The specimens seen appeared to be small Striped Marlin, of sufficient size to have lost juvenile characteristics. They had taken on fully the appearance of an adult fish.

All the Striped Marlin taken by the American Museum of Natural History expedition off Talara, Peru, and Tocopilla, Chile, were found to be sexually inactive females. No small specimens were taken. Nothing is known about their breeding habits; no ripe females, small stages, larvae or eggs have been found.

The Striped Marlin is caught both inshore and offshore. They often congregate in numbers without forming schools and are also often solitary. Kip Farrington mentions very large concentrations, amounting to schools, in the Cape San Lucas-Guaymas run.

BLUE MARLINS

ATLANTIC: *Makaira ampla* (Poey)
PACIFIC: *Makaira ampla subsp.* (as yet unnamed)

RANGE: Atlantic: Cuba, Bimini-Cat Cay, Florida, Cape Hatteras, Long Island, Block Island, Georges Bank. Pacific: Mexico, Japan, Hawaiian Islands, and without doubt many other Pacific areas.

Most numerous: Cuba (April to October); Bimini-Cat Cay (January to July).

It is only recently that the Pacific form has been distinguished, but there are known concentrations off Japan, and off Hawaii.

COLOR: The color varies, but usually the top of the body and upper sides are dark blue and the rest of the body bright silver. Narrow light blue bands run from the ridge of the back, part or all the way down the sides. The color of these bands varies in intensity in individual fish and becomes almost invisible in some. The dorsal fin is vivid dark blue; pelvics black; other fins purplish black. All the colors are greatly intensified when the fish is hooked and become particularly vivid when it is dying, at which time large powder blue patches appear, particularly below and behind the pectorals.

Amer. Mus. Expedition photograph
Three Striped Marlin taken by Michael Lerner.

DISTINGUISHING CHARACTERISTICS: This fish is larger and heavier and has a stouter spear than the other Atlantic form, the White Marlin. Its body is about five times as long as it is deep, whereas that of the White is more than six.

FOOD: Fishes.

SIZE: The average Blue Marlin taken weighs between 200 and 300 pounds. The present record is 780½ pounds which was made off Puerto Rico.

HABITS: Blue Marlin are reported, as the range shows, from many points on the Atlantic coast. The major concentration area lies between the north coast of Cuba and the western edge of the Great Bahama Bank. Off Cuba, they are taken commercially as well as by anglers from a quarter of a mile to four miles offshore.

Off Cuba, females taken in August and September have been found to be in condition to spawn within two days. No free eggs or identified larvae of Blue Marlins have been taken, but juveniles are known of the Atlantic form. Up to a few years ago, it was generally believed that Blue Marlin existed only in the Atlantic, although several anglers insisted that they had seen Blues in Mexico and other Pacific spots. Examination of specimens not fitting into other Pacific categories, showed another marlin, closely related to the Atlantic Blue, but showing certain consistent scale and body-measurement differences. This would appear to be a Pacific Blue Marlin, a subspecies of the Atlantic Blue, but as

Amer. Mus. Nat. History

Blue Marlin group in Fish Hall, Bahamas.

yet its scientific name has not been determined. It is particularly abundant off Kona, Hawaii.

Although it is known that spawning grounds must be near Cuba, there is a complete lack of knowledge of the egg, larval, and small growth stages of this fish.

SPEARFISH *Tetrapturus*

There is little definite information regarding this fish due partly to the small number of specimens reported, and also to misidentifications and the ease with which it is confused with other speared fishes.

The specimen from which the original description, *Tetrapturus belone* Rafinesque, was made, was taken off Sicily. Since that time this fish, under numerous specific names, has been reported from the waters of Europe, Asia, Africa, and North America. Some of the descriptions are obviously of marlins. However, there have been well authenticated occurences off Florida, France (Brittany), Formosa, and Japan. The Brittany specimens were taken off Finistère in the open ocean.

The fish is blue or greenish-blue on the upper sides, silvery below. Its most easily recognizable characteristic is the long, dorsal fin which is of approximately the same height throughout its length. The fish has pelvic fins, scales, and two keels on the caudal peduncle. Little is known of its habits.

SWORDFISH
BROADBILL SWORDFISH
BROADBILL

Xiphias gladius Linnaeus

There is only one species of Swordfish. It is world wide in range and without doubt is present in many localities from which it has not as yet been reported. It is at home in a variety of depths and temperatures.

Authenticated reports of occurrence: Iceland (one reported—July); Baltic Sea; Atlantic coast of Scandinavia; Firth of Forth (one washed ashore). British Isles; France; Spain (both Atlantic and Mediterranean coasts of France and Spain); Portugal; Gibraltar—particularly in the Straits; Italy; Sicily; north Africa (Mediterranean); Sea of Marmora; Bosphorus; Black Sea; Sea of Azov; from Gibraltar down West African coast in the Cape Spartel-Casablanca region; Canary Islands; Mauretania and Rio de Oro; Senegal; up coast of South and East Africa to vicinity of Durban; Madagascar; east of Madagascar near Réunion Island; Ceylon; Japan; Philippine Islands; Australia; New Zealand; the island of Rapa; Hawaiian Islands; California north to Santa Cruz Island; Mexico; Peru; Chile south to Calderá; Rochedos de São Paulo; Canaries drift between Puerto Rico and French West Africa; Cuba; Florida; New York; Connecticut; Rhode Island; Massachusetts;

IGFA

Young 95 mm. Swordfish.

Amer. Mus. Nat. History

Skeleton of Swordfish.

Georges Bank; Cape Breton, Nova Scotia; Newfoundland.

The fish is reported from other places but the reports are unconfirmed.

CONCENTRATIONS, BOTH ANGLING AND COMMERCIAL:

Straits of Gibraltar, between Algeciras and Tarifa, Spain, and Ceuta and Tangier: Commercial fishing at night with hooks set on a heavy main line. It is reported that most of the fish are dead when picked up. The Algeciras fleet fish during April and May and resumes fishing from September to December. The average weight is low because many of the fish are young (small). They run up to 500 pounds, however, and an 800 pound fish is reported. It is also reported that the commercial tackle is not adequate to handle large fish.

In 1947, Mr. Max R. Borrell from whom this information comes, tried his luck angling in the Straits, but when south of Tarifa had to turn back. This is obviously a place for very experienced anglers with well equipped boats.

Northwest Atlantic coast of Africa in the Cape Spartel-Casablanca area: No angling is reported from here. The fish run into the two mile long nets set for tuna and are taken in some quantity. This inshore run appears to be breeding behavior, and it would not be surprising to find spawning grounds in this general region.

Southern Italy and Sicily, concentrating in the Straits of Messina: Swordfish are spawning here and all stages from egg to adult have been taken. They are present from April to December. Eggs are found from June to September; young fish from ½ to 5 kilograms from October to December. Adults are present in all months except January and February. The fish, ready to spawn, swim inshore in pairs or threes. It is at this time that they get into the stationary tuna nets where eggs and young stages have been collected and studied.

This is a long established commercial fishery and while some sports angling has been considered, there are as yet no facilities.

Bosphorus-Black Sea area: The fish are in the Sea of Marmora from March to May gradually passing through the Bosphorus to the Black Sea. In August they are back in the Bosphorus and go into Marmora again from that time to January. There is a commercial fishery in the Bosphorus both for adult and the smaller fish from 10 pounds up. This is largely carried on at night and fish are taken from the surface down to 100 fathoms. Swordfish are also fished by sportsmen in the Bosphorus and in Marmora.

Cuba: Swordfish are taken off the north coast of Cuba almost all year. They are also reported off the south coast. Off the north coast, in the general vicinity of Cojimar, specimens from 4 inches to large adults are found. In August and September females have been examined which contained eggs

Amer. Mus. Expedition photograph

Michael Lerner, the late Capt. W. D. Hatch, and two Swordfish taken off Tocopilla, Chile.

Fish & Wildlife Service

Swordfish.

ready to be deposited within a few hours, showing that spawning grounds are near this locality.

There is much sports fishing off Cuba and also a commercial fishery. They are taken from the surface to 90 fathoms and fishing is particularly good at night. No free eggs or larval fishes have been found here.

Montauk-Block Island-Georges Bank: Both adult males and females are present. The great majority of those examined were adult, inactive females (Long Island); those from Block Island to Georges Bank were all adult inactive females.

Commercially they are taken from the surface to 125 fathoms, by deep trawls, and by harpoon. They range from 20 to 100 miles offshore, from June to September, the season beginning later as one goes north. One 4-foot, 3-inch specimen was picked up by commercial fishermen 80 miles due East of Newport, and one ripe female was found off Massachusetts. The Montauk-Block Island region is one of the spots most favored by Swordfish anglers.

Cape Breton Island, Nova Scotia: Up to a few years ago the historic town of Louisburg was a center for angling and for a large commercial fleet. This fleet made large catches there despite the uneven weather, but because of this and the short season, the number of fish caught by the comparatively few anglers able to sit out the bad weather was low. Suddenly a few years ago, the fish shifted location and deserted the Louisburg grounds.

Japan: Off Japan, the Swordfish runs in quantities sufficient to have supported a good export business. The fish are both large and small.

New Zealand: There are sufficient numbers off New Zealand for a commercial fishery, but it is also a favorite angling locality. The concentration does not seem to be as large as in some other areas and all fish reported are adults.

Peru-Chile: Both commercial and sports fishing exist in Peruvian waters which are one of the finest grounds. The season extends from January to June. From June to December, high winds make fishing uncomfortable. Residents of Cabo Blanco, near Talara, say that the fish are present all year and are sometimes within four miles of shore. In late April, 1940, they were about 80 miles offshore, feeding where the warm current, El Niño, met the Humboldt and food was plentiful. The fish are large, weighing 300 to 400 pounds.

Off Chile, Swordfish run in large quantity as far south as the general region of Calderá. Commercial fishing is small. The best known angling grounds are off Tocopilla and Iquique, the fish averaging over 300 pounds with larger individuals occurring frequently. The specimens examined were all inactive females and no small ones were found.

In this region, the swordfish run both close inshore and offshore. The season is yearlong off this desert coast of Chile, and the run is quite irregular. The best season is March to October, with the months of May and June perhaps the best. The quantity of fish both off here and the Peruvain coast can only be estimated because of the small size of the commercial fisheries and because angling is also not concentrated. The former world's rod and reel record of 860 pounds was taken by one of Tocopilla's pioneer anglers, Mr. W. E. S. Tuker, off Tocopilla. The present world record, weighing 1,182 pounds, was taken off Iquique, Chile, in 1953.

California: The season is May to October, but the fish are often present in small numbers as late as December. There is both commercial and sports angling. No small stages or young have been recorded.

Hawaiian Islands: Adults, and small fish from 6 to 8 pounds are caught commercially on lines set from 6 to 30 fathoms. The season is August to November, and good angling is available.

COLOR: The Swordfish is dark above and about three-quarters of the distance down the sides. This color is usually a dull bronze, sometimes with a silvery underlay. The lower parts of the sides are sometimes the same color, but usually whitish or slightly silvery getting lighter on the belly. The head, fins and sword are dark. The half grown fish resembles the adult in color but larval fishes are very different in color as well as in appearance.

DISTINGUISHING CHARACTERISTICS: The Swordfish has no pelvic fins and no scales (in the adult). The sword is heavy and flat underneath. With this weapon it has been known to ram and pierce the heavy oak planking of a boat. There is a single keel on the caudal peduncle. The dorsal lobe is short and high.

FOOD: Other fishes, squid.

SIZE: The record rod and reel catch weighed 1,182 pounds, but the fish undoubtedly runs heavier. The average size is between 250-350 pounds.

HABITS: The Swordfish runs both inshore and offshore. It has been taken one hundred miles offshore and without any doubt also can be found farther out. The Atlantic fish are not, as seems to be a prevalent opinion, one group of fish that cross the ocean, but consist of different population units.

From all observers and from examination of stomach contents, it is obvious that the fish usually feeds fairly deep, but it is also to be seen at or very near the surface, especially in sunny weather. It is taken both by day and at night, and is a very profitable commercial species. The flesh is white and firm in the adult, less so in the young. Occasionally a pink-fleshed specimen is taken. The liver is sold for its oil content.

When hooked, or harpooned, the Swordfish makes powerful, swift runs, and is also in the habit of suddenly sounding deeply. It can stand more variation in temperature than many ocean fishes.

When the spawning season arrives, the Swordfish head inshore in pairs or threes, otherwise they are solitary fish. Its life cycle is the best known of the speared fishes, as in the Straits of Messina the fish swim into the large stationary Tuna nets where eggs and larvae have been collected and studied.

The egg is minute. Larval Swordfish are whitish with orange and black markings. In larval fish of less than an inch, both jaws are extended and equipped with widely spaced and sharp teeth; the body is covered with glassy, spike-like scales. At a slightly later stage, the jaws are still longer and toothed, the back fin is very long and is higher toward the tail than in front. At a length of about 3¾ inches, the jaws still have teeth and scales are still present on the body. They persist until the fish reaches a length of over 4 feet. The dorsal fin gradually becomes even in height, and then increasingly high in front, and shorter. In a four-foot specimen, the skin has overlapping, triangular scales, each armed with small transparent spines.

As stated, Swordfish spawn off southern Italy and Sicily, particularly in the Straits of Messina, and somewhere near the coast of Cuba.

Single specimens of larval and very young Swordfish have been found in the following places: A series measuring from 10 millimeters to 46 millimeters was collected many years ago and described by Lütken. These were collected in the open Atlantic south of Rochedos de São Paulo; east of Puerto Rico in the Equatorial Current; between Puerto Rico and French West Africa in the Canaries Drift; east of Madagascar near Réunion Island, and about 150 miles south of Cape Hatteras in the Gulf Stream.

Other single specimens were found in "the south Atlantic" (12½ mm.); Port Sewall, Florida (¾"); Gulf Stream off Florida (41 mm. and 87 mm.); Rochedos de São Paulo (6 inches); It must be remembered that small larvae could

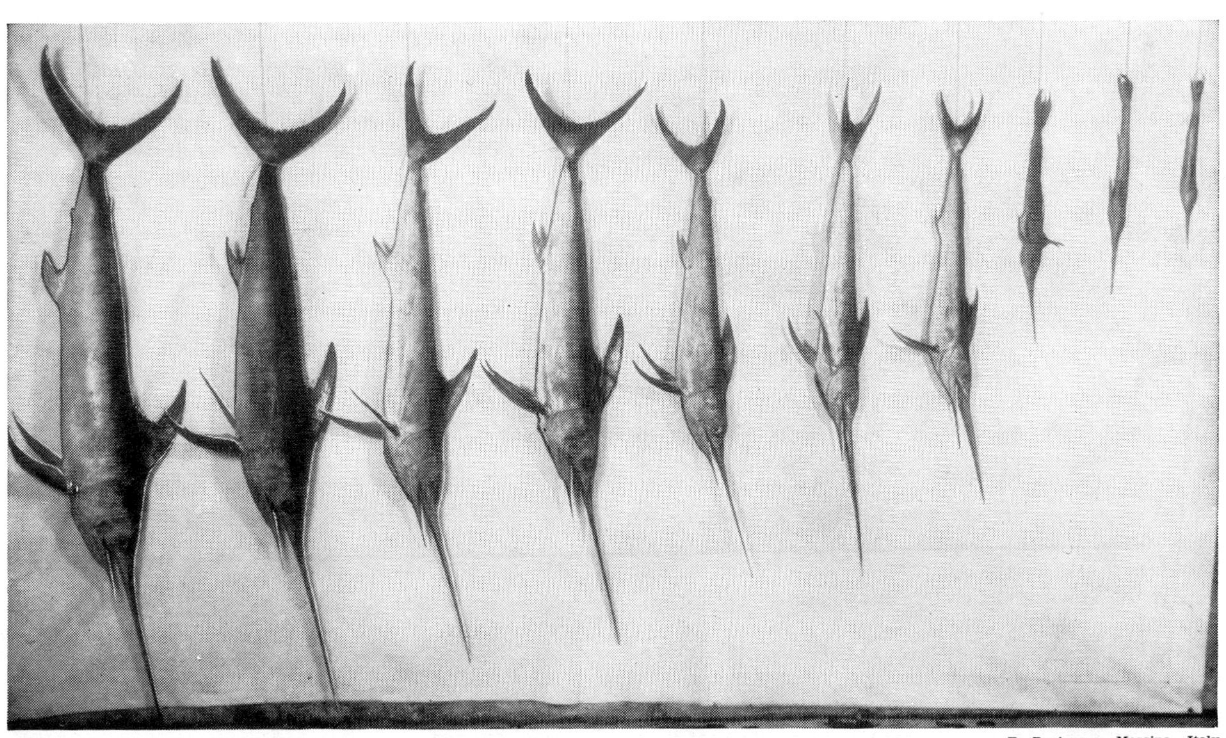

F. Benincasa, Messina, Italy

Growth series of the Swordfish.

Amer. Mus. Nat. History

Pacific Sailfish Group in American Museum of Natural History, New York.

easily drift long distances. Some have stuck to the leader of fishing tackle.

SAILFISH *Istiophorus*

Numerous species of Sailfish have been described and possibly there are sufficient differences to justify geographical races. However, for practical angling purposes it is enough to recognize two species, the Atlantic Sailfish, *Istiophorus americanus* (Cuvier & Valenciennes), and the Pacific Sailfish, *Istiophorus greyi* Jordan & Hill.

The chief difference seems to be in the size of the adult. The Pacific form reaches twice the size of the Atlantic.

Both fish appear to be present all or nearly all year wherever they occur in numbers, and are probably not as migratory as other speared fishes. They are normally a fish of warm seas, though individuals occasionally straggle north of the usual range. They are an outstanding light-tackle favorite and one of the most spectacular of existing game fish.

RANGE: Sailfish very probably occur in all warm seas.

Well authenticated occurrences are: *Atlantic:* Sicily, Senegambia, Gold Coast, Venezuela, Brazil, Tobago (rare), Puerto Rico (a rod and reel catch was made in December 1948 only six miles off San Juan), the Bahamas, British Honduras (March to May over the reefs), Texas, Alabama, Atlantic coast of Florida, North Carolina, Maryland (July and August especially), New York to Rhode Island (stragglers). *Pacific:* South Africa (the Cape; rare), Tanganyika, Mombassa, Natal, Red Sea, Ceylon, Japan, Philippine Islands, Cocos Island (Keeling), Australia, Guam and vicinity, Fiji Islands, Hawaiian Islands, California, Mexico, Panama, Costa Rica, Colombia, Galapagos Islands, Ecuador.

Most numerous: Florida, from Jacksonville to Key West and to the Bahamas from January to May, especially off Palm Beach where, in January to April, they run close inshore due to the proximity of the Gulf Stream to the coast. North Carolina, where they are reported as far north as Hatteras; Southport, N. C. from June to October, is rapidly becoming well known as an angling center. Bimini to Cat Cay, B. W. I., November to April. Texas (Gulf of Mexico), with centers at Port Isabel, and from Galveston to Freeport. The season is May to November and the fish run fairly close inshore over the reefs. Gold Coast, Africa, where Sailfish are reported to run in quantity from 12 to 14 miles offshore and to run to one hundred pounds and over, which is distinctly large for the Atlantic Sailfish. Gulf of Panama, April to December, with the best months July and August. The Perlas Islands are a center and Colonel Leon Mandel who has studied this fish reports that they are plentiful in the channel between the islands of Coiba and Jacarón. Mexico: present all year from Acapulco north. The Guaymas run starts in May and June and the fish are largest in October. Off Acapulco they run very large in February, March and April. Hawaiian Islands: here they are numerous and running fairly close to shore but appear only in small sizes from present reports. Philippine Islands: abundant, but no angling reported although it is probable that the fish has been taken there on rod and reel for many years. Sports fishing has long been practiced in these islands and a well organized Game Fishing Association has existed in Manila for at least ten years. Tanganyika: Sailfish are said to be plentiful, but rarely caught by anglers. A fine individual of 101½ pounds was caught there in March, 1943. Costa Rica: reports plenty of Sailfish that are caught for fun, though not on rod and reel due chiefly to difficulty in securing tackle.

COLOR: The upper part of the body is bright, darkish blue; the remainder very bright silver. Occasionally there are rows of large light spots from the back about half way down the body. The dorsal fin varies from cobalt blue to purplish blue and is sometimes deep purple. This fin is often more or less ornamented with dark spots. The tail fin may be either dark blue or black; other fins are dusky or dark; the head is dark and the spear very dark. There is a bronzed color phase but the colors described are more normal.

DISTINGUISHING CHARACTERISTICS: The most outstanding characteristic is the sail-like, high, vividly colored dorsal fin, which can be folded down into a groove on the back. The body and the spear are slender. As in other speared fishes, the spear extends far beyond the tip of the delicate lower jaw. The scales of the adult are long and thorn like. Pelvic fins are present and the caudal peduncle has two keels.

SIZE: The Atlantic adults are smaller than those of the Pacific, averaging fifty pounds and often weighing much less; the Pacific fish averages 90 to 100 pounds.

FOOD: Fishes, squid, copepods.

HABITS: A fish of warm seas and open waters. In the Atlantic it is found in or near the Gulf Stream.

Little is known of the breeding habits, although a number of larval specimens have been secured in various places; some near areas suspected of being spawning grounds, and others in places to which such small individuals might easily have drifted. There is a persistent belief that it spawns off Florida during June, July and August, and female fish with roe spilling have been reported. There is also an unconfirmed report that ripe females have been taken off Acapulco. Sailfish have been taken late in the year off Brownsville, Texas, with spawn running from them when they were boated. This last report is amply confirmed, so there must be spawning grounds off Texas.

The larval and very young Sailfish is quite different from the adult. Small larvae are chunky bodied, with only slightly extended toothed jaws of even length. Their body is covered with sharp, transparent, spikey scales; the head is equipped with long, sharp, barbed spines; the dorsal fin is low. When the fish has reached the length of 16 millimeters, the dorsal is much higher and the jaws longer, but still toothed and even in length. A 20-inch specimen much more closely resembles the adult; the sail is high as in the adult and the spear has developed. In the adult, only denticles remain of the jaw teeth, and the scales have become like long, sharp thorns. Larval and very small Sailfish are definitely known as follows:

When not otherwise noted, only one specimen has been reported.

5.5 mm. from the South Atlantic;
9 mm. from Tortugas, Florida, very dark above, paler below, fins colorless (S. Hildebrandt);
9 mm. from French West Africa;
14 mm. from 30° S. Lat. 25 W.;
16.5 mm. from 9° N. Lat. 119 W.; 20 mm. from Cuba; 25 mm. from Messina, Sicily;
1⅝ inches from Costa Rica, body shining blue with 6 wide bands, belly silvery white, dorsal black with yellow streaks and three jet black spots at base (W. Beebe);
38.1 mm. from the west coast of Mexico;
3¼ inches taken on surface attracted by night light, west coast Lower California (W. Beebe);
101.9 mm. west coast of Africa;
4.5 inches, two specimens, taken 25 miles southwest of Cape Malo, Panama (L. Woods);
4¾ inches, two specimens taken off Cocos Island, one of which was kept alive in aquarium for several days. Dorsal with yellow markings and large dark brown blotches on the fin. (L. Mandel). The American Museum of Natural History has a strip of color film of this fish in the aquarium.
127 mm. taken off Western Province, Ceylon;
151 mm. from Great Abaco, Bahama Islands, found in the mouth of a bonita so that the locality is uncertain;
7 inches, Charleston, South Carolina;
8 inches to 1 foot, Tarpon Springs, Florida;
289 mm. from Nagasaki, Japan;
18 inches from Djetta, Red Sea;
20 inches from Aransas Pass, Texas;
several specimens from 25 to 30 inches from Galveston to Freeport, Texas;
17½ ounce fish from Freeport, Texas;
several fish from 2 to 10 pounds (the latter weight quite frequent), from the Gulf Stream off Miami, Florida;
three young from the Turks Island, Bahamas, region;
a 7 pound fish from Freeport, Texas.

This strikingly colored fish swims with its sail folded into the groove of the back, but when sunning, the sail is raised, and when fighting the hook in a series of spectacular leaps, the sail is also usually unfurled.

Like other speared fishes, it appears to use the spear to stun other fishes upon which it feeds. Whether, when it gets into a school of fishes, hungry or not, it strikes out with the spear does not seem to be known. Dr. L. A. Walford reports that the launches of the "Haida" were attacked by hooked sailfish.

THE CREVALLES *Caranx*

This is a large group with a wide distribution in warm seas. Most of the Crevalles are tough fighters when hooked, despite their relatively small size.

They are found both inshore and offshore; in the surf; around reefs, wrecks and pilings. Those offshore are usually larger than the inshore specimens. They school near the surface.

The genus is characterized by keeled bony plates on the lateral line, which toward the tail are each armed with a sharp spine; peduncle, very narrow; first (nearest the head) dorsal fin short and made up of delicate spines (fin rays that are not branched at the tip); second dorsal longer and

IGFA
Sailfish weighing 128 pounds taken by H. G. Lapham while still fishing with live opelu for bait.

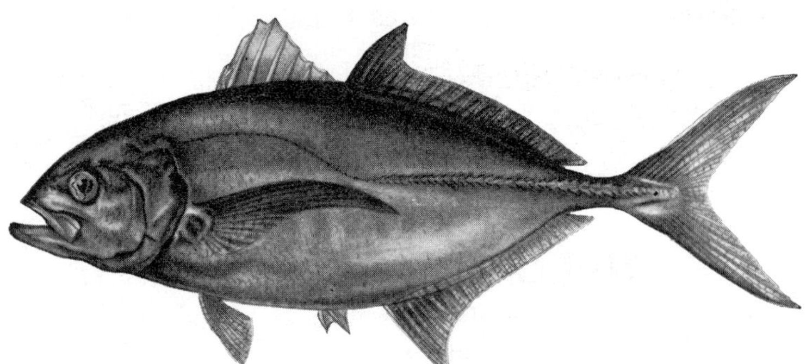

From: "North American Game Fishes" by Francesca LaMonte. Copyright 1945 by Francesca LaMonte, reprinted by permission of Doubleday & Co.

Blue Runner.

without spines; scales small and smooth; teeth present in the jaws, on the roof of the mouth and on the tongue; tail forked; color greenish or bluish above, silvery below, frequently with yellow on the sides, and there may or may not be cross bars. Cross bars are more apt to appear in young fish, a fighting fish, or after it has been landed.

Crevalles occur on both Atlantic and Pacific coasts of the Western Hemisphere; in Oceania; both coasts of Africa, and in Asia. Several species usually occur in each range, most of them being somewhat similar in appearance. Nearly all species are taken for sport wherever they occur in numbers. Without doubt, various Crevalles not mentioned here are caught by anglers in other parts of the world. There are so many species that it is impossible to distinguish between them without careful use of a key to their classification. A short discussion of the more familiar forms will cover most of the characteristics of this genus whose breeding habits are not known.

JACK CREVALLE *Caranx hippos* (Linnaeus)
also known as CREVALLE

This is the common Jack from the warmer parts of the Atlantic coast, from the West Indies as far north (as a straggler) as Massachusetts, and also in the Pacific, from Guatemala to Cape San Lucas, both shores of the Gulf of California, and Guaymas. It, or a very similar species, is also found in Hawaii, and other parts of the Pacific and in the Indian Ocean.

COLOR: Dull greenish on the upper sides; a dull silver gilt below; and yellowish on the belly, a conspicuous black spot on the back of the gill cover, and an inconspicuous one at the base of the pectoral fins.

DISTINGUISHING CHARACTERISTICS: The breast is scaled only in a small triangular patch in front of the ventral fins. Black spot on the gill cover; broadly forked tail.

SIZE: Averages 2-3 pounds; reported to reach 20 pounds.

FOOD: Fishes.

HABITS: Like others of the genus, this is a schooling fish. It is found in large numbers in the southern part of its range. The Jack Crevalle is usually seen around reefs, beaches, pilings, inlets, and even in the surf.

BLUE RUNNER
Caranx crysos (Mitchill)

RANGE: Brazil to Nova Scotia where it is a rare straggler, the concentration areas being to the south as is usual in this genus.

COLOR: Back greenish, shading into yellowish silver; fins almost colorless; no dark spot on the pectoral fin base.

DISTINGUISHING CHARACTERISTICS: The breast is covered with small scales. If present at all, the dark spot on the gill cover is very small. The pectoral fins are long and curved. 24 gill-rakers.

SIZE: Runs as high as 6 pounds, but averages 2.

FOOD: Fishes, shrimps, crabs.

HABITS: Longley and Hildebrand observed that the young of this fish were common about Tortugas but only a few adults were noted.

SKIPJACK *Caranx ruber* (Bloch)

For some reason, possibly because it has not been recognized as this species, the Skipjack does not usually appear in anglers' lists. However, as it is the common *Caranx* of the western Atlantic, it is safe to assume that it is taken for sport.

RANGE: From the West Indies and Cuba north to Florida. The fish is common off the Bahamas and Cuba, and is recorded as far north as North Carolina.

COLOR: General color dull silver tinged with blue, a dark blue streak along the dorsal fin base to the base of the caudal fin and on to the lower lobe of the caudal. Above this is a conspicuous line of light blue. The color, however, is variable and the fish sometimes looks very light all over. Sometimes the two streaks are not visible.

DISTINGUISHING CHARACTERISTICS: The body and particularly the head are much less robust than those of the Jack Crevalle or the Blue Runner; forehead, instead of being convex in profile, showing a concavity between the nostril and eye; breast fully scaled.

SIZE: Said to reach a length of 1 foot, but usually much smaller.

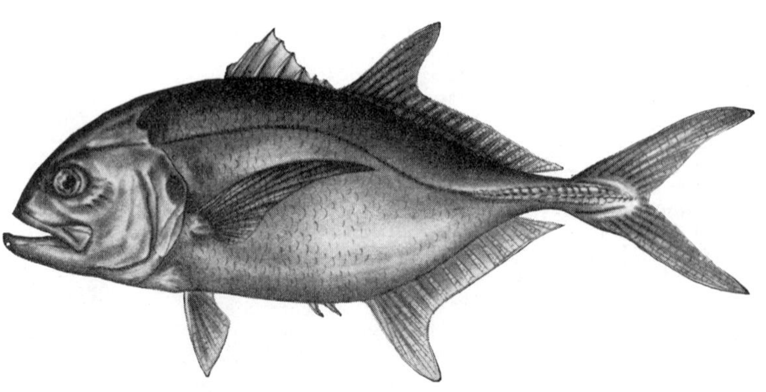

From: "North American Game Fishes" by Francesca LaMonte. Copyright 1945 by Francesca LaMonte, reprinted by permission of Doubleday & Co.

Common Jack Crevalle.

FOOD: Fishes, shrimps.

HABITS: This fish is very common in summer off the Florida Keys. Quantities of small and medium sized ones have been reported at Tortugas over all types of bottom. It is, however, less coastal than some of the other crevalles. It is thought that there is a nursery ground for this fish in the center of offshore currents.

From: "North American Game Fishes" by Francesca LaMonte. Copyright 1945 by Francesca LaMonte, reprinted by permission of Doubleday & Co.

Rainbow Runner.

YELLOW JACK

Caranx bartholomaei Cuvier & Valenciennes

This fish is common off Cuba, and, during summer off the Florida keys. It ranges from the West Indies to Florida and the Bahamas and straggles slightly farther north. It usually stays nearer the bottom than the Skipjack.

The Yellow Jack is deeper bodied than either the Blue Runner or the Skipjack. It has no black spot on the gill cover, and the breast is completely scaled. The dorsal and the anal fins are also completely covered with scales. In color, it is yellowish, with yellow fins. A yellow stripe runs down the middle of the sides, on which more or less faint blue lines may also be seen.

HORSE EYE JACK *Caranx latus* Agassiz

RANGE: Brazil to South Carolina, straggling north to Virginia. Abundant in the West Indies and on the Atlantic coast of Panama. There have been reports of this from the Pacific but most students believe these to be other species of *Caranx*.

COLOR: Typical blue and silver color of this genus; a small back spot on the gill cover; another, smaller spot at the base of the pectoral; young, like the young of other species of crevalle, often with dark cross bars.

DISTINGUISHING CHARACTERISTICS: The forehead profile is strongly convex. Some of the outer teeth are large and canine-like. The breast is completely scaled. There is a low sheath of scales at the base of the dorsal and anal fins. The tip of the dorsal fin is black; the tail is yellow.

SIZE: This fish, if correctly identified, has been reported to weigh as much as 35 pounds but the average fish is usually under 20.

FOOD: Fishes, crabs, shrimp, etc.

HABITS: Travels in large schools; young from 50 to 125 mm. in length reported as not uncommon in summer around Tortugas, Florida.

GREEN JACK *Caranx caballus* Günther
also called JUREL

RANGE: San Diego, California to Peru. Abundant around Cape San Lucas, and off the coast of Central America.

COLOR: Blue-gray or greenish above; silvery or silver gilt below; and a black spot on the gill cover.

DISTINGUISHING CHARACTERISTICS: The Green Jack looks much like the Blue Runner, from which it may be distinguished by its range. It also has a more elongate body, a smaller mouth, and more gill rakers than the Blue Runner. The breast is fully scaled. The other Pacific species are different in color pattern.

SIZE: A small species; rarely over 15 inches long.

FOOD: Fishes.

OTHER CREVALLES

Among other crevalles mentioned by anglers as very gamey when hooked is the Big Eye Jack, *Caranx marginatus* Gill, a fish which is present from Mazatlán to Panama, and off Hawaii. This fish reaches a length of 3 feet or more and is recognizable by the dark dorsal and anal fins of which the highest rays are white tipped. The Blue Crevalle, *Caranx stellatus* Eydoux & Souleyet, has the general bluish color of the crevalles, but is covered with black spots on the back and sides and has bright blue patches at the base of dorsal and anal fins. This fish runs as much as 20 pounds in weight and a length of from 2 to 3 feet. It has been taken off Lower California, Panama, and Cocos, in March and April, and is said to put up a very fine fight. In Hawaiian waters the average size is 4 to 10 pounds, and a recent Hawaiian publication also lists it as being present in the tropical Atlantic (possibly an error), the East Indies, and Tahiti.

RAINBOW RUNNER

Elagatis bipinnulatus (Quoy & Gaimard)

RANGE: World wide. Red Sea, Indian Ocean, Oceania, Australia, Hawaiian Islands, Cape San Lucas to the Galapagos Islands, Long Island to the West Indies, both coasts of Africa. The fish is not abundant anywhere.

COLOR: The color is very striking. The back and upper part of sides are dark blue margined with light blue. Below this, the body is yellow to the mid-line of the body where there is another horizontal light blue line. The remainder of the body is silvery-yellow. The fins are yellow.

DISTINGUISHING CHARACTERISTICS: This is a long, slender fish with pointed nose and small mouth. The profile from tip of jaw to beginning of dorsal fin is almost straight. The outstanding characteristic is the single small finlet following both the second dorsal and the second anal fins. These fins are long and are preceded by the first dorsal and anal fins which consist of five or six fragile spines. The tail is forked. There are bands of fine teeth on jaws, roof of mouth and tongue.

Fish & Wildlife Service
Permit or Great Pompano.

SIZE: About 1 foot; known to reach a length of 3 feet and a weight of over 12 pounds.

FOOD: Fishes, crustaceans.

HABITS: Aside from the fact that the fish is nowhere common and is a pelagic, warm sea species, nothing seems to be known of its habits.

THE POMPANOS *Trachinotus*

Some of the species of this genus are very difficult to distinguish. Further confusion is caused by the fact that the young are common in many localities, but without adult fish. It is not easy to identify the young without knowing the parents. Anglers also continually dispute the question of separate identities for the Permit and the Round Pompano. Ichthyologists at present are studying this problem. It must be remembered that fish are distinguished by a combination of characteristics rather than by a single one and, therefore, identity can not be established by the presence or absence of a single bit of evidence.

The Pompanos are characterized by a smallish mouth; rounded upper and lower profiles; lack of keels or keeled scutes; smooth scales; first dorsal made up of low spines not connected by a membrane and almost invisible in the adult fish; and an anal fin preceded by two short almost separate spines, a third spine being attached to the fin following it. As the fish grows older, the dorsal and anal fins grow longer and more pointed.

All of these fish are fine eating, and many of them are well-known sports fish.

In North America the best known of these fishes are the Pompano, the Round Pompano, and the Permit or Great Pompano.

There is little chance of mistaking the Common Pompano for either of the others, because of its more numerous dorsal and anal rays. It has 25 dorsal and 23 anal rays, in contrast to the 19 to 20 dorsal and 17 to 19 anal rays of the other two.

However, the Round Pompano and the Permit are sufficiently alike to make identifications difficult, particularly from photographs. The Round Pompano is deeper bodied than the Permit; the depth measured on a vertical line dropped from the dorsal to the ventral margin is contained 1.7 times in the length of the fish measured from the tip of the snout to the base of the tail. This measurement in the Permit is 2.6. The Round Pompano also has a strongly arched profile and a long dorsal fin lobe. The profile of the Permit is not strongly arched; and the dorsal lobes are low.

POMPANO *Trachinotus carolinus* (Linnaeus)

RANGE: South Atlantic and Gulf coasts, Brazil to Cape Cod. Abundant in Florida from January to April. The young are reported abundant in the West Indies.

COLOR: Bluish above; silvery with golden tinge below. The anal is light orange yellow, sometimes with blue traces.

DISTINGUISHING CHARACTERISTICS: Depth of the body is about 2/5 of the length from the tip of the snout to the base of the tail. Dorsal lobes are low; profile is not strongly arched; there are no crossbars as in a rather similar species, *T. glaucus;* dorsal fin has 25 rays and the anal 23 rays.

SIZE: An average market size is 1 to 2 pounds; an average angler's size is 4 pounds; maximum appears to be 8 pounds.

FOOD: Crustaceans, mollusks, fishes.

HABITS: In Texas waters, it is known to spawn in the open Gulf during April, May and June; the females usually being found some distance beyond the surf, and the young in the surf.

This pompano is found most frequently in inlets, in small schools. It is abundant around Key West and Indian River, Florida, in winter and appears in Chesapeake Bay in May. Small specimens are abundant in Chesapeake Bay from summer to fall.

It is caught in large numbers for the market in Texas, from mid-winter to mid-spring.

E. T. Ragsdale
A former all-tackle record Permit. The fish weighed 39 pounds, 8 ounces and was caught off Bimini, B. W. I.

Smithsonian Institution

Round Pompano.

ROUND POMPANO

Trachinotus falcatus (Linnaeus)

RANGE: Cape Cod to Brazil; most abundant in the southern part of its range. Young found as far north as Woods Hole.

COLOR: Light greyish-blue above; silvery below. Dorsal rays black; anal rays orange except at tip which is black; tail yellow with black margin.

DISTINGUISHING CHARACTERISTICS: Dorsal has 19-20 rays; the anal 17 to 19 rays. Depth of body 1.7 times in the length from tip of snout to base of tail. The profile is strongly arched and the dorsal fin lobe long. The fins are usually blue with light tips. When the mouth is closed, the end of the jaw bone (maxillary) reaches to below the middle of the eye.

SIZE: Reaches 3 pounds in weight.

FOOD: Fishes, crustaceans.

HABITS: Little seems to be known about this fish, but its habits are presumably rather like those of the others of its genus.

PERMIT *Trachinotus goodei* Jordan & Evermann also called GREAT POMPANO

RANGE: West Indies to Florida.

COLOR: Dusky blue over silver. Fins dusky.

DISTINGUISHING CHARACTERISTICS: 19 to 20 dorsal and 17 to 19 anal rays. Profile not strongly arched. Fins with dusky tips. When the mouth is closed, the end of the maxillary reaches to beyond the middle of the eye. The dorsal lobe is not prolonged.

SIZE: The all-tackle rod and reel world record weighed 47 pounds, 12 ounces, taken off Boca Grande, Florida. This is the largest of the pompanos and a number have been taken weighing more than 30 pounds, although the average weight is well under 20.

FOOD: Fishes, crustaceans, mollusks.

HABITS: The Permit is taken on the edge of the Gulf Stream and also in shallow water and in the surf.

OTHER POMPANOS

There are a number of additional species of *Trachinotus,* some of which are occasionally taken by anglers; others like one species, *T. glaucus,* are usually too small to be of much interest. This fish taken from Virginia to Panama and once reported from Uruguay, is marked with dark crossbars; the lobes of the dorsal and anal in the adult fish reach past the middle of the tail fin. It has the familiar formula of 19 to 20 dorsal and 17 to 19 anal fin rays and the usual bluish and silvery color. The young are very difficult to distinguish from the young of the Permit. All these species, however, are easily distinguishable as Pompanos.

THE AMBERJACKS *Seriola*

This genus is characterized by its first dorsal fin which is composed of six to eight fragile spines connected by membrane. The adults have a low keel on the stem of the caudal.

Seriola is found in southern marine waters: from California to Chile; from Massachusetts to Brazil; off Europe, Africa, and the east coast of Asia.

From the many species of this group, the greater proportion of which are gamey, a comparative few are plentiful in North American waters.

The Amberjack, *Seriola lalandi,* is believed by many ichthyologists to be the same as the Mediterranean species, *Seriola dumerili.* The Bermuda fish locally called Bonito, *Seriola falcata,* may be the same as another Mediterranean form, *S. rivoliana.* The young are difficult to distinguish unless one is very familiar with all the forms.

AMBERJACK *Seriola lalandi* Valenciennes

RANGE: Both eastern and western Atlantic coasts. Found from Cape Cod to Brazil. Abundant off Florida where it is usually fished in spring and winter although apparently present all year. It is most abundant south of Cape Hatteras.

COLOR: Although the Amberjack probably got its name from an amber-tone color phase, its more usual coloring is blue on the upper part of the sides near the back; blue with a silver undertone to below the lateral line where the body becomes silvery. The fins are dusky with a pale yellow band near or on the edges. The tail is frequently yellowish. The young are banded, like the young of some other species.

DISTINGUISHING CHARACTERISTICS: 30 to 34 dorsal rays. The maxillary (hind bone of upper jaw) extends to a perpendicular dropped from the middle, or past the middle, of the eye. The scales are small. There are very fine teeth on the tongue, roof of mouth and in bands on the jaws.

SIZE: The average size is from 10 to 15 pounds. A 146-pound Amberjack was reported hand-lined

Fish & Wildlife Service

Amberjack.

off Bermuda in November 1938, but the identification was uncertain. The rod and reel record weighed 106 pounds and was caught off Passagrille, Florida. Other catches of fish from over 40 to over 70 pounds have been made off Florida and Bimini, B.W.I.

FOOD: Fishes.

HABITS: This fish is to be found in loose schools about offshore reefs. The presence of various stages of young off the North Carolina coast have indicated that the spawning season there is summer and that it occurs at sea. Young are often found in sargassum weed. Other spawning grounds which doubtless exist have not been found.

As occurs in many other fishes, a hooked Amberjack is often followed for some time by its companions.

PACIFIC AMBERJACK

Seriola colburni Evermann & Clark

RANGE: Cape San Lucas south to Mexico. There is a fish in Panama which is either this or a very similar species. Abundant throughout its range. This fish was not named scientifically until 1928; therefore Pacific records made before that time may be confused with other species.

COLOR: The body has a bronzed general tone, tinged with green which deepens on the upper part of the sides near the back.

DISTINGUISHING CHARACTERISTICS: The first rays of the soft dorsal and anal are at least two-thirds as long as the head measured from the tip of the snout to the back margin of the gill cover. These rays are longer than in other species. There is no yellow stripe along the side. There are 28 to 31 dorsal rays, and 13 to 16 gill rakers on the lower branch (below the angle) of the first gill arch.

SIZE: Averages 25 pounds. Dr. Walford reports that several weighing over 100 pounds were taken on the cruises of the "Haida;" the largest, taken at Cape San Lucas, weighing about 112 pounds.

FOOD: Fishes, crustaceans, mollusks.

HABITS: From the fact that the food of the Pacific Amberjack includes bottom living mollusks, it may be assumed that the fish spends some time, or at least feeds partly, near the bottom. It is reported to spawn in spring and early summer on or near the surface.

PACIFIC YELLOWTAIL *Seriola dorsalis* (Gill)

RANGE: Monterey to Mexico. Abundant off California from March to June.

COLOR: A general grey-green, with a gleaming yellow stripe from the eye to the tail, which is yellow. The back and upper part of the fish are peculiarly silky.

DISTINGUISHING CHARACTERISTICS: Yellow stripe. 15 to 17 gill rakers on lower branch of first gill arch. The front rays of the soft dorsal are less than half as long as the head measured from tip of snout to hind margin of gill cover.

SIZE: There is disagreement about this: some anglers estimate the average size at 20 pounds; others say from 8 to 15. Fish from 30 to 50 pounds are by no means uncommon.

Fish & Wildlife Service

Pacific Yellowtail.

The rod and reel records may be confused in localities outside of America due to the uncertainty about species, but the American record is undoubtedly the 105-pound fish caught at Topolobampo, Mexico, on April 30, 1955. Other large fish have been taken off Catalina and San Diego.

FOOD: Fishes, crustaceans.

HABITS: This is an important fish both to commercial fishermen and anglers.

It schools inshore, often around rocks, and may be observed driving smaller fishes into shallow water. In California there is quite a regular run, off San Diego from March to early May, and off Los Angeles about a month later. In fall and winter they are present off Lower California and in the Gulf.

They are known to spawn in spring and summer.

BERMUDA AMBERJACK

locally called BONITO

Seriola falcata Cuvier & Valenciennes

This fish was originally described from the Gulf of Mexico. It is common off Bermuda and is also found from Florida to Cape Lookout, North Carolina, and probably occurs farther north. Small ones have been taken off the east coast of Florida in Gulf weed, and also off North Carolina. Little is known of its life history.

The Bermuda Amberjack is greyish above and pale or faintly silvery below. The fins are dark. The tail is not yellow. There is sometimes a faint dark band from the eye to the front of the dorsal fin.

It is distinguishable by a soft dorsal fin with 29 rays and the height of its front rays contain 1 2/3 times in the length of the head from snout tip to hind margin of gill cover. The maxillary (back bone of upper jaw) reaches to a perpendicular dropped from the front of the pupil of the eye. There is a low keel on top of the head.

MAZATLAN YELLOWTAIL

Seriola mazatlana Steindachner

This fish has been confused with the Pacific Yellowtail and the Pacific Amberjack for so long that at present there is no accurate account of its habits. It is known to run abundantly off Mazatlán, Mexico, and off the Galapagos Islands. It is listed here solely on the possibility that someone fishing in those localities may hook one. There seems to be no color description of the living fish, a contribution which an angler might sometime supply.

CALIFORNIA HORSE MACKEREL

Trachurus symmetricus (Ayres)

There are several species of this genus in various parts of the world. Some ichthyologists believe that most of these belong in the one species above. Others believe that there is a different species, *T.lathami* Nichols found in the Atlantic.

Whether or not the California Horse Mackerel is a game fish is a matter of opinion. Off California it is said to be caught from piers and barges.

RANGE: Pacific: San Francisco to Chile. Walford reports it as most abundant in the Los Angeles region, where it occurs all year, but very irregularly. It is also found in the Galapagos Islands, Peru, and Chile. Atlantic: Florida Keys and West Indies straggling north to Massachusetts. The young have been reported in numbers off Key West. It is also found off Sweden and south to Spain, Italy and the Mediterranean.

COLOR: Metallic dark bluish-green above, shaded with lighter; silvery below.

DISTINGUISHING CHARACTERISTICS: The fish is mackerel-shaped; the lateral line sharply down curved above the vent, and armed with bony scutes its full length. The scutes of the straight part of the lateral line are spiny. There is a keel on the caudal peduncle. There are no finlets, but the last ray of the dorsal and anal fin in adult fish is nearly separate. The two dorsals are close together and the spines of the dorsal are nearly as high as the first soft rays. The lower jaw projects slightly. The teeth are very small and in a single row on the jaws; there are fine teeth in bands on the roof of the mouth and tongue.

SIZE: In the Pacific, this fish is reported to reach 18 inches in length. In the Atlantic, the maximum length of 9 inches is reported for *T.lathami.*

AFRICAN POMPANO

also called CUBAN JACK

Hynnis cubensis (Poey)

Another species, *Hynnis hopkinsi* Jordan and Starks, known in the Pacific as the Goggle-eye, is very similar to this fish.

RANGE: Rare everywhere, both Atlantic and Pacific. West Indies and Cuba to Florida and the Bahamas. The Goggle-eye has been taken off Mazatlán and Panama.

COLOR: Bluish or purplish-blue above; pearly or silvery below, with a metallic sheen over all color.

DISTINGUISHING CHARACTERISTICS: The extreme flatness of the body which looks like that of a Pompano, but much flatter. The front of the head is steep, and the top of the head is keeled. On the hind part of the lateral line there are bony scutes.

SIZE: Reported to reach a length of over 3 feet, and one taken on rod and reel off Miami Beach weighed 39 pounds; another 35 pounds, 12 ounces; and another, from Bimini, 31 pounds, 8 ounces. The Goggle-eye is reported to reach a length of at least 2 feet.

FOOD: Fishes, so far as known.

HABITS: The life history of this fish is not known. Some ichthyologists believe it to be the adult of the Threadfish, *Alectis ciliaris* (Bloch). The Miami Herald Fishing Guide for 1948 reports that up to 15 pounds it has long streamers on the dorsal fin, as in *Alectis,* also that it is present the year around, but best fishing is off the upper keys in winter when it is "taken trolling or drifting near Amberjack holes."

CALIFORNIA POMPANO

Palometa simillima (Ayres)

This is not a Pompano despite its common name, but one of the Butterfishes. It is said to put up a good fight on rod and reel, although it does not usually appear in game fish lists.

RANGE: San Diego to Puget Sound. Most abundant in the Los Angeles region. Present the year round, but very irregular in numbers. More abundant in winter and spring.

COLOR: Metallic shiny green or blue above; silver below.

DISTINGUISHING CHARACTERISTICS: The convex curve of the upper and lower profiles of the body are almost alike. The dorsal and anal fins are also almost alike in height and length. The tail fin is widely forked. The mouth is small and the teeth are small. The scales are small. This fish reaches a known length of 10 inches. It is a good food fish.

DOLPHIN

Coryphaena hippurus Linnaeus
Coryphaena equisetis Linnaeus

The occurrence of this offshore, blue-water fish is very widely but scatteringly reported, due to the fact that it is an open-water fish, but does not occur in commercial quantities, and therefore is not as easily observed as fishes closer to shore or brought in commercially.

Although once, ichthyologists considered that there were as many as nineteen different species, this number was gradually reduced to two, of which *C.equisetis,* a southern species only, runs consistently smaller than *hippurus.* Further study may prove these two to be the same species.

The two species look so much alike that in southern areas where either or both may be present, fishermen have made little effort to distinguish between them. Each occurs in both Atlantic and Pacific; both have been identified as far north as Cape Lookout, and both occur off southern California.

The Dolphin of heraldry is a combination of this fish and the mammalian dolphin.

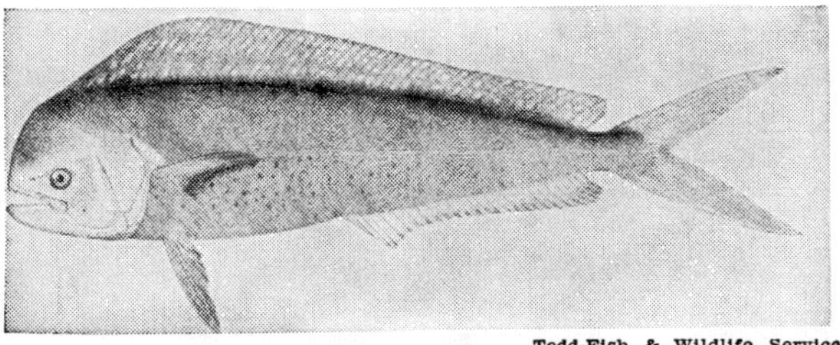

Todd-Fish & Wildlife Service

Dolphin (male).

RANGE: (Both species are included, as it is impossible to tell to which species most authors refer).

Atlantic: Usually near or in Gulf Stream. Recorded from Brazil to southern New England, including the Gulf of Mexico. Plentiful: Ocean City, Maryland (July and August in large schools of small, and some large bulls, about 35 to 50 miles offshore); Florida (moving north in summer); the flying fish grounds off Diamond Shoals, North Carolina; Bermuda (common offshore); Cuba. Azores. Southern Italy and Sicily. Gold Coast.

Pacific: Oregon to Peru, including the Hawaiian Islands. Common off Mexico. Japan. India. East Indies. South Africa from the Cape to Delagoa Bay.

COLOR: The Dolphin is one of the most brilliantly colored fishes, and equally shifting in color. The color pattern tends to two basic phases, one with bright yellow, golden and green as ground colors ornamented with blue, purple, and green spots and patches; the other with an intense medium dark blue as ground color with silvery splotches and markings. The colors are so varied and so evanescent as to make descriptions completely inadequate.

DISTINGUISHING CHARACTERISTICS: The Dolphin is high at the head and tapers toward the tail. In the adult males the profile above the snout mounts almost vertically for some little distance until it turns sharply to ascend to the beginning of the dorsal fin. In the female this vertical rise is less marked but present. The southern species, *equisetis,* apparently does not have such a blunt, steep forehead. The long dorsal and anal fins are almost the same length and height.

SIZE: Averages under 25 pounds. The rod and reel record, caught September 24, 1957, off Acapulco, Mexico, weighed 76 pounds. Several good sized specimens have been caught off Florida and Tahiti. A previous world record was caught off Waianac, Hawaii.

FOOD: Fishes. The Dolphin is particularly fond of flying fishes. As these fly above the water, the Dolphin pursues them in the water below, striking its prey as it hits the water.

Smithsonian Institution

Roosterfish.

HABITS: This is an oceanic fish, generally found near the surface. Little is known of its breeding or spawning habits. Norman writes that a female Dolphin was estimated to contain 500,000 eggs, and further says that the eggs are probably shed in the open sea. Hildebrand quotes the Mission report that a number of females with large swollen ovaries and almost ripe ova were taken off Callao, Peru, in February. Breder reports that in the West Indies, the Dolphin spawns in the spring. Young have been taken in Hawaii. The young are quite different in appearance from the adults. Their foreheads are normal, and there are dark bands on fins and body.

The fish schools, particularly the smaller specimens.

ROOSTERFISH

also called PAPAGALLO

Nematistius pectoralis Gill

RANGE: Southern California and Gulf of California to Mexico, Central America, Panama and Ecuador. Abundant off Mexico and the Pacific coast of Panama, and reported as abundant off Ecuador. Its appearance anywhere is very irregular. Within its range, it appears to be present all year.

COLOR: Light grayish-blue with metallic sheen, shading into lighter on the lower part of the sides. Occasionally there are green reflections. The long dorsal filaments are yellow, with black bands. There are rather indistinct dark-bluish bands across the snout, from below the front of the first dorsal down and backward to below the pectoral where it curves toward the tail, and beginning below the two last rays of the dorsal curving down and back to the tail. The fins are greenish gray; the tail darker than the other fins.

DISTINGUISHING CHARACTERISTICS: The Roosterfish is rather like the Jacks in general shape. The profile of the back rises fairly rapidly from snout tip to beginning of dorsal fin. The mouth is large, the scales small, and there are no scutes or keels on the lateral line. The tail is forked. This fish is easily distinguished by the greatly prolonged dorsal spines, the longest of which is equal to more than half of the total length of the body. The membranes joining the dorsal spines extend up only about one-seventh of the length of the spines. Beyond this, the spines are free, and consist of delicate filaments. The fin can be folded down into a fleshy groove on the back. The second dorsal is low and long. The anal is about one half as long as the second dorsal. The pectoral extends to a point about mid-way in the length of the base of the second dorsal.

SIZE: The Roosterfish averages about 20 pounds, but catches of 74 and 72 pounds are recorded from the Pacific coast of Panama, and present world record, taken in 1960 off La Paz, Mexico, 114 lbs.

HABITS: The Roosterfish seems to be an inshore fish, generally taken over sandy bottom or around rocks. Nothing is known of its breeding habits, but schools of young Roosterfish have been seen breaking the surf inshore off Lower California. From observations of the condition of adult fish, the spawning season would appear to be sometime between July and December. (Walford).

When hooked, the Roosterfish makes a strong, spectacular fight. Its flesh is good eating.

BLUEFISH

Pomatomus saltatrix (Linnaeus)

Small specimens of this fish are sometimes called Tailors. It is also the Shad of the Cape Province, South Africa.

RANGE: The Bluefish is very widely distributed in temperate and tropical waters, but appears irregularly, sometimes being absent for long periods from waters where it has previously been very numerous. Where present, it may be found in various sizes almost all the year round.

Eastern and Western Atlantic; Indian Ocean; Mediterranean. Argentina to Nova Scotia. Sicily to Constantinople. Gold Coast and Senegambia. South and East Africa, especially from the Cape to Durban. Australia.

Abundant almost everywhere within its range and usually in commercial quantities. Uncommon off Bermuda, and not reported in the Bay of Fundy or off the Nova Scotian side of the Gulf of St. Lawrence.

COLOR: Iridescent dark greenish-blue shading into lighter which in turn becomes silvery on the belly. The base of the olive pectorals is dark. The ventral fins is light and the base of the anal is light. Otherwise the fins are dusky or olive.

DISTINGUISHING CHARACTERISTICS: This well known fish has a rather long head, large mouth, strong, uneven teeth in both jaws, and a forked tail. There are two free spines in front of the anal fin. The first dorsal fin consists of very fragile spines. The scales are small, thin and numerous, about one hundred or more in a row from shoulder to base of tail fin. The only fishes with which this could be confused are Jacks, from which the teeth distinguish it.

SIZE: The market size averages 1 to 4 pounds; the average size is usually considered to be 3 to 6 pounds, with a 10-pound fish not unusual. The fish runs to 25 pounds or more.

FOOD: Fishes, particularly menhaden which it pursues with great vigor; crustaceans; squid; worms.

HABITS: The finest fishing months for this fish are spring and fall. There is a big run off Hatteras, North Carolina, which begins in May, and in the New Jersey-Long Island region large ones are to be caught in July, August and September. Smaller ones up to a pound can be fished from shore and in inlets in the fall. The bluefish begin to pass North and South Carolina in March or April; enter the Chesapeake later in those months and are still there in large quantities in October. They begin off New Jersey in April and reach Massachusetts later in the summer. The larger fish run offshore.

The Bluefish is believed to spawn in most of its range in spring and summer offshore. Larvae have been found at sea. Free eggs have not been reported.

N. Y. Zoological Society

Cobia.

This voracious fish runs in huge schools, pursuing its food in the same savage manner in which it takes the hook. It is one of our best known food fishes.

COBIA

also called CABIO and LEMONFISH

Rachycentron canadus (Linnaeus)

The young of this fish look very much like the Remora or Sucking Fish, but, according to Dr. William K. Gregory, a comparison of anatomical characteristics lends no definite support to the view that there is any relationship; he thinks the Cobia is merely "a somewhat mackerel-like offshoot of the true percoids."

RANGE: Atlantic: Brazil to Cape Cod; Gulf of Mexico. Cape Verde. Senegal. Guinea. False Bay, South Africa. Pacific: not on our Pacific Coast. South Africa around from False Bay and north to Delagoa Bay. East Indies. Japan. Australia (where it is known as the Black Kingfish and is rare.)

The Cobia is fairly frequent in Chesapeake Bay from May to late summer; most common in June. It runs irregularly and in small numbers on the North Carolina coast; one of the most numerous occurrences was in June, 1945, when sixteen were taken off Roanoke Island. It is reported from the Bahama Islands as a rare visitor, which is also true of Jamaica. Although it occurs on both coasts of Florida, it is not frequent and has been reported only as single individuals. This fish, so rare elsewhere, occurs in very large numbers off Mississippi. Mr. Anthony V. Ragusin, of the Biloxi Chamber of Commerce, reports that hundreds of Cobia are seen in outside waters, particularly around the buoys, just before and at the crest of the incoming high tide.

COLOR: Varies from dark to very light brown or buff. The color becomes paler on the lower part of the sides and on the belly. There is a dark stripe, varying in intensity, running from the snout to the base of the caudal fin. The fins are dark. In the young, this dark stripe is very conspicuous and is margined with white. White is also present on top of the head and on the first dorsal and anal fin rays.

DISTINGUISHING CHARACTERISTICS: The Cobia is a fusiform fish with a long flat head, wide mouth and projecting lower jaw. There are bands of sharp teeth on both jaws and on the roof of the mouth and tongue. The first dorsal fin consists of seven or eight short strong spines which can be depressed in grooves. The scales are very small. The lateral line is wavy in the region above the pectoral fin. The tail of the young Cobia is very convex; that of the adult is forked or lunate.

SIZE: The average size is from 10 to 15 pounds. Fish of well over 30 pounds are common in Chesapeake Bay, and fish of 70 pounds are said to be fairly common in the season in the Gulf of Mexico where much larger specimens have also been seen. The all-tackle rod and reel record weighed 102 pounds and was 5 feet, 10 inches long. It was taken off Cape Charles, Virginia, on July 3, 1938.

FOOD: Fishes, crabs.

HABITS: The Cobia is an offshore fish found around wreckage, rocks and buoys. In South Africa it enters estuaries. It is believed to spawn in or near Chesapeake Bay in summer. Other population units are also believed to spawn in summer in localities as yet undiscovered. Young a few inches long have been taken in the Gulf of Mexico in July and August.

This fish is temperamental about taking bait at which it usually snaps. Sometimes it will take whatever is offered, and at other times it is completely uninterested. It is a hard fighter on the hook.

The fish is a good food fish both because of the white flesh and because the nature of the flesh does not alter with the size of the fish.

SNOOK

Centropomus undecimalis (Bloch)

This fish is closely related to the basses and the perches. There are a number of species, but as far as anglers are concerned the chief variance is in the maximum size. Some of the species reach a maximum at one foot; others between three and four feet. As anglers do not distinguish the species, the range as here given includes all of them. This is not the Snoek of South Africa, which is one of the snake mackerels.

RANGE: Florida to South America. Gulf of Mexico. Mexico to Peru. Occurs plentifully but irregularly off Texas in large schools. Rather common in all of the Cuban coastal rivers; in the Panuco River, Mexico, and in the White River, Jamaica. Not uncommon off both coasts of Florida and formerly very abundant in the Everglades. Present almost all year where it occurs.

COLOR: Upper half of body dull green or sometimes brown; lower half dull silver or white. The dorsal fins are dusky; the ventrals yellowish. The lateral line is black.

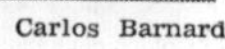

Carlos Barnard

Robalo or Snook leaping.

J. Mahony

Snook.

DISTINGUISHING CHARACTERISTICS: The black lateral line and projecting lower jaw. The dorsal fins are separated from each other by an appreciable distance. There are small fine teeth on the roof of the mouth and in bands on the jaws.

SIZE: Averages between 4 and 8 pounds. The rod and reel record of 50½ pounds was caught in Gatun Spillway, Canal Zone, January 2, 1944.

FOOD: Fishes, crabs, shrimp.

HABITS: This popular game fish is an inhabitant of saltwater inlets, or the lower reaches of rivers, where the water is brackish. Smaller ones sometimes go quite far up rivers. This fish are frequently to be found around pilings, and under mangroves. It is a very strong, violent fighter. It is a good food fish, with white, flaky flesh.

THE SEA BASSES

The Sea Basses form a very large group which includes some of the best known food and game fishes, both fresh water and marine.

These fishes must be distinguished from each other by a combination of characteristics, not by any particular one. They are all spiny-rayed; in nearly all the two dorsal fins are continuous, not separated, and all have teeth in their jaws. Many of them, however, are very difficult to distinguish because of their ability to change color and color pattern with great speed and variety. Dr. C. H.

Townsend's "Records of Changes in Color Among Fishes" discusses these color phases and shows many of them in its splendid color plates.

STRIPED BASS
also called ROCK or ROCKFISH

Roccus saxatilis (Walbaum)

RANGE: Atlantic: Cape Breton Island, Nova Scotia to Florida. Most common between Cape Cod and Cape May. Pearson: The Life History of the Striped Bass or Rockfish *Roccus saxatilis,* Walbaum. Bull. U. S. Bur. Fisheries, 1940, XLVIII, #28 approved for publication, July 28, 1937, gives the most distant Atlantic inland fresh-water range as Quebec.

Pacific: Striped Bass were brought from New Jersey and planted in San Francisco Bay in 1879 and 1881. Their Pacific range is now from Columbia River, Washington, to Los Angeles County, California. They are rarely taken south of Monterey and are most abundant in the San Francisco region. Pearson gives their furthest Pacific inland range as 250 miles up the Sacramento River, California. The best seasons are spring and fall.

This famous food and game fish is very plentiful in Chesapeake Bay in May and June. A well known run begins around the first of May off Massachusetts, in the Cape Cod Canal, around Martha's Vineyard, and among the Elizabeth Islands of which Cuttyhunk is a famous grounds. This run lasts all summer. In September and October there is a Striped Bass derby in Vineyard Sound. In the fall, they are abundant off the New Jersey coasts.

In the Gulf of Mexico, where the fish seem to run only in the coastal rivers, they are especially abundant in the region of Mobile, from June to January.

COLOR: Greenish or brownish on the upper part of the sides; silvery or brassy below; white on the belly. Seven or eight dark, well defined stripes run from the back of the gill cover to the base of the tail. One of these follows the lateral line, and three or four, fainter and more interrupted, are below the lateral line. In the young, the stripes are often absent. The fins are dusky.

Amer. Mus. Nat. History
Striped Bass or Rock-fish.

DISTINGUISHING CHARACTERISTICS: The dorsals of the adult Striped Bass are definitely separated from each other. This characteristic, and the longitudinal dark stripes mark the fish at once as a Striped Bass.

SIZE: Size varies greatly in the individual runs and in various localities but may be said to average from one to 10 pounds, with 15- to 25-pounders not rare. The record rod and reel catch, taken in Vineyard Sound, Massachusetts in 1913, weighed 73 pounds.

FOOD: Fishes, crustaceans.

HABITS: In general, the spawning area of this fish on the Atlantic coast is from New Jersey to North Carolina. Chesapeake Bay is probably a nursery. An area in the Roanoke River, North Carolina, 100 miles above tidewater, and one 12 miles upstream in the Susquehanna River are thought to be spawning grounds. On the west coast, Stripers are believed to spawn in the deltas of the Sacramento and San Joaquin Rivers. The adults migrate from the sea, brackish, or fresh water and go up the rivers to spawn.

Female Striped Bass are mature by the fourth year and males by the third. Quantity of eggs in a 2-pound female were calculated as 14,000; in a 12-pound fish as 1,280,000 and in a 50-pound fish as 3,220,000. Survival of eggs and young are

Amer. Mus. Nat. History
Anatomy of Striped Bass.

of course dependent on vicissitudes of temperature, salinity, drift, etc.

In colder weather, for example, November and December in New Jersey, the Striped Bass go into the deeper river waters. In summer in the north they go into the sea, but in southern waters they seem to prefer fresh and brackish water all year.

There is a great fluctuation of abundance of this fish from year to year and place to place, and also great variation of the age group which may dominate the schools in various localities for several years and then disappear. An example of this is found in the situation in Nova Scotia. Larger Striped Bass appear every year in the Annapolis and Shubencadie Rivers and Grand Lake, and (spottily) further north. However, in 1941, '42 and '43, there were very large runs in the southwestern section of Nova Scotia (Yarmouth-Shelburne-Queens) of small Striped Bass, up to five pounds. By 1944, the runs were greatly decreased, and have since tapered off so that almost none of this size are seen.

GIANT BLACK SEA BASS *Stereolepis gigas* Ayres

Range: Mexico north to San Francisco Bay. Most common around San Diego.

Color: Body and all fins except ventrals dark brownish black. Light patches under chin and tail. The ventral rays are dark, but the membranes between them are white.

Distinguishing characteristics: There are more dorsal spines than soft rays. The slope of the body from about the middle of the bases of dorsal and anal fins toward the tail forms a rather sharp angle. Large size. Dark color.

Size: The fish runs to 500 pounds, and is said to have been taken at 1000 pounds. It averages between 3 and 6 feet in length and usually weighs over 40 pounds.

Food: Fishes, crustaceans.

Habits: The Giant Black Sea Bass is a bottom, inshore, non-migratory fish, present all year. The most favored angling season is summer. The fish is also caught commercially in considerable quantity.

Amer. Mus. Nat. History

Sea Bass.

N. Y. Zoological Society

Sea Bass and Tautog.

On the hook it is a heavy, rather than a spectacular or interesting, fighter, and by the time it is finally raised, it is too exhausted to fight further.

Young Giant Black Sea Bass have been taken inshore in from 4 to 15 fathoms in December, April and September. They differ in color from the adults, and are red with dark spots and light patches.

JEWFISH *Promicrops itaiara* (Lichtenstein)

RANGE: Brazil to Florida, including the Gulf Coast. Present all year. Another species of *Promicrops* has been recorded for Central America.

COLOR: This fish has a number of different color phases, the most usual of which is a dark greenish gray ground color with small, dark and irregularly placed spots in the head region which is lighter in general than the rest of the body. There are widely spaced, reticulated dark bars and saddle marks near the ridge of the back and upper part of the sides. The fins are dusky with darker bands; some of the spines are light. The pectorals are lighter than the other fins. This fish also has a white phase in which the fins are conspicuously margined with black, and a grayish phase in which there are large black blotches on the sides.

DISTINGUISHING CHARACTERISTICS: Very large head which is broad between the very small eyes. Large size. More rays than spines in the dorsal and the spines of the dorsal all lower than the highest soft dorsal rays. Eight soft rays in the anal. The inner teeth can be depressed backward into a nearly horizontal position.

SIZE: A 750-pound Jewfish has been taken, but it averages much less although seldom taken under 25 pounds.

FOOD: Fishes.

HABITS: A heavy, sluggish fish frequenting rocky areas. It does not school and is not migratory.

SEA BASS *Centropristes striatus* (Linnaeus)

RANGE: Maine (as a straggler) to northern Florida. Abundant off New Jersey (May to November); off New England most of July to September; offshore in North Carolina waters in winter; present most of the year farther south. There is a fairly general movement north in the spring.

COLOR: Almost a checked pattern: the grayish or greenish or bluish ground color is criss-crossed by very narrow dark lines running from the back of the gill cover to the base of the tail and by dusky greenish scale marks which form vertical

Todd-Fish & Wildlife Service

Spotted Jewfish.

Al Johns, San Pedro

Sand Bass.

lines. As the rest of the scale is whitish, a white dot appears in the centre of each square thus formed. There are also often about five dusky or brownish bands from the ridge of the back to slightly below the lateral line. The fins are rather light and often spotted or barred with white.

DISTINGUISHING CHARACTERISTICS: Spiny and soft dorsal fins are continuous and equal in length. The fish, however, is particularly distinguished by its tail which is rounded on the hind margin with a prolonged ray at the upper edge.

SIZE: Averages ½ to 2 pounds and is rarely over 4 pounds. The males are said to run larger than the females.

FOOD: Fishes, crustaceans, barnacles. A bottom feeder.

HABITS: This is a bottom fish, often found among rocks both inshore and offshore, although more often the latter. Due to its size and the fact that the rocks it swims among are hard on tackle, it is not one of the most popular game fish. The meat is white and the fish is good eating.

The Sea Bass spawns in May on the North Carolina coast, and from mid-May to late June off New Jersey and Long Island.

Two species have been reported; occurring to some extent in the same range.

ROCK BASSES *Paralabrax*

In addition to the Rock Basses discussed here, species of this genus have been recorded from Panama, the Galapagos Islands, Peru, and Chile. As they are all called Rock Bass, it is inevitable that there should be uncertainty about just which species has been caught by anglers, just as there appears to be uncertainty about the southern limits of the range of the various species.

The state of California requires marine fishing licenses for most of the Rock Basses.

ROCK BASS
also called CALIFORNIA SAND BASS
Paralabrax nebulifer Girard

RANGE: Southern limit unestablished. Runs north to Monterey, California.

COLOR: Greenish above; darker on top of back and head. Silvery below. There are some indefinite dark greenish bands extending from the ridge of the back to below the lateral line. The fins are dusky. In the young, there are spots on the head region.

DISTINGUISHING CHARACTERISTICS: No spots in the

adult. The third dorsal spine is higher than the others; the first two spines are very low. The top of the head between the eyes is scaled as far forward as the front margin of the eyes.

SIZE: Reaches a length of over 1 foot.

HABITS: A shallow water fish often found over sandy bottom.

KELP BASS *Paralabrax clathratus* (Girard)

RANGE: Mexico to San Francisco. Most plentiful around Los Angeles. Present all year, but most abundant from May into September.

COLOR: Very much like the Rock Bass, but the head is lighter and there are indistinct dark bars and splotches above the lateral line. The fins are yellowish brown or yellowish green.

DISTINGUISHING CHARACTERISTICS: The third, fourth, and fifth dorsal spines are about the same length. There are no dots. The top of the head is sparsely scaled. The snout is rather pointed.

SIZE: Averages under 5 pounds, which is about the maximum.

FOOD: Small organisms found in the kelp beds.

HABITS: This is a rather common fish off California and is fished commercially. It is frequently found among kelp beds.

RED SPOTTED ROCK BASS also called SAND BASS

Paralabrax maculatofasciatus (Steindachner)

The Red Spotted Rock Bass is an inshore fish of undetermined southern range but coming north as far as the Santa Barbara Channel. It is frequently confused with other, more commonly fished species.

The fish is gray or greenish, darker above than below, and with dark reddish spots on the sides. The general color of the fins is lighter than that of the body. It is distinguishable by the spots, and the facts that the third dorsal spine is longer than the others, and that there are few scales on the top of the head.

THE GROUPERS

Mycteroperca and Epinephelus

There are many species in both genera of groupers. Because of their enormously varied colors and color patterns, and their generally similar appearance they are almost impossible to identify without the use of a technical key. C. H. Townsend in his "Records of Changes in Color Among Fishes," published by the New York Zoological Society, gives some beautiful color plates showing many of these color phases.

Smithsonian Institution

Grouper.

Calif. State Fisheries Laboratory

Broomtailed Grouper.

They are found from Florida to Brazil, occasionally straggling farther north, and from the Gulf of California to Central America. One of the most popular as a game fish, the Black Grouper, is abundant about the Florida keys and Cuba and has been taken off Woods Hole, Massachusetts in the fall.

They swim in groups, rather than in schools, and are apt to stay, not only in one locality, but in one spot, for long periods. They are especially fond of rocks and reefs where line is easily tangled or cut. Groupers are present all year on their grounds. They are good eating.

DISTINGUISHING CHARACTERISTICS FOR THE GROUP: A single, continuous dorsal fin. There are always at least 10 dorsal spines and 10 dorsal rays. The mouth is large with a projecting lower jaw and with canine teeth in front. The top of the head in the genus *Mycteroperca* is broad between the eyes; that of *Epinephelus* is narrow.

Despite the many species of groupers, only a few are considered sporty enough to be classed as game fish. These are the Black Grouper, the Nassau Grouper, and the Red Grouper. Others, however, have afforded pleasure and sport to a sufficient number of anglers to warrant their inclusion, and still others are of interest to anglers not only because they have occasionally taken the hook but because of a very striking appearance.

BROOM-TAIL GROUPER

Mycteroperca xenarcha Jordan

RANGE: Mexico to Peru, where it is uncommon, and where it is the only *Mycteroperca* recorded.

COLOR: Gray, brown, or greenish with irregular dark rings and blotches. Head, body, and fins sometimes covered with small brown spots.

DISTINGUISHING CHARACTERISTICS: The seventh anal and the tenth dorsal rays are longer than the others. The membranes between the rays of the tail fin are deeply indented, giving it a jagged appearance. There are from 20 to 23 gillrakers on the lower limb (below the angle) of the first gill arch.

SIZE: Reported to reach 60 pounds or more.

LEOPARD OR GOLDEN GROUPER

Mycteroperca pardalis Gilbert

This grouper is mentioned here because of the confusion of its common name, Golden Grouper, with another fish that has been fairly often taken off the Galapagos Islands and is also known as the Golden Grouper, *M.olfax*.

RANGE: Gulf of California.

COLOR: This fish has two distinct color phases. One is brown or green ground color with small brown spots. The other is golden, with black saddle marks and blotches across the back and on the upper part of the sides.

DISTINGUISHING CHARACTERISTICS: Color. About 21 gill rakers on the lower branch of the first gill arch.

SIZE: 2-3 feet.

FOOD: Fish and small oceanic organisms.

HABITS: Frequents rocky shore waters. Has been reported as having "ovaries full of developing eggs" in March and April.

COLORADO GROUPER also called GOLDEN GROUPER

Mycteroperca olfax (Jenyns)

RANGE: Panama to the Galapagos Islands.

COLOR: The fish has two phases. One is a dark greenish-brown with purple and brown dots which vary in number and intensity and may be entirely absent. The other phase is all yellow—a very brilliant yellow, almost orange. Several such fish have been hooked off the Galapagos and have been called Golden Grouper.

SIZE: Said to reach a length of at least 3 feet.

BLACK GROUPER *Mycteroperca bonaci* (Poey)

RANGE: North to Massachusetts (as a straggler), but rare north of Florida from whence it runs south to Brazil. Abundant around Key West.

COLOR: Brownish, or dark orange with light shadings, or dark gray with interrupted dark stripes. There are other color phases with blue and brown bars and green dots, and a white phase with indefinite dusky markings. Townsend gives excellent plates of this.

DISTINGUISHING CHARACTERISTICS: About 110 scales in a line from the hind margin of the gill cover to the base of the tail.

SIZE: Reaches 50 pounds, but averages between 5 and 10.

FOOD: Fishes, crustaceans.

HABITS: A popular game fish taken both offshore and inshore around reefs.

GAG *Mycteroperca mircolepis* (Goode & Bean)

RANGE: The southern limit of the Gag is not established. It runs north to North Carolina and is found on both coasts of Florida.

N. Y. Zoological Society

Yellowtail. One of the Groupers.

COLOR: Like the other groupers, the Gag has several different color phases. The most usual is a greenish-brown. The dorsal usually has a white edge; the caudal is black with patches of bright blue and a white edge. The anal is a purplish blue with white margin.

DISTINGUISHING CHARACTERISTICS: Very small scales; about 140 from the back of the gill cover to the base of the tail.

SIZE: Averages about 3 pounds.

FOOD: Fishes, crabs.

HABITS: A reef fish, found both in and offshore.

ROCK GROUPER also called YELLOW GROUPER

Mycteroperca venenosa (Linnaeus)

RANGE: Florida Keys and probably farther south.

COLOR: Upper body and head light greenish; lower part of body rosy. Large black spots on upper part of body; smaller ones on head and lower part of body. Fins dusky. Soft dorsal and tail fin have black margins. This fish may also be pure white with faint dusky markings or with black dots. The color changes very rapidly and completely.

DISTINGUISHING CHARACTERISTICS: Heavy body. Very small scales, about 125 from hind margin of gill cover to base of tail.

SIZE: Reaches a length of 1½ feet.

FOOD: Fishes, crabs.

HABITS: Typically offshore, but also taken in shallow water.

Epinephelus

The groupers of the genus *Epinephelus* are distinguished from those of the genus *Mycteroperca* by the narrowness of the top of the head between the eyes and the fact that this species has either 8 or 9 anal rays and not 11 anal rays as does *Mycteroperca*. They have a very wide distribution.

The various species, like those of *Mycteroperca,* cannot usually be distinguished from each other by color, but must be sorted on the basis of other characters, such as number of spines and rays in the fins, number of gill rakers, etc. It is necessary to use a scientific key in making accurate identification of a grouper.

The eggs and larvae of some species of *Epinephelus* have been taken in the Straits of Messina where the fish are present all the year. These have been studied by Dr. Antonio Spartà. The spawning season there is from July to September. The round and transparent eggs are easily mistaken for eggs of several other fishes. The larvae differ very much from the adult in appearance. Larval fishes measuring 3.60 millimeters show the second dorsal spine and the ventral spine tremendously lengthened; reaching to or beyond the tail, and sharply toothed. By the time the fish are 22.12 mm. the ventral spine has become almost like that of the adult and at 28.20 mm. the dorsal too has shortened and the fish is more like the adult.

FLAG CABRILLA

Epinephelus labriformis (Jenyns)

RANGE: Cape San Lucas, Lower California to the Galapagos Islands.

COLOR: The ground color varies from gray-green to dark brown, always shaded with darker. The body is, however, always covered with white dots. The lining of the mouth is red.

DISTINGUISHING CHARACTERISTICS: Short ventral fins, not reaching the vent; 11 dorsal spines.

SIZE: Reaches a length of about 20 inches.

HABITS: Despite the fact that this is quite a common fish within its range, little is known of its habits except that it frequents rather shallow water.

SPOTTED CABRILLA or CABRILLA PINTA *Epinephleus analogus* Gill

RANGE: Galapagos Islands to Lower California.

COLOR: The ground color is pinkish, with red dots scattered copiously on body and fins and especially conspicuous on the bases of the fins. There are a few indistinct broad dark bands from the back to the lateral line.

DISTINGUISHING CHARACTERISTICS: The spiny dorsal is evenly rounded. There are 10 spines.

SIZE: This is the largest of the Pacific cabrillas, reaching, according to Walford, a weight of 15 to 20 pounds.

HABITS: The Spotted Cabrilla is a very fine and abundant food fish. Because of its tendency to make for the rocks, it is more popular as a food than as a game fish. However, when found over a sandy bottom, it puts up a fairly good fight.

NASSAU GROUPER *Epinephelus striatus* (Bloch)

RANGE: Brazil north to the Florida Keys, including the Gulf waters both of the United States and Mexico. Present all year. Abundant in the Bahamas, Key West, and Puerto Rica.

COLOR: Very changeable but a black spot at the tail base remains through all color variations; and in all the variations except those without any bands, there is a dark band running from the eye to the beginning of the dorsal fin. There are no spots other than the one at the tail base. The color varies from pure white, with a faint saddle mark on the upper caudal peduncle, to plain dark brown.

DISTINGUISHING CHARACTERISTICS: The first dorsal spine is low but the second is as high as the others. The lower jaw projects very slightly if at all beyond the upper. There are no spots.

SIZE: Averages between 5 and 10 pounds.

FOOD: Fishes and crustaceans.

N. Y. Zoological Society

Nassau Grouper.

HABITS: An outside fish of coral reefs. Usually solitary except in the breeding season which is reported to be May and June.

RED GROUPER

Epinephelus morio (Cuvier & Valenciennes)

RANGE: Rio de Janeiro to Virginia. Common off Key West and on the west coast of Florida and off Havana. Present all year.

COLOR: Not spotted except in the brown and white phase in which the fins are light red blotched with white. There are also some small white dots chiefly in the region of the pectoral fin and a few indistinct dots on the upper side. In this phase the dorsal and caudal are margined with black as in all phases of this fish except the darkest, in which the caudal is white rimmed. There is a light red color phase; a light brown phase, and a white phase; also a dark almost black, phase. In some there is darker color in an indistinct and rather broad area running from snout to base of tail. The inside of the mouth is orange red.

DISTINGUISHING CHARACTERISTICS: The membrane between the dorsal spines which are not very stout runs to, or nearly to, the spine tips. Lack of spots.

SIZE: Usually not as large as the Nassau Grouper. A Red Grouper is very heavy at 40 pounds.

FOOD: Feeds like other groupers.

HABITS: An abundant fish of offshore waters, particularly on reefs and banks.

ROCK HIND *Epinephelus adscensionis* (Osbeck)

RANGE: From Brazil to southern Florida and straggling north to Massachusetts. Abundant at Key West. Noted as uncommon off Bermuda. Also present off Ascension and St. Helena Islands, and listed by Professor J. L. B. Smith (The Sea Fishes of Southern Africa) as present from the Cape of Good Hope (eastward) to Knysna.

COLOR: Greenish gray with darker markings and red spots with light centers on body, dorsal and anal fins and on the basal half of the pectorals. The ventral spots are larger and more orange in color. The spots are largest on the breast. There are also some pale spots on the body and the dorsal and anal fins. In some color phases in addition to the red spots a number of large white spots appear on the body and smaller ones on the fins. In other color phases there may be dark bands from the back to the ventral outline. The ground color varies but in general is rather light greenish. The fins are usually green.

DISTINGUISHING CHARACTERISTICS: The first and second dorsal spines are lower than the others. The lower jaw projects noticeably beyond the upper. There are no scales on the hindmost bone (maxillary) of the upper jaw.

SIZE: Reaches 16 pounds but averages between 2 and 3.

FOOD: Like that of other groupers.

HABITS: This fish shares with the others of its group, the habit of making for the rocks when hooked. It is not fast but is a strong fighter.

RED HIND *Epinephelus guttatus* (Linnaeus)

RANGE: Brazil to the Florida keys, and straggling to the Carolinas.

COLOR: A very beautiful fish. Its general tone is light; olive above, reddish below. There are three oblique dark bands on the sides and the body and fins are everywhere covered with small red spots. The inside of the mouth is also sometimes red-spotted. In one color phase, the body is white, with red spots. The fins are greenish yellow, spotted with dark red.

DISTINGUISHING CHARACTERISTICS: The lower jaw projects little if at all beyond the upper. There are scales on the maxillary. The red spots are characteristic.

SIZE: This fish averages about 2 pounds.

FOOD: Like that of other groupers.

HABITS: This is a small reef fish and is not very common anywhere.

GRAYSBY

Petrometopon cruentatus (Lacépède)

RANGE: Florida keys to Brazil. Abundant in Bermuda. Acapulco to Panama (rarely taken in this range. Either the same or a species closely resembling *P.cruentatus.)*

COLOR: This fish has several color phases. A rather common one is a reddish background speckled with darker. Another color phase has a brown background with darker specks and four or five white spots at the base of the dorsal fin. A very pale phase has a white ground color, speckled with yellowish-brown over the whole body including the fins. The four or five dots at the base of the dorsal are dark in this color phase.

DISTINGUISHED CHARACTERISTICS: Although the characteristics by which ichthyologists distinguish this fish are the structures of the skull bones, the angler will probably recognize it by its rather large and very rough scales and its convex tail.

SIZE: Specimens of 1 foot are not rare.

FOOD: Fishes.

HABITS: The Graysby frequents rocks and reefs, and is rather difficult to capture, but in Cuba it is a fairly important food fish.

CONEY *Cephalopholis fulvus* (Linnaeus)

RANGE: Florida to Brazil. Caribbean coast of Panama (not abundant). Common in the West Indies, and Bermuda.

Another species has been reported from Cape Lobos, California, and as having been seen in the Panama City market.

COLOR: Varies in pattern, color, and intensity. All the color phases are speckled with light blue. The ground color varies from light brown or pinkish to dark green. The fins are usually margined with light blue, and there are frequently saddle like blotches running across the ridge of the back.

DISTINGUISHING CHARACTERISTICS: Eleven dorsal spines. No stripes. Light blue dots. Teeth easily depressible toward the back.

SIZE: The maximum is about one foot in length.

FOOD: Chief item of its diet appears to be crustaceans.

HABITS: Usually found inshore. Aquarists who have kept these fishes in tanks find them very combative.

Calif. State Fisheries Laboratory

Tripletail.

SANDFISH

Diplectrum formosum (Linnaeus)

RANGE: North Carolina to Uruguay. Common. There are four or five species of this genus, some of which are present from California to Ecuador.

COLOR: Very changeable. Possibly some of the species may prove to be color phases. The color is apt to be grayish with blue and brown stripes and with a blue-striped head. There are frequently dark cross bars and a stripe from snout to base of tail where there is a black spot. There is another black spot on the end of the dorsal base.

DISTINGUISHING CHARACTERISTICS: No notch between spiny and soft dorsal. Ten dorsal spines and 12 rays. Area on top of the head smooth. Clusters of strong spines on the preopercle.

SIZE: A small fish, under a foot in length.

HABITS: This is a shore fish, frequenting channels, lagoons, and water over sand and mud bottom. It is good eating, and puts up quite a fight when hooked.

TRIPLETAIL

Lobotes surinamensis (Bloch)
and *Lobotes pacificus* Gilbert

RANGE: Uruguay north to Cape Cod. Gulf coast (April-October): Florida (north to around Fort Myers), Alabama (abundant), Mississippi (abundant), Louisiana, Texas (abundant), Mexico (Campeche Banks). Although recorded to Cape Cod, this fish is not abundant above West Palm Beach, Florida. Also found in the Mediterranean and off West Africa (Cameroons).

Smithsonian Institution

Tripletail.

A Pacific species, *L.pacificus,* is fairly common off Panama. The Tripletail has also been reported from Japan.

COLOR: Ranges from pale tan to dark greenish; darker above and on head. Soft dorsal, ventrals and pectorals lighter than the other fins which are dusky with dark green or blue margins. The young, and sometimes the adults, are marked with yellow and brown.

DISTINGUISHING CHARACTERISTICS: Short snout, small eye, no teeth on roof of mouth. Outer row of backwardly directed conical teeth in the front of the jaws with narrow bands of very fine teeth behind it. There are twelve dorsal spines, depressible in a shallow groove. The fish gets its name from the fact that the rounded margins of soft dorsal, anal and caudal fins give the appearance of a three lobed tail. This is partly due to the shortness of the caudal peduncle which brings the posterior part of these fins close to each other.

SIZE: Averages 7-10 pounds. Known to reach slightly over 40.

FOOD: Fishes, crustaceans.

HABITS: The Tripletail does not make regular appearances on its grounds, but is apt to be absent for one or more seasons. The runs also vary in abundance and in composition as to sizes. The fish may school or may be solitary. Although more usually in open fairly deep offshore water, it also enters river mouths and may be found in very shallow water. Near the Yucatan coast, both adults and young have been taken as deep as 25 fathoms. In some localities it is found inshore in spring and in deeper water later in the year.

Small *Lobotes* have been taken in various places, both inshore and offshore: Campeche Banks (Yucatan), Puerto Rico, Key West, Bermuda (in gulf weed), Panama (Colon). Specimens less than 3½ inches long were reported by Baughman from Aransas Bay, Texas in August 1939, and are said to be there also in summer.

Fish nearly ready to spawn are reported off Florida; Biloxi, Mississippi (July-August); Freeport, Texas (June, July, August); and in Sargassum weed off Bermuda.

The Tripletail is edible although not frequently seen in markets.

THE SNAPPERS *Lutjanidae*

There are about two hundred species in this world-wide family, many of which are important food fishes. Because of their large number and the fact that most of them will take a hook, only those most frequently taken, and those which may be confusing are discussed here. As in the case of the groupers, the only sure method of identification is the use of a scientific key.

In general, the group has large scales, deeply divided dorsal fins, two nostrils on either side of the snout, strong teeth, large head, and concave or forked tail. Ventral fins are present, and the anal fin has three spines.

The snappers are schooling fishes of warm shores, generally found over banks, among rocks, around mangroves, or even in the surf. Some species enter fresh water estuaries. They feed on fishes and crustaceans. The ranges of the species are frequently identical or overlapping. Little is known of their younger stages or of their breeding habits.

The color changes of which the Snappers are capable add to identification difficulties. Their common names are also confusing; the favorite name is Red Snapper, due to the fact that many have a reddish color.

STRIPED PARGO *Hoplopagrus güntheri* Gill

This fish is sometimes put in a separate family.

RANGE: The Striped Pargo is only found on the Pacific Coast, where it ranges from Lower California to Panama. It is nowhere abundant, but has been taken most frequently off Cape San Lucas, Guaymas, and in Panama Bay.

COLOR: Green above; reddish below. There are dark bars across the body and the stem of the tail. The spiny dorsal and the ventrals are a light reddish tan; the other fins are green. The iris is red.

DISTINGUISHING CHARACTERISTICS: The front nostril is tube-like and is on the upper lip; well separated from the rear nostril. A projection of the gill cover fits into a small notch in front of it.

SIZE: Reaches a length of 2 feet.

FOOD: Fishes and crustaceans.

HABITS: A fish of deep, cold waters.

THE "RED SNAPPERS"

Several different fish are known locally as Red Snapper, and several others have reddish color phases which have led to their being confused with these Red Snappers. The Outdoor Writers Association of America, in its Standard Check List of Common Names for Principal American Sport Fishes, uses the name Red Snapper for *Lutjanus blackfordi* Goode & Bean, for which other authorities use the more definite name Pensacola Red Snapper, as there is another Red Snapper *L.campechanus* (Poey), also called the Caribbean Red Snapper. Overlapping the ranges of both is still another snapper often confused with one or the other, the Silk Snapper, *L.vivanus,* and still another *L.buccanella,* less common but also found in the Caribbean and the Gulf of Mexico. This last has a jet black spot at the base of the pectoral fin.

The Pensacola Red, Caribbean Red, and Silk snappers are closely related and very easily confused—so easily that information on any is unreliable, as it may have been based on one of the others.

For an article dealing with these three species, interested anglers are referred to a paper by Isaac Ginsburg, "Commercial Snappers (Lutianidae) of the Gulf of Mexico", Bulletin Bureau of Fisheries, 1930, volume XLVI, pp. 265-276.

RED SNAPPER or PENSACOLA RED SNAPPER

Lutjanus blackfordi Goode & Bean

RANGE: Gulf of Mexico east to Key West, Florida, and straggling as far north as Long Island. Common in the Gulf of Mexico, where it is taken commercially.

COLOR: Deep red, including the fins.

DISTINGUISHING CHARACTERISTICS: There are 9 rays in the soft anal fin. The iris is red.

SIZE: Reaches about 2½ feet in length.

FOOD: Fishes, crustaceans.

HABITS: Although this fish is known to take the hook, it is famous as a food rather than as a game fish. It occurs most frequently around rocks and is taken commercially in fairly deep water. Ginsburg believes it probable that this fish spawns in deep water as the young are very rare in shallow water.

RED SNAPPER or CARIBBEAN RED SNAPPER

Lutjanus campechanus (Bloch)

RANGE: Gulf Coast; Florida keys, and possibly as far south as Brazil. Straggles north to Long Island. Abundant off Florida and in the Caribbean.

COLOR: Deep red including the fins. Margin of tail is black. Iris red. Not much yellowish in the color pattern.

DISTINGUISHING CHARACTERISTICS: There are 8 rays in the soft anal fin. Not much yellow on the tail. Iris red.

SIZE: This species has been so confused with the preceding one that data on its size seem highly unreliable.

FOOD: Fishes and crustaceans.

HABITS: This fish is reported to spawn in schools on its feeding banks, but this may actually be some other snapper. At such times it is said to refuse the hook. The Caribbean Red Snapper is found in deep water and has been taken in about 73 fathoms. It is usually taken commercially on lines set to a depth of about 40 fathoms.

SILK SNAPPER

Lutjanus vivanus (Cuvier & Valenciennes)

also known as YELLOWTAIL, and PARGO DE LO ALTO

RANGE: A southern form found in the West Indies; common in the Caribbean. The fish is red, darkest on the back, silvery on the belly and streaked with lighter. The tail fin is yellow. In smaller specimens the iris is bright yellow, but becomes reddish with growth. The anal fin has 8 soft rays. The fish is said to reach a weight of 40 pounds. It is a common market fish in the West Indies and often confused with one or more of the other species. It feeds on mud bottom and often has a muddy taste.

Another closely related group of four Snappers is the Cubera, the Mangrove Snapper, the Dog Snapper, and the Schoolmaster. For definite determination of these species, anglers should refer to a recent publication by Luis R. Rivas "A record of Lutjanid fish *(Lutjanus cyanopterus)* for the Atlantic coast of the United States, with note on related species of the genus." Copeia, 1949, No. 2, June 30.

These four Snappers look much alike and exhibit similar color changes, usually from the more frequent color phase of a greyish background to a very light or a very dark ground color.

All except *L.cyanopterus,* are common in Florida, especially about the keys.

CUBERA also called RED SNAPPER

Lutjanus cyanapterus (Cuver & Valenciennes)

RANGE: Brazil to Florida. Common in Cuba.

COLOR: Background grayish with indistinct bars on the younger specimens. Fins grayish except the anal which is reddish and the pectoral which is almost without color.

DISTINGUISHING CHARACTERISTICS: Upper and lower canine teeth equal in size and very strong. Teeth on the roof of mouth in a crescent shaped patch, with or without a very slight backward projection.

SIZE: Reaches 100 pounds, but averages 30 to 60 pounds.

FOOD: A bottom feeder; fishes, crustaceans.

HABITS: Usually found in water of less than 20 fathoms depth. Small specimens have seldom been seen.

MANGROVE SNAPPER

Lutjanus griseus (Linnaeus)

RANGE: Brazil to the West Indies, straggling north to Cape Cod, and common around the Florida keys and the Bahamas.

COLOR: Very similar to that of the Cubera. Grayish background with faint bars not always present in the larger specimens.

DISTINGUISHING CHARACTERISTICS: The upper canine teeth are much larger than the lower. The patch of teeth on the roof of the mouth is anchor shaped with a distinct background projection.

SIZE: Averages under 5 pounds; rarely over 20 pounds.

FOOD: A bottom feeder on fishes and crustaceans. This fish has been offered bread, potatoes, and beans, which it eats voraciously.

HABITS: A very common species usually found in water of less than a fathom over muddy bottom or around mangroves, and occasionally in estuaries. It has been found, also over offshore reefs. In some localities it feeds entirely at night.

DOG SNAPPER

Lutjanus jocu (Bloch & Schneider)

RANGE: Brazil to Florida; straggling to Cape Cod. Less abundant than the Mangrove Snapper.

COLOR: A lighter and more brightly colored fish than the two previous species. The ground color is a reddish tone with some olive or yellow admixture. The bars are more conspicuous and the fins orange or yellow. There is sometimes a light patch on the cheek.

DISTINGUISHING CHARACTERISTICS: The patch of teeth on the roof of the mouth is as in the Mangrove Snapper. There is a whitish area between the eye and the end of the upper jaw bone. The pectoral fin is longer than the distance between the tip of the snout and the hind margin of the preopercle.

SIZE: Reaches 20 pounds but rarely over 5.

HABITS: Found in shallow water. The larger ones are seldom in more than 20 fathoms.

SCHOOLMASTER SNAPPER
also called SCHOOLMASTER

Lutjanus apodus (Walbaum)

RANGE: Brazil to Florida; sometimes straggling farther north. Common around Bahamas.

COLOR: Yellowish orange tinged with red and frequently silvery. Fins yellow. Smaller specimens are barred. The fish also has a brown phase with bands. The fins are yellow in this phase also.

DISTINGUISHING CHARACTERISTICS: Color. The patch of teeth on the roof of the mouth is as in the Dog and Mangrove snappers. There is no whitish bar below the eye.

SIZE: Rarely over 20 pounds; usually less than 5.

FOOD: Fishes, crustaceans.

HABITS: Most frequently found in open water over reefs or sandy bottom.

LANE SNAPPER *Lutjanus synagris* (Linnaeus)

RANGE: Brazil to Florida and the Gulf coast.

COLOR: Red or gray above shading to greenish gray or silvery below. A dark blotch on the side. The fish sometimes shows bars or yellow stripes. The dorsal and tail fins are red; other fins yellow.

DISTINGUISHING CHARACTERISTICS: Dark blotch. Lower jaw projects beyond the upper. There are about 60 scales from the back of the gill cover to the base of the tail fin.

SIZE: Usually under 4 pounds.

FOOD: Fishes, crustaceans.

HABITS: Found around reefs, and coral heads. Less numerous than the Mangrove or Schoolmaster.

MUTTONFISH SNAPPER
also called MUTTONFISH

Lutjanus analis (Cuvier & Valenciennes)

RANGE: Brazil north to the West Indies and Florida; straggling farther north. Present all year on its regular grounds.

COLOR: Usually olive above: pinkish below; sometimes barred. Smaller specimens streaked with light blue. Dark spot on sides. Dorsal fin yellow; other fins red.

DISTINGUISHING CHARACTERISTICS: Dark spot on sides. Red fins. Small scales.

SIZE: Reaches a weight of 25 pounds; averages around 4 pounds.

FOOD: Fishes, crustaceans.

HABITS: A fish of the outer reefs, feeding at night.

The centre of abundance of the Pacific Snappers is Mexico and Central America.

PACIFIC DOG SNAPPER
also called PARGO PRIETO, PARGO NEGRO, and PARGO MORENO

Lutjanus novemfasciatus (Gill)

RANGE: Mexico.

COLOR: All red usually, but also has a darker phase which is almost purplish above and brownish red below. The back and about one fourth of the upper sides in the red phase are brownish and the anal caudal fins are darker toward the margins.

DISTINGUISHING CHARACTERISTICS: The rear nostril is round. Teeth in jaws conspicuous. The patch of teeth on the roof-of the mouth is crescent shaped with a very slight, if any, backward projection.

SIZE: Reaches a weight of 80 pounds.

COLORADO SNAPPER
also called PARGO COLORADO and RED SNAPPER

Lutjanus colorado (Jordan & Gilbert)

This fish is so similar in appearance to the Pacific Dog Snapper that it is often mistakenly identified. It is found from Mexico to Panama. In general the color tone is lighter than that of the Pacific Dog Snapper, and the rear nostril is long and narrow. Its pectoral fins are also longer than that of other species.

JORDAN'S SNAPPER *Lutjanus jordani* (Gilbert)

This is a reddish fish; red above; silvery below; sometimes barred. It is found from Mexico to Panama, and reaches a length of 3 feet. It may be distinguished by the diamond shaped patch of teeth on the roof of the mouth.

MULLET SNAPPER *Lutjanus aratus* (Gilbert)

This fish is listed here only because of the rarity of information about the breeding habits of the family. Walford reports that a specimen of Mullet Snapper taken at Cerralvo Island in early April was sexually mature and a female was becoming so. The fish is reddish, narrowly striped with brown. It reaches a weight of 40 pounds, but is seldom taken as a game fish.

SPOTTED ROSE SNAPPER

Lutjanus guttatus (Steindachner)

The Spotted Rose Snapper is found from Mexico to Ecuador. It is a reddish fish with some silver and sometimes yellowish tinges. There are oblique dark or yellow lines above the lateral line formed by dark or yellow dots on the scales; below the lateral line these lines are horizontal. The ventral and anal fins are yellow; the dorsal and pectorals pinkish and the tail fin red. The patch of teeth on the roof of the mouth is anchor shaped with a small backward projection. The fish reaches a length of about 30 inches.

YELLOWTAIL or YELLOWTAIL SNAPPER
also called PARGO AMARILLO

Lutjanus argentiventris (Peters)

The Yellowtail is found from the Gulf of California to Panama and south to Ecuador. It is very abundant around the Tres Marias Islands and off Panama.

This fish may be recognized by its color which is rose on the front part of the body; yellow on the rear. Below the eye there are bright blue spots which sometimes form a streak. There are a number of variations on this color pattern but the back part of the body remains yellow. The fish reaches a length of 2 feet.

YELLOWTAIL *Ocyurus chrysurus* (Bloch)

RANGE: Brazil to Florida where it is very abundant around the keys.

COLOR: Bluish gray with spots and lines of yellow. Some of the stripes join before the base of the caudal fin. The fins are yellow.

DISTINGUISHING CHARACTERISTICS: Caudal fin is deeply forked. Spots on upper half of the body. No scales on top of the head.

SIZE: Averages less than 1 foot in length although it is known to reach a length of over 2 feet.

FOOD: Fishes, crustaceans.

HABITS: The Yellowtail is very common in inlets, channels, and lagoons of medium depth. In winter it goes into deeper water. It also occurs on the surface and on the bottom. It feeds both during the day and at night.

THE GRUNTS *Haemulidae*

The grunts are closely related to the snappers, but may be distinguished from them by their lack of teeth on the roof of the mouth; their scaled dorsal and anal fins, and the fact that the scales near the lateral line do not run parallel to it.

These fishes normally move singly and in small groups, although at breeding time they form large schools. They feed almost entirely at night on very small fishes, crustaceans, sea urchins, starfish, etc.

The name Grunt comes from the ability of these fish to make sounds by grating the upper throat (pharyngeal) teeth against the lower. During this motion, the edge of the lower pharyngeals presses the end of the swim bladder which acts as a resonator.

The family has a world-wide range in warm waters. In the Western Hemisphere grunts occur in the Atlantic from Argentina to North Carolina and are most abundant from Florida south. They are also present on the Gulf Coast. In the Pacific they are found from California to Ecuador, but although common in markets, are not generally considered a sport fish.

There are many species of grunts, most of which are used as food, and many of which are regularly caught by anglers.

SAILOR'S CHOICE *Haemulon parra* (Desmarest)

RANGE: Brazil and Panama to Florida. Abundant off the Florida keys and Puerto Rico (summer).

A very similar fish, the Mojarra Prieta *(Haemulon scudderi* Gill), is found from Guaymas to Ecuador.

COLOR: Unevenly gray, sometimes with darker stripes and a dark spot at the base of the tail. Above the eye there is apt to be a yellowish patch or streak. The inside of the mouth is orange-red. There are indistinct dark streaks below the lateral line.

DISTINGUISHING CHARACTERISTICS: The rays of the dorsal, anal, and pectoral fins are closely covered with scales. The outline of the body from the tip of the snout to in front of the eye is very steep.

SIZE: Averages about $\frac{1}{2}$ pound. Reaches a weight of 2 pounds and a length of 1 foot.

FOOD: Mollusks, algae, worms.

HABITS: Frequents reef or rocky bottom, channels, inlets, and mangroves. In Puerto Rico, this fish is known to spawn over rocky bottom in July and August.

N. Y. Zoological Society

French Grunt.

FRENCH GRUNT
also called YELLOW GRUNT

Haemulon flavolineatum (Desmarest)

RANGE: Brazil and Panama to the Florida keys. Abundant in the West Indies and Puerto Rico. Quite common on the Atlantic coast of Panama.

COLOR: The ground color is a light greenish or bluish gray. There are wavy yellow stripes on the body and head. Below the lateral line these stripes are wider and oblique. A bright yellow stripe runs from the head to the end of the dorsal fin. There are yellow streaks and patches on the head and black patches near the lower angle of the gill cover and at the posterior end of the mouth. The inside of the mouth is bright brick red. The fins are yellow. In some specimens, there are blue stripes in addition to the yellow ones.

DISTINGUISHING CHARACTERISTICS: Scales below the lateral line are very much enlarged toward the front of the body. Yellow stripes.

SIZE: Reaches a length of 1 foot, but averages much less.

FOOD: Chiefly invertebrates.

HABITS: This fish is to be found most often around large coral patches.

GRAY GRUNT *Haemulon macrostomum* Günther

RANGE: Colombia and Panama (Atlantic) to Florida. Especially abundant on the Atlantic coast of Panama.

COLOR: Dusky blue on upper part of body and sides; brown below. There is a green bordered black stripe on the back. Dark and light blue stripes alternate on the sides of the body above the lateral line becoming less distinct or disappearing below it. There are no stripes in front of the eyes or on the gill covers. The dorsal fin is greenish, its spiny portion bordered with yellow; its soft portion dark at the base. The tail fin is yellowish or greenish. The first rays of the anal fin are dark; its last rays and its margin are yellow. The ventral fins are very dark at the base, becoming lighter toward the margin. Unlike most fishes, the young and the adults have the same color markings.

DISTINGUISHING CHARACTERISTICS: Large mouth. Second anal spine very long. Color pattern.

SIZE: Reaches a length of about a foot or slightly more.

FOOD: Very small fishes, crabs, starfish, sea urchins, etc.

HABITS: Abundant about coral reefs.

MARGATE GRUNT

Haemulon album Cuvier & Valenciennes

RANGE: Brazil to the Florida keys. Abundant around Key West. The Mojarra Almejero, *Hae-*

mulon sexfasciatum Gill, found from Lower California to Panama is very much like this fish.

COLOR: The Margate Grunt's color changes frequently and rapidly. The most usual phase is light gray with dotted dark horizontal lines above the lateral line, light greenish fins, yellow lips and a very bright orange-red lining of the mouth. There is sometimes a dark band on the sides. Another color phase is greenish with seven dark stripes.

DISTINGUISHING CHARACTERISTICS: The back of this fish is higher than in other grunts, resulting in a very steep profile. The scales above the lateral line run obliquely.

SIZE: Averages from 4 to 6 pounds or smaller, and reaches a weight of 8 to 10 pounds and a length of over 2 feet.

FOOD: Like that of other grunts.

HABITS: This fish is most abundant around reefs in rather deep water. It comes into more shallow water to feed. It spawns in early summer.

BLUE STRIPED GRUNT also called YELLOW GRUNT

Haemulon sciurus (Shaw)

RANGE: Brazil to the Florida keys. Abundant throughout its range, especially about the keys.

COLOR: Very changeable. Its most striking color phase shows stripes of blue and yellow from the back of the gill cover to the tail, and blue lines on the head. In this phase, the dorsal fin is very dark, its spiny portion margined with yellow; the caudal margin is yellow, and the other fins are yellow. In another color phase the fish is grayish and the fins light.

DISTINGUISHING CHARACTERISTICS: The horizontal blue stripes, and general yellow color. The fish in the grayish color phase must be distinguished by means of a scientific key to its body proportions.

SIZE: Reaches a weight of 3 pounds. Averages smaller.

FOOD: Like that of other grunts.

HABITS: Dr. Longley who observed this fish at Tortugas, writes that in the day it stays in schools near the bottom, around large coral stacks, but at dusk these schools break up and scatter. Various authors have noted that cold seems to affect this fish seriously.

WHITE GRUNT *Haemulon plumieri* (Lacépède)

RANGE: This fish is found farther north than other grunts. It is generally present all the year from Brazil and the Atlantic coast of Panama as far north as Cape Hatteras, North Carolina. It is abundant off Puerto Rico and very abundant in the fall off Key West.

COLOR: Changeable. Olive with wavy golden or brassy stripes and thin lines of light blue, or entirely olive or brown with light and dark patches. The inside of the mouth is red.

DISTINGUISHING CHARACTERISTICS: The scales above the lateral line are larger than those below it. In the striped phase, there are about 12 wavy blue lines on head and body.

SIZE: Averages less than 1 pound; rarely weighs over 2 pounds; known to reach a weight of 4 pounds and a length of about 18 inches.

FOOD: Like that of other grunts.

HABITS: Frequents sandy shores, but the best fishing is said to be over rock bottom. This grunt gathers in large schools for spawning which takes place in August and September, after which the fish scatter.

PIGFISH *Orthopristis chrysopterus* (Linnaeus)

RANGE: Gulf coasts of Mexico and Florida; Atlantic coast from Florida straggling to Massachusetts; uncommon north of Virginia. Taken frequently as far north as North Carolina. Other species are found in the Pacific from the Gulf of California to Peru, but are not usually listed as anglers' fishes.

COLOR: Silvery blue ground color with dark dots on head and dorsal fin and a blue line on the side of the upper lip. The mouth is white inside. There are blue and brownish stripes above and below the lateral line; those above it run obliquely; those below horizontally. The pectoral fins are yellow with dark tips and there is a yellow patch at the base of the tail.

DISTINGUISHING CHARACTERISTICS: A longer body and head and more pointed snout than the other grunts. The second anal spine is not noticeably larger than the others. The soft rayed dorsal and anal fins are not closely scaled. The scales above the lateral line are not parallel to it.

SIZE: Reaches a length of 15 inches.

FOOD: Small fishes, mollusks, etc. A bottom feeder.

The Pigfish frequents shores, sounds, and estuaries from March to November. It spawns off North Carolina from March to June. Its buoyant, transparent eggs are hard to tell from those of the White Perch. They hatch within 36 to 72 hours. The fish is sexually mature at about the age of two years and very few are known to live longer than four years.

POMPOM also called BLACK MARGATE

Anisotremus surinamensis (Bloch)

The two species of this genus usually considered as game fish are the Pompom and the Porkfish.

The Pompom occurs from Brazil to Florida and is not very numerous anywhere. It is grayish or brownish fish with darker fins and with dark spots, averaging from 1 to 2 pounds, and frequenting deep holes, channels, coral heads and rocks. It eats crabs, sand fleas, crustaceans, and small fishes. It is considered a good food fish.

PORKFISH *Anisotremus virginicus* (Linnaeus)

RANGE: The Porkfish is found from Brazil to Florida and is common in the West Indies.

COLOR: The ground color is silver, over which there are about eight light yellow stripes on the sides. The belly is whitish-silver. One broad black band runs from the beginning of the dorsal fin to the base of the pectoral fin; another runs from the top of the head through the eye to the angle of the mouth. The top of the head and all the fins are bronze. There is a yellow patch covering the scales which form the sheath of the anal fin.

THE PORGIES

The porgies are small food fishes, chiefly found in southern areas. They have a single dorsal fin of spines and rays, a three-spined anal fin followed by soft rays; the teeth in the front of the mouth are conical or incisor and there are none on the roof of the mouth or on the tongue.

NORTHERN PORGY

also called SCUP *Stenotomus chrysops* (Linnaeus)

RANGE: North Carolina (in offshore waters in winter) to Maine where it is a straggler. Introduced into Bermuda. Abundant in summer and fall off New York and southern New England.

COLOR: Back and upper part of sides dusky or brownish; silvery below. Fins brownish.

DISTINGUISHING CHARACTERISTICS: Front teeth narrow and incisorlike. Front profile very steep. Snout short. Pectoral fin shorter than head.

SIZE: Averages less than a foot and about 1½ pounds. Said to reach 1½ feet and a weight of 3 or 4 pounds.

FOOD: A bottom feeder. Crabs, squids, clams, fry of fishes, worms, mollusks, and some vegetable matter.

HABITS: Spawns in June and July at about the third summer of its life. The eggs are transparent and buoyant.

SOUTHERN PORGY

also called SCUP

Stenotomus aculeatus (Cuvier & Valenciennes)

RANGE: Virginia to Florida and Texas. Very rare off Florida. Not very abundant anywhere.

COLOR: Very closely resembles the Northern Porgy.

DISTINGUISHING CHARACTERISTICS: Front teeth narrow and incisorlike. Front profile not very steep. Pectoral about as long as head. Snout long.

SIZE: Reaches a length of about one foot; usually smaller.

FOOD: Crabs, squids, worms.

JOLTHEAD PORGY

Calamus bajonado (Bloch & Schneider)

RANGE: Brazil to Florida, including Bermuda and the West Indies. Very abundant and present all year.

COLOR: Metallic yellowish with brassy spots. Blue marks on the head and a blue stripe below the eye. The angle of the mouth is yellow and purple. Fins dusky.

Stickney-Fish & Wildlife Service

Southern Porgy.

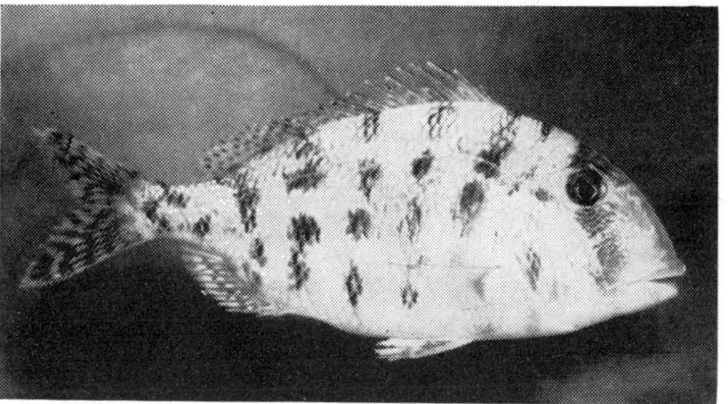

N. Y. Zoological Society

Grass Porgy.

DISTINGUISHING CHARACTERISTICS: Front teeth conical; the outer one on one or both jaws is larger than the others, and canine-like. There are 54-59 scales in a row from the back of the gill cover to the base of the tail. The body is not as deep as that of the Saucereye or Littlehead Porgy, and the color is distinctive.

SIZE: Averages below 5 pounds; recorded up to 14 pounds and a length of 2 feet.

FOOD: Feeds in the daytime on crabs, squid, mollusks, and small fishes.

HABITS: An inshore fish, usually to be found schooling over smooth rock bottom but also present over sandy bottom. Reported to spawn in July and August.

SAUCEREYE PORGY

Calamus calamus (Cuvier & Valenciennes)

RANGE: West Indies and Bermuda to the Florida keys. Fairly common at Bermuda.

COLOR: Silvery blue with brassy horizontal stripes formed by spots on the scales. Golden spots on the head. A light streak on the gill cover. The head in front of the eye, the lower jaw, and a streak below the eye are dark purplish blue. The fins are light, blotched with orange.

DISTINGUISHING CHARACTERISTICS: Deep body. Steep profile. Outer tooth on one or both jaws a large canine. Color is distinctive.

SIZE: Averages less than a pound, which is about its maximum weight.

FOOD: Like that of the Jolthead Porgy.

HABITS: This is a good food fish, but not as plenitful as the Jolthead or Littlehead Porgies.

LITTLEHEAD PORGY

Calamus proridens Jordan & Gilbert

RANGE: West Indies to the Florida Keys.

COLOR: Very bright silvery with lavender blue horizontal stripes on the upper sides and light orange spots below.

DISTINGUISHING CHARACTERISTICS: Very much like the Saucereye from which it may be distinguished by its color.

SIZE: Averages less than a pound.

FOOD: Like that of the Jolthead Porgy.

GRASS PORGY *Calamus arctifrons* Goode & Bean

RANGE: West Indies to Florida. Not abundant anywhere.

COLOR: Dull greenish with dark bars and some

Al Johns, San Pedro

California Sheephead.

dark spots. A few light spots on the scales. Six yellow spots along the lateral line, and yellow lines in front of the eye. The fins are barred and spotted. Sometimes there are dark bars across the sides.

DISTINGUISHING CHARACTERISTICS: There are 45 to 52 scales in a row from the back of the gill cover to the base of the tail. The pectoral fins are short.

SIZE: Averages under a pound.

FOOD: Small crustaceans and mollusks.

HABITS: This very small porgy is to be found in shallow water where there is vegetation. It is a good food fish but not abundant anywhere.

PINFISH *Lagodon rhomboides* (Linnaeus)
also called BREAM

RANGE: Cape Cod, Massachusetts to Bermuda and Cuba; also on the Gulf coast. Not abundant north of Delaware; common from Virginia south and on the Gulf coast of Florida. Present the year around.

COLOR: Sides bluish-silver; back dark and greenish. A prominent black spot just behind the upper end of the gill cover. Often has four to seven dark bands across the body, and horizontal narrow gilt stripes which converge near the tail base. The dorsal fin is blue with an indefinite gilt band; the anal fin is blue with a yellow stripe; caudal and ventral fins are yellow; the pectoral fins transparently dusky.

DISTINGUISHING CHARACTERISTICS: This fish has a small mouth and conspicuously notched incisor teeth. There are eleven or twelve sharp spines in the dorsal fin, preceded by a very small, sharp, forwardly-directed spine and followed by eleven soft rays. The anal has three spines and ten or eleven soft rays. There are 67 to 70 scales in a line from the back of the gill cover to the base of the tail.

SIZE: Averages about 6 inches in length, but reaches 10 inches.

FOOD: Fishes, clams, mollusks, copepods, shrimps, worms.

HABITS: A schooling fish of commercial importance in the south. It is found chiefly in inlets and bays where it feeds around pilings, mangroves, etc. Although young have been taken in offshore waters, apparently heading in, the spawning grounds are not known.

SHEEPSHEAD
Archosargus probatocephalus (Walbaum)

RANGE: Cape Cod to Tampico, Mexico. Another species is found south to Brazil. The fish is abundant throughout its range, and is present the year around. It moves in and out with the tide, and sometimes runs up rivers.

COLOR: Dull green above; dull silver below. Wide dark bands around the body. No shoulder spot.

DISTINGUISHING CHARACTERISTICS: Deep body; dark bands; small mouth and notched incisor teeth in front; crushing molar back teeth; forked caudal; long dorsal fin with strong spines preceded by a forwardly directed and imbedded spine.

SIZE: Averages between 1 and 2 pounds but not uncommon up to 5 pounds. Reported to reach a weight of 30 pounds, but very unusual over 12 pounds.

FOOD: Chiefly crustaceans and mollusks.

HABITS: Swims in groups but not in regular schools. Gathers in large groups when feeding. Spawns in the Gulf of Mexico in March and April on sandy shores in 6 to 8 feet of water. The eggs are round and buoyant. Except when spawning, the Sheepshead spends its time around rocks, wrecks, and mangroves. It is a good food fish and is caught commercially.

GIRELLAS

OPALEYE *Girella nigricans* (Ayres)

RANGE: Present all year from San Francisco to Cape San Lucas, Lower California; most abundant in winter. Another species is found off the Cape Verde Islands off the coast of West Africa.

COLOR: Upper part of body olive; lower greyish brown. The eye is opalescent blue. Young specimens have a light spot on the side near the dorsal fin.

DISTINGUISHING CHARACTERISTICS: Soft dorsal and anal are not scaled. Very few scales on the head. Bands of teeth in the jaws, the outer of which are tricuspid and easily movable. Very small teeth on the sides of the roof of the mouth; none in its center.

SIZE: Reaches a length of about 17 inches.

FOOD: Herbivorous.

HABITS: Frequents inshore waters around rocks.

RUDDERFISHES or CHOPAS

BERMUDA CHUB *Kyphosus sectatrix* (Linnaeus)

RANGE: Massachusetts to the West Indies and the Atlantic side of Panama. Also reported from Madeira and the Canary Islands.

Another species, *K.elegans* (Peters), is found from Guaymas, Mexico, to the Galapagos Islands, and another, *K.analogus* (Gill) from Guaymas to Panama.

COLOR: Ground color brown, becoming lighter on the lower part of the sides. Ventrals whitish; other fins brown. *Kyphosus elegans* is brown with lighter spots and a black margin on the gill cover.

DISTINGUISHING CHARACTERISTICS: Outer teeth are incisorlike and immovable, followed by a band of very fine teeth. There are no molar teeth. The soft rayed dorsal and anal fins are closely scaled. The head is scaled except between the eyes.

SIZE: Averages between 3 and 4 pounds.
FOOD: Herbivorous; chiefly algae.
HABITS: A shore fish.

CROAKERS, DRUMS, and WEAKFISHES

This group is characterized by an anal fin with either one or two spines, and a lateral line which runs out to or nearly to the end of the tail fin.

In most of the species, a croaking noise is made by means of the air bladder acting as a resonator.

CROAKERS AND DRUMS

SILVER PERCH *Bairdiella chrysura* (Lacépède)

This fish is often confused with the White Perch, *Morone americana* (Gmelin) (see Fresh-Water section). It is not generally considered a game fish although some local lists include it as such.

RANGE: New York to Texas.

COLOR: Dusky green above with small black dots on the body but not on the head. Silvery with pinkish tones below. Fins light brown.

DISTINGUISHING CHARACTERISTICS: Anal fin with 2 spines (the White Perch has 3); outer row of teeth in upper jaw are canines. Margin of the preopercle (bone directly in front of the gill cover and overlapping it) serrated.

HABITS: Found on sandy shores in summer; probably moves offshore in winter.

CHANNEL BASS
also called RED DRUM and PEZ COLORADO

RANGE: New York to Texas and Mexico. Not common north of Virginia. Abundant Chesapeake Bay, North Carolina, Gulf Coast. Present all year off North Carolina but best fishing is in spring and late fall. Resident in the Gulf of Mexico off Texas. This is one of our finest and most abundant fishes and both adult and young are sought by anglers.

COLOR: Lighter or darker tones of coppery red or yellowish red with deeper red or brown spots on the scales forming longitudinal stripes. Conspicuous black spot on the upper part of the tail base.

DISTINGUISHING CHARACTERISTICS: Black spot; color; no barbels; long head; outer teeth of upper jaw large.

SIZE: Reaches a weight of over 80 pounds and a length of over 5 feet. Sold commercially at 5 pounds; 15 pounds not uncommon.

FOOD: Fishes, crabs, shrimp.

HABITS: Swims in large schools. Is found in inlets, channels, along sandy shores. Spawns in the mouths of passes in the Gulf of Mexico. The height of the spawning season off Texas is known to be October. In Chesapeake Bay, it probably spawns somewhat earlier.

BLACK DRUM *Pogonias cromis* Linnaeus

RANGE: Long Island to Florida and Texas and said to run to Argentina. Resident and abundant.

COLOR: Gray or dark silver or copper above; lighter below; fins dusky; in small specimens there are dark vertical bars.

Calif. State Fisheries Laboratory

Opaleye

DISTINGUISHING CHARACTERISTICS: Profile of the back is humped. A row of barbels under the chin. Very large blunt throat teeth. Long, very strong second anal spine. Dorsal spines high. Mouth set very low in profile.

SIZE: Averages 3 to 6 pounds, but a number of catches have been made of over 50 pounds.

FOOD: A bottom feeder on fishes, crustaceans, and mollusks.

HABITS: Occurs in large schools in bays, inlets and also in the surf, spawning in the Gulf of Mexico from February to May. Especially during the breeding season, the fish makes a loud drumming noise.

The Black Drum is edible although the flesh is rather coarse.

SPOT *Leiostomus xanthurus* Lacépède

RANGE: Massachusetts to Texas and the West Indies (rare). Abundant Chesapeake Bay, April to November; in past years there have been very erratic large runs in New York harbor (1902, 1907, 1917 and 1925).

COLOR: Blue gray above; silver below. There are 12 to 15 narrow oblique, yellowish bars from the ridge of the back to slightly below the lateral line; the first bar is below the fourth or fifth dorsal spine; the last two are on the caudal peduncle; a dark spot on the shoulder; fins light yellow, except the caudal which is dusky.

DISTINGUISHING CHARACTERISTICS: Rounded snout with mouth set low in the profile of the head. The profile from the eye to the beginning of the dorsal fin is steep. Teeth very small in bands in jaws and none in the lower jaw in many adults. Anal with 2 spines. Scales small and ctenoid (toothed on their open margin); dorsal spines high in front, highest in the middle, the last two very low. Soft rays of almost the same height throughout the length of the fin.

SIZE: Reaches a length of a foot and a weight of 3/4 of a pound. Averages between 6 and 10 inches and around 1/2 pound.

FOOD: Small fishes, crustaceans, worms, some vegetation.

HABITS: The male of this fish makes a drumming sound, but it is not so loud as that made by some other croakers. The abundance varies greatly from year to year. Adult Spots, and to some extent the young, appear to make migrations to and from inshore and offshore water. The young also go

Fish & Wildlife Service
Spotfin Croaker.

up into fresh water. Spawning takes place in fall or winter not far offshore.

SPOTFIN CROAKER

Roncador stearnsi (Steindachner)

RANGE: San Francisco to Mexico. More abundant from Pt. Conception southward. Present all year; most abundant in summer.

COLOR: Metallic steel blue or brassy on upper part of sides; silvery below; faint oblique dark lines across the sides; conspicuous black spot on the pectoral fin base; fins dusky.

DISTINGUISHING CHARACTERISTICS: Two anal spines; pectoral spot; dorsal fin deeply notched between spinous and soft rayed portion; caudal margin straight; upper jaw longer than lower; dorsal and anal fins scaled; pectoral fin reaches past the end of the ventral; no barbels.

SIZE: Reaches a weight of 5 pounds

FOOD: Fishes, crustaceans.

HABITS: A popular sport fish taken both in shallow water and surf.

CALIFORNIA KINGFISH

Genyonemus lineatus (Ayres)

RANGE: British Columbia to Mexico. All year. Most abundant in winter and spring.

COLOR: Metallic whitish-silver; upper part somewhat brassy; fins yellowish; faint dark wavy lines on sides.

DISTINGUISHING CHARACTERISTICS: The range; no teeth on roof of mouth; upper jaw slightly longer than lower; no barbels.

SIZE: Usually under one pound.

HABITS: Apt to be found in mixed schools near shore.

CROAKER *Micropogon undulatus* (Linnaeus)

RANGE: Cape Cod to Texas where it is abundant but runs small. Abundant New Jersey to North Carolina and quite common off the Gulf coast of Florida. Other species of *Micropogon* are found in the West Indies, South America, Mexico, Panama, and the Gulf of California.

COLOR: Brassy above becoming lighter below; body irregularly spotted with brown; short, dark bars cross the lateral line.

DISTINGUISHING CHARACTERISTICS: Very small barbels on lower jaw; outer teeth of upper jaw enlarged.

SIZE: Reaches a length of about 20 inches and a weight of about 4 pounds.

FOOD: Mollusks, crustaceans.

HABITS: Present in summer feeding in shallow water over grassy bottom; spawns in the fall and early winter but disappears with low temperatures. Free eggs have not been taken, but a specimen 15½ inches long, taken in Chesapeake Bay, contained 180,000 eggs.

A very popular fish with bait fishermen in Chesapeake and other bays to the south.

YELLOWFIN CROAKER

Umbrina roncador Jordan & Gilbert

RANGE: San Francisco (occasional only) into the Gulf of California. Common from San Diego south. Present all year but most abundant in summer. Other species of *Umbrina* are found in the Atlantic but have never been recorded as taken for sport.

COLOR: Metallic gray and gold; silvery below; oblique wavy lines across body are dark; dorsal fin dark; other fins yellow.

DISTINGUISHING CHARACTERISTICS: One short barbel on tip of the lower jaw; second anal spine long and very strong; upper jaw slightly longer than lower.

SIZE: Reaches about 15 inches.

FOOD: Presumably like that of other croakers.

HABITS: A fish of shallow sandy shores. Also taken in surf.

WHITINGS *Menticirrhus*

The fishes of the genus *Menticirrhus* are long and slender with a small, single barbel at the tip of the lower jaw. One weak anal spine is present. These fishes have no air bladder and consequently do not croak. The species are not generally distinguished by market dealers.

WHITING

Menticirrhus saxatilis (Bloch & Schneider)

RANGE: Maine (rare) to Florida and introduced into Bermuda. Most common from Cape Cod to Chesapeake Bay in summer and fall.

COLOR: Ground color gray, varying in tone; about 6 oblique bars on sides, one across the back of the head; the next two meeting at their lower ends to form a V; a dark bar below the eye.

DISTINGUISHING CHARACTERISTICS: The longest dorsal spine is prolonged into a filament reaching nearly to the middle of the soft rayed dorsal. There are 91 to 96 scales in a row from the back of the gill cover to the tail base. The anal usually has 8 soft rays. The pupil of the eye is vertically elongate.

SIZE: Averages ½ pound; reported to reach a weight of 3 pounds.

FOOD: Small fishes, crabs, squids, shrimp.

HABITS: A fish of sandy bottom and surf. Spawns

Fish & Wildlife Service
Cero or Kingfish.

Todd-Fish & Wildlife Service

Croaker.

off New Jersey in June, July and August; in Chesapeake Bay and off Beaufort, North Carolina probably in April and May. The eggs are buoyant and transparent. At a very small size, the young resemble the adult in external appearance. The fish is mature when two or three years old.

SOUTHERN WHITING

Menticirrhus americanus (Linnaeus)

Another very closely related form occurring from the West Indies to Argentina is regarded by most ichthyologists as a southern form of this species.

RANGE: New Jersey to Texas. Abundant Chesapeake Bay southward. Most plentiful in spring.

COLOR: Ground color dull silver or gray with indistinct oblique bars; a few dark dots on the spinous dorsal and soft anal fins.

DISTINGUISHING CHARACTERISTICS: Dorsal spines not prolonged; anal usually has 7 soft rays; there are 86 to 90 scales from the back of the gill cover to the base of the tail; the pupil of the eye is round.

SIZE: Averages about ½ pound in weight but reaches 2½ pounds.

HABITS: Found with the Whiting off New Jersey in late summer. It spawns later than *saxatilis* off New Jersey—sometime in August—and later still in Florida. Both young and adult are found both in inshore and offshore waters near the bottom, and are frequently caught in winter.

GULF KINGFISH

Menticirrhus littoralis (Holbrook)

RANGE: Chesapeake Bay to the Gulf Coast.

COLOR: Usually plain silver; a few fine dots on the membranes of the first few spines of the dorsal fin.

DISTINGUISHING CHARACTERISTICS: Dorsal spines not prolonged. Anal usually has 7 rays. There are 70 to 75 scales in a longitudinal row from back of the gill cover to the base of the caudal fin. The pupil of the eye is vertically elongate. The color is plain.

HABITS: Known to spawn off North Carolina from May to August.

CALIFORNIA CROAKER

Menticirrhus undulatus (Girard)

RANGE: San Francisco (rare) to Mexico. Present all year. Most abundant in summer from Pt. Conception southward.

COLOR: Metallic steel on back, growing lighter below; white on belly; indefinite oblique dark lines and black dots on lower part of sides; fins dusky.

DISTINGUISHING CHARACTERISTICS: Dorsal spines not prolonged. The range. Otherwise the characteristics are technical, and a key must be used.

SIZE: Reaches a length of 20 inches.

FOOD: Fishes, crustaceans.

HABITS: Usually taken by surf casting.

BLACK CROAKER *Sciaena saturna* (Girard)

RANGE: Present all year from Pt. Conception to Cerros Island. A number of other species are found off Panama, Peru, and Chile, but they are not fished by anglers.

COLOR: Dusky blue on the upper sides; dusky silver below with a copper overtone; dark dots on scales; a vertically elongate blotch on the back of the gill cover; fins dark; sometimes there is a pale band on the base of the dorsal fin across the body, and occasionally there are dark lengthwise stripes.

DISTINGUISHING CHARACTERISTICS: Humped outline from head above the eye to the beginning of the dorsal fin. Two spines in the anal fin. No teeth on the roof of the mouth. No barbel. Snout reaches beyond the tip of the lower jaw. The range.

SIZE: Reaches a length of about 15 inches.

FOOD: Fishes, crustaceans.

WEAKFISHES

There are many species of weakfish found world-wide in warm seas, but many are never caught by anglers.

Their general characteristics include a lateral line running to the end of the tail fin; 1 or 2 anal spines and 8 to 11 anal rays; canine teeth in the jaws; a spiny margin on the preopercle; and a very metallic color. The name refers to the very tender mouth.

WEAKFISH also called SEA TROUT

Cynoscion regalis (Bloch & Schneider)

RANGE: Massachusetts, and straggling farther north, to Florida. Reported in Gulf waters as far as Mobile. Present all year from North Carolina southward. North of that state it comes inshore from May to October at which time the large Long Island and New Jersey runs occur.

COLOR: Dusky silvery blue above, thickly dotted with black; pinkish silvery below; fins apt to be either pink or yellow, but sometimes greenish.

DISTINGUISHING CHARACTERISTICS: The soft rayed dorsal and anal fins are scaled. There are two large canine teeth in the upper jaw and the lower jaw is longer than the upper.

SIZE: Averages under 6 pounds; usually 1 to 5, but frequently caught at 10 pounds, and reported to reach 30. The rod and reel record was taken in Mullica River, New Jersey, and weighed 17 pounds 8 ounces.

FOOD: Fishes, squid, shrimps.

HABITS: This schooling fish is found most frequently in channels, inlets, surf, and tide rips. It spawns from May to September from South Carolina to Cape Cod, near the bottom. The eggs are deposited in 3 to 5 fathoms of water and float to the surface, drifting until they hatch, which is in

Calif. State Fisheries Laboratory
Totuava.

approximately 1½ days. Off North Carolina, where the Weakfish has been most intensively studied, it was observed that the larger individuals leave in fall and return in spring.

SPOTTED WEAKFISH
also called SPOTTED SEA TROUT

Cynoscion nebulosus (Cuvier & Valenciennes)

RANGE: A permanent resident from New York to Texas, common south of Delaware. Not abundant on the Gulf Coast.

COLOR: Very much like that of the Weakfish, but with more conspicuous black spots on the body, dorsal, and caudal. Those on the body are concentrated on the upper side from the beginning of the dorsal to the tail. The anal fin is dusky.

DISTINGUISHING CHARACTERISTICS: Dorsal and anal not scaled. Color.

SIZE: Said to reach 16 pounds. The rod and reel record, taken off Fort Pierce, Florida, weighed 15 pounds 3 ounces.

FOOD: Fish, shrimp, squid.

HABITS: Found in shallows, and into brackish water. Sometimes schools of this fish become numb with cold and are picked up inshore. In Texas, the fish goes deeper in cold weather. It is reported to spawn in that state from May to October in bays, depositing the eggs on the bottom.

SAND WEAKFISH *Cynoscion arenarius* Ginsburg

RANGE: Gulf coast.

COLOR: Dusky yellow above; silvery below; sometimes indistinctly spotted; tip of snout and lower jaw dark.

DISTINGUISHING CHARACTERISTICS: The color. Middle rays of tail fin longer than the others. Snout long. Not less than 10 soft rays in the anal fin.

SIZE: A small fish of 1 pound or less.

HABITS: Occurs in shallower water than the Silver Weakfish.

SILVER WEAKFISH *Cynoscion nothus* (Holbrook)

RANGE: Maryland to the Gulf coast; rare on the Atlantic coast of Florida. Less common than the Weakfish or the Spotted Weakfish; abundant off Alabama, Louisiana and Texas in winter in from 3 to 10 fathoms.

COLOR: Silvery; somewhat brownish or tan above; sometimes there are irregularly scattered dark dots on the upper parts of the sides.

DISTINGUISHING CHARACTERISTICS: The anal fin usually has 9 rays; seldom 10. The soft rays of the dorsal and anal fins are scaled.

SIZE: 9¼ inches is about the maximum length.

HABITS: More often found in open water than either the Weakfish or the Spotted Weakfish. Like the others, it is a good food fish.

CALIFORNIA WHITE SEA BASS

Cynoscion nobilis (Ayres)

RANGE: Puget Sound to Mexico, but not found commonly north of San Francisco. Most frequent from Santa Barbara to Mexico. Present all year but most abundant May to September.

COLOR: Metallic blue-gray above; whitish silver below.

DISTINGUISHING CHARACTERISTICS: Dorsal and anal rays not scaled. Canine teeth, if present in adult, are small. Lower jaw longer than upper. No enlarged canines. No stripes or bars.

SIZE: 20 to 30 pounds. Reaches 60 or more. The rod and reel record fish of 83 pounds, 12 ounces was taken on August 29, 1955 off San Felipe, Mexico.

FOOD: Fishes, especially flying fish and herring, crabs, squids, shrimps.

HABITS: An inshore fish, frequently found around kelp beds. Believed to spawn from March to August. A good food fish as well as a hard fighter on the hook.

TOTUAVA *Cynoscion macdonaldi* Gilbert

RANGE: From the top of the Gulf of California to Guaymas. In past years they have been abundant in the Guaymas region in winter, but recently they have been scarce around Guaymas and more numerous near the mouth of the Colorado River. They are most abundant at that point in March. In April and May they begin to move to an unknown destination.

COLOR: Dull iridescent silver and copper; the inside of the mouth is dirty yellow.

DISTINGUISHING CHARACTERISTICS: No scales on the membranes of the soft rayed dorsal, which has 24 to 25 rays. The middle rays of the tail are longer than the others. There are no dark stripes or bars.

SIZE: Reaches a weight of 225 pounds. Very common between 50 and 100 pounds.

FOOD: Fishes, crustaceans.

HABITS: A very much prized game fish, usually found near the bottom.

BLANQUILLOS

OCEAN WHITEFISH

Caulolatilus princeps (Jenyns)

RANGE: Point Conception to the Galapagos Is-

Calif. State Fisheries Laboratory
Halfmoon.

Smithsonian Institution
Halfmoon.

lands. Present all year; most frequent December to April.

COLOR: Pinkish or reddish-brown, darker on the upper part of sides; fins pale greenish.

DISTINGUISHING CHARACTERISTICS: A single, low, undivided dorsal fin consisting of 9 spiny rays and 24 soft rays. This fin is almost even in height throughout its length. The anal fin consists of 2 weak spines and 23 soft rays and is also long, low and even in height. The scales are very small. No teeth on roof of mouth. The teeth in the back part of the jaw are large canines.

SIZE: Averages 10 to 12 pounds and 25 to 35 inches, and reaches a length of 40 inches.

HABITS: Usually taken around rocks.

HALFMOON

Medialuna californiensis (Steindachner)

RANGE: Present all year from Point Conception to Cedros Island.

COLOR: Dark metallic-gray above; lighter below; a black spot on shoulder; fins dusky; there are sometimes faint oblique dotted lines on the sides and occasionally a dark lateral band bounded above by a lighter area.

DISTINGUISHING CHARACTERISTICS: Small mouth. Lateral line runs much above the center of the side. The dorsal fin has 9 low spines; its soft rays are higher than the spines. The anal has 2 low spines. The rayed portions of dorsal and anal are scaled. There are small teeth on the roof of the mouth. The scales are not even in size.

SIZE: A maximum of 1 foot.

Scheffer-Fish & Wildlife Service
Rockfish. Known in some localities as "bass."

FOOD: The fish is herbivorous and feeds chiefly on algae.

HABITS: Found around rocky coasts.

ROCKFISHES *Sebastodes*

There are over fifty species of Rockfish on the west coast of North America, the majority of which are found off California where they are all year residents but most abundant in winter and spring. Some of the species are found as far north as Alaska and some are also found in Japan. Many are fishes of very deep water.

The Rockfishes are recognizable by their single, long, dorsal fin which is very distinctly notched between its spines and rays. It has 13 strong spines; the anal has 3 spines. There is a bony ridge under the skin running back across the cheek from below the eye.

Many of these fishes are very bright shades of red or yellow; others are black. They vary in size from 5 to 10 pounds.

The Rockfishes are more important commercially than as sports fishes, although they are sometimes taken by anglers. The one most frequently caught by anglers is the Priestfish, also called the Black Rockfish, *sebastodes mystinus* Jordan and Gilbert. This is a dull blackish fish, white on the belly. The dorsal fin has 13 spines none of which are higher than its soft rays. There are no spines on top of the head. The fish reaches a length of over 20 inches.

These fish are important to ocean fishermen whether trolling or bottom fishing, and furnish a considerable part of the catch of hook and line fishermen off the northern California and Oregon coasts.

SCORPIONFISHES

CABEZON *Scorpaenichthys marmoratus* (Ayres)

Although there are several species of this genus found off the west coast of North America, this is the one chiefly valued by anglers. It is also the only one of any size, reaching a weight of 25 pounds although averaging less. It is a scaleless fish, varying in color from red to green. There is a flap of flesh on the snout and similar flaps in back of the eyes. In front of the eyes there is a heavy spine. The dorsal fin has 11 spines; the anal none.

The Cabezon weighs from 10 to 15 pounds and is a shallow water fish. It is found from British Columbia to San Diego.

SABLEFISH and GREENLING

SABLEFISH
also called BLACK COD and CANDLEFISH

Anoplopoma fimbria (Pallas)

RANGE: Monterey Bay to the Aleutian Islands. Most common in Puget Sound and southeastern Alaska.

COLOR: Dark gray or green; lighter on the lower part of the body.

DISTINGUISHING CHARACTERISTICS: The two dorsal fins are separated by a considerable space. A bony support runs across the cheek below the skin, beginning below the eye.

SIZE: Reaches a weight of 5 pounds.

FOOD: Fishes, crustaceans.

HABITS: Usually caught in from 2 to 15 fathoms. The fish is marketed as food, but its flesh is rather dry.

ROCK TROUT

Hexagrammos decagrammus (Pallas)

RANGE: Kodiak Island to Point Conception (fall and winter).

COLOR: Brown or gray above; greenish blue below; brown or yellow dots on head and body; fins brown or yellowish; in darker colored specimens, the flesh is green.

DISTINGUISHING CHARACTERISTIC: There are no anal spines. The dorsal is long and notched, with spines and soft rays. There is only one lateral line.

SIZE: Reaches 30 or 40 pounds, but averages 10 to 15.

HABITS: The liver oil is valuable for its vitamin content.

ATKA MACKEREL

Pleurogrammus monopterygius (Pallas)

RANGE: The Aleutian, Pribilof, and Shumagin Islands, particularly around Atka and Attu where it is very abundant from April to October.

COLOR: Gray or yellowish with black bars of varying width which run from the top margin of the dorsal fin across the body; the dorsal fin is yellowish except for the last few rays which form the upper part of a broad dark bar crossing the body; the upper part of the pectoral fins is pinkish, the lower dark; the anal and ventrals are dark and the tail is reddish brown.

DISTINGUISHING CHARACTERISTICS: The fish has five lateral lines and no anal spines, the color striking.

SIZE: Averages about 2 pounds and is known to reach about 4 pounds and a length of 1½ feet.

FOOD: Chiefly crustaceans.

HABITS: The Atka Mackerel is usually fished through kelp in from 2 to 4 fathoms. Large schools are to be seen inshore. They feed and spawn in kelp patches. The spawning season is June, and July, and at that time the fish are in the inter-island passes. After spawning they return to the ocean. It is a good food fish.

SURF FISHES *Embiotocidae*

The Surf Fishes occur in the Pacific ranging from Alaska to Lower California, with one fresh-water representative. There are about 20 species. They are present all year and are caught both for food and for sport. They are small fish of about 6 to 18 inches.

Calif. State Fisheries Laboratory
Barred Perch.

Calif. State Fisheries Laboratory
Striped Perch.

These fishes may be recognized by a long dorsal fin with up to 11 spines; an anal with 3 spines. Neither fin is heavily scaled. The mouth is small and there are no teeth on its roof.

They are to be found over sandy or rock bottom and in surf.

The Surf Fishes all bear live young.

BARRED SURF PERCH

Amphistichus argenteus Agassiz

RANGE: San Francisco to San Diego.

COLOR: Metallic-blue on the upper part of the sides; pinkish silvery below; the body is crossed by about 12 dark, irregular bars, a more or less continuous bar alternating with one composed only of three or four dots; these bars are most conspicuous from the lateral line downward but do not reach the lower margin of the body; there is a dark streak on the gill cover; the fins are greenish.

DISTINGUISHING CHARACTERISTICS: Two series of slender, conical teeth in each jaw. Lower lip with a broad fold. Rays of the dorsal fin higher than the spines. Small scales. The color pattern.

BLACK SURF PERCH *Embiotoca jacksoni* Agassiz

RANGE: Vancouver Island to Cedros Island.

COLOR: The scales are bluish, edged with brown; the lips are brown.

DISTINGUISHING CHARACTERISTICS: The teeth in a single series in both jaws. The lower lip with a fold. A patch of scales between the pectoral and ventral fins are larger than the others. Thick brown lips.

SIZE: Reaches a length of 14 inches, but is generally smaller.

STRIPED SURF PERCH

Taeniotoca lateralis (Agassiz)

RANGE: San Diego to Vancouver Island; more abundant in the northern part of its range.

COLOR: Metallic; the body color consists of alternating orange or brassy and blue horizontal stripes, less distinctly marked but present on the head; the fins are tan or brassy.

DISTINGUISHING CHARACTERISTICS: The color pattern. The lower lip has a fold. The teeth in one series in both jaws. The short deep caudal peduncle. The soft rays of the dorsal fin are much higher than its spines. The tail is concave in its marginal outline, but not forked.

SIZE: Averages 7 to 8 inches long.

PACIFIC WHITE SURF PERCH

Phanerodon furcatus Girard

RANGE: Vancouver Island to San Diego.

COLOR: Silvery, darker above; a dark line runs along the base of the dorsal fin; the tail fin is light, with a broad dark margin.

DISTINGUISHING CHARACTERISTICS: Teeth in a single series in both jaws; lower lip with a fold. No bars or stripes. A long slender caudal peduncle. A deeply forked caudal fin.

SIZE: Reaches a length of 12 inches but is generally smaller.

HABITS: The breeding season of this fish is indicated to be February to April.

WALL EYED SURF PERCH

Hyperprosopon argenteum Gibbons

RANGE: Washington (State) to Lower California. Present all year.

COLOR: Steel blue above, shading to silver; faint dark bars.

DISTINGUISHING CHARACTERISTICS: Two series of teeth in each jaw. The lower lip has no fold. The mouth cleft runs almost parallel to the outline of the body below it. The scales are small; 72 in a line from the back of the gill cover to the tail base. There are 3 spines and 29 to 32 rays in the anal fin. The eye is large.

SIZE: Reported to reach 12 inches, but usually smaller.

HABITS: The breeding season is apparently March and April.

POGIE *Holconotus rhodoterus* Agassiz

RANGE: Central California north to Oregon. Frequently caught in surf off Oregon.

COLOR: Greenish above; silvery below, spotted and blotched with orange and red, some of the spots forming bars; caudal, anal and ventral fins red.

DISTINGUISHING CHARACTERISTICS: Teeth in two series in each jaw. No frenum on lower lip. Short blunt gill rakers.

THE WRASSES

The wrasses are chiefly tropical fishes with small mouths, prominent lips, and strong canine teeth sometimes fused at the base. They have powerful

Fish & Wildlife Service

Tautog.

N. Y. Zoological Society

Hogfish.

throat (pharyngeal) teeth. The scales are smooth. The spinous portion of the dorsal fin is longer than the soft rayed part. Individuals in the southern part of the range are apt to be very brilliantly colored. They frequent corals and rocks in the south.

TAUTOG
also called BLACKFISH

Tautoga onitis (Linnaeus)

RANGE: New Brunswick to South Carolina. Common from Cape Cod to Delaware. Present all year but not often seen in winter.

COLOR: In general the Tautog is a dark gray or greenish fish; large uneven black reticulations cross the sides of the body; the fins are dark.

DISTINGUISHING CHARACTERISTICS: Small scales. The preopercle (the cheek covering in front of the gill cover) is not serrated on its hind margin. The upper profile of the body is more convex than that of the Cunner with which it might possibly be confused, and the fish in general is a larger, heavier fish.

SIZE: Reaches a length of over 3 feet and 23 pounds, but individuals weighing over 10 pounds are unusual.

FOOD: Mollusks and crustceans, which it is able to crush with its throat teeth.

HABITS: This is a well known and plentiful fish found around rocks and seaweed in rather shallow water inshore. It spawns offshore in June and July. It is popular with hook and line fishermen.

CUNNER *Tautogolabrus adspersus* (Walbaum)

RANGE: Labrador to New Jersey and straggling south to Chesapeake Bay. Present all year. Abundant off Long Island in summer.

COLOR: Brown or greenish above with some bluish or green mottlings on the side and occasionally metallic brown spots. Gives the impression of a very smooth dark fish.

DISTINGUISHING CHARACTERISTICS: The preopercle margin is serrate and the snout is rather long. There are about 60 scales from the hind margin of the gill cover to the tail base.

SIZE: Usually under a foot long and under a pound in weight. Reaches a weight of about 2½ pounds.

FOOD: Crustaceans, small fishes, fish eggs, sea weed.

HABITS: Found over rocky bottom, and around

wharves and pilings. Goes as deep as 35 fathoms. Spawns offshore in June and July.

HOGFISH *Lachnolaimus maximus* (Walbaum)

RANGE: Windward Islands, Puerto Rico, West Indies to Florida. It is common from Florida south.

COLOR: Very changeable. Usually the basic color is red or yellow. The fish may be entirely pale straw color with pinkish shadings, or yellow with faint reddish scale margins and a bright orange-red area from just above the tip of the snout to the beginning of the bright yellow dorsal fin, and a green spot at the base of the soft rayed dorsal. It may also have light blue dorsal margins and a light blue caudal band. In another phase the fish is bright orange-red with irregular conspicuous spots and interrupted bars of white all over the body and fins. If the Hogfish is disturbed when in its pale straw color phase, it instantly changes to this striking phase.

DISTINGUISHING CHARACTERISTICS: The profile from snout to back is high and steep. The snout is pointed and the mouth low set. The dorsal has 14 spines the first three of which in the adult fish are prolonged into long streamers. The first few soft rays of both dorsal and anal fins are long, and the outer rays of both upper and lower caudal lobes are very long.

SIZE: Reaches a length of about 2 feet.

FOOD: A daytime feeder, chiefly on mollusks.

HABITS: This is a reef fish of open spaces, moving around in groups of two or three; not schooling. It is most often found among gorgonians.

CALIFORNIA REDFISH
Pimelometopon pulcher (Ayres)

RANGE: Monterey Bay to Mexico. Another species runs from the Galapagos Islands to Peru. The California Redfish is most abundant around Catalina Island, in winter.

COLOR: The male is an extremely striking fish. The head is rosy-black except for the lower jaw which is whitish. From the shoulder to below the last two dorsal spines the body is bright light rose; the remainder of the body is black over rosy. The margin of the tail is white as are the margin of the soft rayed dorsal, the last few rays of the ventrals, and the spines and last few rays of the anal. The dorsal spines are white and pinkish. The females lack black markings.

DISTINGUISHING CHARACTERISTICS: The color pattern. Very blunt head especially in the male fish, with profile from upper jaw tip to back a vertical line. Small scales, 50 to 60 in a line from the gill

Todd-Fish & Wildlife Service
Silver Hake or New England Whiting.

Scheffer-Fish & Wildlife Service
Alaska Cod.

cover to the base of the tail. There are 12 low dorsal spines followed by soft rays of which the middle ones are long.

SIZE: Averages around 10 pounds or less. Reaches a weight of 15 pounds.

THE HAKES

SILVER HAKE *Merluccius bilinearis* (Mitchill)

RANGE: Grand Banks to Maryland. Abundant in summer as far south as Cape Cod and the edge of the Continental Shelf off southern New England.

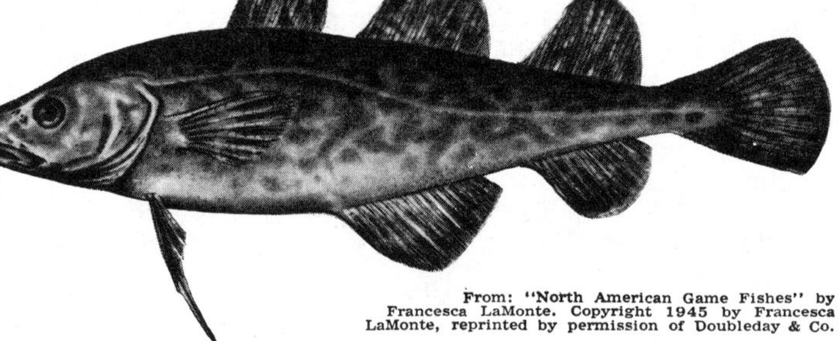

From: "North American Game Fishes" by Francesca LaMonte. Copyright 1945 by Francesca LaMonte, reprinted by permission of Doubleday & Co.

Tom Cod.

A Pacific species, *M. productus* (Ayres), is found from Puget Sound to southern California but does not appear to be an angler's fish.

COLOR: Brownish-gray above; the lower sides silvery; inside of mouth dusky.

DISTINGUISHING CHARACTERISTICS: Long body and long head and mouth. Two dorsal fins, the second much the longer, its rear part much higher than its front. A long anal similar to the second dorsal. No spines in the fins. No barbels. Large smooth scales. W-shaped ridges on the top of the head. A prominent lateral line.

SIZE: Reaches a length of 2 feet.

FOOD: A voracious fish, eating fishes, crustaceans, and squids.

HABITS: Usually found over sandy or pebbly bottom from the surface to a depth of 300 fathoms. It spawns in summer at moderate depths.

COD *Gadus callarias* Linnaeus

RANGE: Greenland to Cape Hatteras. Very abundant off Newfoundland and Massachusetts all year. Not common south of New York. In Europe it runs from Spitzbergen to south of Great Britain and straggles into the Bay of Biscay.

COLOR: Brown or grayish on back and upper sides; blotched and spotted with brownish; dirty

MACKEREL
Scomber scombrus Linnaeus

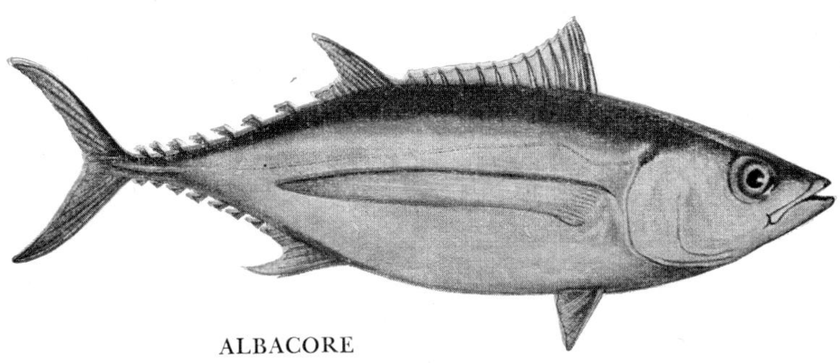

ALBACORE
Thunnus alalunga (Bonnaterre)

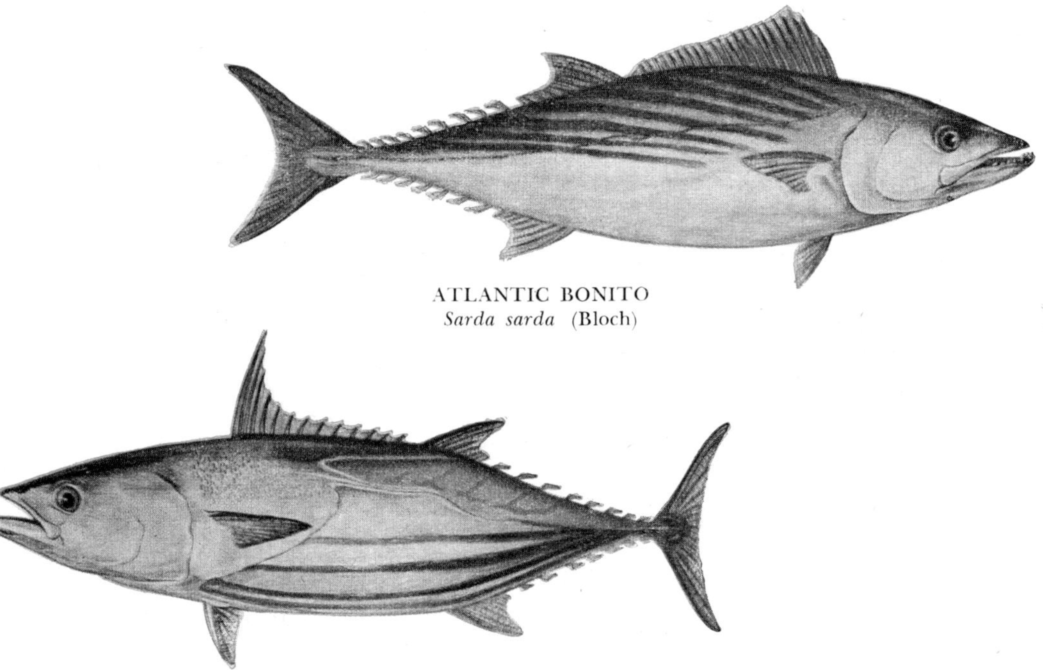

ATLANTIC BONITO
Sarda sarda (Bloch)

OCEANIC BONITO
Euthynnus pelamis (Linnaeus)

WHITING
Menticirrhus saxatilis (Bloch & Schneider)

WEAKFISH
Cynoscion regalis (Bloch & Schneider)

CALIFORNIA WHITE SEA BASS
Cynoscion nobilis (Ayres)

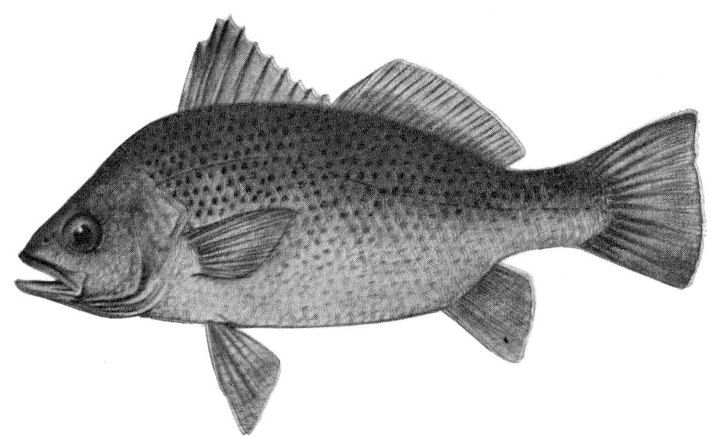

SILVER PERCH
Bairdiella chrysura (Lacépède)

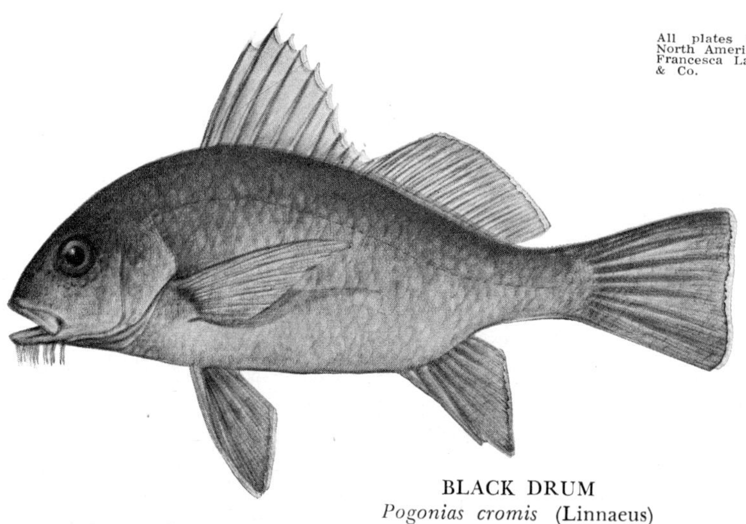

BLACK DRUM
Pogonias cromis (Linnaeus)

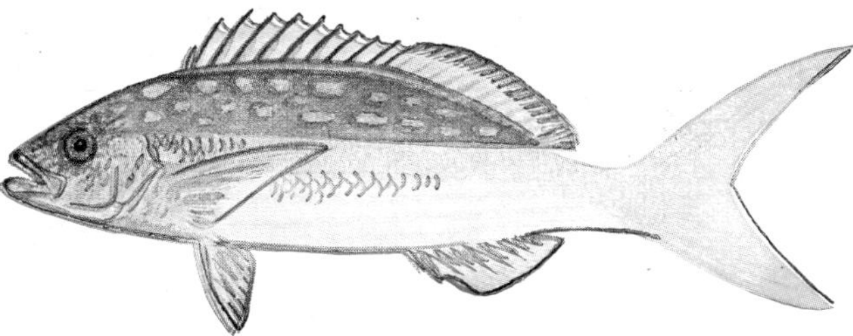

YELLOWTAIL
Ocyurus chrysurus

COMMON SEA BASS
Centropristus striatus

BLACK MARGATE
Anisotremus surinamensis

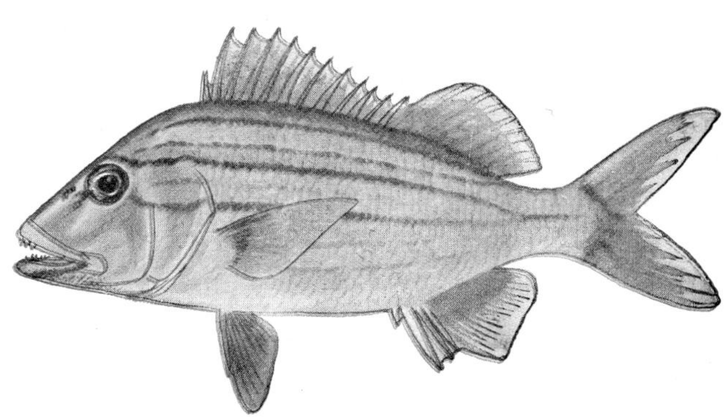

GRAY GRUNT
Haemulon macrostomum

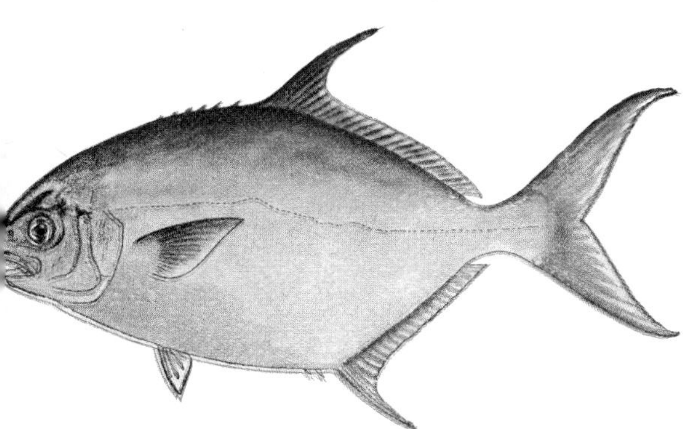

COMMON POMPANO
Trachinotus carolinus

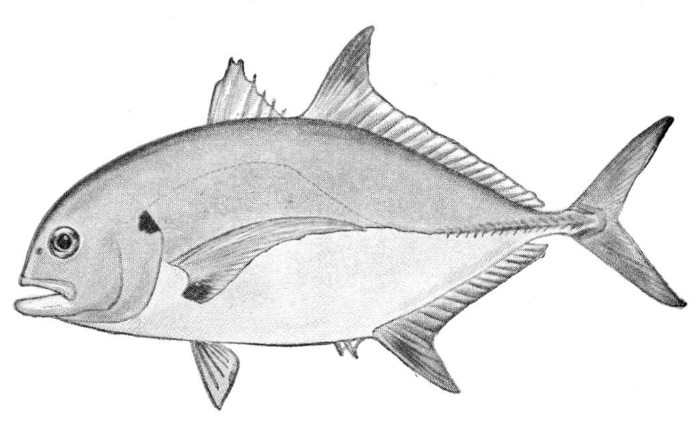

COMMON JACK
Caranx hippos

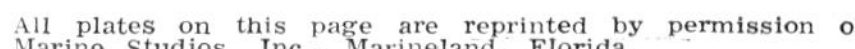

All plates on this page are reprinted by permission of Marine Studios, Inc., Marineland, Florida.

SEA DRUM
Pogonias cromis

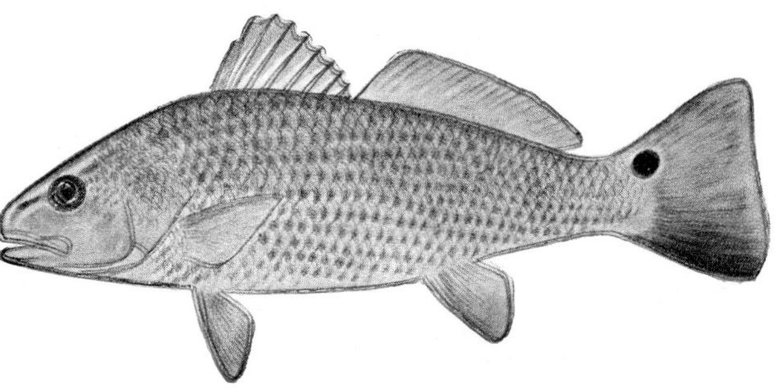

CHANNEL BASS
Scioenops ocellatus

RED GROUPER
Epinephelus morio

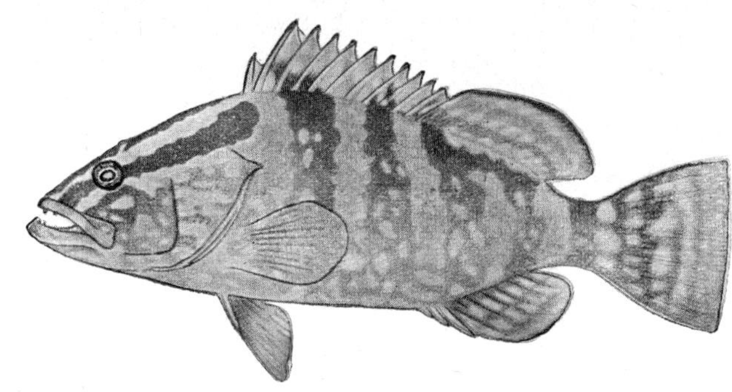

NASSAU GROUPER
Epinephelus striatus

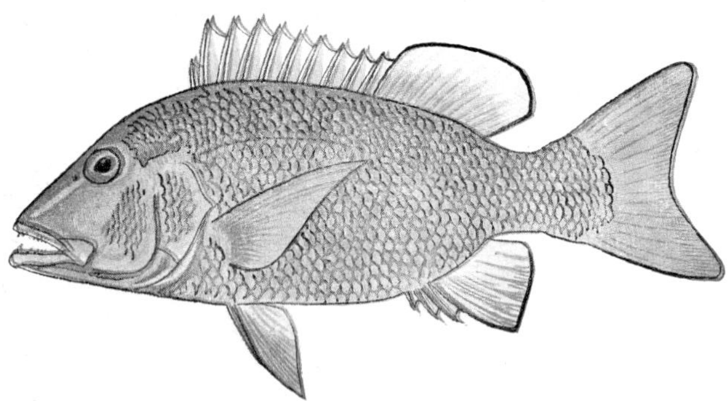

RED SNAPPER
Lutianus blackfordi

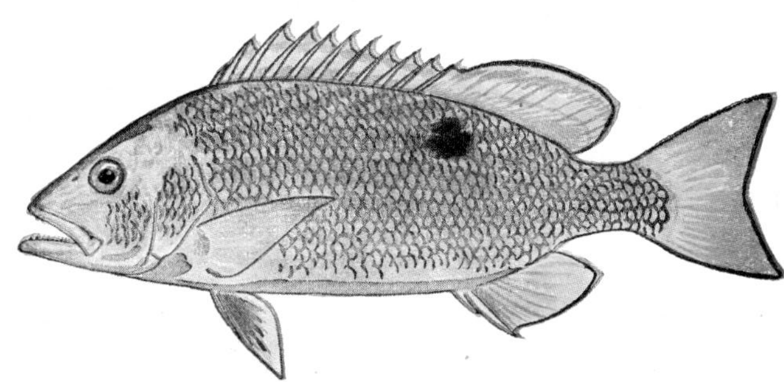

SPOT SNAPPER
Lutianus synagris

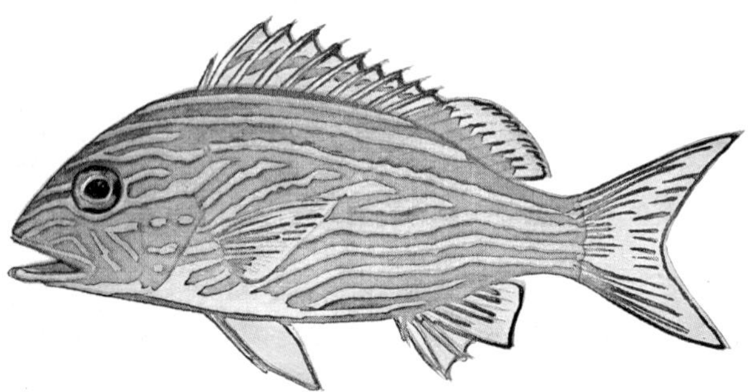

YELLOW GRUNT
Haemulon flavolineatum

SHEEPSHEAD
Archosargus probatocephalus

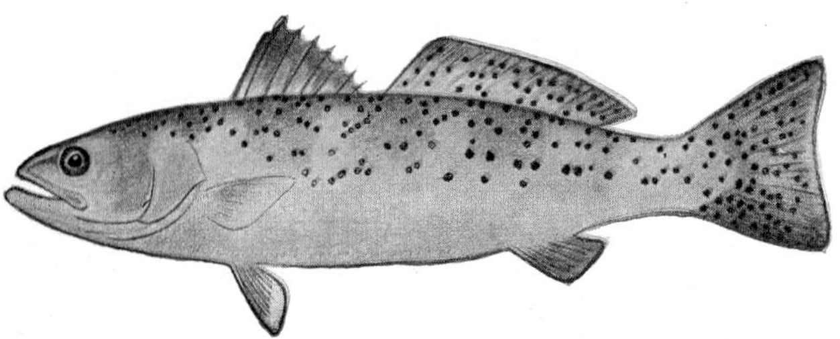

SPOTTED WEAKFISH
Cynoscion nebulosus

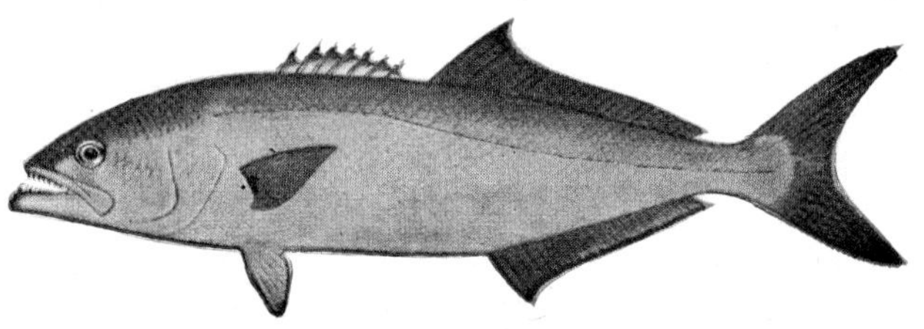

BLUEFISH
Pomatomus saltatrix

ATLANTIC SALMON
Salmo salar Linnaeus

CHINOOK SALMON
Oncorhynchus tschawytscha (Walbaum)

LANDLOCKED SALMON
Salmo salar sebago Girard

SILVER SALMON
Oncorhynchus kisutch (Walbaum)

LAKE TROUT
Cristivomer namaycush (Walbaum)

HUMPBACK SALMON
Oncorhynchus gorbuscha (Walbaum)

BLUEBACK SALMON (spawning male)
Oncorhynchus nerka (Walbaum)

DOG SALMON
Oncorhynchus keta (Walbaum)

BLUEBACK SALMON
Oncorhynchus nerka (Walbaum)

All Salmon undergo a remarkable physical change during the spawning season. These changes are especially marked in the male Pacific Salmon. The jaws become hooked, the teeth large, the body more or less humped, and red or reddish blotched. All salmonoids tend to take on some red coloring in the spawning period but in Trout this color is confined to the lateral line and belly.

LARGEMOUTH BLACK BASS
Micropterus Salmoides (Lacépède)

SMALLMOUTH BLACK BASS
Micropterus dolomieu (Lacépède)

WALLEYED PIKE
Stizostedion vitreum (Mitchill)

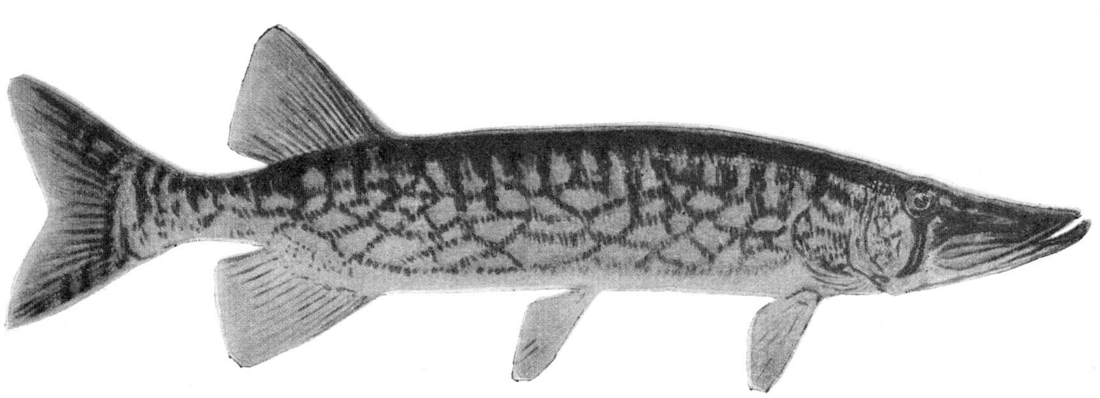

PICKEREL
Esox niger LeSueur

CHAUTAUQUA MUSKELLUNGE
Esox masquinongy ohiensis Kirtland

CALICO BASS
Pomoxis nigro-maculatus (LeSueur)

ROCK BASS
Ambloplites rupestris (Rafinesque)

YELLOW PERCH
Perca flavescens (Mitchill)

BLUEGILL SUNFISH
Lepomis macrochirus Rafinesque

SUNFISH
Lepomis

Scheffer-Fish & Wildlife Service
Alaska Pollack.

white below; lateral line paler than the rest of body; fins brownish.

DISTINGUISHING CHARACTERISTICS: Three separate spineless dorsal fins. Two separate spineless anal fins. Single barbel under the tip of the lower jaw. Small scales.

SIZE: Averages 10 to 12 pounds and up to 25 on the Banks. 50 and 60 pound Cods are not uncommon and it is known to reach a weight of 200 pounds.

FOOD: Small fishes, crustaceans, and all small invertebrates. A very voracious fish.

HABITS: Usually keeps close to the bottom over rock or sand. The Cod spawns from October to April. A female of around 70 pounds is said to produce over 9,000,000 eggs in a season. These are not all released at the same time. Out of the enormous number of eggs deposited, it has been calculated that it takes 72 to produce 1 larva, such is the dependance of survival on natural conditions. This is one of the most abundant and profitable food fishes in the world and the support of large commercial fleets and canneries.

There is a regular migration of some of the enormous schools of Cod. Others, however, are present all year. Extensive tagging experiments have been carried on for years, and the interesting results and methods are presented in Document No. 1081 Bull. U. S. Bureau of Fisheries, vol XLVI, 1930, by W. C. Schroeder.

"Rock Cod" is a term applied to small, usually reddish colored cod taken near shore and rocks.

POLLACK *Pollachius virens* (Linnaeus)

RANGE: A cold water, all year round resident off both coasts of the North Atlantic, running south to Cape Cod and straggling to New York and even as far south as Chesapeake Bay. Reported to have been seen off Cape Lookout, North Carolina. It is very abundant in winter.

COLOR: Dark green, shading to silvery gray on the sides: the lateral line is lighter than the rest of the body; ventral fins are pinkish, the other fins green.

DISTINGUISHING CHARACTERISTICS: Three dorsal and two anal fins. Projecting lower jaw; concave caudal fin; tiny chin barbel.

SIZE: Averages around 4 pounds; known to reach a weight of 35 pounds.

FOOD: Fishes; small crustaceans.

HABITS: May occur anywhere between the surface and the bottom but is more frequently found near the surface than is the Cod. It moves in very large schools. The larger specimens are more abundant in fall and winter offshore and in spring inshore. The Pollack spawns from October to December in from 15 to 50 fathoms. The usual number of eggs produced is about 200,000 but a maximum of more than double that number has been known to occur.

THE FLATFISHES

This group includes the Flounders, Halibuts, Turbots, and Soles. They are widely distributed geographically and comprise more than fifty genera and five hundred species, many of which are good food fishes and a few of which are caught for sport, or for sport and food at the same time.

In appearance the Flatfishes cannot be mistaken for anything else. Their bodies are extremely flat, and except in very young fishes, both eyes and most of the color are on the upper side of the body.

Flatfish larvae are eyed on both sides, colored on both sides, and live and swim normally. Very early, however, one eye migrates over the top of the head and reaches a position beside the other. The fish then takes up a one-sided life. The blind side is whitish or lightly colored, and in some species the mouth becomes distorted.

Many of these fishes live on the bottom, depending on the small organisms there for their food; others, like the Halibut, are more active and pursue their prey.

These fishes may be roughly divided into Flounders, Halibuts, Turbots, and Soles. None of the Soles are considered game fish, and none of the North American Soles are good food fish. The fish served in North American restaurants as "fillet of sole" is usually Winter Flounder.

FLOUNDERS

The Flounder mouth is not symmetrical; the jaws on the eyed side are straight; those on the blind side curved. The teeth are all, or almost all, on the blind side. The ventral fins are alike.

From: "North American Game Fishes" by Francesca LaMonte. Copyright 1945 by Francesca LaMonte, reprinted by permission of Doubleday & Co.
Pollack.

Fish & Wildlife Service

Rusty Dab or Yellowtail Flounder.

Kubichek-Fish & Wildlife Service

Starry Flounder.

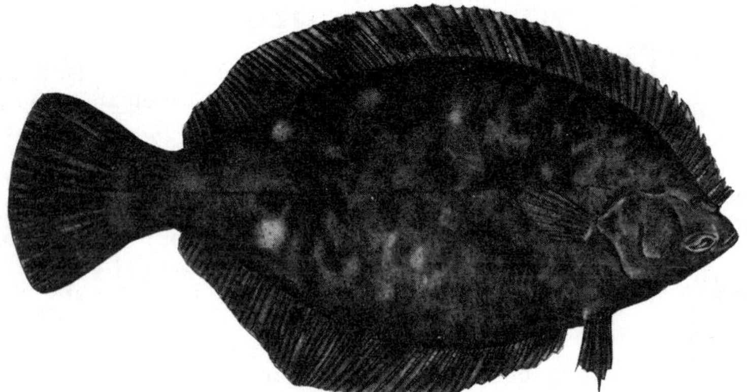

Winter Flounder.

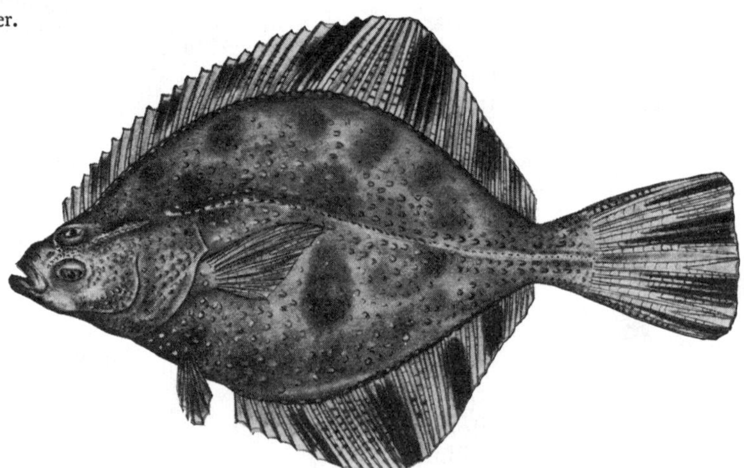

Winter Flounder and Starry Flounder from: "North American Game Fishes" by Francesca LaMonte. Copyright 1945 by Francesca LaMonte, reprinted by permission of Doubleday & Co.

Starry Flounder.

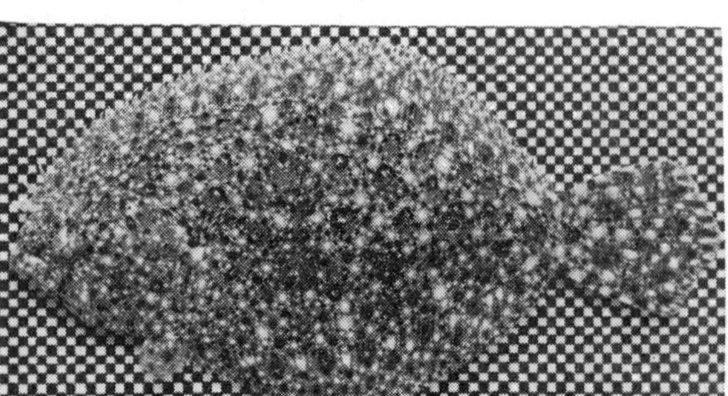

Fish and Wildlife Service

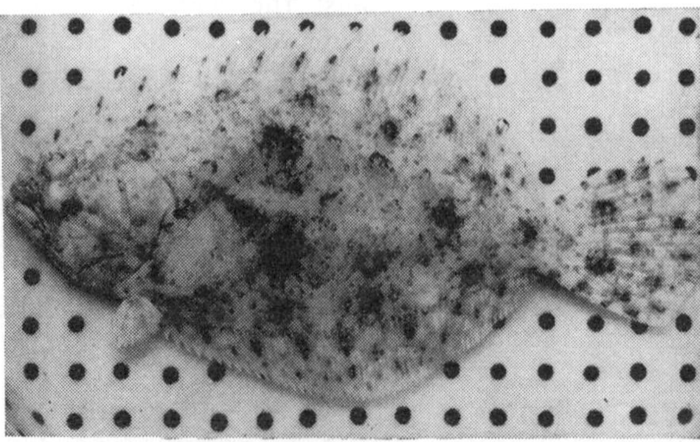

Fish & Wildlife Service

Gulf Flounder on black and white background.

RUSTY DAB *Limanda ferruginea* (Storer)

RANGE: Labrador to New York.

COLOR: Brown with dark spots on body and fins; the blind side of this fish is lemon yellow, brighter near the body edges.

DISTINGUISHING CHARACTERISTICS: The eyes are usually on the right side. The blunt teeth are chiefly on the blind side, but there are always at least six teeth on the eyed side. There are 10 to 12 gill rakers on the lower branch of the first gill arch. The upper profile is concave above the eyes. The lower eye is slightly nearer the snout than the upper.

WINTER FLOUNDER

Pseudopleuronectes americanus (Walbaum)

RANGE: Labrador to Cape Hatteras. Abundant Massachusetts and New York.

COLOR: Dark brown; sometimes with reddish spots.

DISTINGUISHING CHARACTERISTICS: Eyes usually on the right side. A small mouth with close set, incisor-like teeth of which there are never more than 6 on the eyed side. There are 7 or 8 short gill rakers.

SIZE: Reaches a length of 15 inches.

FOOD: Crustaceans and mollusks.

HABITS: Bottom living; inshore in winter and spring.

DIAMOND FLOUNDER

Hypsopsetta guttulata (Girard)

RANGE: From central to southern California (Cape Mendocino to Magdalena Bay).

COLOR: Brownish, usually without markings.

DISTINGUISHING CHARACTERISTICS: A deep bodied fish with eyes usually on the right side and separated by a narrow bony ridge. The upper eye is close to the dorsal edge of the body. The mouth is very small and has thick lips. Small slender teeth in bands on the blind side in both jaws and very few if any on the eyed side. No canine teeth.

SIZE: Reaches 4 pounds but is generally smaller.

HABITS: Found in bays and surf.

STARRY FLOUNDER *Platichthys stellatus* (Pallas)

RANGE: Southern California to Alaska. Abundant all year and widely distributed in Alaska. Also occurs off Japan and Korea.

COLOR: Body is dark brown or blackish, sometimes with pale markings; the dorsal, anal and caudal fins are orange alternating with black.

DISTINGUISHING CHARACTERISTICS: Eyes may be on either right or left side. The scales are replaced to a very large extent by spinous tubercles. There is a row of these tubercles at the bases of the dorsal and anal fins. On the blind side, the tubercles are found almost entirely near the edges of the body and around the lateral line. The teeth are better developed on the blind side. There are 8 to 10 gill rakers on the lower limb of the first gill arch.

SIZE: Averages 2 to 5 pounds. Reported to reach 20 pounds.

HABITS: A bottom fish of shallow water. Sometimes goes up large rivers.

HALIBUTS

In these fishes the mouth looks fairly normal, and the teeth are the same on both eyed and blind sides of the body. The ventral fins are alike.

The Halibuts are active in pursuit of their food which consists of small fishes and more quickly moving organisms than does the food of the bottom living flatfishes.

ATLANTIC HALIBUT

Hippoglossus hippoglossus Linnaeus

RANGE: Greenland to New Jersey. Spitzbergen, Ireland, Bay of Biscay.

PACIFIC HALIBUT

Hippoglossus stenolepis Schmidt

RANGE: Alaska to California. Bering Sea to Okhotsk Sea.

The body of the Pacific Halibut is more slender than that of the Atlantic, and more often mottled with paler tones. Otherwise they are very much alike.

COLOR: Dark brown; sometimes mottled in the Atlantic form; usually so in the Pacific.

DISTINGUISHING CHARACTERISTICS: Long body; eyes on the right side and separated by a wide space; large mouth and jaws and teeth similar on both sides of body; the scales of the eyed side are round edged and often bounded by smaller scales.

SIZE: Reaches a weight of 400 pounds and is reported to reach 700 pounds and a length of 8 feet.

CALIFORNIA HALIBUT

Paralichthys californicus (Ayres)

RANGE: San Francisco to the Gulf of California. The largest commercial landings are around San Diego. Present all year. Most abundant north of the Mexican border from February to May; south of it from July to October.

COLOR: Greenish-brown, sometimes mottled, and the head sometimes speckled with black.

DISTINGUISHING CHARACTERISTICS: The upper profile of the head is straight. The upper eye is a little bit nearer the snout than the lower. The teeth are strong canines. Scales partly rough on the eyed side, and almost entirely smooth on the blind side. There are about 20 gill rakers on the lower limb of the first gill arch.

SUMMER FLOUNDER also called FLUKE

Paralichthys dentatus (Linnaeus)

RANGE: Maine (only present as a straggler north

Fish & Wildlife Service

Common Halibut.

Scheffer-Fish & Wildlife Service

Halibut.

of Cape Cod) to Texas and probably occurs off Florida.

COLOR: Pale uneven brown with paler spots on the body and fins.

DISTINGUISHING CHARACTERISTICS: Upper profile of head is straight; the lower jaw does not project; the dorsal fin begins directly in front of the upper eye. The teeth are strong canines. There are 14 to 17 gill rakers. The jaws and teeth are about alike on both sides of the body.

SIZE: 2 to 8 pounds. There is a rod and reel record, taken off Oak Beach, New York, of 20 pounds.

FOOD: Crabs, shrimps.

HABITS: Found in bays over sandy bottoms.

SOUTHERN FLOUNDER

Paralichthys lethostigma Jordan & Gilbert

GULF FLOUNDER

Paralichthys albiguttus Jordan & Gilbert

These two fish may be the same species. *P. lethostigmus* is abundant from South Carolina south and on the Gulf Coast and may run as far north as New York. *P.albiguttus* is abundant on the South Atlantic coast.

The technical characteristics by which they are distinguished from each other are not always present. Both also closely resemble the Summer Flounder from which they are distinguishable, however, by the number of gill rakers. The Summer Flounder has 14 to 17 gill rakers; these two have from 8 to 12.

The Gulf Flounder appears to have consistently somewhat larger eyes and larger scales than the Southern Flounder.

COLOR: Both are mottled brown with paler spots.

HABITS: The Southern Flounder is believed to spawn in November and December. The young of the two are exceedingly difficult to tell apart.

TURBOTS

The eyes and color of the Turbots are apt to be on the left side. The ventral fins are not symmetrical nor similarly attached to the body. The one on the eyed side is attached to the abdominal ridge; that on the blind side is attached to the side of the ridge.

SAND DAB *Citharichthys sordidus* (Girard)

RANGE: British Columbia to Lower California. Present all year.

COLOR: The ground color is brown; the male has orange blotches and dark edged scales; the dorsal and anal fins are black or dusky margined with yellow and blotched with orange, the females are lighter in color and the fins are generally without markings.

DISTINGUISHING CHARACTERISTICS: The unsymmetrical ventrals. The upper profile of the head is straight or may be slightly concave above the eyes. The teeth are not distinctly canine but are slightly larger in front. There is a single series in both jaws and both jaws and teeth are almost alike on both sides of the fish. There are 15 or 16 fairly long gill rakers on the lower limb of the first gill arch.

SIZE: Reaches a length of 12 inches.

SOLES

None of the Soles are game fish, but for the sake of distinguishing these fishes from other Flatfishes, it may be said that the teeth are rudimentary or entirely lacking; the eyes are very small and lie close together, and the small mouth is distinctly twisted.

Part 3. Fresh Water Species

LARGEMOUTH BASS

Micropterus salmoides (Lacépède)

In some sections of the South this fish is erroneously called Trout and is sometimes known as Linesides.

RANGE: The Largemouth Bass is now found in almost every state in this country due to extensive transplanting, and also in Canada and Mexico. Within this century, it has been introduced into the waters of Germany, France, Spain, and South Africa; and this transplanting has been particularly successful in South Africa.

In this country, Largemouth Bass are abundant in the new impoundments in the South and West.

COLOR: As with many fish, the color of the Largemouth is influenced by the color of its surroundings. Clear lakes with sand bottoms usually produce lighter colored fish than do dark colored waters with mud bottoms. Aside from the above, the general color of this fish is dark green on the back, shading into a lighter green on the lower sides and a greenish-silver or yellowish-white on the belly. It usually has dark blotches along lateral line, although in clear waters these are not always present. In all cases, a thin black line or stripe runs along the sides from the top of the gills to the middle of the tail.

DISTINGUISHING CHARACTERISTICS: The Largemouth Bass is frequently confused with the Smallmouth Bass, but is readily distinguished from it, due to a number of marked differences. The most easily recognized of these is that the jaw joint of the Largemouth extends back beyond the eye while on the Smallmouth it ends directly beneath it. On the cheek of the Largemouth there are 9 to 12 oblique rows of scales, whereas the Smallmouth always has more than 12, and usually 12 to 17 rows.

SIZE: The average size of the Largemouth Bass caught in northern waters will be from 1 to 2 pounds, but in the South, and especially in Florida, the fish run larger. In the North, a 5- or 6-pounder is considered an unusually large fish, but in the South, it would take an 8- or 9-pounder to qualify in this category. The official world record is 22 pounds, 4 ounces.

Fish & Wildlife Service

Largemouth Bass

FOOD: The Largemouth will strike almost anything that moves, such as snakes, small birds, field mice, etc., but its favorite foods are minnows, worms, insects, frogs, and crawfish.

HABITS: The Largemouth is noted for its pugnacious disposition and is admired by anglers for its willingness to strike their offerings. From the time the water starts to warm up in the spring until late fall, they are in a striking mood. Slow moving rivers and streams as well as lakes are the favorite haunts of this fish, and they are generally found around lily pads and weedy points as well as over weed beds.

Largemouth Bass spawn in the spring; the male prepares the nest and then after the spawn is deposited, guards it. The average nest will hold from 4,000 to 5,000 eggs, but nests holding over 10,000 are not rare. Eggs will hatch in from 2 days to a week, depending upon temperature of the water, and after remaining in the nest for a few days, the young forage for themselves.

SMALLMOUTH BASS

Micropterus dolomieu Lacépède

The Smallmouth Bass is considered by many to be our greatest freshwater gamefish, and is at times referred to as a bronzeback bass.

RANGE: Like its cousin the Largemouth, the Smallmouth Bass is now found in nearly every state of the Union and in southern Canada, due to transplanting. Prior to its introduction in other parts of the country, it was native to the area from Georgia to southern Canada and from the East Coast to the Mississippi Valley.

COLOR: Golden-bronze green or brownish-green, depending upon water conditions. Usually lighter in color than a Largemouth. Shades to a yellowish-white on belly. Darker brown or bronze markings, at times forming vertical bands, usually appear on sides. Usually a dash of red is present in the eye.

DISTINGUISHING CHARACTERISTICS: One of the chief differences between the Largemouth and Smallmouth Bass is the position of the maxillary or jaw joint. When the mouth of the Smallmouth is closed, the rear end of the jaw joint is directly below the eye, whereas on the Largemouth, it extends back of it. The cheek of the Smallmouth has from 12 to 17 rows of scales, but the Largemouth never has more than 12. In the Smallmouth, the dorsal fin is not deeply notched, whereas the dorsal of a Largemouth is so deeply notched that it often appears as two separate fins.

SIZE: Generally, the size of the Smallmouth is a little under that of the Largemouth and the average throughout the country is about 1 pound to 1½ pounds. Four- and 5-pounders are not rare, but 10 and over are most unusual. For years a 14-pound bass, caught in Florida, was officially recognized as the world record. Most ichthyologists now believe this bass was a subspecies of Largemouth Bass and not a true Smallmouth Bass. In view of this, an 11 lb., 15 oz. fish is the recognized record.

FOOD: At times, the Smallmouth appears to be more choosey in its selection of food than the Largemouth, but quite often, like the Largemouth, it will gobble up anything in sight. Its preference, however, runs to minnows, worms, insects, frogs, crawfish, and hellgrammites.

HABITS: It is the concensus of opinion among anglers that the Smallmouth is a better fighter than the Largemouth. This is due to some extent to the fact that the Smallmouth prefers cooler, cleaner, and faster moving waters than the Largemouth. Fast moving streams with sand or rocky bottoms are preferred to slow moving rivers, and sand bottom lakes to ones with mud bottoms. In streams, the favorite spots to find Smallmouths are around semi-submerged boulders and in pools at the foot of rapids or riffles. In lakes, they are found over gravel bars and along rocky shorelines, especially if they have a fringe of weeds.

Smallmouth spawn early in the spring, and prefer a sand or gravel bottom. The male prepares the nest, carefully clearing away all debris so that the eggs will adhere to the clean stones or gravel on the bottom. In a few days the young hatch, and after spending several days hiding in the crevices of the nest, until their yolk supply of food is exhausted, they leave the nest and are on their own.

SPOTTED BASS

Micropterus punctulatus (Rafinesque)

The Spotted Bass has some of the characteristics of both the Largemouth and Smallmouth Bass. It was formerly known as Kentucky bass.

RANGE: The Spotted Bass was first identified in the state of Kentucky during 1927, and for some time, it was believed to be more or less local to that vicinity. Then it became recognized throughout most of the South. While some have been taken north of the Ohio River, it is more plentiful in the South, and found in good numbers in the states of Florida, Georgia, Alabama, Louisiana, Oklahoma, Arkansas, and Texas.

COLOR: Same general coloration as Largemouth and Smallmouth Bass, generally a combination of both. Between the lateral line and dorsal fins the sides are studded with a series of more or less diamond-shaped dark markings which tend to form a definite pattern. The longest row of these markings runs along the lateral line and gives it the appearance of a broad saw-toothed band. Below the lateral line the color shades into white.

DISTINGUISHING CHARACTERISTICS: The Spotted Bass is so similar to both the Largemouth and the Smallmouth that it is easily understandable why it is not readily identified by the angler. Although coloration in fishes is not an accurate guide; nevertheless, a Spotted Bass does have distinctive markings. The diamond-shaped markings, which appear just below the lateral line and run lengthwise along the sides, are not found to be so clear and pronounced in either the Largemouth or Smallmouth. The jaw joint of the Spotted Bass does not extend beyond the back of the eye nor end at a point directly beneath the center of it—but rather at a point between the back and center of the eye. The mouth of the Spotted Bass is not as large as that of the Largemouth, but is larger than that of the Smallmouth.

SIZE: The average size of the Spotted is from 1 to 2 pounds, although it will average larger in the southern part of its range than it will in the northern part. Five- and 6-pounders are not rare, and catches have been reported running as large as 10 and 12 pounds and over, but have not been identified by competent authorities.

FOOD: In its choice of food, the Spotted Bass resembles the Smallmouth, inasmuch as it prefers minnows and insects, but it also feeds on crawfish, hellgrammites, and other crustaceans, as well as worms, frogs, and grubs.

HABITS: The Spotted Bass does not prefer cold water like the Smallmouth, nor warm water like the Largemouth, and as a result, will be found in typical Largemouth waters in the northern part of its range and in those frequented by the Smallmouth in the southern part. It prefers flowing water to still water, and when encountered in lakes, it will be found around rocky shores and around rushes and lily pads.

The spawning habits of the Spotted Bass are similar to those of the Smallmouth in general, but there are two very important differences. The spawn hatches in about one-half the length of time required for the spawn of the Smallmouth, and fry develop at a uniform rate so that there are no large ones to prey on the smaller ones.

The Spotted Bass appears to be a hardier fish than either the Largemouth or Smallmouth, and thrives better than either when transplanted in suitable waters.

ROCK BASS *Ambloplites rupestris* (Rafinesque)

This fish, a popular panfish, has characteristics of both the bass and sunfishes, and is often known as a "redeye."

RANGE: It is found in the greater part of the United States and southern Canada. It inhabits the section west of the Alleghenies from Vermont to Florida, thence westward to the Dakotas and south to the Gulf Coast. They are most plentiful in the Midwest.

COLOR: Olive-green on back, becoming lighter and tinged with yellow on sides. Sides have a darker mottled appearance, due to dark spots on individual scales. Yellowish-white on belly. Red eye.

DISTINGUISHING CHARACTERISTICS: Chunky body, with single dorsal fin, the front or spinous portion of which contains 10 to 12 spines, anal fin contains 5 to 7 spines. Mouth is large in comparison with body, and when closed, the jaw joint extends back past the middle of the eye. Usually has a black spot on gill cover.

SIZE: Average size, the country over, is about ½ pound. In the South, this average is higher and reports of Rock Bass reaching a foot in length and weighing from 2 to 2½ pounds have been made.

FOOD: Prefers insects, such as crickets and grasshoppers, and grubs, catalpa worms, and other worms. Also small minnows, crawfish, hellgrammites, larvae, and various small crustaceans.

HABITS: Rock Bass are school fish, and when one is caught, there are usually many others in the immediate vicinity. While they prefer cool, clear water, they will also be found in sluggish creeks and streams and mud-bottomed lakes. In streams. look for them in deep holes and under overhanging banks, and in lakes around stumps, logs, and lily pads.

Like the Largemouth and Smallmouth Bass, the Rock Bass spawns in early spring, and the male prepares and guards the nest. Usually nests are in shallow water and poorly made. Rock Bass are very prolific, and in smaller ponds and lakes, unless they are heavily fished, there is a danger of these fish multiplying so rapidly that their number becomes too great for the available food supply. This results in stunted fish.

Sacramento Perch

The Rock Bass has a Western relative which is found west of the Rockies, known as the Sacramento Perch *(Archoplites interruptus).* The range of this fish is confined to the Sacramento-San Joaquin Basin, and tributary waters. It reaches a larger size than the Rock Bass, and is darker along the back, and lighter along the belly. The average size would be from 8 inches to 1 foot, but specimens have been reported up to 2 feet in length.

WHITE CRAPPIE *Pomoxis annularis* Rafinesque

BLACK CRAPPIE *Pomoxix nigro-maculatus* (LeSueur)

These two fishes, the largest panfishes, are so similar that they are treated together. The Black Crappie is frequently called Calico Bass.

RANGE: Both the White and Black Crappie have been transplanted extensively, with the result that they are now found in nearly every state. Originally, these fish were only native to the area from southern Canada and the Great Lakes to Florida, and Nebraska to the Gulf Coast. The White Crappie is more numerous in the South, and the Black Crappie more abundant in the North.

COLOR: The over-all appearance of both crappies, White and Black, is a dark mottled olive-green clouded with darker spots which in some cases appear to almost black. The lower part of the fish is lighter and has fewer markings. The markings on the Black Crappie are more pronounced and give the fish an over-all darker appearance.

C. R. Gutermuth

White Crappie

Fish & Wildlife Service

Crappie

DISTINGUISHING CHARACTERISTICS: While they closely resemble each other in shape, the Black Crappie is heavier than a White Crappie of the same length, due to its body structures being more robust. The Black Crappie has 7 or more dorsal spines, whereas the White Crappie has 7 or less.

SIZE: The average size of both White and Black Crappies will vary from ½ to 1 pound, although in some sections, the average will be much higher, at times around 2 pounds. A number of White Crappies caught in Southern reservoirs have been reported that weighed slightly over 5 pounds; the largest Black Crappie was 5 pounds.

FOOD: While both White and Black Crappies may be caught on insects, worms, larvae, crawfish, and other crustaceans, their principal choice is small minnows which will average from an inch to an inch and a half in length.

HABITS: Both White and Black Crappies are school fish, and once a school is located, usually a goodly number of fish are caught until the school sounds or moves away.

They are primarily lake fish, but are also found in streams and rivers, especially where the bends in these streams and rivers form deep holes. In lakes, they are generally found close to the shore among the lily pads, but they are also inclined to school out in the lake some distance from shore.

In the South, Crappies spawn in the very early spring months, even as early as January, provided weather conditions are not severe, but in the North, they spawn in the late spring and early summer.

The male prepares the nest by fanning out a slight depression in the bottom, and then after the spawning occurs, remains to guard the eggs. Crappies are quite prolific, and a large female has been known to produce more than 100,000 eggs in one spawning season.

BLUEGILL *Lepomis macrochirus* Rafinesque

The Bluegill is one of our most popular and best known panfishes, and in the South is often erroneously called Bream.

RANGE: Originally, the Bluegill was native to the Great Lakes region, the Mississippi Valley and the South Atlantic states, but due to successful transplanting, it is now found in nearly every state, and also in southern Canada.

Ben East

Bream fishing provides real satisfied customers.

COLOR: As with so many fish, the color of the Bluegill varies greatly, depending upon the existing water conditions. Generally, it is dark greenish-olive on the back, with a purple iridescent cast, and chainlike, transverse greenish bars. The cheeks are an iridescent blue, and the gill cover is jet black. Belly varies from a reddish copper color to a brilliant scarlet.

DISTINGUISHING CHARACTERISTICS: While the Bluegill is very similar to other members of the sunfish family, it does have a few distinctive characteristics such as the jet black ear flap with no margin showing, and the rather indistinct black blotch at the rear of the soft dorsal fin. It does not have orange or reddish spots on its sides which are so characteristic with other sunfishes.

SIZE: The average size of Bluegills caught throughout the country will be less than ½ pound, and one over a pound and a quarter or a pound and a half is unusual. There is an authenticated report of one weighing 2 pounds, 10 ounces, and in 1950, one was caught in Alabama that weighed 4 lbs., 12 oz. Largest specimens are caught in the deep south.

FOOD: The Bluegill will take almost anything that it can get in its mouth, but its favorite foods are small crustaceans, insects such as crickets, grasshoppers, etc., small minnows and worms.

HABITS: The Bluegill is a schooling fish, and when the various spots that the school inhabits are located, they can always be counted upon to produce a good catch. Bluegills are equally at home in streams, rivers, and lakes, and prefer rather thick "cover" such as around brush piles, pond lilies, and weed beds. Favorite places are also around stumps, dead trees, bridges, docks, and deep holes.

In spawning, the Bluegill has one characteristic that differs from other members of the sunfish family. It does not keep its spawning bed segregated from those of other individuals, but is inclined to keep them in a colony, usually in comparatively shallow water. The male prepares the nest, which is a small depression in the bottom, from 1 to 2 feet in diameter, and approximately 6 inches deep.

As with other sunfish, the male guards the eggs until they hatch and stays with the young for a few days, after which they shift for themselves.

Bluegills are prolific spawners, and unfortunately are inclined to feed upon the spawn of other fish. These two factors work together to produce a condition which is often detrimental to good fishing. There are many lakes throughout the country that contain practically nothing but Bluegills, all stunted in size. This is due to the fact that there is not enough food to go around. In lakes like this, the removal of a majority of the Bluegills will actually produce larger fish.

PUMPKINSEED *Lepomis gibbosus* (Linnaeus)

The Pumpkinseed is one of the most beautiful of freshwater fish, and is known by many different names, the principal one being sunfish, which is generally applied to all small members in this family.

RANGE: The original range of the Pumpkinseed was from Maine westward throughout southern Canada to the upper Mississippi Valley, and south to the Gulf Coast and Florida. Since then, it has been successfully transplanted to nearly every state and also to Mexico.

COLOR: Coloration varies considerably with the Pumpkinseed, but generally it is a greenish-olive on the back with an overcast of purple. A series of darker vertical bands or stripes run from the dorsal fin to slightly below the lateral line. The sides are dotted with orange spots, and the belly is orange colored. Cheeks are deeper orange with wavy blue lines radiating from the mouth to edges of gill cover.

DISTINGUISHING CHARACTERISTICS: The Pumpkinseed may be distinguished from other sunfish by the red spot on the gill cover; and its body is usually heavier in proportion to its length than other sunfishes.

SIZE: Average weight is less than ½ pound and the average length is in the neighborhood of 7 inches. In some waters, Pumpkinseeds are inclined to run larger, and have been reported to reach 2 pounds in weight.

FOOD: Insects, flies, worms, leeches, small minnows, and small crustaceans.

HABITS: Pumpkinseeds do not prefer swift waters, and are generally found in slow moving streams and in canals, lakes, and ponds. In streams, they will be found in deep holes and under overhanging

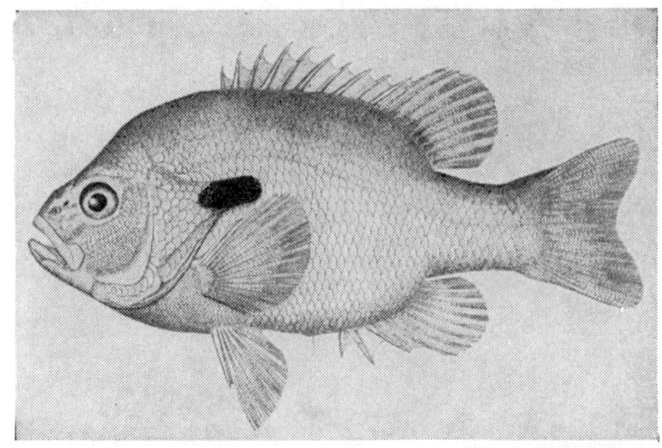

Fish & Wildlife Service

Longear Sunfish

C. R. Gutermuth

Green Sunfish

banks, where the water is comparatively deep. In lakes, they are found around weed beds and pond lilies, and also around old docks, boat landings, and tree stumps.

The spawning habits of all sunfish are quite similar, inasmuch as they spawn in the late spring and early summer. The male prepares the nest and then guards the eggs until the young are ready to leave the nest, and it is the rule rather than the exception for Pumpkinseeds to spawn more than once during the season.

Due to their similarity in spawning, and the close proximity of nests, hybrids are quite common among all these smaller members of the sunfish family.

Other sunfish which are quite similar to the Pumpkinseed and are also caught with regularity are the Green Sunfish *(Lepomis Cyanellus)* which is found in nearly every state and has a larger mouth than the other sunfishes, more like that of the Rock Bass. The average length is 6 to 8 inches.

Another very popular sunfish is the Longear Sunfish *(Lepomis megalotis)* which is identified by its large ear flap with a narrow pale blue or red margin. This fish is especially plentiful in the Mississippi Valley eastward to the Atlantic Coast.

The Redbreast Sunfish *(Lepomis auritis)* is identified by its long black narrow ear flap, and is sometimes called Yellowbreast Sunfish. This fish is most abundant west of the Alleghenies and south of New York State.

The Shellcracker *(Lepomis microlophus)* is one of the most popular and largest sunfishes of the South, and prefers snails as a diet. It is identified by the scarlet edge of its gill cover.

C. R. Gutermuth

Shellcracker Sunfish

Another popular southern panfish is the Stumpknocker *(Lepomis punctatus)*. Its color is similar to that of a Bluegill, but it has numerous dark brown specks covering the body which give it a brownish or olive-green appearance.

The Warmouth *(Chaenobryttus coronarius)* prefers slow-moving streams and lakes with mud bottoms, and is also known as a Mud Bass. It is very similar in appearance to the Rock Bass, but is not so chunky in build.

KING SALMON

Oncorhynchus tschawytscha (Walbaum)

The King Salmon, one of the great gamefish found on the Pacific Coast, is often called Chinook Salmon.

Range: On the Pacific Coast, the King Salmon is found from Monterrey Bay, California, to Alaska. On the other side of the Pacific, it ranges from the Bering Straits south through Russia and Japan to northern China. It has also been introduced in Chile and New Zealand.

C. R. Gutermuth

Warmouth

Color: The appearance of fresh, sea-run Salmon is an over-all silver color, which shades into a darker blue or bluish-olive on the upper sides, and becomes still darker on the back. Small dark spots are profuse on the dorsal and caudal fins, and also appear on the upper part of the body, above the lateral line.

Distinguishing characteristics: The King Salmon are the largest of all of Pacific salmon, and are identified by the profuse spotted markings on the dorsal and caudal fins, as well as the body. The anal fin has 14 to 17 rays. Teeth are absent in the mouth of the male fish, and the teeth on the roof of the mouth of the female are very small.

Size: While the average size of King Salmon throughout its range would probably be in the neighborhood of 20 to 25 pounds, it is not unusual to catch much larger fish, and reports of 40- and 50-pounders are not rare. A catch of 92 pounds was made on rod and reel, and King Salmon have been caught in a trap by commercial fishermen, weighing as much as 125 pounds.

Food: Small Salmon, before they have migrated to sea, feed on flies, insects, worms, and crustaceans;

but upon reaching salt water, they prey on small fish such as herring, anchovies, and sardines and also shrimp, squids, and crustaceans.

HABITS: The life cycle of the King Salmon is the strangest of all fishes, and while the statement that Pacific Salmon never see their young is questioned by some, scientists who have made a study of the Salmon, accept it as a fact. The life history of all Pacific Salmon is practically the same, inasmuch as they spend the majority of their lives at sea and then ascend fresh water streams to spawn. Of all the salmon, the King Salmon makes the longest migratory ascension of these streams.

When they leave the sea and enter the tidewater, they stop feeding, but due to instinct will occasionally strike artificial lures or natural bait presented attractively, but no actual food is taken into the stomach.

The energy they store up while in salt water provides them with the strength they need for this spawning migration. At last when they reach the headwaters of the stream which they have ascended, battered and beaten from leaping waterfalls and being thrown against rocks, they feebly scoop out a bed in the bottom of the stream and spawn—and die. The spawning takes place in the fall, and the eggs hatch in about 50 days, depending upon water temperatures. Some of the young make their way to the sea at once, but others remain in fresh water until the following year.

Upon reaching salt water, their whereabouts are unknown, until after a lapse of 4 to 7 years they return to freshwater streams to complete their life cycle of spawning and dying.

Other Pacific Salmon which are worthy of mention are the Silver Salmon *(Oncorhynchus kisutch)* which is also known as the Coho. While this fish does not reach the size of the King Salmon, it is very popular with sportsmen, due to the fact that it will readily strike artificial lures. The average weight is 9 to 10 pounds.

The Humpback Salmon *(Oncorhynchus gorbuscha)* is also known as the Pink Salmon, and is the smallest of the Pacific salmon, averaging from 3 to 7 pounds.

The Dog Salmon *(Oncorhynchus keta)* is also called the Chum Salmon. It will average from 8 to 10 pounds, but is not very popular with anglers, for it does not show much inclination to take a hook.

The Sockeye Salmon *(Oncorhynchus nerka nerka)* is also known as the Blueback Salmon, and will average 5 to 8 pounds. While it is a fish of commercial importance, it does not readily strike bait or artificial lures.

Kokanee Salmon

The Kokanee Salmon *(Oncorhynchus nerka kennerlyi)* is also known as Kennerly's Salmon, and is considered to be a dwarf form of salmon, inasmuch as it reaches maturity when it is less than a pound in weight. It is believed by many that the Kokanee is simply a sockeye that never leaves freshwater. Its principal range is from Idaho to Oregon, hence north to Alaska.

ATLANTIC SALMON

Salmo salar salar (Linnaeus)

The Atlantic Salmon differs from the King Salmon found on the Pacific Coast and is sometimes referred to as Kennebec Salmon.

RANGE: The present range of the Atlantic Salmon, on this continent, is confined to a few rivers in the state of Maine and rivers and streams in Nova Scotia, New Brunswick, Quebec, and Labrador. Previously it was found in good numbers from Delaware to Labrador, but due to pollution and dams, it is now practically extinct in these waters. On the other side of the Atlantic, it is found along the European coast from Greenland to Spain.

COLOR: It is not a simple matter to describe the coloration of the Atlantic Salmon, for it is really necessary to describe four fish. A sea-run Atlantic Salmon, which means a fully matured Salmon that has just left the ocean to start its migration into fresh water, is a steel blue with silvery sides. It is marked with numerous dark spots on the body, head, and fins. Red spots appear on the sides of males. A brownish-reddish cast develops after the adult has been in fresh water for some time.

When young salmon are hatched in the headwaters of streams, they remain in fresh water for several years. These salmon are known as parrs and the color is brownish on the back, marked with dusky or bluish cross bars and red and black spots. After remaining in fresh water for several years, the parrs begin their migration to sea, and when they are in the tidewater, they are called smolts. At this time the brownish cast leaves their backs and is replaced with a greenish-blue which blends into light silvery-gray on their sides. This merges into a silvery white on the belly. Sometimes, smolts, after remaining at sea for a year or more, migrate back into fresh water before reaching maturity. Those who start this premature migration are known as grilse. The backs of grilse are a lighter steel blue than the adult salmon, and the sides are a lighter silver. Black spots are scattered irregularly over the body, mostly above the lateral line.

DISTINGUISHING CHARACTERISTICS: Unlike the Pacific Salmon, the Atlantic Salmon rarely die after spawning, but return to sea to live to spawn again. Another difference between the Atlantic and Pacific Salmon, and one that is greatly appreciated by sportsmen, is that Atlantic Salmon do feed to some extent after leaving salt water, and as a result will take a fly more readily.

SIZE: The average size of a fully matured Salmon is between 10 and 15 pounds, although catches of Salmon weighing over 20 pounds are quite frequent. The world record was caught in Norway and weighed 79 pounds and 2 ounces, but there are no records of any taken from the waters of this continent that are as large as this, and a 55-pounder taken in Quebec is still considered the American record.

FOOD: Parrs feed on larvae and insects; smolts on sand fleas, small crabs, shrimp, and minnows. Grilse and mature salmon when at sea feed on small fishes, such as herring and smelt and also crustaceans.

Habits: Atlantic Salmon are anadromous fish, which means that they are equally at home in fresh or salt water. Anadromous fish are those which spend most of their time at sea, but ascend streams to spawn. Each spring, Atlantic Salmon start their annual migration, but do not reach the spawning grounds until fall. During this migration, they are found only in clear open streams, and prefer to lie at the lower ends of the deeper pools. Other favorite places are at the edge of eddies and pockets behind rocks or other obstructions, where the force of the current is broken.

Spawning is not usually accomplished until the fish reach about 5 years of age. In the fall of the year, eggs are buried, usually in clean gravel, during the months of October and November. The young are hatched the following spring, usually in March, and slowly work their way through the gravel to start their lives as parrs.

LANDLOCKED SALMON

Salmo salar sebago Girard

The Landlocked Salmon resembles the Atlantic Salmon in everything except size, and is frequently known as Sebago Salmon.

Range: Due to successful transplanting, Landlocked Salmon are now found throughout the New England states and Canada, and also some parts of New York State. It was first identified at Sebago Lake, Maine, and was thought for some time to exist only in that lake and a few neighboring lakes.

Unsuccessful attempts have been made to introduce this fish into some of the Pacific Coast states; in contrast to this, transplantings in South America have been highly successful.

Color: The color of the Landlocked Salmon ranges from a deep black on the back to a dark olivaceous shade, depending upon water conditions. This darker coloration ranges into greenish or bluish-silver sides which further merge into a silvery-white belly. The upper sides are marked with irregularly placed and cross-shaped black spots.

Distinguishing characteristics: While the general appearance of the Landlocked Salmon is similar to that of the Atlantic Salmon, they have larger eyes and scales and longer fins. They also possess the migrating instinct of the Atlantic Salmon, and ascend tributaries of the lakes they frequent. After migrating up these streams and spawning, they return to the lakes from which they came.

Landlocked Salmon will only exist when the water conditions are 70° F. or below, and the water contains a large percentage of dissolved oxygen. Coupled with this, it is necessary for the water to be extremely low in acid content.

Size: The average size of Landlocked Salmon varies greatly with the various lakes they inhabit. A general over-all average would be from 3 to 5 pounds, although 10- and 12-pounders are not rare. The world record Landlocked Salmon weighed 22 pounds and 8 ounces, but there is also an authentic record of a Landlocked Salmon taken by commercial fishermen that weighed 35½ pounds.

Food: Smelts are the favorite food of this fish, but they also will feed on flies, insects, worms, and minnows.

Habits: Deep, clear, cool lakes are a prime requisite of waters inhabited by Landlocked Salmon. Just after the ice goes out in the spring, they will be found in the shallow water near shore, and also in the inlets of tributary streams. Later in the year, when the shallow water is warmed by the sun's rays, they go to the deeper parts of the lake where the water is cooler.

In October, Landlocked Salmon start their migration to the headwaters of streams where they will breed during October and November. The redds, or nests, are made in clean gravel, and the eggs are then covered. This procedure is varied somewhat, due to the fact that occasional nests are made in shallow water or shoals in the lakes which they inhabit.

OUANANICHE SALMON

Salmo salar ouananiche McCarthy

The Ouananiche Salmon inhabit waters which give them access to the sea, but they do not migrate to salt water. They are sometimes called Dwarf Salmon, and are frequently confused with the Lake Trout.

Range: Ouananiche Salmon are found principally in the Province of Quebec. They have also been reported from the lakes and streams of Labrador, but the maximum extent of their range is not definitely known.

Color: There is very little difference between the Ouananiche and the Landlocked Salmon, except the black-cross markings on the Ouananiche are deeper in color and more numerous than those on the Landlocked Salmon. They have bluish-silver sides, which merge into a darker coloration along the back.

Distinguishing characteristics: Do not reach as large a size as do Landlocked Salmon. While the Ouananiche are not Landlocked, nevertheless, they do not possess an instinct to migrate to sea, although they could readily do so, if they so desired. They do, however, migrate up tributary streams, from the larger bodies of water which they inhabit, for spawning purposes.

Size: The average Ouananiche will run from 2 to 4 pounds, although catches up to 8 and 10 pounds in size have been reported.

Food: The Ouananiche Salmon show a marked preference for flies, over that of the Landlocked Salmon, and also feeds on insects, worms, crustaceans, and minnows.

Habits: While numerous Ouananiche are taken from deep, clear, cold water lakes, they really prefer rivers and steams.

Like the Landlocked Salmon, the Ouananiche ascend streams to spawn. The spawning occurs in the fall, and the young are hatched in late spring, usually around May.

LAKE TROUT *Cristivomer namaycush* (Walbaum)

The Lake Trout, also known as the Mackinaw Trout, is one of the largest fresh-water gamefish.

Range: Its range extends from Labrador, Hudson Bay, and Alaska, south to British Columbia, the Great Lakes region, and New England.

COLOR: Usually a dark gray, with an olivaceous overcast, but in some waters, it is a lighter gray, without the overcast. The body is profusely covered with spots which are often tinged with pink. With this fish, the color is inclined to vary with age and the nature of the water in inhabits.

DISTINGUISHING CHARACTERISTICS: Lake Trout are closely related to the true trout family, which includes the Brook Trout and Dolly Varden Trout, and like these fish, have teeth on the roof of the mouth.

SIZE: Lake Trout when caught in shallow water average around 3 to 5 pounds, but when taken from deep water, the average is higher, from 5 to 15 pounds. Individuals of 20 pounds and over are by no means rare, and it is believed that these fish reach a weight of over 100 pounds.

FOOD: When in shallow water, Lake Trout prefer flies, insects, and crustaceans; but when in deep water, they will feed on smaller fish such as whitefish, herring, smelts, and minnows.

HABITS: Lake Trout only thrive in lakes where the water temperature does not exceed 65°F., and they prefer water between 40° and 50°. They are never found in lakes where the depth is less than 40 feet. During warm weather inhabit only the deeper parts of the lakes, but in early spring and late fall, they are found over underwater reefs or ledges, or along shorelines where the water may be only 10 feet in depth. During the warmer months, they are found near the bottom and are inclined to frequent the deepest slopes of underwater reefs.

Lake Trout spawn in the fall, usually depositing their eggs, which sink, on rocky underwater reefs; although at times, they will deposit them in shallow water which has a gravel bottom, and at other times ascend tributary streams for this purpose.

RAINBOW TROUT *Salmo gairdnerii* Richardson

The Rainbow Trout is frequently referred to as a Steelhead or Steelhead Trout, but they are the same fish.

RANGE: The original range of this fish was on the Pacific slope of the Sierras, from California to Alaska. Due to the fact that its eggs can be transported with little difficulty, it is now found in most states, except some of the southern ones bordering the Gulf. Transplantings to Europe, Asia, Africa, Australia, New Zealand, and South America have also met with marked success.

COLOR: While the color of Rainbow Trout inhabiting fresh water varies greatly, it generally has a bluish or olive color above the lateral line, which shades into a silvery green on the sides. The dorsal fin and tail as well as the sides are profusely sprinkled with small dark dots. A characteristic marking is a broad band of purplish red that extends along the sides from head to tail. Lower fins have a dusky whitish cast.

When this same fish comes in contact with salt water, and remains for any length of time, the brilliance of the fresh-water coloring fades, the dark spots become lighter and the bluish cast changes to a light steel blue with a silvery sheen. The vividly colored lateral band of purplish red becomes lighter and the sides take on a pinkish cast. Upon its return to fresh water, the darker markings return. During spawning season, the males assume a bight red cast.

DISTINGUISHING CHARACTERISTICS: Aside from its characteristic markings, the Rainbow Trout can be distinguished by the zig-zag rows of teeth on the roof of its mouth. The Rainbow can survive in warmer water than any other of the trouts, and this is one of the main reasons for its wide range.

SIZE: In small streams, the Rainbow Trout average around 1 pound in weight; in larger streams, or larger bodies of water such as lakes, the average will be higher, around 2 to 4 pounds, and 5- and 6-pounders are not rare. Generally, the larger the body of water, the larger the fish. Rainbows that have migrated to sea, or to large inland lakes, such as the Great Lakes, are larger in size than those that have not migrated. These fish will average 6 to 10 pounds, and 15- to 20-pounders are taken in limited numbers. The world record Rainbow Trout weighed 37 pounds.

FOOD: Flies, insects, worms, minnows, crustaceans, salmon eggs, and smaller fishes.

HABITS: The Rainbow Trout is a favorite of the angler, due to its splendid fighting ability and its tendency to break water when hooked. The Rainbow does not like to stay in one location, and, as a result, migrates to a greater degree than do other members of the trout family.

While Rainbows have been known to inhabit waters where the temperature reached 80° F., they prefer a cooler environment, such as streams and lakes where the temperature does not get over 70° in midsummer.

Although Rainbows are plentiful in lakes, they really prefer fast, turbulent waters. In streams, they will be found in stretches of swift-flowing water, rather than in the slow-flowing portions, and at the edge of strong currents and at the head of rapids.

The spawning habits of the Rainbow differ slightly from those of other fish. The female prepares the nest by digging a depression in the clean gravel bottom on a pool, usually at the lower end. Into this nest or depression, two males, instead of one, spawn the female. After the spawning is accomplished, the female moves slightly upstream and washes loose gravel over the eggs until they are covered.

This spawning takes place from early winter to late spring, depending upon the elevation of the water. In water temperatures of around 45° F., the eggs hatch in about 48 days.

* * * *

During recent years, the extremely large Rainbow Trout caught in Lake Pend d'Oreille, Idaho, have attracted national attention. These trout were often called Kamloops or Kootenay Trout, and believed to be a different trout or a subspecies of Rainbow Trout. Scientists are now agreed that, like the Steelhead Trout, it is a true Rainbow Trout and does not differ from it, except as it may be affected by water conditions, environment, and abundant food supply. The huge size of the rainbows caught in Lake Pend d'Oreille (20- and 30-pounders are not rare) is due to the abundance of small Blueback Salmon, upon which the Rainbow Trout feed.

BROWN TROUT *Salmo trutta* Linnaeus

The Brown Trout was introduced into this country from Europe, during the past century, and is often called the Loch Leven Trout or German Brown Trout.

RANGE: Due to the fact that the Brown Trout is easily transplanted, it is now found in all but the southernmost states (where the temperature of the water is too warm) and Canada. The first of these trout were imported from Germany in 1803, the shipment coming from a scientist by the name of Von Behr of the German Fisheries Society. For some time, the names, Von Behr or German Brown Trout, were in common usage. Later, a shipment of a subspecies of Brown Trout, known as Loch Leven Trout, was received from Scotland and transplanted in the West. These two immigrants have now interbred and the characteristics that were supposed to separate one from the other have not persisted; so it is now practical to designate Brown Trout in this country as one species.

COLOR: The color of the Brown Trout varies with the environment it inhabits. Its general overall color is dark brown with an olivaceous cast along the back and upper part of the sides. This darker cast blends into a lighter brown on the lower sides. Along the back, it is heavily marked with black or brown spots, and on the sides with black or brown and red spots.

DISTINGUISHING CHARACTERISTICS: This fish has rather large scales, larger than those of the Brook Trout, and also has an overly large adipose fin. The red spots on the sides are encircled by light rings. Older fish develop an extended and hooked lower jaw.

SIZE: When taken from small streams, Brown Trout average from ½ to 1 pound, but in larger streams, the average increases from 1 to 4 pounds and 7- and 8-pounders are not rare. A Brown Trout weighing 39½ pounds, reported from Scotland, is considered to be the largest ever taken.

FOOD: Prefer flies and insects, but also feed on minnows, worms, snails, crawfish, and other crustaceans.

HABITS: The Brown Trout is the most wary and cautious of all the trouts. This, coupled with the fact that it can live in waters uninhabitable for Brook Trout, allows it to survive where Brook Trout would become extinct. Brown Trout can live in warmer waters than most trout and despite the inroads of civilization, seem to hold their own better than many native trout.

Some time ago, considerable antagonism toward the Brown Trout developed, for it was felt that its introduction into streams containing Brook Trout depleted these native trout. It is now felt, however, that in time these streams would have become barren of Brook Trout due to deforestation, which raises water temperatures, and if it were not for the introduction of the Brown Trout, there would be no trout fishing.

Brown Trout prefer the larger streams and are also found in rivers and lakes. They like waters where there are submerged obstacles and crevices under overhanging banks. They frequent the lower ends of pools and like to lie just ahead of rocks in the current.

The spawning of Brown Trout takes place from fall until early spring, depending upon the locality. The female prepares the nest, a hole in the gravel bottom of the stream. The pit she scoops out is usually slightly larger than her body. Into this, with the help of a single male, the eggs are deposited, after which she moves upstream and churns gravel down to completely cover the eggs. Depending upon the temperature of the water, the eggs hatch in from 4 to 5 weeks.

CUTTHROAT TROUT *Salmo clarkii* Richardson

The Cutthroat Trout is the native trout of the West, just as the Brook Trout is the native trout of the East. Local names are frequently applied to this trout such as Columbia River Trout, Colorado River Trout, etc.

RANGE: Unlike other trout, the Cutthroat has not been transplanted extensively; but it has a wider natural range than any other trout. It is found from northern Mexico to southern Alaska, but not east of the Rocky Mountains.

COLOR: So many subspecies of trout have sprung from the Cutthroat, each having various shades of coloring depending upon their environment, that color varies to a greater extent than it does with other trout. Generally, the color is an olive-green along the back and upper sides, which shades into a yellowish cast on the lower sides. The body and fins are profusely sprinkled with spots, sometimes large, sometimes small; sometimes golden in color and sometimes black. At times there is a wide lateral band along the sides which is sometimes pink and sometimes a purplish pink. One marking or characteristic color that does not change is the red streak or gash on both sides of the lower jaw. It is this marking that gives the fish a cut-throat appearance, hence its name.

DISTINGUISHING CHARACTERISTICS: The red stripes on lower jaw. Spots on jaws. Unusually large mouth with teeth in jaw and roof of mouth.

SIZE: Here again the larger the body of water, the larger the fish. The average from the smaller streams is ½ to 1 pound; larger streams, rivers and lakes, 2 to 4 pounds, or even 6 pounds. Fish taken from tidewater will average still more. The world record stands at 41 pounds.

FOOD: Flies and insects, shrimp, crawfish, and other crustaceans. Worms, minnows, small fish, and salmon and trout eggs.

HABITS: The Cutthroat Trout, together with a dozen or more subspecies, inhabit waters from sea level to mountain lakes having an altitude of 10,000 feet. Cutthroats with access to the ocean are inclined to migrate to sea, and these sea-run fish attain a much larger size.

When frequenting the smaller mountain streams, Cutthroats are found in riffles, around rocks and under logs and overhanging banks; also in deep pools. In the larger bodies of water, around rocks and rocky and sandy shores, and also over underwater ledges in lakes.

Cutthroats spawn in the spring, shortly after the ice has gone out, but in the "high country" this spawning is usually delayed until midsummer. Spawning beds are made by the female in gravel bottomed streams, females producing from 3,000 to 6,000 eggs or more, depending upon size.

GOLDEN TROUT *Salmo agua-bonita* Jordan

The Golden Trout of the West is considered the most beautiful of all trout and was known at one time as Volcano Creek trout.

RANGE: Originally, the Golden Trout was found only in Volcano Creek high in the Sierras of California. Now, due to successful transplanting, it is found in other creeks, streams, and lakes in the adjacent high country. This fish should not be confused with the Eastern Golden Trout, which will be mentioned later.

COLOR: Olive-green on back, shading into a golden yellow on sides which shades into a yellowish white on belly. A broad rose-colored lateral line, which is marked by 10 or so round dark olive-colored spots, runs along the sides from the cheeks to the tail. The upper portions of the sides, above the lateral line, and the dorsal and caudal fins are sprinkled with black spots. A reddish stripe runs along the under side of the belly.

DISTINGUISHING CHARACTERISTICS: Exotic coloring. Broad dorsal fins and tail. Extremely small scales. Found only in restricted range of high altitudes.

SIZE: In small creeks, it will average around ½ to 1 pound. In larger bodies of water, where it has been introduced, and especially in lakes, the average will be larger. There have been reports of 6- and 7-pounders and an 11-pounder taken in 1948 is considered to be the world's record.

FOOD: Principally insects, larvae, midges, and flies. Also worms and spawn of other fishes.

HABITS: The Golden Trout is definitely a fish of the high country and only inhabits from choice the clearest of streams and lakes. It will readily take a fly, and its fighting ability is of the highest order.

In creeks and streams, it prefers pools below rapids, and likes to lie close to high banks where the water is deeper than it is in other parts of the streams. In lakes it is found along rocky shores, especially where the water is deep.

The Golden Trout spawns in late spring or early summer, usually in June, depending upon when the ice goes out. Spawning is usually done in streams and in both the inlets and outlets of lakes. Depending upon temperature, the eggs hatch in about 6 to 7 weeks; and at the end of the first summer, the young are usually approximately 2 inches in length.

* * * *

The Golden Trout of the East *(Salvelinus aureolus)* is an entirely different fish from the Golden Trout of the West, and is also known as Sunapee Trout and American Saibling. This trout is native to Sunapee Lake in New Hampshire and a few other nearby lakes, but has been transplanted in the adjacent territory to a limited extent.

The Golden Trout of this area are not comparable to the Golden Trout of the West. They prefer deep lakes and frequent the deep water. Intensive fishing has depleted their numbers to such an extent that 2- and 3-pounders are rare; whereas in the past, reports of these trout reaching 15 and 20 pounds were common.

An 11½-pounder caught in recent years is believed to be a record that will not be equalled for some time.

BROOK TROUT *Salvelinus fontinalis* (Mitchill)

The Brook Trout is the native trout of the East and a favorite with fly fishermen. It is also known as the Speckled Trout.

RANGE: Before deforestation and civilization made inroads into our wilderness, it was found from Labrador west to Saskatchewan, and south through the Alleghenies to northern Georgia. With the exception of the states of Iowa and Minnesota, it originally was not found west of the Mississippi River. Due to transplanting, it is now found in the waters of the West from California to Alaska.

Yearly, the range of the Brook Trout is diminishing, due to deforestation and pollution. Streams that afforded excellent fishing years ago are now barren of this fish, for it must have pure, clear, cool water to exist.

COLOR: The general color varies greatly with environment. It is usually darker on fish taken from dark, shaded streams, and lighter on fish taken from unshaded streams and lakes. The background color of the upper sides and back varies from an olive-green to an olivaceous brown. Lighter markings of irregular shape appear against this darker background. The sides are sprinkled with red spots which are interspersed with lighter whitish spots. The front of the lower fins and the lower edge of the tail have a distinctive white border.

DISTINGUISHING CHARACTERISTICS: The Brook Trout is actually a charr, rather than a trout, due to the bone structure of its mouth. While a charr actually does differ from a trout, it need not concern the angler, for the general characteristics are the same. What classifies the Brook Trout as a charr is the fact that the teeth in the roof of its mouth are only in the front part of the mouth and do not extend to the rear portion. The scales are so small that they are hardly visible to the eye. Tail is square, rather than forked.

SIZE: The average size varies with the waters it frequents and the abundance of food present in those waters. In small streams and creeks, the average will be less than ½ pound, but in larger waters, the average will be higher, dependent upon the food supply. Numerous 5- and 6-pound catches are reported yearly, and the world record stands at 14½ pounds.

FOOD: Smaller fish, such as those weighing ½ pound or under, prefer flies, insects, worms, small minnows, and small crustaceans. In addition to the above, larger fish feed on small fish, crawfish, mollusks, and even frogs.

HABITS: To survive successfully, Brook Trout must have colder water than is necessary for other trout, and will not thrive in water where the temperature exceeds 70° F.

Trout inhabiting streams and rivers which flow into larger bodies of water, such as the ocean or the Great Lakes, at times migrate into these larger bodies of water, and as a result, greatly increase in size. These migrants are frequently called "coasters."

In creeks and streams, trout are generally found in riffles and in back of rocks and obstructions in the current. Deep pools are also favorite haunts, in which the trout will be found lying close to the bottom.

Brook Trout spawn in the fall, and, depending upon the section of the country and weather conditions, this spawning may take place from September to February. The female prepares the nest by scooping out a depression slightly longer and wider than her body. After the eggs are laid, the male and female both fertilize them, and the female then covers them with sand and gravel. The nest is then deserted, and the eggs hatch in from 7 to 8 weeks, depending upon water temperatures. During spawning season, the males develop a hooked lower jaw.

DOLLY VARDEN TROUT

Salvelinus malma spectabilis (Walbaum)

The Dolly Varden Trout, like the Brook Trout of the East is a charr rather than a trout, and is also known as Bull Trout.

RANGE: The Dolly Varden is native only to the Pacific slope from Sacramento northward to Alaska. It is most plentiful from British Columbia north, and has never been transplanted to any great extent.

COLOR: The color varies in intensity, depending upon the waters inhabited. Sea-run Dollys are much lighter in general appearance, and the entire body has a silvery cast. The over-all color of these fish in fresh water is a greenish brown with small red and orange spots covering the back and sides. These spots become larger as they extend down the sides. Lower fins are edged with a light colored stripe.

DISTINGUISHING CHARACTERISTICS: The Dolly Varden Trout is a western relative of the Brook Trout, and resembles it in appearance, but does not have the worm-like markings on its back. It has teeth in the forward part of the roof of its mouth, thereby distinguishing it as a true charr. Has an unusually large adipose fin and well-forked tail.

SIZE: In small streams, the average size of the Dolly Varden is from ½ to 1 pound; but in larger streams and in rivers and lakes, the average is increasingly larger, and will be in the neighborhood of 2 to 4 pounds. Dolly Vardens that have migrated to sea or to large lakes get even larger, and catches of from 10 to 15 pounds are not exceptional. The world record individual came from Pend d'Oreille in Idaho, the same lake that supplied the world record Rainbow. This record-breaking fish weighed 32 pounds.

The Dolly Varden is the glutton of the trout family, and large ones will eat almost anything, even including pieces of cut up fish or raw meat. Those of smaller size, however, frequenting small streams, feed mostly on flies, insects, worms, and small crustaceans. The larger ones, inhabiting rivers and lakes, feed on minnows and small fish, including young trout and salmon, as well as the eggs of trout and salmon.

HABITS: The Dolly Varden is destructive, due to its fondness for the spawn of other fish, and also its willingness to prey upon them. These destructive and cannibalistic tendencies are largely responsible for its being held in ill repute. When taken from fast, clear, cold water, the Dolly Varden has fair fighting ability, but in general it does not put up the battle which is characteristic of other members of the trout family.

With the exception of the Rainbow Trout, it possesses to a more marked degree the migrating instinct common in the trout family. As a result, where it is possible, it usually migrates into the sea or large lakes. In certain streams, regular downstream migrations occur in the spring, which are followed by upstream spawning migrations in the fall.

In the smaller streams, Dolly Vardens are found around rocks, logs, and other obstructions in the current, as well as in eddies, riffles, and deep pools. In pools, they are usually found lying on the bottom. In lakes, they are found along the lowermost edges of underwater reefs and also where sand bars drop off into deep water.

Dolly Varden Tout spawn in the fall and winter in the same manner as do other trout. The female prepares the nest, and after the eggs are deposited and fertilized, she covers them with gravel. When they migrate from salt water for spawning purposes, they usually return to the ocean after this is accomplished, or seek out large deep pools in the lower stretches of the stream in which they spawn.

MONTANA GRAYLING

Thymallus signifer tricolor Cope

The Montana Grayling is one of our really great game fish, but due to its scarcity and restricted range, is little known. At times, the Rocky Mountain Whitefish is confused with it.

RANGE: Only three species of Grayling inhabited this continent, and only two were native to this country. These two were the Montana Grayling and Michigan Grayling; however, the Michigan Grayling is now extinct.

The Montana Grayling was originally found only in the Missouri River above Great Falls,

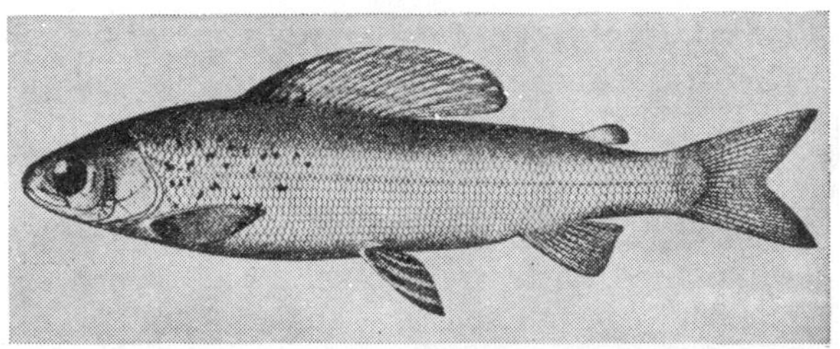

Fish & Wildlife Service

Montana Grayling

Montana; but its range has been somewhat extended, due to transplanting, and it is now found in waters adjacent to Great Falls, and also in the waters of the Yellowstone National Park.

The Arctic Grayling is the third member of the Grayling family, and is found in the streams of northern Canada and Alaska, and its range extends as far north as the Arctic Ocean. This is the most plentiful of all the graylings.

COLOR: A most beautiful fish, rivaling in beauty the Golden Trout of the West, the head is a combination of blue and bronze, the back a purplish blue which blends into a lighter silvery purple on the sides. The forepart of the body is sparsely sprinkled with small black spots. The upper part of the dorsal fin has a greenish hue, and is dotted with brilliant red or purple spots.

All three species are readily identified by the long, high, sail-like dorsal fin. It has an unusually large eye for the size of its body, but its mouth is small and rather square shaped. Scales are larger than on a trout of comparative size, and all of the fins are soft rayed.

SIZE: The Grayling does not reach a large size, and the average would be considerably less than a pound, but specimens have been reported weighing up to 4 and 5 pounds.

FOOD: It feeds mainly on insects and flies, but will also feed on midges, larvae, and occasionally worms.

HABITS: These inhabit only the clearest, coldest, and purest of streams, which have not been polluted, and have sand or gravel bottoms. In these streams, they frequent the deeper pools.

Unlike members of the trout family, Graylings spawn in the spring, usually in shallow parts of streams with gravel bottoms. Redds have also been reported in shallow water on the gravel shores of lakes. As with trout, a depression is scooped out in the gravel or sand, and after the eggs have been laid and fertilized, they are covered and the nest deserted. Approximately 2 weeks are required to hatch the eggs when the water temperatures are above 50°F.

* * * *

As previously mentioned, the Michigan Grayling, despite all attempts to propagate and preserve it, is now extinct; and while it is hoped the Montana Grayling will be preserved for the anglers of this country, but it is infrequently taken.

The Arctic Grayling is most abundant, due to the fact that it exists in unpolluted waters which have not received the questionable benefits of civilization. This Grayling *(Thymallus signifer)* has the largest dorsal fin of all the Graylings, and its coloring is more vivid.

MUSKELLUNGE *Esox masquinongy* Mitchell

The Muskellunge is the largest member of the pike family, and also one of the largest fresh water fishes. It is also known as Great Lakes Muskellunge.

RANGE: In addition to the Muskellunge *(Esox masquinongy)*, there are two subspecies which are frequently encountered by anglers, and whose range extends beyond the range of this Muskellunge. These will be dealt with later.

It ranges from New York and Vermont west through southern Canada and the Great Lakes Basin to northern Michigan and Wisconsin, also in the Mississippi Valley and northward.

COLOR: The back varies from a dark slate gray to a greenish-brown. This darker coloration on the back blends into a silvery gray on the sides, but at times, the entire body has a brownish olive sheen. It is often called the Spotted Muskellunge, due to dark spots and irregular shaped markings which appear on the body and fins from the gill covers to the tail.

DISTINGUISHING CHARACTERISTICS: All of the Muskellunge are frequently confused with other members of the Pike family, but can be readily distinguished by the distribution of scales on the cheeks and gill covers. The Muskellunge has scales on only the upper halves of the cheeks and on the upper halves of the gill covers. The lower halves of the cheeks and the lower halves of the gill covers are devoid of scales. The Northern Pike differs from this in that its cheeks are completely covered with scales; but its gill covers, like those of the Muskellunge, do not have scales on the lower portion. The cheeks of the Pickerel are entirely scaled, and so are its gill covers.

The belief that Muskellunge shed their teeth during warm weather is erroneous; it possesses the ability to grow new teeth when the old ones become broken or worn out.

SIZE: The average size varies from 15 to 25 pounds. A Muskellunge weighing over 75 pounds was reported by the Wisconsin Fish and Game Commission as being netted in Minocqua Lake, Wisconsin, and it is believed that a weight of 100 pounds may be reached by this fish, due to specimens seen but not caught.

FOOD: They feed principally upon other fish, such as suckers, perch, minnows, and even its own kind. In addition to this, they will take frogs, mice, squirrels, snakes, and almost any kind of moving object that strikes their fancy.

HABITS: The Muskellunge is a solitary fish, and likes to lie in concealed spots to await the appearance of its prey. Temperamental to a marked degree, it will often spurn the choicest food and ignore any form of offering. It has the annoying characteristic of stalking its prey like a cat would stalk a mouse, and then instead of swallowing it the minute it is seized, it will hold it in its mouth for a long period before doing so.

While these fish have been taken from small streams, nevertheless, they are found principally in larger bodies of water, such as rivers and large lakes. They prefer to lie in pockets in weed beds and lily pads, and a favorite spot is along the edges of submerged weed beds and underwater reefs. Also, they frequent the edges of channels and sand bars.

Muskellunge spawn in the spring, usually in April or May. At that time, both males and females move into shallow water, and prefer to spawn over a soft bottom, sometimes even in marshes. Practically no preparation is given the nest, and the eggs are scattered more or less promiscuously on the bottom. The number of eggs, which are small in size, deposited by each female is tremendous. Depending upon the size of the fish, as many as 300,000 eggs may be produced in a single season. These eggs hatch in from 10 to 15 days, provided the water temperature is not below 50°. No protection is given to the fry, who start to forage for themselves as soon as the yolk sacs are absorbed. They are carnivorous from birth, which of course holds true during the entire life of the fish.

* * * *

While reports are constantly being made of new species of Muskellunge, these have never received scientific approval. In addition to the Muskellunge dealt with above, there are two other subspecies which are recognized by scientists, but the various hybrids produced by the Muskellunge themselves or in combination with the pike will not be considered.

The Chautauqua Muskellunge *(Esox masquinongy ohiensis)* is also called the Barred Muskellunge, and is found principally in Lake Chautauqua and the Ohio River, although they have been taken from as far south as northeastern Georgia and Tennessee. This fish is bronze colored on the back, which shades into a lighter silvery bronze below, and it is marked with a series of dark spots, appearing vertically on the sides of the fish, which tend to give the appearance of bars.

The Northern Muskellunge *(Esox masquinongy immaculatus)* is also called the Mississippi Muskellunge and is most plentiful in the lakes and streams of Wisconsin and Minnesota, and the waters of Canada which are tributary to Hudson Bay. Coloring with this fish varies greatly, but it has a decidedly bluish-gray cast with an olive tinge, and like the Chautauqua Muskellunge, the dots on its sides tend to give the appearance of rather obscure vertical bands.

CHAIN PICKEREL *Esox niger* LeSueur

The Chain Pickerel is the largest member of the pickerel tribe, which are the smallest members of the pike family. This fish is frequently known as the Eastern pickerel, and in many sections of the country is called Jack or Jackfish.

RANGE: From Canada south to Florida, thence west to Texas and northward through the Mississippi Valley.

COLOR: The Chain Pickerel is a dark greenish-black along the back, which shades into a brownish-green along the upper portions. This fades into a greenish-yellow on the sides and belly.

A chain-like pattern is formed by a network of dark lines along the sides; the fins are unmarked; and there is usually a vertical black mark below the center of the eye on the forward part of the cheek.

DISTINGUISHING CHARACTERISTICS: Both the cheeks and gill covers are entirely scaled, which distinguished it from the Northern Pike on which the lower halves of the gill covers are not scaled and the Muskellunge, which is barren of scales on the lower halves of both its cheeks and gill covers.

SIZE: The average size is from 1 to 3 pounds. Four and 5-pounders are rare, and while few authentic records are available, a 9 lb. 3 oz. fish was taken in New Jersey in 1957.

FOOD: Small fish and minnows constitute the principal diet, but like other members of the pike family, it feeds on almost any object that moves, such as frogs, worms, insects, flies, crawfish, mice, and even fish of its own kind.

HABITS: It possesses all of the savage characteristics of the pike family, and is a carnivorous fish. Like other members of the pike family, it usually seizes its prey in the middle of the body, and after crippling it, will release it, only to turn and swallow it head first.

Pickerel are found in streams, rivers, and lakes, preferring stretches of water in streams and rivers where the current is not swift. They frequent weed beds in lakes, and lurk around logs and lily pads, or any place where there is good cover.

As a general rule, these fish spawn in the early spring, although evidences have been found of their spawning in the fall as well. No nests are prepared, and spawning usually takes place over soft bottoms and in quiet water. The male and female swim side by side and the eggs are fertilized as they fall to the bottom.

The eggs are deserted as soon as they are laid, and in a week or two, depending upon the temperature of the water, they hatch, and the young start their search for food.

* * * *

The Barred Pickerel *(Esox americanus)* is a subspecies often encountered by anglers. It is dusky green in color, and has curved dark bars on its sides. It seldom reaches over a pound in weight, and is found east of the Alleghenies from Maine to Florida.

The Grass Pickerel *(Esox vermiculatus)* is also called the Mud Pickerel. The body is dark green, marked with long wavy lines, and it also seldom reaches over a pound in weight. It is generally found south of the Great Lakes district, and its range extends through the Ohio Valley and through the lower Mississippi Drainage.

NORTHERN PIKE *Esox lucius* Linnaeus

The Northern Pike is one of the most voracious fresh-water fish, and in some sections is looked upon with disfavor, because of its cannibalistic tendencies.

RANGE: The Pike is of world-wide distribution, inhabiting the cold fresh-waters of the world. In North America it is found from Lake Champlain westward to the upper Mississippi Valley, and the Lake of the Woods, thence northward to Alaska.

COLOR: The over-all color of the Northern Pike varies from a greenish cast to one of olive-gray which shades into a lighter color on the lower sides, and becomes yellowish white on the belly. The body is profusely covered with lighter oval or bean-shaped spots, and the fins are usually spotted with darker markings.

DISTINGUISHING CHARACTERISTICS: The bean-shaped light colored markings are a quick way of distinguishing the Northern Pike, although not always infallible. The one sure way is by the scale markings, for the cheeks are fully scaled while only the upper halves of the gill covers have scales, which readily distinguishes it from the Muskellunge and Pickerel.

As with the Muskellunge, there is no foundation to the belief that Pike shed their teeth during hot weather. New teeth are merely nature's way of replacing ones which are broken or worn.

SIZE: Northern Pike average from 2 to 4 pounds in size, but 10- and 15-pounders are not rare. The world record stands at 46 pounds, 2 ounces, and there is an unauthenticated report of one caught in Germany which weighed over 100 pounds. However, this is not accepted by scientists.

FOOD: Like all Pike, the Northern Pike feeds on nearly anything that moves. Small fish, even those of its own kind, are its preference, but it readily strikes minnows, frogs, field mice, insects, and worms.

HABITS: It is a voracious feeder, and it has been estimated that it daily consumes one-fifth of its own weight in food. Inasmuch as this consists mostly of other fish, the introduction of Pike into waters containing less savage species is frowned upon.

Like the Muskellunge, the Pike is a solitary fish, and likes to conceal itself in sunken weed beds, around logs, and other places, where it may remain hidden to pounce upon anything that comes its way. It also frequents lily pads and the edges of rushes, and in hot weather, prefers deep holes and channels. From early spring until June, Pike migrate into shallow waters for spawning. They prefer soft bottoms and marshes for this purpose. Like other pike, they do not prepare any nest, but merely drop the eggs on the bottom, and fertilize them.

* * * *

During recent years, a blue pike has been reported. This fish does not have any of the characteristic pike markings, and is a light silvery blue on the sides, which blends into a darker blue on the back. This "sport" is believed to be a cross between the Muskellunge and the Northern Pike, but is more closely related to the Pike than it is to the Muskellunge. Furthermore, it will successfully breed with others of its kind, and when this occurs, it produces a fish similar in all respects to its parents. In view of this, it is reasonable to believe that a new subspecies may be in the making.

YELLOW PERCH *Perca flavescens* (Mitchell)

The Yellow Perch is one of the most popular panfishes. It is also known as Ringed Perch.

RANGE: The original range was from southern Canada to the Carolinas; and from the eastern seaboard westward to Minnesota. In recent years, it has been introduced on the Pacific Coast and elsewhere.

COLOR: Dark olive-green on back which blends into a golden yellow on sides. This shading becomes lighter as it reaches the belly, which is white. While coloration in a fish cannot be taken as an accurate guide to its identity, the Yellow Perch is an exception to this rule. Its sides are prominently marked by 6 to 8 broad vertical dark colored bands of an olive-green color. These bands run from the back to below the lateral line, some of them almost to the belly. The lower fins and tail are shaded with reddish orange.

DISTINGUISHING CHARACTERISTICS: Peculiar to this fish are the distinctive markings described above and a humpbacked appearance due to the head being concave above the eyes and before the beginning of the dorsal fins. The two dorsal fins are distinctly divided, classifying this fish as a true member of the perch family and distinguishing it from the sunfish family.

SIZE: The average size is less than 1 pound, although there are many lakes noted for extra large fish, which sometimes average around 2 pounds. A recognized record for Yellow Perch was established in New Jersey in 1865 of a 4-pound, 3½-ounce fish. In view of the fact that nothing has been reported to approach it in size in over three-quarters of a century, it is wondered if the proper identification was made.

FOOD: Favorite foods are worms, small minnows, and crawfish, but Yellow Perch also feed upon crickets, grasshoppers, various grubs, insects, and flies.

HABITS: It is a school fish, and usually when one is caught, there are others in the same location. The spawning migration in the Great Lakes is similar to that of various salmon and trout elsewhere, for in early spring they ascend streams emptying into these lakes, in huge schools.

While primarily a lake fish, it is also found in slow moving streams and rivers. In these waters, it prefers the quieter stretches, and is especially fond of the deep holes around bends. In lakes, the larger fish prefer the deeper parts, and are often taken at depths of 30 feet and over.

Spawning occurs in the spring after the water temperature reaches 50° F. or over. No nest is prepared, but the female produces the eggs in a zigzag gelatinous string which the male fertilizes as they appear. These egg ropes drift to the bottom or become lodged upon logs, roots, bullrushes, or other obstructions. The young hatch in a week or so and immediately start forging for themselves.

Perch are quite voracious, and no respecters of other fishes' spawn, nor of their own. This characteristic often in disastrous to other less prolific fish.

WALLEYE

Stizostedion vitreum vitreum (Mitchill)

The Walleye is one of the more popular sportfishes, and is known by a great many different names, the most common ones being Walleyed Pike, Walleyed Perch, Pike Perch, and in Canada Doré.

RANGE: The native range was from Labrador to Alberta, southward through the Mississippi Valley and the Great Lakes Basin. Due to the ease with which it can be transplanted, it is now found in almost every state, with the exception of those in the far West and extreme South. It is particularly plentiful in such new lakes as the TVA impoundments.

COLOR: While the color varies, with environment, it is generally a dark olive green on the back, which shades into a lighter color on the sides. This darker color is mottled with a lighter color of a decidedly yellow cast, and this lighter color often forms indistinct oblique bars. The lower fins, especially the forward parts, have a pinkish cast.

DISTINGUISHING CHARACTERISTICS: The Walleye is easily distinguished from true pike, inasmuch as it has the two clearly separated dorsal fins, characteristic of the perch family. Pike have only one dorsal fin. The Walleye has an exceptionally large eye, which has a glassy cast, hence the name Walleye. It has strong, canine teeth, and the upper jaw extends to a point beneath the rear margin of the eye. It has a dark blotch at the lower rear end of the first dorsal fin.

SIZE: Walleyes vary considerably in size, dependent upon the section of the country where they are caught, and a general average would be from 2 to 5 pounds. The world record is 22 pounds, 4 ounces.

FOOD: While the favorite foods are minnows and small fish, they also apparently relish worms, crawfish, frogs, crustaceans, and insects of all kinds.

HABITS: To a great extent, Walleyes are a school fish, and inclined to congregate in large numbers in certain locations. They prefer deep waters to the shallows, but as night approaches, come into the shallower water to feed, particularly on sand bars and flats.

They prefer clear water, and in rivers and streams, are usually found in deep bends and pools below rapids or falls. In lakes, they will be found in the deep water along rocky ledges, and at the lower slopes of rocky reefs. They spawn in the spring, both in lakes and rivers. Where the rivers are tributary to a large lake or body of water, there is a spring spawning migration up these rivers, similar to that of the Yellow Perch. These fish do not prepare a nest; the eggs are dropped in shallow water, preferably on a clean, hard bottom, and are fertilized by the male while they are being laid. When the water temperatures are above 50°, they hatch in about three weeks. After the yolk sac is absorbed, which takes about 10 days, the fry begin to feed on minute organisms. Walleyes are extremely prolific, the average female laying between 50,000 and 60,000 eggs during the spawning season.

The Sauger *(Stizostedion canadense)* is often confused with the Walleye, and is frequently called a Sand Pike or Jack. While its color duplicates that of the Walleye, it is an inferior fish, and has a slimmer body, the average weight being under 1 pound.

C. R. Gutermuth

Sauger

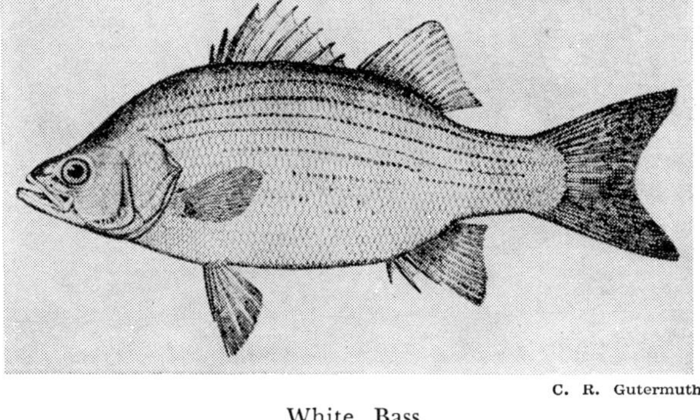

C. R. Gutermuth

White Bass

WHITE BASS *Roccus chrysops*

Due to the restricted range of the White Bass, it is not widely known, but it is one of the largest panfishes, and is frequently called Striped Bass and Silver Bass.

RANGE: It ranges from southern Ontario and New York State, westward through the Great Lakes region to Minnesota, thence south through the Mississippi Valley to eastern Texas and Louisiana.

COLOR: The over-all color is silver, with a golden cast on the lower sides. From the head to the tail, along each side, narrow dark lateral lines run the entire length of the fish. Four or 5 of these dark lines usually appear above the lateral line, and 3 to 5 below it.

DISTINGUISHING CHARACTERISTICS: The White Bass is distingushed by the dark lateral lines mentioned above, and this is an indication of its close relationship to the salt-water Striped Bass, which is similarly marked. Many authorities believe that this fish is a descendant of the salt-water Striped Bass, and that sometime during the spawning migration, the salt-water Striped Bass became landlocked, and that the White Bass is now but a small edition of its original forbears. The White Bass has two distinct dorsal fins which are separated, and has teeth on the base of its tongue.

SIZE: While numerous reports have been received of White Bass weighing 4 and 5 pounds, these represent exceptionally large fish, and the average for this species is from 1 to 2 pounds.

FOOD: The favorite food is the small fresh-water minnow commonly called shad. In addition to this, it will feed on minnows, small fish, worms, insects, larvae, mollusks, crawfish, and other crustaceans.

HABITS: These fish are equally at home in streams, rivers, and lakes, but show a decided preference for clean water. In rivers and streams, they prefer the swifter water, and frequent the turbulent water below dams. In lakes, they are usually found in open water, away from the shoreline.

They are school fish, and while occasionally located in deep holes in rivers and lakes, they are more apt to be found cruising close to the surface in large schools.

The White Bass spawns in the spring, close to the shore, in rivers, lakes or streams. No nest is prepared, but the eggs, together with the milt are deposited in shoal water and then deserted by the parents.

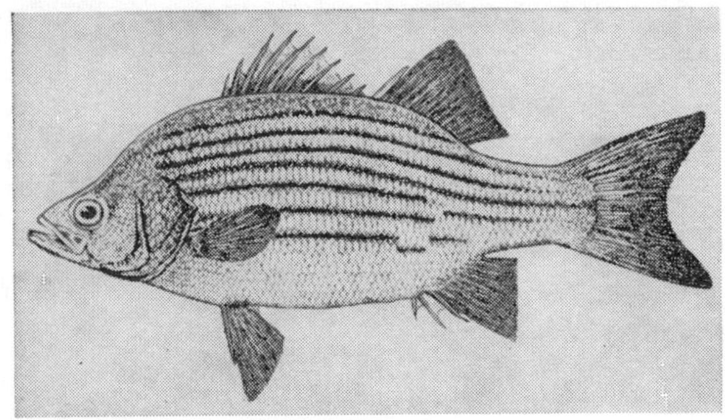
C. R. Gutermuth

Yellow Bass

YELLOW BASS *Roccus interruptus*

The Yellow Bass is closely related to the White Bass, and is a member of the sea bass family. As a result it is frequently called the Striped Bass. It is also known as Barfish.

RANGE: While the Yellow Bass is found as far north as southern Minnesota, Wisconsin, Illinois, Indiana, and Ohio, it is primarily a southern fish. From the states mentioned above, it is found south to Texas, Louisiana, and Alabama. It is most plentiful in the Mississippi Valley.

COLOR: The Yellow Bass has a yellowish brassy cast along the upper two-thirds of its body, but this color is darker towards the back, and is tinged with a greenish cast. This yellowish or brassy cast becomes lighter as it reaches the belly. From the gill covers to the tail, there are usually 6 or 7 distinct black longitudinal stripes. Below the lateral line, these stripes are interrupted, giving them an offset appearance.

DISTINGUISHING CHARACTERISTICS: The broken stripes mentioned above, appearing below the lateral line, are one of the definite characteristics that identify this fish; the two dorsal fins are definitely joined, whereas the dorsal fins on the White Bass are not; the Yellow Bass does not have teeth at the base of its tongue, as does the White Bass; and the lower jaw of the Yellow Bass recedes rather than protrudes as does the lower jaw of the White Bass.

SIZE: The average size is from 1 to 2 pounds, but 2- and 3-pounders are not rare, and reports have been received of individuals running slightly over 5 pounds in weight.

FOOD: The favorite food, like that of the White Bass, is shad minnows, but it will readily take other minnows, as well as smaller fish. It also feeds on worms, flies, insects, shrimp, and other crustaceans.

HABITS: It is a school fish, and while it is found in rivers, it prefers lakes. In the spring, it will be found in the shallow waters of lakes and rivers, and especially frequents bars and shoals where the water is clear.

Like its salt-water relative, it is inclined to make spawning migrations in the spring, and will ascend streams which are tributary to the body of water it inhabits. It prepares no nest, but the female deposits the eggs on clear gravel or sandy bottoms, and they are simultaneously fertilized by the male. Depending upon water temperatures, the eggs will hatch in a few days, and after the yolk sac is consumed, the young immediately start feeding on minute organisms, or any life that is small enough for them to consume.

WHITE PERCH *Roccus americanus*

The White Perch is a member of the bass family, rather than the perch family, and is one of the larger panfishes. It is frequently called Silver Bass or Silver Perch.

RANGE: The range is from Nova Scotia to South Carolina and east of the Alleghenies.

COLOR: The sides of this fish are a brilliant silver color, which assumes a darker greenish cast on the back. It often has pale streaks along the sides, and when caught in tidewater, the color is lighter than it is with fish landlocked in fresh water.

DISTINGUISHING CHARACTERISTICS: The White Perch has a smaller mouth in proportion to its size than either the White or Yellow Bass, and has no teeth on the base of its tongue.

SIZE: These fish are larger in salt or brackish water, but the general average is less than a pound. Two- and 3-pounders are not rare, and reports have been received of specimens running slightly in excess of 4 pounds.

FOOD: In fresh water, White Perch feed on flies, insects, minnows, worms, and crustaceans, and in salt water, small eels, crabs, shrimp, and minnows. They are also not above consuming the spawn of other fishes.

HABITS: Not only is the White Perch a school fish, but it is also an anadromous fish. Anadromous fish are those which are equally at home in either fresh water or salt water, but which make migrations from salt water to fresh water for spawning purposes. In some cases, these fish have become landlocked in strictly fresh water, and while they do not reach the size of their salt-water brothers, they apparently are perfectly at home. They actually prefer brackish waters, and are generally found in shallow bays and tidal lagoons. In fresh-water lakes or rivers, they frequent deep holes, and are also found around the edges of shoals and bars. In early spring, White Perch start spawning migrations into the shallow water of fresh-water streams, although they will also spawn in brackish water or even in salt water.

In brackish and salt water, they spawn in April

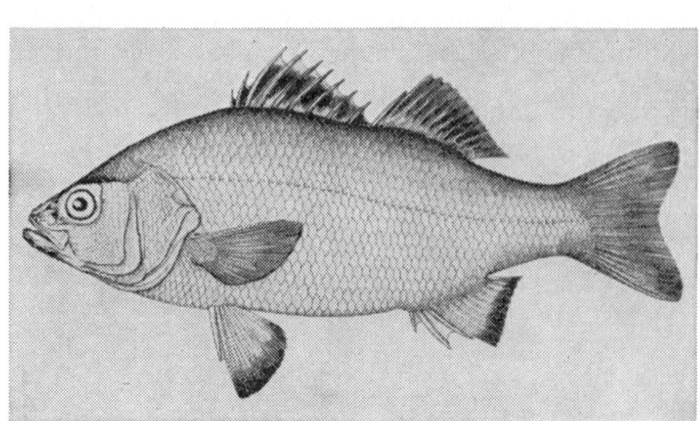
Fish & Wildlife Service

White Perch

and May, but in fresh water, this is delayed for a month or so. The eggs are scattered on the bottom, and receive no parental care. When the water temperatures are above 60°, they hatch in about two days.

ALLIGATOR GAR *Lepisosteus spatula*

LONGNOSE GAR *Lepisosteus osseus*

SHORTNOSE GAR *Lepisosteus platostomus*

SPOTTED GAR *Lepisosteus oculatus*

The gars are considered obnoxious fish, and prey on other fish to the detriment of these fish.

RANGE: With the exception of the Alligator Gar, which is found only in the South, gars are generally distributed from southern Canada to the Gulf, and are particularly plentiful in the extreme South.

COLOR: Depending upon water conditions, the color of gars varies from a dark olive green on the back to a light olive green. This greenish shade becomes lighter on the sides, and shades into a dirty white underneath.

DISTINGUISHING CHARACTERISTICS: The scales of the gar are extremely hard, and appear to be covered with an enamel-like substance, which is so tough that it will often turn the blade of a knife. The Alligator Gar has a broad, triangular shaped head, resembling that of an alligator, while the other gars have extended upper and lower jaws, approximately 1/5 to 1/6 the length of their bodies. These jaws are filled with sharp needle-like teeth.

SIZE: Alligator Gars attain a huge size, and specimens have been reported as long as 7 or 8 feet in length. The other gars, depending upon the section of the country in which they are taken, may reach a maximum length of 4 to 5 feet, including the snout, but the average will be approximately 2 feet.

FOOD: Gars are most destructive fish and prey mostly on any smaller fish, including game fish. They will also take insects and crustaceans, and are scavengers to some extent.

HABITS: While gars have no generally recognized value as sport-fish, and certainly none as food fish, some fishermen find sport by using a light springy wire which is formed into a loop, employing this means of snagging them around the bill.

Fish & Wildlife Service

Mooneye

C. R. Gutermuth

Mudfish

They prefer warm, sluggish, or stagnant waters, and are usually found in muddy bottomed streams and lakes. During spawning season, schools of gar can be readily detected due to their peculiar habit of thrashing on the surface, at which time the female deposits the eggs, which sink to the bottom.

MUDFISH *Amia calva* Linnaeus

The Mudfish is one of the most voracious and destructive fresh water fishes and is known as Dogfish and also as Bowfin.

RANGE: It is found from southern Canada to Florida and the Gulf Coast; also found from west of the Appalachians to the Mississippi Valley and north along the coast to the Carolinas.

COLOR: The over-all color is an olivaceous brown which shades into a lighter or muddy brown on the belly. Irregular shadings give the fish a mottled appearance. The male has a black spot encircled with orange at the upper base of the tail.

DISTINGUISHING CHARACTERISTICS: The Mudfish is readily distinguished by the low, long, uninterrupted dorsal fin which contains no spines and covers about two-thirds of the body. It has small, beady eyes, and a rounded tail, and is equipped with powerful jaws and teeth.

SIZE: The average size is from 2 to 5 pounds, but 8- and 9-pounders are not rare, and individuals up to 20 pounds have been reported. The female is much larger than the male.

FOOD: Almost anything that it can seize in its jaws; its favorite diet being smaller fish, minnows, worms, frogs, insects, crawfish, and crustaceans.

HABITS: It is a solitary fish and likes to lie in thick weeds over muddy bottoms. It avoids swift flowing waters and prefers the sluggish parts of lakes and rivers, and particularly shallow swamps. They are able to live in waters that are unhabitable for other fish, due to stagnation or pollution, and show a preference for warm muddy waters rather than waters that are clear and cool.

They spawn in the spring. The male prepares the nest in shallow water having a mud bottom, by scooping out a circular depression. Into this nest the male usually spawns several females until 100,000 or so eggs have been deposited. He then remains on guard until the eggs hatch, which requires from 8 to 10 days.

An excellent parent, the Mudfish remains with the young fry, which are coal-black until practically the end of the first summer.

GOLDEYE *Hiodon alosoides* (Rafinesque)

The Goldeye is related to both the whitefish and herring, and is frequently called Mooneye.

RANGE: The Goldeye is found from an area extending eastward from the upper Mississippi Valley through the Great Lakes region, and northward into Canada.

COLOR: A steel blue iridescence along the back, which blends into bluish silvery sides, with a golden luster underneath. A pearly iridescence appears towards the tail.

DISTINGUISHING CHARACTERISTICS: The Goldeye has a short, chunky, compact body, with a decidedly forked tail, exceptionally large in proportion to its body.

SIZE: Average size is from 8 inches to 1 foot.

FOOD: Grubs, mollusks, grasshoppers, and other insects.

HABITS: The Goldeye prefers the lakes and larger streams, and is usually found in swift water, when encountered in rivers and streams. During the spring months, it will strike readily at artificial flies, but during the warmer weather, seeks the deeper water.

FRESHWATER DRUM

Aplodinotus grunniens Rafinesque

The Freshwater Drum is one of the few fishes that have the ability to produce sound, and it is frequently known as the Sheepshead.

RANGE: The range of this fish extends from southern Ontario through the Great Lakes region to Manitoba, thence south to the Gulf States. It is most plentiful in the Great Lakes and Louisiana and Texas.

COLOR: The Freshwater Drum has a silvery olivaceous shade to its back, which blends into shining silver sides. When taken from muddy waters, the sides are not so bright and have a metallic grayish shade. At times, the sides are marked with faint oblique stripes.

DISTINGUISHING CHARACTERISTICS: Located on each side of the head and slightly back of and above the eyes are located two ear bones which are known as "lucky stones." These "stones" vary from 1/4 inch to 1/2 inch in diameter, depending upon the size of the fish, and plainly etched in each stone is the letter "L." The Freshwater Drum has a deeply notched, though continuous, dorsal fin, which extends from the uppermost portion of its back to near the base of the caudal fin. The lateral line extends from the gill covers to the end of the tail. The lower throat bones are covered with coarse blunt teeth which give it the ability to produce sound, like its salt-water cousins, the croakers.

SIZE: Depending upon the waters from which it is taken, this fish averages from 1 1/2 to 3 pounds, although catches of 9- and 10-pounders are not rare. Commercial fishermen have reported Drum up to 60 pounds in weight.

FOOD: Mussels are the principal food. The teeth in its lower throat are used to crush the shells, which are then discarded and the mussel consumed. This fish also feeds on worms, small fish and minnows, crawfish, and other crustaceans.

HABITS: They prefer the quieter waters and are usually found over mud bottoms where they travel at a leisurely gait in search of their favorite food.

In the spring, they forsake these mud bottoms to move into shallow water with gravel or sand bottoms, where they spawn. No nests are built, but numerous eggs are scattered over the bottom and remain there until hatching, with no protection from the adult fish.

CHANNEL CATFISH

Ictalurus punetatus

Of the huge catfish family, which contains over 1,000 odd species, the Channel Catfish is considered the sportiest member. It is also known as the Silver Catfish.

RANGE: The Channel Catfish has a greater range than any other member of the family, in this country. It is found in Canada from Ontario to Manitoba, thence south to Florida and the Gulf States and also in northern Mexico.

COLOR: It usually is a slate gray along the back, which shades into a silvery gray along the sides. In some waters, the entire fish has a decidedly light olive cast instead of a gray cast. The belly is lighter than the sides. Irregularly shaped black spots are liberally sprinkled over the entire body along the sides from head to tail. In some southern states, albinos are occasionally caught; these fish have pink eyes and are creamy in color.

DISTINGUISHING CHARACTERISTICS: The single spine of dorsal and pectoral fins is extremely tough and sharp, with the result that care must be exercised in removing catfish from the hook, or a painful injury to the hand will result. The barbels, or whiskers, on channel catfish are quite long and the adipose fin, near the tail, is smaller than that on other catfishes. Like all members of the catfish family, the Channel Catfish has no scales. The tail of the Channel Catfish is forked to a greater degree than it is with other members of the family.

SIZE: It averages from 1 to 2 pounds in weight, and catches of 10-pounders are rare. The world record stands at 55 pounds.

FOOD: It would probably be simpler to list the foods that a catfish will not take (if it were possible to think of a single item) than it would be to list those that it will. Without mentioning the various concoctions used by fishermen, some of the favorite natural foods are minnows, worms, crawfish, frogs, insects, and anything else that moves and is small enough for the catfish to get into its mouth. It is also a scavenger, and will feed on dead animal and fish life. Also algae and other types of aquatic growth.

HABITS: While it will be found in slow moving,

C. R. Guthermuth

Channel Catfish

C. R. Gutermuth
Blue Catfish

mud-bottomed waters, it actually prefers clear, clean, swift-moving streams and rivers. In lakes, it is generally found over clean sandy or gravel bottoms and frequents the deeper portions.

Although these fish do feed during the day, most of their feeding is done at night. When night comes, they are inclined to leave the deeper parts of the rivers and lakes and move into the shallows over bars or close to the shoreline.

Channel Catfish spawn in the spring, usually in the flowing waters of rivers and streams. At this time of the year, there is a definite upstream migration.

BLUE CATFISH

Ictalurus furcatus (Cuvier & Valenciennes)

The Blue Catfish, the largest catfish in this country, is sometimes miscalled Channel Catfish.

RANGE: It is found from southern Canada and the Great Lakes region to the Gulf States and from the Appalachians west through the Mississippi Valley; it is most plentiful in the Mississippi and its tributary streams.

COLOR: Rather a dark bluish-gray on back which fades into a lighter slate gray on sides. Silver white on belly. Has no dark spots, which are a characteristic of the Channel Catfish.

DISTINGUISHING CHARACTERISTICS: The head of the Blue Catfish is smaller in comparison with the size of its body than is the head of other catfishes. Its uniform blue color and the absence of spots distinguish it from the Channel Catfish. Like the Channel Catfish, it also has a deeply forked tail.

SIZE: Although it becomes extremely large, the average size is from 2 to 5 pounds in most waters. Catches of fish weighing from 10 to 20 pounds are so numerous in certain waters that in those waters they can almost be accepted as average. Blue Catfish weighing as much as 160 pounds have been reported.

FOOD: Like other catfishes, the Blue Catfish will feed on practically anything that it can get into its mouth.

HABITS: The Blue Catfish prefers larger lakes and rivers, and slow moving or quiet waters to those that are fast flowing. It is mostly a bottom feeder and like other members of the family, feeds more at night than it does during the day.

C. R. Gutermuth
Flathead Catfish

Among other species of catfish that are worthy of mention is the White Catfish *(Ictalurus catus)* which is about halfway between the Channel and the Blue Catfish. It is found from Pennsylvania south to Texas and has a dull grayish or greenish cast along its back which blends into lighter gray sides. It also has a deeply forked tail, which, together with its coloring, frequently causes it to be confused with the Channel Catfish. The White Catfish does not get as large as either the Channel or Blue Catfish, and averages around 1 to 1½ pounds in weight. It is also found in brackish water more frequently than are other fresh water catfishes.

The Flathead Catfish *(Pilodictis olivaris)* is another of the larger members of the family. This fish is found from South Dakota to western Pennsylvania, and fom Texas along the Gulf States to Alabama. It is most plentiful in the Mississippi and Ohio Valleys. The color is an olivaceous brown, mottled with a lighter muddy yellow. In addition to color, it differs from the other catfishes previously dealt with by having a very large head and a rounded instead of a forked tail. Fish up to 30 to 50 pounds in weight are not rare, and specimens of 100 pounds in weight have been reported. It prefers slow moving, sluggish, mud-bottomed rivers.

C. R. Gutermuth
Brown Bullhead

BROWN BULLHEAD

Ameiurus nebulosus (LeSueur)

The Brown Bullhead is the largest member of the bullhead tribe and is a most popular panfish. It is also known as Horned Pout.

RANGE: The native range was from southern Canada to the Gulf of Mexico, and east of the Mississippi Valley. Due to the ease with which it can be transplanted, it is now found in nearly every state.

COLOR: The color varies from a light brownish yellow to a black-brown, but it is generally a dark brown with mottled markings of a darker shade. The coloring of the sides of the fish becomes lighter on the belly.

DISTINGUISHING CHARACTERISTICS: Like the Catfish, the Bullhead has no scales, and the forward spines of the dorsal and pectoral fins are extremely sharp and have a sawtooth edge. The barbels under the jaw of the Brown Bullhead are dark in color.

SIZE: The average size is less than a pound, but

C. R. Gutermuth

Yellow Bullhead

catches of 2-pounders are not rare. There have been reports of Brown Bullheads reaching 4 pounds.

FOOD: Bullheads readily feed on worms, minnows, or crawfish; but like other members of the family, they draw the line at nothing as far as food is concerned—just so they can get it into their mouths.

HABITS: The Bullhead can live in waters in which other fish cannot survive. Stagnant waters, polluted waters, and shallow muddy waters are all taken by the Bullhead in its stride, and in addition to this, it can live out of water for an extremely long time. Fish being transplanted from one pond to another have been kept out of water for 3 or 4 hours with apparently no ill effects.

While not strictly a school fish, the Bullhead is gregarious, and when one is found, there are usually others present.

It prefers slow moving, muddy streams, or muddy ponds and lakes. It is a bottom feeder and feeds mostly at night.

Bullheads spawn in late spring and early summer, and extreme care is spent in the preparation of the nest, which is built by both the male and female.

The nest is sometimes constructed in a place that nature provides, such as a hollow log or a depression in the bank or a natural hole in the bottom. If a natural nest is not available, they will dig one of their own, using their stiff spines as picks and their mouths as shovels to carry away the dirt. The eggs are then deposited in the nest, which is cared for by both parents.

After the eggs hatch, the young are carefully guarded by both parents, who keep them "rounded up" in a compact school. Should one of the small fry make a mistake and leave the school, it will never be repeated—for the male will instantly pursue it and swallow it in a gulp. While such extreme methods are not to be recommended to modern day child psychologists, nevertheless, there is a middle course.

C. R. Gutermuth

Black Bullhead

Two other species of Bullheads are frequently confused with the Brown Bullhead, but there is so little difference between them that they are rarely recognized by the angler. One is the Yellow Bullhead *(Ameiurus natalis)* which has practically the same range as the Brown Bullhead. It is lighter in color, having a brownish-yellow cast which is mottled with darker markings. It has a shorter more compact body, and its head is larger in comparison to its body. It rarely reaches 2 pounds in weight.

The Black Bullhead *(Ameiurus melas)* can be identified by the light colored band at the base of its tail, and its very dark greenish brown color. Its belly is never white, but usually a dirty yellow. This Bullhead is not found as far south as the others. It has no mottling on the body, and does not reach the size of the other two species.

Fish & Wildlife Service

Carp

C. R. Gutermuth

Mirror Carp

CARP *Cyprinus carpio* Linnaeus

The Carp was originally a native of Asia, and from there transplanted to Europe. From Europe, it was brought to this country in 1877, and now furnishes angling pleasure to many whose local waters are not inhabited by gamefish.

RANGE: Since its introduction, the Carp has been so widely distributed that now it is found in practically every state.

COLOR: The color varies greatly with the type of water it inhabits. When taken from clear water with a sand or gravel bottom, it is a light brassy silver on the upper sides and back. The belly is a silvery cream. When taken from muddy waters, this color varies from a muddy green to brown or black.

DISTINGUISHING CHARACTERISTICS: There are no

teeth in the mouth of the Carp, but it does have teeth or grinders in its throat. On each side of its mouth are two barbels. Its dorsal fin is single and placed in the middle of its body. Both the dorsal and anal fins have a single stout saw-edged spine.

SIZE: Carp average from 1 to 6 pounds, and catches of 15- and 20-pounders are not rare. Weights as high as 55 pounds have been reported in this country, and in Europe it grows even larger.

FOOD: While it prefers to feed in the mud on vegetable matter, it is really omnivorous, in that it will also consume animal matter, such as worms, insects, larvae, crawfish, and crustaceans.

HABITS: It is usually found in rivers, streams, and lakes having mud bottoms. It likes to "root" up aquatic plants and feed on tender roots. In rivers and streams, it prefers the quieter stretches.

Carp spawn in the spring and move into the shallower waters for this purpose. After the eggs are deposited, the parents leave them with no

Haddon-Fish & Wildlife Service

Carp

protection. Female Carp are unusually prolific, and one weighing around 20 pounds will produce as many as 2,000,000 eggs in a season.

WHITE SUCKER

Catostomus commersonii (Lacépède)

The sucker family is extremely large, and the White Sucker is selected as being the best-known member.

RANGE: The White Sucker is found from northern Canada, south to the Gulf States and Mexico, and from the East Coast to the West Coast.

COLOR: The body varies from a creamy white to a silvery white. The back is darker, usually having an olivaceous silvery cast. During spawning season, the color of the back of the male deepens, and a black lateral line appears on its sides, which is bordered by a broad pinkish stripe. Due to this change in coloration, it is sometimes mistakenly called a Black Sucker or Rainbow Sucker.

DISTINGUISHING CHARACTERISTICS: The mouth, which is located under, rather than at the end of, its enlongated head, is a true identification of this species. The Sucker can protrude the thick lips of

Fish & Wildlife Service

Carp Sucker

its mouth so as to produce a perfect suction cup, which enables it to suck up food from the bottom.

All of its fins are soft rayed, and it has a forked tail. Its scales are larger on its under side than they are on the upper sides and back.

SIZE: The average size is from 1 to 2 pounds, although larger ones of from 3 to 4 pounds have been caught.

FOOD: They feed on aquatic plants, insects worms, and mollusks.

HABITS: They are found in streams, rivers, ponds, and lakes and prefer clear water, and in streams and rivers are usually found in pools, and along the edges of the current. In the spring, they congregate in great numbers at the foot of waterfalls and dams.

Suckers spawn in the spring, and usually a definite upstream migration occurs at this time. The spawning is done in shallows or riffles which have a gravel bottom, and the eggs are buried in the loose gravel. The fry hatch in about three weeks in water above 50° F. and after the yolk sacs are absorbed, shift for themselves.

ROCKY MOUNTAIN WHITEFISH

Prosopium williamsoni (Girard)

This fish should not be confused with the Whitefish caught commercially in the Great Lakes *(Coregonnus clupeaformis clupeaformis)* for it is an entirely different species. Due to the high dorsal fin of the Rocky Mountain Whitefish, it is frequently mis-identified as a Grayling by inexperienced fishermen.

RANGE: It is found from Colorado to British Columbia on the west slope of the Rocky Mountains.

COLOR: This fish has a medium to light bluish-silver cast to its back and upper sides which becomes silvery white on the lower sides and white on the belly.

C. R. Gutermuth

Redhorse Sucker

C. R. Gutermuth
Spotted Sucker

DISTINGUISHING CHARACTERISTICS: It is readily identified by its large, oversize dorsal fin, and its large adipose fin, which extends beyond the anal fin.

SIZE: It averages between 1 and 2 pounds, and specimens weighing as much as 4 pounds have been reported.

FOOD: Its favorite foods are insect larvae, insects, and flies, but it also feeds on worms and small minnows.

HABITS: Rocky Mountain Whitefish prefer waters similar to those occupied by trout. In streams, they will be found in the fast water, and in lakes in deep water along ledges or rocky shores. During the spawning season, which is fall and early winter, these fish make a spawning migration up the streams which are tributary to the waters they inhabit.

There are many other species of Whitefish which are close relatives of the Rocky Mountain Whitefish. One is the Pilot or Round Whitefish *(Prosopium cylindraceum quadrilaterale)* found in the East. Another is the Great Lakes Whitefish previously mentioned, which is of no interest to the angler.

The Cisco *(Coregonus artedi)* is closely related to the Whitefish of the Great Lakes, and is found in lakes in the northern part of the Middle West, especially those adjacent to the Great Lakes. During the latter part of spring, when the mayflies hatch, these fish furnish excellent sport to anglers, who take them on the surface with flies.

SHEEFISH *Stendodus leucichthis*

This is a little known fish of the Arctic waters, and considered to be one of the finest gamefish by those who have caught it. Sometimes it is known as Inconnu, which is the Eskimo word for unknown.

RANGE: While the exact range is not definitely known, they are most plentiful in Alaskan waters from the Aleutian Islands north to Kotzebue Sound. They appear in lesser numbers north and east of there, and have been reported from the mouth of the Mackenzie River and farther east in extreme northwest Canada. They also ascend the tidal rivers into the interior of Alaska, and are reported to be present in Siberia.

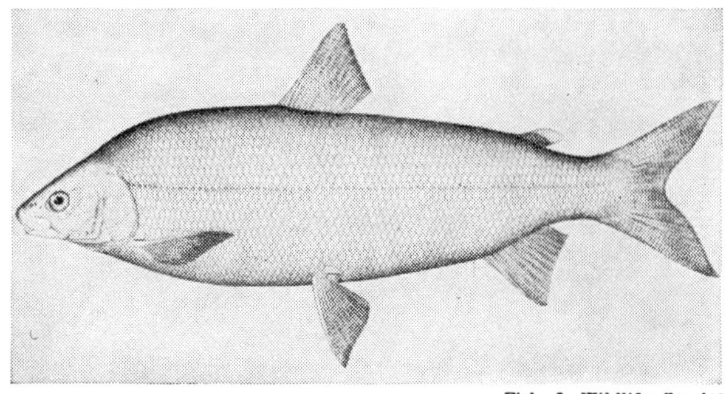
Fish & Wildlife Service
Whitefish

COLOR: General over-all color is a clear silvery white with a pinkish overcast on upper portion, shading to a pearly gray on belly. Back has a darker greenish olive cast.

DISTINGUISHING CHARACTERISTICS: The Sheefish is devoid of markings and has large coarse scales, and an extended tarpon-like under jaw. Mouth contains numerous small needle-sharp teeth.

SIZE: Average size is 10 to 20 pounds, but catches of 40-pounders are not rare. Fish of up to 85 pounds in weight have been reported.

Fish & Wildlife Service
Shad

C. R. Gutermuth
Hickory Shad

FOOD: Smaller fish, especially smelt.

HABITS: The Sheefish spends most of its time in the brackish waters at the mouths of rivers, but is anadromous in that it migrates up fresh water rivers for spawning purposes. After this is accomplished, it descends these rivers to the sea.

SHAD *Alose sapidissima* (Wilson)

The Shad, while basically a salt-water fish, comes up into fresh water for spawning purposes, and at times furnishes splendid sport for anglers. Ofttimes, the name of the river in which Shad are taken is joined with that of the fish, such as Delaware River Shad, Susquehanna River Shad, etc., etc.

RANGE: The Shad is found on our Atlantic Coast from the Gulf of St. Lawrence in Canada to the St. Johns River in Florida. During the past century, this fish was transplanted to the Pacific Coast, and it is now found from southern California to southwestern Alaska, but is most plentiful from Monterey Bay, California, to the Columbia River.

COLOR: Bluish or bluish-green along the back, which blends into silvery white sides. A dark spot or spots are present just above the upper gill cover. These spots often extend back as far as the dorsal fin.

DISTINGUISHING CHARACTERISTICS: The short dorsal fin has no spines, and the tail is deeply forked. The center of the lower jaw rises to form a small peak which fits into a corresponding notch in the upper jaw.

SIZE: The female is larger than the male, and an average size for females would be 4 to 5 pounds, and for males, 2 to 3 pounds. A Shad of from 6 to 8 pounds is considered large, but commercial fishermen have reported Shad weighing as much as 13½ pounds.

FOOD: Insects, insect larvae, crustaceans, minnows, and small fish. Also minute plant and animal life.

HABITS: Shad spend most of their lives in the ocean and only come close to shore in the spring when they start their spawning migration. Practically nothing is known of their life while at sea. While on this spawning migration, they take no food, but will strike at flies and spinners and even at minnows occasionally. This striking is due to a lifelong instinct to strike at any object that resembles food, and despite the fact that they are not feeding, this instinct is so strong that it in reality becomes a reflex motion.

Shad start to ascend rivers for spawning purposes when the temperature of the water reaches the neighborhood of 60° F. The spawning is accomplished while the fish swim side by side, and the eggs sink to, and are scattered over the bottom. After spawning, the spent fish immediately descend the river to the sea.

The young hatch in 6 to 10 days, and after the yolk sac is absorbed, they begin feeding at once. The fry remain in fresh water until the cool weather of fall arrives; by that time they are 3 to 7 inches long, and start their migration to salt water.

North Carolina Wildlife Resources Commission

Fishing a stream in the Great Smoky Mountains

SECTION II

FISHING EQUIPMENT AND FISHING METHODS

Part I. Fishing Tackle

HISTORY

Tackle used by today's sportsmen is the culmination of centuries of experimenting and testing. Some of the most fundamental parts of tackle were developed so early there is no certain record of what man or even which peoples first used them. Other tackle units are so modern they still are being tested in actual practice.

There are artifacts which show how one tribe developed the fish hook from a simple gorge. But back of such records in point of time, we find references to hooks being used in other countries. Simple reels with no genuine difference in principles from modern single action fly reels were used by the Egyptians long before they were mentioned in English publications.

In contrast, there is the recent introduction of glass fiber rods. Synthetics also have produced a new leader. Better tackle is still being sought and produced.

Reaching back to seek beginnings of fishing equipment in use today reveals an interesting situation. Many types of tackle units considered "new" were either actually in use many years ago or were being experimentally tested. A rod with the reel within the grip has been presented recently as something new. But a book titled *The Art of Angling,* published in London in 1651, and written by Thomas Barker, contains an illustration of a "wind" which was a spool-type reel seated in a space *in* the butt section of the rod—basically the same idea as the reel-in-grip so recently "introduced."

Pioneer construction often embodied principles nearly identical with the "newest" thing in today's tackle catalogs. Dry flies were used in England soon after 1800. Steel rods were tested as early as 1848. The history of artificial flies tells of the Red Hackle being in use on the river Astracus, at least as long ago as the third century A.D., catching "speckled fish," which were close relatives of our Brook Trout.

It's trite, but in fishing tackle one wonders if "There's nothing new—."

What device appeared first as a means of catching fish is not clear. The net and the spear were in use as earliest references to fishing were recorded. Just where the hook, the fishing pole, and the line appeared, and thus set up the first assembly of tackle which was the multiple-great-granddaddy of that used today, is lost in dim centuries. From that point, tackle improvement is the running record of the evolution of the oldest sport unless hunting antedates fishing. Refinement of tackle has been the very basis for more highly developed sportsmanship.

Primitive anglers undoubtedly were concerned almost wholly with the objective of landing something to eat. Tackle supplied a means of getting it. Even the first artificial lures were someone's idea of being able to hook fish and not have to spend time gathering bait.

Somewhere along the line, anglers became proud of their skill. They probably showed the "big one" they had caught on tackle lighter than other members of their tribe had used. The element of skill, and pride in ability and better tackle emerged. The genesis of sport fishing, of being able to do a neater, more skillful act, began at this point.

Just when the recognition of fishing as a sport took precedence over merely securing food cannot be determined. Well before Walton, there was a definite trend toward angling as sport. The earliest books on angling in the English language, and in some earlier French writings treated fishing as a sport.

By the time Walton wrote of pleasure in angling and the ethics that should govern, sport fishing was well established in England. Tackle and how to use it was a much discussed subject. Artificial lures were recognized as more sporting than bait fishing. Fishermen were boasting that they could land the heaviest trout or salmon on a leader formed of a single strand of horse hair, while others were contending that a sane angler would not risk losing a fish on such tackle and should have a three-hair leader on the line.

Anglers still argue this way—and as they experiment and test their tackle, working toward more sporting equipment, sportsmen still give the motivation for manufacturers to continually seek improvement in equipment.

Tackle that can now be purchased at any counter is a heritage from millions of anglers. In tracing the history and development of each segment of tackle assembly one can develop keen appreciation for the present background and standing of sport fishing.

HOOKS

Fish hooks are seldom given a second thought. They are as common as carpet tacks, needles, or knives. Yet some angler of ancient days fashioned a hook and his tribesmen probably hailed him as the "inventive genius of the age."

The hook is the most fundamental unit in sport fishing. Without its invention, rules governing netters, spear handlers, and other methods of landing fish might well have developed. But the hook was developed and on it rests the entire structure of modern sport fishing.

Some form of hook and line had been in use, perhaps for centuries, before records of fishing began. The hook may have appeared in a number of places at about the same time or in different eras at widely separated locations. Evidence of the hook developing spontaneously in fishing areas is found in the earliest records of primitive tribes. Some reports of first explorers visiting primitive peoples mention fish hooks made of shell or bone—hooks with all essentials of bend, point, and barb.

How the hook thus may have developed in many places is well illustrated in artifacts archaeologists have secured from sites of the old communities of lake dwellers of Switzerland.

The antiquity of these Lacustrine communities is not certainly established. It is believed that

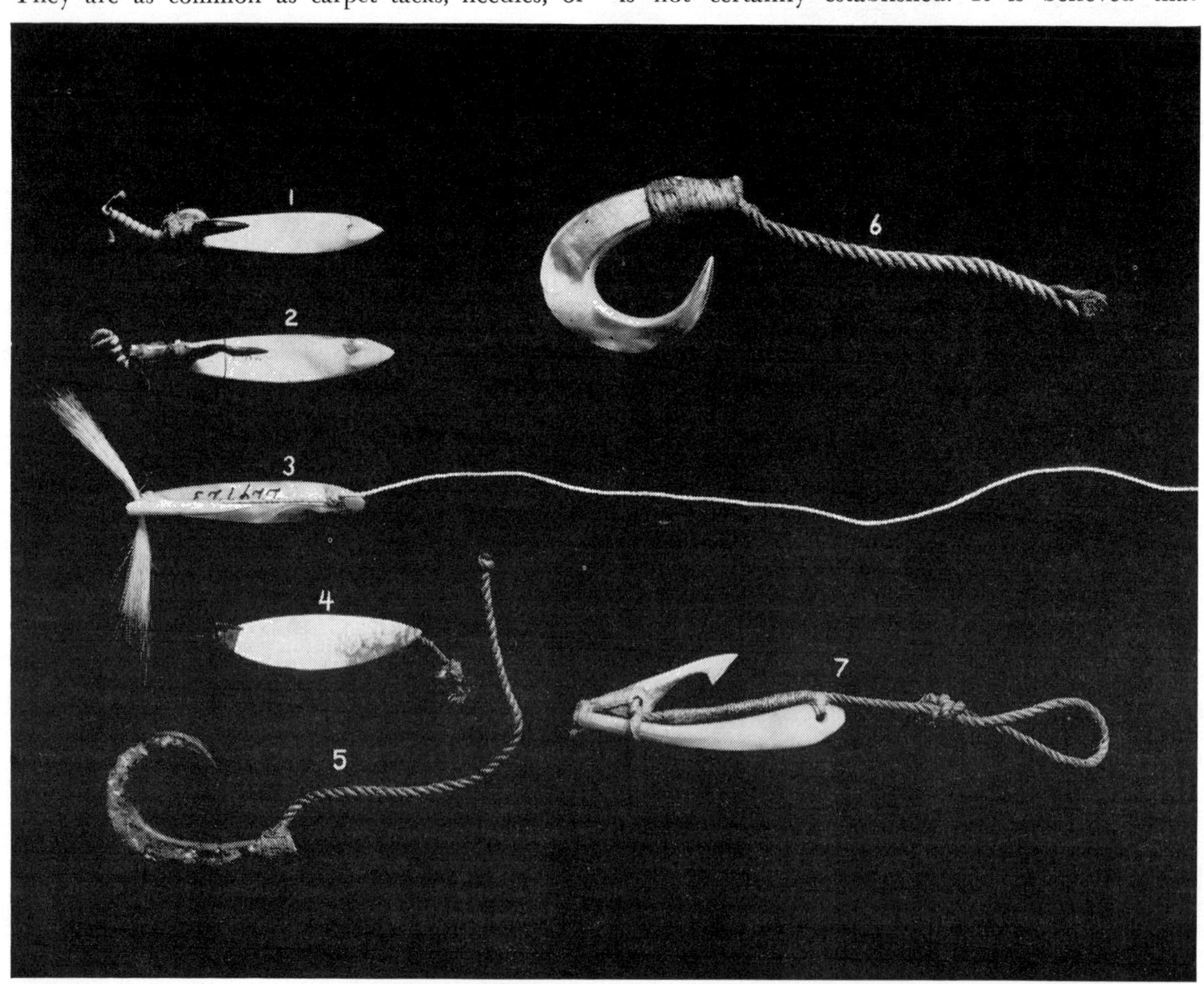

Smithsonian Institution

Stone, Horn and Shell hooks from South Pacific.

1) Solomon Islands stone hook, mother-of-pearl shank, head feather. 2) Solomon Islands horn hook, mother-of-pearl shank. 3) Hawaiian bone hook, mother-of-pearl shank, feathered. 4) Kingsmill Island, shell hook with mother-of-pearl. 5) Penrhyn Island mother-of-pearl hook. 6) Polynesian mother-of-pearl hook. 7) Marquesas Islands hook.

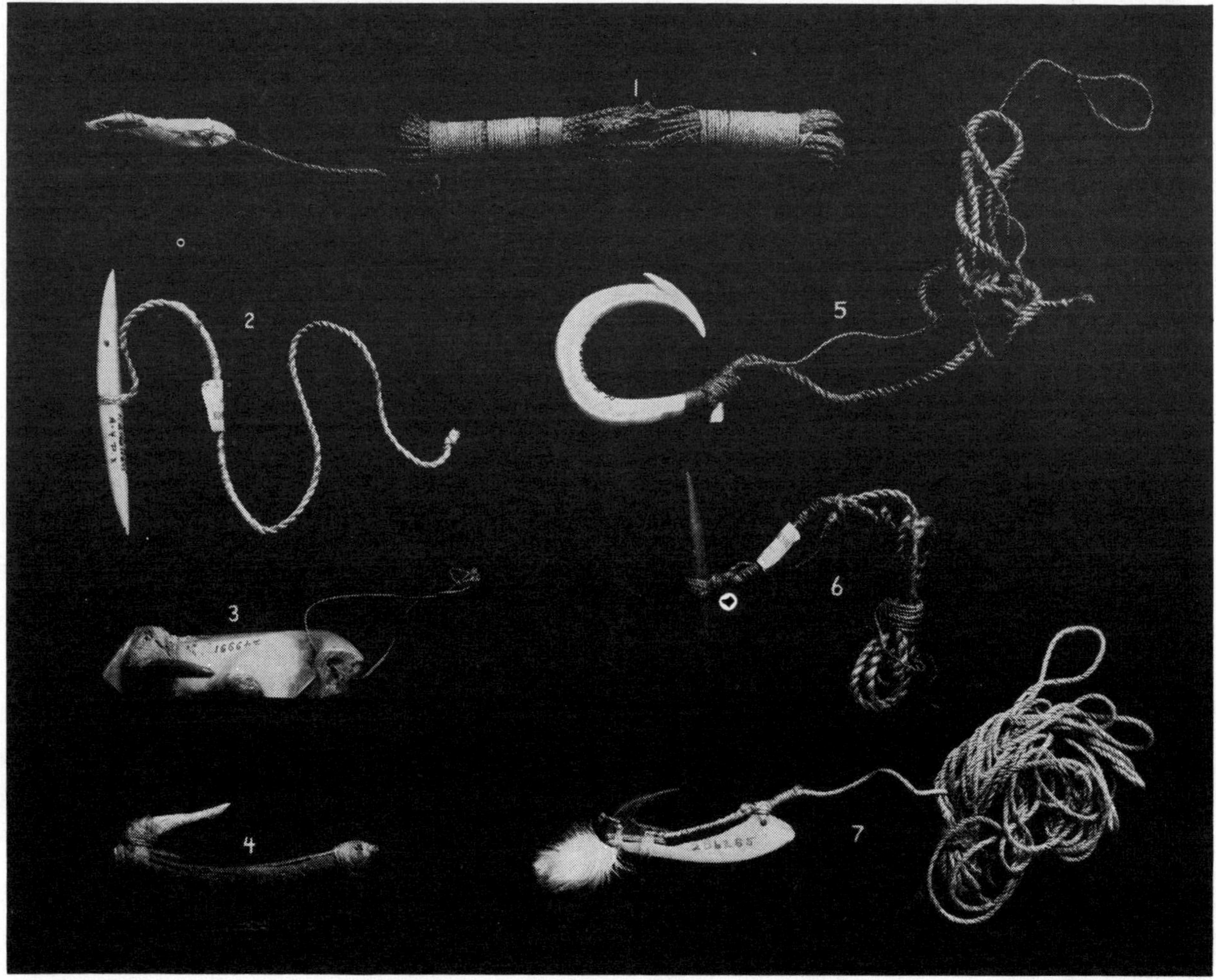

Smithsonian Institution

Polynesian Shell and Bone Hooks and Gorges.

1) Samoan, shell hook, mother-of-pearl shank and line. 2) Hawaiian fish gorge (shell) and line. 3) Marshall Islands, mother-of-pearl hook and shank. 4) New Zealand bone hook, shod with mother-of-pearl. 5) Hawaiian shell hook, barbed, and line. 6) Hawaiian fish gorge and line. 7) Funafuti, Ellis Island "Paa" shell hook, pearl shank, and line.

they were in existence more than 2000 years ago. Herodotus wrote about them in the 5th century B.C. All that now remain are the foundations of their dwellings, stone platforms located out from lake shorelines or the remnants of piles on which houses stood above the water.

These artifacts are not the oldest antecedents of the fish hook, but do illustrate the way the hook was developed.

Far earlier than the existence of this Lacustrine civilization, fishermen had fashioned a gorge. This was a simple cross-bar affair, made of stone, bone, or wood. It was tapered toward both ends and had a groove cut around the middle where a line could be fastened.

Such a gorge was attached to the line, and thrust into bait. The line's end paralleled the gorge. As the fish swallowed the bait, a tug on the line would pull the gorge out of the bait. Because the line was attached in the center, the gorge would seat crosswise in the fish's gullet and it could be dragged in.

A gorge found under 22 feet of earth in a French peat bed, in the valley of the Somme, was estimated to be as much as 30,000 years old because of the over-lying depth of peat. It was estimated by other scientists as not so ancient but at least 7000 years old.

The early craftsmen used the materials at hand in shaping the gorges. They were made of thorn, bone, stone, or shell. Even before the appearance of metal gorges, some ancient gorges had slight curves from the middle toward the points, for better holding of the catch, and thus forecast the curves which were to develop into hook shapes as metal entered the scene.

As an incidental observation, the gorge has been found in many places and in use within comparatively recent times. Tribes of the Arctic, bushmen of South Africa, American Indians, and fishermen of the South Sea Islands, have used gorges only a few decades past. Gorges still are used in certain types of eel fishing in Scotland.

Two thousand years ago, the dwellers around Lake Neuchatel in Switzerland probably knew all about the gorge and its uses just as we accept the fish hook of today. They were workers in bronze and some inventive cuss among them, developed the "bricole"—a simple section of bronze wire with a slight hump in the middle where the line could be attached. It was a metal wire gorge, with just that little hump, the beginning of the eye of the hook, bent into the middle.

The next step was to twist the wire so instead of the hump an eyelet was formed in the center. The two arms probably bent a bit as the early artisan twisted the eyelet into the wire and he saw that was a smart idea. He found a bent wire so fashioned held better than a straight wire.

So he decided to put more bend in the wire. He formed two hooks, one on either side of the attachment of the line. This was still better for holding fish. Somewhere the idea occurred that if the point of the hooks were barbed, they could penetrate but not slip out so easily, and fewer fish would get off the hook. So the barb, probably an idea adapted from the spear or the arrow, was added to the double hook.

One day in all probability, an old Lacustrine fisherman broke one of his double hooks and decided he could keep on fishing with the single one he had left. He tried it. It held just as well as the double hook. Fish would swallow it easier. As stress was put on the line the tip of the hook sunk the barb better.

The hook, as it is known today in all of its essential features, has come out of the modification of the simple bar of bone or wood or shell—a wire hook, of tempered bronze or copper, and so like the modern hook it jolts one to compare them.

The lake dwellers probably fished from their back porch. They lost gorges and hooks. Scientists have used these to demonstrate gorge-to-hook evolution. However, this tribe should not be credited with being the first to fish with the hook.

For there is mention of a bent hook that was barbless in use in the First Egyptian Dynasty, which reaches back into yesterday to between 5702 to 2700 B.C. The exact time of this dynasty is not positive but it was within that stretch of years. The Egyptians had improved this hook by 1200 B.C., which was during the Twelfth Dynasty, by adding a barb.

So the array of artifacts found on the Swiss lake can be considered as a demonstration of the evolution of fish hook but someone, long before, had shaped a hook, and had given it a barb.

The hook form has been found in many widely separated places, in different cultures uncovered by archaeologists, and constructed of many substances. The hook as such, probably appeared in the late paleolithic period, or more likely in neolithic. Tribes of later times, with cultures comparable to these periods, used hook forms that are typical of those ancient eras.

An ancient shell hook from Santa Barbara, California, is a genuine hook, even with barb, although this was on the exterior side of the point. The Mohave Indians fashioned hooks of cactus thorns. In New Guinea the spur of an insect leg supplied the point. And in some Pacific islands, human bones were material for hooks.

Even currently, some hand-fashioned hooks, tied together with fiber are in use in some Pacific islands. Those that are especially successful actually have names given them and are treasured.

Whether or not there were artisans in England specializing in making fish hooks at the time the first English book dealing with angling was published, is debatable. This book, by the Abbess of Sopwell, Dame Juliana Bernes, published in 1486, considered the hook as an accomplished fact. It is probable that there were craftsmen who turned out hooks for British anglers of the time, each individual hook a hand product and a project in itself.

The books which followed the first treatise by Dame Juliana stimulated a growing interest in angling, and participants increased in numbers. The slow process of hand fabrication had to be supplanted by some sort of volume in hook production.

The steel needle is the direct ancestor of the volume-produced fish hook.

The use of an eyed awl for sewing probably far antedated the first fish hook. Just when the first steel needles were produced is unknown, but the Chinese are credited with the invention. From that country, the steel needle traveled through trade channels into the Mediterranean countries, and then into France and Germany. They had achieved a degree of standard manufacture and some volume by the latter part of the 15th century. About 1470 Nuremberg was the center of needle production.

The needle industry of England centered around the town Redditch. There is a published statement in an old British magazine to the effect that by 1560, some of these needle manufacturers also made fish hooks. It was a logical source for hooks; a hook is essentially a needle bent at one end and with a barb added. Even as late as 1900, catalogs of the famous Alcock Company of Redditch, founded in 1803, listed fish hooks and other tackle, plus needles.

The volume production of fish hooks boomed after 1800. In 1826 the first stamping machine that drilled eyes in needles was put in operation. In this period English manufacturers turned to the Scandinavian countries for artizans to work in the needle-and-hook factories. Some of these craftsmen later returned to their homelands taking their know-how in making hooks with them.

The famous Mustad Company, still making fine fish hooks, was founded in Oslo, Sweden, in 1832. English producers had not mechanized hook making as much as they might. The Scandinavians introduced a number of machine methods replacing much of the hand finishing then current in England. Even today, there is considerable remainder of the hand finishing of hooks persisting in many European factories.

From the middle of the 19th century, the world production of fish hooks was in England and Scandinavia. Although a high degree of mechanization had been reached, when compared to the production of a hook entirely by hand, the process remained rather laborious and somewhat uncertain until after 1850.

The processes then used, at the beginning of the production of hooks at low cost and in volume which has made them so cheap and common, should be of interest to the modern sportsman, for they persist in many establishments and they are the foundation for the most modern of all hooks those entirely machine-produced in the United States today.

A book by Henry P. Wells, *Fly Rods and Fly Tackle,* published in 1883, gives an excellent description of the method of making hooks at that time.

Round steel wire was fed through a hole in a steel block until the cut end met a stop. It was then sheared at the hole-end of that length, and the process repeated. The length required for various sizes and patterns of hooks was determined by the distance between the hole and the stop.

An individual cut length then was laid on an iron bed, and a steel tool with a chisel-like cutting edge was applied, the bevel edge being up. This cut incised the barb. The bevel of the cutting tool determined the "rankness" of the barb—the degree of angle between it and the body of the hook.

The next step was to anneal the wire; make it soft by application of heat. The point tip of the wire then was placed under a drop hammer which struck that end in such a way as to nearly or quite shear off the blunt end beyond the barb, to form the hook's point. Two or three strokes of a hand file smoothed off that cut side of the point and further shaped it.

The hook now was ready to receive the bend between point and shank. This was done by laying the hook on a block which had a peg against which the point was seated, and a raised form against which the softened wire was bent. This raised form on the block would be different in shape according to the type of hook to be produced, such as the Sproat, Pennel or Round.

The hooks, softened by the preceding heating, were then hardened. This was done by putting them in a sheet-iron dish and heating them in an oven until they were cherry red. When the worker handling this step believed they were at the proper temperature, the whole batch in the pan was dumped into oil. They came out brittle and hard.

The hooks were then drawn to a spring temper by being placed in a pan full of sand that was heated to produce the proper temperature. The worker stirred these around, judging by the appearance of the steel when the proper heat was reached. When he believed this accomplished, he removed the batch and allowed it to cool.

It is perfectly obvious that, if the craftsman missed on his judgment of the heating in either of the two tempering steps, the batch of hooks handled in this manner was worthless. If they were heated too much in the hardening, the steel would "burn" and no later measures would make them springy and tough. Also if the tempering heat was misjudged, they would be lacking in springiness, likely to straighten out when subjected to a strain.

A perusal of the angling books written in the last half of the 19th century will reveal the hook troubles of anglers in those years. Hooks were too brittle, or would straighten out, always when playing a goodly fish.

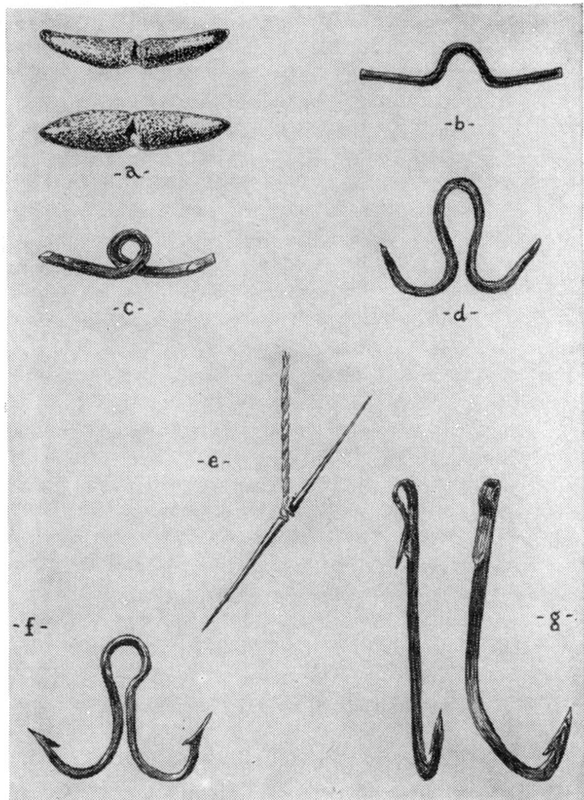

Drawing by James B. Trefethen after "Sport with Rod and Gun" by Alfred M. Mayer, Appleton—Century—Crofts

Primitive Fish hooks.

a) Stone fish gorge from the Valley of the Somme, used about 7000 B.C. b) Bronze bricole from the Lake of Neufchatel, Switzerland. c) Bronze bricole of later period. d) Double hook from the Lake of Neufchatel. e) Needle gorge, a modification of the Neolithic form, used in modern France for taking eels. f) Double-hooked barb from the Swiss Lakes. g) Bronze fish hooks from the Swiss Lakes. All above with exception of (g) are approximately same size as the original. g) is shown approximately one-half size.

A final factory inspection tried to guard against such troubles. Each hook was laid on a block with pegs which would hold the bend and point. The shank then was pulled around to a specified point and released. If it broke, the hook was discarded; if it didn't spring back to the original shape when released it was equally worthless.

With some advances, this general system of hook production persisted into the period of World War I. Then American manufacturers began seeking a better, more exact, means of mass-production.

The Enterprise Manufacturing Company of Akron, Ohio, developed a machine which would feed wire in one side and tumble hooks ready for tempering out of the other side. Types produced were spearpoint designs.

During the later 1920's, Wright and McGill of Denver began machine production of hooks. Two features of their process represented steps toward better hooks. One was the mechanically hollow-ground point. The other was a new bend, christened the "Eagle Claw." It is so formed that the line of traction set up by the line is directly coincident with the line of penetration of the point.

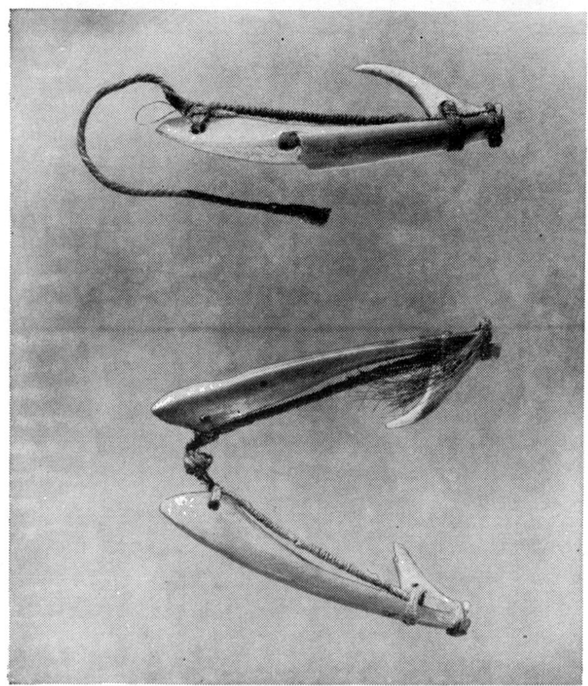

Amer. Mus. Nat. History

Fish hooks from Fiji Islands.

This was the major advancement in hooks in the half century between 1885 and 1935. (See page 172.)

In addition to securing typical American mass production, with uniformity in shape in any one batch, two other factors were added. One was a precise chemical formula of steel used for the hook. With this, tempering by controlled heat in an electric furnace supplied an exact process to replace the "good guessing" of the craftsman who supervised the tempering in former methods.

The net result of these developments is that today hooks are as nearly identical in each batch as mechanized methods can make them, with identical composition in the steel and precision tempering. Because this country produced all hooks during World War II and thus built up its production potential, the center of fish hook production today is in the United States.

The American companies now producing fish hooks are Wright & McGill of Denver, The Enterprise Manufacturing Company of Akron and Bill DeWitt Baits, Auburn, New York. Other manufacturers further process the basic hooks, to form doubles and trebles and other forms such as weedless.

While the hook had long ago advanced to the fundamental form—the bends, the points and other details used today—did not emerge as recognized patterns until the 19th century. Earlier, it is certain, each artisan designed hooks according to his ideas. By 1880, when the mechanization of hook making had advanced to some degree of standardization, there were heated discussions of the proper style for the best hook.

Leading patterns of that period included: the Round, Kirby, Limerick, Sneck Sproat, O'Shaughnessy, Aberdeen and Kinsey. And while the "invention" of the barbless hook has been credited to others of later years, it was a recognized type on the market in 1885. If we wish to be exceptionally exact, the Egyptians had the "first" genuine barbless of record!

One of the more prominent figures in this controversy regarding hooks, was Mr. H. Cholmondely Pennell of England. He held forth at length on the mechanics of the simple fish hook in his book *Modern Practical Angler,* published in London in 1870.

Pennell lays down some of the more important considerations in the forms of hooks, and how they function, and his observations are worth inclusion here. Hook shapes which he analyzed and criticized are still in use.

Mr. Pennell wrote: "Extraordinary as it may seem in such a mechanical age as ours, we cannot go into a tackle shop, and buy a hook in which one or more glaring defects, or offenses against first principles of mechanics, cannot be pointed out. The most common fault of all, perhaps, lies in the shape of the bend. I have shown—how great is the difference in the penetrating powers of different bends. Between the two extremes it amounts to no less than cent. (100) per cent; and yet the best of these fall below the point of efficiency which ought to be attainable.—

"The theory of hooks, as based simply on mechanical principles should probably run somewhat as follows:

"1. What are the objects to be aimed at in a perfect hook?—
   "a. Penetration.
   "b. Holding power.
   "c. Strength.
   "d. Lightness and neatness.
"2. How are these to be attained and combined?"

He then goes on to state that the greatest penetrating power of a hook occurs when the line of penetration is coincident with the direction of the force applied. He remarks that the Kirby and Sneck forms of hooks, with their points at an angle, do not penetrate in the line of traction, and the greater the bend in such a type, the more the line of the point of penetration deviates from the line of pull.

Pennell analyzes the mechanics involved when various types of hooks are sunk in a fish's jaw through pull on the line and clearly presents the shortcomings of a number of standard hook styles. He then presented diagrams showing graphically how far the line of penetration deviated from the line of traction in most hooks. In comparison he offered his own design of hook bend and point, showing that among those illustrated it more nearly approached the coincidence of line of traction and line of penetration. Pennell was arguing for his pet design; it was sound argument.

Those controversies and dissertations of the 1870-1885 period went far toward bringing about the acceptance of certain designs in hooks and undoubtedly discarding many others. Hook styles that became "standard" at that time remained so, and are used today.

When Mr. Henry P. Wells' book *Fly-rods and*

Fly-tackle, appeared in 1885, he reprinted much of the Pennell discussion, added four new diagrams of hooks to show the penetration-traction relationship, and further discussed the mechanics of hook construction.

The Hutchinsons, of Kendal, England, were the manufacturers to whom Pennell assigned his design. Pennell's hook has, however, its own faults. The bend has two accented "angles," one as the bend leaves the shank and one as it turns toward the point. The bend between these points rather "flattens out." The sharp "angles" at these points in the bend are more likely to break under stress than where there is a smooth, continuous curve in the bend.

The "eagle claw" type of hook, actually very recent in its entrance into the tackle field, achieves what Pennell was trying to secure. The bend of the "eagle claw" type begins well up on the shank, this curve being part of the mechanics which keeps the point of the hook in line with traction pull as the point sinks. The curve "flows" in a bending line all the way to the point itself. In addition to that the hollow-ground point is precisely curved, so the point and barb as it shears into the cartilage of a fish's mouth continues to be in the line of traction.

Whether or not any present hook is the final word in its design is open to question. In looking over the long history of the hook's development, anyone would be rather rash to prophesy that never will there be another fish hook which will surpass present types. It is easy to visualize the old Lacustrine fisherman on a Swiss lake with his precious "bricole" of tempered bronze wire holding it up and saying, "Now, fellows, that's the real answer to sport in fishing. You can say all you want to about its faults,—I say nobody ever will improve on a bronze bricole. I ought to know; I'm the champ fisherman on this lake!"

Any person attempting to search more recent records to give credit to manufacturers who "introduced" the compound hooks—the doubles and trebles now placed on so many bait casting lures—would certainly be trying to gild the lily. One glance backward would make such claims ridiculous. Bronze age artisans made double hooks before they began to use single ones.

It's the same when the "new barbless hooks are discussed. The hooks of antiquity were barbless before some bright angler, who probably lived before 2000 B.C., looked at a spear or arrow and mused, "If I fashion the point of my hook with a barb like my spear, it will sink in and not slip out."

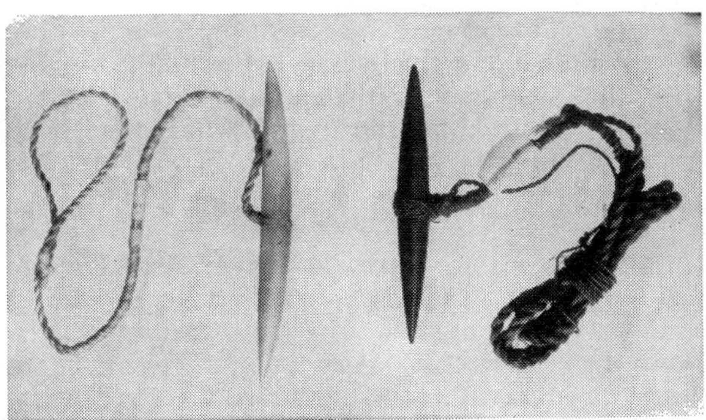
Smithsonian Institution

Polynesian fish gorges and lines.

In the history of tackle development, and as the most vital point in all tackle assembly, the fish hook deserves full recognition. Thanks are due those fellows in the dim yesterdays who labored with skill and high ingenuity for their time in fashioning the first hooks, the multiple-great-grand ancestors of the fine hooks of today.

LEADERS

In considering tackle assembly from the hook toward the angler the next bit of tackle is the leader or trace. One type of leader made of gut is used in fly fishing; another, generally of metal filament or braided wire is used for bait casting.

Leaders have two fundamental functions. The leader used by fly fishermen is filmy, and its purpose is to achieve deception. It affords a less visible connection as the fly is laid out on the waters between lure and line. The objective of using such a leader then is deception and lightness in handling.

The other leader or trace, used in bait casting or trolling, supplies a section of line near the lure, which will take strain and roughing in a place where that is most likely to occur. The bait casting leader of such material as braided bronze wire or single strand piano wire can meet the sawing of rough gill edges or teeth of a caught fish, or of ledges or sunken logs better than any line.

How far back a primitive leader was used is lost in antiquity. Perhaps the strengthening of the line near the hook end was so logical and desirable that no fisherman of early days thought of it as something of note; it was just accepted as a common-sense thing to do. Also, whatever material may have been used as leaders in early days it being more perishable than bone or metal, disintegrated while the gorge or bricole remained. Thinking speculatively, if a fisherman with a line of some sort of fiber attached a leader of some animal gut to strengthen the line at the hook end, such gut would have rotted away centuries before primitive hooks were dug up by scientists. The fact that a filament leader from the silk-worm was called "gut" strongly indicates that some animal gut had been used previously as a leader.

The leader used for fortifying the line near the hook, if it was a part of pre-history tackle, simply came onto the stage as an established facility when the earliest records were made.

By the time of Walton, it appears that the leader was an accepted method of fortifying the line above the hook. In his instructions on tying flies, he refers to "arming" the hook, which is to tie or whip the line around it. Later in giving instructions on fishing with a frog as bait for the pike *(Esox lucius)*, which is the fish we call the "northern pike," Walton writes:

"Put your hook into his (the frog's) mouth:—I mean the arming wire through his mouth and out at his gills."

The wire leaders today are undoubtedly the outgrowth of very similar leaders that were in general use perhaps from the earliest period when wire was hammered out of metal. The modern materials are, of course, far superior.

The history of the deceptive leader is somewhat clearer than the one used to fortify the line near the hook. The line of the early days was in general effect a "leader." We find in the *Book of St. Albans* (Berners) that the Prioress recommended a braided line of horse hair, three strands. Capt. Richard Franck, author of *Northern Memories,* and a contemporary of Walton who disagreed with "Ike" on many points of sport angling, goes all out to claim that he could land any salmon on a *single* horse hair strand. Certainly a single horse hair approximates a leader of fine Nylon so far as fineness and need for expert playing of the catch is concerned.

At least over the century and a half between the first book in English regarding the sport of angling and Walton's time, the principal connection between the line and the hook was a leader of hair. Juliana recommended a braided hair line, which approximated a leader in effect, and in the early part of Walton's dissertation on fly fishing, of which he knew not too much, being a bait man primarily, he wrote:

"I shall next give you some other directions for fly-fishing, such as are given by Mr. Thomas Barker, a gentleman that hath spent much time fishing; but I shall do it with a little variation.

"First, let your rod be light and very gentle. I take the best to be of two pieces. And let not your line exceed, especially for three or four links next the hook,—I say, not exceed three or four hairs at the most, though you may fish a little stronger above in the upper part of your line; but if you can attain to angle with one hair, you shall have more rises and catch more fish."

The "natural gut" which has been used for leaders by fly fishermen for years, and still is preferred by many, is tied in with the history of silk as closely as fish hooks are related to the story of the steel needle.

Silk comes from the cocoon of the "silkworm," the larval phase of a moth, *Bombyx mori.* The first growing of silkworms is credited to the Si-ling, wife of Emperor Hoang-ti, of China, in the year 2609 B.C. Within forty years groves of the mulberry, on which the silkworm feeds, were established as "pasture" for the "worms." The big expansion of China's silk industry occurred in the time of emporer Twang-Ti, in the 18th century B.C.

Authorities differ as to the year when the first silkworm eggs were brought to the Mediterranean countries, to initiate the silk industry. But the story of smuggling silkworm eggs out of China seems well authenticated, whether this was in A.D. 530 or 555.

Since China had a monopoly through control of silkworm culture, it was a capital offense to take eggs or other stages of growth of the moth out of the country. Anyone attempting this would if caught have a chop-chop ending—by an ax.

Silk had been sold in trade much earlier than this, reaching Europe through Phonecian and Persian routes. Aristotle mentioned silk in the hands of the natives of Cos, from which the fabric found its way to Rome.

The Roman Emperor Justinian sent two monks to China to bring eggs of the moth to the Mediterranean. Concealing the eggs in the hollows of bamboo staffs, the monks delivered these at Constantinople—A.D. 530 or 555, whichever you like best as a date.

The Saracens brought sericulture to Spain in the eighth century, and even at that time, there may have been some "gut" produced by experimenting Spaniards, and even used as leaders—there's no way of telling.

There are early references to silkworm gut, which give some indication of when it may have been used first in England as leader material.

In his "Diary," under the date of March 18, 1667, the famous Pepys mentions a "Mr. Caesar" showing him "gut" string which is—beyond any hair for strength and smallness." The specific comparison to hair, which then was used for lines, suggests that Pepys may have been thinking of this gut in connection with sport fishing—but there is no proof in mere reference.

However, James Saunders, in his *Compleat Fisherman,* the 1724 edition, makes the first direct mention of silkworm gut as something used by fishermen.

By the middle of the 19th century, the demand for silkworm gut for fishing leaders had grown to a modest industry. These were the steps in its production at that time.

Just before the silkworm weaves its cocoon, it ceases feeding. The fluid in the two sacs within the worm is ready to be spun, and the tiny beginnings of the thread are visible in the worm's mouth.

At this stage, the worms were placed in a vinegar solution for some hours, and pickled. They were removed from the solution, seized by the head and tail, and pulled apart. The two sacs containing the fluid from which the worm would have spun the cocoon, were then grasped, and pulled apart. The viscous fluid stretched into a single filament, hardened on contact with the air, and produced a length of "gut."

The speed with which the stringy fluid was stretched, determined the thickness of the gut. If pulled out rapidly, it hardened into a thinner diameter. Heavier gut was produced by slow pulling. Although the Spanish peasant doing the job might be fairly expert, it's readily evident that this action inevitably produced gut which varied in diameter and strength.

After the gut dried, with the residue of the sacs still adhering, it was bundled and sold to dealers in this material for further processing and cleaning. Cleaning in earlier days, was done by women and girls drawing the dirty gut between their teeth. One writer remarks that the spectacle of these workers using teeth and lips to scrape off remains of the pickled worm, the gut sometimes cutting lips, and the women spitting and pulling gut, was a wholly gaggy sort of a business. Chemicals were soon substituted for the teeth-cleaning process but much of the other procedure is essentially similar today.

The fact that there were attempts to develop the silk industry in America are largely lost to general knowledge. But as early as 1732 the Colonial government of Georgia allotted land for the planting of white mulberry trees on which silkworms feed, and land grants were made to settlers provided they planted 100 such trees on every 10 acres cleared, and kept them in cultivation for 10 years.

In 1759, 10,000 pounds of American raw silk were produced, and of such quality that it brought three shillings a pound premium on the London market. Other states initiated silk culture and it continued up to the Revolution. The last spurt in producing silk in the U. S. occurred just before 1837, when wildly speculative promotions took place. In that year a financial depression put an end to large-scale silk production in America.

However, this interest in the production of silk tied in to some extent with the tackle developments of the time, and furnished a background for the efforts of a number of American anglers and manufacturers to produce "Spanish gut." This interest carried past 1850, and the enthusiasts of that day not only tried to work out methods of producing gut from the Chinese silkworms, but prospected the chances of securing gut from certain closely related cocoon-spinning native "worms."

The Chinese silkworm required the leaves of the mulberry tree as food, and in addition the handling of the worms was a ticklish business. American sericulturists sought a "native worm" that was more hardy. This led to experiments with the larva of the moth entomologists then knew as *Attacus cecropia* and later named *Samia cecropia.* By all reports, the cocoons of this moth produced more yardage and a stronger silk fiber than that of the Chinese species.

The pioneer fly dresser, Orvis, had attempted to produce gut from the Chinese worm. He had also tried producing it from the native moth larvae. Others were at work on the same problem.

One of these was Dr. Theodatus Garlick of Bedford, Ohio, one of the American pioneers in the field of fish culture.

Working with the cecropia moth and three other closely related species Dr. Garlick mated these moths, placed the fertilized females in paper boxes, hatched eggs, and fed young larvae on young plum, pear and apple leaves. As larvae grew to about an inch in length, he placed them on fruit trees and watched the worms until they were ready to spin cocoons. He did not pickle the worms before he drew the gut, believing the acid solution would do damage. He wrote in a letter, July 17, 1884, addressed to Henry P. Wells:

"I have drawn this gut eight or nine feet long, and strong enough to hold a salmon. There is no more difficulty in drawing this gut from *Attacus cecropia,* than from the ordinary silkworm."

Although these angler-experimenters apparently produced a natural gut which could be drawn

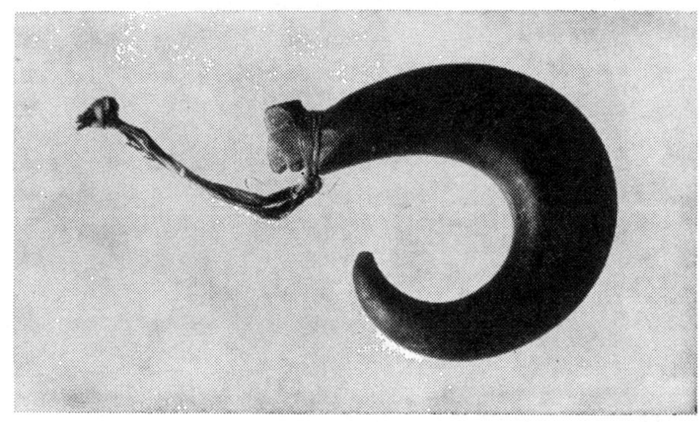

Smithsonian Institution

Easter Island stone fish hook.

out much longer and in heavier diameters than Spanish gut lengths, American gut never became a stock item on tackle counters.

The Spanish gut had and has faults. There are spots where the gut is thinner; some points have imperfections. The lack of uniform diameter can be overcome by drawing the strands of gut through dies which shave off outer layers so the thickness is the same throughout each length. But the outer layer of the gut is the strongest portion of the strand and strength suffers as uniform diameter is secured. The finer tapered leaders are made of gut lengths which require slight "drawing" through dies to produce uniform diameter in each length.

Between World War I and World War II, experiments designed to produce a synthetic leader material were undertaken.

In the 1930's "Japanese gut" appeared on the market. It was made by binding fibers of raw silk together with a gelatin material. This served fairly well, but long use wore off the surface binding material and the gut became fuzzy. It also had the fault of becoming sleazy when wet. It was a cheap material, giving fair service for the cost.

Just before World War II, Nylon was introduced as leader material with its many advantages.

A level leader of any length, even whole lines of Nylon filament can be produced. Nylon offers the same facility for long, tapered leaders that natural gut does, by tying different diameters of Nylon in step-down taper.

The next step was to attempt a Nylon leader that was tapered from line to lure, in solid knotless filament. Unlike natural gut, the Nylon material is uniform in cross-section, the inner portion being equally strong with the outer surface. A tapered leader of Nylon drawn down progressively would decrease in strength in direct proportion to decrease in diameter, but removal of the surface would not take away its greatest layer of strength. If such a continuous, tapered leader of Nylon could be fashioned, it would be still another step toward finer tackle.

In 1947, the Whitney Sporting Goods Company of Denver began developing a knotless tapered Nylon leader. The first tests of this leader were made that year. Among those giving the new leader a try-out was Ted Trueblood, former fishing editor

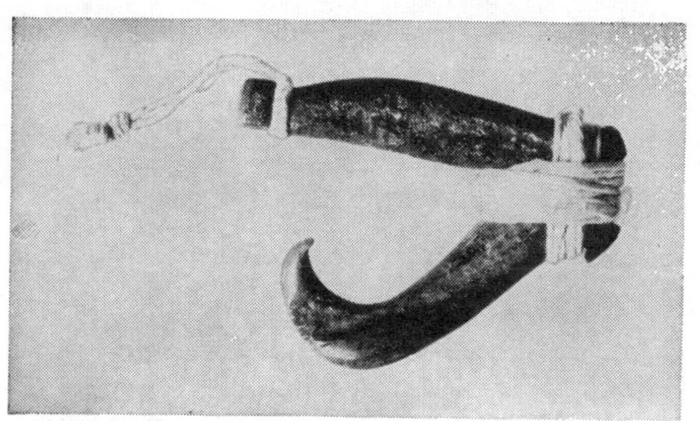

Smithsonian Institution

Human bone fish hook from the Easter Islands.

of *Field & Stream.* Trueblood fished the Rogue River in Oregon. Members of the Whitney staff which included Jim Haywood, a noted fly caster, also tested the leaders in many western waters.

Early in 1948, trade samples of this tapered Nylon leader were released by the Whitney Company. Almost at the same time, the Welch Tackle Company, of Altadena, California, distributed samples of a tapered Nylon leader basically the same as that which Whitney had been developing.

The Welch leaders of knotless Nylon, tapered in a continuous reduction of diameter comparable to similar natural gut leaders, were offered by Welch in 1949 in one length: 7½ feet. In the same year, Whitney offered knotless Nylon tapered leaders in three lengths: 6, 7 and 9 feet. The taper on the Whitney leaders was from OX to 4X.

Whether these are the final answer to the demand for the finest possible leaders remains to be proven; but it appears that here is a final word in leader construction for the most delicate type of fly fishing. With one exception—and that is total invisibility in the water. Total invisibility always has been an objective of tackle makers, a goal they probably never will achieve.

Various stains have been used to cut down the visibility of lines and leaders. Years ago anglers were experimenting to achieve this end. Here is the process for giving a hair line a dun color, as given by John Jackson in his book *The Practical Fly Fisher,* published by Gribbings & Company, London, in 1853. It is significant that Jackson, at that time, was still arguing for the braided horse hair line as against the oiled and enameled lines which were beginning to appear. From this, it would appear that the line of braided hair had held a high position in the field of fly fishing to the middle of the 19th century. Jackson's method of coloring the leader was—

"To stain gut or hair a dun colour; boil a handful of walnut tree leaves and a little soot, in a quart of water for half an hour; then steep the gut in the liquor till it acquires the colour." For a blue stain, he used ink. To secure a yellowish green "colour" he boiled the hair leader or gut in water to which an onion peel had been added.

Jackson's book, with hand colored plates of trout stream flies and the artificial flies fashioned after each species, was sufficiently standard for English fishermen, that it reached a fourth edition, in 1899, nearly a half century after the first printing had been run, and after the death of the author.

Henry P. Wells, in his book *Fly-rods and Fly-tackle,* also gives space to methods of dyeing gut to reduce the visibility. He states that ink-dye is the one he prefers. He makes the point that coloring gut leader material is desirable because without this when sun strikes it, the gut appears in the water as a silver strand.

Thaddeus Norris in his book *The American Angler,* published earlier, outlines a method of dyeing gut by putting one drachm of ground logwood and six grains of powdered copperas in a pint and a half of cold water, boiling this for five to six minutes, removing the pot from the fire, and after the liquid has stopped bubbling, immersing the strands of gut in the solution for two to three minutes.

All these dyes had some corrosive effect on the gut. Wells reports but does not authenticate, a process recommended by Mr. Fred Mather, leading fish culturist of the time. Mather stated that the juice of the milk-weed would remove the gloss from the surface of the natural gut, and thus cut down the visibility without injury to the gut. The removal of the surface allowed penetration of color without too long exposure of the gut to detrimental chemicals.

As a matter of observation, which has some pertinent relationship to the history of tackle development, Charles F. Orvis, in *Fishing With the Fly,* published in 1883, remarks, "'Mist colored' or stained leaders are, by many, thought to be better than the clear white gut; but I must say I never have been able to see that they are, or that there is any difference, practically." The pertinency of this bit lies in the illustration of how anglers argue, experiment, and wrangle among themselves as to which is "best" in any portion of their tackle assembly—and out of just this basic trait, or argument, testing, and trying for something better, has come much of the tackle advancement over the centuries. Probably if the first fisherman had been satisfied with his tackle, or his fishing partner had been the same, there would have been little progress in tackle design.

Wherever and however leaders began, there is now available fine material in leaders for bait casting, trolling and those designed for the most delicate type of fly manipulation.

LINES

The use of lines to land fish surely antedated the hook. We have the evidence of this in the gorge which was ancestor of the hook. That little groove around the center of a gorge is where the line was tied.

Shreds of ancient lines, made of plant fiber, used on gorges, have been found, also braided and spun lines of such fiber, and even of human hair. But the genius who tied a chunk of bait to the first line, perhaps a tough vine, allowed a fish to swallow it, then yanked the fish out, has never been given credit in the records.

The line is the second primary part of tackle assembly which underwrites all sport fishing. Although the line may have come first, the addition of the hook was the step which made possible fishing as a sport.

As reported previously, the use of hair, braided in three strands, was the "sporting" type of line used in the time of Juliana of Sopwell. Linen came into the picture when thread, was spun from this fiber. Perhaps far earlier, in China, silk lines had been developed, for the step from thread for sewing with those early steel needles to braiding, twisting or spinning threads into fishing lines seems very logical.

The record shows that the line of horse hair was still in use by the advanced fly fisherman in the middle of the 19th century; John Jackson's advocacy of such a line appeared over three and a half centuries after the *Book of St. Albans,* and two centuries after Walton's *The Compleat Angler.*

Lines of fiber were beginning to take the place of the hair line by the middle 1800's. The transition period saw lines made of a mixture of horse hair and silk. It was perhaps a compromise to induce die-hard anglers to quit the hair lines. There was sound argument for the inclusion of silk fiber with the old, standard hair lines. The added silk did lend strength and reduce the roughness. While the earlier hair lines were twisted, they were later braided to overcome the tendency of twisted lines to kink and possibly "unwind."

By 1880, the silk line had taken over the market. There were two types of line offered in that period: the "raw" silk and the "boiled." The former was the silk fiber as it was unwound from the cocoon with the gum which bound the cocoon together still present. The boiled silk was cooked to remove this gum before spinning.

Italian silk was considered the best obtainable. It was shipped to this country in hanks, similar to hanks of yarn now offered in drygoods stores. This raw silk had a golden color, and was as harsh as linen. Lines made of raw silk were rough, and those made of raw Chinese silk carried the trade label of "grass line." No grass was in this line; it was all raw silk.

Boiling the silk removed the surface gum and reduced weight by nearly a third. The color was deepened by the process. Smoothness and flexibility resulted. While raw Italian silk of that period brought about $5 per pound, the boiled silk cost $7 or more. The reduction of the diameter of each silk thread through boiling does not take away any of the tensil strength; so lines of smaller diameter of boiled silk have the same tenacity as those of larger size of raw silk.

One of the grievances of anglers of the 1880's was the inclusion of "shoddy" in fishing lines. Old silk fabric, from worn-out dresses, stockings and other sources, was put through a machine which fluffed up the fiber, and this was then spun into lines. Because the fibers were worn and broken, such cheap lines gave out sooner than those of virgin silk. The one best guarantee that the fishing lines of that period were of good silk was the integrity of the manufacturer. It's a good guide to quality merchandise at any time.

When used on a fly rod the untreated silk lines were as flexible and "snakey" as bait casting lines are today. The limber line was always getting half-hitched around the tip of the rod. An angler had to wade to the bank of the stream to untangle—since rods of the time were generally in excess of ten feet in length and the tip could be reached only when the butt was on solid ground.

The time and place at which line dressing was first used is indefinite. But since there had been experimental fishing with dry flies, in pioneer forms, as early as 1800, the greasing of lines was already an established practice in some types of fishing. The next step was toward impregnating the limber lines with linseed oil. American manufacturers as well as European firms were offering this type of "oiled" line. It is a process still used on cheaper fly lines.

The "enameled" line which appeared about the middle of the 19th Century was an American introduction. The secret of the "enameling" was carefully guarded, and while the European tackle makers attempted to copy it, they were behind the parade in this development.

Henry P. Wells goes all-out in recommending the enameled lines available in the 1880's. Charles F. Orvis in discussing lines, wrote:

"Enameled, or water-proof, braided silk, tapered, American fly-lines, are the best made for fly-fishing. It is important that the size of the line should be adapted to the rod. A heavy line on a very light rod would be bad. A very light line on a heavy rod would be worse.—It is impossible to cast well against or across the wind, with a very light line; and very light lines do not 'lay out' as easily or accurately as heavier ones."

Fundamentally, then, by 1885, American manufacturers had produced a fly line of enameled silk, in a *taper,* and in different calipers and weights. The weight of the impregnated line added that essential of having the weight of line flex the rod on the back cast, so that the pent-up power in the rod will shoot line, and with it the light fly, on the forward cast.

Essentially, the fly line that emerged in this period is the silk, enameled fly line of to-day. All added qualities are refinements of this original introduction.

The single recent development in lines for fly casting and the closely allied spinning type of fishing is Nylon. Lines of this material and related synthetics have the same advantages which this synthetic has when used in leaders.

One specific improvement in lines which arrived with Nylon was the production of a continuous, uniform, high-tensil strength monofilament line. This is practically "leader" material from one end to the other and its highest value has shown up in the adaptation of monofilament to the stationary-spool spinning reel.

Today the use of letters is generally accepted to denote the caliper of lines. Numbers were used before the turn of the 20th century. Their progression was in reverse of the standard letter designation of today. For example, a line we designate as "C" was numbered 1. That is the heavier line. What we know as "D" was No. 2 line, and our "G" size line, was No. 5, the standard smallest line of that day.

While there had been lines of fiber material developed for various types of fishing before the appearance of the "Kentucky" or multiplying reel, it was the introduction of this reel, with the line paying off the spool as the cast is made, which brought the type of line used for bait casting today.

Credit for making the first lines for bait casting has been given to Elisha J. Martin, of Rockville, Connecticut, who was a silk handler and a fisherman. Lines he had been able to purchase for his bait casting fell short of being adequate. So in 1884, Martin took home some silk strands and braided a few lines for himself and for some fishermen friends. They were specifically built for the hard wear of a line paying out through rod guides at each cast, and rubbing the same guides as the line was retrieved.

Martin soon found himself in the business of making silk casting lines. When Elisha died, a son, A. Leroy Martin took over the business and carried it on until December of 1919. At that time the Horton Manufacturing Company, of Bristol Conn. took over the Martin enterprises, and the Kingfisher Silk Lines on the market today are direct descendants of the lines Elisha Martin braided for bait casting in 1884.

The finer casting lines now are braided so that they are "four sided" around a silk core. In contrast, a fly line is round. The squarish cross-section of the bait casting line has its value; it tends to lay on the spool in "flatter" layers as it is reeled in, and does not wedge in between other strands already retrieved. The paying-out of the line as the cast is made is thus facilitated. Although fishermen plagued with back-lashes may silently dispute the statement, the squarish line does tend to cut down these troublesome tangles.

Here again, Nylon has entered to give competition to the braided silk casting line. Earlier Nylon casting lines were dressed with a compound which had a tendency to become sticky after some use; these lines "mushed" on the reel. Other dressings which prevents this trouble have been developed. And while the anglers who have had good service from braided silk have been slow to change from this tested line. Nylon, achieving an equal handling quality, adds those other advantages of being non-rotting, stronger in any unit fiber, and uniform throughout in tensil strength of each fiber braided into the line.

In other lines, the braided copper line for such fishing as deep trolling for Mackinaw Trout, with an ancestry far back, still is standard. As metal wire of high tensil strength and resistance to corrosion was developed, lines of such compounds came into the market with Monel metal, used in salmon fishing and other salt water angling as an example. This type of line came into the tackle shops between World War I and the second conflict of that name.

Who first used a line to catch a fish, and of what material? There is no record. Somewhere in the far past and even before the invention of the fish hook, lines were in use. The long, experimenting trail over the centuries has brought the superb lines of today, each specially adapted to certain types of fishing, and giving high quality service.

Perhaps the logical attitude is to give blanket credit to the old timers who fished with braided horse hair, with sinews from animals or birds before that, or with tediously braided lines of fiber. Then, with the advent of the silk industry into the European theater, with its by-product of both leader and better lines, give thanks for all the testing and trying and arguing that went into the present fine lines for sport fishing.

REELS

The earliest rod-and-line tackle assembly merely had a length of line tied to the end of a pole. Thus tied, the line was of fixed length during any period of angling. The pole, or rod, was better than merely holding a line in hand. The hook with its bait or lure could be cast through the leverage of the pole as it was swung; the same pole gave leverage as the angler set the hook and hoisted the fish; and it is probable that some early anglers preferred a somewhat pliant pole to aid in playing the catch—and perhaps to give greater pleasure in angling.

The "running line" preceded any primitive reel. With some guides along the rod or pole, an angler could hold extra line in his hand, in coils, to give line when necessary, and retrieve it as he worked the fish in. Anglers of today who snarl into a backlash can appreciate that the old angler who tried to make the hand, holding coiled extra line, serve as a reel had even greater trouble when these coils fouled while battling a sizable fish.

There are reports of the Egyptians using some sort of a spool affixed to the pole as a place for storage of extra line. The history of those reels which were the antecedents of modern reels begins in England and can be fairly well fixed as to date.

There is no mention of anything resembling a reel in *The Book of St. Albans* by Dame Juliana. At that time, and as late as the years when Walton fished, the practice followed when a fish was too lusty to snub and hold was to throw the whole outfit into the water. The early English rods, if they could be called such, were big, wooden affairs, that would float. After the catch became tired of towing the pole around, the angler seized it again, if possible, and completed the landing of the fish. This probably was the only possible line of action if it is remembered that the line used in that period (1496) was of three braided horse hairs.

Either the idea of a spool affixed to the base of the rod on which extra line could be stored came to England through travelers who had seen it elsewhere during the one hundred and fifty year lapse between Juliana and Walton, or some inventive fellow devised such a "wind." It was not in general use at the time of Walton's first edition in 1653 for he made no mention of it.

However, Barker, in his *Art of Angling,* 1651, two years before the first *Compleat Angler* came from the presses, did mention a "wind" for line storage. Barker described this first crude reel thus: "Within two foot of the bottom of the rod there was a hole made for to put in a wind to turn with a barrel to gather up his line, and loose at his pleasure."

Walton's second edition, 1655, mentioned such a reel on page 189; he called it a "wheele."

The reel idea was rather a long time in becoming a part of the sportsman angler's equipment: Radcliffe estimates that between 3600 to 5000 years elapsed between the use of the first "running line" assembly of tackle and what might be considered the first reels.

After Walton had mentioned the "wheele" in 1655, Barker published a revised edition of his book in 1657, and in it is the first illustration of a fishing reel. In essential details of principle and use, the "wind" or "wheele" of this period is the single-action reel of today. The "click" has been added; the materials of which the reel has been made now include light metal alloys and plastics, the width between side plates has been much narrowed and high precision in construction has made single-action reels most serviceable and generally more attractive. They're still a "wind," however, on which to store excess line.

A watchmaker and the "black bass" are the combination which produced the second type of reel for angling equipment.

Anglers of Kentucky, using a cane pole, and probably a "running line" technique in their casting, discovered that about the sportiest fishing in their home waters was "bassing." Single action reels could be used for storage, but in the cast, the bass fisherman, flinging a frog or a "crawdad" into a likely bass hole, had to hold line in loops to release as the cast was made. A single action reel would pay out a bit of line on a cast, but not enough to get to the spot where the big bass was waiting.

Sometime between 1800 and 1810, George Snyder, who lived at Paris, Kentucky, conceived the idea that if he could construct a reel with a spool which would spin and pay out line directly on the cast, he would avoid a lot of current bass fishing difficulties. Snyder was a watchmaker, a silversmith and significantly, he was President of the Bourbon Angling Club.

Snyder's first reels were made in his watchmaker's shop, for his own use and for his friends. He never progressed to the point of engaging primarily in the commercial production of reels.

The Hon. Munson Brown, a Kentucky judge, residing at Frankfort had the distinction of owning a Snyder reel. Someone stole it in 1833. About that time Jonathan Flemming Meek, another watchmaker, had transferred his business from Danville to Frankfort and Judge Brown persuaded him to construct a reel similar to the lost Snyder reel.

That started Meek into a new business, but he didn't throw watchmaking overboard. It was his principal occupation until 1840, when B. F. Meek,

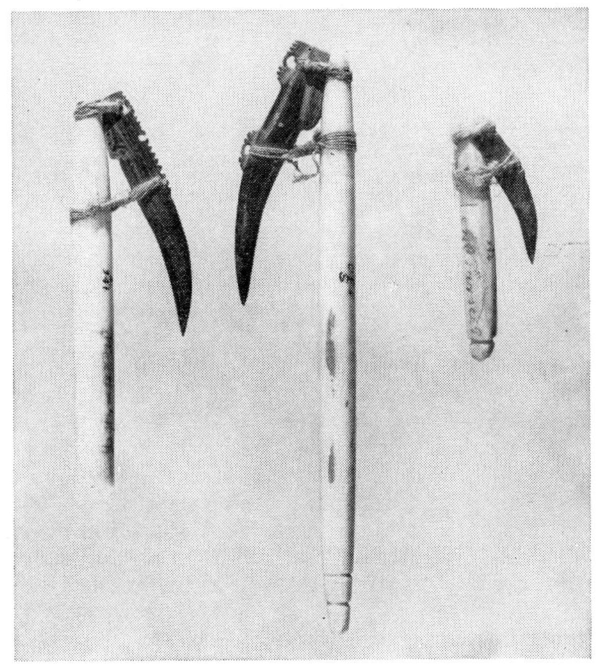

Amer. Mus. Nat. History

Huon Gulf, New Guinea fish hooks.

brother of J. F., became a partner. They continued making watches in one portion of their establishment, but another section of the building was the first multiplying "reel factory."

The Snyder reel had a ratio of one turn of the handles to four revolutions of the spool. Meek's product, like most multiplying reels of today, held to approximately the same ratio.

The Meek reels had a click and also a drag, operated by sliding buttons on the outside plate. The reel was further improved by adding a collar around the crank shaft and the spool shaft which had protruded in earlier models was housed.

The first reels were riveted together. When anything went wrong, they had to be literally torn down. J. W. Hardman, of Louisville, Kentucky, introduced the use of screws to fasten on the head and tail plates of the reels so they could be more easily taken apart for repair or maintenance. He also shortened the spool. Benjamine C. Milam, an apprentice of the Meeks, in 1863 is credited with further improving the multiplying reel.

Rights to manufacture the Meek reel were transferred to the Horton Company, Bristol, Conn., and the improved Meek reel, with its long history of service, was produced until the beginning of World War II. It was the advancement of over a century of refinement which persuaded Horton's executives that it was time to retire the pioneer reel of this type.

The first multiplying reels were made for the purpose of casting bait such as frogs, crayfish, and similar bait lures. The development of the reels which were to handle the lighter artificial lures, was an outgrowth of outright bait casting.

The early models, made by the watchmakers, had jeweled bearings to take the wear of fast turning parts. As late as 1920, O. W. Smith, angling editor of *Outdoor America,* was expressing preference for bearings of sapphire. Phosphor bronze and other new alloys, now supply materials for bearings which have practically replaced the "jewels". The alloy bearings don't crack; they are precision made, cheaper and certainly supply as high a level of service.

The improvements added to the original basic design with its click and drag that the Meeks introduced, are the anti-backlash "snubbing" of the spool to prevent line tangles, the free-running spool, the star drag especially used in the salt water types of the multiplying reel, and the level-wind mechanisms.

The multiplying reel with the line that Martin made to fit the reel's demands are the key units of equipment in "bait casting" tackle. Early rods were modifications of fly casting types; but use and need brought the "casting rod" after the bait casting reel and line had been established.

The whole bait casting field of sport fishing is American—initiated by the "black bass" and some Kentucky watchmakers. As late as 1881, Dr. Henshall, in his *Book of the Black Bass* wrote, "It (the multiplying reel) has not been used there (in England) within my recollection. For a century the British angler has used the single-action reel for all branches of fishing."

Henshall gives Julius vom Hofe credit for making the first "take-apart" reel which was called "The President." Hardman, introducing screws for rivets, in 1843, may have a better claim. O. W. Smith relates that Shakespeare should be credited with the first level winder, the Marhoff fitted with single propelling screws.

Meek's advertisement in *Outdoor Life,* February 1900, offers their reel "No. 10" for tuna and tarpon. The same advertisement features their automatic drag and spiral gear. In the May issue of that year, the Meeks state that their reel was "originated in Frankfort, Ky., in 1835," which may indicate that there was some commercial production of this reel by J. F. Meek before his brother B. F. became a partner in 1840.

But the genesis of the whole business of bait casting must be credited to Snyder and the "black bass"—for the record is clear.

As an interesting sidelight, illustrating how anglers continue to use the "good old stuff" even when better is on the market, R. B. Roosevelt, in his *Game Fishes of the North,* published in 1862 under the pen name of "Barnwell," declares against the multiplying reel. He defends the old single action reel, with a click, and a big spool, fastened to the rod—but by a leather strap!

In spite of such resistance, the multiplying reel and the American-made sport of "bait casting" had come to stay.

The "automatic reel" for fly fishing met the same resistance as the multiplying reel did in bait casting. The spool or drum of an "automatic" is equipped with springs which "wind up" as the line is payed out. It merely is storage space with the convenience of pressing a trigger and allowing the spring force to wind back on the spool line which was pulled off as line was cast.

The first "automatic" ever made has been in continuous manufacture since 1884 except for the period of World War II when all tackle production was stopped. This is the Martin Automatic Fishing Reel, made by the company of that name, located at Mohawk, N. Y. (See page 139.)

Many other manufacturers have developed reels of this type, and these are standard representatives of such reels now available. Although the automatic reel has thus been on the market for nearly three quarters of a century, there still is some resistance to its use, the purists claiming they are not so "sporting" as the old single action reel which go back to Walton's time.

The third type of reel, the stationary spool, used extensively in spinning, came from England. While spinning and the use of this type of reel had begun to make headway in North America before World War I, the conflict put a halt to its progress and acceptance. After this war ended, spinning took a new impetus and within a few years many American adaptations of the stationary spool type of reel came on the market.

The first general use of the modern spinning reel was in England, about 1900. An original patent on such a reel was allowed to Illingsworth in 1905. Although there were some beginnings of spinning in England in the two decades following, not enough impetus developed to bring it across the Atlantic.

Bache H. Brown tells of entering a sporting goods store in New York City in the early 1930s, and seeing there an Illingsworth No. 3 light salmon reel, that had been in stock for some years —the clerks knew nothing about using it and hadn't been able to sell it.

Mr. Brown had been in England between 1923 and 1935, and had been spinning. He brought with him in 1935 a number of the small Hardy reels of this type, and gave a number, with suitable rods, to friends in the U. S. and Canada. The interest shown persuaded him to begin importing spinning equipment, starting with Luxor, which Mr. Brown thought was the best then available.

The outbreak of war forced Bache Brown to develop his own reel, the Mastereel. When war stopped manufacture of the reel in 1941, production was delayed, until in 1946 this American-made reel again came on the market.

Almost simultaneously the Humphreys reel, developed by I. B. Humphreys of Denver, an engineer-fisherman, was introduced. It immediately spurred interest since it was a marked departure from the spinning reels that had come from Europe. Thus, from two different points in the nation, this "new" classification of sport fishing began to capture interest across the country.

But again the records show that some fishermen had been prospecting this type of reel some years before it began to be used in England. A dig into the patent files shows that on March 23, 1875 Thomas Winans and Thomas D. Whistler received patent No. 161,314 which was for a reel in which the spool remained stationary as the line went out. It has some of the fundamental features of the spinning reels found on the market today. It developed at a time when the attention of anglers was caught by the multiplying reel combined with the typical bait casting rod and when the bamboo six-strip rod was in the spotlight for fly fishing. That might explain why this pioneer reel with the spool stationary as line strung out failed to achieve popularity, catch interest, and start spinning as a type of angling a quarter century earlier.

The single action reel was in use at an unknown early date, but started its development toward American use after it was used about the middle of the 17th century in England. The multiplying reel, making bait casting types of fishing possible, is an American type of tackle unit, associated with definite types of lines, leaders, rods and reels. It appeared soon after the beginning of the 19th century. The automatic reel for fly fishing appeared in America in 1884, and the fixed or stationary spool reel came to the North American continent from England, between the two World Wars.

These are the types of tackle units for storing extra length of line, giving greater facilities for playing a catch, and in the case of the multiplying reel and the fixed spool type, entering into the actual casts by paying out line when the lure is shot at a target.

RODS

The first angler who used a pole that was light enough, and sporting enough to step over from a "pole" to classification as a "rod" is unknown. It probably is hair-splitting to try to designate the line separating a "fishing pole" and a "fishing rod." We might suggest the rod designation enters when it is used as a facility for playing a hooked fish as contrasted with using a pole of sufficient strength to immediately hoist the catch out of the water.

Perhaps the point of designation lies as much in the tactics employed as in the construction of the tackle. One fisherman may use a light rod as a "pole" to yank a fish out of the water as soon as hooked, while another uses the same rod to play the fish.

Progress toward the lighter, sporty modern rod models can commence with the type used by Dame Juliana Bernes, which is described in her *Book of St. Albans.* This tackle unit was, by modern standards, a whopping clumsy affair. Nevertheless, Juliana, and those who followed her in writing of sport angling, give emphasis to the use of this "pole" in a sporting manner—as a means of playing the fish rather than merely yanking him into the atmosphere. Their three-hair braided lines dictated the playing of the fish.

The rod of Juliana's time was of two parts. The butt was called the "staffe" while the tip was named the "croppe."

Juliana gave specific directions about the wood to be used. It must be cut between Michaelmas and Candlemas, in the winter. There was less sap in it at that time. It should be heated in the oven, and tied to a piece of straight, dry wood to prevent it warping. It should be finally dried in smoke.

The woods recommended for the butt or "staffe" should be willow, or rowan, six feet long, thick as an arm, and evenly tapered. The pith was burned out of the butt to form a hollow with even taper inside. The butt was fitted at each end with a broad ferrule of iron or brass and the large end had a spike of metal—that could be thrust into the bank, probably, for set-line fishing. It could be removed so the tip could be slipped into the tapered hole running lengthwise in the butt.

With the tip nicely sequestered in the butt, a "Sunday fisherman" could sneak out for a walk, carrying his "staffe" and when he quite accidentally ended up on the brink of a good fishing spot, he was prepared to take advantage of any opportunities confronting him. The practical purpose of the hollowed "staffe" was to reduce weight, for those old rods were heavy stuff; and as a protection and carrying place for the tip.

The tip was of two parts, spliced together. The lower part, wrote Juliana, should be made of green hazel, while the upper portion was made of

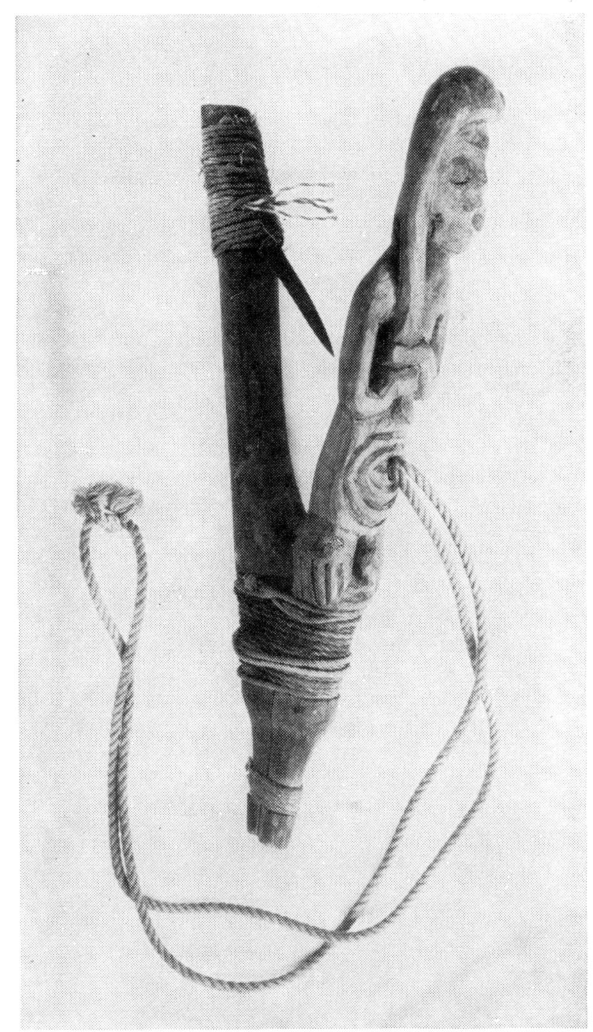

Smithsonian Institution

Southeastern Alaska carved two-section fish hook. Iron barb lashed on.

Oriental Institute

Fish and hunting scene. From Davies-Gardner, "Ancient Egyptian Paintings," Vol. II.

"a fair shoot of blackthorn, crabtree, medlar or juniper."

The butt section nine feet long, suggests what a lumbering affair served as a rod in those days.

The over-all length of the St. Albans rod was at least fourteen feet. Wells observes that while this was a little on the heavy side for use in fishing it had other advantages; it could be used as a vaulting pole over small rivers, a foot-log or a mast for a small boat when one got weary of rowing!

The heavy rod prevailed for years. Whether it was the type of angling or the disposition of the British to change slowly from some article that has proven serviceable to something different, this persisting early influence may explain why British fishermen still hold to rods of greater length and weight while American anglers have shifted to the far lighter, shorter fly rod.

Cotton, who wrote the section on fly patterns for Walton's fourth edition, used a rod that was from 15 to 18 feet in length. Undoubtedly there were anglers and makers who experimented with lighter rods, different woods, other lengths, but not a century ago, Francis listed British rods, by leading makers, with a range of from "13 ounces, 4 drachms" to "14 ounces, 6 drachms" in weight, and a length of 11 feet, 7 inches as a minimum, 12 feet, 8 inches as a maximum.

Francis recommended that rods be two-hand. It took a good man to whip one of those mastodonic affairs, if he used only one hand. Francis did try single-grip rods of this weight and length, and wrote: "But to fish a whole day with a single-handed rod is very trying to the forearm and more particularly to the grasp of the right hand. Many a time has my hand and arm ached so after a long spell of casting, that I have been compelled to leave off to rest them."

Search for a better rod material apparently took on impetus at the beginning of the 19th century. For practically 100 years, the development of fly rods, moving erratically toward what we have today, was in a state of extreme flux. By 1900 the split and glued, six-strip bamboo rod had fought to dominance. But in intervening years there was controversy between anglers as to which woods in what weights and lengths made the best rods.

The height of this argument was reached about 1880, for in the two decades before that bamboo rods began to move toward supremacy. Commercial production of such rods became established in this time.

A variety of woods were being tested and used in the first half of the 19th century. Henry P. Wells, in 1885, when the "bamboo vs. the field" was near climax, declares that his choice of rod wood was greenheart, from British Guiana. He wrote, "In my opinion it takes first place among rod woods." But he does say that the tip should be of some lighter wood.

Charles Orvis, in 1883, declared that in his estimation, bamboo ranked first as a fly rod material, lancewood second and he was a bit uncertain about greenheart—whether it rated third or not. He believed paddlewood, which was not available in rods, might rank high—no telling.

In the same period, Bethabara was being touted as the premier material for fly rods. Thaddeus Norris, author of *The American Angler,* had voted for Ironwood, the "hornbeam" which grows as a small tree in the forests of eastern states.

Red cedar, not the sort from which lead pencils were made, but straight grained and seasoned by lying in swamp water for some years, was considered the rod wood for the dilettante. Mahoe, a Cuban wood, used in that country to make springs for the "volante" cart, and resembling straight grained black walnut, was advanced as being as good as the cedar.

Wells reports hickory as being still held in high esteem in England. It should be second growth, from the shag bark variety, cut in December or January with the sap out of the wood. The sticks then were squared and immersed in water for from six to eight weeks, which soaked out the starch. Wells warns against kiln-drying or boiling the wood. After the soaking period, the squared sticks were hung up to air-dry, and weighted to prevent warping. This took eighteen months.

The question of who made the first split bamboo rod, and started this wood toward dominance in the construction of sport fishing rods, still can stir up hot argument. For when the bamboo rod stepped into the lead, there was a rush of those who said, "I knew it! I'm the one who 'discovered' the bamboo rod."

The facts seem to be, that a whole flock of anglers and manufacturers had a considerable part in the evolution rather than the discovery of the bamboo rod.

Although Wells declares his preference for ironwood for rod material, he concedes that in his time, the 1880s, American anglers had begun to show a definite preference for the split and glued bamboo.

While bamboo grows in many sections, including the southern part of North America, it came into the fishing scene from the Calcutta region in India. Why bamboo lengths from this section always arrived with fire-stained surface was a matter for speculation. Some said it was a religious requirement to slightly char the cane, or that it was to kill larvae of boring insects, or ornament, or that jungles were fired to clear clinging vines before bamboo was cut, or that it was a straightening process. The scorched surface of bamboo was the "Calcutta cane" trade-mark.

This was a "soft" cane compared to that which is now used. For a few years it was the only material put into the rived-and-glued rods. Then one William Mitchell, who was given to pioneering in the tackle field, made the first rod of Chinese bamboo, in 1869. There then was a struggle between the Indian and the Chinese bamboo to see which would take precedence.

Today our best cane for the superior rods, comes from the Tonkin province of China. It has a tenacity of fiber, a "backbone" superior to other bamboos that have been used in rod construction.

It was Mitchell, searching for the better rod wood, who showed Wells samples of sections taken from South American bamboos, which seem to have given considerable promise, but which, for some reason, dropped out of the race. Mitchell had been given a bow made by South American Indians, which was six feet long and without one joint or node in the entire length. The value of such a section of bamboo, without knots or joints, in making strips uniform throughout, is obvious, if it has the "life" of Tonkin cane. Whether this possibly better material, without joints, was passed over because Tonkin cane took leadership and brushed it aside, or whether it was tested adequately and could not compete, is not clear. Tonkin did take the lead.

Who made the first "bamboo rod?"

Between 1875 and 1900, that question would bring up a dozen partisans with twelve emphatic answers. Each would say a different pioneer tackle man "invented" the split bamboo fly rod.

What seems to be one of the earliest references to such a rod being in an experimental form, is in a book published in 1801, in Newark, England, titled *Practical Observations on Angling in the River Trent.* The author was Charles Snart, an attorney.

Apparently, most of the confusion as to "who made it first," is due to whether the "first" was a tip for a rod with butt of other wood, or a three strip rod, or four strip, or six strip entirely of bamboo. Henshall, for example, gives the palm to one Samuel Phillippi, a gunsmith, living in Easton, Pennsylvania. This rod, produced in 1848 had three sections, the upper two rived-and-glued bamboo, but the butt was of ash. There is a claim that Phillippi never made a complete rod of bamboo before his death about 1878. Another claim is advanced that Phillippi did make a three-section rod of bamboo in 1866.

The first mention of a split bamboo rod in a book, following the one by Snart, 1801, was in the *Handbook of Angling,* by "Ephemera," (Edward Fitzgibbon) in the 1847-1848 edition. There is some dispute about the date of the book and a further dispute as to an earlier edition in 1844.

The fact is authenticated by the records, that the first three-strip bamboo rods were being offered to anglers before the 1851 Crystal Palace Exhibition in London. The firms of Ainge & Alred, J. Bernard and J. K. Farlow, had such fly rods on display there that year.

There was some professional pride (or jealousy) involved in rod making at the time, for one Mr. Little, 15 Fetter Lane, rod maker to his R. H. Prince Albert, stood up about that time, and said: "I am prepared to prove that there are not more than three men in London capable of making, perfectly, rods of solid cane, rent, glued and then correctly finished with the bark lying on the outside."

Mitchell, in *The American Angler,* states that the first split bamboo rod was made by Wm. Blacker, 54 Dean Street, Soho, London, to order for one James Stevens, of Hoboken, N. J., in 1851. Mitchell probably meant the first such rod to reach an American angler's hands. If the reference is correct, that may have been the first fly rod entirely of split bamboo to throw flies on American waters.

By 1860, E. A. Green, of Newark, N. J., was making a three-strip, entirely split bamboo rod for the trade. Green's first four-strip rod was on the market by mid-September in 1863.

Between 1863-64, another New Jersey rod maker named Charles E. Murphy had entered the field with a four-strip bamboo rod.

Harold H. (Dike) Smedley, in his excellent little *Fly Patterns and Their Origins,* 1944, throws in a touch of human interest, by telling of Murphy rods being sold in 1863, across the counter of the sporting goods firm of Andrew Clerk and Co., of New York City, by one Charles Abbey. Abbey was one of the partners of the famous firm of Abbey & Imbrie, succeeding Clerk in 1875. Clerk's concern had been "purveyors of fine tackle" from 1820. After 55 years Abbie and Imbrie were bought out by Horocks-Ibbotson, of Utica, New York. The direct succession of continuous service to fishermen, through three managements and ownerships, still continues by H-I after more than one and a third centuries.

Probably the best approach to the question "Who made the first bamboo rod?" is to view the 1800-1870 period as one of rod evolution. It was about 1870 that H. L. Leonard of Bangor, Maine, put his six-strip bamboo fly rod on the market. From that point on, the six-stripper took the field —and there are many anglers today who cherish a "Leonard," not only for its performance but somewhat for the "name" of the rod, as many have cherished a "Meek" reel.

From the entrance of the "Leonard" type of rod into the markets, the progress has been through better materials, better design and fittings, and other refinements. The fairly "cheap" rods of today probably would have been hailed as marvels three quarters of a century ago. The superb rods of the present, would have been miraculous.

The split bamboo rod became so dominant, that any rod of competing material had a rough field to enter. The alloy metal rods, for example, fought a tough battle for recognition.

As early as 1883, Henry P. Wells devoted several pages of his book to urging rod makers to consider a tubular steel rod. The suggestion was never followed until after World War I when new alloys with lightness plus toughness came into the field. In 1936 the writer stood beside a canal at Geneva, Ohio, near the True-Temper plant, with the late Karl Kinnear who put an experimental tubular "steel" rod in his hands—It was within a fraction of an ounce of the weight of bamboo of similar dimensions, and with good "life" in its action. This company and others, offering exceptional metal fly rods, have not been able to break through the allegiance to the "good old bamboo" so dear to anglers' hearts.

The same sort of bid for reception by "glass" fly rods began in 1948-49; Shakespeare, having produced a "glass" casting rod which did catch on, offered a fly rod of the same material, and the glass rod has made heavy inroads in the popularity of the traditional bamboo.

Its greatest assets are durability and longevity of life. No pampering or special care are necessary, as is the case with bamboo. When set in motion, rod action is similar to that of bamboo. Because a supply of cane is no longer available, it seems reasonable to expect glass to supplant bamboo.

The typical bait casting rod is the legitimate child of the six strip bamboo fly rod and the "Kentucky" multiplying reel. Without the reel which pays out line directly from the spool, as the lure is cast, there would have been no search for a rod which would fit in with the thrown lure and the unwinding line.

Dr. Henshall is the early evangelist of bait casting and his *Book of the Black Bass* blazed the way for this type of sport fishing. It turned attention to the game qualities of the Largemouth and the Smallmouth Bass. It gave methods of handling the new reel and associated tackle.

Henshall was genuinely a bait caster. He may have tinkered with artificial lures but his method was to hook a frog or other bait lure on his line, and offer the bass actual food. The Kentucky bass fisherman generally fitted the multiplying reel to natural cane rods that had been used in the "running line" technics which preceded the advent of the multiplying reel. Henshall sought lighter tackle.

The rod that the Doctor used, was an adaptation of fly rods of the time, with a heavier tip, to handle the weightier bait. Henshall makes no mention of a shorter rod and the one he advocated was the type he used, 8¼ feet long.

O. W. Smith is the source of the statement that the first short bait casting rod was made for a fisherman named J. M. Clark, who resided in Chicago at the time, and later moved to Kansas City. Clark stated that this rod, of lancewood, 6 feet, 3 inches long, was made in 1885, by Fred D. Divine, later of the Divine Company of Utica, New York.

The development of all modern rods, for "bait" casting, which has persisted as the name for this type of fishing after artificial plugs were accepted by sportsmen, parallels the phases of change in the fly rods. There was the decade or so of argument over bamboo replacing lancewood, greenheart and other woods that had been used for rods, with bamboo taking precedence. Then the steel rods, and far more recently the "glass" rods, made their bid for acceptance as a proper rival or replacement for bamboo. The question of supremacy of any one individual type of bait casting rod material may not be settled with any one type at the top of the heap. They all have their virtues and their shortcomings, their advocates and their critics.

The use of steel in rods reaches back to 1842. One Giles Little then made a rod which was the trail-blazer for later rods to come. It was merely a tapered spring—a forecast of the "rapier" casting rod.

Others may have experimented with steel as a material for rods. Henry P. Wells was appealing for consideration of steel as a material as his book was published in 1883. One of the early records of steel rods has been supplied by M. C. Treadway of the Horton Company, Bristol, Connecticut.

Everett Horton was a fisherman. He lived in a community where church-going on a Sunday was the proper behavior. Everett preferred to go fishing. He made a rod of tubular steel, which

Smithsonian Institution

"Their manner of fishing in Virginia." John White drawing.

would telescope. By shortening it he might slip the rod down his pant-leg, and walk, a little stiff-legged perhaps, out to the river to commune with nature. His communion involved unlimbering the rod and philosophically fishing. The rod was hollow, and the line was threaded within the hollow tubing—a feature which has shown up as late as the 1930's and 1940's as a "new idea."

In the flux of development, manufacturers have produced the "rapier" rod of solid steel, four sided, hexagon or round. As alloys of high tensil strength and lightness appeared we have been offered the newer tubular steel bait-and fly-casting rods. They are smoothly tapered as round rods are "drawn" or with the distinctive "step-down" construction in another type. One of the first of the "step-down" models was put on the market by the True-Temper Company in the late 1920's.

As methods of steel making improved about 1900, there appeared not only whole rods of steel, but producers were attempting to add steel resilience and spring to rods of bamboo.

In the 1899 edition of John Jackson's book, *The Practical Fly Fisher,* Hardy Brothers of Alnwick, offer "cane built, steel centre and greenheart rods—lighter and most powerful—over 44,000 in use." In the same book D. & W. H. Foster of Ashbourne, Derbyshire, ballyhooed a steel rib-

Dale Henning
Stone hook found at Fish Mound group near Lansing, Iowa.

bing for their cane rods, challenging the world to a test by any able angler—the maker of the losing rod to donate a specified sum to charity. The Fosters offer to make a "steel-rib" of any rod, so it might be "converted thereby into a *modern* dry fly rod."

The thread of alloy steel in the center of a rod appeared again, as something rather new, in the "Cunningham" model of the Horrocks-Ibbotson "Hexi-Super" series of about 1930.

Also, there has been an offering in more recent years of the "double-bilt" rods; two layers of "cane" to supply more of the tougher, springier "cuticle" of the bamboo in rod construction. However, the 1899 advertisement in Jackson's book, shows a cross-section of just such a "double-bilt" rod, which was being offered by Hardy in the years just before 1900.

The first glass-and-synthetics casting rod to be introduced in quantity production, was the Shakespeare "Wonder-rod," to be followed swiftly by other manufacturers using the same material. The introduction of the solid "rapier-type" glass rod followed swiftly with several of such construction on the market by 1949.

Trolling rods were a collateral development of the casting rod, marching along in the same steps of improvement in materials, fittings and similar refinements. Incidentally, this act of paying out line and lure behind a slowly moving boat, which we call trolling, is an adaptation of the French word, *troler,* meaning to "lead about." The trolling rod is merely a shorter, stiffer type of casting rod, built heavier to take the constant and sometimes heavy drag of the lure and line as the boat moves.

Fittings of rods have kept pace with the other phases of rod development. The first guides, for example, were merely wire. They abraded the line and the line in turn wore them particularly when gritty substances clung to the lines. Agate, and simulated agate, were used as guide material in earlier bait casting rods; and still are. They have the fault of being subject to cracking or chipping; certain to cut the line if not repaired. German silver has been used; it has been too soft to stand hard usage. Top quality in guides, both for bait casting and fly fishing, has been secured by the Perfection Tip Company, of Denver. By a secret process they make metal guides and tips as hard in metal as agate, and they do not crack.

The grips of rods, the reel attachments, have been modified to fit use requirements better. The screw-locking reel seat is one example; the off-set reel base in the modern casting rod grip which brings the line down parallel to the rod as it runs toward the lower guide, is another. All are refinements toward better angling service.

The history of the rods used in sport fishing is somewhat of a gauge of the progression in technics and ethics of sport fishing. Juliana of St. Albans' nunnery, fished with a "rod" at least 14 feet long, with the joints bound with long "hoopes of yren" (iron). There had not been much change over the century and a half between her time and that when Walton, Cotton and their contemporaries angled. The real spurt in development of a light, lively rod began toward the end of the 18th century. With the advent of the split-and-glued bamboo rod, actually coming on the scene in six-strip construction about 1870, there has been a swift movement toward lighter rods.

The sportsman-angler of today probably would take a willow pole in preference to those very first "rods" of the 17th century and for years later. But it isn't necessary.

Like a pageant unfolding, the development of sport fishing rods highlights the steady movement toward tackle which gives more sport and the fish more of a fighting chance.

LURES

Of the three artificial lures—spoons, plugs, and flies—it is a question which was first used by the early anglers who substituted such contraptions for food baits. One of the earliest mentions of an artificial lure, was by Theocritus, who was writing over two hundred years before the Christian era. He did not define what sort of lure this was, merely stating that it was "the bait fallacious suspended from the rod."

The record does show that in the third century, artificial flies were in use in the Middle East. And while we may thus be inclined to credit artificial flies with being the first such lure used, it is far more likely that some other type of lure preceded them.

The basis for such supposition lies in the artifacts unearthed by archaeologists. Parallel to these are the gadgets in use during comparatively recent times by peoples whose cultural development is comparable to that of very ancient tribes. There is also the continuance of the use of home-made lures of this type, by primitive peoples in isolated sections of the world.

With only such indications to guide in speculations, the best guess would be that the spoon-type of lure in some form, was the first "bait fallacious" used in angling. It may have been added to primitive hooks as a charm, the user finding he needed nothing except the charm. Or he may have reckoned rightly that what he fastened to the hook would attract the attention of a fish.

The primitive lures of this type, like their more recent relatives made by primitive people, probably were what we know as spoons. They would be of shell, bone, or some other curved-surface material to produce a wobbling or whirling action when drawn through the water.

As an example of how the spoon-type of artificial lure was used in ancient angling, Captain James Cook, visiting the islands we now know as Hawaii, then called the Sandwich Isles, 1772-1778, made note of the natives using a spoon-type lure, fashioned from shell. In several volumes of annual reports of the Bureau of Ethnology, published prior to 1900, there are illustrations of primitive fishing lures of bone or shell which had spoon action, and other references to such lures used by native tribes.

No specific references to the English anglers of early times using the spoon type of lure have been located although it seems almost certain that some such lure would be in the equipment of those pioneers.

There is one definite bit of information that came through Harold Dahl of Denver, an ardent angler, which indicates that the spoon was in use in Europe and probably generally so, well ahead of the commercial introduction of this type of lure in America. Dahl spent his boyhood in Stockholm, Sweden. Some time shortly before 1900 he paid visits to a farm where there was good Northern Pike fishing. On one of these visits, he was scouting around an old log barn and found an old, brass-bladed spoon, of the wobbler type, stuck away in a corner. When questioned, his farmer friend who then was well advanced in years, stated that he had no knowledge of the spoon being there, and no recollection of its having been used within his lifetime. While this is no proof of the age of this spoon, which resembles several of the more modern spoons of the type, it strongly suggests that when found this lure may well have been most of a century old.

The commercial introduction of the spoon-spinner type of lure in America is credited to Julio T. Buel, born in 1812, near Lake Bomoseen, Vermont. The story of his "invention" of the spoon follows many another such legend-tale of how a "new" lure came into being.

As a child, Buel loitered along a stream one day, idly tossing bright pebbles and bits of wood into the water. He saw trout rise and strike at these bits of material, and this gave him the idea of soldering a bit of bright tin to a hook which successfully attracted the fish.

Later, when he had reached the age of 18, he was fishing on the lake, and as noon-time arrived, began to eat the lunch he had brought along. He accidentally dropped a tablespoon over the side of the boat while lunching, and as he watched it wobble down through the water, he saw a large fish rush at it.

These incidents led young Buel to a raid on the family silverware. He cut off the handle of a spoon, affixed a hook to the bowl, and went fishing—with success.

This led him to make spoon lures for himself, and for other sportsmen. A furrier by trade, a fisherman by choice, Buel began to make these lures as a sideline. He entered this field in 1848, but still considered himself as a furrier after he moved to Whitehall, New York, in 1854. The demand for the lures led to his assigning full time to this business, and in securing the first patents in the United States on this type of artificial lure. The letterhead of the J. T. Buel Co., still producing the Buel pattern of lures, carries the statement "Established in 1848" which fixes the year of a first commercial production of the spoon-type of lure in this country.

Another of the early pioneer manufacturers of the spoon-spinner type of lure, was William T. J. Lowe of Buffalo, New York. He was in commercial production at least as early as 1883. The Lowe lures were the type in which the blade spins around a shaft, while the earlier Buel lures were the spoon-wobbler type. After Mr. Lowe's death in 1915, the Enterprise Manufacturing Company, of Akron, Ohio, bought out that company, and still offer a series of "Lowe" lures.

There is no telling—the artificial lure that is now classed as a "plug" may have been used by primitive people as early as they made and used the first crude wobbler-spinner "spoon." Again there are artifacts found by anthropologists which were used as fish lures, which have "body" rather than "blade" construction and would thus be in the "plug" class rather than the "spoon" division of artificial lures.

There is a fairly good indication of how the name "plug" came to be applied to the lure of this type. Buel undoubtedly tagged the wobbler-spinner-blade type of lure with the name "spoon" when his first gadget was made from a spoon. So the name "plug" actually became a general term for this type of lure, because one of the first of this type was just that—a whittled plug of wood.

British anglers had been using the Devon and Phantom artificial minnows before 1800. They were constructed of wire and some fabric, variously fashioned, and represent a stage in the development of the modern "plug." They were and still are called "artificial minnows," with some fine-line differentiation from our "plugs."

The commercial production of the wooden plug lure in America, began shortly before 1900. There is some uncertainty as to whether the Dowagiac lure of this type came on the scene first, or the Rush Tango preceded it. Application for patents on these lures were filed in the Patent Office within a matter of hours of each other.

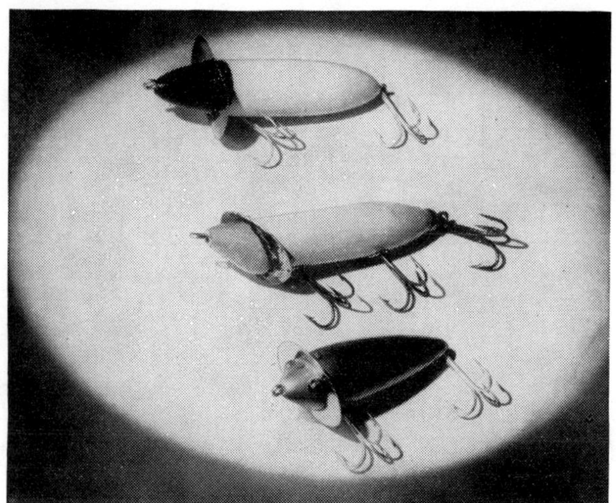

James Heddon's Sons

This photograph shows a replica of the first Heddon plug manufactured for the trade. Modern adaptations of the same are shown above and below.

Lou Caine, fisherman, and official of the James Heddon's Sons company, has supplied the following story of how the first Dowagiac lure came into being, and while Lou doubts if it is possible to determine the first use of a "plug" type of lure, this does recount how one of the first to be commercially produced arrived on the market.

Just as Julio T. Buel idled by a stream and threw pebbles and fragments of wood in the water, so James Heddon loafed beside Dowagiac Creek, waiting for a fishing partner to come by. Heddon whittled. He tossed the bit of wood he was whittling into the creek. A big bass lunged at it, knocking it high into the air.

At home that evening, Heddon whittled out several similar plugs, jammed the metal cap from bottles on each, and the next day tried them out. They worked. Bass hit them. They were *surface* plugs, and Lou Caine believes this is the first time a bass ever had been caught on such a surface plug lure.

This happened in 1896. Two years elapsed before Heddon put his plug lure on the market. The barn behind his residence was his first factory. In 1902 the business had grown to such size that it moved into a plant built for the production of lures. The new type of lure took hold so that many fishermen referred to this type as "Dowagiacs." The Heddons continue to manufacture a lure, No. 210, which is the current representative of the first "plugs" the founder of the company whittled out for bass fishing.

While the record of the development of the first lures which would be classed as spoons or as plugs, is not clear beyond the relatively recent beginnings of commercial production, the history of those lures called "flies" can be traced back some eighteen centuries.

Theocritus' reference to the "bait fallacious" may have been to an artificial "fly." There is no question about the first description of an artificial fly and where and when it was used.

Claudius Aelian, lived between 170 and 230 B.C. He was a writer and something of a naturalist. His *De Natura Animalium* contains the following passage:

"I have heard of a Macedonia way of catching fish, and it is this: Between Boroca and Thessalonica runs a river called the Astracus, and in it there are fish with spotted (or speckled) skins; what the natives of the country call them you had better ask the Macedonians. These fish feed on a fly which is peculiar to the country, and which hovers over the river. It is not like the flies found elsewhere, nor does it resemble a wasp in appearance, nor in shape would one justly describe it a midge or bee, yet it has something of each of these. In boldness it is like a fly, in size you might call it a bee; it imitates the color of a wasp, and it hums like a bee. The natives call it Hippourus. As these flies seek their food over the river, they do not escape the observation of the fish swimming below. When, then, a fish observes a fly hovering above, it swims quietly up, fearing to agitate the water lest it should scare away its prey; then, coming up by its own shadow, it opens its jaws and gulps down the fly, like a wolf carrying off sheep from the farmyard; having done this, it withdraws under the rippling water. Now, though the fishermen know of this, they do not use these flies at all for bait for the fish; for, if a man's hand touch them, they lose their color, their wings decay, and they become unfit for food for the fish. For this reason they have nothing to do with them, hating them for their bad character; but they have planned a snare for the fish, and get the better of them by their fisherman's craft. They fasten red wool round a hook, and fit on to the wool two feathers which grew under a cock's wattles, and which in color are like wax. Their rod is six feet long, and the line is of the same length. Then they throw their snare, and the fish, attracted and maddened by the color, comes up, thinking to get a dainty mouthful; when, however it opens its jaws, it is caught by the hook and enjoys a bitter repast, a captive." (Translation from *De Animalium Natura,* book XV, chapter i.)

The first artificial fly of record—by description accepted by authorities as the original Red Hackle—and the fish it caught pretty certainly a member of the char group, blood relatives of our Brook Trout.

By what route artificial flies reached England is not defined. Whether the use of such lures traveled with the returning Crusaders, or by other routes, we find our Dame Juliana in her discourse on "hawkynge, huntynge and fysshynge," listing a dozen fly patterns with instructions as to tying.

Among these is a pattern of which she writes: "In the begynning of Maye a good flye, the body of roddy wull and lappid abowte wyth blacke silke; the wynges of the drake of redde capons hakyll." The Red Hackle had arrived in Britain.

About a century later Mascall pirated the list of flies which Juliana had described, changing the name of four. And a half century after that, Walton, who it must be remembered was a bait fisherman for the most part, gave the same list as Mascall.

In his discussion of *natural* lures for trout, Walton lists "the dun-fly, the stone-fly, the red-fly, the moor-fly, the tawny-fly, the shell-fly, the cloudy or blackish fly, the flag-fly, the vine-fly."

When he comes to the paragraph given to artificial flies, he states that the directions were given him, "by an ingenious brother of the angle, an honest man, and a most excellent fly-fisher." He then wrote:

"You are to note that there are twelve kinds of artificial made-flies to angle with upon the top of the water. Note, by the way, that the fittest season of using these is a blustering windy day, when the waters are so troubled that the natural fly cannot be seen or rest upon them. The first is the dun-fly, in March: the body is made of dun wool; the wings of the partridge's feathers. The second is another dun-fly: the body of black wool, and the wings made of the black drake's feathers and of the feathers under his tail. The third is the stone-fly, in April: the body is made of black wool, made yellow under the wings and under the tail, and so made with wings of the drake. The fourth is the ruddy-fly, in the beginning of May the body made of red wool, wrapped about with black silk; and the feathers are the wings of the drake, with the feathers of a red capon, also, which hangs dangling on his sides next to the tail. The fifth is the yellow or greenish fly, in May likewise: the body made of yellow wool, the wings made of the red cock's hackle, or tail. The sixth is the black-fly, in May also; the body made of black wool, and lapped about with the herle of a peacock's tail; the wings are made of the wings of brown capon, with his blue feathers in his head. The seventh is the sad yellow-fly in June: the body is made of black wool, with a yellow list on either side; and the wings taken off the wings of a buzzard, bound with black braked hemp. The eighth is the moorish-fly, made with the body of duskish wool, and the wings made of the blackish mail of the drake. The ninth is the tawny-fly, good until the middle of June: the body made of tawny wool; the wings made contrary one against the other, made of the whitish mail of the wild drake. The tenth is the wasp-fly in July: the body made of black wool, lapped with yellowish silk; the wings made of the feathers of the drake or of the buzzard. The eleventh is the shell-fly, good in mid-July: the body made of greenish wool, lapped about with the herle of a peacock's tail, and the wings made of the wings of the buzzard. The twelfth is the dark drake-fly, good in August; the body made with black wool, lapped about with black silk; his wings are made of the mail of the black drake, with a black head. Thus have you a jury of flies likely to betray and condemn all the trouts in the river."

The "mail" Walton refers to, is the mottled type of feathers, their markings resembling a coat of mail.

He goes on to say, "I shall next give you some other directions for fly-fishing, such as are given by Mr. Thomas Barker, a gentleman that hath spent much time in fishing; but I shall do it with a little variation."

It was Charles Cotton, who regarded Walton as his "father" who apparently touched off the parade of many fly patterns. Cotton was a fly fisherman, and in the fourth edition of *The Compleat Angler,* he listed and described upward of sixty patterns. This edition was printed twenty-two years after the first "Angler" had appeared. While Mascall and Walton apparently had helped themselves to the information Dame Juliana had put in her book on flies, without much change, there were undoubtedly other than the twelve fly patterns being developed and tested. Cotton rounded up those which had achieved some standing and gave us the beginning of the parade of the artificial flies.

Walton is credited with giving the name to the "palmer" types of flies. For he wrote: "And yet I will exercise your promised patience by saying a little of the caterpillar, or the palmer-fly or worm–." Here he was referring to the caterpillar as natural bait.

Later, after having given the twelve patterns which Juliana listed, Mascall repeated, he discusses the palmer type of fly, giving credit to Barker for the information on this style. So this is confirmation of the fact that while Walton listed the "original twelve," there were other recognized, named flies, and Cotton had these to draw on as he wrote his section of the fourth edition of *The Compleat Angler.*

Patterns still used are so close to Juliana's original twelve that they can be identified as slight modifications. The first dun-fly is today's Dun; the second dun fly is the Olive Dun. The Stone Fly has retained its style and name. The Red Spinner has also. The yellow fly is our Little Yellow May Dun. The dun cut is the Yellow Dun, the Maure and Tandy are two different stages of the May fly, the wasp is the Wasp; the Drake is today's Alder; the Shell fly has kept its name, and the black louper is not greatly different from the Black Palmer.

The first flies used by American anglers were from England or dressed by those who had learned the art of fly-making abroad. We still import English flies although the American manufacturers are capable of producing as dainty and effective flies as can be found.

To attempt to give the history of trout fly patterns would require a volume in itself. But there are some most used that should be so recognized. Along with them, is the record of the early fly dressers who established that art in this continent.

Midway in the 20th century realistic ties of nymphs; streamer flies and bucktails, which are impressionistic imitations of small fish; flush-floating opaque models of the terrestrial insect forms, and garish fish-finder dry flies were in common use. Popular favorites of yesteryear, however, are important because of history and tradition, and because they still take fish. Against the background of the "original twelve," the following have been preferred flies.

The Royal Coachman is an American fly. A customer of John Haily, a professional fly dresser of New York City, asked him in 1878 to tie a fly on a Coachman pattern, but to make them "extra strong." Haily wound the central part of the body with red silk to protect the peacock herl and added the barred feathers of the wood-duck as a tail. He sent one of the flies to Charles Frederick Orvis, a friend and another pioneer in fly manufacture. Orvis and his brother L. C., were in a party of friends a few evenings later, "disputing the fly question," as Orvis puts it. One of the group said that it would be better merely to number the flies being produced, not name them, and thus avoid some confusion. Others in the group disagreed.

"What can you do?" protested the one who argued fǒr numbering. "Here is a fly intended to be a Coachman, yet it is not a true Coachman; it is quite unlike it, and what can you call it?"

"Oh, that is easy enough," said L. C. Orvis, "call it the Royal Coachman, it is so finely dressed!"

So the currently most popular fly in America was made, and so named.

The Gray Hackle, peacock which stands second in the survey list, and its variations in body color, the yellow bodied type standing fifth, have such a long lineage they reach back to the very beginning; to the Red Hackle of Aelian's time. Also the Brown Hackle, peacock, with stands fourth in the survey list. It could well be, that those anglers who originated the Red Hackle in the third century, wanted to go fishing one day, couldn't catch a red-feathered cockrel to pluck a hackle with which to tie a fly, grabbed a gray or brown bird instead, tied the flies for the day's expedition, found these flies good, and the Gray Hackle or Brown Hackle entered the scene.

The Black Gnat came from yesteryears in England, with no record of who "invented it." It was a copy of a natural fly, made in England with lead colored wings, and modified by American fly dressers; so now it is generally tied with black wings.

The Mosquito, which stands 6th in modern purchase preference, is another fly derived from natural insects. It also apparently is a natural adaptation from live fish food, with no "inventor" to credit—except the mosquito himself.

The Coachman is another matter. Tom Bosworth was coachman for the royal family of England; for George IV, William IV and Queen Victoria. David Foster, who wrote *Scientific Angler,* was a contemporary of Bosworth, and paid high praise to his fishing skill. Foster states that Bosworth developed the Coachman fly particularly for night fishing. The Leadwing Coachman and other little bits of fancying as the fly is dressed, are merely variations from old Tom's original.

The McGinty pattern, standing eighth, in the survey, apparently came on the scene in 1889 or a little later. Dike Smedley suggests that it derived its name from the popular song, "Down Went McGinty to the Bottom of the Sea" which was first sung in that year, but Dike declares all research has failed to locate the person who first tied it or gave it that name.

Ninth in the order of preference, is Professor. The "Professor" was a Scotchman, John Wilson, who wrote articles, many of which were on angling, for Blackwood's Magazine, under the pen name of "Christopher North." A selection of these articles with a number about angling, were published in two volumes, titled *Recreations of Christopher North.* Wilson was actually a professor of Edinburgh University, starting with 1820. He was born in 1785, died in 1854. He devised this fly pattern, and it became "The Professor." With a slight change, body orange in place of yellow, hackle palmer style and no tag, we have Queen of the Waters, which stands eleventh in the survey list. The King of the Waters is another variation from the basic Professor. And to round out the Wilson story, his brother, James, author of *The Rod and Gun: The Treatises on Angling and Shooting,* published in 1840, tied up the original Grizzly King, another popular fly but not in the first dozen of the survey list.

Number ten in the famous rating of old is Cowdung. It seems to be another of those flies which began its career as an imitation of a natural insect, with Nature being the designer, and no record of who first tied it.

The twelfth in this list is Parmachene Belle. It is rated as a "fancy fly"—resembling in no reasonable degree any natural insect. It is an interesting comment on the list of twelve current favorites that it begins with a "fancy fly," the Royal Coachman, and closes with another "fancy fly," the Parmachene Belle. If they had been numbered, as the friend of Charles and L. C. Orvis argued during the moments when the Royal Coachman was christened, they may never have reached such high popularity. But the appeal of casting something "royal" and of tossing a "belle" about could have had something to do with the success of these patterns. There's something in a name. Both flies, naturally, catch trout—or they never would have reached a footing among the first dozen preferred as shown by the survey of quantities of each pattern purchased.

The story of the "Belle" is well authenticated. Henry P. Wells, who wrote those several excellent angling books in the 1880's, was on a fishing trip with his brother, John, angling in favorite Maine waters. They were concocting fly patterns one day, preparatory to the evening's fishing. The "Belle" was tied; it proved itself; it's been a favorite since, coming close to taking the lead in preference over the then-favorite Coachman, in that period just before 1900. Undoubtedly it was Wells' own emphatic cheering of this fly pattern in his books and magazine articles which gave it the initial push toward wide use, and then the fly proved itself. It is named after Parmachene Lake in Maine.

A quick glance back over this survey list shows that half of them are "fancy flies," with the "inventor's" name known except in the case of

McGinty. The others are reasonable imitations of the "natural" flies, even the hackles stemming first from that fly which buzzed over the River Astracus. And with these, the inventor was Nature herself—and no record of who first made the copies of her patterns.

The list of flies is seemingly endless. Some come and go; others hang on. Each has some interesting history if it can be uncovered. In these sketches of the twelve patterns most bought in the middle of the 20th century, is the general shape of those stories; their histories and how they came into being.

Wet flies have been thought of as being the first used. That is probably true. But Walton speaks of keeping the flies well on the surface, although they may have been "sinkers" if not held so they rode the ripples. The first flies of record which were designed specifically to ride the surface were mentioned in Mascall's book. They were fitted with "corke" bodies and were more like the smaller "bass bugs" of more modern times. That was toward the end of the 16th century.

The first mention of a fly that floats is in a book by George Scotcher, *The Fly-fisher's Legacy,* published at Chepstow, England, in 1800. The next discussion of such a fly is in George P. R. Pulman's *Vade Mecum of Fly Fishing for Trout,* which ran through three editions, 1841, 1846, and 1851. In the first two editions, Pulman merely discusses the use of a fly which was built to float. In the 1851 edition, he gives instruction on "switching" the fly to dry it between casts.

One James Ogden, of Cheltenham, a professional fly-dresser, in a book published in 1879, states that he made floating flies in 1839, and gives an account of using floating "May flies," on Derbyshire Wye River, near Bakewell, June 15, 1865.

Thus we have the record of where the two major divisions of artificial flies began to be used, and by whom. Wings had appeared on fly patterns when Juliana wrote, but the hackles were and still are a dominant type. Actually, when she wrote her book, a century and a half before Walton angled, fly fishing had passed its infancy. There were named and recognized patterns, tied to specifications, and a technic developed for the use of each type, and a season when each brought best success.

Martin Automatic Reel Co.

View from the bottom of the original Martin reel showing crude arrangement of gears and shafts as compared to modern techniques.

Probably ever since the first Red Hackle caught fish very similar to our Brook Trout in that far away day on far-distant River Astracus, there have been modifications of fly patterns, each "new, better, sure-fire." And it probably will go on.

We have the streamers, the buck tails, the hair flies, the nymph patterns, and a host of other modifications and variations. But back of it all is the thing that happened near Thessalonica—some fisherman copied a natural fly and the rest of the fellows took it from there.

Anglers are an experimenting lot, aren't they!

Martin Automatic Reel Co.

Side view of the original Martin reel shown with the present-day type.

PRESENT DAY TACKLE

It really makes little difference to the actual angler, who first devised which lure. It can be taken for granted, that those that survived and are offered to fishermen today have had their testing and have proven themselves. But back of each lure in use, there is this interesting, engaging panorama of yesterday's fishermen and the lore they developed, which brings the lures used today.

It makes no difference, either, whether the spoon came first, or the plug, or the artificial fly. Someone found each type fitted to some kind of fishing, and found fun in using artificial lures and artifices in technics, to land fish on these fraudulent concoctions.

And in the final analysis, starting with the hook, the little-changed counterpart of the first fish hook made, whatever has been developed in tackle has been a steady progression toward those kinds of equipment which make fishing the most universal sport in America.

Fishermen have cause to become a bit nonplussed as they approach a tackle counter. Arts and sciences in angling have become so diversified that the equipment presents a baffling array.

The fellow who lets impressions and impulses direct him, or who listens to the insufficiently informed salesman, buys something that "looks good" and misses fundamental features which make a tackle unit good or otherwise. A bit of snappy-colored winding on a rod may even be the factor which determines a selection. The "paint job" on a lure may attract and lead to purchasing a lure—but it may not be the one which will do the most business when presented to fish.

It must be recognized that the manufacturers of tackle have tried to "keep up with the Joneses" in some degree. One recently said that unless his company brought out "new" lures each season, his competition would steal the show with other "new" lures. So there is a tendency to fancy-up various items to make the article "something new." Dress-ups do not materially change the basic functions of the article. In some measure, this sort of a situation leads away from producing equipment functionally better. On the other hand, we should recognize that the questing for new things does result in genuine, basic advancements.

This section offers a somewhat analytical approach to each division of the tackle assembly, sorting out the different *basic types* in each unit, and thus supplying a foundation for the average angler to look beyond the "paint job" and see structural and functional features.

The various portions of tackle assembly, starting with the lure are in this sequence: Lure, Hook, Leader, Line, Reel and Rod. Those are basic. An additional grouping should include minor accessories that are fairly universal in their use; such as sinkers and swivels.

Starting with the lure as a main division of tackle they can be separated into major subdivisions. There are Spinners and Spoons, Plugs (lures with body), "Bass Bugs" and Jigs, with their partial body and feather or hair streamers, artificial flies, doodads that are artificial representations of natural bait such as rubber frogs and the like and natural bait.

The different types within the Spinner and Spoon division can be further segregated into spoons that wobble on the retrieve, and spinners that whirl. Then, in spinners where the blades revolve, there is the Colorado Spinner the blade of which is attached to a split ring, and the two general types of attachment where the blade revolves around a shaft. One of these is the "Indiana Spinner" type which has an attachment by a small clevis, and the other the "Star-Lowe" type in which the attachment of the blade is a loop of wire around the shaft or a hole in the end of the blade. In further analyzing the structural-functional features of the spinners, there are differences in the shape of blades, some long and narrow, others more roundish with varying degree of dish in the blade.

Each of these steps in analysis of structural-functional features of a bit of tackle, leads quite definitely to estimating how that unit will perform in use.

There's the point. The color job on a lure has nothing to do with the action. In trying to decide color first, one may not get into the analysis of the structural-functional features. The varnish job on a rod is not necessarily the basis for determining its quality, action, and stamina.

The very specialization of equipment for specific types of fishing does two things. It increases the potential confusion on the part of the angler-purchaser. But if he has the ground work to fit the type of tackle items selected to the sort of fishing to be done, he can fit the best equipment available to the job ahead.

So what may be done here without becoming too highly technical is to set up an approach to classifying types of each unit of tackle assembly available with attention to the structural-functional way they will perform in action. As this is done there will be presented the wide array of various tackle items from which the angler may select equipment to fit his fishing needs.

Such a review also will serve as a reference check-list of what tackle is available.

LURES

One may approach the classification of lures somewhat on the same basis that a biologist uses in sorting living things into their proper relationship to each other and to the whole field of biology. In some measure each lure is made to simulate natural food for fishes. It is not too illogical to parallel the biologist's methods of classification in considering the lures.

Living things are sorted into "families," on the basis of major characteristics common to all so grouped. Using the same approach a line may be drawn between each major division of lures.

We have the Spoon-Spinner "family" of lures, the Plugs which are definitely baits with body, the "bug family" which has some body and usually some feather or hair streamer fittings, the artificial flies and that conglomerate group of lures which contains such things as whirly-gig jiggers revolving around a shaft, hair mice, rubber hellgrammites, and gutta-percha frogs.

The Spoon-Spinner family is probably the oldest of all artificial lures. It is the simplest in much of its basic construction. It includes all lures in which the action is the result of water resistance created on a blade of metal or other substance as the lure travels through water. The simple wobbler spoon is probably the most universal of all fish-getters.

There are two sub-families in this main division. The first is the Wobbler Spoon group, in which there is no shaft. The blade of the lure is attached to the leader at one end, causing it to whip and wobble from side to side as it is drawn through the water. The other sub-family is the Spinner group, in which the blade of the lure whirls continuously in a circular fashion, clockwise or the reverse, around the axis of the line of traction.

SPOONS

(See color plate)

WOBBLERS

The fundamental construction of these spoons is a dished blade, symmetrical or unsymmetrical over the central axis of the spoon. A hole in the forward end usually is fitted with a split ring or split ring and swivel, with the hook or hooks either solidly attached to the blade itself, or free-swinging on a split ring through a hole in the rear end of the blade. The dish in the spoon supplies the "planing surfaces" which give the spoon action as it moves through the water.

The impact of the water pressure on the dished surface throws the blade from side to side. In a symmetrical, oval spoon, evenly dished from all sides toward the center, the action pivots to some extent across the middle of the spoon. A deep dish will throw the blade from side to side in wider dives and wiggles than the blade which has a shallower dish.

The Dardevle is a symmetrical blade, its sides and dishing uniform over the long axis. However, the blade is not of uniform width, the "bulge" of the spoon occurring near the rear end in the shape of a "shoe spoon." The deepest point of dish is at the widest part of the spoon near the hook end. Also, there is a small "planing surface" at the very forward end of this spoon which bends back slightly away from the dished side. This throws in an additional "planing" force at the forward point, which adds to the erratic action of the lure in the water. With the most pronounced dishing rather deep at the rear end, the greater width there, the lure is impelled by water forces on the planing surfaces, to "whip" more at the rear end than forward.

These features of shape in the typical "shoe spoon" design produce the erratic darting, diving action in the water. Combine that with the slight counter force that occurs at the forward end because of the small turned-back planing surface at the point of attachment, and we have the complete picture of the forces that supply action to this sort of spoon. It is a good example of the modification that can be introduced in spoon shapes, depth of dishing, point of deepest dish, to supply a chosen type of action.

Pursuing the step-by-step classification as a biologist would with living things, the Spoon-Spinner "family" has been divided into the two sub-families. The next step in classification would be to segregate groups which have common major features of structure. In the world of living things these divisions are called "genera." For example, the fish called trout all belong to the salmon family, but because of their differences in certain physical features, the Atlantic Salmon, the Rainbow, Brown and Cutthroat Trout are in one genus, while the Brook and Dolly Varden Trout are in another.

The differences in wobbler spoons because of the physical features found in hook attachment can be considered as a basis of putting the fixed hook in one "genus" and those with free-swinging hooks in another.

Within each genus of living things, taking the Salmon trout as an example, there are species; Atlantic Salmon, Rainbows, Browns and Cutthroats. So in the divisions of wobbler spoons, there can be "species" of fixed and free swimming hooks.

If this line were followed as a biologist might in his field, there could be varieties within species. Stepping into the garden for illustration, a whole group of roses may be of one species, but different varieties, have different colors and some slight differences physically. That would be comparable to the lures which have the same physical assembly but a different enamel or dye job.

It is unnecessary to attempt to sort out "varieties" in lures since the principal objective is to sort out the structural-functional features of lures, and weigh their affect on performance. After determining these primary considerations the pattern or "variety" preferred is up to the individual fisherman.

On such a basis, let's sort out and group spoons and spinners.

Fixed-Hook Wobblers

The typical fixed-hook wobbler spoons may have the hook attached by solder, or constructed so the hooks are attached by a screw and are removable. As typical of this group there are:

The Cayuga, an old, standard wobbler.
The Canandaigua, also an old standard.
The modern Johnson "Silver Minnow."
Some of the Dardevles.
Pflueger "Record."

And there are a number of other spoons of this group with fixed hooks.

Free-Swinging Hook Wobblers

The hooks in this group are usually attached to the rear end of the blade with a split ring. Typical are:

Dardevle thus fitted with hooks.
K-B.
Finlander.
Old Lob, an old standard.
Oneida.
Onondaga,—and many others.

The second appraisal of structural-functional features of wobbler spoons can be on the basis of shape of the blade.

Symmetrical Oval-Elipse Spoons

The most typical representative of this shape of wobbler is the Cayuga. The outline is uniformly oval, each quarter being identical with the other quarters over long and cross axes, and the dishing is uniform from the center to the rim.

Symmetrical Blades Over Longitudinal Axis But Not Over Cross-Axis

These are the wobblers which are "egg shape" or "shoe spoon" in outline. The deepest dish usually occurs in the center of the spoon at its widest point and the rear portion of the spoon is usually the widest. Typical are:

Seneca
Oneida
Old Lob
Dardevles,—and many others.

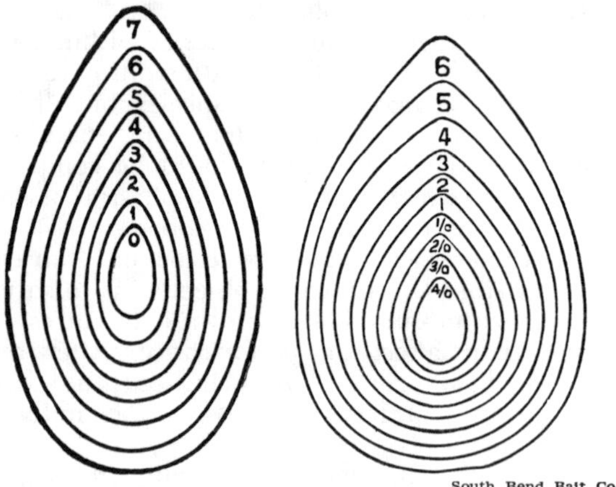

South Bend Bait Co.
Representative spoon sizes.

Blades Not Symmetrical (Often Fish-Shaped)

Probably the first representative of this type is the "Old Style C" lure produced by Julio Buel. Horrocks-Ibbotson's "Del-Rey" and Pflueger's "Limper" are other spoons, not symmetrical across either axis.

One other wobbler type that deserts the basic oval or "shoe spoon" outline, is represented by South Bend's "Trix-Oreno;" a flat, somewhat oblong blade, with head weighted and angled planing surface at the rear.

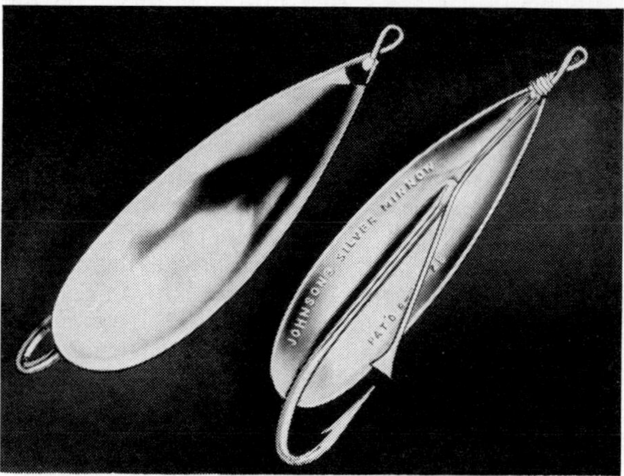

Louis Johnson Co.
The Johnson Silver Minnow—typical of the wobbler type.

Still another modification, which does not enter into fundamental differences in shape related to action, since it is uniformly eliptical, is the "Sun-Spot" produced by South Bend. Holes are punched in the body of the spoon, and these are made into "windows" flashing various colors, by fitting the inside of the spoon with a layer of tinted plastic.

Fundamentally, then, the wobbler spoon is a blade of metal, usually following somewhat an oval or shoe spoon shape in outline, dished to supply planing surfaces, so it will dart and wobble in the water as retrieved. The depth of dishing, the place it occurs, combined with the outline is what determines the action. The more pronounced the dishing, the wider will be the darting; the more the dishing is toward the rear end of the lure, the wider will be the darting divergence from the line of traction which is the retrieving line.

Finally there are apparently two factors that causes fish to hit these lures. The first is the movement, the action. The second is the finish. How much any game fish reacts to given colors is a question. The red and white "Shoe-spoon" lure seems to have high attraction to the Pike family as against other color combinations.

Experience also indicates that right at the top in finish for these spoons, is the silver, gold or bronze surface and more recently the gunmetal finish. Generally, even though there is an enamel finish in some color combination on one side, the other side (usually the dish) is metal. It then would indicate that the predominant feature in attracting fish is the action plus the erratic flashing of reflected light.

The selection of such a lure should first take into consideration the action the shape and planing surfaces of the wobbler will supply, at varying rates of retrieve, with the consideration of the finish to follow, and with emphasis on the type of finish which will give additional flash and change in appearance as the spoon travels.

The wobbler spoon has top rating as a lure for either casting or trolling for any of the Pike family, Muskies, Northerns and Pickerels. In early spring it is a good Walleye lure. It casts well in the medium sizes for bass. Smaller sizes fitted with a bit of pork rind will take pan fish and trout. There is a growing use of the medium size wobbler in fishing deep holes in trout streams and in trout lakes. In larger sizes it is used for some salt-water game species.

Some of the most experimenting and persistent anglers say that if they could take only one lure in a kit, he would select one of the simple wobbler spoons.

SPINNERS

(See color plate)

This sub-family is characterized by being constructed with thin blades of metal or other substance, which whirl with a circular motion around the axis of the line of traction. The same general system of sorting these into groups can be followed as with the wobbler spoons.

SINGLE-BLADE SPINNERS

Within this sub-division of the spinner subfamily, the rotating blades are single units, attached at one end, each blade turning independently. There may be two or more blades on a lure, but they have no attachment to each other.

Classification by Method of Attachment

1. Blade attached to split ring to which the hook (or hooks) also is attached; no shaft. The universal example of this type is the Colorado Spinner.
2. Blade or blades rotating freely around bearing on shaft.
   a. Bearing either a hole in attached end of spoon or eyelet of wire soldered or welded to end of spoon and encircling shaft.
      (1) Star-Lowe (Pflueger)
      (2) Ontario (Buel)
      (3) Pflueger Bearcat.
      (Plus many, many others)
   b. Attachment by a clevis-shaped "collar" or "saddle."
      The type-name generally accepted for this group is "Indiana Spinner" with many trade names in many makes.
   c. Attachment to shaft by hole or loop bearing in the upper end of the spoon blade, with a fixed-arm also with bearing on the shaft which holds the blade out from the shaft at constant angle.
      "June Bug" is the type name most used for this spinner.
   d. "Flasher" or Multiple series; a series of spoons several in number, simple blades, on shafts, the shafts linked in line.

Classification in blade forms.

1. Circular or broad oval.
2. Narrow oval.
3. "Shoe spoon" or egg shape, symmetrical over center axis but wider toward one end, usually rear portion.
4. Willow leaf; sides symmetrically curved segment of circle, ends pointed.
5. Kidney shape.
6. Fluted; a modification which can be applied to any blade shape, but usually to rear portion of egg-shaped ovals.

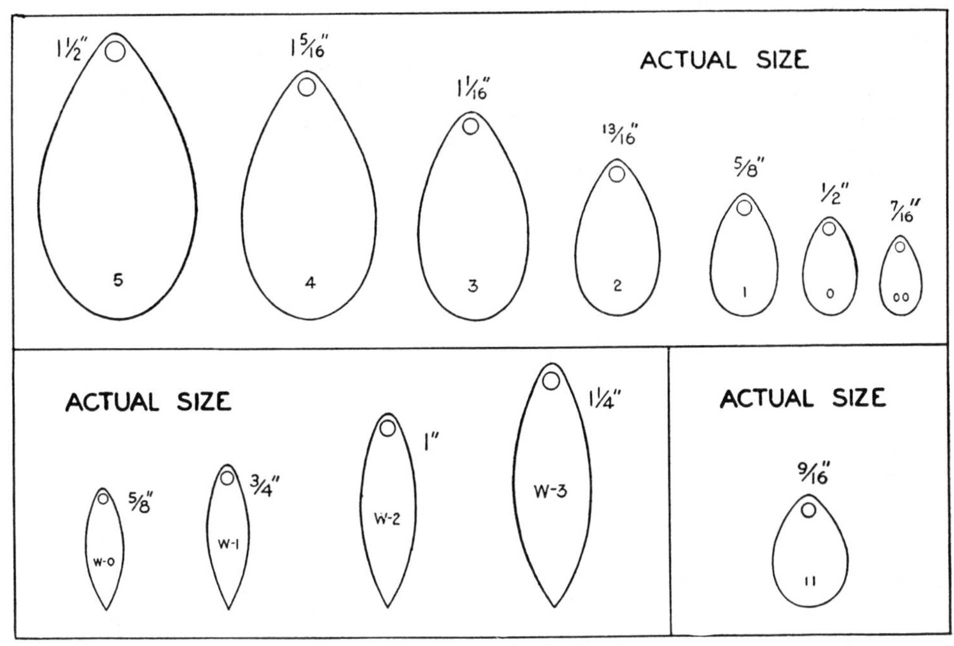

Types of spoons and relative sizes.

There are infinite numbers of small variations in the shapes of blades both between manufacturers' lines and the individual "name" patterns they produce. Those points that should be kept in mind in selecting any lure in this class are the approximate basic shape of the blade, whether wide or narrow; the degree of dishing, both of which affect the speed of rotation and the angle at which the blade will stand out as it spins. Other features are: Narrow blades, faster spinning, closer to shaft; wide blades turning slower, standing out farther. It takes more rapid retrieving to activate narrow blades while wider blades will start spinning at slower speeds.

PROPELLER-BLADE SPINNERS

This group has double blades, propeller-shaped, rotating around the shaft on a bearing in the center.

1. Simple propeller type.
   This group has one or more "spinners" often two on a shaft rotating in opposite directions to neutralize line twisting. The "propeller" is the moving unit, unattached to any other portion of the lure.
2. Additional portions of the lure rotate; attached to and activated by propeller blades.
   a. Pflueger Cyclone
   b. Buel Spinners
   Many others.

There are a number of additional applications of the spinner function to give flash and movement to lures. Spinners are placed before flies. Some plugs have spinners fore and aft. Still other lures of the plug type have been fitted with propeller blades so the head or the entire body will turn on a central shaft. These are hybrid types of lures, falling within the classification of their predominant features. Thus, while the spinner principle may be used to whirl the body of a plug, it is, in fact, an accessory to the plug, and such a one probably should be considered a plug first, with the spinner feature added.

The spinning-blade lures are not so readily cast as either the wobbler spoons or plugs. The "joints" in a spinner-blade lure, at the attachment to the line or leader where a swivel makes a double joint, and at the far end of the shaft where either the gang hooks with feathers or buck-tail or bait such as pork rind are attached perhaps with another swivel, tend to "buckle" while handling. They are used for casting, often ahead of some "bait" type of body lure; often natural bait.

Their principal use without additional accessories is in trolling. Here the question of speed of rotation needs consideration. The Pike family, for example strikes swiftly and the lure can be moving faster with fewer "short strikes." The slower moving lure, requiring less drag to set blades in motion is suited to Lake Trout, an example of a fish with more deliberate strike.

One main use of the "June Bug" spinner is for Walleyes. Their strike is somewhat slow. Since a free blade will not start spinning until a certain velocity of movement has been attained, that could be too rapid a rate of travel for a deliberate Walleye. So the "June Bug" with its fixed arm, with the blade already standing out from the shaft, solves the problem by being in a position to start whirling with a very moderate movement.

The smaller, lighter, whirling-blade spinners have a high use in fishing somewhat turbid trout waters, particularly in early season. This is a lure used by many in the West for early trout fishing. This, and other whirling blades are also a good lure type for pan fish.

Particularly in trolling, the spinning-blade lures, of a size suited to the fish to be taken, fitted with buck-tails, feathered gangs, a flapping pork rind, or similar addition, are probably second only to the wobbler in universal appeal to all game fish.

In selecting a lure that is a member of the Spoon-Spinner Family, look first at the structural features; shape, dish of the blade, where the impact of water will hit the planing surfaces. After that, consider color or finish needed for the type of water and the species of fish and then choose the additional fittings to follow the primary feature of attraction which lies in the wobbling or spinning blade.

Some of the most effective lures in all types of fishing are found in the simpler forms of both the wobblers and spinning-blade lures. Don't miss having a few of these basic fish-getters in the tackle box.

PLUGS: LURES WITH BODY

(See color plate)

The classification of subdivisions within this "family" of lures may be approached from several angles. One of the most understandable methods of sorting out fundamental types is on the basis of whether they are designed to float on the surface, dig under the surface on the retrieve but float when traction is stopped, or sink because they are weighted so they will get down into deeper fish-feeding zones.

All of the lures in this family are characterized by having a "body" as a main structural feature, which in some degree usually resembles a small fish or other live bait. The first commercial offerings of such lures had woven hair or wire bodies. The modern "plug" began as a wood-bodied lure, but since its introduction plastic has become predominantly the material used and has proved to be an excellent material.

Some of the features of construction will be found common to all groups, surface, sub-surface or deep. Planing surfaces designed to make the plug wobble, may be found in all types. The principle that the center of weight which if forward in a plug will give it a faster "wiggle" and a slower action if weight center is farther to the rear, applies to all. So while the separation most easily made is on the zone in which the plug will "fish," consideration of structural features such as planing surfaces and center of weight should apply to all sub-divisions of this family.

FLOATERS AND SURFACE-DISTURBANCE PLUGS

Plugs in this group remain on top of the water on the retrieve. They can be weighed to be "sinkers," but their function is to simulate something struggling or moving on the surface. Some are fitted with planing surfaces which tip them slightly, so they will dig into the water a little, creating a disturbance. Others have planing surfaces to make them dart from side to side; others have spinner or flapping blades to agitate the water.

SURFACE-DISTURBANCE LURES

A. Somewhat fish-shaped bodies or small animals.
  1. Propeller equipped; no side action.
    a. Pflueger Scoop Minnow.
    b. South Bend Surf-Oreno.
    c. Horrocks-Ibbotson Injured minnow.
    d. South Bend Crippled-Oreno.
    e. South Bend Nip-I-Diddee.
  2. Spoon-spinner attachments.
    a. Heddon Flaptail.
    b. Pflueger Tandem.
  3. With planing surfaces that cause darting-wobbling motions. Planing surfaces either body shape or attached plates.
    a. Heddon Creek Chub "2000" Darter.
    b. South Bend Dash-Oreno.
    c. Arbogast Jitterbug.
    d. South-Bend Teas-Oreno (Curved body)

B. Popper lures.
  1. Resembling small fish; body lure. Dished head in lure.
    a. Wright & McGill Pop-o-Lure.
    b. Heddon Chugger-Spook.
  2. Partial body; supplement of trailing feathers, hair or other material. Head dished for "popper" effect.
    a. P&K Walkie Talkie
    b. Arbogast Hula Popper
    c. South Bend Plunk-Oreno
    d. Horrocks-Ibbotson Feather-O-Minnow.

We have here the illustration of gradations between definite classes of lures of one type toward those of another. The feather or hair streamer of the popper lures gives it a status somewhat between actual plugs and streamer flies. However, they fall more within the plug than the fly family, because of the portion of the solid body they have, plus the fact that the streamers, in water, tend to resemble a body shape, merely giving the lure a degree of flexibility in its action—an appearance of more "living thing" action.

SUB-SURFACE LURES

These can be segregated into groups by the method of supplying the surfaces which cause the lure to dig a bit under the water when traction is applied.

A. Planing surfaces found in shape of lure head.
  1. South Bend Bass-Oreno
  2. Horrocks-Ibbotson Rush-Tango
  3. Pflueger Mustang Minnow Series 8600
  4. Heddon Lucky 13

B. Planing surfaces supplied by body shape. Planing surface in head; body curved to supplement.
  1. Flat Fish

C. Planing surfaces a metal "diving" plate, recessed in plug head.
  1. Pflueger Mustang Minnow Series 8900
  2. Wright & McGill Miracle Minnow
  3. Shakespeare Pup

D. Plate not recessed; exterior; attached near "throat" of lure body.
  1. Makinen Wonderlure.
  2. Heddon Vamp Spook.
  3. South Bend Pike-Oreno
  4. P&K Amazing Mazie.
  5. Horrocks-Ibbotson Krazy-Krab.

DEEP OR SINKING LURES

A. Not designed to wobble; lure follows line of traction without much side-to-side motion; "Flash" and motion supplied by propeller spinners.
  1. Heddon Torpedo, and Dowagiac Minnow.
  2. Pflueger Peerless Minnow.
  3. Devon Minnow, having propeller blades that spin entire "body" around shaft.

B. Planing surfaces causing lure to dart and wobble.
  1. Planing surfaces in head form.
    a. South Bend Fish-Oreno
    b. Shakespeare Wiggle Diver
  2. Planing plates attached.
    a. Heddon River Runt in "sinker" patterns.
    b. Phantom Minnow
    c. South Bend Dive-Oreno
  3. Planing surfaces in head and also in body shape.
    a. P&K Bright Eyes; body is curved
    b. South Bend Peach-Oreno; body with scooped-out areas.

Classification of the zone, whether on the surface, sub-surface or deep, a generally accepted way of segregating plug lures, is merely one factor of where and how such a lure will perform. It determines the vertical zone where the lure will be fished. Having determined that, the action of the lure within that zone depends on either the planing surfaces are for darting motion, propeller, or flapping spinner blades. Also, the disposition of weight in the lure combined with contour of body will affect action. So, in choosing a plug type of lure, these are the points to examine after the zone in which they will be fished is determined.

Plugs may be used in all types of game fishing—correlating the size, the zone of fishing, the species to be fished, and the best action in one's judgment, which will attract fish. Appraisal of structural-functional features can go far in determining choice.

After that, color pattern can be a consideration. Again, there is some question as to how much time a Bass or Northern Pike will take to look at the colors. If action and flash are there, they may be dominant in the lure's value. Since Brown found in his experiments on color selectivity of Largemouth Bass that they would jump at "their color" even when it was still slightly above the surface, and that red was the most potent in its attraction, there is little question that color should be something to consider.

In the experiments referred to, it was found that as colors progressed from the relatively longer wave-length portions of the spectrum, beginning with red, toward the deep blues, the ability of bass to differentiate colors decreased. It is then well proven that so far as bass go, a pattern with vivid red stands at the top, bright yellow and orange tones next, with deep greens and blues definitely less attractive.

There seems some logic in giving higher consideration to the factor of color in the sub-surface lures than either the surface-disturbance or deep lures. In the case of the surface lures, action and disturbance would appear to be the predominant elements in causing fish to hit; the body of the lure being seen in silhouette. A darker bodied lure in the deep zone would not receive much sunlight to be reflected as color rays. Here action and body shape would dominate in the fish's response.

In the sub-surface lure, working near the surface, sunlight usually does penetrate in abundance. The lure itself is far enough under the water to be within reasonably clear vision of a fish if water is not murky, and color can be seen clearly.

In other words, more consideration should be given to action, shape and size in the deep and surface group than to color. In the sub-surface, color would step up to take a point of near equality with functional-structural features.

The principal use of plug lures is in casting, but they can be trolled. While we think of bass as the principal fish caught on plugs, the pike family next, use can extend under certain conditions, to Walleyes, trout and many other species. In the medium-small lures of this group, one of the most rapidly extending uses is in the pan-fish group—Bluegills, Crappies, and their kin and associates.

The plug family has its appeal based principally in its simulation of "a chunk of meat" in the form of a small fish, animal, or bird. The attractiveness therefore, to a game fish, is in proportion to how it looks like a belly-full of food. An approach to selection of the lures in this class is to weigh out how ably it will do just this—appear as a likely mouthful of fish food. And how well it does this, is determined by its structure. This classification has attempted to give the steps which may result in appraising plugs on that basis.

FLIES

(See color plate)

The fly family, simulating insects or "bugs" in most patterns, but more nearly resembling small minnows in the streamer-types, contains the greatest number of subdivisions because of differences in construction features. Within these subdivisions there is a bewildering list of named patterns, some so nearly identical with others that only the addition of a tag at the tail, a shading of color in material, supply the reason for different names.

One chance for confusion is the occurrence of named patterns in each of the several groups. Thus we may have the Silver Doctor pattern, appearing in salmon, bass, pan-fish, steelhead and both wet and dry fly types for trout. The basis of naming this or any other fly in several type-groups, is in the combination of materials and colors and where they are tied into the pattern—how they are "dressed up." Just remember that this is the explanation for the occurrence of the name in the different type-groups; that there is some structural difference, for example, between a Silver Doctor tied for salmon fishing and one tied for dry-fly trout angling, and that the structural differences adapt them to the type of fishing to be done.

The most universal basis of separation of flies is whether they are "wet" flies or "dry" flies. This separation is principally in trout flies.

Also, as general divisions, there are trout, salmon, steelheads, bass, and pan fish flies.

In considering the trout flies, anglers are accustomed to a division between "dry" patterns and "wet" patterns. Actually a "wet" fly can be made a "dry" fly by treating it to float on the surface. A "dry" fly can become a "wet" fly quickly as it loses its floating qualities.

The members of the dry-fly cult who quibble about the ultimate in details, will lift horrified voices over this statement. But the truth is, that in quite a major portion of the flies, there is no great fundamental constructional difference between those for dry fly fishing and those classed as wet flies.

The viewpoint that there is a radical difference between wet and dry flies has been nurtured somewhat by manufacturers. They list dry and wet flies separately. One of the most expert commercial fly dressers states that while there may be a little more hackle on a "dry fly" tied spread-wing, there is little else different from the same pattern "tied wet," or between most of the wing types of the same patterns.

It is a fact, however, that some types of construction fall definitely into one class or the other and cannot be interchangeably used. The nymphs are all wet; the variant flies may inadvertently be fished wet but they are a dry fly in construction and use. Most winged patterns, that can be separated by the way they are formed, with the exception of the wet double wing construction, may serve either wet or dry.

That's heresy—but it's pretty much fact.

In making a break-down on structural differences, flies with heavier dressing are more suited to dry-fly fishing, while those more sparsely dressed work better wet.

NYMPHS

Wingless, without hackles or sparsely dressed with hackle "feelers" with the body usually fairly slim, "nymphs" are supposed to simulate the larval stage of water insects. There is a wide range of construction features, some being fitted with quill "legs" to further resemble the larval and imago stage of the insects. There is no such standardization of structural form in this group as is found in other wet flies, each manufacturer dressing them in accordance with individual ideas. They are particularly characterized by their lack of wings, the body being the principal portion of the lure, and any other appendages being lacking or sparse.

Insects which lay their eggs in the water pass through the larval or nymph stages there. The nymph fly is predominantly an artificial lure of early season. They may be good at any time, however.

When it is realized that the hellgrammite, which is the larval stage of the Dobson Fly, passes thirty-five months in the water in this form, and only about one month as the adult fly out of the water, and that other insects also go through considerable time as "water worms" of this type, one can see that a nymph fly may be effective at any season if it approximates the current stage of some water-dwelling form. Nymphs are a principal food of trout. They may be in any level of the water, surface to bottom. The most likely time for them to be taken, however, is shortly before the time some local species of fly is approaching its adult stage. Then the nymphs have detached themselves from rocks, snags and other dwelling places, and are wiggling up toward the water surface. When feeding on nymphs, trout will not give much attention to winged flies or other lures.

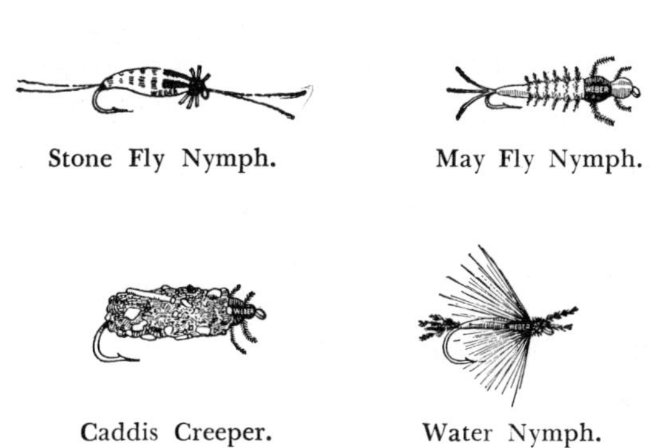

Stone Fly Nymph. May Fly Nymph.

Caddis Creeper. Water Nymph.

Weber Lifelike Fly Co.

A selection of nymph patterns is good insurance against hitting a stream when trout are feeding on this type of food, while passing up other lures.

HACKLES

The hackles are, in fact, a nymph form; wingless, with heavier winding on bodies in most cases, more hackle around the "head" of the fly. The first artificial fly of record was a Red Hackle. The entire group derives names from the color of the hackle feather, preferably from the neck of a cockrel for stiffness and durability, with the designation of the body dressing added to further identify it. Thus a Grey Hackle takes its basic name from the color of the feather wound around the head, and all Grey Hackles have such dressing. The body made of peacock herl is the Grey Hackle peacock; a red silk body is Grey Hackle red; and so on as other windings may be used. Some fly dressers add a tag for the tail of the hackle flies; others do not.

All of the hackle patterns are basic lures for the fly book. They are all-season equipment. Their greater use is as wet flies but with heavy hackles they become a good fly for dry use.

HAIR FLIES

These closely resemble the hackle construction. Since the hackle is specifically a feather, and the "hackle effect" and often the body of the hair flies are hair, they are set apart on the basis of the material used in their making. They have the advantage of having stiffer, more durable material in the hair than softer feather hackles. Manufacturers are inclined to give their series of hair flies names other than those of similar standard feather-dressed flies. It is logical, since no greater differences are the basis for specifically different names where other materials are used. Actual construction, with bodies of woven hair, gives additional reason for pattern names differing from somewhat similar flies in other categories.

Weber Lifelike Fly Co.

Spinner fly.

PALMERS

The palmer type may be any pattern in which a "palmer body" is constructed. The name "palmer" is derived from the old English name of the "palmer worm" which was applied to caterpillars. To get this caterpillar effect, hackle feathers are wound into the body of the fly so the barbules stick out, all fuzzy, the length of the body. Strictly speaking, the palmers are made up in hackle type of construction, wingless. Of course caterpillars don't have wings. If, however, any fly were made up with hackle wound in to make the body bristly with barbules, it would very likely be referred to as a fly that has a "palmered" body. Quite a few of these palmer patterns are specifically members of this group not found in other pattern lists, such as the Soldier Palmer or Claret Palmer.

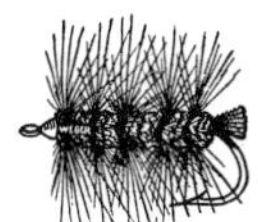

Weber Lifelike Fly Co.

Palmer type fly.

SPIDERS

The tying of the spider type closely follows the construction of the hackles. They are wingless. The hackles used have extra long barbules and the hooks usually are somewhat lighter for their size than in other flies. They are mostly fished dry, the wide-spread hackles supplying good floating qualities when oiled.

VARIANTS

The variants are tied like the spiders, usually with hackle barbules somewhat shorter, but two small wings are added. They are considered one of the best dry-fly types. They are named, like the hackles, in accord with the color of the hackle—Red Variant, Ginger Variant and Rusty as examples.

Weber Lifelike Fly Co.

Closed wing fly.

Weber Lifelike Fly Co.

Typical "dry fly" construction with thick dressing.

Weber Lifelike Fly Co.

Fan wing or divided wing fly.

Weber Lifelike Fly Co.

Typical "wet fly" construction.

Weber Lifelike Fly Co.

Bivisible Type Fly.

It is but a step from the variants to the flies in which the wings are the basis for the type names; how they are tied to the fly body, and how they stand with reference to the rest of the fly.

Many anglers may not know of the care taken in matching the feathers used in constructing the best grade of winged flies. Take the wings of mallard feathers as an example. Mallard wings come in pairs; supposedly from the same bird. As the fly dresser clips one fly wing from, say the second feather on the right mallard wing, the other fly wing is clipped from relatively the same spot on the same feather in the left mallard wing. Thus they are matched, in color, texture and all other features.

CLOSED WING

The standard closed wing fly is tied with two bits of feather placed with the convex side out, the wings standing upright on the upper side of the fly. These flies also are given the class name of Upright Wing. They serve wet or dry, but are of the construction often referred to as "wet."

FAN WING

Materials and assembly of these flies are the same as the Closed Wing for each pattern, with the exception that the curve of the wing feather is reversed and therefore they flare outward. Generally the wings are formed more roundish and somewhat larger than in the closed wings.

SPENT WING

The pattern materials remain the same, they are slightly less heavily dressed, but the wings are longer, narrower, and are tied so they extend out from the body of the fly more nearly at right angles to the plane of the hook.

BIVISIBLES

These are tied with hackles of two colors intermingled as the fly is dressed. Otherwise they follow standard pattern assembly. The theory is that two colors wound into the hackles increase visibility; lighter tones being seen more easily by trout under some light conditions, dark tones more readily under another sort of lighting.

DOUBLE WING

The one type of winged fly which is distinctly constructed for dry fly fishing has two feathers, tied close together in each wing. This is a great buoyancy factor. Fly oil on two such closely parallel feathered wings, actually in contact on most of the surfaces, increases the ability of such a fly to stay on top.

STREAMER FLIES AND BUCKTAILS

Streamer flies and bucktails are artificial flies which imitate a minnow or any of the other fish on which game fish feed. As such, streamer flies and bucktails usually are "long flies" and normally are dressed on long-shanked or tandem hooks or occasionally on short-shanked hooks when tied with a long "wing". Streamer flies and bucktails are all in the wet fly category. The line of demarcation between flies of the streamer and bucktail type and the shorter winged flies commonly termed "wet flies" is not an arbitrary one. Many of the "short flies" may be taken by fish to resemble either a food fish, a nymph, a drowned insect or merely something they wish to attack, to play with, or to strike at from curiosity. Conversely, streamer flies and bucktails are not always taken by gamefish because they are dressed to re-

Rainbow Trout (Steelhead)

Tahoe Cut-throat Trout

Kamloops Trout

Brown Trout (Loch Leven)

Roosevelt Golden Trout

Eastern Brook Trout

Coastal Cut-throat Trout

Canadian Red Trout

Yellowstone Cut-throat Trout

Dolly Varden Trout

PRINCIPAL TYPES OF FLIES
(OTHER THAN TROUT TYPES)

(Reading from left to right and from top down)

First Row.

STEELHEAD TROUT FLIES: Red Parmachene Belle, Claret Red Bird, Jock Scott, Phenian, Rail Bird.

Second Row.

SALMON FLIES: Thunder and Lightning, Dusty Miller, Durham Ranger, Silver Doctor, Jock Scott.

Third Row.

BASS FLIES: Manchester, Polkadot, Scarlet Ibis, Premier, Yellow Miller.

Fourth Row.

PANFISH FLIES: Silver Doctor, Black Rio Grande King, Scarlet Ibis, Parmachene Belle, Royal Coachman, Yellow May.

Fifth Row.

HAIR FLIES: Jock Scott, Dark Caddis, Golden Demon, Royal Coachman, Rail Bird.

Sixth Row.

STREAMER FLIES: Glory, English Admiral, Dragon.

Seventh Row.

STREAMER FLIES: Golden Glow, Brown Sedge, Perch.

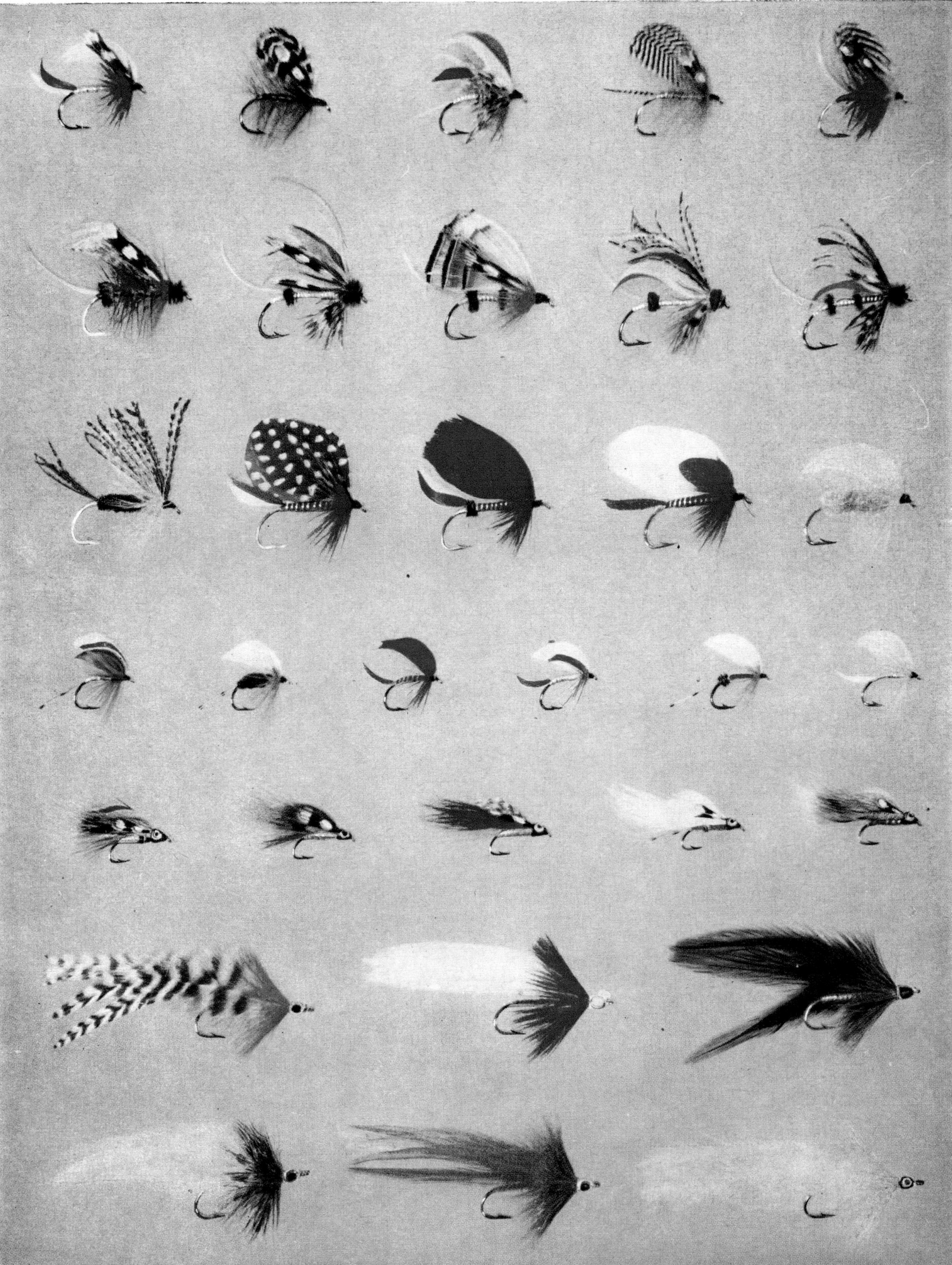

TYPES OF TROUT FLIES

(Reading from left to right and from top down)

First Row.

REPRESENTATIVE NYMPH PATTERNS. No attempt has been made here to name these nymphs. Very similar nymphs are produced by all manufacturers to which they give their own catalog name.

Second Row.

HACKLES: California Hackle, Brown Hackle Peacock, Grey Hackle Peacock, Grey Hackle Red, Grey Hackle Yellow, Orange Asher.

Third Row.

BIVISIBLES: Badger, Ginger, Brown Claret, Grey, Skunk.

Fourth Row.

VARIANTS: Rusty Variant, Grey Variant, Red Variant. PALMERS: Laramie Spinner, Caddis, Beaverkill.

Fifth Row.

CLOSED WING: Black Gnat, Royal Coachman, Parmachene Belle. UPRIGHT WING, single divided: Parmachene Belle, Royal Coachman, Black Gnat.

Sixth Row.

DOWN WING: Black Gnat, Royal Coachman, Parmachene Belle. 4-WING DIVIDED: Parmachene Belle, Royal Coachman, Black Gnat.

Seventh Row.

FAN WING: Black Gnat, Lead Coachman, Royal Coachman, Scarlet Ibis, Professor, Brown Ant.

Eighth Row.

SPENT WING: Spent Gnat, Adams, Horse Fly, House Fly, Deer Fly, Special Mosquito.

In the fifth and sixth rows, four of the most common types have been repeated to illustrate the constructional difference between these closely-allied types. This explains the repetition of the pattern names.

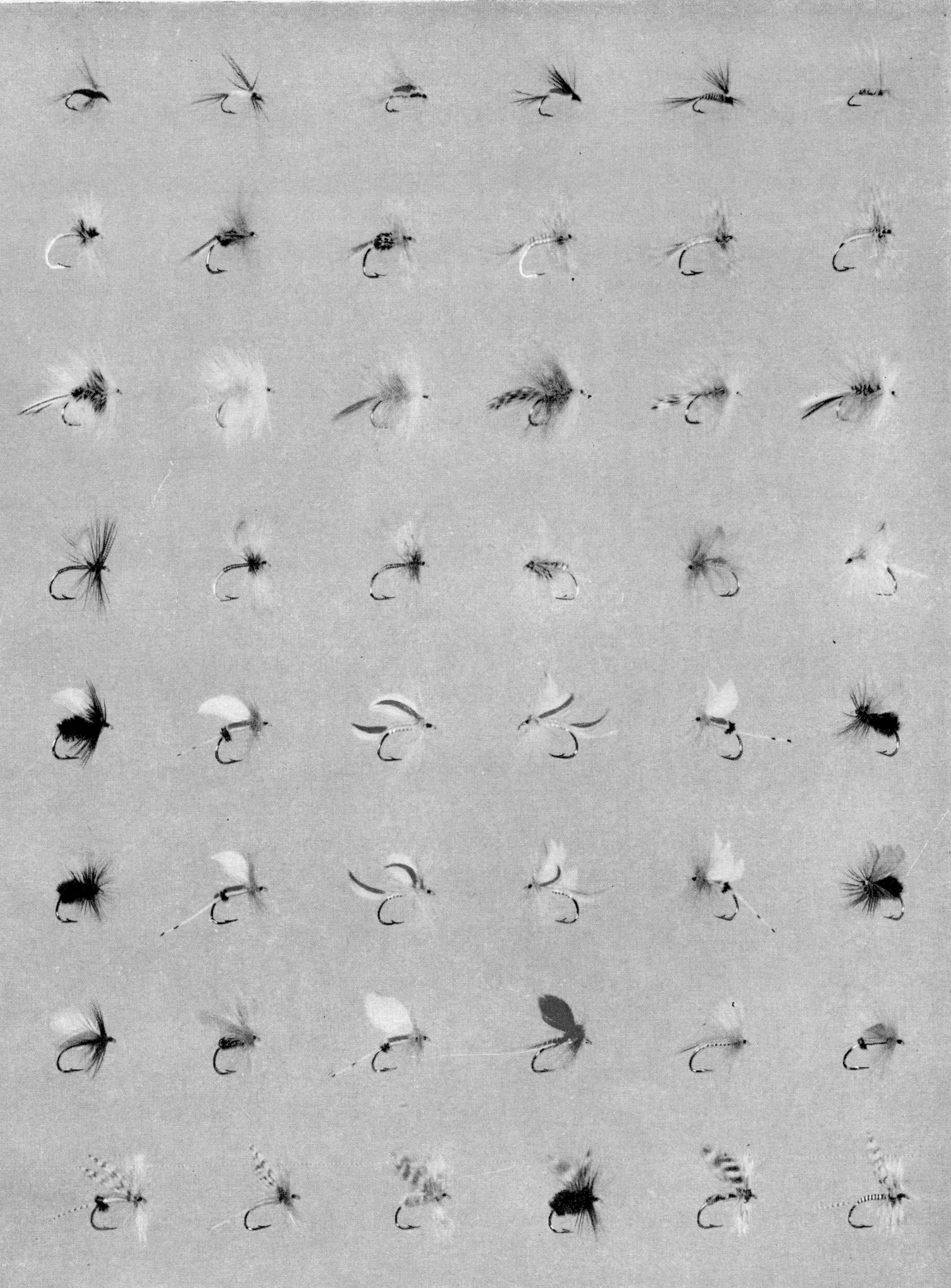

THE TWENTY-FOUR TROUT FLY PATTERNS MOST USED THROUGHOUT THE UNITED STATES

(Reading left to right)

First Row.

Royal Coachman, Grey Hackle, Grey Hackle Yellow, Black Gnat, Brown Hackle, Mosquito.

Second Row.

McGinty, Ginger Quill, Coachman, Cow Dung, Professor, Silver Doctor.

Third Row.

Queen of the Waters, Red Ant, Rio Grande King, Cahill, Western Bee, Parmachene Belle.

Fourth Row.

Montreal, Blue Quill, Blue Bottle, Jock Scott, Yellow May, Grizzly King.

FAVORITE FLIES USED IN THE THREE PRINCIPAL TROUT REGIONS

(Listed in the same relative order as the illustrations)

NORTHEASTERN		ROCKY MOUNTAINS		PACIFIC COAST	
Light Hendrickson	Dark Hendrickson	Pink Lady	Mormon Girl	Flying Caddis	Yellow Forktail
Gordon Quill	Olive Quill	Hell-grammite	Cut Throat	Dusty Miller	California Mosquito
Olive Dunn	Adams	Blue Upright	Orange Asher	California Coachman	Calif. Grey Hackle Yellow
Alexander	Governor	Trout Killer	Barber Pole	Captain	Brown Hackle Yellow

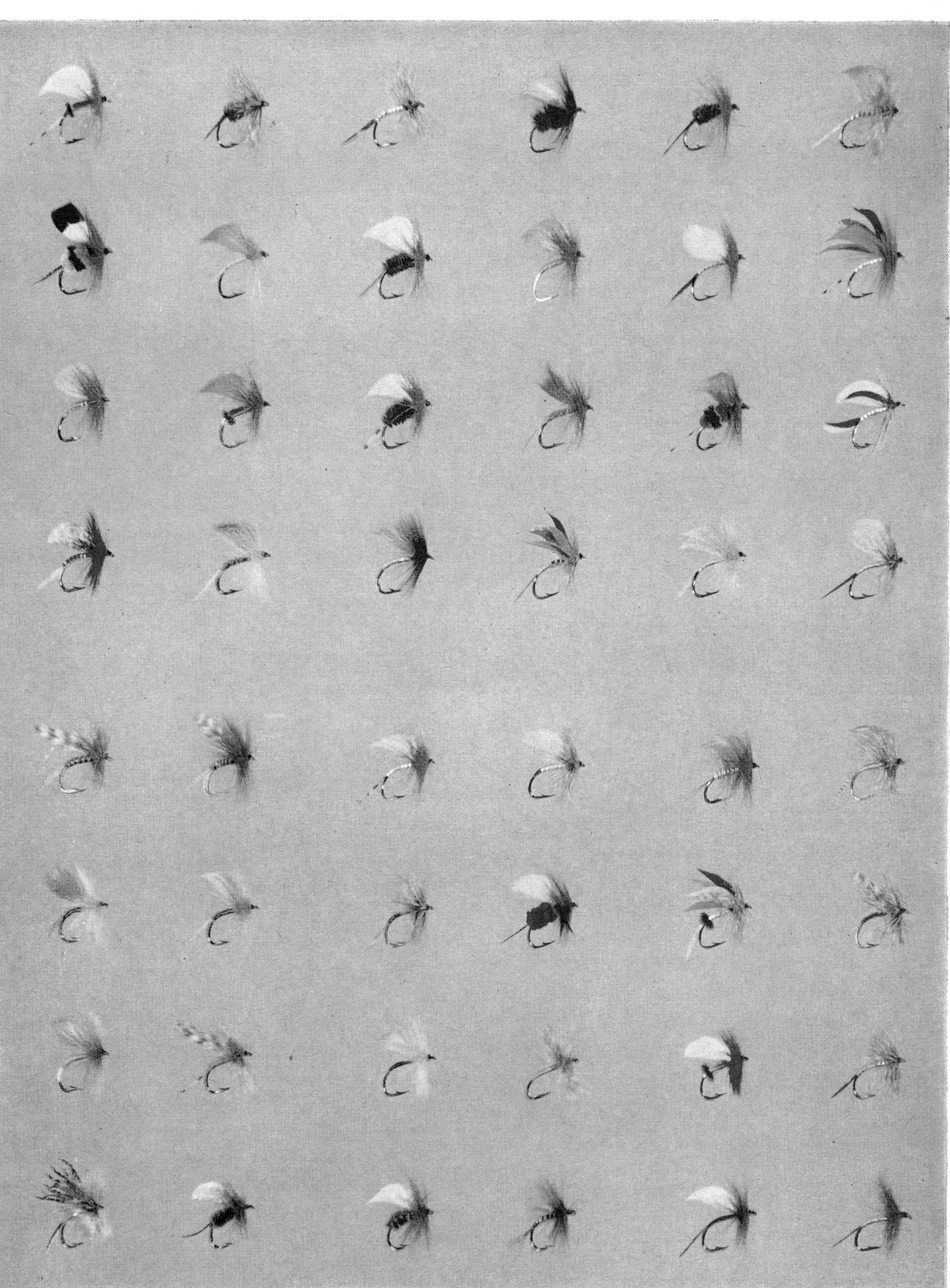

BUCKTAIL AND STREAMER FLIES

First Row

Left, Alaska Mary Ann Bucktail. Center, Ballou Special Streamer. Right, Blackbird Bucktail.

Second Row.

Left, Governor Aiken Bucktail. Right, Black Nose Dace Bucktail.

Third Row. (left to right)

Bonbright Streamer, Colonel Bates Streamer, Edson Dark Tiger Bucktail.

Fourth Row.

Edson Light Tiger Bucktail, Eight-ball Bucktail, Grey Squirrel Silver Streamer, Family Secret Streamer.

Fifth Row.

Black Ghost Streamer, Grey Ghost Streamer, Jane Craig Streamer.

BUCKTAIL AND STREAMER FLIES

(Reading left to right)

First Row.
Jesse Wood Streamer, Lady Doctor Bucktail, Mickey Finn Bucktail, Rose of New England Bucktail.

Second Row.
Nine-Three Streamer, Silver Garland Marabou Streamer, Sanborn Streamer.

Third Row.
Supervisor Streamer, Welch Rarebit Streamer.

Fourth Row.
Royal Coachman Streamer, Gordon Dean Beadhead Streamer, Shangs' Special Streamer.

Fifth Row.
Gibbs Striper Bucktail, Palmer Diller Bucktail, Chesapeake Bay Shad Fly.

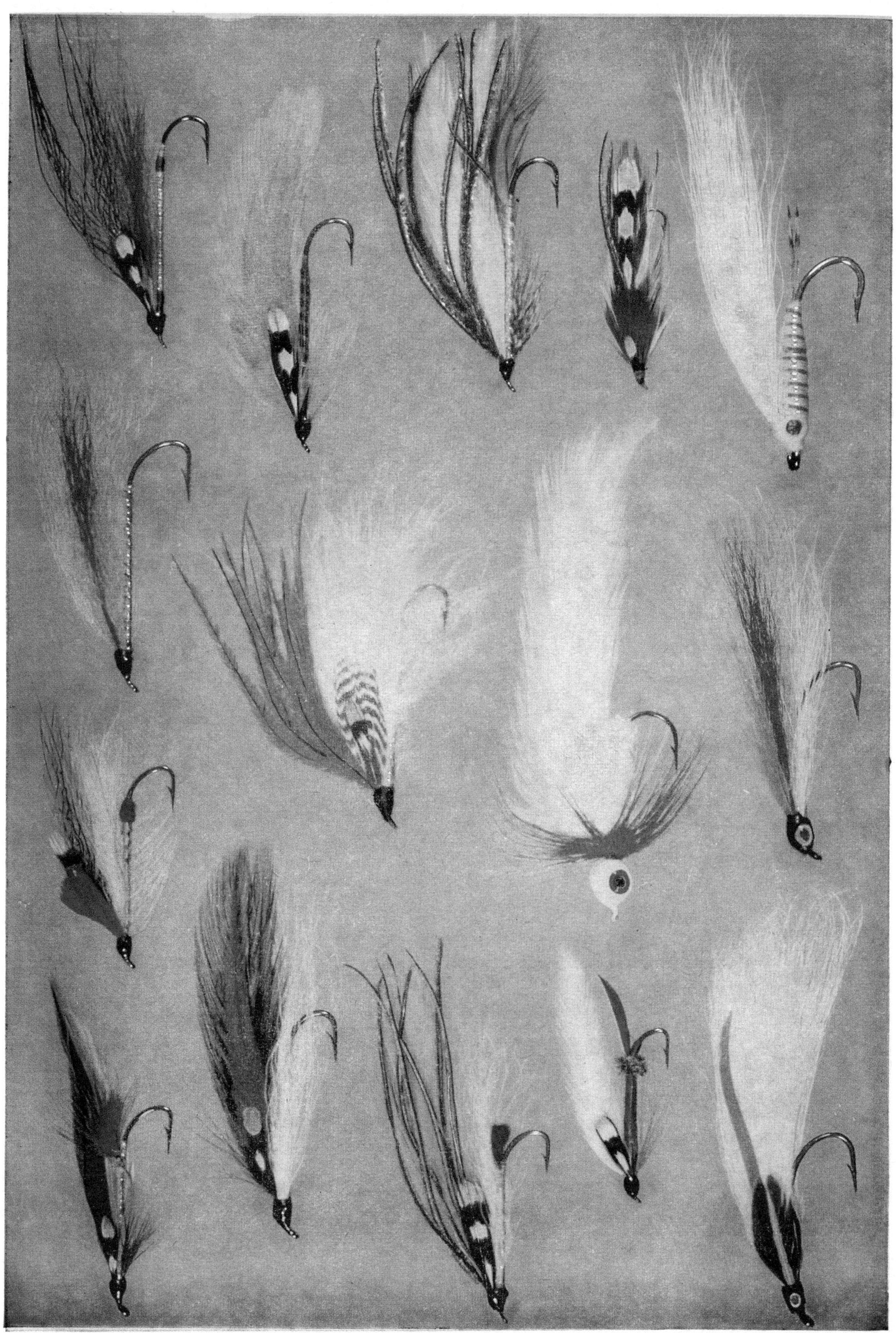

PLUG TYPE LURES

(Reading from left to right)

First Row.

Plugs with cavities in the head as planing surfaces: Pop-O-Lures, Wright & McGill; Walkie-Talkie, P&K; Lucky 13, Heddon; Swimming Mouse, Shakespeare.

Second Row.

Propeller-equipped plug: Nip-I-Didee, South Bend. Metal planing wings attached to head: Waddle Bug, Makinen.

Third Row.

Plugs with planing surfaces in head, surface action: Wizzard Wiggler, Pflueger; Chugger Spook, Heddon, Plugs with planing surfaces in head but also curved shape in body; Super Snooper, South Bend; Holi-Comet, Makinen; Bright Eyes, P&K.

Fourth Row.

Plugs with planing plates attached exterior to head; first two are Miracle Minnow (panfish size), Wright & McGill. Plug with planing plate recessed in head: Pal-O-Mine, Pflueger.

Fifth Row.

Various body shapes, sub-surface, planing surfaces attached exteriorly to head: Whopper-Stopper, Whopper-Stopper Co. (Actual "head" of lure in action is "tail."); Dive-Oreno, South Bend; Magic Minnow, Zeigler; Lil-Rascal, South Bend; Miracle Minnow, Wright & McGill.

Sixth Row.

Planing surfaces exterior, attached to head, underwater: Pumpkin Seed, Heddon; Fish-O-Bite, South Bend; Spook, Heddon; Go-Deeper River Runt, Heddon; Fish-O-Bite, South Bend.

Seventh Row.

Under-water, planing surfaces of flat metal in body: Trix-Orenos, South Bend.

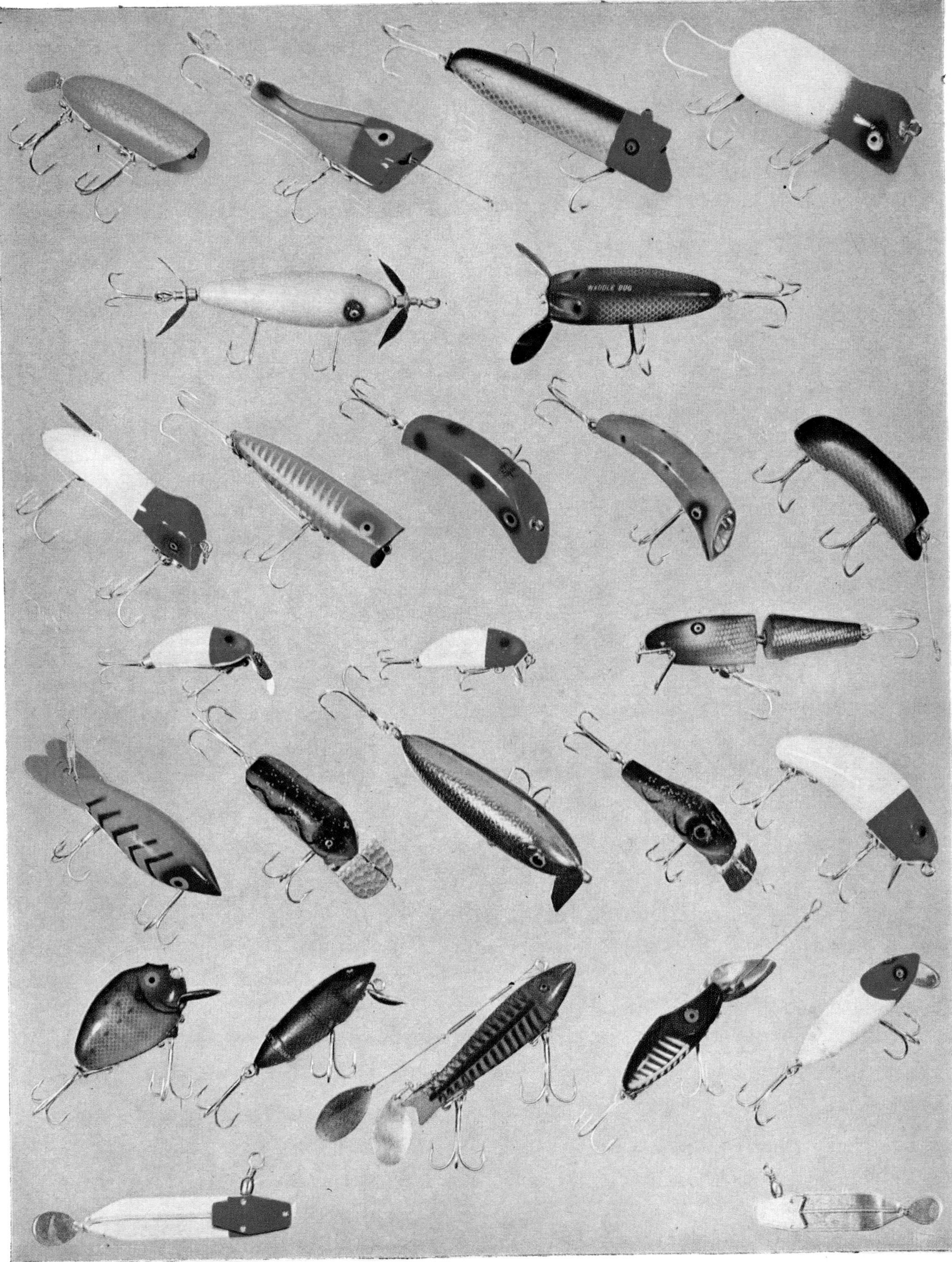
WADDLE BUG

TYPES OF SPOONS AND SPINNERS

First Row.

Symmetrical spoons showing different sizes and finishes, with fixed hook. All Johnson spoons.

Second Row.

Symmetrical spoons, hook stationary but removable: Sun Spot, South Bend; Record, Pflueger; Johnson; Chum, Pflueger.

Third Row.

First four are symmetrical spoons with free-swinging hooks, the last two unsymmetrical with free-swing hooks: Old Lob, Buel; K-B, Superior; Johnson (with bucktail added); Dardevle, Eppinger; Del Rey, Pflueger; Limper, Buel.

Fourth Row.

First spinner, blade and hooks attached by split ring: Colorado Spinner. Four spinners revolving around fixed shaft: Muskill, Pflueger; Willow Leaf Blade, Buel; Kidney-shape Blade, Buel; Fluted Blade, Pflueger.

Fifth Row.

Large and small "shoe-spoon" type of spoons, plus added "propeller" spinner at fore-end. Third one is Lucky Spinner (so-called June-bug), spinner blade is held at fixed angle to shaft by arm, Mille Lacs.

Sixth Row.

Propeller type of spinners. Tandem Spinner, Pflueger; Buel Spinner.

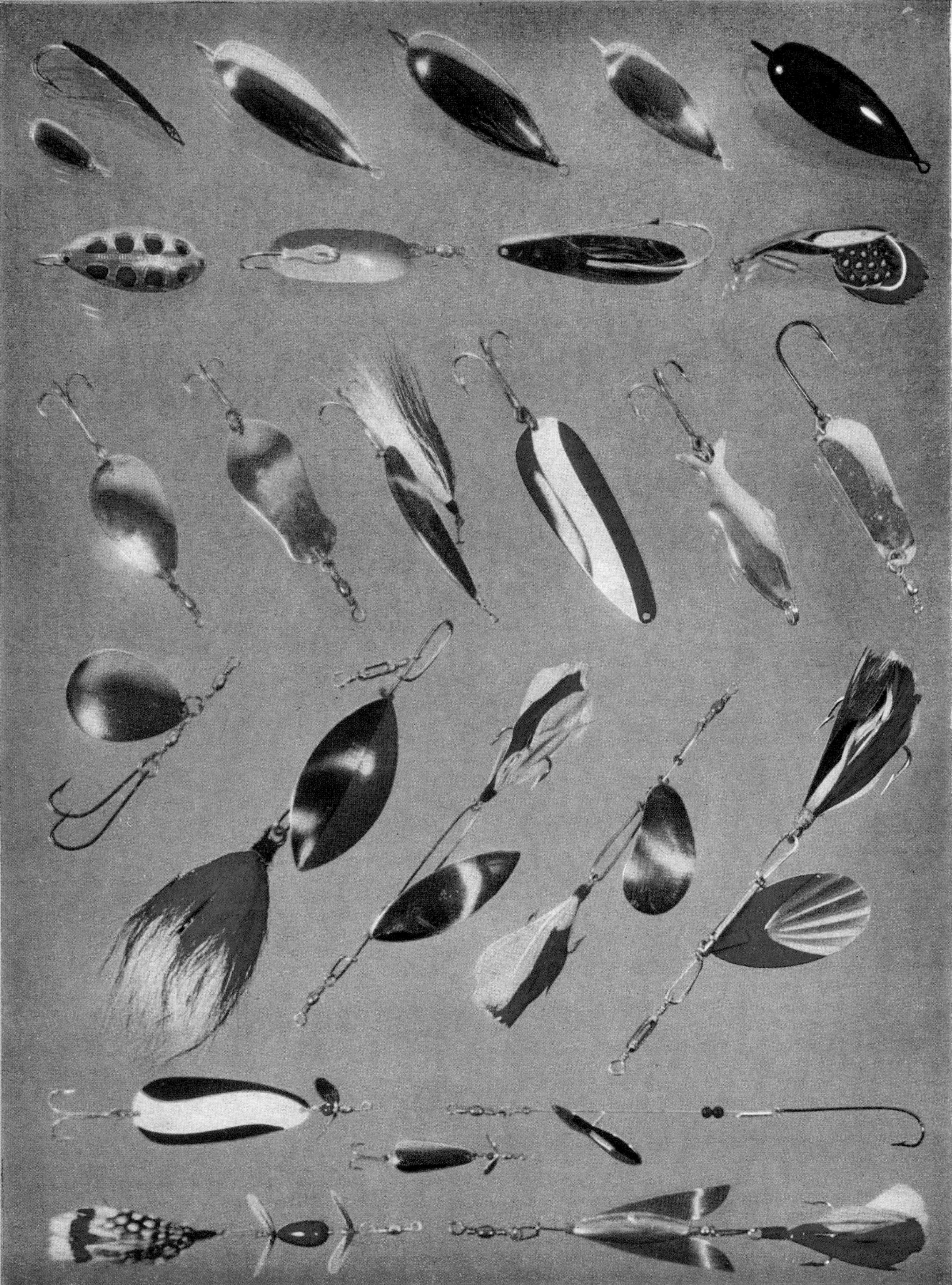

ODD LURES

(Reading left to right)

First Row.

Rubber composition imitations of natural bait: grasshoppers, worms and minnows, P&K.

Second Row.

Weezels, Weezel Bait Co.

Third Row.

Frog-Oreno, South Bend; Wonder Frog, P&K; Crayfish (an old pattern); Hellgrammite, P&K.

Fourth Row.

Swimming mouse, two sizes, P&K; hair mice, two color types, (maker unknown).

Fifth Row.

Tumblebug, two colors, P&K; Cork-bodied fly-rod "popper" bugs, Buel.

Sixth Row.

Series of South Bend Oreno "bass bugs"; Guinea, Yellow Sally, Mallard, White Miller, Golden, Black Gnat.

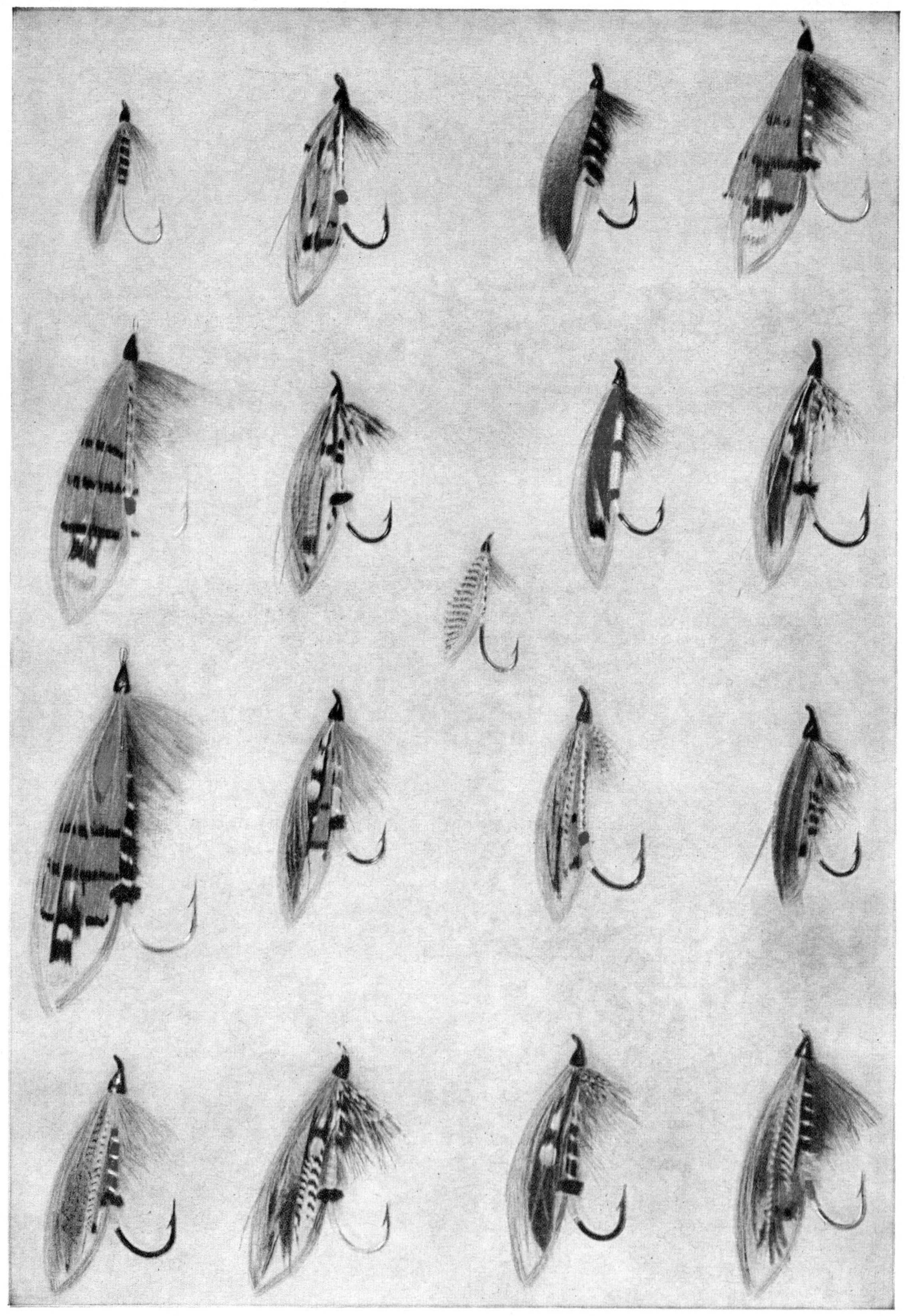

Reprinted by permission from "Fishing Flies and Fly Tying" by William F. Blades.

SALMON FLIES
Painting by Wm. F. Blades

SALMON FLIES

(Read top to bottom, left to right.)

No. 1 KATE

Tag: Silver tinsel, light yellow floss.
Tail: Topping.
Butt: Black herl.
Body: Two turns of crimson floss, remainder, crimson seal fur, palmered with crimson hackle; entire body ribbed with silver oval tinsel.
Throat: Yellow hackle.
Wings: Grey Mallard, tippet strands, Golden Pheasant tail, yellow, crimson and blue swan, brown Mallard; Golden Pheasant topping.
Shoulder: Jungle Cock.

No. 2 JOCK SCOTT

Tag: Silver twist; yellow floss.
Tail: Topping, and Indian Crow.
Butt: Black Ostrich herl.
Body: Two equal parts; No. 1, yellow floss; ribbing, silver twist; veil with Toucan breast feathers. No. 2, Ostrich herl butt black, black floss; ribbing, silver oval (larger than twist) palmered with black hackle.
Hackle: Guinea fowl.
Underwing: Two strips of black Turkey, white tipped, married strands of blue, yellow and red swan, Bustard, Florican and Golden Pheasant tail, two strands of Peacock sword, narrow strips of Teal and Wood Duck.
Wing: Brown Mallard, with Golden Pheasant topping.
Sides: Jungle Cock.
Cheeks: Blue Chatterer.
Horns: Blue and yellow Macaw.

No. 3 THUNDER AND LIGHTNING

Tag: Gold twist yellow floss.
Tail: Topping; Indian Crow.
Butt: Black herl.
Body: Black floss; ribbing, gold oval tinsel, palmered with orange hackle.
Hackle: Blue Jay.
Wings: Brown Mallard with topping.
Shoulders: Jungle Cock.
Horns: Blue and yellow Macaw.

No. 4 BLACK DOSE

Tag: Silver twist orange floss.
Tail: Topping; Teal; Ibis.
Body: Three turns of blue seal fur; remainder, black seal fur palmered with black hackle; ribbing, silver oval tinsel.
Throat: Claret hackle.
Wings: Two tippets veiled with Teal, light mottled Turkey, Golden Pheasant tail, Wood Duck, Peacock sword herl, Ibis, green Parrot, brown Mallard, Golden Pheasant topping.
Cheeks: Blue Chatterer.
Horns: Blue and yellow Macaw.

No. 5 BLACK RANGER

Tag: Silver tinsel yellow floss.
Tail: Topping, Indian Crow.
Butt: Black herl.
Body: Black fur; ribbing, silver tinsel.
Hackle: Black, palmered.
Throat: Light blue.
Wings: Four Golden Pheasant tippets doubled, two projecting Jungle Cock feathers between tippets, topping, Golden Pheasant.
Cheeks: Blue Chatterer.
Horns: Blue and yellow Macaw.
Head: Black

No. 6 GREEN HIGHLANDER

Tag: Silver twist canary floss.
Tail: Topping; Teal; Ibis.
Butt: Black herl.
Body: One third yellow floss; remainder green seal fur palmered with green hackle; rib entire body with silver oval tinsel.
Hackle: Yellow.
Wings: Two tippets veiled with Bustard, light and dark, Golden Pheasant tail, dark mottled Turkey, green Swan, brown Mallard; and topping.
Shoulders: Jungle Cock.
Horns: Blue and yellow Macaw.

No. 7 SILVER DOCTOR

Tag: Silver twist and yellow floss.
Tail: Topping, blue Chatterer.
Butt: Scarlet wool.
Body: Flat silver tinsel; ribbing, silver oval.
Hackle: Blue and Guinea fowl.
Underwing: Tippet, Summer Duck, Pintail, Golden Pheasant tail, yellow and blue Swan, Bustard.
Wing: Brown Mallard, and topping.
Horns: Blue and yellow Macaw.
Head: Scarlet and black.

No. 8 BUTCHER

Tag: Silver twist and yellow silk.
Tail: Topping, Teal and blue Macaw, optional.
Butt: Black herl.
Body: In four equal parts, first light red claret seal fur, light blue, dark red claret, and dark blue seal fur.
Ribbing: Silver tinsel.
Hackle: Natural black, palmered from light red claret seal fur.
Throat: Yellow hackle followed by guinea fowl.
Wings: Golden Pheasant red breast feathers and two tippets, sides small strips of Teal, Golden Pheasant tail, guinea fowl, Bustard, Peacock wing, Parrot, and yellow Swan; topped with two strips of brown Mallard.
Horns: Blue Macaw, Cheeks: Chatterer. Head: Black.

No. 9 DURHAM RANGER
(Silver)

Tag: Silver twist and yellow floss.
Tail: Topping; Indian Crow.
Butt: Scarlet wool or fur.
Body: Silver, ribbed with silver oval tinsel; last two thirds palmered with scarlet hackle.
Hackle: Scarlet.
Wings: Two large Jungle Cock, then two pairs of Golden Pheasant tippets, doubled.
Topping: Golden Pheasant crest.
Shoulders: Jungle Cock (optional).
Cheeks: Blue Chatterer.
Horns: Blue and yellow Macaw.

No. 10 MAR LODGE

Tag: Silver twist.
Tail: Topping and Jungle Cock.
Butt: Black herl.
Body: Three parts; flat silver, black floss, flat silver; ribbing, silver oval entire length.
Hackle: Guinea fowl.
Underwing: Yellow, red and blue Swan, Golden Pheasant tail, Peacock wing strips, Wood Duck, grey Mallard, dark mottled Turkey.
Wing: Brown Mallard and topping.
Shoulders: Jungle Cock.
Horns: Blue and yellow Macaw.

No. 11 RED SANDY

Tag: Silver twist.
Tail: Topping; Indian Crow.
Butt: Scarlet wool.
Body: Two parts; silver oval tinsel; centre butt, Indian Crow and scarlet wool; front half palmered with scarlet hackle.
Wings: Four Indian Crow feathers, doubled, over-lapping each other and enveloping two large Jungle Cock feathers.
Topping: Two Golden Pheasant crests.

No. 12 DUSTY MILLER

Tag: Silver twist and yellow floss.
Tail: Topping, Indian Crow.
Butt: Black herl.
Body: First two thirds; embossed silver tinsel. Balance, orange floss. Ribbing, silver oval tinsel entire length.
Hackle: Guinea fowl.
Wings: Two strips of dark white tipped Turkey; over these place married strands of Golden Pheasant tail, yellow, red and orange Swan, Florican, Bustard, Pintail, Wood Duck, brown Mallard.
Topping: Golden Pheasant.
Cheeks: Blue Chatterer.
Horns: Blue yellow Macaw.

No. 13 LOGIE

Tag and Ribbing: Silver tinsel.
Tail: Golden Pheasant crest.
Body: Claret floss.
Wings: Brown Mallard.
Cheeks: Jungle Cock.
Hackle: Silver Doctor blue.

No. 14 SILVER WILKINSON

Tag: Silver twist.
Tail: Topping and tippet fibres.
Butt: Scarlet wool or fur.
Body: Silver tinsel; ribbing silver oval.
Hackle: First, blue, then magenta.
Wings: Two Jungle Cock feathers, veiled with barred Wood Duck and red Swan; topping with small tippet over it.
Shoulders: Jungle Cock.
Cheeks: Blue Chatterer.
Horns: Blue and yellow Macaw.

No. 15 BLACK FAIRY

Tag: Gold Tinsel, yellow floss.
Tail: Topping.
Body: Black seal fur; ribbing, gold tinsel.
Throat: Black hackle.
Wings: Brown Mallard.
Head: Black.

No. 16 DURHAM RANGER

Tag: Silver twist and yellow floss.
Tail: Topping and Indian crow.
Butt: Ostrich herl, black.
Body: Two turns of orange floss, two turns of orange seal fur; the front half black seal fur.
Ribbing: Silver lace and tinsel.
Hackle: From orange fur, palmer with claret hackle.
Throat: Silver doctor blue hackle.
Wings: Two large Jungle Cock, then two pairs of Golden Pheasant tippets, doubled.
Topping: Golden Pheasant crest.
Cheeks: Blue Chatterer
Horns: Blue and yellow Macaw

No. 17 SILVER AND BLUE
Centre fly
(Low Water Salmon Fly)

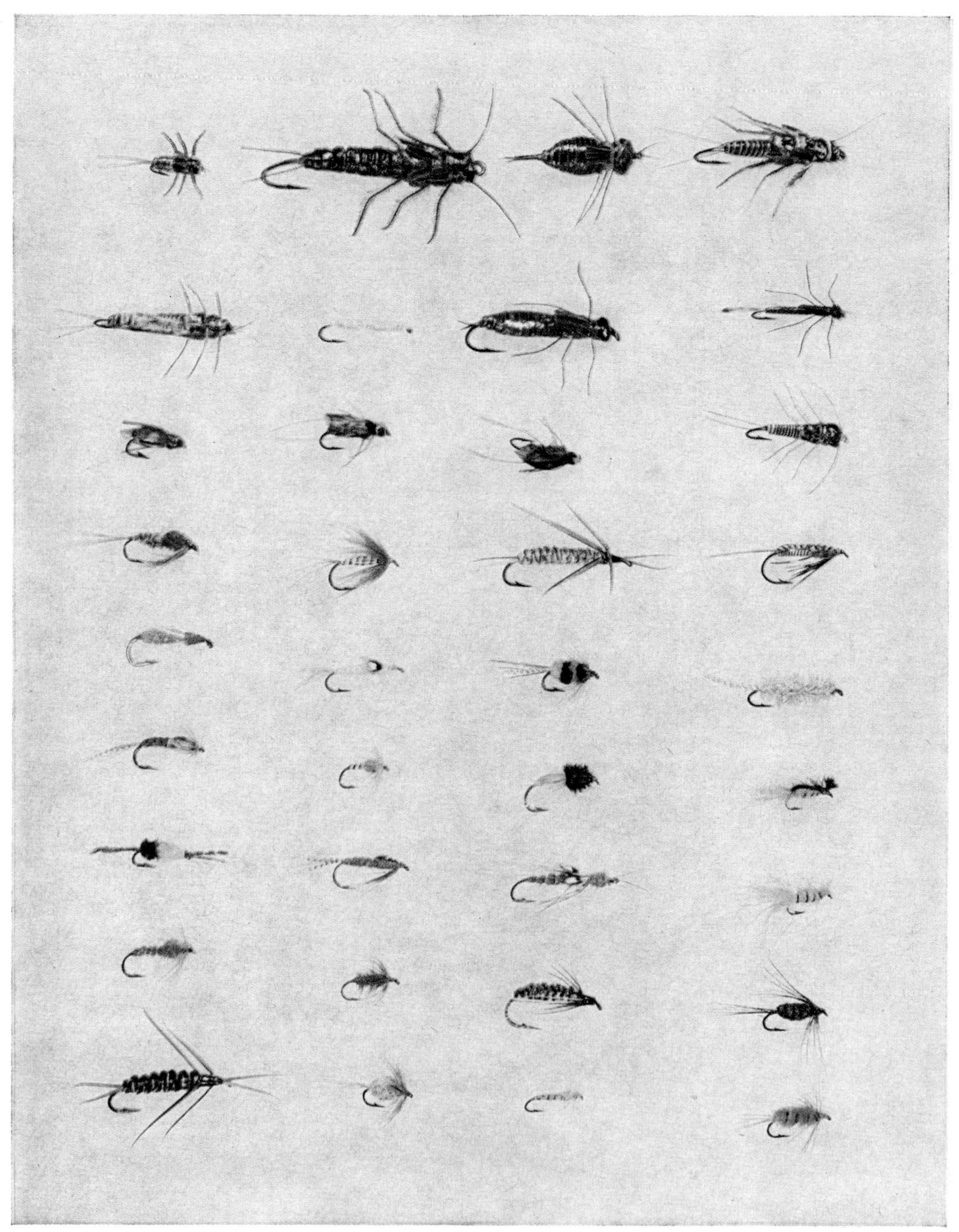

Reprinted by permission from "Fishing Flies and Fly Tying" by William F. Blades.

NYMPHS.

SELECTED NYMPH PATTERNS

No. 1
BLADES' MAY FLY NYMPH
STENONEMA FUSCUM

Tails: Three trimmed brown hackle stems.
Body and Thorax: Tan raffia; ribbing brown raffia. Under body moulded plastic.
Wing cases: Two Turkey wing quill fibres dyed tan.
Legs and antennae: Trimmed brown hackle stems, legs marked with dark brown enamel.

No. 2 May Fly Nymph Hexagenia

No. 3 Back Swimmer Nymph No. 1

No. 4
BLADES HACKLE NYMPH

Tail: Brown hackle fibres.
Body: Yellow and brown hackle clipped to shape; thorax, orange hackle clipped to shape; crown, grey goose quill fibres.
Hackle: Blue dun on throat only.

No. 5 CADDIES NYMPH

Body: Light grey wool; silver tinsel
Legs: Six white fibres from goose wing outer feather, sharpened on both ends.

No. 6 CARROT NYMPH

Tail: Wood Duck or Mallard.
Body and thorax: Orange seal fur or wool saturated and flattened.
Ribbing: Gold tinsel.
Crown: Red floss (stiffen with cement).
Hackle: Badger hen, two or three turns.

No. 7 CADDIS GRUB NYMPH

Tail and horns: Peacock sword strands.
Body: Black and white chenille.

No. 8 DARK OLIVE NYMPH

Tail: Blue dun hackle fibres.
Body: Olive seal fur mixed with brown bear, heavy at the thorax.
Ribbing: Fine gold tinsel.
Hackle: Pale blue dun.
Crown: Purple floss.

No. 9 DARK MOSSBACK
(Dan Bailey)

Tail: Feelers, and antennae are from the Turkey wing feather, dyed brown.
Body: Pale yellow floss under body, over this is a woven horsehair body with brown and green on top and brown and yellow on the underside.

No. 10 Large Stone Fly Nymph

No. 11 May Fly Nymph
Ephemera guttalata

No. 12 Back Swimmer Nymph No. 2

No. 13
DRIFTING MAY FLY NYMPH

Tail: Pheasant tail fibres.
Body: Pale yellow floss; ribbing, silver tinsel.
Hackle: Olive hen.

No. 14 GREEN DRAKE
(C. M. Wetzel)

Tail: Honey dun, very small tips.
Body: White fur, picked out for legs.
Wing cases: Jungle Cock.
Hackle: Pale honey dun.

No. 15 HALF STONE NYMPH

Body: Primrose silk; ribbing, gold tinsel.
Thorax: Mole fur, grey.
Hackle: Blue dun hen, two or three turns.

No. 16
HENDRICKSON NYMPH
(Art Flick)

Tail: Mandarin flank feather.
Body: Fur dubbing a greyish brown shade, made from grey fox belly fur, beaver, and claret seal.
Ribbing: Fine gold wire.
Wing case: Blue heron wing section.
Legs: Partridge hackle.

No. 17 IRON BLUE NYMPH

Tail: Soft white hackle fibres tied short.
Body: Mole fur spun on crimson silk, expose a few turns of silk at the tail.
Hackle: Two or three turns of blue dun hen, or Jackdaw throat hackle, short.

No. 18 IRRESISTIBLE

Tail: Brown deer tail.
Body: Grey deer body hair.
Hackle: Soft grizzly.

No. 19 DRAGON FLY NYMPH

No. 20 DRAGON FLY NYMPH
Nasiaesehna

No. 21 BACK SWIMMER No. 3
Ready for flight

No. 22 LIGHT MOSSBACK
(Dan Bailey)

Tail: Feelers and antennae are from the turkey wing feather, dyed brown.
Body: Cream floss under body, over this is a woven horsehair body with brown and pale green on top and white on the underside.

No. 23 MCGINTY NYMPH

Tail: Mallard and red hackle fibres.
Body: Yellow and black chenille.
Hackle: Brown.

No. 24 MIKE

Body: Yellow floss.
Legs: White polar bear.
Thorax: Peacock herl.

No. 25
MIDGET BUCKTAIL NYMPH

Tail: Antennae and throat hackle; fibres from the Partridge body feather, grey mottled, brown tipped.
Body: Brown mink fur dubbing; ribbing, Peacock quill.
Wings: Brown bucktail (about 15 hairs). Small Jungle Cock at thorax.

No. 26 MOSSY CREEPER
(Dan Bailey)

Body: Cream floss under body, over this is a woven horsehair body with dark green on top and white on the underside.
Hackle: Badger hair.

No. 27 OLIVE NYMPH

Tail: Blue dun hackle fibres.
Body: Olive seal fur; ribbing, flat gold tinsel.
Thorax: Olive seal fur; crown, orange floss.
Hackle: Honey Badger.

No. 28 STONE FLY NYMPH

No. 29 DAMSEL FLY NYMPH

No. 30 SMALL STONE FLY NYMPH

No. 31
STONE FLY CREEPER
(Art Flick)

Tail: Two strands from cock pheasant tail, half inch long.
Body: Large ginger cocks hackle stem.
Thorax: Seal fur dyed amber.
Wing case: Wide barred flank feather from Mandarin drake, tied flat extending full length of body.
Legs: Grouse hackle.

No. 32 STRAWMAN NYMPH
(Paul H. Young)

Tail: Barred grey Mallard.
Body: Grey deer body hair, clipped.
Ribbing: Yellow floss.

No. 33
YELLOW AND BLACK MARABOU NYMPH

Tail: Yellow marabou.
Body: Yellow marabou over soft copper wire, black marabou on back.
Ribbing: Soft maroon colored enameled copper wire.

No. 34
YELLOW MARABOU NYMPH

Tail: Yellow marabou.
Ribbing: Soft maroon colored enameled copper wire.
Body: Yellow marabou over copper wire.

No. 35
WEIGHTED ORANGE NYMPH

Tail and hackle: Black.
Body: Orange seal fur, saturated with liquid cement and flattened.
Back: Black enamel.
Ribbing: Soft copper wire.

No. 36
WEIGHTED YELLOW NYMPH

Tail and hackle: Orange.
Body: Yellow chenille.
Ribbing: Dark enameled soft copper wire.

Reprinted by permission from "Fishing Flies and Fly Tying" by William F. Blades.

HACKLES FOR FLY TYING.

HACKLES

(Read left to right and top to bottom.)

1. NATURAL RED: This is a brown or reddish brown.
2. FIERY BROWN: A shade of fiery mahogany.
3. COACHMAN BROWN: A dark, flat brown.
4. LIGHT GINGER: This is a pale tan shade.
5. DARK GINGER: Same as above, only a darker shade.
6. BADGER: This has creamy white fibres, with a natural black center marking.
7. YELLOW BADGER: These fibres are a yellow ginger, or pale gold color with a natural black center marking.
8. GRIZZLY: This is a pure-bred Plymouth Rock chicken, and the markings are barred black and white.
9. BLUE DUN: This is a light blue dun dyed hackle, which is pale grey and hard to procure in the natural feather in dry fly quality.
10. BLUE DUN: Natural hackle which is a little darker.
11. IRON BLUE DUN: This a similar hackle, much darker, and blue grey in color.
12. CHINCHILLA: Marked the same as the Plymouth Rock, only in dun grey and white.
13. FURNACE: This is a brown hackle with a black center marking.
14. COCHY-BONDHU: This hackle is a furnace brown with black on the edge of the fibres, and has a black center marking.
15. HONEY DUN: Pale honey color with brown or brownish grey center markings, which can be broken or solid.
16. FIERY VARIANT: Fiery brown hackle with cream and grey markings.
17. MULTI-VARIANT: This hackle is barred in dark and light grey, ginger to fiery brown; in other words, a mixture of many colors.
18. GINGER VARIANT: This hackle is ginger, barred similar to the Plymouth Rock with cream and tan markings.
19. NAROBI: Brown with white tips, and also black with white tips. White hackles are found on the same neck.
20. FURNACE HEN HACKLE: Brown hackle with black center. These are very soft feathers used for wet flies and nymphs.
21. ENGLISH GROUSE: Soft hackle for wet flies; the colors are dark grey, tan and brown, mottled.
22. BLUE DUN HEN: Soft, for wet flies.
23. GREY PARTRIDGE: Breast feather for wet flies. Grey with black markings; also grey with brown markings. Used on March Browns and Sedges.
24. BROWN SPADE: Excellent for spider and variant flies.
25. BADGER HEN: For wet flies. White on tips, dark center markings.
26. ENGLISH BLUEJAY: Used on several English salmon flies.
27. BADGER SADDLE HACKLE: White to cream sides, with black center.

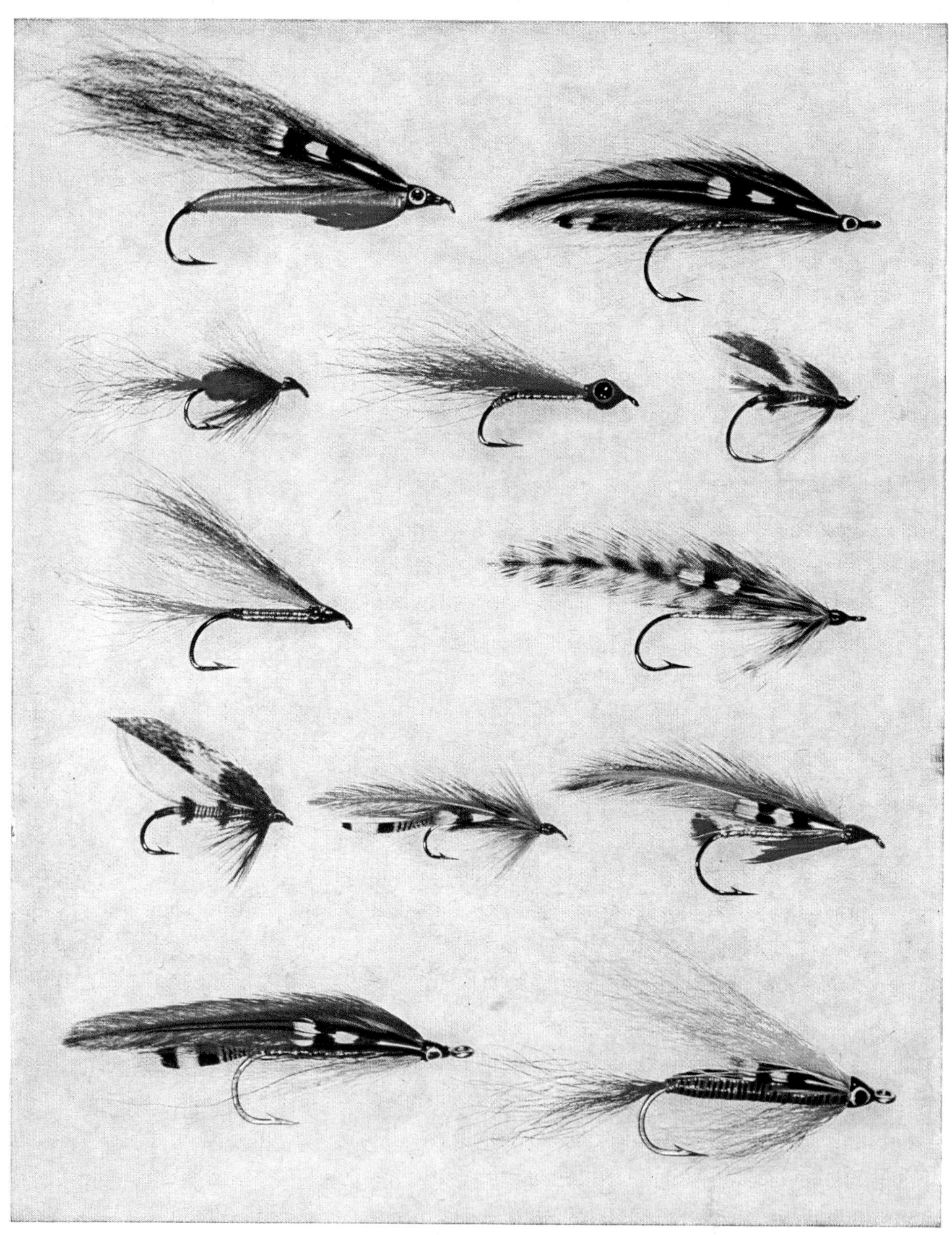

Reprinted by permission from "Fishing Flies and Fly Tying" by William F. Blades.

STREAMER AND STEELHEAD FLIES.

semble a fish. Instead, they often are taken for another of the reasons given above. Their normally distinctive long shape and the fact that they usually are successful because they resemble a fish does, however, put them in a separate category. Eastern streamer flies and bucktails follow this line of demarcation more closely than do Canadian streamer flies and Western bucktails, both of which are somewhat shorter types.

Sometimes the words "streamer flies" and "bucktails" are used synonymously and occasionally their meanings are interchanged. In recent years these two related types have been given distinctive sub-definitions. Streamer flies have feathered wings while bucktails have wings of hair or fur which may be and usually is the hair or fur from some animal other than a deer. Although bucktails may have a topping of herl, such as peacock or ostrich, they have predominantly hair wings. Although streamer flies may have an underwing of hair or fur, their predominantly feathered wing (usually of two or more complete hackle tips) distinguishes them.

THE MAINE STREAMER FLY

Although this type of fly was not conceived in Maine, as is sometimes supposed, it did obtain a large amount of its impetus, development and renown in that state. Eminent anglers, such as Herbert L. Welch, who originated the Black Ghost, Jane Craig, and Welch Rarebit; and Joseph S. Stickney who developed the Supervisor, Lady Doctor, and Warden's Worry—learned that the new "long flies" frequently were more successful than the usual wet fly patterns, dry flies, or even live bait. Sportsmen visiting the teeming trout, bass, and Landlocked Salmon waters of Maine were quick to see the advantages of the new patterns; to try them in their own waters, and to send back to the fly dressers of Maine for more.

The fly dressers soon learned that, while simple bucktails and plainly dressed streamers invariably caught as many fish as did the more ornate patterns, the angler usually preferred the elaborateness of the fancy flies to the relative drabness and the economy of the simpler ones. Mrs. Carrie G. Stevens, who originated the nationally famous Grey Ghost and who was one of the earliest and best of Maine's streamer fly dressers, would say that her beautiful creation would catch just as many fish if it possessed only half of its wide variety of feathers. But she would be quick to add that the fishermen would not like it half as well.

Realizing the desire for variety and elaboration in streamers, the fly dressers gave the angling public what it wanted. Famous Scotch salmon patterns were adapted to the streamer type by Gardner Percy, long the dean of Maine fly tyers, and by Bert Quimby, generally considered to be the runner-up in quantity and quality of his state's streamer fly production.

Independent of the stimulus given to the streamer fly and bucktail in Maine, and often influenced by it, this new type was developed by other anglers and fly tyers in far-flung places. New patterns both good and bad, sprang up as rapidly as dandelion blossoms on a lawn in Spring. Today, if the inconsequential ones are disregarded there would still be about three hundred productive streamers and bucktails, or important variations of them, worthy of note.

At this time, the streamer fly surpasses the bucktail in popularity in Canada. The use of the two types is about equal in the eastern United States, but the bucktail is vastly more acceptable in the West. Nearly all western Steelhead flies

Weber Lifelike Fly Co.

Streamer Fly.

are dressed with bucktail wings; dressed more fully and somewhat shorter than their eastern counterparts. This may partly be due to the feeling of confidence of western anglers in their flies and partly for the reason that the western method of dressing bucktails has proven successful; their shorter wings offer less wind resistance, allowing them to be cast greater distances across the wide and deep western rivers. Be that as it may, eastern fishermen who have used Grey Ghosts, Black Ghosts, Mickey Finns, and Edson Tigers in western lakes and rivers affirm that they are equally as productive as the western varieties and that they will catch fish consistently anywhere. An example of this is the Ballou Special, a white marabou streamer with a bit of peacock herl and a few additional frills, originated by A. W. Ballou of Litchfield, Maine. This fly is not unlike the equally famous series of Silver Garland Marabou streamers originated and popularized by E. H. Rosborough, the well known fly dresser of Chiloquin, Oregon, for western use. From Maine to Oregon and from the Canadian northwoods to the Florida keys, streamer flies and bucktails have reached prominence at least equal to artificial flies of other types.

SIZE AND COLOR SELECTION

When one remembers that there are more than three hundred locally or nationally well-known patterns from which to choose, it is obvious that the novice streamer or bucktail fisherman may have difficulty in making wise selections unless he depends almost wholly upon the experience of local anglers. There are certain basic rules which may make this selection easier. The first is to imitate as closely as is possible in size, shape, and color the food-fish which are in the water to be fished and upon which the larger fish usually feed. In Maine, for example, Trout and Landlocked Salmon use the Smelt for a large part of their diet particularly when the spawning runs of Smelt are in force in spring. Since the Smelt is a relatively large food fish, the fly used is in the larger sizes also, normally dressed on a number two, four or six long-shanked hook. Among the well known streamers dressed to imitate the Smelt are the Supervisor, Grey Ghost, Black Ghost, Jane Craig, Ballon Special and the Nine-Three. One of these flies is almost sure to account for a maximum number of large fish, if it is manipulated in a proper imitation of the swimming of a Smelt. The brighter colored of these flies are preferred when the water is turbid or when the sky is overcast. The darker ones are for clear water and bright days. On some occasions when fish are feeding actively they may strike at almost any fly, streamer, bucktail or otherwise. On other occasions greater care must be used in the selection of the fly and in the method by which it is fished.

The minnows and other bait fish vary widely in size and in coloration. Some of them have a pronounced dark stripe down their sides. When these food-fish are in the water, a fly of the Black Nosed Dace or Mickey Finn type may be preferable to any other because this type of fly also has a pronounced stripe. In other waters the minnows may have a dark back and light belly but no pronounced side stripe. Here, it is possible that a fly such as the Edson Light or Dark Tiger may be the one to use. Clear waters or places where the food-fish normally are very small may call for streamers or bucktails in the smaller sizes. Other waters and conditions may require something larger. Although these few general rules may be of help, a bit of experimentation often is advantageous. When the practice of natural imitation fails, an entirely different approach to the method of fly selection may be needed. When a fish is hungry he may strike at a wide variety of flies and particularly at flies which imitate the food-fish for which he is searching. When he is not hungry, he often may be made to strike at a fly because the fly makes him angry or excites his curiosity. He may also strike at it in a spirit of play. This explains why fish strike at flies which are so colorful and garish in design that they in no way resemble a food fish in color, even if they do so in shape.

When flies are selected with these purposes in mind, they usually are extraordinarily bright and colorful, such as the Lady Doctor (originally tied in small sizes to imitate a bee) or the Bonbright (often called in Maine the Dana or the Ross McKenney). The method of fishing them under such circumstances often may be far from orthodox. Frequently they will excite a fish's curiosity and anger, or coax him to a spirit of play, when they are slapped down on the water and fished in as erratic a manner as is possible.

ANGLING METHODS

The proper manipulation of the streamer fly often calls for angling methods somewhat different from those used in fishing with other wet flies or dry flies. Since the streamer or bucktail is made to imitate a food fish, it usually should be fished in a manner as similar to the swimming of a food-fish as is possible. In learning this method it will pay the novice to sit beside a quiet pool and to watch the behavior of the minnows in it. They will drift about or move forward a few inches at a time with a short, jerky motion when they are undisturbed. If a pebble is thrown among them, they will dart away with quick, spasmodic haste.

In fishing a stream it is normal to fish the streamer fly across the current and to allow the force of the water to give it what motion is necessary. When the fly has reached a position downstream from the angler the flow of the current beside the tight line will work the fly with a quivering motion, closely approximating the behavior of a minnow when he starts to combat the current after drifting with it for a time. At this moment, just before the fly is retrieved, most of the strikes will occur, either on eastern or western rivers. Therefore, at this point the fly should be allowed to pause and work in the current for a few moments. Following this the fisherman may elect to retrieve it in short spasmodic jerks, occasionally allowing it to drift back and sink deeper in the current before regaining it and starting a new cast.

When streams are turbulent, it often is difficult to get the streamer fly down to the fish, which may be feeding deep in runs and glides behind rocks and other obstructions. One method is to cast the fly quartering upstream so that the relatively slack line thus obtained will sink it to a greater depth than if it were cast directly across the current. Another method, when fish and game laws permit it, is to weight the fly. This can be done by adding one or two BB shot to the leader immediately above the fly. It also can be done by winding the hook with lead or copper wire before body dressing is applied. Many western Steelhead bucktails, notably those patterns originated by the famous angler Peter J. Schwab, are dressed in this latter manner.

When streamers or bucktails are used in the quiet water of lakes or pools, it is necessary to put them in motion immediately upon their touching the water, and to keep them in motion until the cast is fished out. The method of their retrieve may be varied between a slow, jerky recovery obtained by slowly recovering line while the rod tip is twitched and a faster spasmodic retrieve occasioned by a more pronounced raising and lowering of the rod tip while line is stripped in at the same time. When fishing from a slowly moving boat, the fly should be cast to the shore line (often as close to it as possible) and to tree stumps or other obstructions and rocks which shelve off steeply.

TROLLING WITH STREAMERS

Ultra-long streamer or bucktail flies, frequently dressed on tandem hooks, often are used for trolling. This method is successful throughout the country, whether it be for trout and Landlocked Salmon in Maine or for Silver Salmon in the Pacific Northwest. If one rod is used (heavy fly rods normally are employed) about forty feet of line is let out so that the fly will troll not far behind the wake of the boat. As many as three rods can be used from a single boat. In this case, the two outboard rods are trolled with about sixty feet of line out and one of the flies usually is weighted to make it ride deeper than the other. The inboard rod is trolled with just enough line to keep the fly beyond the wash of the boat. Many anglers prefer to have the inboard fly troll directly in the wash of the boat on the theory that fish are attracted by it. When a fish comes to the inboard fly but does not take it, it is possible that he may take one of the two outboard flies as they pass by. Normal practice is to run the boat fairly fast; at the fastest possible rowing speed or, if a motor is used, about as fast as a man can run. Unless there be reasons to the contrary, it usually is most advantageous to closely skirt the shoreline, taking in all the bays and coves and passing as closely around points of land as is possible.

SIMPLE BUCKTAILS AND STREAMERS

It has been noted that the elaborateness of a bucktail or streamer fly is not necessarily an index of its ability to take fish. Simple bucktail patterns are successful in all waters wherein there

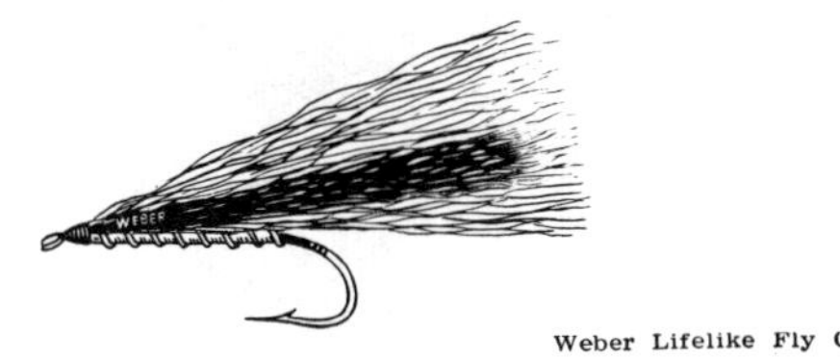

Weber Lifelike Fly Co.

Bucktail Fly.

are game-fish throughout the North American continent. Basically, these simple bucktails are made in all sizes with long-shanked hooks wound with silver or gold tinsel or perhaps with peacock herl or chenille. Wings are of one or more colors of natural or dyed bucktail, polar bear, squirrel, or other hair or fur and should be only slightly longer than the hook. The wings may be in plain colors of white, yellow, brown, or black. Preferably, they are in two or more colors, usually with the darker color uppermost (or in the case of triple color patterns with the darker color in the middle). Some of the favorite patterns are: brown over white, yellow over white, red over white, green over white, black over white, red over yellow, brown over yellow, black over yellow, black over brown.

These simple patterns may be embellished to any extent desired by the angler. A few strands of peacock herl as a topping often add to the effectiveness of the fly. Jungle cock cheeks are considered to contribute an added fifty percent to its effectiveness. A ribbing over the metal tinsel body adds to its glint in the water. A tail or tag of red, yellow, or some other color may be added and so may a throat of hackle fibres. Eastern bucktails normally are dressed rather sparsely, while those used in the West are haired more fully, frequently with the wing raised to an angle of about forty-five degrees. Four saddle hackle tips may be substituted for the hair, thus converting the bucktail to a streamer. The outer two hackles may be of a different color than the inner two and plain or dyed barred or furnace hackles or other variations may be used. A few strands of hair may be placed under the wing if desired, and, for really fancy flies, shoulders, toppings, horns, tags and butts may be included.

SALT WATER STREAMERS

Recent years have seen a pronounced and most successful practice of fly fishing with streamer flies and bucktails for salt water game fish. Bonefish, small Tarpon, Channel Bass, Spotted Weakfish, Ladyfish and many other species are taken successfully by this method in southern waters; and Bluefish, Mackerel, Striped Bass, Weakfish and other varieties now are sought by the fly fisherman in the North. Both streamer flies and bucktails are used for this purpose, either dressed in the orthodox manner as single wing flies or dressed as divided wing patterns so that the hair or feathers splay out to form a "V". This makes the wing open and close in the water, a motion considered by many well known anglers to be of added value in taking fish.

Streamer flies and bucktails for salt water fishing normally are in combinations of colors of white, yellow, or red—such as the Bonbright (when dressed on salt water hooks) or the Gordon Dean Bead Head patterns originated by Gordon Dean of Miami, Florida. These streamers usually are dressed on silver or chenille bodies with extra long saddle hackles and occasionally with hackles of a different color tied on as a collar. Flies in these same colors of dyed Plymouth Rock hackles often are used, especially for Bonefish. Northern streamers are normally of conventional length and are more often of the bucktail type, such as the Gibbs Striper and the Palmer Diller, which are favorites for Striped Bass. In this type of fishing sturdy nine, or nine and a half foot rods are most popular with large reels equipped with torpedo tapered lines and one hundred and fifty yards or more of backing.

SEASONAL ADVANTAGES

Since streamer flies and bucktails imitate food-fish rather than insects or nymphs they normally are more attractive to larger fish than are the smaller flies because, as fish grow larger, they depend more and more on a diet of food-fish for their subsistence. These two types of flies are used almost exclusively in salt water fly fishing since other food taken by salt water fish, such as shrimps and bottom feed, can not be imitated with hair or feathers as successfully. Streamers and bucktails in inland waters are more productive than other artificial flies in the early Spring because at that time insect life in many northern waters has not begun to hatch, thus causing the gamefish to depend either on minnows or bottom feed for their livelihood.

The development of the streamer fly and the bucktail has long since passed through the experimental stages. Patterns of this type now have become as well established as the famous wet and dry fly standards created in earlier years. With the perfection of this relatively new type of fly, torpedo taper fly lines and longer, stiffer streamer fly rods have been developed in order to cast it more advantageously. Today the streamer fly and the bucktail offer angling advantages unduplicated by any other lures obtainable for fly fishing. As such, they are now considered indispensable in the equipment of every versatile angler.

When it comes to named patterns in the various types of flies, there is an indefinite array. Some will be tied only in one of the construction types listed above, while many other names will be listed in several types. A popular pattern such as the Royal Coachman will be tied in upright wing, fan wing, spent wing, salmon flies, bass flies, and other types. It will be "tied dry" and "tied wet."

Every angler has his preferred selection of patterns in the types he uses. The more ardent devotees will carry unnamed flies of their own invention, or that of a friend or one particular fly dresser, or one that is locally noted for its fish taking qualities. Others will prefer flies of longstanding use. As a basic check list, without trying to differentiate between different types of flies, the following are patterns most purchased across the country. This does not mean that they are the best in any locality or even country-wide; merely that they stand in the upper brackets in numbers used.

Grey Hackle, in peacock, yellow and red body
Royal Coachman
Coachman
Black Gnat, male and female
Brown Hackle
Mosquito
McGinty
Professor
Cowdung
Queen of the Waters
Parmachene Belle
Cahil
Silver Doctor
Grizzly King
Montreal
White Miller
March Brown
Wickham's Fancy
Blue Quill
Pink Lady
Red Ant

FLIES FOR FISHES OTHER THAN TROUT

Fishing with artificial flies is not used exclusive for trout. There are instances of Whitefish, Walleyes and even some of the pikes rising to flies. The most common fly fishing besides that of trout is for bass, salmon and the panfishes. While Steelheads definitely are trout, a different series of flies, somewhat differently constructed than commonly used for other trout species are made for catching these fellows.

STEELHEAD FLIES

Many of the standard trout patterns may be tied as flies for Steelheads. The typical Steelhead fly, however, is tied with an upright wing, the wing feather usually a darker tone, plus a small, supplementary wing feather and a palmered body. Since the Steelhead generally is a much larger fish than average up-stream trout, these patterns are on larger hooks.

SALMON FLIES

Many of the trout fly patterns originated as salmon flies; Silver Doctor is a typical example. The salmon flies are larger, gaudier. Wings are multiple, often of several bright colors; hackles are as multiple and varicolored. Wing feathers are comparatively narrow and long, tied openwing or actually "sprawly" to get the colors to show. Sizes are proportionately large and in scale with size of fish caught.

BASS FLIES

The standard bass fly is tied in many of the usual patterns, closed-wing. Wing feathers are relatively large, roundish in outline, and dominate the pattern assembly. Hackles are less in amount in relation to wing size; bodies are of materials similar to those used on trout flies.

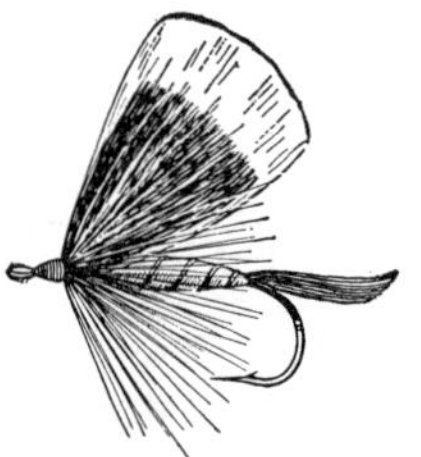

Weber Lifelike Fly Co.

Bass Fly.

PAN-FISH FLIES

These, as would be expected for species closely related in the Sunfish family to the bass, are similar to the bass flies, but reduced in scale. They are tied with wings off the body, width much less in proportion to the length than bass flies, sides of wings parallel.

OTHER ARTIFICIAL LURES

(See color plate, page 169)

We have in the spinner-spoon, plug, and fly families, the three principal main divisions of artificial lures. There is no strict boundary between them, for manufacturers borrow fittings of one family and apply them to forms which have the major features of the other groupings. A wisp of feathers has been added to some models of the Dardevle. It still is a shoe-spoon wobbler; not a fly by any means. Or a propeller spinner is placed at the fore and aft ends of a plug. It still is a plug and not a spinner.

There are, however, two additional groups of lures, much used, which must be included in any coverage of the lures, and cannot be classified in the three major divisions.

(Continued on Page 171)

BUGS

The bug lures stand in an intermediate position to plugs and flies. They have body, but they generally have bodies made of materials such as used in bodies of flies; hair, wool, silk, and the like. Some types have solid "popper" heads, with fly-like feathering. They are a popular type of lure, much used in bass fishing. In attempting systematic classification of lures, they may be considered either as a hybrid group, or a sub-group of the plug family.

Beyond a general setting-apart of this type of lure there is no chance to extend into any reasonable classification of subdivisions. Every season, every manufacturer produces "new" bug lures, sometimes quite extravagant in their makeup, sometimes close to fantastic. The simpler types certainly are established as a standard form of bass lure. And that's not saying the wildest concoctions may not catch fish; they are very likely to do just that.

NATURAL IMITATIONS AND WEIRD LURES

Perhaps these should not be grouped together. The natural imitations, in rubber or other material, of hellgrammites, mice, frogs, fishworms, and any other natural prey, have a semblance of legitimate food. Some of them are genuine fish-getters. But beyond this point of reasonable resemblance to natural food, there is a spread of lures which come nigh to being piscatorial nightmares. Whether the fish strike at them in fright, anger or just don't give a whoop and try anything once, is something an angler never can prove. If fish believe they're taking a run at something to eat, they disprove all angler belief that a game fish is canny, tricky and sly.

In this far extension of lure design the fundamentals are that movement, action and perhaps color, regardless of shape and construction that resembles anything that any fish could regard as food, will attract fish. So while these extreme doo-dads may be considered in one respect, and with reason, as being produced to appeal to the gadget-loving sportsmen first, nobody should discount their probable likelihood of catching the fish.

This division of what may be called "weird lures" simply does not fall into any pattern of classification. Anything can and does happen. It can only be pointed out that there is a spread of fish lures, entirely outside the generally recognized divisions and sub-divisions of artificials, remotely resembling natural fish food if resembling it at all,—and that regardless of any inclination to scoff at them, they more often than not, catch fish.

FOOD BAITS

Our concern has been principally in sorting out the various artificial lures which fishermen may purchase, point out what makes the difference in such lures, in construction, action and appeal, and give groundwork for intelligent selection of the best lure for fishing to be done.

It goes without saying, that anything in the field of genuine food can be considered at least on a par with any artificial lure, and often more effective. Angleworms, grubs, grasshoppers, meats, dough-balls—the whole list of genuine foods must come in for consideration and use by the intelligent angler, fitting such bait to the type of fish, type of water, season and all other factors which go into selecting the sort of appeal which will be attached to the hook, the business end of the tackle.

HOOKS

A hook is the catching instrument; the business end of the tackle assembly. The highest efficiency of a hook occurs when the line of penetration of the point coincides with the line of traction. The curve of the hook, from shank to point, influences the degree of divergence of the line of penetration and line of traction; the length of shank, the straight part of the hook, also has an effect.

The anglers of the middle decades of the 19th century were experimenting with various bends and shank lengths to secure a greater coincidence of these two lines. While the simple round bend, which is a segment of a true circle, did not go out of use, and still remains in use, the modified bends

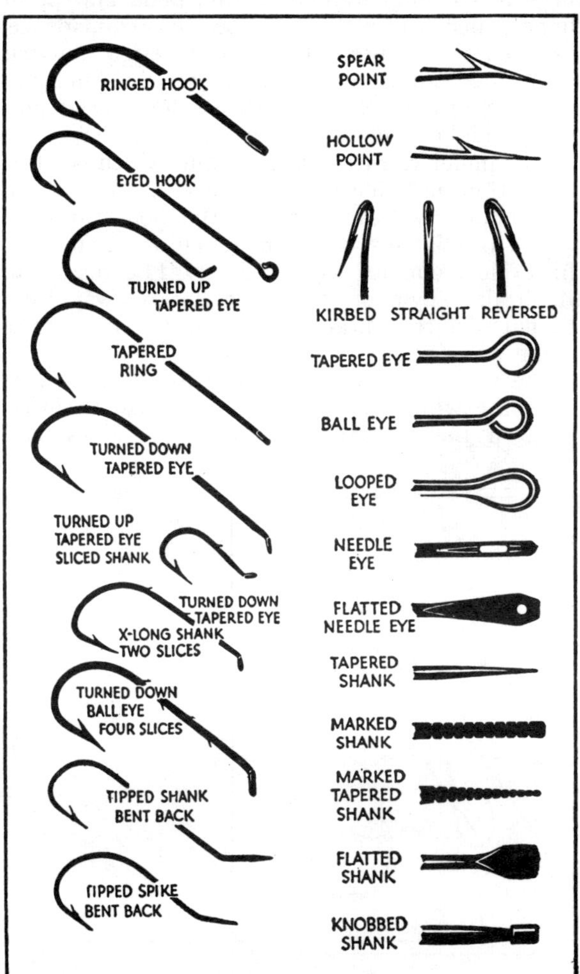

Weber Lifelike Fly Co.

Shapes and styles of present-day fish hooks.

READY REFERENCE TABLE SHOWING THE COMPARATIVE SIZES OF HOOKS

Kirby, Limerick, Sneck and Sproat	No.	9	8	7	6	5	4	3	2	1	1/0	2/0	3/0	4/0	5/0	6/0
Carlisle and Aberdeen	No.	9	8	7	6	5	4	3	2	1	1/0	2/0	3/0	4/0	5/0	6/0
O'Shaughnessy	No.	9	8	7	6	5	4	3	2	1	1/0	2/0	3/0	4/0	5/0	6/0
New York Trout		–	–	–	–	8	7	6	5	4	3	2	1	1/0	2/0	3/0
Cincinnati Bass		–	–	–	–	26	25	24	23	22	21	20	19	18	17	16
Chestertown		–	–	–	–	12	11	10	9	8	7	6	5	4	3	2
Virginia		–	–	–	–	10	9	8	7	6	5	4	3	2	1	1/0
Kinsey		–	20	19	18	17	16	15	14	13	12	11	10	9	8	7
Sheepshead		–	–	–	–	–	–	8	7	6	5	4	3	2	1	1/0
Kirby Sea Hooks		–	–	–	–	16	15	14	13	12	11	10	9	8	7	6
Pacific Bass	No.					8	7	6	5	4	3	2	1	1/0	2/0	3/0

Courtesy Horrocks-Ibbotson Co.

reached some standardization. Thus we have the named shapes of hooks, such as the Sneck, Sproat, and a number of others. The Pennell hook, coming into general use during the fourth quarter of the 19th century, was the nearest approach to coincidence of line of traction and line of penetration up to that time.

During the 1920's, the "eagle claw" type of hook, developed by Wright & McGill, in which there is a combination of shank, bend and point shape which brings the two lines into coincidence, made its appearance. This type of design now has taken the lead in most hooks used in American tackle except for those which are for special purposes and best met by older standard shapes.

The angler can test the degree to which the line of traction and line of penetration are coincident in a hook, by "standing up" the hook, at right angles to a flat surface, point touching at one end, the eyelet touching at the other. The degree to which the angle of the point stands away from the flat surface indicates the amount of divergence of the two lines.

There are special hooks made for specific types of fishing which have shapes other than those offered in the standard patterns. The hooks used for salmon egg fishing for trout, for example, are short-shanked, almost round, so they may be sunk into the globe of the egg bait and conform to it almost completely.

Another type of modification is the combination of hooks in multiple. The three-hook gang, used so generally on spinner and plug lures in the past, is merely a group of standard hooks combined in a fixed position.

The Kirbed hook has an off-set bend of the point to the right as the hook is held verticle, point to the front. The reverse hook has a point bent to one side in the opposite direction; to the left.

Spear point hooks have a straight side on the barbed side of the hook; the hollow ground hook has a curved surface at this point.

There are also standard designs of hook attachment; ball eye, tapered eye, knobbed, and several other types are in use.

The best presentation of the features of hooks, their shapes, types of points, and types of attachment is by charts. These which follow show the features of hooks and the names they commonly carry in the tackle business.

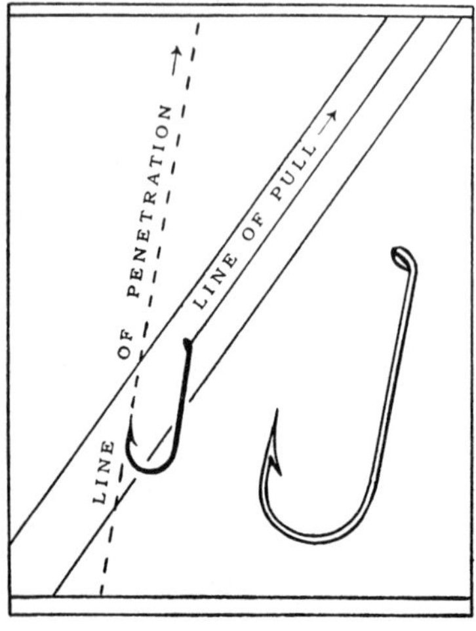

Ordinary bend and point.

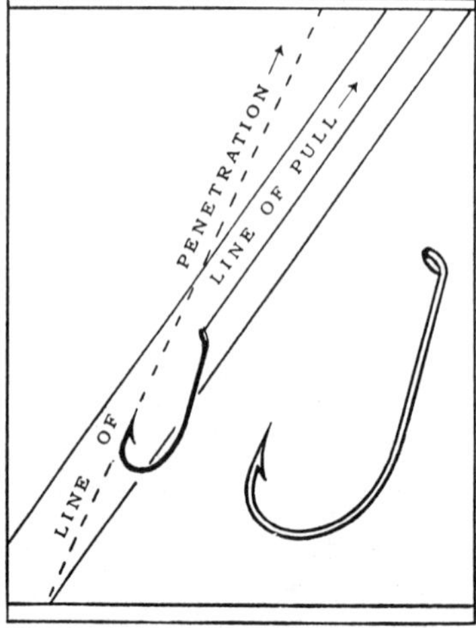

Eagle claw bend only.

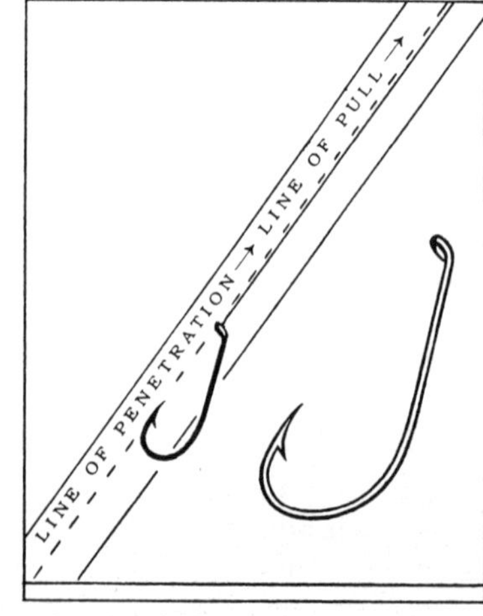

Eagle claw bend plus eagle claw point.

Diagrams illustrating the relation between direction of line of pull and line of penetration.

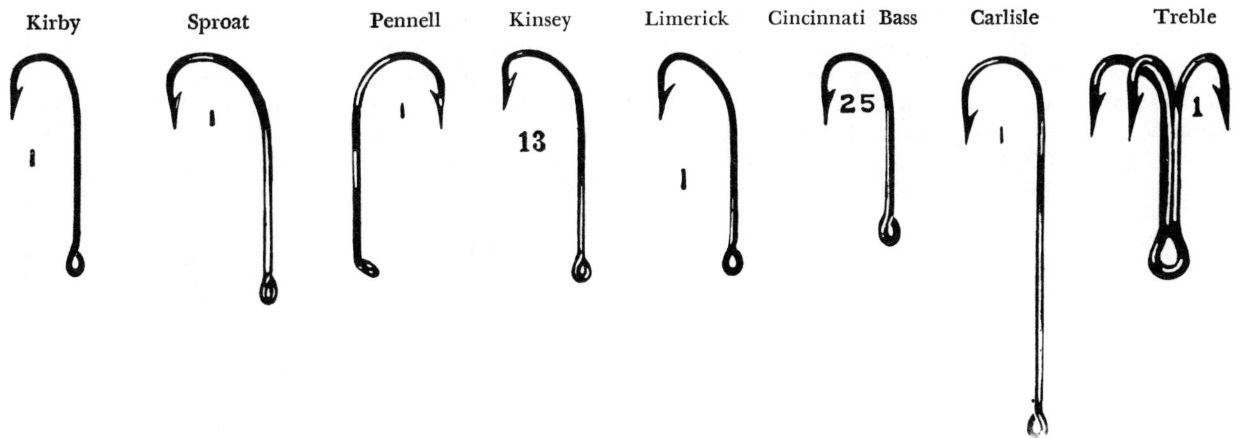

Horrocks-Ibbotson Co.

Common names and size number for various types of fishhooks—Shown actual size.

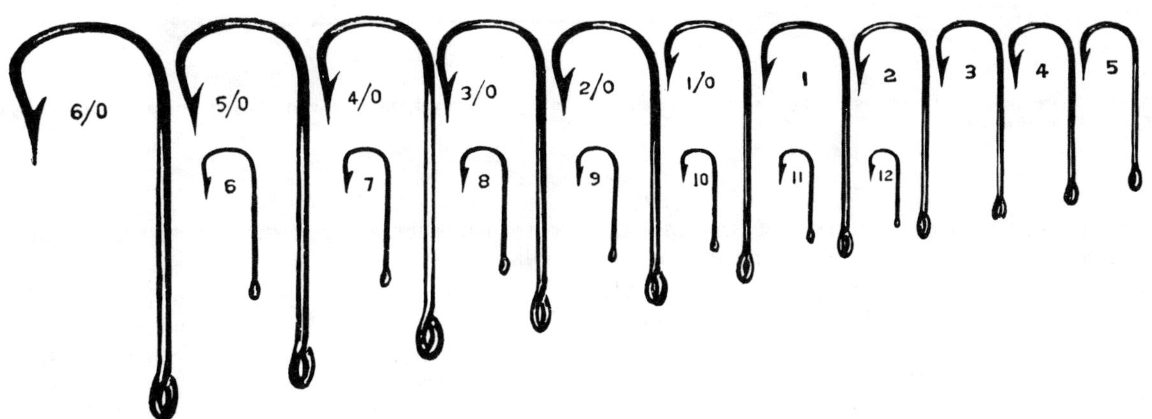

Horrocks-Ibbotson Co.

Chart showing actual sizes of the Sneck hook.

LEADERS

Next in the units of tackle assembly from lure to angler, is the leader. There are two functions of leaders, and two general types.

The leaders used in bait casting, between the line on one end, lure on the other, are principally reinforcement at a point where breakage or severance is most likely to occur. They are therefore made of material to resist cutting or breakage. The most common types of long standing are of piano wire, braided bronze wire and occasionally of heavy natural or synthetic gut. Some anglers who wish to add a degree of deception to their bait casting have used synthetic gut of fairly heavy size, in lengths of up to about 5 feet. But the average leader in use on bait casting rigs is 9 to 12 inches in length. Trolling leaders of the same material are offered in lengths up to 30 inches.

Some very large fish have the capacity to totally engulf the lure, their teeth-armed jaws closing beyond it. When this happens, the section of stouter material that is the leader guards against the line being bitten in two. Another typical service of these leaders is when a fish, trying to free itself from the hooks, rams its head under a bit of rock or other obstruction. If then the leader section is rubbing against a cutting edge, it can take the punishment where line would shear.

The other type of leader has the principal function of making the connection between the lure and fisherman less readily discernible to the fish. It is principally used in fly fishing.

The original leaders of this type were horse hair. With the introduction of what is known as silkworm gut, this material became standard. In the 1930's "Japanese gut" was introduced. It is made of raw silk fibers, the same basic material as the silkworm gut, bound together with a type of gelatin compound. It has the disadvantages of becoming extremely sleazy and limber when wet and use wears off the outer surface of the gelatinous compound, exposing the silk fibers, and the leader becomes fuzzy.

Nylon gut, introduced just before World War II, has met acceptance by a large portion of anglers. It has the advantage of being a continuous filament, no knots, and uniform in strength in proportion to the diameter.

Leaders for fly fishing are made in two subtypes. The level leader is of uniform diameter throughout its length. The tapered leader is heavier at the line end, and the diameter decreases toward the lure end. This was secured in the natural silkworm gut leaders by tying lengths of different diameters in reducing sequence from the heavier toward the lighter, lure end. Any leader of natural gut has the disadvantage of being knotted to secure the length required, since the gut, which is not gut but the hardened fluid of silkworm sacs pulled apart, rarely is over a foot long for each length.

In the earlier use of Nylon leaders, they were level; uniform monofilaments. Tapered Nylon leaders had to be made up of cut lengths of different diameters knotted together. In 1948 two tackle firms developed methods of shaping the Nylon filament so it tapers from one end to the other, following the diameter specifications of the tapered leaders made up of tied lengths of natural or Nylon gut. This eliminates knot troubles of tapered leaders tied out of lengths of different diameters.

Leader lengths for fly fishing run to extremes. Some super-expert tackle handlers will select a tapered leader which will be 9 feet long, some running to 20 feet or more. The theory is, that this extreme length, used almost exclusively in dry fly fishing, helps present a light, airy dry fly more deftly to the fish, has less tendency to drag a fly under because of the filmy extreme end section, and cannot be seen nearly so readily by the fish. As a matter of average requirement in the tapered leader for dry-fly fishing, one of 7 feet is entirely adequate in most locations.

The level leader of 3 to 6 feet, is usually used in wet fly fishing where the water conditions are not so critical in the way of clearness. Such a leader generally has an end loop, and one or two "dropper" loops along its length, where additional snelled flies may be attached. Thus one fly at the extreme end may be fished fairly deep, while the one or two on the dropper loops above will cover the upper levels of the water, offer additional chances of catching a fish, and in some degree, indicate when fish are working in the upper levels as against the deeper level. Also, offering three different fly patterns often will uncover which is most effective at the moment.

The extreme detail in leader lengths, calipers and all other features is something the ultra-super tackleist will worry over for hours; in fussing with them, in making them or in use, or in arguments over which is "best." A fairly standard midground 7½ foot tapered leader will have a diameter of .016 at the line end, decrease .002 of an inch for the next three sections, reduce to .009 in the section next the tip, and the tip will be about .008 in diameter. An extra-special 20-foot tapered leader will be .018 in diameter at the line end, and progressively reduce to a diameter of .007 at the tip.

The National Association of Angling and Casting Clubs has worked out a standardized table, showing the designations of leader diameters, the diameter in decimals of an inch and the minimum permissible breaking test. This is their standard table.

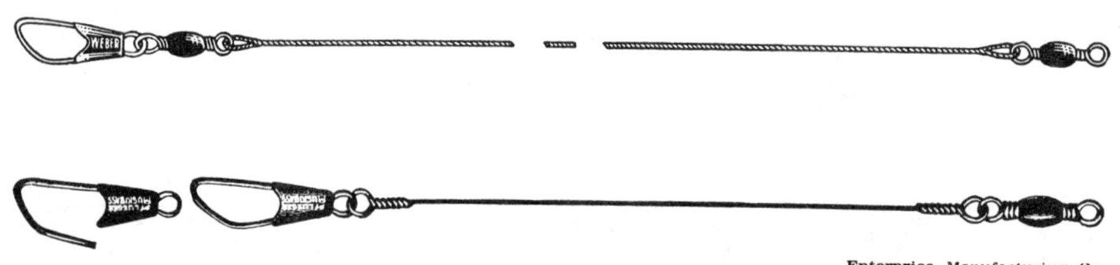

Enterprise Manufacturing Co.

Piano wire leaders, Upper, snap and swivel on terminal end and swivel on line end; Lower, snap on termi'al end and swivel on line end.

7X—.004½—¼	10/5—.001—2½
6X—.005—⅜	9/5—.012—3
5X—.005½—½	8/5—.013—3½
4X—.006—⅝	7/5—.014—4
3X—.007—¾	6/5—.015—4¾
2X—.008—1	5/5—.016—5½
1X—.009—1½	4/5—.017—6¼
0X—.010—2	3/5—.018—7½
	2/5—.019—8¾
	1/5—.020—10

The breaking test of the above applies to natural gut of that diameter. Nylon is stronger in equal diameters. The following table gives the size in decimals of an inch of Nylon leader material, and the Test in Pounds.

Inches in diameter	Pounds Test
.012	4
.014	6
.015	8
.017	10
.019	12
.021	15
.023	20

The greater strength of Nylon is apparent when the diameter of equal size is compared with natural gut listed, and the break test strength of each is compared.

Leaders serve the two purposes; in the bait casting type of angling, they supply added strength at the point where greatest wear or tear may occur, and in the fly fishing they are added to aid in deception. One or the other type of leader will be found in most types of angling for all species in all waters.

LINES

Lines can be classified in general groups by the type of fishing to be done. There are lines made for bait casting with the multiplying reel and lines for salt-water angling also used with the heavy-duty multiplying reel built for that sort of fishing. Others are made for fly fishing and for spinning, and the reels and rods used in those divisions of the angler's sport.

Within these main divisions, the break-down can be based first on materials of which the lines are made, and second on the structural features.

For example, the salt-water lines are made of metal or fiber; Monel metal deep-trolling line representing one material-type of line, "Cuttyhunk" line of Irish linen as representative of the other type. Or bait casting lines which have been universally of braided silk in the past, now also are made of Nylon.

In structure the fly line that is "level," which means of uniform diameter from end to end, can be separated from the "tapered" line, which has a thicker portion in the "body" of the line, with tapering diameter toward the end where the gut leader is attached. A modification in the tapered group is the "torpedo" line, with an increased diameter in a section near the head and back of that a lesser, uniform "shooting line."

LINE STRENGTH

In actual fishing a line of a given test will handle a catch far greater in pounds than the pound-test rating. The test applies a direct force to the straightened line, while a fish will have the bend of the rod, the handling of line by the angler, the friction of water and more or less stretching of the line itself, small as it may be, to absorb the shock of jumps and lunges.

Some lines have slightly less strength when wet while the linen lines become 50 percent stronger.

Monofilament lines for spinning are used commonly in ranges from 2 to 30 pound test. Tournament silk casting lines are made with as low as 4½-pound test, and up to 9-pound. The average bait casting line used in fishing may be as light as 9-pound test, with a 20-pound test line about the heaviest for good handling. Lines do run into higher test brackets, to 40-pound and more, but when they get into their heavier sizes they're more likely to be used in trolling than for casting. With reasonable handling of reel, giving and taking line, and the spring of the rod, there is every reason to land a record fish with a 20-pound line or less; any line failure is likely to be due to a damaged line or the wrapping of line around the cutting edge of an obstruction—and any line will cut through under some circumstances.

BAIT CASTING LINES

Casting lines, as well as trolling and other lines, and in some cases leaders and snells, are rated by their "pound test." Various methods have been used to denote the amount of strain which may be put on a line before it breaks. A direct tension test may be made by attaching one end of line or leader to an accurate spring-type scale and then increasing tension until it breaks. The more modern and accurate method of testing lines is a machine known as the "Scott Incline-plane Tester." This is fitted with an automatic recording chart which not only gives graphic data on breaking of the line under test, but also the stretch of the line as tension increases. Most manufacturers give their "pound" rating for dry lines and usually such rating is well under the actual amount of strain which causes a break.

Lines for use in this division of angling are braided around a core of silk fiber and are somewhat four-sided. This can be felt by rolling the line between thumb and finger. This square cross-section aids in preventing line reeled in from wedging between turns already on the reel. Snarls and back-lash often are caused by "mushed" line.

Nylon casting line is stronger than silk of equal diameter. It also has resistance to rot, alkali water and other conditions that weaken silk lines. Early Nylon lines were inclined to "mush" on reels, but later types have been treated so this is largely avoided.

Nylon when first used in fishing lines had a "stretch" of as much as 30 per cent. With such a stretching factor, when an angler attempted to sink the hook as a fish struck, much of the force applied merely stretched the line and was not delivered at hook-point. The makers of Nylon line now have a process of heat treating, with a trade name of "Thermoset." It is done with infra-red rays. Treated Nylon line has a maximum stretch of 12 percent, with somewhat less "give" in actual use. When this is compared with the stretch factor in the finest "Coutrai" linen lines, 50's lea, which is 8 percent maximum, the Nylon performs about as well as any line.

Silk lines are braided both "soft" and "hard." The hard braided lines will stand more wear running through rod guides but lack the greater flexibility of the soft lines. For average casting the hard braided line will handle satisfactorily and give better service. The very soft line has some tendency to throw half-hitches around rod tops and snarl in other ways.

Since it is impossible for the average angler to judge the quality of silk used in making a line, the best guarantee that it is made of first-grade, pure silk and not of cheaper grades or even shoddy, is in purchasing a line which is backed by a reliable trade name.

SALT-WATER LINES

Standard salt-water lines were formerly made exclusively of Irish linen and of fine cotton, and measured on the basis of threads, each with a breaking point of 3 pounds. Thus, a 9-thread line was rated arbitrarily at 27-pounds test. With the encroachment of Nylon and other synthetic fibers into this field, the A. G. F. A. now rates lines on breaking test alone. Nylon, Dacron, Orlon, and other synthetics, either braided or monofilament, have all but replaced natural fibers except in the heavier tests, and they have been making heavy inroads there. Their advantage lies in their resistance to rot. For deep trolling solid Monel metal lines have all but replaced the braided metal lines formerly used.

TROLLING LINES

Any type of line suitable for casting can be used for trolling provided it possesses the strength required to meet existing conditions. Monofilament Nylon, Dacron, and other synthetics have earned great popularity.

FLY-CASTING LINES

These are treated lines, impregnated with oil or "enamel" not only to supply the desired degree of flexibility for fly casting, but to add weight. In fly casting, the lure itself does not possess the weight necessary to "spring" the rod, and thus supply the propelling power. The weight is in the line. When a fly is cast, one actually casts the line, the weight of that line carrying the cast out, the fly with it.

The oil impregnation process is the less costly; the objection is that in time such treating is affected by exposure and tends to become sticky.

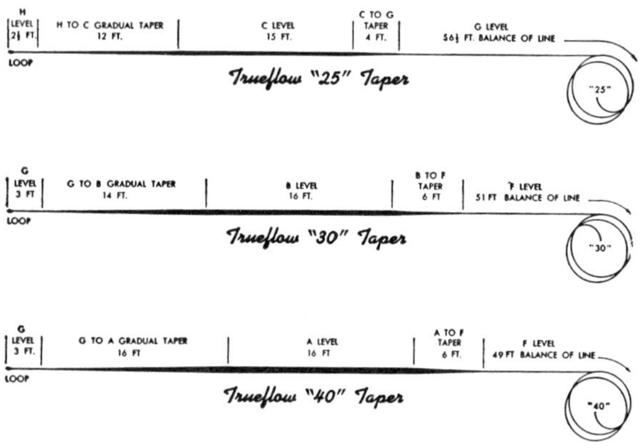

Typical tapered fly lines.

The enameled line, of somewhat higher cost, does not have this trouble, but may crack after long use, with the covering finally shelling off and exposing the threads.

The pliability of the enameled line is an important factor. One way to check on the quality of the line and the dressing is to unroll several yards and cast it out on the floor. A line which has the top quality should not kink but lay out fairly straight, even though it has been rolled in a circle on the display card.

The enameled line is most used for fly casting. It is subdivided into groups on the basis of constant or varying diameters. The level line has a uniform diameter throughout. Tapered lines have varying diameters.

"Weights" of fly casting lines are given in letters of the alphabet. The heavier lines are designated with letters at the beginning of the alphabet, the lighter ones by letters farther along in sequence. The level fly line designated as "C" size, has an approximate pound-test rating of 38 pounds; and "H" line has about a 14-pound test.

The double tapered line is designated by the letters which show the thickness at the end, at the middle, and again at the far end. Thus a tapered line which is designated as "HEH" has a 14-pound test tip, and tapers from that to the "body" of the line, "E" thickness, with a pound test of about 28, and then tapers down again to the "H" size at the other end.

The point where the taper begins, how rapidly it decreases in size, where each thickness occurs, is regarded as very important by those who are extremely critical tackle manipulators. They demand the location of the weighting of the line at specific points. There is also a definite relationship between this weight of line and where it occurs, to the "action" of the rod used. No small part of the many variations in fly line weights is related to the varying preferences of rod weights, lengths and actions. This is not all ultra-finnickyness, for the "matching" of rod and line, to secure the best inter-action, have enough fly-line weight to spring it properly, not too much, not too little, is important. A stiff rod will not put out a light line properly; a limber rod will be over-weighted and sluggish in handling a line that is too heavy.

The tapered line, becoming smaller at the end, aids in putting out a fly lure more delicately than the uniform level line, with constant weight per foot.

The "torpedo" line recognizes the need for extra weight in that section which enters into the springing of a rod as a fly is cast, and no need for such a heavy, reel-filling line back of that section. The tip of a torpedo has the general structural features of the tapered line; light at the end, increasing in diameter for some distance back of the end which is level for some feet, and then, after adequate weight is supplied by the "swelled section" there is a reduction to a lesser diameter back of this weighted section. That long, level portion back of the torpedo head is used as "shooting line," the torpedo weight carrying it out on the cast. Because such construction throws the weight at a point where it is needed, and supplies a lighter line to be pulled out by

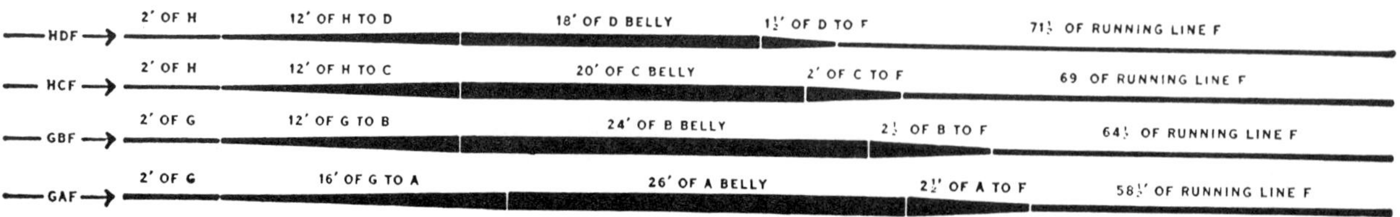

Diagram of Cortland Stratoline Shooting Taper Fly Line. (Torpedo type)

such weight as it is cast, it is claimed that the length of casts may be increased as much as 50 per cent.

There always is the temptation to shoot the cast far, wide and handsome. The "other side of the fence" is greener; the far riffles of a stream look "fishier." There are situations where the torpedo head is the one answer to reaching the spots where fish lie. But in the majority of cases, distance in cast is far less important than intelligent and thorough working of the near by water.

In order to better illustrate the distribution of diameters on both tapered and torpedo lines, manufacturers have resorted to graphic charts showing the way tapers occur.

REELS

The direct progression of tackle assembly from lure to angler puts the reel as the next unit after the line. There are four major divisions among reels, namely, the single action, the multiplying reels, the automatics and the spinning type. They are differentiated principally by their construction, method of manipulation and type of fishing for which they are suited.

SINGLE ACTION REELS

This is the simple progenitor of all reels; essentially a spool fitted with a crank, usually directly attached to the spool. One turn of the crank causes one turn of the spool. This type of reel has a primary function of serving for line storage. It does not pay out line on the cast. Its use is almost wholly confined to fly fishing. Line is stripped off to lengthen the amount beyond the tip of the rod, reeled into shorten the length on the cast line, and during the landing of the fish the reel enters as a means of winding in the line that is out until the catch is within landing distance.

Weber Lifelike Fly Co.

Single action reel.

Because of its simplicity of construction, (no gears, springs or other more intricate mechanical features). Good single action reels can be purchased within a moderate price range. There are however, reels of this type, finely made, superbly fitted and finished, which do get into higher price brackets.

In addition to reasonably good materials, construction and finish, there are some points to check in selecting a single action reel. It should be fairly narrow, its diameter supplying the storage capacity. The narrowness prevents, somewhat, the chance of tangling on the spool that might occur if wider. The sides of the spool should be smooth, perhaps with slight curved surface to aid in free unwinding of any turn of line next to the sides. Four posts between the sides of the spool instead of a single hub shaft will give some better assurance of those sides remaining parallel; if one of the sides were out of line with the other and with the side plates, difficulties in operation would result. A sprung side would not fit close to exterior plates of the reel at one point and would rub at another. The little gap where the side plate was sprung open would allow line to get in there and jam. That also is a point to check; see that the plates of the spool are so constructed there is no crack between them and exterior side plates where line might slip in. The cranking handle should be a smooth, rounding cone with the point out rather than level or slightly spool shaped. This avoids a line getting looped over the crank and fouling the operation of the reel.

AUTOMATIC REELS

These serve the same purpose as the single action reel. As the line is stripped out, it winds up springs within the reel. Tension thus supplied will draw line back on the reel spool when the force is released by a finger trigger on the reel.

Good reels of this type are fitted with a winding device which can turn tension into the springs, and also with a release which will throw off all such tension. The same points of barrel and hub construction as in a single action should be checked in selecting one of these automatics.

Since the function of either the single or automatic is identical, being line storage, it would seem that there would be no contention as to which was the more "sporting." However, some fly fishermen do hold that the single action reel is more sporting—and it supplies a good subject for argument.

The automatic reel is not supposed to be used as something to "play the fish" directly, letting the fish work against the tension of the springs. The spring facility is there to take up the line as it is brought in. The automatic reel with the winding trigger under a finger of the rod hand leaves the other hand free to manipulate the line between the reel and the first guide. This other hand strips out line to a running fish, strips in to retrieve line. The automatic wind does much to avoid excess line tangling between reel and lower rod guide.

Thus the automatic reel allows one hand to do what two hands must do when operating the single action reel; leaves one hand free to manipulate the line during the playing of the catch. Also, when the catch is ready for landing, it is possible to be ready with the rod hand and trigger finger to take slack quickly at the last moments

Martin Automatic Fishing Reel Co.
Martin "Flywate" Upright Reel.

if the fish makes a lunging run toward the angler; one point at which the automatic reel may enter directly into landing the fish, and legitimately so. Conversely, line will pay out automatically if the fish starts to run away at the very point of a netting.

An unbiased approach to the automatic versus a single action reel argument would seem to indicate that the automatic reel, serving as a place of line storage, gives a higher facility for such service—merely an advancement of our mechanical age over the direct-wind spool which first showed up centuries before the Christian Era in Egypt.

MULTIPLYING REEL

The "Kentucky" or multiplying reel, devised originally for bass fishing, differs essentially from the "line storage" reel, in that the weight of the lure, cast from near the tip of the rod, pulls the line from the reel spool for the length of the cast. The other fundamental difference lies in the gears between the crank handles and the spool. The spool turns several times as the crank makes one circle. The usual ratio is close to one crank turn to four turns of the spool.

One side of the reel contains bearings; the other the gears to the spool and additional attachments that have been fitted to some reels. Pillars between the ends hold these apart. The spool width is greater than the single action reel. A representative reel with a spool diameter of 1½ inches, with length between pillars of 1¾ inches will hold about 100 yards of 20-pound test line.

Since the line pays out from the spool at each cast, and at a high speed, the ease of turning is of considerable importance. The length of time a reel will turn with a quick, flip-twist of the crank handles has been accepted rather generally as an indication of the action quality of the reel. However, it is more important to judge the ease of the spool *starting* than the *length* of time it will spin. The length of spinning time may be due more to the weight of the spool itself than to the lightness of operation of the mechanism. The instant of most importance in getting a cast out is in that first split second when the inertia of the spool has to be overcome. If the turn of the spool responds swiftly, smoothly to that first tug of the line, and continues to pay out with light pull on the line, that is the desired objective. A spool that will spin longer because of its weight in motion, will do two things contrary to the best results in its use. Weight means more inertia to be overcome in the first tug; more force required to start the spool spinning inevitably diminishes the out-pull force of the pitched lure. Also, the spool of heavier weight, once in motion, may continue to spin under its own momentum, faster than the lure is pulling line through the rod guides, "over-running" the line pull beyond the tip, stacking up line between reel and lower guide—and causing a nightmare of backlash.

As a first consideration, selection of a multiplying reel should begin with checking the general quality of construction, the type of metal alloy bearings, the "smoothness" of assembly, sturdiness, and the quality of hardened metal in gears—for these gears take a terrific beating. With the quality of material and smoothness of assembly first considered, then test the factor of inertia to be overcome in *starting* the spool spinning.

Construction of the main features of these reels is well standardized. Manufacturers have added attachments to aid in handling. One of the most serviceable in actual fishing is the "level-wind." This is a guide, traveling back and forth, its movement caused by spiral gear cuts in a shaft running the width of the reel and operating inside of a partial hood. With the line threaded through the guide, it is laid on the turning spool in uniform layers, largely avoiding the tangling and "mushing" which contributes to backlash. As the line pays out, it also is guided off the reel by the traveling guide.

Anti-back-lash devices put a bit of tension on the reel spool, to prevent it from full, free turning, so it will not over-run the drag on the line by the out-soaring lure. They reduce length of cast, but they also reduce over-run by the spool and resultant tangles.

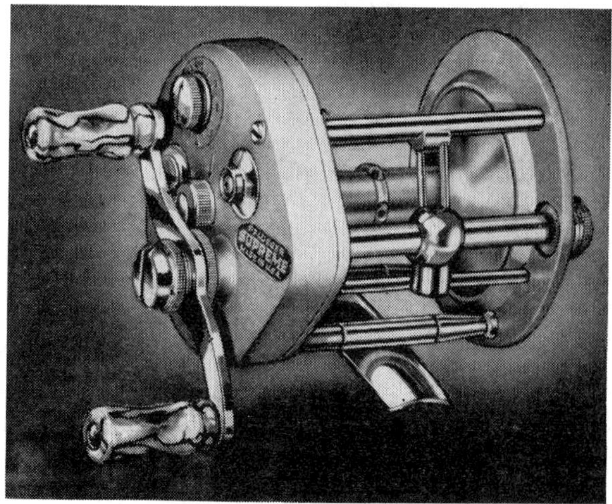

Pflueger
Pflueger's Supreme Multiplying Reel.

Another anti-back-lash device is constructed so the spool is allowed to run entirely free, without any drag on it, until the line slackens, which is the point where line may stack up on the spool. Then the brake on the spool is automatically engaged.

The post of the reel spool is relatively small; it is built to handle as much line as possible. However, one quick thought will call attention to the fact that a harder tug is required to set a spool in motion if the diameter of the spool plus line is smaller, than if it is fairly well filled out toward the outer edges of the spool. It is the same principle as any lever; the longer the lever

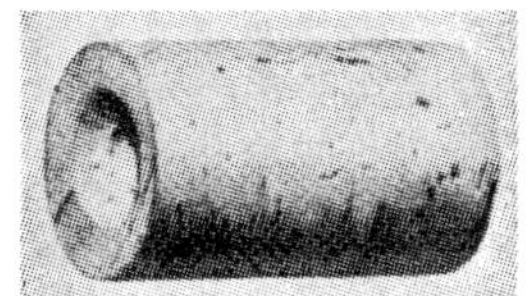

Horrocks-Ibbotson Co.

Cork Arbor.

the less pressure is required to exert a definite force over the fulcrum; or, taking another example, it is easier to start a jacked-up automobile wheel spinning by touching the outer edge of the tire than to twist the hub.

There are two ways to increase the diameter of the hub of the spool, so the advantage of "leverage" is secured in starting the spool turning. One is to put on "line backing;" that is, winding a length of line, perhaps an old casting line, on the hub to build it up, with the advantage of more line available if it is necessary to "give line" to a large and obstinate fish. This has the disadvantage of adding more weight to the spool, and while it does give great "leverage" in starting, it also tends to maintain the spinning beyond the point where the lure is pulling line from the rod tip—and with potential snarls resulting. The other method of increasing hub diameter is to put on the standard "cork arbor," two halves, hollowed on inner sides to fit the spool hub, fitting together over the hub so the outer sides are level-round between spool ends. This "builds up" the hub, so that a lesser amount of line then is wound out nearer the maximum diameter of the reel, without adding the weight that is in "backing line."

Modern multiplying reels have been so developed that those of moderate price assure high service. In older reels, construction failure was not so rare. Particularly, the ends of the spool often did not fit well into the end assembly, cracks between these and the ends let in line, and there it jammed, cut or snarled. Today's reels are far better made in all price brackets.

While the principal use of the multiple reel in fresh-water fishing is for bait casting, it serves fully for the pay-out and reel-in needs of trolling.

Reels of this type with a "free spool" have the means of throwing off the gear assembly and allowing the spool to turn all by itself. After a cast is made tripping the lever or button back re-engages gearing.

SALT-WATER REELS

Models for salt-water fishing are of both types; single and multiple action. The principal difference between these and their counterparts used in fresh-water fishing is a greater capacity for line. Many of the multiplying reels used in salt-water fishing are fitted with a "star drag." This is a fixture between the crank and the reel body, with five "spokes" having rounded ends, and within reach of fingers of the reeling hand. The star drag acts as a friction clutch between the crank and the barrel of the spool. By tightening it the clutch takes hold of the hub so the full force of winding is transferred to the spool. Loosening allows the spool to "slip" in ratio to the tension of the drag even though the crank is constantly turning. Thus by setting the drag at a moderate tension, it is possible to keep up a continuous

Pflueger

The Pflueger "Templar" multiplying reel.

reeling, and if the fish exerts more force in pulling on the line than the slipping clutch transfers, the line will unwind, giving line. It serves to give line if a run on the fish requires it, takes up line when there is any available, and keeps a continuously tight line on the catch. Salt-water spinning reels are fundamentally large-sized versions of standard fresh-water models.

SPINNING REELS

While the type of angling which has come to be known as "spinning" derives its name from an initial use of light spinners as the lures, it now is more predominantly associated with a type of reel which makes the use of intermediate weight lures possible. Prior to the spinning type of tackle, rods, reels and lines such a gap existed in lure weights that they could not be handled. The quarter-ounce or less "bug bait" did not have enough weight to spring the average bait casting rod nor the weight at the end of the line to pull out that line. The same lures were too heavy for the fly rig assembly.

The reels we now term as "spinning reels" have stationary spools on the cast, and the line unwinds by slipping off over one side of the spool.

Garcia Corporation

Salt-water Spinning Reels, like the Mitchell 302 are essentually large-sized versions of fresh-water models. It has a reel capacity of 500 yards of 10-pound test monofilament line.

The common illustration of this action is to hold one end of a spool of thread between the fingers and pull thread off over the other end.

By providing extremely smooth surfaces over which the line will slip, the friction factor is reduced to a minimum. There is no spool inertia to overcome. There is no momentum of reel spool to keep on paying out line in an over-run as the lure slows at the end of the cast. Backlash therefore is eliminated. Light lures can pull line from such reel assemblies.

The rewinding of the line on the spool of these reels generally is accomplished by a "finger" or bail, which "picks up" the line and just as a finger would wrap line back, rewinds it on the spool. Some few reels that have stationary spools on the cast engage gears to turn the spool as line is brought in. This tends to twist the line; it is payed off the end of the spool, wound back by the turning motion, and twisting is certain.

Spinning reels are classified on the basis of the mechanism for the rewind. One, represented by the Bache Brown "Mastereel," one of the first quality spinning reels manufactured in the United States, produced by the Airex Corporation, has the reel spool seated at right angles to the rod-grip, the winding finger or bail being open and exposed, and the reel mounted directly below the casting hand. When the bail is opened, the line is controlled by the index finger in the casting operation. On the retrieve, the bail closes automatically and rewinds the line on the exposed spool.

The closed-face reel is typified by the "Abu-Matic," manufactured by the Garcia Corporation. This type of reel is mounted on the rod like a multiplying reel, but the spool is at right angles to the grip and is covered by a metal cup. On the cast, the line, which flows through a hole in the center of the cup, is released by a thumb trigger. On the retrieve, the line is engaged by retractable pins on a shallow dish-shaped inner cup, which revolves as the handle is turned.

The open-faced reel requires special over-sized guides, since the line leaves the reel in coils. The closed-face reel may be used with standard casting rods.

Both types of reel have adjustable drags and anti-reverse mechanisms.

Many modifications of these basic types are being offered. The fundamental identification in all cases is the stationary spool, line slipping off the side, as the cast is made.

The standard lines used in other styles of casting may serve in a spinning reel, but the extra smoothness of the Nylon lines, either fine-braided or mono-filament, are emphatically recommended. The mono-filament is especially indicated in the closed-face reels. Bache Brown recommends such line up to 6 pound test, but above that he prefers braided Nylon. Since a major portion of the lures that will be used with a spinning outfit are light in weight, the 6-pound or less, test mono-filament line will give the best results. A lure under a quarter ounce will hardly have the weight to pull out the heavier line.

The first function of any reel is storage for length of line beyond that which is possible in fixed-line angling. In one main division, the line pays out directly from the revolving reel on the cast; the multiplying reel. In the second division the single action reel, it is wholly a facility for line storage. In the third division, the spinning reel, the line pays out from a spool which does not turn. Those are the essential structural and use features which form the basis for classification.

RODS

Fishing rods have three major functions. They give leverage and length in putting out lure or bait. This is true even in fixed-line still-fishing

Airex Corporation

The Bache Brown Mastereel, one of the best known American spinning reels.

with a cane pole. They supplement the length of an angler's arm, so while the bait or lure is in the water he can manipulate it with greater facility. While this is not generally stressed, the movement of the rod in guiding a lure into likely spots or imparting motion to the lure, is a part of the service a rod supplies. Third, the rod becomes a major part of the play in landing a fish, absorbing much of the shock when the strike is fierce, bending to pit its resilience against the tug of the fish as it fights.

The separation of fishing rods into types is based on functions in each type of fishing, and the particular species sought.

Therefore, a first segregation is on the basis of the type of fishing; fly casting, spinning, bait casting, trolling, salt-water surf fishing and deep-sea fishing. Within each class there is a further subdividing on the basis of species for which the rod is best suited; for example, in fly rods there are those particularly designed for dry-fly trout fishing, for bass, for Steelheads, or for salmon. The materials of which rods are constructed furnish a further basis of separation. For example, in the bait casting group there are rods of split bamboo, of solid steel, of tubular steel and of glass.

Since legal game fish range from trout measuring six inches or so and weighing perhaps 4 ounces to such lunkers as the Bluefin Tuna, rod construction has as great a correlated spread. At one extreme then is the thready little 6-foot trout rod weighing less than 3 ounces, and at the other the stout, tough deep-sea rod capable of landing a catch four or five times the poundage of the angler.

FLY RODS

The principal material which dominated the trout rod field for half a century was bamboo in the six-strip construction and only recently has it found a serious competitor in glass fiber. Some years past there was a classification of such rods as being built in "dry-fly action" and in "wet-fly action." The former was stiffer than the latter. Dry fly rods were built to have the "action" nearer the tip. Today improved construction has generally erased this differentiation. Lines now available, suited to the rod action, can bow the rod so it will serve well in either dry-fly or wet-fly fishing. The tendency is toward the live, springy action, resembling that formerly considered a dry-fly type.

Action in fly rods is determined by the material used and the "taper" from butt to tip. Early construction produced a constant taper from one end of the rod to the other. Then makers found that by shaping the rods so the exterior surfaces were not straight but slightly curved, they could throw the "point of action" at any point throughout the length. By carrying a slightly greater diameter toward the tip, and then smoothing into the lesser diameter by following a flowing curve, the rod carried greater strength, stiffness and power to that point, with enough "whip" in the tip as the diameter blended to that point, to put out the flies.

There are several common methods of determining the "action" of a fly rod as it is examined in the sporting goods store. Weighting the end of the rod and holding it out horizontally will show the bend in some degree. Others hold the tip, bend the rod, and watch where the "flow of the bend" occurs. A third way has been to hold the butt of the rod solidly on a horizontal counter surface, and flip the rod so it vibrates in a vertical plane.

The best method to demonstrate "where the action falls" in a fly rod is to stand with the rod held out horizontal in front. Whipping the rod back and forth, checking each lateral motion at the *end* of the whipping impulse, will bend the rod in a *continuous* flowing curve from butt to tip. This gives some indication of the "feel" of the rod. However, it does not reveal the "break" in the action, the "point of action," any more than the other tests cited.

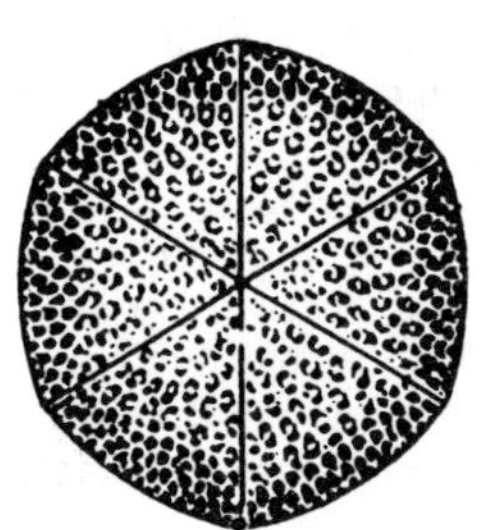

SINGLE BUILT.

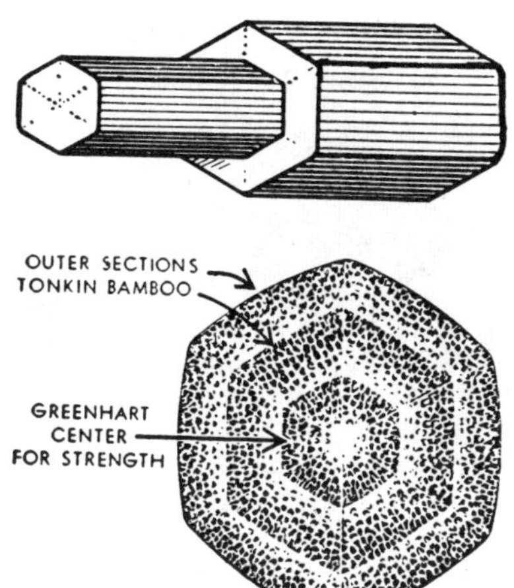

Cross-sections of built-up bamboo rod.

If, as the rod is whipped horizontally, the side-whipping impulse is stopped before it has reached its full side bending, the rod can be thrown into two curves at the apex of motion. For example, the impulse to the left will throw a curve into the bottom portion of the rod which bellies out in the left direction. But somewhere along the rod, the curve will be in the opposite direction with the tip pointing to the right. As the rod is whipped, actually almost "wiggled" in this horizontal plane with two curves alternating in opposite directions, there is a point on the rod which will approximately stand still; a "pivot point" on which the end of the two curves meet. This discloses the point of action in the rod, high or lower down.

Bamboo rod construction follows this general pattern.

The best bamboo cane comes from Tonkin Province of China, but the supply has been seriously curtailed since World War II, a fact which gave glass rods an additional impetus. The resiliency and stamina of bamboo lies in the outer layers—the "rind." Bamboo growing on sandy hillsides in Tonkin Province has a higher content of the substance called lignin in the rind than other bamboo. Lignin contains a silica compound and silica (principal constituent of sand) is the substance from which glass is manufactured.

Shipments of bamboo come in suitable lengths for rod sections, all grades mixed. Experts can judge the quality of each piece by a quick look and quick tests. Those which are the most nearly perfect and of high quality are set aside for the higher grade rods. Since there is a small percentage of such pieces, this is one factor which enters into the difference between the higher priced rods and those of lesser cost.

The pieces are split (not sawed) into strips suitable for each rod length. Some manufacturers construct each rod section out of strips from one piece of bamboo in order to assure the same resilience and flexing quality in all six parts of that section. Others "match" strips within a section, taking three strips from one piece of bamboo, three from another.

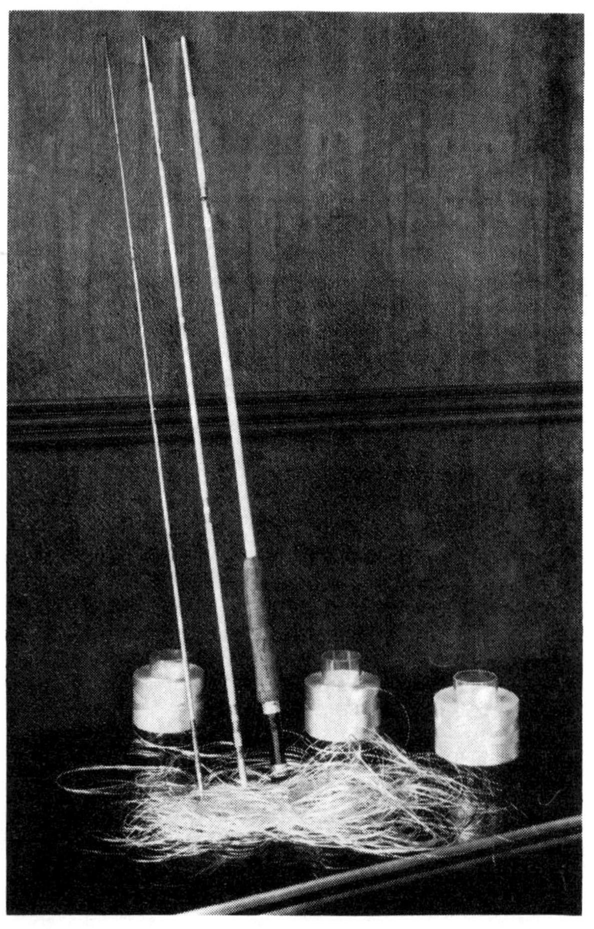

Shakespeare Company

A glass fishing rod (Shakespeare) and the material from which it is made.

Strips are then roughed into wedge shape. All cutting is done on the inside, removing the pith and softer wood, so there will be no loss of the strength which lies in the rind. Once selected for a section, all six strips are kept together for the finished rod.

With the cutting all occurring on the inner side of a strip, this must be done to exact templates, each section, to secure the precise, slight curve which will be in the outer surface to insure the action at the point desired.

The outer surface of the strips is cleaned up; two superficial layers above the hard rind are cleaned off. The strips are chemically dyed to secure the golden or brown tone of the finished rod. The final shaping follows, the strips are glued together under pressure, a filler is put on the wood, the fittings (grip and ferrules) are added, another filler coat is put on, the exterior is dressed down to the last shaping of the taper, windings and guides are put on and lined up, and the varnish job completes the rod.

This is a rough outline of what happens in fly rod manufacture. There is constant checking of each step, minor adjustments all the way through such as heat-straightening sections if necessary, before final finishing, singeing of wrappings to remove fuzz, and the like. But even this quick summary of steps involved in the construction of a three section fly rod with extra tip, containing 24 pieces of bamboo strip, indicates the work that goes into the production of such a rod.

Emphasis was formerly put on the weight of a rod, even to small fractions of an ounce. There have been several reasons for accenting the weight of a fly rod. Before bamboo took over in this field, rods were made of other woods; greenheart, lancewood, and many other materials. All of them produced heavier rods than can be made of bamboo giving equal strength and service. Lighter weight was therefore an important talking point as bamboo came into the picture. Even then, bamboo construction had not reached the refinement now existing. The present methods of shaping action into a rod, throwing it where it will be of most effectiveness, has allowed more reduction in the weight of rods over earlier ones. While weight still is a factor in rod selection, and will be in proportion to the length and diameters, the way the action is "thrown" into a rod somewhat takes precedence in making a selection. There is assurance that the manufacturer has cut the weight to the minimum for the type of rod, has preserved the layer of strength which lies principally in the rind of the cane, and in some degree substituted live, effective action for mere diameter or bulk.

Trout rods range from the 6-foot, super-light ones, weighing 3 ounces or less, which are delightful things in fishing small brooks and light fish, to those made to cast flies, bucktails and similar lures, for salmon, Steelheads, and bass. The salmon and Steelhead rods may exceed 11 feet in length and weigh 7 or more ounces. English rods for these fish will be even longer and heavier.

The all-around trout rod is one with dry-fly action, 8½ feet long, weighing some 4⅞ ounces, and handling a "C" level line, or "HDH" in a double-taper. A 9-footer will weigh 5¼ ounces and will spring best with a "D" level line or a "HDH" double-taper.

In contrast, a 9-foot rod built for Steelhead and bass fly fishing, will weigh 6¼ ounces and require a "C" level line or "HCH" taper to give the best results.

In purchasing a fly rod, the extra price for the higher grade rests on the superior quality of cane in the rod, the care with which it is brought to the most exact taper in the cutting and finishing, and in finer fittings. After the most nearly perfect cane is selected for these high priced rods, the grades of lesser quality have some slight imperfections in them, but are still of very good substance. Much of the deficiency which might lie in any such slight imperfections is offset as the manufacturer "matches" the strips in each section, making certain that any slight flaw is not coincident in the rod with any similar one in another strip.

On a general basis, the rods obtainable in the middle bracket range offered by reliable manufacturers are full of fight, stamina and satisfaction. For the average angler, there may be more dollar-service in obtaining two rods of medium cost than placing all the rod-money in one very superior article. The selection of two rods, medium cost, would be, one of the 7½ or 8 foot length for smaller waters, lighter fish, and one in the 8½, 9-foot or greater length which could handle the weight and battle of big bass or trout of Steelhead size.

In any case, it should be emphasized that in fly fishing, it is the weight of the line which bows the rod on the cast. It is therefore important that the line used with the rod should be in the size fitted to that rod; a line too heavy makes the cast sluggish, while a line too light in weight will not

Abercrombie and Fitch

(Reading from top to bottom): Glass spinning rod with Mitchell Reel; Steel Bait Casting rod and Langley Bait Casting Reel; Orvis bakelite impregnated bamboo salt water trolling rod with Penn Senator 9/0 reel; glass surf casting rod with Penn Squidder reel; A & F split bamboo fly rod, 8½ feet with extra tip equipped with Ocean City Plymouth fly reel.

bring the rod to a full bowing and the full power of the rod will not be developed.

A modification in bamboo fly rods is found in the "double-built" construction. They merely are rods in which the inner sides of strips are shaved off until it is possible to incorporate two layers of strips into each of the six segments, thus making what amounts to a thin inner rod of mostly cane rind with another of the same material over it. The objective is added strength and resilience.

Another modification which was offered as early as the 1890's, is incorporating a thin, high tensile wire in the center of the rod.

A word should be said about wrappings. In the past, these wrappings were put on rods in addition to those which hold on guides and dress the end of ferrules, to hold the strips together. The glue of those times was not the superior type now available. Water entering through a chipped place in the varnish would seep into the bamboo, spring it a little, mildew would start, and the sections would separate. The wrappings were designed to prevent this. Today there are types of glue, and methods of putting the rod together with high pressure which secures a joining between strips rated as water-proof.

Two other materials have been used in recent years in the construction of fly rods. With the advent of super-tensile steel alloys, of light weight, several companies built and offered tubular rods of steel. They are slightly heavier than bamboo and there is some difference in action. Although they have some points which recommend them highly, such as not being subject to such deleterious effects of climate as bamboo sometimes suffers, they have not secured any great acceptance.

Following the introduction of glass fiber rods for bait casting, many companies began to offer glass rods for fly casting. Glass rods are essentially of synthetic bamboo since the fiber which gives bamboo its "life" is comparable to that of the glass rod.

It took the bamboo rod most of a half century after it was first made available in the rived-and-glued form, to take over the field from green-heart, lancewood, and other woods used in early rods. As it competed for first place, the bamboo rod had many refinements and improvements built into it. The same pattern of development and improvement, on a much accelerated scale, permitted glass to take its place along with bamboo. Glass rods already have made obsolete the cheaper rods that were made of Calcutta cane, and the better-quality glass rods are surpassed in feel and beauty only by hand-made rods of Tonkin cane produced by the best rodmakers. Since fiberglass rods may be mass-produced, their cost is much less than that of bamboo rods of the same quality.

SPINNING RODS

Since spinning stands between fly fishing and bait casting, the rods which have been developed for it are somewhat intermediate. The preferred lengths are in the neighborhood of 7 feet, the weight running between 4 and 5 ounces. The "contour" of the rod, that is the shape from butt to tip, follows the design of good, "dry action" fly rods. There must be lively "spring" in such a rod to handle lures which may weigh as little as 1/16th of an ounce.

Rods to be used with the Bache Brown type of reel require a much larger lower guide than found on fly rods; it must be ¾ of an inch in diameter and set up about that distance from the rod. It should not be closer to the reel than 20 inches. The reason for this lies in the lateral motion of the line as it unwinds from the reel spool or is rewound. With the spool of the reel setting at a cross axis to the rod, the "throw" of the line, back and forth, is the diameter of the reel spool. The guides are decreased in diameter to the tip, but this assembly is necessary to add to the full freedom of the line movement as it is cast. The grips on these rods are also somewhat different than in trout fly rods, being 12 to 14 inches long.

Basic construction of good spinning rods follows closely that of the standard fly rod, with those of glass fiber dominating the field.

CASTING RODS

There are two main divisions in this group, which are associated with the multiplying reel and its facility for paying out line on the cast. They are the fairly standardized bait casting rod for fresh-water game fish, and the much longer, heavier rod used in surf casting.

The bait casting rod of more or less standard type is from 4½ to 6 feet in length. The difference in length combined with type of material used in its construction, and the "action" of the rod, whether stiff or limber, make the main difference between one such rod and another.

The bamboo bait casting rod is built in essentially the same way as the fly rod of the same material; six strips of bamboo cane, selected, fashioned, joined and finished. The same considerations of quality of bamboo goes into the making. Such rods are made in one length which fits into the handle, or of two lengths, a ferrule in the center, with the bottom section permanently fitted with the grip. Rods of this material are usually considered somewhat more "sporting," but the main reason they are preferred by some is that they are somewhat lighter than comparable rods of other material.

Taper again, in this type of rod, determines the place "where the action falls." However, it is not possible to whip the shorter, somewhat stiff casting rods into the double-bend rhythm which reveals the point of action in a fly rod. A check of the taper, a bending of the rod, whipping it a bit with a dummy plug attached to the tip, will have to serve in checking a casting rod's action.

A spring steel rod, crude and the forerunner of the fine steel rods of the present day, was under test before 1850. The real antecedent of present steel rods made its appearance as a commercial product a little before 1900. Since the improvement of steel alloys, the steel casting rods have become the dominant sort in general use.

The "rapier" type of casting rod is so named because of close resemblance to the type of sword bearing that name, which has a thin blade and principally used in thrusting. Rapier rods are solid, alloy steel and may be four or six sided or round. The taper determines whether they are of light or limber action, medium, or stiff. They are the type of rod which will generally stand up under the most punishment.

Tubular steel rods are just that; hollow. Some are drawn in a continuous taper, while others have a "step-down" construction, in which the decrease in diameter takes place in a series of reductions, with the tube of uniform diameter between these points. The step-down construction is supposed to give somewhat better action. Selection between rods of the two sub-types, smooth or step-down, and in rods within each group is up to the individual.

Glass rods are a comparatively recent innovation, made possible by the development of synthetic resin binder material during World War II. The basic construction principle is binding together with such resins, a great number of almost microscopic glass fibers to form the rod. The tensile strength of such fibers exceeds that of steel. They are so very fine, that each fiber in itself, is as flexible as silk.

It has been pointed out that the resilience of bamboo, found in the hard rind, is due to a glass-like substance in the fibers. The glass rod approaches a synthetic replication of the natural process occurring in growing bamboo. Because it is a controlled mechanized and chemical process, it can achieve the advantage of uniformity in texture, elimination of such flaws as inevitably occur in nature-grown bamboo, and approach the flexibility which makes the bamboo rod a favorite.

Early models of glass rods and some cheap imitations of the better products, possess a major defect. Glass fiber rubbing against glass fiber very quickly cuts in two. In the body of the rod there are tremendous numbers of such tiny fibers which, if not insulated against such abrasive action as the rod flexes, will cut the rod to pieces. In early hours of use the rod behaved excellently. But unless there is protection against abrasion around *each individual fiber* within the body of the rod, cutting takes place, and sudden failure shows up because the rod "has its insides cut to pieces."

Most glass rods are now produced by a process which spreads an ultra-thin but protective resin sheath over each of the tiny fibers. This can't be determined by superficial inspection of the rods themselves. It can be ascertained by determining the process of manufacture. Those companies which employ this advanced and long-life process are pretty sure to reveal it as a talking point in favor of their rods, while those which do not possess this protective feature will pass it over. But make no mistake; if glass fiber rubs against glass fiber, it cuts, and quickly.

Glass rods are made solid, with a core of such material as balsa wood and hollow.

All steel and glass rods for bait casting are usually made with the "blade" of the rod itself without joints. A ferrule fits into the handle which contains the reel seat. A distinct difference between fly rods and those for bait casting is the position of the reel in reference to the grip. In the fly rods, the reel seat is below the grip; in the casting rods it is above the hand.

The types of grips for casting rods are divided into straight and off-set. The straight grip is in line with the rod in all its length, the reel standing out from the seat. The off-set has a dip in the handle, which drops the reel down in relation to the axis of the rod. The advantages of the off-set reel lie in bringing it down to where the reel spool is more easily reached by the thumb, and putting the line more in direct alignment with the guides, thus reducing wear. The grip of the off-set handle may be in direct line with the axis of the rod as in most models, or there may be a slight angling of the grip.

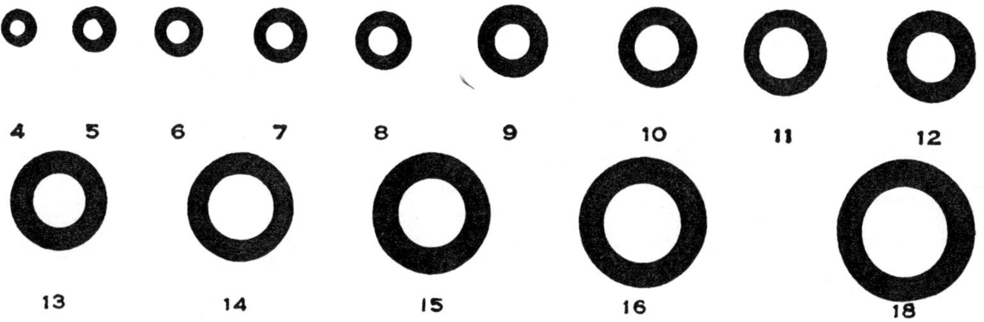

South Bend Bait Co.

Agate guide sizes. These guides are shown actual size and are measured in millimeters.

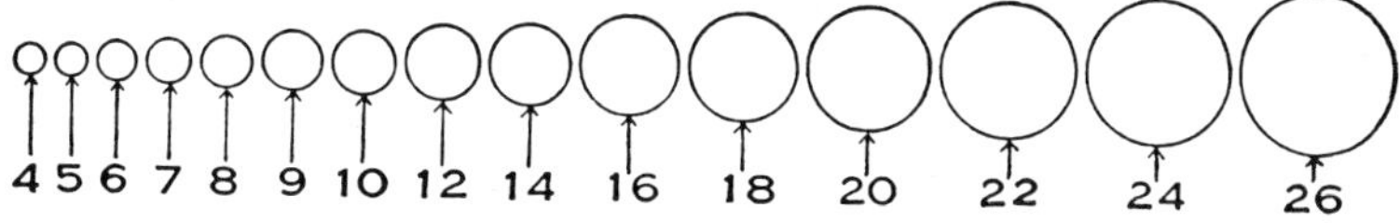

South Bend Bait Co.

Rod tip sizes. These rod tips are shown actual size and are measured in sixty-fourths of an inch.

The grip itself is usually of cork. Cork has small tubular openings running parallel to the trunk of the tree on which it grows. Ordinary bottle corks are cut across this grain and these tubular openings can be seen. The finest cork for rod grips is cut with the grain, so no such tube gives an opening for moisture to go directly to the center of the grip and loosen the cork. Cork so cut is termed "jug cut." Generally this cork is put on in rings and compressed. A number of shapes are made so the contour fits the hand and that is a matter of personal preference—which fits your grip best.

Formerly the guides for better casting rods were fitted with rings of agate or simulated agate. A cracked guide could play hob with the line. With the introduction of the extremely hard steel ring, with those made by the Perfection Tip Company as examples of this construction, the shift has been to these equally hard and smooth, noncracking guides.

In selecting a casting rod, give attention to the device which is supplied to insure the reel remaining tight on the rod. There are several types; a sleeve that screws down over the upper part of the reel attachment, a plate screwed down to hold this end of the reel with the other fitted into the slot, and some other variations. Still another feature on some rods is a locking device which insures the male part of the ferrule remaining tight in place; cinching it in place so it will not let the rod shoot out on the cast or while landing a fish.

SALT WATER RODS

These are, in major features, stout "big brothers" of the casting-trolling, and spinning rod groups. Those for trolling for heavy fish usually are from 6 to 7 feet in length. Two indications of their suitability are in the weight of the tip, which will run from 4 to 12 ounces, depending upon the type of fish sought and the weight of line required.

Other types are genuine casting rods, used in surf casting. The heavier models have long grips, for added leverage and two-hand casting, and overall lengths of from 8 to 12 feet. For lighter fishing, such as for Weakfish and Bluefish, the rods are lighter, and many anglers use standard fresh-water rigs for these species where they regularly come within casting distance of this tackle. Long, double-handled spinning rods with light tips provide casting distance where needed and provide much more sporting fishing for these smaller species than the heavy casting rods formerly used universally as surf tackle.

Fiberglass has now replaced almost entirely all other materials for salt-water use, and bamboo rods are found only in the most expensive models.

In rods, as in nearly any product, the integrity and reputation of the maker are always guides to a good product.

TACKLE ACCESSORIES

The standard tackle assembly for sport fishing, is lure, hook, leader, line, reel and rod. Those sections are common to all rod-and-reel types of fishing.

There are, however, some accessories for the tackle assembly itself, which are used in various types of sport fishing, and any discussion of tackle units should include mention of these.

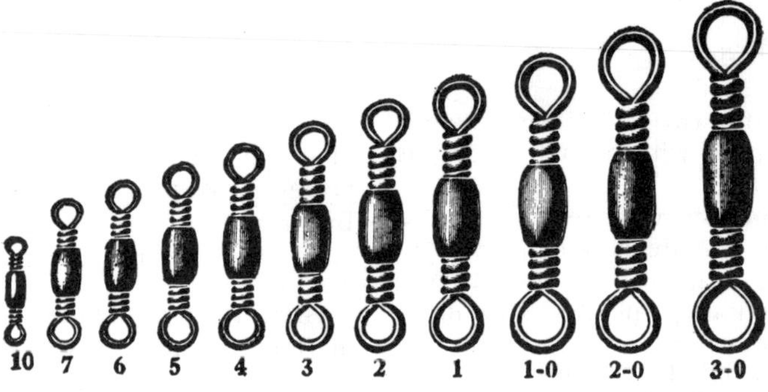

Actual sizes of swivels.

The two most common minor additions to the tackle assembly are swivels and sinkers, with snaps a third bit of convenience.

SWIVELS

There are no essential differences in swivels. They are of metal, usually in three parts. A wire loop at one end has a short shaft inserted in a "barrel" with the end of that shaft spread to prevent it slipping out of the barrel cavity. The eyelet can revolve with the widened end of the little shaft as the bearing. The other end of the swivel is a duplicate. With such a double joint, allowing free rotation, a lure attached at one end which is twisting can turn without imparting that motion to the line at the other end of the swivel.

That is the function of the swivel—to prevent the twisting of one unit from being transmitted all along the remainder of the line.

In spite of everything, a spinning lure will tend to twist line. Many of the spinner lures are fitted with swivels at their line end as they leave the factory to incorporate this "universal joint" in the assembly. Any lure which will turn consistently in one direction requires a swivel to prevent this

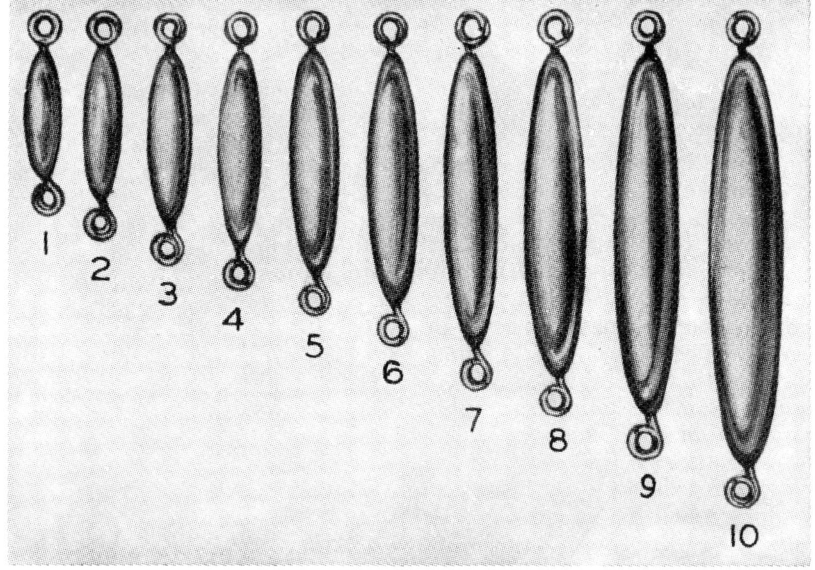

Courtesy Horrocks-Ibbotson Co.

Common ringed sinkers.

motion being built up in twist of the entire line—and a twisted line on the reel spells trouble.

Swivels are more used in trolling with spinning spoons than in any other sort of angling. There is one lure when used with a trout rod that is a super-spinner-twister. That is the Colorado Spinner. Since the spoon blade is attached to a split ring and there is no shaft for it to revolve around, the entire hook-up must turn. In single-blade Colorado spinners, there is a swivel above the split ring, another below. A double-bladed lure of this type has a total of *four* swivels to allow free turning of the lure without line twist.

Swivels may be either closed-barrel, in which the enlarged end of the shaft is entirely covered, or another type which has open sides, somewhat like an enlarged link. Swivels are made in a variety of sizes to fit the size of lure and other tackle. The big ones are produced for heavy duty in salt-water fishing. The material is hardened brass or bronze. Ball-bearing swivels provide the greatest insurance against line twist.

While there isn't much to be checked in selecting a swivel, it is well to know that the knobs on the end of the shafts are sufficient to prevent pulling out.

SINKERS

The purpose of the sinker is to get the lure down deeper when desired. The simplest application is to put a bit of lead on the line so that the portion below the bobber will hang down as you are fishing for bottom feeders. Another use is to add a bit of lead to a lure which is of light weight, to supply weight for casting. Still another use enters in some salt-water fishing, where a flattish sinker is used, to "anchor" the end of the line and hold the lure in position so it will not be whipped about by currents. A sinker which is of the "keel" type, with one side larger than the

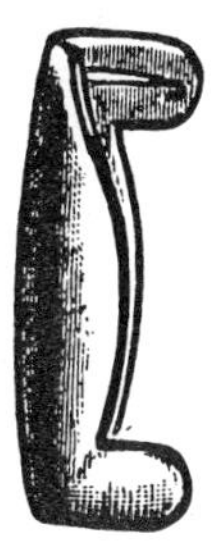

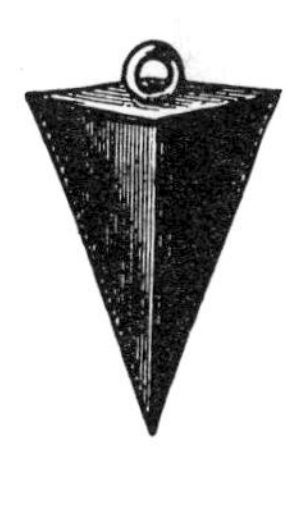

Courtesy Horrocks-Ibbotson Co.

Three types of lead sinkers.

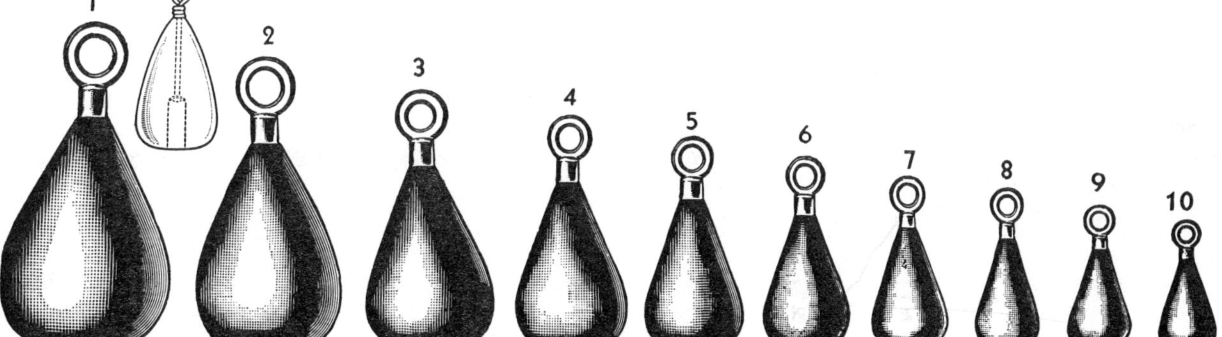

South Bend Bait Co.

Actual sized swivel dipsey sinkers.

other, will tend to travel with that side down all the time, and if placed above a swivel, will aid in preventing any line twist that might occur in spite of the swivel.

Sinkers are shaped to fit the type of fishing to be done. They generally are of soft lead.

The simplest sort of sinker is a lead shot, with a cut in one side, into which line or leader may be inserted, and by squeezing the crack shut, fasten it to the line. Sizes run from BB to buck shot. This type enables the fisherman to put on one or more, depending on the depth to which the lure is to be carried, and how much current has to be counteracted to "get the lure down." The disadvantage of split shot lies in its bulging out from the line and forming a point where it may hang-up in a rock crevice or a submerged snag.

Spindle-shaped sinkers reduce this tendency to get caught in under-water obstructions. They are made with a slot along the side into which the line may be laid, with lead "ears" at each end which may be bent to hold the sinker in place. They are fitted with a bit of close-coiled wire at each end, which has been molded into the sinker. In the coiled-wire end, the line is merely slipped in between two of the coils to secure attachment.

A third type of sinker is merely a strip of thin lead, which may be wrapped around line or leader in a spiral. It has the least bulk of all, and can be used best where there is need for a relatively light sinker.

The fourth type is the "dipsey," a squat, cone-shaped bit of lead. This is an end-of-the-line sinker. It usually is rigged to drag along the bottom in trolling. As an illustration, the lure is put on the line's end, and the dipsey is attached by say three feet of old casting line to a point on the main line a couple of feet above the lure. In action then, the dipsey drags along the bottom, the lure strings out behind a foot or so above the bottom and in a position not likely to get snagged. If the dipsey gets caught in bottom snags, the stouter main line can snap the old casting line, the dipsey is lost, but the lure is saved. Since a dipsey costs but a few cents and the lure a dollar or so, there's economy in that. At the same time the lure is held in the right position for deep, near-the-bottom trolling.

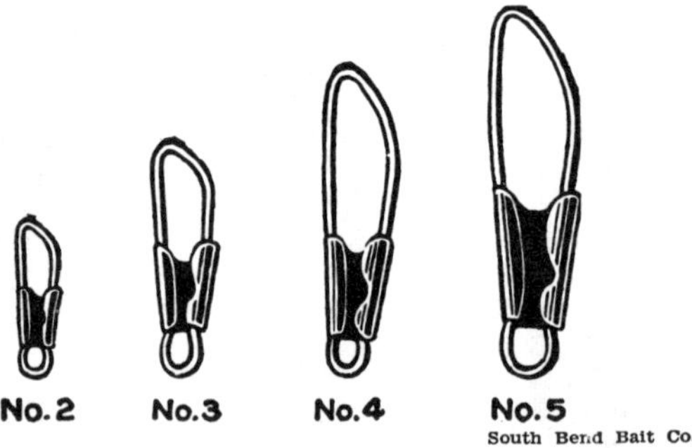

South Bend Bait Co.

Typical snaps used in assembling tackle.

Another use of the line-end dipsey is to carry out the cast, sink to the bottom, and supply a light "anchor" at that point. With baited hooks a foot, two feet, or similar distances back along the line, the line then can be tightened until it is pulling slightly against the dipsey and the bait is held just above the bottom so anchored it will not whip around in currents.

Dipseys are made in various sizes; a standard range from No. 10 which weighs 1/8 ounce, to No. 1 weighing 3½ ounces. Weights heavier than that are designated by a number, a diagonal mark and a zero back of that; the 3/0 dipsey for example weighs 8 ounces.

SNAPS

Snaps work in about the same fashion as a safety pin. They are of spring wire, without the point of course, with one end of the wire solidly seated, the other readily depressed to "open" the snap. It is easy to slip the eyelet of a lure or a leader over the wire of the open snap, and close it—far easier than untying and re-tying a knot. That is the value of a snap on leaders or other point of attachment at the lure end of the line. They are used mostly in bait casting, and trolling in either fresh-water and salt-water fishing.

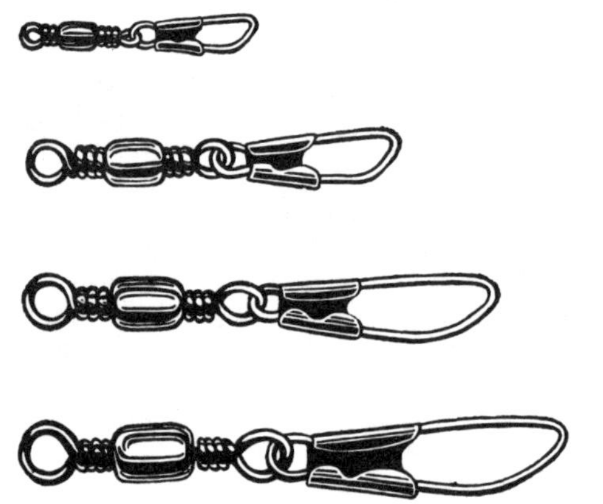

South Bend Bait Co.

Typical snap and swivel.

For convenience, tackle makers often make combinations of swivels, leaders, snaps and sinkers, combining any one unit with another; for example, a leader which has a swivel at one end, and a swivel and snap at the other.

Individual anglers and manufacturers experimenting and testing, will cook up other attachments and gadgets which may be added to the basic tackle assembly.

MISCELLANEOUS FISHING GEAR

In addition to regular angling equipment, there are almost innumerable gadgets available, and anglers are inclined to stock up with such articles. Many are standard equipment for certain types of fishing. Only those used regularly by a considerable number of fishermen will be listed, as the list could be stretched out almost endlessly if variants offered were included.

BAIT BOXES

The original bait box, and still the most widely used, is a tin can used to carry the earth worms or grasshoppers. The flat, tin tobacco boxes are also widely used. For bank or boat fishermen, they serve the purpose as well as a special article, and they can be discarded at the end of the fishing trip.

For those wading to fish, bait boxes or live-bait cages designed to fasten on the belt are available in various sizes and shapes. They keep crayfish, frogs, grasshoppers, worms, crickets, and similar baits alive and in a convenient place for use. They offer a real advantage when the hands are needed for something other than holding a bait can while fishing out another bait.

BAROMETERS

An increasing number of fishermen are carrying barometers in order to be able to forecast weather conditions for at least a few hours. There are reliable barometers on the market which will accomplish that purpose. They are valuable not only to give some indication as to the kind of clothing to be worn on a particular day, but many fishermen believe that fish respond to barometric changes.

Anyone purchasing such an accessory should get one that is reliable, compact, and easy to carry. Some on the market are too bulky to pack around, the most easily carried being made the size and shape of a watch.

CREELS

The classic creel and the one most often seen is the creel basket usually woven of willow to a definite shape and size. These are slung over one shoulder and hung under the arm at the waist on the opposite side of the body. They are used mostly by stream fishermen, since those fishing from boats have less need for such a device.

In recent years various types of canvas bags, some of them with waterproof innerlining that can be taken out and washed if necessary are on the market. Collapsible fish bags and creels are also available in several styles and shapes, all of them serving the same purpose—providing a convenient way of carrying fish when walking or wading to fish.

It is easy to wash the willow creels by rinsing them in the stream. Anyone purchasing a canvas creel should find out first whether it is easily washed or not. A bag that cannot be cleaned becomes a smelly accessory in a comparatively short time.

Some of the more fancy creels have outside pockets for tackle and have other accessories useful to fishermen.

FLY BOOKS

Fly books are made in a wide variety of styles and shapes. The ones for snelled wet flies contain plastic leaves with springs and clips to hold flies with felt drying pads between. Usually within the leaves are pockets for other bits of tackle. Those designed for dry flies may contain a series of small, flat compartments in an aluminum box. A combination will have both these and plastic envelopes with dryers attached or just plastic sheets with felt drying pads between for holding wet flies. Almost any one that suits the fancy of the individual is satisfactory, and all will carry many more flies than any fisherman can use in one day.

Most fishermen make a selection for the day's fishing and keep a reserve supply of other lures in the tackle box, changing those in the book as the occasion demands.

FLY BOXES

With the development of various plastics, a whole array of fly boxes and fly containers have been placed on the market. Many of these are trans-

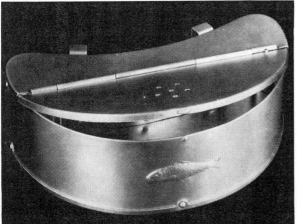

Abercrombie and Fitch

Bait box.

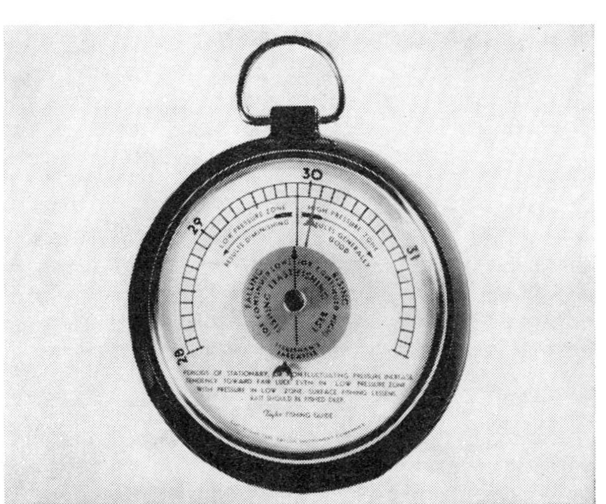

Abercrombie and Fitch

Barometer.

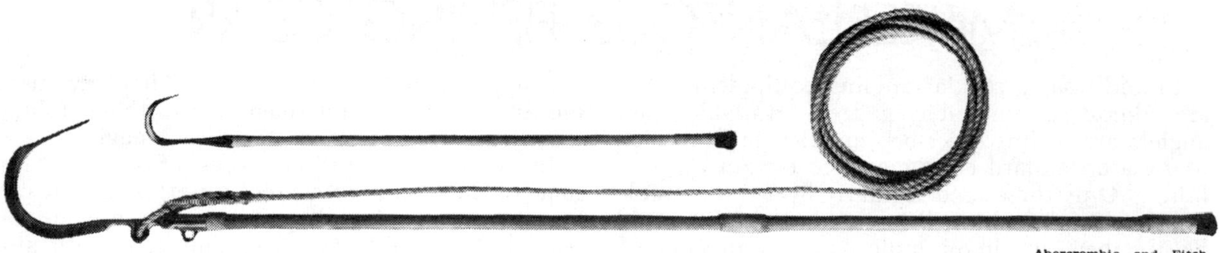

Abercrombie and Fitch

Gaff hook.

parent and give the angler the advantage of being able to see what is in the box before it is opened. They also keep the flies from being pressed out of shape, something that frequently happens in the fly book. Some are divided into small compartments; others have various combinations so the flies can be stored loosely in the pokets or attached to cork rods or strips provided.

These boxes have the disadvantage of being somewhat more bulky than a fly book; the larger ones are so big that they will only fit into a large pocket.

GAFF HOOKS

Gaff hooks are boat equipment only. Fishermen fishing the banks or wading do not carry such equipment. Large, long-handled ones are used on the sea-going cruisers for landing big game fish. Smaller hooks with shorter handles are used largely by those fishing for Lake Trout or Northern Pike inland, or for the medium-sized salt water fish.

While they are on the market in a number of different designs, all have heavy, sharp hooks with a handle and a hand grip. The newer ones with metal handles are built with a screwed-on handle so that the hook can be taken down and stored in much less space when not in use or when traveling.

KNIVES

Any knife will do for fishermen, although those designed especially for that purpose sometimes have an advantage. The blade should be of good steel to hold an edge; it should be heavy enough for general use and have a sharp point. A blade that locks in position is also a great advantage.

Fisherman's knives can be purchased which provide a complete set of little tools, but the essentials are a strong, sharp blade and point, heavy enough so it will not break when it is needed. One of the best contains one blade, together with another tool that is a hook disgorger and fish scaler. Sometimes the latter is put on the back of the single blade, and the end of the handle itself made into a hook disgorger. The choice rests largely with the fisherman, but the advantages of a knife designed especially for the use of fishermen are great enough to justify the purchase of such a utensil if a great deal of fishing is to be done.

LANDING NETS

Landing nets, like other accessories, come in a variety of shapes and styles but are largely boat or lake equipment. The most easily carried are the collapsible ones that can be folded together into a small, compact bundle when traveling.

Abercrombie and Fitch

Fabric creel.

L. L. Bean

Basket creel.

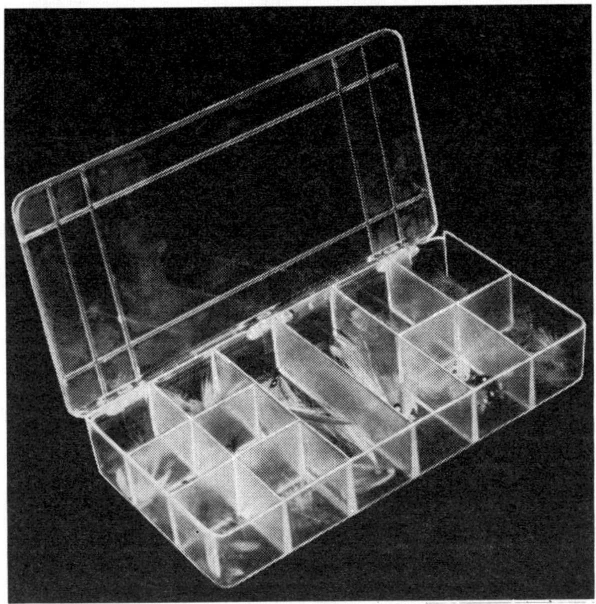

L. L. Bean

Plastic fly box.

Abercrombie and Fitch

Line drier.

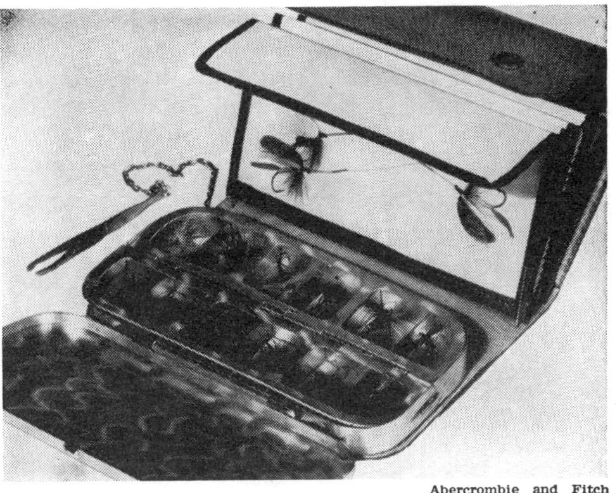

Abercrombie and Fitch

Combination fly book.

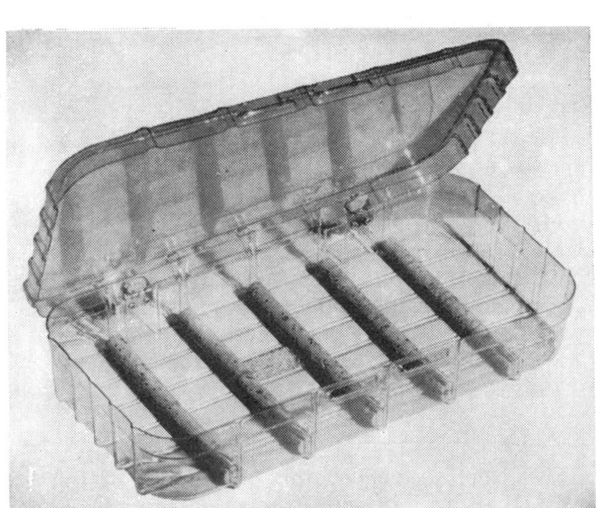

Abercrombie and Fitch

Bass plug box.

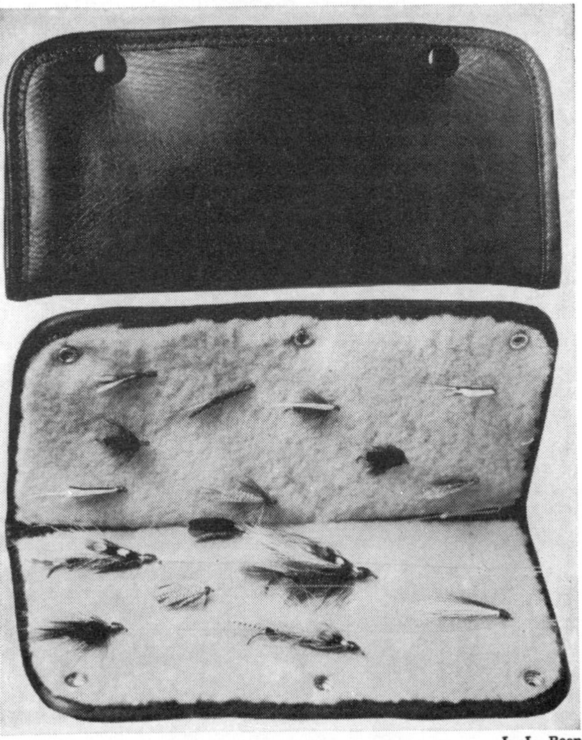

L. L. Bean

Fleece-lined leather fly book.

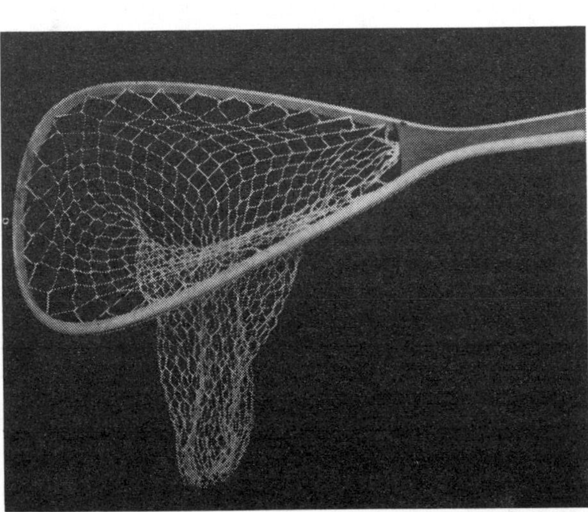

L. L. Bean

Landing net.

Many trout fishermen also carry a landing net that can be carried slung over the shoulder or from the belt. Some fishermen dislike to carry them because they get between their legs when wading, but many fish are lost for lack of a landing net.

LINE DRYERS

Most fishermen dry lines by stretching them between the chairs in the house or between trees on bright, sunny days. If there is no one around to interfere with this practice, it gets results. However, there are wooden or metal reels available which can be used when it is inconvenient to use more primitive methods. Whatever their design, all are small reels on which the line can be wound until dry and then rewound on the reel. Some provide a clamp on which the reel can be fitted while the line is being run off on to the dryer. This is simple, convenient, and economical of space and also time when at home, but is another gadget to carry when in the field. For field use, a vest pocket line dryer that is no bigger than a fountain pen has been designed and put on the market. Those who like gadgets will undoubtedly be fascinated by this one. It is useful and usable, and can be purchased for a nominal sum.

MINNOW BUCKETS

Buckets designed to carry minnows for those who use this type of live bait have long been on the market. The standard design has an outer shell, together with a wire screen or perforated metal bucket which fits into it and may be lifted out. A clamp top insures the minnows staying in place when the bucket is placed in the water. Normally it is hung over the side of the boat when still fishing. It is kept in the boat and the water renewed from time to time when trolling.

There are also more elaborate ones fitted with little aerating pumps and in which minnows can be kept alive without the bother of putting them over the side or changing the water.

Buckets are standard equipment for those who habitually use this type of bait and often one means the difference between success and failure. Dead minnows are usually no better than cut bait so that one expecting to use this lure should keep it alive as long as possible.

Some of the newer buckets are provided with inner buckets of porous plastic, in place of the wire mesh or perforated metal.

MINNOW NETS

Minnow nets for the taking of live bait are also carried by many fishermen, particularly when in remote areas where there are no regular bait suppliers. The most common is a folding net which can be packed into small space. It consists of a square of small mesh net measuring approximately three feet each way, extended by two crossed rods from corner to corner. The cord by which it is lowered is attached to the point where the rods cross, and lifted when minnows are attracted to the bait placed in the net.

Other fishermen carry a small length of fine mesh net and make small minnow seines by cutting a couple of poles at the point where they wish to secure bait. This type requires wading, which means a shallow place inhabited by a sufficient number of minnows must be found before the gear can be successfully used.

MINNOW TRAPS

Minnow traps are also used to secure bait. The older, conventional type is a barrel-like, galvanized mesh wire container with a funnel on each end through which the minnows can enter. It is lowered into the water with a cord and has the advantage of being fishable at any depth that minnows are likely to occur. There are similar traps made of transparent plastics.

REPAIR KITS

Repair kits for fishermen are as varied as fishermen themselves. Some of them carry tools enough to do a complete job of tackle mending. A minimum should consist of small, blunt-nosed pliers; small screwdriver; small pocket oil can with a screw cap; small flat stone for sharpening hooks or knives; and a small roll of tape. Many other small tools that are useful occasionally can be added, if desired, but it should be remembered that all add to the weight of the gear.

SCALES

Fishermen's exaggeration of the size of fish are proverbial, and in self-protection many fishermen now carry small scales to weigh their larger catches. Those desiring such equipment should look for accuracy and small size, since every gadget adds to the amount of weight on a fishing trip.

A gadget appropriately named the *Fisherman's Deliar* is on the market. It weighs the fish and also has a 24 inch steel tape for measurements. The unit is little larger than an ordinary cigarette lighter, but can be bought in several sizes. Those anxious to know the accurate size and weight can purchase this one.

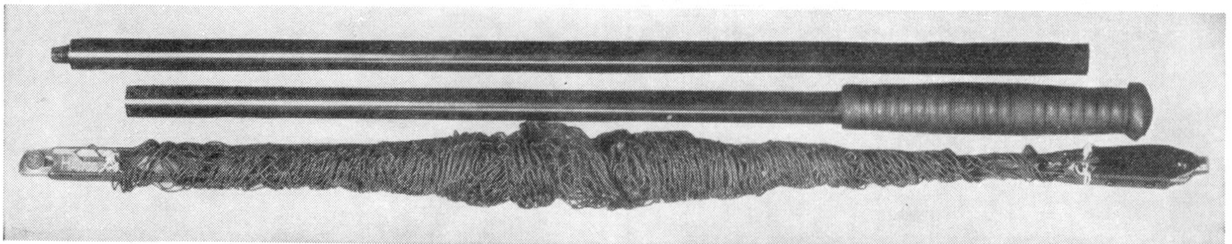

L. L. Bean

Live-bait net.

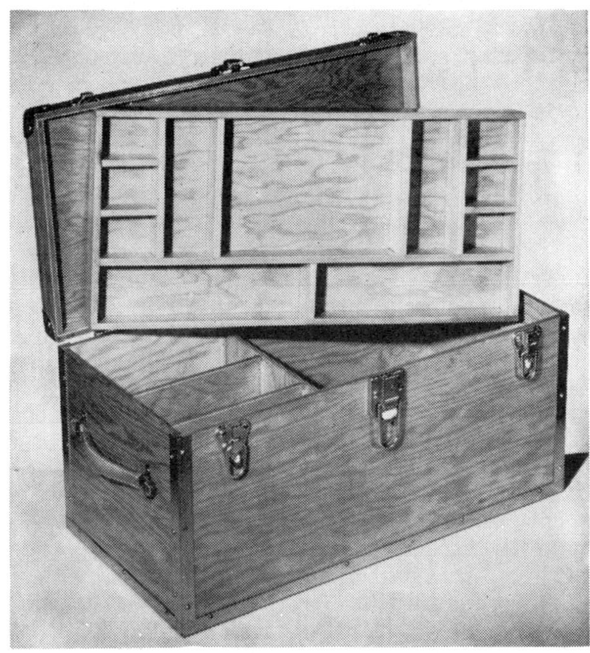

Abercrombie and Fitch

Reinforced wood tackle box.

Abercrombie and Fitch

Metal tackle box.

FISH STRINGERS

The country boy has always taken home his catch by cutting a willow fork; so that fish could be strung on one or both of the long twigs. Another common practice is to use a short length of line with small three or four inch sticks tied around the center; one stick is used in threading a fish on the stringer through the gill opening, the other to hold the fish on the end of the line.

There are light chain stringers, each with several safety pin-type hooks that will hold several panfish or one larger fish. They are mostly valuable for use in lake or stream fishing from a boat. Those fishing by wading or from a bank prefer creels or bags to stringers.

There are also mesh nets in which fish can be kept alive. These have the advantage of keeping the fish uninjured and in better shape than those put on stringers.

TACKLE BOXES

Tackle boxes are available in a wide variety of styles and complexities. A cigar box is a convenient tackle box for the average small boy and the angler who only fishes occasionally. There are metal, plastic, and leather tackle boxes on the market, usually about 16 to 20 inches long, six inches deep, and about the same width. Cheap boxes can be a nuisance in having a single tray that lifts out; if it does not fit too well, it usually spills the hooks and other material into the bottom.

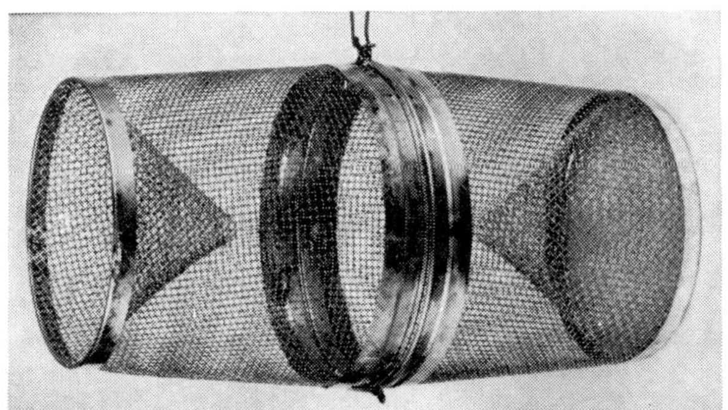

Abercrombie and Fitch

Minnow trap.

The better ones have one or more trays which are hinged to lift out as the box lid is opened. Those that open out flat are better than those in which the lid stands up, as the latter are too easily upset. Some that do not open out flat have a heavy handle as a prop to hold the lid steady.

In purchasing a box, be sure that there is no place into which a hook or leader can work itself while being carried about in a car or a boat.

Metal boxes have the disadvantage of rusting quickly around salt water but are the ones most commonly available. There are tackle boxes of plastic which lack this disadvantage, but which are not as strong as the metal boxes. The tackle box takes a good deal of punishment in the course of a season, when carried in a car or boat.

Those who go in for expensive cases can buy English leather cases made to hold rods, reels, leader books, fly books, boxes in a great variety. They can also spend a lot of money in purchasing such units if their inclinations run to gadgets.

THERMOMETERS FOR FISHING

Many fishermen believe that the temperature of the water has much to do with the success or failure of their fishing trips. An increasing number of them are carrying thermometers. As in buying a barometer, anglers should get an accurate one if they invest at all. It should also be easy to read and light and compact, if it is to be handy when needed. Some made in a fountain pen style are both convenient to carry and easily read.

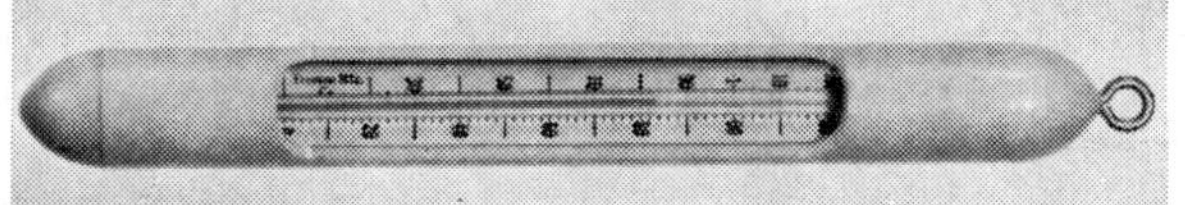

Abercrombie and Fitch

Thermometer.

Part 2. Fresh Water Methods

HANDLING THE TACKLE

Able manipulation of sport fishing tackle requires a reasonable amount of practice and skill. Certainly, the ability to put the business end of the line where a fish will grab the lure is fundamental.

There is a tendency on the part of some interested in sport fishing to throw so much emphasis on niceties in tackle handling that it becomes the dominant theme. It's granted that it is pleasant to watch someone who so handles tackle that it performs with exactness in every move. It also is granted that those who can find enjoyment in thus handling their tackle, acquiring increasing skill, have an added return from their angling activities.

Good tackle handling actually is a means to an end. Its real objective is to permit the angler to lay his lure so it will attract fish. When one loses sight of this and puts form and finesse ahead of the act of angling, he becomes a "tackleist" instead of an angler. When this develops into a sort of cultism it veers away from fishing as such, and tackle manipulation overshadows the true goal of using fishing equipment.

There is no condemnation of the super-tackleist. The enjoyment derived from contest casting, the pride in being expert, are things to be sought and cherished. Many anglers could use more of the practice and study of better tackle handling. But when such skill is acquired, it must be recognized that it is a means for securing the tangible return from skills acquired—fish in the creel or on a stringer.

Fundamentals covered here are groundwork for going on toward tournament casting. Far more important, they are the foundation for greater enjoyment and success in angling. Two types of skills separate the dub from the able angler. The first skill is a certain smooth, well controlled handling of the tackle assembly. The other is waterlore: the knowledge of fishes and the place to put which lure for the game species sought. Tackle skill and waterlore combine to produce results.

The first hours, almost minutes, in which the tackle assembled is in hand are of utmost importance. The goal sought is to become wholly unconscious of the series of moves made to put a lure in the desired spot. One wants to be so proficient that merely thinking of placing a lure at a certain spot in a certain way, sets in motion the smoothly blended sequence of motions that accomplished the objective.

When that point is reached, the tackle, in the way it responds, becomes almost a living extension of oneself and all attention can be given to the pleasures of fishing.

Whenever any action is first undertaken, it must be thought through, move by move.

Psychologists have called the channels which thought commands follow "neuronic tracts." Every time the sequence of an act is repeated these "tracts" are deepened or what might be called "grooved." This is the way habit is formed; the process by which good or bad habits in tackle handling are established. Ultimately, all that is necessary to place a lure in a chosen spot is to start the thought of such action; and the resulting sequence of action zips through from the mind, automatically accomplishing the act.

Those who start their fishing careers by slam-banging line and lure invariably set up awkward and troublesome habits of tackle manipulation. It's harder to break down "habit channels" that are bad and re-learn the right way, than to start along good lines and follow through. If casting habits have been formed on the slam-bang, let's-get-fishing routine, new habit channels must be developed to become a more expert angler.

Many of the fundamentals of manipulating bait and fly casting rigs are so nearly similar that what is applicable to one closely parallels the other. Most important of all is the in-graving of the correct "habit channels."

The use of the wrist, the motion of the forearm, the spring of the rod on the back cast (which provides the power for the forward cast), the points at which motions take place are quite similar in both types of casting. The super-expert will argue the points, perhaps, but there is enough similarity to make it easier for one who has handled one type of casting rig to learn the use of another than if he had no experience whatever.

Therefore, by a reasonably thorough discussion of one type of casting much of the ground work for others can be laid. Major differences between fly, bait and other technics of casting can then be pointed out.

While there may be points touched which will cause anyone who has done some casting, to remark, "Even a dumbell knows that!" it won't hurt to review essentials. There always is a tendency to get away from basic stuff too fast and give too much attention, too soon, to details. These following paragraphs are instruction to beginners, and certainly review for others.

BAIT CASTING

ASSEMBLING THE TACKLE

The rod is the first unit to be put together. It should be unnecessary to warn against trying to align the line guides in the different sections or with the reel, by twisting the rod after ferrules are together. But some do it. No rod is built to take such torque.

Thrust the male portion into the female portion of the ferrule by a direct, straight thrust. If guides are out of alignment, loosen the parts and firm them together again. Ordinary light oil may get gummy on the contact surfaces of ferrules, and the advice is against using it. If oil is used, only the highest grade, very light oil, should be applied thinly with a rag slightly moistened with oil. Many lay the male part of the ferrule alongside the nose, and give it a twist or two to pick up the natural skin oil, or rubbing it through the hair will supply good lubrication.

Sight the guides in; be sure they are in a straight line from reel to tip. Off-line guides wear as line shoots through them and they wear the line.

In setting up a new bait casting rod, one is likely to notice that the ferrule at the grip end does not seat fully down. On good rods, such ferrules are made for very close fitting, and the male part is purposely slightly over-size. It has a very light taper. It will wear a little as it is used, and the tiny bit of over-size and taper are provided so there will be tight joining at this part throughout the life of the rod. If the ferrule is fully seated at the start, wear would finally be sufficient to make it loose. The rod would wobble slightly on the cast or it would be loose enough to go shooting out from the handle with the cast. So if the ferrule at this point does not fully seat at first, simply thrust it in firmly and put it in use. It will "wear in" fast enough to seat entirely.

Now seat the reel. Any locking devise to hold it should be comfortably tight. Pull the line through the guides. Slip on the reel "click" to prevent excess line running off the spool. Some tie a six-inch loop in the end of a casting line; it gives double line just above the leader, and it is a facility for threading the double line of the loop through the eyelet of leader or swivel, passing the loop over and bringing it up taut. The leader can now be attached, say a 6 inch piano wire type, to the end of the line loop, the snap of the leader at the outer end, and a plug snapped on. The standard ⅝ ounce rubber, plastic or wooden practice plug, without hooks, is a convenient gadget built for non-fishing casting. The rubber type can be pitched indoors without knocking all the plaster off a wall but it isn't guaranteed not to crash a window. If such a plug is unavailable any old plug with hooks removed, medium weight, will do. Or a little sack filled with sand can be used, although this isn't the shape used in actual castiig.

THE ACT OF CASTING

The over-head (straight back, straight forward motion of the rod) is the basic one to learn. Fundamental moves in the over-head cast embody the essence of most other casts.

To take a grip on the rod, hold it in the left hand, so the rod balances. If the rod is held free, the weight of the reel will turn it underneath. A right-handed caster, will want the reel, handles up, on the side of the rod to the left. Reels are located on the bait casting rod just above the hand grip. Turn the rod so the reel takes this position, and grip the rod with the left hand to hold it there. Now let the right hand drop naturally over the grip. The thumb will be in a position to touch the reel spool. That's the place for it. One of the bits of coordination to be developed is the use of the thumb to control the rate of turning of the reel in relation to the rate at which the cast lure is carrying out line.

There are two ways to brake the reel by using the thumb. One is on the line wound on the reel. The better one is by lightly touching the flange

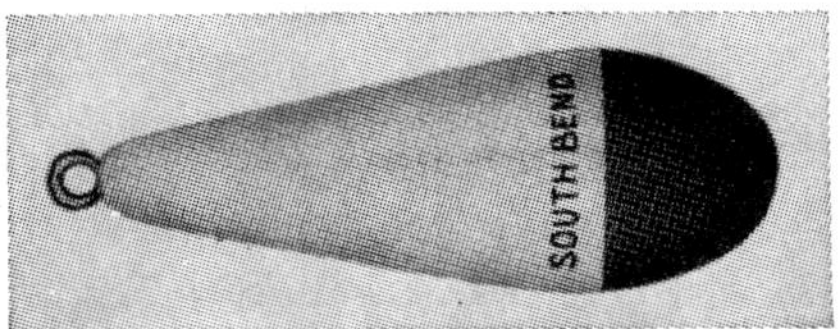

South Bend Bait Co.

Practice Casting Weight.

or side of the reel spool. In the cast, one needs to get the "feel" of how the line is traveling out in relation to the turning of the spool. Practice will develop this. The touch of the thumb as a brake on the spinning reel spool should be just enough to prevent it from "over-running" the line.

Now, with a grip on the rod, the thumb on the reel to hold it from letting out line, try whipping the rod back and forth. Hold it out at about the "ten o'clock position" as though you were standing beside a big clock dial, with that dial to the right. Bring the rod up over your shoulder in a straight swinging motion, describing a vertical arc. Check the rod when it is slightly passed the perpendicular. The weight of the plug on the end will bend the rod back. It isn't a bad idea to let someone do this also, while you watch the way the bow goes into the rod as you check it and the plug weight bends the tip back. Actually on a medium limber 5 foot casting rod, the tip will bend back almost toward the three o'clock position even though the axis of the grip has not gone any farther than the one o'clock point.

There are those who have figured out just how many degrees of a circle one should swing through in this back-sweep motion. They'll fix the exact point to check the rod and even diagram it. The fact is that there is no precise point on the circle that applies to all casters, all casts, all rods, all lure weights. One fellow will let this back sweep go very little beyond perpendicular. The next one will let it drift back to near one o'clock. One rod will not let the tip bend much beyond two o'clock; another rod will bend so the tip points to three o'clock. One will develop the feel of the point at which the back sweep should be checked for the tackle in hand and the lure to be cast.

Still keeping the thumb on the reel, "play" with back and forth rod-whipping. Get the feel of the power the whipping motion develops. That feel of life in the rod is part of the whole effort to link together all the movements as a good cast is made.

One should "fuss around" quite a little while with this preliminary playing with the rod. To

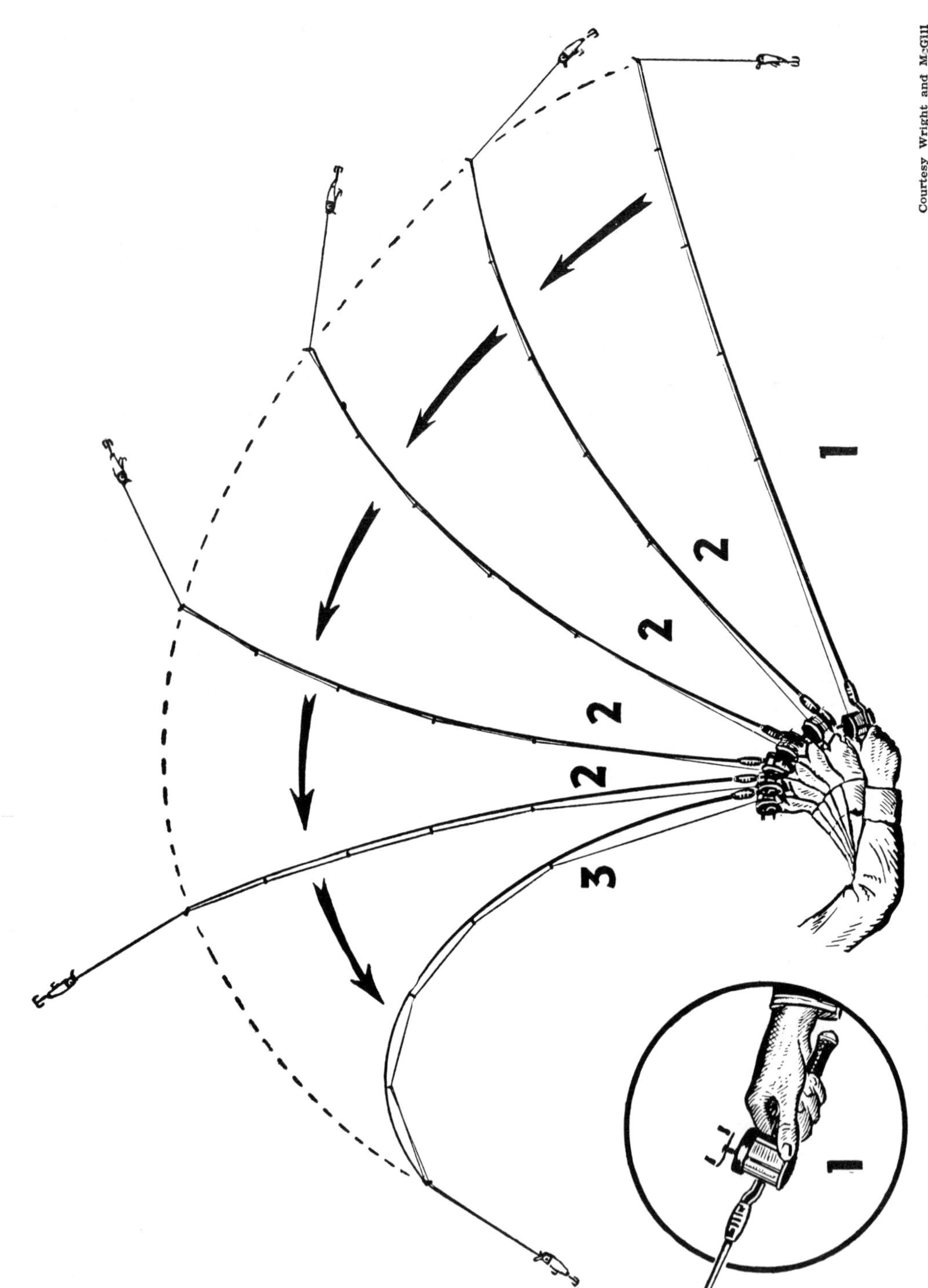

Courtesy Wright and McGill

Backward motion of the wrist, forearm and rod preparatory to making a cast.

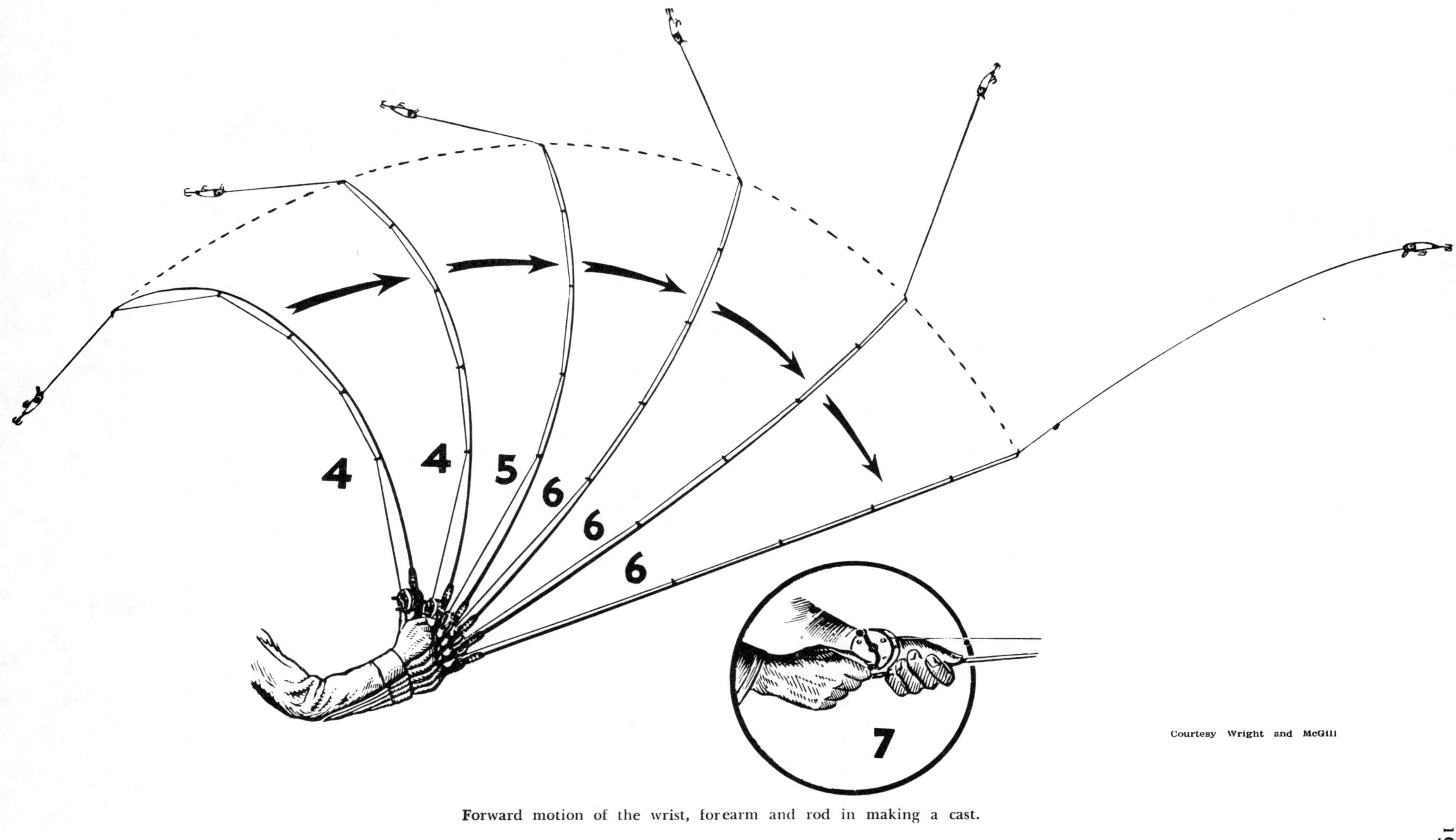

Courtesy Wright and McGill

Forward motion of the wrist, forearm and rod in making a cast.

start making trial casts, place a newspaper or cardboard a foot to two feet square about 12 steps away. Now step back to take up the rod in casting position. Generally the right foot will instinctively be placed a little ahead. It gives a little easier position.

The mistake most commonly made by beginners is to try to make the cast through application of muscle power. It's the wrong approach. The power lies in that live body of the bent rod. The power to bow the rod is applied through the wrist; rocking back and forward.

A handkerchief or folded newspaper can be placed under the upper arm if it will help. Keep it close to the body in these preliminary stages. Form this habit. Holding something between the upper arm and body directs action into using the wrist to whip the rod. There is a slight movement of the forearm up and down, but in this over-head cast, the arm from the elbow up should be kept immobile.

Slip the click off the reel if it is on. The casting plug should be 5 or 6 inches beyond the tip of the rod. A short leader will insure the distance of this "tip end swing" that goes into this casting.

Now do this slowly—at least comparatively slowly. Hold the rod pointing out to about ten o'clock. Bring it back easily, with increasing speed, past the perpendicular a little, and check it.

As this is done, if the grip is not held too tightly, the handle of the rod will rock slightly over the fulcrum of the web between the thumb and first finger. The lower fingers will pry out a little.

As the rod bends back and reaches the farthest bend beyond the point where it is checked, the lower fingers should be closed in a squeezing motion rather than by a quick clutching. Simultaneously the forearm is moved down a little, and at the same time the gripped hand is rocked forward on the wrist hinge, propelling the rod tip in a forward-sweeping arc.

As the rod springs forward, reaching a point slightly beyond eleven o'clock, check the sweep of the rod, and release the thumb pressure on the reel flange. The plug shoots out. It takes line with it. The reel whizzes under the lightest touch of the thumb. The plug is nearing the end of its flight. The lightest increase of thumb pressure on the reel will slow it down so the spool will turn in proportion to the flight of the plug and the latter's ability to carry out the line that is leaving the reel.

All right, that wasn't very good. Try again. Line the rod up and sight over the rod tip at the target. Swing the rod back—maybe not cast, but bring it down to sight in and see if there is good alignment in the forward sweep. Try again, not too much power. Release the reel; make the cast. Check the reel smoothly as the plug reaches the outer end of the flight.

There's a snap application of power just before the forward motion of the rod is checked that should be learned. It's the last flip of throwing the power of the bowed rod into the cast. One begins to do it somewhat instinctively, but it's good business to think it through in practice.

That handkerchief under the arm just above the elbow has fallen. That's a warning that the upper arm is getting into the cast. No good. Put the handkerchief back and don't let it get away. Hold it there as a reminder to keep that upper arm motion out of this practice.

Some stylists insist the elbow should be glued to the side even in actual fishing. It's too much attention to style. The fact is, that as one becomes accustomed to handling the tackle the upper arm is moved, but it will not move as a major portion of putting power into the cast. It will be more to get the desired position of forearm, wrist and deviation of the rod from the straight up-and-down, horizontal-to-vertical direction of these practice casts.

Don't be stiff and tense. If the handkerchief is hugged, this is evidence of two much stiffness. If the rod grip doesn't "rock" a little in the hand there is tension. Relax. One can't get a smoothly flowing coordination of motion if all keyed up. Don't put too much practice time in any one period. Break it up into more short periods.

The objective is, to get the plug out and *drop* it on the target. A plug that is "shot" out will hit the water surface with a shooting run. There might be occasions when this would be desirable. More often the plug should reach the target, with just enough force, to seem to pause in flight about a foot off the proper spot, and then drop in on the bulls-eye. Sighting in on the target, and then "thinking the lure" to a point *above* it helps develop this method. The cast is aimed at that spot a foot above the target—where the lure should halt and settle. The lure is likely to slam into the target with a forward impulse instead of hovering and dropping, if the rod is allowed to travel too far down on the forward cast before the reel is released.

A backlash means the reel was turning faster than the out-flying plug could drag the line through the guides. There was too little thumb pressure on the flange of the spool. If too much pressure is applied, the plug will end the flight short of the target with a jerk and tumble, rather than drop.

As the line is reeled in for the next try, it's a good bet that the left hand has been brought up under the reel and cupped around it. The grip of the right hand has been shifted to take hold of the handles of the reel. The rod and reel are given a quarter turn to the right as this is done, and the reel handles are at the right of the rod grip. In actual fishing, as well as retrieving a dry line during dry land practice, some tend to have the line running between the first finger and the thumb of the left hand which is cupped under the reel. A light pressure of thumb and finger keeps a constant tension on the line so it will wind on the reel snugly, without snarling, but not so tight it fouls up the next cast. This requires a left-hand grip under the reel, cupped, with thumb and finger circled around the rod above the reel. Or the grip is farther toward the butt end, with fingers around the grip below the reel, the thumb lying naturallv along the left side. Try both ways; pick the one preferred.

Those "habit channels" are being cut with every move. The more concentration on "thinking" the cast, the more swiftly those channels will be grooved. If they are thought through they'll be grooved right. One is not troubled by the chance that a fish will hit the lure and can give all attention to the actions involved in a good cast. Keep at it, establishing those habit channels.

A good illustration of how a thought finally will set the whole coordinated series of motions in action is a typist. As a stenographer learns the "touch system" in typewriting, all keys are blank. A chart above the typewriter shows the location of the keys. The student looks at the chart and telegraphs the thought to the finger to hit the key which imprints the letter selected. It is hard, concentrated thinking at first. But the whole process leads to a typist seeing a word, that word setting up the impulse and without any conscious thought, nerve centers telegraph the correct fingers into action to pound that word onto the paper.

The same degree of habit reaction can be developed in casting.

There are a couple of points to stress in addition to those covered above.

The flight of the lure is far higher than most anglers realize. It appears to bow up a little in its trajectory but actually its curve is higher. Concentrate on that a bit, for here is the means of sensing that higher arching trajectory. Such a trajectory allows the lure to drop in on the target. While the flatter, "bulleting" trajectory will deliver the lure in a skidding splash.

The lure pulls the line through the guides in bait casting. If the guides remain in alignment with the lure at all points of its flight, there is not the side friction of line against the guides that otherwise would occur. There is less line and guide wear, and the cast travels farther with the same effort. Also, if the initial whirl of the reel spool has been started on first impulse, with the lure and line in alignment with the guides the full pull of lure weight is applied. If, as the line goes out, there is friction of the line on guides, while the reel spool has spinning momentum, the friction slows the out-shooting of line through guides, the lure doesn't pull it from the tip, and there is more of a potential for backlash—the guide friction is a sort of barrier against which the whirling reel throws excess line.

Therefore, point the tip of the rod at the lure throughout the flight. That is the nearest possible alignment between guides, line, and out-flying lure. Follow the lure down. Aim the rod at it all the way.

Now the lure reaches the target. The upward bow of the line settles and there is slack line to the amount of difference between a straight line between rod tip and lure and the bow of the trajectory. One of the most potent moments for a fish to strike is when the lure has just landed. If there is slack in the line when a fish hits, it may be free before the line can be tightened enough to give that little flip-jerk which sinks the hook.

When the coordination of movement is mastered to the fullest, the lure is cast, and is followed with the pointing of the rod, with the trajectory ending (either by a very accurate judgment in application of force or of gentle thumb-braking of the reel) at a point just above the target. There it falls.

In that fraction of a second between the time that the lure is hovering over the target and the moment it hits the water, the left hand is moving to cup and grip under the reel. The right hand is still on the rod handle, ready to release it and take hold of the reel handles as the left hand grips the reel. At that time, both hands on the rod, bring the rod up to a 45 degree angle. The lift of the rod should just take up the slack of the curved line. If a strike comes at the moment the lure settles on the water, there are four things in readiness for such luck; the line is taut, two hands are gripping the rod, the rod is at an angle where its spring will take the shock of the striking fish, and the rod is in a position to give that flip-jerk to sink the hook. If the rod is not brought up from its level position at the end of the lure flight, to set the hook, both the weight of the fish and the tautening of the line are taken on the line. With the rod up, a few inches of sharp flip will set the hooks with the shock factor mostly absorbed by the live rod instead of by a jerk on the line.

This upward lift of the rod should be made at the moment the lure is delivered on all practice casts until it becomes a habit.

The group of coordinated actions, which begins as the reel flange is released are: the lure and line shoot out, the rod points to the lure in flight, the lure shows to a point above target, the left hand swings in under the reel, grips, and the rod is raised to 45 degrees or half way between horizontal and vertical, in the moment when the lure is dropping to the water surface.

All the groundwork of pounding the sequence of casting action into habit channels can be laid in dry-land practice. If it is possible then, move to a practice casting pool and put in some time casting over the water. The more this coordination can become instinctive reaction following a mere thought, the more attention can be given to interpreting the water factors and the fish habits, in order to place the lure in the best spot.

In playing a fish the spring of the rod should be pitted as much as possible against the catch. That means the tip has to be kept fairly well up. There will be the give and take of line as your right hand manages the reel. (The objective is to keep a steady, moderate force that is in the spring of the rod against the strength of the fish.) In rare instances, the full shock of a lunging fish may come against the tensile strength of the line. It cannot easily happen if the fish is played against the bow of the rod. A tug of a fish which would snap even a fairly strong line can't break it if there is bow of the rod which will absorb most of the shock.

The over-head cast is the fundamental one. The wrist-hinge action is the most important application of power and direction in this, as it is in any other cast. The bow of the rod is the force, developed through wrist-hinge motion. If the overhead cast is fully mastered by pounding in the "feel" of all the coordinated moves it requires, the foundation is laid for all bait casting.

After it has become a habit to use the wrist as the principal power and directing point, with the supplementary moves of closing fingers on the grip as the cast starts its forward or outward motion, and the forearm moves easily to aid in the direction of the cast, and this all comes smoothly as the result of thinking the lure on target—forget the handkerchief under the upper arm. That part of the arm will be habitually kept close and without too much thought it will be moved, to get position for the forearm and wrist when it is necessary to put the lure to some particular spot.

OTHER CASTS

There are two principal casts with a bait outfit besides the overhead. They are the side cast and the flip cast, both of which shoot the lure out with the rod sweeping through an arc parallel to the water surface.

The over-head cast is the safest when two men are fishing from the same boat. Either the flip or side cast which requires the rod to traverse an arc which sweeps parallel to the boat have a good chance of sinking hooks into a fishing partner. Even though the caster is in one end of the boat, aiming the lure at a point out from the bow or stern, and the rod grip is checked short of right angles to the long dimension of that boat, the bow of a limber rod will pull it around so it may hit or come very close to the other fellow.

Both the flip and side casts have the advantage of shooting the lure out more nearly level with the water surface, so it can be put in under overhanging branches.

Both are described here as being made by a right-handed angler.

SIDE CAST

The rod is held level, thumb on reel flange. The reel in this cast is on the upper side of the rod. The forearm is a few degrees below level, the wrist hinge giving to hold the rod parallel to the water. The rod is held out straight to the fore from the wrist.

Rock the wrist sharply to the right. The forearm will swing a little in coordinated movement. The sharp swing, mostly activated by wrist movement, bows the rod to the right. The counter-action brings the rod sweeping back in a level plane, in front of the caster. It is checked as it is in the back-cast, with the final power-flip just before the check and the release of the reel.

One fact should be brought out, and that is that the point at which the cast is checked and released determines the direction the lure will take in outward flight. In the overhead cast, a degree or so of difference in the point at which the lure is released will influence merely the height of the trajectory. If the over-head cast is "lined in" straight enough, it will go in line toward target. In the side cast, point of release determines direction the lure will shoot—out at an angle toward the point the caster is facing, out at right angles, or slightly beyond that, at an angle back of the caster and to the left.

The supplementary motion of the forearm enters more in the side-to-side motions of the side-cast than the up-and-down motion in the over-head. The wrist-hinge moves in a different plane—from side to side instead of up and down. But with these differences, the fundamentals are the same as established in the over-head cast.

FLIP-CAST

The flip-cast, also used in getting in under overhanging obstructions, is in the opposite direction from the side cast. In the latter, there is a swing of the forearm, right to left, to more or less come in toward the abdomen and end near paralleling the body. In the flip-cast the forearm moves little and is held fairly straight out from the elbow which is at the side.

Hold the rod out level, directly in front, or pointing slightly to the left. Entirely with a quick wrist motion, with no back-cast motion to the left but from a "standing start," snap the rod to the right. The wrist motion puts a moderate bow into the rod; the force which will pitch the lure. The release point again determines the direction of lure flight. The rod does not swing through nearly as much of an arc as in the other two casts. It is a flip-pitch cast, for middle and shorter distances, to shoot the lure in under over-hanging branches which may lie to the right of the angler.

Between these two casts, which are made somewhat in the plane level with the water surface, and the straight over-head cast, there are many planes in which one will make casts, utilizing slightly different movements. But the important point is, that if an angler has ground in the essential of the wrist action powering and directing the cast, and all the other coordination with it, he'll never think of "now-I-must-do-this-or-that," but merely think "I want the lure to land *there*," and all the motion will go into the attainment of that result.

After accuracy and the "feel" of the whole business are attained, it is time to try for distance. However, until that point is reached, good casting develops faster by concentration on coordination and accuracy.

As a final word— the rhythm of bait casting is "one-two." There is no pause between the back-cast and the forward motion. The weight is at the end of the rod, pulling it into a bow, and the application of forward power puts the full bow, bending against the weight, into the rod. The rhythm of casting with the fly rig is "one-two-three." The reason for this difference lies in the fact that it is the weight of line beyond the rod tip, looping to the rear on the back cast, which must be strung out before the forward-cast power is thrown into the rod. This extra count in fly casting is to give that moment required to allow the line to string out behind. The need of this will be clarified in the instructions on handling fly tackle.

FLY CASTING

The essential differences between casting a fly line and lure and bait casting lies in these points: you cast the line when you pitch a fly; the weight to bow the rod is in the line, not the lure. Line is strung out, therefore, beyond the tip of the rod all through the cast. The reel does not enter into the cast but is strictly a storage facility which al-

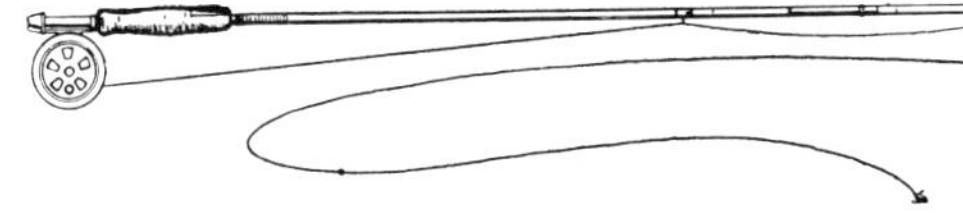

lows lengthening or shortening the line as required.

In many essentials other than these, whatever applies to handling a bait-casting rig has a counterpart in fly casting. Particularly is this true of establishing the "habit-channels" of good casting. So all that has been said about starting with the right sequence of handling in bait-casting goes every bit as emphatically in learning to handle a fly rig.

In assembling a three-section rod, it's good practice to insert the ferrules of the two upper sections first. Then seat the bottom of the middle section into the lower section. Remember not to twist the rod but align the guides by loosening the ferrules, lining guides and then thrusting home.

The reel is below the hand grip and hangs on the under side. The grip is a natural closing of the hand down over the rod handle. There are three positions of thumb and fingers used. The one in which the hand is closed naturally around the grip, thumb around one side, four fingers around the other, gives a greater freedom of wrist movement and is least tiring. A second position in the grip is to lay the thumb out along the handle to do two things; to make more certain that in bringing the rod up in a back cast, it will not swing too far over the shoulder, and to give the benefit of thumb pressure in putting the forward snap-throw into the rod. The third position is to wrap the thumb around, but lay the fore-finger out parallel on the rod grip. The claim for this position is that it gives more accuracy, since the finger is somewhat instinctively pointed at the target.

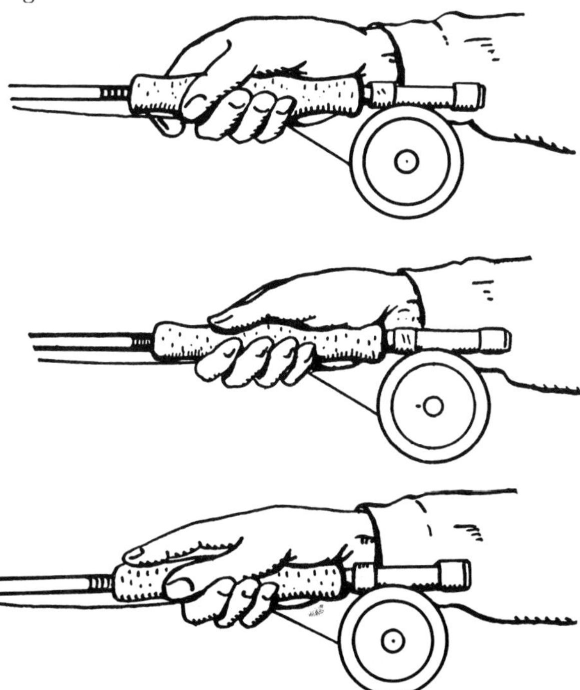

Three methods of holding the rod.

A tightly rolled strip of paper, about 3 to 4 inches long, a quarter inch wide, tied into the end of the line in dry-land practice, simulates in some degree the air resistance a fluffy fly will have. It isn't quite the same, but it gives a bit more of the feel of actual casting.

Now, find an open space. Strip out between fifteen and twenty feet of line beyond the rod tip. Flip this line either to the right or left. Pick it up from where it lies with a rocking motion of the wrist, moving the rod, in a plane at right angles to the point faced. Before the line has settled from the pick-up, and still is at least a little above the level of the tip of the rod, swish the rod lightly in the opposite direction. Keep it up, back and forth, in rhythmic sequence.

The rod tip should be stopped sharply at the position of about one o'clock on the right, eleven o'clock on the left if facing an imaginary clock dial. Play with this line and rod swinging them from side to side. Don't let the line's end touch the ground on either side. Try to start the reverse movement in either direction while the line is nearing the conclusion of a high, rather wide, open loop, right or left.

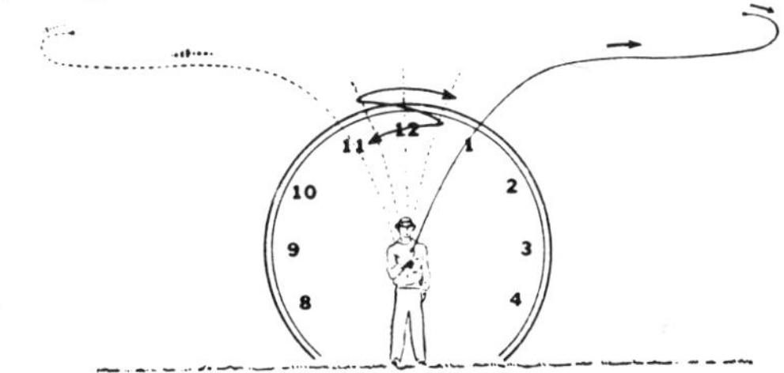

To secure the wide-swinging loop, the pick-up as direction is reversed should be rather quick, decisive and light as the line is "unrolling" in the direction the rod tip has just been whipped. The counter movement of the rod should begin briskly but not too "snappy." As the tip of the line turns out of the loop and as the tip of the rod is just approaching perpendicular the wrist should put a tiny "power-flip" into it. This will throw the line fairly high, and it should be kept so.

This "playing" with the rod, sweeping it back and forth, will give the "feel" of the rod—how it bows, where to start the reverse in movement, how long to pause at the point where the sweep is checked to let the looping lines unroll sufficiently to bow the rod as the reverse move is made. Get that "feel" of the action of muscles, rod, and line. Watch what is happening as the rod is moved from side to side, and "think" this into coordination with the "feel" of the tackle.

The odds are that there will not be enough of this "watching the feel" of rod and line in this side-to-side play. But ground will be gained if it is practiced for some time before trying to make a cast. For when an actual practice cast is made at a

-----

All drawings illustrating this article on Fly Casting are used through the courtesy of the Ocean City Mfg. Co.

target, the "thought channels" and the feel of the muscle-motion and joints in the wrist and forearm have to tell what is happening in line and rod as the back cast over the shoulder cannot be watched to see if it is being kept high. Since the sequence of events can be watched by this side-to-side "play," one gets a mental image of what happens when the rod is in front-back-front motion.

The over-head cast, front-to-back-to-front, is the basic one in fly casting as it is in bait casting. If one has a reasonable mental picture of what happens in rod and line on the side-to-side "play" the next step can be some dry-land casting practice.

Pace out about ten steps from the casting point and place a cardboard or other target on the open ground. There should be forty feet of clear space behind as well as in front. Lay the line out in front. Pick up the rod and hold it horizontal.

The old handkerchief trick comes into practice again; place it between the upper arm and body. Just as in bait casting, the wrist, supplemented by some forearm action puts the power and direction into the rod.

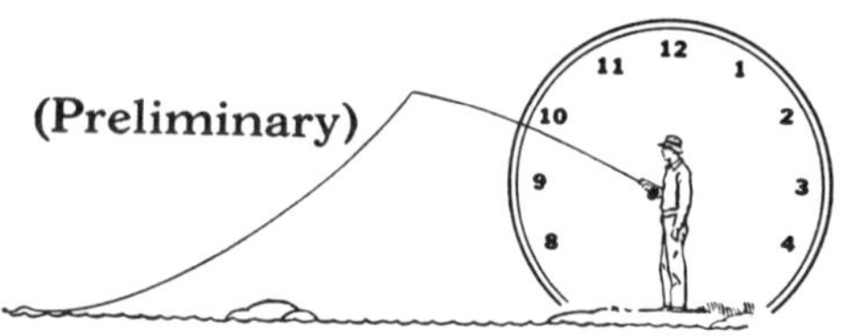

The rod should be raised smoothly, from horizontal to about ten o'clock when ready for the first practice cast. In actual fishing it will be at ten o'clock or a little above before starting motions which will be the beginning of the cast. If the arm is held so the upper section is close to the body, the forearm horizontal, and the wrist, with the hand in thumb-side-up position, it will be evident that any straight stick gripped in the hand will not point out level, because the hinge of the wrist is incapable of moving to a full right angle to the forearm. That means, with the forearm horizontal a rod held as near towards horizontal as easily possible still points up around ten o'clock. To get it fully horizontal, the forearm must be dropped below level.

The line is out in front, across the open ground. Hold the elbow to the side and sweep the rod up through a vertical arc with the wrist and forearm until the rod is at least vertical in a line in front of the shoulder. At about 11:15 position in the up-sweep, put a definite "power-flip" into the rod, wrist action. This bows the rod tip forward, giving

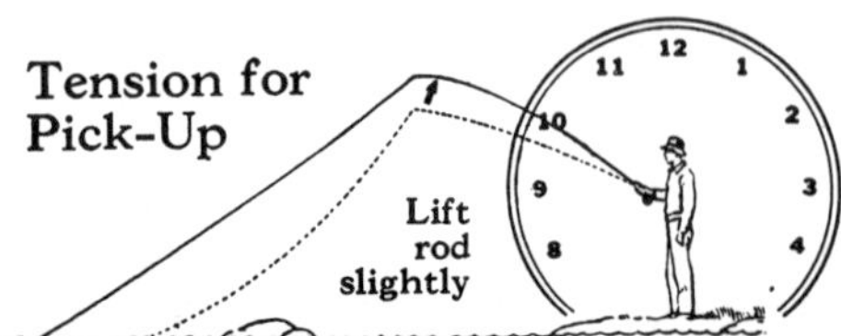

the pick-up power to throw the line back, rather high, over the shoulder.

Some able fly casters tell you not to allow the main axis of the rod to pass beyond the vertical. Check it at the twelve o'clock position. Others will advise bringing it back as far as one o'clock or slightly beyond. A check that far back tends to allow the line to "sink" farther behind, and it should be kept high. It is suggested that the rod axis be allowed to drift slightly after the power

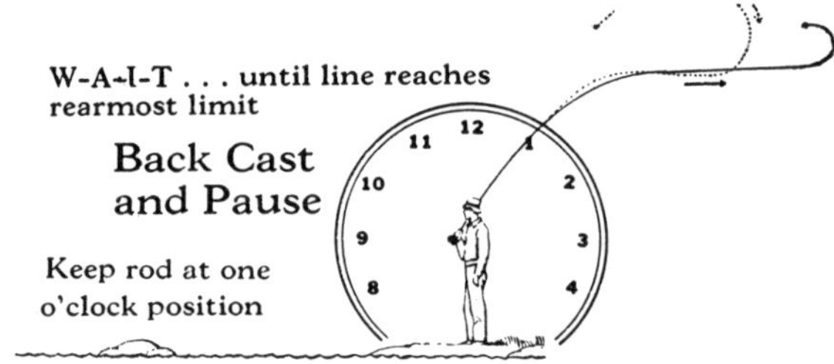

flip at 11:15, to between 12:15 and 12:30. Just where it will stop is dependent on the rod length, its action, length, and weight of line. Again one must depend on the "feel" of what is going on.

The rhythm of fly casting is "one-two-three." "One" for the upsweep, "two" for the check and moment when the line is rolling out in the loop back, well up over the shoulder, and "three" for the beginning of the forward sweep.

Start with a moderately brisk forward motion, straightening the rolling loop, so the weight of the line will be opposed to the spring of the rod as it sweeps forward. Don't make this start so fast that the loop is pulled tight to make the end a sharp turn, and get a "snapper, whip-crack" effect. That effect can come from the loop being pulled out of the turn too swiftly, or from the line getting too low on the back cast or from allowing the loop to unroll just a bit too much before "pulling it out" by beginning the forward motion.

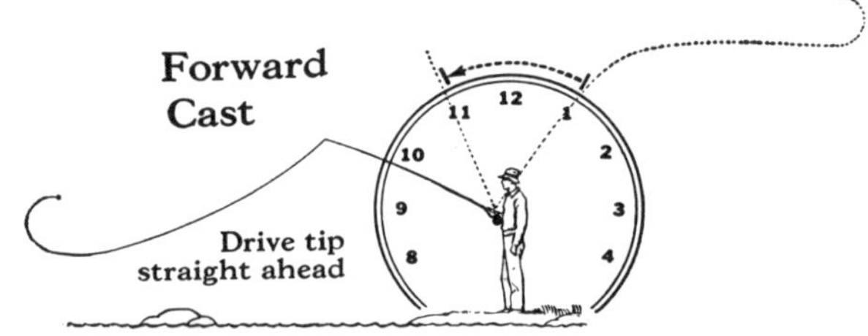

The power of the wrist is applied progressively as the rod reaches the 11:15 position on the forward sweep. Between 11:30 and 11:15 put the forward "Power flip" into the line. It should be all straightened out, the "corner" or the turning loop should be passed, and the full weight of the line bends and puts power into the rod. That last little flip in the forward sweep shoots the line.

Just as the objective of casting a plug bait with a "bass" rod is to have the line all strung out and the lure halting *above* the target; so the fly should be put into a spot *above* the point where it is to fall. If the rod comes too far down and continues to put on power beyond the 11:15 "flip" point, the line and lure will be lashed down on the water. The weight of the line should level it out; so that the last pull *it* exerts, will put the final throw into the fly, straighten out the several feet

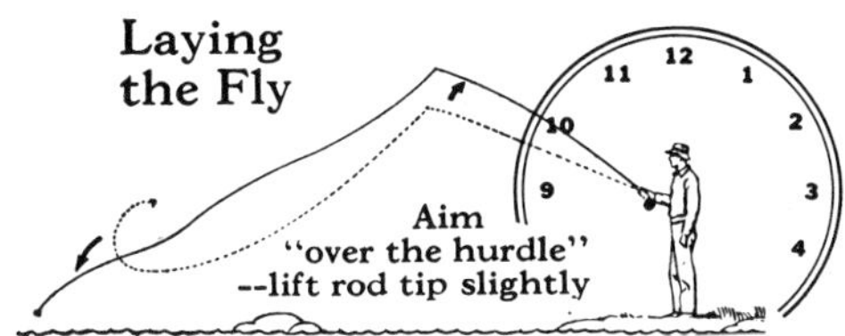

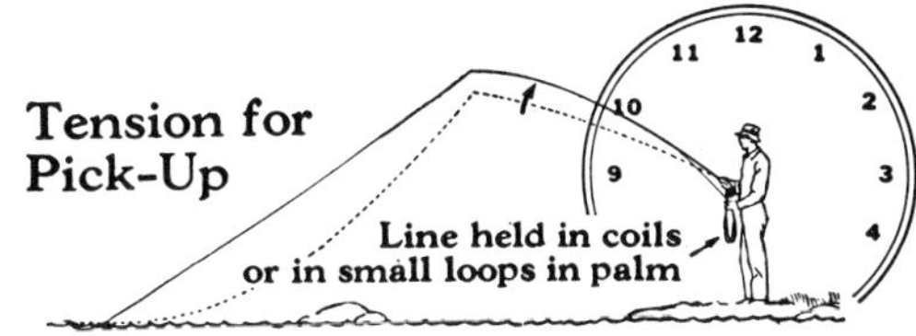

of filmy leader and allow the lure to settle as lightly as possible. The ideal cast straightens to let the line, leader, and lure *settle* on the water.

Practicing, the line has been shot at the target. The line is out in front. Repeat the sequence of motion in the back-stop-forward cast. Don't try for distance; try for accuracy. *Think* the sequence into a smooth, rhythmic continuity.

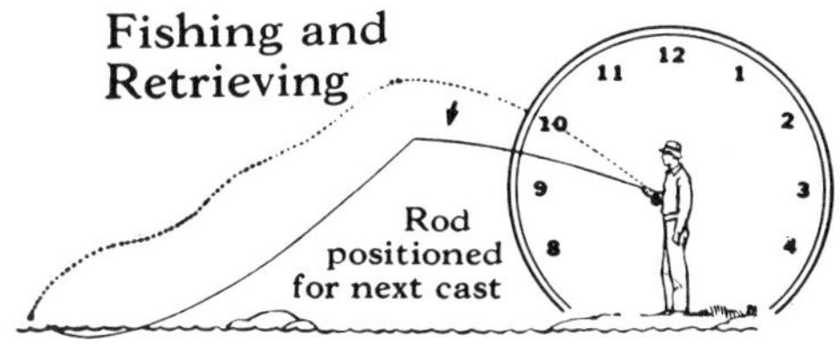

Don't try to do the job by muscle. It is timing, and the light, precise application of the little snap-power of the wrist that does the job neatly.

Periods should not be more than fifteen minutes in any of this ground-work practice. It is far better to get some segment of the whole sequence of motion and action worked out smoothly a few times, than to keep on, tire, begin to do something wrong, undo all that has been accomplished, and start toward bad habits.

The next step is to practice on water where one more important element to handling a fly rig can be added. Put on a 4 to 6 foot leader and say a No. 8 fly—and snip off the hook point to avoid possible injury. That does happen; even with experienced casters through a sudden gust of wind or bad timing.

Now get into the "false cast" to get line out from the shore. This is used in actual fishing not only to get the line out, but also to dry a fly to some extent; a false cast before actually laying the lure on the water often gives better control over direction and distance factors of the subsequent actual cast.

With a few feet of line pulled beyond the tip of the rod, use the left hand to "strip" some additional line from the reel, holding it in loops. Sweep the rod back, as in a back cast, let the loose line in the left hand go, and the weight of the line beyond rod tip will pull it out. Strip more line from the reel as the rod is swung, let it go on the next false cast, either at the apex of pull of the back cast or at the end of forward cast when the line is tugging out near full forward extension. Several false casts will get out the amount of line needed beyond the rod tip. Let the line, leader and lure settle on the water when enough line is out.

This false cast also can serve in changing the direction in which the line is laid. A couple of such casts, changing the direction of each forward cast toward the spot where the lure is to be dropped is often a handy way to do this.

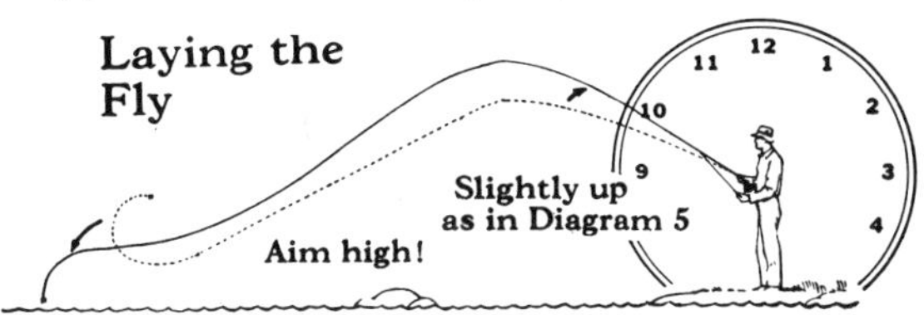

Now the line is cast out and in the water. Here are two more factors to work out. There is some slack in the line as it alights. Part of this is taken out by raising the rod tip—for the same reasons slack is taken to have a tight line in bait casting. With the line straightened out, the water will "grip" the line. Take the line between reel and lower rod guide loosely in the curve of the fingers or the left hand. By moving the hand toward the left, allowing line to move through hooked fingers, pull slack out of the line, and if it has sunk, this,

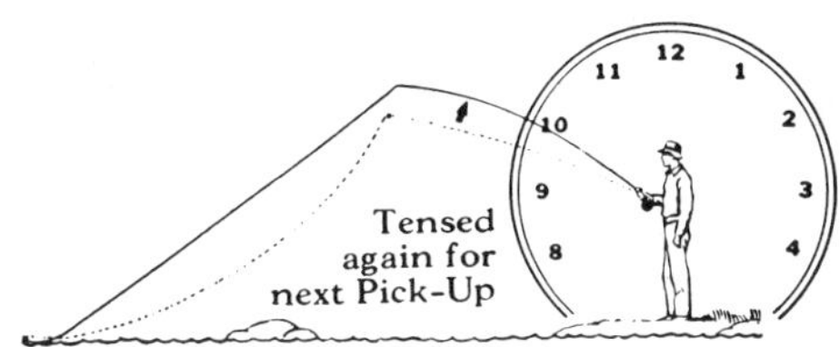

with raising the rod tip to ten o'clock or above, will largely free the line from the water. The far end should be right on the surface, although four to eight feet may still be in contact with the water. Start the back cast with those conditions. A bit of "grip" of the water remains on the line, and this contributes to bowing the rod in that direction as the back-cast starts, adding force and stacking up rod-power in the remainder of the cast.

Free the line from the water with a swift "pick-up" with the line getting free in time for that

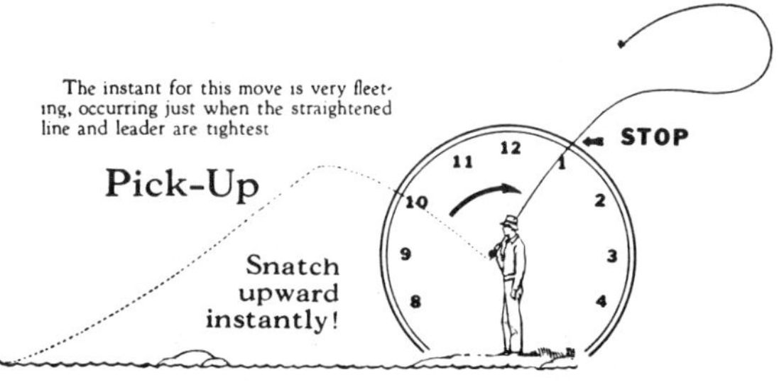

"power-flip" point on the back cast, at about 11:15. The rest of the cast is like that followed in the dry land practice.

In actual fishing, the left hand, dealing with the line between reel and lower rod guide, is important. As the current puts slack in the line, or as it is drawn in to keep it from sinking below the zone where the fly is to be presented, strip in line below the lower guide. That line looped in the left hand should go out in the next cast. In playing a fish in some stages and under some conditions, the line at this point should be controlled by the left hand to take or give line quickly. When using an automatic reel, this line stripped in as a fish is played can be taken up by pressing the take-up trigger. If applying most of the control of in-and-out movement of the line while landing a fish by line stripping instead of directly reeling, the line should either be looped in the hand, or gathered in by what has been called the "hand twist retrieve." In the latter, grasp the line between thumb and forefinger, rocking the hand counter-clockwise. Catch the line thus pulled in by clamping the third and fourth finger over it. When it is gripped under these fingers, release the thumb and forefinger, twist the hand clockwise, get another loop in, twist the hand back, lay it under the fingers, and grip it. There will then be a sort of "hank" of line lying in the palm of the left hand, held there by fingers.

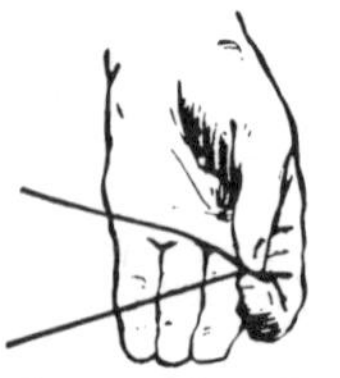

Grasp the line with the thumb and first finger of your left hand, palm facing up.

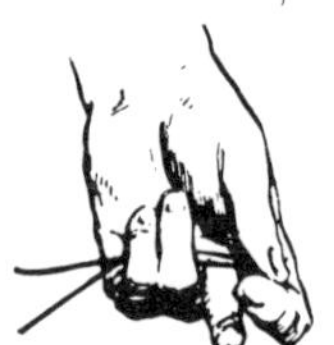

Close the other fingers firmly over the line lying across the palm.

Turn your hand palm-down and take another "bite" of line with thumb and first finger.

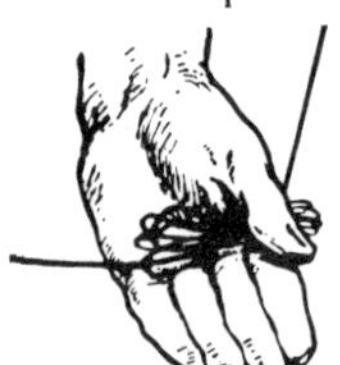

Turn your hand palm-up. Repeat these movements smoothly.

The "hand twist" retrieve.

Another method of taking in line as a fish is played with a single action reel, is to shift the grip of the rod to the left hand and work the reel handle, give and take, with the right hand.

Fingers of the hand gripping the rod have something to do with the line also. If the pick-up is with the full line out and the tip of the rod has been lifted to free line from deep in the water, use the two upper fingers, or perhaps all, to grip the line against the handle of the rod just above the reel. This is to prevent the pull of the line as you sweep the rod from taking more line from the reel. If there is no such grip, the force of line-pull will be delivered directly to the reel spool, line will pay out, and some of the force that packs into the rod as it pulls backward against line weight will be lost.

Keep at this over-head cast until it is mastered. The motions involved are basic in all fly casting—meaning in essence, that the manipulation of the rod lies in wrist action supplemented by forearm.

In some degree, once good "habit channels" are formed in this cast, casting in any plane and in any direction can be developed.

There are, however, a number of "named" casts which have been developed to meet conditions in actual fishing. These mostly stem from the fact that unlike bait casting, where there is no extension of line to the rear in fly casting, there must be clear space to the rear for the line to straighten in over-head casts.

SIDE CAST

A side cast with a fly rod is useful not only for getting under overhanging branches but to keep the line low in strong winds. The line must be out to the left, at the beginning of the side cast with a fly outfit, perhaps carried there by current action on a stream. Otherwise it is an adaptation of the over-head cast, with sequence of motion parallel to the side-cast with a bait outfit. When the rod is up at about a 15 degree angle from parallel to the water surface, lift the loop on the back cast so it unrolls well above the water; then shoot it to the left, with the forearm swinging across the front of the body somewhat parallel to the water surface, with the forward-cast loop unrolling to the right of the straightening-out section of the line.

FLIP CAST

There is a cast in fly fishing which is somewhat comparable to the flip cast with bait rigs. The line has been pulled down current and it is desired to shoot it up current to let the fly traverse that section of the stream again. The line is well straightened out down stream. Get it properly free from water grip and then with a quick wrist motion put the bow power into the rod with a flip, to throw the line up stream, somewhat parallel to the water surface. It's a handy maneuver when on a brushy stream of narrow width. A line tossed into a riffle will carry down, pay out a little line from the reel as the current drag takes hold, and then flip-cast, up the main axis of that section of the stream, strip line in as the current carries it down, pay out as it travels on down current, and repeat. Its best use is in such small stream fishing, where one must fish from the bank, where the only open space through which a line can be shot is back and forth along the center of a stream so encompassed with brush that there is no chance to get the lure to the desired spot except by such tactics.

STEEPLE CAST

This is merely a modified over-head cast. It is used when bushes, trees, or cliffs directly behind prevent the usual unrolling of line on the normal back-cast.

In this cast the upper arm comes in play. Start the back cast with the wrist pick-up, but thrust up the whole arm to near vertical. The check is made right there, with the rod vertical. This will throw the line high, with the unrolling loop above instead of back and above the shoulder. As the loop unrolls in this area, thrust your full arm out, forward, in a way that has been described as a "spear-thrust-motion." At the last part of this full-arm thrust, apply the wrist motion to give the power flip.

ROLL CAST.

This is a straight forward cast also developed to meet conditions where obstructions behind prevent normal manipulation of rod and line. When the line is out, lift the whole arm with moderate

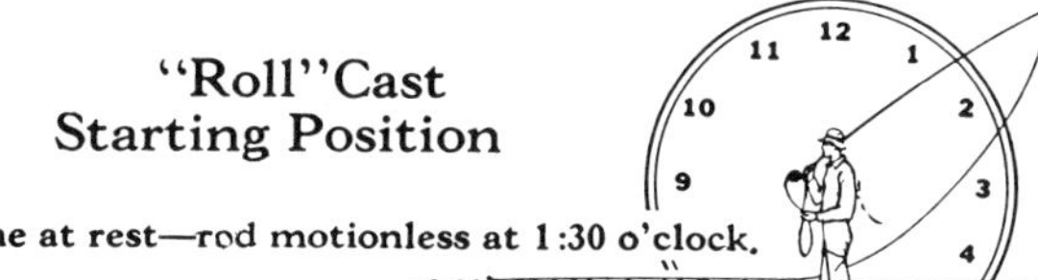

motion to full extent, rocking the wrist so the rod points back of the shoulder to the one o'clock position. As this is done with progressively increasing speed, the line at the far end, still in the water, will remain level. But between the point where it still is in water-grip, and the tip of the rod which is now high and back, there will be a great sweeping curve of line.

At this point, bring the rod, the arm, and even the body, swinging forward in a great-circle sweeping motion. If it's done correctly, the drag of the line in the water will cause the line to shape into a great curving arc, with its "belly" pulled high

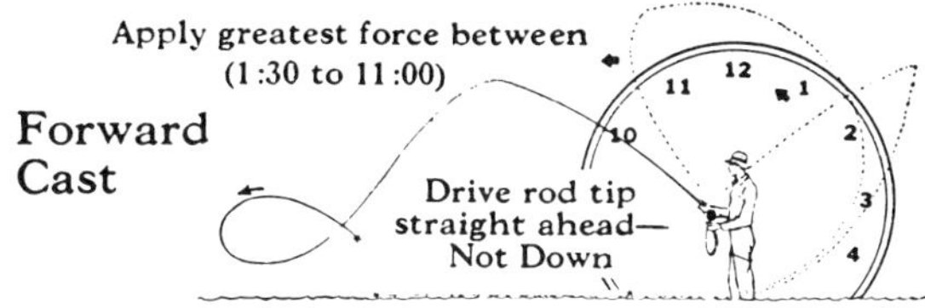

in front of and bulging toward the caster at the end of the application of power in the cast. The arm is full out, the body bent forward. Just as the wide loop of a standard forward cast unrolls, this line will come up, over, and roll out, propelled by the bow-power of the bent rod.

GALWAY CAST

Again this is an adaptation of the principles of the over-head cast. It is a facility for seeing where the line is unrolling in the direction opposite from which the following forward cast is made. It can be used when there is an opening in the brush where the back-cast can unroll, but be sure it unrolls there instead of into trees.

The line is out. Make a quarter turn of the body, shifting foot position, so the body is "facing" at right angles to the axis of the rod. The rod hand is out to the right side. The opening in the brush is to the left.

Look sidewise toward the place where the line lies. Pick up line, and as it leaves the water, swing on the ankles and turn the body, enough to *look* left, in the direction the line is to unroll. It goes into the open space there. Pivot again, feet not moving, and make the forward cast normally, except that the feet remain planted in that right-angle position to the rod motion.

The reel will remain under the rod; at the start it is to the right side, at the end of the back cast it is to the left, and as the forward cast is made it swings back to the right side again. This is due to the hinge action of the wrist; a half turn into which the body pivot also enters.

DART CAST

This cast is for small streams with overhanging brush. It is most easily accomplished with a rod not over 7½ feet. Do not swing the rod and line in this cast. The bow-power of the rod is used to shoot the fly as one would bow the stick in shooting a dart such as youngsters make out of narrow pieces of wooden roof shingles.

Encompassed with brush; the only open space lies in front; a fly is to be placed across a narrow stream under brush or an over-hanging bank. The line is about the length of the rod. Grasp the fly between the thumb and forefinger of the left hand. Point the rod at the spot where the fly is to be placed. Pull the line back, putting bow-power into the rod. Release the fly to shoot out approximately level with the water just as a dart would be shot. And that's it; a handy cast for a small stream with brushy banks when using light tackle.

OTHER CASTS

Experts who have devoted their knowledge and analytical attention to refinements of fly casting, have assigned names to many variations of fly rod manipulations. Even the angle in which the rod deviates from the straight over-head cast supplies a specific designation for some such deviations. For those who become immersed in the technics of casts, there is a considerable field of further study and practice. All of these various casts are useful under specific conditions. They're "nice to know."

But the essentials of most of these modifications and adaptations lie right in the fundamentals of the straight over-head cast. However, if those fundamentals are so well mastered, so thoroughly pounded into the habit channels of rod and line handling that all one has to do is "think the lure on target," almost instinctively adaptations will be made to fit the situation faced. And no one will care whether or not it has a name. Establish habits of casting into smooth, rhythmic coordination that needs nothing but a thought to set the whole sequence of motions in action, and most situations will then be met as they occur.

SHOOTING THE LINE

This is a means of getting out more line than can be pitched with rod-bowing where the weight of the unrolling line loop in the back cast alone puts pull on the rod. It is more effective with the heavier fly-tackle assemblies, including a fairly heavy line.

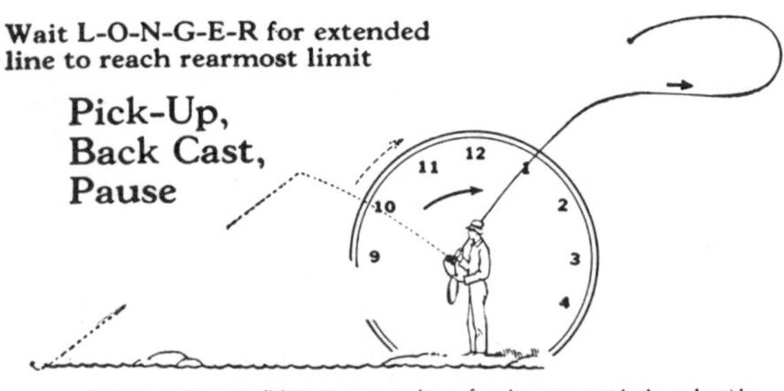

Hold the coils or small loops in your palm in fair alignment with the rod guides that the line will encounter the least resistance in shooting.

The left hand, which already has stripped line between the reel and the first rod guide, grasps the line fairly close to the lower rod guide. As the rod comes close to the full bow of the back cast which the straightening line will impart, the rod is thrust up sharply and the left hand grasping the line is swept down and back, putting an additional pull on the line. The two actions put more pull on the rod tip, increasing the bow-power. This farther back-bowing gives the necessary "push" to send the line out with more force on the forward cast. Not only will this take out the line which has been stripped, and that which has been pulled

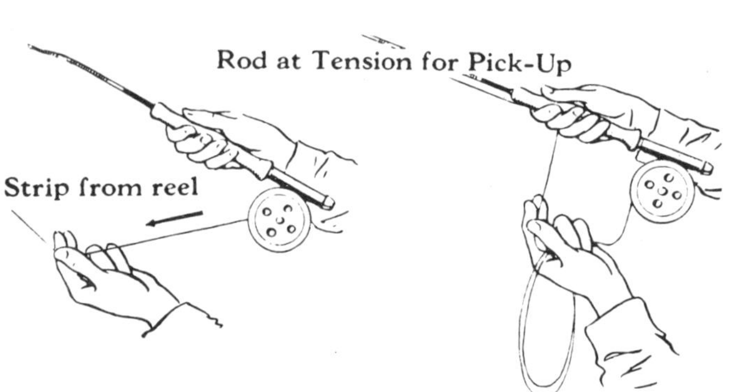

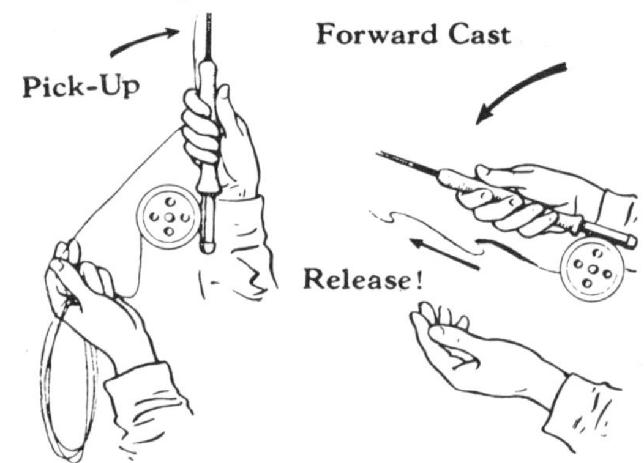

down in the sweep of the left hand, but additional line which may have been pulled from the reel and looped in the left hand to go out on the shoot. This can be especially effective in handling the "torpedo" type of line, with the line of lesser diameter which is the "shooting line" back of the "torpedo head."

MENDING THE LINE

This is not a cast. It is a move to get the most out of a cast already made. The fly is out. The current takes hold of the line, and it bellies down stream. The pull of the water forming the curve where the drag is on the line, threatens to drag the dry fly under, or if fishing wet, the current will begin to pull the fly faster than any natural insect would travel.

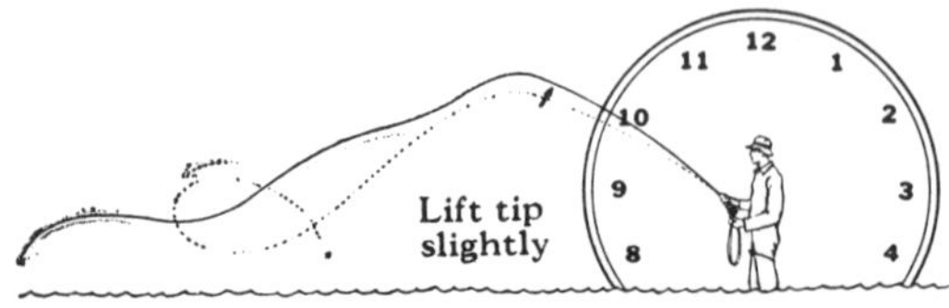

To counteract this down-stream belly in the line, make a quick circular motion with the tip of the rod—lift the curve of the line and flop it over so it is up-current. Sort of like putting a spatula under a flapjack and flopping it over. It will give more "float" to the fly for that cast.

Expert fly casting can be a joy in itself. The ground-work outline will start the beginner toward able fly fishing, and open the way to further exploration of the niceties which the expert demonstrates. There has been some tendency to represent the manipulation of fly tackle as a difficult art. Those who have accepted this idea may have shied away from fly casting, thinking it beyond their sphere. Certainly anyone who will not try to jump the necessary first steps, some thinking practice, can master what is needed to become a good fly fisherman in a few hours. Neglect of such preliminary application of thought and practice may prevent one from ever progressing beyond being a slap-dab operator.

Fishing with a fly lure usually is associated with trout. That is a major field for this type of angling. But all of the pan-fish, the basses and even chubs, can be taken with a fly. With light tackle, the opportunity to enjoy a type of fishing for such fish besides bait and casting lures can be found in fly fishing.

Angling should be enjoyed in all its phases. Differences in waters, in species of fish and in tackle rigs used, offer a tremendous spread of many variations of this, the greatest American sport. If one fails to develop fly casting, one of the most interesting of all sport fishing is missed.

SPINNING

The method of sport fishing known as "spinning" differs widely in the United States from the sport of the same name practiced in European countries. Spinning in Europe (and in many other part of the world) is defined as "a method of light tackle angling wherein live or artificial baits or lures which spin or revolve in the water are cast with a revolving-spool, multiplying reel." In fact, spinning in Europe is very similar to bait casting in America, although baits which spin in the water are used more commonly than plugs or spoons. Ordinarily, larger rods (more like American salmon or streamer fly rods) are preferred and the revolving spool reels are somewhat different in design from the bait casting reels used in the United States.

Through common usage in America, "spinning" is defined as "the sport of angling with a light lure and a thread-like line on a fixed-spool reel." In Europe, this is termed "fixed-spool angling" or "threadline fishing," or, translated into French, "lancer leger," which means "light casting." Thus, "spinning" in America is synonymous with "threadline" fishing or 'fixed-spool" fishing in England and "lancer leger" in France, and should not be confused with the method of angling called "spinning" practiced in England.

In this article, "spinning" will be discussed under its commonly used American connotation; the sport of light casting in which a fixed-spool reel is used, thus making possible longer cast with finer lines and lighter lures.

SPINNING REELS

A spinning reel has a spool which does not rotate in casting. The axis of the spool is parallel to the rod so that the line can uncoil over the lip of the reel-spool. The difference between the operation of a spinning reel and a rotating spool reel can be observed easily by holding a spool of thread in the fingers. If the spool is held by both ends between the thumb and forefinger, the spool will rotate when thread is pulled from it. This is the principle of the rotating spool reel. When the spool is held between the thumb and forefinger by one end, the thread can be pulled off the other end in a spiral without rotating the spool. This is the principle of the spinning reel. If this is done, it will be observed that the thread uncoils from the lip of the spool much more easily in the second instance than it unrolls from the spool in the first. Thus, in spinning, line uncoils from the spool with less drag, making longer casts possible. Even more important, since the spool of the spinning reel does not revolve, the cast line can not override or "backlash" as it does on the multiplying spool type reel. For this reason, backlashes are eliminated entirely from spinning.

After casting, the line is replaced in the spool by a mechanical pick-up finger, pick-up wheel, or bail, which is affixed to a cup built around the reel spool. The cup rotates around the fixed spool when the reel handle is turned. The pick-up finger or bail is opened in casting but closes automatically with a partial turn of the handle. When the pick-up finger or bail closes, it automatically engages the line and winds it back onto the reel spool. Most spinning reels have a multiplying

Wright and McGill

"Break-down" of the Fre-Line Spinning Reel.

French Centaure Spinning Reel.

action which causes the pick-up finger or bail to revolve three or four times for every turn of the reel handle, thus aiding in quick recovery of the line.

The reel spool of a spinning reel is mounted on a spindle which usually moves in and out as the reel handle is turned, thus cross-winding the line and aiding in the smooth casting of the reel. If the line was wound onto the spool in a level manner instead of being cross-wound, it would be possible for a tightly wound coil to pick up loosely wound coils and thus cast out too much line at once, making a snarl.

Although the reel spool does not revolve in casting, it does revolve when the run of a fish removes line from the spool. To regulate the drag on the spool, there is a wing-nut brake which usually is screwed to the spindle of the reel and which thus is located normally on the front face of the reel spool. By adjusting this wing nut, any degree of tension may be put on the line, from a nearly free-running line to a locked spool. Usually, the tension on the reel spool is set rather lightly and added braking power is provided by the angler placing his fingers or thumb against the lip of the revolving spool, when need be.

This method of braking the spinning reel allows much lighter lines to be used because, since the brake always is set to a lighter tension than the strength of the line, the line cannot be broken by the sudden run of a large fish unless it be through an error made by the angler in setting the brake too strongly or in holding the reel spool too tightly. It will be noted that the brake is not influenced by turning the handle of the reel. The angler may be reeling in even when a fish is taking line from the spool. Reeling under such circum-

Mitchell 300 Spinning Reel.

stances is a bad practice because it only serves to put a twist in the line. It is better to control the run of the fish by using the pressure of the fingers on the spool, if the power of the brake is insufficient, and not to attempt reeling until the fish has completed his run, or is stopped by the pressure exerted by the angler.

To allow freedom of the reel hand by the fisherman, most spinning reels have an anti-reverse lock which can be snapped on when a fish is hooked. This anti-reverse lock prevents the reel from backwinding and allows the angler to remove his hand from the reel handle during the run of a fish.

All open-spool spinning reels have a large "leg" which joins the "foot" of the reel to the reel proper and keeps the reel at a distance from the rod grip. The purpose of this is to allow free uncoiling of the line, which would slap against the rod and impede the cast if the reel was situated too close to the rod grip. All open-spinning reels are slung under the rod grip; this being a natural position most comfortable for the angler. Most closed models mount like standard bait-casting reels.

RODS

Just as a plug casting rod is not adapted to fly fishing, and vice versa, so is a special type of rod required for spinning. Spinning rods usually are between seven and eight feet in length and are distinguished by a long cork grip on the length of which the spinning reel may be affixed by means of a reel seat or, in some models, by two sliding rings in whatever position best suits the angler and best balances the rod.

The action of the ideal spinning rod is quite different from that of a fly rod in that the tip should be stiffer and the butt more limber so that the action of the rod is distributed more uniformly from tip to butt. In choosing a spinning rod it is important to note that, upon oscillating it, the tip must come quickly to rest. A rod with abnormal tip action impairs the distance of the cast and impedes accuracy.

Line guides also are different in a spinning rod. The butt (or gathering) guide is very large, usually nearly an inch in diameter, and is set on the butt section near the ferrule of the two-piece rod. It is also offset about ¾ of an inch from the rod; these requirements allowing the line to uncoil from the reel and to be gathered by the butt guide without unnecessary friction and without allowing the uncoiling line to slap against the rod. In addition to the butt guide, there usually are four more line guides, each diminishing slightly in diameter and in offset from the rod for the purpose of keeping friction to a minimum. Although the best American and foreign spinning rods have been of split bamboo, rods of glass fibre, prove to be equally satisfactory and most American rods now are made of this material. Length is as important in a spinning rod as in a fly rod. Added length, within reason, provides added "whip" which casts light lures to greater distances. It gives more even tension to the line and adds to the sport of handling fish. When angling on brushy streams, however, the long rod is at a disadvantage. The ideal brush rod should be about six feet in length to provide a maximum variety of casts from under and beside obstructions.

LINES

All spinning lines are (or should be) of braided Nylon or Nylon monofilament. Nylon being a mineral substance, does not lose strength with age and cannot be impaired by leaving it on the reel spool wet or dry. Since spinning lines are very light in strength and very fine in diameter, it is obvious that the tendency to rot and lose strength, as in lines of animal or vegetable fibre such as silk or linen, would be disastrous.

In Europe, spinning lines of Nylon monofilament are used almost exclusively; one reason for this being that braided Nylon has not been developed to the state of perfection attained in the United States. Nylon monofilament has the ad-

A typical steelhead, taken on Oregan's Deschutes River with a Record Spinning Reel and a wobbling spoon.

vantage of being extremely sturdy and wear resistant, true to strength, maximumly smooth for distance casting, and of ideal stiffness when properly stretched. Some lines have the disadvantage of setting in coils when left on the reel spool for any length of time. This wiriness easily can be eliminated by attaching the lure to a branch and walking away, allowing the castable length of line to pay off from the reel. When this length of line has been paid out, a slight pull on the tackle will stretch the line and remove the coils, at the same time testing the tackle for abnormal weakness. If it is not convenient to do this, the line automatically will become stretched after a bit of casting or after handling the first fish.

Braided lines usually are made without a core in order to decrease weight and diameter in proportion to strength. They should be treated to make them water repellent and to give them proper stiffness. Braided lines are available in several colors, usually black or dark green. Nylon monofilament lines normally are dyed in green, grey or "invisible blue." Braided and monofilament lines are available in strengths of from two to 50 pounds test, although Nylon monofilament can be obtained in even lighter strengths. Lines in excess of eight pounds test normally are not recommended for fresh-water spinning because they require ultra-heavy lures to make long casts. Heavier lines usually are unnecessary, even in handling very large fish. The lighter the line used, and farther the lure can be cast so it is important that the lightest line be employed commensurate with the weight of the lure and the strength of the rod. For average spinning, lines testing three or four pounds should be adequate; the stronger and larger diameter lines only being necessary in fishing near underwater obstructions or in handling ultra-large fish. Spinning essentially is light tackle fishing. One of its greatest appeals is that with it anglers may enjoy the added sport of handling large fish on extremely light and fine lines, with ultra-light lures and wand-like rods.

BAITS AND LURES

Lures for spinning comprise a wide range of both natural and artificial baits. Worms, hellgrammites and similar foods used to attract fish may be cast much farther and more accurately with spinning tackle than with any other type of fishing gear. When extremely light baits are employed, a bit of lead attached on the line just above the hook may be needed to make sufficiently long casts or to get the lure deep down in the current. Spinners may be attached to the bait if desired. In float fishing, the plastic ball is superior to cork or wood floats because it casts extremely well and its weight can be varied by filling it partially or fully with water making it adaptable to a wide variety of angling uses. This colorless plastic ball is about one inch in diameter with holes on its rim for attaching line and leader and with a plugged aperture for adding water. Minnows may be used with the plastic ball by hooking them through the lips or dorsal fin, using a very small amount of lead between lure and float to keep them down in the water, yet allowing them a reasonable freedom of movement. More often, however, minnows are attached to a minnow gang, which is a set of hooks tied to gut and with a nail-like bit of lead for insertion into the minnow's mouth, thus weighting him for casting. The hooks are fastened to both sides of the head, with a trailer hook inserted near the tail to provide a curve to the bait, thus giving it a spinning or oscillating movement in the water.

While natural baits are very popular in the European version of spinning, they are much less popular than artificial lures in America because the artificial type are easier to use and offer an extremely wide selection. This selection comprises plugs, spoons, spinners, wobblers, and weighted or unweighted flies. Nearly any kind of artificial lure may be used providing it offers a minimum of air resistance and a reasonable amount of weight in proportion to its volume.

Streamer flies or bucktails may be used advantageously with spinning tackle if enough weight is added a foot or two above the lure to enable them to be cast properly. This type of fly may be tied on a leaded hook or a hook weighted with wire, but many experienced anglers feel that the excess weighting of the hook gives an unnatural, deadened action in the water. For this reason, they prefer unweighted flies with lead added to the leader or line. The plastic ball float is very useful as a substitute for lead, particularly when it is filled with water so that it will sink. Since this float (when filled) has a specific gravity nearly the same as that of water it is less liable to sink too deep in the current and cause the tackle to become caught on the bottom. The plastic float method of fly fishing utilizes stream currents, even on the opposite side of the river from the angler. As the float drifts and then swings in the current as the cast is fished out, motion is imparted automatically to the trailing fly. Float fishing with flies is especially successful on western steelhead rivers; even more so, at times, than fly fishing with the fly rod or using more conventional methods with spinning tackle.

Ordinary wet flies may be used in the same

Chas. C. Ebbets, Miami News Bureau

Largemouth Bass taken in Florida on an American-made Bristol Spinning Rod and Reel and a Quilby minnow lure.

manner as above described. Dry flies also may be used with spinning tackle by employing the floating plastic ball. These latter two types of fishing, however, are better adapted to the fly rod than to the spinning rod. While spinning is a third and major method of angling, competing with fly fishing and plug casting in importance, it is most successful when it is not used where one of the other two methods would be preferable.

Suitable weights of spinning lures vary with the power of rod and the strength of line employed. Lures of one-sixteenth to one-eighth ounce are best used with ultra-light rods and lines testing not over two pounds in breaking strength. Lures of one-eighth to three-eighths ounce are ideal with medium strength rods and lines testing between two and five pounds. Lures over three-eighths ounce are used with even stronger rods and with lines of from five to eight pounds test. Lures over one ounce in weight rarely are cast with spinning tackle because the advantages of the spinning method and of the tackle diminish as the weight of lures used approaches that which ordinarily is better suited to plug casting equipment or to heavy salt water gear.

SELECTION OF EQUIPMENT

While the majority of imported and domestic spinning tackle now is properly made and suitable to purpose, there is and probably always will be certain items sold for spinning which are unsuited to the method. It is as true in buying spinning tackle as in buying any other kind of angling equipment that care must be taken to obtain well recommended rods, reels, lines and lures which match in sets suitable for the kind of angling they will be called upon to do.

Ordinarily, the novice at spinning buys tackle which is too heavy and too strong. Greater pleasure is obtained with tackle so light that the angler is repaid in giving the fish an even chance (or better) by the added thrills which light tackle affords in catching him. It has been noted that lures, lines and rods should be matched in sizes, just as fly rods and fly lines are matched. Reels, also, must be chosen with purpose in mind. Ultra-light, moderate line capacity reels are available for the tiny rods and thread-like lines normally used for pond or stream fishing where large fish and obstructions usually are not encountered.

Average sized reels holding about two hundred yards of medium diameter line are ideal for use with rods in the medium strength class. Heavier and sturdier reels with spool capacities of three hundred yards or more of eight pound test line can be obtained for handling heavy salt water fish and rods of similar power can be bought to go with them. Ordinary tackle usually is considered quite satisfactory, however, for Striped Bass, Bonefish, small Tarpon, Weakfish, Bluefish, Mackerel and similar species when they are fished for in relatively unobstructed waters.

The fishing of brushy streams calls for a relatively short rod, of six or seven feet, to allow it to be handled easily in congested places. In lakes or open waters, rods of eight feet or even more furnish better sport. If one chooses to use spinning tackle among lily pads or in fishing around rocks and logs, the moderate power rods with five to eight pound test lines are preferable. This type of tackle is adequate for steelhead, many varieties of salmon, and for all but the largest surface fighting salt water fish. It is difficult and misleading to recommend rods by length, size or weight because the long cork grips and the hardware, as well as the quality of bamboo in the rod itself, will influence the sturdiness and power of the rod.

Spinning tackle is a long-term investment, as is any other type of good tackle, and in buying it it is well to seek the advice of others who are experienced in its use on the waters to be fished, and then to buy the best of the recommended gear that one can afford.

ASSEMBLING TACKLE

When spinning tackle is purchased, it usually is necessary to wind the line on the reel spool. This is done by removing the spool from the reel and by winding on the line by hand. When line is wound onto the spool by cranking the reel, the line twists in being wound; a condition which hand-winding can eliminate.

To put the line on the spool, a Perfection Loop knot should be tied in the end and a noose formed with the loop; the noose being placed over the spool. If the noose slips, it should be reversed. The line spool is placed on an axle, such as a pencil or gun cleaning rod, so that it will revolve when the line is unwound. When the line is attached to the reel spool it is wound on in a clockwise manner with a moderate amount of tension; the reel spool being held in the left hand and the line being wound on with the right. (A few reels, such as the Mitchell, require winding line in a counter clockwise direction but these reels are in the minority.) The reel spool occasionally is rotated slightly to assist in winding the line evenly. When a twist is noticed in the line the reel spool should be reversed in the left hand until a reverse twist is noted. The reversal in holding the reel spool should be made about every twenty turns. The spool should be filled to the lip of the reel only. A spool insufficiently filled will impede casting distance. A spool too full will cause the line to cast off in coils. Backing may be used to help fill the spool if need be, but it is preferable to fill the spool completely with line. The line then can be reversed when it becomes worn and there always is enough for emergencies. Lines should be of continuous length but if splicing is necessary, they can be joined by a Barrel Knot. The normal reel spool holds two hundred yards of line of five pound test; less with heavier lines and more with lighter lines. For the large salt water spinning reels, a continuous length of three hundred yards is the safest to use. When the line is placed on the spool it is held in place by a clip on the spool, or by a wide rubber band if no device for securing the end of the line exists. A knot may be tied in the rubber band to aid in removing it from the reel spool. When the spool is replaced on the reel, the reel is ready for use.

After joining the rod, the reel is placed anywhere along the long cork grip where it seems to

Record Rainbow Trout of 1948 weighing 31 pounds 12 ounces, taken at Lake Pend Oreille, Idaho on a Rumer Spinning Reel and 8 pound test monofilament line.

best suit the angler and to best balance the tackle. It is held in place by the two sliding rings on the rod grip. (Spinning rods ordinarily do not have locking reel seats.) The best position for the reel is forward when casting heavy lures and nearer the butt (to lengthen the rod) when lighter lures are used. In addition to this purpose the long grip serves as a support to the angler's forearm in casting and allows the butt to be placed against the angler's stomach when handling a heavy fish. The spinning reel always hangs in a downward position (as does a fly reel); this being most comfortable for the angler.

When the line is threaded through the guides and the lure is affixed to the end of the line, the brake on the reel should be checked to be sure that the tension is light enough so that the line will not be broken by the strike of a fish. Leaders are not used with monofilament Nylon, since the entire line is a continuous leader. The knot which fastens the lure to the line is the weakest spot in the tackle and the line should break at this point if it is necessary to pull loose in case the lure becomes caught on an obstruction.

A Nylon leader as long as desired may be used with braided Nylon line. If the leader is attached to the line by a Barrel Knot, it is unnecessary to use a swivel, which might become caught in the line guides. Tiny snap swivels may be used between line and lure when it is desirable to change the lure frequently. Swivels of bead chain, or other swivels, aid in preventing line twist when rotating lures are used.

Most spinning lures do not twist the line. When line twist is noted, the lure should be changed to one which revolves in the opposite direction. Line twist is easily avoided if the reel is not cranked when line is not being retrieved and if lures are separated into non-twisters and those which twist to the right and to the left. Lures which develop a pronounced twist in the line should be marked "R" or "L" to indicate the direction of spin and then kept separated in the tackle box so that one type can be changed for another when line twist is noted.

Upon disassembling the tackle, if the line has become twisted in fishing, the twist can be stroked out with the fingers, or it can be straightened by trolling it in the current of a stream or behind a moving boat. Line twist should not concern the angler because it develops to excess only due to the angler's fault, and thus easily can be avoided.

CASTING

(See detailed illustrations, on page 213)

In casting with spinning tackle, the lure is reeled in to about a foot from the rod tip. The rod is held (with the reel hanging downward) in the right hand so that one or two fingers are in front of the reel "leg" (the post which joins the reel to the rod) and the rest behind. On some reels it is more convenient to place one finger in front; with other reels, two, or occasionally three. This depends upon the construction of the reel and is decided by holding the rod so that the tip of the forefinger easily can be placed against the lip of the reel spool to aid in braking the reel if greater tension than that afforded by the brake is needed in controlling the run of a fish.

The reel is wound forward or backward by the reel handle, or by turning the cup with the left hand, until the pick-up wheel (over which the lines passes) is nearest to the rod grip. The line is picked off the pick-up wheel (sometimes called "roller-pickup") by the *tip* of the forefinger and is held in this position while the cup of the reel is turned backward to get the pick-up out of the way of the forefinger which holds the line. The pick-up is then opened (disengaged) and the angler is ready to cast. The operation is simple to accomplish, although detailed to describe.

In casting, the rod tip is brought downward to the right and is instantly cast forward and upward with an accelerating sweeping motion which utilizes the whip of the rod. The rod is stopped over and above the target and the line is released instantly by straightening the forefinger which holds it. The lure will then shoot toward the target and can be stopped instantly, if need be, by turning the reel handle forward (counter clockwise) or by placing the tip of the forefinger against the reel spool. In turning the reel handle, the pick-up closes automatically and engages the line. The lure can be slowed down in flight by bringing the forefinger near enough to the whirling line to impede its progress.

The cast above described is the easiest to master and is the most practical because it shoots out the lure and line in a low trajectory which is less influenced by wind. The overhead cast is made in the same manner except that the rod is cast from an overhead position. The overhead cast is more accurate because the lure is cast in a single plane, allowing the direction of the target to be measured more accurately. It has the disadvantage of shooting line and lure in a high trajectory which causes the line to belly in the wind. It usually does not permit as long a cast as does the side cast.

If trees or other obstructions are present, the side cast from the left may be desirable. In this cast the forearm of the angler is held in front of him, parallel to the ground, or nearly so, with the rod tip pointing downward to the left. From this position the lure is cast with a forward motion.

Reels are available for anglers who habitually cast with the left hand. These reels have the reel handle placed on the right side of the reel. A few reels are obtainable wherein the handle can be changed from one side to the other. In any case, casting for left handed anglers is in reverse of the methods above described.

After the cast, the lure may be allowed to sink or may be retrieved on or near the surface, at the discretion of the angler. In fishing shallow streams it is necessary to start the retrieve almost immediately and oftentimes to select lures which do not sink rapidly. Keeping a lure on or near the surface is easy to master if no slack line is allowed when the cast is completed. Obviously, the overhead cast prevents quick controlling of the sinking of the lure when fishing shallow waters because it causes a greater belly in the line, which must be recovered before the lure can be retrieved.

Only a slight twitch of the rod tip is required to hook a striking fish. In fast water, or when the lure is being recovered rapidly, even this may not be necessary. The line must be kept tight at all times, as in any other kind of fishing. Reeling should be stopped when the fish is taking line from the reel because it has been noted that reeling, without recovering line, only serves to put a twist in the line. If the brake is not tight enough to control the fish during a run toward an obstruction, added braking power can be obtained by placing the forefinger of the right hand against the reel spool or by using the thumb and forefinger of the left hand to brake the spool.

If it is found that a heavy fish, or a moderate sized fish in a heavy current, can not be brought in by reeling under the light tension of the brake, it may be necessary to regain line by "pumping." This is done by braking the reel spool manually with as much force as is thought advisable while the rod tip is raised. When the rod tip is raised as high as desired, line can be recovered as the rod tip is lowered. This "pumping" operation can be repeated as often as is necessary. If an anti-reverse lock is included in the reel, the lock should be snapped on soon after the fish is hooked so that the left hand can be used on the rod or to aid in braking the reel without allowing it to back wind.

In stream fishing the lure usually is cast across stream and is allowed to swing with the current until it is retrieved from a position downstream of the angler. In casting to rocks, or other hiding-places for fish in the current, the lure should be cast far enough above or beside the position to allow it to work as deep down into the water as is desired.

One of the important advantages of spinning is that it makes possible long casts, even when obstructions are present which would make the use of the fly rod impossible. With these long casts more water can be covered. Since no false casts are necessary, the lure is in the water for a greater proportion of time. A wider selection of lures is possible than with any other type of tackle. The fisherman can fish the surface or search the depths with his lure, as he chooses. Properly used, spinning is acknowledged to be one of the sportiest methods of angling; a method which may take larger fish, but a method which gives every fish a fair chance and which gives the angler maximum enjoyment in his chosen recreation.

SKITTERING

Skittering is generally associated with still fishing; it usually is a type of bait fishing. However, it involves casting the lure. It actually is the antecedent of modern bait casting. It was the limitations of the fixed line used in skittering that led to the development of the multiplying reel, which would pay out line and thus increase the distance to which the lure might be pitched.

Skittering is done with a long pole, usually 15 to 20 feet long, with a fixed line 2 to 4 feet longer than the pole. The lure used is usually live bait; frog, crayfish, or similar lure. There may be the addition of a spinner or spoon to attract attention of the fish.

Just as in all casting, the pole (rod) becomes a lever which gives added facility for throwing the lure out to where the angler wishes it to land.

The lure is pitched out by the throw of the rod, and the line is tauted to keep the lure well up on the surface. The rod tip then is swept from one side to the other, pulling the lure along on the surface in much the same sort of position as a surface lure is manipulated with bait casting tackle. As the end of the side-sweep is completed, one side or the other, the lure will be more or less in front of the angler, out about the length of the rod. The rod is right or left, as far as it can be swung. The rod is swept up and over in the opposite direction. The lure is picked up by the action. The line describes an arc which allows the lure to drop at the end of the line length in the direction in which it is propelled. The action of the pole in this maneuver is not unlike that in "mending" line in fly casting. It is exaggerated and the lure in this case, is lifted entirely out of the water, to travel in an arc to the limit of the fixed line.

The other plane in which the skittering lure may be cast is more or less directly forward. The lure has been pitched out and the pole tip rises to keep it "skittering" across the water surface, being drawn toward the angler.

When the pole nears the vertical, it is in a position not unlike the fly rod in the initial position of the "roll cast." The skittering assembly is handled in just that way. The pole is thrust toward the vertical, the tip is swept forward, the drag of the lure and line that lie forward pull a bow in the line, the pole tip describes a forward-thrusting circle, and the bait flips up-and-over to fall directly ahead.

FRESHWATER TROLLING

Fishermen, in general, give less thought to trolling than to other methods. Although some look upon trolling as an unsporting way to take fish,

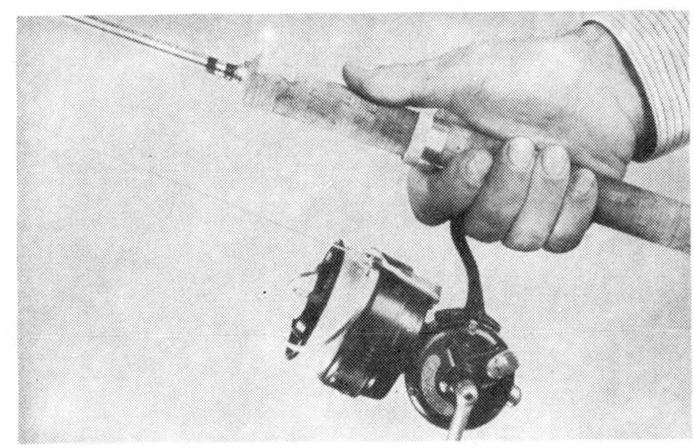

1. Hold rod and reel this way. Thumb along top of rod aids in control and casting accuracy.

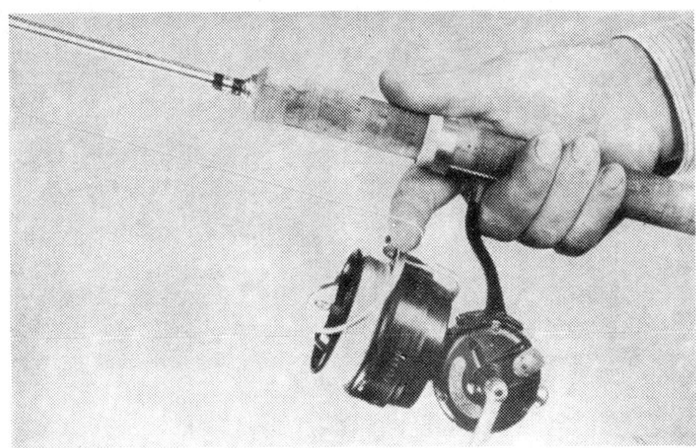

2. Pick up the line with tip of index finger. Now move pick-up arm in reverse to the bottom of the reel.

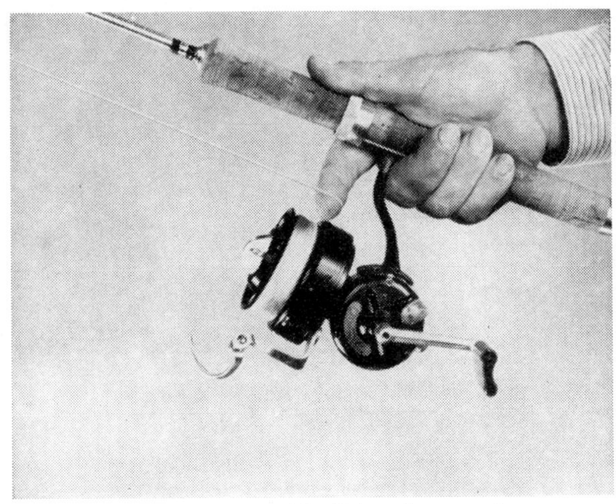

3. Pull pick-up open with light downward movement until it is in position shown here for casting.

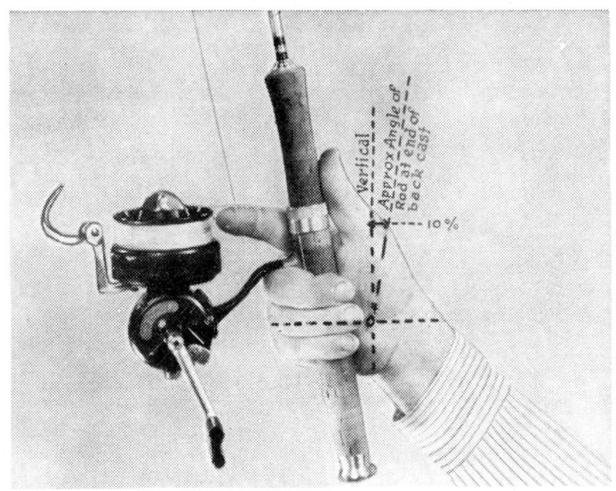

4. Cast with the wrist movement shown. Let line slide off the finger on forward cast to make lure fly straight out.

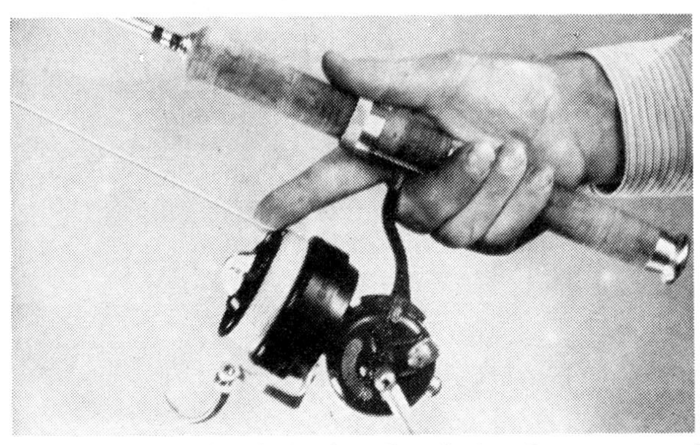

5. Stop the flight of the lure by placing finger on spool flange to drop lure in water with minimum disturbance.

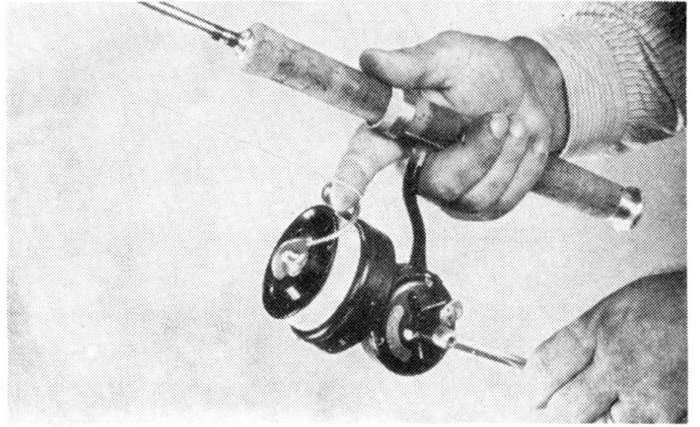

6. Start the retrieve by cranking with left hand; the pick-up will automatically close and pick up line from the finger.

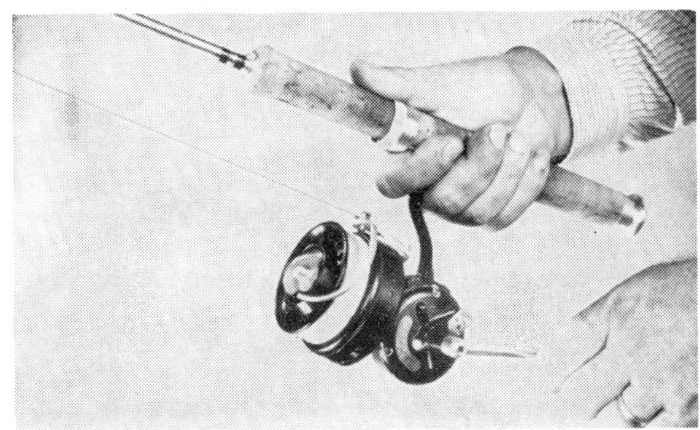

7. In retrieving, crank the handle at a speed desirable for the type of lure you are using and for fishing conditions.

All photographs used on this page were furnished through the courtesy of The Ocean City Manufacturing Company.

THE OPERATION OF THE SPINNING REEL

Frank B. Wire

Oregon has good Bass fishing in addition to its highly publicized Trout and Salmon fishing.

many an otherwise barren fishing trip has been turned into a successful one by trolling.

Wise anglers who have cast all the usual types of cover such as weed beds, shorelines, lily pads, logs, moss beds, etc., without success, know that the fish either are not feeding—or, they are in deep water. Trolling at such a time is the only method for locating them.

Trolling is also valuable in locating those underwater holes which are not visible to the fisherman. Trolling will locate these and once an angler has them spotted, he can be assured of spots known only to himself, or a few other trolling-wise fishermen. These little-fished, invisible holes pay off regularly when the heavily fished cover is producing nothing.

No one method of trolling will take all species of fish. The proper procedure and type of tackle varies because of nature, habitat, and size of the fish. The major freshwater game fish will be covered individually or by groups.

Those species which can be taken regularly while trolling are Muskellunge, Northern Pike, Pickerel, Lake Trout, Kamloops Trout, Steelhead, Cutthroat, and Rainbow Trout, the Largemouth, Smallmouth and Spotted Basses, Walleye, Black and White Crappies, Yellow Perch, White Bass, Striped Bass, Yellow Bass, and the popular members of the sunfish family, Bluegill, Pumpkinseed, and Longear Sunfish.

Logically, the most popular species should be given preference. This places the initial spotlight on the Largemouth and Smallmouth Bass, and would include their lesser known cousin, the Spotted Bass. The first two fish, especially, are widely distributed and rank high with sport fishermen.

LARGEMOUTH BASS

Praised for its fighting ability and cussed because of its habit of outwitting the unseasoned angler, the Largemouth Bass is undoubtedly, the most popular choice of trollers. Its wide distribution, great numbers, and willingness to strike any moving object make it a natural for trolling tactics.

Tackle. Any good casting rod, 5 or 5½ feet long, of medium or sturdy action is best for it will allow a quick setting of the hook. A limber rod is not as good for this purpose because much of the power applied is lost when the rod fails to take up the line fast enough.

The reel should be sturdy, of 100 yard capacity and equipped with 15 to 18 pound test line. A three- or four-foot Nylon monofilament leader should be used to prevent line fraying and to make a nearly invisible connection ahead of the bait.

The lures depend upon the waters to be fished. For shallower weedless waters from 3 to 6 feet in depth, a floating-diving type of lure which travels 2 to 3 feet deep is best. This takes in spoons, plugs, bucktails, pork rind-spinner baits, and allied combinations. Make certain that the lure runs straight and does not turn over; such a miscreant is useless for any kind of fishing.

For deeper weedless waters 6 to 10 feet in depth, a sinking type lure will travel 4 to 8 feet deep, depending upon its weight and design. After a few trips, a studious angler will be able to tell the approximate depth covered by each lure. This is important, for a lure should swim just above the cover without fouling in it.

For extreme depths of 15 feet and over, deep-diving lures should be used. These have large collars which offer more resistance to the water and this takes them down much farther than the conventional collar.

In trolling, the speed of the boat should be regulated, together with the length of the line, so that the lure is wiggling along just over the bottom, or cover.

For weedy waters a weedless lure should be used, particularly if the angler finds his regular lures are fouling constantly.

Weedless spoons, plugs with weedless hooks, and the various weedless bucktails and spinner-pork rind types work best.

In some waters where the weeds are not too heavy, some anglers merely snip off the bottom hook on the front treble. This makes the plug practically weedless for sparse cover.

METHODS. The Largemouth is a predator and by nature hides around cover such as logs, weed beds, lily pads, moss pockets, etc.

Therefore, for best results troll as closely as possible to all types of cover, being careful not to get in close enough to disturb the cover or get fouled in it.

Try different colors in baits. Often one certain color will do the trick where others fail. Troll at various speeds; some days the Largemouth wants a fast moving bait, other times just the opposite.

Learn to "feel" the bait. The vibrations given off by the swimming motion of the bait are noticeable through a casting rod. If it cannot be felt working, it's probably fouled with leaves or moss which prohibit proper action. A fouled lure does not catch fish, so, be sure to keep the hooks clean at all times.

When permissible, two rods are recommended, one on each side of the boat. In this manner two different types of lures can be used, thus increasing the angler's chances for success.

When trolling live minnows, frogs, crawfish, etc., try to make the bait work as naturally as possible. This requires some study as to how it should be properly hooked. If the lure has a tendency to spin by all means use a swivel between the lure and line. Otherwise, a badly twisted line will result.

Special harnesses are available for frogs and minnows at nearly any sporting goods store. For live bait trolling these items are a good investment.

Immediately upon hooking a fish, stop the motor or cease rowing. If the fish is a large one, clear the outside of the boat of all obstructions such as oars, stringers, etc. Raise the motor out of the water; this gives a clear field of action and prevents a good fish from fouling the line.

Play the fish completely out; never "horse" a big fish, as many are lost this way. After it is boated, make shore sightings to locate the exact spot where the fish was caught.

Swing boat in a large circle and troll through this spot again. If another fish is caught, take the boat up wind, drift to a spot just above the hole, anchor quietly, and cast it thoroughly with various lures.

Don't use any larger sinker than is absolutely necessary to take the lure down. Ordinarily, sinkers are necessary only with live bait; as manufacturers of artificial lures have these already weighted for various depths. A heavy sinker takes away much of the sport of playing and feeling the fish.

There is no trick to hooking a Largemouth for in most cases it hooks itself when it strikes. However, due to the flex of the rod and the stretch of Nylon line, it is best to set the hook vigorously once or twice *after* the fish has been hooked. This drives the hook in past the barb and will save many otherwise lost fish.

When a Largemouth dives into moss, weeds, or other heavy cover, do not "horse" it; you may tear the hook loose. Let it sulk for awhile, then move the boat directly over the spot where the fish is snagged. Gently tug in different directions until the bass comes loose.

One of the most effective rigs for trolling, at a slow speed, is as simple as it is effective. Use a floating-diving plug at the end of the line; attach a keel sinker about 18 inches from the plug. The sinker should be only large enough to stay on the bottom while the boat moves at a slow speed.

This rig permits the sinker to drag on the bottom and is practically weedless, even over logs and rocks. Above and behind it will be swimming the floating lure, never fouling and being very attractive to all gamefish.

SMALLMOUTH and SPOTTED BASS

All of the foregoing information applies to these two fishes, plus these tips. Both the Smallmouth and Spotted Bass prefer a faster-wiggling, generally smaller lure than the Largemouth.

Lures in the 1/4, 3/8 and 1/2 ounce class will produce better average results. Keep the hook points sharpened and when a strike is felt, set the hooks solidly.

Both of these fish are extremely fast and acrobatic. They will bounce out of the water and quickly throw a loose bait. Once the hook is set, keep the line tight until the fish is played out.

WALLEYE

This fine eating fish is not an outstanding fighter but is worth the attention of all trollers. The Walleye is essentially a deep water fish and the basic methods used on the Largemouth apply.

Here are additional tips. Walleyes prefer a very fast wiggling lure with as much commotion as possible. Sinking plugs with spinners fore and aft are very effective.

A June bug spinner with nightcrawlers or a minnow behind produces excellent results. Once a number of holes where Walleyes bite regularly are located, always try these first on each trip out; more Walleyes will move into a hole when previous occupants have been caught. A 6 to 12 inch wire leader is recommended.

On moonlit nights, troll over sand or gravel bars using an all white, slow wiggling plug, preferably a floating-diving type. Walleyes are great nocturnal feeders, and the largest ones will be caught at this time.

NORTHERN PIKE and PICKEREL

These two members of the pike family can be considered together because of their close similarity in habits and weaknesses for similar lures.

TACKLE. Wire leaders 12 to 18 inches in length are recommended because of the sharp teeth of these two fishes. The rod for larger Northern Pike should be about 5 feet in length and of sturdy action; the reel, any good make holding 100 yards of 20 to 25 pound line. A gaff hook or large landing net should always be a part of the equipment because these fish are dangerous to handle. They have dozens of large, sharp teeth and hundreds of tiny ones; if no gaff or net is available, never reach for a pike or pickerel until it has been played out completely. When the fish is exhausted, place the index finger on top of the fish's head, with the thumb and middle finger in the gill openings. Once it is gripped, hold it tightly until the fish is unhooked with pliers, and safely on the stringer.

METHODS. Troll slowly around sunken trees, logs or moss beds, or through scattered weed fields, using the same basic tactics as for Largemouth.

Red and white spoons are particularly effective; June bug spinners and floating-diving plugs are a close second.

Once a pike is on, strike hard and be sure the hook is set past the barb. When using live bait, such as frogs or minnows, wait a few seconds after the initial strike before setting the hook. This gives the fish time to get the bait well into its mouth.

The Northern Pike and Pickerel are lively, rugged customers; keep a tight line, play the fish cautiously, particularly if it is a large one. These fish have a nasty habit of coming in with hardly any fight; then, when the angler reaches for it, suddenly dashing under the boat. Many broken rods and more lost fish attest this fact.

Play a large fish from the end of the boat, this will reduce the possibility of the broken rod and lost fish. Never underestimate the instinctive cunning of a Northern Pike or Pickerel and always be prepared for that last unexpected dash for freedom.

MUSKELLUNGE

Here is the giant of the Pike family and the fish nearly every freshwater troller hopes to land. They are a solitary fish and moody in nature.

Once a musky is seen in a certain area, it should be trolled repeatedly until the fish is in the proper mood.

TACKLE. The rod should be 5 to 5½ feet in length, very stiff. The reel a regular casting model holding 100 yards of 25 to 40 pound test line. A wire leader 12 to 18 inches in length is necessary because of the large, vicious teeth of the Muskellunge.

The lures should be large editions of those used for bass. Floating-diving plugs weighing 1 to 2 ounces and 4 to 6 inches in length, giant bucktails and spoons, and surface commotion lures get the largest muskies. Live bait falls down in bagging big muskies.

METHODS. Muskies habitually live in the deeper waters and here the trolling should be done. Large holes surrounded by weeds, and old logging camps are natural hangouts.

Troll slowly and repeatedly in areas where Muskies are known to live; ask the natives and camp owners for best spots.

Muskies are moody and sometimes sulk for days without feeding. Persistency is the keynote, for on some trolling trips the Musky will cooperate.

Try the various lures mentioned, different color combinations, different depths. Use the same basic suggestions as for bass.

Large top water plugs with spinners for creating commotion should be trolled 50 to 75 yards behind the boat, very slowly, just fast enough to work the spinners.

If the deep water doesn't produce, try these top water commotion plugs in the shallower water. Try night fishing, particularly, when the moon is bright and the lure will make a good silhouette against the sky.

When a Musky strikes, set the hooks hard, then set them again for a safety measure. Stop the forward progress of the boat, and if the Musky is of sufficient size and strength, follow it until it starts to tire. Then play it out and land as described for large Northern Pike.

LAKE TROUT

Here is another large fish that has plenty of followers. It is a strong fish but, unfortunately, because of the methods necessary for taking it, much of the fighting qualities are nullified.

It lives in deep water and special tackle is necessary for taking it.

TACKLE. Heavy rods with extra long butts are necessary for proper leverage. Correspondingly large trolling reels holding 250 to 500 yards of 30 to 50 pound test wire line are used.

Large sinkers are used to take the lure to the extreme depths necessary and because of them the fight of the Lake Trout is reduced.

Large wobbling spoons and live bait account for more trout than any other types.

METHODS. The metal line is payed out until the lure is barely skimming the bottom. Trolling speed is varied for at times a slow-moving bait is successful; at other times the trout prefer a fast-moving bait.

When the trout strikes, strike back hard, and then there is not much to do except reel and tug.

Due to the fact that these trout are found far out in the larger lakes, it is usually necessary to form a party and charter a boat. This is wise for the beginner because these charter boatmen know the habits and hangouts of Lake Trout.

At any rate, do not make the first Lake Trout fishing trip alone; go with an experienced troller for it's unlike other trolling.

KAMLOOPS and STEELHEAD TROUT

These two trout are treated together because both are giant Rainbow Trout. The Steelhead is a Rainbow that migrates and grows to large proportion.

The Kamloops is a Rainbow made famous in Lake Pend Orielle, Idaho. Because of ideal conditions it has broken all world's records for size, 15 to 25 pounders are just ordinary.

TACKLE. The same tackle used for Lake Trout is best for Kamloops except that metal line is not always used, and the recommended lures are wobbling plugs.

For Steelhead, the same tackle used for bass is satisfactory, although the line should be 20 to 25 pound test, because here is a big, very rugged fighting fish.

METHODS. Kamloops first; although the reported man-hours-per-fish in famous Lake Pend Orielle is over 200, anglers still flock there to take their chances.

Trolling is done with motors, from 3 to 5 horsepower, and at unusually fast speeds. This lake is exceedingly deep and various depths are tried in an effort to locate the big fellows.

Curiously enough, although practically all Kamloops are taken deep, a former world record 36 pounder was taken while trolling a surface lure. This is one of those unexplainable catches; the fish just happened to be there at the right time and in the proper mood.

When a fish is hooked the fight is fast and spectacular, the Kamloops clearing the water in beautiful leaps. It is a rare and unforgettable thrill.

The Steelhead is taken mostly by trolling in larger streams. The popular procedure is to troll regular bass plugs upstream, pausing at each deep hole to allow the plug to swing back and forth as it wiggles.

Trolling is also done in close to brush piles, fallen trees and logs. When the Steelhead is hooked, a battle ensues that the angler will never forget. Here, again, it is wise to go with an experienced Steelhead troller for the first trip.

PANFISH

This includes various sunfishes such as the Bluegill, Pumpkinseed, Longear, etc.; and the Yellow Perch, Black and White Crappies, Striped Bass and Yellow Bass, and Cutthroat and Rainbow Trout.

Few anglers realize that larger panfish can be taken regularly if trolled for properly. It is an easy and efficient way to locate these smaller species which travel about in schools.

TACKLE. There is no standard recommendation beyond this; the outfit must be lightweight for the best sport.

Cane poles, heavier fly rods, spinning rods, casting rods—all these are satisfactory.

The reel can be single action, automatic, or the standard casting models.

The best lures are small wiggling plugs, spoons, bucktails, flies, June bug spinners, and worms, or live bait such as minnows, worms, leaches, crawfish, wigglers, etc.

METHODS. Trolling can be done with motor, oars, or just drift-trolling with the wind, if sufficient to keep the bait off the bottom.

Once a fish is taken, circle around and troll repeatedly through the same area. Panfish usually travel in schools and when one is located the limit can be taken in short order.

Trolling demands patience and study. Patience to locate the deeper holes, channels and drop-offs; and repeated trips to these spots until the fish sought is found in a feeding mood.

Study is necessary to determine the proper depth, type of lure and color. Once an angler learns the tricks of trolling, he rarely comes home empty handed. The results and thrills are worth the effort.

STILL OR BAIT FISHING

Despite the growing interest in plug casting and fly fishing, more angling is still done with bait than with any other method. Fishing from the banks of a stream or lake or from an anchored boat is the most common method of using bait, although it is also used in trolling and to a more limited extent in casting. There are two broad groups into which baits naturally fall: those used in fresh and those used in salt waters. Natural foods usually head the list, but many substances that can by no means be so classified are successfully used in bait fishing. Only the baits most widely used, together with methods of securing, preparing, and using them can be presented. Those used in fresh water will be discussed in this section; those for salt water will be found on page 252.

FRESH WATER BAITS

ANGLE WORM

Undoubtedly the most popular bait of all is the common garden worm, found most anywhere in North America where the soil is black or fertile. There's hardly a fish that won't bite on it. There are many ways to put them on a hook. One school of anglers advocate running the hook into the large end and continuing until the bend and the shank are covered, letting the remainder of the worm trail out behind. Others prefer to bunch the worm by inserting the hook through about a half-inch from the head, then again and again at one inch intervals; this leaves the worm hanging in loops and the point of the hook can be kept covered. Either method is good for most panfish and for trout. Sometimes if the fish are fussy, two or even three worms can be placed on a hook.

Worms should be kept in an open or ventilated-top can with plenty of good dirt. Worms are apt to bunch and coil around each other, so it's well to shake them up at least once a day if they are to be kept for any length of time.

Those who dig their own worms, look for little mounds of soil in the shady sections of gardens, around manure piles, or anywhere the earth is moist. These are worm "droppings" in the shape of small balls. When dry seasons start the worm patch can be preserved by putting a pile of leaves or lawn cuttings—six inches to a foot thick—on the spot.

Worms are also used on hooks behind spinners, or as an extra lure on streamer flies and trolled.

When casting a worm bait, swing it out without a sharp jerk as the latter will snap most of the worm off the hook. With a little practice one can cast a worm baited hook for a considerable dis-

---

Drawings illustrating "Fresh Water Baits" are used by courtesy of Ollie Rodman.

tance with a fly rod, bait casting rod, or spinning outfit.

NIGHT-CRAWLERS

These giant worms, four to six inches long, and as big as an ordinary lead pencil, are good bait used whole for bass and big trout, or cut or broken in inch long pieces for pan fish such as Sunfish, Perch, Bluegills, Bream and Bullheads. Yes, they're good for eels, too; fished on or near (about a foot) the bottom.

Hook a whole crawler through from side to side at about one inch intervals, letting it hang in loops. Or for the pan fish inch long sections strung over the #8, 10 or 12 (the smaller the better) hook so as to leave the point hidden will do well.

Catching night-crawlers is almost as much fun as fishing! They get their name from their habit of emerging at night (dewy nights are best) from their holes for almost their entire length. Tread softly with a bright flashlight and when one is seen grab it quickly before they can get back underground. If one is caught by the head only, pull steadily and gently; his holding power will soon tire and he'll come loose; pull too hard and he'll break in the middle and will not keep. They are easily found on lawns, or in the space between the planted rows of the garden. It is well to let the neighbor know in advance about night-crawler-collecting trips. To anyone not informed on the subject, a man gathering night-crawlers, hopping quickly, then treading gently and flashing a light, looks like a raving maniac.

CRAYFISH

This vest pocket edition of the lobster, from an inch and a half to three inches long, can be found in and around rocky sections of shallow streams. And hellgrammites are there too. Hook crayfish through the tail; when the bass (or other fish) hit them, let the fish run for a bit so the fish has a chance to mouth and swallow the bait. Keep them off the bottom as otherwise they'll crawl under rocks and foul-hook the line to the bottom; okay to bottom-fish with them in sandy or muddy bottom.

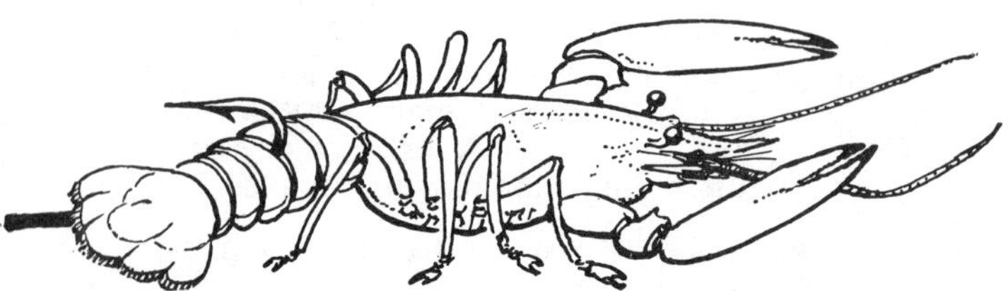

HELLGRAMMITES

Available from fresh water bait dealers or they can be caught in and around the rocks of shallow, shady streams. Hook under—as shallowly as possible—the pronounced "collar," and run the point of the hook out again; and fish them off the bottom unless it's sandy or, like the crayfish, they'll get on the under sides of rocks which is their natural home, hook or no hook.

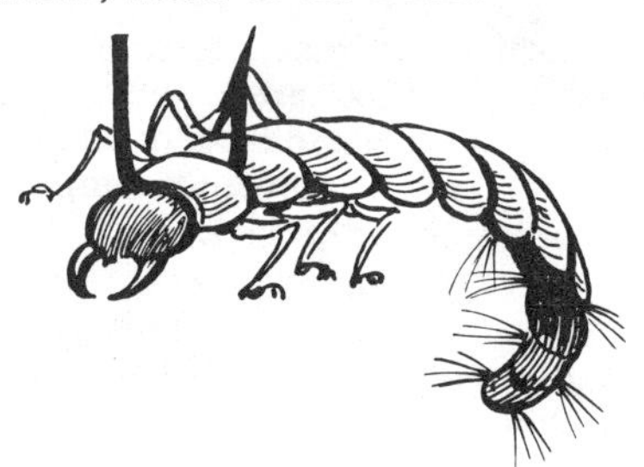

Great bait for both Largemouth and Smallmouth Bass, they keep best in a cool spot; placed in a pail or can with a mass of grape leaves or grass.

CRICKETS

These black insects live under stones, old boards, piles of discarded lumber, wood piles, especially near patches of long grass. Handle them gently as they should be as lively as possible. A good container is a ten- or twelve-inch mason jar with a screw top, ventilated. Or regular live bait containers can be purchased from tackle dealers.

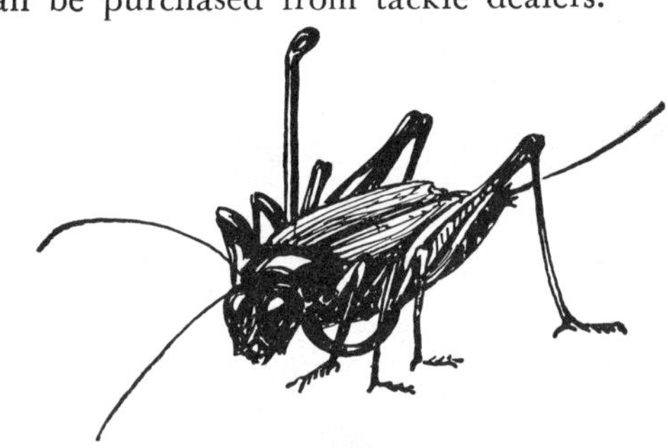

This "bestest" of Smallmouth Bass baits—good also for most all fresh water pan fish from Trout to Perch—should be hooked just under the "collar" or through the hard part of the body, letting the hook point come out again. They're tender and take careful handling both in hooking and in getting them to the fish. Use a very gentle cast, or better yet, just let them down into the water with a split shot for weight.

SHRIMP

This paragraph refers to the small salt water variety about an inch to an inch and a half long. One can catch them and it's more fun to fish with bait obtained in this way. Run a long-handled net with very fine mesh along the edge of the bay, inlet, or tidal creek. Or better yet, get a ten-foot, fine-mesh seine and haul this very close to the bottom—a two man operation.

Keep in sawdust mixed with wood shavings and keep cool—on the cement or damp cellar floor or in the ice chest (if the lady of the house does not object). Have the top of the box open or perforated; a shoe box is just the thing; make a layer of sawdust and shavings on the bottom of the box about an inch deep; then put in a layer of shrimp about an inch deep; then alternate an inch of each as long as the shrimp last. If, however, there is more than four inches in all, get another box so that the weight does not suffocate or crush the bottom layer of shrimp.

While fishing, keep the box of shrimp out of the sun. Under the boat seat is a good place. A wet towel loosely draped over the box will help.

Hook shrimp on singly or if they're very small, use two or three, placing the barb through the big part of the body. Small hooks are important here, as they are in all panfishing and for Smallmouth Bass too. Change the shrimp if the fish doesn't bite before they turn white or red. Also keep dropping a shrimp or two overboard now and then (this is known as "chumming") to attract fish.

Shrimp are one of the best of baits for panfish, especially killing for Smallmouth Bass, Yellow Perch, White Perch, Eels, and Hornpout. Once again, use a small sinker or split-shot about two or three feet from the hook—use at least three feet of light (six pound test) Nylon or gut leaders. Lighter and longer leaders catch more fish!

FROGS

Smallmouth and Largemouth Bass, Pickerel and Northern Pike love small frogs. Best are the little black fellows called "leapers," found in the grass along a marshy shore, under rocks and logs; or they can be caught at night using a flashlight. Tread softly and quietly, move a hand toward them until very close and then grab quickly but firmly. Open the frog box carefully as they'll all jump out if given a chance.

Hook through the lips; cast out gently and let them swim around; or troll slowly with forty or

fifty feet of line. There are also many frog harnesses on the market, designed to hold the frog without hurting him and with an especial eye to making him live longer. (See page 573).

To digress from the bait angle, if frogging and some big old bullfrogs are found, just remember that frogs' legs (fried) are one of the world's leading delicacies for humans!! Dangle a bit of red flannel in front of a bullfrog's eyes and he's practically in the bag. Trout or Bass flies work too.

GRASSHOPPERS

Use same as crickets for Smallmouth Bass and panfish. Hook through stomach with point coming out the back, and in the large part of the body. Same applies to wasps, hornets, bees or other small insects for panfish or trout.

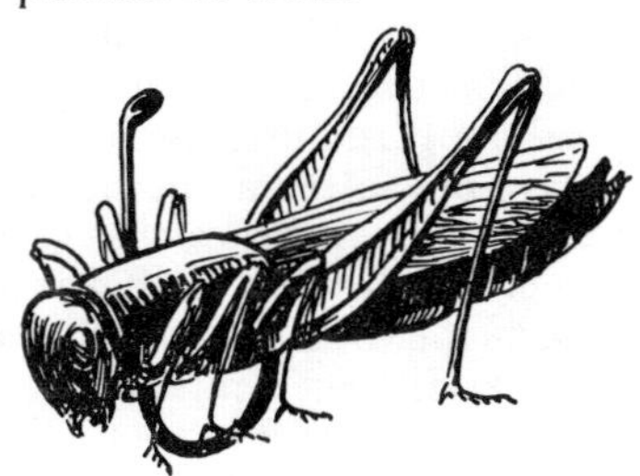

MINNOWS

This is an inclusive term that is intended to cover small fish, one to four or five inches long, or any species. Remember that most all fresh water game fish are cannibalistic; that is, they will eat small fish. In fact, Largemouth Bass have been known to try to eat fish so near their own size that they have been found choked to death with most of the intended victim sticking out of their mouth!!

Probably the most popular minnow is the fresh water shiner. They can be caught in a drop net, baited with corn meal, chunks of bread, bread or cracker crumbs. Lower the net gently from a dock or quiet boat; wait—again quietly—for several minutes and then lift slowly but steadily. Or minnow traps can be set—and there are several good makes in about any well-equipped tackle shop.

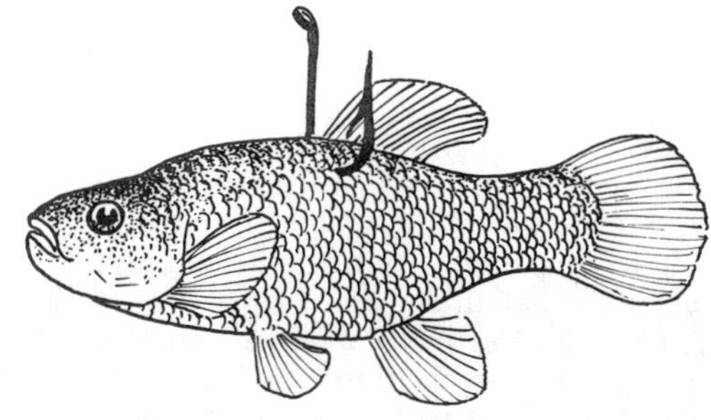

One needs a minnow bucket with an aeration device—also commonly found at fishing tackle and hardware stores—to keep shiners for any length of time. They have been held for several days by stealing the laundry tub where there is plenty of water. A friend used the family bath tub—that is, until his wife took one look! But shiners carried in an ordinary can or pailful of water will soon be dead and belly up. They're still good for trolling by hooking through the lips but they're no use for still fishing when a live, swimming bait is needed. Those dead ones are death on eels fished on the bottom; best time for eels is at night although they can be caught, especially in salt water, in the daytime.

Place the live shiner on the hook (handle him gently, squeezing him just enough so he won't flip out of your hand) by carefully inserting the hook just under the skin under the dorsal fin; if you go deep and hit his backbone, he'll die almost instantly. This method of hooking applies to any live minnows whether shiners, smelt, mummies, small perch, or any small fish; that is, if you want to use them alive while still fishing. More wiggle, more strikes, and more fish in the creel.

For trolling, hook any minnow, through both upper and lower lips. To troll and have the minnow whirl (a killer behind a spinner for many game fish from Walleyes up to and including Landlocked Salmon) requires a bit more effort, but a fairly easy one after a bit of practice. For this result follow these instructions: use a snelled hook; pass the hook through both the upper and lower lips (and just enough behind the outer edge of the lips so that it won't pull out easily); pull the hook through until there is about three or four inches of leader between hook shank and the lips; then insert the hook through the same spot in the lips to make a complete loop through both lips;

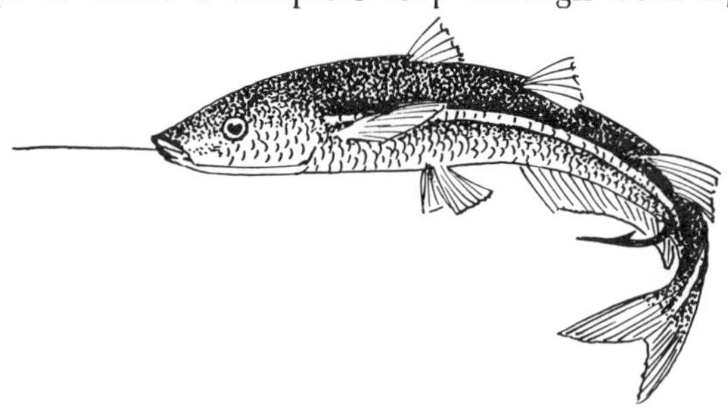

then insert the hook upwards from alongside the anal fin, close to the backbone of the minnow, and bring the barb out the back; make a slight bend in the minnow between head and tail, lay the hook shank flat alongside the minnow and tighten the loop in the lips to retain the curve or bend in the minnow; pull through the water and make sure that the minnow is making even revolutions; if it does not, try a little more curve in the minnow by changing the loop through the lips. This is called "sewing" on a minnow and is a real fish-getter. Yes, the minnow is dead, but the trolling action gives it a spinning, wounded action. One of the best minnows for this type of rig is the fresh water smelt. Heavier, deeper bodied minnows are harder to handle in this fashion. Incidentally, be sure to have a small swivel or even two between the line and leader.

Under "Frogs" mention was made of "frog rigs" as something that could be secured at a tackle shop. It is possible to buy minnow rigs too.

If near salt water, "mummies" (mummychaugs) are good baits—small ones for panfish; large ones for Pickerel or Pike. These will keep for days by spreading a wet gunnysack on the cellar floor, laying the mummies out on it and merely sprinkling with water once or twice a day.

NOTE: Perhaps now is as good a time as any to break into listings of baits with a bit of general information which is most important. This concerns the hooks and leaders to which the baits are attached.

Remember that in the first place, hooks are cheap; that despite their cheapness they are the vital link which will connect with the catch. So be sure to have a goodly supply of hooks in the tackle kit.

And keep them small: trout and panfish have very small mouths. Too many fishermen use too-large hooks. The largest size that should ever be used is # 8 either long or short-shanked with # 10 and #12 being strong enough and big enough in ninety-nine cases out of a hundred. Light tackle is used for panfish to begin with; most baits are too small to impale on a large hook, and so small hooks are needed. They're less conspicuous and easier to use with such small baits as larvae, grasshoppers, crickets, shrimp, etc.

Small hooks call for light leaders; less see-able by the fish; easier to insert and tie to the small eye; stronger than needed even if as small as four pound test. Nylon monifilament is ideal as it is not only always full strength, but it does not need to be soaked like the old-fashioned gut leaders to make it pliable; and it does not rot out. And it is dirt cheap. Fine leaders and small hooks mean more fish deeply hooked, so just snip off the leader at the fish's mouth and bend on another hook. You can retrieve the hook when the fish are cleaned. Six pound test leader should be the heaviest used, and three feet of it should be used for the shortest leader.

Use small sinkers. A couple of split shot, bent onto the leader two or three feet above the hook should answer to carry the bait to the deepest level under most any condition. Big sinkers can scare fish away.

Before leaving the minnow category, it should be pointed out that some of the smaller panfish are also good bass, pickerel and pike baits. Small yellow perch up to three inches are one of the best. Little Sunfish up to two inches are "not bad." Again, hook them just under the back fin, use # 4 short-shanked hooks such as the "Eagle Claw" as these short hooks do not weigh down the live minnow as the longer ones do. Check the local laws to make sure that use of small panfish is legal.

Not to be recommended as a conservation measure, but if fishing a wild river area where there are lots of trout and where few fishermen go, here's a tip. Small trout are "hot stuff" for really big trout. Once in New Brunswick, fishing the Nepisquit, some seventy miles of trout water (every inch of it), a fishing companion hooked a trout of about six inches. It was at the tail of a deep pool where the fast, heavy water swirled under a jutting ledge whitened at the edge with a bit of foam—one of those really trouty looking places where one feels sure a big one lives. And one did. Hardly had the little trout grabbed the fly and been lifted to the surface when a huge Brook Trout rose and took the helpless six-incher into a maw that looked as big as a bucket. Unfortunately, the angler got "buck fever" and tried to set the hook immediately, something which should not be done with live bait. One needs to give the fish time to take live bait into his mouth, run to a spot he feels is safe, mouth the new-found meal, and possibly turn it around in his mouth for easy swallowing then and not before is the time when the hook should be set. Such fishing takes practice, patience, and steel-cold nerves on the part of the angler, things which the average man does not have when he sees a big fish take hold. That trout got away but it taught a lesson that has helped take some big ones in the wild, well-populated trout streams of the north country.

CUT BAITS

Artificials will sometimes take more fish than live or real bait, but at other times the opposite is true. Then is when knowledge of live and cut baits, plus a bit of ingenuity, comes in handy to give that wanted sag to the creel.

A New Brunswick guide demonstrated that the big ones, trout in this instance, really went for the pectoral fin of a trout, floated down in the current and given a twitch now and then to keep it off the bottom and impart a fluttery motion.

A house painter in southern Rhode Island who spent more time fishing than painting, showed that the throat latch of a fish was a good bait for any minnow-feeding fish; that the white strip of a pickerel's belly was a killer for Pickerel and for Largemouth Bass; that a cut piece of any fish, usually off the belly or throat, and trolled or skittered through or on top of the water would take surface and near-surface feeders when the artificials failed.

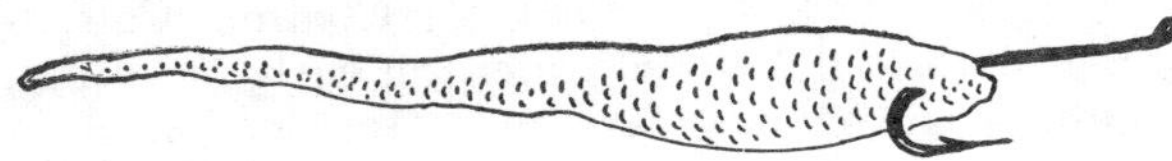

Perch and pickerel belly is especially effective in weedy or lily-padded waters if used on a weedless hook and skittered over the top of the weeds and pads. Those big ones will come after this bait and provide some fishing in waters where an artificial plug would be hung up all the time.

GRUBS, SMALL WORMS AND LARVAE

Through the courtesy of Mark Burlingame, author of *Trout Secrets, Bass Secrets* and *Panfish Secrets* we borrowed the following reliable information on the following:

"A. Cockroaches. (Very, very good!) Just exactly as good in the north as the south. Use small hooks, light wire, as roaches are fragile. Main trouble, even where plentiful, is to catch them. *The Sporting Goods Dealer,* 10th & Olive Sts., St. Louis, Mo., might tell you where to get traps if postage is sent. Some catch roaches in hollowed loaves of stale bread, dampened inside by several brushings of greasy (not soapy) rinsings from cooking pots. A little sweetening helps.

"Corn ear worms, found in the ears while they're still soft. (Excellent).

"Horseweed worms, found in common horseweed, and split out with a knife. (Excellent.)

"Bonnet worms. Lift lily stalks from water and peel out little green, juicy worms. Use tiny short, short Eagle Claw No. 14 hooks. (Exceptionally good.)

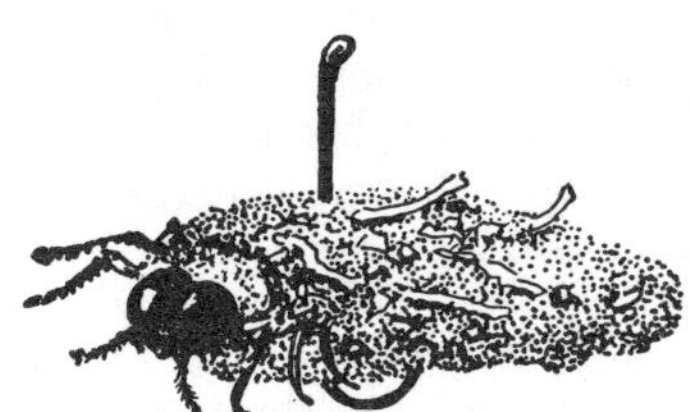

"Catalpa worms. Found wherever you can find catalpa trees. (Ugh! But grand bait!)

"Wigglers catch Bluegills through the ice when nothing else will! Look for these mayfly larvae in deep mud, where plenty of little "blow-holes" perforate surface. Scoop up a patch of mud, digging down and under at least six inches. Rinse and slosh around in a wire bucket of ¼" gravel screening 'til only worms and weeds remain. Then set weeds and worms in screen bucket in slightly larger regular bucket of water so they won't freeze stiff. Any strong scoop set on a six-foot handle will bring 'em up from muddy bottom, but wire scoops on metal frames are best. (Wonderful bait.)

"Goldenrod grubs for winter Bluegills. Collect a bunch of goldenrod stems with plenty of gall swellings. Hang in cool, dry spot in basement. When you need 'em, split galls with jacknife and take out grubs. Keep three or four dozen in cardboard Quaker Oats box, half full of dry rolled oats. (Simply scrumptuous bait!)

"Corn borers, in winter corn fields. Collect stalks. Split out borers. On small No. 14 or No. 12 hooks they'll take Bluegills through ice most any time."

When using borers, grubs, or wigglers—use tapered leaders about six feet long—made of a length of four-pound test Nylon tied to one of two-pound test. Much better than all four-pound test! A single split BB will take bait down. If results are not too good, go down to a finer tippet, say, 4X. A nice limber rod is needed in order not to break the fine tippet when the strike is made.

MICE

Not the kind of bait that everyone wants to handle. However, they have been known to take some big bass and trout when floated or cast over the proper spots. Personally, we'd pass them up as we dislike the idea of even hooking them on, whether alive or dead. But they had to be mentioned—or did they? They do make some very lifelike artificial mice in both fly rod and bait casting sizes.

CARP AND CATFISH BAITS

Again quoting from Mark Burlingame's fishing *Secrets,*

"B. For Carp: Use enough bait to cover only the barb of the hook—and don't use big hooks. It is ridiculous to fish for carp with big one and two hooks. Even a twenty-pounder can be easily landed on an eight, six or four, provided you have plenty of line on the reel.

"Chum spots you intend to fish a day or two in advance with small, boiled-til-soft green peas, corn, barley, oats, wheat, cheese bait, whole rice, dough balls, clam bait, scattered hamburger, or ground horsemeat.

"Then bait with the same material. Use just enough to cover the barb of a No. 4 hook, or slightly more on No. 8 or No. 6 hooks.

"Hook should be very near bottom in eighteen to twenty-four inches of water. Use a very small quill float.

"Strike quickly if using dough bait, whenever the quill moves, as dough comes off the hook easily in the fish's mouth.

"After June, carp go into four or five feet of water, and in very hot weather can often be found in from ten to twenty feet depths. To bring them up where you can reach them with fly rod throw out a handful of chum into deep water, then another several feet nearer you, and so on, until you end up nearby. Carp will follow 'til within reach.

To make carp bait and chum:

(1) Parboil well-soaked green peas, white corn, lima beans, oats, wheat, barley, or unpolished rice 'til soft. Put in a teaspoon or two of bicarbonate of soda to keep from souring.

(2) Mix approximately half cornmeal and half flour into firm dough, and roll or cut into small pea size hunks. If dough crumbles knead flour with water. If you still can't keep it on your hook work into it a wisp or two of cotton batting. A dash of diluted honey helps.
(3) Boil and mash potatoes in their jackets. However, when about half done save out two or three to use as bait. Half done they'll stay on small triple hooks (# 12) worked into small chunks shank first, then tied to leader.
(4) Knead a pound of meal, a pound of ground beef or horsemeat, and a pound of flour together into a stiff dough. Make into separate little pellets with a wisp of cotton batting for each as you need bait or chum.
(5) Put a bowl of bran under a good size chunk of "high" meat hung in the shade on a hot day and hatch yourself some maggots. Ideal carp bait, one or two on the point of an eight or ten short, short shank Eagle Claw hook.

"Here's tops in all 'stink' baits. Get a couple of quarts of fresh water clams. Chop 'em up into lima bean size and hang in the sun in a milk jar. When they begin to smell high throw some out the night before into the carp water you expect to fish. Bait up next morning with small pieces of this same bait. You'll get action galore!

"Two or three days before fishing clean off slime and weeds from bottom in space about six feet square. Chum this a couple of days. Then bait up with same bait, and fish cleared area on bottom—no sinker, no quill. This must be in still water.

"For Channel Cat: Channel cats are the gamest, sportiest, fastest, cussedest of the catfish tribe! Here are a few pointers: Keep shadow off stream where you fish. Look for spots where there's cover for cats in daylight, i.e. stumps, drifted weeds held by logs or brush, roots, rocks, overhangs. Put on enough lead to keep bait well down toward bottom, but not so much it can't keep off snags, etc., as you drift down current.

"Fish deeper water daytimes. Best night spots are riffles above deep pools and holes. Best method, night or day, is to keep bait near or on bottom, yet shift along from time to time with current, or occasionally pump rod to lift off bottom.

"Use at least four-foot leader, eight or ten pound test, with tiny swivel on each end—a "snap" swivel (very small) at terminal end facilitates changing lures or hooks (on twelve-inch snells). Put dipsey sinker 1/8 to 1/2 ounce depending on the current, on the line just above the snap swivel.

"Channel Cats are not dainty feeders. They like a real "gob" of worms. However small, one to two inch frogs are better than big ones. A No. 1 hook is big enough. And many like No. 2s better.

(1) Tops in channel Cat baits is coagulated chicken blood, allowed to dry in the sun for a couple of hours, This won't stay on hooks too well, but you can increase tenacity by drying narrow strips of mosquito netting in each bait, and hooking barb through end of netting.
(2) "High" baits are good for all kinds of "cats", including channels. These include "stink" minnows, sour claims, and Limberger cheese. "Stink" minnows are prepared by drying approximately four-inch chub or shiners in the sun or both sides 'til they rattle when tossed around in a tin dish. Then bury them in closed jar for about three days, to ripen and bring out scent and oil. Another good bait is unhatched chickens, hooked through the head—the chickens that have died in the shells, being too weak to break out.
(3) Chicken, rabbit, beef, pig, lamb livers are good baits, the first and second considered "bestest because strongest".
(4) Hellgrammites, crayfish, grasshoppers all good Channel Cat bait. "High" crayfish tails are especially good.
(5) Last, but not least, are live minnows, allowed to drift down stream naturally with one or two split buck shot clamped on leader. Some channel fanatics claim this is the best way of all to get results.

"GENERAL RULE: Look for Channel Cats in rising, slightly discolored water, on early mornings, evenings, and cloudy days, in current channels, in two to five feet of water. At night (black nights best) they're in one to three foot depths . . . sometimes even shallower, best spots then are riffles above and below pools. Best daytime hours are early dawn 'til around ten o'clock A. M.

"For Yellow Cats and Blue Cats: Number one bait is black sunfish—two and three inchers taken from shady waters. They live long, are very active and attract all catfish! Other good baits are hard head minnows and cockatouche or "stone-bull heads".

"A swell cheese bait is good sharp (aged) New York or Wisconsin cheese, mixed with comb honey and flour to a tough consistency. Use a bit about the size of a marble moulded around a No. 1 or No. 2 hook.

"Most any of the Channel Cat baits mentioned previously are just as good for all other catfish, and "bullheads".

"For Bull Heads (Pout): Contrary to many ideas it's not necessary to fish on the bottom for pout. Use a small float, and two or three BBs for sinkers, and fish about a foot above bottom.

"Small pieces of cut bait, either fish or meat, and small dead shiners, or chubs, are all good.

"All still baits described above for catfish will take pout, when used on #4 hooks in smaller portions. Grass shrimp, dead or alive, are also excellent bait.

"Many times in ponds one can have wonderful luck fishing for pout if they are "tolled" to boat or bank. Throw a scant handful of chopped dead grass shrimp, chopped fish or chopped meat, as far from you as possible. Then scatter some all the way in, 'til the final batch is around the area fished.

"Wind narrow strips of calico rags into about an inch ball. Loop a leader around this, and stitch it firmly to the rags. Then thread worms along stout thread, leaving only heads and tails to wiggle. Wind thread around rag ball 'til whole ball is about two-and-a-half inches in diameter.

"Lower to bottom. Pull up slowly and steadily when you feel a bite. Lift quickly but without jerking into boat—and pout won't let go 'til you have 'em safe and sound. (You'll often get two or three at a time!)

"Use raw chicken gizzards—they're tough. Tie one on the line. Sink to bottom. When bullhead tugs, pull him out steadily. The stubborn critter won't let go 'til he's on bank or in boat.

"Crow and other baits are good for pout: With your .22 pick off one or two crows. Dress 'em, and use all internal organs for bait, cut into small pieces.

"White garden grubs, bark grubs, one-inch to one-and-a-half-inch grass frogs, crayfish, grasshoppers, crickets, grass shrimp, salamanders, water-beetles, fish entrails, beef brains, any and all of 'em are good pout bait."

ICE FISHING

The onset of real winter in the north sets in operation one of the oddest of all forms of angling —ice fishing.

It holds scant charm for the angler who demands comfort with his sport, but for the hardy fisherman who does not shrink from moderate hardship, it has unique appeal.

The setting itself is novel, and attractive to those who like winter. The level white plain of the frozen lake, the swirling fog of wind-driven snow, the bare trees and black underbrush along the shore, the grey storm clouds or the high blue vault overhead—all these together constitute an atmosphere quite unlike that found in other angling.

Unless local laws interfere, ice fishing starts as soon as the lakes are frozen and lasts until the ice grows unsafe in the spring. The winter angler has available a surprisingly long list of fish that may be taken successfully with the right lures and methods. Northern Pike, Bream or Bluegills, Perch, Lake Trout, Walleyes, and other fish bite as readily in January as in June. In general, however, ice fishing lacks one element that characterizes summer angling, that of spectacular gameness on the part of the fish. The cold water seems to slow them down and, in consequence, they offer a less showy battle in winter. Even the most ardent ice fisherman will concede that there is little resemblance between the tactics of a 10-inch Bluegill on a winter line and the performance of the same fish on a flyrod or slender cane pole six months later. The Pike gives a fair account of himself on ice tackle but is not capable of the headlong, slashing fight that marks him in summer. And to a large degree the same thing is true of other fish caught in the cold months.

Many of the details of bait and gear differ locally, but the tackle, bait, and methods used in New England and the Lake States of the Middle West are those used by the greatest number of fishermen. They are, with local modifications, applicable to other sections.

IN NEW ENGLAND

Oddly enough when going ice fishing in the southern section of the northeast sector of the United States, one doesn't use fishing tackle, as a rule, but uses "traps" or "tilts". These names are used for the equipment needed to establish contact with the fish by those hardy souls who fish in the cold, icy weather. Three inches of ice are minimum for safe travel; and even then it is well to make sure that good hard ice is always underfoot. This is especially true for those who ice-fish where there is any current or in the brackish tidal rivers where the ice is not as hard and reliable as in the fresh, still waters. But it takes only normal intelligence to determine whether or not ice is safe for travel. In fact, many northern lakes freeze so solidly that they're safe for auto travel.

Certain equipment is needed, other than warm clothes, ear muffs, and enough socks inside insulated boots to keep the pedal extremities warm. The ice fishing trap or tilt is, for its purpose, the complete rod, reel, line and hook. Almost invariably with this "tackle" live bait is used. Tilts or traps can be made at home, bought at the local store or from mail order outfits specializing in such rigs. They are simple affairs. Some are made to set into a slanting notch, cut into the ice in such a manner

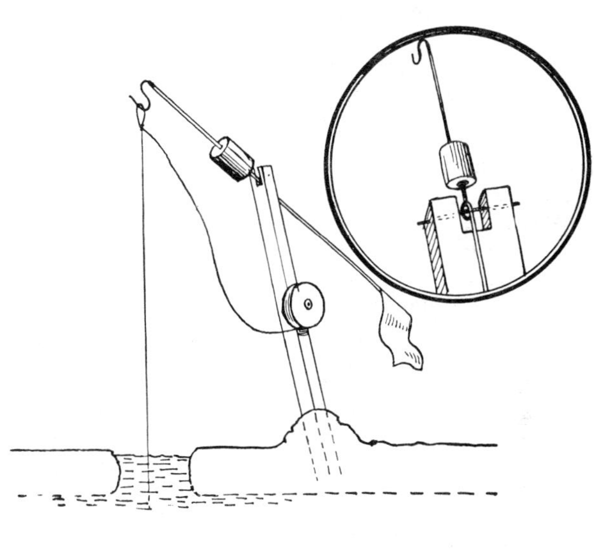

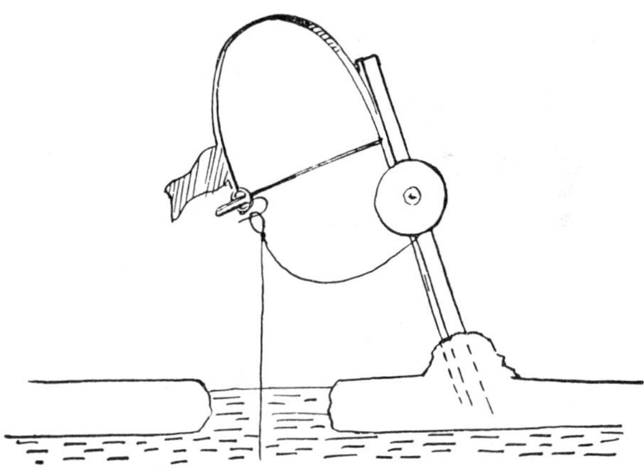

"Tackle Tinkering" by H. G. Tappley (A. S. Barnes & Co.)
Two Methods of Constructing Ice Fishing Traps or Tilts.

that the top of the trap comes over, or near, the center of a hole a foot in diameter cut in the ice; the line lays out on the ice either in coils that will unwind handily when there is a strike, or, if there are no careless skaters around to cut them, in one long loop. With this kind of a trap or tilt, lines should not be allowed to freeze into the ice. If they do, the fish is brought up short and pulled off the hook. A good ice fisherman makes a continual round of his tilts or traps to see to this point and other things.

Once the hole is cut and the trap snugly set into its notch so the line will fall straight into the middle of the open hole, the next job is to determine how deep the live bait should swim. If the depth is known, set the bait about a foot or two off bottom; if it is unknown, drop a sinker with a loop on the top into which a hook is inserted is dropped to the bottom; then lifted about a foot and the line marked for the proper depth.

A loop in the line fits over the top V in the wire. This loop is merely a tightened slip knot which will hold its loop when a fish strikes, pulls down the top of the wire, allows the sinker or weight to slide up to the V and raise the flag on the opposite end. Make the flags any desired color.

Now with the loop of line over the V the hook is ready to bait for action. In New England, fresh water shiners from two to three inches long or mummies (Mummychaugs, from salt water) are the most used baits. Shiners are kept in a minnow bucket with some kind of an aerating device; but all that mummies require is a market basket lined with newspaper. The mummies lie in a wet gunnysack with its ends folded over, or another gunnysack is thrown over the top. A handy trick with this bait is a five-inch wide, twelve-inch long piece of sacking, moistened, and containing a dozen or so mummies carried in an outer coat pocket.

In ice fishing a lively bait, one that will wiggle just as long as possible, is necessary. This means hooking either the shiner or the mummy about half-way from head to tail, just under the skin at the dorsal fin, to make your live bait ride evenly in the water. Hook that bait carefully so it will live and it will pay dividends. This hooking job is easier if hooks are used which have a thin wire, which are not rusty and have sharp points.

After hooking, the baited hook is lowered into the icy water, and the loop is hung on the V of wire at the top of the tilt.

Ice fishing is more fun with a partner or two than alone. On the way to the lake it's a good idea to portion out the duties that are ahead. The holes must be cut, and even if the long-handled ice chisel is sharp as a razor, it is still work. The fairest way is to take turn and turn about until all the jobs are finished. As can be seen, ice fishing is a sort of "community affair," something which requires teamwork to win over those fish below.

A big strainer from the local hardware or five-and-dime store is excellent for skimming loose ice. The ice in the hole after cutting is finished must be removed and dumped where it will not interfere with the free running of the line.

A fish usually takes a live bait in the front of his mouth, runs a short distance, stops to turn it around and then makes another run. When the flag goes up it is a great temptation to grab the line and try to set the hook. Don't do it! Let the fish run; give him time until there is a chance to set the hook and have it hold.

Hook sizes for ice fishing depend entirely upon the kind of fish sought. In many lakes and sluggish rivers of Rhode Island, Massachusetts and Connecticut, New York (southern) and New Jersey, Pickerel, Smallmouth and Largemouth bass and Perch are primary objectives. If the water is a good perch producer, use #6 and #8 hooks and small sizes of shiners or mummies, or if available in midwinter, worms. If the lake is primarily best for Pickerel and Bass, both of which have larger mouths, long-shanked #4 hooks are better.

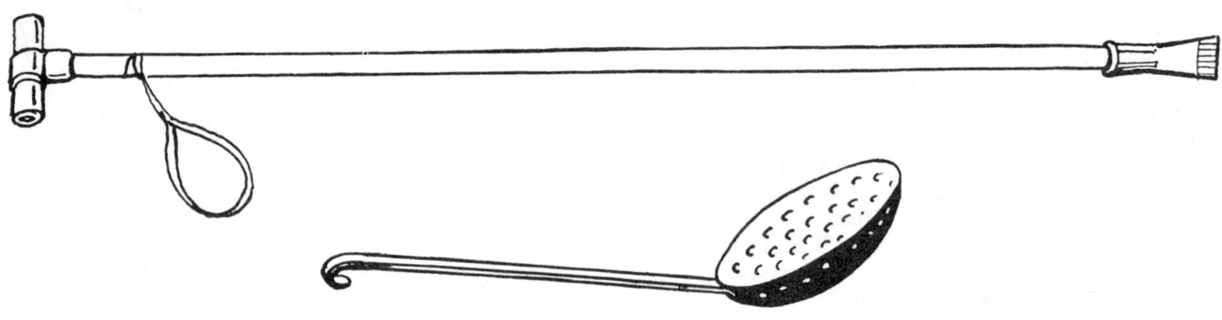

"Tackle Tinkering" by H. G. Tappley (A. S. Barnes & Co.)
Ice Chisel and Skimmer.

Another extra dividend of ice fishing, if night fishing is permitted, is catching eels. These bottom feeders go for dead minnows or shiners, or cut pieces of fish if the traps are left in over night and with the lines lowered until the bait rests on the bottom. Eels are not the most appetizing looking creatures in the world, but cut in three inch sections, rolled in flour or crumbs, and fried to a golden brown, they're food fit for a king.

Any lake has varying depths of water. Perch may be found in the deeper holes; but Pickerel can be taken through the ice in water of only a foot or two. Even in winter Pickerel prowl the shoal waters. So knowledge of water depths will determine where the ice fishing trap should be set. A party fishing a number of traps should set several lines of traps. One in water two to three feet deep, near shore and in a fairly straight line, parallel to the shore; about fifteen to twenty yards apart; a second line about ten yards farther from shore spaced in such a way that the traps are between the traps of the inshore line; and then for the third line, move out another ten yards or so setting these in line (looking from the middle of the lake to shore) with the inshore traps. This should give, on an average lake or pond, a good coverage of shallow, medium and deep waters. It also concentrates fishing so that in "tending" the traps one doesn't have to walk too many miles to reach them.

Too many ice fishermen feel that once the holes are dug and the lines baited all that remains is to wait for the fish to bite. That's a mistake. Instead, it is smart to cut a small stick about four feet long and trim off the branches. The party then takes turns in making continuous rounds of the set traps, tapping the line of each tilt with the stick. As the line is touched and stirred the minnow will become more active; if it doesn't, put on a livelier one. On cold days, it will be necessary to skim out the ice as it forms in the fishing holes. Otherwise, if it is really cold, the hole will quickly freeze the line so that a fish cannot move it to pull down the flag. Also "tending" means watching those lines to make sure that they are not frozen into the ice, or that the underwater reels are really in working order. Incidenally, if there is snow on the ice, clear a space to make it possible to see whether or not the lines are free. And don't walk on those lines, as this will push them into the ice and cause them to freeze all the faster—and frozen lines mean lost strikes.

An ice chisel, preferably made of tubular piping with a sharp cutting edge (like the blade of an axe) at the lower end is "must" equipment. On the top end there should be a wide leather thong attached, which can be slipped over the wrist, to prevent loss of the chisel in case it slips from the hand. In ice no more than four or five inches thick, an axe will do the job. Fishing traps or tilts, skimmer, bait in moist burlap or in a minnow bucket, extra hooks, lunch adds up to a lot of luggage for a couple or trio to carry. But there's a way around all that. A big, rugged market basket with a handle can be placed on runners (two or three) and can be hauled over the ice with a six- to eight-foot piece of clothes line. Two men can carry it from the car to the edge of the ice, and once on the ice, it's a cinch.

Perhaps the traps purchased will have lines on them but if they are being made at home or the line needs to be replaced it's well to know how it's done. The length will depend on the depth of the water and the size of the fish expected. For the Massachusetts to Jersey area, in which the main objective is apt to be bass, pickerel or perch, about thirty feet of line is enough. It can be of braided Nylon, braided cotton or cuttyhunk (linen) and testing about twenty-seven pounds. Too small a line is hard to handle when hands are wet and cold and it can also cut into the fingers. Once a fish is hooked it is a "keep-'em-coming" proposition unless the fish is really heavy, in which case the line can be allowed to slip back through the hands when the strain feels as though it might tear out the hook or break the line. Lines should be checked for frayed or cut spots and if skaters are present they must be warned gently but firmly that if they skate too closely, they'll cut the lines.

There's a good stunt that keeps fish fresh and even alive during the course of the day's fishing. If the ice is five inches or more thick, chip out with ice chisel or axe a place about three feet by two feet, about three inches deep, choosing a spot near the center of fishing activities. After chipping and cleaning out the chips, a narrow channel is cut off one corner for about a foot and a hole driven straight down through the ice. The water coming through the hole, will run down the narrow channel, and fill the depression in the ice with water. Fish, fresh from the hook, placed in this well, are apt to stay alive all day. It is called a "fish well".

One of the most popular kinds of ice fishing in the northeast is for salt water smelt. These little fellows, seldom more than five to eight inches long and built like a cigar, are one of the most toothsome of all fishes.

In more northern waters (Maine, New Hampshire and Vermont) where zero temperatures, plus night fishing, which is very effective for smelt, are not uncommon, the fishing is usually done from an ice fishing house. Maybe "house" is gilding the lily a bit, but with a little heater plus protection from the cold biting winds, it is a good shelter, even if it does resemble a glorified out-house on runners. Even though they are merely frame shacks covered with wallboard, some of them have windows, hooks for clothing and equipment, and a comfortable seat for at least two people. The houses are pulled over a hole in the ice, leaving only enough room for the anglers to get in and out without falling into the icy depths below.

The house itself should have a peaked roof so the heavy snows won't cave it in. Remember that it should be built on runners so that it can be pushed around on the ice, either by man power or towed behind the family car when the ice gets really thick as it does in northern states. Once it is in position, slip some boards under the runners so they cannot sink into the ice and freeze tight. The walls should have hooks, on which to hang things, like a pot and frying pan for a hot bit of broth or even a fresh fish fry on top of the little but efficient stove; spare clothing when the shack gets really hot, and extra fishing gear. Those desiring extra comfort can hang a folding table so that it lies flat against the wall—handy for quick use for lunch or for a game of cards if the fishing's slow. Most important for the business at hand are at least two steel springs, bent up sharply at the ends so the loop in the handline, set at the preferred depth, can be hung on them. As the weight of the line will bend these springs, the slightest touch on the bait (a third to half of a fresh water smelt) will attract attention—but the hook should not be set until the fish is really bearing down. If fish are cleaned in the fish or bob-house, drop the entrails and other remains down into the water as chum for more fish.

The salt water smelt run in tidal waters of northern New England during the late fall with the first heavy frosts and stay to spawn, leaving about the time spring thaws call a halt to ice fishing. This same section also has ice fishing for the big fresh water smelts in many of its larger lakes.

Ice fishing is permitted in Vermont on lakes not inhabited by trout, but there are many exceptions to this because of zones in which fishing is

Ben East

A typical ice fishing area.

permitted in certain waters inhabited by trout. The best fishing is in Lake Champlain, Lake Memphremagog, Lake Bomoseen, and certain others.

The bulk of the ice fishing in Vermont is done by use of tip-ups, bobs, hand-lines, or by the method known as gigging which is a wooden stick with two lines attached, or when done in a shanty, it may be an arrangement that has so many strings attaching from a cross member that they look like the strings on a harp.

The most common baits are the eye of a fresh-caught perch, a strip of salt pork, or a piece of smelt, either flesh or skin, live minnows or a piece of perch skin, flesh or brightly colored fins.

The most sought-after fish are Perch, Walleye, Northern Pike, Pickerel, Saugers or Rock Pike, Smelt, with occasional catches of Cusk, Bowfin, Whitefish, and other species being taken.

Considerable fishing for Trout and Togue is done in more northerly Maine ponds by sportsmen who fly in there. Moosehead is quite a spot for Togue fishermen. Pickerel in Washington County and most of the other coastal counties are sought by an appreciable number.

Pickerel fishing is done the same as elsewhere, with "traps" (a short stick with a red flannel flag that flies up when the fish takes a minnow or other bait). Lake Trout (Togue) are caught with minnow tails, cut bait, etc. The Squaretail and Salmon fishing is pretty much restricted but still possible in some places. Live baits and cut baits are used. Considerable smelt fishing is done in the late winter, both fresh water and on tidal streams. These salt water smelt are caught with bloodworms, clam worms, etc., for bait from smelt shanties rigged with a number of lines.

IN THE MIDDLE WEST

For the ice angler interested in big fish, something above the panfish class, the Northern Pike stands at the head of the list.

True to the gluttonous ways that are the hallmark of his clan, he suffers little loss of appetite with the arrival of cold weather and the winter freezeup. Other fish may grow more selective at this season, requiring special baits offered in special ways, or they may turn cautious and wary of leader and hook. Not so the Northern. He was spawned hungry, he lives hungry, and he dies the same way, often betrayed by his own hunger. It makes no difference to him whether his lake dances under the July sun or is locked beneath a heavy seal of February ice. Food is food. Put it within his reach and he will smash into it with reckless savagery, kill it, bolt it, and take the consequences. All of which makes him a natural for the ice fisherman.

Because he prefers fish smaller than himself to any other fare, a live minnow or an imitation of one is the surest way to lure him to the hook.

Winter pike fishing is sometimes done with handlines, but more commonly with the tackle known as the tip-up. Tip-ups vary in design from home-made contraptions that tilt vertically when a fish pulls the line tight under the ice to elaborate spring devices on which the striking fish releases a trigger and causes a small red flag to fly up, warning the angler that there is business needing attention.

Live minnows, usually chubs or shiners three to six inches long, are the standard bait for use with tip-ups. Since the line is not held in the hand and often is not even under immediate control, there is no way to impart action to a spoon or other artificial lure, and for that reason artificials cannot be used. If the fisherman prefers a hand line and is willing to keep the bait in motion by jigging, special ice spoons are sometimes used successfully.

Small goldfish may be substituted for other minnows, but this practice is now generally frowned upon and is prohibited by law in some states; the goldfish is a member of the carp family and the escape or dumping of goldfish used as bait may result in the establishment of carp in game-fish waters where they are not wanted.

One other method of taking Pike through the ice rivals tip-up fishing in popularity and even outranks it in some sections, despite the disapproval of many anglers on grounds of sportsmanship. That is spearing the fish from the shelter of a dark-house after they have been lured within range by a large live minnow or artificial decoy.

The dark-house is a small shanty, light and easily portable, usually built of canvas, tar paper, plywood or similar material, often movable from one place to another on the ice by runners attached to one side. Its basic requirement is that it be completely light-proof.

A square hole or an oblong one at least two feet wide is left in the floor, and this is placed directly over a corresponding hole spudded in the ice. The dark-house is used in shallow water, rarely more than 10 or 12 feet deep, and the spearman, sitting in total darkness, has a clear view of the scene under the ice, illuminated by the pale green, luminescent light that filters through the ice.

If a live decoy is used it is often a chub or sucker as large as 12 inches in length. Artificial decoys are of about the same size, shaped and painted to resemble minnows, made of wood with metal fins, and weighted with lead so that they will sink slowly through the water, swimming in a circle.

The decoy is lowered into the hole on a hand

line. Live lures are allowed to "work" of their own will, the artificial variety kept in motion by being repeatedly pulled up and allowed to sink again.

The spear has a short handle, usually a metal rod, attached to the roof of the dark-house by a stout cord. When a fish is lured within range, the spear is lowered carefully into the water until it is poised only a few inches above the quarry, then driven home with a hard thrust. The spearman releases his hold on the handle at once and the weight of the spear carries it to the bottom, where the struggles of the fish spend themselves futilely. When things have quieted down, spear and fish are pulled up together.

Many fishermen practice ice spearing and defend it vigorously. Others contend it should be outlawed as a destructive and unfair method of taking fish.

It is difficult to believe that a man can be accused fairly of poor sportsmanship because he resorts to it. Winter spearing is not angling in the sense that bait or fly casting are, but it is a good lively outdoor pastime, packed with action. The dark-house is usually equipped with a small stove that insures complete comfort. It's a pleasant place to be on a day when the winter wind is wailing across the ice. The under-ice world, with its weeds and fish and strange illumination, is a fascinating world. And the ice fisherman who spears a big pike tastes some primitive pleasure, the satisfaction of hand-to-hand combat with his prey. Presumably the cave man got the same delight out of the creatures he subdued with his crude weapons. It may not be fishing in the fine sense of the word, but a man is hardly to be condemned for enjoying it.

The spear and dark-house, equipped with an oversized decoy, are sometimes used for taking Muskellunge as well as pike. Curiously enough, there are few or no instances where muskies have been taken through the ice on handlines or tip-ups, but several lakes regularly yield big 'lunge to winter spearman, including fish exceeding 40 pounds in weight. These big muskies can be brought either to live or artificial decoys. There is no obvious reason why they could not be taken on tip-ups if they were offered large minnows and if the ice fisherman had the necessary patience to wait for them to come along.

Walleyes rank close to the Northern Pike in popularity as a winter fish in many places. Like the pike, they regard minnows as their natural food and are taken on both tip-ups and hand-lines.

Now and then, on lakes where state laws do not give the black bass protection during the winter months, the ice fisherman makes a killing on bass, especially Largemouths.

This is not a regular occurrence, however, for the reason that bass are strongly inclined to retire into semi-hibernation with the arrival of cold weather and ice. They do not become completely dormant and their period of inactivity cannot be compared with the true hibernation of certain mammals. But they do lose interest in food, retreating into sheltered places under stumps, logs, submerged brush and in other crannies, and in consequence rarely pay much attention to any offering the winter angler may lower beneath the ice.

Ben East

Ice fishing results.

Occasionally, however, they continue feeding after the lakes are frozen, especially in the early part of the winter, and the ice fisherman who makes contact with them under such conditions and tempts them with medium-sized minnows on a handline is likely to take a highly satisfactory catch. Black bass are inclined to school at that season, and the angler who encounters a feeding school is reasonably sure of lively action.

The Lake Trout is another popular fish on the ice angler's list. He feeds voraciously the year around, moving into deep water for the winter months but passing up no meal that comes his way. Lake trout are sometimes taken with spear from a dark-house, where they can be enticed into water sufficiently shallow. Either an artificial or live decoy of large size can be used.

Most winter fishing for Lake Trout is done with handlines, however, using minnows or jigging with a strip of cut herring.

On the Straits of Mackinac, connecting Lake Michigan and Lake Huron, Lake Trout jigging is often done two or three miles offshore, in water more than 100 feet deep. A special tarred line is used which will not stretch when a fish takes the bait and the angler attempts to set the hook. With a hundred feet of line down, the stretch of ordinary linen or silk would result in "delayed action" and afford the trout time to get rid of the herring before the hook could be driven home.

The method of landing trout in that area is novel. Once the fish is hooked the angler throws the line across his shoulder, wheels, and races across the ice at top speed. He keeps going until the trout is flopping on the ice behind him, too. It's much faster and surer than hauling 'em up hand over hand.

Leaving the category of large fish and moving into the panfish class, the perch stands high in popularity among ice anglers wherever he is found. He suffers no loss of appetite in winter, and tends to gather under the ice in large schools, a trait that makes him relatively easy to catch. On the platter winter perch are hardly outranked among the common fishes of inland lakes.

Small minnows are the standby bait for taking perch through the ice, and a handline or short winter rod is the standard gear. In recent years fishermen have learned that the creature commonly known as the wiggler, the larva of the burrowing mayfly, a highly effective bait for winter Bluegills, also is deadly on perch at certain times and in certain waters. Perch occasionally take other Bluegill lures, too, such as corn-borer grubs and meal worms, but in general they show marked preference for minnows not more than two inches long. Small artificials of the type known as the Russian spoon also are effective on perch in some localities.

Winter fishing for perch is done chiefly on the open ice, although a few fishermen operate from the warmth and shelter of a shanty or dark-house.

Another small but tasty fish that has recently gained popularity among ice fishermen in the few sections in which it is found is the smelt. Ice fishing for smelt has reached the proportions of a winter carnival on certain lakes in Michigan, following the establishment and rapid increase of the fish in that state more than twenty-five years ago.

The smelt are taken on small minnows in deep water, usually biting best at night, and the fishing is virtually all done from roomy and well-equipped ice shanties that have such comforts as gas lanterns, beds, stoves and cooking utensils.

Last on the list of winter fish, but by no means least in importance, is the Bluegill or Bream.

He is relatively a newcomer to the sport, having gained the attention of ice anglers within the last quarter century. Yet in many places he is now the backbone of ice fishing, attracting sportsmen in greater numbers and yielding larger catches than all others taken together.

Up to about twenty-five years ago few fishermen considered it possible to catch Bluegills through the ice. It was commonly believed that this fine little panfish retired into inactivity with the approach of cold weather, and winter Bluegill fishing was an unheard-of sport.

It took a strange assortment of unorthodox lures to bring the Bluegill out of his pseudo retirement and into the limelight. The simple fact is that his vigorous summer appetite undergoes a marked change in winter. He becomes more dainty in his feeding habits, scorning food that would appeal to him at other seasons. Once fishermen learned his winter requirements and began to cater to them, the Bluegill proved cooperative to an astonishing degree.

Among the successful baits now in use for winter Bluegill fishing are such tidbits as corn borers, the mayfly larva known as the wriggler, the tiny white grubs found in goldenrod galls, wood grubs, meal worms, and ordinary red or manure worms served in very small portions on the point of the hook.

Somewhat curiously, one of the most deadly of all winter lures for these fish is the ice fly, a small artificial tied in a variety of solid colors and patterns, with very soft hackle and having a small split shot pinched onto the hook at the bend to carry the fly down to the proper depth.

Good ice flies in the hands of a skillful fisherman who knows how to manipulate his line will take Bluegills without the aid of any natural bait. Most fishermen prefer to combine the two, however, impaling grub or wriggler on the hook of the ice fly, relying on the latter to get the attention of the fish and the live lure to close the deal. Properly used, this combination is really a deadly one.

Because the Bluegill is far more wary in winter than in summer, greater care must be used in the choice of line and leader. Lightweight Nylon lines are close to standard equipment, and most fishermen use short, stiff ice rods. Some like a float or bobber, others prefer to judge the bite of the fish by feel. If a bobber is used, it must be small and extremely sensitive, since the Bluegill is a confirmed nibbler in winter, taking the bait in a very delicate and cautious manner.

Bluegills display a marked tendency to gather in large schools under the ice, usually in moderately shallow places in coves and bays. Normally these schools can be looked for in water averaging about twenty feet deep, but on spring-fed lakes and under other unusual conditions they sometimes move close inshore and are found where there is less than twenty-four inches of water under the ice.

All the members of the school feed at the same time. Consequently, once the ice fisherman strikes "pay dirt" in a Bluegill lake, he can expect fast and continuous action until the feeding period ends. Other experienced anglers know this, and as soon as one fisherman starts landing Bluegills, he is almost sure to have company. Concentrations of ice fishermen ranging up to two or three hundred, clustered elbow to elbow in one spot, usually means that a winter Bluegill schooling ground has been located and the fish are biting.

These excessive concentrations of fishermen and the heavy catches they make on productive lakes have resulted recently in considerable agitation for stricter regulation of winter Bluegill fishing.

Nothing about his outfit is more important to the ice angler than his clothing and footgear. Whether he fishes for Bream or Pike, he is engaging in a rugged sport where his comfort depends almost entirely on whether or not he is properly clothed.

He needs wool from the skin out, of course, and the warmest is not too warm. Wind-proof parkas or down-lined jackets, worn over wool shirts and pants, and quilted Dacron underwear, are an excellent protection against severe weather. Galoshes over shoes large enough to take two or three pairs of wool socks will go a long way to insure warm feet. Some winter anglers prefer heavy felt socks, flying boots or other special equipment.

If the weather is really bad a small shelter, augmented by a fire on the ice, is worth consideration. A square of canvas rigged on three poles will do much to fend off wind and snow.

One final word of caution to the winter angler: *take no chances on unsafe ice.*

Ice is likely to be dangerously thin when the lakes are first frozen. Test it thoroughly before venturing over deep water. There is another period, when the spring breakup is getting under way, that brings even more treacherous conditions.

And in the coldest weather of midwinter ice is not dependable around the shores of spring-fed lakes, in the vicinity of inlets and outlets and along the margin of marshy or swampy shores.

Many fishermen now drive their cars onto the ice and fish from the shelter of the car or from a spot nearby. Remember, it takes far thicker ice to support a car than a man.

Ice fishing claims lives needlessly each season. These mishaps, like most accidents connected with angling and hunting, could be prevented by following a few common-sense rules.

In winter fishing, as in any other outdoor sport, *play it safe!*

FLOAT FISHING

Down in the Ozark Hill region of southern Missouri and northern Arkansas, folks have developed a way of fishing that is as different and flavorful and full of tradition as the Ozark way of life itself. They call it "float fishing," or sometimes just "floatin'." Whatever it is called it is an experience never to be forgotten.

A float trip is unique in its combination of so many of the elements that fishermen enjoy. There's that continual promise of discovering something new just around the next bend; in float fishing, this promise is satisfied repeatedly and effortlessly. There's the knowledge that one can get a real work-out, casting at every attractive spot and do it all day long; or, with a good guide and a good companion, one can just drift along until tired, on a beautiful, ever-changing stream and let the other fellow do the work. And, there is the supreme experience of a feeling of being absolutely free from the annoyances of civilization, tempered with the feeling of security that civilization—if it must be sought—is never more than a few hours away.

The Ozark rivers run through the remote backcountry. They are the ancient highways of a region too rough to have many roads; one can float some of them for a week and never see a highway bridge. To fish one of these streams is an experience; to float-fish it, is to know it at its best. Picture this spring fed, clear blue water flowing sometimes fast and sometimes slow, sometimes through large deep pools or "eddies," over beds of sand or gravel or rock. Magnificent scenery, from rock bluffs looming tall in varicolored patterns above slow, deep eddies or slashing chutes, to tree-clad slopes and occasional smooth bottomlands. Flashing bits of color and song from the bird life that makes the stream its community center. Huge springs boiling from deep caves or bursting out of flat ground; the chattering of squirrels from the water's-edge tree line; the splashing of a startled deer in the shallows; and on a rare occasion even the thrilling gobble of a wild turkey. With these as background, there is the sharp slashing strike of willing Smallmouth, the flurry of eager goggle-eye, the powerful run of Walleye, or the dogged tugging of Channel Cat. Cool nights on dry gravel bars, the subtle odors of woods and waters pierced with the tang of wood-smoke, boiling coffee, and frying fish—an experience so full and rich that to partake once, means to become an addict.

Like any sport different and appealing enough to become a tradition, float fishing has developed a pattern of equipment and methods adapted through long experience to get the best results. Yet there is variety in this pattern; plenty of room for individual preferences. For example, one can take his own canoe or boat and camping equipment, start wherever one wishes, fish where and when and stop at one's own pleasure. All one has to do is to arrange for transportation at both ends of the float. Or one can rent a boat from one of many rivermen and do the same thing. In the end this usually proves to be the simplest and most economical. At the other extreme is the deluxe float trip, in which outfitter furnishes boat, guide, cook, camping equipment, provisions—everything but clothes, tackle, and personal needs. Costs for such a trip run up to $16.00 per person, per day. In Missouri, most float trips are conducted by arrangement with a regular operator, who furnishes boats and guides.

A float trip can be arranged for one day or for two weeks; alone with a guide in a single boat, with a companion and guide in one boat, or as a member of a party requiring a whole flotilla plus a commissary boat. One river or several can be fished in Missouri or Arkansas or both.

The "johnboat" is the standard craft developed for Ozark stream travel. A typical "johnboat" is long and narrow, with a light taper or none to both square-cut ends, shallow of draught and light in weight. The bottom is flat and often reinforced to withstand the rocks in the fast chutes or riffles. In many ways it is a practical compromise between a rowboat and a canoe. Handled with pole or paddle, it is surprisingly stable and maneuverable. In quiet water, a steady man can stand up to cast with confidence.

It must always be kept in mind that, if the water is in best fishing condition, it is not at high-water stage, hence, one must step out of the boat frequently to pull it over shoals. Again, unless one is thoroughly familiar with every riffle or is an experienced fast-water boatman he is bound to bump into rocks and logs. That is why the canoe may prove too fragile and the ordinary river or lake keel-boat too deep of draught. Besides, if really doing an Ozark float trip, why not do it in the Ozark way and in the Ozark boat? Long experience has taught the native Ozark dweller that the "johnboat" is the thing.

On a float trip, the practice is to drift downstream. The boatman regulates the speed of travel according to the distance that has to be covered to the over-night stop-over, or—if a one-day trip—to the taking out place. He will call attention to the most productive spots, lingering to let them be covered thoroughly, making up time in the less productive stretches. There are favored places for stop-overs, for lunch or a stretch. Since most operators try to give their customers the longest float possible in the time available, most fishing is done with the boat on the move, but don't make the mistake of being too ambitious to cover long stretches and make time and go far. If this is done,

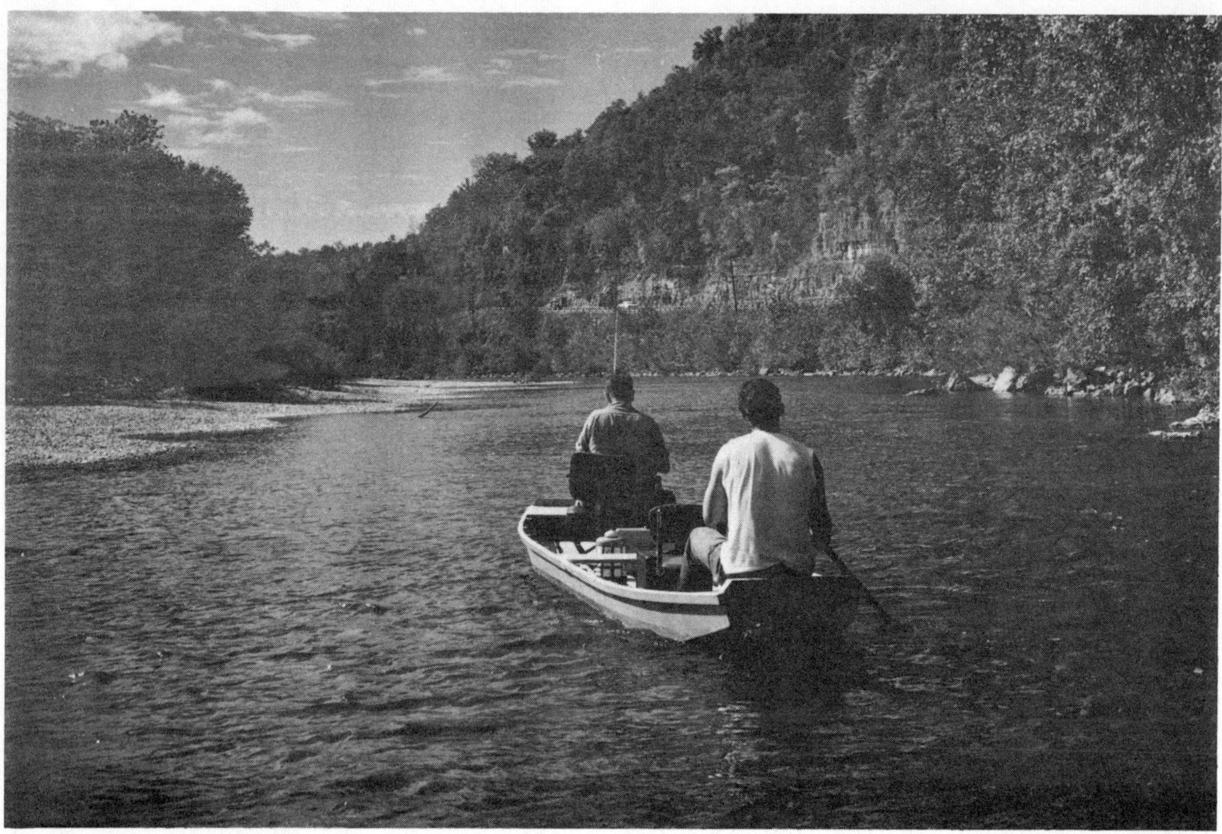

Missouri Conservation Commission

Float-fishing is Missouri's own fishing method. Born in Southwest Missouri at the turn of the century, it is not the most productive angling method but it is one of the most pleasant.

leisure disappears, fishing results are poor and it hasn't really been a float trip. Many customers take time along the way to still-fish, wade and fish, or set baited night lines during the overnight stop.

Plug, fly-casting and "popping-bug" or surface bait casting are the most common fishing methods. Though Ozark streams offer a variety of fish, the Smallmouth Bass is the species for which they are famous. Therefore, Smallmouth rods and lures are the ones that will be used most. In plugs, both the surface lures and the deep-running types are good. Fly fishermen find fairly large flies with medium-sized spinners a good combination. Some of the most successful fishermen on the White River use almost nothing but floating bugs or "popping-bugs." It is always safe to bring lures that have proved themselves elsewhere, and then to pick up locally any needed extras according to "what they're hitting." The various river runt plugs, feathered minnows, and Hawaiian wiggler type baits are old standby's, as are streamer and buck-tail flies.

Since float fishing is a combination of down-stream travel and casting, it isn't always possible to stop the boat to retrieve a hung lure, especially in the fast, rugged stretches. When that happens, it's better to have a leader pop than to lose the line (or even the rod) in addition to the lure. There is also a chance of hooking on to a big Walleye or a heavy Channel Catfish that can't be handled on a light leader in a fast, rock-filled channel. For these reasons, most experienced floaters prefer a fairly stout rod and line, and a leader heavy enough to hold any reasonable fish, but enough lighter than the line to break before anything really disastrous happens.

The type of fishing suggests the most suitable clothing; it should be durable and able to resist a possible wetting, or at least something that will not be ruined if it gets wet. Midsummer days are likely to be hot, the nights just pleasantly cool. A light jacket is useful at this period; in spring and fall the nights on these spring fed streams are likely to be quite crisp, and a heavier jacket is a comfort. Light-weight, rubber-soled shoes or sneakers are comfortable in the boat, and an extra pair—together with several changes of socks should be carried, since it is easy to get wet feet. In fact, foot-wear should be of a type that can be "dunked" frequently, because on shoals there isn't time to take off your shoes and socks, and besides the gravel is very sharp. Rubber boots and waders are a nuisance, except for wading and fishing during stop-overs, but most anglers prefer old shoes and trousers. A good flashlight is very useful on over-night camps. It is advisable to carry a raincoat or poncho; even if it doesn't rain, the raincoat makes a good cover for valuables on dew-drenched nights. While the woods on shore may be humming with mosquitoes at night, few if any of them bother out on the bars where camps are usually located. During the day they are no problem. Nevertheless, a square of cheesecloth might be needed.

No one without previous experience with Ozark streams or in boat handling should try his first float trip without a guide. The country is lone-

Missouri Conservation Commission

Putting in. The john-boats have been brought by trailer to a convenient "putting in" place to start the float. Scene is Bryant Creek, tributary to White River.

some in stretches; the streams are swift and—in spots—a little ticklish to navigate. A stove-in boat and lost equipment in strange back-country can be anything but a joke. Also, a heavy thunder-shower on the watershed can send the stream booming over the gravel bar camp in a hurry and one might get trapped in a dangerous way.

Although the Smallmouth Bass typifies Ozark waters, a variety of other fish can be caught in most streams. Other Bass include the Kentucky, Largemouth, White, and Yellow. There are Walleyes (jack salmon) and Channel Cat; Bluegill, Crappie, Rock Bass or Goggle-Eye and Green and Long-ear Sunfishes. In the upper current and middle Niangua Rivers, some surprisingly large Rainbow Trout not infrequently provide an added thrill.

Squirrel season opens May 15 in Missouri, and some floaters like to take along a .22 or a .410 with the thought of varying the menu with young squirrel. Later in the fall, float fishing can be combined with duck hunting.

Floating has become an organized business in Missouri. There are nearly 100 registered operators, most of whom employ several guides. A few of the larger outfits are prepared to run a number of completely-equipped floats, on different streams, at the same time. Arrangements can be made to travel any of the floatable streams in the Ozarks. The major streams include such famous rivers as the Current, Black, White, Eleven Point, Gasconade, Niangua, Meramec, James, and their many tributaries. Because of the popularity of this kind of fishing, it is seldom possible to engage boats or guides without considerable advance notice. Many reservations are made in the previous winter and most operators like to be contacted at least a month in advance. A list of the operators, showing available services and equipment, can be obtained from the Division of Resources and Development, Jefferson City, Missouri.

It would be difficult to say which of the Ozark streams is the most popular for float fishing; impossible to say which is the "best." They all offer the condiments of opportunity and enjoyment that have made this kind of fishing a tradition in the Ozarks, a by-word in the Middle West, and a seldom resisted temptation to devotees from all corners of the nation. No two of them are alike. It's a way of fishing that defies description; it has to be experienced to be understood. In the words of one old-time Ozark native—a guide for many years—"If you ain't floated, you ain't fished."

LIMNOLOGY

Limnology is the study of the behavior of lakes and other inland waters and of the various physical, chemical, meteorological, and biological conditions existing in them. Little was known of this subject prior to the beginning of the twentieth century, but since the development of the microscope and other scientific instruments progress has been rapid.

This discussion of limnology is confined to that part of the science which is of the greatest value in guiding fishermen to the fish in lakes during the changing seasons. It is important to observe that the waters in all deep lakes which freeze on the surface in the winter and grow warm in the summer undergo a nearly continuous temperature change. This change at certain times varies radically between the water temperatures near the surface and those at varying depths underneath. Because cold-water game fish are extremely susceptible to this change, and vary their locations and feeding habits accordingly, a knowledge of this behavior is of the greatest value in helping

Missouri Conservation Commission

Smallmouth Water. Fast current rippling over rocks and gravel; weed-beds and over-hanging vegetation. Smallmouth Bass grow fast and powerful in such waters. Bryant Creek.

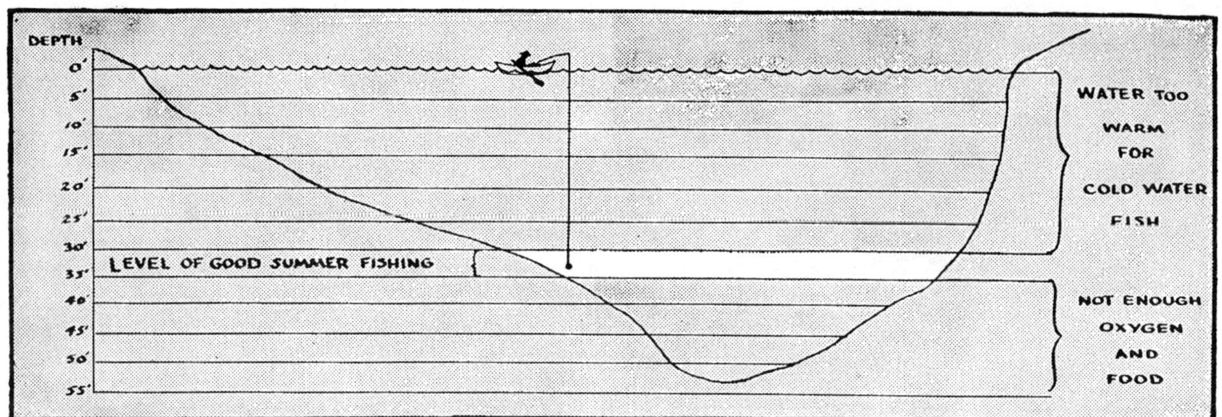

In this typical small lake, experience has shown that best fishing in summer for cold water fish is near the 35 foot level, which is the level of the thermocline here.

the angler to fish at the right places and depths at the right time and thus to catch more fish. It provides definite guides to the catching of cold-water fish; where to fish; how deep to fish, and, to an extent, what kind of tackle to use to obtain best results.

WHY WATER TEMPERATURES AFFECT FISHING

To understand how the seasonal variations in lakes influence the movements of fish, anglers first must be reminded that Trout, Landlocked Salmon, Smallmouth Bass, and many other species of cold-water fish shun water which is too warm or too cold for their comfort and seek what might be called "optimum temperatures." If these optimum temperatures are near the surface of a lake, the fish will be feeding on top. If these temperatures are deep down, one must troll or still-fish at these depths or go somewhere else where water temperatures are more adaptable to surface or near-surface fishing. Gamefish feed actively at these optimum temperatures but feed with increasing passivity as the water grows warmer or colder than the temperatures which they prefer. It is therefore obvious that temperature plays a prominent part, in determining where fish may be found and how readily they will take a lure.

The ideal temperature for Brook Trout, for example, is generally considered to be about 58° F., although it may vary slightly with the local characteristics of the fish and the water conditions to which they have grown accustomed. The ideal temperature for Brown Trout and Rainbow Trout is approximately three degrees higher than this, and for Smallmouth Bass about seven degrees higher. Lake Trout and Landlocked Salmon prefer

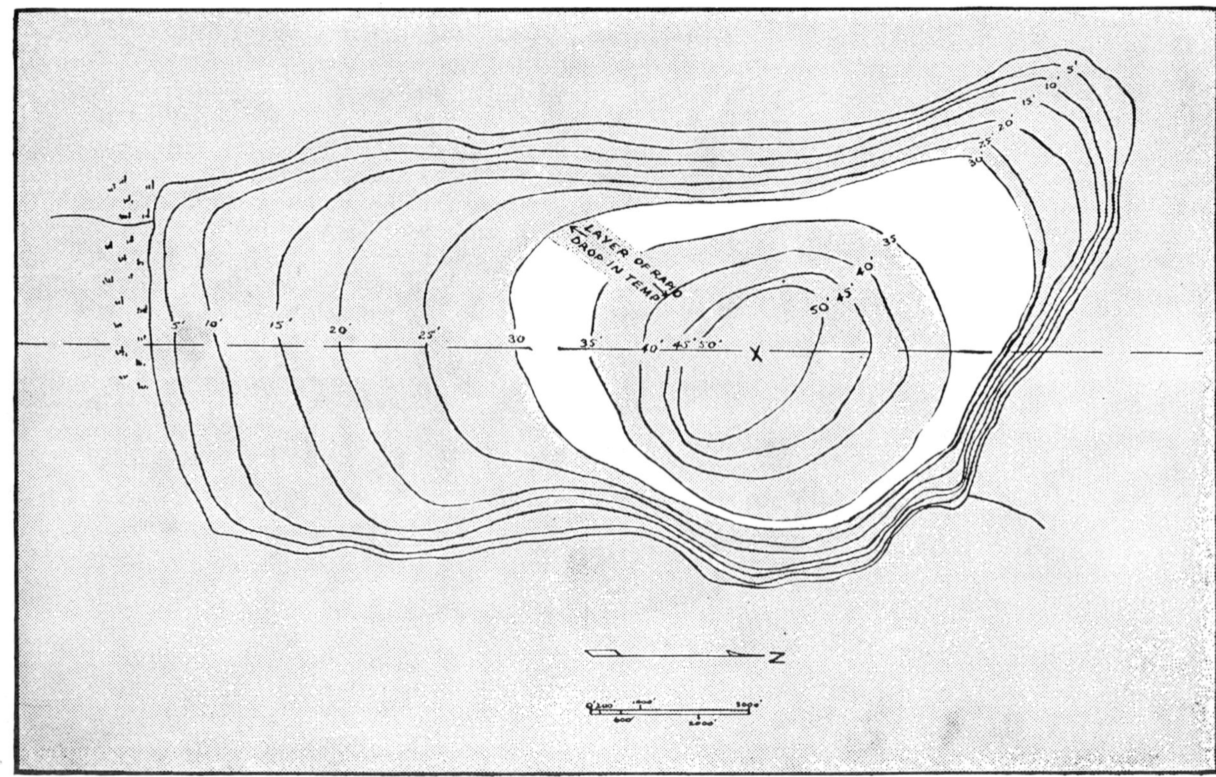

Since fish seek the shoreline at the thermocline level in summer for food, best trolling in this lake is at this depth. White area is the path of good fishing. Other areas and depths do not offer good summer trolling or bottom fishing.

colder temperatures of about 45° F. The optimum water temperature range for these fish is about ten degrees above and below the ideal temperatures just listed. Thus when fishing for Brook Trout it may be taken as a rule that they will feed with greatest activity and will live with greatest comfort in water which is between 48° F. and 68° F. This general rule is influenced by food conditions and other requirements such as oxygen, protection, and freedom from pollution in the water. Lake Trout and Landlocked Salmon desire temperatures within ten degrees of their ideal of 45° F., or water in the 35° to 55° range. This condition occurs on the surface of lakes in the early spring when the ice breaks up, and therefore these fish may be taken on the surface at that time. As the surface waters reach the maximum optimum temperature of 55° F. these fish will seek deeper, colder water and will not feed on or near the surface to a marked extent until water conditions again change.

WATER TEMPERATURE PREDICTION

Fortunately, the science of limnology provides seasonal and predictable rules for forecasting water temperatures in lakes during the four seasons. It teaches why water is coldest near the surface in the early spring; why it is warmest near the surface in the summer and why cold fall nights again reduce temperatures and thus induce gamefish to return to the upper level where they may be caught with top-water lures again. If an angler elects to go to Maine for Lake Trout or Landlocked Salmon, for example, he learns that surface fishing will be best in lakes directly after the ice leaves. However, if he prefers to catch a big Brook Trout he knows that his luck will be better a few weeks later and that this same cyle will repeat itself in the fall. If the fisherman's vacation is only possible in the summer, it warns him not to attempt to catch these species near the surface unless he is in a part of the country where favorable temperatures for the species of gamefish he wants to catch exist near the surface during that period.

It suggests that he will have better luck trolling in the lake for these fish, and it indicates approximately how deep he should troll. If he does not wish to do this, limnological conditions invite him to do his fishing in brook or stream mouths or in spring holes where more suitable water temperatures induce gamefish to congregate. To understand how limnology predicts water temperatures and what the fisherman should do about it, it is helpful to trace the behavior of a cold water lake through the four seasons, starting at the time when the ice covers the lake in the winter.

WINTER STAGNATION PERIOD

The cycle of annual water temperatures in a lake begins when it is ice covered and dormant. The key to the cycle is the fact that water reaches its maximum density (is heaviest) at a temperature of 39.2° F. Since it is heaviest at this temperature, all water which is warmer or colder than 39.2° F. will rise to the top. Thus, in a deep lake in the winter the water at the bottom of the lake is at a temperature of 39.2° F. and the water above it all is colder and lighter, with the lightest water at the top, just under the ice, at a temperature very close to that of freezing, or 32° F. Since this range of temperatures is too cold for trout and bass they will be relatively inactive at this time and disinclined to feed. Since it is better suited to Landlocked Salmon and Lake Trout, they will roam more widely and feed more actively. These fish, however, will seek the deepest (and warmest) level in which they can obtain a sufficient amount of oxygen and food. In some lakes this may be in the deepest parts. In other lakes an abundance of microscopic or tiny animal and vegetable life may make the water so turbid as to prevent sunlight from reaching the depths, thereby preventing the photosynthesis of plant life. This biochemical process causes plant life to absorb carbon dioxide from the water and to give off oxygen in exchange. Since the presence of sunlight is necessary for this reaction, it can be seen that in deep lakes clouded with an overabundance of organic matter there will be too little food and oxygen in the depths and these deep parts may be devoid of fish life.

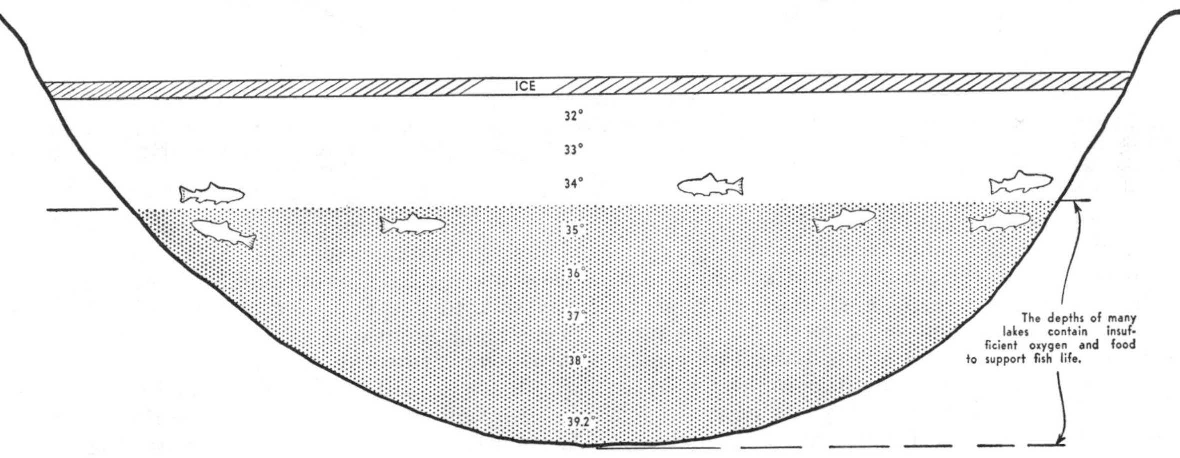

Winter Stagnation Period

Water at 39.2 F. is heavier (denser) than water which is warmer or colder. At this temperature it settles to the bottom and both colder and warmer water rise to the top and mix. Cold-water fish go to lowest level containing oxygen and food.

SPRING TURNOVER STAGE

When the ice breaks up, a pronounced change takes place which has a most favorable effect upon fishing. The sun warms the surface water rapidly. As its warmth approaches the temperature of maximum density of 39.2° F. these surface waters, which become heavier as they become warmer (up to this point), sink and mix with the lighter, colder waters below. This mixing or displacement process is hastened by wind action and continues until all of the water is at its maximum density of 39.2°. At this point the waters have mixed to such an extent that they may literally be said to have "turned over."

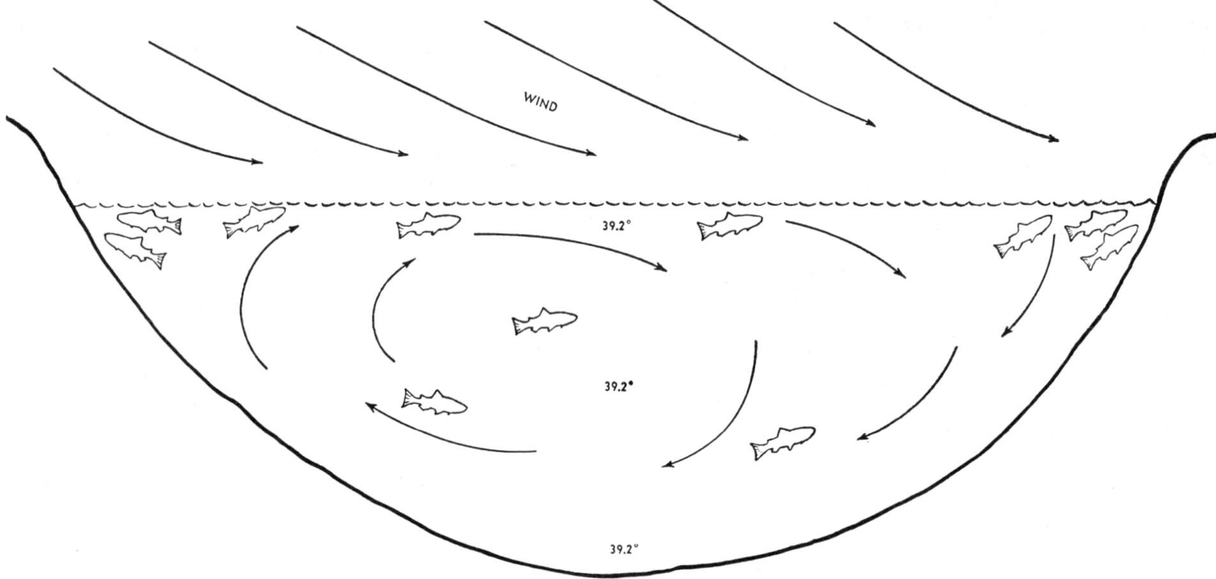

Spring Turnover Stage

The warmth of the sun heats surface waters, causing them to sink and mix with the colder water below, until all of the lake is at maximum density of 39.2 F. Cold-water fish come to surface for the more abundant supply of oxygen and food.

The sun and wave action fills the surface waters with a new and abundant supply of oxygen, putting new life into the gamefish and bringing them to the surface to find more satisfactory temperatures, more oxygen and more food. At this time, the Landlocked Salmon and the Lake Trout roam the surface and are avid for the top-water fly or lure. Fishing for these fish is at its best. Anglers flock to the northern fishing resorts, usually to bring home exciting stories of the "big ones that didn't get away." At this time, in the earliest part of the season when surface waters are in the neighborhood of 39.2°, the water is still too cold in most areas for trout to feed actively. As the sun keeps on warming the water, Brook, Rainbow, and Brown Trout, as well as Landlocked Salmon and Lake Trout, begin to feed on the surface and may be taken in any part of the lake where food is abundant. Since the waters along the shorelines of the lake are warmest, and provide an abundance of oxygen and nearby food, gamefish often are taken very close to shore. Early in the season it is customary to take all these species in water so shallow that a boat could be operated in it only with difficulty. Usually, best fishing is enjoyed on the windward shore because fish seek this shore to find food which the wind drifts in to them. At this time schools of baitfish ascend the rivers and brooks to spawn and the gamefish begin to follow the migrating schools, intercepting them at the stream mouths or following them up the rivers.

SUMMER STAGNATION PERIOD

After the spring turnover, the sun continues to warm the surface waters as the season progresses. When the critical point of 39.2° has been reached, further warming of the surface waters makes them lighter than those underneath, rather than heavier, and thus the warmer and lighter water stays on top and no longer mixes with that which lies below.

Rising temperatures soon make the top water too warm for Lake Trout and Salmon. They gradually sink to deeper and cooler levels or stay near the stream mouths where snow water still maintains temperatures to their liking. The other trouts (both trouts and charrs are included in this term for convenience) stay near the surface after the Landlocked Salmon and Lake Trout have gone to the depths, but whenever surface water reach their maximum tolerant range of about 70°F., the Trout also seek colder water. They may go to stream mouths and to spring holes and, where the water stays cold enough, they may remain all summer.

With the warming of the surface waters, deep lakes become divided into three layers each with different temperature ranges. The warm water being lighter, stays on top. The cold water, being heavier, remains at the bottom. In between this warm and cold layer is a relatively thinner "cushion" which is a dividing layer of water with a rapid drop in temperature, known as a "thermocline," separating the warm water above from the cold water below. Thus, in summer, there is relatively little vertical motion in the waters of a lake. It is a period of summer stagnation which exists until the reverse of the temperature change occurs in the fall.

In their constant attempt to find water conditions which are to their liking, gamefish usually will not live in the upper warm layer (known as the "Epilimnion"). They may not live in the lower cold layer (known as the "Hypolimnion") because this layer may be lacking in sufficient oxygen and food. Commonly they will be found in the region of the thermocline (which is defined as the layer or zone where the drop in temperature is at least one degree Centigrade per meter of depth) because it contains the most favorable conditions of temperature, oxygen and food supply. Since these conditions usually are more favorable nearer the top level of the thermocline, or just above it, here is where the fisherman will find best summer fishing if he does not elect to fish the spring holes or stream mouths.

The depths of these three layers vary somewhat with the size and depth of the lake and the amount of wind action upon it. A small lake in Oregon, for example, is fifty-five feet deep, with the thermocline at the thirty to forty foot level. Angling tests proved that the greatest number of fish (Rainbow Trout) are taken in summer at this depth. Fishing tests below the forty foot level indicated that no fish exist in this part of the lake in summer. In a very large lake in Idaho, with a depth of over one thousand feet in some places, the thermocline is at the sixty to seventy-five foot level. Catch records prove that best success is enjoyed by fishermen who troll at this depth during the summer period.

Taking the locations of the thermoclines in these two lakes of very small and very large sizes as examples, it may be assumed that the thermocline generally lies between thirty and seventy-five feet in all lakes in the normal size range in which stratification occurs. Since the approximate size of the lake on which the angler is fishing is known, this information should provide the basis for an intelligent guess in determining thermocline depth. In making this guess it should be remembered that pronounced wind action drives the thermocline deeper while little or no wind action will cause it to be nearer the surface.

Determining the level of the thermocline, or the level of good summer fishing, by this means will seem to some to be a rather rough approximation. Some anglers will prefer an approximation to practice of determining it more accurately by taking water temperatures at five foot intervals until the level of rapid drop in temperature is found. It should not be difficult for any fisherman to estimate thermocline depth within an error of ten feet. Since the location of fish will vary by this amount, or more, above or below the top level of the thermocline, the approximation has been proved satisfactory in fishing tests in widely separated areas. Equally important with determining thermocline depth is the matter of knowing exactly how deep the angler is trolling. This usually is greatly over-estimated by fishermen who assume that, because they have several hundred feet of line out, they must be trolling their lures at a considerable depth. Trolling depth can be checked by going nearer and nearer to shore until the lure becomes caught on the bottom. By backing up the boat until it is directly over the lure and marking the line at the surface at this point, the actual trolling depth easily can be ascertained and corrections can be made accordingly. It is obvious that a knowledge of the proper depth for good fishing is of no value if the fisherman does not make sure that he is trolling at that depth.

Most of the food for deep water fish usually is on or near the lake bottom. Trolling at the point where the thermocline intercepts the bottom of the lake should produce the best deep water fishing. On a contour map, this ring of lake bottom would appear as the path of good trolling. If the fisherman's knowledge of trolling depths and his knowledge of the formation of the lake bottom is accurate, he should enjoy maximum summer fishing success by following this path.

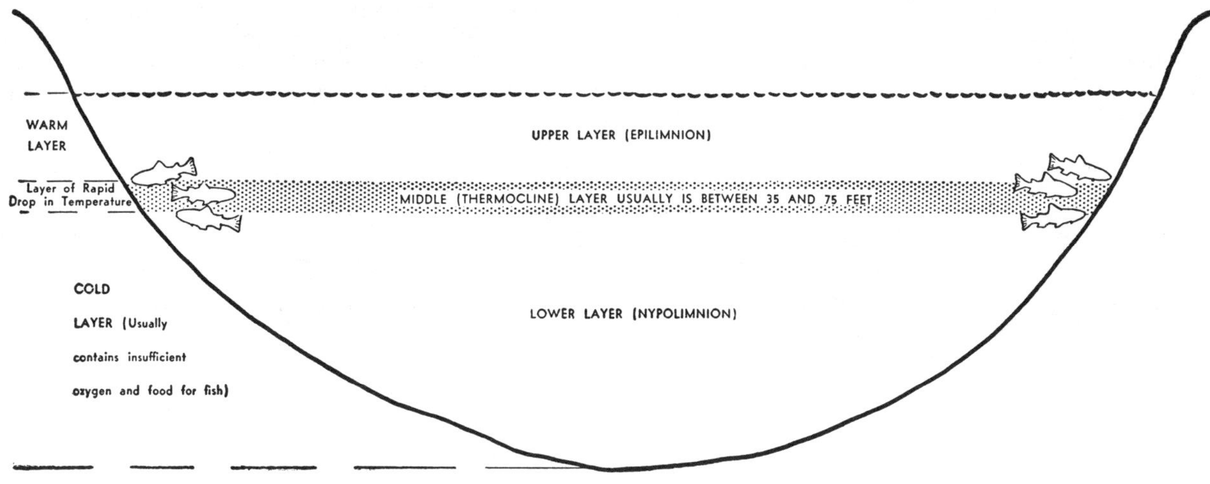

Summer Stagnation Period

When surface waters heat to more than 39.2 F. they are lighter and stay on top. Colder water, being heavier, sinks to bottom, and a layer of rapid drop in temperature divides the two. Cold-water fish usually are in or near the middle layer because the best combination of temperature, oxygen and food is to be found there.

The point should be stressed that all lakes are not deep enough to have a thermocline. In such lakes all of the water is made up of the upper layer, which may be too warm for cold water gamefish and only suitable for Largemouth Bass, Walleyes, Pickerel, and panfish. In such waters the cold water gamefish, if any, will be compelled to remain in spring holes or to travel up or down tributary streams until the summer stagnation period is over. There are other lakes wherein a part is too shallow to have a thermocline but where there is a deeper "bowl" at one end where complete stratification takes place. In such lakes it is obvious that gamefish will leave the shallow part and will remain in the deeper part in summer. This may offer a suggestion to anglers who troll in a certain part of a lake and catch only snags and weeds while, at the same time, fishermen in another part of the lake are returning with their limit of fish!

of the winter stagnation period occurs and, one by one, the gamefish again seek the level of most suitable temperatures until the ice leaves the lakes in the spring.

Until recent years anglers have scoffed at the logic (or inconvenience) of considering water temperatures as an aid to good fishing. Experience is beginning to show that the temperature factor is one of the vital aids in finding fish, regardless of the time of year. Only the behavior of temperate zone lakes has been discussed since polar lakes and tropical lakes, which behave somewhat differently, are less interesting to the majority of anglers.

The knowledge of water temperatures and temperature changes is being applied to fishing practices by an increasing number of fishermen. Many use the temperature of the water directly as a guide. While any type of instrument will do, a fisherman's thermometer is best because it is more convenient. Quick-acting fishing thermometers en-

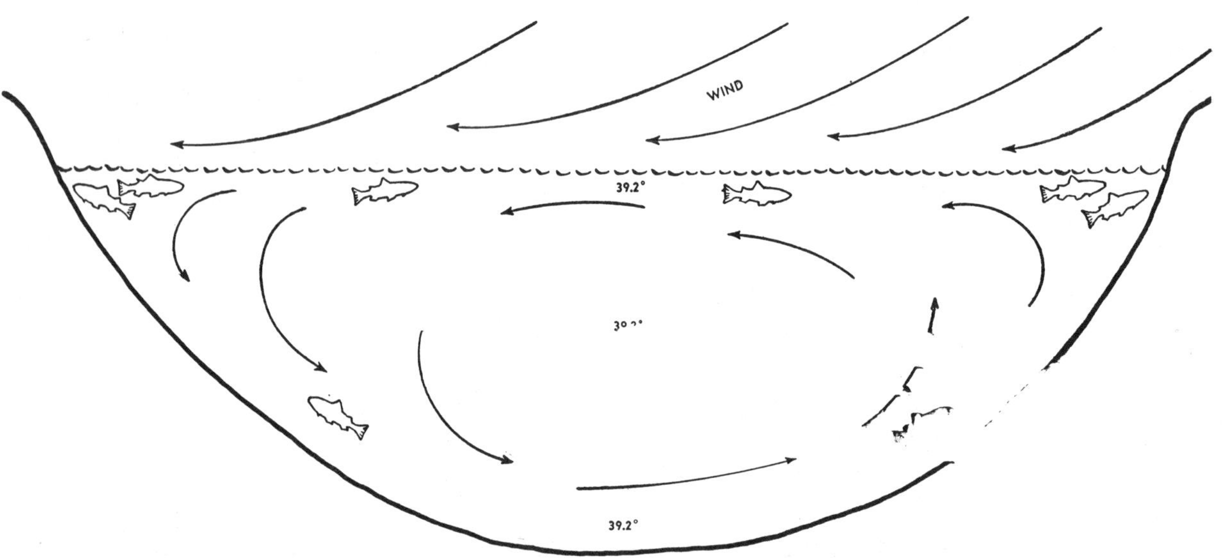

Fall Turnover Stage

When cold fall weather cools surface waters, the colder water sinks and mixes with the warmer water below until all of the lake again reaches maximum density of 39.2 F. With the mixing of the water, fish again come to the surface as they do in the spring.

FALL TURNOVER

The cold nights of fall bring on the reverse of the spring turnover process. As cold air reduces surface temperatures the colder and heavier water sinks to mix with the warmer water below. When this sinking and mixing process reaches and includes the thermocline level all of the water again gradually reaches its point of maximum density of 39.2°. At this point, the action of winds again mixes the waters thoroughly. The colder surface waters and the increased oxygen and food again bring gamefish to the surface. First come the bass and other species which enjoy cool temperatures but which will not tolerate the excessively warm surface waters in the summer. Then come the various species of trout, and finally the Lake Trout and Landlocked Salmon. As the surface waters draw nearer and nearer to freezing the beginning

closed in a plastic cover and with six waterproof plastic charts to show the locality of the fish at each range of surface water temperatures are on the market. One widely known is called "Steel's Fish Locator," and most sporting goods stores carry it.

Even though water temperature is an important and quick guide in locating game fish, do not make the mistake of thinking it is the only condition that governs the whereabouts and actions of game fish. Barometric pressure, availability of food, stage, and condition of the water (whether clear or muddy or "in bloom"), cover for the fish, wind direction, solunar feeding periods, and many other factors also affect the lives and habits of fish. Fish are like robot planes. Their actions are governed by the conditions—water, food, and cover conditions—and of these conditions perhaps the most important is water temperature.

LARGEMOUTH BASS

Largemouth Bass are so inactive in water under 50°F. as to be practically hibernating. They usually do not feed until the water gets above 55°F. If in early spring or late fall on a Largemouth lake or stream, the thermometer indicates the water is under 50°, it is useless to fish. As the water warms to between 55° to 60°, the fish get more active and begin to look for food—minnows, frogs, crawfish, and nymphs of aquatic insects. In this temperature bracket the best fishing will be during the warmest part of the day—between 10:00 a.m. and 4:00 p.m. and on the warmest and sunniest days, look for the bass in medium depth water —from 5 feet to 10 feet down on mud bottom near deeper water. Bass are cover fish and even though they will be partly "cruising" in these conditions, they will likely be in brush cover or near underwater logs, fallen tree tops, or under water weed beds. Another favorite hangout in 55° to 60° water is the outer edge of deeper weed beds or rushes—in places where the water is from 5 to 10 feet and where there is either a deep water bar or rather deep underwater weed beds within 100 feet of the outer edge of the rushes. The stems of the rushes will be covered by nymphs and larvae of aquatic insects. Minnows feed on these nymphs and the bass feed on the minnows.

In this 55°-60° F. water, bait casting or spinning with medium depth lures is very successful. By medium depth lures is meant baits that run from 3 to 5 feet under the surface. Drifting or still fishing a live minnow, frog, or angle worms near the bottom in 5 to 10 feet of water has a good chance of success, as does medium depth trolling. Both should be done in the same cover positions as for bait casting. Fly fishing is not usually too successful at this temperature, but if streamers, bucktails, or nymphs are used and fished wet and deep, by the action retrieve method, some fish will be taken.

Bass go to the shallows—from 2 feet to 4 feet deep—when the water is between 60° and 62°. At 62° they begin to spawn—the Largemouth in shallow nests on mud bottom. Spawning continues up to 65°. This does not mean, however, that bass in water between 62°-65° bracket are always spawning. In the 60°-65° bracket bass range widely over the shallow feeding grounds. They will be present on shallow bars, near the shorelines in brush and sunken log cover, around roots and tree tops, close to or under overhanging banks, in the edges of shallow rushes and near or over weed beds. Mud-bottomed, stumpy bays are particularly good spots.

All gamefish go deeper with a low or falling barometer or in stormy weather, and to slightly shallower water with a high or rising barometer. As a rule, other conditions being equal, gamefish feed and strike somewhat better on a rising or high barometer. Again, other conditions being equal, they feed better during solunar periods. (See page 244)

There are two seasons—the "change-over" periods in the early spring, and in the fall—in which the water temperature of lakes and deeper streams is practically the same at all depths. At such times the usually dominant effect of water temperature in causing fish to go to a certain depth or location doesn't apply because all depths have about the same temperature. In these conditions—rising or falling barometric pressure—solunar feeding periods and the easy availability of food really come into their own as factors in determining the location and feeding activities of fish.

The 65°-75° bracket, especially from 70° to 72° is the favorite condition for the Largemouth Bass. With this temperature the fish range widely into the shallow and shore line feeding grounds going often into water not more than 1 foot deep. From one to 4 feet is usually the best depth with this surface temperature. In this shallow water, bass can see an angler or a boat far off, and the larger bass, especially, won't strike when they can see the fisherman. That means that casts should be fairly long (35 feet or longer in fly casting, and 50 feet or more in spinning or bait casting).

The fly or bait should be put down lightly. Small lures should be used in bait casting in shallow water and thumping or scraping of feet around in the boat should be avoided. Bass bugs often work nicely in this 65°-73° range, as does bait casting with surface or medium depth lures.

The 73°-80° temperature range is one often found in early summer in vacation country. In it Largemouth Bass will be in medium depth water—from 5 feet to 12 feet on mud-bottomed bars, the edges of lily pads and near deeper weed beds. If the shore line is fairly deep, and especially if there are overhanging tree branches, then shore lines around logs and brush cover are good spots. Deeper rushes and other feeding grounds with water from 5 to 12 feet deep, but preferably nearer even deeper water, are also favorite haunts. Rather deep-running lures are needed in casting. In 73°-80° water these fish often feed in the shallows in the evenings and early mornings. They go into these feeding grounds because there are more frogs, small minnows, crawfish, and aquatic insects. When in the shallows the bass will be in the same cover locations as in the 65°-73° and the 60°-65° water brackets.

As the water gets close to or above 80° the bass will begin to feed more and more at night, going to shallow-water feeding grounds after dark. Bait casting especially with surface lures, will bring fish at night where none will come to the landing net in daylight. A noisy lure that struggles on the surface attracts the bass. Weedless lures are good if there are weeds, brush, or logs in the water being fished. A flashlight should be carried preferably hung around the neck on a cord, but it should not be used except to put on or take off a lure or when unhooking a fish.

When the surface water passes 90° the bass will be deep down in water of from 12 feet to 25 feet—looking for cooler water (between 70° and 72°) if they can find it. When just resting, as they often do in 80° to 90° water, they will be in the 15 to 25 feet depth. Spring holes and spots near the mouths of colder feeder streams make good warm water fishing spots. The bass in warm water can be tempted with very deep running bait casting or spinning lures, or by drifting or still fishing with live bait—minnows, worms, crawfish, or frogs. In 80°-90° surface water, cast out, let the lure sink within a foot or two of the bottom and retrieve slowly enough to keep the bait at that depth.

Largemouth Bass in Streams

Largemouth rivers are mostly slow and fairly deep mud-bottomed streams with much weed growth in them. Often they are largely marshy channels between lakes. In rivers having both Largemouth and Smallmouth Bass, the Smallmouth will be in the faster sand and gravel-bottomed parts of the stream, while the Largemouth will stay in the slower mud-bottomed eddies and sloughs.

In water under 50° F. this fish will not feed. Between 55° and 60° they take natural bait fairly well if it is drifted carefully and skillfully into the deeper mud-bottomed holes, eddies and deep under-cut banks. Minnows, frogs, or worms all work. They must be fished slowly and close to the bottom as the bass are a bit lazy at such temperatures. The warmer parts of the day—between 9:00 A.M. and 4:30 P.M. will probably provide the best fishing.

At 60° river bass range out of the deep water winter quarters into the shallow riffles where aquatic nymphs, larvae and adult aquatic insects and crustacae abound. They will be found hunting minnows, frogs, and crawfish along the edges of rushes, along the shore lines where there are overhanging trees or grass-covered under-cut banks or shore line weed beds. Underwater brush, stumps and logs, also make fine spots.

In 60°-73° water, all kinds of artificials are taken freely. A bass bug floated over their feeding grounds by the "rest-and-twitch" method so successful with these flies will give a lot of action. Bucktails and streamers in the deeper feeding places and nymphs in the riffles will all get fish.

Bait casting and spinning with surface or medium depth lures works well and good fishing may continue through the day as well as in the evenings and early mornings. Night fishing is neither necessary nor particularly successful.

One of the real delights of an angler's life is a well managed "drift" down a good bass river after either Largemouth or Smallmouth, or both. Just to place a fly delicately alongside a log or to slip a bait casting lure accurately to that brush pile where the current swirls under an overhanging bank as the boat moves along the alder and hardwood timbered shorelines is a joy in itself. Then the smashing surface strike of a bass, the fast play of a fighting fish, and the contentment of a river battle won is added satisfaction. These things and a hundred more make a river "float trip" one of the happy times that are long remembered!

At water temperatures of 73°-85° Largemouth Bass begin to return to the deeper, cooler water, in the shade of trees, heavy lily-pad areas, and to spring holes and near the mouths of cooler tributary streams. Especially in the upper 70's and above 80°, the bass get lazy in the daytime. They feed mostly in the evenings and early mornings, and in the warmest water temperatures will do almost all feeding at night. During these night feeding periods the bass range on to the shallow feeding grounds on the riffles and around the weed beds, rushes, and underwater logs and take commotion-type surface lures avidly.

In water above 76°, except for the late evening and night periods, more success is likely with natural bait—frogs, minnows, worms, or crawfish—than with anything else. A spinner-and-natural bait rig will do good work for the bait caster or spin-fisherman in these conditions.

SMALLMOUTH BASS

Smallmouth Bass are less of a warm-water fish than Largemouth. They do some feeding, although not much, in water between 40° and 52° F. Bass are lazy at these water temperatures, all their bodily processes including digestion being much slower; but they will take lures, especially natural bait (minnows, crabs, frogs, and worms). Smallmouth Bass stay in deep water—12 feet to 30 feet—in this cold bracket. During the winter and early spring the deeper water is warmer than the surface water and at this time the fish stay deep. As the water warms, they become more active, and at 48° they even rise to the surface occasionally to feed. Live bait, drifted or still fished, is the best fishing method.

This fish likes clear water, over sand, gravel, or rock bottom. In 40°-52° water they are on deep rock or gravel bars and around deep rock ledges. Bottom springs, if present, are likely places for bass because they are usually warmer in cold weather than are the other parts of the lake.

Smallmouth usually come into medium depth water—5 feet to 12 feet deep—when the surface water reaches 52° or 53° F. Up to 60° they become more lively and go into the sand, gravel, or rock-bottomed shore lines on which there is log, brush, or rock ledge cover. The outer edge of deep rush beds that are close to deeper sand-bottomed bars are also good fishing spots in both this and the next temperature bracket. Bass can be taken in this water range by bait casting with deep running or medium depth lures—especially the smaller baits. Still fishing and drifting with live bait (minnows, crawfish, frogs or angle worms) also works well.

Sixty to seventy degrees is the most comfortable water temperature range for Smallmouth Bass. They move into shallow water at 60° F and prefer 67° water to any other temperature. They will find this temperature if possible. If there is food together with cover, they will stay. If such water has no food, the fish will make feeding trips into warmer water when they become hungry enough, but these forays will be made at times when the water is as close to 67° as may be found.

In this range Smallmouth feed in water from 2 feet to 10 feet deep—on sand, gravel, or rock bottom along rocky shore lines, around under water logs, brush cover, rock ledges, rock or gravel bars, or shore line boulders where the bottom drops away fast to deeper water.

There are three fine sporting methods of fishing

in this bracket—bait casting and spinning with surface or medium-depth lures and fly fishing with either bass bugs or wet flies, streamers, or bucktails. While Smallmouth take artificials of all kinds best in this range, there are times when these temperamental and moody game fish will take only natural bait. In these conditions a live frog, minnow, or crawfish on a Nylon leader worked over the feeding grounds thoroughly by careful bait casting or spinning methods is usually successful.

In clear water the fish can see both fisherman and boat a good ways off (unless there is a riffle on the water). There the fish should be stalked cautiously, using small lures. Small dark colored baits are best. In this bracket Smallmouth usually feed through the day, although the evening hours may still be the best feeding times.

Bass will be found in medium depths of from 4 feet to 15 feet at these 70°-80° temperatures. Cover and bottom will be similar to those mentioned previously but in deeper water. This is for normal weather. In stormy conditions or when the barometer is low or falling rapidly, Smallmouth go to deeper water (12 feet to 20 feet), especially to deep rock ledges and rock and gravel bars near still deeper water.

Bait casting with medium depth or deep running lures on a spinner-and-natural bait rig is an excellent method. Especially in the lower temperatures Smallmouth occasionally feed in the shallows in the evening and early morning hours and under these conditions take bass bugs and bucktails or streamers quite freely.

When the surface water is above 78° F. this fish searches out really deep water if it is to be found. They will try to find 67° water even if it is from 20 feet to 40 feet down. Sometimes it is necessary to fish as deep as 73 feet to get this fish when the surface temperature reaches 90°. In such cases, water temperature taken at that depth with a maximum-and-minimum thermometer were found to be 67° F.

In warm surface waters, Smallmouth are likely to do most of their feeding *at night*. The fish go to shallow or medium depth feeding grounds and while there will respond to spinning or bait casting with surface lures. Strikes at night are explosion strikes. Bass hit at night as much by sound as by sight. Any one who cannot get bass in the daytime in warm water conditions should try night fishing. It's a real thrill!

Smallmouth Bass in Streams

Rivers do not have the great variation in water temperature that is found in lakes because there isn't as much difference in depth and also because the current mixes the various water temperature layers. However, the same type of temperature patterns apply to streams as to lakes except for stratification patterns in lakes. In addition, water temperatures control the hatch of aquatic insects and determine whether bass will be in the riffles, in the pools, in the eddies, or along the rock ledges.

In 40°-52° temperatures, the fish will be in the deeper pools and stillwaters, where they will take natural bait better than artificial lures. Drifting a minnow, crawfish, hellgrammite, or worms into these deep pools or deeper under-cut banks and eddies will probably take more Smallmouth in these conditions than any other method.

Stream Smallmouth become more active in 52°-60° temperatures and edge into faster and more shallow water. The fish also begin to respond to artificial lures more freely, both in bait casting and spinning, and in fly fishing. For spinning and bait casting use medium depth lures chiefly. In fly casting, wet flies, streamers, bucktails, and nymphs are usually the best.

Water temperatures between 60° and 70°, especially 67° water, are optimum in streams, just as they are in lakes. At 60° the bass go to the shallow water feeding grounds. This means the riffles, the ends of current tongues at the heads of pools, rock ledges, under-cut banks where the bottom is sand or gravel, boulder-strewn rapids, and the shallow flats at the lower ends of pools. Here, bass bugs, as well as underwater flies, streamers, bucktails, and nymphs work well. In bait casting or spinning, small dark surface or semi-surface lures are best. By assuming that the fish won't strike if they see the fisherman by fishing carefully more strikes are certain.

Smallmouth gradually retire to the deeper pools and deeper eddies, deeper rock ledges, shaded deep under-cut banks and highly aerated shaded waters as water temperature rise above 70°. Also, they feed more in the evenings and early mornings, and, in still warmer water, feed almost entirely *at night*.

TROUT

Trout, unlike bass, are a cold water fish. But even trout do not like water colder than 40° F. even though they can get along in water only a few degrees above freezing (32° F). As 40° (actually 39.2° F.) water is more dense than either colder or warmer water, the deepest holes always tend to approach a temperature of 40° F. If the air remains colder than 40°, then the shallow water will be colder than the deeper water. For the same reason, if the air remains consistently warmer than 40°, the shallow water will be warmer than the deeper water. That is the reason water is colder as depth increases in summer, but gets warmer as it increases in winter.

Eastern Brook, Rainbow (including Steelhead), Cutthroat, Brown, and Dolly Varden Trout all react enough alike to water temperatures to be safely grouped together.

When surface water is between 33°-50° F., trout will be in the deepest water. They will be found in the deep pools, the slower current, and the deep-water pockets beneath undercut banks. Spring holes will usually be warmer than the surrounding water and for that reason, will be good places for trout in this ice-cold water.

In water under 50° trout digest their food more slowly and are less active than in water in the upper fifties and the sixties. Also, below 50° F. there are few hatches of aquatic insects in the streams. Probably these two items account for the fact that trout seldom take artificial flies in water below 50°. Below that temperature it is best to fish with a fly or spinning rod with natural bait and during the middle of the day. Worms, grubs, very small minnows, hellgrammites, or (if they can be kept on the hook) nymphs or larvae of aquatic insects all make good natural baits.

The angler must keep out of sight, and drift the bait on a light leader with a small hook into the deeper holes where the trout are hiding. This method will take trout in cold water. A small wobbling spoon on a spinning outfit or bait cast with a very light rod will also take trout—and big ones.

Trout take wet flies well in water from 50°-55° F. but do not take dry flies well under 55°. At this temperature the trout, especially the larger ones, will be close to the bottom in medium depth water of 3 feet to 6 feet under the current tongues at the heads of pools, in the deeper water of the riffles and beneath under-cut banks, around sunken logs, and in medium depth water below and above boulders lying in the current. If the water is high and murky, natural bait will be needed, but in clear water, wet flies, nymphs, bucktails, or streamers should be good.

Dry fly water temperature is 55°-68°. At 55° trout begin to feed on the surface more freely. More insect hatches occur than in other temperatures, and this range therefore makes the best dry fly water. Trout are on the active feeding grounds in the shallow riffles, surface feeding at the edges and ends of current-tongues, at the shallow tails of pools, in the eddies, close to under-cut banks, in the broken water above and below rocks, and in all sorts of log and brush cover. Gravel bars at the mouths of creeks are likely spots. Any place where fish food floats by is a good place for trout. Trout strike best as a rule when the barometer is rising and in solunar feeding periods. Evenings are usually the best fishing times in this water.

Above 68° trout begin to be uncomfortable. Fairly good trout fishing can be had up to a temperature of 70° F. and for Brown Trout and Rainbows in fast highly aerated water, a temperature of 72° F. may occasionally be fishable. Brown Trout have been caught in water as warm as 83°, but this is very unusual. In warm water, trout feed mostly at night and natural bait is most successful. Night is then the best time to fish, especially for Brown Trout.

Trout in Ponds and Lakes

Fishing for Brook Trout, Rainbows, Cutthroats, and Brown Trout in ponds and lakes is much like fishing the deepest stream pools. When near the surface they take flies and also casting baits or spoons. If the trout are down deep, then deep fishing methods are needed. This usually means still fishing or drifting with natural bait. It can also mean deep trolling. Spinning with a light monofilament Nylon line works well and is a favorite method in these conditions. Where the trout will be found is determined chiefly by water temperature, slightly modified by barometric pressure.

In water from the freezing point up to 50° trout stay down from 10 to 25 feet in ponds and as deep as 40 or 50 feet in some mountain lakes. Still fishing with natural bait—worms, grubs, salmon eggs (in the West) or small minnows—is the method by which most of these trout are caught. Deep trolling will also get them in these conditions. Spinning with deep running lures is also somewhat successful.

Trout will withdraw to deep water in temperatures above 68°, especially over 70° and will be down from 12 to 30 feet. As in other deep water fishing live bait works best—but here again fish can be taken by spinning.

LAKE TROUT

Lake Trout are one of the most selective fish in regard to water temperature. They like water between 40° and 45°F., and prefer a temperature of 41° F. As a matter of fact, they practically refuse to stay in water other than that between 40° and 45°. As 40° is just about the temperature at which water is the densest, this 40°-45° water is usually found very deep in lakes in late spring, summer, and early fall, this means going down from 100 to 200 feet to get Lake Trout. At these depths, deep trolling with metal line and wobbling spoon is usually the best method.

The thermometer will tell where to fish for Lake Trout—just locate 40°-45° water, preferably 41°—and fish there. It doesn't matter whether this 41° water is deep or shallow 200 feet, 100 feet, 50 feet of 10 feet—that's where the Lake Trout will be.

In very early spring, just after the ice goes out, and in the late fall, just before the freeze-up, the surface water of northern lakes is between 40° and 45° F. At that time there is very exciting bait casting with medium depth lures—mostly wobbling spoons. Wet flies, streamers, and bucktails, fished deep by the action method, will also take Lake Trout in from 6 to 12 feet of water during this period.

It is interesting to note that the explanation for taking Lake Trout at the surface in Great Slave Lake in the Northwest Territory in Canada, in late July and early August, is that the temperature of the surface water in midsummer is between 40° and 45°, usually 41° F. This is a spectacular proof of the statement that 41° water is a magnet for Lake Trout.

At 40°-45° Lake Trout will be on rock bars and rock ledges off islands and points in from 5 feet to 12 feet of water. Bait casting with medium depth lures—especially wobbling spoons, is the preferred method of fishing, but wet flies, streamers, bucktails, and a small spinner-and-fly handled on a stiff fly rod will also work.

When the temperature goes above 45° the Lake Trout immediately leave the surface and go to the necessary depth to reach 40°-45°. This will be found to gradually work down from a depth of 12 to 18 feet at a 45° surface temperature, to one of 40 to 60 feet when the surface is 60°, and to 60 to 90 feet with the surface at 70°. The depth at which the Lake Trout find the 40°-45° layer varies in different latitudes and different lakes. For this reason, the better way to pick Lake Trout fishing spots is to locate the 40°-45° temperature layer with a thermometer. For taking deep water temperatures, a "maximum and minimum thermometer" is the best, but it can be done fairly well with a fishing thermometer. For all fishing except at the 40°-45° surface temperature, the most successful fishing method is deep trolling with metal line and a big wobbling spoon. Monofilament Nylon lines are also beginning to be used with success.

With a surface temperature of 70°-80° such as is common in many northern lakes in summer, the desired temperature may be down from 90 to 160 feet and sometimes as low as 200 feet. The 41° water will usually lie below 90 feet in water of a total depth of 160 feet or more. In northern lakes in which the water is 100 feet or less in depth there is usually no water under 50°—*and no Lake Trout will stay there.* This means that if you are fishing in surface temperature of 70°-80°, look for water over 160 feet in depth, preferably off the rocky bars and ledges where the Lake Trout come to the surface in early spring. Even then it is advisable to check the temperature to find a layer between 40° and 45°. If it is 41°, that is fine.

ATLANTIC SALMON

This most renowned of all game fish—the royal standard bearer of all fish that take a fly in fresh water—has about the same water temperature habits as Brook, Rainbow, and Brown Trout. Like Steelheads, Atlantic Salmon usually lie in the deeper pools and rapids of the rivers in which they spawn.

In water from 40°—50° F. they stay in the deepest parts of the pools. In 50°—55° water they usually move into medium depth water. Above 55° they will take any fly to some extent although they take underwater flies a larger percentage of the time than trout.

Landlocked Salmon in most lakes follow somewhat the same tactics as the Lake Trout. In the spring with a surface temperature up to 48° F., they stay in the upper 10 feet of the lake's surface. Here they take either dry or wet flies very well.

When the surface water gets much above 48° they go deep and stay there during the summer.

When in streams, Landlocked Salmon follow the same temperature ranges as the Atlantic Salmon.

KING SALMON

King Salmon (Chinook), the big Pacific Salmon, is a great fresh water game fish except that they do not take a fly in fresh water. In the tremendous power of its runs the Chinook has no equal among fresh water game fish. Its spectacular jumps are only equalled by the Atlantic Salmon and the Steelhead—and the Chinook averages almost twice as large as either of these fine fighters.

Very little is known of its water temperature habits while in the ocean. They enter Pacific Coast rivers, on their spawning journey, when water temperature is from 50° to 65° F. and stay in the deeper, fast-flowing pools and rock-ledged currents where the water temperature is between 50° and 63°. Shallower and slower water in which the temperature rises to 70° at the surface seldom holds Salmon. As with Trout, productive spots are the current-tongues at the upper ends of deep pools, especially just below rocky ledges with deeper water under the main current flow. It was in just such a beautiful pool in the Umpqua River in Oregon—in 54° water—that the world's record 83 lb. Chinook Salmon was taken. This fish was landed after 45 minutes of the wildest kind of a battle. During the fight this Salmon hauled the boat, containing two fishermen, down through three boisterous rapids. An 83 lb. salmon ramming and jumping all over the fast tumbling water is not soothing to jittery nerves. The fish was finally beached and gaffed in the fourth pool. This occurred in 1910 and the record still stands.

Trolling with large spoons, (about 4-inch blade) is the universal method of fishing for Chinook in the rivers. One rows upstream but in the strong current, actually backs zig-zag downstream with the revolving spoon a hundred feet ahead. Between dawn and sunrise and between sunset and dark are the best times; in fact, about the only times when salmon strike well in these rivers above tidewater.

Of the other four salmon, only the Silver is of much importance to anglers. In the Northwest Pacific Coast rivers, Silver Salmon furnish good trolling, bait casting, and fly fishing in about the same water temperatures as for King Salmon. Silver Salmon run usually from 3 to 15 pounds and are a splendid game fish.

THE PIKES

There are three species of true pikes: (1) Muskellunge, (2) Northern Pike, (3) Pickerel. They are widely distributed and furnish fishing for vacationists in the northern United States and in Canada.

MUSKELLUNGE

This pirate of lonely weed-grown northern sloughs and lakes moves from his winter lair in the deep water under the ice in the early spring (or just after the ice breaks up in the spring) to the summer feeding ground. The favorite winter resting grounds for Muskellunge is in water from 40°—45° F. at a depth of from 20 to 50 feet depending on the depth of the lake. Smaller Muskellunge often winter in shallower water than the big ones. Still fishing with large live minnows is the most successful fishing method under these conditions.

In the spring, when the surface temperature is from 35°-50°, Muskellunge pick spots, usually in water of 5 to 15 feet, under or alongside old sunken logs, fallen trees, or stumps, or in the edges of heavy weed-covered spots or thick underwater weed beds. Pockets in the swale or muskeg areas and the tiny pine-hidden lakes with weed fringed shore lines, lonesome lily pads and drifted windfalls are favorite spots for Muskellunge. These lairs or hide-outs are selected for concealment so that a Muskie can be in position to move out and devour any unwary smaller fish or larger minnow that comes his way. All the pikes are solitary hunters, and do not travel in schools or even in pairs except at spawning time. They lie in wait for their prey without so much cruising around when feeding as bass, trout, walleyes, or panfish. Large Muskellunge—called "Mossbacks" in the north—

lie alongside their sunken logs and weed beds so quietly that tiny aquatic vegetation actually grows in the dark slime along their backs. This helps their camouflage, particularly as one of these giants will lie motionless for hours and even days after capturing a big Walleye, large Sucker, Redhorse, Bass, Northern Pike, or other fish. The Muskie swallows his prey whole and then retires to his weed-and-log-protected lair to digest his meal much as a tiger lies dormant for hours or days after a heavy meal. Bait casting with medium depth lures is the most successful method.

Muskellunge go into shallow water, of 4 to 8 feet deep—at a temperature of 50° to 60° F., to spawn. Mud-bottomed inlets, bays, and overflow areas with plenty of weeds, brush, and stumps are favorite spawning grounds. Spawning is from two to four weeks later than the Northern Pike. The time varies with the water temperature but is usually in April or May. Casting with surface lures is the most successful method at this time.

After spawning, when the water is at about 60° F. (and until it reaches about 80° F.), they return to their hunting lairs in water from 8 to 15 feet deep. They will be found in weed covered pockets, and in slow current spots clogged with driftwood. It is in this 60°-80° water that most good Muskellunge fishing occurs.

If the Muskellunge can be located in their solitary lurking places and a lure cast to them without their being aware of the fisherman, they may be receptive. At this temperature they are neither numbed by the cold, as in the winter, nor stupified by the heat, as in mid-summer. However, they may be gorged with food, and a Muskie that is stuffed with food is less liable to strike than a bass under the same circumstances.

Bait casting is the preferred fishing method and either artificial lures or large, live minnows or suckers can be used. Many are also taken by trolling with wobbling or spinning spoons, and by drifting with a live sucker or big chub minnow.

While Muskellunge are not a "cruising" fish, like bass or trout, they do leave their lairs and cruise for food in the evening. They go to reefs in the larger lakes and to gravel or rocky bars in other waters to feed on the smaller fish and larger minnows which congregate there. Few fishermen know this, and many guides fail to tell them because they like to work from seven in the morning to five in the afternoon and then lay off for supper. Bait casting is the best method of taking these cruising muskies.

When the mid-summer temperature rises above 80°, especially in the high 80's, Muskellunge get rather sluggish from the heat (contrary to some fishermen's opinion, it isn't their teeth). In these temperatures, they drift to water of 15 to 40 feet deep. Live bait, still fished or drifted, is the way most Muskellunge are taken in warm water.

During warm water periods Muskellunge also do some cruising on the reefs and bars but usually *at night.* Here bait casting with medium depth lures or natural bait and spinner is the best technique.

NORTHERN PIKE

While many bass, trout, and muskie fishermen look down upon the Pike, this is not at all justified. When caught in cold water on light tackle, the Northern Pike is a thoroughly good fighting fish. They have another advantage for most vacation fishermen in their habit of striking lures more freely than any other game fish.

Northern Pike are caught through the ice in from 10 to 20 feet of water at temperatures of 33° to 38° F. Still-fishing with live minnows is the accepted method. The fish are pretty torpid with cold but will take bait half-heartedly.

In temperatures of 38°-60° Northern Pike go to the shallows both to feed and to get ready for spawning. Even before the ice has entirely gone from the lakes, the smaller Pike commence to go inshore to water from 2 to 3 feet deep, either in pairs or in groups of one female and several males. They enter shallow weedy mud-bottomed inlets. This migration occurs at a water temperature of about 38°, usually in March.

When the spring is far enough advanced so that lakes are free of ice and low-lying marshes and meadows are under spring flood waters, the larger Pike start to spawn. This will commonly be at temperatures running from 45° to 55°. Spawning, for each size of Pike, continues through a range of about 7 degrees of temperature. The smaller individuals spawn the earliest and the largest ones last. This usually lasts through March and April and sometimes into May. The last Pike usually finish spawning when the water is at 60° F. in the shallow breeding grounds.

The surface temperature over the deep underwater weed beds, in which the Pike feed on minnows, will be from 50°-60° during this period. Shortly after spawning is finished they return to their normal hunting function. When on the feeding grounds over the underwater weed beds in about 8 to 12 feet of water, the Pike are often mixed with Walleyes. Natural bait of minnows or frogs, attached to a spinner or deep running artificial lures works well at this time.

When the surface temperature is between 60° and 80° Pike are along weedy, rush-lined shores in water of 3 to 12 feet. Pike on the shorelines, like Muskellunge, hunt alone. Each fish takes over a particular weed pocket or rush covered inlet and defends that spot against all comers (except Muskies).

At mid-day in water in the higher seventies Pike frequently go to water of 10 to 20 feet near their normal shoreline feeding grounds. Pike generally roam more than Muskellunge but are less inclined to feed after dark.

In warm water, above 80°, the larger pike drift out to deeper water of 15 to 40 feet just off the weed and rush pockets where they make their lairs in late spring and early summer or to deep bars and reefs extending from rush covered points or weed-bottomed bays. These bars may be from 15 to 50 feet down and the fish found on them are liable to be big ones of from 8 to 25 pounds. Deep trolling with a spinner and minnow or deep drifting with a large live minnow (4 to 6 inches) is usually the best method of fishing these places. Large, deep running artificial lures also take these pike. Bait casting can also be used if the lure is allowed to sink to the bottom and then reeled in very slowly.

PICKEREL

There are three species of Pickerel—the Eastern or Chain Pickerel, the Western, and the Banded—but only the former attains a size to make it of much interest to anglers. The Chain Pickerel is a favorite of the New England ice-fisherman and may attain a length of 25 inches and a weight approaching ten pounds, although the average fish is below 3 pounds. They are found in weedy, muddy lakes, and their habits are similar to those of the Northern Pike, except that they rarely venture into really deep water. In northern waters when Bass and Trout are more difficult to catch, Pickerel fishing remains good. Pickerel will strike at anything that moves, and are taken with plugs, spoons, spinners, popping bugs and live bait.

WALLEYES

Walleyes or Pike-Perch belong to the Perch family. The Walleye—next to the Brook Trout, Grayling, and Salmon—is probably the best eating fresh water fish. Its firm flaky white meat, fried, broiled, or baked in the open beside a cold stream or lake is one of the real joys of a northwoods fishing trip.

Walleyes are school fish. Where one is found, there are likely to be several or many more. As Walleyes are free biters, it is especially important for the fisherman to know enough of their habits to be able to locate a school. This fish prefers sand, gravel, rock, or at least clay bottom—*not* mud bottom—and they like clear better than murky water.

At 33°-40° temperatures there is little difference in water temperature at all depths and Walleyes, practically released from temperature control, may be found from 5 to 50 feet deep over sand or gravel bottom. Still fishing or drifting with live minnows, is the best fishing method. Bait casting or spinning, deep trolling, or for that matter, trolling at any depth with mid-depth or deep-running artificial lures, spinners, wobbling spoons and pork-rind or spinners and natural bait may produce results. The warmest part of the day is the best time to fish. Many Walleyes are also caught through the ice.

At 40°-55° Walleyes go to the shallow sand and gravel-bottomed waters of streams and lakes (if no suitable stream is available) to spawn. In lakes they may go to the spawning grounds even earlier—in water temperatures between 35° and 40°. In lakes, gravel and sand bars at a depth of 7 to 15 feet are good feeding grounds. In streams, Walleyes will be in the medium depth water in pools and in the deeper water of the riffles. Clear water and sand or pebbly bottom is favored. Mid-day remains the best time for fishing in the early part of this period, gradually changing over, in higher temperatures to the evening. Bait casting and spinning with mid-depth and deep-running lures and with spinner and live bait work well.

Walleyes like the 55° to 70° range. In it they circulate widely looking for food, mostly minnows and crawfish, in water of 12 to 20 feet. They still prefer sand, gravel, or rock-bottomed areas, especially bars and inlets. The best fishing hours are usually between 9:00 A. M. and 5:00 P. M. but in water above 60° the evening hours become better. When this happens the fish will be in shallower water of 10 to 12 feet in lakes. Good feeding spots are over the underwater weed beds.

In streams, the fish will be in the deep pools, deep strong runs, in the faster current at the heads of the pools, the mouths of feeder brooks, at sharp bends (on the deep side) and in the deep water below falls. In the evenings, in water above 60°, they work out to the shallower areas. Bait casting and spinning with artificial baits of the deep-running types, especially minnows and crawfish lures, are good methods. Also a spinner and natural bait works well at these temperatures and drifting live bait and trolling also are successful.

Walleyes work to deeper water as the surface gets warmer. In the 70°-80° bracket they will be down 15 to 35 feet. Bottom and cover conditions will remain the same and methods of fishing are also the same except the baits are fished. In this period, however, the fish feed more in the evenings and early mornings in the shallower water, less in the mid-day except in quite deep areas. Also, they feed more *at night.* After sunset and while there is a red or orange moon is a fine time.

Walleyes do not stay in water above 80°, so as the surface of the water rises, they withdraw to deeper cooler water or to spring holes. In lakes the fish will be down 30 to 50 feet. The only time they return to shallower water, 12 to 15 feet, will be at night, especially during the dark of the moon. Still fishing or drifting live minnows or crawfish or deep trolling, with spinner and natural bait, are the most successful warm water methods of fishing for Walleyes; but deep running artificial lures that act, look and feel like minnows or crawfish do a good job.

In July and August, when warmer water has made bass, and to some extent, pike fishing uncertain, the free-biting Walleye will save many an otherwise fishless day.

PANFISH

If a mid-summer vacation spot doesn't offer Walleyes and the bass or pike aren't biting well in the warm water, panfish can prevent an otherwise fishless vacation. Panfish—Bluegills, sunfish, Crappies, Rock Bass, perch, Bullheads, and catfish provide much sport when taken on a fly rod or light spinning rod. Except for the bullheads and catfish all will take flies at times—and a light rod with live bait will turn in plenty of thrills.

Panfish, like Walleyes, are school fish. If one is taken there are probably others present. Also, panfish are slow current or still water fish. For this reason, they thrive best in ponds or lakes. If in streams, they stay in the slack water eddies and still water pools. They also like brush, weed and reed cover.

Under 45° panfish stay in water 10 to 25 ft. deep. Bars and bays with brush or weed cover or both are favorite spots. Still fishing or drifting with angle worms fished close to the bottom is a good method for this deep fishing.

Panfish roam over the medium-depth (5 to 15 ft.) weed beds and brush cover of a lake or pond at 45°-60°. As the water warms, the panfish go into shallow water and 55° to 60° will usually put the panfish into 5- to 10-foot depths. Sunken logs, roots, log jams, under water brush piles, old docks, swimming floats, as well as weed beds and lily pads all make excellent panfish feeding grounds. drifting and still fishing with fly rod or light spinning rod and live bait catches the most panfish. In addition to angle worms (the standard bait for panfish), other good baits are small minnows, small crawfish, hellgrammites, weed worms, grubs, crickets, and nymphs. Panfish also take wet flies, small streamers, small bucktails, and nymphs, fished deep by the action method, very well.

Sixty to eighty degrees is the dry fly and small bass bug temperature for panfish. In it these small cousins of the bass take floating hair bugs, tiny poppers, and trout-size dry flies beautifully. With a light fly rod, a royal good time can be had with panfish in this water. The fish will be in from 6 inches to 5 feet of water—and, when a school in feeding mood is located, they'll almost jump out of the water for the flies.

When the surface water rises above 80°, panfish return to deeper water—first to the 7- to 15-foot depth, and later to really deep water at 15 to 25 feet. At these depths drifting and still fishing with live bait usually works best. However, spinning with small, deep-running lures will also catch panfish.

PERCH

Yellow Perch is one panfish that belongs to a different family and has different feeding habits. They are widely distributed in ponds, lakes and streams and like other panfish, are school fish. They belong to the same family as the Walleye and like it are delicious eating.

Many Yellow Perch are caught through the ice. They spawn in the early spring on a rising water temperature of about 47° F. Perch frequent moderate depths, and early in spring, are found in the edge or foot of riffles when feeding. As the water warms, they are found in the deeper water of both streams and lakes—deep pools, below mill dams and around submerged timbers of bridges, beneath undercut banks, and in eddies near logs and boulders. Drifting, still fishing and spinning, with worms and other live bait, are standard methods. These fish will take wet flies, fished deep by the retrieve action. On a light fly rod or light spinning rod, Yellow Perch are a great vacation fish and furnish much sport in thousands of summer resorts.

THE SOLUNAR THEORY

The Solunar Theory, like most innovations, was discovered accidentally. Actually this natural law is in no sense new. Scientists, market hunters, and some of the tribes of American Indians have long known about its manifestations. What was not known, however, was the formula for the calculation of the schedule of solunar periods a year or so in advance.

Miami Beach News Bureau

John Alden Knight, outdoor writer and editor. Leading exponent of the Solunar Theory.

The market hunters of Florida and Georgia (back in the days when market hunting was allowed) planned their fishing and shooting trips according to daily moon positions. They had learned that wildlife usually was active and feeding when the moon was directly overhead or directly underfoot. At these times game was out of hiding and readily available, and fish were feeding actively.

This bit of folk lore was picked up while on a fishing trip in Florida in 1926 with the grandson of a Georgia market hunter. It did not take long, however, to discover that the "moon up-moon down" method of approximation was far from being accurate or satisfactory. At certain times of the month this method brought the forecasts fairly close to the true schedule of activity periods as shown by the behavior of wildlife itself, but at other times of the month there would be a variance of as much as an hour and a half or two hours.

It was quite evident that the loose approximation used by the old market hunters was not accurate enough to qualify as the formula for a reasonably exact schedule. After all, a schedule of this sort should function as a time saver and as a reliable guide to the best fishing that each day has to offer. There must be a reason for accuracy at some times of the month and inaccuracy at others.

The problem was solved, after a fashion, by the process of elimination. First a list was made of the factors which influence or control the day-to-day behavior of both fresh- and salt-water fish. Everything was taken into account which could possibly have any bearing on the matter. The reaction was in no sense local as it had been well established that the phenomenon manifested itself at the same time in several widely scattered bodies of water.

This list was a long one, including thirty-three possibilities. Gradually, one by one, they were examined and rejected. After three of them, however, question marks had been placed, indicating the advisability of further examination. These three were "sun", "moon", and "tides".

Surely the sun could have little effect. Its cycle was the same day after day, whereas the activity periods of fish were apt to be evident at most any time of day or night. The moon already had been weighed in the balance and found wanting. Tides? Surely there could be no tidal movement in a trout stream.

The fact remained, however, that tides had always guided salt-water fishermen to good fishing. Could it be that the prompting stimulus lay in the influence of the sun and the moon, which cause ocean tides, instead of in actual tidal stages or flow?

This line of reasoning led to a rather intensive study of tides, in which the New York office of the U. S. Coast and Geodetic Survey was extremely helpful. For several years the Atlantic Tide Tables served as the basis for the calculation of the theoretical "inland tides", and the schedule that was set up for further experimentation was called, more for the convenience of giving it a name than for any other reason, the "inland tide tables".

For two years this schedule was investigated but it, too, showed too much variance from the true schedule at certain times of the month. Only after actual tidal times had been disregarded and the daily positions of the moon and the sun alone considered was it possible to forecast a schedule that was reasonably accurate.

Along about this time the theory was given a new name. From the words "solar" (Sun) and "lunar" (Moon) the word "solunar" was coined and the theory was labeled "The Solunar Theory".

"The Solunar Theory" was first made public, in two articles that were published in *"Sportsman"*. These articles were titled "Ocean Tides and Fresh-Water Fish", and they appeared early in 1935. The response on the part of the readers was indeed surprising. About a thousand letters were received by the editors, all asking for more information. The eventual result was the publication of the first edition of *The Solunar Tables* in 1935.

When the original research was being done in working out the fundamentals of the solunar theory, only the approximate times of "moon up-moon down" were considered. Gradually, however, it became increasingly evident that there were also intermediate periods of activity that occurred about midway between the two major activity periods of each day. Thus, the more evident periods were called "major solunar periods" and the intermediate periods, which were of shorter duration, were called "minor solunar periods". When *The Solunar Tables* for 1936 were published, both major periods and minor periods were listed.

It has ever been one of the frailties of human nature that things which are not readily understood are automatically condemned. The solunar theory was such a radical departure from the general run of fish lore that it came in for more than its share of ridicule. It was called "the looney theory", "the solunatic tables" and so on, while John Alden Knight, the originator, was labeled a nature faker, a charlatan, a swindler, and one who used the mails to defraud.

Gradually, however, sportsmen took the trouble to investigate its workings for themselves. To the surprise of many, the daily set schedule of activity periods and rest periods was found to exist, and their fishing was greatly improved through the intelligent use of this knowledge. As the years passed more and more people came to believe that *The Solunar Tables* would do for them exactly what was claimed—guide them to the best sport that each day of fishing had to offer.

To substantiate the solunar theory, insofar as fish are concerned, a systematic inquiry was instituted to acquire complete details surrounding the capture of record catches of fish. By "record catches" is meant both individual large fish and large numbers of fish. All reported record catches were investigated. Sometimes these details were easily secured; more often complete information could be obtained only after a great deal of correspondence.

Approximately two hundred of these catches were investigated. As had been suspected, more than ninety per cent of them were made during the dark of the moon (when the effects of the solunar periods seem to be of maximum intensity) and, more important, they were made during the actual times of the solunar periods.

Throughout the initial stages of the development of the solunar theory, only the behavior of fish was considered in working out the schedules from year to year. Of course, it was known that the "moon up-moon down" system was used by the market hunters as a guide to good hunting as well as good fishing. However, it seemed the wiser course to proceed slowly and not to make the matter too all-inclusive at the start. Thus, from 1935 to 1939, *The Solunar Tables* were offered simply as the "Forecast of Daily Feeding Times of Fresh- and Salt-Water Fish". During this time, however, intensive observations had been made of the relative behavior of game birds and animals. As had been suspected, these, too, responded to the prompting stimulus of the solunar periods as completely as did the fish.

Game birds, such as pheasants, grouse and quail, were observed to move into the feeding cover at the beginning of a solunar period and to stay there, filling their crops, for about two hours. At the close of the solunar period the birds returned to the safer protection of the swamps and briar patches, or in the case of grouse, to the hemlock groves. While the birds were feeding, they showed two decided characteristics. They seemed to display a pronounced lack of fear during the feeding periods; also, if disturbed, they were reluctant to leave the feeding cover and were content to hide, thereby rendering themselves available for dog work and the attendant good shooting.

Rabbits and squirrels showed the same tendencies. The former, like the birds, came out of hiding and made themselves available to the gunner in the open fields. The latter scampered about on the ground or among the limbs of the trees in search of food.

Having established this point, *The Solunar Tables* for 1940 were offered as the "Forecast of the daily feeding times of fish and game" and each subsequent annual publication has been thus labeled.

Observation of the behavior of song birds, squirrels, domestic animals, rodents, and even insects and plants indicated that all reacted as typically as did fish and upland game.

Of course, *The Solunar Tables* are of interest mainly to the fishermen and hunters of the world. Foreign editions are published in Canada, France, Holland, and Germany as of 1950.

Every fisherman knows that fish do not feed ravenously all the time. He knows also, that for some reason fish often go on the feed and take readily almost any offering, be it a live bait or an artificial lure. This sort of thing is apt to happen most any time of day. To be sure, fish usually feed actively at dawn and again at dusk, but generally the real fishing of the day is during the "odd-hour" feeding periods. If weather and water conditions are favorable the fish are active at these times for from one to three hours. These "odd-hour" feeding periods are what are now called solunar periods.

As is true of game, fish seem to lose much of their natural caution during solunar periods. They feed readily at the surface and have no hesitation in leaving the safety of the deeper water and cruising about in the shallows, thus exposing themselves to their natural enemies. Then surface baits are taken more readily than the underwater varieties.

It is not uncommon for bait fishermen, to complain that *The Solunar Tables* are useless and that more fish are caught between solunar periods than during the scheduled feeding times. While these criticisms are no doubt well-founded, the explanation is not difficult. Fish, particularly game fish, find most of their food in the shallows. When a feeding period arrives, game fish leave the deeper water and move into the feeding grounds. Bait fishermen, who almost always make it a point to anchor their boats in fairly deep water, actually are fishing in practically barren water during the solunar periods. Only after these periods draw to a close and the fish leave the shallows to return again to their resting stations, do the bait fishermen find a market for their wares in deep water. Naturally, they feel that *The Solunar Tables* are valueless.

While most of the field work was done in fresh water during the initial research in the development of the solunar theory, it does not follow that the usefulness of the information ends there. Salt-water fish respond as readily to the solunar periods as do their fresh-water cousins.

Today, the uses of the tables are many and varied. Commercially they have been put to the test and found satisfactory. Trappers, commercial fishermen, party-boat captains, professional guides for both hunting and fishing plan their days so that the solunar periods shall not be wasted. Professional biologists make use of the schedule in their field work. Bird lovers find that it pays to keep track of the solunar periods. Men, whose spare time is limited, use the tables when they plan to take a few hours off to go fishing or shooting. In addition, thousands of sportsmen have learned that it is wise to check up on the times of the solunar periods when planning their days in the open.

For best results, the *Solunar Tables* must be used intelligently. Sometimes they must even be used "in reverse", so to speak. Take crow shooting for example. The ideal time for this sport is in the winter months when the birds congregate in huge flocks and use a central roost each night. Then the ardent gunner can find pass shooting that is truly excellent.

Crows answer the solunar periods as readily as do other birds. They feed during the feeding periods, and they move into the resting cover when these periods are over. Normally they fly to the central roost during the final hour of daylight. If. however, there happens to be a solunar period in progress at that time, they will postpone their homeward flight until the last moment. Thus, the shooting, although fast and furious, probably will last only fifteen or twenty minutes before darkness puts an end to the day.

Conversely, if the day is stormy and if there is no solunar period in progress, the birds will come in early and the good shooting often will last for a matter of hours.

Of course, it must be remembered that every day does not show clean-cut reactions to the solunar periods. This is especially true in the case of fish. Barometric fluctuations, particularly when the trend is downward, often will ruin the fishing completely, solunar periods or no solunar periods. How fish manage to know what the barometer is doing is anybody's guess, but the fact remains that they do. For that matter, all wildlife knows what to expect on the part of the weather, and any bird, animal or fish can sense the approach of a storm well in advance of the information from sensitive instruments.

Adverse temperatures, abnormal water conditions, all sorts of things, will offset the effects of the solunar periods. However, every sportsman knows that it is beyond all reason to expect good fishing or good shooting every day. Such a Utopia did not exist before the introduction of the solunar theory, and there is no reason to expect that tables will alter that basic truth in any way. The solunar theory will point the way only to the best in sport that each day has to offer, but it is in no sense a guarantee of a full creel or a heavy game bag.

Another thing to remember is that the promptings of the solunar periods—"solunar influence" is a good term for it—seems to vary in intensity according to the position of the moon. The time of new moon—"the dark of the moon," when there is no moon in the sky—evidently is the time of maximum intensity. "South moon under," the market hunters used to call it, and that was the preferred time for them to plan for their best catches of fish and their best kills of game. As stated earlier, a very high percentage of the record catches of fish and most of the individual record fish are taken during the dark of the moon. Then the earth, the moon and the sun are approximately in line. Ocean tides reflect this intensity in their magnitude. This maximum intensity lasts for about three days, and wildlife responds with maximum activity. Thus, fishing or shooting generally is better at this time than at any other during the month.

Thereafter the degree of intensity of activity seems to taper off until it is at its minimum during the third quarter phase of the moon. Of course, weather and water conditions may alter this general rule. If conditions are good, excellent sport can be found during the solunar periods when solunar influence is at its minimum. Conversely, adverse conditions will result in indifferent sport when ordinarily the best should be expected. There are entirely too many variables involved to attempt to lay down hard and fast rules.

On two occasions the behavior of fish was observed during an eclipse of the sun. This being the time that the earth, the moon, and the sun are approximately in line, there is, of course, a solunar period in progress when the eclipse occurs. In each case the fish evinced a tremendous amount of activitiy, feeding ravenously and affording excellent fishing.

Intensity of activity also varies from day to day, according to conditions in general. If the barometer happens to be steady or rising, if the temperature arrangement is favorable, with air temperature about fifteen degrees higher than that of the water, then long and active response to a solunar period may be expected. If, however, the weather is cloudy, the barometer unsteady or falling, or the temperature arrangement of air and water abnormal, there may be no noticeable response to a solunar period so far as the sportsman is concerned. For that matter, conditions can and do change so completely in a matter of hours that a major solunar period will be of little value while a minor solunar period some six hours later may show excellent fishing. Generally, however, a change in the weather, be it for better or worse, is apt to be a deterrent to good fishing.

Another variant of the manner in which solunar influence affects living creatures is what might be termed "physical lag." As stated earlier, the scope of the solunar theory includes all living things. However, the order of development of the creature in question influences the speed of response. In other words, the higher the order of development, the slower the creature or organism is to feel the effects of the prompting stimulus, whatever that may be.

This may be seen quite easily by watching a pool of any good trout stream as a solunar period "comes in." In the interests of clearer visibility, it is better to select a day which is windless and sunny. Too much stress cannot be laid upon the importance of selecting the observation post well before the scheduled time of the solunar period, and then remaining there quietly so that the aquatic life will not be in any way disturbed.

When a position is taken, well in advanace of the scheduled solunar period, the pool will probably be quiet, with no dimples of feeding fish showing at the surface. As zero hour approaches, particular attention should be given to the stream bottom. Usually the first creatures to show signs of activity are the stream-bottom insects, the nymphs. These come out of hiding and crawl about over the rocks in shallow water in search of food. Crawfish and minnows materialize where none were before. Perhaps a hatch of May flies will develop in the riffle, and the fish will then rise to them, the small fish first and later, the larger ones.

If the day is fair, with weather and water conditions favorable, feeding and general activity sometimes will continue for a couple of hours. Then, gradually, the creatures discontinue feeding, having had their fill, and retire once more to the safety of their resting stations as the period draws to a close.

Meanwhile, on the banks and in the trees overhead, small animals and birds will have been moving about and the air has been filled with bird song.

The larger animals, such as dogs, deer, and domestic livestock, react more slowly than do the aquatic creatures. Last on the list come human beings. Their physical lag, built up by systematic dulling of the perceptions down through the centuries, requires as much as an hour or so of cumulative solunar influence to make itself felt. Thus, in setting up the annual *Solunar Tables,* allowance must be made for physical lag with the result that the published times of the solunar periods are, at best, only averages, designed to suit the response of the various creatures of interest mainly to the sportsmen.

As a matter of interest and curiosity, check the *Solunar Tables* by watching the behavior of your dog. He does his real sleeping during the inactivity periods. He may lie down during the solunar periods, but you will find him alert and ready for action at these times.

Some dog trainers have learned that they get far better results with their dogs in training if they follow the solunar schedule and take the dogs afield during the solunar periods. Not only are the dogs more keen and active, but they find more birds at these times.

During periods of inactivity, goldfish and tropical fish spend much of their time resting quietly near the bottoms of their aquaria. With the arrival of solunar periods, they become more active. Goldfish, in particular, rise to the surface and move about, "blowing bubbles." If goldfish and tropicals are fed at the beginning of solunar periods, little of the food will be wasted, and the aquaria will need cleaning less often.

Plants, in common with other living things, are more "alive" during solunar periods than at other times. The effects are most evident in the flowering plants. Careful counts have been taken, and it is quite well established that more buds will burst into full bloom during solunar periods than at other times. Horticulturists will find this phenomenon an absorbing study.

Should one wish to check personal reactions against the solunar schedule, do not look up the solunar times in advance. If the time is known behavior will be affected, subconsciously. Instead, keep track of reactions from time to time, and then check this record against the solunar times in the tables.

Sleep, being an unconscious reaction, is a good guide post to the extent of your susceptibility to solunar stimulus. Many people do not sleep well during solunar periods. If troubled in going to sleep, or staying asleep, check the experience against *The Solunar Tables* the following day. Often a tendency to stay awake during solunar periods is evident, particularly during the dark of the moon, when solunar stimulus is at its peak.

Evidence of solunar effects often is quite noticeable in groups of people—theater audiences, meetings, church services, large offices, and so on. Increased activity often is plainly evident when large gatherings are observed. With the arrival of a solunar period, a large group becomes more responsive; laughs more easily and applauds more readily.

There has been much conjecture as to the cause or causes which are responsible for the well-established reaction of wildlife to the urgings of the solunar periods. In view of the fact that the daily succession of activity periods, and rest periods among wildlife is in approximate rhythm with the movements of the tides, it was only natural that the tides should be considered as the possible explanation of the phenomenon. In due course, this was found to be an error, but not before mistakes were made which, in the long run, were bound to be obvious.

Having eliminated the tides themselves from the calculations, the next step was to investigate the gravitational pull of the moon and the sun which causes tidal action. Gradually, a new formula of calculation was evolved. While this came closer to the mark, this method was not perfect.

It must be remembered that this was an attempt to solve the riddle by working from known effects back to probable cause, always a difficult process. Then one day, quite by accident, some new evidence showed the problem in an entirely new light.

Present indications are that the solunar phenomenon is electronic in nature and that the moon and the sun function merely as catalyzers instead of principals. There is not space here to go into the ramifications of this newer conception. In addition, the information in a work of this sort should be exactly that—information, not conjecture.

At present it is known that there is a daily fixed cycle of alternate activity periods and rest periods, and that all living things, whether they realize it or not, pattern their behavior to some extent to conform to this cycle. This cycle is in approximate rhythm with the moon and the sun. It manifests itself in many and various ways—not now and then, but *always*. One trained in the observance of the effects of the cycle invariably can point to clear evidence of the presence of these manifestations. After all, a natural law, to qualify as such, must function invariably, not once in a while, and the solunar theory is exactly that, a new natural law.

The present method used for the calculation of the forecast of the daily times of the activity periods of this cycle—the solunar periods—will produce a set of tables that is surprisingly close to the true schedule as shown us by the behavior of wildlife itself. Many uncontrollable factors, of which weather and water conditions are outstanding, can, and do bend or retard this cycle temporarily, but basically the cycle is as fixed as those of the moon, the sun and the earth. There exact information ends.

If a fisherman or a hunter will take the trouble to keep account of the daily solunar periods and plan his days in the open so that these times of probable activity will not be wasted, his foresight in so doing will pay him big dividends in sport during the course of a year.

Part 3. Salt Water Methods

BOTTOM FISHING

Bottom fishing is practiced by more anglers than any other salt-water fishing sport. There are several reasons for its popularity, the main ones being first, that more kinds of fishes will take a bait on or near the bottom, and second, it is a comparatively simple method of angling that can be pursued almost anywhere at little cost.

Bottom fishing is accomplished mainly from piers, docks, sea walls, jetties, causeways, bridges, and small boats. Nearly every salt-water angler has indulged in this form of fishing at one time or another, especially if, as a child, the angler resided near or visited localities where salt-water fishing was available.

In its simplest form, bottom fishing requires little tackle. A line, a hook, and a sinker suffices. Such rigs can readily be prepared by the angler, or can be purchased for a small sum at the nearest store handling fishing tackle. If the rig is already made up, it is known as a "made line."

The majority of these "made lines" consist of 50 feet of green line, a two-ounce kedge sinker, and a 1/0 hook, wrapped neatly on a wooden frame. For a slight additional cost, the angler can obtain a "made line" that includes a cork or balsa wood float. While the float is not absolutely necessary, it is handy and worth while.

These rigs can be made into better fish attracters by adding a short length of leader wire between the hook and the line. If the fish sought possess teeth, the addition of the wire leader will save many that might otherwise get away by cutting the line. If the fish are not of the toothy varieties, a Nylon gut leader is an even better camouflage than the steel wire.

The chief reason for using a leader is that fish can see a line more easily than the leader, and many are wary enough to refuse a bait with a line plainly in view. Some bottom fishermen scoff at this, but it definitely has been proved in many tests that drop lines equipped with leaders will catch fish in localities where lines not so equipped will not.

One of the recent innovations in bottom fishing is the use of monofilament line. This, in a mist color, is practically invisible in water and great claims are made for it. It apparently completely fools the fish and that even the most wary individuals show no hesitation in picking up a bait when this line is employed.

It has been proved also that certain other artifices may be employed to take bottom feeders. For instance, in Florida, anglers bottom fishing for various kinds of snapper frequently use a crawfish feeler to fool the fish. This feeler, usually from 12 to 14 inches in length, is slipped over the leader just above the hook.

The supposition is that the snapper, seeing the feeler with a piece of bait protruding from it, figure that a live crawfish has lost the appendage. Without hesitation, they take the bait and are hooked. The feeler, incidentally, is prepared by letting the little meat it contains rot out. This leaves a hollow tube that is easily slipped over the leader.

Another dodge frequently employed is to drop several pieces of bait into the water at the same time the baited hook is let down. The idea of chumming the water in this manner is two-fold. It attracts more fish and, also, the fish get excited at the presence of so much food and tend to lose their natural wariness.

The generally accepted meaning of the term "bottom fishing" is fishing for the smaller salt-water fishes with line, sinker and hook, on or near the bottom. However, fishing for these fishes on or near the bottom also can be, and frequently is, accomplished through the use of rod and reel. As a matter of fact, many large fishes, such as shark, Warsaw Grouper, Halibut, Jewfish, and others, usually are caught bottom fishing with rod and reel. Likewise, it is one of the accepted methods of fishing for giant Blue Marlin.

One of the former presidents of Cuba expressed the opinion that anglers who used rods and reels in bottom fishing were sissies. He maintained that a man should be stout enough to hold, play, and land any average fish on a plain line and hook, and he used to prove the truth of the assertion by hooking, fighting, and landing fish that weighed in excess of 100 pounds in that manner.

The majority of bottom fishing, however, is for the smaller fishes, and most of it is practiced in bays, inlets, and other inland salt waters. There are two kinds of bottom fishermen. One type is the casual angler who fishes infrequently, dropping his bait into almost any kind of water and hoping he will be lucky enough to catch a fish or two.

The other type is one who specializes in this method of fishing and who carefully studies various localities, fishing conditions, the phases of the moon, the tides, the various kinds of bottom, the prevalence of bait fishes, and other natural fish foods. This type is generally more successful in his "take" due to his application of his observations.

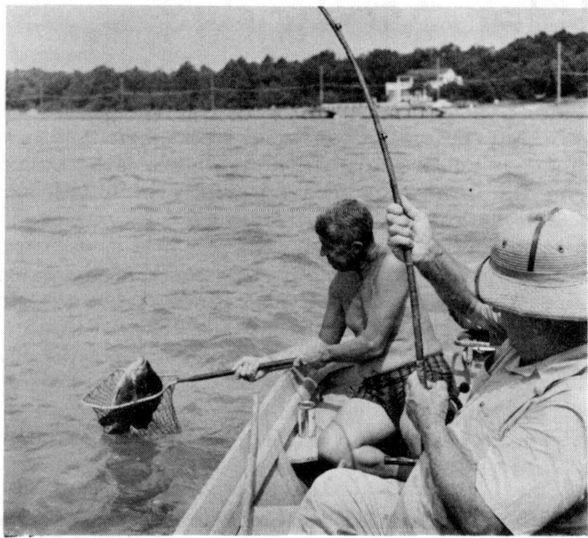

Paul Kalman

Boating a Tripletail near the seawall at Waveland, Mississippi.

In bottom fishing it pays to know the habits of the fish as certain kinds will grab a bait and run with it, others will take it quietly and with little commotion, while still others will nibble at it nervously and warily. In fishing for the first kind, almost anyone can make a goodly catch. With the other two kinds the expert will take fish while the non-expert will lose ten baits to catch one fish.

In many cases, it is better to keep the bait a foot or so above the bottom. This is particularly true when the majority of the fish are of the nibbling variety. Thus, the delicate nibbling can be more easily felt by the angler, as the fish is forced to jerk the bait slightly to obtain any part of it; and with the bait suspended in the water the jerk is more readily discerned than when the leader, hook, and sinker are resting on the bottom.

It is natural for the angler to jerk back on the line when the nibble is felt. However, this is the wrong technique to use with the majority of the nibblers. The strike should not be made until the angler definitely feels the fish moving away with the bait. Some anglers cannot overcome the tendency to strike immediately and, if this is the case, it is better to place a float on the line.

Naturally, the float should be so fastened to the line as to allow the bait to reach within a foot or so of the bottom. The angler can see the float and can watch its bobbing up and down as the fish nibbles at the bait. When the float starts to move away, the time to hook the fish is at hand and that is the time to jerk back smartly and hook the nibbler.

Sometimes there will be many small fish around a bait. These fish, too small for sport or for the pan, can consume a bait in quick order and as each takes a little bite, the size of the bait is reduced rapidly. However, the presence of little fishes usually indicates the presence of larger fishes.

The larger fishes are much more wary than the smaller ones and they swim close to the bait, seemingly watching to see what happens to the smaller fishes. If one of the smaller fishes is hooked, the larger ones will not take the bait as a usual rule. If, however, the big fish see that the smaller fishes are getting a meal without coming to any harm, they will move in and take the bait.

At such times it is well to let the smaller fishes eat bait, replacing it as needed. The larger the bait, within reason of course, the more attractive it is to the larger fishes, thus the saying, "the bigger the bait, the bigger the fish." This is not always true, for it is quite possible to take fair-sized fishes on a small bait and small fish on large bait.

For the best results in bottom fishing it usually is good practice to use live bait, such as shrimp, small crabs, sand fleas, minnows, or other small bait fishes. Considerable care should be taken in placing such baits on the hook so that they may live and present a lively appearance as long as possible.

In hooking a live shrimp the hook should be thrust through the shell just forward of the point at which the tail joins the body. It should be hooked from the underside with the point of hook protruding above the back. A little mercurochrome, about six drops to the gallon of water, will keep the shrimp alive longer in the bait bucket and at the same time make them livelier.

Crabs should be hooked at either end of the top shell, where the shell ends in a point. In that triangle the shell is harder than most other parts and, also the flesh of the crab usually does not extend all the way to the point. Most anglers remove either one or both claws from the crab before using it as a live bait. This, they reason, is practically inviting the fish to an easy meal.

Sand fleas are a small, white crustacean, that come in with the waves on some of the southern beaches, immediately burying themselves in the sand as the wave recedes. They are an excellent bait for Pompano and Bonefish, and most other fishes will take them willingly. They should be hooked at the tail end through the shell, but they do not remain alive long regardless of how they are hooked.

Minnows and other bait fishes should be hooked at the hump in the back, a short distance back of the head. A study of the bone structure of these bait fishes will enable the angler to learn the best way to hook them so that the hook will remain firmly imbedded through the fish without undue irritation or injury to a vital portion of the body.

Worms should be hooked through the tail, the middle portion of the body and just back of the head. Care should be taken to leave enough of the head and tail end to allow the worm to wiggle and thus present a more natural appearance. Thrice hooked, worms will remain firmly attached yet live a considerable length of time. In many areas they are an excellent bait.

Dead shrimp, minnows, and other bait fishes can be used whole, hooked in the same manner as when alive. However, the majority of anglers using dead shrimp remove the head and the shell, employing only the body meat as a bait. The flesh of lobsters and their cousins, the southern spiny lobsters or crawfish, is used in the same manner.

In preparing cut bait from fishes, the fish are scaled and filleted. The less bones in the fish flesh, the better. The fillets should be cut into strips

Erl Roman

Two nice Mangrove Snapper comprise this angler's catch.

about one-half inch wide and two or more inches in length. The point of the hook is thrust through one end of the strip, which is then doubled back and again pierced by the hook. This method of hooking hides the hook quite well and leaves an inch or more of tempting bait protruding.

Squid, when used as bait in bottom fishing, is cut into strips and attached to the hook in the same manner as fish flesh. Clams are used by anglers in some localities and make a fine bait. Oysters also are regarded as good bait. However, they are soft and do not remain on the hook very well. In Alaska, Washington, Oregon, and the northern portion of California, salmon eggs singly and in clusters are used in bottom fishing with excellent results.

Strip baits prepared from fish flesh, and the flesh of shrimp, lobsters, and crawfish, can be hardened and kept indefinitely by placing it in jars and adding a level tablespoon full of powdered borax to each pint-sized jar. Baits prepared in this manner should be tightly sealed and kept in a cool place. It is an excellent way to prepare shrimps, lobster, and crawfish especially. The hardened flesh remains on the hook better.

Drop lines for bottom fishing can be of almost any reasonable size and length, but it is always better to use the lightest line possible consistent with the weight and fighting abilities of the fishes to be caught. Leaders should be light also, and it is well to use them of sufficient length, say from two to five feet. Lines may be of any material, although most anglers prefer twisted linen as it does not lose strength by being immersed in salt water over long periods. Twisted Nylon also is good and is gaining many adherents.

It is good practice to take care of lines. Although salt water does not harm either Nylon or linen, they should be washed or rinsed in fresh water and dried on a line dryer in the shade. Exposure to the sun will ruin a linen line in time. They should never be dried in the sun. Keep them wet while in use, then dry in the shade. In use, the end of the line near the leader will become worn, and it is well to check frequently in this connection. If the line is worn or nicked, cut that portion off.

While the majority of "made lines" are furnished with kedge sinkers, these are of little value where the bottom is rocky, grassy, or strewn with debris such as sunken pilings, sunken ships, etc. The kedge sinkers tend to become tangled or wedged in the rocks, grass and other obstructions, thus allowing the hooked fish to pull free and usually causing the angler to lose not only the fish but also the hook and leader.

Two better sinkers when fishing under such conditions are the egg sinker and the almond sinker. These derive their names from their shapes. The egg sinker is somewhat egg shaped, only more nearly eliptical. The almond sinker is shaped somewhat similar to the almond nut. Both have a hole running longitudinally through the center. In rigging for bottom fishing with either sinker, the line is run through this hole just above the leader.

The egg and almond sinkers not only do not tend to become tangled or wedged in the rocks or other obstructions, but when the fish bites at the bait the action is felt more quickly and distinctly by the angler. This, of course, is not true if the angler is fishing above and not on the bottom. The kedge sinker, when used, is fastened to an extra loop of line just above the leader usually. However, some anglers place it at the end of the line, fastening the leader about 10 inches back of the sinker.

In bottom fishing, as in all fishing, good results depend largely on the presence of numbers of fish in the waters fished. There is an old saying that

Erl Roman

Bottom fishermen glory in their chosen sport. This one displays some Grouper and Snapper.

"you have to keep your bait in the water if you expect to catch fish." It is likewise true that fish must be present in the water fished if fish are to be caught. Some waters are barren, while others have goodly fish populations. The angler who knows where the fish are is more apt to make the best catches.

In this connection, it is well to remember that fish usually congregate where food and shelter are readily available. The great majority of fish frequent rocky or grassy areas, and they also can be found around submerged wrecks, old pilings, piers, jetties, and seawalls. Infinite numbers and varieties of minute marine life attach themselves to rocks, grasses, and other bottom obstructions; and these attract small fish, crabs, etc.

This, as readily can be imagined, provides a convenient sort of marine cafeteria for the larger fishes, which, of course, attract still larger fishes. They find both food and shelter from their enemies in such places, and by getting behind a rock they can find a little rest from the otherwise ceaseless battle of swimming against the tides and other water currents.

The best way to locate such places is to obtain a map of the bottoms to be fished. These maps, made up and printed by the Federal government, are obtainable at practically all marine hardware establishments at a small price. On them is indicated the depths of the water and the type of bottom, such as rocky, grassy, sandy, and muddy. The locations of submerged wrecks and other obstructions to navigation are clearly marked.

If it is inconvenient to secure one of these maps, the next best bet is to consult the bait man nearest to the area to be fished. These men usually keep quite well informed on the fishing in their immediate neighborhoods and are willing to share this information with their customers. In fact, it benefits their business to keep such information on hand at all times, as it puts them in a good position to give out fishing tips that apply to the area in which they are located.

SALT WATER BAITS

Salt water baits, used largely in still fishing, are almost entirely natural foods or imitations thereof. The number of baits used locally is almost innumerable, but there are a more limited number widely used. Some are used as cut baits, other entire. The following discussion covers only the most important and widely used items. It also provides information on the manner of preparing, placing on the hook, and handling the baits.

CLAM (SOFT SHELL)

This is the ordinary clam, the kind over which we humans ooh and aah when they're steamed, baked or fried—and of course, there's clam chowder too. But oddly enough most all the salt-water fish also smack their lips over this particular shellfish.

This is a bait which one can easily dig but be sure to know the local laws. Most east coast towns which have shellfish beds within their environs require a shellfish license (it may be as low as twenty-five cents a year), have a minimum length limit and also a limit on the amount to be taken; in some places one has to be a resident of the town. If able to dig, use a short-handled clam hoe (from any local hardware store). Clams prefer gravelly spots and they have holes which run about six inches down, where they live. In fact, if one walks close to a clam hole he's apt to see a squirt of water shoot up. Dig rather gently unless only bait is wanted as the clam will not live long if the shell is broken. Low tide is the time to dig.

The best part of the clam for bait is the hard snout and the rim which runs around the stomach; the latter is so soft that it will not stay on the hook even when lowered into the water gently.

Maybe there's a salt-water fish which won't take the clam but it is yet to be found. Chaughshead or Cunners, Tautog, Striped Bass, Eels, Mackerel, Scup, or Porgies—in fact, any fish that lives near the bottom will take this bait. Great for Tommycod too; and a natural for Founders and Rock Bass.

Those with neither time nor inclination to dig them can usually find them for sale near their home haunts on the tidal fronts at about two bits per quart.

CLAM (HARD SHELL)

Usually called quahog, known more generally as a restaurant delicacy under the name of Cherrystone and Little Neck. These are much rounder and have harder shells than the common clam. Also they are found just under the surface of the sand or mud flats; easy and fun to find for bait (or for the table). Low tide is best.

One needs a special quahog knife or one with a fairly stiff thin blade to open these clams. Look carefully and it will be seen that they have a wider opening at one end of their curved front. Place the big part of the quahog against the heel of the left hand; place the edge of the blade of the knife gently in the edge of the wider side of the clam; fold the fingers of the hand holding the clam over the back edge of the knife and press firmly to wedge the shell apart; as it opens slide the point of the knife upward under the top side of the shell; cut the muscles at both ends of the clam; twist off the top shell; drop it overside as an attractor to any fish below; scoop out the meat of the clam. Insert the hook through the hard part of the quahog—twice, if a big clam.

Great bait for all bottom fish including Haddock, Hake, Cod, Tautog, Cunners, Rock Bass. Also for Striped Bass. In fact, most any fish will take this bait if still fishing. After a nibble or two, it's well to look to see if the quahog is still on the hook as this is a soft bait.

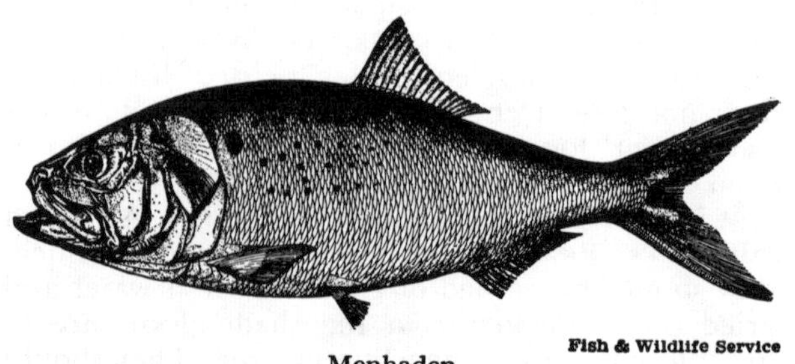

Menhaden. Fish & Wildlife Service

Fish & Wildlife Service

American Smelt or Icefish.

If one can't open quahogs easily with a knife, hit them with a hammer!

Like the soft shell clam, this is a bait that can be taken home to eat if no fish are caught.

SEA, BLOOD, AND CLAM WORMS

These worms are found in the mud flats and can be dug or bought at local bait dealers. Check local laws.

This is really an all-round bait. An inch or so on a #10 hook is tops for smelt; a similar amount on a small hook (#6 or #8) is just as good for flats or small Flounders; a whole one hooked through the head, just behind the pincers (on blood-worms, the many-legged ones) and on a hook behind a spinner, or even without a spinner is an excellent trolling bait for Striped Bass, Weakfish, Scup or Porgies; threaded on a hook they're the best for Porgies when still-fishing, for Tautog, Cunners, Rock Bass. Go back to small hooks again and they're okay for Tommycod. Offshore a big hook, (10/0), with a big worm threaded on, will take Haddock, Hake, Eels, Codfish, Halibut, and Fluke. In fact, few fish which will refuse them. Thousands of dollars worth are shipped southward from Maine each year.

For trolling, hook them through the head. Sometimes two worms will take fish when one won't. For still fishing, they had best be threaded. Hard to loop if a hook is put through them about halfway from head (big end) to tail, they're so brittle that they'll break off. Use a second hook trailing about five inches behind the head hook.

Keep them in rockweed in a shoe box and where it's cool. The family icebox is a fine place if the women-folk don't catch on.

SQUID

Squid is available from most bait dealers along the North Atlantic. Look like a small octopus and vary from six inches in length to over a foot. If up early one may find them at the edge of the beach or on the tidal flats—that is, before the gulls get there. Winter squid are a pale flesh color and the larger; summer squid are smaller, a spotted, golden brown when fresh—and probably the better bait of the two species.

The use of squid depends upon the type of fish sought. If it's Bass (striped), use a whole squid and let it lay on the bottom weighed down with a sinker (pyramid, if sandy); or fishing the same way, some anglers claim that just the head is a better bait. This same method will take other bottom feeders like Codfish, or even an occasional Weakfish or Bluefish.

If trolling, hook them with the tail toward the eye of the hook and they're wonderful for anything that will take a trolled bait from Tuna on down to Blues, Weaks, or Bass.

Used as a cut bait, depending on the size of the fish, they're good for most anything that swims.

Another good use is in thin strips (half an inch wide and three or four inches long) hooked on a feather jig or barracuda, on a bare hook behind a spinner, or even on the tail hook of a top-water plug to give extra wiggle and attraction.

This bait is cheap and in the areas where is it plentiful a ten-quart bucket full can be secured for a small sum. In view of this, it can be used as chum. If still-fishing from a boat, drop cut pieces overboard occasionally; if in a tidal current, do likewise. If surf-fishing, cut in inch-long pieces and throw out into the surf as far as possible. This latter practice has brought Striped Bass more than once; as proven by looking in the stomach of the fish caught and finding some of the cut pieces.

If tuna-fishing offshore, one might have as much as a barrel, or even two, of squid along just to use as chum; that is, to drop one or two of them overboard every few minutes to bring the big fish near the boat looking for more and especially—as far as the angler is concerned—for the squid on that big 12/0 hook.

Squid have to be kept cold or they'll spoil quickly. If on very good terms with the wife, freeze some in the ice trays of the electric refrigerator or in the deep freeze.

HERRING

One of the most plentiful bait fish in the Atlantic and Pacific Oceans; also one of the most sought-after natural foods by all salt-water game fish from Tuna to Striped Bass or almost any other fish which has a mouth big enough to take them whole and alive, or cut in pieces. Used as bait from the three-inch size (often called sardines) up to their full maturity of twelve or fourteen inches.

If off Bald Island in Soldiers Rip at Wedgeport, Nova Scotia, world-famous Tuna grounds and former scene of the International Tuna Matches each year; if fishing Tuna in Casco Bay from Bailey's Island, Maine; or if offshore of Ipswich Bay or Provincetown, Mass., there is apt to be a whole herring on the big tuna hook. It may be hooked through the back for still fishing; or it may be sewn on the hook with the point coming out of the vent and pointed down and the mouth sewn up to make the bait troll with a natural wiggle. And beside the one on the hook, there may be two or three barrels of herring to be cut or dropped overboard whole as chum.

Or one may be fishing Striped Bass and letting a whole herring, hooked just under the dorsal fin, drift in the tide; or it may be half a herring rolling around in the surf or on the bottom for the same fish; or just a chunk for Pollock, Cod or Haddock. Or one may have filleted the Herring and might be using one side of the fish as a trolling bait for surface feeders. Any way it's used, it's great bait.

Fish & Wildlife Service

Common Herring.

It also is great chum for Bluefish, using a big meat grinder and dropping the chewed up result overside to create a slick and chum line. For this, a strong stomach is needed, especially if out where the waves roll high.

MULLET

Most common from Jersey to South America, usually about one foot long and a popular natural food for most game fish. Also called Striped Mullet. A school-fish taken usually in nets and seines; especially common in Florida waters. Used as cut bait for Channel Bass; drifted whole for Tarpon; most commonly trolled as a strip bait where each side of the fish is sliced off lengthwise next to the backbone—commonly called filleting—and placed on the hook so that it flutters through the water looking like a small, live fish.

To make a strip-bait of this sort really lifelike, it has to go through the water without looping or doubling which will make it spin. To get this straight, swimming action, use a small bit of copper wire passed through the eye of the hook and with one end long enough, to make a twist around the leader wire which is attached to the hook. Lay the big end of the cut or strip-bait along the hook shank so that the front (big) end is even with the eye; then pierce this end of the bait with the copper wire and fasten firmly by making a twist or two around the leader wire; before this has been done, the barb of the hook has been passed through the bait in such a way that the strip lies flat along the shank. Good for most any fish that will take a trolled bait, be it Channel Bass, big Weaks, Amberjack, Bonita, Pollock, Grouper, Kingfish, Spanish Mackerel, Tarpon, etc.

This bait-fish also common along the Pacific Coast, south from Monterey, California.

The Mullet really takes the place of the Herring in our more southern waters.

EEL

Here is a bait which has not yet been fully appreciated nor used generally. Commonly known as a killer on Striped Bass and Blues, either whole when rigged with hooks fore and aft, or by using the skins over hollow-headed eel-skin rigs both for trolling (light) or casting (heavy).

Big Weakfish, Pollock, school Tuna, and even ambitious Codfish are taken on whole eels or eel skin rigs. Eels have a tough hide that will withstand even the sharp teeth of Bluefish; they are a natural resident of the entire Atlantic coast and they have a wriggling, enticing motion when reeled or trolled through the water that is irresistible.

Small eels, eight to ten inches long, can be hooked through the back or the lips and fished as live bait—especially on bottoms that are sandy or muddy—and are found good for Striped Bass, Blues or Weakfish.

Eel skins come in jars, packed in salt or brine and will last indefinitely if the screw top is kept tight. Eels can be caught at night using #6 long-shank hooks. (Eels will swallow a bait and the long shanks are easier to unhook.) They should be baited with small minnows or worms (sea or garden). Or if one knows where to look in the muddy tidal creeks, they can be speared. If the whole eel is not wanted for bait, skin them out; keep the skins for bait and eat the flesh. For cooking, cut the eel in three-inch lengths, roll in flour or cracker crumbs and fry in hot fat to a golden brown. They're a dish fit for a king.

In pulling and fixing an eel-skin over a rig, which is obtainable at local dealers, be sure that there are no loose folds between the point at which the forward part of the eelskin (inside out, incidentally) is tied on the head of the rig and that part where the hook pierces the skin. Such a fold will make the eel-skin run through the water in a whirling fashion when it should ride smoothly. Jerk the rod now and then while trolling or retrieving to give a wounded, darting action. Troll fairly fast unless the head of the rig is a very light

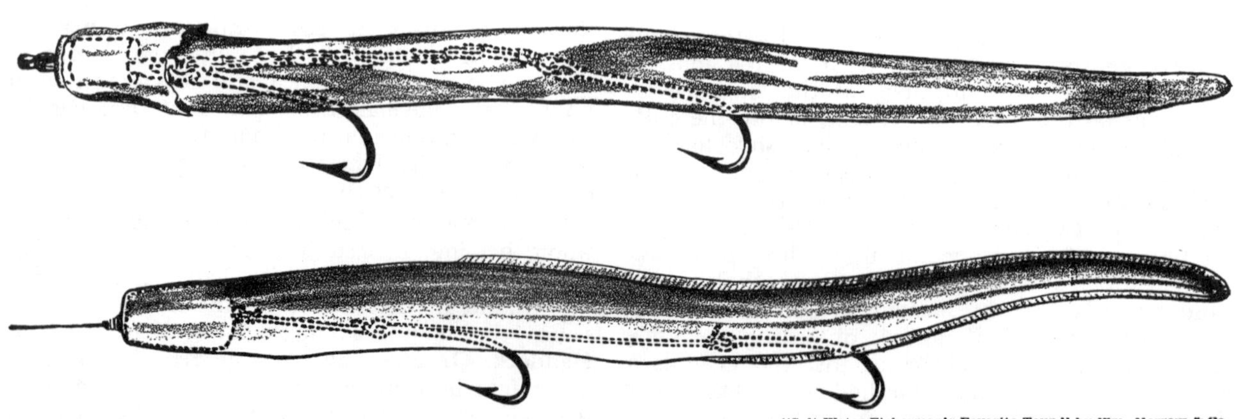

"Salt Water Fisherman's Favorite Tour," by Wm. Morrow & Co.

Eelskin rig.

one, in which case an eel-skin two feet long can be trolled very slowly—a popular method at Cuttyhunk for Stripers.

There's room for experimenting with whole eels and their skins in many waters of both the Pacific and the Atlantic. If local dealers do not have these lures, write to most any sporting goods dealer in New England where this is a standard and proven lure.

SAND EELS

The correct name is the Sand Launce. A small three-to seven-inch fish which looks like an eel and burrows into the sand when frightened or hiding from its natural enemies. Travels (and netted or seined) in schools. Good bait when cut or used whole for all bottom fishing; also for game fish such as Weaks, Mackerel, Blues, Pollock, Striped Bass when used as bait behind a smooth-running spinner, such as the June Bug or Northern (shaped like a willow leaf).

Common to more northern waters, south only to Cape Cod, Mass.

CRABS

There are so many different kinds of crabs—approximately one thousand in all—that they must be grouped together. Some of the more common ones used as bait are Green Crabs, Fiddlers, Paddlers, Hermit, Rock, and Blue—the latter being the one commonly considered such a delicacy and when soft-shelled and cooked whole are served at fancy prices in restaurants.

The section of coast being fished will determine the kind of crab used for bait. Any of the larger crabs from the size of a hand down to the silver-dollar sized ones are good when cut up for all bottom fish. Turn the crab upside down, breaking his claws off first for insurance against a hard and painful nip. With the crabs legs to the left and right sides, cut in half directly and horizontally from top to bottom; if the crab is a big one, cut again, this time from left to right in the middle of each half as it lies after your first cut. The crab is now in quarters, with some legs on each piece.

Then hook on by inserting the barb between the legs of the cut pieces and out again; this leg section is the toughest part of the crab insuring the hook holding against nibbles of smaller fish. If the crabs are the size of a two-bit piece, then put on whole, again running the hook through between the legs and out again through either the back or under sides.

If using Fiddler Crabs, found in temperate or tropical climates, put them on whole, again inserting the hook between the legs and out the front or back. Great bait for Rock Bass, Tautog, big Porgies, Cunners, and other bottom feeders. Virginia hooks are especially good with this bait and in sizes from #2 to #4. These crabs can be dug out of their holes between the high and low tide mark in sandy or marshy areas. On the low tides they'll gather in great crowds on the mud flats in open marshy spots, especially on sunny days. One has to grab fast to catch them as they can reverse their direction with the agility of an All-American half-back with first down and goal to go.

Green Crabs are found along the rocky shorelines of bays and inlets, in tidal rivers, and marshy creeks. Use an old fish head for bait or several of them scattered along the shore and they will appear out of nowhere. Dip them up in a crab or landing net—almost as much fun as fishing. This fish-head bait is good also for catching other crabs. Or get them at local bait dealers along the seacoast.

Shedder Crabs are crabs in the state of changing or shedding their shells, at which time the shells are soft. Especially desirable for bait then for Channel Bass, Stripers, Tautog. Hard to keep on the hook and must be handled gently.

SHRIMP

To the northern fishermen this word "shrimp" refers automatically to the small inch to inch-and-a-half long (big as a pencil) ones which are known as Grass, Harbor or "Pin" Shrimp. To the southerner it means the big jumbo shrimp, big as your middle finger and commonly found fresh in the fish market or canned at the local grocer—a table delicacy either way.

Looking at the two, one would think that while they belonged to the same family they must be two different species; but good authority holds them to be one and the same "animal."

While the Grass Shrimp has been discussed for fresh water fishing and its efficacy as an all-round fresh water bait pointed out, it is only fair to give him the same rousing send-off as a salt-water bait too. In fact, if one devoted a lifetime to finding out what fish would and what fish wouldn't take the Shrimp when properly presented, a good guess would be that the score would be 100% in the affirmative, that not a single species would refuse this bait. Off hand one might think that a fifteen pound Striped Bass would not bother with a shrimp no longer than an inch and a half, but Bass that big have been caught with them in their stomachs. Big Weakfish, able to take in a six-inch fish will follow a chum line of shrimp dribbled out of your boat in the running tide and nip them off one at a time with apparent relish; dropped to the bottom the Grass Shrimp, or cut pieces of the jumbos, make a top-taker for most all bottom fish from Cunners in New England waters to Snappers in Florida. If one on a hook doesn't do the trick, run the hook through the middle of three or four.

In Florida and other southern waters of the Gulf it would be almost impossible to name the various fish that will take either whole or cut pieces of jumbo Shrimp which are apparently as much of a delicacy to fish as they are to men, the only difference being that fish like them raw.

SARDINES

On the Atlantic coast these fish are small (three-to four-inch) herring. The true sardine of the Pacific, the Pilchard (common from California to British Columbia), yields the largest volume of canned fish produced in the United States. It is also widely used on both coasts as bait.

SURF FISHING

Surf fishing immediately connotes high, rolling seas breaking on and over a rocky promontory, foaming across the offshore bars and onto the sandy beaches toward a man armed with a thirty-inch butt, topped with a six- to seven-foot tip to form a complete and powerful casting rod capable of hurling a three- to four-ounce lure eighty to one hundred yards offshore. The reel is a free spool, star-drag affair holding at least two hundred yards of cuttyhunk (linen) or Nylon (braided) line. But surf casting has come to mean more than that. It now includes not only casting artificial or fresh bait lures into the open ocean or in the bays where there are waves breaking on a beach, but also casting from a boat. Those on shore cast out as far as their tackle and strength will allow; those in boats cast in as far toward the beach or rocky shoreline as they can and dare, with much depending on the ability of the boatman to handle his craft in white water, his knowledge of the rocks jutting up from the bottom, and the set or run of the tide. This isn't as foolish as it sounds, as both beach and boat fishermen are working the inshore waters where surf fish live.

The surf area of a beach or shoreline extends from the lap of the high tide out beyond the longest cast. Long casts are not always necessary; in fact, they can be a waste of energy and time if the fish are close inshore. When a wave washes up the beach and recedes under the break of the succeeding wave, it creates a trough or quick drop-off which is a constant boiling spot where the sand and anything in it (crabs, shellfish, sand fleas, small bait fish) is churned up. So don't be surprised when surf fishing to find that big fish—up to forty or more pounds—may wander in close to the beach. Many a time Bluefish or Stripers take lures as they come through the wave nearest to the dry beach.

At other times and places long casts are necessary. When there is little or no wind and the sea is flat as a millpond, the fish are apt to move offshore. High surf and onshore winds drive in the small bait fish and the game fish follow. In calm water, these bait fish move offshore and the fish again follow. Just how brainy a fish may be has yet to be determined by the ichthyologists, but they certainly have enough sense to follow their food supply. This does not mean that fishing is best during a high onshore wind, such as a stiff easterly on the Atlantic outer beaches; but it does often mean that some fish will be taken then and as the easterly subsides. In surf casting those able to cast a fairly long line (seventy to eighty yards) have a greater chance to take fish under more variable conditions. The man who can average one hundred yards is "hot stuff."

But before considering when and how to take fish from the surf, let's have a look at the kinds of fish involved. The *Salt Water Sportsman,* the only magazine devoted entirely to the sport of salt-water fishing, once made a survey to determine the preferences of twenty thousand Atlantic Coast readers. These men represented a good cross-section of anglers interested in all kinds of salt-water fishing with rod and reel, from the lowly bottom-feeding Flounder up to the giant Tuna. This survey disclosed the following:

Prefer to fish for:	*1st*	*2nd*	*3rd*	*total mention*
Striped Bass	232	39	9	280
Weakfish	51	84	14	149
Flounders	17	5	4	26
Fluke	15	15	0	30
Bluefish	13	39	5	57
Fresh Water Trout	9	13	3	25
Channel Bass	8	2	3	13
Tuna	7	12	3	22
Kings	7	6	1	14
Tautog	7	14	2	23
Mackerel	6	21	2	29
Cod	6	4	0	10
Salmon	5	5	2	12
Croakers	5	4	1	10
Fresh Water Bass	4	20	5	29
Any and all and seasonal	4	2	0	6

The following were mentioned also but not frequently enough to quote figures: Sailfish, Sea Bass, Cobia, Lake Trout, Pollock, Tarpon, Panfish, Bonefish, Porgy, Swordfish, Scup, Bonita, Marlin, Haddock, and miscellaneous fresh water fish.

This section is concerned with the methods used in surf casting, where to look for fish, the tides to work, and the over-all technique, but it is also well to know what fish might be caught. Surf casting is an inclusive term and is a method of fishing used wherever there is a beach or shoreline of any character facing the ocean or open sea.

If there is one logical starting point in telling how to surf cast, it is by warning that one should not start out with the idea that his first cast will break the world's record or reach the coast of England, Hawaii, or South America, whichever is directly ahead. The first cast should be a short one to wet down the line. A bit more energy can go into the next one, if the first cast goes well. Increase the effort with each succeeding cast until distance is secured without too much effort. It is well to emphasize that surf casting, especially with an artificial lure is an hour-after-hour performance which requires a lot of energy. Many short casts will often bring in more fish than a lesser number of long, back-straining ones. The latter soon wears

Martha's Vineyard Steamship Line

Surf fishing.

the caster down and the fish may decide to bite while the angler is resting.

To begin with, surf casting is not an easy sport. To an ardent follower of this type of fishing, no hour is too early or too late; even the slipperiest of rocks offer no obstacle in the daylight or dark as many surf fishes are night biters. The only time fish are caught is when the lure is in the water, so the wise angler starts easily and keeps at it for as many hours as are at his disposal. Perseverance pays off here.

MAKING THE CAST

There are dozens of schools of thought on how to cast but most agree on the basic principles. The first important point is the position of the feet. As with a good hitter in baseball or a good golfer, the proper position of the feet places the body in such a position where the natural actions of the muscles are most efficient. If Babe Ruth were digging in for a lusty swing at a fast-coming baseball, he'd have his feet in the right spots: left foot parallel with the front side of home plate; right foot directly behind, so that the left shoulder is pointed at the pitcher and the right shoulder—we're batting right-handed now—directly behind. This is exactly the foot and body position of the surf caster: only the left foot is parallel with the edge of the beach, left shoulder pointed toward the offshore spot at which the lure is aimed. Try this in the living room; get the swivel feeling that exists in the waist. When making a cast, a follow-through is needed: the pressure of making the cast is on the left foot; the right foot and leg are pulled by the momentum of the cast; the right foot comes forward, directly (or nearly so) in front of the left foot, and takes the weight of the body as the cast ends. If this sounds complicated, drop this volume and try it out. This is a graphic way of telling that the cast is not made by the wrists, the arms, or even the shoulders, but by the coordination of all of those plus the whole weight of the body from the toes up. These motions made slowly will demonstrate that all the body muscles are utilized. No. It's not complicated; it's easy. And it is easier to put weight into a cast, long or short, than to rely on arms and shoulders alone.

So much for the general stance and swing of the body, but even before becoming good at that, one must also learn the proper position of the hands. Too many people like to make the so-called "art" of surf casting sound as though it were a game only for experts. Such is not the case. First, a whip-socket or rod butt rest, strapped around the waist, has a leather or canvas cup into which the butt end of the rod can be dropped. The butt is probably thirty inches in length, and designed to space the hands well apart to give more leverage and power to the cast. With the butt of the rod in the whipsocket, the right hand is folded around it with four fingers under the reel, and the thumb resting on the left hand side of the reel spool and applying enough pressure so that the reel spool cannot turn when the left hand throws off the free spool lever. Then the left hand slides down to the end of the rod butt, lifts it out of the socket; the right thumb still holds the reel spool from turning.

Now the rod is brought around until it is pointing directly behind the angler. The lure or baited hook is next dropped about four feet from the rod tip. The rod is held in such a position that the right and left hands are about level with the shoulders. The lure or bait is next dropped onto the beach, and the rig is ready to make the forward cast. This actually starts slowly and gathers momentum until the rod is pointed about straight up. At this point, one *pulls down hard with the left hand and pushes forward with the right.* This throws a bend into the rod tip which, as it straightens to normal position, gives an extra forward flip or thrust. A fraction of a second after—the right thumb releases the reel spool so that the forward and outward pull of the lure pulls the line freely off the reel. Here is the critical moment at which backlashes occur. Even on anti-backlash reels a slight pressure of the thumb, just the faintest touch against the left side of the reel spool is helpful in lowering the frequency of birdnests or backlashes. Why the pressure on the reel spool rather than the line? Because if the line is thumbed, two things happen: first, unless the line is wet, one can burn a thumb as the spool revolves rapidly; secondly, the diameter of the reel spool diminishes so rapidly as the lure flies seaward, that the thumb must be shifted to keep an even pressure, and that takes a lot of practice. On the other hand, if the side of the reel spool is thumbed, there is an unchanging surface upon which to exert the needed control. A few practice casts made without trying to reach the coast of Spain will tell more than a thousand words. One must get the feel of it; just as with the swing of a shotgun on a flying bird, so the surfcaster finds the swing which is most natural and productive for him.

Surf casting can be done from behind and around to the side or by an overhead cast. The latter school states that the rod should be brought directly up and over the top of the right shoulder; the "sidewinder" swings his rod almost parallel to the beach instead of perpendicularly. Both methods get distance for their advocates. But the method which gives the most distance with the greatest ease and least effort is the one to follow and practice.

But here the surf caster has been left with the lure flying seaward. What then? Most surf casters will agree (a remarkable thing) that the reel should be thrown back into gear (reverse the free spool lever) and the angler should start reeling the plug or metal jig (or other artificial lure) the instant it touches the water. This is sound as the first sight of the artificial lure by the fish should be that of a moving, perhaps wounded, living thing. One never knows, unless casting into a breaking school of fish, just how close the lure may land to a fish. If it happens to be close and is allowed to sink without any movement, it may scare rather than attract a fish. It takes very little practice to throw the reel back in gear, and start reeling in time to move the lure the instant it hits the water.

With top-water, popping plugs this immediate action may not be as important. In fact, more than one fisherman patiently picking out a backlash with such a plug resting immobile on top of the water has had a big Striped Bass hit it hard. But action in plugs is important too. Some are made to take fish with a straight swimming motion; by watching the action of a plug at varying retrieving speeds one can soon tell the speed that gives the lure the most action. That speed may vary from a slow deliberate inching around of the reel handle to spinning it as fast as possible. If surf casting with a top-water, popping plug, take about four complete turns of the handle, then give the plugs hard "pop" by bringing up the rod tip—or moving it sideways—sharply for about a foot or two. This sudden speed of the plug will make it splash and throw water, a commotion which seems to attract most surface feeding fish, especially Striped Bass. Even with the underwater swimming plugs a short sudden jerk now and then gives an extra dart-dive action to most lures.

The speed of the retrieve of metal jigs, plugs, weighted spoons or any artificial casting lure will also depend on the strength of the tide. If casting from the end of a jetty where there's a tidal river pouring into the bay or ocean the rush of the tidal current will give extra action almost without retrieving it. It pays to experiment.

Using live bait is one of the most effective methods of taking fish from the surf, even though on occasion artificials will out-catch the live offering. The choice of baits is governed by the kind of fish and the kind of water being worked. A good general rule is to use a live bait that is a natural food of the fish sought: a Fiddler or cut crab for Tautog or Cunners; a seaworm or perhaps a whole squid for Striped Bass; cut mullet for Fluke or Channel Bass. Again the size of the bait is cut to fit the size of the fish's mouth.

If casting out on a rocky bottom, a sinker which is round or perhaps the Newport type, both less apt to catch in rocky crevices should be used. For this type of fishing, the hook or hooks should be about a foot above the sinker; then with a taut line the least touch on the bait can be felt. This also keeps the hook off the bottom and makes for better visibility of the bait.

When fishing from a sandy beach and over a bottom of sand or mud, the pyramid sinker rigged on a fish-finder is needed. In bait fishing in the surf where there is no particular hole or slough, one casts well out and brings the line taut. The rod tip is held high to keep the line out of water as much as possible; the incoming waves will wash the bait gradually toward the beach if there is a sizeable surf running. When the bait is washed in so that the line goes slack, it is taken up carefully to obtain a taut line again. Or if the surf is still, every few minutes the bait is moved in closer. This movement stirs up the bottom a bit and might catch the eye of a fish when a still bait would not.

When using a whole herring, squid, or other bait which is heavy enough to cast well no sinker is needed; also such baits washing around in the waves range a lot of territory to increase fishing coverage.

The line should be the best obtainable, as a surf line takes a beating not only from the pressure of casting but from rubbing against the sand, possible contact with rocks, bridge or pier pilings or other obstacles. It is a good rule to buy a nationally advertised one, and one designated by the manufacturer especially for surf casting. It can be either linen, commonly called cuttyhunk, or braided Nylon which has come into increasing popularity. The cuttyhunk needs to be really wet down with several casts before it will run out smoothly; Nylon soaks up little water but even so casts better after it has been wet.

A line that has been used for trolling should never be used in surf casting. If the same reel must be used (it's better to have one for each method of fishing) purchase one reel with two spools. Put the trolling line on one spool, the casting line on the other—and never, never mix 'em up. Trolling a line, even with straight running lures, cuts down its value for casting.

Another important thing to remember is that the line should be reeled back onto the spool evenly: if it is allowed to build up in one spot it will slide off the top of this "heap," loosen other winds and is almost certain to snarl on the next cast. Surf reels do not have level winds but after a bit of practice, the thumb will become an almost automatic level winder. As the line comes in, the left hand is held directly under the reel, so that the left outer side of the reel is braced against the heel of your thumb. The thumb is free to direct the line back and forth across the face of the spool.

Small diameter lines spool on more evenly than the larger sizes. The best for an all-round surf casting line is either the nine-thread cuttyhunk which tests twenty-seven pounds, or its equivalent in braided Nylon. It's strong enough to take a fifty-pound or even heavier fish if the rod tip is kept up so that the spring of the tip takes up the sudden strain of a hard strike or an unexpected rush of a fighting fish. In fishing rocky shoreline one may want a thirty-six or a forty-five pound test line. Or if using a fine running line to get greater balance (the smaller the line, the more distance with the same amount of effort) then one can splice on about fifty feet of heavy line next to the leader and lure.

By and large, Nylon lines are smaller in diameter for a given test than the linen. Nylon does not absorb water and therefore does not have to be dried to prevent rot or mold.

As one may hook fish that will run a hundred yards on their first rush, at least two hundred yards of line is desirable with one hundred and fifty yards the absolute minimum. A line will last an entire season, or maybe more, for the average surf caster. Lines carried over from year to year should be removed from the reel, wrapped around a hat box and stored in a cool dry place during the off-season months. However, it is better to invest a few dollars for a new line each season than to suddenly find a weak line when the fish are biting and the nearest replacement miles away. One can get longer wear and more service out of a line by reversing it on the reel when one end begins to show signs of getting "tired."

WHERE TO CAST

Where to surf cast? Well, there are telltale signs along the coast, either rocky or sandy, that once learned will reveal the shallows, bars, channels and deep cuts near the beach. Watch for terns and gulls feeding: they're after small bait fish or they may be watching a school of big fish and waiting for the fish to drive small bait to the surface. Terns and gulls usually scream when they are feeding so keep both your ears and your eyes open. Watch for rips which mark hidden rocks or bars around which fish feed. If the water, even the turmoil of the surf is watched carefully, a definite pattern to the waves will be noted. A school of fish, just under the surface, may break that pattern. Or small bait may be surfacing, even leaping out of water. Sharp eyes can detect fish in the clear water under the breaking crest of a wave or a swirl of a single fish may guide the cast. All these things go unobserved by the lazy, careless fisherman but fishing the surf is no sport for the languid. Or one may note that on certain tides the fish bite best in one spot; that when that place is not good, there's another slough down the beach that is.

Surf fish are not afraid to come close to the beach. Weakfish, Blues, Fluke, Channel, and Striped Bass sometimes chase bait practically up onto the sand. It is well to watch for a place where there is a deep hole or channel well in toward the beach. Outside of it there may be a long arching bar: when the incoming waves hit that bar they lift up, break, or show a white crest, then subside to regular size when they hit the deeper inshore water. If there's a long point on a beach, one may find just such a condition there. Fish the offshore bar if possible on the high tide when the fish come up out of the deeper water and look for food washed out of the sand on the shoal. Fish the deeper water on the low tide and remember also that these bars and sloughs change, especially after heavy storms. Polaroid sun glasses help spot holes and shoals.

Another hot spot is where two tides meet. On Nantucket Island, for example, the tides do not rise and fall as much as they run east and west, along the shores. At Great Point, the northern tip of the Island there is a great shoal, barely one hundred yards wide which runs offshore for several hundred yards. When the tide covers this shoal, the fish work in on it, even if there's only a few feet of water; and when there's a tide running against a goodly wind, this rip really cuts up. Bass and Blues are the surf fish here and they love really rough water, being completely at home in the foaming white water. Whether sandy or rocky, any promontory with some depth of water at high tide is apt to be good for surf fishing. Also areas where there are offshore weed beds are good spots to seek out. Those fishing a rocky shore should look for offshore rocks and fish around them. And, most of all, watch where the local fishermen go and what tides they fish. These men know; they may not be too eager to impart information to strangers but a humble, I-need-help-came-a-long-way approach can work wonders with the most grizzled natives.

In surf fishing the fish may be heavy. There are innumerable places in the inner waters of the Gulf or the inland waters of Florida in which one can catch small to medium size Channel Bass, otherwise known as Redfish or Red Drum; but the big ones—including the world's record fish (such as the Channel Bass record taken from the outer beach of Cape Hatteras, North Carolina) have come from ocean waters. Inshore waters provide fast fishing for school Stripers up to fifteen pounds or more; but the old tackle-busters are taken from the surf. The same goes for Weakfish, Bluefish, and the big Fluke or Croakers. Therefore, surf tackle should always be kept in good shape, just in case one of the giants happens to pick up the lure. In fishing in an area where there are Bluefish, a wire leader should be put next to the jig or lure. At other times Nylon leaders, being more flexible, get all the action there is out of the lure.

There is one surf-fishing lure that has not yet been mentioned. That is the eel-skin casting rig, or the whole eel called an eel-bob. These are killing lures for Blues and Bass and probably for Channel Bass, Weaks or anything else that will take a moving lure. Either whole eels rigged and pickled in tight glass jars or eel skins packed in similar containers and ready for use can be purchased. (See Striped Bass.) If they cannot be found locally, write to New England where they are common and productive to boot. In buying an eelskin rig for surf casting, specify the ones with the weighted heads; the trolling eel rigs are too light to cast.

Probably no bit of fishing equipment takes a greater beating than the surf reel, so it pays to get a good one—and take care of it. It should be oiled after each trip and kept out of the sand. A good split bamboo, hollow steel, or berrylium copper rod are all satisfactory and the even newer glass rods are tough and gaining fame for themselves. The choice of surf rod should be governed by the stature, weight, and strength of the user. A very short person will find a twenty-eight inch butt and a six or six-and-a-half foot tip big enough. A husky six-footer weighing a couple of hundred pounds or more and with not too much of the weight pushing out the belt buckle may want a seven-foot tip backed by thirty inches of butt. Beginners might try out a rod or two borrowed from surf casting friends, rather than to walk into a store and take what the salesman may offer. The trend is toward lighter tackle—and it's more fun.

Another detail but an important one is the manipulation of the star drag with which all good surf reels are equipped. It should never be screwed up as tight as it will go. It is better to have a slight drag and then adjust it with the finger tip as a fish is played than to work in the reverse way. Enough drag to help set the hook in a fish's mouth is all that is needed at the start. Thumb pressure can help out if needed. Then set according to the weight of the fish.

Mass. Div. of Fisheries and Game

Surf fishing is rugged on the New England coast. Many fishermen use plugs to catch Striped Bass.

After all this instruction, it's about time to actually catch a fish. Let's make it a twenty-pound Striper taken from a sandy shore with the great white combers crashing onto the beach so hard that one can feel the sand tremble under foot. The gulls and terns are wheeling and dipping about fifty yards out. Bait fish jump frantically out of water, and behind them a great swirl and then another as the Stripers slash into the bait school. This is it. No time should be wasted in sending a lure sailing out and beyond the school. As it hits the water, it is reeled steadily in. The jig should be in those fish by now—and it is!! There is a terrific strike that makes one brace his feet. The rod tip dips; the line runs off; the tip is lifted to strike once, twice, not too hard but firmly to make sure the barb of the hook has sunk home. It apparently has and the big fish is headed straight to sea.

With the bobbing rod tip well up in the air, added pressure is put on the running fish by pressing the thumb on the spinning reel spool. The fish slows now and his broad tail flashes as he breaks water at the end of his first long run. The reel is spun fast to keep the line taut, to keep a constant pressure on the fish, to tire him out as soon as possible. The fish starts to parallel the beach now, gathering speed again. The angler walks along in the same direction, to keep as much line on the spool as possible. Five or six minutes pass and the fish is well in toward the beach. But the outgoing rush of a wave takes him off again and line goes out grudgingly but wisely as that's a big fish and the test of the line is not much more than his dead weight. This is the critical moment, that brief portion of the fight when the fish is pretty well licked, but still must be brought through the last breaker and held against the outrush of the wave. Steady does it: do not run back up the beach; better to have it out right here, heel to fin, win or lose. When the fish rolls over on his side in the trough behind the nearest breaker, it is time to bring the fish through that crashing surf. The rod tip is up; the reel grinds steadily; then as the waves lift the fish to wash him on the beach, a step or two backwards, reeling furiously to keep the line taut, will hold that fish inshore. The pressure is heavy but the tackle, in good shape, takes the strain and the fish is flopping on the sand. No time is wasted in grabbing him under the gill covers and lifting up the beach well beyond the reach of the biggest waves.

The surf fisherman standing close to the breakers is taking chances against terrific odds when the small area his lure or bait reaches is compared to the miles of beach on either side of him. What he catches, he earns through perseverance and often hard work, but in fishing it's called fun. Surf fishing may be no sport for softies, but it pays off in fish, health, and satisfaction to those who pursue it.

PLUG CASTING

Casting artificial lures with a casting rod for salt-water game fish is a comparatively new branch of angling. Anglers had been casting plugs for fresh-water fish for many years before it occurred to them to try this same method in bays, inlets, estuaries, canals, and the oceans. They found the salt-water fishes willing and co-operative, and casting in salty waters has gained in popularity rapidly.

While salt-water plug-casting now is practiced along both coastlines of the United States, the sport received its greatest impetus in south Florida. This is due to the fact that the fishes in the Florida Keys, in the Bay of Florida, the Shark river area, the Ten Thousand islands, and north to St. Petersburg, seem to be greatly attracted by plugs and other artificial lures.

This should not be taken to mean that fishes of other areas will not strike at plugs, for the reverse is true. Plug casting in salt water is popular all around the coast of the Gulf of Mexico, along the Florida west coast thence westerly to Texas and on to Point Isabel. It is claimed that the sport received its initial impetus at Corpus Christi, Tex., in the early 1920's.

However, regardless of its history, salt-water plug-casting quickly has gained in favor. Many articles regarding it have appeared in nationally circulated magazines—mainly fishing and hunting publications—and northern fresh-water anglers visiting southern states now bring their plug rods and tackle boxes. They find, as have other anglers before them, that various salt-water gamesters strike harder and battle more strongly than their fresh-water cousins.

In most other coastal states the varieties that will strike a plug are limited to such fishes as Striped Bass, Channel Bass, salt water Trout or Weakfish, and salt water Catfish. Some Tarpon, Mackerel, and Bluefish are taken on plugs out of the south Florida range, but the sport has not progressed in those areas as it has in south Florida where anglers catch the famous Bonefish, Tarpon, Channel Bass, Snook, Snapper, Chiro, Grouper, Barracuda, Dolphin, and many others throughout the year.

It is a revelation to northern plug-casters when they first try casting plugs for Tarpon. Accustomed to catching Black Bass weighing not more than five pounds, and usually not more than two pounds, they are non-plussed when they hook their first Silver King. If it is a big one, weighing 50 pounds

Paul Kalman

Spotted Weakfish are rated as the Gulf's most popular species of fish and are favorites with thousands of anglers. Here, a big Spotted Weakfish puts up a last ditch fight in brackish Lake Pontchartrain near New Orleans.

or more, they feel that they have something to talk about the rest of their lives, even though they may not be successful in landing it.

The biggest Tarpon will strike a plug at times. Thus, the angler never knows whether he will hook a 200-pounder or a 10-pounder. This, of course, adds to the thrills and excitement of plug casting for them. The majority of Tarpon weighing in excess of 50 pounds will break the line or throw the hook within a few minutes after being hooked. But the thrill of the strike and the sight of the silvery fish leaping high in the air is recompense enough.

Dolphin also are mighty battlers when hooked on casting rods. These blue-water fish are usually encountered by anglers trolling the offshore waters. They travel in small schools as a rule, and when one is hooked on trolling tackle the others will remain close by. Anglers, knowing this, keep a casting rod close at hand, all ready to cast.

When Dolphin are encountered, the angler quits trolling and starts casting. Dolphin will strike at almost any kind of lure—plugs, feathers, spoons, tin squids—but it is more fun and sport to try for them with a surface plug. Seeing the strike is an added thrill. Even a two- or three-pound Dolphin will put on a leaping, dashing, fight on casting equipment, while a 20-pounder will keep the average angler busily employed for an hour.

The newest salt-water innovation is casting for Bonefish. It was formerly believed that these fish, famed for their speed and power, would take natural baits only. Within the past fifteen years, however, it was found that they would strike a plug under certain conditions or when in the humor. Since then many have been taken and casting for Bonefish has become a recognized branch of salt-water angling.

Occasionally, in casting for Bonefish on the shallow banks adjacent to the Florida keys, the angler will tie into a Permit or Great Pompano. These are amongst the toughest of all fish to fight and land on casting tackle. They are speedy, tricky, and possessed with wonderful staying powers. Lucky, indeed, is the angler who is successful in fighting one weighing in excess of 10 pounds. Like the Bonefish, Permit do not indulge in aerial gymnastics.

Barracuda ramble all over the Florida keys water areas, and the angler is apt to encounter them in shallow as well as the deeper waters. When taken on casting tackle, these tigers of the sea are very worthy opponents. They smash hard at a plug, run with more than average speed and sometimes leap high and frequently. They are equipped with sharp and long teeth and should be handled carefully when removing them from the hook.

Snook are favorites with most plug casters, for they are quite plentiful, run fairly large in size, leap frequently when hooked, are found in bays, rivers, inlets and canals that lead to salt water, around piers, bridges and seawalls. In addition,

Homer Rhode, Jr.

Barracuda are plentiful in the shallow waters of southern Florida. This one struck a plug and staged a fine battle before it was landed.

they are mighty good eating when properly prepared and cooked. Granted that they are not the mightiest battlers when taken on plugs but usually, they are more than willing to hit either a surface or underwater lure and they put up an interesting fight when hooked.

Although none of the size have been recorded as caught, Snook probably reach a top weight of 70 pounds. Many of them tipping the beam between 20 and 30 pounds have been successfully fought by casters, but the average weight is around seven or eight pounds. They usually do not clear the water when they leap at the end of the line. It is more of a half-leap, accompanied by a wicked shaking of the head, in an effort to free themselves from the hook.

Chiro, also known as Big-Eyed Herring and sometimes mis-called Ladyfish, are plentiful in south Florida's inland salt waters. They run small in size, the average being about one and one-half pounds, but they stage the type of fight that casters like. Chiro will strike almost any kind of artificial lure, are fast and powerful swimmers for their size, and they leap high into the air frequently when hooked. The first run of the Chiro after being hooked is extremely speedy and a four- or five-pounder will give the caster all the fight he can handle.

Channel Bass, known as redfish in Florida, have much the same distribution in that state as the Chiro. Plug casters seek them in all the inland salt waters. They strike hard and fight a dogged battle, never leaping and never giving up until they are thoroughly whipped down. Jack Crevalle are another species that are very plentiful in south Florida. They are both strong and tricky and have a habit of gathering up some last minute strength and dashing off just about the time the angler thinks he has them licked. This trick has earned them the nickname of "rod busters."

Snapper, of which there are several kinds, stage a fight quite similar to that of fresh-water bass. Like the black bass, too, at times they will smash at a plug without hesitation, while at other times they pay no attention to any artificial lure. If they are in a fighting mood, however, they are lots of fun when hooked. Mainly weighing a pound or two, the larger ones up to eight and ten pounds, are strong, tricky, and fairly speedy and provide great sport.

Grouper, Gag, and Jewfish of the smaller sizes can be listed together so far as the plug caster is concerned. The big ones usually live in fairly deep water but those under 10 pounds in weight are found in the shallow inland salt waters. They are strong but are neither speedy or tricky. However, they do strike either surface or underwater lures willingly, and they are top table varieties.

Plug casting along the eastern seaboard north of Florida and on the Pacific Coast is not as popular as it is in the Gulf Coast states. However, it is rapidly gaining favor, especially amongst anglers fishing in the bays and inlets. Fish mainly sought by plug casters on the Pacific coast and the Atlantic coast include Striped Bass, Channel Bass, Trout or Weakfish, and Bluefish. Pollack also have been taken on plugs when encountered in comparatively shallow offshore waters, while Shad frequently are caught.

Most of the plug casting along the Pacific Coast is concentrated around San Francisco Bay. Both plugs and spoons are used by plug casters there, the plugs generally being of the jointed, surface varieties, red and white in coloring. Some fair-sized Stripers are caught, the usual weight being up to 10 pounds, but occasionally larger ones are taken. Feather and bucktail lures should produce good results with Stripers in that area, especially those equipped with silver flash spinners. Spoons of the Dardevle type, in chromium plate of red and white, are good.

In the bays and sounds north of Georgia, plug casters seem to favor spoons, feathers, and bucktails of various designs and colors. Also, they catch more fish on the underwater plugs and lures that retrieve under the surface. The deep-diving clothespin-type plugs are held in esteem, and nearly every plug manufacturer makes some of these types under various names and shapes. In the upper Chesapeake Bay sector bucktails with spinners have proved their worth in attracting Striped Bass and Shad.

In the New York-Massachusetts area plug casters practice chumming the water with natural baits, then cast or let their lure drift back into the chum line. Spoons are used in this sort of fishing to a certain extent, but the bucktail with spinners is more favored for Striped Bass, with spoons the favorite for Bluefish. In the northern waters, Weakfish are better attracted by deep-diving lures, excepting when they are encountered in comparatively shallow areas.

Popping with a plug casting outfit is practiced by practically all southern plug casters. In popping, the lure used is a combination of the natural and artificial, but the cast and retrieve is made the same as in casting some of the plugs. Popping is resorted to when casting for Trout or Weakfish that are in fairly deep water, from eight to 18 feet, and will not rise to surface plugs. It receives its name from the popping sound made by the lure.

Many plug manufacturers now make special popping lures, but the old way of popping with homemade lures is still a favorite with the majority of plug casters. The operation is quite simple. A short length of leader wire, about eight inches, is pierced through a cork of about one and one-half inches diameter and perhaps two inches long. A loop is made in the leader wire at the tail end, or small diameter end, of the cork. Another short length of leader wire, about six inches in length, is looped to the first loop so that it swings freely. The hook, generally about 2/0 in size, is fastened to the end of the second leader wire.

A swivel is fastened to the upper end of the leader wire that runs through the cork, then the line is fastened to the other eye of the swivel, a bait is placed upon the hook, and the plug caster is ready for action. The cast is made in the usual manner, but the retrieve is made in extra-hard jerks. This causes the cork to pop and splash in a noisy manner and the trout seem to love it. They can be attracted by a popper when ordinary plugs and other lures fail.

Tackle used by anglers casting plugs and other artificial lures in salt water has undergone several changes since this branch of the fishing sport started. At first, it was thought that rods, reels, and lines should be heavier and stronger than those used in plug casting in fresh waters. Salt-water casters went in for stiff and heavy rods, 30-pound test lines of silk or nine-thread linen lines. Small free-spool surf casting reels were customary.

Today, however, the trend is toward lighter casting equipment, with regulation quadruple-multiplying casting reels the rule, and 15-pound test casting line the maximum. Salt-water casters favor light and fairly whippy rods with an overall length of from four and one-half to five and one-half feet. Rod manufacturers have progressed rapidly in the ability to turn out these light rods with plenty of backbone and whip to shoot plugs farther than ever, plus the strength and stamina to withstand considerable punishment.

Whereas it formerly was customary to mount agate or some glass imitation guides on casting rods, now the rule is plain metal guides that will not rust in salt water. Many casting rods were made in two or more sections, necessitating one or more ferrule joints. Now the great majority of these rods are made in one-piece tips that eliminate the stiff spots caused by ferrules. In fact, some of the plug casting rods now turned out have the tip and butt integral, with the tip extending all the way through the butt.

Good casting depends, in a large measure, on the uniformity of bend in the rod tip. If the tip has alternate stiff and limber spots, it is next to impossible to cast properly with it, and the tip naturally is weakened. Good rods should have considerable backbone near the butt end, getting uniformly more whippy toward the top or tip end. Manufacturers of good plug-casting rods have realized this and have practically perfected their product in this connection.

Reel manufacturers also have done well in meeting the desires of salt-water casters. Not only have they made, at reasonable prices, quadruple-multiplying, level-winding casting reels that will stand up under the severe punishment given them in salt water fishing, but they have also sought for and found better and lighter metals and parts. However, it is still necessary for salt-water casters to make sure that the reels purchased are made to withstand salt water use, keeping away from reels that are especially made for use in fresh water.

This does not mean that any of the salt-water casting reels will give maximum service without some care. Casting reels, regardless of the price paid for them, should be frequently taken apart, cleaned and oiled. Extra pawls for the level-wind mechanism should be kept conveniently at hand, generally in the tackle box, for replacement of worn ones. The level-wind mechanism should be oiled frequently when casting. This chore takes only a few seconds, permits better casting and saves trouble that is almost sure to develop if this frequent oiling is omitted.

The oiling and greasing of a piece of machinery as small and as delicately adjusted as a plug casting

Homer Rhode, Jr.

It takes a good fisherman to hook, fight and boat a Tarpon of this size on a plug and plug casting rod.

John Mahony

Barracuda taken on a plug off Marathon, Florida.

reel should be done with oils and greases especially made for the purpose. Occasionally, the reel should be taken completely apart, cleaned carefully in mineral spirits, and carefully oiled and greased. This kind of care will enable the reel to give the maximum service that the manufacturer has built into the product. Better still, it will insure better casting, more fish attracted and landed, and less fish lost.

Good rods need very little care. Generally, the best treatment is to wash them in fresh water after fishing in salty water. Metal parts on the butt should be kept well cleaned and polished. If the rod is of the kind that consists of tip and butt, the male ferrule on the tip should be kept clean and polished, and the same with the female ferrule in the butt. In joining the two together, always wipe the male ferrule with an oily rag or, better still, revolve it alongside your nose or through your hair to obtain a slight oily deposit. Never put a lot of oil on it with an oil can for that will cause a vacuum and make the tip difficult to remove from the butt.

If the tip does stick in the butt and the two do not come apart easily, do not try to force things by using one of the guides as a fulcrum. Take the rod by the butt near the ferrule and place it behind you. Then reach back with the other hand and secure a firm grip on the rod tip near the butt. This should be done at knee height. Then bend the knees outward so that they press against both arms just above the wrists. A little pressure will cause the butt and tip to separate without injury to either. Another good way is to face a companion. One should take a good hold on the tip; the other in the butt near the ferrule. Then each person grabs the other's arm near the wrist and both push together with the free hands.

Lines mostly used in salt water casting are of Nylon. Some anglers still stick with silk casting lines, while a few prefer twisted linen. Silk lines cast somewhat smoother than Nylon and lots smoother than linen. However, they lose quite a bit of strength when immersed in salt water. Nylon lines have too much stretch, but they are very little affected by water. Linen lines gather strength when wet but do not cast smoothly. All lines should be rinsed in fresh water after using in salt water, then dried in the shade. There are many good line drying mechanisms available for running off and drying lines.

It might be repeated that Nylon and linen lines are not adversely affected by immersion in salt water. Nylon loses a little strength, while linen picks up strength when wet. However, while in salt water and used in fishing, all lines get fish slime and other foreign matter on them that is apt to be injurious. Consequently, the advice to rinse all lines in fresh, clean water after using in either fresh or salt water.

Constant casting with a line tends to wear the line, especially at the end next to the leader. This part of the line should be inspected frequently during a day of fishing. If the line shows nicked or rough spots, cut that portion of the line away. Many a good fish has been lost through failure to properly care for line. Many salt-water casters periodically treat their lines with a line dressing or with beeswax. Several kinds of line dressing are available at tackle stores and these are meeting with increased favor.

Leaders can be made with either light leader wire or from Nylon gut. The gut is to be preferred if the fish sought do not have teeth. If, however, the fish are Mackeral, Bluefish, Barracuda, or other toothed varieties, it is better to use wire. The leader need not be long, most casters prefer them from six to 10 inches in length, and they should be as light as possible. This is desirable because the thinner the leader the less it will interfere with the action of the plug or lure.

Swivels and snap hooks should be eliminated when fastening the leader to the plug and the leader to the line. They add weight and serve no especially good purpose. However, many salt-water casters use a snap hook at the end of the leader for convenience in the quick changing of plugs and lures. Care should be taken in knotting Nylon gut and line. The blood knot, or half-barrel, is best for the purpose. When properly tied it not only holds securely but will not cause the line to cut on itself. *(For knots used in tying Nylon see Section VII.)*

Many kinds of plugs and other lures are available to casters and more of them are making their appearance every day. It would be impossible to list all of the artificials or assay them for their worth. Suffice it to say that it costs real money to introduce a new plug or lure and manufacturers would not invest if they did not have faith in their product. Boiled down, this means that any plug or lure will catch certain kinds of fish under certain conditions. The plug or lure that will catch all kinds of game fishes under all conditions has yet to make its appearance.

The main point in the use of any plug or lure is to put the action in it that the manufacturer desired it to have. There are many ways of retrieving a plug or lure after it has been cast. Some should have a slow retrieve, others fast, while certain kinds should be retrieved at a medium speed, and still others at alternating speeds—first slow, then more rapidly. Most of them should be given a jerk at frequent intervals during the retrieve. A good caster can make a surface plug fairly dance on the water. He knows just what to do to give it the right action to attract the fish for which he fishes.

Generally speaking, plugs can be divided into several types. Of the surface plugs, there are darters, wigglers, wobblers, injured minnows, injured shad, poppers, and crawlers. Darters can be made to do their stuff—dart—by a rather fast retrieve, with frequent jerks while winding in. Wigglers need slower retrieving, with the jerks not so pronounced. Wobblers and crawlers should be retrieved slowly and without jerking. Injured minnows and injured shad should be retrieved by a series of slow jerks, with a trifle of rest between each jerk. Poppers should be jerked hard, rested, then a repeat on the sharp jerk. That makes them pop, which is what the manufacturer intended them to do.

In the underwater plugs there are wigglers, wiggle divers, porkrind gadgets, and darters with and without spinners. The wigglers require a medium speed retrieve, with a jerk now and then to put more action in them. Wiggle divers should be allowed to sink, then should be jerked sharply to cause them to wiggle rapidly toward the surface. The porkrind gadgets should be retrieved with a series of easy, slow jerks. Darters, with or without spinners, should be retrieved with a series of rather sharp, short jerks.

There are several kinds of spoons, squids, and feather lures available. However, they can be divided into wigglers, wobblers, darters, wiggle divers, and those made to be used with porkrind strips. They should be retrieved accordingly, and the advice that goes for plugs goes also for them. It might be remarked, however, that bright nickel, chromium, or silver produces better results in salt-water casting than gold or bronze, while yellow feathers usually are to be preferred to white or any other color or color combination.

In casting underwater plugs or lures, with the exception of wiggle divers that should be allowed to sink, then be jerked, the retrieve should be started as soon as the plug or lure hits the water. With surface plugs, however, it is better to let the plug lie still for a few seconds before starting the retrieve. To the fish, the surface plug is some land critter or object that dropped into the water. He eyes it, startled at first, then with considerable curiosity. If it moves away immediately and quickly, the fish figures it can get away.

If, however, it makes a slight movement as though it was still stunned, the fish becomes interested and moves toward it. Then it moves more freely, and the fish darts after it to catch it before it gathers higher speed. This, of course, is the usual rule, determined by actually watching the action of fishes after a plug. However, there are variations. For instance, sometimes a fish will hit a plug even before the plug hits the water. At other times, the fish will follow the plug a considerable distance before striking at it.

While they are not better as fish catchers, surface plugs generally are preferred by anglers. The reason for this is that part of the thrill of casting comes from seeing the fish strike. It generally is better, therefore, to start with a surface plug. If it fails to attract fish, try an underwater plug or lure. It is sometimes possible to observe what the fish are doing by watching the water carefully, or listening if it is night time. Fish feeding on the surface make a disturbance in the water that can be seen as well as heard.

It pays good piscatorial dividends to study the water before casting. Note if there is any surface or near surface action. Study in this connection, if pursued attentively, can mean a lot. For instance, there are many anglers who can name the species of fish by the movements or sounds made while feeding. In fact, there are some anglers who have become so expert through observation that by listening, even on the darkest night, they can name the fish and tell whether they are or are not feeding.

To the inexperienced ear, the ripples and splashes made by fishes feeding on or near the surface, or moving through the water, have no meaning. However, close observation reveals that certain fish make one kind of splash or ripple, while other fish make quite different splashes and ripples. For instance, the popping noises made by Snook when feeding easily can be distinguished from the roll and slight splash made by Tarpon. Likewise, the hurried skittering of Jack Crevalle as they close in on luckless minnows is certainly not the same sound as is made by Channel Bass when feeding.

A close study of fishing localities is tremendously worth while, too. For example, when the tide is coming in, fish usually will be on the inner side of a bar at an inlet. They will be on the outside when the tide goes out. Along a salt water stream or

Erl Roman

This Tarpon really "hit the air."

canal, the fishes will be found mostly around the rocky and deeper areas, and they will seek the shade and comparative darkness where trees and bushes grow close to the bank or overhang the water. In channels, most fish will stick close to the edges rather than the center. Shallow banks where crabs, clams, and other crustacea, and shellfish make their homes, are good for wading and casting on the incoming tides.

It pays, also, to be quiet as well as observant when fishing. Talking or singing, even in loud tones, does not disturb fishes, but stomping around a boat or being carelessly noisy with the oars will, and this is especially true in shallow waters. The approach to a fishing locality should be made quietly, the boat motor being shut off before reaching the spot. Clothing worn on plug casting trips where fish can be seen and can see the angler should be of neutral colors, such as gray or tan. White never should be worn.

Casting should be practiced long and frequently if the angler expects to perfect himself in it. Good casters attain a smooth and easy action which sends the plug or lure the required distance without apparent effort. Such casters will automatically keep backlashes to a minimum and will not put the lure more than a few inches off the spot they desire to hit. Experienced casters are rarely at a loss as to what to do and when to do it. It takes lots of fishing practice to gain the necessary experience.

One of the indispensable items needed by salt-water casters is a tackle box. Fishing tackle dealers feature a large number of tackle boxes of various shapes and kinds, made of wood, metal and plastics. Lightness, strength, and durability is what the plug-caster should look for in selecting a tackle box. In most cases it is well to have two tackle boxes—a very small one that can be fastened to the belt or slung over the shoulder for carrying a few plugs and some extra leader material, and a large one to have handy in the automobile.

What to carry in the average tackle box puzzles most casters. Usually, they start with a small box and a like amount of plugs, lures, et cetera. This they keep adding to until a new and larger box is needed to accommodate all the things they have collected. This ends sometimes with the angler having too many unnecessary items, making the necessary ones difficult of access. A tackle box should be kept so well arranged that the angler can find the object he seeks almost automatically.

A list of necessary items for the tackle box should include some extra plugs and lures; hooks of the kind and size to replace those that might be lost, broken or damaged; hooks to be used in case one wants to try bottom fishing; sinkers for bottom fishing; a coil of leader wire and a coil of gut leader; a knife that can be used for filleting and scaling fish; a small pair of scissors; a pair of square-nosed pliers with a cutter for wire leaders and a pair of round-nosed pliers; a small screw driver; an oil can filled with good reel oil; a tube of reel grease, a clean rag and a small sharpening stone.

Then there should be a spare reel with line; an additional spare line; one complete level-wind mechanism and two spare pawls; a small but fairly complete first-aid kit; a tightly corked bottle of insect repellent; and a good flashlight. If swivels are used, it is well to carry a supply of these, and if fishing in poisonous snakes territory, take along an anti-venom outfit, and by all means have some ammonia to apply to insect bites.

What one angler deems necessary may be just more junk to another, and vice-versa. In any case, however, it pays to review the contents of the tackle box frequently to get rid of items that are not necessary, to restock items that have been used or lost, and to re-arrange all items more conveniently. Items that are used constantly, such as extra plugs, knife, scissors, screw driver, and pliers, should be contained in the top part of the box where they can be reached easily and quickly.

FLY CASTING

Despite the fact that salt-water fishing with flies and fly rods was a subject of a book published in London in 1851, this sport failed to take hold in a large way until very recently. This is doubly surprising in view of the present and rapidly growing popularity of fly casting in salt waters. Just a few short years ago, it would have been possible to count the number of salt-water fly-casters on the fingers of one hand.

It is even more surprising when it is realized that two very famous anglers employed fly rods and flies for catching Tarpon in the salty waters of Florida back in the early '80s, later writing about it in a book which enjoyed wide distribution. "The tarpon meets every demand the sport of fishing can make," the book relates. "He fits the light fly rod as no trout even dreamed of doing and leaps high out of the water a hundred times for every once that a trout clears the surface . . . To one who has known the tarpon, the feeble efforts of the salmon to live up to its own reputation are saddening."

One would think that, after reading such a glowing tribute to fly-casting for Tarpon, anglers everywhere would have unlimbered their fly rods and had a fling at it. However, nothing of the sort occurred, and years passed with little or no mention of fly fishing in salt water. True, a few brave souls tried their fly rods in Gulf Stream fishing off Miami around 1930, and two rod manufacturers made what was known as an ocean fly rod. While this fishing enjoyed a measure of popularity for a few years, it was short lived.

It could be said, with truth, that fly casting in salt waters did not come into its own until sometime after the close of World War II, when a few anglers in south Florida proved beyond doubt that the smaller salt water game fish would take a fly in preference to any other artificial lure; that at times they would take a fly when natural baits failed to attract them; and it not only was possible but also a lot more fun and sport to catch them with fly rod tackle. Once that was demonstrated and publicized, the anglers took up salt water fly casting in a big way.

Homer Rhode, Jr.

Snook will strike a fly willingly, as this one did to its sorrow.

Fly casting in salt water is a fascinating form of angling. The necessary tackle is light in weight, limited in amount, reasonable in price, and a pleasure to use. All the equipment a fly caster needs is a fly rod, a large size fly reel, a dozen or so flies, some line, and leader material. That, and a knowledge of fly casting which can be gained in a few hours, and the angler is set to fish the salty waters and actually catch fish. The rod weighs but a few ounces, the reel with its line and leader can be carried in a convenient pocket, while the flies can be decked around the brim of a hat. That really is packing a lot of potential fun and sport in a small space.

Of course, the angler who takes fly casting seriously does not stop with the small amount of equipment described. Chances are that he owns and uses from three to a half dozen fly rods, has at least one reel for every rod, two lines for every reel, buys leader material a dozen coils at a time, possesses more artificial flies than there are real ones around a molasses factory, has numerous gadgets in which to carry the flies, has a tackle box or two to accommodate reels, lines, fly tying equipment and other tools, and is ready to argue that every item he owns is essential and could by no means be discarded!

The list of fishes that can be taken on flies in salt water is not complete. Nearly every day some salt-water fly-casting enthusiast adds a new one. However, it is known that all those that will strike at a plug will also take a fly, plus several others to be added to that list. Generally speaking, the fish caught range in weight from a few ounces to 60 or more pounds, and if you think they put up a good battle on a plug rod, just try them on a fly rod for new thrills and a new idea of their fighting abilities. The results have been so amazing that old salmon and trout anglers have taken a new lease on life and are wondering why they did not take up with Tarpon and Bonefish long ago.

The best part is that fly fishing in salt waters can be successfully practiced by almost anyone and almost anywhere. All that is necessary is some fair fishing localities, some equipment, and some practice, The art of casting a fly is easy to learn. Of course, one cannot become expert in a few easy lessons, but the average angler who has never had a fly rod in his hands can, with proper coaching, learn to get a fly out creditably in a short while. Naturally, it takes much practice and a lot of fishing to reach the top ranks, and some who do not have the knack never will become expert. Distance, accuracy, and know-how in salt-water fly casting takes careful application, but the promise is there if one perseveres.

It might be thought that, inasmuch as salt-water species are larger, wilder, and stronger than their fresh-water brethren, a heavy fly rod is necessary if the angler is to successfully hook, fight, and land them. However, the majority of salt-water fly-casters are using rods weighing from five and one-half to six and one-half ounces, and measuring from eight to nine feet in length. Glass fly rods are meeting with general favor, but those made of cane, bamboo or steel are holding their own. A good rod is a thing of beauty and joy forever if it is built for the intended work and is cared for properly. In selecting a fly rod for salt-water use, the angler should keep several things in mind.

In the first place, the rod should have plenty of backbone. By this, it is meant that the "soft" bending rod is not to be considered. The rod should be springy and quick—not soft and logy. It should have strength enough to withstand the strong and numerous rushes of salt-water game-fish, and power enough to shoot a line a considerable distance. It should be made to take a whipping without taking a set. Several kinds of salt-water fish have a habit of reviving just as they are about to be netted or lifted from the water. It takes quick action on the part of the angler and inbuilt goodness in a rod to handle such fish without disaster.

If the angler is not sure of his rod and its ability to take punishment when giving the fish the butt, it is much better to take things easy and make sure that the fight is over before trying to gaff, lift, or net the fish. Permit, or Great Pompano, and Jack Crevalle are particularly noted for their trickery when apparently all in and ready to be landed. They'll be flat on their sides, fins moving very weakly, if at all. Then, quick as a flash, they'll

Homer Rhode, Jr.

Crevalle Jack, even the small ones, put up a tough battle when taken on a fly rod.

gain a last measure of strength and dart downward or sideways at great speed. If a fly rod has any weakness, it will reveal itself at such times.

All metal parts of the fly rod, but particularly the guides, should be of material that is not adversely affected by salt water. It has always seemed odd that manufacturers of fishing tackle have seemed slow in adopting rust and corrosion-proof metals in rods, reels, tackle boxes, and other angling equipment. This same tendency also has been noticeable in boatbuilders, who lagged miserably in adopting modern metals and sound-proofing materials. After all, it makes good sense to use materials that will not rust or corrode in any item that is always around water, either fresh or salt.

Metal guides that rust, do so quickly when in contact with moist, salty air or salt water. Not only do they ruin a good fly line quickly, but it is impossible to do a good job of casting through rusty guides. Salt-water fly-casters would do well to refuse to purchase rods with plain steel guides. If, inadverdently, such a rod is purchased, the first thing to do with it is change the guides. These can easily be made with No. 12 stainless steel leader wire, but it is a nuisance to have to wind new guides on a rod that should have been equipped with non-rusting ones at the factory.

After fishing with a fly rod in salt water, the rod should be washed carefully with fresh water. A rubbing down with some good polishing wax—tip, guides, ferrules, and butt—also is a help.

In salt-water fly-fishing the reel plays a rather important part. It takes a long line to play some of the larger and stronger salt-water game-fish, and it pays to have some in reserve. This means that the reel must be of a large size, and it often means that it is necessary to use the reel to get in line rather than looping it over the head as it is stripped in. The majority of salt-water fly-casters frown upon the use of the automatic reels, claiming that they are not practical for their purpose. However, some anglers use and like them. It is a problem that the individual will have to work out to his or her own satisfaction.

The reel should be able to accommodate the fly line plus 150 yards of backing line, generally six-thread linen. Some anglers prefer to use 15-pound test Nylon, while others use nine-thread linen. As it usually is rather windy around salt water, the preferred fly line is the torpedo head. Due to the way it is proportioned, this line works out well, being much easier to cast under windy conditions than either the usual tapered line or the level lines. However, it is not absolutely necessary, and the tapered and level lines can be used.

The majority of beginners fail to realize the importance of balancing the line to the rod. If the line is too heavy or too light for the rod, good casting is impossible. Some manufacturers signify the weight of line that should be used with each rod, and this at least gives the angler an idea of the line size to use. On the other hand, many anglers find that they cast better if they use a line a size larger than the manufacturer recommends. This is apt to be a bit tough on the rod, but it pays off in better casting and more fish in the creel. At any rate, other lines should be tried if the one used seems awkward to cast.

In fly casting, the line should be kept in good condition. Salt water does not seen to affect good fly lines adversely, but fighting salt-water fish subjects line to tough punishment. This usually shows up in little nicks in the finish of the line. Of course, if the line has too many of these frayed spots, it is best to discard it. On the other hand, if the line is treated with a good line dressing each time it is used, nicks will be largely avoided. In other words, if the angler properly cares for his line it will reward him by lasting longer and giving better service.

The same thing applies to the rod and reel and, for that matter, to all equipment used. If the angler expects to get the use out of fishing tackle that manufacturers have tried to build into it, the tackle must be treated and cared for properly. A fly reel is a rather simple mechanism, and it is easy to keep clean and well oiled. Rusty guides on a fly rod, nicked, or frayed lines, and a dirty reel, do not lead to good results. Tackle should

Miami News Bureau

A pair of nice ones taken on fly rods.

be kept in top condition because even under the best use it takes a real licking.

Brilliant colors in flies do not seem to add to their attractiveness for salt-water fish. Plain white, yellow, and dominique flies seem to be preferred. Two types seem to be outstanding in southern waters. They are the divided-wing streamer with hackle, and the popper bugs usually employed in taking Black Bass in fresh waters. The best divided-wing streamer flies are about two and one-half inches in length, with a hackle of the same or different color. One of the favorites is the dominique with white hackle. White with yellow hackle is very good.

Flies made with bucktail or white polar bear hair, with a dab of red paint near the eye of the hook, are good in most fishing areas. In northern waters, from the Virginia capes to and including the New England coastal states, these flies have found considerable favor. Some anglers like the addition of a small flash-spinner, and some also like a mixture of white and black hair instead of all white. This mixture of white and black, combined with a spinner, is used a lot in fishing for shad.

In the salt waters from the mouth of the St. Johns River north to the New England States, salt-water casters say that the addition of a spinner to any adaptable kind of fly lure is a big aid in attracting and catching fish. This, it seems, is not true south of the St. Johns. Also, it has been noted by anglers in the inland salt waters of south Florida that while the divided-wing streamer fly is best in the Florida keys, the popper bugs catch more fish in the Ten Thousand Islands. Snook are particularly attracted by popper bugs.

Dry flies work well on some of the Florida fishes. The Mullet, which will not strike at a plug and usually are caught by anglers fishing bottom with small hooks baited with a very small piece of salt pork or the white part of bacon, will rise to several kinds of dry flies and are especially intrigued with the black gnat. When fishing for Mullet with dry flies, it is best to lay the line and leader right out so there will be no straightening out of the leader in the current after the fly hits the water. Mullet usually take the fly at the time it hits the water or very shortly thereafter, and they tend to shy off from a fly where the current has shown a slight riffle due to the leader.

Undoubtedly, as the sport of catching gamesters on flies in salt-waters becomes better known and more practiced by anglers, more will be learned concerning the reactions of the various species to flies and fly lures of various kinds. Anglers, finding a fly that catches fish, are apt to favor that one and fail to try others. However, trials have been made with fly lures, such as the miniature spoons, Colorado spinners, and bead combinations, artificial minnows and propellor spinners. These have proved fairly successful, especially the spoons with a fly porkrind attached. Miniature plugs also will take fish, and some anglers maintain that they will do the work when flies of feather or hair fail.

Boiling it all down, the divided-wing streamer flies seem to be preferred by most salt-water fly-casters. These usually are made with three feathers to each wing and two feathers for the hackle. Properly retrieved, they present an enticing appearance in the water, the hackle alternately flattening and standing up and the wings spreading and closing. Nearly every kind of fish is attracted by this action, it appears, and as time goes on more and different varieties of fishes are reported in the catches.

Although Tarpon are attracting their share of attention, anglers are showing a preference for Bonefish. This does not mean that the leaping, flashing fight of the Tarpon is growing less popular. It is rather that the wariness of the Bonefish is a distinct challenge to fly casters, making it a more difficult species to cast to successfully. Unlike Tarpon, Bonefish do not break the water when hooked. A small fish—10 pounders are whoppers—the Bonefish is both strong and speedy. A seven- or eight-pounder will run off 100 yards of line before the angler really is aware of what is going on, and many nationally-known fly-fishermen have declared the Bonefish tops of all fishes, fresh- or salt-water, that can be taken on a fly.

Practically all the salt-water fly-casters carry a tackle box well filled with fly casting equipment. A day in good fishing waters usually ends up with the loss of from a dozen to three dozen flies, broken leaders, and, sometimes, broken rod tips. In order to meet this loss, the angler keeps 100 or more flies and fly lures in the tackle box, along with extra guides, tools, oil cans, hook sharpeners, sharpening stone for the bait knife, bait knife, a flashlight, an extra reel, a couple of extra lines, coils of leader material, small weighing scales, and tape measure, some spools of silk or Nylon thread, a bottle of clear lacquer, and other useful items and gadgets.

An extra fly rod or two is considered a "must," and some fly-casters also go in for a fly-tying vise, feathers, hair, cork, chenille, gold and silver braid, and practically everything that goes into fly making. A number of these anglers make their own flies, and some have managed to attain considerable skill in this connection. On the other hand, some of the homemade products resemble nothing that anyone ever has seen before. However, they all seem to catch fish, and anglers finding a fly that seemingly is more successful in luring fish, stick with it regardless of its weird appearance. Salt-water fly-casting has created a large demand for fly-tying vises and materials, and stores that never before handled these items now have them on their shelves as a regular item.

Fishing tackle dealers also are handling feathers, bucktails, polar bear hair, and other materials used in making flies. This demand came about because salt-water fly-casters fancied the idea of making their own flies. At first, they were unable to find the types of flies needed on the shelves of the dealers. In addition many anglers had their own ideas concerning the kind of flies to use in salt-water fishing and proceeded to make their own.

Some of these flies proved to be excellent for the purpose, and it was not long before manufacturers began producing them. In the meantime, however, the anglers had found out that making flies was not difficult and that it provided a spare-time diversion. As a consequence, many anglers are making their own flies, and there is a steady demand for the necessary materials and tools. The majority of these flies are tied on No. 1/0 Mustad-O'Shaughnessy tinned hooks, the anglers maintaining that the Norwegian hooks are superior to the American-made product. Mustad hooks are manufactured in Oslo, Norway.

The fact that so many fly casters make their own flies is an indication of the special interest they take in the new sport. Very few plug casters make their own plugs, although occasionally one who does will be found. Practically no equipment is necessary in making plugs at home, and excellent fish-getters can be, and are, made from old-fashioned wooden clothespins. However, the great majority of plug casters buy their plugs and other plug casting lures, whereas a goodly number of fly casters take a special delight in making their own flies despite the fact that the investment in tools and materials is considerable.

Tarpon on a fly rod in the flats off the lower Florida keys.

Erl Roman

"Yep," the angler seems to be saying, "that fly will catch fish."

The discovery that many fish will take flies when they will not strike at other lures or take a natural bait is of great importance to salt-water anglers. Shad and Mullet, for instance, are common fishes that before World War II played a very minor part in rod and reel fishing. They were not thought of as game fishes, yet both put up a worthy battle when hooked and played on a fly rod.

Both Shad and Mullet are common on the Atlantic and Pacific coasts and the coast of the Gulf of Mexico, Shad running the more northerly waters and Mullets in the south. Through fly fishing, the Shad, in particular has become popular as a game fish, and there is little doubt, that this same thing will apply to other species not ordinarily included. At the very least, this would seem to open many new avenues of piscatorial enjoyment to anglers who take up salt-water fly-fishing. It likewise broadens the fields in which good fishing may be enjoyed conveniently and at little expense.

What the future holds for salt-water fishing is anybody's guess. Whether it will continue to grow rapidly in popularity, or is just a fad that will prosper for awhile and then be forgotten, remains to be seen. The present outlook, however, is most favorable for continued rapid growth. A shorter work-week, more leisure time, longer vacations brought about by automation, and greater significance attached to outdoor recreation will exert influences. There will be no let up in the promotion that sport of this nature is physically and mentally beneficial. Then, too, there is that strong pull out of the past, the latent desire to follow in the footsteps of primitive ancestory.

SPINNING IN SALT WATERS

Although the fixed-spool reel used in spinning made its appearance in England in the early years of the present century, it was practically unknown in the United States until 1935. Of course, the principle of stripping line from a reel instead of letting it unwind from a revolving spool has been common knowledge for a long time, and it is claimed that the Siwash Indians used a square wooden device embodying that principle in the 17th century.

Even after the fixed-spool reel and spinning rods and lures were introduced in this country, they did not make an immediate appeal to anglers. An attempt to popularize them in salt-water fishing in Florida, following actual fishing tests made during World War II, failed to achieve its object. However, the idea of employing spinning tackle for salt-water fishing around Long Island, Massachusetts, and Rhode Island gained some headway. Progress also was noted in Maryland, New Jersey, and Virginia.

Until 1949 the use of spinning tackle in salt-water fishing in Florida showed a very small increase. But after that year the popularity of this tackle leaped ahead in a very remarkable manner. Plug-casting in salt waters already had become a popular form of the angling sport, and fly-casting had gained adherents by the thousands, before the quick pick-up occurred in spinning tackle casting, or spin casting.

On the Pacific coast, the use of the fixed-spool

Erl Roman

Bonefish have fallen a ready prey to anglers using spinning rods, reels and lures. These gamesters put on a terrific battle when hooked on this light equipment.

Erl Roman

This Florida Bonefish struck at a spinning lure, probably a weighted bucktail, and was landed. Yellow or white bucktails, weighted slightly at the head, seem to be preferred by these gamesters.

Mass. Div. of Fisheries and Game

The ability to land lunkers like this big Massachusetts Brown Trout, just fresh from salt water, on light rods and a wispy line lends appeal to spinning tackle.

Erl Roman

Spinning tackle accounted for this mixed string of salt water Trout and Crevalle Jack.

Erl Roman

A mixed catch, mainly Channel Bass, made in the Florida keys on spinning tackle.

reel and spinning rods and lures also experienced slow growth. Until 1950, spinning tackle was still unusual enough in American waters everywhere to elicit curious inquiry from users of conventional tackle whenever one of its enthusiasts appeared on the fishing grounds.

The first spinning tackle used in this country was imported primarily from France and Great Britain where "thread-line" fishing had been popular for years. Soldiers serving overseas in World War II and on subsequent occupational duty became familiar with spinning, and many brought European equipment home with them. The reels were of the standard open-spool type familiar to all anglers today. The rods were primarily of split bamboo from 7 to 7½ feet in length, which had been developed by the Europeans as ideal for use in fishing for Pike, Trout, and Salmon. In North American waters they worked equally well for these species as well as for fresh-water bass, Pickerel, and panfish.

Spinning offered two innovations over conventional tackle. The light line gave the small reels a great capacity while the adjustable drag prevented line breakage, much as the star drag of conventional saltwater reels prevented a fish in the 500-pound class from breaking a line testing no more than 50 pounds of breaking strength. The almost frictionless release of line permitted unbelieveably long casts with lures weighing only a fraction of an ounce. Publicity attending the catching of heavy fish on lines with a breaking test of only 4 pounds won additional converts. It was not long before American spincasters began looking for new fields to conquer and took their thread-line tackle to salt water. For taking Striped Bass, Salmon, Bluefish, and Bonefish, the new equipment proved ideal.

Shortly before 1950 great improvements were made in the tackle that was available to American anglers. One of the most important was in the development of the monofilament line. The development of Nylon had made the use of synthetic leader material possible, and it soon all but crowded expensive silkworm gut out of the market. The new material came in long unspliced lengths. Used in place of conventional braided line on spinning reels it demonstrated many advantages over braided line. It was practically invisible in the water, and it did not pick up water on the retrieve. The first monofilament lines, however, had some disadvantages of their own. They were inclined toward stiffness in the coil and toward excessive stretchiness under the stress of a fish strike. While manufacturers and importers of spinning tackle emphasized in their advertising the indisputable fact that the fixed-spool reel "eliminated backlashes," they seldom played up the equally indisputable fact that improperly spooled monofilament line, especially that of poor quality, can result in a "bird's nest" of massive proportions. Other difficulties arose be-

Erl Roman

This Miami angler did quite well with his spinning tackle. The fish are Channel Bass.

cause some of the early models of reels had a tendency to catch the line in their working parts or to impart an excessive twist in the line. These faults are still inherent in many of the cheap reels and lines made by fly-by-night manufacturers, who are more interested in quick profits than in building a reputation for quality. They are no bargain at any price. These early faults have been largely eliminated from their reels and lines by reputable manufacturers.

Modern monofilament line in Nylon, Orlon, and related synthetic material is as soft and as pliable as the finest silk, and it has the added advantage of being non-absorbant and rotproof. Unlike braided line, it does not carry water to the line on retrieve. It retains just enough stretch to provide a valuable shock-absorbing buffer against the lunge of a heavy fish. The development of the monofilament line undoubtedly was the most important single factor in launching the spinning boom of the early 1950's and in establishing the method as one of the most popular methods of fishing.

Simultaneously with the development of the good monofilament line was the development of the fiberglass rod in various weights and sizes. Fiberglass provided precisely the right action for obtaining casting distance with light spinning lures. American manufacturers soon were offering rods that were equal in action, strength, and serviceability to imported rods of split bamboo costing ten times as much as the mass-produced product.

In addition to fresh-water fishing, spinning tackle soon was found to be ideal for taking the smaller salt-water game fishes. The pioneers in salt-water spinning used standard fresh-water equipment, and tackle of this kind still is excellent for fishing for Mackerel, Bluefish, small Striped Bass, and similar fishes. As spinning came into its own, however, American manufacturers began offering tackle designed especially for salt-water use. Reels were made corrosion-proof and rods were equipped with rust-proof guides and reel-seats. The rods and reels also were offered in various sizes for handling larger and heavier fish, up to and including 100 pounds in weight.

Fresh-water rods with tips of from five to seven feet in length are entirely suitable for most fish up to 10 pounds, but for salt-water fishing where larger species may be encountered regularly a two-handed rod will provide greater casting distance and more leverage in fighting the fish. Such rods are ideal for fishing for Snook, Bonefish, small Tarpon, and Salmon. Where great distances in the cast are required, the angler can obtain surf-casting models, with tips up to 10 feet in length. A spincaster using tackle of this kind can cast a 2-ounce lure as far as a surf-fisherman with conventional tackle can cast an 8-ounce lure. Not long ago, nine-thread linen line with a breaking test of 27 pounds was considered light for use in fishing for any but the smaller of the salt-water game fishes. Today fish

Erl Roman

A Channel Bass and some Crevalle Jack taken on spinning tackle.

up to one hundred pounds are taken regularly on monofilament line with a breaking strength of 10 or 12 pounds. The spincaster is at a decided disadvantage over the caster using conventional tackle only when casts must be made into a heavy wind, where heavy sinkers or lures must be used, or where the fish has access to jumbled rocks, coral reefs, and similar hazards. Spinning tackle also is not suitable for large bottom-dwelling fish, such as a heavy Grouper, that attempt to thwart the angler by skulking in caves and wrecks and which must be "horsed in." Spinning tackle is at its best when used for battling the free-swimming gamefish, like Salmon, Mackerel, Bluefish, Tarpon, Striped Bass and other species that depend upon strength and speed rather than seeking shelter on the bottom. There are few species, however, that have not fallen victim to spinning tackle, and considering the apparent frailty of the equipment, the size and weight of individual specimens is all but unbelievable to those who are not familiar with the use of such tackle.

The majority of the rods made for salt-water fishing with fixed spool reels are equipped with reel seats locked with screw rings. These are a decided advantage over the once universal sliding bands which are still used on many fresh-water rods, since they hold the reel more securely. Reels used in salt-water fishing usually are of greater line capacity and therefore heavier than those designed for light fresh-water service. If fresh-water tackle is employed in fishing salt water, care should be taken that all metal is rinsed thoroughly in fresh water after use since salt water is highly corrosive to steel and aluminum.

As this form of angling sport gained in popularity in the United States, a bewildering array of spinning lures appeared on the market. Nearly all plug manufacturers began to produce light-weight models of their old standbys for use with fixed spool tackle. Other manufacturers, as well as most of the old-line companies, produced many new models designed specifically for spinning tackle. Nearly every locality has its own favored lure for specific seasons of the year, and the proprietors of all tackle shops usually have their own "killer lure" for the local fish. Usually their recommendations are sound, although if the fish are known to be there and fail to respond to the recommended lure, it may pay to experiment. Not infrequently a popping surface lure will produce results when feather minnows, bucktails and other deep-working lures fail to take fish.

Nearly every form of lure that has been designed for fishing is available in light-weight spinning sizes, and nearly all will take fish of some species under certain conditions.

The fixed-spool principle, which permits long casts with exceptionally light lures, has made it possible to cast large streamer flies by adding a few split shot, pinched onto the monofilament line several inches from the fly. By doing this, the angler provides enough weight for casting without unduly disrupting the action of the streamer fly. Weighted flies may also be cast with spinning tackle, although these usually lack the lively action of those weighted independently or of the bucktail or feather jigs in which the head of the lure rather than the body is weighted.

Spinning tackle also is ideally suited to bait fishing, the size and weight of the tackle being selected according to the prevailing conditions. A favorite method on the banks and flats of the southeastern coast, which is covered in greater detail in the following section, is to rig a hook directly onto the monofilament line, without sinker, float, or swivel, and to bait with a single medium-sized shrimp. Nearly all of the many species that frequent these waters—Bonefish, Barracuda, Permit, Jack Crevalle, and similar species—are taken regularly on such

Mass. Div. of Fisheries and Game

A beach-buggy fishermen's camp on Cape Cod. These are trucks or carry-alls, customized to travel on packed sand and containing all the necessities of the beach fisherman.

simple rigs. With Barracuda a light wire leader is required since the razor-like teeth of the fish usually cut the line on the strike except when the fish is hooked in the lip so that the shank of the hook provides a bearing against the teeth. Similar rigs, with or without swivels, leaders, and sinkers are used for all forms of salt-water bait fishing. A single seaworm, minnow, or strip bait provides adequate weight for casts of medium length with light-weight salt-water spinning rods. When fishing from an anchored boat in a tidal current, the angler can cover much water merely by releasing the line gradually and permitting the tide to take his bait or lure in a natural drift and retrieving it slowly. The depth of the drift can be regulated by the use of the nearly invisible plastic bubble float, designed specifically for fishing with fixed spool tackle, and by using various numbers of split shot. The plastic bubbles may be filled with water to reduce their buoyancy, and very little weight is required to drift them below the surface.

The sport of spinning in salt water, although of relatively recent origin, has gone far in winning new converts each season. Spinning for salt water fishes has become one of the favorite methods, especially with anglers who like to fish for free-fighting species in weight classes below fifty pounds with ultra-light tackle.

FISHING SHALLOW BANKS

In many salt-water fishing localities there are extensive shallow areas, generally referred to as banks or flats, and some of these furnish excellent fishing for the smaller sport fish. In fact, this fishing has proved so attractive that a number of anglers specialize in it to the exclusion of all other kinds of sport fishing. This is especially true in extreme southern Florida from Miami to Key West, and in the Bahama Islands.

Covered with but a few feet of water at high tide, these banks usually are composed of mud or silt with salt-water grasses and other marine plants growing profusely. This makes an ideal set-up for various kinds of other marine life, such as shellfish and crustacea. It also provides food and shelter for tiny fishes, and these, along with the shellfish and crustacea, attract the larger fish. These visit the shallows with the incoming tides.

Fishes that are not at all afraid when in deep water become both wary and scary on the flats. Not having enough depth of water to maneuver and thus escape their enemies, they must depend upon watchfulness and speed. Thus, they are alert to every sound and movement, which means that anglers must exercise extraordinary caution to get the lure to them. Also, it means that fish hooked under such circumstances put up a much stronger and speedier fight than when hooked in deeper waters.

The most noted of these is the Bonefish, a fish of medium size that is plentiful in the Florida keys and the Bahama Islands. Rarely caught in weights of 10 or more pounds, this fish is held by many to be the gamest of all fishes, pound for pound. In fact, the angler who caught the first one on rod and reel said, "I verily believe that, pound for pound, the Bonefish is, far and away, the king of all swimmers; and the only objection I can urge against him is that an experience with him forever spoils one for all other fishing."

Another worthy foe, the Permit or Great Pompano, is sometimes encountered on the flats where Bonefish feed. It runs larger than the Bonefish and has also been described by enthusiasts as the gamest of all fishes. However, whereas the Bonefish usually caught on the flats weigh from 6 to 8 pounds, the Permit run from 12 to 16 pounds. They are wary, speedy and strong, and stage a very tricky battle when hooked.

Permit are not as plentiful on the flats as the Bonefish, and consequently are not as well known to anglers, thousands of whom engage exclusively in bonefishing and count the catch of a Permit as an extra piscatorial dividend. Since the first Bonefish was taken on rod and reel in Bear cut, near Miami, in 1893, anglers have built up a technique for fishing shallow banks that qualifies this form of angling for special mention.

Fishing the shallow banks combines casting and bottom fishing. Two methods are used, one of which is to select a location, anchor the skiff, chum the surrounding area, cast out baits and await whatever may develop. The other is to pole over the flats until the quarry is located, then try to cast the bait near the fish, and hope that they will find and take it. Anglers following the latter method consider it the most sporting, and they resent any other sort of fishing on the flats, especially the rather recent invasion by fly and plug casters. Being specialists, they look upon others as interlopers and usually do not hesitate to express their opinions.

Many anglers have become so engrossed in bonefishing on the flats that they have skiffs, rods, reels, lines, and hooks made especially to their specifications, and friends of long standing frequently have serious arguments over some minor difference in tackle or technique. In other words, so engrossed have they become in this form of angling, and so seriously do they pursue it, that they actually sell themselves on the idea that their technique is the only right one, and their equipment is the only correct rig.

Contrary to what one might think, this is a healthy attitude. It encourages competition on the highest level—honest competition in its highest sense in which the competitors not only express their opinions but stick to them with all the tenacity that is attributed to the Scots. Due to this condition, there has emerged over the years excellent tackle and other equipment built especially for bonefishing, and this sports fish has received recognition out of all proportion to its size.

Inasmuch as fishing the shallow waters includes casting as well as still-fishing, the rod is a sort of double-handed casting rod. It usually consists of a one-piece tip and a separate butt, the tip being from 61 to 62 inches in length and the butt about 18 inches. The tip weight is from three and one-half to four ounces, while the butt is made light but strong, with the handgrips of cork. The forward grip usually is part of the butt and is not placed on the tip.

The rod tip must have plenty of backbone to withstand the speedy runs and strong pull of the Bonefish, Permit, or large Barracuda encountered on the flats. However, it must have enough whippiness near the tip to allow maximum casting efficiency. Usually the tip is furnished with four or five intermediate guides in addition to the tip guide, and the tip guide must have line guards, to prevent the line from becoming entangled around the guide. This may appear to be a small item, but many fish have been lost when the line has whipped around the tip guide and failed to slide free.

The reel preferred by these specialists is a small and light free-spool reel without brake or level-wind mechanism and with a carrying capacity of about 150 yards of nine-thread line. Anglers who employ a reel with a star drag, or with a level-wind device, are generally looked down upon by the bonefishing gentry. They claim that the angler should be able to control the battle with thumb pressure and that in so doing he is giving the fish a more sporting chance, and he also is doing a more creditable and more enjoyable bit of angling. Also, they maintain, a level-wind device tends to reduce casting distance, and good anglers do not need these contrivances.

The line should be of monofilament or of nine-thread linen in natural color. However, some Bonefish specialists dye their lines in an assortment of colors calculated to make the line less visible when lying on the vari-colored bottom. The method of accomplishing this is quite simple. The line to be dyed is wrapped around a stick 12 inches long. It is wrapped lengthwise of the stick so that the loops are approximately 12 inches in length. Then three inches of one end is dipped in brown dye and three inches of the other end in green dye. This leaves six inches of white in the middle.

When the dye has dried and the line is unwound the result is six inches alternately of brown, white, green, white, brown, to the end of the line. The white, of course, is the natural color of the linen line—a sort of off-white. When cast and lying on the bottom of the majority of shallow areas, it is almost impossible to see this line even at a short distance. It is a type of camouflaging that is really effective and, seemingly, worth while. The cost of dyeing is negligible. Two small and inexpensive packets of dye will prepare a number of lines.

The hook employed usually is of the O'Shaughnessy type, with a medium shank, in a 1/0 or 2/0 size. This is tied to a Nylon gut leader of about 8 to 12 inches, which is then tied to the line. Some specialists double the line for a couple of feet, while others frown upon the practice. Also, tied to the line is another length of gut or fine line with a one-ounce sinker on the end. In other words, at the end of the line there are two lengths of gut, or one of gut and one of fine line, with a hook on one leader and the sinker on the other.

Bonefish specialists insist that the sinker should extend a couple of inches past the hook so that it hits the water first when cast. The bait should slide into the water right behind the sinker to eliminate noise and splash. To further eliminate noise and splash, a special sinker was designed for bonefishing. This is somewhat the shape of a tear drop, with a pointed end and an extended neck. There is a hole in the neck to permit tying. Being extremely streamlined, this sinker goes through the air like a bullet when cast and enters the water with an almost imperceptible splash.

Lately, there has grown up another group of Bonefish specialists who decry the use of any sinker and who overcome the disadvantage in casting by employing a six-thread linen line, or using 10 to 15-pound test Nylon, instead of nine-thread linen. They maintain that the Bonefish taken in shallow waters is handicapped by being forced to drag a sinker around. This practice is rapidly gaining adherents, although the old-timers still stick with the sinker and say that the six-thread line is too easily nicked and broken when it comes in contact with shells, rock, coral or mangrove shoots that are usually part of good bonefishing flats.

The boat, or skiff, used in bonefishing is an important feature, and it has been refined to an almost unbelievable degree in the Florida keys. Usually about 12 feet in length, it is beamy and somewhat full-cheeked. It is light in weight, comparatively speaking, yet of strong construction and with good seaworthy abilities. It tows beautifully behind a powerboat at either high or low speeds, poles almost as easily as a canoe and requires only a few inches of water to float. Inasmuch as the boat must be poled in most instances, and the use of an outboard motor or oars is unheard of amongst bonefishermen except in reaching the flats, the fact that the bonefish skiff poles very easily makes it a desirable craft.

Baits used in fishing the shallows should correspond with the marine life that inhabits the bottoms. In Florida, where this fishing is highly specialized, the anglers use hermit crabs, finny crabs, and shrimp. Naturally, live bait is preferred. In the Bahamas, the favored bait is conch meat, the native guides tenderize it by chewing before placing it upon the hook. If live crabs are used, the claws are broken off before the crab is placed upon the hook. This is supposed to make the bait even more attractive to the Bonefish or any other fish happening upon it. In using hermit crabs, the creature is relieved of its adopted shell before being made a bait.

A study of the shallow waters to be fished is advisable. If the water is clear and the bottom plainly visible, it is comparatively an easy task for competent anglers to figure where the greatest concentration of fishlife will be found and the routes the fishes will take over the shallow areas. This is particularly true in Florida and the Bahamas, where the bottom is visible even in the deeper spots, and the marine life on which the larger fishes feed can be observed even by the casual angler. For purposes of a quick survey it can be assumed that the most fish will be found where the plant growth is the thickest.

Knowing this, anglers who specialize in such

fishing usually pole their craft to the edge of the heaviest underwater growth, drop the anchor as carefully and quietly as possible, thrust the poling pole down deeply at the stern and tie a rope to it. This tie at the stern and anchor at the bow keeps the craft from swinging in the tide and wind. The next move is to throw the chum, which is ground up crabs, shrimp, conch, or other bait items into the water where the baits will be cast. Then the angler casts the bait, winds in a few turns on the reel to be sure the rig is straightened out, and awaits the strike, or "take," as some describe it.

If no fish are sighted, or the bait remains untaken, the angler moves to another spot and tries it again. This procedure is followed until a good area is located, the angler and his guide in the meantime scanning the water for signs of fish. Sometimes the upper lobe of the tail fins will be visible to the close observer, or it may be the dorsal fins, according to whether the fish are swimming along and looking for food, or rooting along with their heads down and tails up trying to locate various crustacea, shellfish, or other marine life. Sometimes the fish will concentrate on a certain area, rooting so deeply that the silty or muddy bottom is stirred up, causing the water to appear muddy.

In the other method of fishing the shallows, the skiff is poled along until finning fish or a "mud" is seen. Then the movement of the skiff is stopped by thrusting the pole down deeply enough to hold well, and the angler casts the bait toward the fins or toward the muddy area. If the bait is cast too near, the fish usually are frightened or startled. Thus it is better to place the bait a little to one side or the other, depending upon which direction the fish are moving or the direction the angler thinks they will move after a quick survey of the bottom. In this kind of fishing no chum is used.

Some of these specialists applied themselves so closely and studied the ways of fishes in shallow waters, so carefully and the types of bottom most attractive to them that they can almost unerringly put their bait nearer the point the fish will pass. To the tyro this may sound impossible, but to the angler who specializes on shallow water fishing such wizardry is an everyday matter, so simple that they do not speak of it unless questioned directly about it. Also, during the years of specializing, these anglers have invented terms to describe certain conditions of wind, tides, bottoms, and fish behaviorism, that only another specialist can quickly grasp.

All these things—the application and study, the pursuit of fishes by sight or other sign, the invention of convenient terms to describe certain conditions—have drawn the specialists together into a sort of clique, into which the non-specialists cannot fully enter until they prove themselves. On the other hand, these men are friendly and glad and willing to aid the tyro in gaining the knowledge they worked so hard to obtain. First, however, they must assure themselves that the seeker of knowledge is serious and not merely making conversation out of curiosity. Most of the specialists are

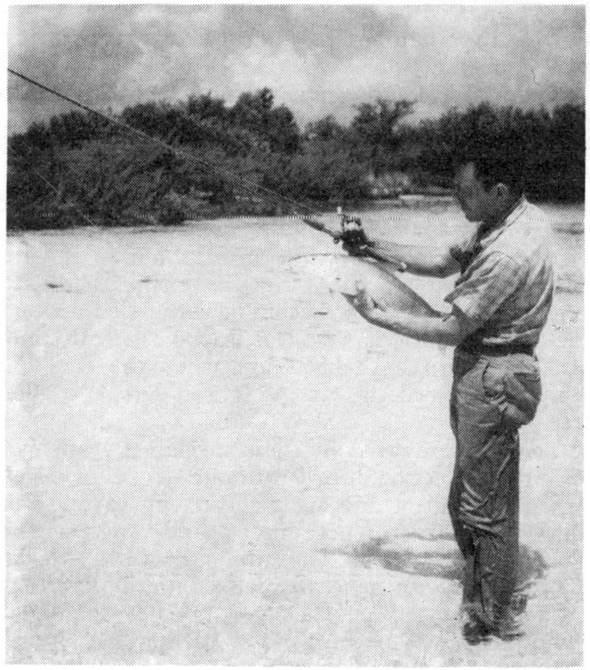

Homer Rhode, Jr.

Bonefish are noted for their speed and fighting ability when taken on light equipment.

anglers intent on their sport and do not take it lightly. They are somewhat akin to the old golf pro who expressed the opinion that a certain club member would never make a good golfer "because" he explained, "he thinks it's a game!"

The cast usually used in fishing the shallows is the side or low cast. In making this cast, the rod tip is held low and to the side, then swung forward. With a good rod and two-handed grip the bait can be easily cast from 100 to 150 feet, skimming through the air just a foot or two above the surface of the water and entering it with a barely audible splash. Shallow water specialists keep low in the skiff while awaiting the "take," and they wear clothing of neutral coloring to make themselves less visible. Most now wear Polaroid glasses to permit better visibility of the fishing area. They fish quietly, speaking in lowered tones and being careful not to scrape their feet or equipment on the bottom or sides of the skiff, or otherwise make noises or cause vibrations that might startle the fishes. Some refuse to use the click on their reels lest it frighten the quarry.

When they have their bait out, they take a few turns on the reel handle to straighten out line and rig. The rod is held low so that it may be raised quickly to set the hook in case a fish takes the bait. Also, very little slack line is allowed between the angler and the bait. If the skiff is swinging slightly, causing the distance between the angler and the bait to shorten and lengthen alternately, the line is taken up or let out to correct this condition. When the "take" or strike is felt, the rod tip is raised sharply almost instantly and the fish either hooked or lost. The reason for this quick action is that fish feeding on the flats usually take the bait firmly by the time the "take" is telegraphed up the line to the angler. At times, even large fish take the bait so easily that it is difficult for the angler to feel the action at his end of the line. At other times, there will be a quick tug that is unmistakable.

In many of the shallow waters the fish usually caught possess plenty of sharp teeth. This is true on most of the flats in south Florida, where the casual angler often hooks such fishes as Barracuda and Snapper. Nylon gut leaders can easily be parted by fishes having teeth, so the average angler fishing the shallow waters uses a light wire leader instead of gut. The specialists, however, does not cast his bait until he sees his quarry and makes sure they are Bonefish or Permit. He has no interest in others when he is fishing for Bonefish, with Permit the only exception.

Of course, there are many anglers who fish the shallow waters without special preparation, tackle, or equipment. Mostly, they employ whatever tackle they may have that is suitable for the purpose. They use ordinary plug casting rods, casting reels of the quadruple-multiplying kind, Nylon or silk line, light wire leaders and any 1/0 or 2/0 hook that suits their fancy. Bonefish and Permit can be handled on this tackle, but it is not entirely suited for the purpose. The equipment used by the specialist has been perfected over many years of shallow-water fishing, and ideas of many excellent shallow-water anglers are expressed in it.

Along the sandy beaches of the Florida Keys on the ocean side there are many places where the shallow waters extend to a considerable distance offshore. These are usually fished by wading. Specialists fishing in this manner practice a method described as "scenting." They cast seaward in a diagonal direction. They will then retrieve the bait and move along the beach, making another diagonal cast that crosses the line of the first retrieve. They then retrieve the second cast until it is just across the line of the first one.

Bonefish, they claim, can follow a line of scent made by retrieved bait. In making two casts three scent lines are provided. The Bonefish follow this fresh scent and eventually find the bait. This has been demonstrated to be good angling practice time and again, although it is not known whether the fish actually follow the scent or are guided by the marks made by retrieving the bait. If no action comes while casting from the beach, the specialist wades out several feet into the water and re-commences operations. The Bonefish may be found either close in or farther out.

This action is, of course, practiced when wave action makes sighting the fish practically impossible. If the shallow area happens to be smooth, the anglers walk the beaches or wade the waters trying to sight their quarry. When the fish are sighted, the cast is made as it would be from a skiff. These shallow water artists have practiced their favorite sport so often and have observed so closely that they can see fish or recognize signs indicating their presence when the average angler would be at a total loss. It emphasizes the difference between studying a sport until every item bearing upon it is learned, and just fishing casually and depending upon luck.

REEF FISHING

The law of the underseas is "fish eat fish," and nowhere can the operation of this law be better observed than on the coral reefs where the water is clear and even the smaller fishes can be plainly seen and identified at depths of 35 or 40 feet. Drifting over a reef for the first time, when the sea is calm and the surface smooth, introduces the angler to a new world. It is a world that is startling in its beauty, with the fantastic shapes of the various forms of coral, the sea fans and sea plumes, the odd vegetation of the salt waters, the delicate and brilliant colorings, the bizarre shapes and many kinds of marine life—all combining to delight the eye of the beholder.

Looking down into the depths, the angler sees tiny fishes as colorful as butterflies swimming about apparently unmindful of the larger fishes swimming nearby. For example, in addition to the tiny fishes, there may be Rock Hind, Grouper, Snapper, Porgy, Triggerfish, Amberjack, Barracuda, Shark, and many others. It looks like the ideal life where the lion lies down beside the lamb, where there are no snobs nor aristocrats, and everyone gets an even break. But suddenly something happens. The peace and calm is shattered, the tiny fishes disappear as if by magic, the larger fishes dart into favorite hiding places, and the brilliant coloring fades as colorful sea worms and other marine life fold themselves into almost invisible protuberances.

This usually happens so quickly that it is difficult to perceive what has caused it. Maybe it was the approach of an enemy or, more likely, some unlucky fish became sub-normal in its movements and was attacked and eaten by one or more of the larger fishes. Then, almost as suddenly as the peace and calm was broken, everything again becomes as it was before the incident occurred. The sea worms and similar life have re-opened or re-emerged to exhibit their odd forms and beautiful colors; the tiny fishes swim around pecking at microscopic life in the coral as if they didn't have a care in the world; the Rock Hind and Grouper slide out of their hiding places; the Barracuda, Amberjack, Shark, and other fishes move to and fro, and everything again is "six, two, and even."

Fishing the reefs on a calm day is like angling in a gigantic fish bowl. The angler can see the fish take the bait, observe what kind of fish it is, strike the hook home, then sit back and prosecute the battle. However, the fish the angler hooks is not always the fish that is boated. For example, the angler may hook a Grunt or a small Rock Hind. Suddenly the fight stiffens and the angler wonders how such a small fish can tug so hard or run so strongly. When the fish is boated, the angler finds, greatly to his astonishment, that he has been fighting a good-sized Grouper.

The answer is that while the fight was in progress the Grouper pursued the Rock Hind or Grunt and swallowed it, becoming hooked in the process. Sometimes, the angler will start out with a small fish, have a larger one take it, a still larger one take that, and end up fighting a big Shark, an oversize Grouper or a hard-battling Amberjack. The angler is too busy with the business end of the tackle to observe the various changes in opponents as the battle progresses. The guide usually can clearly see what transpires and sometimes tells the angler to slow up. "There's a big Barracuda after your fish," he may say, or it may be a Shark that is after a Barracuda the angler has hooked.

Three methods are used in reef fishing. In one, the boat is anchored and the angler still-fishes. Drifting and slow trolling are the other two methods. Still-fishing is practiced over shallow reefs where the majority of the population is made up of the smaller sport fish, and the chances for catching larger fishes is remote. In this fishing the angler employs lighter tackle, such as plug casting rods and reels, bonefish rods, double-handed casting rods, or light trolling tackle. The bait usually is live or dead shrimp, conch, or the flesh of lobsters or crawfish.

This is an excellent form of fishing, especially on a calm day when the actions of the fishes can be clearly observed and the angler can place his bait temptingly near a fish. It is good, also, in that it permits use of lighter tackle and enables the angler to have a satisfactory fight even with a small fish. Of course, even here there is always the possibility that a larger fish, say 25 to 50 pounds, may take the bait directly or pursue and swallow a smaller fish that has been hooked. Such an occurrence always heightens the excitement and usually provides another story about the "big one that got away."

In drifting and slow trolling over the reefs, cut baits are used. The best are cut from the undersides of Bonito, Albacore, Dolphin, Barracuda and Amberjack. The Bonito is best for this purpose, the silvery skin and red flesh being especially attractive to reef fishes. The bait is cut and trimmed to a streamlined shape, pointed at both ends. It is from eight to 12 inches in length and about one and one-half inches wide at the widest part, and about one-quarter of an inch thick at the thickest part. It must be carefully proportioned so that it will troll smoothly without twisting or untwisting the line.

If cut bait is used, some care must be exercised in making up the rig. In this rig the leader is usually No. 8 stainless steel leader wire and is from eight to twelve feet in length. A loop is twisted in one end of the leader, while on the other end the leader is placed through the eye of the hook, bent twice or three times around the shank, then brought back through the eye. It is then twisted around itself three or four times and formed to make a sort of safety pin to hold one end of the bait.

The hook usually is a 7/0, 8/0 or 9/0 O'Shaughnessy or Martuna type. After one end of the bait is pierced and fastened to the safety pin device of the leader, it is measured against the length of the hook, pierced in the right place and placed

Erl Roman

Fishing the reefs is productive of good catches. The fish shown is a Grouper. Note keel sinker on rig at right.

upon the hook. This part of the job should be carefully done so that there is no looseness or tightness between the safety pin and the part of the bait pierced by the hook. If it is too loose or too tight the bait will twist or untwist the line when it is trolled.

Sometimes artificial lures such as spoons, tin squids and feather minnows, are used in slow trolling over the reefs. Sometimes these are baited with a strip of fish flesh or porkrind especially prepared for salt water fishing. If a tin squid is used, it is not necessary to add a sinker to troll it slowly at a depth of several feet. However, if the lure is a spoon, cut bait, or a combination of spoon and cut bait or porkrind, a sinker is required. The sinker usually employed is known as a keel sinker, generally one weighing eight ounces, and it is placed between the line and the leader. The feather minnow is of the lead head type and usually of sufficient weight so that the rig requires no sinker.

During the past 20 years many reef fishermen have been using a stainless steel or Monel metal wire line instead of the customary twisted linen line. The reason is that with the wire line no leader is required, nor is a sinker necessary. The wire line sinks of its own weight. However, wire lines have not come into general use for reef fishing, and the majority of anglers look upon it as unsporting in reef and other ocean fishing. Some anglers use it because no sinker is needed and it does not tend to chafe and break when a hooked fish causes it to scrape over a coral rock. This is one of the reasons why other anglers condemn it. They maintain that it does not give a hooked fish a sporting chance.

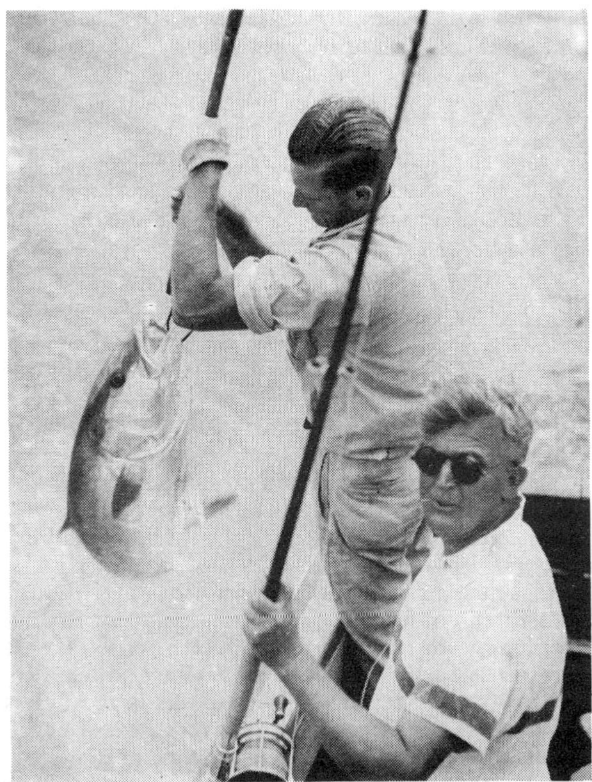

Erl Roman

The Amberjack stages a sturdy battle. This one was caught on the Florida reefs.

Generally speaking, reef fishing rods are of medium or heavy weight. The tips measure from five to six feet in length and weigh from nine to 16 ounces. The butt is the customary trolling butt, about 21 inches in length. Trolling reels varying from 4/0 to 6/0 in size are used, while the linen lines are from 18 to 24-thread. Some anglers, however, prefer to use lighter tackle, with rod tips weighing from four to six ounces and lines from six to nine-thread. On such light tackle the trolling reels are usually 3/0 or 4/0 in size. Practically all reels used in drifting or slow trolling over the reefs are equipped with star drags.

Gamesters sought by anglers drifting or slow trolling over the reefs include, Amberjack, Grouper, large Snapper, Barracuda, Jewfish, African Pompano, and Sharks. Of these the Amberjack is considered the best battler, pound for pound. The average Amberjack caught weighs about 35 pounds, although many smaller and larger ones are taken. However, a 35-pounder is a tough customer when taken on light tackle. Amberjack are quite speedy in their runs when hooked. They fight a strong and tricky battle and are noted for their ability to stage a last-moment fight just when the angler figures he has them whipped.

This trick of the Amberjack should be remembered by anglers trying reef fishing for the first time. The fish will be swimming weakly on its side, apparently all in. In the flick of an eyelash, it will dart strongly downward. If the angler is not prepared for this maneuver, the rod tip is forced down across the transom of the boat and broken. This same trick is practiced by the Crevalle Jack, noted as one of the trickiest of all game fish. Because of it, these two fish have earned the name of rod busters.

Comparatively few African Pompano are caught by reef fishermen. They are deep and flat of body in proportion to their length, somewhat on the order of Crevalle Jack and Permit, or Great Pompano. Usually, they fight a typical Pompano battle, keeping broadside to the pull of the rod, running strongly and sounding frequently. Average size of those caught is about 20 pounds and African Pompano of this size are fine fighters when taken on light tackle.

Grouper of various kinds are plentiful in the coral reefs. When hooked, a Grouper will immediately try to dodge into a convenient hole or crevasse in the coral rocks. Sometimes they succeed before the angler can stop or turn them. If the Grouper does succeed, the angler has three courses open to him. One is to cut the line and fasten on a new rig; the second is to let the line go slack and try to fool the fish into thinking it is safe to emerge from its hiding place; and the third recipe is to hold a tight line and strum on it as on a guitar string. This vibration sometimes frightens the Grouper and causes it to dash out of the hole or crevasse.

If the angler can stop or turn the Grouper before it reaches a safe hiding place, the ensuing battle is not at all strenuous. For a few runs the Grouper is a fairly strong opponent. However, after that it resorts to pulling and tugging, finally giving up and allowing itself to be taken alongside and boated. Grouper attain weights in excess of 100 pounds, and the Warsaw variety taken on deep reefs triple that. The average weight, however, is about 30 pounds. They are difficult to take on light tackle, due to the exceedingly strong first run.

Several kinds of snapper are caught on the reefs, but the kinds mainly sought are the Mutton Snapper and the Dog Snapper. The latter have been caught weighing more than 100 pounds, but the average is much less. Dog Snapper weighing between 20 and 30 pounds are regarded as good catches, while the Mutton Snapper averages about the same. Both kinds fight hard, being rather speedy on the take-off and fairly tricky. They are good fighters when taken on light tackle, as are all of the snapper family.

Barracuda, known as "tigers of the sea," run large on the reefs. Average size is about 18 to 20 pounds, although much larger ones are sometimes caught, and it is not at all unusual to take individuals of 40 pounds. These fish probably gained their nickname due to their rather ferocious appearance and large teeth. They will strike either an artificial lure or trolled bait readily and put on a fairly speedy battle when hooked on light tackle. They are not generally regarded as a top game fish, but this is due to the fact that they usually are hooked and fought on heavy tackle.

Jewfish run large and lazy. Attaining a weight of 600 pounds or more, they resemble the grouper both in appearance and in style of fighting. If the angler can stop them before they dive into some hiding place in the coral formations, they tend to give up rather easily. If, however, they reach the safety of the hideout, the angler might as well cut the line, rig up anew, and start fishing operations again. Smaller Jewfish, weighing under 100 pounds, are speedier and more stubborn when hooked, and the very small ones of 10 or 12 pounds prove themselves excellent fighters when taken on plug casting equipment.

Most of the shark taken trolling over the reefs are Sand and Leopard Shark, with an occasional Mackerel Shark. Of the three, the latter are by far the best fighters. Mackerel Shark leap frequently when hooked, are fairly speedy and tricky, and are stubborn to the last twist of the reel handle. Those taken on the reefs average about 150 pounds, although much larger ones sometimes are caught. Mackerel Shark are listed as one of the top game fish by most anglers who have tied into them. Sand and Leopard Shark are not nearly as speedy, nor are they as tricky. They do not hit the air in great leaps. On the other hand, they are strong and stubborn to the last notch, and Leopard Shark run large as an average.

Reef fishing is not as popular as it deserves to be. This is probably due to the publicity achieved by the blue water Marlins, Swordfish, Tuna, Wahoo, Sailfish, Dolphin, and Bonito. The great majority of salt-water anglers who fish the offshore waters are sold on these highly publicized game fish that deserve all the publicity they receive. On the other hand, reef fishing is an enjoyable and exciting form of angling and it should be more popular than it is. When guides hit a slow day in the blue waters, they often try the reefs where they know they can always tie their customers into some kind of a fighting fish.

John Mahony

A good Barracuda.

OCEAN TROLLING

Trolling the blue offshore waters has been a favorite sport with salt water anglers for many years. Books on salt water fishing published around the middle of the 19th century sometimes refers to this sport as trailing, as well as trolling. Trailing was, perhaps, more correct, for in this form of angling the bait, or lure, actually is trailed behind the boat to attract fish. However, trolling now is the accepted term, and it is so listed in dictionaries. Perhaps the sport took its name from troll, the early name for the reel used for trailing.

Ocean trolling now is practiced throughout the world and with many kinds of angling equipment, known generally as extra light, light, medium, heavy, and extra heavy tackle. During the past 35 or 40 years, however, the trend has been toward the lighter equipment. This is largely due to improvements in fishing craft, which has become more speedy and more easily maneuverable. Also, as the sport has become more popular both anglers and fishing guides have become more experienced and more familiar with the fighting habits of the blue water game fish. Last but not least, fishing equipment, especially lines and reels, have been considerably improved.

Trolling rods usually consist of a one-piece tip measuring from 60 to 62 inches in length, with a separate butt generally measuring from 14 to 26 inches in length. Some of the extra light rods have butts measuring as little as 12 inches, while the extra heavy rods used in big game fishing have butts longer than 26 inches, according to the make, the preference of the angler, and the type of fish sought. Some butts made for fishing for giant fish have a special cradle arrangement to hold the reel, thus making the reel part of the butt. A recent innovation in big game fishing rod butts is one that curves sharply midway between the butt cap and the reel seat. It is claimed that this butt aids the angler in pumping in line when a large fish is hooked.

Trolling rod butts of the better grades usually have an indentation in the butt cap to fit the rod gimbal with which fishing chairs aboard fishing cruisers are equipped. This indentation prevents the rod from turning to either side while a fish is being fought, which is a real aid especially in big game fishing where the reel is heavy and maintaining it in the proper position causes additional strain.

Trolling rod tips usually are equipped with a tip guide and four intermediate guides. This number sometimes is varied according to the weight of the rod tip in relation to its flexibility. The tip guide may be a plain guide or a roller guide. In the roller guide the line moves over a freely running wheel, somewhat like the wheel in a pulley, thereby eliminating friction on the line. Some of these roller guides have wheels that rotate on an axle, while others are provided with roller bearings. Both types are rather expensive as compared to plain tip guides, due to the work involved in making them.

The majority of intermediate guides are somewhat elevated to aid in keeping the line from rubbing on the rod tip. Some rod makers lay great stress on this point, elevating the guides considerably in a sort of bridgework arrangement. Usually this bridgework is made of a springy material, mainly stainless steel, and the claim is made that through this arrangement the line is not only prevented from rubbing against the rod tip but also that the strain on the line and the rod tip is more evenly distributed. The effect of such strain is cushioned, it is claimed, and direct shock strain prevented. When first introduced, the bridge type guides appeared only on the heavier rods. Now, however, they may be obtained on trolling rods of almost any type or weight.

Rules and regulations for salt-water trolling at first limited the weights of rod tips and the length of rod butts, at the same time specifying the kind, size and breaking strength of the line to be used with different rods. Some angling clubs still adhere to such rules and regulations, but the trend during the past 10 or 15 years has been to make these rules more or less elastic with the main emphasis placed upon the breaking strength of the lines.

Had these rules and regulations continued in force and been expanded in general use, it is possible that trolling rods of stated dimensions,

John Mahony

The angler standing is using light tackle, while the angler seated has a heavy rig. Note outriggers and elevated control deck.

weights and sizes would have become standard. Drifting away from the rules has acted against standardization in trolling rods and also in trolling reels. Likewise, where previously these rules acted as a sort of guide to salt water anglers, enabling them to balance the rods with the reels and lines, the reverse now is true. Many anglers regret this condition, and it is possible that a return to the former regulations, or something similar may occur in the future.

Rod tips are made of various materials, such as cane, wood, steel, beryllium-copper, glass, and a combination of cane and woods. The cane, or bamboo, rod tips usually are formed from six strips of the material firmly glued together. Rod tips made in this manner are known as single built. Other cane rods are double or triple built, using double or triple the number of strips, the inner six strips forming a core over which the other strips are glued. Due to the care with which these double- and triple-built rod tips must be made, and the amount of time and labor involved, they are more expensive than the single built tips.

Some wood rod tips are made in one piece, while others are laminated. Usually white hickory or greenheart is used in the one piece rod tips. In the laminated rods various combinations of wood or wood and cane are used. Usually the lamination is made up of flat strips of wood and cane, these strips being glued firmly and planed down to shape after the glue has set. Cross sections of most laminated rod tips resemble the cross section of a bow, this form having been found best for the purpose.

Erl Roman

Angler fighting a Bluefin Tuna off Bimini. Note the red flag denoting "Fish On—Keep Away."

Steel rod tips are made both in solid and seamless tubular steel. Beryllium-copper rod tips are made in seamless tubular design. Manufacturers of steel rod tips base their claim for superiority of their product on the theory that steel is more uniform than other materials from which rod tips can be made. In addition, it is stronger and can be shaped and tempered to produce a rod tip of any desired flex. The main claim advanced for beryllium-copper rod tips is that they will not rust or corrode. These tips also can be made in any desired weight or flex, such as whippy, medium or stiff.

Glass rod tips are a new product, introduced since World War II, but they have made considerable progress in angler acceptance since their introduction. Mostly they are made tubular or round with a wooden core. However, some are made square instead of round. All are made of thousands of glass fibers about the thickness of human hair welded together in a mold with plastics or other resinous products. Considerable improvement has taken place since they first were introduced. These tips require no particular care, do not have to be painted or varnished, and are not adversely affected by exposure to salt water, or damp or dry weather.

Erl Roman

Note the fishing chair—or "fighting chair" as they are sometimes called. This one was built to the owner's specifications.

The majority of tips for trolling are made in 4- ounce, 6-ounce, 12- and 16-ounce weights, with heavier tips for trolling for giant game fish. These heavier tips usually weigh from 22 to 45 ounces, of which weight the guides, forward grip and the male ferrule represent a considerable portion. Mostly, all metal parts of salt water fishing rods are made of stainless steel or chromium plated brass. Both have proven satisfactory in salt water use, although the stainless steel generally is preferred, being stronger and requiring less care. It does not rust, corrode, or discolor.

Clubs maintaining certain tackle regulations applying to rods and lines classify their tackle as three-six, four-six, light, heavy and extra-heavy. The three-six tackle gets its name from the rod weight and length and the line used with it. The rod is six feet in length, fully assembled, and weighs six ounces complete. The line used is six-thread linen. The tip of the rod must measure not less than five feet, and the butt not more than 12 inches. Originally, three-six tackle was intended for holding the rod with only one hand while fighting the fish. Later on, however, anglers began using two hands, through the placement of a removable forward grip on the rod just forward of the reel seat. It was made removable so that its weight would not be counted as part of the rod tip weight.

Four-six tackle consists of a rod with tip measur-

Erl Roman

Fighting a big fish. Note heavy rod and big reel, also the padded harness attached to the reel with heavy straps.

ing not less than 60 inches in length and weighing not more than four ounces. The length or weight of the butt is not specified. This rod is used in combination with six-thread linen line, and the tackle derives its name from the weight of the rod tip and the threads of line specified. As in the case of the three-six tackle, anglers try to get as much strength in the tips as possible without exceeding the weight limit. Thus, many anglers using three-six and four-six tackle have their rods built to order, getting away as much as possible from heavy guides and ferrules and putting as much material in the tip as possible.

Light tackle means one thing in one club and another thing in a different club. However, three specifications are more or less general. One calls for a tip measuring not less than 60 inches and weighing not more than six ounces, with a butt measuring not more than 14 inches in length. This rod is used in combination with nine-thread linen line. The second is almost identical, the only difference being that the butt can measure 18 inches in length. The third is the same as the second, except that it allows the use of 12 thread linen line.

Heavy tackle specifications include rods with a 12-ounce tip, no regulations applying to the butts, and lines up to 18-thread linen permitted. The extra-heavy tackle calls for 16-ounce rod tips, butts not specified as to weight and length, and 24-thread line as a limit. In big game fishing with rods heavier than the extra heavy being used, no rod regulations apply. However, in this fishing as well as in fishing with lighter tackle in salt water trolling, the International Game Fish Association has laid down rules and regulations governing the taking of fishes that must be adhered to if the catch is going to be eligible for recording. Salt water trolling records are kept by this organization.

Formerly, all salt water trolling was done with linen or cotton lines. Then linen became the popular line and for many years had this field to itself. More recently, however, Nylon lines have entered the field and became increasingly popular as they improved. Nylon is made of coal, air, and water by some chemical wizardry. When first introduced, Nylon lines had too much stretch, curled badly when over-stretched under the strain of fighting a large fish, and when wound tightly on a reel expanded against the side plates of the reel spool and put the reel out of commission. However, many improvements have been made in this line until practically all of the objection has been overcome. More recently monofilament has enjoyed increasing popularity for salt water trolling.

Following World War II, linen line became very scarce, whereas Nylon could be obtained. This gave the latter an opportunity for trial that might otherwise not have been presented. One of the advantages claimed for Nylon is that it is little affected by salt water and is not at all affected by foreign substances in the water or encountered in salt water fishing, such as minute marine organisms, fish blood, and fish slime. Nylon loses a small percentage of its strength when wet, whereas linen line becomes stronger when wet than when dry.

More service can be assured from all lines if, after fishing, they are run off the reels onto line dryers and carefully dried. They should not be exposed to the sun but should be dried in the shade. When winding lines onto the dryer, it is well to look for fish blood, slime, bits of seaweed, and parts of fish scales. It also pays to note the condition of the line. Often, nicks will be found that will weaken it. The line nearest the leader gets the worse wear because it is in the water longer than the rest of the line.

In ocean trolling, the line nearest the leader is also subjected to considerable friction from the

John Mahony

Bait for big Marlin and Tuna—a combination feather lure and cut bait.

Erl Roman

Scene at Cat Cay, Bahamas, during the Tuna Tournament. The Tuna season there runs from about May 6 to June 28.

water. It picks up considerable seaweed and marine life. In addition, it is let out and reeled in through the line guides frequently. When fighting a fish this portion of the line is more apt to come in contact with the fish and therefore is more likely to collect slime and blood. The minute marine life, invisible to the naked eye, quickly rots on the line and causes it to deteriorate.

In fighting large game fish, a ticklish part of the battle comes when the fish is close to the boat, almost whipped, but still as stubborn as a mule. It is at this time that the angler usually tightens up on the drag. A few yards of line is gained, then lost, and regained only to be lost again. That is when the line next to the leader is under the greatest strain, as it is reeled in and pulled out through the line guides. That is the main reason for the invention of the roller tip guide, to do away with a large amount of friction in times of greatest stress.

Trolling reels have kept up with the improvement in other fishing tackle. Starting from a simple spool and handle arrangement that made it convenient to let out or wind in line, reels now are as smooth and dependable as any other piece of small machinery. Even the less expensive trolling reels are well made and serviceable. As in other items, fine reels requiring fine metals and careful workmanship naturally are expensive merchandise. However, it pays big piscatorial dividends to use these better quality reels.

Perhaps the biggest boost to improvement in trolling reels came with the discovery of the big game fishing grounds in the Bahama Islands. Anglers fishing those waters in the early 1930's found their reels lacking when they tied into big Bluefin Tuna and giant Blue Marlin. However, American ingenuity proved equal to the emergency, and it was not too long before manufacturers were turning out reels that could take the punishment involved in a fight with these big fish.

At that time, comparatively few anglers specialized in big game fishing, and few reels large enough to accommodate the length and size of line required were available. Most of the big reels at that time were made on order. With the discovery of the Bahama big game fishing grounds, however, the popularity of fishing for giant fishes grew rapidly and reel manufacturers not only improved their product, or developed new types of reels, but also managed to meet the unprecedented demand.

Trolling reels generally are geared two-to-one, which means that the spool revolves twice for each complete turn of the reel handle. A few of the larger reels have been made with a one-to-one gear ratio but have not proved popular. Another innovation, reels with a handle on each side, failed to become widely used. The idea was to reel in line with both hands. However, big game anglers found that it was better to use one hand and arm pumping in line, employing the other in turning the reel handle to spool the line gained by this maneuver.

Reels used in trolling have a throw-out lever, or other throw-out device, that frees the spool and allows it to run unimpeded. Some of them

Erl Roman

The battle is over. The Bluefin Tuna is being boated over a roller built into the boats transom. Part of the transom has been removed.

have two levers, one to free the spool completely and the other to maintain just enough brake on it to prevent backlashing of the line. The majority of the trolling reels are equipped with a star drag, while others have an automobile type drag or brake. Big game fishermen usually employ the latter, claiming that it gives them a more dependable and smoother brake. This type of brake is adjusted with a lever that also serves to put the reel in the free-spool position.

Regardless of the type of brake with which a reel is equipped, the main test to determine if it is practical is the smoothness with which the drag or brake operates. This can be accomplished by putting on a heavy drag then pulling out the line against the drag. If it pulls evenly and smoothly, the reel is worth while. If the pull is uneven, the reverse is true. Another test that should be made is to put the reel in free-spool and then revolve the spool rapidly. A good reel will run quietly and without noticeable vibration in such a test. A third test to determine the worth of a reel is to note the smooth and quiet engaging and disengaging of the gears as the free-spool lever or other device is operated.

All trolling reels should be maintained in excellent working condition. This is true with all fishing tackle items. A weakened rod, a poor reel seat, a nicked line, or a reel that is not kept clean and well oiled and greased may mean the difference between losing or landing a fish. Failure of some item of tackle is usually the reason for the stories of the "big one that got away,"; it's tough enough to lose a good fish under any condition, but it's still more sad when the failure is due to the carelessness of the angler or fishing guide.

Trolling reels should be fitted to the reel seat snugly and firmly. There is nothing much more exasperating than to have a reel work loose while fighting a fish. To eliminate this possibility, the reel seat should be capable of firmly holding a reel under all stresses, and the reel should be fitted to it. Most reels will fit good reel seats without alteration. However, the angler will occasionally find that the reel base is too broad or arched too high to fit the seat. These faults can be overcome by a little judicious filing of the reel base so that a perfect fit results.

Through proper care, most reels will serve for many years in salt water trolling. Some of the more expensive reels will easily outlast the angler and can be passed on to the younger generation. Following each fishing trip, unless the angler is fishing for several days in succession, the line should be run off on a dryer, the reel should be removed from the rod and be cleaned, polished, and oiled; and the rod should be washed with fresh water and carefully dried. If the angler is fishing for several days in succession, it is all right to leave the tackle assembed. However, even then it pays to give each tackle item careful inspection to make certain that it is in good condition.

In recent years, many salt water anglers have tried very light tackle in ocean trolling. For example, they use a trolling rod with a tip that weighs but two or three ounces, employing with it a two or three thread linen line or a Nylon line of comparable strength. Some very creditable catches have been turned in by these anglers, but it is unlikely that such light equipment will ever come into general use. The use of such light equipment requires a combination of good angler, a good fishing guide, and an exceedingly speedy fishing craft that can be "turned on a dime."

Three-six and four-six tackle, employing a 2/0 or 3/0 reel to hold the six-thread line, is more practical. This is used by a goodly number of salt water anglers who get an extra thrill out of battling hard fighting fish on this light equipment. Such gamesters as Sailfish, White Marlin, and the smaller of the Striped Marlin usually leap more frequently when hooked on light equipment, and it is possible to bring them alongside without too much aid in the way of a speedy boat and a fishing guide who can, through expert handling of the boat, anticipate and somewhat counteract the desperate runs of the hooked fish.

In most of the fishing, both on the Atlantic and Pacific coasts, regular light tackle consisting of a six-ounce tip, 9 or 12-thread line and a 4/0 reel, is considered just about right for sporty trolling. This equipment is light enough to provide an enjoyable fight with even a small fish, yet is strong enough to battle almost any fish weighing up to 125 pounds. Of course, larger fishes have been taken on such tackle, but it is the exception rather than the rule. Anglers specializing in light tackle trolling soon learn the niceties of handling such equipment and some do wonders with it. Its use does not impose a heavy strain on the angler through weight or tough pumping, and its lightness causes the angler to use his "fishing brains" in order to make good catches.

Among the many species of fishes that should be fought on this light tackle are White Marlin, Sailfish (both Atlantic and Pacific), Tarpon (when taken in offshore waters of ocean or gulf), Pacific Yellowtail, California White Sea Bass, Wahoo.

Barracuda, Dolphin, Albacore, False Albacore, Atlantic Bonito, California Bonito, Oceanic (Arctic) Bonito, Striped Bonito, Kingfish, Spanish Mackerel, and Cobia. Also, if they are not running too large, say in excess of 180 pounds, Striped Marlin. There are several other species not usually taken in offshore waters that are great fighters on light tackle, such as big Channel Bass, Striped Bass, and Bluefish.

It has been the experience of light tackle anglers that billed fishes, such as Sailfish and Marlin, leap more frequently when hooked on lighter tackle. These fishes can be, and are, taken on three-six and four-six tackle and have also been successfully fought on 2- and 3-thread line. This same thing applies to Tarpon hooked in the Gulf of Mexico and short distances offshore in the Atlantic Ocean. These fish tire quickly when they leap repeatedly, and they can be brought to boat within a reasonable length of time by anglers expert in the use of light and extra-light angling equipment.

Fishes that bore deeply when hooked, such as the Bonitos and Albacores, fight stubbornly against light tackle. The larger ones stage a tough battle, especially Albacore which attain weights as high as 50 pounds, the small Bluefin Tuna, small Yellowfin Tuna, and small Allison Tuna of the same weight. These fishes put a big strain on lightrods and lines, and it is much more sensible to hook them on heavier tackle.

Pacific Yellowtail, California White Sea Bass, Wahoo, and Great Barracuda are logical light tackle gamesters, although they take lots of line on their first runs after being hooked. This is especially true of the Wahoo, reputed to be the speediest of all ocean gamefish. The smaller Dolphin, weighing up to 20 pounds, put on a brilliant, leaping fight on the lighter kinds of tackle, while the larger ones, up to 60 pounds, actually present a light tackle problem. When hooked, they will leap awhile, then swim at a different angle from the pull of the rod and line until they have regained strength. In this manner, they manage to make themselves hard to beat on light tackle.

Rods with 16-ounce tips have come into increased favor with big game anglers. These rods are used in combination with 24-thread line wound on a 10/0 or 12/0 reel. Many giant fishes have been taken on this line-up of fishing gear in both the Atlantic and Pacific Oceans, including Blue Marlin, Bluefin Tuna, big Yellowfin and Allison Tuna, Mako Shark and Striped Marlin. Some of the better known anglers and guides are outspoken in their praise of this tackle and claim that heavier tackle is not necessary in hooking and fighting the biggest of big game fishes.

Quite a number of anglers throughout the world specialize in trolling for giant game fish weighing in excess of 350 pounds. In fact, some of these specialists have been known to order their guides to pull the bait away from fish that look smaller than 500 pounds. They do not want to spend their time fighting any fish weighing less, figuring that the time thus spent might more profitably be employed looking for larger game. Also, there are several big game anglers who like to fight the big ones on a rod tip weighing from 9 to 12 ounces, 15-thread line, and a 9/0 or 10/0 reel. Some big fish have been taken on that rigging.

This trend toward lighter equipment in hooking and fighting ocean game fish is growing rapidly. Where big game anglers formerly used 54- and 72-thread line, with very heavy rod tips, they now use 24- to 39-thread line, with rod tips in proportion. Many anglers who formerly boasted of their catches on light tackle have now adopted three-six, four-six and even lighter equipment and are employing it regularly in the taking of Sailfish and White Marlin. This has created a problem for rod and line manufacturers, for anglers are demanding super-flawless merchandise that will withstand punishment that such light equipment never was made to endure.

Fishing cruisers and other motored fishing craft have kept pace with the rapidly growing popularity of ocean trolling. In the early days of the sport these boats were slow, undependable, and uncomfortable. Today they are speedy, completely dependable, and as comfortable and convenient as a fine private office. Where the average fishing cruiser was a smelly nose-diving or water-pushing monstrosity, they now are clean and seaworthy. The majority of them are equipped with twin motors and two rudders, with motor driven pumps and good air circulation assuring a dry bilge.

The fishing equipment also has rapidly improved. This is especially true in the seating arrangement of one, two, three, or four fishing chairs in a roomy cockpit. Some of these chairs, known as "fighting chairs," have been built especially to the specifications of the boat owner. Others come as regular equipment on the cruisers. Each chair is furnished with a gimbal arrangement that holds the rod securely, preventing it from twisting, yet permitting the angler to move it up and down or

Erl Roman

Mackerel used as trolling bait, rigged on piano wire leader with hook projecting from the side.

sideways, a great aid when fighting a big fish. The back of the chair is removable to permit the angler to pump the rod more efficiently and with less strain. Also, there is an adjustable foot rest that allows the angler to brace himself in a more comfortable position.

Some of the cruisers have a removable section in the transom, with a roller placed below it so that big fish can be hauled into the cockpit with a minimum of effort. All cruisers used in big game fishing have a block and tackle arrangement for hoisting the giants aboard, and some have a roller at the side instead of the stern to facilitate the boating of fish. The majority of the cruisers have dual controls, with one set in the cockpit and the other top the cabin. This elevated control deck is useful in many ways, but mainly it allows the guide to more surely sight fish, watch the progress of the battle after the fish is hooked, and operate the craft accordingly; see a greater expanse of ocean and watch other craft in the vicinity.

Naturally the cabins of the modern cruisers also have been improved. In the larger ones, the crew quarters are entirely separate from those of the owner and his party. Excellent accommodations are provided, some with a shower bath and nearly all with a electrically-flushed toilet. Bunks are as comfortable as fine beds and now have inner-spring mattresses instead of cotton filled canvas bags. Full advantage is taken of the convenience of electricity for lighting and also for refrigeration in the galley and the operation of small electric fans. The efficient galley stove is operated handily with bottled gas or other convenient and odorless fuel.

Perhaps the greatest advance of all has been the installation of the ship-to-shore radio-telephones in the modern fishing cruisers. Through the use of this little contraption, communication can be quickly and easily established not only from one boat to another, but also to the angler's home or office. It mainly is used, however, in communicating with other fishing cruisers to find out how the fishing is in various localities and thus locate the best areas. Introduced as a sort of innovation, the ship-to-shore telephones now are regarded as just about the most important piece of equipment on the modern cruiser, increasing safety and convenience.

Outriggers now are standard equipment. These outriggers usually are from 35 to 40 feet in length. They are lightly built, generally of aluminum and bamboo, and are hinged to the boat so that they can be fastened in an upright position when the boat is at dock. In fishing, they are dropped to a 45 degree angle, extending outward from the sides just aft of amidships.

Outriggers are useful in keeping the trolled baits out of the wake of the boat, and also in giving a more natural movement to the baits. They have a small pulley or glass ring at the end, with a cord passing through it and extending back into the cockpit. A spring clothespin is fastened to this cord and the fishing line, after it has been let out the right distance, is placed between the

Erl Roman

The White Marlin is strong, graceful, tricky and speedy. This one is indulging in what is known as "tail walking" or "dancing on the wave tips."

jaws of the clothespin. It is then carried to the end of the outrigger through manipulation of the cord, in the same manner as a flag is hoisted on a flagpole.

In use, the fishing line runs from the reel to the tip of the outrigger, thence back into the ocean with bait attached. As the cruiser rocks with the wave motion, the outriggers flex and recover alternately, causing the bait to leap, wiggle and dive. When a fish strikes, the line is pulled from the clothespin by the force of the strike, and the fish is hooked as the line straightens out. By keeping two of the lines out of the wake of the boat and a considerable distance apart, the outriggers make it possible to fish two flat lines directly behind the boat, which are separated a distance equal to the width of the cruiser plus the length of the rods. It is also possible to fish a flat line from the center, making a total of five lines and baits trolled.

Of course, when a large or active fish is hooked, it usually is necessary to reel in the idle lines to prevent them from becoming tangled or fouled in the line that has a fish. In fact, most anglers reel in their lines when another angler has hooked a fish, so that he may fight it without the extra hazard of trying to keep clear of other lines. Sometimes more than one will be hooked at the same time, and there have been several instances of three Sailfish being hooked at the same time, all three being fought successfully. Instances of hooking one, two, or three fishes, in addition to the fish that struck first, are frequent enough to be classed as not rare, and in such instances the anglers, the guide, and the mate all have their hands full. There is enough excitement at such a time to create a pleasurable piscatorial milestone in the memory of even the most blasé angler. It is one of the high spots in the thrills of ocean trolling.

In fishing with light or extra-light trolling tackle, some anglers like to stand while fighting a fish. This, of course, takes them out of the fishing chair with its gimbal for resting the butt of the rod. Some anglers equip the butt end of the rod with a rubber arrangement made especially to fit, somewhat on the order of a rubber tip used on a crutch. In fact, some anglers use this rubber crutch tip, while others use a regular rubber butt rest shaped like a flattened ball. Another, and better, form of butt rest is made of leather. This is fastened by a belt arrangement around the waist so that the butt rest is in a convenient position. Other butt rests, to be used either as a belt or with a belt, are available. Most of these are made of metal, with a backing of foam rubber.

In fishing with extra-heavy tackle a harness is required. These usually are made to go over the shoulders and are then fastened to the reel. Thus equipped, and with the butt of the rod in the chair gimbal, the angler is enabled to distribute the strain of the fight to his back, in addition to the arms and legs. Some of these harnesses are simply made of leather, while others are fashioned of heavy canvas, foam rubber and leather. The latter are much better as the foam rubber and canvas fits the back from just below the shoulder blades to the hips, giving wider and more comfortable distribution of the strain in a long drawn out, tough battle.

Alongside of each fishing chair in correctly equipped fishing cruisers, there is a rod rest attached to the coaming of the boat. They usually are made of metal pipe and lined with a short length of rubber hose. Rests provide a convenient place to hold the rod in case the angler wishes to leave the fishing chair, or if the angler wants to eat or drink, or for any other reason does not wish to be bothered with holding the fishing rod. These rests are placed in a slanting position, so that when the butt of the rod is placed in them the tip is slanting to a safe degree, and the rod will not be broken if a fish happens to strike.

In big game fishing, the strikes are usually few and far between. In addition, the guide nearly always sees the big fish before they strike. So, the angler usually leaves the rod in the rod rest and is thereby relieved of holding the weight of the rod, plus the pull of the trolled bait. He is, however, always on the alert and prepared to grab the rod, fasten his harness to the reel, hook the fish, and then carry on the battle. A good mate also is in the alert to aid the angler in getting set for the fight by helping him fasten the harness to the reel, adjusting the harness, and removing the back from the fishing chair.

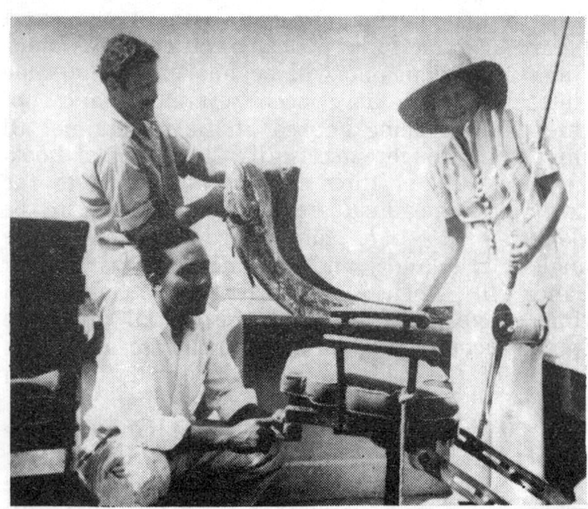

Erl Roman

Female Dolphin taken on 12-ounce tubular steel rod and 15-thread line.

In the majority of cases, fighting such giants as Broadbill Swordfish, Blue Marlin, Black Marlin, Striped Marlin, Mako and Bluefin Tuna, puts a great strain upon the angler. Of course, there are instances where the hook happens to strike home in a vital spot, and the fish is not able to put forth normal effort. Also, it is well established that Bluefin Tuna taken in shallow waters do not require the same amount of effort by the angler as those taken in deep waters. Generally speaking, however, hooking and fighting giant fish is a tough game—one that not only requires skill and knowledge but also a lot of hard work.

Even with the aid of a butt rest or gimbal, a harness, and a chair especially designed for fighting big fish, the weight of the tackle is partly supported by the angler. This weight, when extra heavy equipment is employed, is considerable. Holding the rod against the pull of the fish, with the reel brake set as it must be, is a strain. Pumping in line when the fish tires or takes a rest gets to be hard duty when the fight lasts from one to several hours. It is during such times that the angler learns that a poorly adjusted harness, or a poorly constructed one, can be mighty uncomfortable and annoying. It is then, too, that the angler finds himself wishing that the forward grip on the fishing rod was thicker and better padded, or thinner and with less padding.

Every little item that might be wrong with the tackle, the chair, the cruiser or the guide—or might be right and still not suitable to the angler—reveals itself during a tough battle. This condition, however, has served an excellent purpose in bringing about improvements in fishing tackle, from fishing hooks to complete fishing cruisers. This improvement has continued through the years, with anglers and fishing guides demanding and manufacturers supplying the demand.

Sometimes the supply has come woefully behind the demand, and that was especially true in the case of big game angling. There have been times when rods and reels suitable for fighting big Marlin, Broadbill Swordfish, and Blufin Tuna were actually unobtainable. In the emergency, local inventors exercized their ingenuity and produced tackle that to this day has not been equalled by the larger fishing tackle manufacturers. Many items of big game fishing gear even now must be made to order.

This condition came about largely through the failure of the manufacturers to test under fishing condition the practicability of the items they offered. While much improvement has come about in the past 25 years, there still is room for more. In the opinion of the majority of anglers, fishing tackle manufacturers could do a better job if they or their representatives kept in closer contact with the sport of fishing.

Many big game anglers are now using heavy

John Mahony

Sailfish tail-walking.

piano wire for leaders. This wire, generally a No. 12 size, is strong enough for all practical purposes, does not tend to kink and break easily, and can be made up into leaders without too much trouble. At this time, however, the majority are still employing twisted cable, despite the difficulty encountered in properly fastening hooks and swivels to it. In light, medium, and heavy trolling, the piano wire has always been the favorite.

In the lighter kinds of trolling the leaders are made up according to the kinds of bait to be used. Mostly they are made so that the hook is fastened stiffly, rather than free-swinging. The main object to be achieved is to prepare the leader and place the bait upon the hook so that it "swims" naturally when trolled. If the bait does not present this natural appearance, it not only will fail to attract fish but will also untwist or harden the twist in a line. Likewise, it will troll heavily, putting too much strain on the line instead of slipping easily through the water.

In big game fishing the bait usually is a dead fish of medium size. In preparing these fish for bait, it is necessary either to remove the backbone or break it in several places in order that it may have a natural wiggling motion when trolled. The usual bait rig has the point of the hook protruding from the underside of the fish, although some guides prefer to have the hook protruding from the side. In one rig, known as the New Zealand rig, the fish is placed behind instead of on the hook. This is contrived by a short line tied to the bend of the hook on one end and to the mouth of the fish on the other.

Artificial lures are successfully used in ocean trolling. Under a slow troll, spoons of various kinds make good lures. However, the favorite artificial lure is the feather minnow, an importation originally from Japan. This lure, made in a number of sizes and weights, consists of a lead head to which is attached a considerable number of feathers. The head has a hole running through it lengthwise. The leader is passed through the hole and the hook drawn tightly against the rear of the head, where it is almost hidden by the feathers.

Feather minnows and bucktails are available in variety and all will attract fish. However, most anglers and fishing guides prefer the yellow or white color, a combination of white and yellow, or either white or yellow with a few short red feathers just behind the head. These feather deceivers are specially good in fishing for Bluefin, Yellowfin or Allison Tuna, White Marlin, the Bonitos, Albacore, and the mackerels. Their fish-attracting efficiency can be increased by adding a strip of porkrind to the hook, or a strip of fish flesh, of sufficient length to provide a wiggly tail to the lure.

One of the old standbys for trolling on a flat line is the tin squid. Most fishing guides troll one of these lures from the center line, mainly to catch bait fish, such as Mackerel, Bonito, and Albacore. The size usually employed is about four ounces in weight. At regular trolling speed, about six miles per hour, this size tin squid will troll several inches below the surface and will pick up a considerable number of fishes during a day. Originally these metal squids were made of block tin but now are made of lead. A little judicious sandpapering now and then will keep them bright and attractive.

Wooden lures are not much used in ocean trolling. However, large wooden lures minus hooks, known as "teasers," are quite frequently trolled to make a commotion in the water and thereby attract fish to the other trolled baits or lures. One of the recent innovations in artificial trolling lures is fashioned of a slim piece of rubber that has wonderful swimming action when trolled. Another, better known because it has been available for several years, is the ocean size porkrind. Neither has become a favorite with anglers, although the porkrind frequently is used in combination with feather minnows.

Listed among the big game fishes mostly sought are Swordfish, Black, Blue and Striped Marlin, Mako and Bluefin Tuna. Thresher Shark and White Shark are seldom encountered by anglers trolling North American coastlines. Black and Striped Marlin, Swordfish and Bluefin Tuna, are caught along the Pacific coast, while Blue Marlin, Swordfish, Mako and Bluefin Tuna are the piscatorial prizes taken by anglers on the Atlantic side who enjoy tussling with the giants.

Big game fishermen have argued long and loudly concerning the comparative fighting qualities of these fish, pound for pound. The Black and Blue Marlin so closely resemble each other in structure and appearance that it is difficult to tell one from the other. Very few Black Marlin are caught within the Pacific range usually visited by American big game anglers, and tales of their gameness may very well be exaggerated. However, it seems reasonable to believe that Blue Marlin stage just as game a fight as the Blacks. Both leap frequently when hooked, greyhounding over the surface of the ocean in a truly remarkable manner and trying every trick to rid themselves of the restraining influence exerted by the angler.

While this is the usual style of fight of all the Marlin, many have been hooked that have failed to do any leaping. These are the ones that bore consistently toward the bottom from the time they take the bait, despite the best efforts of the angler to stop them. An individual of this sort really puts the angler at a disadvantage by stubbornly refusing to be led in any direction. This means that the angler not only has a terrific job battling the fish while it is heading for the depths, but he also has the backbreaking task of getting it up from the depths when it finally tires.

Mako stage a beautiful fight as a usual rule. When first hooked they start on a fairly long and speedy run, terminated with a gigantic leap that is actually startling. It is difficult to understand how such a larger fish can cleave the air to such a height. As the fight progresses, the length and speed of the runs, and the leaps, grow less. But the Mako is a game fish of unusual qualities and of great beauty of shape and appearance when alive and fighting. It seems a shame that they are so infrequently encountered by big game anglers.

Bluefin Tuna are tough opponents when taken in deep water. They're plenty tough in comparatively shallow water, but when they get their heads down and bore steadily toward the bottom in deep water, they really give the angler fits. They are speedy in their runs, and have been clocked at an estimated 56 miles per hour. They run very large in size, averaging better than 450 pounds. Prior to the advent of speedy and easily maneuverable cruisers, and before anglers and guides had familiarized themselves with the habits of hooked Bluefin Tuna, these fish were breaking more lines and rods, and freezing more reels, than any other.

Swordfish are considered by the lucky anglers who have caught them as the gamest of all the giant fishes. These anglers point out the difficulty in locating this fish and the many hours spent trolling the ocean before encountering one. One big game fisherman actually figured that it cost him $10,000 in boat and guide fees to catch his first Swordfish. Even after the Swordfish is sighted, there is no assurance that he will take the proffered bait. Added to this, Swordfish have a rather tender mouth, and the angler never knows just how well the fish is hooked, or how much pull he can exert without having the hook pull out.

Taking all this into consideration, it is no wonder that so few Swordfish are taken by anglers fishing from Mexico north on either side of the continent. When hooked, the Swordfish is a tricky, speedy, and stubborn fighter. He conserves his energy, never leaping high out of the water as does the Mako, and never greyhounding over the waves. When he comes up, he breaches the surface in a half leap. When he goes down, he bores speedily toward the bottom. Swordfish possess great strength and staying powers.

The majority of the fishes taken by trolling are automatically hooked by the power of their own strike and the speed of the boat. This, however, is not generally true with Sailfish and Marlin. These fish slash at the bait with their rounded bills—snozzles, some anglers call them. The bills are covered with small but sharp denticles, and when a small fish is the victim of such slashing tactics, it is injured and stunned. The Sailfish or Marlin then mouths and swallows it.

Thus, when one of these fish slashes at a trolled bait, the angler immediately puts the reel into a free-spool position, letting the line run out and causing the bait to settle on the water's surface in resemblance of a stunned fish. Occasionally, a Sailfish or a Marlin will grab a trolled bait and make off with it without further ado. However, in the majority of instances they slash first and swallow the bait later. The interim between the slashing and actually taking the bait varies from a few to about 10 seconds. Some anglers let the line run free for the full 10 seconds. Others, more experienced, strike and set the hook when the free running line picks up speed, indicating that the fish has the bait and is running with it.

Marlin, and especially the White Marlin, are more apt to take the bait without the preliminary slash than are Sailfish, and nearly always Marlin are quicker to take the bait after slashing than the

John Mahony

Sailfish off Miami Beach.

Sailfish. With the larger Marlin, the guide usually can see just what is transpiring and can inform the angler when to strike and set the hook.

Sometimes, even though the angler strikes at the instant that would seem right, the fish is not hooked. The thing to do then is to reel in rapidly. This maneuver usually brings the quarry back to the bait, to start the slashing process over again or to grab the bait and run. Often this performance will be repeated as many as three or four times. In at least one case a Blue Marlin slashed at the bait five times before being hooked, the angler reeling in rapidly after each unsuccessful strike and finally hooking the big fish not more than 40 feet from the boat.

It is well to remember that while fighting a big game fish a tight line should be maintained. This is particularly necessary when fighting a leaping fish. The best thing to do is to keep an eye on the line when the fish is running. When the line starts coming to the surface, indicating that the fish also is coming up, the rod tip should be dropped to just a trifle above horizontal so that it can be lifted when the fish leaps, thereby gaining line quickly when the fish hits the air. In addition to quickly raising the rod tip when the fish leaps, the angler should be prepared to reel in line quickly. Sometimes, if the rod tip is raised quickly enough, the fish is pulled off balance and falls on the water in an awkward position.

Handling a fish in this manner usually shortens the battle, for when the fish falls awkwardly, it often is strained or shaken up considerable and sometimes injured. It could be compared to a tumbling act, where the trained performers know how they are going to fall in order to do so gracefully and without injury. If someone had a line tied to the tumbler and yanked upon it while he was in the air, the resulting fall might prove fatal even though the fall was on a yielding substance.

Many anglers, in striking back the rod to set the hook, tend to bring the rod tip back too far. The best method is to strike hard but not to raise the tip of the rod past perpendicular. The same rule is true when pumping the rod to regain line. The rod tip should be stopped before it reaches perpendicular. When the rod is in an upright position, or past the perpendicular, the greatest part of the strain is on the tip end. At all times, the angler should endeavor to keep the rod in an arc that best distributes the strain on both line and rod.

At times, some anglers allow the rod tip to reach horizontal, with a practically straight line between the rod tip and the fighting fish, thus putting all the strain on the line. This is as poor form as raising the rod tip past the perpendicular, for the fish should always be made to fight the bend of the rod as well as the strength of the line. If the angler allows all the strain to go on the line, some sudden movement of the fish can cause a break.

John Mahony

The critical moment—leading in a Sailfish.

Erl Roman

Sailfish being photographed before being released.

When the fight is nearly ended it is more necessary than ever for the angler to keep his wits. More fish are lost close to the boat than at any other time. The angler should be on the lookout for a last flurry on the part of the hooked fish. Even after the guide has taken the leader, the angler should hold the rod in good position to renew the battle, just in case the fish is not as tired as it appears. Many times guides have grabbed the leader on a "green fish," or one that is not thoroughly whipped, and has been forced to relinquish his hold on the wire by some sudden activity on the part of the fish.

There is a certain code of ethics governing the actions of anglers who troll the ocean that should be followed in the name of good sportsmanship. First and foremost, release all fish that are not unduly injured, unless they are wanted for food, mounting, or photographs. Good sportsmen do not kill fish unnecessarily, and they should be glad and proud to spare the life of a worthy opponent. To release fish is also good conservation practice. After the fight is finished, let the fish go, so that it may recover and furnish thrills for some other angler—or even for yourself, should you happen to hook the same fish at a later time.

It is unethical to troll close to a boat aboard which an angler is fighting a fish. In big game angling the guide runs up a red flag signifying the fact that a fish is hooked and is being fought. Keep away from the immediate vicinity. In trolling, do not run close to, or over, another angler's line. If an angler fishing from the same boat hooks a fish, start reeling in line unless the guide says it isn't necessary.

It is well, also, to remember the old saying: "Don't count your chickens before they're hatched; don't fry your fishes before they're catched." Some anglers are superstitious and are apt to lay the blame for the loss of a fish on some other angler who may have been unduly optimistic while the fish was being fought. You may draw one of these superstitious anglers for a fishing companion, so, in the language of a rather prominent big game fisherman, "keep your mouth off the other guy's fish while he's fighting it!"

STRIP FISHING OR SPINNING FOR PACIFIC SALMON

Strip fishing or spinning, as it is called in the Northwest, is a popular and highly efficient method of taking feeding salmon. Developed in Puget Sound it has spread north through the coastal waters of British Columbia and into southeastern Alaska.

It is the light tackle means of catching the sporty Pacific Salmon and requires considerable skill and experience; not only in the preparation of the bait, but in boating the fish after it has been hooked.

The technique of spinning was evolved by studying the feeding habits of the salmon; particularly the King and the Silver. The King Salmon after a few months in salt water feeds almost exclusively on small fish—Herring, Pilchard or Candle Fish. Silvers when mature feed on the same bait although the diet of the younger Cohoes is primarily plankton.

The Herring or Candle Fish travel in schools within the protected coastal waters and are active, darting fish of from three to twelve inches. A salmon will rush into such a school, swim through it thrashing at the bait with its tail, thereby crippling a number of the small fish. It then turns back and leisurely picks up the slowly swimming cripples.

The spinner fisherman's object is to prepare a bait or lure that imitates as realistically as possible the actions of the crippled minnow. Normal fish swim upright and in a straight line except when changing its course. An injured minnow swims erratically, swaying from side to side, not turning completely over but swerving back and forth within a narrow plane.

Four species of the Pacific Salmon; the King Silver, Humpback and Dog may be caught by spinning if sought for at the proper season. But the King (Chinook, Spring, or Tyee as it is called in the Northwest), and the Silver or Cohoe form the greater part of the sports catch.

Spinners take most of the Kings landed during the winter from December through March when these fish are feeding in accessible waters on schools of Herring and Candle Fish. These immature Kings are called Blackmouth and run from six to twenty pounds in weight. During the summer and early fall, mooching—another form of spinning—will take mature Kings that usually run from 18 to 35 pounds. However an occasional Chinook ranging up to 50 pounds may be boated by this method. Landing a 50-pounder on mooching gear with a line testing 10 to 12 pounds is a feat the angler may rightfully brag about the remainder of his fishing career.

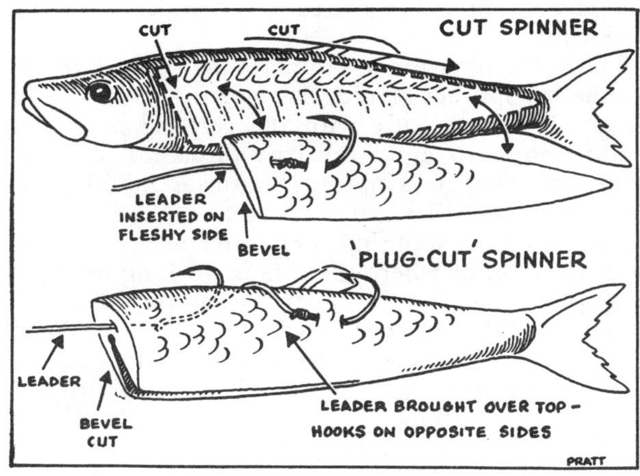

Allen Pratt

The Silvers are taken by spinners from late spring until October. The early feeding Cohoes are small going from two to three pounds. But by mid-summer they will have grown up to six pounds. Then in September the big spawners come in and fish weighing 10 to 14 pounds are common with an occasional twenty pounder being boated.

The cut spinner is prepared in virtually all cases from salt water Herring, the most readily available bait. The larger Herring are caught in traps or brush weirs usually between January and March. These are frozen, stored in deep-freeze lockers and sold by the dozen to fishermen throughout the season. Smaller size Herring will be netted during the summer season, kept alive in bait boxes, and retailed on the dock to the prospective spinner.

When fishing during the hot days of summer, the Herring must be kept cold by packing in sawdust and on ice, as a soft fish will neither cut well or stay on the hook.

Although old-timers may have a special knack for preparing a cut spinner, their technique is uniform in principle. These spinners are usually cut in the boat. A flat one-inch board about 12 by 15 inches, or the seat of the boat (if one doesn't mind the mess) is used as a working base. The spinners are cut as used during the fishing day so as to keep the bait as fresh and firm as possible. The most efficient knife is one with a single, narrow blade about six to seven inches long. The blade should be honed rather thin and kept as sharp as a razor.

Herring ranging from 6 to 10 inches cut into the best spinners. Whenever obtainable fresh Herring are preferred. Such Herring will keep firm and not burn during a hot day if they are allowed to purge themselves of all food by being held in a live box for at least 24 hours.

After the angler has carefully maneuvered his kicker boat over the "spinning hole," he drops anchor and starts preparing the bait. The Herring is laid flat on the cutting board and a firm cut is made just back of the gills at about a 45 degree angle; not straight down but slanting towards the tail. Then holding the fish by the thumb and forefinger of the left hand a second cut is made along the back of the fish from the top of the first incision to the base of the tail. This cut should slant along the back of the fish from the top of the first incision to the center of the tail. One should cut evenly, clear to the back bone.

Now a third cut is made along the belly of the Herring, starting at the bottom of the first incision and slanting to the tail. This forms a pennant shaped slice out of the side of the Herring, one side of which is covered with the shiny scales of the fish.

Next the knife is inserted in the first incision back of the gills and is pushed down to the bone. It is then pushed along the back bone of the fish from the head to the tail, and the spinner can be lifted free. A nicely cut spinner should be beveled along its upper edge, thinning off a bit to the point.

The second type of spinner; the "plug-cut" was originally devised to make use of the smaller Herring which would not turn out good spinners. However, it has come into general use and at times is a more efficient lure than a cut spinner. It may be made either from a small or large bait and very often a small plug-cut will take more Salmon than a large spinner.

To prepare a plug-cut the angler places the Herring on the cutting board with its back up, holding it with the thumb and forefinger of the left hand. Starting about an inch back of the gills for the larger fish, slice off the head with a bevel cut that slants towards the tail. This cut should be beveled at such an angle that it will impart a crippled twist to the bait as it is pulled through the water.

If the angler is using a small Herring he may complete the operation by simply pulling out the insides of the fish. With a larger bait one must trim off the edge of its belly before removing the entrails. If the "plug" has been cut correctly, it should now spin nicely without further slicing.

Both single or double hooks may be utilized with either type of spinner. A Seely or Mustad type of hook made of round silver wire usually off-set with a large bite is used. Sizes range through 2-1-1/0 to 2/0; the larger hooks preferred when the big Chinooks are running.

Leaders are usually six to eight feet long of selected clear Nylon in tests of six to eight pounds. For small Silvers one may use four pounds, but during the fall run of Kings, eight or ten pound test leaders are customary.

When using a single hook on a cut spinner, the hook should be inserted on the flesh side of the bait near the point at the wide end of the pennant shaped slice and pulled all the way through. Then with the point of the hook towards the tail of the spinner and its own length away, it is pulled through the spinner and out again. Thus when the leader is pulled tight the hook will lie down along the scale side of the bait, with its eye pulled into the hole of the first entry.

When using two hooks the second one should be fastened onto the leader so that there is about 2½ inches of Nylon between them. Any type of knot that will hold well on Nylon may be used. These double hooks may be tied at home in various sizes and leader weights, and then fastened onto the leader needed for the type of salmon the angler is after.

Both hooks should be pulled through a hole

made in the head end of the spinner. Then the top hook is fastened, as described, for the single hook-up. The second or terminal hook is fastened in a like fashion near the tip of the cut spinner. A properly hooked up spinner will always have the point of the hook towards the top of the bait and the bend of the hook pointing towards the tip of the cut spinner.

When using a single hook on the plug-cut Herring, the hook is first inserted through the flesh side of the Herring at the bevel cut near its top. Then it is pulled all the way through and fastened onto the scale side of the bait in the same manner as with a cut spinner.

With a two-hook leader the simplest method is to pull both hooks through the same hole near the top of the bait. The top hook should then be fastened as with a single hook-up. Now the hook on the end of the leader may be crossed over to the opposite side of the Herring and inserted into the lower end near the tail and the leader pulled tight thus placing a hook on either side of the bait.

If the angler wishes he may fasten both hooks on the same side of the bait inserting one below the dorsal fin with its point extending up beyond the bait. The terminal hook is then fastened near the tail of the Herring pointing down.

One should be very careful to fasten the hooks in the bait to give it a slight curve, so that when it is pulled through the water, it will "spin" or rotate like a crippled fish. In all cases the spinner should be dragged alongside the boat to watch its action before allowing it to drop back into the trolling position.

The preferred type of spinning rod has a springy tip, and is 8½ to 10 feet in length. Its butt should have a double grip finished in cork for easier handling. A level wind or free spool reel may be used—one of large line capacity and rugged enough to stand the strain of playing heavy fish.

Monofilament Nylon line is universally used for stripping, in weights of six- to fifteen-pound tests; the lighter line for feeding Silvers and Blackmouth, and the heavier line for the mature salmon of either species. A crescent-shaped sinker weighing from ½ to 3½ ounces is utilized with a swivel at either end. The line is looped onto one end of the lead, and the leader with another swivel and snap fastener is attached to the other end of the sinker.

When casting a spinner the angler first strips the length of line he expects to use into the boat at his feet. Then he pulls the sinker up to the tip of the rod and holding the line with his thumb against the rod—with a side sweep of the arm—he casts the bait from the boat in an overhead arc. As the leader pulls on the tip, the line is released and it slips through the guides until all the loose coils are pulled out. The bait is then allowed to sink to the bottom or as far down as the line in use will permit.

After leaving it for an interval, depending on depth and the speed of the tide, one strips it back into the boat. This is done by reaching up to the lower guide on the rod with the left hand and with an even downward pull strip the line down into the bottom of the boat between the feet. Pull in lengths of line that are easy to handle with the left arm.

This stripping process imparts the desired action to the cut spinner or plug-cut Herring. One should learn to do it evenly with the correct speed and timing so as to move the bait through the water with the proper crippling erratic action. By experience one will learn the exact tempo to use.

When one is spinning over water where there is a fast run-off or where the tide is working or swirling past, the "dead-spinner" technique may be practiced. This is done by resting the rod against the side of the boat so as to allow the bait to work just off the bottom. The angler then just sits and watches the bobbing of the rod tip.

When the tip is pulled down with a couple of little jerks the angler should grasp the rod and be ready to hit the Salmon with a sure heavy set of the hook as soon as he feels the strike.

A variation of the spinning technique which has come into great favor on Puget Sound waters is called mooching. In its simplest terms, this is trolling the spinner from a moving boat instead of casting it from an anchored one. The same gear is used for both types of fishing, and the angler may spin or mooch on the same trip, as fancy dictates.

Moochers prefer the protected waters such as bays or estuaries where the tides are not extreme; where bottoms are fairly uniform; and the depth ranges from 75 to 125 feet. A rowboat is used when the angler is alone. He allows his cut spinner to run off the stern of the boat until the sinker bumps bottom. He then picks it up for a few feet and rows along at the speed that will impart the correct action to his bait.

He works the spinner along usually trying to keep close to bottom unless he is bothered excessively by bottom fish, such as Cod, Snappers, or Sole. He can raise the bait either by shortening the line or by rowing faster. Moochers like to vary the action of their bait by ceasing to row for a bit and then speeding up. This will alternately drop and raise the bait along an inclined plane.

One must watch the rod at all times for the telltale twitching of the tip. Sometimes the Salmon strike viciously and run off line in a screeching dash. At other times they simply tap it and the angler must hit hard to set the hook.

In less protected waters and in the more remote fishing grounds, motor mooching has superseded the ordinary rowboat method. A regulation kicker boat is used and the anglers usually fish in pairs. The one handling the motor will use a rod holder while his partner may hold a rod in his hand to feel the strike.

Each angler runs line off the reel until the lead reaches bottom. It is then pulled up several feet depending on the bottom terrain or amount of weeds and the fishermen sit back and troll at the speed necessary to keep the spinners working properly. Usually the speed that works well with a plug will be about right for the cut spinner.

When a Salmon is hooked by this method, it is given its head and allowed to run without checking. Should it be a heavy King, it may be necessary to chase the fish with the motor. At all times it is well to keep out as short a line as possible and attempt to keep well up on the Salmon.

The spinning group at first limited themselves to rather restricted fishing grounds. The popular locations were usually close to resorts or in protected bays or harbors. But with the development of mooching these light tackle artists have spread out and now take salmon at virtually every spot the troller does.

Within recent years the moochers have successfully moved into the trolling grounds in the Strait of Juan De Fuca. Off the rocks at Sekiu and Midway; near Cape Flattery and Tatoosh Island at the mouth of the Strait are spots that are high producers of Kings during July and August. Should the salmon be feeding off this rock-bound shore, or in one of the near-in "bait holes," a cut spinner trolled through such waters is extremely effective.

The inveterate spinner may follow his sport all year in the inner waters of Puget Sound or along Vancouver Island. He has learned that during December he can take late run Dog Salmon weighing up 10 to 16 pounds that are fast runners and good sport fish on a light rod.

From January through March he will be seeking Blackmouth, the young Kings that will not mature for six months or a year. These Salmon school where ever bait such as Herring or Candle Fish have congregated. Among the better known spots in Puget Sound are Elliott and Shilshole Bays at Seattle; Holmes Harbor and Possession off Whidby Island; Anderson Island; Gig Harbor; Quilcene Bay and Bald Point in Hood Canal; and Sekiu and Port Angeles in the Strait.

The Blackmouth is full of dynamite and fast as lightning. It puts up the sort of fight that makes the angler forget the cold mornings that chill him to his very marrow; and help to maintain his interest through a raw foggy, clammy winter day.

A prime Blackmouth may tap the spinner lightly, but when the hook is set, it runs like a scared antelope. It can take out 200 to 300 feet of line in a sizzling run, swirl to the surface, and then head for the boat. At such times the angler is hard put to keep a tight line.

Salmon will often run under a boat and it takes fast footwork to get the rod tip swung around. The anchor rope is a bad hazard when a lively fish is circling the boat and many a good salmon has gained its freedom by looping the leader around the anchor rope and then snapping it off.

The mature Kings which are taken during the late summer into September provide a rugged tough slam-bang battle that will test the resource of light tackle to the utmost. They substitute power for speed and know how to pour it on. They surge off like a runaway locomotive and with mooching gear, the angler must follow immediately so as to get line back on the reel. A forty-pound King on a ten-pound test leader won't stand snubbing. If the angler can't follow, a broken or lost line will result.

Silvers, on the other hand, are the acrobats of the salt water. They make a fast initial run and then often leap repeatedly when the line tightens. They tend to be surface feeders while the King is inclined to sound.

Cohoes often appear to come in quickly as if already whipped. But on sighting the boat they will jump almost in one's face and then take off again just under the surface. On four- to six-pound test leaders a Cohoe is a regular leaping dervish; one that is capable of throwing the hook before its prancing is over.

But whatever Salmon the spinner is seeking, he knows that he will have good sport whenever he hooks a fish. For his rod tip is flexible; his line is light; his reel free running without star drags. He gets every possible ounce of fight out of his quarry and when the silvery fish lies netted between the seats of the boat he knows that all the skill he possessed went into the boating of this Pacific Salmon.

SPEAR FISHING AND SKIN DIVING

No phase of fishing sport has grown more rapidly since World War II than skin diving and spear fishing. The development of spinning, which zoomed upward during the same years, was a modification of techniques that had been used for many years in Europe. Skin diving was something radically new, opening vast new frontiers to the angler. Traceable to the Japanese in their development of the culture pearl industry, it received a tremendous shot in the arm through the release of information on the activities of the ultra-secret "frog men" of

Lamar Boren

Preparing for their underwater adventure, these skin divers put on their swim fins. These webbed appendages permit the swimmer to utilize the tremendous driving power of his leg muscles to the fullest. Each man is also equipped with a special iron for prying abalone off the rocks, and wears a face plate—one of them is wearing his mask over his own glasses. Note the specially moulded earplugs, built from wax casts made of the divers' ears, and constructed from plastic denture material. These plugs distribute the pressure over the entire ear on dives into deeper water.

Lamar Boren

Two goggle fishermen emerging from the surf with two Giant Black Sea Bass. One fish weighed 125 pounds and the other 112 pounds. Note gun spear with line and paddleboard which comprises the fish equipment.

the war. The techniques used by the members of these hardy forces were adopted for underwater exploration, and eventually for fishing.

In the culture pearl industry, the Japanese found it necessary to improve on the eye goggles that pressed dangerously on the eyes at the great depths at which the divers operated. To overcome this hazard, they developed a single glass plate, tightly encased in a rubber housing which fitted tightly over the face, enclosing the eyes and nose. It served the double purpose of improving vision and distributing the water pressure over a wide area of the facial bones. The face plate, or diving mask, is the single indispensable piece of equipment for underwater travel.

The real impetus to spear fishing, however, came with the development of the rubber swim fin, which is used to "torpedo" the body through the water. Such fins, attached to the feet, were developed and designed by Owen Churchill, a Los Angeles sportsman who had observed natives of the South Pacific islands using grass fins to provide amazing underwater speed as they procured their food through spearfishing. Today, that basic design has been perfected to a high degree of efficiency, and swim fins have become standard equipment for spear fishermen.

Another development was that of the "snorkel," a plastic breathing tube equipped with a flanged mouthpiece, which permitted the fisherman to cruise and breathe with his face submerged.

The first spear fishermen, as the name implies, used simple spears, tridents, or five-pronged forks propelled by muscle-power alone. It was soon discovered, however, that Giant Black Blass, Jewfish, and Groupers were too heavily fortified with scales and thick skin to be taken readily with such weapons. To handle fish of this kind, slip-point spears, powered by high-tension springs, rubber tubing, compressed CO_2, and even gunpowder were developed. Released by a trigger, these will hurl the point of the spear at high velocity for several yards and drive the barbed projectile deep into the flesh of the fish.

The spear fisherman holds a line attached to the spear point. When the spear strikes, he surfaces to fight the thrashing fish. In this manner many giant fish have been landed.

An experienced skin diver can travel as far as 100 feet under water in half a minute. Because of the limited amount of time he can remain underwater in search of his prey, the ability to travel great distances within a matter of seconds is of prime importance. Most spear fishermen are able to remain under water less than a minute. The development of the self-contained underwater breathing apparatus, however, has expanded these early horizons greatly. SCUBA equipment permits the spear fisherman to cruise at much greater depths and to remain underwater for an hour or more.

In warmer waters, such as California, the Gulf Coast, and Florida, skin diving may be enjoyed the year around without discomfort. Latex rubber "frog suits," copied from those used by underwater demolition teams in World War II and which cover the body completely permit northern sportsmen to enjoy this sport even in the winter months.

Abalone fishing is popular in Southern California. The abalone, a large mollusk which clamps itself to a rock is taken by prying it loose with a tire iron or similar tool. The safest means of attaching the iron to the wrist is with a strip of innertube rubber, which can be stretched to permit release of the iron should it become inextricably wedged under a stubborn abalone. Skin divers who have used leather thongs for this purpose have had their lives endangered when they were unable

Lamar Boren

A couple of bull lobsters caught by hand underneath a reef at a depth of 30 feet.

immediately to escape from the suction grip of an abalone on the prying iron.

Several abalone at one time may be brought up in a single dive. Occasionally a skin diver returns

Lamar Boren

A morning's catch of two experienced goggle fishermen—63 pounds of fish and two "limits" of abalone of five each.

to shore with a paddle-board full of these mollusks after only a short period of diving.

Also readily caught by goggle fishermen are lobsters, which are brought up with bare hands. The deeper a skin diver goes—and 35 to 40 feet is considered a depth only the most proficient dare—the larger the lobsters he may find. They "hole up" in underwater caves and crevices.

Some fish also are captured with bare hands principally sharks. These, of course, are the comparatively smaller relatives of the man-eaters. They are shovel-nose sharks, which attain a length of 4 feet; and "horned" bullhead sharks, which have powerful teeth, designed for cracking hard-shelled prey. Although they are not man-eaters, they have prodigious strength, and real courage and skill are requisites in their capture.

Goggle fishermen are faced with constant dangers. Moray eels, up to 6 feet long, will follow skin divers with teeth bared, and have been known to snatch the meat of an abalone out of a diver's hands, leaving him with the bare shell. Rays, with saw-toothed barbs and poison glands, are hazards along the sandy bottoms where hunting is good for skin divers.

Lamar Boren

Giant Black Sea Bass or Jewfish speared off La Jolla, California. Note slip point spear that went all the way through the fish.

Using spears for fishing is illegal in California waters, except for skin divers, indicating the recognition which has been given this new sport, where the divers give themselves no such advantage over their prey as do other fishermen, safely operating behind rods and reels.

With such legal encouragement, a host of skin divers are exploring the strange, fascinating underwater world off southern California alone, and the sport is rapidly gaining in popularity along other coasts and on the larger lakes of the interior.

→

Ross Hall

Porcupine Lake, located in the Cabinet Mountains of Idaho, produces good Rainbows and Cutthroats.

SECTION III

CRAFT FOR FISHING

The origin of the fishing boat, like that of the fishhook, is hidden in the archaeological past. Many centuries after some prehistoric man first discovered that a dry log lent buoyancy and safety to his attempts at crossing streams, another obscure genius lashed two logs together with flexible vines, and the raft was born. This innovation permitted the operator to sit or stand upright and relatively dry as his craft drifted down the stream. By paddling with hands or feet he gained some control over the direction of drift. Later one of his descendants learned to shove the raft with a pole and still another flattened one end of a pole to form a paddle. With the development of the first crude fishhooks, the prehistoric angler found that the raft gave him a firm base of operations in waters too far from shore to reach with his thrown bark or sinew line. Ever since that time, the boat has been as indispensable as the fishhook for many kinds of fishing.

Dugouts have been used by primitive people for thousands of years. This development was a logical step from the single log as a means of transportation. Large trees were felled by fire and stone axes, and similar tools were used to hollow the cavity and shape the exterior. The birchbark canoe of the northern Indian tribes probably evolved as a modification of the dugout, which was used by other North American tribes. The kayak and umiak of the Eskimo probably originated in a similar manner, but the lack of suitable woods for boat building forced the arctic aborigines to utilize other materials. Sealskins and walrus hides became the standard covering for these seaworthy little boats in which the Eskimo still braves the icy waters.

Boats of fitted planks and timbers were developed soon after the invention or introduction of the metal saw into each country. Boats of this construction combined the stability of the well-built raft with the maneuverability of the dugout, and they extended the range of the fisherman into offshore waters. Such craft are as old as civilization itself.

With the merging and fusing of various civilizations, and as one people borrowed and developed the inventions of another, most boats lost much of their regional and local flavor long before sport fishing became popular. For the most part, the modern sport fishing boat is merely an adaptation of craft developed long ago for other purposes. The development of gasoline engines for marine use has been responsible for the most radical changes in boat design within recent decades; both inboard and outboard motors demand boats of special design and construction to bring out maximum efficiency of the power unit.

The ancestors of the modern, sport fishing boat were the dugout, the birchbark canoe and kayak, the whaleboat, the jolly boat and longboat of the sailing ships, the dory and seaskiff of the commercial fisherman, and the punt and pram of European rivers and canals. Practically all of these craft reached present type before the middle of the last century when good boat design frequently meant the difference between life and death to the whaler, the handliner, or the sailor.

PICKING THE RIGHT BOAT

Features from many types have been merged to meet the specific requirements of sport fishermen. As a result, the prospective boat purchaser can find nearly every kind of a craft imaginable, and the choice of the right boat for his use often is a confusing one. The two primary considerations in purchasing a boat are: What do I need? And how much can I afford to pay?

The answer of the second question is largely a matter of personal consideration; that of the first frequently is more difficult. Fish have been caught for sport from practically everything that will float, from the most elementary of rafts to ocean liners. Good fish are taken regularly from sail boats of all descriptions, but that fails to make the sailboat a first-class fishing boat. Tarpon are taken regularly from canoes in the tidal inlets of Florida and large tuna are taken from dories, but this in itself does not make the canoe the best boat for tarpon fishing or the dory the ideal tuna boat.

What characteristics distinguish the fishing boat from the pleasure boat? Often the difference is a subtle one or there is none at all. The craft selected by the wilderness camper and the wilderness fisherman probably would be identical; the boat selected by the yachtsman and the offshore big-game fisherman, however, might differ materially. Fishing boats are utilitarian craft and anything which interferes with their primary function must be eliminated or modified. Fixed awnings over the cockpit protect passengers from the sun and rain, but they also interfere with rod action. Large cleats on the after deck may be handy for mooring purposes, but they may snag a leader and cause the loss of a large fish.

Sport fishing covers such a broad field that no one boat can be called the perfect fishing craft. There are, however, boats which are near perfect for each principal type of angling. Selection must be governed primarily by the type of water in which it will be used and the kinds of fish which will be sought.

Boats for Wilderness Lakes. The angler who plies the lakes of the roadless back country away from the crowd and confusion that often prevail nearer civilization, enjoys sport fishing at its best. Usually he fishes from the bank or wades the shallows, but not infrequently the biggest fish lie just outside the range of his longest cast. Some wilderness lakes have their shorelines and shallows clogged with windfalls, snags and vegetation that make casting difficult and playing a fish on light tackle all but impossible. The answer, of course, is some sort of craft to carry him into deeper and more open water, but if everything must be brought in on his own back or on pack animals, the weight and bulk of even the lightest rigid boat would make an impossible addition to his load.

Unless he can arrange to have an outfitter bring in a light boat or canoe by air or by jeep, as many wilderness fishermen do on waters accessible to aircraft or four-wheel-drive vehicles, he must rely on his own resources or do without. The true wilderness lover disdains such assistance, and many fine lakes can be reached only on foot or horseback and are too small to permit the landing of a float plane. On others, lying in officially designated national wilderness areas, the entry of planes and vehicles may be prohibited by regulation or law. The choice then narrows down to the collapsible boat, the inflatable raft, or that grandfather of all fishing craft, the primitive raft constructed on the spot.

Rafts. The raft is the most elementary of all fishing craft, and floating platforms were used by man soon after the first dawn of human intelligence. They still offer the least expensive and least troublesome method for the back-packing wilderness fisherman to reach fish lying beyond reach of his casting ability.

Log rafts are heavy, cumbersome, and unwieldy to maneuver, but these qualities are of minor importance when no other craft can be found. The simplest raft consists of two or three dry logs tied together with rope or cross members nailed to the floats. Such a craft can be poled, drifted, or paddled out where the big fish rise. All that is required for their construction, other than native materials, some basic axemanship, and applied ingenuity, is a few yards of light rope or a handful of heavy nails, whose total weight adds only a few ounces to the back pack. They may be made as large or as small as need and safety dictate, and a well-constructed one will permit from one to three fishermen to cast erect and dry-shod in waters that would otherwise be inaccessible.

On short back-packing trips or when pack animals are used, weight and bulk are less important but still major considerations. Under such conditions inflatable rafts, designed originally by the Air Forces for life-saving purposes, weigh about 20 pounds and, complete with collapsible plastic oars or paddles, pack into a bundle occupying no more than a cubic foot. Cheaper models are of Vinyl plastic, the better ones of rubberized rayon or other fabric. The latter, while slightly heavier, are much more durable and more easily patched in an emergency. Nearly all of the inflatable boats

Old Town Canoe Co.

For fishing headwater lakes and streams the canoe has not been surpassed.

have more than one air compartment to prevent the complete collapse of the boat if the fabric should be snagged.

Designed for keeping a man afloat in the most severe oceanic storms, they are all but unsinkable, easily maneuvered on sheltered waters, and moderately comfortable, although they will not permit the angler to stand to cast or play a fish.

A refinement of the oval liferaft is the inflatable skiff. These have most of the advantages of the older type of craft and a few of their own. Only slightly heavier than the life-raft type, they are more easily maneuvered and are equipped with seats, mooring attachments and brackets to accommodate motors weighing up to 30 pounds.

Heavier and bulkier when broken down than the inflatable boat or raft, the folding or collapsible boat makes up into a more rigid craft that provides the angler with more freedom of movement. Most of the larger models are too heavy to be backpacked for any distance, but they are ideal for use in the pack train. The typical model consists of an aluminum frame over which is fitted a rubberized fabric cover. Most employ a locking slip joint, which permits the boat to be assembled from a small package into a full-size skiff in a matter of minutes.

Boats for Wilderness Cruising. The angler who needs a boat both for fishing and as a means of transportation on swift wilderness streams has special requirements. A boat used for such purposes must be light enough to carry around or over obstacles, rugged enough to take the battering that such travel involves, and stable enough to support duffel and sufficient equipment to supply the needs of one or two men for a week or more.

The canoe, which was developed expressly for use on such waters by the Indians of the what is now Eastern Canada and the northeastern United States, has not been improved upon in basic design. It draws only a few inches of water, even with a full load, and carries a surprising amount of cargo for its weight and size. It may be paddled, poled, pushed with a light motor, or dragged through rapids with a towline. It may be portaged overland for a mile or more without taxing the endurance of a man in good physical condition.

A 70-pound canoe, 16 feet long will accommodate two adults and all their camping and fishing equipment for a one-week trip without crowding, and on shorter trips it will accommodate a third person. If three people will be carried regularly, however, the 19-foot model offers greater carrying capacity, wider beam and greater stability. The larger models are to be preferred where open lakes lie along the course of travel. The 15-foot models offered by some manufacturers are ideal where much portaging will be encountered. Most are as broad of beam as longer models, and their short length and light weight make them easy to handle on portages.

Here is the height of portability in a rigid boat-outboard motor combination, an 11-foot fiberglass canoe and a 3-h.p. motor. Two men can easily portage the canoe, motor and fuel enough for a day's fishing a quarter of a mile or more.

The challenge of local wilderness has given rise to other boats that are used to tap otherwise inaccessible fishing waters. Along the Colorado and Columbia River and their canyon-walled tributaries where fishermen once were excluded by some of the most vicious rapids in the world, large rubber boats of the life-raft design are used by professional guides. Their flexible construction and innate stability permit them almost literally to flow with the water through boulder-studded rapids in which no rigid craft could live.

In Florida, the airboat, a light craft pushed along by an aircraft propeller will skim the angler deep into the Everglades in an hour or two to fishing grounds that no conventional motorboat can reach. Airboats were designed for and are used primarily in marshes and shallow lakes that are clogged with vegetation where an ordinary outboard motorboat would become hopelessly entangled. Since they draw almost no water at all when under way they can literally skim over mudflats where even a canoe would bog down. In the Everglades, they have just about replaced the ages-old pirogue which formerly was the only practical means of navigating the sawgrass jungles. Most airboats are homemade, but commercial models are available with strong fiberglass hulls and reliable powerplants. They require a skilled operator to handle them, however, and they are not adaptable to choppy, windswept waters.

The true pirogue is still used widely in much of the South, for navigating the swamps and streams of the Gulf Coast. The typical pirogue of Louisiana, once hollowed laboriously from a solid log, is now almost universally constructed of planked lumber. Low of silhouette, narrow, double-ended, and from 8 to 15 feet long, it is ideally adapted to cruising the swamps and bayous for which it was designed. Many now mount light outboard motors, but all handle well with paddles or the traditional pushpole.

In the Ozark Mountains of Arkansas and Missouri a specialized craft called the "john-boat" was developed long ago for cruising the wild streams of that region. Originally the john-boat was a simple keelless, flat-bottomed craft, narrow of beam and square cut at bow and stern, developed by the farmers as a means of getting produce to market. The loaded boat was floated downstream to a town where the boat usually was sold for firewood along with the corn, poultry and other farm goods that made up its cargo, the owner returning upstream on foot. When sport fishing developed in the region, fishermen adopted the john-boat as their own, and "float fishing" was born. (See Section II.)

Modern john-boats are not as disposable as their ancestors, and the development of the outboard motor makes upstream travel feasible and easy. Usually the Ozark fisherman still prefers to travel downstream, carrying his boat back on a truck or trailer. As the metal canoe has made inroads into waters that once knew only john-boats, the john-boat may be encountered on eastern rivers that once knew only canoes.

Excellent light-weight aluminum craft based on the john-boat design are produced by many boat builders in and out of the Ozarks. Lighter than traditional planked models, they are equally as rugged and much more easily handled in the shoals. They are unexcelled for fishing waters where extensive portages are not necessary and where snags, shallows and rocks make the use of other craft impractical.

Boats for Permanent Camps on Small Lakes. The fisherman who owns a camp on a small lake need not be overly concerned with the portability of his boat, and he needs only the lightest of motors to meet his requirements for trolling. Electric models are ideal on lakes under 100 acres where most of the fishing will be by casting, still-fishing, or drifting, or no motor may be required at all. Almost any stable shallow-draft easy-handling boat between 10 and 16 feet in length will fill the bill.

Johnson Motors

A light aluminum boat and a 10-h.p. Johnson motor, make an excellent combination for the man who wants to tap widely separated fishing waters. It can be carried on a light trailer or even an auto-top rack and it takes up little storage space.

The canoe, the modern metal version of the john-boat, the larger prams or the time-honored flat-bottomed skiff will all satisfy his needs.

Since camp-based boats usually are beached frequently on rocky shores, they take a lot of abuse. Boats used at small camps often must be stored outside over winter and the metal, molded fiberglass, or plastic hulls stand weathering better than those of wooden construction. They are also ready to go in the spring with a minimum of maintenance when camp is reopened.

Boats for the Traveling Fisherman. The choice of the fisherman who wishes to tap widely separated fishing grounds from his own boat will be governed by several considerations. If the predominant fishing that he plans to do is on streams and small lakes, the likelihood is that he will prefer a light-model canoe, skiff or pram carried on a car-top carrier.

With larger boats, storage space will be a major consideration, unless the owner wishes to pay rental at a marina. The suburbanite with a two-car garage and one automobile can use and store a large trailer-carried runabout weighing up to 350 pounds, but the apartment dweller must be content with more compact models. For the latter, there are folding boats that break down into full-sized skiffs from bundles that store readily in a closet or luggage compartment. They will permit the angler to fish any sheltered waters and to use light outboard motors.

The development of well-designed mass-produced boats of light weight, the expansion of launching facilities by state agencies under the Federal Aid to Fish Restoration Program, and the development of sturdy light-weight trailers have been major factors in developing the boating boom. Light A-frame trailers are available that will handle boats weighing nearly a ton behind ordinary automobiles. Most fishermen, however, will be quite satisfied with much smaller models.

Since the boat used by the traveling fisherman will be out of the water more than it is in, it must be of a material that is not affected by drying. Light-weight boats of molded fiberglass, plastic, or metal, available in a wide range of sizes and styles, are ideal for use with trailers or car-top carriers.

Boats for Lakes and Deep Rivers. The angler who fishes the larger rivers and broad, open lakes needs a more stable craft than the one who confines his fishing to sheltered ponds and shallow rivers. His fishing excursions may take him ten or more miles from his base camp, he will spend more time trolling for Lake Trout, Salmon, or Walleyes, and there may be times when he will have to make a run for it before a vicious line squall strikes.

Any boat that gives good service on smaller waters will serve on the protected bays and coves of the larger lakes, but if the angler wishes to venture far from his camp, he will want a boat that will handle motors of ten horsepower or more. Flat-bottomed boats, suitable for use in shallow rivers and on small lakes, handle poorly where the wind gets a sweep because they tend to slam and pound in bucking waves, even at trolling speeds. Boats with V-type or round bottoms take such surface conditions in stride.

Since most boats used in this type of fishing are kept in the water throughout the fishing season at a dock or marina, they may be of conventional wooden construction, which is stronger than any other material except welded metal. Boats of the run-about style, with windshields, remote control steering, and decking over the bow are excellent for waters of this kind.

Evinrude Motors

This light but roomy pram powered by a 3-h.p. Evinrude Lightwin motor, is safe and comfortable for fishing sheltered lakes.

Boats for the Bay Fishermen. Light 10 and 12-foot skiffs and runabouts are used regularly by anglers on Chesapeake, Cape Cod, and Buzzards Bays on the East Coast and in San Francisco Bay, Puget Sound and other large, partly sheltered bays and estuaries in trolling for Salmon, Striped Bass, and Bluefish. Such craft are suitable if the operator watches the weather, knows the waters well, and does not stray too far from land. A change of tide and a shift of wind, however, can turn these seemingly protected waters into snarling challenges to seamanship and seaworthiness. The fisherman caught far from port during one of these sudden changes of oceanic mood may well wish that he had a lot more boat and a larger reserve of power. When these waters start to kick up, they are no place for a landlubber in a sluggish underpowered tub.

Even on relatively calm days there is likely to be some chop or wave action in these waters, and on many of them the tides run strongly with dangerous rips. Boats used reguarly on such waters must be seaworthy and have a reliable power plant, whether inboard or outboard. Coaming around the cockpit, decking at least over the bow, and windshields, conveniences on boats used on quieter waters, become near necessities in rough water. Since much of the fishing will be done in the early spring and late fall, a deck house or, on the larger models, a small cabin, will prove real conveniences. Cockpits, however, must be roomy, and rear-facing or swivel fighting chairs can add to the usefulness and comfort of the craft.

Bottoms should be of the round, V-type, or semi-V-type design, and solid wood construction, either in lapstrake or strip-planking will take the pounding that these waters can give. The lighter fiberglass and aluminum hulls have the edge in getting the most in speed and efficiency from motors of equivalent horsepower, but solid wood hulls give a stability that the newer and lighter materials lack. Boats used for bay fishing must be capable of throttling down to a bare two or three miles an hour but of running in fast when a sudden line squall or storm shakes its fist on the horizon. Sometimes even a fast-stepping boat may be caught in the open by a sudden storm, so a good seaworthy craft is required for safety. A minimum of 16-feet length with plenty of beam, smooth flaring lines, and single or paired 40 horsepower motors will prove none too large for the bay angler.

Boats for the Bonefish Flats. The bonefishermen along the Florida coast and in the West Indies and the Bahamas have developed craft specifically suited to stalking the wary Bonefish, Tarpon, and Permit that frequent the white marl flats that hem the Peninsular State and the nearby islands. Many types of craft are used by visiting sportsmen, but the professional bonefish guides prefer modified skiffs of broad beam and shallow draft of from 16 to 20 feet in length mounting motors of from 35 to 50 horsepower. Power is used only in moving from the dock to the fishing grounds or from one flat to another with a minimum of wasted time. On the flats, propulsion is by means of a pushpole, the guide or boat handler usually standing on the after thwart or decking, the angler standing in the cockpit. Casting usually is done only to fish that are visible, and the higher vantagepoint increases the range of vision.

Most of these boats are of light construction with flat or shallow semi-V bottoms. Some are equipped with fighting chairs, but these are used predominantly while trying for Tarpon when the tides are not suitable for bonefishing.

Since the waters in which these boats are used are shallow, free of the rocky hazards that concern the northern coastal fisherman, and as clear as dew, and since bonefishing is entirely a fair-weather sport, ruggedness usually is sacrificed for lightness, quietness, stability and comfort.

Any commercially built runabout of from 12 to 18 feet in aluminum, fiberglass or wood will prove ideal for this type of fishing, provided it is stable enough to permit the fisherman to stand erect. A high vantagepoint is essential for success in bone-

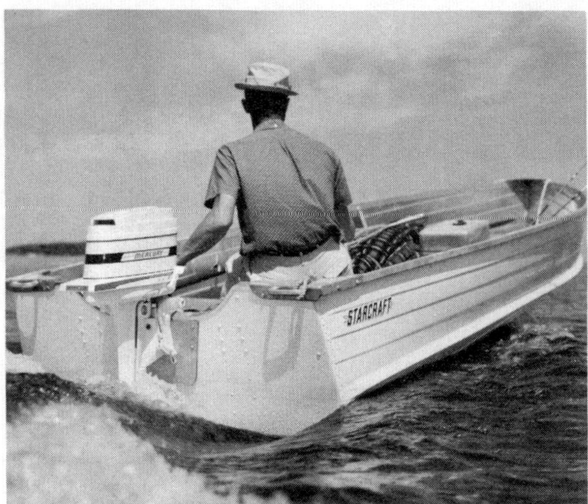

Kiekhaefer Corp.

A boat like this Starcraft skiff is well designed for fishing exposed waters of open bays and estuaries and the 10-h.p. Mercury will provide adequate speed for a run back to port ahead of a storm.

fishing since the lure or bait must be presented with great accuracy to the feeding fish.

Boats for the Rocky Coast. At the opposite pole from the bonefisherman, who plies the sun-drenched marl flats of the warmer coasts, is the Striped Bass angler of the Northeast. From Montauk north to the Maritimes, the shore is studded with glacial boulders that provide shelter for the big "bull" bass ranging from 20 pounds to near the 73-pound record set by Charles Church back in 1913. Between this rugged coast and Europe there is little to break the seas that beat against it, and some of the best fishing is enjoyed when the sea is churning and boiling in against the land. The fish lie close in to the breaking surf, and the professional guides long ago developed a specialized technique for taking them.

The boats are worked close to the rocks, and often among them, the fisherman trolling or casting inshore toward the breaking surf. As often as not, the guide joins in the sport, wielding from a standing position a long surf rod armed with a huge plug or a two-foot eel bob, while nonchalantly guiding the boat with the pressure of his knee against the tiller.

Needless to say, these are not waters for the lightly built boat, and a specialized craft has been developed to cope with them. The ancestor of these boats probably was the time-tested motorized life boat, like those used by the Coast Guard, and some are still to be found in service in these waters. The Montauk or Cuttyhunk striped bass boat, however, is a lusty descendant of its work-a-day progenitor. The majority of them are from 18 to 30 feet long and of heavy lapstrake or strip-plank construction both for stability and to take the pounding that they receive in the waters where they are used. High of bow and with plenty of freeboard at sides and transom these boats are built to take seas in which ordinary pleasure craft would be battered to pieces. The larger ones give excellent service in deep-water Swordfish and Tuna fishing far from land. The smaller of these craft are usually devoid of superstructure except for windshield and coaming inside a narrow decking; the larger ones may have a small wheelhouse, and combined galley, cabin, and head.

Nearly all have two sets of controls, one forward and the second aft, and many have a tiller as well as a wheel. The standard boat of this design is powered by one or two inboard engines. The high transom is to foil following seas. Twin outboards in stern wells are used in boats patterned after the Cuttyhunk bass boat, but they are more satisfactory for open-water fishing. Similar outboard boats will be seen in the open ocean in the mooching fleets of the Pacific Northwest.

These are among the purest of fishing boats. They were designed only for fishing, and in the prototype everything that interferes with the casting operation, the fighting of the fish, or the action of the angler is dispensed with or modified. While designed primarily for inshore fishing, they are among the most seaworthy of craft, capable in the hands of a competent sailor of weathering all but the worst storms on the open sea.

Craft for Offshore Fishing. The fisherman who ventures out into the open ocean, often far from the sight of land, requires a seaworthy, stable craft with sufficient fuel storage capacity to troll all day and, if necessary, to run for harbor at full speed ahead of a threatening squall. It must also be able to ride out foul weather if caught unawares. Boats for big-game fishing are beyond the reach of the average fisherman, except on a short-term charter basis, but the angler who can afford the luxury of purchasing and maintaining a yacht of from 32 feet and up, suitable for blue-water fishing, can attain horizons of recreations of which his less fortunate brothers can only dream.

Boats in this class are much more than mere fishing platforms. The larger of them are literally floating homes. By cruising the coast, the owner can enjoy tidewater fishing for Striped Bass or venture out to the open sea for Marlin and Dolphin. He can anchor in a sheltered estuary and with an outboard-powered dinghy or tender probe up rivers for fresh-water angling. He can literally follow the fish.

While the outboard motor with its revolutionary development in recent years is making inroads into all realms once dominated by the inboard power plant, the heavy-duty marine inboard engine still reigns supreme for cruisers designed for offshore ocean fishing. The big 80-100 H.P. outboard, paired and mounted in tandem, will move even a large boat at a lively clip, but they use fuel less efficiently than the marine inboard engine. The location of the motor, on the transom, makes the outboard cruiser less suitable for opensea fishing than the inboard. The transom must be lowered to use the engine at full efficiency, which may make the boat vulnerable to swamping in a heavy following sea, or if the drive shaft of the power plant were made long enough to permit mounting on a high transom, the engine housing would be in an inconvenient position for trolling and raise the center of gravity of the boat. Most outboard cruisers of modern design compromise by using a false transom, mounting the motors in a well aft, or on a stern bracket but a heavy following sea can drown motors mounted in this fashion just when they are needed most. If a motor needs servicing while trolling is in process, the mechanic cannot make the needed adjustments without getting, literally, under the feet of the anglers.

The inboard engine is mounted low, providing a high degree of stability to the boat. It is out of sight in its own housing, which is usually well forward of the fighting chairs and it can be serviced or adjusted by the operator without the fishermen being aware of the fact. The decking above the transom usually is used as a bait well on inboard cruisers; on outboards this must be less conveniently located. The use of inboard engines permits the incorporation of high transoms in the design, making a more sea-worthy craft.

Outboards, however, have certain advantages. Since the drive shaft and propeller can be swung up above the line of the keel, they can run into much shallower water than the inboard with its fixed shaft. They are highly maneuverable, since they are steered by the changing of the angle of the propeller, which shoves the stern of the boat immediately to the right or left. Inboards are steered by rudders while the angle of the propeller remains fixed and respond much more slowly to the wheel. Since they may be removed easily as a unit, they are much easier and economical to service at dockside, although the advantage is reversed when a mechanical failure occurs while the craft is in use.

In order to seek a compromise between the advantages of both types of motors, the manufacturers have developed the outboard-inboard. The power plant is placed inboard, while power is transmitted to the propeller by means of a drive shaft linked at right angles by gears. This permits the use of a 4-cycle inboard engine with its reliability and economy and ease of servicing, eliminates the high-riding power head of the standard outboard engine and provides the maneuverability of the outboard. As in the standard outboard, the propeller and lower drive shaft may be raised or lowered, and the unit can be mounted on boats with high transoms. Its disadvantages lie in the fact that an additional set of gears are required over the standard outboard, adding a point at which break-down is possible. On large boats, they are more suitable for general marine use than the standard outboard engine, but not as suitable nor as economical as the inboard marine engine.

For all-around reliability, economy, and efficiency the marine diesel engine has not been surpassed,

Massachusetts Division of Fisheries & Game

Rugged strip-planked boats like these at Buzzards Bay, Massachusetts, are used in fishing for Tuna and Striped Bass.

MacKenzie-Gray Boat Co.

The rugged Cuttyhunk Bass Boat was designed for fishing the rocky coast of New England. This custom-built 26-footer, powered by a 225-h.p. V-8 engine has a frame, keel and stem of white oak and planking of solid mahogany. Note the high stern, capacious cockpit, and tiller supplementing the forward wheel. Its cabin will sleep two and contains a bed. This is purely a fisherman's boat, designed by fishermen. The model shown was built by the MacKenzie-Gray Boat Company.

particularly for use in craft over 30 feet in length. The diesel engine is ideal for those planning long excursions along the coast, especially to foreign ports, since high-grade marine gasoline is not always available while diesel fuel can be found at any port.

Whether outboard or inboard, engines for marine fishing should always be paired. Commonly, only one is used while fishing, with the second held in reserve, but when full speed is required both can be operated. Paired engines in addition to increasing the speed and decreasing the time needed in running out or into port, are insurance against a disabling power failure far from land or the loss of a good fish if even a minor stall occurs after a fish has been hooked. In big-game fishing, boat handling often plays an important part in the fight. With two engines, if the operating one stalls, the other can be started immediately. With only one motor, the boat could be dead in the water long enough for a heavy fish to break free.

Boats built specifically for marine fishing have several features which set them apart from craft designed only for pleasure cruising. Cockpits must be roomy and free from obstructions, and flying bridges which permit the boat to be controlled from a high vantagepoint are essential. Not only does the flying bridge, with its second complete set of controls, permit the boat operator to spot fish that would be invisible to him from the lower vantage point of the deck house, but it provides a better view of the action when a large fish is hooked so that the boat can be maneuvered to the best advantage.

Nearly all boats used in offshore marine fishing are equipped with ship-to-shore telephones, or short-wave radios, which are a major convenience in locating school fish, provided the operator is in good standing with his fellow fishermen. In some waters, a boat skipper, finding a school of fish will use every subterfuge to keep other boats away. The most gregarious anglers are found in the salmon mooching fleets of the Pacific Northwest. When a school of salmon is located, the skipper who finds it usually uses his short-wave radio to call in all of his friends, and the air crackles with calls from one boat to another when the action is at its height. In addition to convenience, such equipment has obvious safety values.

Another new convenience, now used on all well-equipped fishing boats, is the fathometer which measures the depth of the water. Models are available even for small outboard runabouts. These are invaluable for locating reefs and submerged wrecks where bottom fishing is usually at its best. They also are used to locate dense schools of bait fish and game fish lying above the bottom. These are electronic devices similar to radar, the depth being indicated on a dial by a "blip" of light. Earlier models are not a reliable substitute for the old and infallible lead line in obtaining soundings, but they are useful gadgets on any fishing boat.

Boats used for deep-water trolling are, or should be, equipped with outriggers. These are flexible poles extending out from the gunwales of the craft, usually amidships. They are equipped with pulleys at their tips which permits the hoisting of a spring clip which holds the fishing line. When a fish takes the lure, the line is pulled from the clip, and the released slack gives an automatic dropback to the bait, giving the angler time to throw his freespool release lever, if a longer pause is needed between the strike of the fish and the setting of the hook. Outriggers also impart a natural darting motion to the bait and when rigged with short lines make the bait simulate the darting skipping motion of a flying fish, the natural quarry of Marlin, Sailfish, and Dolphin. In addition, they permit the use of four or five rods being used at one time in trolling without danger of tangling lines.

Pulpits, narrow catwalks extending out from the bow and protected by rails are used predominately for harpooning fish. This practice is frowned upon by the AGFA and outlawed by many local angling clubs, and in some quarters the boat without a pulpit will receive a warmer welcome than one equipped with a harpooner's platform.

All boats used for blue-water fishing should be equipped with fighting chairs. They are conveniences even when fishing predominantly for smaller species of school fish such as Mackerel, Bonito, and Bluefish. When fighting Tuna, Marlin, Sailfish and other larger species, they are indispensable. Well-made fighting chairs are comfortable to sit in for long hours between strikes, and the best usually are made of mahogany or other attractive woods and are lightly upholstered on seat and back for comfort. They may be locked in position but released to swivel easily so that the angler always faces his fish. A chromed brass or stainless steel rod-butt socket on the fore-edge of the seat, permits the angler to bring leverage against the fish, and an adjustable foot rest, which is an integral part of the chair, permits him to keep a firm footing throughout the fight.

The cockpits of all boats designed for marine trolling are equipped with rod holders. These are fixed sleeves of brass, stainless steel, or chromed brass into which the butts of the rods may be set. They permit the angler to rest with his line still in the water, counting on the momentum of the boat to hook any fish that takes the bait. This is less sporting than hooking the fish with the rod held in the hand, but it does permit the fisherman to continue fishing while stretching his legs, eating, or even catching a catnap.

All boats used for marine fishing should have a capacious icebox for preserving the catch in good condition and for keeping baits fresh. The most convenient are located just above the stern of the boat and are flush with the decking. Where live bait is used regularly most boats have live-fish wells automatically supplied with a continuous change of water to maintain the bait in perfect condition until used.

When fishing for really large specimens, such as Tuna or Broadbill Swordfish, a winch, hoist, or similar mechanical contrivance is needed to boat a catch in the 400-1000 pound class. Boats designed specifically for such fishing often are equipped with rollers. Large fish of this kind can be towed to port when the boat is not equipped to lift the catch aboard, but fish dragged behind a boat are exceedingly vulnerable to attack and mutilation by sharks.

All boats used in offshore waters, of course should be fully equipped with all standard navigation and safety aids.

HAND PROPELLED FISHING CRAFT

In this age of mechanization and gadgetry, the ages-old crafts of rowing, paddling, and poling have become all but lost in our preoccupation with motorized travel. To most members of the present generation these methods of propulsion are only for emergency use when the motor fails or the gas tank runs dry, an ordeal to be endured until the trouble can be corrected.

For the fisherman, however, these primitive means of locomotion still have many uses other than the therapeutic value of exercise. In some types of fishing they are unsurpassed. In deep waters, motors will not bother fish, and in some instances the wake of the propeller seems to serve as an attractant to game fish. Sailfish usually are hooked only yards behind the stern of the boat, and spring trolling for Lake Trout and Land-locked Salmon is done from power boats on lines that seem startlingly short to the uninitiated.

But when Trout or Bass are rising to a hatch of flies on a silent and glass-smooth lake over a rocky bottom an approaching motor would be likely to end the action while the rowboat or canoe can glide into their midst little noticed by the feeding fish.

Rowboats. If a boat is to be propelled primarily by oars, it must be designed for rowing. Good rowboats do not handle well under power, nor do well-designed powerboats—even light ones—handle well with oars. The reason lies in the basic design of the two craft, especially in that of the stern. Boats designed to hold outboards must be broad across the stern to support the weight of the motor and, in motor skiffs unequipped with remote controls, that of the operator. The transom must be heavily reinforced to take the strain and vibration of the power plant. The broad stern, which rides high when the motor is removed, forces the bow deeper in the water and imparts a drag to the boat when oars are used. Rowing such a boat for any distance can be a fatiguing process.

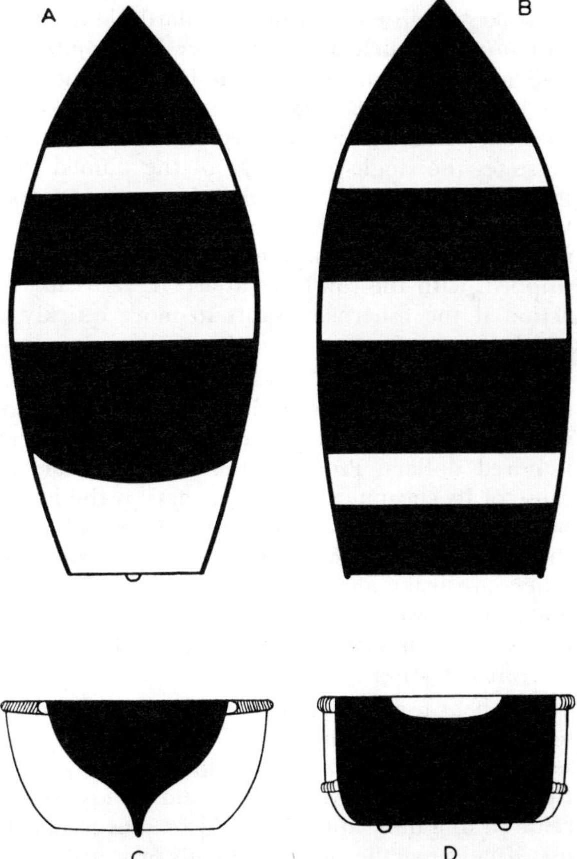

Comparative lines, seat plans, and transom designs of (a) a typical rowboat and (b) a typical outboard motorboat of the same length; three reasons why the rowboat cannot be used effectively with a motor and why the outboard motorboat handles poorly with oars. The stern of the rowboat (c) is not broad enough to support adequately the weight of a motor and operator sitting on the after seat. The broad stern, and wide transom of the outboard motorboat (d) causes the boat to drag heavily when rowed.

A well-designed rowing craft on the other hand is literally streamlined below the waterline. The transom is shallow and narrow at least on its lower edge and the bottom flares up to meet it, eliminating the drag that is evident in the hand-propelled outboard boat. In the banks dory the transom is reduced to a tiny "tombstone" of wood. In some light canoe-built rowboats, the boat is double-ended and the transom is eliminated completely.

Boats of this kind are a pleasure to row, and oars properly matched to handle them will propel them at a surprising rate of speed. For casting on small lakes where little trolling will be done, for bottom fishing in bays, on deep, slow-moving rivers, and lakes, and for drift fishing, boats of this kind are near-ideal.

Oars should be matched to the length and weight of the boat. Short, stubby oars burn up energy, and, for proper feathering, the oars must be free in the rowlocks. Pinned locks are rarely positioned properly, and nothing is more fatiguing than trying to row against the wind with oars pinned permanently in locks set too far apart. Since they cannot be turned so that the edge of the blade is parallel with the water on the up-stroke, or feathered, they act as brakes against any wind. Standard U-type locks will provide much more efficiency and comfort as well as freedom of action, but for the fisherman, the ring lock is near ideal. This permits all of the freedom of action of the open U-lock, but it also possesses the single advantage of the pinned lock, insurance against loss, provided the oar is equipped with a leather sleeve with a collar larger than the ring. In drifting or still-fishing, the oars can be shipped, with the row-locks attached, yet ready for action if the fisherman wants to move quickly to another spot.

Rowboats come in a variety of models, from simple wooden prams and punts to cedar- and mahogany-planked, or plastic craft costing several hundred dollars. Probably the most popular, because of its cheapness and ruggedness, is the locally built flat-bottomed skiff. Since much depends upon the competence of the builder, some are excellent, others are leaky abominations. They are not built for exposed waters, but a good one will give excellent service on a small lake or in sheltered coves, even in salt water.

Any boat used in salt water must be constructed with rustproof fastenings and metal fittings. Salt water is exceedingly corrosive to iron, and a boat that might last for years on inland ponds will be reduced to a hulk in two or three seasons of marine use, if held together with iron nails or screws. Even heavily galvanized steel is not impervious to the action of salt water, since exposed fastenings and fixtures usually are subject to wear, and as soon as the coating goes, disintegration is rapid. Stainless steel is the one exception to the rule, but bronze, copper, and brass are more commonly used.

Many excellent boats are now made without fastenings of any kind, the hull being molded in a single piece from plastic or literally welded together with the new epoxy glues. These newer types of construction are ideal for rowing craft since they permit the design of feather-light hulls of capacious size. Boats of conventional strip-planked or lapstrake construction, like the Old Town rowing skiff and equally rugged Ipswich Bay skiff, both of which are based on the seaworthy dory, are ideal for saltwater use or for large lakes. Since boats of this type depend upon the swelling of wood fibers to keep them water-tight, they cannot be carried far on trailers without drying out and leaking. But they are among the most stable of rowboats for use at a permanent camp, and they can stand rugged use. A number of excellent mass-produced fiberglass, metal and plastic hulls are based on this design.

Canoes. The fisherman's canoe should be selected on the basis of the waters that the owner is most likely to fish, and the material is largely a matter of personal preference. The conventional canvas-over-cedar planking models are still available, although aluminum, fiberglass and other plastics have made heavy inroads into the field. Canvas requires more annual maintenance, but it is the easiest to repair if the shell is punctured by a snag. Fiberglass stands weathering much better. Aluminum will take a heavy battering in snags and rocks and is almost impervious to weather, although if used much around salt water it should be protected by a specially anodized coating, applied by the manufacturer, or by a good grade of marine enamel applied over a primer.

Aluminum has the advantage of lightness for use where much portaging will be done, or when the boat will be carried regularly on an automobile top. Grumman produces a 13-footer weighing only $39\frac{1}{2}$ pounds, which is ideal for knock-about use on overnight trips or for reaching ponds not readily accessible by road. A canoe of this size can be

Rex Gary Schmidt, U. S. Fish and Wildlife Service

The pirogue, evolved from the dugout canoe, is still used to navigate the shallow swamps of the Southeast.

portaged easily for a mile or more with ease by anyone in good condition.

At the other extreme is the big 100-pound, 20-foot Guide's Special produced by Old Town. These big rugged canoes are heavy-duty boats of great capacity, designed and built primarily for use by guides and wilderness freighters. They will give excellent service for fishing on open lakes or on rivers where white water will be encountered frequently. They are not designed nor suitable for knockabout use by fishermen who want to travel from one stream or lake to another using an auto-top carrier rack since they are excessively long. They are easily portaged only by a strong man in good physical condition. For use from permanent camps, where portability presents little or no problem, however, they are excellent because of their stability, ruggedness and capacity and their ability to weather a sudden squall.

Canoes can be used to good advantage with light outboard motors, provided they are equipped with brackets that clamp to the gunwales. Such accessories cost only a few dollars and are indispensable if motors are to be used. Light-weight gasoline motors or electric motors can be mounted directly on the gunwale of a large canoe, but this practice is not advisable because of possible damage to the finish and, in prolonged use, to the structural members of the craft itself. With brackets a 16- to 18-foot canoe can employ an outboard motor of up to 4 horsepower without strain. When motors will be used regularly, square-sterned models designed to mount the motor directly on the transom should be selected.

Most modern canoes of aluminum or fiberglass are equipped with flotation chambers that prevent the craft from sinking when swamped, although canoes of conventional wooden construction have an inherent bouyancy. Some old models may still be encountered with flotation chambers running the length of the gunwales in the form of external blisters called sponsons. Sponsons add greatly to the buoyancy of the canoe and they were designed primarily for use at children's camps. They add greatly also to the weight; sponson models weigh about 25 pounds more than canoes of conventional design, and they are totally unsuitable where much portaging must be done.

In addition to paddling, poling, and motor, the canoe can also be rowed if equipped with detachable outriggers to hold the rowlocks. Canoes are too narrow to permit the mounting of the locks directly on the gunwale, but when the outriggers are used, canoes handle beautifully with oars on rivers or lakes. If much trolling will be done these accessories are ideally suited to this type of fishing since the rower faces the stern and can keep an eye on his rod and line while the paddler must face forward. Trolling from a paddled canoe is a rather awkward business at best.

The canoe fisherman will find a light anchor a very useful accessory, although it is an item that is usually dispensed with by those who use canoes entirely for transportation. They permit the fisherman to stop and cast or to work a particularly productive area. Because of the small surface presented to the wind and water by an anchored canoe a very small weight will hold the largest canoe in position against a strong wind or current. With wooden or fiberglass boats grapnel anchors are unsuitable because their sharp points tend to mar the finish or even puncture the fabric when carelessly handled; mushroom anchors in the smaller sizes are much more suitable. Many canoe fishermen make their own anchors by filling a tin can with molten lead in which an eye-bolt has been set. Concrete is also used, but it makes a bulkier weight. The can may be stripped away for a more professional appearance, or it may be left in place. Light-weight patented anchors are much more compact and lighter and have great holding power and can be packed with the duffel on portages for wilderness travel, although most wilderness anglers prefer to improvise their own anchors on the spot from properly shaped stones. Except for such emergency use, however, a permanent anchor of proper design and weight will prove more satisfactory.

In travelling across open exposed water an anchor can be a valuable safety device since, in the event of capsizing, it will hold the boat in place, if the line is long enough to reach bottom, rather than permitting it to drift beyond the reach of the operator. In deep swift rivers, however, the opposite is true, since it will hold the canoe in place while the operator, unless he is able to grasp the canoe as it goes over, drifts downstream. When anchors are carried aboard on rivers of this kind they should be lashed to a seat or thwart when not in use. In travelling either type of water, some form of approved life preserver should be carried aboard.

The canoe is one of the oldest fishing craft in America, and, in its proper element, it is still one of the most versatile. (See also, Section VII).

OUTBOARD BOATS FOR THE FISHERMAN

Up until the late 1940's nearly all boats were built individually by hand, and even boats turned out by the same builder on identical forms often developed an individual personality of their own. Boats of the same design, made of the same materials by two different builders often varied greatly in maneuverability and performance for reasons that only master marine engineers might fathom. Each individual section of the coast, and each geographic region of the interior developed time-tested models so distinctive and dissimilar from those of other areas that the experienced waterman glancing at a picture which showed nothing but water and a few boats could spot the locale immediately.

Today, thanks to technological progress, this is no longer true. Small boats, and some larger ones, are mass-produced in hundreds of shapes and sizes, their hulls moulded of plywood, plastic, fiberglass and metals. Boats from the same form produced by the same builder are as alike as the members of a school of tadpoles, varying one from the other not one iota in weight, line, or workmanship.

The majority of these mass-produced modern craft are designed for power with outboard motors.

Modern boat designers have borrowed the best features of all of the regional designs that have developed in various waters over the centuries. The john-boat, once confined to the rivers of the Middle West, may be encountered on streams and lakes all over North America. Modifications of the Ipswich skiff and banks dory ply the waters of Lake Mead and the Pacific Northwest.

Catamarans, which originated in the East Indies and in India, many centuries ago, are double-hulled boats with a platform deck straddling the two halves. Until recent years they were rarely seen on American waters. Around 1960, however, a few boat designers recognized the inherent stability of such craft, modified the original design to gain greater cockpit capacity and began producing them for use on rivers, lakes, and even the open ocean. The modified modern catamaran, called by the name of their primitive prototype, or by such descriptive names as sea sled, enjoyed ready popularity among fishermen.

The sea sled usually is constructed of fiberglass or metal and from the side resembles a standard broad-beamed outboard skiff or runabout. Its bottom, however, is recessed along the keel line, which permits much more speed and efficiency than would be possible with a standard hull of the same beam. In moving through the water any boat creates a certain degree of drag, and this is especially true

Evinrude Motors

This Penn Yan Cartop boat weighs only 57 pounds and the 3-h.p. Evinrude Lightwin motor adds only 33 more pounds, an excellent combination for the lone fisherman who wants ease of portability.

of hulls designed for use with outboards, since the after portion of an outboard must have a broad bearing to support the power plant. The divided hull of the modified catamaran eliminates much of this source of friction. At the same time, the generous size of the cockpit permits the fisherman much more room in relation to the overall length of the hull. Since trolling must be done at low speeds at which wave motion exerts its greatest influence on a boat, they are adapted to fishing in offshore waters or on exposed lakes where moderate seas may be encountered.

The angler selecting a new outboard boat and motor now has a bewildering array of equipment from which to choose. Assuming that a boat will be used entirely for fishing, rather than for pleasure cruising, water skiing, and other water sports, the choice will depend entirely upon the type of fishing that he wants to do, which is governed, in turn by the local water conditions. If the fishing will be primarily for Smallmouth Bass on rocky rivers with many rips and shallow rapids, the prospective buyer would be silly to consider an 18-foot cruiser mounting a 50-plus horsepower motor. One of the modified aluminum john-boats mounting a 5-horsepower kicker would prove near ideal for such purposes. On the open sea or on large choppy lakes, however, the user of the john-boat with its low freeboard and square ends would be courting disaster; the cabin cruiser could take such conditions in stride.

The majority of outboard motor boats used in fishing are employed on lakes of more than 25 acres, in relatively sheltered bays and estuaries, and on broad and relatively deep streams. The skiff, runabout, and cruiser are all used to good advantage on such waters depending upon the needs and finances of the owner. The larger craft provide more roominess and comfort since the better equipped models have a sleeping cabin, galley, refrigerator, running water and a chemical toilet, or head. They can be used for cruising long distances without returning to the home port, and they are much more seaworthy than smaller craft of similar hull design.

While very large boats can be towed easily behind an automobile on a modern boat trailer, boats over 16 feet in length are much more difficult to handle on the roads and require more elaborate launching sites. If the fisherman plans to transport his craft regularly by trailer to far distant fishing grounds, a model of 16 feet or less should be selected. A light trailer-and-boat combination permits the touring angler to launch anywhere he can drive within parking distance of a sloping riverbank or beach.

The majority of the mass-produced fiberglass, metal, and plywood outboard motor boats today are built with planing hulls—flat aft and with V-shaped bottoms forward. Boat hulls are classified by marine engineers in two types—displacement or planing. Displacement hulls, as the name implies, displace water when under power. They are designed to move *through* the water by pushing it out of the way. All rowboats are displacement craft, since no rower has the strength and energy to propel even a light boat fast enough to plane. Nearly all large cabin cruisers and other large inboard motorboats also are designed on the displacement principle. Although designed to plane at normal cruising speeds, all planing hulls operate as displacement hulls when used at low speeds.

From the standpoint of the fisherman, the displacement hull has advantages that often are overlooked by many boat owners. Planing hulls are designed for maximum efficiency at high speeds, to "get up on their step," and skim *over* the surface of the water instead of making their way through it. No one in his right mind would attempt to fish while his boat is planing along at 20 knots or more. When the hull designed for planing is propelled at slow speeds, such as those that must be used in trolling or casting, the boat is likely to pitch and toss heavily in any kind of a sea. Displacement boats with their rounded or deep V-bottoms were designed principally for riding through water of this kind at lower speeds, and they are much more comfortable to fish from when the going is rough.

The advantage of the planing hull is its ability to move fast when a school of fish is sighted working on the surface a few miles away, their presence indicated by a feeding flock of terns or gulls. The planing boat can also move ahead of an approaching squall rather than being forced to weather it. But when heavy weather overtakes the boat, the displacement hull has all the advantages. When the going gets rough, even the advantage of speed is lost to the planing boat, since their hulls are designed primarily for maximum efficiency on calm waters, and a heavy chop can cause them to pound, slam, and porpoise not only uncomfortably but even dangerously. If caught out of harbor in a squall or in heavy chop, the prudent skipper slows down if his hull is of the planing type. Under such circumstances he is likely to be passed by the owner of the theoretically slower but much more stable displacement boat. Not infrequently, if the storm is of relatively mild intensity the owner of the displacement boat may continue fishing while his swifter planing neighbors scurry for cover.

Ideally, outboard fishing boats for open waters should be of a semi-V bottom construction, with the V carried all the way to the stern. Under full power these boats will plane nicely, but they can be slowed down to trolling or casting speeds without discomfort even when the water becomes choppy. Most of the inboard motorboats designed for coastal or offshore fishing are of such design; outboard boats with similar bottoms are not always so easy to find among the mass-produced models on the market, which have been designed

This roomy Lone Star runabout, powered by twin Gale outboards of 40-h.p. each is popular with Gulf Coast fishermen. Note the roomy clutterless cockpit. Controls, operator and accessories are all out of the way of the fishermen.

primarily with the pleasure boater rather than the angler in mind. But a number of local builders and some of the larger manufacturers offer such models, and they are the ideal choice in hull design for the fisherman. The sea sled offers many of the same advantages as well as a higher degree of roominess.

In any fishing boat, or boat of any kind, the builders' specifications for power should be followed carefully. Displacement boats, which are designed to slip smoothly through the water, have a maximum speed, or "hull speed," that is approximately equivalent to 1½ times the square root of their length. No matter how much power is added, once hull speed is attained, the boat will not go faster. If attempts are made to exceed hull speed, by adding power, the boat will perform crankily and often dangerously, waste fuel, and handle sluggishly. All displacement motor boats operate most efficiently and economically at speeds considerably less than the hull speed, another factor to consider when contemplating the purchase of a boat that will be used primarily for trolling.

A planing hull, on the other hand, operates more efficiently and more economically as it gathers speed. At maximum speed at which control can be maintained friction with the water is reduced almost to zero, and standard models have been pushed to speeds of up to 80 knots. Theoretically there is no limit short of actual flying to which a planing hull can be moved on calm water. But if the planing hull is overpowered or the water is rough there is danger of it breaking up under the strain of the power plant and the pounding of the water, which at high speed can assume an astounding solidity. The operator is in constant danger of losing control, and a spill at maximum speeds can be lethal. When slowed down, the weight of a too-heavy motor will cause the boat to squat and flounder heavily. Safety, economy, and commonsense all dictate that the horsepower rating of the manufacturer of the boat not be exceeded.

Motors of less than the rated horsepower capacity of the hull can, of course, be used, but only at the sacrifice of efficiency. The one exception is that boats with tandem motor mounts can be used with two motors of different horsepower, a large heavy-duty engine which will generate full power for fast travel to and from the fishing ground and a smaller motor for slow trolling or shifting position for drift fishing.

From a safety standpoint, if for no other reason, boats used for offshore fishing on the open ocean or on very large lakes should mount two motors. As a common practice, only one of the two motors is used at one time, but the second motor provides excellent insurance against a power failure which, on exposed waters, could lead to disaster. Needless to say, an adequate supply of fuel should be carried in the reserve tanks before venturing out into exposed waters.

Except on small craft used primarily for casting and still fishing on sheltered waters, outboard motor boats with remote controls are a major convenience if not a necessity. They are indispensable in craft used regularly for trolling for the larger fresh-water and nearly all salt-water game fish. The remote control permits the operator to control the boat from the forward portion of the cockpit where he is out of the way of the trailing line or lines, which with direct control he must constantly duck whenever the boat makes an abrupt turn. If a heavy fish is hooked, the operator is also in a more strategic position to maneuver the boat promptly and accurately if the controls are located forward. In many types of fishing, skillful boat handling may mean the difference between a trophy fish brought to gaff and another empty story of a big one that got away.

Outboard boats used for heavy-duty trolling are best equipped with stem brackets or false transoms to form a well in which the motor can be mounted with the power head lower than the after coaming of the cockpit. This not only eliminates another potential hazard to the lines while trolling or fighting a fish but is an important safety factor in blue-water fishing. Outboard boats of the larger classes must carry their power heads relatively close to the surface of the water if the propeller is to be submerged to the proper depth for optimum efficiency. If the motor were mounted on the main transom at a level with the deck of a large deep-hulled boat, the drive shaft would have to be awkwardly long to reach the water. The alternative, which most manufacturers employ, is to cut down the height of the transom. This arrangement works well enough for general cruising on calm waters, but boats used in fishing spend much of their time traveling at greatly reduced speeds, often in rough water. If the fish are working in a relatively small area, the boats of necessity must circle and travel at least one-fourth of the time with the wind and with a following sea. On the open ocean large combers can sweep in rapidly,

Evinrude Motors

Big rugged lapstrake outboard runabouts and cruisers like these, mounting motors of 40-h.p. or more, singly or in tandem, are essential for use of the open ocean. The runabout in the foreground mounts a single 75-h.p., while that in the background is powered by paired 40-h.p. motors. The latter method has many advantages over the former for fishing use.

and the boat with a cut-down transom is highly vulnerable if it is overtaken by one of these great white-capped waves while the operator is preoccupied with fighting a fish or in maneuvering into position for a strike. The recessed motor mounted in a well overcomes much of this hazard. One of the great advantages of the inboard motor, and a major reason why most professional deep-water fishing guides use inboard motors almost exclusively lies in the greater seaworthiness of the inboard, which is traceable to the more efficient mounting of the power plant and the high transom that its design permits.

It was to combine the principal advantages of the inboard and the outboard motor that the so-called "inboard-outboard," was developed. Advantages of the outboard, over and above the basic purchase price, are its portability, its ease and economy of servicing in port, and its ability to run through shoal water, since the entire drive-shaft and propeller can be lifted to clear obstructions or when running in to a beach. Its disadvantages lie in the difficulty of servicing or adjusting the motor on the open water, its relative cost of operation on a miles per gallon basis, especially at slow trolling speeds, and the inefficiency of its usual mounting in relation to the stability of the boat. Since outboard motor boats are steered by changing the position of the propeller rather than in response to a rudder, however, they are much more maneuverable than inboards. An outboard boat can be turned, at low speeds, within a space little wider than its length. No standard inboard can match this performance, especially at near-stalling speed, since it must be moving ahead in order for the rudder to take hold. Outboards can be reversed and maneuvered through obstructions much more readily than inboards.

Inboards, with their less exacting fuel requirements, on the other hand, are much more economical to operate and use fuel more economically, especially at usual trolling speeds. The two-cycle outboard, which is standard for most outboard motor models, operates most efficiently in terms of gas consumption at its maximum speed. The inboard motor, like the closely related automobile engine, gives maximum economy at slow speeds, and it does not have to be fed a mixture of gasoline and oil in carefully measured proportions.

The outboard-inboard, which was introduced on the American market around 1960, has the power plant located inside the cockpit, where it can be reached easily for adjustment, even while under way. It can be of 2, 4, or even 8 cylinders and operate efficiently on raw gasoline unmixed with oil, or even diesel fuel with its great additional economy. Yet it can maneuver in deep water or shallows with the facility of the outboard, since it steers on the same principle, and the drive shaft and propeller can be lifted out of danger. For the same reason it carries more easily on a trailer, since the drive shaft and propeller hinge up out of the way for carrying.

The major disadvantage of the outboard-inboard, aside from its higher capital cost, lies in the additional mechanical complexity of the drive-shaft, which must be of indirect drive through a set of gears rather than directly from the power plant as in the case of the standard transom-mounted outboard or the conventional inboard.

Except for minor refinements, the outboard motor appears to have been developed close to its maximum potential, at least from the standpoint of the fisherman. Outboards above 50 horsepower are so heavy that they require a semi-permanent mounting and a winch to remove them, eliminating much of the advantage of portability over the inboard, and without its basic economy of operation, especially for the fisherman who will operate his engine much of the time at trolling speed. Below the 50-horsepower mark, however, the outboard is considered an almost indispensible piece of equipment by fishermen who ply any fishing grounds not readily accessible by wading or a few strokes of the oars or those that are best reached by large inboard motor boats designed specifically for marine use.

No piece of fishing equipment developed more rapidly in the decade between 1945 and 1955 than the outboard engine. Part of the spurt was due to the boating boom in which the mass-produced boat replaced the hand-made product of individual shops. The water-skiing craze gave it further impetus. Before 1940, most outboards were single-cylinder models of less than 10-horsepower and anything much larger was considered a monster. Starting had to be done by a separate pull-rope on an exposed flywheel, although many manufacturers had housed the wheel under a streamlined hinged hood. Propellers were unguarded and had a tendency to clog in weeds. Most of the models lacked a reverse, although some smaller models could be reversed by turning the motor completely around, and reserve tanks, self starters and remote controls were unheard of. Performance of even the better models often was cranky, requiring precise adjustments of many valves before they would start and function properly. Carburetors were generally cranky and unreliable.

The pull-rope starter is still standard on most motors of low horse-power today, but the rope is self-winding on nearly all recent models. Almost all low horse-power motors have been designed with the fisherman in mind, and the majority can now be driven through beds of heavy weeds without entangling the prop. For the angler who likes to fish for Largemouth Bass, Pickerel, Northern Pike and other denizens of weedy, shallow lakes, this is a major improvement. So is the slip clutch, a more recent innovation to re-

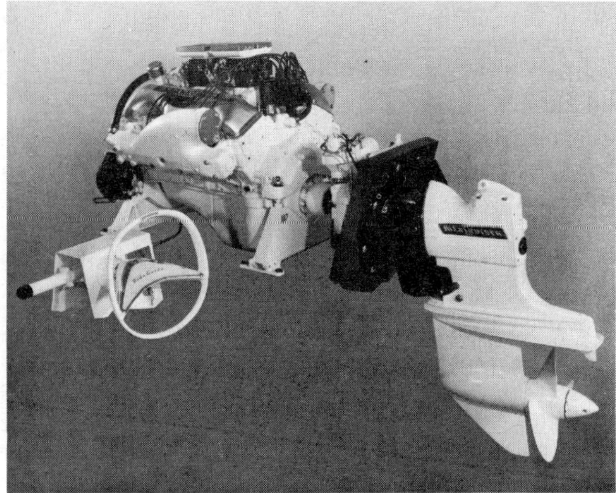

Kiekhaefer Corp.

The outboard-inboard combines economy of operation and power of the inboard with the maneuverability of the outboard. The 310-h.p. MerCruiser stern-drive power package is a four-cycle V-8 with the MerCruiser II stern-drive unit. A manual crank, or optional electrical pushbutton mechanism, operates from inside the boat to invert the unit 180 degrees.

place the shear pin for boats used where rocky ledges, stumps and snags present major hazards. These new safety clutches permit the propeller to slip on its axle whenever a solid obstruction is hit but to reengage as soon as the boat is in the clear. The older shear pin provided the same insurance against a broken propeller, stripped gears, or a bent drive shaft, but the boat had to be stopped and the motor shipped while the pin was replaced. In rough water, such as a tide rip or a swift-moving current, the operation often was a hazardous one, and even at best it was time-consuming. On larger models the push-button starter and remote control are now standard, with obvious advantages to the fisherman which have been discussed earlier.

A few years ago all outboard motors were equipped with integral and usually skimpy fuel tanks that had to be refilled frequently with a funnel and fuel can. In rough water, this operation, too, was often a hazardous one. It was necessary for the operator to stand, sometimes in a badly pitching boat, and there always was danger of a fire resulting from spilled fuel, a bleak prospect for any fisherman on a wilderness lake or river or on a choppy bay some distance from land.

This problem is overcome by the use of separate tanks that are connected to the motor by tubes and with visual fuel gauges. When the operating tank begins to go dry, the reserve tank can be put into operation in a matter of seconds. The danger of spilled fuel is practically nil.

The underwater exhaust has been with us for many years. This eliminated much of the objectionable noise that was generated even by light models in earlier days. A number of late models supplement the underwater exhaust with mufflers and rubber powerhead mountings.

Nearly all outboards except the smaller models are now equipped with gear shifts which enhance the already great maneuverability inherent in the outboard principle. Most of these have three positions—forward, neutral, and reverse. The neutral gear permits the boat to stop the propeller without stalling, another major safety factor and one with great application for the boat angler.

The fisherman selecting a motor today has a wide range of models from which to pick, ranging from compact models weighing less than 20 pounds and generating less than 3-horsepower, up to huge power plants with the energy of 100 horses packed under their streamlined bonnets. They are amazing examples of engineering efficiency and ingenuity.

All motors, of course, must be matched to the weight and design of the boat, and the specifications of the manufacturer should be followed both for the sake of safety and efficiency.

For light skiffs, cartop boats, square-sterned outboard canoes, or standard canoes used with motor brackets, motors between 1½ and 3 horsepower are excellent. Not to be overlooked for such craft, most of which will be used primarily on small lakes and sheltered rivers, are the electric outboards. These operate on rechargeable storage batteries and require no fuel. Even with the weight of the battery considered, they are exceptionally light, and, in comparison to the internal combustion models, almost silent. With the rise in popularity in boating, several states have zoned their waters for various types of craft. In some states only hand-propelled boats and those powered by electric motors are allowed to be used on ponds below specified acreages. The electric motor will move the light craft for which they are designed at a lively clip with maximum economy and as silently as oars.

Motors rated between 5 and 10 horsepower are suitable for use with displacement craft up to 16 feet in length—for heavier skiffs, dories, and other boats used in relatively sheltered lakes or on broad deep rivers. For the boatless fisherman who wants a motor for use with rented boats available at most liveries and marinas, the choice of a motor in this horse-power range will prove most practical. It will combine adequate power for most rental boats with ease of portability; most 10-horse-power motors are compact enough to pack in an automobile trunk. The majority weigh less than 75 pounds, and 5-horse-power models less than 50 pounds.

Motors rated at a horse-power between 10 and 35 horsepower are used primarily with runabouts and other planing models and the larger displacement hulls. These are heavy motors and usually are fixed semi-permanently to the transom since winches and special motor dollies are required to remove them for storage or servicing. For the coast-based fisherman who wants to run out into open exposed water, they provide a good reserve of power for speed in an emergency, or for reaching distant fishing grounds. Larger motors are for the heavier runabouts and cabin cruisers.

Matched to the craft with which they will be used and given routine maintenance, the modern outboard motor will provide long and economical service.

Care and Servicing of Outboard Motors. A new outboard motor, like a new automobile engine, requires careful handling during its breaking-in period. The modern outboard is a precision instrument, and present-day machining methods have reduced this formerly long and tedious initial period to a minimum. During the first 20 or 30 hours of use, however, up to 50 per cent more oil must be used in the fuel mixture than would be used under normal operating conditions. Speed during this time should not exceed one-half the maximum. During the recommended breaking-in period, specifications of the manufacturer should be followed to the letter. Running a motor fresh from the factory at full speed with a mixture designed for normal use may cause serious damage or shorten its life.

After the motor has been run at half speed for the time recommended by the manufacturer or dealer, it should be given a general check-up. The extra oil used while breaking in may have fouled spark plugs, and these should be removed and cleaned. The skirts should be removed and all nuts and bolts tightened. Since less oil is used under normal conditions, an adjustment of the idling jet usually must be made after the breaking-in has been completed.

The proper ratio of oil to gasoline to use in preparing a mixture for an outboard motor depends upon the kind of motor and its horsepower. Again, the specifications of the manufacturer should be followed religiously for best results. Highest automobile gasoline, containing large amounts of tetraethyl lead, creates lead oxide upon combustion in low-compression engines and the use of heavily leaded gasoline will cause constant fouling of spark plug points. So-called "regular" gasolines contain very little lead and may be used without trouble.

In most outboard motors, lubricating oil mixed with the gasoline is distributed under pressure to all moving parts in the power unit. Because this system differs radically from that used in automobiles, heavy-duty oils containing detergents are not satisfactory. The lowest priced bulk oils carried by reliable gasoline stations will give universally good service in outboards. Some oil companies produce canned oil especially labeled for use in outboard motors. While canning assures protection against adulteration or error, any "straight-run mineral-type" motor oil purchased in bulk containers will give good service at low cost. Most standard motors use either oils of number 30 or 40 SAE viscosity. Customarily, ratios of one-half pint to each gallon of gasoline for motors up to 5 H.P. and three-quarters of a pint to each gallon for motors between 5 and 8 H.P. are recommended. In larger motors guesswork and approximations may prove costly, and the manufacturer's specifications always should be obtained and followed. Motors used much at high speed and those used at high altitudes require more oil than those used at trolling speeds at sea level. Accuracy in preparing fuel mixtures is essential to the best performance. In this respect, a metal quart measure will pay for itself many times over. While no more accurate, it will usually be found more convenient and less subject to breakage than the milk bottles often used for this purpose.

A standard outboard motor gasoline can with a flexible snout is the most satisfactory utensil for mixing and carrying fuel. The fuel *never* should be mixed in the tank of the motor itself. In mixing, components should be poured into the can gradually, a half-gallon of gasoline first, a little oil, a little more gasoline and then the rest of the oil, and finally, the rest of the gasoline. To mix the ingredients thoroughly, the can should be shaken vigorously and should be shaken again each time the motor is refueled. A funnel equipped with a filter will prevent inpurities or foreign matter from entering the system.

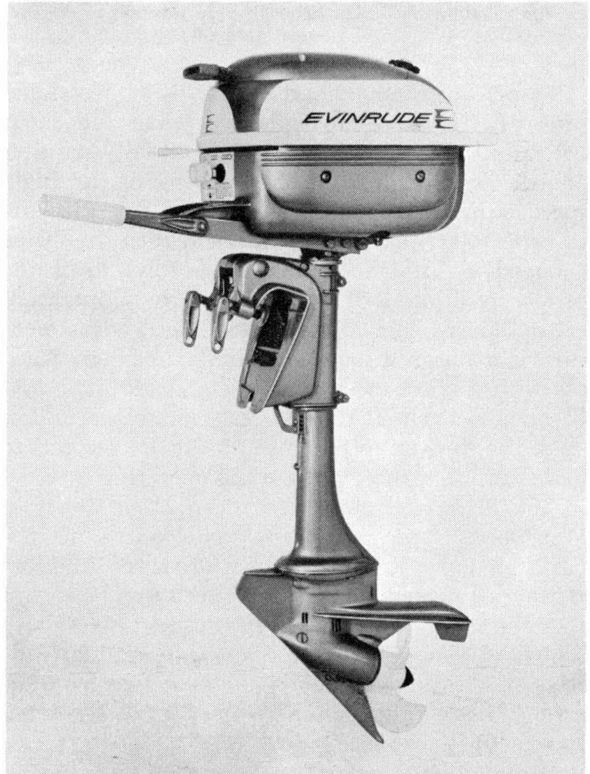

Evinrude Motors

The 3-h.p. Lightwin is the bantam model in the line of Evinrude Motors. An economy motor, the Lightwin will run at full throttle on a small dinghy for 1½ hours on a half-gallon of fuel. Weighing 33 pounds, the Lightwin features an integral fuel tank.

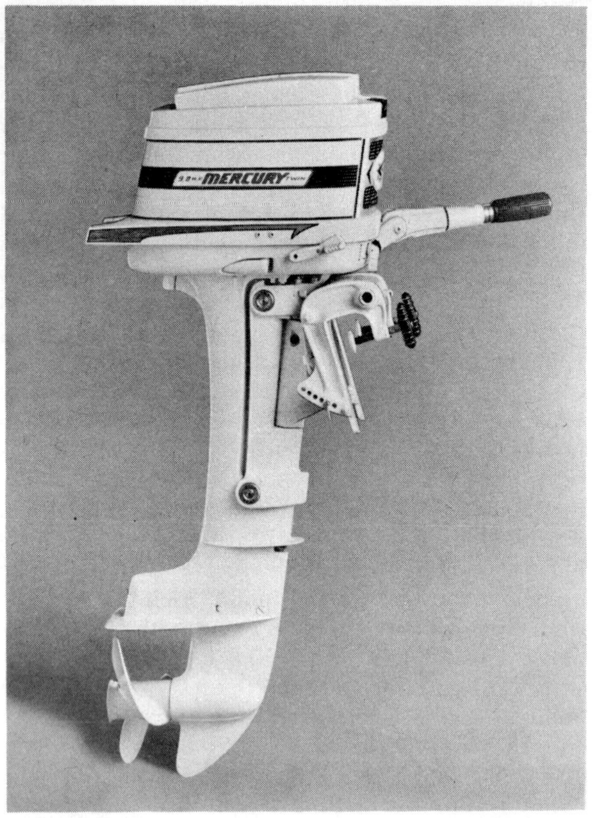

Kiekhaefer Corp.

The Merc 110 is a 9.8-h.p. fishing motor weighing just 55 pounds, 20 percent lighter than any previous outboard motor in the ten-h.p. class, and even lighter than competitive 5½-h.p. models. Its design helps it glide through weeds and over stumps. There are no shear pins or drive pins.

Simple adjustments and check-ups at occasional intervals may save an expensive repair bill later. Adjusting the carburetor properly usually requires a little experimentation. The setting of the high-speed adjustment should be checked first with the throttle wide open. The adjustment then should be changed—a little at a time both ways until the proper position is found for smoothest operation at top speed. The idling or low-speed adjustment then is made in a somewhat similar manner. Starting with the low-speed adjustment closed, it should be opened one-half turn. After starting the motor, open the throttle to full speed for a few seconds to make sure that there is a normal operating mixture in the firing chamber before throttling down to low speed. If the motor spits and coughs, set the adjustment for a slightly richer mixture. Frequent stalling or ragged firing at low speed usually means that the mixture is too rich. Adjustments for both high and low speeds must be made gradually by trial and error, although a study of the manufacturer's instruction manual will save much wasted effort and lost motion.

Most modern motors are equipped with chokes instead of primers and do not flood easily. In old motors, if flooding occurs, the main carburetor adjustment should be set "full lean" and the starter cord pulled until the motor starts. Once the motor has "caught," the carburetor should be adjusted until the proper setting for the main carburetor adjustment is found. Flooding rarely occurs in cold motors.

Water and dirt in the fuel system is a common source of trouble in outboard motors which can be avoided by careful filtering of all fuel before placing it in the gasoline tank. Most outboard motor dealers can supply a funnel containing a filter of fine wire mesh which will remove any dangerous foreign particles. Where water in the gasoline gives trouble it can be separated and removed by running the supply through a chamois pad folded into the funnel. Gum, sometimes evident as a sticky, semi-fluid mass in the fuel system, may be avoided by using approved kinds of oil and gasoline in the correct proportions.

Occasional cleaning of the fuel system—which consists of the carburetor, gas tank, filter, and gas line—will lengthen the life and improve the performance of most motors. To clean this system the fuel first should be drained from the tank by removing the fuel line. The fuel filter, which strains impurities from the mixture in the tank, should be removed and washed thoroughly in clean gasoline. If gum is present, acetone may be needed to dissolve it. The tank then should be sluiced with fresh, clean gasoline. If the fuel line is obstructed, a wire run through it will clear it completely. Merely blowing through the line usually will remove any light foreign matter or moisture. To clean the carburetor, remove the plug in the side or at the bottom and let the fuel drain.

Fishermen who use motors for trolling sometimes will find that the porcelain around the center electrodes of the spark plugs are covered with oil. If this happens, a dealer should be consulted to obtain a slightly hotter plug. If the proper plug is used, the porcelain insulation should be dry and light brown in color. If the porcelain is white or covered with a black, crusty substance, a cooler-running plug should be used. The latter conditions are more commonly found in motors which are run frequently at high speeds. When plugs are checked, a feeler gauge should be used to be certain that the gap recommended by the manufacturer is maintained. For most motors this is approximately .030 inches although the products of different manufacturers vary a few thousands of an inch either way. Any carbon deposited on electrodes may be removed by scraping with a knife.

To check the spark, remove the plugs and ground all but one lead wire by holding them against the motor. Then hold the ungrounded wire about three-eighths of an inch from the motor and pull the starter cord. A plainly visible blue spark should jump between the end of the ungrounded wire and the motor. Each of the other lead wires then should be tested in the same way. The wire being tested should be held with the fingers away from the end to avoid shocks, and those wires not being tested should be properly grounded before the cord is pulled.

Loss of grease from the lower unit of the motor may permit water to come in contact with gears and bearings and cause damage. New alloys and better tooling methods have made this source of trouble much less serious than it was in earlier models. Gear housings now are made so tight that grease loss is kept at a minimum. When using a new motor it is wise to check the grease supply in the gear housing every month or so until the proper checking interval is found. In most new motors this will be only once or twice each season. In most motors two screw plugs will be found in the housing. The lower is the grease port and the upper a vent to permit the entrance of air so that water and grease will not be held by vacuum. Removing both plugs will allow any water which may have leaked in to escape. In refilling with grease, use approved outboard gear lubricant, which comes in tubes, and squeeze some into the lower hole until grease is forced out through the upper. In replacing screws, be certain that they are fully tightened to prevent further leaking.

Motors used in salt water require much more care than those used in fresh. The lower unit in particular should be checked frequently to see that grease loss has not permitted the entrance of water. Although most motors today are made of alloys which are highly resistant to corrosion, salt left in gear housings will quickly ruin the motor. To avoid damage, the motor should always be cleaned with fresh water immediately after use in tidal waters. To remove salt water and crystals, the motor should be sluiced or hosed thoroughly with fresh water immediately after it is removed from the boat. It then should be run for a few minutes with the lower unit set in a barrel of fresh water to remove any salt. Occasional greasing of the spline connections between drive shaft and crank shaft in the power head may prevent subsequent damage to these parts after exposure to frequent use in salt water. Use an oily cloth to polish the outside of the motor after all salt has been removed inside and out.

If an outboard motor is dropped overboard while running, it probably will need the attention of a skilled mechanic as soon as possible after it has been raised. Under such conditions, damage to pistons, rings, crankshaft, or connecting rod is commonly suffered and replacement parts will be needed. If it is impossible to raise a motor within a day after it is dropped overboard, it is best to take it, after recovery, to a competent mechanic for servicing even though it may not have been running when it went overboard. The unskilled amateur mechanic may do more damage than good since the motor must be completely disassembled and each part thoroughly cleaned and dried. If the motor can be raised within a day after it has been dropped and if it was not running when it was submerged, it can usually be put in running order within a short time. The gas line should be removed and all fuel drained from the tank, which then should be rinsed out with clean fuel. The ignition system may be dried by removing the spark plugs, grounding the wires against the power head and pulling the starter cord several times.

To remove water from the carburetor, put a little fuel in its intake and turn the motor over by hand until all water seems to have been pumped out. If the motor still will not start after it has been reassembled, the spark plugs should be removed and dried again.

Motors always should be stored during the winter months in a clean dry place. In most homes the attic probably is the best location although a completely dry basement or garage will serve. Metal stands for use in storage may be obtained from most dealers or a serviceable stand may be made easily from scrap lumber and pipe. The base always should be large enough so that there will be no danger of someone knocking over the motor. A canvas covering will keep out dust and dirt.

Before storing a motor for long periods of time certain precautions should be taken. The fuel system should be thoroughly drained and cleaned, and the lower unit drained of any water and greased. Remove the propeller and clean and oil the entire shaft. Examine the shear pin for flaws and replace

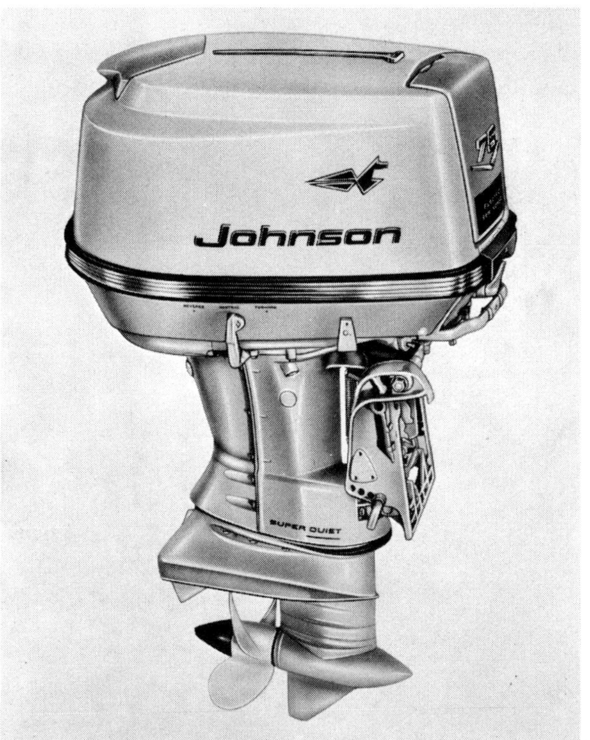

Johnson Motors

The Super Sea-Horse V-75A. Johnson has a factory-installed, high capacity, fully transistor, regulated alternator-type generator. Other features include fixed high-speed carburetor jets, fully sealed wire harness from motor to junction box, temperature warning lights, new needle-thrust bearing, safety interlock switch to permit starting in gear but only at slow throttle settings, and additional sound silencing.

it if necessary. To protect the carburetor, remove the spark plugs and squirt lubricating oil into the carburetor intake while pulling the starter cord. This will distribute oil to all working parts and inner surfaces and keep them from rusting. Spark plugs should be cleaned and checked for proper gap.

A motor may be transported safely by laying it on its back or side in an automobile luggage compartment. Be certain that there is no space between the powerhead and the forward wall of the luggage compartment or a sudden stop may send it sliding forward. Padding the motor with an old rug or blanket will prevent damage from shocks and jars. Care in packing other gear should be taken so that nothing will fall on the motor when traveling over rough roads, and better protection may be assured if a carrying case is used. Some carrying racks are equipped with small wheels for convenience in transporting the motor from car to boat.

BOAT TRAILERS

Boat trailers have developed nearly as rapidly and as spectacularly in the last 20 years as boats and motors. Before World War II the heavy wooden boats then in use were not readily portable with the exception of the smaller canoe-built dinghies and lighter plywood skiffs. Newer materials such as fiberglass aluminum, and light-weight steel alloys have made even fair-sized cabin cruisers light enough to move on suitable trailers behind an ordinary passenger car.

Early trailers were mostly hand-made of old automobile axles, springs, and wheels with cradles of wood, padded with scrap rubber. They were, at best, inelegant, heavy and usually difficult to tow and to use in launching. Except for carrying very light boats, they were used primarily for moving boats from storage to water in the spring and back again in the fall.

Modern trailers are handsome, efficient, and provide maximum protection both for the boat and the automobile. For their load capacity they are remarkably light, and those made for heavy boats are equipped with winches to facilitate launching and loading. The trailer is backed down a launching ramp or firm beach directly into the water to a level slightly below the depth of the axle. The winch is slacked off, and the boat is launched. In removing the boat from the water, the process is simply reversed; the winch hauls the boat quickly back on the trailer where it is cradled surely and gently on rubber pads, strapped in place, and ready to move on its way. Trailer hitches are sure, strong, and reliable, and most of the better models of trailers are equipped with shock absorbers in addition to springs.

One point of maintenance that sometimes leads to trouble is the failure to give the trailer the same maintenance and care that is given the motor and boat. Axles should be kept greased, since they are exposed frequently to water, inviting rust. Ungreased axles can result in a dangerous and costly accident. Paint should be touched up as needed to prevent any weakening of the frame, and padding should be checked for damage to prevent gouging or scarring of the boat. The wiring also should

Washington Department of Game

One of many public access sites, complete with launching ramps and parking facilities, available to anglers in Washington State.

be checked carefully, since a loaded trailer without lights on a modern high-speed turnpike is not only illegal but a highly dangerous vehicle. Hitches should be inspected regularly for any wear or chafing that could lead to breakage and the loss of all equipment on the highway.

As with boats and motors, the specifications of the manufacturer for carrying capacity should never be exceeded when loading the trailer. Neglect of this commonsense precaution has caused more than one boat owner to end up with a costly pile of junk by the side of the highway.

THE OUTBOARD BOATING CLUB OF AMERICA

Most of the nationally advertised manufacturers of outboard motors, outboard boats, and trailers are members of the Outboard Boating Club of America. This organization requires that member manufacturers submit their products to the club engineers for accurate and unbiased tests of horsepower and capacity at scientific laboratories. The "OBC Certified" rating stamped on a product is an absolute guarantee of the quality of the product and the limits of its practical use.

The Club with offices at 307 North Michigan Avenue, Chicago 3, Illinois, accepts no advertising in its publication as an added insurance against partiality in the evaluation of equipment.

The Outboard Boating Club also evaluates legislation affecting boaters, provides comparative engineering data to its members in the industry, and offers low-cost insurance against fire, theft, collision, loss, and storm damage to owners of boats and motors. The coverage is complete, whether the equipment is in use, being transported, or in storage. Also available is liability insurance to cover damage that the operator may cause to the property of others. Coverage of this kind should be carried by all boat owners.

BOAT REGULATIONS AND LAWS

Federal and State regulations governing the use of boats commonly used by fishermen are relatively simple, and there is little excuse for violating them. Copies of the complete federal laws or abstracts applicable to small craft can be obtained from any U.S. Coast Guard office. State laws and regulations can be obtained from the respective state conservation department. Aside from the legal penalties involved, violation of any of these laws can involve the risk of serious physical injury or financial loss. Federal law embraces coastal waters and tidal tributaries, the Great Lakes, and connecting waterways, interstate waters, such as rivers and lakes bordering more than one state, and any inland waters under the jurisdiction of any federal agency.

Prior to 1958, only a few states had adopted regulations applying to boats used on state-controlled waters, and these often were in conflict with federal regulations or with those of other states.

In order to overcome this confusion as well as to encourage more states to enforce boat safety regulations, Congress enacted the Federal Boating Act of 1958. Effective on April 1, 1960, this law extended the provisions of the Motor Boat Act of 1940 to cover all boats propelled by power aggregating over 10 horsepower regardless of length, when used on waters under the control of the U. S. Coast Guard. Under the earlier law, boats under 16 feet in overall length had been exempted. The new law also authorized the state to assume the function of registering power-driven boats at fees set by the state and to assign numbers, which must be displayed on each bow of every registered boat. Nearly all states have enacted enabling legislation bringing their boaters under the terms of the federal law, even though the boats will be used primarily on waters on which the Coast Guard has no jurisdiction. Information about the various state numbering systems may be obtained from the state conservation agency, any Coast Guard Office, and most boat dealers and marine supply stores.

The Coast Guard will not issue a certificate of number to a boat that will be used primarily in the waters of a state having a numbering system under the terms of the Federal Boating Act, but in states not having enabling acts, the cost is $3.00, renewable every 3 years, with a $1.00 charge for the reissue of a lost or destroyed certificate of number. Most state fees conform to the federal rates but some have slightly higher fees. Unpowered boats and those using outboard motors of less than 10 horsepower also may be registered, a wise precaution if the owner expects to use rented motors or to step up his power rating at a later date.

The number awarded to the boat must be displayed in numerals of plain block design, in a color contrasting with that of the hull—black letters on light colored hulls, white ones on dark-painted hulls—and script, scrolls, shading, or other embellishments are illegal. These numbers must be at least three inches in height. Numbers assigned under the Federal Boating Act have a prefix indicating the state of principal use. In numbering the alphabetical prefix and suffix must be separated from the numerical portion by a hyphen or a space; i.e., **NJ-1234-AB,** or **NJ 12345 AB.** When a boat is lost, destroyed, abandoned, or transferred, the certificate must be surrendered within 15 days. Applications for renewal must be made at least 90 days before the expiration of the original registration. Each state participating in the Federal Boating Act will recognize the number issued by another state or by the Coast Guard for a period of 90 days. Boat numbers and certificates of number are not transferrable, although the administering agency may reassign the existing number to the new owner when boats are sold.

All boats operating under waters coming under the jurisdiction of the Coast Guard or of a state agency participating in the Federal Boating Act are required to stop immediately or to maneuver in such a way to permit a boarding officer to come aboard upon being hailed by a patrol boat. Failure to comply may subject the operator of the boat to a fine of $100.

When a boat is boarded, the inspecting officer will look for several things. He will check the certificate of number to ascertain that the assigned number is displayed properly on the boat and he will make certain that approved safety equipment is carried aboard and is in serviceable condition.

At least one approved life preserver must be aboard for each passenger and crew member carried. These may be of three different types: jackets or vests or "horse-collar" designs fitted with pads of kapok, plastic foam, or fibrous glass in a cloth or vinyl plastic-dipped covering; buoyant cushions; or ring buoys. Approved equipment carries a white tab or a stamping indicating the approval of a Coast Guard inspector.

Ring buoys may be constructed of cork or balsa with a canvas cover, or may be of plastic foam. These must be fitted with a grab line and must be either white or orange in color.

Buoyant cushions must be equipped with grab straps but may be of any color.

Buoyant vests and jackets come in sizes for children and adults, and those manufactured since 1949 have been required to be orange in color. Equipment made before that date will be accepted provided it is in safe and usable condition. Effective July 1, 1963, however, kapok and fibrous glass life preservers and buoyant cushions are required to have plastic-covered pad inserts.

A fire extinguisher must be carried on all inboard motorboats regardless of length, but outboard motorboats of less than 26 feet without decking or compartments in which gases could accumulate are not required to carry fire extinguishers unless the boats are used to carry passengers for hire. Fire extinguishers may be of the foam, carbon dioxide, or dry chemical type. Carbon tetrachloride extinguishers were withdrawn from approval effective January 1, 1962, and are no longer legal. Outboard cruisers or runabouts with cabins, compartments or decking that prevent the free circulation of air must carry approved fire extinguishers. Carburetors on all inboard motorboat engines built after April 25, 1940 are required to be equipped with flame arrestors. The inboard boats also must be equipped with two or more ventilators for removing gasoline fumes from the bilges in engine and fuel-tank compartments. Motorboats, whether inboard or outboard over 16 feet in length must carry a hand-, mouth-, or power-operated whistle or horn capable of producing a 2 second blast audible for one mile.

Lighting requirements are quite exacting, and they vary between inland waters and coastal waters or the high seas. The regulations of primary interest to boat-owning fishermen are:

Rowboats, including canoes, must have ready at hand a lantern showing a white light which must be exhibited in adequate time to prevent collision when traveling at night. On inland waters all pleasure boats under 26 feet in length using power must display on the bow a combination red-green running light mounted on the bow and visible for one mile, and a white light on the stern visible in all directions for two miles. Those 26 feet and over must use separate red and green side lights, each visible for ten points of the compass from the side from a distance of one mile, a white bow light visible for 20 points for 2 miles and a white stern light visible all around for 2 miles.

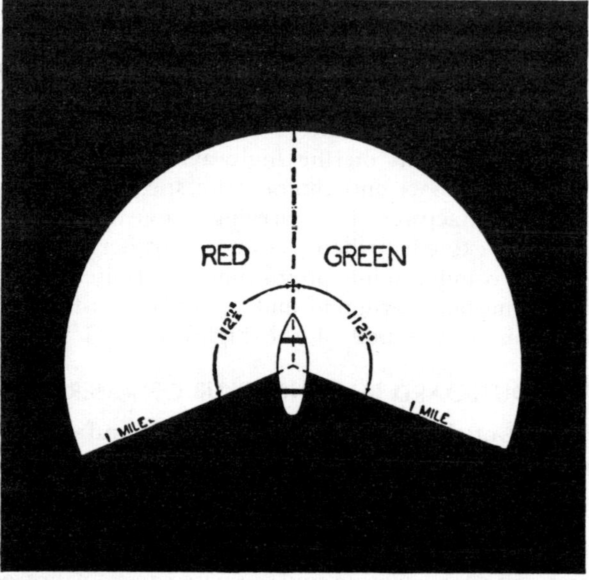

Power boats under way at night must display a combination red-and-green bow light, visible through an arc of 225 degrees for a distance of one mile, according to Federal law. These lights are screened so that the red half shows to port and the green to starboard. A boat approaching head on will show both green and red. Also, they must show at the stern and higher than the front light a white light visible for 2 miles in all directions.

Boats used on the high seas under power are required to display either separate sidelights of red and green or combination red-and-green bow running lights, both visible for one mile; a white stern light visible from astern through an arc of 12 points for a distance of 2 miles and a white bow light visible through an arc of 20 points forward for a distance of three miles.

Boats lighted under International Rules may be used on inland waters, the Great Lakes, and Western Rivers but those lighted under Inland Rules may not operate on the high seas.

Another feature of the Federal Boating Regulation is the penalty for reckless and negligent operation of any boat on waters under the jurisdiction of the Coast Guard. Failing to obey the rules of the road can lead to a fine of up to $2,000 or up to a year in prison. All boat operators should familiarize themselves with these regulations, which can be obtained upon request from any office of the U. S. Coast Guard.

COAST GUARD DISTRICT COMMANDERS AND MERCHANT MARINE ACTIVITIES

District	Title	City	State	Address
1st	Commander, 1st Coast Guard District.	Boston	Massachusetts	1400 Customhouse.
	Marine Inspection Officer	do	do	Do.
	Officer in Charge, Marine Inspection	do	do	447 Commercial St.
	do	Portland	Maine	Post Office Box 108, Pearl Street Station.
	do	Providence	Rhode Island	409 Federal Bldg.
2d	Commander, 2d Coast Guard District.	St. Louis	Missouri	224 Old Customhouse, 8th and Olive Sts.
	Marine Inspection Officer	do	do	222 Old Customhouse, 8th and Olive Sts.
	Officer in Charge, Marine Inspection			
	do	do	do	216 Old Customhouse, 8th and Olive Sts.
	do	Cairo	Illinois	425-427 New Post Office Bldg.
	do	Dubuque	Iowa	Room 301, Post Office and Courthouse Bldg.
	do	Cincinnati	Ohio	748 Federal Bldg., 5th and Main Sts.
	do	Louisville	Kentucky	254 Francis Bldg., 4th and Chestnut Sts.
	do	Memphis	Tennessee	426 Falls Bldg.
	do	Nashville	do	670 U.S. Court House, 801 Broadway.
	do	Pittsburgh	Pennsylvania	1215 Park Bldg.
	do	Huntington	West Virginia	328 Federal Bldg., 5th Ave. and 9th St.
3d	Commander, 3d Coast Guard District.	New York	New York	650 Customhouse.
	Marine Inspection Officer	do	do	626 Customhouse.
	Officer in Charge, Marine Inspection	do	do	720 Customhouse.
	do	New London	Connecticut	302 Post Office Bldg.
	do	Albany	New York	313 Federal Bldg.
	do	Philadelphia	Pennsylvania	801 Customhouse, 2d and Chestnut Sts.
5th	Commander, 5th Coast Guard District.	Norfolk	Virginia	Box 540, U.S. Post Office and Court House.
	Marine Inspection Officer	do	do	Do.
	Officer in Charge, Marine Inspection	do	do	204 Customhouse.
	do	Wilmington	North Carolina	Custom House Wharf.
	do	Baltimore	Maryland	209 Chamber of Commerce Bldg.
7th	Commander, 7th Coast Guard District.	Miami	Florida	Pan American Bank Bldg., 150 SE. 3d Ave.
	Marine Inspection Officer	do	do	Do.
	Officer in Charge, Marine Inspection	do	do	410 Calumet Bldg., 10 NE. 3d Ave.
	do	Tampa	do	406 Federal Bldg.
	do	Charleston	South Carolina	32 U.S. Customhouse.
	do	Savannah	Georgia	205 Customhouse.
	do	Jacksonville	Florida	210 Federal Bldg.
	do	San Juan	Puerto Rico	Post Office Box 3666, 302 Federal Bldg.
8th	Commander, 8th Coast Guard District.	New Orleans	Louisiana	328 Customhouse.
	Marine Inspection Officer	do	do	309 Customhouse.
	Officer in Charge, Marine Inspection	do	do	310 Customhouse.
	do	Mobile	Alabama	563 Federal Bldg.
	do	Port Arthur	Texas	General Delivery.
	do	Galveston	do	232 Customhouse.
	do	Corpus Christi	do	101 Federal Bldg.
	do	Houston	do	7300 Wingate Ave.
9th	Commander, 9th Coast Guard District.	Cleveland	Ohio	Main Post Office Bldg., West 3d and Prospect Sts.
	Marine Inspection Officer	do	do	Do.
	Officer in Charge, Marine Inspection	do	do	1055 East 9th St.
	do	Buffalo	New York	440 Federal Bldg.
	do	Oswego	do	205 Federal Bldg.
	do	Detroit	Michigan	430 Federal Bldg.

District	Title	City	State	Address
	.... do	Duluth	Minnesota	311 Federal Bldg.
	.... do	Toledo	Ohio	401 Had Bldg., 429 Summit St.
	.... do	Saint Ignace	Michigan	Municipal Bldg.
	.... do	Chicago	Illinois	10101 South Ewing Ave.
	.... do	Ludington	Michigan	National Bank Bldg.
	.... do	Milwaukee	Wisconsin	551A Federal Bldg.
11th	Commander, 11th Coast Guard District.	Long Beach	California	706 Times Bldg.
	Marine Inspection Officer	.... do	.... do	1105 Times Bldg.
	Officer in Charge, Marine Inspection	.... do	.... do	Do.
12th	Commander, 12th Coast Guard District.	San Francisco	California	903 U.S. Appraisers Bldg., 630 Sansome St.
	Marine Inspection Officer	.... do	.... do	Station B, Box 2129.
	Officer in Charge, Marine Inspection	.... do	.... do	Do.
13th	Commander, 13th Coast Guard District.	Seattle	Washington	618 2d Ave.
	Marine Inspection Officer	.... do	.... do	Do.
	Officer in Charge, Marine Inspection	.... do	.... do	Do.
	.... do	Portland	Oregon	Room 202, Lincoln Bldg., 208 SW. 5th Ave.
14th	Commander, 14th Coast Guard District.	Honolulu	Hawaii	Post Office Box 4010.
	Marine Inspection Officer	.... do	.... do	Post Office Box 2997.
	Officer in Charge, Marine Inspection	.... do	.... do	Do.
17th	Commander, 17th Coast Guard District.	Juneau	Alaska	Post Office Box 2631.
	Marine Inspection Officer	.... do	.... do	Do.
	Officer in Charge, Marine Inspection	.... do	.... do	Do.

STATE AGENCIES RESPONSIBLE FOR STATE BOAT NUMBERING AND SAFETY LAWS

* Indicates states which have boat numbering systems that do not comply with Federal Boating Act of 1958.

** Indicates states which do not have a boat numbering system.
In states marked by asterisks, local Coast Guard District Office should be consulted regarding numbering of boats over 10 horsepower on navigable waters.

ALABAMA
Department of Conservation
Water Safety Division
State Administrative Building
Montgomery 4, Alabama

**ALASKA

ARIZONA
Motor Vehicle Division
Highway Department
1739 West Jackson
Phoenix, Arizona

ARKANSAS
Game & Fish Commission
Game & Fish Building
State Capitol Grounds
Little Rock, Arkansas

CALIFORNIA
Division of Small Craft Harbors
State Office Building #1
Sacramento 14, California

COLORADO
State Park & Recreation Board
221 State Services Bulding
Denver 3, Colorado

CONNECTICUT
Boating Safety Commission
Dept. of Agriculture, Conservation & Natural Resources
State Office Building
Hartford 15, Connecticut

DELAWARE
Small Boat Safety Division
Commission of Shell Fisheries
Dover, Delaware

FLORIDA
State Board of Conservation
P. O. Box 551
Tallahassee, Florida

GEORGIA
Game & Fish Commission
401 State Capitol
Atlanta 3, Georgia

**HAWAII

IDAHO
Department of Law Enforcement
State of Idaho
P. O. Box 34
Boise, Idaho

ILLINOIS
Conservation Department
Boat Licensing Division
400 South Spring Street
Springfield, Illinois

INDIANA
Enforcement Division
Department of Conservation
605 State Office Building
Indianapolis 9, Indiana

IOWA
State Conservation Commission
East 7th & Court Avenues
Des Moines 8, Iowa

KANSAS
Fish & Game Commission
Pratt, Kansas

KENTUCKY
Department of Public Safety
Division of Boating
Frankfort, Kentucky

LOUISIANA
Wild Life & Fisheries Commission
Wild Life & Fisheries Building
400 Royal Street
New Orleans, Louisiana

*MAINE
Dept. of Inland Fisheries & Game
State Office Building
Augusta, Maine

MARYLAND
Boating & Recreation Division
Department of Tidewater Fisheries
State Office Building
Annapolis, Maryland

MASSACHUSETTS
Division of Motorboats
100 Nashua Street
Boston 14, Massachusetts

MICHIGAN
State Waterways Commission
1004 Cadillac Square Bldg.
Detroit 26, Michigan
Department of State
Capital Building
Lansing, Michigan

MINNESOTA
Department of Conservation
Boat & Water Safety Division
State Office Building
St. Paul 1, Minnesota

MISSISSIPPI
State Boating Safety Committee
Game & Fish Commission
P. O. Box 451
Jackson, Mississippi

MISSOURI
State Boat Commission
P. O. Box 603
Jefferson City, Missouri

MONTANA
State Fish & Game Department
Water & Hunter Safety Section
Helena, Montana

NEBRASKA
State Game, Forestation & Parks Commission
Lincoln 9, Nebraska

NEVADA
Department of Motor Vehicles
Motor Boat Section
Registration Division
Carson City, Nevada

*NEW HAMPSHIRE
Division of Safety Services
Department of Safety
State House Annex
Concord, New Hampshire
Boat registration issued by:
Division of Motor Vehicles
Department of Safety
State House Annex
Concord, New Hampshire

NEW JERSEY
Department of Conservation & Economic Development
Division of Resource Development
Bureau of Navigation
137 East State Street
Trenton 25, New Jersey

Department of Conservation & Economic Development
205 West State Street
Trenton, New Jersey

NEW MEXICO
State Park Commission
P. O. Box 958
Santa Fe, New Mexico

NEW YORK
Division of Motorboats
State Conservation Department
New York State Campus
1220 Washington Avenue
Albany 1, New York

NORTH CAROLINA
Motorboat Registration & Licensing Section
Wildlife Resources Commission
Box 2919
Raleigh, North Carolina

NORTH DAKOTA
State Game & Fish Department
Bismarck, North Dakota

OHIO
Department of Natural Resources
Watercraft Division
1800 West 5th Avenue
Columbus 12, Ohio

OKLAHOMA
Planning & Resources Board
Boat & Motor Licensing Division
533 State Capitol
Oklahoma City, Oklahoma

OREGON
State Marine Board
Public Service Building
Salem 10, Oregon

PENNSYLVANIA
Fish Commission
South Office Building
Harrisburg, Pennsylvania

RHODE ISLAND
Department of Public Works
Division of Harbors & Rivers
216 State Office Building
Providence 3, Rhode Island

SOUTH CAROLINA
Wildlife Resources Department
Division of Boating
P. O. Box 360
Columbia, South Carolina

SOUTH DAKOTA
Dept. of Game, Fish & Parks
State Office Building
Pierre, South Dakota

**TENNESSEE

TEXAS
Highway Department
Motor Vehicle Division
40th & Jackson
Austin, Texas

UTAH
Boating Division
State Park & Recreation Commission
19 West South Temple, Room 255
Salt Lake City 1, Utah

VERMONT
Department of Public Safety
Marine Division
Montpelier, Vermont

VIRGINIA
Game & Inland Fisheries Commission
P. O. Box 1642
Richmond 13, Virginia

**WASHINGTON
Boat numbering exists at county level, and county commissioners should be individually consulted regarding numbering on local waters.

WEST VIRGINIA
Department of Natural Resources
Boat License Section
State Office Building
Charleston, West Virginia

WISCONSIN
Conservation Department
Madison 1, Wisconsin

*WYOMING
Game & Fish Commission
P. O. Box 378
Cheyenne, Wyoming

BASIC NAVIGATION FOR THE FISHERMAN

Some knowledge of navigation is indispensable to the owner of any boat that will be operated on any waters except small lakes where the operator is rarely out of sight of his home dock. On large open waters a basic knowledge of the principles of navigation by "dead reckoning" may save lives and, of less vital importance, it can help a boat operator locate fish. In its more advanced ramifications navigation is a highly complicated field of study involving higher mathematics, trigonometry, astronomy and electronics. With equipment, costing little more than ten dollars, and a knowledge of plane geometry, however, anyone can locate his position within practical limits nearly anywhere except on the high seas, where the boat operator unschooled in navigation should not venture in the first place.

The needed equipment consists of an accurate liquid-filled compass, preferably one mounted in a binnacle, a chart of the waters where the boat is being used, a ruler or straight edge, and a pair of dividers. A sounding line, or lead line, to determine depths and bottom conditions, and binoculars will also prove useful.

Charts of all coastal waters, large navigable rivers, estuaries, and bays, including the Great Lakes and other waters under the jurisdiction of the Federal Government, can be obtained from the U. S. Coast and Geodetic Survey, Washington 25, D. C., and from many marinas and marine supply houses.

These charts show all features of inshore waters of interest to the boat handler—shorelines and their character; water depths; bottom types; navigation aids, such as buoys, lighthouses, radio beacons, and lightships; and navigational hazards, such as reefs, shoals, wrecks, and military bombing ranges.

During the daytime, with good visibility, the boat operator should be able to plot his position at any time on the chart by triangulation. The chart must be oriented in relation to true north (See Maps and Compasses, Section VII). A bearing, or compass reading is then made to a prominent landmark—lighthouse, buoy, water tower, or similar structure—and a line drawn through the symbol representing it on the chart to represent the line of sight. Either a protractor or parallel rulers are useful for this work, although the compass face and straight edge will give fairly accurate readings.

A second bearing is taken on another landmark, widely separated from the first, and a second line representing this bearing drawn on the chart. The point at which the two lines intercept should indicate on the chart the exact position of the boat. It is wise to take one or more additional bearings as a check against error. The boat, of course, should be dead in the water for accurate readings, but an approximate location can be determined while the boat is moving at reduced speed, provided the two readings are made quickly. This system of triangulation is also an excellent method of locating reefs, submerged wrecks, and sandbars that are the natural concentration points for fish.

Once the position of the boat is known, the boat operator can tell exactly what course to take to reach his destination or to run back to port. If he has kept a good record of the fuel consumption of his motor he knows exactly how far he can venture out before returning for fuel.

With basic equipment such as this, the boat operator is not entirely blind, even when he is caught out after dark or in a heavy fog. On clear nights, villages, highways close to shore, lighthouses, and lighted buoys can give similar bearings by their patterns of light. Each official lighthouse, light ship and light buoy has its own distinctive pattern of light flashes, and these are recorded on the navigation charts.

Fog is a much more formidable opponent, since it can obscure all normally visible landmarks. The boat handler caught in this, especially in navigation channels used by large vessels, must be exceedingly careful to avoid collision. Running lights should be kept operating, and the horn, whistle or bell should be sounded at the required intervals. At the same time, the operator should be on the alert for signals from approaching vessels.

Navigating in the fog requires that the operator take his bearings by sound rather than by sight, although a powerful lighthouse may still be pinpointed through fog by its distinctive flashings as well as its fog horns. Bell buoys, whistle buoys, and other navigation aids can be identified by their distinctive sounds and bearings taken on them. The same procedure is used for locating the position of the boat by sound as by visible landmarks. Not infrequently shore sounds, such as music from a dancehall, highway traffic, and similar distinctive sounds can be heard far at sea on a foggy night. All of these give clues to the position of the boat in relation to the land.

In shipping channels, can buoys, nun buoys, or similar markers may be passed. The number painted on any buoy will provide its identification on the chart and give the exact location of the boat.

Interpreting Navigation Aids: Most prominent of the navigation aids on coastal waters are the lighthouses, usually manned structures located on or near points especially dangerous to shipping. The largest are the familiar masonry structures, up to and sometimes exceeding a hundred feet in height. Other light structures consist of cylindrical towers, caissons, and skeleton iron structures, all of which may either be manned or unmanned with the lights, horns and radio signal equipment operated automatically. Other lights are unmanned structures consisting of a small skeleton steel structure or even a group of pilings supporting the signal equipment. Each of these structures, however, is distinctively colored and transmits sound, light, and radio signals that are readily distinguished from all others in the vicinity. The navigation charts locate all such structures and indicate the signals that they transmit. One light may flash alternately red and white, another white at designated intervals, and so on, in endless conbinations. Standard colors, however, always are in white, red, or green.

Another light structure is the lightship, which serves the same function as the lighthouse and transmits similar signals. Lightships are always painted red and carry the name of the station in large white letters on their sides. They usually locate the mouths of broad estuaries or dangerous offshore shoals. Some of the former famous lightships have been replaced in recent years by "Texas towers," skeleton steel structures permanently fixed to the bottom of the sea.

Fog signals are produced by all of these structures, and each produces a distinctive pattern of sound. Bell buoys and whistle buoys are activated by the action of the sea and do not produce a distinctive pattern of sound that identifies them with absolute accuracy unless only one or two of them are located in the area.

Buoys are maintained by the Coast Guard in nearly all navigable marine waters to warm the navigator of dangerous shoals, obstructions, or changes in the sea bottom, or to indicate safe channels.

Channel-marking buoys are of five general types —spar, can and nun, and lighted and unlighted whistle. At times all of these types can be found in a single vicinity.

Buoys marking the borders of a safe channel are always either solid red or solid black. The black buoys always carry odd numbers, while the red are always numbered in sequences of even numbers. In approaching a marked channel from seaward, the boat operator keeps the black, odd-numbered buoys on his port, or left, side, the red, even-numbered buoys on his right. In running out to sea, the relative position is, of course, reversed. In unfamiliar waters keeping in the marked channel is always a safe precaution, even though the boat may be a light outboard motor runabout drawing only a few inches of water. The channels, however, are usually marked for much larger craft drawing ten feet or more, and the small boat will be safe in most of the waters outside the channel. In narrow channels where shipping traffic is heavy the small boat may actually be safer outside the marked channel. A glance at the chart will inform him whether or not he can deviate safely from the marked area.

Spar buoys are the simplest type and usually, but not always, mark relatively shallow secondary channels. No distinction can be made between the odd- and even-numbered spars by shape alone. These are simply long poles, weighted so they float

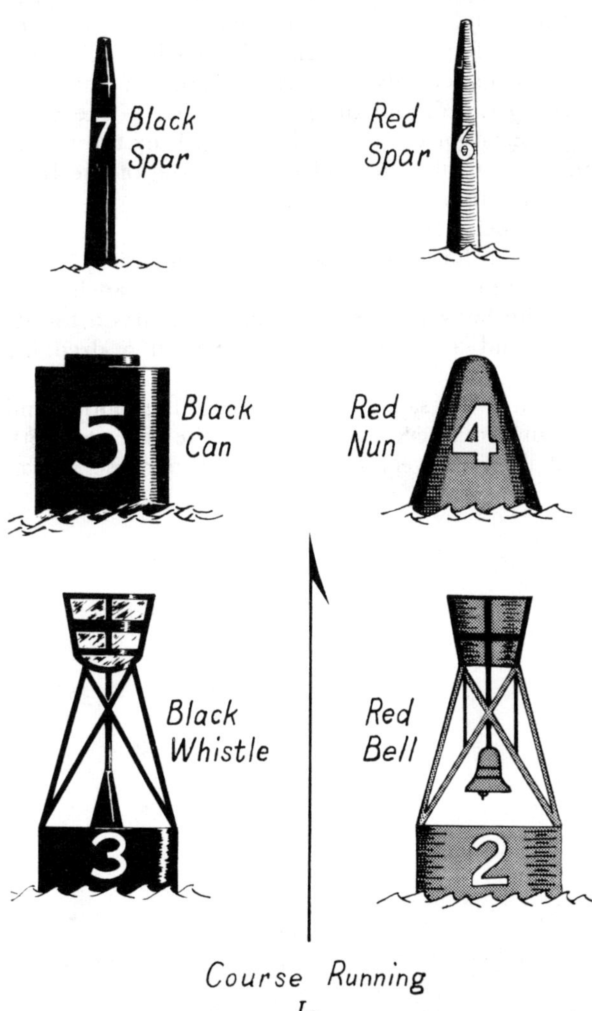

Samples of the most common navigation aids. In running into a harbor or up a navigable stream, red buoys are always passed to the left, black buoys to the right to assure a clear channel. Can and nun buoys usually are used in combination and can be distinguished by shape alone. Whistle or bell buoys usually mark turns in the channel or special hazards and may be either red or black, depending upon the side on which they may be passed.

up-right in the water and anchored in position by their submerged end.

Can and nun buoys are sometimes used in combination and can be distinguished from one another at a distance in poor light by their shape alone. Can buoys are upright floating cylinders, and they are always black and odd-numbered. Nun-buoys on the other hand, are always red and even-numbered and appear as cones above the water line.

Lighted buoys or unlighted bell, and whistle buoys, usually mark turns and special hazards. They may be black or red, depending upon which side they should be passed on, and those of both colors are essentially can buoys carrying a skeleton steel structure which supports the light, whistle or bell housing.

The exception to the color code for channel-marking buoys is that all of these types of buoys may be found vertically striped in white and black or horizontally striped in red and black. Buoys of either kind mark the mid-channel and may be passed safely on either side. The red-black combination marks only channel junctions or entrances from seaward, and the preferred side of the channel for larger craft is indicated both by the uppermost band of color and by the shape of the buoy in the can-nun combination.

Distinctively colored special-purpose buoys of various color combinations will sometimes be encountered. A solid white buoy marks an anchorage, a white buoy with a black band indicates a fishnet area, and a white-green combination a dredging area.

Nearly all salt-water fishermen use buoys and channel markers to locate favorite fishing spots, and they are very useful for this purpose. Never moor a boat to any floating navigation aid, however, since this is a violation of federal law and may subject the violator to severe legal penalties.

Further information on this subject in a more comprehensive form may be found in *Aids to Marine Navigation of the United States* (CG-193), which is available from the Commandant of the Coast Guard, Washington 25, D. C., from the Government Printing Office, and from various sales agents in boating areas.

The most recent development in navigation aids, as it applies to small boats of interest to the fisherman, is that of "loran." This coined word is derived by combining the first letters of "LOng Range Aid to Navigation." In principle it works exactly like the system of triangulation by compass on sights or sounds, but since it employs radio beams it is effective even in the densest fog. The development of low-cost compact loran receivers has brought these reliable navigation aids within reach of most small-boat owners. Loran is effective up to 800 miles by day and 1,400 miles by night.

Transmitting stations, located along the shore, send out distinctive radio signals 24 hours a day, in a series of pulses or short bursts at regular intervals, so that each signal can be distinguished from all others. Loran differs from the older radio beacon system in that it is based on the difference of time of arrival of radio signals from two separate stations. An indicator on the loran receiver permits the operator to take an exact bearing on each station and compute his position exactly. Special loran charts and tables, however are required for this purpose and are available from the U. S. Navy Hydrographic Office, Washington 25, D. C., and a detailed booklet on the subject can be obtained from the Coast Guard.

→

Joe Mears

Tenaya Lake, at 8000 feet in the Yosemite National Park, is renowned for its roadside fishing.

SECTION IV

Fish Conservation

Provision of optimum sport fishing opportunities for an ever-increasing host of anglers is the task of fish conservationists. The fish conservation field is a small one, but it faces squarely one of the greatest challenges to confront American civilization today. If it has the needed guts, intelligence, and imagination, it can in the next few decades establish the profession as a vital factor in the national welfare. That challenge is: How shall our society make proper use of increasing amounts of leisure time brought on by a rapidly decreasing work week? The 40-hour work week is standard in industry—if not among fishery workers—and many people already work only 35 hours per week. Indeed, with the rapid growth of automation, the 30-hour week is close at hand. Some economists predict that Americans of the next generation may yet find themselves yielding up their switches and push buttons to relief crews after working perhaps only 3 days per week.

At the same time there is growing evidence that the stress of modern living and the decreased physical activity accompanying it is wreaking havoc upon our society. The incidence of psychosomatic and of coronary and other physical ills has risen to near-epidemic proportions and is approaching the level of a national crisis. Leading medical authorities in these fields, such as Dr. Paul Dudley White, heart consultant to former President Eisenhower; Dr. Campbell Moses, associate professor of medicine, University of Pittsburgh; Dr. Robert S. Kesel, College of Dentistry, University of Illinois; and many others, have testified before Congress or reported to leading medical groups their findings to this effect. The solution to this serious problem is to provide an acceptable antidote. It must be not only painless but also attractive and eminently worthwhile. It must be completely relaxing of mind and body, yet it must require modest physical exertion; sport fishing provides a near-perfect answer. Few people wish to loaf openly, yet angling has the unusual advantage of being a socially acceptable dignified way of "doing nothing." Yet, most anglers will insist for many years that the added zest of playing and landing a fish—and taking it home as proof of prowess—is an important part of the fishing trip.

Already, fishing is well established as one of the most popular of all participation sports and the prospect is that, where one out of every four "walking Americans" now fishes for sport, perhaps every other American may do so tomorrow. This could mean a three-fold increase in fishing pressures in the lifetimes of many readers of this encyclopedia. Such a growth of angling participation should be actively encouraged. We shouldn't be so concerned over increasing fishing pressure that we strive to suppress it. More than one great nation crumbled with the growth of leisure time which failed to develop a form of outdoor recreation or some other philosophy requiring proper husbandry of its natural resources. It does not seem too far-fetched to suggest that outdoor recreation such as sport fishing may hold the very salvation of free nations with high living standards. In thinking of fishing as a key recreational outlet and therapy, it must not be envisioned merely as a vacation sport to be indulged at infrequent intervals. Rather, it should be regarded and encouraged as a continuing activity during any week of the year. Ideally, perhaps, there should be both inclination and opportunity for almost daily fishing excursions close at hand.

In any such event, it would appear likely that two current major fish management problems—super abundance of under-utilized pan fish and abundant unharvested rough fish—will become important assets. By this time, too, it should be apparent even to newly-matriculated biologists that the sportsman is an ally and not an enemy. College professors may finally recognize the need for fishery students to study the social sciences—psychology and human relations. There may even be a new academic course in personal courage and how to use it. Fortunately, most fishery biologists "discover" at relatively tender ages that the purpose of fish conservation is to benefit large numbers of people who are called anglers. Sportsmen are not stupid. They have a right to their ideas, a right to express them, and a right to have them respected and thoughtfully considered. Nevertheless, the sportsman has a vital role to play in creating suitable working conditions that make conservation efforts on his behalf possible. The fact is, anglers and professional conservationists cannot get along *without* each other. Creation of proper working conditions constitutes a continuing and important challenge to the organized sportsmen. In most states low salary scales are a serious deterrent to progress in fish conservation. The average pay of professional fishery workers is below that of laborers in the building trades. If it were not for dedication to the job, and confidence in the future, few men would remain in the field.

A few states are beginning to realize that this is a serious problem. In one north-central state, for example, the sportsmen took positive steps a few years ago to correct this inequity. They realized that their fish and game director was grossly underpaid at the current $5,000 figure set by statute. He administered annual budgets of over $1,500,000. Even more important, his work strongly influenced the condition of a recreation business amounting to over twenty times as much. No industry of comparable size would think of paying such a ridiculously low salary to its chief executive officer. Consequently, the organized sportsmen set up a statewide, nonpartisan action committee to rectify the situation. It was dedicated to bringing about statutory changes to raise the Director's salary to some figure between $10,000 and $15,000. This is still "peanuts" by industrial standards. But it did much to help solve the salary problem for fishery and wildlife scientists in that state. It rates as one of the outstanding conservation achievements of the decade.

People are the most important part of fish and game management. All research and management activities should have as their ultimate objective to benefit people as a social unit in some way. Such a philosophy rejects a single-use concept of natural resources. It definitely embraces a broad multiple use concept, and it demands greatly enhanced and broadened outdoor recreational opportunities. Conservation needs a cause that is more appealing to the general public than ill-defined and vague "intangible values." It needs a cause that is more influential at the conference table than mere dollar volume of business generated.

Outdoor recreation provides that cause.

If the emphasis in conservation planning continues to be placed only on the maintenance of suitable conditions for fish and game itself, there will continue to be fought a losing battle of attrition against the stronger forces of resource exploitation in the utilities and industrial fields. If, however, there is emphasized the creation, development, and maintenance of optimum outdoor recreational opportunities for the benefit of the general public—in the forms of people needs for fishing, boating, hunting, etc.—conservationists gain new and potent muscles. Fish must be placed in their proper perspective—as a means to an end, not the end itself.

Outside of religion and taxation, very few peacetime issues other than the recreational use of leisure time can rally so many people to a common interest. The sport of angling, for example, provides a bond of mutual interest that cuts across all racial, social, economic, religious, age, and sex distinctions. If you have red blood in your veins it is almost inevitable that you will like to fish—given the opportunity. Furthermore, fishing is good for you—mentally, socially, physically, and morally. If provision of maximum recreational opportunity for leisure-time use by people becomes the goal and the guiding force for fish conservation efforts, the natural resources *must* of consequence become properly managed for wise multiple-use purposes. This provides the new cause, together with the potential weapon—mass public opinion—needed to prevail in that cause.

RECREATIONAL FISHING AND ITS BASE

Two national surveys of fishing, conducted at 5-year intervals, sponsored by the United States Fish and Wildlife Service, have established that sport fishing is of great national significance both sociologically and economically, and that participation is increasing at a rate twice that of the growth of the population. About 25 per cent of Americans participate in fishing for recreation. One in every four men, and one in every ten women, fish regularly for their outdoor relaxation. These men and women spend an average of more than 18 days annually out fishing. Including children of all ages, nearly 32 million Americans fished twice each or more often in 1960 (another 10 million fished only once), totalling something over a half-billion recreational days of fishing, driving nearly 19 billion miles, and spending almost three billion dollars for needed goods and services in the process. About one-fourth of these totals were attributable to saltwater sport fishing—the "growing giant" of angling—the rest to freshwater sport fishing. The average annual increase in numbers of freshwater anglers is about 3.3 per cent; for saltwater anglers it is about 6.7 per cent. In some areas saltwater anglers were taking as many fish of jointly used species as were commercial fishermen. Over-all, the sport catch of all kinds of fishes in both fresh and salt waters considerably exceeds one billion pounds, and the catch by marine anglers alone is equivalent to nearly 20 per cent of the United States commercial harvest of marine food fishes. Combined with the freshwater catch, the angling harvest of edible fishes amounts to about half the total commercial catch of food fishes.

In 1959, the United States Congress passed an Act creating a bi-partisan Outdoor Recreation Resources Review Commission. After three years of intensive study, the Commission reported its findings and recommendations to the President and to the Congress, in an historic report entitled *Outdoor Recreation For America*. The report confirmed that sport fishing is one of the most significant forms of outdoor recreation, that water is the principal kind of environment around which outdoor recreation centers, and that fishing is the leading participant form of water-borne recreation. ORRRC Special Study Report Number 7* provides a detailed analysis of fishery resources and future needs. It reports that the inland freshwater sport fish habitat of the 50 states comprises about 73,590,000 surface acres of water (5,812,000 acres of streams, 9,330,000 acres of natural lakes, plus 35,878,000 acres of U.S. waters in Great Lakes, and 10,163,000 acres of reservoirs, all in the 48 contiguous states; 12,403,000 acres of streams, lakes, and reservoirs in Alaska; and 4,000 in Hawaii). The saltwater sport fish habitat adjacent to the 21 contiguous coastal states, extending offshore for a distance of three miles, comprises about 24,724,000 acres. The report predicts that numbers of anglers will increase 50 per cent by 1975, and 150 per cent by the year 2000. The population is expected to double, but demand for recreational fishing to triple by century's end. It concludes that the resulting fishing demand *can be met* with only slight reductions in the present average catch, *provided* there are greatly accelerated research and management efforts.

New reservoirs are expected to add 10 million surface acres by 2000, doubling present impounded waters. These new waters will supply about one-third of the expected increase in fishermen-trips. *Improvement of existing waters* through better management (including control of pollution) and the capacity of existing waters to absorb more fishing effort is anticipated to meet an additional one-third of increased demand. *Marine waters* can absorb the remaining one-third, provided that estuaries are not damaged or rendered unfit as spawning and nursery grounds, and anadromous species are not blocked by more man-made structures.

Siltation and pollution must be prevented and controlled more effectively, fishery research must be expanded to provide bases for improved management, and the problem of getting adequate funds for these conservation programs must be solved. At least 75 per cent of the angling activity in 1960 occurred on public waters, and this percentage will rise in the years ahead. The problem of assuring adequate public access to these waters is large scale and urgent. Management responsibilities of the governmental fishery agencies will grow proportionately, and the future of sport fishing depends on how well they are permitted to do their job, and whether adequate financing is provided for the purpose.

A Developing Science. In the post-World War II decades there has emerged—as a function of the burgeoning demand for recreational fishing—a broad field of activity, known as fish conservation, that is evolving gradually into a recognized profession. It is concerned with the increased understanding of fishery resources and their environment, to the end that they may be successfully and deliberately modified in order to effect maximum sustained yields of desirable crops of fish, for the benefit of human beings (either as recreation or food products or both). A commonly accepted definition of the word *conservation* is "The wise utilization of natural resources for the greatest good to the greatest number." Taken literally this might seem to mean that majority uses or interests are or should always be paramount. However, democratic principles applied to conservation programs require that minority interests be taken into consideration. Thus, a strong force making for variety is at work. It also means that utilization and change is counterbalanced to some extent by protection and preservation.

The science—perhaps more properly—the art of fish conservation embraces many elements. Among them, *fishery management* attempts to apply previously accumulated knowledge and experiences in programs of action designed to produce predetermined results in terms of improved fish production and fishing. Long before this stage can be reached there must be many years of *research* to learn about fishes, how they live, why they do the things they do, and precisely what role is played by various aspects of the environment in which they live including associated kinds of fishes. This is *basic research,* a searching for knowledge for its own sake with no other immediate goal. The product of basic research is new ideas. As an increasing body of information is accumulated, various possibilities for influencing the fish populations toward desired goals become apparent and suggest themselves. These are tried out as controlled experiments, to see if the theoretical results can be obtained, and how well, in *applied research* projects. The difference between this and *experimental management* is only in degree, with promising new "tools" being employed in large scale projects. An essential aspect is evaluation of results of the project, a form of specific short-term research that might best be called *management investigations.*

It is after demonstrated success of a series of experimental management projects that the science or art of fishery management matures into established procedures and the "handbook" stage is reached. Notable progress has been made in all aspects of fish conservation, especially since World War II, but the field has been handicapped by a dearth of funds to support basic research. This has reflected an inability of information-education programs to convince the public and legislators alike of the vital urgency for research expansion. Consequently, the post-war pace is slowing down. Needed new conceptual breakthroughs that can be trans-

* King, W., J. Hemphill, A. Swartz, and K. F. Stutzman. 1962. Sport Fishing—Today and Tomorrow. ORRRC Special Study Report No. 7, 130 pp., U. S. Gov. Printing Office, Washington 25, D. C.

lated through improved management into better fishing have not been forthcoming. The pre-existing small capital stock of raw knowledge is becoming depleted more rapidly than it is being replenished. Thus, the "handbook" stage is many years away in most aspects of fish conservation. Outstanding exceptions are found in pond reclamation or rehabilitation of small northern lakes for Trout and management of Bass-Bluegill combinations in southern farm ponds. Even in these instances many troublesome questions remain. In both cases, however, several decades of intensive basic research, followed by more years of applied research and experimental management, preceded the attainment of the "handbook" stage of sophistication in fishery management. For most fishes, however, not even the broadest outlines of life history information is available. It is estimated that these are known for less than one-half of one per cent of the world's known 25,000-odd species of fishes! Of the latter, of course, probably fewer than 1,000 are of possible importance either directly or indirectly to sport fishing.

Fish life has been classified popularly along a number of functional lines. People speak of game fish or commercial fish, sport fish or food fish, rough fish or weed fish, pan fish, etc. All of these terms have currency and all are significant, if arbitrary, means of expressing useful connotations as well as prejudice. These distinctions are constantly subject to change, although they may be expected to persist for some time. A *sport fish* is one of whatever species that may be taken on sport fishing tackle, usually some form of fishing rod and reel with line attached to a hook. It may be a saltwater or freshwater fish of any kind, so long as it may be caught with this type of gear. The object of capture is recreation by the angler. The fishes taken in this way are not generally sold as food by their captors, although this may be customary with certain kinds of saltwater fishing. A *commercial fish* is one of whatever species in freshwater or saltwater that is caught with additional harvesting machinery such as a multiplicity of hooks per line, or various types of nets or other gear designed for mass capture. The object is to harvest protein production for marketing as food. In salt water there is frequently heavy exploitation of the same species by both sport and commercial fishermen. In fresh water, with some exceptions, sportsmen generally utilize the predatory kinds of fishes (the so-called *game fishes*) and commercial fishermen generally exploit the species (the so-called *rough fishes*) that are non-predatory upon other fishes in their feeding habits. Here, commercial fishing is often used to benefit sport fishing by removing fishes that compete heavily for the food supplies of young game fish, which compete for space, and which through their feeding habits muddy the water to the detriment of most sport species. Thus there will be constant regrouping as to species included in these arbitrary classifications. From a management standpoint as well as angling, certain group recognitions on the basis of biological requirements are rather well fixed and should be remembered. These divide fishes into fresh water, brackish water, and salt water groups, on the one hand, and into warm water and cold water groups on the other hand. Recognition of elementary biological limitations has a profound bearing both on angling and fish management.

Origin and development. Our earliest ancestors in Europe and Asia did certain things and followed certain practices which would, today, be deemed sound management of a fishery resource. The Chinese were conducting experiments in fish-breeding as early as the fifth century B.C. In A.D. 1411 the taking of a Scottish Salmon in closed season was, by royal edict, punishable by death. Indeed, the fish and game of the realm were generally considered the property of the crown, despite the terms of the Magna Carta which had been forced upon the king by his landed nobles several centuries earlier. Among other things, the nobles secured some fishing and hunting rights for themselves, although these did not extend to the common people who continued to poach at their peril. Thus it was that common folk fleeing the tyranny of the Old World settled in the New and established common rights of ownership to the fish and game resources. This they granted by Colonial statutes but also vested custody of those resources in the government as a trust for all the people.

It is well established that the North American Indian was no conservationist in the modern sense. He took what he needed and was able to harvest with little thought for the future; his means of capturing fish were primitive. There was an abundance of fish and he made no profound changes in the landscape of which he was a part. He was an aboriginal and knew nothing of the simplest machinery with which the colonists were equipped. Almost overnight, the advent of Europeans to the North American continent upset the balance of nature—the ecological climax—of which the Indian was a part. The colonists didn't like the dark, towering forests from which savagery threatened constantly to erupt. They set about to remake the land in the image of the old country with ax, plow, and fire. They built mills, dammed and polluted waterways, harvested anadromous fish runs relentlessly, and soon eliminated the Atlantic Salmon and almost eliminated Atlantic Shad from the rivers south of the St. Lawrence in Canada. At an early date it became apparent that fishery resources were dwindling, even though the reasons were not understood. Edicts governing the use of saltwater fish made their appearance in the Massachusetts Colony as early as 1639. Cod, Haddock, Hake, Pollack, and Mackerel became the dubious beneficiaries of a closed season during their spawning period as a result of legislative enactment as early as 1652. As Englishmen, the Colonists had already become accustomed to such restraints in the mother country.

Thus, one traditional element of present day fishery management—regulation of take—became by transfer and evolution an ingrained method of administering our fishery assets. As new areas were settled, the citizenry frequently deemed it wise to impose a few simple "thou-shalt-nots" with respect to the taking of fish. This occurred in spite of the fact that the adjective "inexhaustible" was commonly applied to the fishery resources during the period of settlement. Restraints upon excessive wasteful fishing were a usual first step in the gradual acceptance—locally, by states, and nationally—of a policy of "doing something" to conserve fish. It was an easy second step to recognize a need for some administrative mechanism to execute or enforce protective measures.

The outcome was the establishment of official state agencies which included among their diverse duties the responsibility of protecting fish and shellfish. The states led in creating these early prototype conservation departments because then, as now, the states rather than the federal government exercised the legal jurisdiction. Massachusetts pioneered by setting up such an agency in 1856. New Hampshire and Vermont took similar steps in 1865. Thereafter, other states in fairly rapid succession gave official recognition to the need for conservation of fish and game. Even so, as late as 1920, several states left this important job to the counties. Now, all of the states and the Canadian provinces include in their official governmental structure some sort of an agency assigned the responsibility for conserving the fishery resources.

In 1871 the Congress established the United States Fish Commission with the broad mandate to "look into the cause of depletion" and take steps to foster and promote the fisheries. The federal government had no direct domestic administrative authority or responsibility with respect to the details of safeguarding the fisheries except in the territories. Therefore, the new agency seemed principally destined to exercise a research function. However, the ink had hardly dried upon the record of its birth before it was embarking upon an extensive program of artificial propagation which has continued to grow to this day. The U.S. Fish Commission ultimately evolved into a technical and scientific organization which exercised a profound influence on the trends of state fishery policy. Its present-day counterpart, the U. S. Fish and Wildlife Service, formed by combining the Bureau of Fisheries with the venerable Bureau of the Biological Survey—stands in the role of a partner with the states. This is a reflection of the fact that these have been the only agencies which can adopt and apply the soundest technical practices available.

The original functions and responsibilities of the state fish and game organizations were obviously to protect and increase fish stocks and to assure that good fishing would continue and improve. The approach to this worthy end was for many decades purely by trial and error—mostly error. The state fish commissioner and his colleagues looked around and observed what other states might be doing. They seized upon what seemed to be obvious self-evident "facts" of fishery biology, which often were not facts at all. These examples and pseudo-facts then served as basis for arbitrary regulations and policies which might be tailored to fit local conditions—and often might not. An example of the fallacies which went into the earlier attempts at fishery management was the mania for planting Pacific Salmon and Atlantic Shad—both being species which spend the major part of their life in the ocean—into all types of inland waters. In these cases, no harm resulted aside from the waste of money and effort. In marked contrast, transplantation of Striped Bass and Atlantic Shad to Pacific Coast salt waters paid off handsomely at very small expense. For example, two plants of fingerling Striped Bass in 1879 and 1882, aggregating 432 fish, were made in San Francisco Bay, and Suisan Bay. By 1889 they were abundant throughout the Bay area.

Unfortunately, many stocking efforts were decidely harmful. A classic example of such damage to existing fish populations was the frequent transfer of White Perch, a close relative of Striped Bass, from coastal estuarine areas into many inland waters of the New England states in particular. Like all of the Striped Bass transplants, some of the White Perch transplants slowly died out, but others "took" almost immediately. Repetitive stocking generally succeeded in establishing White Perch in almost any inland lake. It is now evident that early failures were due to transfer of fish of one sex—usually males—owing to their habit of schooling by sex in different areas in the early spring. Although their establishment is often deemed desirable at first by anglers, the end result has often been the near-elimination of other kinds of fishes probably through a combination of very successful spawning and resulting overwhelming competition for limited food supplies, followed by a gradual stunting of the White Perch as their numbers multiplied. These and other unwise trial-and-error introductions of non-native freshwater fishes have wreaked costly damage to fish populations in many areas. In Massachusetts, for example, it has been estimated that this practice had contributed materially to the causes of poor fishing in well over half of that state's lakes and ponds by 1952,* and led to the recent spending of several hundred thousand dol-

* Stroud, R. H. 1955. Fisheries Report for Some Central, Eastern, and Western Massachusetts Lakes, Ponds, and Reservoirs, 1951-1952. Massachusetts Div. Fish. & Game, Boston. 447 pp.

lars for corrective measures to restore good fishing. A misguided though well-intentioned crusade to distribute the European Carp throughout the nation had after-effects which will continue to plague fishing in the forseeable future. Fairness requires stating that federal rather than state authorities actively promoted this tragic error. It is probable that this one project has damaged more native fish production than any other facto except water pollution. However, good intentions, an honest recognition of mistakes, and open-minded attitudes on the part of many of those in responsible positions opened the way for gradual improvement in policies and in their implementation. Only in the post-war II period has the hatchery become recognized in its proper perspective as but one of an array of fish management tools, useful only when employed to fill scientifically demonstrated needs. Otherwise, tragic errors could cause virtually permanent destruction of thriving sport fisheries instead of enhancing recreational opportunities. No less important is the danger cited by Dr. Robert R. Miller, University of Michigan ichthyologist, at a recent meeting of the Michigan Academy of Science, Arts and Letters. He reported that the establishment of 36 species of exotic fishes in southwestern states (where he has studied the fish fauna extensively) has seriously displaced a number of less aggressive native forms having considerable scientific interest.*

Among the new ideas which developed in the post-Civil War period, one had a tremendous effect upon fishery management. This was the requirement that those who engaged in certain types of angling be licensed. This was an unwelcome limitation upon traditional freedoms adopted as a necessary evil. The policy of licensing anglers was not based on any theory that possession by the fisherman of a piece of official paper would conserve or increase fish populations. Licensing actually arose from realization that it was necessary for the state to spend money in various ways in order to maintain fishing. Civilization, urbanization, and industrial developments were here to stay to the detriment of fishing. Charging the fisherman for the cost of maintaining his sport in the face of these handicaps seemed so logical that soon the chief arguments related to the amount of the charge.

The sportsmen quickly developed very active interest in the manner and purposes for which their dollars were to be spent. It was this interest that led to development of modern scientific fishery management by professional fishery biologists. Regulations were increasing in volume and complexity. Catch limits, size limits, and closed seasons were being applied—species by species—and these differed between limited areas within a single state. It required larger organizations, more fish wardens to carry on this policing. A booklet of 100 pages devoted entirely to fishing regulations was not—and is not now—unusual. Yet, the result, in terms of the individual fisherman's catch, was increasingly unsatisfactory. Eventually, it dawned on many of the more thoughtful and progressive minded anglers that the regulations were more or less arbitrary and their questioning led to initiation of biological surveys—the first resource inventories by biologists.

However, the major cause for seeking additional funds for the support of fish and game departments was due to the steady expansion of artificial propagation, widely heralded by politically-appointed administrators, as a "sure fire" means of maintaining good fishing. In the middle 1800's European scientists demonstrated beyond doubt that Salmon and Trout could be bred by artificial fertilization and rearing. During the pre- and post-Civil War periods several Americans undertook the refinement and perfection of these discoveries. Their experiments led to the wholesale adoption of hatcheries as the assured means of guaranteeing good fishing not only for salmonids, but for warm-water fishes as well. As indicated previously, the federal government became active in this field in 1872. A few states had already started to operate hatcheries in a small way. Massachusetts was operating the first public fish hatchery in 1867. Thereafter, artificial propagation of fish was an accepted —and increasingly costly—core of fishery conservation programs. It still occupies an important niche in state and federal programs. Even though its efficacy has been sharply questioned, and the use of the hatchery product curtailed to scientifically demonstrable needs in most instances, it continues to account for the lion's share of fishery expenditures.

The Role of Research. The next and most important development in the evolution of modern fish conservation was the introduction of scientific research. Prior to about 1870, fishery biology was largely the prerogative of individual "naturalists" who were chiefly taxonomists or classifiers of what they saw. Many of them thus helped brilliantly to develop one of the tools for more sophisticated research later on. The early program of the U. S. Fish Commission (established 1871) centered upon extensive research of fish populations and environment by means of reconnaissance biological surveys of waterways. Taxonomy or the scientific classification and identification of aquatic organisms was strongly emphasized. Limited experimental studies of common trial-and-error procedures were undertaken especially concerned with problems of artificial fish propagation. The Commission soon became heavily involved in the development of methods of artificial propagation and the operation of fish hatcheries. Up to the turn of the century, the states had done relatively little in the way of organized research with respect to

* Miller, R. R. 1961. Man and the changing fish fauna of the American Southwest. Pap. Mich. Acad. Sci., Arts, Letts., Vol. 46 (1960):365-404.

their fishery resources. Human curiosity is a powerful stimulant, however, and able men in a few universities and colleges soon ventured into the poorly charted field of fishery research as individual investigators. The same curiosity about the fundamentals of their problems arose in some of the state conservation agencies, and by 1920 the voice of the biologist—or "expert," as he was disparagingly labeled—was being heard more loudly, even though the problems being faced were ones for "practical" men. Usually, the biologists were university professors, employed during their summer vacations. It was a rare state that utilized the services of biologists for more extensive periods. About this time some of the more imaginative biologists recognized that they were dealing with diverse natural laws, forces, and reactions which could be analyzed and brought together to serve as a basis for a course of action, which could be called "fishery management."

The last thirty years have been a clarification of this concept, step by step, to recognizable form. Educational institutions have recognized and accepted their responsibilities in providing the manpower trained to produce, disseminate, and utilize facts about fish. The University of Washington (Seattle) established a College of Fisheries in 1919. Its graduates are active in all phases of fishery administration, research, and management, especially of the commercial fisheries. Other schools such as Cornell University and the University of Michigan were among the first to generate strong fishery courses in their curricula, especially at graduate level. Their graduates have had a profound influence in many conservation agencies. A few research institutes, comparable to industrial research organizations, have been established, principally with the support of the conservation agencies and the schools.

One of the most important stimulants to progress in fish conservation through research resulted from the advent of the Federal Aid in Fish Restoration Program which began when Congress passed the Dingell-Johnson Act in 1950. Under this program, the states for the first time, generally, had modest funds for research (and development) at their disposal. Roughly half the funds (derived from manufacturers excise taxes on certain items of fishing tackle) have been invested in investigational work of some kind—mostly applied or "practical" research, designed to develop, test, and refine theoretical management procedures. In a few years the states, collectively, were investing between two and three million dollars annually through this program in investigational work. Because of public pressures to keep the work "practical," relatively little attention was paid to replenishing the dwindling stockpile of fundamental new knowledge upon which "practical" or applied research is wholly dependent. In addition to the limited funds available, this was and remains the chief weakness and deficiency of research efforts by most state fishery agencies. The D-J program was oriented toward the sport fisheries. A somewhat comparable grant-in-aid program for research soon developed for the commercial fisheries (utilizing a portion of tariff revenues realized on importations of foreign-produced commercial fish) through the passage by Congress of the so-called Saltonstall-Kennedy Act in 1954. Some of the finest quality research to come out of that program concerned the reproductive physiology of Channel Catfish, carried out at the University of Oklahoma.

In 1956, a reorganization of the United States Fish and Wildlife Service led to a broadening of its research authorities, especially in the sport fisheries field. The Fish and Wildlife Act of 1956 was followed in quick succession by the Marine Game Fish Research Act of 1959, which clarified the intent of Congress that the Department of the Interior should undertake continuing basic research on saltwater species of fishes of importance to sport fishing. Stimulated by introduction of several bills into the Congress directing that the federal government undertake similar research on reservoir sport fishes, the Department of the Interior requested appropriations for this purpose under its broad new authorities, and research on reservoir fishes and fish habitat was initiated.

Sport fishing is now recognized to be one of the nation's leading forms of active participative outdoor recreation—even by non-fishermen. It is well documented that more people find needed relaxation in sport fishing on more days annually and spend more money in the process than in any other form of outdoor recreation. The responsibilities of state fish and game agencies to many millions of anglers are clear. In simplest terms, they are to provide an abundance of places to fish and good fishing in those places. This is simple to say and difficult to accomplish. For one thing, it means provision of facilities or places to fish—where these may be scarce—and assuring perpetual accessibility to existing waters—where these may be abundant. This takes money and lots of it. The second aspect of the agency responsibility—good fishing—is dependent upon deliberate management of fish populations themselves.

Good fishing just doesn't happen any more—it must be developed by competent fishery biologists. An example of this is near-doubling of fishing opportunity through the widespread liberalization of sport fishing regulations—an outstanding dividend from research. Prior to 1945, annual closed seasons were in vogue during the spawning period of most species. In 1962, 36 states permitted essentially year-round fishing in all or most of their waters for Bass and other predatory warmwater game fish; 45 did so for pan fish. Interestingly, 9 states did so for Trout, as well. Another example is the improvement of fishing through extensive rehabilitation, principally by chemical means and restocking, of unbalanced lakes and streams. All states now make use of fish toxicants in some manner. Chief impetus came with the advent of the Dingell-Johnson (federal aid) program and the new funds it made available. Through 1960, an estimated 2,000 lakes (larger than farm ponds and up to 30,000 acres) had been rehabilitated by total or partial removal of undesirable fish. By this means, often coupled with restocking, good fishing is restored to nearly 100,000 acres of poor fish water annually.

These management activities were not developed without prior accumulation of knowledge acquired through research. Basic research is the fountainhead of all management and development. Not long ago a leading industrialist stated that less than 5 per cent of his company's research "paid off." But he emphasized that it was that important 5 per cent that kept them out of bankruptcy. Fishery research plays the same vital role in assuring continued fishing. Its batting average, however, is far higher. Indeed, it's one of the best investments an agency can make. What appears to be needed is greater emphasis on basic as distinct from applied research. Promising areas for basic sport fishery research are detailed life history and ecological studies, and behavior studies. What do fishes do from day to day, hour to hour, and what are the factors influencing their activities? These are neglected and potentially fruitful areas of study. A great deal of activity now glibly called research is in reality routine management, most akin to checking inventory and sales of canned goods in a supermarket. Careful study of available published records shows that *all* government and private agencies (including state and federal conservation agencies, and the four great federal research grant agencies) are spending less than $500,000 annually on *basic* sport fishery research. Probably less than 2 cents of the state fish conservation dollar is spent on basic research, though upwards of four-fold that amount is spent in applied research and its companion activities, routine management, inventory and trouble-shooting.

This appears to be the weakest aspect of fishery programs. Apparently, few states have found it "climatically" or "politically" possible to engage directly in basic research programs. Progress could be made, however, if a sum of $20,000 to $30,000 were given annually to an appropriate university or college of choice in each state to permit unencumbered research in the areas cited above. Neither immediately practical results nor short-term applied research should be sought from such a program—this would fail to meet real needs. The objective should be, simply, acquisition of new knowledge about fish life, for the product of basic research is new ideas. It is precisely to help meet this need that the Congress has commenced appropriating modest sums both for reservoir and for marine game fish research. The programs are designed to help the states—not by providing more federal grants—by providing needed new knowledge. Pressure for immediate results at the state level has largely limited state activities to applied research and management inventories. This is fine, but has become increasingly difficult as the stockpile of basic knowledge has been drained away without replenishment. The situation badly needs correcting. Unless this is done, the nation's anglers cannot be properly served by the states in their traditional management functions.

The value and the volume of scientific analysis of fishery problems is limited by the availability of well-trained, imaginative and resourceful men. Training of fishery workers is improving constantly. In the 1940s considerable stress was placed on technical training in fishery specialization at the undergraduate level, which tended to emphasize a trade-school approach. It was felt—partly in response to demands by politically appointed conservation administrators—that the universities should turn out fish technicians, already pre-skilled in handling gill nets, seines, water chemistry analysis, fish identification, stream and lake improvement, etc. They wanted employees who already knew the answers and would undertake management at once. Unfortunately, the hours devoted to technical courses to teach these skills were hours that could not be used to acquire a depth of knowledge about biological functions and processes, chemistry and physics, to say nothing of English and other languages, economics, social studies, and the humanities in general. All too often, the results were disappointing and the "technicians" proved inadequate to the real needs. They were seldom able to analyze the constantly changing problems, both biological and sociological, with which they were confronted because they were neither trained in the scientific method nor equipped with a depth of background sufficient to provide insight into the problems.

Not everybody who works in fish conservation is a fishery biologist. To avoid confusion on this point it may be helpful to define him. Here is how the committee on professional standards of the American Fisheries Society does it:

> 1. A fishery biologist is a professionally trained person capable of defining and investigating problems related to fisheries, and of proposing scientifically sound solutions of the biological problems in sport and commercial fisheries.
>
> 2. The fishery biologist can be expected to have a working knowledge of basic biology, chemistry, physics and mathematics as applied to aquatic biology and fisheries. He must also be capable of presenting results and recommendations in suitable written and oral form.

This definition seems reasonably satisfactory so long as it is recognized that "professional training" should not dominate undergraduate courses so much that it precludes sound education in the humanities. It seems increasingly evident that many of the deficiencies or attributes that may be apparent in the work of practicing conservationists—be they fishery biologists or game technicians—are closely correlated with the depth of liberal arts *education* that provides the foundation for the superposed specialized (professional) *training*.

Some administrators and anglers, alike, may fail to appreciate that biologists are the necessary kind of people to employ in fish management positions as well as in research. Fishery biology consists of two main divisions of effort and responsibility. One of these is in *research*—for the discovery of new fish facts and new ideas. The other is in *management*—for the proper application and development of new discoveries in terms of improved sport fishing. There must be a capacity among fish managers for understanding of biological limitations and potential. There must be a close working relationship with research. Unless biologists are utilized in these important fish management positions, many helpful research findings will undoubtedly be allowed to "wither on the vine," as a result of scientific ignorance and incompetence.

It has long been established that there is far more to fish management than blind stocking of baby fish to curry temporary local publicity, or enforcement of arbitrarily-made regulations. These things—reminders of a more primitive period in fish conservation—have long since been widely discredited, though these practices still persist in a few states. Admittedly, there may still be a few old-fashioned administrators who are striving to preserve the status quo. Their purpose is to keep qualified professionals out of positions of responsibility and authority, simply because it is simpler not to make program changes! Fortunately, this will be rare; should it occur, the sportsmen affected can count on many more years of empty promises, "political stocking,"—and poor fishing.

In the 1950s, as in medicine and engineering, academicians and administrators both commenced to see the need for broader based training giving greatly increased emphasis to the liberal arts at the undergraduate level with major concentration in the biological sciences rather than in technical fishery courses. Specialization in the narrower field became increasingly postponed to the graduate level with greater numbers of students attaining graduate degrees at the Master's level and some at the Doctorate level. On the whole, this has greatly benefitted fish conservation, by producing a supply of better qualified fishery workers—biologists rather than technicians. These people were able to attack the new problems, analyze them, set up experimental management procedures, evaluate results, modify methods to meet changing conditions, and even undertake continuing basic research where need and opportunity combined. Most of the measurable progress in fish conservation has been attributable to these better trained individuals in whatever decade they appeared.

By the 1960s, at least 90 universities or colleges were offering one or more courses in fishery biology. Included were ichthyology, fishery research, management, limnology, aquatic biology, fish diseases, fish genetics, biological oceanography, marine ecology, pollution, aquatic entomology, and fish parasitology. These were offered in a variety of academic departments and at undergraduate as well as graduate levels depending upon local educational circumstances.* The courses involved the special services of more than 250 professors engaged in teaching and research in the general fishery field, the vast majority of whom hold the Ph.D. degree. In this period, the Congress began to appropriate funds to establish Fishery Cooperative Research Units at a number of leading universities strategically located throughout the country. The Units are geared to graduate level training of high quality fishery biologists and to undertake continuing research on various aspects of fishery biology, a most promising new venture.

The vast majority (90%) of professional fish conservationists are employed by state and federal agencies, with most of the remainder employed by colleges and universities, only about one per cent being employed privately. A majority of these professionals, in turn, are members of the American Fisheries Society, one of the nation's oldest scientific societies, organized in 1870. By 1962, nearly 2000 professional conservationists held membership in the Society. Of these, at least 78 per cent were biologists with at least a bachelor's degree, or were college biology students committed to the fishery field; six per cent were fish culturists; four per cent were administrators, outdoor writers, interested conservationists, etc.; and the remaining 12 per cent consisted of other interested individuals, library members, official agency members, etc.* An earlier analysis of "technical" fishery workers throughout the United States and Canada revealed that about 60 per cent were engaged principally in some aspect of research or investigations, whereas only about 27 per cent devoted the major part or all of their time to fixed fish management activities including fish culture, with the remainder in administration. Over 90 per cent had secured the bachelor's degree, while about half of these held advanced degrees (Master's degrees by two-thirds, Doctorates by one-third).*

Three other scientific societies are the principal

* Sport Fishing Institute. 1961. Institutions and Professors offering fishery biology and related courses in North American colleges and Universities—1961 Revision. Mimeo, 8 pp. (May). Sport Fishing Institute, Bond Building, Washington 5, D. C.

** Jenkins, R. M. 1962. 78 per cent biologists (AFS that is). Newsletter Vol. 5 (2):2 (April). American Fisheries Society, Washington, D. C.

† Carlander, K. D. 1959. A survey of technical fishery personnel. Transactions of the American Fisheries Society, Vol. 88 (1):18-22 (Jan.)

ones that serve more specialized interests within the fishery field. One of these is the American Society of Ichthyologists & Herpetologists which provides the principal scientific forum and journal for biologists specializing in taxonomy or the classification of fishes. Many of its members are drawn from academic circles and a high proportion hold dual membership in the American Fisheries Society as well. A very young society, known as the American Institute of Fishery Research Biologists, as its name implies, provides a mutuality of specialized interest exclusively for research biologists, principally basic research people. Here again, there is common ground with the American Fisheries Society and broad dual membership prevails. It also cuts across the membership of the American Society of Ichthyologists and Herpetologists. Finally, the American Society of Limnology and Oceanography provides the specialized forum for common interests of those researchers concentrating on exploring and understanding the environment of fishes, both physical and biological, in fresh water and salt water. Cross-membership in the other specialized groups and in the potpourri of related interests represented by the American Fisheries Society is again commonly practiced by the limnologists and oceanographers.

Elements of fishery management. Modern fishery management programs are undergoing continuing change; indeed, lack of change may be regarded as a sign that something may be decidedly wrong. First of all, there needs to be a proper climate in which able professionals can work at the action programs in the water that directly affect fish populations and fish habitat. If the professional fishery workers are subject to political or group pressures to favor certain areas or undertake local pet projects that probably ignore biological principles and limitations, little except chaos can result and almost no improvement in fishing can be expected to result. Because nearly a century of trial-and-error attempts to maintain good fishing has resulted chiefly in continued failure, sportsmen have insisted since the mid-thirties that fish and game agencies be protected as much as possible from political and local interference. Revenues from sale of state fishing licenses and other sources have by law become segregated within the state treasuries of every state in dedicated fish and game funds. To oversee the expenditures of appropriations from the funds and to assure that these go only for intended purposes, all states have adopted some form of policy-making body, to establish and guide fish and game program policy and usually with power to hire and fire the chief fish and game or conservation administrative officer or director.

Periodic national surveys of state fish and game commissions by the Sport Fishing Institute have revealed that their basic structure has remained virtually unchanged since World War II. The size of the commissions varies a great deal but usually include 5 or 7 non-paid commissioners, serving for terms of 3 to 5 years on a staggered basis, whose job is formulation of policy. The most frequent requirements found to determine the selection (by the state governors) of commission members are these: (1) there must be proper geographical representation; (2) the membership must be bipartisan; and (3) the individuals selected must be well informed and interested in fish and game matters. The studies have pointed up a number of weaknesses that are inherent, not so much in the commission system as in the frailities of human nature. It is clear that the majority of commission members want to do a good job. These are some of the apparent weaknesses:

1. A tendency to give personal advancement (political or otherwise) priority over conservation.

2. An inclination to "know the answers" instead of relying on the findings and recommendations of the professional personnel.

3. A tendency toward "taking over" administrative functions that should be handled by the director.

4. An inclination toward "provincialism"—giving prior consideration to their own district—instead of thinking on a statewide basis.

5. A tendency toward feuding with other commission members, or with staff personnel, leading to low morale, confusion, and program deterioration.

6. A tendency to bow to pressure groups regardless of the merits of the proposals of these groups.

7. A tendency to show too little interest in the program, by failing to attend commission meetings, or by failing to keep up on developments.

Many conservation leaders are disturbed that conservation agencies are not yet as secure from political manipulation as some other state agencies—for example, public health. Some of these folks are giving thought currently to the possibility of defining the optimum qualifications of the individuals to be selected by the governors to serve on the state fish and game commissions. It's the people who count rather than the organizational chart. At the same time, a smooth organization can greatly facilitate the work of dedicated staff. Therefore, many lay conservationists feel that busy state governors may sometimes need specific guidelines to help them to make suitable appointments to the fish and game commissions. Fortunately, they have succeeded in making many excellent appointments in many states as the record shows. Rather too often, however, exceptions arise to plague conservation. This usually happens when the Governor fails to appreciate the economic importance of the fish and game resource to his state and/or when he uses commission appointments to pay off minor political debts. In an ideal situation, the commission members realize that they are laymen in what has become a highly complicated field. They will therefore select well qualified personnel to handle the job; they will then back those personnel to the limit and rely on their judgments. The commissioners will make every effort to learn what needs doing and what is being done. A major function will be to act as a "buffer" between pressure groups and the fish and game personnel. It is evident, nationally, that a large number of commission members try to do this.

Despite some weaknesses, the best system yet devised for managing fish (and game) resources provides for a policy-making and budget-controlling commission with an administrator selected by the commission but free to carry on the policies and programs of the commission. Dr. Ira Gabrielson, who has had a long and unique experience studying organizational structure of state conservation agencies, has said:

"By and large [the commission system] has provided the best continuity of personnel, and the best visible results. This is true despite the obvious weaknesses, the most common of which is the almost inevitable tendency of such boards to dabble into administrative affairs and to postpone making vital policy decisions on controversial questions, while messing with operating details that should be left to the director. The best departments are those in which the separate duties and responsibilities are clearly spelled out in law and are observed by both the commission and the director."

Dr. Gabrielson noted further that growing complications caused by the increasingly intensive human use of land and water for purposes other than producing fish and game make it increasingly important that the administration of these resources be in the hands of trained men and that they follow a consistent program, modifying it only as additional information and changing conditions indicate are advisable. "The last thing in the world needed in this present day and age," he has said, "is administration of these natural resources to please the political friends of any governor, regardless of his administrative competence."

Human nature being what it is, it is not surprising to find, in a few states, that political pulling and hauling becomes so bad from time to time that everything possible is done—even in the face of constitutional provisions designed to prevent it—to tie up funds, harass the fish and wildlife interests, delay appointments of key people and otherwise assure inaction in fish [and game] conservation. Nevertheless, most commissions do a fine job, literally because good men—the measure of any system—are appointed. This happens where governors recognize that the importance of the fish and game or conservation department ranks with that of any other in the state. In Massachusetts, for example, with a well-established, officially-adopted fishery policy, the fish and game board (commission) resists pressures to manage the fishery resource on other than a sound biological basis. Tennessee was until recently the only state to choose its fish and game commissioners by a system of popular election. This led to serious administrative abuses. Fortunately, a recent legislative act abolished that wretched system. At the same time it gave to the commission previously lacking authority for autonomous control of employment of necessary personnel.

The majority of states fortunately enjoy much capable membership on their fish and game commissions, and competent administration under them. Nevertheless, it is apparent that no state is immune to a possible change of fortune in this regard. It also appears that political meddling in fish and game is an ever-present danger. The time may have come when sportsmen and conservationists should agree on and define the standards that commission members must meet with regard to fish [and wildlife] conservation affairs, as well as executive and policy-making abilities. Some years ago, as a starter along these lines, the late Dr. R. W. Eschmeyer (first Executive Vice President of Sport Fishing Institute) outlined some basic guidelines to the commission set-up that still apply, in the form of a series of questions, as follows:

1. Does the state have a fish and game commission with staggered terms? If not, there's room for improvement. Nearly all progressive states now have such commissions.

2. Are the men on the commission selected on the basis of ability, or is their selection a matter of paying a political debt? In a few states the commissioners are the major stumbling block to progress.

3. Does the commission have full authority to pass regulations? It should have that authority.

4. Does the commission lean heavily on the advice of its trained fisheries personnel in making the regulations, or in planning the program? If not, new commissioners might be needed.

5. Do the commission members think on a "statewide" basis, or do they want special consideration for their own localities? It makes a difference!

6. Do the individual commissioners themselves pose as qualified authorities on fish conservation? Some of them are, but many are not. If they "know the answers" they will not rely on the trained conservationists for advice.

7. Does your state (if it's a coastal state) have separate fresh water and salt water commissions? If it has two independent set-ups, the chances are much better than even that the saltwater sport fishermen receive little consideration.

Coastal Marine Fisheries. About 20 per cent of all sport fishing is centered on coastal marine waters. Saltwater sport fishing is increasing about

6.7 per cent annually, or twice as rapidly as freshwater angling. By century's end, with overall fishing expected to treble, the proportion to be borne by coastal marine fishery resources is expected to increase from one-fifth, as at present, to one-third of the total at that time. There are those who promote the growth of saltwater sport fishing on the premise that it relieves pressure on inland waters, allegedly already overburdened. Fishing in extensive areas of inland waters is known to be poor—because of pollution, siltation, overcrowding by non-sport species of fishes, overabundance and stunting of pan fishes, ill-advised introductions of unsuitable species through "political" stocking, natural or man-induced warming of waters, and other reasons, but as a rule seldom from overfishing. Nevertheless, a number of factors such as increasing populations, better roads, increased urbanization, etc., are over-riding influences that of themselves assure the rapid proliferation of marine sport fishing. Added to this is an intrinsic appeal of saltwater fishing itself. There is strong basis for doubt that saltwater fishing provides any significant relief of pressure on freshwater fishing because they are different kinds of fishing with different built-in appeals. In comparing the appeal of saltwater and freshwater angling, British angler-philosopher Bernard Venables (*Angling Times,* London) wrote in part as follows:

"Freshwater fishing and saltwater fishing are different, so different that they do not compete. One is close and intimate and soft and sweet-smelling and full of intimate excitements; the other is wide and salty, and with its own different kind of away-from-it-all. A deep sea boat is a world away from all other worlds, as lovely a loneliness, in its way, as that of the river bank . . .

"What fishing means to me, in fresh water, is the same as it always meant. What fishing means to me, in salt water is another thing, a thing so separate from fresh water that, in atmosphere, it has nothing at all in common with freshwater fishing—except that you must be the sort of man an angler is to find the delight of either of them. And, if you delight in one, so almost certainly, you will in the other."

From time immemorial, Man—including anglers, commercial fishermen, landlubbers, and marine biologists, alike—seems to have regarded ocean fishery resources as inexhaustible; at least, until very recently. Perhaps the first serious formal challenge to this cornucopian concept of the seas was delivered by two scientists of the U. S. Fish and Wildlife Service (Bureau of Commercial Fisheries) at the first United Nations Food and Agriculture Organization Conference on Fish Nutrition. They calculated roughly that the world's seas contain about 560 billion pounds of bony fishes all told, of which about half—280 billion pounds—might ultimately become available for use by Man. They estimated present world harvest at about 66 billion pounds, or about one-fourth of the available supply.* The significance lies not in the precision of the estimates but in the fact that it is possible to show that yield is not unlimited, and that judgments of the upper limits of supply and yield are possible. These estimates are equivalent to a total supply of bony fishes equal to about 6 pounds per acre of total ocean area, a maximum potential yield of about 3 pounds per acre, and a current yield or harvest somewhat less than 1 pound per acre. This is comparable to the average harvest per acre in the Great Lakes. It is considerably less than the harvest (over 9 pounds per acre) of fish from Lake Erie, the most productive of those waters.

It is small wonder, therefore, that anglers are coming into conflict from time to time with commercial fishermen over use of the marine fishery resources, particularly in close-in coastal waters, bays, and estuaries. Heads-in-sand attitudes and wishful thinking will not solve these problems. On the contrary, the rapid proliferation in numbers of marine anglers will probably aggravate rather than diminish them. In 1960, there were an estimated 6.3 million anglers who fished regularly in salt water. There were also estimated to be some 3.5 million more who fished occasionally in salt water. Close to 10 million in all! Already, some states have acted to designate some marine species as game fish—Snook in Florida, Striped Bass in California, for example; there are others and the list seems sure to grow in the next few decades. A national survey of saltwater sport fishing, conducted as a supplement to the 1960 National Survey of Fishing and Hunting, revealed a national sport catch of about 633 million fish. If these averaged somewhat under a pound apiece, they were equivalent to about one-fourth of the commercial harvest of food fishes in the U.S. coastal waters. For some jointly exploited species, in some coastal areas, it is known that sport fishing harvest already at least equals the commercial harvest. It is known, too, that sport fish harvest alone may be sufficiently great to utilize the entire annual recruitment of a species.*

Sport fishing effort on coastal marine waters will probably become double current effort by 1976; it may well become quadruple by the last decade of the current century. It seems apparent, for an increasing number of species, that marine bony fish resources are not in sufficient supply for indefinitely carefree joint exploitation by both sport and commercial interests. When harvests are high—and approach or exceed recruitment—overfishing

* Graham, Herbert W. & R. L. Edwards. 1961. The world biomass of marine fishes. Int. Conf. on Fish in Nutrition, UN FAO. Unpub. Ms. (Sept).

** Poole, John S. 1961. Age and growth of the fluke on Great South Bay and their significance to the sport fishery. N. Y. Fish & Game Jour., 8 (1):1-18 (Jan.).

becomes possible and may threaten species abundance. Biological research can determine when rate of recruitment and rates of harvest approach one another. Administrators and legislators, responsive to the best interests of the public, must make the necessary and unavoidable decisions regarding the wisest use of the marine fishery resources. At least one prominent marine fishery scientist has suggested seriously but unofficially that only those peoples who discard the skins of fishes but utilize their flesh for food are true fish conservationists and that those other peoples who discard the meat and save the skins (as mounted trophies) are not. He was, of course, suggesting that sport fishing is a form of waste of scarce protein in a very hungry world. There is some obvious waste in the practice by some anglers, for example, of catching magnificent game fishes like the Marlins only to hang them in the sun to rot after taking a few snapshots. There is far greater—though less noticeable—waste in the failure of some commercial men to use savings gear which would permit the escape of young fishes of a number of species for the greater bounty of the future.

In our envied, sophisticated society, "wise use" does not necessarily imply exclusive use of fish as food. It is trite but nonetheless true to say that "man does not live by bread alone." This philosophy finds its greatest expression and realization, of course, in a modern democratic society. As a point of fact, our chief source of protein is beef, not fish, and monies now spent to purchase commercially-caught fishes for food can as easily be spent on other cheap meats—and are, increasingly. Whatever vital nutritional contribution is made by fish to diet in the United States is readily suppliable from the catches of sport fishermen. Including fresh water, these are already equivalent to half or more of the total U. S. commercial catch of food fishes. Contributions to the economy from purchase of goods and services utilized out fishing on marine waters already amounted by 1960 to some $626 million at retail. This is about half the ultimate value of U. S.-caught commercial food fishes, also at retail; it will equal it by 1976 and double it or more by 1990.

Many marine fishery biologists have neglected ecology and been content to become historians, collecting and charting statistics of catch. They have assumed—until very recently—that catch regulation is the only promising approach to the matter of managing marine fishery resources. One of the nation's best known marine fishery administrators has stated as recently as 1960, for example, that "once you know catch, you know everything!" Freshwater fishery biologists had abandoned this view by the close of World War II. By the late thirties, they had begun to study the fish populations themselves in addition to collecting statistics of catch. It was not long until they discovered that catch alone is a very imperfect mirror of population structure and dynamics. This realization led directly to year-round fishing for warm-water sport fishes and an eventual doubling of fishing opportunity in inland waters, without harm to future supply.

There are many possibilities for managing fish populations beyond regulating catch—in coastal marine as well as inland waters. For example, the Japanese have known much for centuries about attracting marine organisms to artificial points of concentration. The extent of their activity along this line was revealed in this country through a 1961 Tokyo Embassy Dispatch. Americans have been fortunate to rediscover some of what they have known, independently (since World War I), through a happy combination of a lot of accident and a little research. Very limited research on artificial fishing reefs in marine waters has occurred in the U. S. during the past decade. In contrast, use of artificial reefs or "fish shelters" had already become a sophisticated tool of freshwater fishery management by the early thirties. Suffice it to say, now, that marine sport fishery interests in a dozen United States coastal states recognize that previously unsuspected capabilities to manage coastal marine fish resources exist, are needed, and are in actual use to a limited extent. As the number of anglers and the amount of fishing effort grow, these management capabilities must be extended and multiplied manyfold and developed along new lines possibly unsuspected at the moment. With increased knowledge of the detailed life histories and ecology of the fishes, their behavior and population dynamics, together with intimate knowledge of their environments, a multiplicity of new management capabilities seems almost certain to unfold. Many examples from other fields of science give confidence on this score, and it has already been borne out to an encouraging degree in the freshwater fisheries. What is clearly most needed is a broad-scale program of basic and applied research. The latter is dependent upon the former, and in turn produces the fish management tools needed to assure maximum sustained yields with which to supply increasing fishing demand.

As already mentioned, a start has been made toward developing the needed continuing basic research program, in the establishment of an embryonic marine game fish research program within the Bureau of Sport Fisheries and Wildlife, U. S. Fish and Wildlife Service. The national program has a $2.7 million annual *authorization* limit. Initial *appropriations* have been only a small fraction of this amount, but will grow. There is also a very limited program of applied research, experimental management, and development under way at the state level, where it should be, financed principally by a share of the Dingell-Johnsons excise taxes on the manufacture of certain items of fishing tackle. Nationally, nearly 25 per cent of the excise taxes available to the coastal states are spent on marine projects. This is close to the proportion of saltwater anglers among all anglers in those states, so it seems fairly reasonable. What is needed here, again, is a manyfold increase in the amount of funds available for marine work. Obviously, most of it must come from new sources. Only two states now have substantial marine sport fishery programs; these are California and Texas. It is significant that these same states are also the only ones having saltwater fishing licenses with extensive coverage of resident anglers. Alabama and Louisiana have token licensing coverage with correspondingly token revenues. Alaska now has a license covering saltwater angling but population and revenues are low. Adequate financing both of basic research at the federal level and of applied research and development at the state level continues to be the major stumbling block to progress in the marine sport fisheries. Coupled with this is the need for adequate representation of sport fishery interests on regional associations of state marine fishery agencies that deal with jurisdictional matters. Licensing of saltwater anglers would go far toward solving these problems.

Improved financial support for basic research will come principally through increased Congressional appropriations for the purpose. Improved financial support for state programs of applied research and development can probably come satisfactorily only through application of the principle of licensing, as long established in all the states for financing inland fisheries work [and now well established in two coastal states for marine sport fisheries work], or by earmarking to this purpose some related existing tax revenues from the general fund such as marine fuel taxes.* The license is purely and simply a fund-raising device, the best in sight, and a proven one at that. No other practical means of raising substantial funds on a continuing basis for such purpose has been devised to date. Experience with inland fishing licenses shows that an annual state fee of about $3.00 is needed to start. It also shows that administration, information-education and law enforcement, collectively, would require about 25 per cent of the funds in the early program stages, leaving 75 per cent for development and applied research. It shows that the funds can be safeguarded against diversion to non-related purposes through deposit in earmarked funds (all states have them for inland fishery revenues). It shows that licensing is acceptable and saleable to the vast majority of anglers if a budgeted program is presented and if there is a policy-making body or commission representing the anglers to oversee use of the funds (nearly all states have them, usually made up of 5 or 7 members, serving in staggered terms). In one respect, a great improvement over inland licensing could and should be achieved at the outset in the marine field. The principle of reciprocity should be built in so that a license purchased in one state would be valid in the waters of the state sharing a common border.

Such a set-up would yield, collectively, over $18 million annually at the 1960 level of fishing participation—an average of about $800,000 per state. This amount of money would provide about $600,000 for development and applied research with about $200,000 for necessary administration, education, and law enforcement, combined. Initially, much development work could be undertaken to great advantage, as well as experimental management projects. With such a program, great benefit would flow to saltwater anglers.

Freshwater fisheries. Merely to maintain present fishing quality for an army of 30 to 40 million anglers annually harvesting upwards of 1½ billion or so pounds of fish from 93 million or fewer acres of water is a staggering proposition by itself. Unfortunately, it's far more complicated than it might look to the casual observer. Superficially, it would appear that there are about 2½ acres of water for each angler, and that these acres are yielding about 15 pounds of fish per acre. Annually, the total harvest averages out to some 40 pounds of fish per angler. This, in turn, is an over-simplification. For one thing, at least 25 million anglers depend exclusively or in part on fresh water, the remainder on salt water areas. Therefore, there are at most only a little over 2½ acres of inland water per angler, yielding somewhere around 12 pounds per acre. Another consideration is that a significant part of this water is not in a condition to support much angling owing to a scarcity of sport fishes due to pollution or other causes. Otherwise, part of it is not available for angling either because angling is not permitted or because suitable public access is lacking. There are new social problems brought on by growth of conflicting water uses such as water skiing, motorboat racing, and skin diving.

This is the broad outline of the challenge confronting the resource administrators. The problems must be solved for the present; planning must consider probable expansion of angling in the future. For fish conservation programs in 1962, for example, about $60 million were available from sales of fishing licenses and manufacturers excise taxes on certain items of fishing tackle, and from all other sources. The funds have been increasing annually at about the same rate as the growth in the economy. However, actual "demand" in terms of needed conservation programming is increasing much more rapidly. A large proportion of the developments that stimulate expansion of the economy are detrimental to the fishery resource and fishing. Pollution abatement programs are not keeping pace with suburban development or industrial growth. As more trees are cut and marginal lands disturbed, more silt—a form of pollu-

* Twentieth Annual Report of the Atlantic States Marine Fisheries Commission, June, 1962:pp. 51-52. Tallahassee, Fla.

tion—pours into the waterways, further upsetting Nature's balance. Construction of big dams is rapidly decimating remnant runs of irreplaceable anadromous fisheries, or changing habitat for native fauna that may disappear, while creating conditions suited to other replacement species that must be managed differently. At a recent National Watershed Congress meeting in Washington, D. C., the U. S. Budget Director reported that federal expenditures in housing, defense and agriculture were rising at a far greater rate than those for conservation. It is evident, too, that state expenditures for conservation have moved ahead very slowly. In balance, then, conservation interests are losing ground rapidly. This is due principally to the fact that state action programs are forced to operate on shoestring budgets.

Commencing in 1954, the Sport Fishing Institute undertook a series of periodic reviews of the activities of state and federal agency programs affecting sport fishing opportunity. The principal action programs in fish management are carried out by the states or in cooperation with the states in one way or another, such that the prerogative and responsibility for management of fishery resources is recognized to rest primarily with the state fishery agencies. Consequently, in 1954, in 1957, and again in 1960, the Institute analyzed the expenditures of the state fishery revenues used in these management programs for the improvement of fishing. Aggregate fishery revenues available to the state agencies amounted to some $55 million in 1959 and to about $60 million in 1962. Very little change was evident in the pattern of expenditures over the three-year interval among five main categories of expenditures: (1) administration—8%, (2) information-education—4%, (3) law enforcement—23%, (4) manipulation of fish populations —52%, and (5) fact-finding—13%. The fourth functional expenditure category was subdivided into fish stocking (28%) and fish management other than stocking (24%). These items were in turn further subdivided in the survey into principal activity groupings. As a result, it was possible to determine the approximate relative emphasis placed nationally on each major fish conservation activity (based on the amount of money actually spent) as shown in Table 1.

TABLE 1.

	In $ millions	(%)
Administration	4.4	(8)
Information-education	2.2	(4)
Law enforcement	12.3	(23)
Manipulation of fish populations		
cold water fish stocking (trout-salmon)	11.6	(22)
warm water fish stocking (including "salvage")	3.2	(6)
land acquisition and access site development	2.2	(4)
construction of new fishing lakes	4.3	(8)
rehabilitation of old fishing waters	1.1	(2)
fish control to favor sport fishes	1.6	(3)
improvement of fish habitat	2.1	(4)
all other forms of management	1.7	(3)
Fact-finding	6.2	(13)
Total	52.9	(100)

By individual states, there is a considerable range of expenditure both in the major functional groupings and within the panorama of fish population manipulations. This is to be expected in part because problems differ from state to state both biologically and sociologically. Some significant differences reveal themselves in program expenditures, based on geographical regions, as reflected in distribution of expenditures from the 1959 fish conservation dollar. See Table 2.

The total 1959 expenditure for fact-finding reported by 50 states was $6,180,000. About 700 state fishery biologists were involved in these studies, which included creel censuses, population analyses, and general surveys. Some university contract research and special projects were also included. Dingell-Johnson funds (federal aid to fisheries) used for research, out of the total D-J apportionments to the states, comprised 43 per cent of the over-all research investment. An unknown, possibly significant, proportion of the fact-finding effort involved "trouble-shooting." Un-

TABLE 2. 1959 FISH DOLLAR

	West	North-Central	South	Northeast	National
Administration	9¢	9¢	6¢	8¢	8¢
Info. and Educ.	3¢	4¢	6¢	3¢	4¢
Law Enforcement	18¢	23¢	29¢	22¢	23¢
Stocking	41¢	20¢	17¢	37¢	28¢
Other Fish Management	13¢	34¢	27¢	20¢	24¢
Fact-finding	16¢	10¢	15¢	10¢	13¢
Total fact-finding dollars	$1,850,000	$1,570,000	$1,890,000	$870,000	$6,180,000
Total Expend. Est. calendar '59	$17,100,000	$15,300,000	$11,000,000	$9,500,000	$53,000,000
Total income Est. fiscal '59*	$15,600,000	$17,400,000	$13,300,000	$8,700,000	$55,000,000

* Estimated total income of all states is for fiscal year 1959 (July, 1958 through June, 1959), and includes only fishing license income and D-J federal apportionments. Special legislative apportionments, oil royalties, and other special or minor sources of fishery funds are not included. Estimated expenditures of all states for calendar year 1959 are based on calculations from data supplied by the states.

fortunately, "trouble-shooting" does not usually add to the store of new knowledge, being largely in the realm of public relations. To the extent that research biologists are diverted to "trouble-shooting" there is waste of precious research funds. Fact-finding efforts ranged from 4 per cent to 45 per cent of the entire outlay for fish conservation, averaging 13 per cent per state. The top ten states, by percentage were: Alaska, Arizona, Florida, Georgia, Hawaii, Maryland, Nebraska, North Carolina, North Dakota, and Texas. Based on dollars the leaders were: California, Idaho, Maine, Michigan, Minnesota, Montana, New York, North Carolina, Texas, and Wisconsin.

The highest percentages of the fishery dollars devoted to law enforcement occurred primarily in the South. However, disproportionately-high enforcement expenditures also prevail in some North-Central and Northeastern states. Stocking, primarily of coldwater fishes, takes the largest portion of the budget in the West and Northeast. The greatest emphasis on management activities other than stocking is evident in the North-Central states. There and in the South construction of new fishing lakes is strongly emphasized.

The successive surveys of state program activities have revealed encouraging progress recently toward more balanced fish conservation programs throughout the nation. Particularly encouraging has been a significant increase in fact-finding efforts. Evaluation of management procedures, developmental research, and other applied studies are being stepped up to meet pressing needs for answers to long-standing questions. Most states seem to be abandoning blind stumbling and follow-the-leader tactics in the management of their fishery resources, which typified the pre-war years, and are developing sound programs, solidly based on facts. However, six states still spent less than six per cent of their budget on management investigations of all kinds. Fourteen state fishery agencies spent more than 15 per cent of their allocation for fact-finding. In most instances, this was attributable to the need for information in totally new management fields, such as salt water. Some of the state fishery units have been functioning for only a few years. They need extensive studies to correctly guide their management programs. Most other agencies were spending somewhat less than 10 per cent of their total fishery income on these vital activities.

A disproportionate amount of money continues to be spent on law enforcement. With the continuation of the trend toward more liberalized fishing regulations, the need for larger enforcement staffs in the fishery field is not evident. There are obvious needs to check licenses and enforce anti-pollution and certain other laws. However, it is extremely doubtful that these activities should require an average of 23 per cent (up to 60 per cent in some southern states) of the fishery expenditures. More states are adopting intensive pre-employment and in-service training programs for conservation officers. Their efforts in information-education and routine management studies such as creel census may probably be expected to increase under proper professional guidance. Sport Fishing Institute's concept of the model fish conservation budget for a mature agency, and a comparison with the national average in 1959, is as follows:*

	Model	*1959*
Administration	10	8
Information-education	5	4
Law enforcement	15	23
Stocking	20	28
Management other than stocking	35	24
Fact-finding	15	13

To approach the suggested model, increased emphasis appears most needed in management work other than stocking, nationally. Actual needs vary from state to state. Decreases in relative emphasis on law enforcement (except for checking licenses) and on stocking would be productive in most states. The adoption and/or development of more efficient hatchery techniques and stocking procedures could cut stocking costs materially without loss to fishing. Many states with little or no coldwater habitat could properly manage with as little as 5 per cent of the total outlay devoted to stocking. Eight "warmwater" states required less than 10 per cent for stocking in 1959. Over 40 per cent of the budget went for fish stocking in 15 states. Twelve states devoted less than 10 per cent of their expenditures to management activities other than stocking. This would indicate either that they enjoy "near-perfect" fishing conditions (doubtful); little water to manage (possible); or that there is serious siphoning of fishery revenues to other conservation agency activities (also possible). Many states could profitably increase their efforts to acquire and develop public access sites, rehabilitate "unbalanced" waters, construct new fishing lakes near urban centers, and control fish populations in existing large waters.

What the fishery agencies are actually doing to maintain, improve, and create fishing opportunities in their efforts to keep pace both with growing fishing "demand" and to adjust to changing environmental conditions for fish resources—due largely to rapid man-induced changes brought on by pressures of growing population and industrialization, and to a minor extent by slow natural climatic changes—is discussed in the following pages. At the same time, some of the problems and challenges confronting fish conservationists are also discussed. This is preceded by a thumbnail sketch of the function of the fishery biologist

* Stroud, R. H. & R. M. Jenkins. 1960. Fish Conservation Highlights, 1957-1959. Sport Fishing Institute, Washington, D. C. (May.) 44 pp.

(adapted in part from an article written by the late Gordon MacQuarrie, originator of the *Milwaukee Journal's* Outdoor Page, and prominent Wisconsin outdoor writer for two decades),* and a brief summary of the role of the Dingell-Johnson program.

THE FISHERY BIOLOGIST

Yesterday's fisherman got his information about coming seasons from a whiskered old guide who lived a quaint and smoky life back in the cutover. This oracle of the gurgling pipe was an eminent figure of his time. He tested the thickness of muskrat houses and peeled onions in the dark of the moon to forecast weather. A few of them are still around, but not too many. Those that persist are often synthetic, self-made characters upholding an old tradition for the sake of local color. His kind began disappearing as long as 20 years ago when bright young men with university training began getting interested in fish and game.

So it goes in a world of change and progress. The old giveth 'way before the new. The prophet with the whiskers and the gurgling corncob did give something to the world—but not much, except humor. The changing scene of conservation requires trained eyes to prescribe for it. Twenty years ago the word "biologist" was just becoming known in the picture of natural resources conservation, as the public saw it. It was in the 30's, too, when the prophetic old timers who quoted their grampaws began to assume less importance in what is a very scientific and complicated business.

As early as the 30's fishery biologists had learned many new things about fish management. Scientists at the Illinois Natural History Survey, for example, were upsetting old theories of fish management. They put the fish hatchery in its place, a subordinate place. They stressed management of habitat. They urged more hook and line pressure on public waters, less restrictions on sport fishing. These basic concepts had been crystallizing at the University of Michigan from the research conducted under Dr. Carl Hubbs by his bright young doctoral students such as R. W. Eschmeyer, Albert Hazzard, Clarence Tarzwell, and many others. Eschmeyer later directed an unparalleled sport fishery research program in TVA reservoirs that paid off in developing the new concept of year-round fishing for warmwater fish. It has since affected every state to some degree with the result that fishing opportunity across the U. S. nearly doubled. Later there came hundreds more fishery biologists who are going at the business of producing fish by methods undreamed of two decades ago. And yet, they often fail. But they expect it, as doctors expect to lose patients. Then again, they often succeed, gloriously.

* MacQuarrie, G. 1959. Here Come The Biologists. Wisconsin Academy Review (Fall). Wis. Acad. Sci., Arts, Letts, (Madison).

Take, for example, Wisconsin's Big Green Lake which provides lake trout fishing. Since the 90's, when they were first introduced in it, the lake trout have not been able to reproduce themselves successfully there. Fishery biologists in the Wisconsin Conservation Department figured out what was wrong and solved the problem. By skin diving, they learned that the lake bottom was muddy, with no rocks. Lake trout eggs fell to the smooth bottom and were being gulped by thousands of mud puppies. So, the biologists persuaded the Green Lake county board to dump thousands of tons of big rocks and little rocks into 80 feet of water. Thereafter, the lake trout eggs fell between the rock crevices where the mud puppies could not get them. Big Green is now reproducing lake trout; there is no further need to plant it. The biologists also remake fishing waters. Hundreds of them have been brought back to good fish production. Quite often, too, the biologists deflate pompous fishermen by proving that lakes and streams alleged to be "fished out" actually carry big populations of desirable sport fish. A classic example of this occurred in California. Under the direction of Dr. Paul R. Needham, the Trout in a California stream were counted where "nobody was catching any fish." In 10 sections of the stream he counted more than 24,000 Brown Trout of catchable size.

When fishery biologists first entered the conservation picture there was some resentment from some game wardens. It was natural, and it was expected. The game wardens watched them become important men in local communities, asked to speak before the luncheon clubs, too. Mostly, that human difficulty seems to have been resolved. The progressive wardens are now on the team—some of them more vehement than the trained biologists in sticking up for science against guesswork. Tragically, some have remained out of step. Despite the public scorn that is sometimes heaped on them—though less often as time passes—these new scientists just keep on plugging away. They like their jobs because they feel they are being useful; it is not so much a business with them as a way of life.

The biologists are constantly working uphill, against pre-fixed public notions of how fish should be managed. No one goes to a barbershop to have his appendix out, but when it comes to calling the shots on fishing everyone is an expert. Although they may have some public relations difficulties, the men recognize that public information programs are good allies. They work hard at this, with literature, movies, and lectures. It is a fact that, very often, after it has been thoroughly briefed, the public strings along with the biological approach. Half the battle lies in building confidence in this newer breed of conservation men. It takes a trained biologist to say "I don't know." It's only the rank-and-file of weekend anglers in their innocent ignorance who can have glib answers for nature's mysteries. The difference is that the biologist is equipped to find the answers—the average angler is not.

It is increasingly recognized that the word "conservation" involves a people-oriented concept of wise use of natural resources. As such, the fish resources become important principally as they serve mankind in some way. For many citizens, this means they are important principally as objects furnishing vitally needed outdoor recreation—sport fishing, for example. It also has increasing significance for a growing segment of business and industry. Obviously, then, fishery biologists exist primarily because they serve needs of people. The old idea that they were in business purely for the sake of the resource has had to give way to reality. Fishery biologists serve society's needs by studying the resource and applying constantly improved management practices (based on continually expanding knowledge) designed to bring about maximum sustained yields. This is the meaningful basis to people for the support of the fishing activity. This is why they pay license fees to finance needed conservation programs, including vital biological work.

It is clear that most people go fishing only if there is plenty of good fishing available. And it has become equally clear that good fishing no longer just happens—it must be created by the teamwork of fishery research and management biologists. Therefore, the welfare of biologists—key figures in the welfare of recreational fishing—should be of concern to businessmen, conservationists, and recreationists alike. One of the most important aspects of his welfare is the question of appropriate salary schedules. Fishery biologists, in effect, are administrators of fishery resources that are essential ingredients in the nation's most popular form of outdoor recreation—sport fishing. Therefore, it would seem valid to compare their salaries with those received by recognized recreation administrators. In this regard the 1958-1959 Annual Report of the California Recreation Commission (now Division of Recreation, Department of Natural Resources, Sacramento) is helpful. Average salaries for recreation administrators in California ranged from $5,964 in cities under 5,000 population to $13,068 in cities over 100,000 population. The average salary for recreation administrators in 289 counties, cities, and special recreation districts was $8,724. This was 65 per cent more than the average for fishery biologists. Yet, the latter administer sport fishing for units of population having an average size equivalent to cities of 180,000 population!

It is not surprising that professionally-trained and experienced biologists continue to desert the fish conservation field. "Dedication" and "deep interest" simply are not negotiable at the grocery store, in the doctor's office, or with the tax collector. Immediate salary increases must be made if the nation's fishery resources upon which angling depends are to be adequately maintained and improved. Governmental fishery management needs the same degree of scientific application today as is necessary in private business and industry. To achieve this goal, dedicated professional biologists who are qualified and competent to devise and implement sound fishery programs are required. However, it is becoming increasingly difficult to attract promising college students into the field when inducements in other science specialties appear so much more attractive. Prospective employment in private industry has been more financially rewarding to talented people than work in a governmental agency. A recent plotting of the number of D-J program employees against duration of employment on the job indicates a very rapid turnover of personnel. About half the workers stay on the same projects for one year. Only about 10 per cent have remained in a single state as long as five years. A strong conviction has developed that this rapid turnover is closely correlated with economic pressures resulting from low salaries.

In an effort to define reasons for recruitment and retention difficulties in state employment, New York's Governor Nelson Rockefeller authorized a study of salaries of state and private employees in comparable work. The survey (1961), conducted by McKinsey & Co., Inc., conclusively showed that the state's failure to keep pace with rising compensation in private employment is at the core of the problem. Biological positions were included in the "bench mark" categories used in the McKinsey study, and comparison showed that starting state salaries were at least 20 per cent below comparable private employment. In intermediate professional positions, state compensation was 27 per cent lower, and in the higher echelons, 34 per cent lower. Top-level state jobs were 63 per cent under similar positions in private employ. Fringe benefits were found to be equal in state and private employ in New York State. The McKinsey report recommended that salaries in the lower and middle grades be raised to equal those offered elsewhere. Higher state job holders should also be paid more, but somewhat less than in comparable private employment, due to intangible "but real non-cash inducements" resulting from added prestige, and "significant public service" opportunities available in top state positions.

In 1957, upon request of the American Fisheries Society, Sport Fishing Institute undertook to serve as an employment clearing house for fishery biologists. The Institute has developed and maintains a confidential register of fishery biologists seeking employment. Over 300 biologists have registered for the service wholly on their own initiative. That is equivalent to an average of six dissatisfied biologists per state. For the most part, the vast majority of registrants are seeking only added pay—in the minimum amount of about $1,500 annually. Significantly, too, about two-thirds indicate they can be enticed across state lines for as little as $1,000 more pay per year. It would appear, therefore, that the states have a great deal to gain by making an all-out effort to upgrade the salaries of professional fishery workers by about 30 per cent. It's a small price to pay to assure continuity of programs and to avoid the duplication in time and effort needed to "break in" new men over and over.

It seems incredible that one-fourth of the Nation's population would sit idly by and let their favorite means of recreation gradually deteriorate through this kind of default—if they understood the problem. It seems equally incredible that the multi-billion dollar outdoor recreational industries can sit idly by. For fishing's sake—there's a job to be done! It cannot be done unless salary scales are commensurate with qualifications and responsibilities. Good men cannot long be held, and needed well-qualified additions attracted to fish conservation, unless pay scales are increased substantially to bring them in line with comparable pay scales in other professions. The quality of future fishing may well hang in the balance of the decision!

THE DINGELL-JOHNSON PROGRAM

The Dingell-Johnson or D-J program (technically, Federal Aid in Fish Restoration), initiated in 1952, has played a highly significant role in stimulating the development of balanced state programs. It is a program which is nominally federal (administered by the U. S. Fish and Wildlife Service) but is actually run by the states, sometimes with too little federal supervision if anything. The states plan and execute the fishery projects involved and spend the money. The funds themselves are derived from a 10 per cent federal excise tax levied on manufacture of fishing rods, reels and creels, and artificial baits, flies and lures. Fishing tackle manufacturers serve as Uncle Sam's tax collectors in this case, and they continue to support the program because the results in terms of improved fishing are substantial and because their customers want it! The funds are earmarked for distribution by formula to the states on a three (federal) for one (state) dollar-matching basis. They are then used by the state fish and game departments for approved sport fishery research and development activities. Such activities as law enforcement, education, and maintenance fish stocking are not approvable for D-J financing under the terms of the Act. In addition—a vital feature—no state can qualify for aid monies unless it has an inviolate dedicated conservation fund. If diversions from the fund to non-related purposes are made, no further aid will be forthcoming until rectified.

This is a tremendously important program for fishing; most states lacked modern fishery programs before its advent. Sport fishermen have bought big improvements in fishing opportunities through these funds. During 1962, the states and territories had over $7 million available for obligation under the program, with well over $1 million of this representing carry-over of unobligated monies from previous years. Excise tax receipts for 1962 amounted to more than $6 million, forecasting continuance of an upward trend in apportionments.

Most of the 154 research studies approved during 1961 were involved in some way with the improvement of known management techniques and practices or solving problems of limited scope. Determination of fishing pressures and rate of harvest, and general surveys and inventories were also stressed. Interest in and concern for marine sport fisheries continued. Fourteen states and territories studied various aspects of this important segment of their sport fishing resource. These studies involved harvest, food habits, age and growth, spawning, and migration of Weakfish, Fluke, Bluefish, Porgy, and Striped Bass of the East Coast, and Sturgeon, Barracuda, White Sea Bass, Rockfishes, Yellowtail, and Striped Bass of the West Coast. The effects of artificial reefs constructed in coastal waters were studied by two states.

In the initial decade of the program, 45 per cent of the funds have been invested in research, with 200 technical and 1,000 popular reports of findings

TABLE 3. SUMMARY OF NET OBLIGATIONS OF FEDERAL AID IN FISH RESTORATION

Fiscal	Surveys and Investigations		Land Acquisition		Development		Coordination		
Year	Amount	Percentage	Amount	Percentage	Amount	Percentage	Amount	Percentage	Total
1952	$ 945,912	63.1	$ 43,897	2.9	$ 360,668	24.0	$ 149,387	10.0	$ 1,499,863
1953	1,313,188	44.3	259,721	8.8	1,225,860	41.3	165,454	5.6	2,964,223
1954	1,796,311	50.4	266,163	7.5	1,279,002	35.9	219,541	6.2	3,561,017
1955	1,921,761	41.0	353,105	7.5	2,196,387	46.8	220,701	4.7	4,691,955
1956	2,041,601	45.2	782,591	17.3	1,466,675	32.4	229,726	5.1	4,520,592
1957	2,103,830	38.7	493,388	9.1	2,532,743	46.6	304,782	5.6	5,434,742
1958	1,943,374	43.6	353,928	7.9	1,930,656	43.3	225,989	5.2	4,453,947
1959	2,115,141	45.9	450,697	9.8	1,729,058	37.7	305,427	6.6	4,600,323
1960	2,355,491	48.7	675,483	13.9	1,483,469	30.6	326,927	6.8	4,841,371
1961	2,762,817	47.7	536,710	9.3	2,143,821	37.0	346,963	6.0	5,790,311
Total	$19,299,425	45.6	$4,215,683	9.9	$16,348,338	38.6	$2,494,898	5.9	$42,358,344*

* Plus revisions to the U. S. Fish and Wildlife Service required to be used for research amounting to $461,534, bringing grand total to $42,819,878 during first 10 years (state matching funds amounted to $14,273,293 additional)

resulting. The control of fish population composition was approached by many states in different ways. Tests of rotenone compounds to determine if they become selective at certain concentrations, the screening of hundreds of chemicals in the search for "species-selective" compounds, the experimental testing of methods for producing pan fish that are of one sex or are sterile in the interest of preventing overpopulation, the testing of the efficiency and selectivity of trapping and netting, the fluctuation of water levels to destroy rough fish spawn, the mechanical destruction of spawn; these and many others were covered. Hatchery production was continually being studied to increase the efficiency of its methods and the quality of its products. Through development of a compressed-air feeder, feeding has not only been greatly simplified but also has been made less wasteful of feed. Through diet additives, Trout can be grown that are almost indistinguishable from Wild Trout with respect to coloration and "wildness." Through further marking and recovery studies, the best return to the fishermen can be assured by selecting stocking times, and the species and sizes of fish most suitable to the waters to be stocked.

Of all funds obligated in the 1952-1961 period, 38 per cent has gone for development, approved for a wide variety of projects. Rehabilitation of lake and stream fisheries through the use of fish intoxicants has been increasingly emphasized, with 225,000 acres of lakes and 2,500 miles of streams restored to good fishing. Complete rehabilitation of waters having undesirable fish populations continued as one of management's most effective tools. Modification of rotenone application techniques and decreased concentrations permitted reduction of gizzard shad populations without harm to game fish populations. This practice was in use in many states; much of the developmental work was conducted under the D-J program.

Acquisition of land, an essential part of many lake construction programs, to acquire lake basin and watershed areas, and in providing fishermen access to lakes, streams, and marine waters, obligated approximately 10 per cent of all funds. During the first 10 years of the program 37 states constructed 160 fishing lakes comprising 21,043 surface acres of water using these federal aid funds. In addition, 28 states used D-J funds to purchase and develop 632 sites for public fishing access to existing waters. These developments opened up or augmented accessibility to 2,177,800 acres of lakes and reservoirs and to 1,297 miles of streams.

In other activities to develop or improve fishing opportunities, 16 states improved 670 miles of streams for fish life (mostly Trout) by emplacement of channel or bank modifications. Eleven states erected 60 barrier screens to prevent extensive fish losses principally of anadromous fishes, and four states constructed 65 fish passage facilities for Salmon and Steelhead Trout.

The program has been a superior one for getting things done. A certain amount of administration and supervision is obviously necessary to assure that fact. Therefore, the authorizing act allows for administrative expenditures up to 8 per cent by the federal government—but it has hovered around 6 per cent since the outset. The states, themselves, have devoted 5.8 per cent of their total obligations for the first program decade to "coordination" (essentially administration). The record has been outstanding in this regard. Further details of the program, and the full significance of its impact on state programs, will become evident in the pages that follow.

MANAGEMENT OF THE RESOURCE BASE

There is only one purpose for fish conservation program expenditures—to maintain, improve, and expand fishing opportunity. Administrators are needed simply because some orderly method of making decisions and fueling the conservation machinery is needed. Out of a wide panorama of possible approaches to objectives, a selection or selections must be made. Organizational patterns must be established, personnel selected and put to work, supplies and equipment secured and maintained, emphasis of expenditures determined and controlled within budgetary limits, licensing handled and federal requirements met to secure needed revenues, efforts properly coordinated among program phases, etc. The commission (which sets policy) must have agenda prepared, be supplied with staff papers summarizing available information bearing on policy questions, etc. This is an extremely important part of fish conservation and how well the administration is handled can make the difference between good and poor fishing. This requires that capable administrators be employed, preferably able resource specialists with demonstrated administrative capacity as well.

Administration. About eight per cent of national fish conservation expenditures are invested in administration. In all probability, including needed upgrading in salaries to assure employment and retention of the best available men, about 10 per cent should be invested in this vital function. In a talk at the 1959 annual convention of the Izaak Walton League of America in Philadelphia, Missouri Conservation Commission Director William E. Towell outlined three major responsibilities that must be met by conservation agencies if they are to keep pace with the growing demand for recreational fishing. The three agency responsibilities identified and discussed are:

1. They must work for legislative recognition of the importance of recreational use of water resources.

2. They must work to bring a halt to pollution of streams and lakes.

3. They must work to give the public access to our streams and lakes.

There is no question that these are among the major responsibilities confronting conservation agencies. In addition, these two additional items of equal importance must be added to round out the list of objectives that administrators must keep constantly in focus if they are to meet the challenge of fishing demand:

4. They must work to encourage improvement of professional standards among fishery (and game) workers, including establishment of adequate pay scales to retain well qualified employees and to attract needed new ones.

5. They must work to increase the quantity and quality of research, the fountainhead of fish (and game) management.

Usually operating, for purposes of administrative efficiency, as staff to the chief conservation administrative officer (director), who generally has responsibilities for game as well as fish resources, are the functions of information-education and law enforcement. At the same time, it must be remembered that these are not ends of themselves, but merely means to the ultimate over-all responsibility and goal of producing good fishing (and hunting). In proper perspective they are to be seen as tools of resource husbandry, nothing more. At times, unfortunately, there is a tendency for these functions to get out of hand and obscure their real purpose as some of the many tools of resource management. Although these functions will be discussed separately, in the context of their rolls as tools of management, it is not unrealistic to view these functions as a part of general administrative overhead—collectively, absorbing some 35 per cent of the national budget in non-productive (directly of fishing opportunity) overhead. This is probably too much and should and can be reduced to a maximum of about 30 per cent, with most of the reduction in law enforcement expense, though not in essential activities. A good job of fishery administration is closely dependent upon doing a good job of continually informing the public on the nature of fishery programs, and the reasons for them, and upon enforcement of the licensing requirements to assure needed revenues to finance the programs as well as enforcement of any laws and regulations for proper management of fish populations and habitat.

Good administration cannot occur without the cooperation both of the sportsmen who foot the bills and for whom the work is done, and of the agency employees. It is part of the job of administration to assure a good climate for productive work by promoting this cooperative atmosphere, a matter in which the information-education and law enforcement functions are important aids. This cooperation, in turn, depends upon an understanding of their responsibilities by the various groups. For one thing, good administration will see to it that there is an active in-service training and orientation program which provides periodic opportunities for non-biologists to acquire thorough understanding of the fish management program and the reasons behind it. Most states now have such programs, many of them of high quality. At the same time, the good administration sees to it that the in-service training is reciprocal, and that biologists acquire needed insight into the vital people factors that exercise strong influences over the working climate for professional conservationists. For example, Robert L. Jones, Special Resource Projects Director, California Department of Fish and Game, and one of the nation's outstanding conservation administrators, thoroughly appreciates that there is one species about which no one has ever been able to learn enough—people. In a talk he delivered at the Humboldt State College he stressed the need for human understanding by fish and game workers. He put it this way:

"An effort to understand, not to argue, not to shout down, but to *understand,* can often resolve seemingly basic differences.

"People aren't impressed by impersonal statistics, by research data and graphs and charts and tables thrown at them by even the most earnest young wildlife technician.

"They're all from Missouri.

"You have to *show* them!

"But you have to show them in terms of their own experience, in terms of the things they actually know and think about.

"You have to answer questions that are worrying *them,* not the ones that seem most important to you.

"Sometimes their questions may seem irrelevant, way off base, completely unreasonable.

"Answer them anyway.

"Answer them carefully. They're the things that are really bothering people, the things they feel strongly about. And until you've shown respect and consideration for those feelings, everything else you say, your most closely planned logical argument, is a waste of breath.

"You must have people's confidence before you can have their cooperation."

Sportsmen also have responsibilities that contribute toward good administration, although these are not universally recognized or agreed upon by them. Nevertheless, many years of activity by organized sportsmen have revealed areas of strength where they can take effective, responsible action to help the cause of good fishing. Areas of weakness and ineffectiveness have also been revealed, where sportsmen can do comparatively little by themselves but where they must recognize their dependence upon professional conservationists. For example, in an address at an Annual Convention of the Michigan United Conservation Clubs, then Interior Department Assistant Secretary Ross Leffler outlined his concept of the responsibilities of organized sportsmen. They seem equally applicable to the unaffiliated sportsmen, as well. They may be summarized from his talk about as follows:

1. Sportsmen must at all times avoid the local, selfish special interest point of view and give strong support only to those projects which are objectively geared to sound management use of the resources. For example, they should not ask for an expansion of a fish hatchery program for an expensive put-and-take operation when the money can be more effectively used for habitat improvement.

2. Sportsmen should seek and then follow the advice of the professional conservationists who have been hired for the specific task of providing sound management of these resources. Though scientific knowledge is required, we occasionally let the loudest lay "experts" unwisely influence the course of our programs.

3. Sportsmen must—once a program course has been established by the professional leadership—go out and fight the battle to get the necessary legislation and funds to fully implement it. Many states are on the ball in getting license fees in line with program needs; others, unfortunately, are making little or no progress.

4. Sportsmen must endorse and push an all-out conservation education effort by all agencies. This is because the entire conservation program can succeed only with public understanding and support.

Information-Education. About 4 per cent of the national fish conservation expenditure is invested in information-education programs. Probably this should be somewhat increased—to about 5 per cent of the budgets. Statewide dissemination of information on fish conservation fundamentals, fish management problems, fishery potential, economic importance of fishing, angling methods, and problems of water-use conflicts is prerequisite to successful application of a modern fishery program. Essential elements include the willingness of the professional fishery biologists as well as the I&E staff members to make numerous talks before sporting and civic groups throughout the state, and periodic statewide releases to news media. Frequent "show-me" population sampling demonstrations should be arranged for outdoor writers, and recreation and civic leaders. Most states now support a recognized conservation education program, with 44 states publishing a conservation or fish and game magazine. Unfortunately, a half dozen of these are issued too infrequently to be significant. The rapidity of progress which can be expected in bringing about improved fishing by means of an up-to-date fish conservation program depends largely on the scope and effectiveness of the education program. If the latter is weak, progress will be slower than would otherwise be possible.

By whatever means employed, it is essential that the public be kept thoroughly informed about the program, its objectives, progress, and results. The basic concepts underlying the fish conservation program need to be "sold" to the public if a reasonably sympathetic attitude is to prevail. Nationwide experience suggests that these six concepts should form the basis for the education effort:

1. A lake or stream is really an aquatic pasture. We must take the same rational viewpoint toward the production of crops in our waters that we take toward production on the land. (For many years we were rational about our land pastures, but expected our aquatic "pastures" to produce miracles.

2. Angling today is for relaxation, not primarily for "meat." (With present human populations, and the resultant heavy fishing pressure, some waters can no longer provide the anglers with large quantities of meat. But, they can furnish many man-days of healthful, badly needed relaxation. Admittedly, taking home some evidence of success will continue to be important, but the emphasis must be on the enjoyment of fishing. If "meat" is all that is wanted, it can be bought at the corner store more cheaply than it can be caught by angling.)

3. Fish conservation has become a complicated science; we must rely on the trained specialist in the same way that we rely on professionals in medicine, law, engineering, dentistry and other fields. (Fish conservation is a relatively new science; we still lack many of the answers and we sometimes make mistakes. However, we rely on the physician even though he can't cure some ailments and even though he makes errors in diagnosis.)

4. Water areas have a limited capacity to produce fish. Even under the best of conditions, the water cannot be half fish, as many folks firmly believe it should be.

5. Only a part of the possible production of water areas is made up by the kinds or sizes of fish that are suitable or desirable for fishing. This varies widely with the species involved, the state of balance, and other factors.

6. Of the portion of the fish population attractive to anglers, only a fraction can be harvested with hook and line. Again, there is a wide range of variability, depending on a number of factors.

An understanding of many other items on the part of the public will also be helpful to the cause of improved fishing. The first three listed above would seem to provide a sound base that must be developed at the outset. As the program develops, the last three items become increasingly significant and must eventually generate statewide understanding if modern fish conservation is to be established and improved fishing result.

Establishment of a continuing, coordinated information-education program is in the interest of the general public, not just the anglers who would actually be paying for it. An important segment of each state's economy would be greatly benefitted by the improved fishing which a sound educational effort could help to generate. There is little question that if fishing were twice as good, additional millions of dollars worth of business would be generated. National surveys indicate that fishing generates an average of nearly 60 million dollars of business activity per state each year. Presumably, if fishing were substantially better, much more money would be spent. To a decided degree, the rapidity and permanence with which fishing can be improved is dependent on the receptiveness of the angling public to a modern fish program and to its continued support. This attitude can be developed and maintained only through continuing sound education.

The more progressive states in the field of fish management also seem to have more extensive educational programs. Several of these already devote as much as the recommended 5 per cent of their budgets to this work, including publication of a monthly magazine in which articles on all phases of conservation are published. A number of states have magazines with circulations exceeding 60,000 paid subscriptions, although the average is between 30,000 and 40,000 and increasing. Readership is several times the paid circulation, usually estimated to be four-fold circulation. Some of these magazines have 40 pages or more per monthly issue; the average number of pages is about 32. In most magazines no paid advertising is accepted because this often leads to bias in writing that defeats the basic educational objectives. This tendency is readily apparent where paid advertising is the principal source of financial support for the magazine, thereby rendering its educational value minimal. Magazines were distributed free by about half the states and by the rest for fees of 50¢ to $2, intended to help defray costs rather than render the magazines self-supporting. The per cent of state population receiving conservation magazines ranged from 0.7 per cent to 3.3 per cent. Staff members concerned with publication ranged from one to eight with an average between three and four. Cost per copy ranges from 2¢ to 27¢, averaging 10 to 15 cents.

At least 5 per cent of the total fish and game budget should be allotted to education, including publication of a suitable magazine, issued on a monthly schedule. No doubt, the money could be found out of increased revenues derived from license sales. Part of it might be obtained from economies effected from cutbacks that could be imposed on some of the less justifiable activities of the division as they become revised. It must be remembered, too, that a magazine would benefit all phases of the conservation program. Another possible solution to this very important problem is for a state sportsmen's group to publish a magazine, at least until the division or department can establish such a program in its budget. This has been done in several states. A few examples of helpful publications in this class have been: *Illinois Wildlife, Indiana Conservation,* and *The Kansas Sportsman.* Kansas has a state quarterly but most quarterlies are of too infrequent appearance to do an effective job. These three publications, and other similar ones, carry much valuable conservation education material. While they have the disadvantage of needing considerable advertising support, they are extremely helpful, especially in the absence of an official state counterpart issued regularly, at least bi-monthly and preferably monthly.

It is extremely important that there be close liaison and good working relations between I&E personnel and the professional fishery biologists and their staffs. Many I&E people are trained in journalism rather than in biology, although some of the outstanding men in the field were fishery biologists who saw a need in information-education work for people with extensive resource backgrounds and responded to the challenge. In any event, I&E personnel should participate in fishery work in the water under professional guidance at every opportunity in order to gain thorough understanding and thereby become better equipped to tell what's going on and why. Similarly, fishery biologists have a responsibility to participate directly in contacting the public through personal talks to organized groups about the work they are undertaking. The essential thing is that the fishery biologists must work actively with the communications specialists in conveying conservation knowledge to the public. The most important objective may be to generate public confidence in the sincerity and capability of the biologists handling the program. In any event, the means must not become confused with the end; the task is not one of informing people, rather it is essentially one of managing the physical natural resources themselves. Failing this, it will prove impossible to cope with mounting recreational demands against a backdrop of drastic continuing changes in land and water use.

Law Enforcement and Regulations. About 23 per cent of nationwide fish conservation expenditures are absorbed in law enforcement functions. Some states, where filling of enforcement positions is still part of the political patronage system, spend more than 50 per cent of available conservation funds for this purpose—and get very little in return for it. Ideally, this could be and should be reduced to about 15 per cent of the annual budgets. In this day of liberalized fishing, which affects virtually every state in one way or another, the validity of big outlays for law enforcement in fish conservation is open to serious question. With a few obvious exceptions, needs for strict law enforcement of the old style have diminished nearly to the vanishing point. There is a continuing need for enforcement of anti-pollution and certain other laws. There is an obvious vital need to check licenses to assure that anglers buy them regularly. New Mexico reported checking at least 10 per cent of license holders annually, a proportion that should be an effective deterrent to fishing without a license! In essence, this activity boils down to a special sort of fund-raising routine, and any expenditure for the latter function which exceeds five to seven cents on the dollar would seem excessive in view of the legal pressure. *Nation's Business* (March, 1956), for example, reported that all expenses for local fund-raising campaigns (such as enforcement of license buying requirements actually represents) should run between five and seven per cent of the goal to be reached.

This does not imply that there should be wholesale dumping of members of state warden or conservation officer forces. It does imply that new duties should be given this force of potentially constructive conservation workers in many states—especially in the information-education field and in the more routine management study phases of fact-finding—all under appropriate professional supervision and direction, of course. This would necessitate establishing intensive new in-service training programs in many states. It would also mean a redrafting of qualifications at a semi-professional level for new conservation officers. It may be expected, under such circumstances, that conservation officers could then contribute much more effectively to "shortening the time between bites." Some progressive states are well along this route already. Whereas, not too many years ago a game warden was often regarded strictly as a law enforcement agent, by 1950 he was contributing substantially to general conservation programs in many states. Law enforcement is still an important part of his duties and will be in the foreseeable future. But, with fewer and less stringent laws regulating sportsmen's activities, his duties have been considerably broadened to help meet more recently recognized needs.

A good summary of present-day requirements was outlined a few years ago by Don L. Brown, Chief Law Enforcement Officer, Montana Fish and Game Department. For example, 25 per cent of Montana's warden's duties had become concerned with fish and game management. This included creel census, game bag checks, game census, trapping and transplanting, range surveys, climatic and ecological observations, and fish planting. Another 25 per cent of the warden's time was spent on hunter safety training, conservation education, public contacts, speeches, sportsmen's meetings, radio and television appearances. Only 30 per cent of the state game warden's time was involved in enforcement of game law violations. This included investigations, apprehensions, and court procedure. Administrative duties took up 15 per cent of the total time. Included in this category was routine inspection of license dealers, game and fur farms, fish ponds, guides and outfitters, fur dealers, locker plants, as well as monthly reports, equipment and headquarter maintenance, and department meetings. Fur and game damage control took up the remainder. A Pennsylvania Fish Commission analysis revealed that about 42 per cent of a year's duty hours of its 56 fish wardens were devoted to stream patrol and law enforcement, 21 per cent to office routine and paper work, 20 per cent to special details—primarily game work—6 per cent to planting fish, 5 per cent to special investigations such as pollution, and 4 per cent to conservation education. Pennsylvania conducts annual two-week in-service technical training courses for fish wardens and trainees. Subjects include water chemistry, pollution problems, limnology, warmwater fishery management, fish culture, and the warden's role in lake and access area acquisition, construction and development.

In 1944, following less than a decade of research into various aspects of life histories and ecology, behavior, and population dynamics of the prominent sport fishes in the large multi-purpose reservoirs of the Tennessee Valley Authority—principally on 34,000-acre Norris Reservoir—all seasonal restrictions on the catch of game fish were removed. Formerly, the season had opened in late May, but in 1944 the closed season was eliminated and anglers could fish any time they chose—even during the spring spawning season of bass, which hitherto had been regarded as a sure-fire way to wipe out bass populations. This was the beginning of year-round fishing for warmwater sport fishes; the effect it had at Norris Reservoir was to double the fishing and the catch without harm to future supply. A reappraisal of fishing by TVA biologists 17 years later showed conclusively that fishing was just as good as it was in 1944 and better than in previous years for all species. In 1945, year-round fishing was extended to all 600,000 acres of TVA reservoirs and has continued without change ever since. After 1945, when both Nebraska and Ohio became the first states to establish year-round fishing, a number of other states quickly followed suit. The marked trend toward liberalized fishing has since spread to most states, although the changes were fairly gradual and, in most cases, have been based on careful study in each state. Today there is much less evidence of over-regulation and lack of logical uniformity than ever before. Fewer local exceptions, special closed waters, and complicated requirements now confront the nation's anglers.

Some of the northern states, with shorter growing seasons and relatively heavy fishing pressures, have been understandably cautious in adopting the new concept of liberalized fishing seasons for warmwater fish and have chosen to set up a series of test lakes to measure possible effects over a number of years. In some cases they have then opened their larger and/or more southerly waters, usually after preliminary findings have proved encouraging. For example, Wisconsin liberalized seasons and size limits for Bass in southern waters of the state in 1955, after encouraging results on test waters. In 1957 the state's fishery biologists reported that ten years of unrestricted angling had failed to "fish out" the Five Lakes liberalized fishing test group in Vilas County, Wisconsin. The wraps had been taken off, and fish of any size and species were permitted to be harvested the year-round. During the ensuing ten-year period, anglers fished 228,941 hours and removed 119,772 fish without harm to present or future fishing.

The largest lake in the group, 293-acre Escanaba Lake—equal to the combined area of the other four —yielded the most fish, with 84 per cent of fishing effort expended here. Altogether, 93,354 fish (78 per cent of the combined Five Lakes yield) were harvested at Escanaba. The main attraction was Walleyes, not present in the other lakes. Yellow Perch made up the vast bulk of fish taken in some years while Walleyes led in others. Bass were relatively common in the catch some years, less so in others. The catch of Smallmouths during the last three years of the decade was almost identical to the catch during the first three years. Muskellunge and pan fish made up the remainder of the catch. Fishing pressure varied from as low as 21.6 hours per acre to as high as 123.2 hours per acre. The annual yield of fish ranged from 9 pounds per acre up to 26.9 pounds per acre, and from 12.9 fish per acre to 48.3 fish per acre. The lake was opened to ice fishing, but this had little or no effect on open-water fishing. Only 6 per cent of the total fishing pressure involved ice fishing and 91 per cent of that took place on Escanaba Lake. Ice fishing harvest amounted to only 14 per cent of the total yield of fish to anglers.

The fishery biologists in charge of the Five-Lakes research had merely verified for these Wisconsin waters what half to three-fourths of all the states (depending on the kinds of fish involved) had already learned, namely that such lakes are in no danger of being "fished out" under liberalized angling regulations. Furthermore, through mark-and-recapture studies they determined that the fish populations were essentially similar after ten years of liberalized fishing to those present before the study began. Thanks to research such as this, Wisconsin and other northern states can now afford to move ahead more rapidly. The esssential provision to make this possible is to place chief reliance on biology in the fish conservation program. Otherwise, the anglers who "pay the freight" will lose out for many more years on about half the recreational opportunity that is rightfully theirs . . .

By 1960, at least 34 states had adopted liberalized fishing seasons (spring fishing or year-round fishing) for Bass on all or most of their waters, and several more were seriously considering its adoption statewide or on selected waters. A few states differentiated between Largemouth Bass and Smallmouth Bass in this respect. For example, Missouri applied some closed season restrictions on Smallmouth Bass streams, although the biological necessity for this is open to question. In all, 15 states maintained closed seasons of varying length on Bass, primarily for Smallmouths, although several of these were on the verge of liberalization. Alaska was the only state in the Union which had no Bass within its borders. Thirty-four states also did not impose length limits, while 15 still enforced minimum size restrictions. Five states imposed seasons but no size limits; five states reversed it. Creel limits were maintained on Bass by 46 states; only Ohio, Washington, and Wyoming had no creel restrictions on Bass.

Widespread liberalization of regulations pertaining to the pan-sized "bread-and-butter" species had occurred. Four states—Maine, Massachusetts, Vermont and Washington—continued to impose seasonal limitations on pan fishes (Bluegills and other Sunfish, Rock Bass, Crappies, Perch, etc.). Maine's closed season involved White Perch. In Massachusetts the closed season was largely academic; fishing was prohibited largely to protect planted catchable Trout until opening day. Vermont's season involved Smelt only. Special season regulations by counties governed pan fish in Washington; Indiana, South Dakota, and Wyoming also had some local exceptions to year-round pan-fish angling. Alaska had no laws restricting take of pan fishes. No state now imposes length limits on pan fish. Nineteen states had creel limits, but nearly all were very liberal.

Two-thirds of the states permitted year-round fishing for most other warmwater game fishes (Channel Catfish, Walleye, Pickerel, Muskies, Pike, etc.). Hawaii had none of these other warmwater game fishes. No length limits were imposed on such species as Channel Catfish, Walleye, White Bass, Sauger, and Pickerel by 37 states; however, creel limits are enforced on most of these species in over four-fifths of the states.

Forty-four states have Trout (Brook, Brown, Rainbow) in sufficient quantity to warrant regulation. Ten of these states now permit virtual year-round fishing for Trout, while closed seasons are maintained in 34 states, primarily to accommodate Trout stocking programs and procedures. Length limits have been removed by four additional states, bringing the total to 30 which impose no minimum size restriction on Trout. It is notable, too, that the Province of Ontario removed Trout size limits in 1960. Biologists of the Department of Lands and Forests cited the following reasons:

"Because of the large natural mortality, it is believed that trout should be harvested more liberally. In fishing for trout of a specific length, there is mutilation and loss when fish that are not long enough to be 'keepers' are returned to the water. The size and growth of trout varies considerably from lake to lake and stream to stream. Lifting of the size limit is expected to simplify enforcement."

Creel limits were imposed by all states except Ohio. This is an obviously necessary regulation in heavily-fished, put-and-take waters, where an effort is needed to spread out the harvest.

Restrictive regulations governing the non-game

(rough, coarse, or obnoxious) fish are rare. Only five states—Maine, Massachusetts, Pennsylvania, South Dakota and Vermont—now have closed seasons (during the Trout stocking period). Length limits are not imposed on non-game fish. Florida and Missouri have established creel limits on some non-game species, but they are liberal.

It appears that fish conservation is at the end of an era of time-honored, severe restrictions which were generally applied on an arbitrary basis without reference to biological fact. Principal restrictions requiring enforcement now involve: (1) creel limits on most all "game" fishes; (2) defined seasons on Trout and, in about 30 per cent of the states, on Bass and other game fish which occur in Trout waters. The strongest trend toward liberalization has involved elimination of seasons on Bass, panfish, and other warmwater game fish. Any further changes will probably occur at a somewhat slower rate, as state fishery personnel make more detailed studies both on the life histories of important sport fishes and on the fishing patterns and habits of anglers. There may be an increase in fishing-for-fun concepts applied to blue-ribbon Trout streams and possibly to the scarcer big game species such as Muskies (especially on the fringes of their natural range, where they are maintained artificially at great expense as publicity gimmicks).

FISH STOCKING

The earliest Chinese writers referred to fish hatching, some of them alleged to date around 2100 B.C.; one of the earliest Chinese books on the subject, *Classic of Fish Culture,* was published in 475 B.C. Twenty centuries later (1639), Paul Hsu recorded the association of fish in ponds in his *Complete Book of Agriculture.* Very little change was made in methods of propagating fish until early in the 18th century. During the period 1711 to 1784 Ludwig Jacobi of Westphalia observed the fertilization of Trout eggs during spawning and, on the basis of these observations, was able to impregnate Trout eggs artificially. This process of artificial insemination was reported on repeatedly through 1848, and it was used in England for the artificial propagation of Salmon. Early in the 19th century two illiterate fishermen, Joseph Rémy and Antoine Géhin, rediscovered the method of artificial insemination, and their activities were reported by Coste, professor of biology in the College of France, in 1849. Establishment of the first fish breeding station or "piscifactory" at Hüningen in 1850 stimulated the artificial insemination and propagation of various fishes in Europe and North America.

The results achieved by the French Government at the first hatchery in Hüningen drew public attention in France and England. Six or seven reports in rapid succession from these two countries led interested individuals in North America to look into the findings. Then, as now, the feeling was that Rémy and Géhin had hit upon a process superior to nature. The process was hailed as a method of bountifully stocking our streams with fish and "applied to all species of fish might become a source of great profit." W. H. Fry published, in 1854, *A Complete Treatise on Artificial Fish-Breeding,* which included translations of the French reports. In 1853 Dr. Thaddeus Garlick and Professor H. A. Ackley established the first fish farm near Cleveland, Ohio. The beginning of *public* fish culture in the United States occurred in 1856, when the General Court of Massachusetts appointed three commissioners "to ascertain . . . such facts respecting the artificial propagation of fish as may tend to show the practicability and expediency of introducing the same into the Commonwealth. . . ." By 1864 Seth Green had started the hatching of Trout at Mumford, New York, and independently perfected the "dry method" of fertilization developed by Atkins, which he reported on in 1874. In 1867, Seth Green succeeded in fertilizing and hatching *Shad eggs* in Massachusetts; he also propagated Lake Trout in 1870. The first Atlantic Salmon were hatched in 1868 in New Hampshire. In 1872, Maine, Massachusetts, Connecticut, and the U. S. Fish Commission built a joint "Salmon breeding" establishment on the Penobscot River at Bucksport, Maine. In 1873, two million Salmon eggs were fertilized on the McCloud River and shipped east to be introduced into various bodies of water. About 40,000 Shad were transported across the country from the Hudson River; 5,000 were planted in the Great Salt Lake in Utah and 35,000 in the Sacramento River at Tehama, California. The transfer of fish species to new waters all over the world had begun.

By 1870, hundreds of fish-cultural establishments were in existence. To "advance a correct knowledge of the best theory and practice of the science of fish-culture," the American Fish Culture Association was formed in that year (in 1884 the name was changed to the American Fisheries Society). On the recommendation of the American Fish Culture Association in 1872, along with that of the state commissions, Congress made an appropriation of $15,000—its first for such purpose—to stock rivers and lakes with useful food fishes. In 1897, the U. S. Fish Commission issued the first edition of its important *Manual of Fish Culture* as an Appendix to the Commission's Annual Report for that year. It was revised at least twice and for many years thereafter the 340-page third revision, issued in 1900 (with chapters on culture of various species by C. G. Atkins, F. M. Chamberlain, F. N. Clark, J. F. Ellis, H. F. Moore, W. F. Page, G. A. Seagle, L. Stone, J. J. Stranahan, S. G. Worth, and H. M. Smith), served as the definitive work on classical fish culture for both state and federal agencies. In recent years, a number of technological advances in diet, disease prophylaxis and treatment, and in mechanical apparatus for rearing and distributing hatchery fish have served only to refine the basic methods developed and used by these pioneer culturists.

By 1960, about 28 per cent of the states' fishery funds were being invested annually in fish stocking, with nearly four-fifths of the expenditures supporting the production, rearing, and planting of coldwater fishes, principally Trout (Brook, Brown, resident and migrant Rainbows, Lake Trout) and Salmon (Chinook, Silver, Kokanee, Landlocked and Atlantic). Warmwater fish stocking, once widespread and vigorous, has been greatly reduced since World War II, and chiefly confined in the more progressive states to situations and species compatable with demonstrated biological needs or utility. An abundance of biological research has shown for most species of fishes that natural reproduction is generally more than adequate to maintain supplies of fishes suited to the environment in question unless the water is overrun with competitor species that crowd out the desired species. Moreover, in the latter case, stocking with additional young of the same species has proved invariably futile. The numbers of fishes produced annually through natural reproduction is many, many times that produced artificially, except in the case of Trout. Facts show that, with the exception of Trout, the fisherman's success usually depends on the availability of naturally spawned fish. It is not necessary, therefore, to stock such fishes to "reseed" waters or to introduce "new blood." Varying quality of fishes depends, rather, on varying conditions of food supply and population density. Furthermore, repeated stocking of such fishes generally serves only to aggravate conditions of overpopulation, disease, etc. Fishery research has also shown that the introduction of fish in certain circumstances is desirable, and stocking is now known or believed to be practical only in the following instances:

1. To stock new waters or reclaimed waters subjected to natural or artificial catastrophes such as winterkill, drainage, etc.
2. To introduce new species where desirable into suitable waters.
3. To help restore population balances by introducing large numbers of large predatory fish ("concentration stocking"), or to make up for deficient spawning in a few instances in the presence of otherwise suitable habitat.
4. To stock catchable-sized Trout to provide Trout fishing in suitable ponds, lakes, or streams that lack facilities for reproduction, or survival of fingerlings, in order to maintain short-term yields at higher levels than the waters will naturally supply.

In 1960, the United States Fish and Wildlife Service issued a summarization of public fish culture in the United States through 1958.* It revealed that there were 482 state and 95 federal fish hatcheries and rearing stations in 1958, compared to 532 and 97 respectively in 1948. The states had decreased the number of their hatcheries by 10 per cent largely through consolidation of Trout facilities in more efficient plants and through reduction of warmwater facilities. The 577 units represented a combined capital investment amounting to \$50,614,000. The cost of operating this collective establishment in 1958 added up to \$17,652,000. The state hatcheries distributed a little over 13 million pounds of all kinds of fishes in all sizes. Federal hatcheries distributed a little under 2 million pounds. Thus the average over-all cost per pound of hatchery fish distributed was about \$1.17. (Natural mortality after distribution to fishing waters is very great; therefore, the ultimate true cost per pound of fish surviving to the creel is obscured by many factors, including the purpose to which the fish were put by fishery managers.) Nearly one billion individual fish were involved. Of these, nearly 550 million were fry, over 383 million were fingerlings, and less than 58 million were of "catchable" size (6 inches and more). At least 45 species of fish were being cultured although the really big production, nationally, was in Rainbow Trout, Chinook Salmon (over 100 million each), Brook Trout, Coho and Kokanee Salmon (over 20 million each) among coldwater fishes; and in Walleyes (over 450 million), Bluegills (nearly 70 million), Northern Pike and Largemouth Bass (near 35 million each) among warmwater fishes. Among coldwater fishes there was also significant production of Brown, Cutthroat, Steelhead, and Lake Trout and Chum and Sockeye Salmon; among warmwater fishes significant production also occurred among Channel Catfish, Muskellunge, Redear Sunfish, and forage fishes (all around 5 million each). Where large numbers are involved, fry and fingerling production accounts for a high proportion of production.

Most of the Salmon are produced at hatcheries built as partial mitigation for losses of natural spawning grounds due to construction of partially or wholly impassable high dams astride Salmon migrational routes in the Pacific Northwest. Their production is vitally important in helping maintain the reduced runs that have resulted from harnessing the rivers for hydroelectric power production and irrigation. The majority of Steelhead Trout production is used similarly. Most other Trout production goes for put-and-take stocking of catchables in heavily fished waters; fry and fingerling production is generally utilized for restocking chemically rehabilitated waters where good conditions prevail for rapid growth (reproduction lacking) to catchable sizes "on the house" (Mother Nature's), or periodic stocking of single species coldwater farm ponds. Most of these programs are justifiable and individual merits rest both with the cost-benefit ratios involved and with the more

* Hagen, W. & J. P. O'Connor. 1959. Public Fish Culture in the United States, 1958. Fish & Wildlife Circ. 58; 44 pp. U. S. Gov. Printing Office, Washington, D. C.

nearly wild type of Trout finally available for fishing. Most warmwater stocking is in the form of new introductions in artificial farm ponds or community fishing lakes (usually Bass and Bluegills or Redears and/or Channel Catfish), maintenance stocking of predator game fish in waters otherwise suited except for adequate spawning (Walleyes, Northern Pike), attempted introductions or maintenance stocking into various waters either for publicity values or attempted adjustments of predator-prey relations (Walleyes, Northerns, or Muskellunge), or to introduce needed but lacking forage species in order to shorten or improve the food chain for game fishes. Maintenance stocking with warmwater species such as Bass and various others, has virtually ceased almost everywhere on the part of responsible government agencies. Production of most other species by these agencies is negligible for specific limited purposes, or has been abandoned altogether. Hatchery operations for saltwater fish, once widely promoted by the old U. S. Fish Commission, were abandoned long ago. Whitefish production for stocking in the Great Lakes to support commercial fishing was abandoned midway between World Wars I and II when it was demonstrated beyond doubt that no correlation existed between extensive stocking of Whitefish fry and commercial catches of Whitefish at maturity.

Coldwater fishes. Intentional Trout breeding programs have been carried on vigorously in governmental and private hatcheries since the first Trout hatchery was operated on a production basis in 1865. The usual aims have been to produce Trout which grow faster, mature earlier, spawn earlier, produce more eggs, and are disease resistant. Unintentional selective breeding also occurs; Trout that are easier to handle, have a "nice shape," or grow better under hatchery conditions are often unconsciously selected by the fish culturist. Can such Trout, adapted to hatchery-trough living, be expected to prosper under relatively harsh natural conditions? A study of Brook Trout conducted by Robert E. Vincent at Cornell University indicated that they cannot.*

For experimental purposes Vincent chose domestic stock of Brook Trout which had been reared in hatcheries for 90 years, and wild stock from an isolated Adirondack Lake. These stocks were subjected to tests in troughs, streams, and lakes. Eggs from both stocks were reared under identical hatchery conditions, so that any differences observed would be due primarily to inherited characteristics; differences were noted by the fishery biologist while the Trout were still small. Offspring from wild stock were easily frigtened by a moving shadow or a hand in the water; however, domestic fish nipped at a submerged finger and showed almost no indication of fright. Domestic fish would dart at a spoonful of ground liver and bite off large mouthfuls; under the same conditions, the wild fish would retreat to the trough corners and not eat until the spoon was removed. At the end of one year in the hatchery the domestic Trout averaged 5.2 inches in length, compared to only 3.6 inches for the wild; this was attributed to the docile nature of the hatchery strain. Elaborate trough and aquarium tests devised by Vincent showed that wild Brook Trout could withstand higher water temperatures and greater concentrations of fish-body waste products in the water; they also displayed greater stamina in swimming against a current. The tests showed that the domestic Trout would typically move to the surface in a trough or aquarium, whereas the wild Trout would seek lower levels, and concealment if it was available.

Survival trials in a small stream and a pond indicated that wild fish experienced less mortality and similar or faster growth than domestic fish. After 73 days in a stream, 33 per cent of the wild stock survived, compared to 20 per cent of the domestic stock. After 108 days in a pond, 65 per cent of the wild fish remained, compared to 43 per cent of the domestic plant. Vincent concluded that selective breeding has produced a more economical hatchery fish with many desirable attributes. However, artificial selection has not improved wariness, fighting quality, alertness, and ability to survive in the wild after planting. Instead, it may have hindered or reduced these desired traits. The problem posed is complex, and affects directly or indirectly all those who fish for Trout—comprising nearly one-third of the freshwater anglers. Fishery workers are constantly striving to improve their Trout programs, to keep ahead of increasing demand for better fishing, and to provide a better return to the angler for each license dollar spent. If there were no Trout reared to catchable size and stocked, especially in the more populous regions, there would be little or no Trout angling in many areas.

With increasing frequency, biologically-sound and carefully executed Trout management programs, utilizing hatchery production, are producing excellent results, especially where natural spawning is inadequate or lakes have been reclaimed. For example, 290,000 sub-catchable Rainbow Trout were planted in 5,000-acre Crowley Lake, California, in the summer of 1960. During opening weekend, alone, of the following April, 19,000 anglers fishing from 4,500 boats caught over 72,000 (about 25%) of those Trout. The fish averaged 1.1 pounds, with the two-day harvest totalling 81,000 pounds. In fiscal year 1960, a total 171,276 fishing permit tags ($1 each) were sold in Missouri's four Trout parks—a 20 per cent increase over the previous year. To provide fishing, 428,285 Trout weighing 310,583 pounds were released in

* Vincent, R. E. 1960. Some Influences of domestication upon three stocks of brook trout (Salvelinus fontinalis Mitchell). Transactions of the American Fisheries Society, Vol. 89 (1):35-52.

the streams. Such stocking as this is justifiable on heavily-fished waters where a big percentage of the planted fish will be caught, and the program is financially self-supporting. Selectively-bred hatchery Trout are usually suited to this type of put-and-take fishing system. However, as biologist Vincent concluded from his studies, cited above, Trout free from selective breeding may prove more desirable if self-sustaining populations are to be established. Native Trout still provide the great majority of the catch on a national basis, as only about 40 million harvestable Trout are stocked each year from the production of state and federal hatcheries. Expenditures for all Trout rearing and stocking in U. S. public waters in 1960 probably exceeded $10,000,000, requiring up to 58 per cent of total annual fishery funds in the case of at least one "Trout-crazy" state.

Some of the most significant research on hatchery Trout was conducted by the late Professor Richard B. Miller, University of Alberta, while he served as Director of the Alberta Biological Station from 1950 to 1958. It centered on the major problem of Alberta Trout stream management—survival of hatchery-raised fish. Briefly stated, based on very carefully controlled experiments in certain sections of Gorge Creek, that were repeated many times to assure reliability of findings, these facts were demonstrated:

1. Summer mortality of hatchery-raised fish (Cutthroat, Brown, Rainbow, and Eastern Brook Trout) stocked in stream sections containing natural populations of wild fish varied from 42 to 66 per cent regardless of species involved.

2. The mortality was not caused by the experimental procedure.

3. Most of the mortality occurred in the first 10 to 14 days after planting, too soon to have been starvation. This led to the theory that "the fish died of exhaustion becuase the resident trout occupied all the resting places and forced the planted trout to stay in the open current."

4. In stream sections from which all wild Trout were removed, only 8 to 11 per cent of planted hatchery Trout died. This confirmed that it was the presence of wild Trout that was responsible for the poor survival of the hatchery Trout. It did not prove that exhaustion was the actual cause of death.

5. Blood samples taken several times each week from wild Trout, from hatchery Trout without competition, and from hatchery Trout with competition, were analyzed for lactic acid content (a good measure of fatigue from muscular exertion). It was found that the lactic acid was several times above normal in the hatchery Trout with competition, thus clinching the exhaustion theory.

6. Wild fish, transplanted to stream sections containing resident wild fish, did not *die* in significant numbers. Thus some fundamental difference between wild and hatchery fish was demonstrated.

7. Energy reserves (muscle and liver glycogen) were discovered to be only half as great in hatchery-raised Trout as in wild Trout.

Now, experiments are centered on the food problem. Already, although the experiments will have to be repeated many times using different diets and various ages of Trout and degrees of competition, preliminary results indicate that improved hatchery diets are helpful in creating higher energy reserves and greater resistance to fatigue. The old ground-meat hatchery diets are inadequate. Pelleted dry feed of a balanced bound cereal mixture producted a larger Trout of superior survival characteristics. It is believed that results of Dr. Miller's classic researches indicate that hatchery Trout diets may be successfully manipulated to produce vigorous Trout suitable for stream plantings.

One of the significant technological breakthroughs in hatchery production of the more common coldwater fishes has been the development of pelleted dry feeds, scientifically compounded to produce balanced diets. Much of the credit for the basic research on Trout nutrition that eventually led to this development belongs to scientists of the United States Fish and Wildlife Service working at the Service's experimental fish hatcheries. Great progress in this field has already been made and most hatcheries are using various types of pelleted dry feeds, either entirely or partly replacing former traditional wet feeds. Some of the more recent dry feeds have been fortified or enriched to reduce or eliminate much of the former necessity to feed liver in the diet. Advantages of the new enriched dry feeds for Trout, especially, are increased nutritional efficiency with reduced food costs, ease of handling, non-refrigerated storage, and reduced labor requirements. Quantities of food required have been more than halved in many instances with only about two pounds of food required to produce a pound of Trout. Not all experience has been satisfactory; Salmon and Lake Trout do not take well to the dry pellets, and Lake Trout are still dependent upon liver. For some still unknown reason, moreover, some Trout fed on dry feeds obtained from certain sources have developed a non-communicable, non-infectious tumorous-like disease called hepatoma. What the actual cause may be remains unknown, and while it is thought to be related to the presence of minute traces of foreign substances in the particular diet this has not been proven. Hepatoma had been observed in wild Trout earlier, and also found in other hatchery Trout, but never before on the scale recently observed in the affected hatcheries.

Over 100 fish diseases have been identified in hatcheries. Many of them have yielded to improved sanitation measures and use of modern drugs. The once-dreaded furunculosis—a wasting disease of the gills and other membranous areas—is readily controlled today. New diseases are continually being identified, and really excellent research is conducted in this field by the U. S. Fish and Wildlife Service scientists at their various disease laboratories.

An alarming report of a new epidemic was released in 1959 by the Oregon Fish Commission.* It should have been sobering to those gullible souls who think that downstream hatcheries are an easy and sure answer to the problem of maintaining declining anadromous fisheries cut off from ancestral spawning grounds by insurmountable high dams. That principal dependence upon hatcheries is far too slender a thread by which to support those fisheries above the abyss of extinction is underscored by the findings presented. According to the report, tuberculosis is salmonoid fishes was first observed in the 1952 run of fall Chinook Salmon returning to the Bonneville Hatchery of the Oregon Fish Commission. Tuberculosis was also found in adult spring Chinook and in Silver Salmon, Blueback Salmon, and in anadromous and resident Rainbow Trout. Advanced tuberculosis was found in salmonoid fishes held in fresh water for two years or longer, as well as in adults returning from the sea.

The disease was originally observed in sexually-underdeveloped fish, and there is indication that it interferes with sexual maturation. It was found that tuberculosis in marked Salmon known to be of hatchery origin was extremely high—in some cases 100 per cent. Tuberculosis was absent in the small number of Silver and Chum Salmon examined which were known to be progeny from natural spawning. Dissemination of the disease may be due to fish-cultural practices such as the feeding of untreated carcasses and the viscera from tuberculous fish. The disease may also be transmitted to healthy eggs during the process of fertilization. Tuberculous adult spring Chinook were found less capable of surviving to maturity after they reached the spawning grounds than were non-infected fish. It is likely that tuberculosis also influences the ability of Salmon to survive during earlier stages of their life history.

The incidence of tuberculosis in adult spring Chinook entering the Dexter holding ponds on the Middle Fork of the Willamette River in 1955 and 1956 was about 8 and 6 per cent, respectively. The increase in incidence to 58 per cent in 1957 is attributed to the increased dependency of the run on artificial propagation necessitated by the construction of Lookout Point Dam. Among Chinook caught in the Columbia River gill-net fishery in February and in May, 1956, some 12 and 10 per cent, respectively, of those examined were tubercular. Although these were spring Chinook, it is believed that hatchery-reared fall Chinook also entered the catch, especially during May, and may have contributed to the number of tuberculous fish taken.

Proper cost accounting is an important element of fish cultural operations, as in any other business enterprise. Some states have been reluctant to face up to the costs of their Trout stocking programs, while others have been leaders in this regard. New Hampshire has been reporting in detail on its costs for a number of years and for 1961 the state's fishery chief reported that the total cost per pound of 250,000 pounds of Trout and Salmon produced was $1.25. About 83 cents (66%) were attributed to personal services by hatchery personnel, 22 cents (18%) went for food, and 20 cents (16%) for plant maintenance and administration. Planting costs were 3-1/3 cents per pound additional. Landlocked Salmon and Lake Trout have a much higher cost index than do other salmonoids, with those species accounting for about 11,000 pounds (4.4%) of New Hampshire's total production. Similarly, Maine's hatchery superintendent reported that the 1961 cost per pound of Trout and Salmon (194,000 pounds produced) was $1.51. Maine's production included 28,000 pounds (14.4%) of the higher-cost landlocked Salmon and Lake Trout. Other larger states with somewhat warmer water and larger production units might expect to produce Trout at a somewhat lower cost, approximating $1.00 per pound.

Research on the fate of the hatchery products has led to some rather definite policy formulations to guide their use in fishery management, especially with respect to catchable-size Trout, embracing a wide range of considerations. In California, for example, catchable Trout are stocked only in those streams where fishing pressure is sufficient to recover at least 50 per cent of the planted fish. Other salient points dictate that (1) Trout production (excluding fingerlings) will be geared to stamp revenue from Trout anglers for the previous calendar year, and (2) requirements for sub-catchable-sized Trout shall have priority over catchable-sized Trout for put-and-take fishing. The Pennsylvania Fish Commission adheres to these minimum standards for inclusion of new streams on its Trout stocking list (which embraces a total of 4,373 miles of streams): (1) minimum continuous stretch open to public must be two miles, or (larger streams) one mile having minimum of four acres of surface area; (2) minimum average stream width (to June 15) must be at least 10 feet; (3) minimum volume of flow (to June 15) must not be less than two cubic feet per second; (4) maximum temperature (to June 15) must not exceed 74 degrees Fahrenheit; and (5) minimum pH must be at least 6.0. South Dakota takes a somewhat different approach, by means of a study of Trout population densities needed to achieve arbitrary standards of fishing success, as set for the Black Hills Lakes. The minimum standards set as goals of the Trout program there were an angling suc-

* Wood, J. W. and E. J. Ordal. 1959. Tuberculosis in Pacific Salmon and Steelhead Trout. Contribution No. 25, Oregon Fish Commission, Portland.

cess of one Trout for every two hours of fishing effort and a harvest of 75 per cent of the planted Trout.

A 31-month-long partial creel census at Iron Creek Lake and a six-month complete census at Victoria Lake provided a basis for evaluation of the South Dakota stocking policy. Collected data indicated that over 2½ hours were required to catch a Trout during summer angling in 1957. Harvest was 71 per cent during that summer but rose to 92 per cent for the entire year's population of stocked Trout. It was concluded that it was necessary to have three Trout present for each two hours of angling effort to provide an angler success of one Trout per two hours of angling. The anticipated angling pressure for 1958 was calculated at 16,100 hours. After making an estimate of the very small resident Trout population, enough legal-size fish were planted to make available three Trout for each two hours of angling. Evaluation of census data at the end of the 1958 summer phase placed the pressure at slightly over 16,600 hours, the rate of fishing success at just about 2 hours per Trout, and the harvest at 79 per cent. For Victoria Lake the study findings indicated that it would be necessary to have seven Trout present for each eight hours of angling effort to provide an angler success of one Trout per two hours of angling. In early May, at Victoria Lake, a population density of about 45 Trout per acre provided the desired level of angler success; in early August, about 220 Trout per acre were required to reach the goal.

Artificial propagation. Generally, the methods of fish culture used for Trout and Salmon are similar. Primarily, there are two means of securing eggs: adults may be taken in traps set at the time spawning runs of such anadromous species as Salmon and sea-run Trout occur, or brood fish may be reared in hatcheries for spawning purposes as with most of the Trouts. Pacific Salmon, unlike Atlantic Salmon, die after spawning. Therefore, these fish are captured as they come upstream from the ocean, killed, and the eggs collected in a suitable vessel after dissection. The spawntaker holds a ripe female brood Trout at such an angle that the eggs flow naturally toward the vent in response to slight pressure with thumb and forefinger on the belly. The eggs are taken in a moist spawning pan, and milt from a male is extruded over them in the same manner until a sufficient amount is available to fertilize the eggs; the contents of the pan are mixed (dry fertilization). A small amount of water is then added, and the vessel agitated; the excess milt is then washed off and the eggs are allowed to stand in water until they become "water-hardened." The water is then changed and the eggs transferred to the hatchery.

At the hatchery, a single layer of eggs is placed on a tray constructed of a wood or metal frame with a wire bottom, and the trays are submerged in troughs supplied with running water. Standard troughs are 14 feet long, 14 inches wide, and 8½ inches deep and are usually supplied with 8 to 12 gallons of water per minute; however, deep troughs with larger capacity are used at Salmon hatcheries and at some Trout hatcheries. Trays may be placed singly in the troughs or stacked two to eight deep (depending upon the quality of eggs, water, and type of trough) and adjusted so as to allow a gentle flow of water over the eggs, which must be kept clean. Dead eggs (which turn white) are removed daily except during the most delicate stages; if sediment accumulates too thickly, it must be removed, or the eggs will suffocate. From the first or second day after collection until the eye spots appear the eggs are very delicate and may be killed by jarring or rough handling. During this period only a minimum of cleaning is done.

The ideal hatching temperature for Trout eggs is in the neighborhood of 45° to 50° F. Temperatures above 50° are generally not recommended. At 45° F., Rainbow Trout eggs hatch in approximately 45 days, Brown Trout eggs in 63 days, Brook Trout eggs in 71 days, and Lake Trout eggs in 72 days. Generally, for each degree above 45° F. the hatching period is shortened 5 days and for each degree below this temperature the hatching period is prolonged 5 days. Temperatures below 40° (particularly if they approach 32°) may prolong the hatching period to such an extent that the fry may emerge in a greatly weakened condition. When the eggs hatch, the fish are referred to as sac-fry and are unable to swim because they are weighted down by the yolk. The yolk is the food supply for the fry and is gradually absorbed into the blood system in 24 to 50 days, depending upon the species and water temperature. The sac-fry have a tendency to congregate and may pile up and suffocate unless kept separated in small lots. In the late stages of yolk absorption the fry "swim up" in the water in search of food. By the time the yolk has been absorbed entirely, the fry are feeding freely under normal conditions.

The first food generally consists of beef liver or hearts ground into extremely fine particles. Like all very young animals, the fry are fed a number of times a day so that growth and health will be promoted. As the fry grow, they are given food ground to a coarser size. Liver is a relatively good diet and is fed until the fry reach about 2 inches in length when they are called "fingerlings." Liver is rather expensive so the diet is changed to a mixture of dry meals and meat products when the fish reach this size. This mixed diet is scientifically compounded to provide the proper levels of the protein factors, carbohydrates, and various vitamins required to keep fish healthy and to promote growth, and is fed increasingly in the form of dry pellets. A lack of any of the necessary food elements or vitamins results in weakened fish, making them susceptible to disease. Trout properly fed from the beginning are less subject to disease than Trout that receive improper care. They should be fed according to their size and in accordance with changes in water temperature. The ideal temperatures for rearing Trout lie between 55° and 60° F. Landlocked Salmon grow best at about 65° and Lake Trout grow best at about 50° F. The good hatchery manager uses very much the same husbandry methods applied in other fields of animal husbandry. Food is scientifically compounded to prevent anemia, dietary deficiencies, and disease. The fish are held in troughs and ponds with the proper flow of water, proper amount of space for growth, and watched carefully to detect the appearance of any disease. Prophylactic treatments with suitable chemicals may be given at regular intervals to prevent attacks by parasites or disease. Careful observation to detect any unusual actions or conditions is necessary so that disease can be identified early and treated with the proper drugs to prevent outbreaks of epidemics. Should disease appear, aseptic procedures are followed to prevent its spread from one lot of fish to the next.

Dr. C. M. McCay made the first fundamental studies on Trout nutrition in the 1920s and established in 1932 at Cortland, New York, the present nutrition laboratory operated cooperatively by the United States Fish and Wildlife Service and the New York State Conservation Department. At this laboratory were determined for the first time the various aspects of the mineral, protein, fat, carbohydrate and vitamin needs of Trout, with the current work being carried on most brilliantly by Dr. Arthur M. Phillips. Dr. H. S. Davis, recognized the world over for his contributions on fish disease, played an important part in developing fish culture on a scientific basis. In recent years, Dr. Stanislaus Snieszko and associates have made significant findings at the United States Fish and Wildlife Service's experimental fish hatchery and disease laboratory at Leetown, West Virginia. Probably the greatest initial impetus toward development of present-day fish culture was given by Dr. G. C. Embody, renowned fisheries professor at Cornell University. A large number of the country's leading fish culturists and biologists attended his course lectures and profited by his counsel and encouragement of their research both as graduate students at the University and later. In addition to his university courses in fish culture, Embody's ideas on and initiation of stream and lake surveys for the establishment of stocking policies stimulated widespread field investigations and inquiry into the efficacy of existing stocking practices.

Warmwater fishes. The emphasis on warmwater fish stocking, nationally, is somewhat over one-fourth that placed on coldwater fish stocking. Regional climatic differences have influenced this very strongly. Whereas coldwater fish stocking is heavily emphasized in the West (40% of fishery expenditures by 12 western states) and in the northeast (35% of fishery expenditures by 11 northeastern states), warmwater fish stocking is negligible in those areas (1% and 2%, respectively). On the other hand, over-all stocking emphasis in the North-Central (11 states) and Southern (13 states) regions is reduced at least half (20% and 17%, respectively) in deference to other equally or more useful fish management tools for the waters involved. In further contrast, warmwater fish stocking is more heavily emphasized than coldwater fish stocking in the North-Central states (13% of expenditures vs. 7%, respectively) and in the South (10% of fishery expenditures vs. 7°, respectively). Principal emphasis on warmwater fish stocking in the latter regions is related to strong emphasis on farm pond and community fishing lake construction, that typify these same regions in contrast to the rest of the country, coupled with extensive efforts at controlling the size and composition of non-sport fish populations which are especially abundant in the Mississippi River drainage basin.

To a large degree, warmwater fish production is geared to needs for initial stocking of new and renovated farm ponds and community fishing lakes. For the most part, this involves hatchery production of fingerling Largemouth Bass, Bluegills, Redear Sunfish, and Channel Catfish. Considerable emphasis is also placed on hatchery production of some of the larger species of predatory game fishes, especially Walleyes and, to a lesser extent, Northern Pike and Muskellunge. Small quantities of other species may also be cultured from time to time in various federal and state hatcheries, often for experimental planting in controlled experiments, occasionally for introductory plantings of desirable forage fishes needed to fill in vacant ecological niches in the food chain, or to shorten the food chain, and increase production of desirable game fishes. An outstanding example of the latter is the recent transitory culture and widespread transfer of Threadfin Shad—a direct converter of algae and other plankton to fish flesh and then to game fish. Minnows are widely cultured in private hatcheries, for sale as bait, and a significant bait industry has built up around this practice, especially in the big warmwater reservoir states of the great Plains area. Methods of culturing various species of Minnows for bait production are technically advanced and highly sophisticated.*

Since the late thirties much effort has gone into evaluating the utility of warmwater fish hatcheries as tools to permit maintenance stocking of warmwater streams, lakes, and reservoirs. Where adult warmwater fishes are present *and reproducing* naturally, the hatchery product has invariably proved useless at best, wasteful or, in some instances, even harmful through unwitting introduc-

* Dobie, J., O. L. Meehean & G. N. Washburn. 1948. Propagation of minnows and other bait species. Fish & Wildlife Circ. No. 12:pp. 1-113. U. S. Govt. Printing Office, Washington, D. C.

tion of diseases and parasites and undesirable species of fish as well. For example, inadvertent introduction of the usually undesirable Green Sunfish in many waters throughout the country was an incidental result of widespread interstate shipment of fish raised in federal hatcheries. This often resulted in displacement of the more desirable and larger species of Bluegills and Redear Sunfish, and rapid deterioration of fishing in the waters affected, and the ultimate necessity to undertake expensive corrective measures. Another unfortunate result was the widespread distribution of the Bass tapeworm into many waters where it was previously absent. This parasite adversely affects the reproductive organs and is aesthetically undesirable to the angler as well.

The fate of warmwater fish hatcheries for the purpose of promiscuous maintenance stocking was sealed for all practical considerations by findings of a most significant fishery research study conducted immediately prior to World War II. In a piece of excellent research on warmwater fish spawning at Deep Lake, Michigan, fishery biologist W. F. Carbine (under supervision of University of Michigan Professor Carl L. Hubbs) studied egg deposition and fry production in 648 fish nets. He sucked up the fry through glass tubes immediately after hatching and counted all those actually produced in nests of 32 Bluegills, Pumpkinseeds, Rock Bass, and Largemouth Bass. The average number of fry per nest was 17,914 Bluegills, 8,074 Pumpkinseeds, 796 Rock Bass, and 4,977 Largemouths, with upper extremes several times higher in some cases. From this it was calculated that spring spawning had produced an average of 559,500 fry *per acre!** Deep Lake is not an especially productive lake by most standards and could support only a few hundred adult fish of these species per acre. The conclusions were inescapable that Nature normally provides a tremendous surplus of baby fish, that the vast majority must die in order that a few may reach maturity and perpetuate their kind; adding a few hundred thousand more of the same kinds already present in great abundance could hardly increase the angler's catch. It became suddenly clear that more fish to be fed by the lake's food resources could only make things worse rather than better.

About 15 years later, striking confirmation of these conclusions came from another study under quite different circumstances. In this case drastic thinning of the fish population of 184-acre Ardmore City Lake, Oklahoma, in September, 1953, left an estimated 50 adult Black Crappies and White Crappies (combined) as a nucleus of a new population. State fishery workers conducted detailed population studies during the following two years to evaluate the effects of the thinning on reproduction and growth of these popular sport fishes. The combined reproduction of those 50 Crappies in 1954 resulted in an estimated *200,500* offspring, averaging 5.3 inches in length, and one ounce in weight, at the end of the first year. The Black Crappie standing crop equalled 49 pounds per acre and the White Crappie standing crop amounted to 24 pounds per acre. Details of this study, conducted by fishery biologist Robert M. Jenkins, were published in the Proceedings of the Oklahoma Academy of Science. The study clearly demonstrates the tremendous reproductive potential of these two species, and strongly emphasizes that stocking Crappies in lakes where they are already present is little short of stupid.

It has also become clear in recent years that some species have specialized requirements that prevent successful reproduction when their particular needs are lacking. Smallmouth Bass, for example, can spawn successfully and maintain themselves through natural reproduction only in those waters that are well supplied with gravel or rubble-covered shoal areas, either underlying thin silt deposits or already exposed. They generally fail to reproduce in strictly sand or mud-bottomed ponds, although some success has been claimed by some biologists on smooth firm bottoms when no other fish are present. Under such circumstances, however, introduction of Smallmouths is generally wasteful and should not be attempted in the first place. Many waters have scant supplies of aquatic vegetation and Chain Pickerel are and must be at low levels of abundance because of it. Pickerel need pond "weeds" for reproductive purposes. Inexpensive and effective means of controlling excessive weed growths are not yet available. Under conditions of weed scarcity, then, the proper course is not to attempt management of such waters for Pickerel by encouraging weed growths. Instead, management should generally be for another species which is adapted for natural reproduction under the prevailing conditions. If the proper species is not present, stocking to introduce the species is then a valid management tool. However, there are some cases where maintenance stocking of warmwater game fish is valid. That is where, as in the case of Walleyes in states like Minnesota, reproduction may not occur in otherwise suitable waters. The factor that makes such an operation feasible is the fact that Walleyes can be cultured with considerable success at relatively low cost using mass production methods to some extent that are not generally applicable to many other species.

Most states have abandoned their Smallmouth Bass hatcheries. Among the last to consider doing so is Arkansas. A news release, issued by the game and fish commission, discussed the reasons for limited Smallmouth production. Fishery Chief Andrew Hulsey reported that, compared to other hatchery-reared fish, Smallmouth Bass are too costly, require too much space, and have question-

* Carbine, W. F. 1939. Observations on the spawning habits of centrarchid fishes in Deep Lake, Oakland County, Michigan. Trans. No. Amer. Wildl. Conf., 4:277-287 (March).

able value for stocking. Smallmouths can't be fed inexpensive prepared commercial foods, as can Trout; but must have live food. This requires extensive and expensive Minnow rearing facilities; it costs about $10 to raise a Smallmouth up to one-pound size. Finally, Hulsey could find little evidence of actual value in Smallmouth stocking—unless it could be done on a put-and-take basis. At $10 per fish, this is regarded as being far too expensive under any conditions. However, before making a final decision about the apparently dim future of Smallmouth Bass stocking in Askansas, larger (4 to 9 inches) but fewer Smallmouths are being raised and their fate after release studied; at least part of all Smallmouths released are being tagged. Findings of the study will indicate whether any further hatchery rearing of Smallmouths is to be continued and to what extent.

There are many examples of field tests showing the fate of hatchery-reared Bass used for maintenance stocking, especially Largemouths. For example, a 30-acre New Jersey pond containing a "well-balanced" fish population (including an established population of Largemouth Bass) was stocking with 3,000 hatchery fingerling Largemouths in the fall of 1952. The following year, the pond was drained and virtually the entire fish population was recovered. Only one hatchery fish was recovered that had survived from the 3,000 stocked a year before. By contrast, there were 400 native yearling Bass, and 1,400 native young-of-the year, and only two months prior to drainage, 300 hatchery fingerlings had been stocked in addition. Yet, only 30 of these latter fish could be found at the time of the drainage.* The fate of Largemouth fingerlings introduced into existing fish populations previously containing no Bass is ample as a rule to provide for establishment of the species provided the environment is suitable. In the fall of 1952, the year's entire production of Largemouths at the Massachusetts Fisheries and Game Division's single Bass hatchery, numbering 27,500 fingerlings two to four inches in length, were stocked into a 47-acre drainable pond that was closed to public fishing. No other Bass were present. The pond had been drained, poisoned, and restocked the year before with a few Pickerel and Yellow Perch adults. Presumbaby, competition and predation were less than ordinarily encountered by newly stocked Bass fingerlings, and the supply of young fish for Bass food greater than usual. One year later, the pond was drained again, slowly to prevent stranding, and a recovery of 80 per cent or more of all fish present--about 114 pounds per acre—was believed probable under the circumstances. A total of 1,073 Largemouth Bass were recovered, of which 466 were 10 inches or longer. Assuming 80 per cent recovery, about 582 catchable Largemouths and 760 smaller Bass were present. Altogether, then, only about 1,342 Largemouths had survived the year under favorable conditions out of 27,500 originally stocked—5 per cent survival. Well over half of the survivors had not yet reached catchable size and needed to grow part or all of another season to become available to anglers—less those that would die from one cause or another. Even among Bass of catchable or near-catchable size, annual natural mortality is considerable. In the fall of 1950, 66 such Largemouths were tagged and released in other Massachusetts drainable ponds (about 90 acres), also closed to public fishing. When the ponds were drained two years later, 20 of the original fish were recovered (in this instance, recovery was believed to be virtually complete), so that an average of 45 per cent of the tagged fish had obviously died annually, in the two-year interval from one cause or another.* Ultimately, applying these mortality rates to the second year of life of the 760 sub-catchable Largemouths, only about 418 would survive the second year. In other words, only about 1,000 catchable-size Bass would result from the original hatchery planting of 27,500 fingerlings—spread over two years—less than 4 per cent. Statewide studies of angling harvest showed that anglers caught less than 15 per cent of available wild Largemouths. Thus only about 150 fish (about ½ of one per cent) would ever be caught. It cost about 16-2/3 cents apiece to produce the fingerlings at the hatchery; but, by the time the survivors are caught by anglers, they actually represent investments totalling in excess of $30 per fish on the stringer.

It is for reasons such as these that most states have closed most of their warmwater fish hatcheries. The more progressive states continue to operate the better designed, well-watered hatcheries of this type as research or fishery experiment stations. In this role they are commencing to make great contributions to improved fish management procedures, evaluate the specific effects of fishing pressure, experiment with regulations under controlled conditions, etc. Many sportsmen visiting a state fish hatchery have said more than once that it would be ideal to be able to fish *there!* For Virginia anglers it came to pass in 1961, when the state Game and Inland Fisheries Commission opened eight rearing ponds (3/4 to 1 acre each) at its Front Royal warmwater fish hatchery (Waterlick) to daily public fishing (except Mondays). The ponds were opened in a 3-year experiment designed to determine whether a minimum size limit on Bass should be recommended for farm ponds. During May of the second year (1962) of the experiment, the ponds supported an average of 131 anglers per acre who caught about 100 pounds of fish per acre (94% Bluegills, 6% Bass), averaging one fish per hour. Per acre the ponds received 359 hours of angling effort, and yielded 415 fish—

* Smith, R. F. 1954. Fishing the Delaware. Part I. New Jersey Outdoors, 4 (11):5-10 (June).

* Stroud, R. H. 1955. Fisheries Report (1951-1952). Mass. Div. Fish & Game, Boston, 447 pp. (May).

the high production resulting from fertilization. In addition to ponds where anglers are permitted to keep the fish they catch, two others were set up as "fish-for-fun" ponds, at which anglers are required to release back in the water the fish they catch. During the same three week, 129 anglers fished a total of 209 hours at the "fish-for-fun" ponds, and caught and released 575 fish including 337 Bass! It is an important corollary of the study and a truly golden opportunity to determine how important keeping the catch may be to the enjoyment of fishing—after the novelty of fishing in a hatchery wears off.

Yellow Perch hatcheries have been in operation on Maryland tributaries of Chesapeake Bay since 1890. An intensive four-year study* revealed no evidence that hatching and yearly release of millions of fry had any effect on the number of adults available later. The release of 18 million fry in the Severn River in 1955 did not result in greater abundance of juvenile Yellow Perch. Muncy compared egg production, size of spawning fish, and commercial catch data. He concluded that total production is probably controlled by varying environmental factors occurring throughout the life cycle which influences good and poor year-classes. He noted that many states are now concerned with control or elimination of Yellow Perch in lakes, rather than increased production. Repeated evaluations of Yellow Perch and other species by other researchers have also failed to show increases as a result of adding stocked fry to natural production. A somewhat similar problem seems to exist in Tennessee where, as recently as 1958, a spring-dated news release that year from the Tennessee Game and Fish Commission commented upon operation of two Redhorse Sucker hatcheries, one at Shelbyville and one at Caney Springs. Local citizens catch the Redhorse Suckers during their spring spawning runs, strip them of their eggs and milt, rush the fertilized eggs to the hatcheries where they hatch. The small fry are then released into Duck River to grow up—they hope. The Commission provides caretaker and equipment. The big unanswered question seems to have been whether it all does any good for the fishery. Most biologists would favor the belief that it does not. In view of the intense interest in the Redhorse fishery, the Commission decided to initiate a series of evaluations to learn more about the fishery and the effect of the hatchery.

Some outstanding success has been claimed for the practice of maintenance stocking of Walleyes in certain waters; however, it is clear that results are highly variable. Predation and competition from other fishes are considered important reasons for the failure of Walleye fry stocking attempts by conservation agencies. A poll of the 50 state and 11 provincial fishery chiefs conducted in 1961 by a Massachusetts fishery biologist indicated that soft (low total alkalinity), slightly acid waters have probably limited the successful establishment of Walleyes in lakes. However, 70 per cent of the respondents considered that lack of suitable spawning requirements was the most important factor contributing to failure to develop self-sustaining populations. This is borne out by a study of egg survival on different bottom types in Lake Winnibigoshish by Minnesota biologist Fritz H. Johnson. Johnson found Walleye egg survival best on clean, gravel-rubble, and poorest on soft muck-detritus bottoms. Over a four-year period, egg survival averaged 2.4 per cent on muck-detritus, 8.6 per cent on firm sand, and 25 per cent on gravel-rubble bottoms. In a paper in Transactions of the American Fisheries Society 90 (3) July, 1961, Johnson concluded that the quality and extent of spawning areas must be considered as important factors in Walleye reproduction. Of the 42 states and provinces reporting Walleye populations in response to the Massachusetts questionnaire, 6 listed native populations only, 16 had introduced populations only, and 20 had both. Twenty-six agencies reported lakes where plantings showed survival, but Walleyes had not become self-sustaining.

Still, at least one key question regarding the merit of maintenance stocking of Walleyes remains, viz: Does stocking of Walleye fry in a lake increase the population, especially when the eggs are taken from fish already spawning in the lake? The answer to this management question has been pursued by Iowa biologists for 15 years. Some conclusions were presented by Dr. Kenneth D. Carlander (Iowa State University fishery professor) in the November, 1961 issue of *Iowa Conservationist.* The professor described stocking experiments at Clear Lake where millions of Walleye fry were stocked in alternate years from 1948 through 1958. Numbers of fingerlings subsequently taken by seining were higher in years when fry were stocked. Also, 75 per cent of the Walleye catch was made up of year-classes augmented by fry stocking. Dr. Carlander nevertheless pointed out that the alternation of abundant and poor year classes may have been the result of competition and predation, and not fry stocking. For instance, an abundant 1948 year-class (fry-stocked) may have prevented the 1949 year-class from developing. Then the 1950 year-class would be abundant because of little competition from the 1949 year-class, and so on. To test this possibility, he recommends that fry stocking be tried on a three-year cycle, with no fry stocking in the third year. If this results in two abundant year-classes and a poor year-class, he believes that "even the more skeptical will have to admit that the fry

* Muncy, R. J. 1959. Evaluation of the Yellow Perch Hatchery Program in Maryland. Md. Dept. Res. & Ed. Resource Study Report No. 15, 12 pp. (Jan.). Ches. Biol. Lab., Solomons.

stocking is affecting the Walleye population in Clear Lake."

Why is the apparent effectiveness of fry stocking at Clear Lake at variance with that in other lakes where little or no effect could be shown? Dr. Carlander cited the fact that Clear Lake has no suitable tributary streams for spawning, and emerging fry in the lake may be subjected to heavy predation by abundant Bullheads and Yellow Bass. Secondly, 5 to 10 thousand fry per acre are stocked in Clear Lake compared to less than 450 per acre in lakes where stocking showed no effect. He concluded that: "For economic management of the fishable walleye population, the optimum number of fry should be determined, even though this will take several years of careful testing."

Another objective of stocking large-size warm-water predatory game species—in addition to new introductions for angling variety, replacement stocking after lake or stream renovation, or possible maintenance stocking in the absence of adequate reproduction—is to cause changes in the fish population structure in order to increase the rate of predation on undesirable or non-sport species or to increase through predation the natural mortality of overcrowded and stunted panfish. In this way it is hoped that an improved balance between predator species and prey species can be achieved thereby leading to improved fishing by means of natural (biological) control over various species in place of artificial means of control (chemicals and mechanical devices). The stocking of predator fishes to remedy stunted panfish conditions is one of the more popular current theories. Walleyes, Northern Pike, Flathead, Catfish, and other species recommended do eat panfish, reducing their numbers and thus providing more food for those remaining. However, the number of predator fishes required to make significant inroads on the stunted fish is very high, and stocking costs are prohibitive.

Wisconsin fishery biologists John Klingbiel and Howard Snow found that stocking 20 pounds of adult Northern Pike per acre in lakes containing slow-growing Bluegills improved Pike fishing but had no measurable effect on the Bluegill population. Reporting in the March-April, 1962, *Wisconsin Conservation Bulletin,* on fish population control, they recounted that 13 lakes were stocked with Walleye fingerlings for stunted panfish control. Results with stocking rates of 50 to 250 per acre were poor. In only one lake, where fifty 4-6 inch Walleye were introduced per acre, was survival good and Perch size increased. Muskellunge have also been tested many times, but only one trial was effective. The biologists concluded that, in general, stocking of predators to control panfish populations has not been successful. Perhaps larger numbers of adults or larger fingerlings are needed. More evaluations of tests are needed to determine the ultimate practicability of this technique. The biologists believe the best possibility in sight lies in selective panfish toxicants—yet to be developed.

At least one outstanding example of a successful case of natural predation effecting substantial control over extensive rough fish populations, and causing excellent fishing as a direct consequence, is known. It was not, however, the result of deliberate introduction by man. Rather, it resulted from a chain of fortuitous circumstances that led to development of the first known self-sustaining landlocked population of the normally anadromous Striped Bass in the Santee-Cooper Reservoir constructed on the Congaree River in 1943 in South Carolina. The stripers were naturally present in the river and an upstream racial group was trapped above the dam, together with their upstream spawning grounds unimpaired by the reservoir. Starting about 1950, the Striped Bass population virtually exploded in the reservoir, and by 1955 a fabulous fishery had developed. Studies of the fishery by fishery biologists of the South Carolina Wildlife Resources Department revealed that the angler harvest of Striped Bass doubled in 1956 and doubled again in 1957. The total harvest in 1957-58 was an estimated 282,000 Striped Bass or more, averaging 5.4 pounds each in creel census samples. Therefore, the total yield for the reservoir came to more than 1½ million pounds—nearly 10 pounds of stripers per acre. In addition, some 60,000 Largemouth Bass, 256,000 Bluegills, 583,000 Black Crappies, and 23,000 White Catfish were also taken. The Largemouths averaged about 1.9 pounds, Bluegills about 0.3 pounds, Black Crappies about 0.8 pound. All in all, something under 15 pounds of fish per acre were harvested by anglers. Some 181,000 successful fishing trips were made on the reservoir in that year.

Not only the Striped Bass fishing has proved to be phenomenal; the fishing for Largemouths, Bluegills, Crappies, and White Catfish is some of the finest in the world, with an abundance of large fish being caught including record or near-record individuals. It is a type of main-stem reservoir where fishing generally goes sour after the first five or six years, rough fish take over, and game fish sharply decline in abundance. It didn't happen at Santee-Cooper, and extensive biological studies point to the presence of the highly predaceous Striped Bass as the probable reason. Be it noted, however, that Striped Bass fishing in Santee-Cooper Reservoir has declined since 1959, according to the latest research reports of biologist Robert E. Stevens, assigned to the lake. Available data suggest a drop in the famed Striper population of 30 to 50 per cent from the amazing 1958-59 high. In addition, yearly population sampling indicates that the weight of Gizzard Shad collected per acre has declined from 287 pounds in 1954 to

75 pounds in 1961. Stevens noted that Shad have typically represented 90 per cent of the food of the Striped Bass and believes that the drop in Shad has resulted directly from the rapid ascendance of the striper population. He reported an improvement in the plumpness of Striped Bass in 1961, and attributes it to a decrease in their numbers to a point more nearly in equilibrium with the food supply—a readjustment of predator-prey balance, expected and anticipated by many biologists. The South Carolina biologist recommended spring opening of the navigation lock at the dam to encourage the entrance of the anadromous Glut Herring to the reservoir to spawn. Herring provide a supplemental food supply for the landlocked stripers. Meanwhile, fishing continues to be good for Largemouth Bass, Crappie, Pickerel and Bream.

Of many other attempts to introduce Striped Bass into inland waters, only four seem to have some possibility of success. These were all recent attempts and the only ones in which the ecology of the Striped Bass as learned from the Santee-Cooper biological studies seem to have been considered. These are Kerr Reservoir in North Carolina and Virginia, Millerton Lake in California, the Colorado River, and TVA's Kentucky Lake in Kentucky and Tennessee. These all have serious "rough" fish problems, and it remains to be seen whether the Striped Bass populations will develop sufficiently to bring the rough fish under control. All other attempts seem to have failed, presumably because there was no large, fairly turbid tributary river of suitable flow with unobstructed suitable spawning sites 30 to 50 miles or more above the lakes.

Northern Pike were highly popular in the early 1960s and widely stocked in the fry stage as possible biological agents to exercise hoped-for and much needed control over rough fish, especially in the huge artificial impoundments of the upper Mississippi River Basin and the north-central states generally. A native species of the region, it requires extensive marshy sloughs for successful natural reproduction, and the acquisition and preservation of such areas adjacent to natural lakes is aggressively pursued within the heart of its range as a key element of Northern Pike management. In a notable D-J study of natural production, fishery scientists from the Minnesota Department of Conservation and the University of Minnesota concluded that success of spawning and early survival of broods of Northern Pike is greatly influenced by water levels, iron content, wind, and temperature changes in Minnesota sloughs.* Concentrating on 535-acre Lake George and its connecting sloughs, the biologists made detailed observations from 1955 through 1958 on adult fish movements, egg deposition, and embryo and juvenile survival. The observations were compared with variations in chemical content, temperature, and water levels in the spawning sloughs and lake.

They found that increased Pike egg mortality was probably caused by iron precipitation on the egg surface and by rapid temperature depression. Comparative numbers of surviving fry and fingerling Pike did not appear to be influenced by cannibalism, predation by insects, or food shortages. Migration from slough to lake occurred on bright, sunny days when the fry reached a length of nearly one inch. Cloudy weather delayed migration and increased the chances of mortality due to stranding by low water, and cannibalism. On reaching the lake, the little Pike were subject to Bluegill predation (Sunfish made up 75 per cent of the lake's standing crop) until a length of about 1½ inches was attained. Dr. Smith and his co-workers postulated that since the total number of eggs deposited did not determine alone the ultimate number of catchable Pike, nor did the numbers of migrating larger "cannibal" fingerlings, the size of each year's ultimate adult production was set by the total number of fingerlings—both *small* and large—which survive and migrate from the slough. Moral—the "nursery" sloughs are the key to Pike production.

The biologists recommend that sloughs be selected for Pike management which have suitably low natural iron content, sufficient water flow to insure continuous lake access, proper slough basin shape, with the bed above lake level to permit annual reestablishment of terrestrial vegetation, which creates good egg beds. Water control structures including gate and fishway could be installed to provide optimum conditions at critical times. Other possible management practices in nursery sloughs include chemical control of undesirable species. Where the slough can be completely drained after July 1, planting of suitable grasses or grains may be necessary to provide firm vegetative mats for egg deposition. Grasses, sedges, or rushes with fine leaves appear to make the best substrate. Addition of chemicals to alter iron cycles or other conditions may be required for intensive management.

Nebraska district fishery biologist Bruce McCarraher has concluded that adult Northern Pike cannot be "stockpiled" for next year's fishing. In other words, if the anglers don't get them, Mother Nature will. McCarraher concluded from his observations, too, that production of good Pike populations in Nebraska is dependent on favorable natural conditions. Artificial propagation of Northern Pike remains unpredictable of success due to interaction of many complex and largely uncontrollable factors. The weather, egg quality, rearing-pond fertility, and cropping methods all directly influence the total hatchery production.

* Smith, L. L. Jr., D. P. Franklin, & R. H. Kramer. 1958. Determination of factors influencing year class strength in northern pike and largemouth bass. 326 pages (Mimeo). Minn. Dept. Cons.

Artificial creation of adjoining marsh-type areas to lakes where such spawning sites are lacking has often proved to be the difference in Nebraska between good and poor Pike fishing. Stocking alone has been found wanting in Nebraska as a means of providing the answer to improved fishing for Northern Pike.

Muskellunge are also strongly championed by some fishery managers as potential biological agents to control rough fish and panfish in the continuing struggle to keep a favorable balance between predator and prey and thereby create good fishing for all species. Here, again, rather specialized requirements of habitat are evidently required, though its characteristics are as yet poorly defined, even though the approximate extent of Muskie habitat is known in several states. In Minnesota, for example, there are a known 250,000 acres of Muskie lakes and 130 miles of Muskie rivers, most such waters being located in the Mississippi River headwaters area. Dr. John B. Moyle, Minnesota game and fish research chief, says that these fish are never very abundant even in good Muskie waters, being "lone wolves" for the most part. Wisconsin has 268,880 acres of Muskie waters; in 1957 the statewide harvest was reported to amount to 47,700 fish—equivalent to a take of one legal Muskellunge per 5.6 acres of known habitat; thereby supporting Dr. Moyle's contention.

A 1958 publication of the Wisconsin Conservation Department summarized in a few pages what little is actually known about Muskies in the wild. For one thing, Muskellunge populations generally consist of only a few individuals per acre of all sizes. In one lake, a tentative population estimate was one fish per acre. Studies on Gile Flowage in Iron County disclosed a population of approximately 1,300 Muskellunge, or one for every 2.6 surface acres. Another point of special interest concerned relative importance of Muskellunge to fishermen. The article states that a sample of 1957 licensees indicated that about 9 per cent of the residents and 10 per cent of the non-residents had fished for Muskellunge.*

Wisconsin has engaged in the continual stocking of young-of-the-year Muskellunge for presumed maintenance purposes since 1899, but has never undertaken a full-fledged evaluation of its Muskie stocking program in terms of what possible effect it may have upon actual fishing success. Only very limited mark-and-recapture work has been undertaken and the results suggested very low survival to the legal size (30 inches). It has been estimated, accordingly, that each surviving hatchery fish caught by an angler would represent an actual expenditure by the state amounting to about $200.

* Oehmcke, A. A., L. Johnson, J. Klingbiel, & C. Wistrom. 1958. The Wisconsin Muskellunge; its life history, ecology, and management. Wisc. Cons. Dept. Pub. 225 (12 pp.).

If this were charged against public relations for tourist promotion with reimbursement to the Conservation Department out of state general funds, the program might be justifiable regardless of the biological merits.

Ohio is one of several states that have active Muskellunge stocking programs. During the 1950-1960 decade, it consisted of artificial culture of native Muskies starting with the trapping of fish from streams with a view toward introducing Muskies in other waters where they were lacking and where they were deemed biologically adaptable. Refinements in artificial culture methods were worked out, and it was concluded in Ohio that the survival of the Muskie depends fundamentally on an abundance of the right size prey in proximity to the young predator. Disease control also proved important. The initial year's stocking in several new lakes was very successful; however, little success attended additional stocking in following years. After 10 years of effort, it has become recognized that results have been small in terms of extent of established populations. These populations are estimated to add up to about one Muskie per 10 acres of surface water. In terms of fishing results, studies at one of the better Muskie lakes indicated, on the average, that about one is taken for every one thousand hours of angling effort! An angler among the few who achieve the status of Muskie fishing "specialist" may average as high as one Muskie about every 100 hours of angling.

A study of comparative growth rates for native and hatchery-stocked populations of Muskellunge in Nogies Creek, Ontario, was reported by University of Ontario biologist Barry S. Muir in the Journal of the Fisheries Research Board of Canada for December, 1960. He found that hatchery fish, planted as fingerlings, showed similar growth for four summers after which their growth rate fell rapidly below that for the native fish, and that the hatchery fish required three years more than the native fish to reach legal length. The reduced growth observed in hatchery fish after four summers of growth indicated to Muir that the present techniques of hatching and rearing may preclude the possibility of favorable competition with wild populations. The reduced growth rate retards realization of whatever value they may be to the fishery, and subjects them to an increased toll from natural mortality. Since rate of maturity generally appears to be more dependent on sizes than on age itself, these fish would also require a longer pre-spawning period.

Artificial propagation. Warmwater fishes do not generally lend themselves so readily as salmonoids to intensive methods of propagation, to confinement in troughs and tanks, or to hand feeding. Rather, they must be allowed to spawn naturally in ponds and/or to live in open pond waters involving large acreages. As a consequence, they cannot be propagated so easily as Trout, and the whole food chain in the pond must be taken into account. Because indirect methods of study must be used, it is much more difficult to acquire information and develop better methods of propagation. Sunfishes of various species (Largemouth Bass, Smallmouth Bass, Bluegills, Redear Sunfish, Crappies) are nest builders and cannot be spawned artificially without injury to the sex organs. The procedure, therefore, is to place breeders in spawning ponds, where the fish build nests on the bottom and lay their eggs to hatch just as they would do normally elsewhere. Hatchery ponds are generally from ¼- to 1-acre in size but may be 5 acres or more. They are generally stocked with 40 to 120 adults per acre in early spring before the spawning season. A ratio of about 4 males to 6 females is desirable to prevent fighting and the resultant loss of eggs and fry.

Smallmouth Bass spawning ponds are provided with gravel nests, in which the gravel is pea size or larger, either in stalls on the edges of the ponds (shallow boxes with two high sidewalls), or in piles spaced properly on the bottom. The gravel piles should be in 2 to 3 feet of water. Largemouth Bass are not so specialized and spawn on the roots of vegetation, on debris on the bottom, or on clean firm bottom if need be. In either species, by brushing silt and fine material from the site with the tail and body, the male forms a large saucer-shaped depression. Nest-making activities take place when the water temperatures are 60° F. or above; spawning takes place when the temperatures reach about 65°, in a series of convulsive movements of both sexes lasting from 3 to 10 seconds. At this time the eggs and milt are extruded over the cleaned depression. The fish circle and spawn alternatively until the female has deposited all her eggs (is "spent"), when she is driven from the nest. A male generally spawns with one female, but may spawn with more, in any event only one at a time. The eggs hatch in 4 to 10 days, depending on water temperatures. The males of both species guard the eggs, and the fry of Largemouths are guarded by the male for a few days longer. At first spawning a Bass about 10 to 12 inches in length may produce 1,500 to 2,000 eggs, with larger fish producing more eggs. The average fry school ranges from 2,500 to 7,000 or 8,000; due to combination of schools it may become as large as 25,000 on occasion.

Largemouth Bass fry remain in a compact school after they start feeding. The male patrols around the school to keep other fishes away. These schools are captured in a fine-mesh seine shortly before the Bass scatter and are transferred to other ponds for rearing. Smallmouth Bass fry remain on the nest until the yolk sac is absorbed. Gradually, the fry rise higher and higher above the nest until they are actively feeding. The school then becomes a loose swarm which breaks up rather easily; therefore, when the eggs hatch the male is driven off and a wire cylinder extending above the water is placed around the nest. The free-swimming fry can then be readily collected and transferred to rearing ponds. Young Bass do not readily learn to take artificial food, so must be fed on natural food produced in the pond. Rearing ponds are filled with water about 4 to 8 weeks before fry are transferred for rearing, in order to permit natural food production to accumulate. The ponds are fertilized and a food chain established so that microscopic organisms (plankton) upon which young Bass feed are present in abundance. Properly fertilized rearing ponds are stocked at rates dependent upon the size of Bass to be produced. Heavily fertilized ponds may be stocked with as many as 40,000 fry per acre if they are removed at about 1 to 1½ inches in length within about three weeks, usually for stocking farm fish ponds. If 3-inch fingerlings are desired, 15,000 to 20,000 fry per acre are stocked, and allowed to grow for 30 to 45 days; for 4- to 6-inch fingerlings as few as 5,000 may be stocked and permitted 2 to 3 months of growth. These larger Bass are used for new introductions into waters already containing other kinds of fish. Bass have strong tendencies to cannibalism; consequently it is imperative that fry of uniform size be stocked in each rearing pond and that the pond be drained at the first appearance of any unusually large individuals. Otherwise, production may consist chiefly of a very few but abnormally large individuals. Proper fertilization diminishes the danger.

Bluegills are the most commonly hatchery-propagated small species of Sunfish, followed by Redear Sunfish ("shell crackers"), used chiefly for stocking new or renovated farm ponds or municipal fishing lakes in combination with Largemouth Bass. The old style promiscuous stocking of Bluegills (often contaminated with the undesirable Green Sunfish as well as other species) in public waters has been thoroughly discredited in modern fish management. The procedure of hatchery propagation is similar for all the small species of Sunfish, and essentially consists of recreating and intensifying natural conditions under more controllable circumstances. Bluegills (as well as Redears and the other Sunfishes) are gregarious, and when the water temperature rises above 75° F., the males build small saucer-shaped nests in colonies, each male defending his own nest without passing over his neighbor's. The nests are brushed out of the soft bottom, generally located in about one-half to one foot of water, but may be much deeper; in lakes, nests may be in as much as 10 feet of water during warm weather. Spawning occurs throughout the summer when the water reaches 80° F. unless inhibited by lack of sufficient food and consequent overpopulation with young Bluegills. Bluegills are stocked at the rate of 15 or more pairs per acre in well-fertilized rearing ponds and left in the pond until growth has ceased because of low fall temperatures. With this number of breeders it is possible to secure a production of 40,000 to 60,000 two to four-inch fingerlings per acre as well as many others too small to save. By stocking a larger number of adults, more than 100,000 smaller fingerlings may be produced in one crop. Two or more crops of Bluegills may be produced in a year through proper manipulation of the spawning ponds.

Channel Catfish do not usually breed in ponds, being specialized river species. Methods of propagation were originally devised prior to the first World War at the former U. S. Bureau of Fisheries biological station at Fairport, Iowa, but actual spawning remained highly unpredictable until Kermit Sneed and Dr. Howard Clemens researched the sexual physiology of Channel Catfish during the 1950s at the University of Oklahoma. They developed the use of hormonal injections with gonadotropins derived from carp pituitary glands to stimulate sexual maturation and subsequent spawning, with a high degree of certainty. Continuing to work on Channel Catfish spawning at the Marion, Alabama, experimental fish hatchery of the U. S. Fish and Wildlife Service, Sneed has found later indications of possible dietary or other complex factors that may operate to reduce the effectiveness of the new method at times, and is continuing his research in order to perfect it. Adult Channel Catfish are usually taken from streams and rivers for hatchery broodstock; in nature, catfishes normally spawn in a hole in the bank, generally under the roots of a tree. With the new hormone injection techniques handling techniques are undergoing considerable change, and much less space will be needed, with brood fish possibly held in compartments in raceways or small ponds (instead of the normal large brood ponds) equipped with nail kegs, milk cans, earthen jars or other suitable containers. These are furnished with a layer of sand and located back in the bank in not more than two to three feet of water to provide dens for actual spawning. Onset of spawning will be highly predictable; otherwise, procedures will probably be much like they have been for several decades, pending possible further refinements in handling the fry and fingerlings.

In larger hatcheries, the dens are examined daily and the eggs are removed to the hatchery immediately after they are deposited. At smaller hatcheries the eggs are left to hatch in the pond where they were spawned. Spawning occurs at water temperatures of 75° to 80° F. or higher. The male spends considerable time in the container, cleaning out the silt and shining up the inside. After the eggs are deposited, he spends all his time fanning the eggs with his fins, moving them about and picking up stray bunches in his mouth to deposit them back on the pile. The eggs are large and yellow and adhere together in a mass. The male keeps the eggs continuously agitated until they hatch. The average Catfish will produce about 10,000 eggs, which hatch in 7 to 10 days, depending upon water temperature. If the eggs are hatched in the spawning containers, the male is left in the pen to guard them. When the young hatch, they congregate in a tight school at the bottom of the container. The keg is then carefully removed to a tub, transferred to the hatchery, and there is placed in a trough with running water. The keg is left there until the fry swim from it to the bottom of the trough; otherwise, the eggs are removed as soon as they are deposited, and placed in troughs with running river water, which are equipped with a series of paddles. Their purpose is to move back and forth and cause some slight motion among the eggs, simulating the gentle disturbance made by the Catfish tail and fins. Apparently, the eggs will not hatch in running water alone without this supplementary agitation.

Feeding is very similar to that of Trout, and the same diets and methods can be employed. Everything in the hatchery must be kept scrupulously clean, care must be taken to avoid overfeeding, and sufficient water must be passed through the troughs to provide proper exercise. When more space is required, the fry are removed from the troughs to large tanks and held until they are 3 to 5 inches in size. In Nebraska hatcheries the fry are placed in cages (6 feet long, 4 feet wide, and 3 feet deep) made of 1/8-inch mesh wire screen and with a wooden bottom. The cages are placed in a pond supplied with a current of water. The fry are fed in these cages for about 4 weeks. To raise Catfish to a larger size, a pond is filled with water immediately before fingerlings are placed in it in order to keep predation by insect larvae, beetles, and crayfish at a minimum. Catfish are subject to many of the diseases that occur in Trout and must be handled accordingly. Fingerling Catfish will continue to take artificial food until they are removed from the pond.

Walleye brood fish are taken by trap nets in late winter from large lakes as they enter tributary streams to spawn, or by seining shallow water areas of large lakes immediately after the ice breaks up. Eggs and milt are taken from the adults in the same manner as Trout. Walleye eggs are very adhesive; so after fertilization is completed, a handful of muck or cornstarch is added to the pan of eggs and carefully mixed to prevent them from sticking together. Excess water is drained off and new water and muck are added at half-hour intervals until the adhesive stage is passed. The eggs are then washed and placed in a container for delivery to the hatchery. A female weighing 2 pounds or more will usually produce

45,000 eggs per pound of body weight. The eggs in the hatchery are transferred to open-top glass hatchery jars. Water runs through a tube to the bottom of the jar and spills over the top, keeping the eggs in motion as the water flows up through them. The hatching temperature is between 40° and 50° F. At 48° the eggs will hatch in 18 to 20 days. The fry are retained in the jar until the yolk sac is absorbed. More recently, these fish have been grown successfully to fingerling size after transfer into fertilized ponds in the manner described for Bass. Large numbers have been grown successfully to about 3 inches in length.

Northern Pike and Muskellunge have been propagated in a few states. The methods used in hatching and propagation are variations of those used for Walleyes. The young grow much more rapidly, are voracious cannibals, and very difficult to raise to large size in significant numbers. Wisconsin has developed the most sophisticated methods for raising Muskellunge in pond cultural operations (although it has not evaluated the significance of Muskie stocking in terms of improvement of fishing, either for Muskellunge or for associated species) and published an account of its methods in 1958.* Provision of abundant supplies of the right kinds of food organisms at the proper times obviously constitutes one of the more important aspects of raising Muskies. Much emphasis must be paid to production of zooplankton *(Daphina)*, fertilizing with Torula yeast, as well as on production of sucker fry. For every 35 to 40 quarts of muskellunge eggs incubated in the hatchery, some 2,000 to 3,000 quarts of sucker eggs must also be cultured. Water temperatures are critical, and aquatic weed control is important. Even under optimum conditions, artificially created for Muskies during the culture operations, it has been determined that mortality ranges from 70 to 30 per cent (averaging about 65 per cent) in hatchery ponds from "swim-up" stage (fry) through the first 2 to 6 weeks of growth. They are then transferred to special rearing ponds, and kept there for some three to four months, while growing at a rapid rate. Despite optimum supplies of food, the mortality for Muskellunge in these special rearing ponds by the time of final harvest (when the fish are 4 to 5½ months old and 7 to 17 inches long) averages 70 per cent. Out of every 100,000 eggs incubated (assuming a 90 per cent hatch), about 90,000 fry may be hatched. Assuming that all of these would survive to "swim-up" stage (mortality rate unknown for this stage) and become safely transferred to hatchery ponds, about 31,500 fingerlings (1½ to 5 inches long) may survive the first two to six weeks for subsequent transfer to the special rearing ponds. From these ponds, during September and October, the survivors (7 to 17 inches long)—reduced by then to about 9,450 fish—are removed for stocking in Wisconsin's Muskie waters.

Farm ponds. A high proportion of the warm-water fish hatchery operations are aimed toward supplying suitable sized Largemouth Bass, Bluegills or Redear Sunfish, and/or Channel Catfish needed for initial or corrective (after renovation) stocking of farm ponds. Farm ponds are usually around an acre in size but may range on occasion up to 10 acres and be as small as a quarter of an acre. Relatively few ponds under one-half acre in size can be managed to produce any significant amount of satisfactory sport fishing, even though of high natural fertility or are heavily fertilized. As yet there exist only a relatively small number of coldwater farm ponds, so that a correspondingly low proportion of coldwater hatchery operations are devoted to supplying fingerling Trout for such waters. Altogether, although nobody knows for sure, upwards of two million farm ponds of all types may have been built in the United States, but perhaps only about one million or so are suitable for fish production or have been stocked with fish. About 50,000 farm ponds suited to fish management were being built annually during the 1960s. Older ponds built during depression years in the Southwest are known to be rapidly filling with erosion silt, reducing their usefulness and stimulating construction of replacement ponds, so that the rate of construction seems unlikely to lessen in the near future.

A 1960 survey of farm ponds by Dr. Willis King, U. S. Fish and Wildlife Service,* revealed that the ponds were multiple purpose in function, and that they were initially constructed chiefly to provide water for livestock and for recreational fishing. Actual purposes served by the ponds were: watering livestock 80%, fishing 70%, irrigation water 13%, swimming 9%, wildlife (observation or hunting) 5%, other purposes 4%. Dr. King's survey had a representative national application and clearly demonstrated that farm ponds are important recreational resources. He estimated that at least five million persons were furnished some twenty million man-days of recreational fishing by about 200,000 farm ponds that have been stocked by the U. S. Fish and Wildlife Service between 1953 and 1957, and for which stocking records are available. This means that nearly 20 per cent of U. S. anglers found at least part of their fishing enjoyment at farm ponds. Dr. King's study provided a summary of the reasons accounting for the poor fishing attributed to about 15 per cent of the ponds. It was found that 21 per cent of the pond owners had added various kinds of fish on their own and that 30 per cent of the ponds contained wild fish. In ponds where fishing was

* Johnson, L. D. 1958. Pond culture of muskellunge in Wisconsin. Technical Bulletin No. 17 (54 pp). Wisconsin Conservation Dept., Madison.

* King, W. 1960. A survey of fishing in 1000 ponds in 1959. U.S. FWS Fish and Wildlife Circ. 86 (20 pp.). U. S. Gov. Printing Office, Washington, D.C.

unsatisfactory, too many small Bluegills, muddy water, and presence of wild fish were the most common reasons. Other frequent reasons for pond failures included too much water flowing through ponds, low fertility, insufficient fishing pressure, partial losses of water, and partial losses of fish. Less frequent reasons were original overstocking, overabundance of Bullheads, and overabundance of water weeds and algae.

Except for the early work of the U. S. Fish Commission in developing pond culture of warm-water fishes—an important first step toward modern farm pond improvement—no further progress occurred in understanding of underlying principles and development of specific management procedures until 1937. Starting that year, H. S. Swingle and his coworkers at Alabama Polytechnic Institute studied farm ponds for the production of sport and food fishes. As a result of their work and that of other investigators, certain principles have become evident for farm fish pond management, about as follows:

1. *Water produces fish according to its fertility.* Bodies of water on relatively infertile soil have a low productivity, and those on good agricultural land produce well. Poorly fertile ponds may be improved by direct fertilization of the water to insure maximum production. Fertilizer permits greater production of microscopic food (plankton) which increases the production of the insect larvae, these by increasing the food supply for Bluegills and baby Bass. Fertilization is through direct application of commercial inorganic or other fertilizers to water, in the same manner as to soils, broadcast along the edges of the pond in water three to six feet deep.

Sufficient fertilizer should be used at about bi-weekly intervals to produce a water "bloom." A bloom consists of the microscopic algal organisms floating in the water, in sufficient abundance to color the water (usually green), thereby reducing its clarity. About 100 pounds of commercial fertilizer (consisting of eight parts nitrogen, eight parts phosphoric acid, and four parts potassium, or other suitable formulation) per acre should be used for each application or until the bloom develops. When the bloom has become dense enough so that any white object will disappear at a depth of 18 inches in the water, the proper concentration has been reached, and fertilization should be discontinued. The fertilizing program should be resumed when the water begins to clear. Presence of a dense water bloom will prevent vegetative growths in the pond, thereby eliminating hiding places for small fish, and leaving the pond bottom clear so that Bass will be able to prey effectively upon small Bluegills. Bass then grow more rapidly because they get more food, there is more space and food for the reduced number of Bluegills which also grow more rapidly. This reduces the tendency toward overpopulation. Fertilization also increases the total quantity of food produced and available to fish, thereby stimulating Bluegill reproduction and in turn renewing food supplies for Bass. In consequence, the carrying capacity of fish (the amount produced) is increased over that in natural waters of low fertility.

2. *A combination of sport species which will utilize the different foods in the pond to best advantage will be most productive for hook-and-line fishing.* The greatest fish production is obtained from omnivorous species, such as Carp, and the lowest production from carnivorous species, such as Pike. As Bluegills utilize natural food and Bass prey upon Bluegills to complete the food chain, a pond stocked with the proper ratio of predator (Bass or other) and prey (Bluegill, Redears, or other) species provides the predator-prey relationship which is required to prevent overpopulation by the more productive prey species. In order to obtain maximum production of game fish, it has been found essential to maintain a certain "balance" between the predator and prey. Information available now indicates that there should be one pound of predator fish for every four to seven pounds of prey for best results. If the ratio of predator to prey is not within this range overpopulation by prey species is usually indicated or imminent and corrective measures must be undertaken. An estimate of the pond's condition can usually be made with a large, small-mesh seine by checking the ratio of fingerling predator and prey fishes present. Scarcity or absence of the former is indicative of overpopulation by the latter.

3. *Fertilization of ponds built on relatively infertile soil is essential to maintain balanced populations.* The reproductive potential of most warm-water prey fish is so great that they soon overpopulate a pond. Heavy fishing is required to remove fish of edible size before they die of old age. This makes room for faster growth of the smaller fish, increases production by more rapid turnover of populations, and reduces the possibility of overpopulation. Under these conditions 150 pounds or more of fish may be taken annually by hook-and-line fishing per acre. One by-product from experience with farm ponds—since found to have rather general application for other waters—is that size and bag limits for most species of warmwater fish should be liberal if not removed altogether. One pair of fish can amply stock an acre or more of water. It has been demonstrated that hook-and-line fishing alone can seldom remove more than about 50 to 60 per cent of the parent stock. At this point, the effort required to catch a fish becomes so great that the average fisherman loses interest and quits fishing. It has also been demonstrated that a maximum of 90 to 95 per cent can be removed (by nets, etc.) under the severest conditions without harm to future production, at

least in southern waters. Few legal restrictions are, therefore, required to assure maintenance of adequate parent stock for reproduction.

4. *To insure satisfactory fishing in a body of water, the population must not only be made up of the proper ratio of predators to prey, it must also have the proper proportion of catchable-size fish.* The percentage of catchable-size fish in the population may vary over a considerable range and produce satisfactory fishing, but the best fishing is obtained if they make up between 65 and 85 per cent of the total weight of fish in the pond. It is necessary that at least one-third of the weight of all fish be of catchable size (about 0.2 pounds or more each for prey fish and 0.5 pounds or more each for predator fish).

The Bass-Bluegill combination has worked especially well in the South, where it was developed, but has run into some difficulties in the North. It has been found that if southern ponds are stocked with 100 Bass and from 750 to 1,000 Bluegills per acre, satisfactory results may be obtained in properly fertilized ponds that are fished heavily so as to maintain desired balance between Bluegills and Bass. Preferably, Bass should be stocked as fry or small fingerlings about 1 to 1½ inches in length as early in the season as possible. If this is done they will reach spawning size the following spring, possibly as far north as southern Illinois and Indiana; in northern Indiana, however, this could not be expected. Northern ponds probably should be stocked with Bass some time ahead of the Bluegills or stocked at the regular rate with Bass two or three years in succession. In some Midwestern and Western states Bluegills are not favored as a sport fish and fishing in farm ponds is confined to Bass. Preliminary evidence seems to indicate that under these conditions stocking with Bass only would produce better results, by preventing overpopulation with Bluegills. Channel Catfish may be stocked in farm ponds but (like Trout) they will not reproduce and it is necessary to stock them every few years in order to provide hook-and-line fishing. Supplementary feeding holds promise of increasing yields. Although Bullheads will produce in ponds, in a few years they will be eliminated by the Bass. If Crappies are stocked, poor fishing will result, because Crappies will gradually take over small ponds, eliminate the Bass, become stunted, and ruin the fishing.

Beyond making initial plants of fish, it is believed that no more than 20 per cent of the million-plus farm ponds receive further management attention from their owners. Consequently, a large number fail to produce or long maintain the anticipated good fishing. For this reason, many states provide some kind of extension service to assist farmers to secure more benefits through more active management of their ponds. One of the problems is to know what to advise farmers by way of proper pond stocking procedures. These will vary with variations in climate, fertility, and other factors. What works in southern states cannot be expected to work equally well in northern states. An article by two fishery biologists in the *Wisconsin Conservation Bulletin* gave some guidelines for that northern state. For example, where the water remains under 75° and spring flow is at least 50 gallons per minute, they recommended that Trout be stocked. Where temperatures are too high for Trout, the stocking of Largemouth Bass *alone* was recommended. Nevertheless, if a Wisconsin farm pond owner insists on stocking Bluegills, it was suggested that they not be introduced until at least one or two years after the Bass are stocked.

In the naturally fertile soils of the upper Midwest corn belt, the value of fertilizing farm ponds has long been questioned. To appraise this practice more thoroughly fishery biologists of the Illinois Natural History Survey conducted a five-year study of six southern Illinois ponds (each one to one and one-half acres) on the effect of fertilization there. During five years of fishing for both Bass and Bluegills, the total harvest of Bass, by weight, was slightly less from three fertilized ponds than from three unfertilized ponds, and the Bluegill harvest from the fertilized ponds was 2.7 times greater. The ratio by weight of Bass to Bluegills was one to three in the fertilized ponds, one to one in the unfertilized ponds. At the end of the five years, the standing crops of Bass and Bluegills in the fertilized ponds averaged 292 pounds per acre, as compared to 238 pounds per acre (ratio 1.2 to 1), and the number of Bass 10 inches or longer was approximately the same in all ponds. The number of Bluegills 6 inches or longer was 1.3 times as great in fertilized as in unfertilized ponds. The greater yields of fish from the fertilized ponds were obtained at costs estimated to range from $0.71 to $1.18 a pound.

The advantage of fertilization does not appear to be as marked in Illinois as it is in several southern states. Considerable intensive research over several decades at Auburn University (formerly Alabama Polytechnic Institute), has demonstrated that far greater advantages apply in terms of sport fish production and fishing yields in the South. Part of the differences are due to climate, and part are due to differences in basic productivity of the soils. Summarizing the many years of research by himself and coworkers at Auburn, Dr. H. S. Swingle reported that unfertilized ponds in the Southeast yield from 5 to 40 pounds of fish per acre per year to hook-and-line fishing, with average catch of approximately 15 pounds annually. Fertilized ponds yield from 100 to 300 pounds of fish per acre, with catch from such waters averaging about 150 pounds annually.

Several years of research have been spent in New York State to evaluate three techniques of stocking Bass and Bluegills. Trials in 23 ponds since 1952 included stocking one fingerling Bass to every five fingerling Bluegill, of one Bass to ten Bluegills, and staggered stocking (where Bass were planted a year before Bluegills). The fish living in these ponds for periods up to three years were inventoried in the summer of 1956. Results showed that Bass survival has averaged 51 per cent in "staggered ponds" and about 37 per cent in the other ponds (in which Bass and Bluegills were stocked simultaneously). After three years Bass attained lengths of about 12 inches in all ponds.

Growth of Bluegills was best in staggered ponds (where their survival was lowest) and poorest in "1-to-10 ponds" (where their survival was highest). The weight of Bass present was highest in "staggered ponds." However, total weight of all fish present was intermediate in these ponds compared to the other two groups. After three years, too, Bass have reproduced successfully in all "staggered ponds," but not in all the others. And young Bass were most abundant in "staggered ponds." They were least abundant where Bluegills were most abundant. It was tentatively recommended for central New York that the practice of stocking Bass and Bluegills at the same time be abandoned. Instead, Bass should be stocked 12 months prior to Bluegill fingerlings.

Another study of the ecology and management of warmwater farm ponds in New York, by a Cornell University fishery scientist, concluded in 1962 with recommendations for stocking a combination of Largemouth Bass and Golden Shiners. The biologist recommended a trial stocking formula of 100 Bass fingerlings and 400 adult Shiners per acre, introduced simultaneously. He concluded that the Bass-Bluegill combination should be attempted only in larger, deeper ponds where surface temperatures exceed 80° for considerable periods, and where owners are willing to devote the necessary time and money to continuing intensive management. Field experiments indicated that properly managed Bass-Bluegill ponds cost about $40 per acre per year. It was found that most pond owners in New York preferred to fish for Bass and were little interested in catching pan fishes. Bass grew somewhat faster in experimental ponds with Golden Shiners as forage, and their standing crops were higher than in combination with Bluegills. Shiner populations reach a peak, decline, and become extinct in most ponds. However, Bass populations remain high for several years after the decline. What corrective action should be taken then was not determined, but a good bet would be to remove all remaining fish and start the cyle all over again.

Such waters in New York and other northern states are often too cold for warmwater fish management, so Trout are indicated. Long-term studies of New York ponds have shown that Trout must be restocked every other year to provide good fishing. Observations by Cornell University fishery biologist Alfred W. Eipper on 167 ponds showed that if 600 fingerlings are stocked per acre, and no fishing is allowed, an average of 230 Trout would remain at the end of the first year, weighing about 115 pounds. One year later, due to natural mortality, only about 45 fish weighing 41 pounds would be left. If the owner doesn't catch the Trout in the first year, Mother Nature will beat him to them. Restocking is then necessary in either case. The study showed that farm-pond Trout rarely reproduced successfully because most ponds lack suitable spawning sites. Stocked Trout began to die when bottom temperatures reached 74 degrees. However, Trout have survived for very brief periods at a bottom temperature of 80 degrees. Rainbow Trout and Brook Trout are preferred species in ponds; Brown Trout are too hard to catch and, moreover, a few old Browns in a pond prey heavily on stocked fingerlings. New York ponds, which provide excellent Trout habitat conditions, may produce up to 250 pounds of Trout per acre.

Much has been said thus far about stocking fish, in terms of its demonstrated limitations as well as its utility. Partly this has been out of deference to its domination of fishery management for almost half a century. Partly it has been because it still accounts for the lion's share of fish conservation expenditures and therefore merits far more than a cursory review. Chiefly, however, it has been due to its important historic contribution to present knowledge of various sport species, and to construction of a solid foundation for improvement of fish management practices. Failure of some early Trout stocking practices or desire to improve them created a demand for biologists to conduct biological inventories of fishing waters, in turn accumulating knowledge of wild fish populations. Hatchery culture of pond fishes led, after some delay, to studies of farm pond problems and development of current methods of pond management. Farm pond studies demonstrated that fishing with hook-and-line is generally incapable of endangering brood stock of warmwater species, and has shown the general uselessness of length and bag limitations for maintaining good fishing. It has also thrown much light on the relationship between predator and prey species, and on the principles of fish food production, food chains, and basic fertility with respect to fish production. Partly as a result of these findings and partly as a result of some excellent unrelated research, on large impoundments and on natural lakes in the post-War II decades, much progress has been made toward developing a series of sophisticated new management tools for improving fishing in a wide variety of waters.

Acquisition and development of public access to fishing waters. One of the important post-war innovations in fishery administration arose from the realization that the creation of good fishing would be to little avail unless there is permanently assured means of access to the fishing waters, and that this could no longer be taken for granted. A limitation of funds, together with growing recognition that real improvement of fishing requires substantial expenditures, forced administrators to choose their management projects with care and with an eye to maximum benefits to anglers. Obviously, if fishermen could not use some water area —an increasing problem—it would be wasteful to manage it for better fishing. It soon became apparent, too, that many waters were heavily used to the point of crowding, while other waters could not be used at all because there was no way to reach them. With improved transportation and rapidly increasing interest evident in recreational fishing, it became necessary for the state fishery agencies to commence programs of selected land acquisition to provide strategically located sites for public access to fishing waters so that anglers could get to the water to fish, from shore, by wading, or from their boats after launching them from areas specially prepared for the purpose. Accordingly, in recent years, there has been a growing realization that state agencies have a responsibility to assure public access to fishing waters for future generations of anglers. In many states, too, the problem is becoming critical for sport fishermen today. It has been only in the post-War II decades that public access has acquired the status of a national problem. It has followed rapid population and industrial growth; for coastal areas, available shoreline has already shrunk to a great degree. Where waterfront land was once cheap, it now sells at house lot prices for hundreds or thousands of dollars per acre. Yet failure to purchase for public access at today's prices means a "hold-up" tomorrow at industrial-site prices.

By 1960, the states were spending about four per cent of their collective annual fish conservation expenditures, nationwide, for the purchase and development of small parcels of land to provide strategically located sites of public access to fishing waters. Increased use of boats (with or without motors) as items of fishing equipment necessitated acquisition of areas comprising several acres in a unit having considerable water frontage, and its development to provide parking areas for large numbers of autos with attached boat trailers, turnaround space, hard surfaced boat launching ramps extending well out into the water, and possibly some sanitary facilities as well. A 1959 survey by Sport Fishing Institute revealed that the state agencies had acquired or developed through the end of 1958 a total of about 2,650 access sites to some 1,500 lakes and reservoirs comprising 555,000 acres of water surface and to 6,400 miles of streams and rivers, comprising about 44,000 additional surface acres—nearly 600,000 acres in all. An important contribution to the total was made by use of Dingell-Johnson program funds (federal aid to the states in fish restoration financed by revenues from the manufacturers ten per cent excise tax on certain items of fishing tackle). Over the first ten years of the program about $21½ million of these funds had been expanded for the purpose in site acquisition (52%) and development (48%). Under the program, which has accounted for about one-fourth of total expenditures by these agencies for access to fishing waters, and has spearheaded the growing effort nationally, access sites have averaged 24 acres each with land purchased and developed for use at an average cost of a little over $5,400 per site.

The significant aspect is what it costs in relation to the number of anglers using each acre of water made available, pro-rated over some reasonable base—say 50 years. Roughly $10 million of expenditures for developed access to 600,000 acres of water works out to $16.67 per acre of fishing water made accessible. Pro-rated over 50 years, the cost is 33 1/3 cents per acre per year. Current fishing pressure would run about five angler-days per acre if spread evenly over all waters of the country (on many inland waters, it is several times as much). Therefore, pro-rated cost of the program thus far has been at most a little over 6½ cents per angler-day per acre per year. This is a conservatively high estimate because the administrators have concentrated at the outset in areas of greatest needs with greatest fishing pressures. With known annual fishing pressures on many near-urban waters already averaging 50 angler-days or more per year, it is obvious that these expenditures are among the best investments an agency can make to provide more and better fishing. By the end of the century, when fishing pressures are expected to be triple those of today, the pro-rated annual cost per angler-day would have fallen to about 2 1/3 cents per acre of fishing water already made publicly available. No doubt, rising land and development costs will increasingly offset the difference in these estimated pro-rated costs with respect to sites acquired in the future.

It was apparent from the Institute's survey of fishing water access programs that expenditure of many millions of dollars on the part of public agencies would be required to provide minimum perpetual free public access to the nation's inland waters alone. It was indicated by survey findings that one access area of at least 10 acres for each 300 acres of fishing water to be served should be provided as a minimum (if camping were to be permitted the area of land would need to be increased by 10-fold!). On lakes and reservoirs relatively large units of land are needed in a single block. On streams and rivers, because of the elongated nature of the water served, this formula needs subdivision to take into account the long distances, inconvenience, and unbearable congestion that would otherwise result. An acre of stream includes a section one mile long averaging 8¼ feet in width. All natural streams and rivers in the United States south of Alaska have actual surface areas averaging about 7 acres to the mile. Therefore, if one 10-acre site were developed per 300 acres, the sites would average nearly 43 miles apart! Obviously, for streams and rivers, it is more practical to develop 10 one-acre sites to serve the same 300 acres, spaced along the river to average 4 1/3 miles apart. In any event, the ratio of 10 acres of access site to each 300 acres of fishing waters to be served is widely recognized as the minimum formula, and an optimum would at least double that ratio. The California Small Crafts Harbors Commission, for example, has developed a standard "access unit" formula that calls for an area large enough to provide parking space for 125 cars and boat trailers equipped with a boat launching ramp capable of launching one boat at a time, or harbor and mooring space for 100 non-trailered boats, for each 160 acres of water served.

Study Report No. 7 (1961) of the Outdoor Recreation Resources Review Commission, entitled *Sport Fishing—Today and Tomorrow,* confirms the fundamental importance to boat-fishing of adequate access to recreational waters. ORRRC predicts that the amount of fishing in 2000 will be three times what it is today. It is believed that the facility needs of this increased fishing demand can be met satisfactorily, but this optimistic outlook is predicated in large part upon the assumption that adequate access will have been provided to existing waters, both fresh and salt, and to new impoundments as well. The Commission secured data on extent of waters already entirely closed to the public (or subject to arbitrary closure at any time). For example, 140,000 miles of streams (about one million surface acres) are in this category. About 1.2 million acres of public natural lakes other than the Great Lakes are entirely inaccessible (much of the remaining 8 million acres is poorly accessible). Nearly one million acres of large public reservoirs are wholly inaccessible (much of the remaining 7 million acres is poorly accessible). Only 6 per cent of the East coastal and 20 per cent of the West coastal salt waters are readily accessible to the public. The 27 million acres of Great Lakes waters pose a special problem of accessibility somewhat comparable to that of coastal marine waters. Altogether, then, 3.2 million acres of inland water alone, exclusive of the Great Lakes (as well as coastal marine waters), are entirely without permanently assured means of public access. At the average ratio of one site per 300 acres of water, the equivalent of 10,670 ten-acre sites are needed for these waters alone. Present costs of acquisition and development indicate that at least $58 million would be required to meet these barely minimal needs (using the California access unit formula the needed investment would approximate $100 million at 1960 prices).

In addition the ORRRC study recognized that about 20 million additional acres of inland waters other than the Great Lakes are poorly accessible at best. Assuming that the minimum access site water area ratio (see above) would apply to these waters as well, it is evident that the scope of the task confronting fish conservation and outdoor recreation planners is enlarged by at least 6-fold, and total costs approach the $400 million mark (in terms of 1960 dollars) not counting the special problems of the Great Lakes and those of the equally extensive coastal marine waters. If the job is to be completed by Century's end, at least $10 million must be budgeted annually, nationwide, by all the concerned agencies. Therefore, annual expenditures for this purpose must be increased to a level not less than five-fold present outlays by the fishery agencies. Other agencies concerned with opportunity for aquatic-based recreation, and other sources of potential revenues based on use or purchase of supplies, equipment, facilities, or services must contribute a large proportion of the added cost, and other groups of aquatic recreationists must contribute their fair share of the burden of cost of these vital multiple-benefit facilities. The task of meeting the need at federally-constructed reservoirs, especially those built by the U. S. Army, Corps of Engineers, is well under way through Congressional appropriations to the construction agencies out of general funds, recreation having become accepted as a project purpose. By 1960 some $2½ million was being appropriated annually for access site development at previously completed Corps' reservoirs and like sums were being made available for access site development at new reservoirs under construction. Seashore acquisition by means of Congressional appropriations was being sought—possibly foreshadowing a similar approach for the Great Lakes.

Intimately associated with development of access to fishing waters is the parallel growth of acute problems of recreational water conflicts, especially between anglers on the one hand—whether fishing from boats or wading or fishing from shore—and speed boaters and water skiers on the other hand. Up until the mid-1950s, the nation's multi-million-angler army had the nation's waterways pretty much to themselves so far as boat traffic was concerned. With the post-War II advent of nearly maintenance-free aluminum and fiberglass boats and of reliable big outboard motors, the situation underwent decided change. Various estimates suggested that water skiers alone may have numbered two to three million or more by 1960. Associated with water skiing are high speeds of operation and youthful age of operators; also associated with water skiing is the need for large areas of unobstructed water for pursuit of this activity. For optimum water skiing an average minimum area of 50 acres is probably required per water skier and tow boat. Actually, a water skier probably requires a minimum of 200 acres of overall area in which to cavort, but four water skiers can easily use the same area simultaneously without serious danger of accident. By comparison, many more anglers fishing from boats can be accommodated safely in any given area. For example, over 3,200 boats (with two or more anglers per boat) have been recorded simultaneously in use for Trout fishing on a single day at 5,284-acre Crowley Lake, California. For each boat there was an average area of about 1.6 acres, although many boats were actually concentrated more closely than this over favorite fishing "holes." This may represent near-maximum concentrations possible in the presence of good fishing.

Use of boats for sport fishing is an extremely important means of implementing this highly favored form of outdoor recreation. In many instances it is the most practical means of getting at fish populations, especially in large waters as, for example, at 2,000-acre Enemy Swim Lake, South Dakota. There, in the mid-fifties, over 14,000 anglers were using the lake annually, about 80 per cent of all fishing being done from boats. At Oklahoma's 19,000-acre Fort Gibson Reservoir about 40 per cent of nearly 600,000 angler-days of annual fishing effort was carried on from boats. The fishing study which revealed that fact also indicated that water-use conflicts had developed to serious proportions on that important recreation area over a two-year period. The investigators stated in their report that speed boat racing and water skiing *in certain areas* produced "intolerable disturbance" to many anglers. It was noted that fishing effort during the second summer, when this condition developed, decreased decidedly from that experienced a year earlier.

Some 40 to 50 per cent of all anglers now use boats of some kind for fishing; the other 50 to 60 per cent continue to do their fishing from shore, bank, fishing piers, bridges, or by wading in the water. Most boats and boat motors are little more than expensive pieces of fishing equipment supplementary to fishing rods, reels, lines, lures, etc. For example, a survey of his organization by the conservation director of the Izaak Walton League of America revealed that at least 80 per cent of all use of boats (owned or rented) by League members was for fishing. Surveys by the Outboard Boating Club of America, a trade association of outboard boat, motor, trailer, and accessory manufacturers, have indicated that the overwhelming single reason people cite for purchasing outboard boats and motors is to use them for fishing (75 per cent of all reasons reported on survey cards at time of purchase). A 1958 study of the national marine consumer market conducted for *Popular Boating* magazine gives strong support to the contention that the preponderance of actual use of boats *after purchase* is for fishing. Findings of the study (with admitted extensive duplications of unknown extent) indicated for that year that some 14.7 million folk used boats for fishing, 12.1 million went pleasure boating and cruising, 1.7 million water skied and 1.4 million used boats for hunting waterfowl. Among the readers of *Popular Boating,* alone, some 83 per cent of boat owners used their boats for fishing. Thus it is evident that the majority of the folk who own or use boats are fishermen, and that other uses for boats such as water skiing constitute definite minority interests. It is also evident that a single skier requires many times as much water for his activities as an angler. These facts, together with the high operating speeds, have created water-use conflicts of major proportions in many parts of the country. The 1962 Report of the Outdoor Recreation Resources Review Commission, *Outdoor Recreation For America,* confirms the preponderant use of water is for fishing, with twice as much time spent fishing as boating (other than skiing, canoeing, or sailing, but *including* fishing from boats), and ten times as much time spent fishing as water skiing.

A challenging article in *Sports Afield* magazine for May, 1961, written by Homer Circle (long time angler and outdoor writer, and chairman, Waterways Committee, American Fishing Tackle Manufacturers Association) discussed whether a fishing crisis exists with respect to numbers of anglers, place for them to fish, and competition for space from other water recreationists. Although the numbers of anglers have increased twice as fast as the population over the past decade some minor decreases in certain populous states have suggested that fishing opportunity may be shrinking in those areas if not nationally. (Some few folk unquestionably regard this hopefully considering the crowded condition of many waters.) Mr. Circle's article was based on a survey of 50 state fish and game agencies on related questions. A wide variety of reasons were advanced to account for possible decreases in numbers of anglers in certain states. However, the most frequent pinpointed in the five affected states was competition from other water sports such as water skiing, hot rodding, skin diving, etc.

What are these and other states doing to assure reasonable opportunity to fishermen to continue to enjoy their sport, while accommodating other uses on a reasonable basis? Mr. Circle found that 60 per cent have set up restrictions based on zoned areas, times, date, no boating on state-built or state-owned waters, singly or in combinations. Specifically, 36 per cent have zoned certain public waters to provide protected fishing areas and safety for fishermen, 14 per cent have time and/or date restrictions for skiers and fast boats, and 10 per cent allow only fishing (no boating) on lakes built or owned by the state. Sixteen per cent reported they saw "no problem yet," while 12 per cent seemed to be aware of the problem, but had developed no programs to cope with it. Thus, all states seem to be aware of the problems and are either thinking or actively doing something about it. The Outdoor Recreation Resources Review Commission research team studying recreational fishing also sought to appraise this problem and secured the views of the state fishery agencies as to the degree of competition that existed in 1961 between anglers and water skiers and speed boat operators for use of public waters. The poll revealed that some degree of competition was recognized to prevail in 48 states. Of these, 12 states rated the competition as severe, 24 states as moderate, and 12 as slight. Among these, 35 states indicated that some measures had been taken to regulate areas of competition or conflicts of interest, while 15 states indicated to the contrary.

Many local efforts have been made throughout the country in recent years to come to grips with the problem and develop solutions that will permit *reasonable* accommodation of the new minority water sports, while not penalizing unduly the traditional majority rights of fishermen to enjoy their preferred form of outdoor recreation essentially undisturbed. Few of the local trials that have evolved from efforts to solve this problem have as yet been fully evaluated. Nevertheless, a kind of pattern seems to be emerging from these experiences that may be helpful, toward some form of zoning, either in terms of space (area) or in terms of time (hours, days), or some possible combination of these. In any event, the Outdoor Recreation Resources Review Commission has stated in its report to the President and the Congress that "Public action is needed to resolve conflicts between recreation and other uses of water, *as well as among recreation activities themselves"* (emphasis added). Relative to the latter consideration the Commission said, in part:

"The use of such a device as activity zoning can do much to resolve these problems. Unless prompt action is taken, however, dangerous conditions will become even worse, as the demand for water-related outdoor recreation continues to climb."

The greatest contributions to be made toward a resolution of the problems of water conflicts will probably come from an application of the scientific method through research. C. W. Threinen (Wisconsin Conservation Department supervisor, lake classification studies), a close student of the subject of recreational water use, discussed the relationship of boat size and boat speed as factors in water sports conflicts, relative to lake size, wave size, and lake section in a thought-provoking article in the *Wisconsin Conservation Bulletin* for November-December, 1961. He presented these observations as being fundamental concepts of boating as he sees it, viz:

1. The space on big waters is ample for all activities, but on small waters as well as close to shore on all waters the little users and slow users have deathly fear of the fast boat.

2. The water height (feet) on a lake multiplied by 10 is equal to the practical maximum length of a boat.

3. The body of water that develops no more than a 6-inch wind wave should not have foot-high boat wakes.

In conclusion. Threinen stated that harmony, scale, and proportion are all part of our everyday life. He believes, if we can achieve this state of matter and mind on water, that a more peaceful existence seems assured.

Wisconsin has 4,136 named inland lakes which constitute its primary recreational asset. Increasingly-heavy recreational utilization of these lakes prompted the state legislature and Governor in 1959 to require the Conservation Commission to set up a classification of lakes by use. In some of the early (1962) results of the statewide study, it was recommended that one-fourth of the shoreline of every lake be placed in public ownership. A large portion of this amount should be dedicated to fish, wildlife, and esthetic purposes; included would be marshy shores of medium-sized lakes, and marshy bays, spawning bars and steep slopes on large lakes (over 1,000 acres). Threinen suggested specific zoning to save wetlands by requiring platted lots to be at least 3 feet above the high water mark, a 25-foot setback for septic tanks, additional measures to protect marshes and steep slopes, and prohibition of building, filling or alteration of lowlands important to aquatic production. The shallow waters of a lake are a zone of intense human activity, and the lake classification specialist recommended a shoreline activity zone about 200 feet wide within which motorboats would be restricted. Within this area are the spawning grounds for fish, duck rearing sites, anchorages, and swimming areas. Threinen stated:

"The slow-moving swimmer is no match for the fast boat traveling 10 times as fast as he is, nor is it reasonable for the fast boat skimming an entire shoreline to disrupt the fly fisherman carefully working one spot. Zoning and also speed and use regulation of water is very much akin to that on streets and highways. Through the application of zoning of water and land and acquisition of shore frontage, maintenance of prevailing preferred uses should be possible. Without these measures, deterioration of some major areas can be anticipated."

A three-month summer survey was made in 1960 by Wisconsin Conservation Department law enforcement air patrol and fishery personnel relative to recreational activities on 423 lakes throughout the state. Sport fishermen were found to predominate among the users of boating equipment, although the pattern varied as between northern Wisconsin and southern Wisconsin. In all, 31,617 boats were actually observed, with nine to 28 times more boats found on southern than on northern waters. In northern Wisconsin 80 per cent of all boats observed were engaged in fishing, compared to 60 per cent in southern waters. Some 1,000 water skiers and 988 sailboats were seen in the southern areas as compared to about 300 water skiers and 93 sailboats in the north. All in all, boat fishermen outnumbered all other types of boaters by two to one and outnumbered water skiers by 16 to one. Most lakes were found to provide at least 40 acres per water skier and average about 2½ acres per fishing boat. It was concluded, in part, that most northern Wisconsin waters have ample space for the boating public and that, in any case, "boaters usually don't get in each other's way on lakes of 1,000 acres or more."

The first two of an anticipated series of recommendations growing out of the Wisconsin Conservation Department's lake and stream classification studies were issued early in 1962. One proposed that no motorboats be permitted on lakes less than 50 acres in size, which are not part of a connected chain. The other asked that the speed of motorboats be limited to five miles per hour within 200 feet of shore on all lakes. The recommendation for no boats on the smaller lakes was based on the fact that with short distances and limited open water space, motorboats can cause substantial interference with other activities. A circular lake of 50 acres can be crossed in five minutes at a rowing speed of four miles per hour. The speed restriction near shore was based on the fact that this zone is used for swimming, piers, boat mooring, shallow water fishing and duck hunting, and is also a nesting, feeding, and nursery area for fish and waterfowl.

Construction of community fishing lakes. Lake construction for the purpose of creating new recreational fishing opportunities is doubtless the most tangible of all aspects of modern fish management, perhaps even outranking the fish hatchery in acceptability to the general public. It also provides an optimum situation where the fishery biologists can and do demonstrate this new axiom of fish conservation: "good fishing just doesn't happen but must be created through the work of competent biologists." As urbanization accelerates there will be a greater need for new fishing lakes in urban areas. Improved transportation will make it increasingly possible for urban dwellers to reach distant large reservoirs and other waters, but it will also be increasingly necessary to bring fishing to urban areas wherever possible to do so. By 1960, the state fishery agencies were expending eight per cent of the collective national outlay for fish conservation in the building of new fishing lakes. In the north-central and southern states, where this activity was concentrated at the time, expenditures averaged almost twice that much and were still higher in some individual states. It has been largely since 1950 that this activity has become prominent in state fishery programs and by 1960 only nine states—Alaska, Connecticut, Georgia, Hawaii, Louisiana, Maine, Massachusetts, Minnesota, and North Carolina—reported that they had no public fishing lake construction program. There is no apparent urgency in states where natural lakes abound; nevertheless, fishing areas near large population centers are increasingly needed even in water-rich states.

Periodic Sport Fishing Institute surveys of lakes built by state fish and game agencies revealed that 447 lakes totalling over 52,000 acres had been completed prior to 1954; 200 new lakes comprising over 24,000 acres were built for anglers in the period 1954-1956; an additional 228 new lakes were constructed totalling more than 54,000 acres in the three-year period through 1959. The latter is well over twice the lake area built in the previous three years. Eighty per cent of these newest lakes were less than 200 acres in area, averaging 50 surface acres. The remaining 20 per cent averaged 1,000 acres, compared to 580 acres in 1954-56. One-half are less than 20 acres, about as in previous years. In addition to the 875 lakes already completed, 84 more lakes were under construction or in advanced stages of planning, and thus committed, in 29 states at the close of 1959. These added 17,000-odd acres of new fishing water when they were completed either in 1960 or 1961, and averaged about 207 acres, thus continuing the trend of states to build increasingly larger fishing lakes.

The leading states, in terms of surface area of waters created are: Pennsylvania, Arkansas, Michigan, Iowa, Kansas, Ohio, Colorado, Kentucky, and Missouri. Other agencies, primarily federal, are building huge lakes for various purposes which also have great recreation values. The lakes included in these surveys are those constructed by state conservation agencies primarily for recreational fishing. The California Wildlife Conservation Board annually administers $750,000 (allocated from the state's tax on pari-mutuel betting) for lake construction, access and other related programs. This agency's present policy is to "exhaust all possibilities for the acquisition and development of available waters close to the public before embarking on a major lake construction program." North Dakota has been active in a program of rebuilding existing structures (primarily old CCC and WPA dams) in cooperation with the State Water Conservation Committee.

A number of states have very excellent fishing lake programs, but that of Alabama is one of the best documented as well as representing one of the best intensive public fishing lake programs in the nation. Altogether, as of 1962, the Alabama Conservation Department had constructed and was intensively managing 19 public fishing lakes totalling about 1,200 acres of new water. They had been open to fishing from one to eleven years. At the 1959 North American Wildlife Conference, Alabama's chief fishery biologist I. B. Byrd reported

TOTAL NUMBER (ACRES) OF LAKES REPORTED BUILT FOR PUBLIC FISHING*

State	thru 1953	1954-1965	1957-1959	Total
Alabama	13 (1,075)	5 (681)	1 (93)	19 (1,849)
Arizona	2 (770)		5 (270)	7 (1,040)
Arkansas	10 (7,810)	3 (1,682)	11 (10,545)	24 (20,037)
California	2 (115)	5 (524)	1 (35)	8 (1,210)
Colorado	13 (910)	8 (605)	12 (3,052)	33 (4,567)
Delaware	—	7 (250)	—	7 (250)
Florida	—	—	2 (187)	2 (187)
Idaho	1 (90)	—	1 (186)	2 (276)
Illinois	10 (1,471)	8 (417)	3 (91)	21 (1,979)
Indiana	18 (893)	2 (1,730)	1 (195)	21 (2,818)
Iowa	23 (2,708)	7 (4,633)	24 (5,300)	54 (12,641)
Kansas	22 (6,751)	10 (1,070)	6 (702)	38 (8,523)
Kentucky	10 (447)	21 (1,592)	24 (2,616)	55 (4,125)
Maryland	5 (50)	21 (158)	3 (98)	29 (306)
Michigan	16 (360)	5 (1,502)	19 (10,794)	40 (12,656)
Minnesota	1 (40)	—	—	1 (40)
Mississippi	6 (1,379)	3 (260)	4 (501)	13 (2,140)
Missouri	28 (593)	38 (2,759)	13 (567)	79 (3,919)
Montana	2 (6)	—	3 (97)	5 (103)
Nebraska	32 (2,552)	—	8 (456)	40 (3,008)
Nevada	—	—	1 (57)	1 (57)
New Hampshire	23 (1,073)	10 (721)	2 (355)	35 (2,149)
New Jersey	25 (1,988)	1 (100)	2 (37)	28 (2,125)
New Mexico	27 (907)	2 (184)	2 (22)	31 (1,113)
New York	—	—	2 (915)	2 (915)
North Dakota	—	—	5 1,183)	5 (1,183)
Ohio	18 (4,348)	10 (2,263)	7 (507)	35 (7,118)
Oklahoma	7 (144)	4 (500)	4 (720)	15 (1,364)
Oregon	1 (52)	—	—	1 (52)
Pennsylvania	44 (11,827)	4 (359)	14 (10,507)	61 (22,693)
Rhode Island	—	1 (1)	1 (4)	2 (5)
South Carolina	—	1 (40)	4 (385)	5 (425)
South Dakota	17 (1,575)	1 (136)	3 (820)	21 (2,531)
Tennessee	24 (1,320)	4 (800)	1 (325)	29 (2,445)
Texas	—	—	1 (1,200)	1 (1,200)
Utah	—	1 (15)	6 (311)	7 (326)
Vermont	—	2 (200)	5 (120)	7 (320)
Virginia	5 (560)	5 (535)	2 (84)	12 (1,179)
Washington	19 (181)	4 (78)	1 (74)	24 (333)
West Virginia	23 (104)	4 (92)	17 (393)	44 (589)
Wisconsin	—	1 (455)	4 (105)	5 (560)
Wyoming	—	2 (34)	3 (356)	5 (390)
Totals	447 (52,099)	200 (24,376)	228 (54,265)	875 (130,740)
Average size (in acres)	117	122	238	150

* In addition to the lakes listed, Louisiana reports 12 impoundments, totalling 63,190 acres, which were built for recreation purposes between 1932 and 1959. They are now managed by the state or local fish and game commissions. Pennsylvania totals include lakes built by the Fish Commission, Game Commission, and Department of Forests and Waters.

many details of the program* affecting 12 lakes (841 acres) among the 16 in operation at the time, that had been open to continuous (year-round) fishing for periods of two years or longer. Byrd effectively pinpointed and answered key questions about long-term angling success and seasonal distribution of catch in the Alabama fishing lakes. Three lakes (155 acres) had been open for 8 continuous years, three (163 acres) for 7 years, one (40 acres) for 6 years, four (233 acres) for 5 years, and one (250 acres) for 2 years. During the period 1950 to 1958, those 12 lakes supported 695,282 individual fishing trips. Altogether, some 2,530,182 fish weighing 746,598 pounds were recorded as caught—a minimal figure. An unknown quantity of fish were caught and went unrecorded.

* Byrd, I. B. 1959. Angling success and seasonal distribution of catch in Alabama's state-owned public fishing lakes. Trans. No. Amer. Wildl. Conf. (24):225-237. March).

Annually, for the 12 lakes, there were more than 162 fishing trips per acre resulting in an average harvest per acre exceeding 174 pounds of fish. This harvest was made up of about 137 pounds of Bluegills and Redear Sunfish, over 29 pounds of Largemouth Bass, 7 pounds of Bullheads, and less than 1 pound of Crappies per acre. The lowest annual utilization recorded for any of the 12 lakes was 89 individual fishing trips per acre; the highest was 242 trips. The lowest harvest was about 129 pounds of fish per acre; the highest was 248 pounds. The proportion of Bass to other species in the catch varied from about 7.5 per cent to about 38 per cent in individual lakes, but there was no correlation between Bass catch and age or size of the lake, number of fishing trips per acre, presence or absence of small quantities of either Bullheads or Crappies, or total yield.

For a period of 13 to 18 months following initial stocking in newly constructed lakes, no fishing is permitted. The first few weeks of fishing on a newly opened virgin lake—especially the first day—result in a very rapid harvest of adult fish. Byrd reported that this condition occurs only once—at initial opening—under continuous fishing conditions. In one extreme example, the catch on opening day was 58 pounds per acre. The average catch per acre for the first day, first week and first month for the 12 lakes has averaged about 27, 74, and 105 pounds, respectively. About 56 per cent of the opening year's catch for all lakes was taken during the initial three months of their angling history. Mr. Byrd noted that "These same conditions do not occur again during the life of the lake." When the lakes are open to continuous fishing, harvest and recruitment to the harvestable stocks occur simultaneously. At no other time does the population contain such a high percentage of harvestable fish as on the initial opening day, nor are the fish as easily caught. Excepting the high first-year harvest figures, representing a one-time typical condition, it is evident that the lakes have provided a year-round fishery with satisfactory seasonal distributions of catch, although a larger total catch was taken during the spring and summer than at other seasons. However, the catch per fisherman-hour was somewhat higher during the fall and winter.

The number of fishermen and the total poundages of fish caught increased gradually from January to May, with a peak in May and June, and then decreased gradually from June to December. The smallest number of fishermen and the smallest total catch occurred during the months of November, December, and January. The seasonal distribution of the catch of Bluegills and Redear Sunfish was more pronounced than that of Bass. The greatest poundages of Bluegill and Redear Sunfish were taken during the months of April to September with peak catches occurring in May and June. The smallest poundages of Bluegill and Redear Sunfish were caught during November, December, January, and February. The seasonal catches of Bass were fairly well divided among 10 of the thirteen 4-week periods with slightly larger catches occurring during April, May, June and September. The smallest catches of Bass were recorded in November, December, and January; however, the poundages of Bass caught during these three months were about equal to the combined poundages of Bluegill and Redear Sunfish taken.

The average first-year catch was about 224 pounds of fish per acre. After that the average yearly catch per acre remained relatively stable, varying from about 144 to 179 pounds per acre for periods up to 8 years. This evidence disproves a popular belief that lakes stocked with Bass and Bluegill always become unproductive after the first year they are open to fishing. In the Alabama program, intensive management includes regular fertilization to offset naturally low productivity, weed control, population manipulation, occasional renovation, and restocking as needed—*all based on 20 years of research* at Alabama Polytechnic Institute and its successor institution, Auburn University.

New findings from research suggest the possibility that even greater yields may be possible in the future should they prove needed. For example, astounding catches of Channel Catfish in a 12.4-acre experimental lake at the Auburn University Fisheries Experiment Station (Alabama) have emphasized the suitability of this sport species for some managed ponds. Fishermen caught 1,292 pounds per acre of Channel Catfish in one year from the lake, according to a report presented at the Southeast Association of Game and Fish Commissioners. The lake was stocked in February, 1958, with 2,000 three-inch fingerlings per acre, and pelleted fish food was added daily at rates varying from 5 to 25 pounds per acre. The pond was opened to fishing in September, when the Catfish averaged 0.7 pounds each. In the ensuing year, 579 fishermen caught 1,292 pounds of Channel Catfish, 37 pounds of Bass, and 27 pounds of other fish per surface acre. A daily fishing fee of $1 was charged, so the average price of Catfish to the angler was 46 cents per pound. They caught 62 per cent of the Catfish stocked. Deducting costs for fertilizer, feed, fingerlings, and labor, the experiment netted $112 per acre. Experiments are continuing to provide needed data on optimum stocking, feeding, and restocking rates, and the use of other species combinations.

Earliest applications of discoveries such as this may well be made in connection with the commercial development of small privately-owned artificial lakes for recreational fishing on a fee-basis. According to a survey by a University of Michigan graduate student about 1,500 such fee fishing ponds were operating in the United States by 1960. Most of these "catch-out" ponds have been opened since 1945, and are most numerous in Pennsylvania (238) and in California (186); 55 per cent handled Trout only, 16 per cent warmwater species only, and 29 per cent handled both. Operators usually charged 10 cents per inch, or $1 to $1.50 per pound of fish caught, and required anglers to keep all fish caught. Trout were typically stocked at 1,000 to 2,000 per acre, and were from 7 to 15 inches long. It was concluded that catch-out ponds provide recreation, but do not make a significant contribution to the over-all sport fishery of any state. Most catch-out pond operators had less than 3 ponds, totalling 4 acres, with annual incomes under $3,000.

Rehabilitation of old fishing waters. The reproductive potential of most fishes is typically more than adequate to maintain high population levels. When environmental conditions are unfavorable—for example, when waters are muddy or when predators are few in number—hordes of small pan fish or big rough fish may overrun lakes or streams. Sport fishes of desirable size are then scarce, and a fresh start with desired species is required if good fishing is to be restored. One of the outstanding dividends of research has been the development of several chemical compounds now in use to "eradicate" undesirable fish and permit starting over. Both the chemicals employed and the techniques for treating "unbalanced" fishing waters have been much improved since 1956. Nevertheless, it is still very difficult to get complete kills in many situations. In practice this may often be an academic problem since many sources of recontamination exist to plague the fishery manager. Not the least of these is the unthinking angler who dumps his unused bait, thus often reintroducing undesirable fishes. Complete kills are desirable because they lengthen the time interval before retreatment becomes necessary, thereby reducing maintenance costs. Complete draining and refilling is often practiced where feasible to establish a clean slate. Because of possible occurrence of unnoticed pockets of water or thick deposits of muck, where fishes can survive, this practice also has its drawbacks. Nevertheless, rehabilitation is one of the most effective means of improving fishing. A big need is for cheaper chemicals, reduced labor requirements, and especially chemicals that are in-

NUMBER OF AREA OF WARMWATER LAKES REHABILITATED

State	Number in 1957-1959		Total area (acres)		
	with chemicals	by drainage	Thru 1956	1957-1959	Total
Alabama	3		1,572	200	1,772
Arizona			985	—	985
Arkansas		9	1,150	8,000	9,150
California	9		1,709	400	2,109
Colorado	5		581	145	766
Connecticut	4		120	350	470
Delaware			670	—	670
Florida	9		20,403	2,890	23,293
Georgia	200		1,700	1,400	3,100
Illinois	212		951	1,473	2,424
Indiana	1	3	—	71	71
Iowa	24	7	8,250	11,370	19,620
Kansas	97		6,593	829	7,422
Kentucky	2,022		5,070	2,000	7,070
Louisiana	13	1	1,180	1,240	2,420
Maine	1		—	5	5
Maryland		4	1,000	145	1,145
Massachusetts	36		1,483	2,889	4,372
Michigan	55		1,100	4,144	5,244
Minnesota	5		194	2,773	2,967
Missouri	758		1,077	1,535	2,612
Montana			116	—	116
Nebraska	69	2	74	3,379	3,453
Nevada	2		—	157	157
New Hampshire	4		401	551	952
New Jersey			548	—	548
New Mexico	2		4	36	40
New York			39	—	39
North Carolina			94	—	94
North Dakota	31		7,545	8,684	16,229
Ohio	16	7	50	521	571
Oklahoma	75	2	11,335	1,500	12,835
Oregon	8		882	55	937
Pennsylvania	8		394	2,790	3,184
Rhode Island			9	—	9
South Carolina			685	—	685
South Dakota	44	3	1,656	3,510	5,166
Tennessee	125	6	583	150	733
Texas	8		3,665	3,062	6,727
Utah	1		—	28	28
Virginia		50	120	400	520
Washington	5		75	80	155
West Virginia		7	111	40	151
Wisconsin	51		2,279	6,634	8,913
Wyoming		2	727	—	727
Total	3,903	103	87,180	73,476	160,656

NUMBER AND AREA OF TROUT LAKES REHABILITATED

State	Number in 1957-1959		Total area (acres)		
	with chemicals	by drainage	Thru 1956	1957-1959	Total
Alaska	6		1,464	225	1,689
Arizona	3		911	360	1,271
Arkansas	1		—	3	3
California	44	1	2,026	2,500	4,526
Colorado	8		1,268	485	1,753
Connecticut	15		160	850	1,010
Georgia			4	—	4
Idaho	56	6	3,500	21,740	25,240
Illinois			3	—	3
Indiana	1		—	1	1
Iowa		1	—	3	3
Maine	33		2,160	2,189	4,349
Maryland	2	3	—	34	34
Massachusetts	56		2,026	3,609	5,635
Michigan	63		1,551	1,300	2,851
Minnesota	36		359	1,721	2,080
Montana	41		324	4,832	5,156
Nebraska	9		4	70	74
Nevada			850	—	850
New Hampshire	3		5,214	150	5,364
New Mexico	4	3	125	160	285
New York			3,407	—	3,407
North Carolina			94	—	94
North Dakota	10		—	421	421
Oregon	22		7,824	4,800	12,624
Pennsylvania	8		307	164	471
Rhode Island	2		161	405	566
South Dakota	6	2	100	520	620
Utah	19		3,610	6,856	10,466
Vermont	2		45	108	153
Virginia		1	—	50	50
Washington	90		22,539	12,320	34,859
West Virginia		2	83	10	93
Wisconsin	18		1,001	422	1,423
Wyoming	5		1,074	400	1,474
Total	563	19	62,194	66,708	128,902

dividually selective for various species of fish. By 1960, the states were devoting two per cent of their collective fish conservation expenditures to rehabilitating old lakes, mostly by means of fish toxicants to remove existing population (and restocking).

Forty-eight states have reported that they use chemical treatment to restore good fishing to unbalanced waters. Only Hawaii and Mississippi had not utilized this method of complete rehabilitation before 1960. From 1957 through 1959, the state fishery agencies rehabilitated 4,588 lakes, totalling 140,000 surface acres. All prior recorded rehabilitation (1930-1956) included 3,989 lakes comprising 149,000 acres. Obviously, much increased dependence has been placed on this effective fish management tool in recent years. Based on lake rehabilitation expenditure data furnished to the organization by the states, Sport Fishing Institute estimated the average cost of chemical treatment was about $25 per surface acre in 1960. Several analyses have indicated that treatment costs average about $1.25 per acre-foot of water volume treated. The average depth of lakes treated was around 20 feet.

The surface area of warmwater lakes that were rehabilitated during 1957-1959 amounted to 73,476 acres. This was an increase of nearly 10,000 acres over the record for the previous three-year period (total of 63,940 acres). The area of Trout lakes rehabilitated during 1957-1959 totalled 66,708 acres, nearly double the 36,315 acres treated during 1954-56. The five most active states in warmwater lake rehabilitation during 1957-1959, in order of decreasing acreage of water treated, were: Iowa, North Dakota, Arkansas, Wisconsin, and Michigan. Up to 1956 the top five in the same order were: Florida, Oklahoma, Iowa, North Dakota, and Kansas. It should be recognized that much additional water area involving only partial or "selective" treatment was not included in the figures. An outstanding example of this is the treatment during the triennium of lakes totalling 43,000 acres in Florida, including huge Lake Apopka (deliberately treated by plan in each of three successive years), for control of overabundant Gizzard

Shad. California treated streams in the watersheds of several future reservoirs that will contain a total of 7,000 acres when completed. Similarly, the five most active states in reclamation of Trout lakes, in the 1957-1959 period, were: Idaho, Washington, Utah, Montana, and Oregon. Through 1956, however, the corresponding top five were: Washington, Oregon, New Hampshire, Utah, and Idaho. Here it should be recognized that Washington, Oregon, and New Hampshire began utilizing this important tool early and are actually far ahead of most other states. New Hampshire, a very small state, is so far ahead in its work that it has already treated most of its suitable waters. Its program has matured to what is principally a maintenance program. In proportion to available waters suited to this kind of management, Massachusetts and New York should both also be reckoned among the leading users of this sophisticated Trout management tool.

According to figures released by the New Hampshire Fish and Game Department, the average cost of reclaiming nine Trout ponds with chemicals in 1956 was about $1.71 per acre-foot of water treated. This figure was based on total cost of reclaiming nine ponds, consisting of 210 surface acres of 3,748 acre-feet of water volume, given as $6,713. Seven of the ponds were reclaimed at an average cost of $1.23 per acre-foot. In two cases, where dams and fish barriers had to be constructed on the outlet, average cost jumped over 2½-fold—to $3.11 per acre foot. Even the latter figure was within the bounds of economic feasibility. Once reclaimed, the ponds produce satisfactory fishing for several years from plants of small trout, usually of fingerling sizes, that may be produced in large quantities at very low annual cost. Without reclamation, the fishery can be maintained satisfactorily only by raising and stocking catchable-size Trout, a very expensive procedure.

The 210 acres of reclaimed water mentioned above could be stocked adequately with fingerlings costing about $500 per year. The ponds might yield 20 pounds of Trout per acre per year—4,200 pounds in all. With all costs considered it costs about $1.00 per pound to produce catchable-size hatchery Trout for stocking. If recovery were 75 per cent (that's high in the absence of reclamation) of stocked catchable Trout from the ponds in question, a total of 5,600 pounds would have to be stocked to yield a comparable 20 pounds per acre. It would cost some $5,600 annually to achieve it under the conditions described. It actually costs about $6,713 to reclaim the ponds. If stocked with fingerlings for three years, at an annual cost of $500, planting costs would amount to $1,500 for that period. Total costs, including reclamation, bring the total up to $8,213, or about $2,740 annually. This is less than half what would be the cost of maintaining an equivalent fishery by stocking catchable-size Trout. Usually the beneficial effects of reclamation last for a period longer than five years (it has been proven to be longer in many cases). Pro-rated on a minimum five-year base, average annual costs of furnishing good fishing would drop to less than $1,845, or about one-third of the probable costs of depending upon catchable Trout plants to furnish the fishing.

With demonstrated effectiveness of reclamation techniques as a means of creating good fishing a matter of repeated record in all parts of the country, some of the western states are beginning to undertake really large reclamation projects. Some of these are designed to make the best possible use of sections of large rivers that are being impounded by other agencies by treating the rivers to remove existing fish populations immediately prior to closure of the dams. This is considered better than sitting idly by and allowing rough fish to take over the new reservoir from the outset and prevent even temporary development of good fishing in the reservoir later. For example, the Oregon Game Commission recently renovated 3,000-acre Davis Lake by introducing carefully controlled quantities of toxaphene in order to kill off the Roach (a kind of large minnow) with which it was infested. An abundance of Roach in the lake, consuming most of the natural food supplies, prevented successful management for sport fishing. The treatment was delayed because of the unknown destination of the lake outflow which seeps beneath the lava flows. Two years of tests with rodamine dyes failed to disclose reappearance of these waters anywhere in the area. Rainbow Trout and Kokanee and possibly Atlantic Salmon will be stocked in the lake. In another example, the San Juan River above Navajo Dam in New Mexico was treated in 1961 with rotenone by the New Mexico and Colorado fish and game departments, in cooperation with the U. S. Bureau of Sport Fisheries and Wildlife. Purpose was to rid the future reservoir of rough fish for a few years, at least, and thus give desired sport fishing a solid head start. Undertaken under the Colorado River Storage Act as a public works measure, 40 miles of the San Juan, 13 miles of the Pine, and 14 miles of the Piedra rivers, plus additional tributaries, were treated with $63,000 worth of rotenone (12,600 gallons, 5% strength). Recreational fishing is expected to be greatly benefited.

Somewhat similar to that of the Navajo Dam preimpoundment treatment in New Mexico was the 1962 treatment of Wyoming's Green River above the Flaming Gorge Dam site to rid the new reservoir of Trout-food competitor species at the outset in order to be able to create a sport fishery for Trout, predicted to attract 90,000 man-days of fishing the fist year. Funds ($130,000) were appropriated under the Colorado River Storage Act for use by the states of Wyoming and Utah in cooperation with the U. S. Fish and Wildlife Service, as a public works measure. Over 900,000 anglers reside within a day's drive of the area, so that the first year's estimated use may well prove conservative. In this instance, the river flows through a National Monument considerably downstream from the dam site. In order to prevent an unnecessary kill of fish in the Monument by transport of the chemical down stream with the normal flow of the river, an oxidizing agent, potassium permanganate, was introduced to speed up the expected natural neutralization of the rotenone. The use of potassium permanganate as a detoxifying agent was tested in 1955 at Alabama Polytechnic Institute (Auburn) and reported in *The Progressive Fish-Culturist* for January, 1956. About a year later the method was confirmed by research at the University of New Hampshire, which also showed that chlorine could also be used as a detoxifying agent in ponds.

Fish population control. Complete rehabilitation is not yet a practical tool of fisheries management on truly large waters, so that other means of manipulating fish populations in favor of sport fish production and effect a significant degree of control over abundant competing species (generally called "rough fish" for convenience) must be employed to make better fishing. A variety of approaches are available, such as partial poisoning to take advantage of vulnerable habits or various life history vantage points to effect a high degree of selectivity over the kinds of fishes being killed. For example, research has shown that treating farm pond margins with rotenone at mid-day will usually affect large numbers of intermediate-sized Bluegills but very few Bass. At other times of the day many Bass would be killed as well. Some fish are more sensitive to rotenone than others; dilute concentrations of rotenone will kill large numbers of Gizzard Shad but have little effect on other species. Yellow Perch are similarly more sensitive than some other species. Also, thermal stratification in the water may provide useful barriers to dispersal of rotenone below certain depths, thereby in summer simultaneously exposing warmwater species and protecting coldwater forms. Various kinds of nets may be utilized to catch large numbers of fish at certain times under certain conditions. Drainage or partial drainage, or a combination of several methods, may be utilized. All the states combined directed about three per cent of their fish conservation expenditures by 1960 toward improvement of fishing by these means. Such activities were most favored by the north-central states which spent twice that much, and by the southern states which spent a little above the national average.

Rough fish, like Carp, Gizzard Shad, and various kinds of Suckers (Buffalofish, etc.) feed by sucking up food from the bottom along with big mouthfuls of silt. They swallow the food and expel the silt out through the gill cover openings. Large populations of rough fish keep clouds of silt permanently suspended in the water, making it muddy. Studies at the University of Oklahoma have demonstrated some of the harmful effects of this situation. Food production and visibility are drastically reduced so that sight-feeding sport fish like Bass find less food available to them. Growth and survival is reduced. In addition, the muddiness interferes with Bass reproduction but aids reproduction of such fish as Bluegills and Catfish. Result is overpopulation by small pan fish, scarcity of the larger sport fishes like Bass, and poor fishing. Complete removal of competing rough fish often improves fishing for sport fishes. In small waters this is a growing management practice. In large waters, the cost of total removal is prohibitive. Therefore, selective or partial removal of competing rough fish is generally practiced, either by partial poisoning or netting.

Florida has emphasized partial poisoning the most and has treated 30,000-acre Lake Apopka according to preconceived plan in each of three successive years with concentrations of rotenone strong enough to kill the overabundant Gizzard Shad but not strong enough to kill any great numbers of Bass. Results have been good enough to put the fishing camp-guide system back in business after it had collapsed following over-running of the lake by Gizzard Shad and associated collapse of the sport fishery for Largemouth Bass. Up to three million pounds of Shad were killed in each year of the project to rejuvenate the fishing. Other southern states are interested in this approach. Mississippi, for example, has tried this on a smaller scale at 1,2000-acre Bluff Lake on the U. S. Noxubee National Wildlife Refuge. Both states are still evaluating the long-term results. Texas biologists, who first discovered by accident the selectivity of rotenone in low concentration for Gizzard Shad, have been very active in using this new management tool.

Some years ago, Iowa fishery workers discussed their many years of rough fish seining in a meeting of the American Fisheries Society. They concluded that in a few lakes where rough fish seining had been vigorous year after year, game fish populations were large and sport fishing good. On some other lakes with large rough fish populations where use of the commercial gear was not intensive game fishes were not abundant. Sport species like Crappies are so prolific in many waters that seemingly intensive angling scarcely affects their abundance. In such cases intensive commercial fishing assures availability of abundant, fast growing, large Crappies for the angler. Illinois permits commercial fishing for Crappies because of this, with great benefit to angling quality and no ill effect on supply. The properly regulated commercial fisherman can be an important ally to sport fishing on many waters. In South Dakota contracts are awarded annually by the Game, Fish and Parks Commission to commercial fishermen for removal of rough fish from the state's large reservoirs. Large-mesh gill nets and trammel nets are often employed nowadays, rather than hoop nets and seines that had proven too ineffective for this purpose in previous years in waters of this type. It is known that few game fish are taken, and any that are can be returned to the water alive or disposed by law in such manner as to yield no revenue to the contract fishermen. Thus, there is no incentive to attempt to take game fish, especially under proper supervision.

The main idea behind rough fish control programs of state conservation departments is to favor growth and production of desired sport fish. It is or should be largely incidental that the fish removed may have commercial value. Naturally, it is desirable not to waste useful protein whenever possible, but this must be kept strictly secondary to the objective of improving sport fishing. Only then can commercial fishing methods be used properly as a useful tool of sport fish management. In 1954, the Wisconsin Conservation Department began a 10-year program of rough fish removal on 138,000-acre Lake Winnebago, using seining crews aimed principally at overabundant Freshwater Drum. In the first five years, more than 20 million pounds of Freshwater Drum were removed from the lake (about 29 pounds per acre, annually —a 20 per cent harvest). Although no firm conclusions were drawn at the time on the results of the program, accurate records of every net lifted in 1959 showed the following population changes, as compared to 1958: Walleyes, up 43 per cent; Sauger, up 52 per cent; White Bass, up 78 per cent; Perch up 45 per cent.

Based on theory, effective control of rough fish, which compete with game fish for food and space and damage the habitat by muddying the water as they feed, should result in improved populations of game fish. This in turn means better fishing. In practice, this sometimes works and sometimes doesn't. Among possible reasons for failure of rough fish control to be followed by better fishing, these two seem to stand forth as important factors: (1) inadequate fraction of the rough fish are removed, and (2) rough fish were not sufficiently abundant to interfere with game fish production in the first place. A number of states having abundant rough fish populations are making successful if costly inroads on them to the benefit of sport fishing, although success is temporary unless control effects are massive and continuing.

One such state is Colorado, where thousands of tons of Carp threatened fishing in 1,500-acre North Sterling Reservoir. Newspaper reporters of the *Greeley Tribune* wrote of the results of Carp control that they observed by 1960. They reported that 400,000 pounds of the rough fish were removed from the reservoir in 1954, equal to 266 pounds per acre. The average size of sport fish has since increased decidedly; in 1954 the fishermen caught 31,936 fish weighing 4,500 pounds; in 1959, they caught a total of 8,746 fish weighing 6,480 pounds. The number of fish caught by the fishermen was reduced, but the average size and weight of the fish had increased several-fold, resulting in improved quality of fishing. In the fall of 1959, test netting indicated that the remaining rough fish population had been reduced to an average of about 20 pounds per surface acre—less than 10 per cent of the 1954 figure. The value of rough fish control in this reservoir was convincingly demonstrated by the Largemouth Black Bass population. Prior to 1954, those fish were present in the reservoir in relatively small numbers and, although they reproduced successfully almost every year, they could not compete with the rough fish. Accordingly, Bass failed to survive in the numbers needed to supply the fishermen with decent fishing. In 1956 and 1957, the Bass got off excellent spawns. By 1958, the Largemouth Black Bass made up 12 per cent of the total number of fish caught by the fishermen, and in 1959 they made up 24 per cent of the total fish harvested from the reservoir.

Improvement of fish habitat. One of the ever-popular forms of fish management is habitat improvement, but it has traditionally been most popular in the north-central states where it was developed and has been used extensively—sometimes with dubious benefits. Those states spend over twice as much (7%) as any other region but, nationally, such expenditures accounted for about 4 per cent of all fishery outlay by 1960. A great deal of research has been done, especially by scientists at the University of Michigan's famed Institute for Fisheries Research, operated in cooperation with the Michigan Conservation Department. The Institute, first under the direction of Dr. Carl L. Hubbs, later Dr. Albert S. Hazzard, and currently Dr. Gerald P. Cooper, has also been a national center for research on Trout toward which stream improvement has been largely oriented. The practice of installing in-stream structures is designed to utilize the hydraulic digging forces of stream flow to scour silt away from food producing gravel and spawning sites, to create a desired ratio of pools and riffles, dig channels, and otherwise improve the habitat for Trout. Judiciously done, there is little doubt that improvement in Trout carrying capacity can be achieved by these means, *provided* other factors such as temperature and stream flow are suitable. These are matters principally of good watershed management, stream bank shade, etc.

In streams. One of the most recent studies of the value of in-stream structures in Trout management, conducted by fishery biologists of the Tennessee Game and Fish Commission utilizing D-J funds, serves to summarize the value of conventional stream improvement work to Trout fishing.

During the study, which covered a four-year period from mid-1954 through 1958, 13 stream alteration structures were built on a flat shallow half-mile section of North River in 1954. Structures included four basic designs: wedge dam, modified wedge dam, K-dam, and single-wing deflector; total construction costs were about $768, or $59 per structure. The structures have been effective in providing habitat and have been durable. The wild Rainbow Trout in the study area decreased in numbers during the two years following construction, associated with an increase in the number of fishermen. A significant increase in the number of young-of-the-year Trout occurred and the standing crop of year-old Trout gradually increased, in spite of greater fishing intensity in the improved area. These specific conclusions were reached with respect to environmental changes that followed construction of the 13 structures:

(1) The flow of water over low dams will effectively dig pools in the hard, rubble streambeds characteristic of Southern Appalachian Trout streams.

(2) In streams flowing from well established watersheds, the pools formed above low dams will remain for many years.

(3) Single-wing deflectors will successfully divert and accelerate stream flow to cut a deepened channel along the terminal ends of the structures.

(4) A better distribution of the fishing load on a stream can be achieved by installing Trout cover devices in shallow stretches having few pools.

(5) A significant increase in young-of-the-year Rainbow Trout (3-5 inches) may be attributed to the quiet water and shelter resulting from stream improvement.

(6) The standing crop of one-year-old Rainbows (6-8 inches) gradually increased, in spite of greater fishing intensity in the improved areas.

Some pilot studies of watershed stabilization have been conducted by a few states like Michigan, Wisconsin, and North Carolina, confirming the value of this kind of activity in retarding runoff and stabilizing stream flow, reducing harmful silt loads, and improving water temperatures. This sort of fish management is beyond the direct resources of fishery agencies, and depends upon the application of generally good soil and forest conservation practices by landowners. Fishery agencies must rely on education programs, coordinating with other agencies, and must practice the fine art of gentle persuasion at every opportunity. Studies in Ohio suggest that this is also the best approach currently available for improvement of warmwater streams for fishing, a generally neglected aspect of fish conservation.

Another means of improving Trout streams is a by-product of dam construction by other agencies. If high dams are constructed, they impound deep lakes that stratify in summer and store large quantities of cold water in their depths, and fishery agencies can recommend that the outlet be placed near the bottom of the dam. As requirements for minimum flow downstream are met, cold water will then be released assuring that Trout can survive (if oxygenated; some means of agitating the water as it leaves the dam will assure it). One of the nation's best known Trout streams, Arkansas' famed White River, has risen to national prominence in recent years as a direct result of low-level coldwater releases favorably influencing water temperatures for many miles downstream from Bull Shoals Reservoir.

In lakes. The Michigan Institute for Fisheries Research was also a center for early investigational work on lake improvement principles and procedures. Over several decades, it has gradually become clear that installation of artificial structures does not affect the productive capacity of the body of water involved but serves chiefly to make certain species of fish more readily available to anglers when both fish and anglers are led to concentrate at the same places. Some fish are more affected than others, and the structures—fish shelter's, brush shelters, or artificial fishing reefs—are useful principally in waters or areas relatively barren of natural cover. There is some evidence because of conditions and embryonic organisms that prevail in saltwater that the reefs are far more useful for the improvement of saltwater fishing than for freshwater fishing. In fresh water, lake improvement structures are generally in the form of brush shelters. Use of brush is far preferable in fresh waters than use of junked auto bodies (as often employed in salt water) because the latter, long-lasting in fresh water, soon transform fresh waters into semi-permanent junk yards that are especially objectionable in the relatively clear, cold waters of the more northern states. The much more corrosive action of salt water greatly reduces their permanency and thus their objectionability.

It has been estimated that a million or more dollars have been spent nationally in the past several decades constructing and installing brush shelters in freshwater lakes and reservoirs intended to benefit sport fish. Considerable work has been done on how to construct them, where to place them, what depths, etc. They make popular sportsmen projects because they offer tangible activities that small groups can undertake with a minimum of equipment and guidance. Obviously, they're not much good unless they actually benefit fish and, eventually, fishing. Unfortunately, little by way of actual evaluation of the effect of shelters on ultimate fishing success was available until recently. Apart from any biological effects upon fish, brush shelters at the very least give an important psychological lift to anglers. They provided specific goals or locations for the fishing effort. To anglers on unfamiliar waters this can make all the difference between success and failure.

With the advent of federal-aid (D-J) funds in recent years, a few states have set out to determine just how valuable brush shelters are as fish management tools. Among them, Virginia and Tennessee have reported interesting if limited findings.

State fishery biologists installed several brush shelters in 145-acre Holliday Lake in central Virginia in late 1955. They then compared fishing success in shelter areas with fishing success for the rest of the lake during the ensuing 1956 fishing season. A catch record was also secured for the lake in the previous year (1955) when no shelters were present in the lake. Results showed a definite *increase in angler-success for Black Crappies* in the shelter areas over the rest of the lake. Over-all fishing pressure increased over 15 per cent from 1955 to 1956. But the harvest of Black Crappies increased 40 per cent in 1956, after installation of the shelters. Fishing effort at the shelters was only 22 per cent of total effort. However, 57 per cent of all Crappies harvested were taken at the shelters. The average daily catch per angler included three Black Crappies taken at the shelters plus two Black Crappies from the rest of the lake. Successful angling for Crappies was concentrated during April and May. The effect of the shelters was to concentrate the Black Crappies in well defined areas of accessibility for the fishermen. On the other hand no such influence was evident for other species present in the lake. Tennessee fishery biologists studied the problem in Fort Loudon Reservoir near Knoxville with respect to White Crappies. Their findings were at best inconclusive —or suggested that the shelters had little influence on fishing success for this species. Comparing the catch in coves with and without shelters revealed no increase in catch of White Crappies per man-hour in coves where brush shelters were located.

Control of excess aquatic weed growths is an important means of improving lake habitat. Excessive aquatic vegetation promotes overpopulation and stunting by pan fishes by providing too much protection from predation to these prey species. Thus, fertilization in southern farm ponds and larger community lakes has as one of its main objectives the control of rooted aquatic vegetation. It is accomplished by stimulating more or less continuous production of plankton blooms that absorb the sunlight thus preventing the other growths. However, the most commonly used aquatic herbicide is sodium arsenite, a deadly poison dangerous to use where warm-blooded animals might use the water within a few days following treatment. Nevertheless, at least one state uses large amounts of this material; in fact, Wisconsin stands out probably as "most active" among the 48; the State Board of Health used 18,830 gallons of commercial sodium arsenite in 1955 for aquatic weed control, with general interest in aquatic weed control increasing throughout the state. Considerable interest has been shown regarding the use of chemical weed control agents as fish management tools in those waters which have stunted pan fish and tremendous weed populations. Waters of this type also generally offer difficult fishing conditions, and may yield poor crops of fish at times. Nuisance algae were controlled in 1955 in Wisconsin waters with 36,713 pounds of copper sulfate, 400 pounds of Phygon, 185 gallons of Cutrine, and 90 gallons of Delrad. In addition, biologists of the Board applied 1,740 pounds of copper sulphate, 550 pounds of copper carbonate, and 320 pounds of lime to three lakes to control "swimmer's itch"; 125 gallons of Cutrine were used to control leeches in one lake.

Obviously, sodium arsenite (As_2O_3) is one chemical that has been and is widely used for aquatic plant control. One reason is that there is generally regarded to be a wide safety margin with respect to fish when used for this purpose. It has been known that some fish-food organisms suffer from concentrations of the chemical required to kill aquatic plants. Beyond this, little attention has been accorded its general effects on fish production. In 1955, however, the Alabama Conservation Department's Annual Report stated: "Recent tests involving two applications of either 4 or 8 ppm As_2O_3 indicated reductions in bluegill production of 30 and 65 per cent, respectively, and a very noticeable decrease in production of bottom organisms."

From time to time promising innovations in habitat improvement come to light, the product of active imagination working upon newly discovered knowledge about fishes. Such an imaginative development is represented by an experimental management technique of inducing Muskellunge to spawn in protected areas within suitable Michigan lakes. Recognizing that hatchery rearing of Muskies is extremely costly and difficult, Michigan biologists propose to bring about increased spawning in the natural environment. Experimental steps include blocking off two spawning areas located within natural lakes by means of sheet piling barriers; adding alfalfa hay to the areas to provide a spawning matrix and cover for fry; and installation of floating cover devices to protect adults and fry. Following these preparations, existing fish in the areas would be eliminated with 1/10 ppm rotenone, and predacious insects controlled with kerosene, and the spawning bays treated with 10-10-10 commercial fertilizer and torula yeast. Adult Muskellunge would be introduced after injection with 1 cc. pituitary gland extract taken from Northern Pike. If all goes well, the little Muskies produced would be released into the main body of the lake upon reaching two inches in length. Previous attempts to introduce this fabled fish into Michigan lakes and rivers have failed to provide good angling. Fishery biologists believe that failure to reproduce or too few stocked may be the reasons for lack of success. They hope to greatly augment fingerling production through the establishment of protected spawning areas, a technique which has also been advocated for Northern Pike in other north-central states.

In coastal salt waters. Until at least a dozen years ago, little interest existed among marine fishery groups in possible use of artificial fish reefs as fish management tools to manipulate fish populations in U. S. coastal marine waters. It has, of course, been well known at least since World War I that fishing in the vicinity of wrecked ships in coastal marine waters is especially productive. Indeed, it appears to be one of those things that is perfectly obvious, actually not requiring organized research to establish as a general principle, although there is both indirect and direct evidence supporting it. For example, a study of the summer standing crop of fish on a small (2½ acre) isolated Bermuda coral reef revealed a population of fishes amounting to about 420 pounds per acre. This was several-fold that of surrounding sandy areas. A recent Hawaii Dingell-Johnson study (federal aid in fish restoration) revealed a standing crop of fish comprising about 23 pounds per acre on a suitable site selected for the placement of artificial fish shelters in depths of 80 feet in Maunalua Bay, Oahu. A related earlier study indicated a 16-fold increase over pre-construction estimates in the weight of fish on an isolated artificial reef placed in the Yokohama Bay area.

The number of wrecks was greatly increased along our shores during World War II, and the fame of productive fishing grounds off Ocean City, Maryland, and off Morehead City, North Carolina, is associated with that fact. The productivity of ocean wreck fishing undoubtedly was the chief stimulant to early post-war efforts to establish artificial fishing reefs in coastal marine waters. Choice of location was probably governed principally by convenience for anglers rather than by any but the most general biological considerations. Possibly the first recorded example of coastal marine reef construction was that of the so-called "McAllister Grounds," near Long Island. It was built in 1950 following its proposal by marine fishery biologists as a possibly beneficial use of broken masonry building materials then being discarded by dumping at sea over a deep gorge off New York Harbor. Later, a group of charter boat captains prevailed upon the Schaefer Brewing Company to donate 14,000 surplus wood beer cases for a similar purpose. These were weighted with concrete and sunk off Fire Island in 1953. There was little or no tie-in with official agencies in either instance so that results went unevaluated and unrecorded.

Unquestionably the first really substantial effort to construct artificial marine fishing reefs was initiated in Alabama waters of the Gulf of Mexico, starting in 1953. At that time, the Orange Beach Deep-Sea Fishing Association (an organization of party-boat interests), with the approval and encouragement of the Alabama Department of Conservation, began construction of the first of a series of artificial snapper banks, utilizing junked auto bodies. Since then, the Conservation Department has created a number of additional artificial snapper banks at various locations in Gulf waters. Altogether, several thousand auto bodies have been dumped on the Gulf floor off Alabama to make better fishing for marine anglers. There is no question that better fishing for Alabama anglers has resulted. No sport fishing for snappers occurred in the areas utilized before the banks were constructed. Only then, the snapper fishing became phenomenal. Not only snappers moved onto the banks in large numbers. Groupers, jewfish, trigger fish, king mackerel, dolphin, cobia (ling), and other species are often taken abundantly in their vicinity. As a result of these experiences, and the publicity that followed, similar projects were rapidly adopted elsewhere.

Altogether, 12 states have had one or more artificial fishing reefs constructed in their coastal marine waters, dating at least from 1950. The Texas Game and Fish Commission, using funds newly acquired through extension of licensing to the state's saltwater anglers, has embarked on a vigorous program of marine sport fishery development. Creation of artificial snapper banks has received early attention, using many hundreds of old auto bodies cabled together in bundles of four and dumped from barges in each of several locations. California set up evaluation studies under the D-J program to measure the relative effectiveness, durability, and costs of different materials—namely, auto bodies, streetcars, quarry rock, and prefabricated concrete units (5x8x2½-foot dimensions). In short order, Hawaii, Guam, and New Jersey also set up reef evaluation D-J projects. Delaware has organized a similar evaluation project. Alabama has worked out plans for a D-J development project to provide for additional future construction. Maryland has studied some aspects of the problem briefly. Sportsmen's groups in Virginia, North Carolina, and Florida have built one or more reefs out of car bodies in coastal waters of their states. New Jersey party boat interests recently initiated further reef development off the southern coast of that state. Richfield Oil Corporation last year installed an auto body reef for benefit of anglers in cooperation with the California Fish and Game Department.

Currently, the big questions—for which only limited answers are available—seem to be:

1. How much better does fishing become as a result of reef construction, in various situations, using various materials?

2. What are the best materials and methods of construction, including site selection?

3. What uniform criteria if any can be established to simplify administrative procedures?

Seven states, out of the 12 involved in some way, have governmental agencies officially engaged in artificial reef work. Among them, findings from the D-J studies by Maryland and Texas, have at least limited application to these questions.

Hawaii found a 16-fold increase in weight of fishes occupying a single area due to addition of an artificial reef. The reef was constructed of a group of prefabricated concrete box-like shelters each 4 feet by 4 feet by 1½ feet and occupied a previously open area of bottom. Another similar reef adjacent to abundant natural cover attracted fishes to a far lesser extent and only temporarily. Competent observers of Alabama Gulf fishing have cited development of excellent sport fishing for snappers and other species over Alabama's extensive car body reefs in areas of Gulf waters where fishing was not previously productive. Texas biologists have made underwater observations of at least one of their several car body reefs in an effort to evaluate their utility as fish concentration points. Fish counts by SCUBA divers revealed large numbers of red snappers, spanish and king mackerel, and occasional large jewfish, wahoo, and cobia, along with numerous species of small reef fishes such as blennies, butterfly fish and moonfish. These observations are supported by reports from anglers of good catches of a variety of sport species. The biologists also found that water currents undercutting the auto body shells result in gradual burial of reefs which may be deposited on shifting soft sand.

A recent Maryland study concerned oyster-shell plantings as fish attractors, in Chincoteague Bay. Fish populations trapped over reef and control areas yielded 14 species of fish, of which the black sea bass was most abundant. The planted areas yielded about three times as many fish for the same trapping effort as the controls during identical periods in two successive years. The black sea bass was more abundant on the reef area than on control areas, as was the total number of species. In contrast, however, a small artificial fishing reef constructed by an angler's club in Chesapeake Bay, also using oyster shells, failed to produce better fishing than an adjacent bare area in Chesapeake Bay. Underwater fish counts by California biologists show without question that their reefs, whether of streetcars, auto bodies, prefabricated concrete units, or quarry rock, attract many thousands of fishes of a great many species into otherwise barren areas. The biologists report that the "fish showed a decided preference for concrete shelters and quarry rock, followed by car bodies and streetcars." Also, they indicate that disintegration of auto bodies will be complete within five years and that wooden streetcars become seriously infested by *Toredo* within a year's time.

Part of the effort to construct reefs in New Jersey waters has involved the dumping of rubble and broken masonry wastes or other small, low-profile objects. A recent underwater search in exceptionally clear water of one such dumping area, pinpointed by Loran-fix, revealed no trace of these materials. Evidently, the latter were either washed away or were sanded over. The most recent New Jersey activity involves the sinking of weighted old wood boats (40 to 75 feet in length). *Toredo* attacks may be expected to curtail their effectiveness as reefs in a comparatively short time.

These collective recent experiences in U. S. waters appear thus far to have added little to knowledge long available from the work of Japanese biologists, but which has become only recently known to us as a result of a report last year by our Tokyo Embassy. Various measures to improve the environment in Japanese coastal marine waters have been undertaken since ancient times. Such measures involve either of two general types. The first is *tsukiiso* ("constructed beach")—to promote the growth of useful aquatic plants and the occurrence of invertebrate animals such as sea-cucumbers, sea-urchins, and spiny lobsters. According to the report, the provision of additional substrate for seaweeds, etc., (*tsukiiso*) has traditionally been accomplished by simply dumping rocks or substitute concrete blocks into the sea at suitable locations, and by blasting natural rock reefs with dynamite to clear away coralline algae. The second is *gyosho* ("fish reef")—designed to encourage the occurrence of fishes. Improvement of the habitat for fishes (*gyosho*) has ranged from planting timbers on the fishing grounds to sinking old boats, sometimes filled with rice bran or other fertilizing materials. In recent years, large numbers of oil drums and sections of concrete pipe have been placed on the sea bottom in many areas around Japan to serve as "fish reefs."

Now, the standard practice for *gyosho* is coming to be the installation of especially constructed hollow concrete blocks. In a recent example on the Inland Sea, 50 socalled "fish apartments" were installed in one area. These were hollow cubes made of reinforced concrete, 3¼ feet on a side, with walls about 4 inches thick and one large opening in each side. The reported objective is to increase the populations of mullet and porgy. As in the U. S., Japanese biologists have had difficulty in developing techniques for precise quantitative evaluation of the effects of the projects. In general, nevertheless, the experience in Japan has been that small, low objects have proved best for promoting the growth of seaweeds; structures with many holes and crevices have been best for attracting invertebrates; and *for fish, the higher and larger the structure the more effective it will be.*

Based on these various, if limited, experiences these helpful principles presently emerge for the guidance of reef builders, subject to future refinement with added knowledge:

1. Artificial fishing reefs, properly constructed and located, will serve a useful purpose as con-

centration points for marine species in otherwise barren sites.

2. Construction units for reefs should be large and bulky, possess large cavities and several entrance holes, and be piled up vertically and horizontally so as to rise well above the bottom profile over a large area.

3. Reef materials should be durable, for prolonged utility and least pro-rated annual cost; large blocks of quarry rock or large prefabricated hollow concrete shelter units are best, with auto body shells and other similar metal objects being next best, and wood structures such as streetcars and small boats having more limited value as reef materials due to rapid destruction by *Toredo*. Use of rubble, broken masonry wastes, and similar small-size particulate, low-profile materials appear to have little or no value in fish-reef construction.

4. Reefs should be located in generally barren areas (they will have comparatively low utility if constructed in or near areas with abundant existing cover), and should be placed on bare or shallowly overlain hardpan or rock situations, or where they will not otherwise become undercut by current action and buried in soft sand or mud bottom deposits.

5. Water depth over artificial reefs will vary greatly, dependent upon local conditions. In the open ocean, depths ranging from as little as 30 to 125 feet or more may be indicated, governed in part by necessity to prevent movement or destruction by storm-surf. In protected situations, depths as shallow as 10 feet may be indicated. Successful artificial reefs are found throughout this depth range.

6. Reefs should be installed only with the benefit of physical and biological surveys "before-and-after."

Other forms of fish management. A wide variety of special miscellaneous efforts, often tailored to specific local situations or to problems of particular species, are undertaken by various states; these accounted for three per cent of all fish conservation expenditures by 1960. Acquisition of marshlands peripheral to lakes and rivers to assure perpetuation and protection of Northern Pike spawning grounds, together with construction and maintenance of water-level control structures, is a vital measure in the north-central states. Construction and maintenance of irrigation ditch screens in the Pacific Northwest has proven its worth to successful management of Salmon and Steelhead Trout and so constitutes an important activity in those states. Stream clearance to remove temporary splash dams and blocks from old lumbering wastes have required considerable expenditures in many northern states, where anadromous species are involved. Laddering otherwise insurmountable blocks to spawning migrations of fish may be done directly with respect to small projects or indirectly in case of large structures. In either case much time and effort is required in advisory and supervisory capacities. In many cases the active cooperation of federal agencies is required.

Opening of domestic water supplies to public fishing is often at least partly the result of much persuasion consultation and cooperation in fish management by the state fishery agencies. For example, a survey by a Texas biologist of the administration of 163 Texas water supply reservoirs revealed that fishing was permitted on 89 per cent of them. The Game and Fish Commission biologist received information from 97 agencies controlling these reservoirs (up to 20,000 surface acres), which indicated that closures to fishing were due to lack of an adequate filter system or the lake was too small to have a restricted zone near the water intake. Picnicking was allowed at 67 per cent of the impoundments boating at 60 per cent camping at 44, hunting at 42, water skiing at 37, and swimming at 28 per cent. In a talk before the Texas Water and Sewage Works Association, the biologist noted:

"Some cities do not want to get into the 'fishing business.' But few are the cities today that do not provide parks, playgrounds, stadiums and other places for the recreation and relaxation of their citizens. Fishing is also recreation, so why not provide a place for it too? If your city is considering the construction of a new reservoir, plan to include recreation along with municipal water usage. In most cases it is easier and less costly to provide these facilities at the beginning instead of adding them later. Such things as control of native fish, correct stocking of game fish, and harvest regulations are available for the asking. If your city lake does not provide good fishing at present, a fisheries survey can be made and recommendations will be given for improvement. With long range planning cooperation and work, another good fishing hole can be created."

The desirability of using water supply reservoirs for fishing and other recreational purposes is being demonstrated repeatedly. More and more industrial and municipal impoundments are opened to fishing each year, especially near urban centers. A recent study on Forrest Lake, a 700-acre water supply reservoir serving Kirksville, Missouri (population 13,300), has proved that intensive recreational activities there did not endanger the public's drinking water. Dr. Dean A. Rosebery, Northeast Missouri State Teacher's College, in a paper presented at the 1961 meeting of the American Fisheries Society, reported on the extent of recreational use, and the density of coliform and enterococcus bacteria in Forrest Lake in 1958-60. He concluded that high recreational use had little or no effect upon water quality at the intake tower of the water filtration plant. During the three-year period, an average of 298,000 people visited Forrest Lake annually. During the summer months, about 22 per cent were sightseeing, 19 per cent picnicking, 17 per cent swimming, 14 per cent fishing, 11 per cent boating, and 4 per cent water skiing. Almost 90 per cent of the anglers fished from boats, and caught an average of one fish every 46 minutes. From 700 to 750 boats were licensed to operate on the 700-acre reservoir each year. There were over 40,000 swimmer-days each year. Sampling of standard index groups of bacteria with the membrane filter method revealed relatively low densities. Highest counts were noted below the thermocline, and in a cove receiving heavy use from boats, wave action, drainage from a camping area, and seepage from the park sewage septic tank. Dr. Rosebery concluded that the existing condition of pollution in Forrest Lake would need to increase considerably before there would be additional costs for filtration and purification of the municipal water supply.

A report issued by the City of San Diego Water Department, written by Donald A. Hoffman, Associate Sanitary Engineer, and Robert C. Payette, Supervising Recreation Specialist, described the results of treating Hodges Reservoir with rotenone. The object was to improve sport fishing by killing off the abundant Carp population. Until a few years before, 200-acre Hodges Reservoir, a water supply for San Diego, yielded an annual catch of 35 tons of game and pan fish to anglers using it for recreation. Then Carp took over and the quality of sport fishing declined. The San Diego Water Department decided to treat the water supply with rotenone, with the State Health Department and the State Fish and Game Department cooperating. Altogether 105 tons of Carp were removed along with only 4 tons of game fish. The reservoir was restocked shortly afterwards with Largemouth Bass, Crappie, Bluegill, and Channel Catfish, in expectation of creating good angling once again. A post-treatment analysis published in the *Newsletter* of the California section, American Water Works Association, recorded that the treatment resulted in great benefits to the water supply. The amorphous load in the water decreased 500 per cent in the first four weeks following killing of the Carp, and water transparencies showed an improvement of 1,100 per cent! Obviously, this is a case where progressive water works management has combined with fisheries management to bring about great savings in water treatment costs.

The desirability of using domestic water supplies for fishing and other recreational purposes is being repeatedly demonstrated. More and more industrial and municipal impoundments are opened to fishing each year, especially near urban centers. Long experience has demonstrated that "fishing in the drink" is practical, and intensive studies have proved that recreational activities on drinking water supplies do not endanger the public. This has become publicly recognized by an increasing number of responsible public health officials. In a report to Congress on environmental health, the U. S. Surgeon General stated, in part (emphasis added):

"In community planning, requirements for recreation areas and their relationship to community living as a whole are matters of concern to health personnel. For example *the use of domestic water supply reservoirs for fishing and other recreational purposes is feasible* if the public is willing to pay the price of necessary protection. Thus, the interplay of several elements of environmental health is demonstrated once again."

To chart past trends, state fishery administrators were asked to estimate the number of surface acres in industrial and municipal water supplies, how much was open to public fishing, and how much had been rehabilitated. Some states could make no estimate of totals; therefore, national totals were not derived. Some states could not determine exact acreages involved. Florida, for instance, claims 3 million acres of lakes and streams, most of which are classified as industrial or municipal water supplies. However, some significant figures were furnished. At least 93 per cent of all municipal reservoirs reported were open to public fishing. Over 362,000 acres of industrial and 1,080,000 acres of municipal water supply waters were recorded in this category. Reports from the states readily lent themselves to classification in terms of "proportion of acres open to fishing," in these categories:

Virtually All Open	*Majority Open*	*Majority Closed*
Alabama	California	Connecticut (94%)
Illinois	Colorado (75%)	Massachusetts (53%)
Indiana	Kentucky (90%)	Pennsylvania (51%)
Iowa	Maryland (75%)	Rhode Island (90%)
Kansas	Missouri	
Maine	New Hampshire (95%)	*All Closed*
Michigan	New Mexico (86%)	Hawaii
Minnesota	New York	Montana
North Dakota	Virginia (60%)	
Oklahoma		
South Dakota		
Tennessee		
Texas		
Wyoming		

California has many small domestic water supply reservoirs that are closed to fishing. Progress has been made in opening some of them, notably in San Diego County. Pardee Reservoir, a large municipal water supply lake, was recently opened to the public. In Michigan, so far as is known, all major industrial and water supply impoundments have been opened to fishing. New York City has 35,000 acres of impounded water supplies, all open to public fishing by state law, subject to rules and regulations promulgated by the City Department of Water Supply, Gas and Electricity.

In all, 24,106 acres of municipal water supplies and 29,111 acres of industrial waters have been rehabilitated for improvement of sport fishing with chemicals or by drainage. With the development

WATER SUPPLY RESERVOIRS

State	Total Acres		Acres Open to Public Fishing		Acres Rehabilitated	
	Industrial	Municipal	Industrial	Municipal	Industrial	Municipal
Alabama	9,000	3,350	9,000	3,350	0	0
Alaska	—None—		......	......	......	......
California	375,000*		375,000		......	......
Colorado	5,019	10,658	3,579	7,945	0	0
Connecticut	11,000	18,000	11,000	1,000	110	0
Hawaii	1,800	50	450	0	0	0
Idaho	300	......	300	......	10	......
Illinois	5,000	45,000	5,000	45,000	0	700
Indiana	?	11,200	?	11,200	......	0
Iowa	60	1,680	60	1,680	0	0
Kansas	470	6,926	120	6,926	185	2,105
Kentucky	......	1,000	......	900	......	100
Maine	?	?	100%	99%	0	0
Maryland	8,800	9,192	911	6,900	0	20
Massachusetts	?	55,000	?	26,000	547	314
Michigan	?	?	All	All	......	......
Minnesota	?	?	All	All	......	......
Missouri	?	?	......	Substantial	......	300
Montana	3,000	300	3,000	0	0	0
Nebraska	Not Significant		Open	......	......	......
Nevada	0	0	......	......	......	......
New Hampshire	?	108,085	All	103,000	0	0
New Mexico	......	291	......	251	......	30
New York	?	35,000	......	35,000	......	......
North Dakota	......	800	......	800	......	800
Oklahoma	11,000	287,000*	6,300	280,000	0	1,100
Oregon	?	?	......	......	......	2
Pennsylvania	27,529	12,254	24,831	6,087	0	0
Rhode Island	?	6,000	Most Open	600	0	0
South Dakota	0	3,540	0	3,540	0	140
Tennessee	0	1,000	0	1,000	0	0
Texas	17,190	535,185*	12,240	535,185	1,490	11,289
Utah	0	0	......	......	......	......
Vermont	?	0	Open	......	0	......
Virginia	6,700	6,500	6,700	3,850	0	0
West Virginia	?	?	?	?	0	55
Wisconsin	134,991	0	134,991	......	933	......
Wyoming	120,111	9,886	120,111	9,886	25,836	7,151
Total					29,111	24,106

* Multiple use.

of more economical techniques, reclaiming of these waters will undoubtedly increase manyfold. Often, this kind of improvement for fishing, by reducing or eliminating rough fish, results in decided improvement in water quality for drinking purposes with substantially decreased costs to the water departments.

Artificial Salmon spawning channels have increasingly interested Pacific Northwest agencies since 1954 as partial means of mitigating losses due to construction of high dams. Recent spawning channel experiments increased the egg-to-fry survival ratio of Pink Salmon to 30 to 36 per cent, compared to 10 per cent in natural streams. The controlled channels are being used in a number of research projects designed to increase Salmon runs and in the partial solution of problems associated with fish passage at dams. The basic concept of the spawning channel is the improvement of survival from egg to fry through the provision of optimum conditions for spawning and incubation. These conditions include size of gravel, depth of water, removal of silt and elimination of high and low flows. Promising in theory, it should prove to be another helpful tool even if severely limited (due to physical considerations) in application as a general substitute for extensive natural spawning areas.

Natural rearing ponds are being utilized wherever possible to augment fish production. For example, Washington Game Department fishery personnel have reported relatively high returns from Steelhead Trout reared in a natural slough on the north fork of the Stillaguamish River. The slough was planted with fry early in 1958 and 9,755 marked migrants released a year later. During the 1960-61 season, creel census estimates revealed that over 7 per cent of the original migrants were caught by anglers as they returned from the sea. Steelhead fry were given complete protection from predators in the slough. They were provided with artificial food supplements, and a controlled water level and flow to induce migration. Departmental biologists point out that, in addition to supplying about one-third of the angler's catch on the river this winter, normal escapement of the slough-reared fish will bolster future natural stream production.

Abatement of water pollution, which adversely affects a large fraction of river mileage in the more densely populated states, is one of the most important means of improving fishing especially where it is in most demand, near urban centers. Responsibility for water pollution control rests with the State Public Health Departments, and the state fishery agencies assist by investigating and reporting on fish kills caused by pollution, working on coordinating groups or inter-agency committees advising on effects of pesticides and recommending safeguards in their use, developing guidelines to prevent or minimize damage to fish from erosion silt (also a form of pollution) generated during road-construction. In this way, many states make significant progress toward better fishing.

For example, the first summary of nationwide pollution-caused fish kills was issued by the U. S. Public Health Service in 1961, covering the period June to October. It was followed a year later by another. In this one, during 1961, the first full year of operation of the reporting system, the Public Health Service received 411 notifications of pollution-caused fish kills from 45 state fish and game agencies. Nearly 15 million fish were reported killed in the 263 instances (64 per cent) where numbers were estimated. River mileage affected, given in 240 reports, amounted to 1,686 miles. About 83 per cent of the kills were in rivers. Industrial wastes accounted for 44 per cent of the kills from known sources and agricultural poisons, 21 per cent. Fish kills did not occur or were not reported in Alaska, Delaware, Nevada, Oklahoma, and Vermont. The Public Health Service noted that, "although many fish kills have been reported, it is realized that these comprise only a rough measure of pollution. Such reports do not take into account the effects of adding to a stream small quantities of pollutants which may not kill fish but which still have a significant effect on the aquatic food organisms which support fish life. They do not take into account weak pollutants which inhibit fish growth and fish reproduction, nor the effects of pollutants which cause flesh tainting, rendering fish unpalatable for human consumption."

Carefully formulated and well documented *water quality criteria* for aquatic life are essential for resolving pollution problems. In setting these criteria, the extremes of environmental conditions must be accurately delineated because they determine the survival of aquatic organisms, together with the effects of interacting multiple variables, such as oxygen, carbon dioxide, and temperature. The ranges of *most* favorable conditions must also be defined. Dr. Clarence M. Tarzwell, U. S. Public Health Service Taft Sanitary Engineering Center, Cincinnati, states that, while criteria are needed to indicate safe levels for short exposure periods, determination of water conditions not harmful under conditions of continuous exposure are also required. Criteria are essential for the production of adequate crops of organisms in the food chain, and the end product—fish. The development of chemical, physical and biological water criteria for aquatic life will serve to more clearly define pollution control and waste treatment, promote uniform regulations, acquaint the public with the problems and basic aims so that public opinion can be an effective force in pollution abatement, and define pollution so that it can be more readily demonstrated in the courts. Much more intensive research will be required to develop clear-cut criteria.

Some fish kills are truly catastrophic and exert a tremendous influence on availability of good fishing. For example, in the winter of 1959, a lethal slug of zinc-bearing waste water swept through a 36-mile stretch of Virginia's famed Shenandoah River and left an estimated 500,000 fish dead in its wake. Fish food bottom organisms were drastically reduced; mayflies and snails were eliminated. The Virginia Water Control Board ruled that "negligent discharge . . . of a substance or substances" from a rayon-manufacturing plant at Front Royal polluted the renowned Smallmouth Bass stream, and assessed a record fine of $154,700. Fishery biologists of the Virginia Game and Inland Fisheries Commission testified that the fish-kill figures, which excluded minnows and other small fish, were conservative. The Commission placed monetary values on the various sport fishes as follows: 35,000 Bass $68,250, 170,000 Bluegills $7,820, 265,000 Catfish $74,200, 30,000 Suckers and Carp $4,500. In assessing the fine, the State Water Control Board stated that the slaughter was "a terrific economic loss to the state," noting that fishermen spend about $50 million a year in Virginia on their sport, much of it in the Shenandoah area.

Better utilization of more species is being promoted because the available fish crops must be divided up in smaller portions among more anglers than ever before. Result is that each fisherman may expect to catch somewhat fewer fish, even though total yield may be and often is much higher today than it was a few score years ago. Consequently, more and more use must be made of the pan fishes and the non-predatory "rough" fishes if there is to be reasonable fishing success in some waters. Many states encourage and promote fishing for pan fish and for "rough" fish. Actually, the pan fishes currently make up 75 to 80 per cent of all fishes caught nationwide. Extensive statewide creel censuses of Ohio anglers, for example, showed that 78,000 anglers (about 9 per cent of all Ohio anglers) caught over 313,000 fish, of which about 80 per cent were pan fish. One means of encouraging more balanced harvest is encouragement of archery fishing for rough fish, and at least 30 states have made this legal. A few states have tried to inform their anglers of simple ways in which to improve fishing success. Texas biologists distributed small-size hooks at one reservoir to unsuccessful bank fishermen who were using hooks too large for Bluegills and fishing success increased spectacuarly as a result. South Dakota fishery authorities, concerned that considerably less than one pound of sport fish per acre were being harvested by anglers at the huge Fort Randall Reservoir, employed a skilled angler to fish the reservoir experimentally and learn how it should best be done, for the benefit of anglers. Reservoir fishing often requires its own special techniques. The project demonstrated its usefulness within a few weeks, when the experimental angler showed that the abundant Saugers could be caught at any time of the day provided proper methods were used. The findings were soon translated into big strings of Saugers taken consistently by anglers for the first time, as well as good catches of Crappies, and Bass. Estimates of fisherman-use indicated that the reservoir was supporting four times as much fishing one year later. Other promotional approaches aimed at increasing utilization of pan and rough fishes often try to take advantage of the natural tendency for civic organizations to sponsor fishing derbies. However, unless these are held in natural situations and for much longer periods than the usual one-day affair, it is extremely doubtful that any measurably beneficial result could be demonstrated.

Fishing derbies are a popular, probably inevitable kind of activity for sponsorship by various civic and other groups who often have well intentioned desires to do something constructive for youngsters. This is very commendable, for fishing is widely recognized as a desirable leisure-time activity for folk of all ages. It is most unfortunate that the fishing derby idea has become perverted through over-promotion and over-commercialization by some organizations in their unwitting burst of good-hearted enthusiasm; the result more often than not has been to defeat the good purpose. Fishing derbies have usually been sponsored in some artificially contrived setting, with an emphasis on immediate success and commercial rewards for "winners;" in actuality, the latter usually turn out to have been "losers." Real fishing is something quite different—it is a *contemplative* not a *competitive* sport. Some of the unfortunate results that can happen were reported in The New York *Times* during a fishing derby in Central Park one summer. One girl, feeling the need to win, "borrowed" a fish that had already won a prize for someone else and entered it again—for herself. The previous year, a boy entered a fish he apparently bought in a market. On the other hand, one girl experienced exultation when she caught a small Carp on a worm she put on the hook herself!

Results of a 1960 survey by the Washington Department of Game with respect to state fish and game agencies' views on derbies were even more revealing. It was found that six states had legally restricted such derbies in some way, three more were considering such legislation, and at least 17 wished to eliminate them if they could. The vast majority of agencies believe that derbies are *not* in the best interests of the fisheries (36 states), sportsmanship (39 states), the public (35 states), or juvenile training (38 states). Most states refuse to supply hatchery fish either for adult fishing derbies (44 states) or juvenile fishing derbies (32 states). At least 3 states place limitations on the amount or value of prizes given in derbies. However, 26 states reserve special waters for juveniles; and 14 of those states require adult supervision of them. It was concluded that states which require adult supervision, together with associated instructions on fishing methods, ethics, and general good sportsmanship, with emphasis on the recreational rather than the monetary rewards, enjoy the best results of their efforts and support of the derbies.

Fishing-for-fun is another approach in the direction of unlimited fishing with complete restriction on harvest or kill—being applied to *Trout*, specifically, which was first proposed and applied (in Michigan) about mid-century by Dr. Albert S. Hazzard. It has continued there, with occasional modifications, in limited application on suitable waters, and is so firmly identified with its originator that it is commonly called the "Hazzard Plan" of Trout management. It does not apply generally to warmwater fish because of the very much greater reproductive capacity of most warmwater species, and the strong tendencies toward overpopulation by many species in the absence of extensive fishing harvest or natural controls (predation), although there is some experimenting in this direction in Ohio with Muskellunge. To be successfully used with Trout, it is necessary to restrict its application to the better Trout streams, those capable of carrying Trout the year-round and having abundant spawning facilities. In other words, it's no substitute for having good Trout streams in the first place. The National Park Service first applied the fishing-for-fun Trout management plan in the summer of 1954 on two streams in Great Smoky Mountains National Park. On Bradley Fork and West Prong Little Pigeon River, anglers were offered the opportunity to catch all the Trout they could with artificial lures, but were required to release every fish. The idea has spread to a few waters in Pennsylvania and Virginia and to Yellowstone and Shenandoah National Parks. Fishing-for-fun in the national parks was expanded in 1958; it was extended to a year-round basis on the two first-tried streams. Two additional streams were placed under the plan during the "off-season," September to May, but modified to permit fishermen to keep Trout over 16 inches (rare).

Fishery biologists of the U. S. Fish and Wildlife Service commenced studies on the Trout populations in those Park Service waters to which the Hazzard Plan was first applied. Their findings indicated that both the quality of fishing and the Trout populations increased. Anglers caught an average of 4 Trout per hour on the Bradley Fork and 3 per hour on the West Prong. Poundage of Rainbow Trout per acre, in the West Prong, increased from 15 pounds in 1954 to 53 pounds in 1959; numbers of Trout 7 inches and over increased from 48 to 164 fish per acre. Opportunities for angling for wild Trout had increased in this particular stream without diminishing the natural populations—a presumed result of applying the Hazzard Plan. Somewhat similar improvement in quality of angling was also attributed to the Hazzard Plan applied (in this case by Hazzard himself) to the Left Branch of Young Woman's Creek in Pennsylvania. There the plan, instituted in 1958, required fly fishing only with barbless hooks, with all Trout being released. Fishing-for-fun, requiring use of barbless hooks and release alive of all Trout caught was placed on trial on the Rapidan and Staunton rivers in Shenandoah National Park in 1960, by fishery biologists of the Virginia Game and Inland Fisheries Commission. This was an effort to respond to the needs of the less-than-5 per cent of Virginia trout anglers who are styled as the "native" fishermen. The affected streams supported about 600 angler-days of fishing during the 1960 season. Pre-existing natural populations of "native" Brook Trout provided over 54 per cent of the 1,902 Trout landed.

Virginia's fishery chief predicted that there will be an increase in the number of fish-for-fun addicts in future years due to increasing fishing pressure on limited Trout streams. However, he emphasized that the greatest number of Virginia trouters at the present time depend on stocked streams and fish that they can keep. He reported that these anglers comprise well over 95 per cent of the estimated 75,000 Trout anglers in Virginia. Dingell-Johnson (federal aid) studies have revealed that 97 per cent of anglers who fish put-and-take waters prefer live bait over artificial, indicating that they are "playing for keeps." Therefore, the fishery authority contends that, in spite of its drawbacks, put-and-take Trout fishing will probably be in strong demand for a long time to come.

Zoned trout fishing, that is fish-for-fun and fly-fishing-only regulations, produces more consistent and better all-season angling in the face of fishing pressure than it is possible to provide without special regulations. Fatality of returned fish hooked with a fly is negligible, whereas deeply hooked fish, which is often the case when bait is employed, have poor chance for survival. Reduced killing is the key to quality fishing near centers of population.

Trout, Unlimited, a national organization, has two basic goals: (1) to protect and reclaim trout waters, and (2) to bring about more zoned stream sections. In conjunction with the latter, this organization points out that there are those who expect and demand consistent angling for acclimated trout. The hobbyist spends considerable time and money in pursuit of his angling. When he hears of good fishing, he samples it. When he finds what he likes, he periodically returns. Thus the trout towns across the Land could improve their economy by developing, maintaining and promoting quality-fishing by instigating more stringent killing regulations. Trout could be utilized to stimulate tourism.

This organization has issued a sobering warning: if consistent angling is not provided by officialdom for the minority who require it, these avid anglers, individually and in groups, will secure fishing rights, manage water as is seen fit, and limit fishing activity to invitation or club membership. Thus, if the old American tradition and heritage of some free and open trout fishing on blue-ribbon water is to continue, it is vital that zoned-fishing programs be expanded and that Conservation Departments acquire some choice stream sections. It must be recognized that there are two kinds of trout and two kinds of trout fishermen. There are the newly-planted fish which must experiment in their feeding activity, and there are the stream-bred and the acclimated hatchery trout which have established selective-feeding habits. Then there are the fishermen who like to work over concentrations of hatchery fish, their goal being a limit catch; and there are those who revel in the challenge of problems, their goal being personal satisfaction. The interests of the two are inimical. Under fishing pressure, sport fishing cannot exist where put-and-take trout fishing is practiced, and there are those who will not accept temporary quantity fishing as a substitute for consistent quality trouting.

These situations are clarified in *Trout,* the monthly magazine of the organization, Trout, Unlimited.

Fact-finding. Short-term applied studies or management investigations, directed toward developing or perfecting methods or evaluating effects of management activities, required an average of 13 per cent of the fishery expenditures by the 50 states (a few states were invlovd in some long-term basic research as well). Fifty per cent more relative emphasis was placed on this in the western and southern states than in the north-central and eastern states, explainable by the facts of historic development. These are regions where the problems of the anadromous fisheries, and of resident warmwater fishes in artificial lakes, respectively, present a need for relatively more research since less sophisticated management tools are as yet available to meet the pressing problems. To a very considerable degree, the fact-finding programs of the states are designed to produce immediately usable information for solving day-to-day fish management problems. Typical studies are concerned with getting the facts about the kinds and qualities of fish available, age and growth characteristics, the harvest by anglers, effectiveness of fish-stocking (including optimum farm pond combinations) and habitat improvement, etc., and to evaluate degree of effectiveness of pilot-type studies designed to increase fish production and fishing success.

Research is increasingly classified as either basic research or applied research. It's easy to oversimplify and characterize the former as long-term, the latter as short-term. It is equally easy to throw up one's hands and take the attitude that research is research. Nevertheless, agencies that grant funds for research must try to distinguish between these things. An article in *Science* (December 22, 1961) by Doctors Dale R. Lindsay and Ernest M. Allen (Division of Research Grants, National Institutes of Health), concluded by discussing these aspects of research. As they described it:

"*Applied research* has as its objective some achievement that can be put to 'practical' use in some way other than as a step toward further research.

"*Basic research* contributes new variables to science, quantitates them, identifies (and quantitates) new causal relationships between variables, and points out new spatial and temporal groupings of variables and new sequences in their changes in value."

Drs. Lindsay and Allen said further, that the motivation and justification and the basis of evaluation are, respectively, the practical objective and the extent to which it is attained. For basic research, the motivation is scientific curiosity—an almost monastic dedication to the pursuit of learning. The justification (in the eyes of the onlooker, including the one who supplies the funds) is that the stream of applied research dries up unless it is fed by basic research. The merit of any one achievement in basic research is measured by the extent to which it clarifies pre-existing knowledge, contributes toward establishing a new generalization, or simply leads to new research.

Many of the findings of state fishery agency research programs have already been related under other topics of consideration, thus demonstrating much of the value of that research in terms of refinement of many management programs. About one-half of the funds expended by the states for fact-finding are received as federal-aid grants under provisions of the Dingell-Johnson fish restoration program, the rest (including state matching funds) coming from the fishing license revenues in each state. A research project is never complete, unless or until the findings are compiled and analyzed, whether by segments or in a complete package. A stock criticism of research projects is that they never end; depending on the nature of any given study this may or may not be true. Admittedly, basic research is customarily long-term and continuing—and no less desirable as a result. On the other hand, the D-J studies (largely management investigations) are ordinarily of short duration. An analysis of the length of completed and active D-J research projects shows that most completed projects have terminated at the end of three years, although some currently active projects are lasting a little longer, up to twice as long. Considering that most of the D-J projects are applied studies rather than basic research this is about what would be expected. One of the most valuable means for showing benefits of research is through publication of findings; publications illustrate accomplishments. Publications are also invaluable to other scientists, saving time, money, and work by preventing wasteful duplication (not to be confused with needed replication). Research findings which are not reported in permanent form have only very temporary and localized value.

For this reason many biologists report their findings at meetings of scientific societies where they can be subjected to scrutiny and constructive criticism by fellow professionals working on similar or related problems under different conditions in other states—a necessary element of good research —or they may prepare papers for publication in journals or for distribtuion directly to other interested parties. A series of papers were read and discussed at the 1961 Midwest Fish and Wildlife Conference (held in Toronto that year), illustrating how this is done, and providing much useful information to fellow workers; following are summaries of a few of the reports.

A University of Michigan professor emphasized that fish are individuals and behave according to their own likes and to the reactions of their nervous systems. He reported on recent tests that show that fish have demonstrated fairly well developed capacities of learning and retention. In laboratory experiments fish learned to perform faster when food was offered as a reward than when punished with electrical shock or other negative reinforcement. The fishery professor stated that some fish remember what they learn from six months to several years. However, he deduced from available data that a Bass would have to be hooked four or five (perhaps even ten) times within a week in order to remember the experience.

Another paper, presented by a Wisconsin fishery biologist, strengthened the thesis that a lake cannot be "fished out" as long as reproduction occurs, even though exploitation is heavy. After 14 years of liberalized fishing at 290-acre Escanaba Lake, the quality of angling has been maintained with average annual pressure near 100 man-hours per acre. In recent years, the Escanaba Walleye population has remained at a high level under estimated exploitation rates of 13 to 45 per cent. Yellow

Perch harvests of 17 to 26 per cent and Pumpkinseed harvests of 28 to 116 per cent of the standing crop have not affected the size of succeeding yearly populations. However, heavy exploitation (50 to 64 per cent) of Northern Pike, combined with unsuccessful reproduction in some years, has severely reduced the population. With no bag, size or season limitations at 180-acre Murphy Flowage, the Northern Pike population actually increased in spite of 33 to 56 per cent exploitation. Reproduction was successful there every year. High Black Crappie population levels have been maintained with harvests of 12 to 21 per cent. Bluegills increased from 72,000 in 1956 to 188,000 in 1960, despite exploitation rates of 15 to 24 per cent.

The Wisconsin Conservation Department biologist also reported on a new 95-acre reservoir stocked in 1958 with Northern Pike and Largemouth Bass. In the 30 days following opening on June 1, 1960, anglers took 74 per cent of the Pike over 18.5 inches, and 50 per cent of those under 18.5 inches. Two-year-old Bass were reduced 68 per cent during June, when 216 man-hours of effort were expended per acre. Although catch rates were much lower throughout the rest of the summer, anglers' luck improved in the fall as the younger fish grew to catchable size.

In contrast, a Michigan Conservation Department biologist reported at the conference that in the 12 years following opening of eight private lakes to the public, fishing went downhill. Virtually complete catch records on the lakes and ponds in the Department's Rifle River Area from 1945 to 1956 suggest that those waters contained a greater number of larger and older fish prior to heavy exploitation by the public. The two largest lakes on the Area (130 and 95 acres) are unproductive marl lakes which yielded only 6.2 and 3.9 pounds per acre the first year of public fishing. For the succeeding 11 years, average harvests were down 60 and 67 per cent. Yellow Perch dominated the catch, followed by stocked Trout and Smallmouth Bass. The smaller, more productive ponds yielded up to 83 pounds per acre of Sunfish and Largemouth Bass in the initial year, but have typically produced less than one-half of this amount in succeeding years (there were exceptions). It was concluded that "it is unlikely that these lakes will again produce yields equal to those of the first year of public fishing unless improved management procedures are devised."

A unique, long-term effort to control Northern Pike in Heming Lake, Manitoba, was recounted by a fishery scientists of the Fisheries Research Board of Canada at the Toronto meeting. Efforts to remove Pike were begun in 1945 in an effort to improve the quality of Whitefish which were affected by parasitic cysts in the flesh. Pike serve as intermediate hosts for the parasite. About 2 pounds of Pike per acre were removed annually with gill nets from 1945-1949, 3 pounds per acre from 1950-1954, and 4 pounds from 1955-1960. During that time, catches of Suckers, Perch, and Burbot rose phenomenally. The Walleye population declined drastically, and the catch of Whitefish and Ciscoes was the lowest on record in 1960. The average size of most species declined in this far north lake, but the poundage removed annually was the same or greater than in 1945.

Results of stocking yearling Muskellunge in two small Wisconsin lakes (37 and 43 acres) to experimentally reduce existing overcrowded Perch populations were outlined by a University of Wisconsin biologist. His data indicated that adult Perch were reduced from 500 per acre to near exinction within a year in one lake. A similar reduction occurred in the other lake after three years. Largemouth Bass decreased in density and Smallmouth Bass increased following Muskie stocking. About 25 per cent of the Muskies died shortly after introduction, and a relatively constant annual mortality of 10 to 15 per cent occurred thereafter.

Miscellaneous publications issued by conservation departments, news releases based on unpublished administrative reports, annual reports, mimeographed progress reports, etc., all tend to keep the information flowing into circulation and use. Biologists in the states learn by these means, for example, that Ontario biologists have demonstrated that Bass sanctuaries have no effect on Bass abundance. In the course of the research, however, they discovered that certain temperature factors principally determined the strength of Bass year-classes. Tennessee and TVA biologists tagged 18,800 Saugers over a 7-year period in the lower Tennessee River and found that only 11 per cent were being caught by anglers, dispelling fears of possible overfishing. Population estimates based on tag recoveries indicated the presence of well over 500,000 Saugers in the tailwaters of Pickwick Dam alone during peak fishing. Surprisingly, they learned that a third of the fish taken at Pickwick Dam originated below Kentucky Dam, 185 miles distant, thereby indicating that Tennessee anglers were probably dependent in part on Ohio River and Mississippi River production for their catches. Michigan Trout studies conducted since 1949 on flies-only, high-size-limit regulations showed that either a higher size limit or a flies-only restriction greatly reduces fishing pressure. More Trout were present in flies-only sections of the Au Sable River system than in adjacent waters where bait fishing is permitted. However, anglers were sacrificing about two-thirds of the numerical catch and one-third the weight of Trout in the creel in comparison with bait waters. Three other test streams showed no evidence that flies-only regulations and higher size limits have had a significant effect on the Trout populations (except for Brown Trout in one stream).

In saltwater coastal sport fisheries, a tremendous need exists for fact-finding. Only a very few states have paid much attention to those important fisheries because only those same few receive revenues generated by such fisheries, through sale of saltwater fishing licenses or otherwise. Chief among them stands California, which has had such a license for a number of years. Consequently, considerable funds are spent by that state to study its coastal sport fisheries and to manage the resource. An article in *The Salt Water Sportsman* in August, 1960, included observations by the President of the California Ocean Fish Protective Association (a large sportsmen's organization) commenting on the value of research by marine biologists. He pointed to the Kelp Bass as one recent example of what can be done to aid a declining fishery once the facts are secured through research. In a study of the Kelp Bass, biologists found that the Bass move very little, remaining largely in one area. They found that they don't spawn until they are quite large, and that they are slow growing. Once these facts were established, the need for a size limit became evident. Following the recommendations of the biologists, a limit was set and the fish have shown a remarkable resurgence in abundance and size. The OFPA President said: "No fisherman can deny this, and it is only one example of many, many such projects."

Another study, concerning various aspects of the life history and fishery of the Barred Surfperch, a small (under 16 inches and 4 pounds) surf species in southern California waters, was part of a general surf fishing investigations project financed with Dingell-Johnson funds. Barred Surfperch appeared in over 80 per cent of all beach seine hauls, among 71 species and 128,000 individuals taken, and made up over 73 per cent of the catch of the four most important species. This fish carries its eggs and developing embryos internally until birth, the number of young per litter averaging about 33. Strong dependence of Barred Surfperch on sand crabs is evident from the finding that in 90 per cent of several hundred stomachs which contained food, sand crabs made up 90 per cent of the food volume. Fishing for Barred Surfperch is generally good throughout its range and appears to be improving. Movements resulting in mixing of fish between adjacent coastal areas appeared to be slow and of short distance. It was concluded that there is no excess strain at present on the stocks of Barred Surfperch in southern California, and that "the bag limit on this species and the closure to commercial fishing provide ample safeguards."

Sometimes the research may not result in improved management but may provide new information that explains some previously mystifying phenomenon. It may provide the means for predicting future periods of abundance and scarcity, with resultant benefits in terms of fishing time and effort and ultimate trip success as the practical reward. Such a case is illustrated by another California D-J study, this time of the Yellowtail fishery. Fishing for Yellowtail is highly favored by southern California saltwater party-boat anglers, due to their fighting ability and large size, usually 12 to 18 pounds and up to 80 pounds in weight. Decreased sport catches in the years immediately following World War II caused considerable apprehension and a study was initiated by California fishery biologists in 1952. They found that Yellowtail fishing is almost entirely dependent on an influx of fish from Baja California waters each spring. The yearly variations of water temperature and chemistry—and not fishing pressure—currently limit their availability to California anglers. Returns from extensive tagging indicated that Yellowtail normally move north in the early spring and south again in late summer and fall. Young fish appear to stay in one locality; between ages three to eight, they form schools and range widely; older and larger fish apparently take up a sedentary existence. It was concluded that the Yellowtail population was in a healthy state, with no present need for further restrictions; a future increase in their economic value could result in an expanded commercial fishery, and thus seriously affect the local sport fishery.

Several East Coast states have recognized the importance of their saltwater sport fisheries and are investing part of their D-J funds, lacking other sources of funds, in useful but limited research programs. Among them, New York State has studied one of the most intensive in-shore sport fisheries known anywhere. Over 1,500,000 pounds of Fluke were caught by anglers in Long Island's Great South Bay during a six-month period in 1958. An extensive creel census conducted by fishery biologists of the state Conservation Department indicated about 400,000 people were fishing the Bay then, and their numbers were increasing. Many reports by fishermen of declining catches, especially in late summer, prompted a careful study of the age and growth of the popular flatfish to determine if overharvesting was occurring. Few Fluke over three years old were found in Great South Bay, but they were growing rapidly, averaging about 18 inches in length at the end of the third year. Seventy-seven per cent of the 1958 sport catch were one- and two-year-old Fluke; 90 per cent in 1959. Therefore, the great majority taken by anglers were still in the process of adding considerable growth. Potentialities for further growth, which would add significant weight as well as length, were lost. It was concluded that the sport fisherman is almost entirely dependent upon spawning success in the previous year; practically no buffer exists between spawning and catch. Therefore, fishing success will fluctuate directly with the previous year's spawning success. This would not be the case if four-, five- and six-year-old Fluke made up the bulk of the catch. A failure in spawning would be buffered by several years of intervening recruitment in this situation.

THE CHALLENGE OF COASTAL MARINE WATERS

A special survey of saltwater fishing, conducted by the Bureau of the Census for the Bureau of Sport Fisheries and Wildlife (U. S. Fish and Wildlife Service), revealed that there were about 6.2 million regular ("substantial") saltwater anglers in the United States in 1960 (plus 3.5 million occasional sport fishermen)—up 35% in five years. This legion devoted well over 80 million man-days and spent over $600 million while catching an estimated 633 million saltwater fish. The survey revealed that Sea Trout (including Weakfish) are the most commonly caught fishes in coastal waters. The "top twenty" marine fishes reported caught in greatest numbers by U. S. anglers were estimated as follows (numbers of millions caught), comprising over 70 per cent of the year's catch:

Species	Millions	Species	Millions
Seatrout	80.2	Mullet	17.1
Croaker	41.7	White Perch	13.2
Flounder	31.8	Striped Bass	12.3
Sea Catfish	31.2	Bonito	12.1
Mackerels	29.8	Blowfish	10.7
Porgy-scup	27.6	Redfish	10.3
Whiting	25.3	Snappers	9.4
Bluefish	23.8	Smelts	9.4
Spot	23.7	Groupers	9.3
Grunt	19.0	Fluke	9.2

All other species combined were represented by 186 million fish, to make up the total of 633 million. Assuming an average of one pound per fish, the sport fishery catch from the sea was equivalent to more than one-fourth the total U. S. commercial landings of all kinds of food fish in the same year. On the Pacific Coast north of Point Conception, 700,000 anglers caught 29 million fish, while to the south a like number of fishermen took 50 million. On the Gulf Coast, 1.4 million anglers caught 185 million fish. One million anglers took 157 million fish along the South Atlantic Coast, 1.3 million Middle Atlantic Coast anglers caught 115 million fish, and 1.2 million anglers took 97 million fish from North Atlantic coastal waters.

Facts about saltwater fish and facilities for marine angling are both in short supply. The inroads of man's activities on coastal fish habitat are increasing daily. Pollution, industrial and real estate development, and channel dredging are combining to limit fish production. "No Trespassing" signs and high fences are sprouting at great speed. Free public access to coastal marine waters is a crucial problem in many areas, especially near large urban centers. Early and extensive acquisition and construction of "open-to-the-public" beaches, launching ramps, piers, and jetties is mandatory. Otherwise, private development and rising real estate prices will soon place remaining shoreline areas beyond the reach of possible purchase by construction agencies. The future of saltwater angling rests, in large measure, on public facility plans and action programs that may be conceived in the next decade or two. An expanding seaboard population and industrial capacity may severely restrict this enjoyable outdoor activity if remedial action is postponed.

Once at the water, the angler wants to catch fish. An analysis of nationwide creel census statistics indicates that saltwater fishermen catch a daily average of about 4½ pounds of fish; thus expectations are high. Management efforts must be greatly expanded if acceptable standards are to prevail while marine anglers increase rapidly. An outstanding recent development in saltwater fish management has been the construction of off-shore artificial fishing banks. Using discarded auto bodies, obsolete street cars, old ships, concrete blocks, and similar materials, progressive conservation agencies in Alabama, California, and Texas are creating some excellent fishing on a noticeable scale. A few other states, hampered by lack of funds, are making token efforts along this line. The new reefs attract and concentrate fish in otherwise barren fishing waters, indicating that this activity could be increased many fold.

A relatively unexplored possibility in saltwater management lies in the establishment of underwater marine refuges. Limited research has revealed that regular "parasite-cleaning stations" are established at numerous points in shallow coastal seas. Large fish appear frequently at these stations and allow tiny Shrimp and brightly-colored reef fishes to enter their mouths and gill cavities to devour parasites, and refrain from eating the "cleaners" during the process. Such "cleaning stations" may have a vital influence on the movements and distribution of important game fishes. There is some evidence suggesting that such stations can be created artifically. This interesting phenomenon needs a great deal of study. Initial discoveries, however, suggest that the establishment of extensive underwater refuges or fish ranges, to protect these stations, may become an important aspect in marine sport fishery management.

The preservation of estuaries and tide-marsh areas is vital to the survival and growth of most marine sport fishes. These coastal habitats furnish spawning, nursery, feeding, and resting grounds for Tarpon, Striped Bass, Bluefish, Weakfish, Croakers, and many other important species. Destruction of the estuaries and marshes through draining, flooding, dredging, and filling increasingly threatens the future of our fisheries. Outright purchase or long-term lease of these areas by fishery agencies may be necessary for adequate protection in some instances. Constant vigilance and greatly expanded studies of estuarine waters must be instituted to safeguard these vital areas and specifically define their importance. Sewage, industrial pollutants, erosion silt, and the deadly new threats—super-insecticides, detergents, and radioactive wastes—continue to encroach upon clean coastal waters. Protective laws must be rigidly enforced, and new methods of safe disposal devised, or other efforts at management will be wasted.

The protection of our present sport fishery resources in coastal waters by means of habitat preservation and vigorous enforcement of sound laws is a *must,* and greatly accelerated development of adequate facilities for anglers is a companion *must* if we are to keep pace with growing demands. Vast amounts of new knowledge about the fishery resource we are attempting to preserve and enhance *must* be forthcoming to provide the sound foundation underlying the proper application of these important tools. In short, substantial and balanced action programs are urgently needed in most coastal states. It bears emphasis that the success of any fish management program is in direct proportion to its basis in factual information. It bears equal emphasis that we do not know what proportion of the available crop is being harvested now, let alone the rate of replenishment. Little is known about growth, longevity, behavior, or cyclic abundance of most fishes. How can intelligent regulations be formulated under these circumstances?

Obviously, saltwater angling represents an important recreational frontier. Moreover, for every marine angler today, there will be several tomorrow. What must be done to assure sustained high yield? It is evident to many thoughtful anglers and biologists alike that substantial research and development programs and long-range planning to meet future needs must be initiated in the near future. These activities will require substantial funds that are not yet in sight in most states.

Possible sources of new funds. There are few possibilities for raising needed funds for saltwater sport fishery research and development programs. They include general legislation appropriations, increased utilization of D-J excise tax revenues levied on sales of certain items of fishing tackle, or some form of saltwater fishing license. The first proposal has yet to be accomplished except rarely by any angling group. Inability to apply this means to financing of continuing sport fishery programs long ago resulted in adoption of licensing systems to meet freshwater needs; that freshwater anglers benefitted is abundantly clear on the record. Concensus of informed opinion is that an approach through general appropriations just doesn't work.

The matter of increased D-J tax allocations has merit, within certain limitations. Although some additional D-J funds might justifiably be spent in some coastal states to benefit marine anglers, the additional sum to be expected over current expenditures is not large. In 1960, for example, out of a total of about $1,600,000 of D-J funds they received, some $300,000 was already budgeted for marine sport fishery projects. In the 21 coastal states chiefly concerned there were then about 10.2 million licensed and unlicensed freshwater anglers combined. Some 3.2 million saltwater anglers fished exclusively in salt water. This suggested something over a 3 to 1 ratio; on this basis, perhaps not the best, a 25 per cent allocation of D-J funds by the coastal states to saltwater work would seem reasonable. In the over-all, present practice in the state D-J expenditures is not far behind.

A more significant approach to the matter of increased D-J allocations for marine sport fisheries would be to license most saltwater anglers. They could then legally be counted under existing machinery and would serve to allocate additional D-J funds into those states. Most important, however, licensing would raise considerable revenues directly and enable all states to set up the needed programs. If the usual exclusions are made in licensing for youngsters and oldsters, and allow for possible duplications, perhaps 6 million anglers would be eligible. If $3.00 were established as the fee, $18 million would be raised; at a $2.00 fee, $12 million would become available. Alabama, California, and Texas already license most of their marine anglers—who receive big dividends. Louisiana licenses those who fish with rods and reels, chiefly non-residents. It has been charged that license revenues would be lost in general funds and diverted to non-related uses. It need not happen if the specially earmarked fish and game fund already in existence in each state is utilized and if the fish and game agency is charged with administration. This is the way it is handled in Alabama, California, Louisiana, and Texas. A new but similar special fund might also be created and similarly administered. Another charge has been that the money would be frittered away in top-level wasteful overhead. Many years of experience with freshwater fish conservation programs using earmarked license revenues refutes that worry.

Available national surveys show that, on the average, only about 7 cents of each fish conservation dollar expended go for administration, 4 cents go for conservation education, and 21 cents go for law enforcement. This leaves 68 cents out of each dollar for the vital research and fish management activities. In saltwater sport fish conservation programs, we can expect that a similar general pattern of expenditures would develop. Of the 68 cents for research and management, expectations are that 30 to 35 cents or less would be spent on "practical" research in developing beneficial fish management practices. The remaining 30 to 35 cents or more would be used to provide the needed angling facilities—access sites, and parking areas, boat launching ramps, fishing piers, bridge outwalks, artificial fishing reefs, beach areas, etc. The particulars of the individual state budgets would obviously vary in accordance with the specialized needs of each state, but could be expected to approximate the general pattern.

The harvest of fish is increasing rapidly. The current catch of saltwater fish by sport fishermen is equivalent to about 25 per cent of the total harvest of marketable food fishes by commercial fishermen. For some of the more important sport fishes, it is much higher. In 1955, for example, anglers accounted for 44 per cent of the take of 27 species of fish by New Jersey sport and commercial fishermen combined. Moreover, the same five species were the ones of most importance to both groups.

The time is no longer remote when an increasing number of decisions will have to be made concerning who gets to harvest what species and how. It's a matter both of the capacity of fish stocks to replenish themselves satisfactorily and of the wisest use of the stocks for the benefit of the most people. In our beef-eating country, many species of fish have their greatest value as objects furnishing vital outdoor recreation, and a few reservations of former commercial fishes for recreational use have already been made. In California (a state having a saltwater license), the tidal-water White Catfish was subject to heavy exploitation by both sport and commercial fishermen. Biological research demonstrated that the joint harvest exceeded the capacity of the Catfish to replenish itself satisfactorily. This finding, together with economic evaluation, resulted in the elimination of commercial harvest and reservation of the Catfish fishery for sport fishing purposes, properly regulated to assure a high level of sustained yield. In Texas (another state with a saltwater license), biological research indicated that there was a similar need to control commercial netting of Redfish and Seatrout in two large coastal bays; and it was done in order to benefit angling. If we are to keep pace with growing fishing pressures on coastal sport fishery resources, and assure future good fishing, the states must begin soon to provide abundant fishing facilities and to maintain continuing research programs designed to develop and evaluate beneficial fish management practices.

At its 1957 National Convention in Washington, D. C., the National Wildlife Federation adopted a resolution urging that all coastal states adopt saltwater licenses. The Izaak Walton League of America adopted a similar resolution at its 1959 Annual Convention in Philadelphia. Together, these two national sportsmen's organizations represent the vast majority of organized sportsmen, some 1½ million strong. Despite these actions by responsible national sportsmen's organizations, it has been questioned whether such resolutions accurately reflect the views of the organized saltwater anglers. Early in 1960, in an effort to determine what actual views prevail among rank-and-file marine anglers, define it, and solicit any alternatives of substance, the Sport Fishing Institute sent questionnaires to 1,461 known sportsmen's clubs located in 17 coastal states. The 10-item questionnaire was designed to be answered only by those clubs whose angling members fished at least part of the time in salt water. If their fishing was exclusively in fresh water they were not expected to reply. The responding clubs gave figures for their total membership and the number of members who actually fished at least part of the time in salt water, thus determining which of the clubs have an active interest in salt water. Saltwater angling membership in the latter added up to 28,643 individuals—averaging about 20 per club.

The organized saltwater sport fishermen recorded unmistakably that they recognize a necessity for initiating state-administered saltwater sport fish conservation programs (93%), including both research (94%) and facilities development (93%). A strong majority also indicated that the state fish and game departments in close cooperation with the state commercial fishery departments, should be the agencies to administer the programs (64%). There was very little sentiment for having the commercial fishery departments administer the sport fish programs alone (2%). Even greater antipathy was expressed toward federal administration of the coastal sport fisheries (less than 1%), the anglers seeing no insurmountable problems of interstate coordination. Although there was unmistakable recognition that state-administered saltwater sport fishery programs are needed, there was no notable trend either for (23%) or against (21%) the saltwater license as a means of financing. A majority (56%) indicated that they had no set opinion or were open-minded in the matter. Among the one-fifth who indicated opposition, 9 per cent nevertheless voted on a question of the preferred license fee. It was concluded that the majority of anglers appear willing to accept whatever mechanism responsible conservation leaders may judge will best serve to raise the needed funds. Most anglers (89%) would want their licenses to be valid (reciprocally) in the coastal waters of neighboring states, and license fees in the range of $2 to $3 was acceptable to the majority (80%).

Alternative proposals to licensing were solicited by the Institute, but few suggestions were offered, viz: One Connecticut club said needs should be financed "through federal funds." The proposal of one Maine club was to "license charter boats;" another said "use commercial fishing license." A Maryland club recommended "tax the commercial netters and fisherman." A Massachusetts club advocated "put an additional tax on saltwater equipment;" another expressed a belief that "the money is already there to be used." A New York club wanted to "use part of the Duck Stamp revenue." A North Carolina club advised that the "gasoline tax should be used for this." It was obvious that the majority attitude of the organized saltwater anglers was fairly summed up by means of this comment, made by a Louisiana club in response to the Institute poll: "The average U. S. sportsman is ready to pay for value received."

Tentative functional budgets for saltwater sport fishery programs may be visualized based on long experience of states with freshwater programs having certain aspects that present common problems. After many years the pattern of necessary expenditures for such things as administration, public information, and law enforcement has become fairly clear. The special needs for substantial continuing studies of the coastal marine sport fishery resources, angler harvest, and evaluation of experimental management measures have also become clarified. Much recent attention has been focused on specific needs for acquisition and development of a variety of fishing facilities.

Saltwater budgets outlined. Assuming that the 21 coastal states principally involved would issue saltwater fishing licenses costing $3 each annually, and carrying full angling reciprocity privileges among the states, and that about 6 million of them would be sold (after making the usual exclusions for the very young and the elderly), total revenues would amount to $18 million. This works out to an average of about $857,000 per state; obviously, some states would get more and some would get less. By the end of the first decade, we expect that the number of licensable saltwater anglers will have increased by nearly 70 per cent, then numbering about 10 million. Assuming the same license fee, total revenues would then amount to $30 million, averaging about $1,428,000 per state. Based on these average revenues, functional budget set-ups may be visualized for the first and tenth years of the program. In the initial few years, the new saltwater sport fishery expenditures would probably approximate the following broad pattern; however, details within functions would vary in accordance with specific needs of individual states, especially as to angling facilities:

Program Function	*Initial Years*	*Tenth Year*
Administration ....$	60,000 (7%)	$ 142,800 (10%)
Public Information ..	25,700 (3%)	71,400 (5%)
Law Enforcement	128,500 (15%)	214,200 (15%)
Mgt. Investigations ..	257,100 (30%)	285,600 (20%)
Facilities development.	385,700 (45%)	714,000 (50%)
	$ 857,000 (100%)	$1,428,000 (100%)

During the initial years of the program, expenditures for necessary administration and dissemination of essential public information will be at their least. By the time the program has matured and stabilized these expenditures would be expected to have increased proportionately. They should not exceed about 15 per cent of the budget in combination. Expenditures for law enforcement should be relatively constant percentage-wise during any year of the program. They would increase dollarwise in proportion to the number of anglers, and the chief function, initially, will be to enforce the licensing regulation. Enforcement otherwise will involve only those regulations on fishing that are found to be necessary to assure a continuing supply of sport fish at high levels of yield, such as protection from illegal commercial harvest, and regulations governing pollution, disposal of dredging spoil, etc. At the outset, capital investment for needed patrol equipment will be fairly substantial. Future needs to replace equipment can be stretched out over several years. As time passes the emphasis will be shifted increasingly to operations and enforcement of such minimal conservation laws as may prove actually needed for adequate conservation of sport fish stocks.

Management investigations and facilities development, collectively, will account for the remaining 70 per cent of funds. Management investigations include needed resource studies in relation, say, to harbor and channel dredging, pollution problems, real estate and industrial development, engineering projects of all kinds, and continuing evaluations of experimental fish management practices, etc. These may be expected to continue at a fairly constant dollar level, therefore becoming proportionately less as the total budget rises. Facilities development includes acquisition of land that must be made available for access, parking, and sanitary facilities, as well as their development for these purposes. It also includes construction of such things as fishing piers, modification of jetties to aid anglers, construction of artificial fishing reefs, bridge outwalks for anglers, boat launching ramps, etc. Expenditures for different items to meet variable specific facilities needed will vary decidedly in detail from state to state. In time, maintenance of the facilities, addition of new facilities, and replacements of aging structures will be needed. This is a natural program evolution with increasing maturity which, together with continually rising land, labor, and materials costs, means that the dollar-expenditures for facilities must rise significantly. This can be accomplished by devoting a slowing rising and substantial proportion of the budget to facilities development.

Fishing piers and jetties. Many coastal states have need for public fishing piers, and those already in existence are very heavily used, often yield large catches of coastal fish, and are in increasing demand. In 1952, for example, there were a total of five ocean fishing piers operating along the North Carolina coast. The state's Conservation and Development Department claims that "strictly-for-fishing" pier construction was pioneered on the Atlantic Coast in 1923 at Kure Beach, North Carolina; in addition, two piers were built at Nags Head in 1947. By 1961, a total of 28 fishing piers were jutting into famed North Carolina surf casting waters, from Kitty Hawk on the Outer Banks down to the South Carolina line. Piers are longer, stronger, and wider than they once were, and all of them in North Carolina are at seaside resort areas accessible by automobile. All have snack bars, tackle and bait; some have restaurants. Several have bathhouses, picnic tables, beach umbrellas, and surf mats as well as fishing gear available to their patrons. This has been stimulated in part at least, within the past few years, by development of new know-how in fishing techniques. This in turn has added Cobia, Tarpon, and King Mackerel to the dozen or more species for which North Carolina piers have long been noted. Consequently, piers are growing in popularity, not only as fishing centers where record catches have been made, but as family recreational areas and sightseeing objectives. Ocean fishing piers totaled 13 in 1954 before Hurricane Hazel demolished some and damaged others. An upsurge in reconstruction and the building of new piers brought the total up to 23 by the spring of 1957. Within the next three years, eight more piers had been opened, and a number of others extended. The piers range in length from 600 to 1,000 feet and are 20 to 24 feet wide.

In 1959, California's Wildlife Conservation Board approved its first fishing pier project, the reopening of 2,000 feet of the Berkley Pier by replacement of decking and some underpinning. The project now provides approximately 150,000 man-days of fishing annually. In 1960, the Board approved a new fishing pier policy to guide its future decisions with respect to such projects and also approved another project (within the terms of its new policy) to rebuild the end 230 feet of an old 80-foot-wide municipal commercial shipping pier at Santa Cruz and retain this portion exclusively for anglers, equipped with "fishing wells" or openings through the decking for fishing. The end portion, with access thereto, was leased to the state for a 25-year period, with maintenance by the city. The Department of Fish and Game endorsed the project, having a sustained fishery available of Jacksmelt, Perch, Cod, Cabezone, Croakers, Flatfish, as well as Skates, Rays, and Sharks. Total cost of the project was $65,000. The fishing pier policy, which now provides guidelines for using capital funds in the future, reads as follows:

"As part of its program to provide fishermen access to the resources of the sea, the Board believes that the construction and repair of fishing piers can provide opportunity for large numbers of people who would otherwise be unable to participate in their favorite recreation.

"Realizing that although piers can provide much fishing opportunity, they are expensive and the demand for them could soon result in exhausting all available funds, the Board adopts the following criteria to govern their construction and repair.

"1. Projects for construction of new fishing piers or the repair of existing piers to provide fishing facilities will be chosen on the basis of providing the most fishing opportunity for the most people. Accordingly they will be located in areas of greatest need and potential use adjacent to concentrations of populations and where fishing results will be satisfactory.

"2. Proprietary interest should be held by the state.

"3. The pier should provide access to good and sustained fishing and should be recommended by the Department of Fish and Game.

"4. The pier, or portion thereof for which state funds are expended, should be used exclusively for fishing or activities related thereto.

"5. Adequate car parking should be available within a reasonable distance.

"6. No charge for pier access or fishing should be made.

"7. Maintenance and operation will be undertaken by the cooperating agency and without cost to the state.

"8. The design of the pier should be substantial and require minimum maintenance, but the cost of construction should relate favorably to the lineal feet of railing which would provide good fishing.

"9. In the case of repair of an existing pier, the cost of construction should relate favorably to the lineal feet of railing which would provide good fishing. The cost per lineal foot of pier available for fishing should not exceed $50.00.

"10. In the case of construction of a new pier, the construction to be accomplished with a matching fund of at least 50% to be contributed by the cooperating agency, but the state's 50% should not exceed $50.00 per lineal foot of railing avaliable for fishing.

"11. Construction costs to include pier construction and related fishing facilities such as approaches, parking, sanitary facilities, etc."

In other areas, ocean structures such as the South Mayport Jetty near Jacksonville, Florida, are providing needed deep-water access for thousands of boatless fishermen along our coasts. The rubble and large rock jetties attract small fish which feed on many small plants and animals around the rocks. The small fish attract larger sport fishes seeking prey. Sheepshead, Drum, and Yellowtail are common around the jetties; Sea Trout, Mackerel, Snapper and Tarpon are seasonal. About 50,000 man-days of fishing have been recorded annually at the Jacksonville Jetty. High angler use also occurs at harbor and channel breakwaters constructed by the U. S. Army Corps of Engineers at Cape Lookout, North Carolina; Savannah, Georgia; Fernandina, Pensacola, Panama City, and St. George Island, Florida; and Dauphin Island, Alabama. The nearness of most jetties to population centers and the small expense involved in the fishing trip make them highly attractive. "Walking" anglers place a heavy demand on any structure which affords access to deep water. Bay bridge fishing is extremely popular. At least 17 large commercial and public piers are available in Florida. Haulover Park ocean fishing pier near Miami recorded 55,500 paid admissions in 1957. In the past, fisherman-use has not been considered in the design and construction of jetties. Many are made of huge rocks, and the difficulty of clamboring over them, added to slippery, algae-covered surfaces, and a possible soaking from breakers, has often curtailed or prevented fishing. Public use has been prohibited on some to prevent injury. Considering the high biological, economic, and esthetic potentialities of the jetties for fishing, efforts to make them safer and more accessible are highly desirable. Studies by the Branch of River Basin Studies, U. S. Fish and Wildlife Service, Vero Beach, Florida, showed that the jetties can be modified in several ways to provide greater recreational benefits. Concrete caps, smooth spots at intervals, walkways, and handrails have greatly increased angler-use at some jetties. The benefits far exceed the small initial costs. Possible modifications deserve serious consideration by local interests on existing and future breakwaters.

THE CHALLENGE OF RESERVOIR FISH MANAGEMENT

According to recent estimates, about *one-third* of all inland lake fishing water (exclusive of the Great Lakes) is now in man-made impoundments, totalling 13 million acres. Construction has accelerated greatly in the past 30 years, and is predicted to continue at a fast pace for the next 30. The Sport Fishing Institute estimates that there were at least 80 million fishing trips on reservoirs last year, or 20 percent of the grand total in all U. S. inland waters, fostering an angler expenditure in excess of 320 million dollars.

The relative importance of reservoir fishing in various parts of the country varies markedly, being highest in the South. For example, fisherman-use and license sales data from Oklahoma, Texas and Arkansas indicate that about 60 percent of all angling in those three states last year was done on reservoirs—a total of 30 million man-days. These three states experienced nearly 40 percent of all reservoir fishing, nationally. Other extremely important reservoir areas are the Tennessee and Ohio River valleys, the southern coastal region and the northern plains states. Reservoirs are also vastly increasing in relative importance in the Western states.

A report by the U. S. Fish and Wildlife Service (1960) to the U. S. Senate Select Committee on National Water Resources included an estimate that water requirements for sport fishery resources in terms of acre-feet would double in the next 20 years. They base this on an estimated increase in fishermen numbers to 47 million in 1980 compared to 27 million today.

The Fish and Wildlife Service forecast that man-days of fishing will triple and expenditures will equal $4.5 billion by the turn of the century. Where will the anglers fish? The Service believes that new opportunities will come through: 1) the construction and improved management of artificial impoundments, 2) reduction of stream pollution, 3) increased interest in marine sport fishing, and 4) utilization of presently under-utilized fish species.

If fishing pressure is going to double in the next 20 years and triple in the next 40, and if a large proportion of this pressure is to be absorbed through improved reservoir management, the urgent need for new knowledge is obvious.

History of reservoir management. As reservoir construction began to gain momentum in the early 1920s, members of the American Fisheries Society took note of the added water area, and passed the following resolution (in part) at their 1923 meeting:

"Whereas, the creation of lakes by the construction of dams for developing hydroelectric power . . . (or flood control); said lakes open to the public at all times during the open season . . .; said lakes likewise furnishing some of our best egg collecting fields. . . .

Be it Resolved, . . . by the American Fisheries Society that it hereby favors such projects as being the means for conserving surplus waters, affording refuge for birds and fish, and providing recreational pleasures for the American public."

About this time, biologists in the U. S. began to study artificial lakes. One of the first investigations was on Lake Keokuk, a run-of-the-river impoundment on the Upper Mississippi River, Limnological studies and fish population surveys were conducted by the U. S. Bureau of Fisheries and Illinois Natural History Survey biologists on shallow river reservoirs throughout the 1920s in that general area.

Another early center of study was in California on the limnological features of Searsville Lake and several small reservoirs in San Diego County in relation to water supply and fishing use. Viosca described the fish populations of periodically-inundated oxbow lakes in Louisiana in 1927, and drew parallels between these fertile waters and reservoirs which might be designated for optimum production.

The 1930s. Management investigations increased in tempo in the early 1930s. In reporting on newly-impounded Sacandaga Reservoir in New York at the 1930 Society meeting, Dr. Emmeline Moore commented on the state of knowledge at that time:

"The fact is we know little about how nature works on the sudden drowning of a valley, in what manner the biological and other factors operative in the newly created reservoir differ from the normal state of affairs in our natural lakes . . . where the relation between animal and plant life is more nearly in balance."

Two years later, she predicted the important role to be played by gizzard and threadfin shad, as follows:

"In stocking (storage reservoirs) with a suitable minnow, a selection should be made from an "income producing" species, i.e., a plankton feeder . . . that can tolerate the vicissitudes of reservoir life and relish the endless monotony of plankton with which to fill themselves."

In 1932, E. L. Wickliff and Lee Roach began

studying Ohio's impounded waters. Wickliff concluded that the gizzard shad was the key to sport fish production. He suggested that trees or stumps be left in areas to be covered by water less than 15-20 feet deep, and that shorelines underlaid by sand and gravel be plowed up to expose it.

In the second half of that decade, fish conservationists began to express disenchantment with impounded waters. Easy answers to management problems were not forthcoming, and the tapering off of superb sport fishing after the early years portended bad days ahead. Some viewed a reservoir as a sort of natural lake "cut in half" by a dam, and thought the difficulties that desirable fishes were experiencing must be linked with this anomaly. Past techniques employed on natural lakes seemed to fall short when applied to "half-a-lake" impoundments.

The formation of a new reservoir study group by the Tennessee Valley Authority was announced at the 1936 meeting of the American Fisheries Society. A. R. Cahn, in outlining the fishery program, dolefully stated that "It is a familiar fact, which has been emphasized by Mr. Jay N. Darling, Dr. M. M. Ellis, and others that impounded lakes become, after the first few years of their existence decidely lacking in fish productivity. Mr. Darling has referred to the results of dam construction as "biological deserts' . . . There are innumerable examples of aquatic deserts, and to list them would be to name practically every large dam so far constructed. . . ."

Ellis, of the U. S. Bureau of Fisheries, gave a paper at the same meeting in which he attributed the initial high productivity of reservoirs to the fact that the fixed nitrogen, phosphates and ionizable salts content of the water are satisfactorily high. He compared new reservoirs with the hay infusion principle used in laboratory cultures. He concluded that of all the factors producing problems, "the disastrous effects of the draw-down are perhaps the most easily recognized."

In contrast to the generally prevailing pessimistic view, some new and exciting ideas were being advanced by fishery scientists in Michigan. Research at the Univ. of Michigan was in high gear. Carl L. Hubbs optimistically viewed the future at the 1938 North American Wildlife Conference. Said he: "To be sure the fish management of impounded waters is presenting grave problems, but I feel confident that most of these problems can be solved satisfactorily."

A critical new look at restrictive regulations was taken at that 1938 meeting. R. W. Eschmeyer advanced some revolutionary hypotheses based on rotenone sampling of lake populations. (Rotenone was first used in 1934 by Michigan biologists Hubbs and Trautmas as a management measure.) Eschmeyer concluded that "The former notion that a planting of fish together with certain legal restrictions could be expected to assure good angling has been found erroneous, and those management methods which have been adhered to for many decades now are recognized as highly inadequate." This marked the beginning of efforts to greatly liberalize laws and regulations which were initiated on man-made lakes six years later.

Dr. Albert S. Hazzard in summarizing the tenor of the 1939 Midwest Wildlife Conference, stated:

"In general the trend of discussion . . . seemed to question most of the present methods of management. . . . The importance of population studies in management was stressed repeatedly. Population control is coming to be regarded as the most promising of the new methods . . . warmwater lakes."

Thus, new ideas were emerging twenty years ago, and some new techniques had been developed. The TVA fishery team had been formed, led by A. H. Weibe, R. W. Eschmeyer, and C. M. Tarzewell, (with biologists Paul Bryan, Earl Cady, Irving Cantrell, Henry Howell, Alden Jones, Earl Lyman, Lawrence Miller, and C. G. Smith), and was at work on intensive investigations of TVA reservoirs and tailwaters. In Illinois, G. W. Bennett, Sam Parr, and D. H. Thompson were studying the production of small impoundments. Biologists Langlois, Roach, Wickliff, Binkley and Huber were working on Lake Meander and 11 other Ohio impoundments. Albert Weyer was studying Lake of the Ozarks, Missouri. J. K. G. Silvey and B. B. Harris were conducting limnological studies of Texas reservoirs; James R. Simon had worked on the limnology of Wyoming reservoirs, John Greenbank on Elephant Butte Reservoir in New Mexico, Francis Felin in California, Emmeline Moore and G. E. Burdick in New York, and M. M. Ellis in various states. D. S. Rawson had begun impoundment studies in Saskatchewan.

All in all, there were probably less than 50 biologists engaged in reservoir management investigations in North America at the close of the 1930s, and many of these were interested primarily in basic limnological research. However, there were probably more fishery men working on reservoirs per unit area of impounded water in 1939 than in 1959.

The 1940s. Armed with management investigation tools such as rotenone sampling of coves with blockoff nets expanded creel census techniques, age and growth analysis, refined limnological sampling gear, and new biologists R. H. Stroud, D. E. Manges, and J. S. Dendy, TVA Fish and Game Branch personnel attacked the problems presented by Norris, Wheeler, Guntersville, Pickwick, Hiwasse, and Chickamauga Reservoirs in the early 1940s. In a 1940 report on creel census and age and growth studies, Eschmeyer and Tarzwell concluded that there was little reason to believe that those impoundments would become "biological deserts." They recommended increased commercial fishing to keep coarse fish in bounds, and the opening of main stream reservoirs to year-round fishing for most species.

Biologists in Illinois, meantime, were studying some small reservoirs intensively and published findings which disagreed with those of Ellis concerning declining reservoir productivity. Bennett held that "the theory of Ellis that high fish production in the early years of impoundment is the result of organic decay in the new lake basin is largely disproved by the fact that this cycle of production can be repeated as often as the reservoir is completely drained and restocked with small numbers of fish."

H. J. Deason, U. S. Fish and Wildlife Service, rose to the defense of Ellis in a brief article in the *Progressive Fish-culturist* as follows:

"The exact basis for the disagreement with the observation of Ellis that the fertility of impounded waters declines with age, is not evident. It may be stated that Ellis' paper summarized limnological information accumulated over a period of many years by outstanding European and American workers. Overcrowding (of fishes) that results in slow growth may not be the self-sufficient cause for a decline in the fish productivity of impounded waters. A diminution in the fertility of the lake may be an equally responsible cause of poor growth. . . . Additional evidence in support of Ellis' contentions has come to our attention during the last few months in the form of stocking and management questions related to artificial impoundments. . . ."

Deason was referring, in part, to a report on Lake O'The Ozarks by Missouri biologist Albert Weyer. Weyer offered these management recommendations: 1) plant lotus, willows, sweet clover on bare gravelly shores, smartweed and timothy on mud-flats; 2) remove size limits, except on black bass; 3) impose a general "rest" period during January and February by closing season; 4) establish closed spawning sanctuaries in one-tenth of the lake area from January 1-June 15.

Ellis gave a paper at the 1941 meeting of the Society reporting his findings on 33 reservoirs from 1936 to 1939. He concluded:

"The limitations of impounded waters for fish productivity can in part be offset by: (1) Controlling the draw-off so that a fairly constant water level will be maintained during the nesting season of the most desirable species of fish. (2) By judicious restocking from hatcheries with vigorous specimens of the desired species. (3) By the construction where feasible of lateral areas of shallow water of constant level and tributary to the main impoundment in which adult fish can nest, young fish can find refuge and fish food can be produced. (4) By the use of various devices such as floating nests, floating shelters, the planting of exposed portions of the reservoir during low water. (5) By the artificial enrichment of soil and water with (fertilizers) in such limited areas as seem to justify the expense."

Except for the first listed, these procedures have since proved generally unsuccessful in the big reservoirs—in fact, have failed completely. But it illustrates the precarious state of the art only twenty years ago, and indicates that much has been accomplished since.

At that 1941 meeting of the American Fisheries Society in St. Louis, members were incensed over the disastrous effects of dams on anadromous fishes, and by the apparent non-productivity of impounded waters. In an attempt to forestall the creation of more problems before the old ones had been solved, and to get biologists in on the design and planning of dams and reservoirs, the Society adopted the following resolution (in marked contrast to the one adopted in 1923):

"Whereas the immense (high dam) projects, present and planned for the future, wholly ignore the biology of water, existing aquatic biological resources, and the public's right to enjoy them; and there are present threats to blanket the country with high dams;

Therefore be it resolved that the American Fisheries Society . . . oppose the authorization or construction of *any more* high dams regardless of their stated pupose until such time as biologists have an adequate role in the preliminary planning of all such projects. . . ."

Four years later, the Office of River Basin Studies was formed.

World War II curtailed efforts to solve reservoir fish management problems but didn't slow the rate of dam construction. Studies continued at TVA and in a few states at a reduced level. Rough fish removal, which had been employed in northern states since the turn of the century as a management technique, was stepped up, being largely justified as an added food source during the war years. The introduction of sport species not present in some reservoirs was begun, and population, age and growth, and limnological studies continued.

In 1943, Moffett gave a preliminary report on huge Lake Mead, and concluded: 1) the introduction of forage fish is believed unnecessary; 2) there is no closed season, and none should be applied; 3) no further stocking of species present is advisable; 4) the introduction of aquatic plants should not be attempted; and 5) regulate the water level from April through June so that rapid falls in level do not occur. Only the first recommendation has not stood the test of time.

In 1944, Tennessee opened Norris reservoir to year-round fishing, its remaining reservoirs in 1945, and was joined by Ohio in year-round fishing in 1945 as well. Some additional states followed quickly on their heels.

Rounsefell analyzed lake fish production as a guide for estimating production in proposed reservoirs in the first issue of COPEIA in 1946. Available published data on standing crops and annual sport and commercial yields were amazingly skimpy.

Rounsefell could muster only 51 standing crop estimates (mostly based on rotenone recovery in ponds), 39 measures of annual sport fish catch and 12 of commercial harvest on inland lakes. This underscores the very limited extent of knowledge of inland water production only 14 years ago.

Using admittedly weak basic data, Rounsefell computed an inverse logarithmic relationship between production per acre and lake size. He calculated that reservoirs over 5,000 acres would not yield more than 3 pounds of game fish per acre per year, and cited water level fluctuations, silt, and unnatural thermal statification as reasons for even lower yields as the reservoirs aged. This dour prediction has not been fulfilled, as many large reservoirs have since yielded well over 30 pounds of sport fish per acre annually.

The Office of River Basin Studies was organized within the U.S. Fish and Wildlife Service in 1945, and 70 biologists were on the job by 1947. River Basin Chief Rudolph Diffenbach, in commenting on river development program and their relationship to fish and wildlife resources, wrote:

"The relationship of reservoir age to productivity has been observed and to a limited degree studied by technicians. Practically all writers are in agreement that the initial high productivity of impounded waters is not sustained, and that decline, particularly for sport fishing, is generally inevitable under the present methods of control. Management practices effective in maintaining the highest possible initial productivity in large impoundments represent one of the most urgent needs of the nationwide water programs."

Diffenbach endorsed the widely-held, but oft-disputed thesis that productivity in reservoirs declines—a hypothesis that is still without factual base. A safer statement, in view of the existing state of knowledge, might have been that the production and/or harvest of sport fish, and not total productivity, declines with age in many reservoirs as shown by Jenkins. The important point he did make 13 years ago was that effective management methods were an urgent need.

After the war, as biologists emerged from colleges and universities, many state conservation agencies became actively engaged in reservoir studies—notably in California, Kentucky, Missouri, Oklahoma, Tennessee and Texas. By the end of the 1940s stepped-up activity by the states and TVA had begun to fill in many of the more easily-obtained gaps in knowledge about impoundment fisheries. Publications tripled over prewar rates, judging from perusal of a "Reservoir Bibliography" compiled by Pfitzer.

An aura of optimism had again pervaded the field concerning potential sport fish production in Mississippi Valley impoundments. But many of the commonly-posed management problems associated with operation of the reservoir for other purposes (hydropower, flood control, etc.) appeared insurmountable. The cream had been skimmed from the knowledge bucket through "practical" research and short-term management investigations. The well of basic facts, provided in large measure by fish population and limnological studies on natural lakes, had about run dry. Concerning this situation, Justin W. Leonard addressed the Midwest Conference with this admonition:

"And constantly administrators should harp on how little, actually, is known—how little, in fact, could possibly be known in view of the small amount of effort thus far invested and the peculiar nature of the problems. It is impossible to make frequent contacts with fishermen without being struck by the inadequacy of our proven, factual information. Very often he has assumed that the answers are in the back of the book. He expresses keen astonishment when he is assured that the book hasn't even been written."

The 1950s. Hard work, with no promise of immediate success, faced reservoir managers at the beginning of the 1950's. They were not only confronted with years of arduous field work (e.g., dead fish pickup in broiling sun), but with, to many, the more difficult task of analyzing data collected. Few young biologists displayed the mental discipline or desire to sit down and try to draw conclusions from the accumulated information. Fortunately, progress in the "non-doing" phases of management investigation has slowly occurred.

Nearly every plan of management in use on natural lakes, plus a few others, had been tried on the big impoundments. Heavy stocking of indigenous sport and forage fishes, provision for spawning sanctuaries, construction of special rearing ponds, planting aquatic vegetation, rough fish removal, cover and spawning devices, had produced few measurable beneficial effects on the production of sport fishes.

Relatively high costs associated with evaluation of the techniques had discouraged any such concerted studies on the big bodies of water. Of course, many were obvious failures, and needed no evaluation. Stroud's studies showed that reservoir populations had been relatively untouched by angling or commercial fishing, and that the changes which occurred were largely the result of natural biological phenomena.

However, some real successes had been chalked up. The liberalization of fishing regulations had greatly increased the long-suffering angler's fishing opportunity and yields were up. Introduction of sport species not present had produced desired results in many instances. The installation of brush shelters and floating fishing docks had increased harvests of certain species on some warm water impoundments.

Several summaries of the status of local reservoir management were presented in a special 1957 American Fisheries Society symposium. J. B. Kimsey reported on the status of California reservoir management, John W. Parsons on southeastern reservoirs, and James T. Shields on Missouri River impoundments.

The principal implements of attack envisioned in the 1950s were 1) water level fluctuation, principally extreme drawdown; 2) introduction of sport and forage species not present; 3) removal of rough fishes through commercial fishing; 4) partial removal of overabundant species through selective rotenone treatment; 5) concentration of fishes by brush shelters, artificial temperature gradients, and lights; and 6) increased angler harvest through press releases on seasonal depth distribution, proper angling methods, and accounts of successful trips.

Water Level Fluctuation. In 1951, Roy Wood published a review paper on the significance of drawdowns in developing reservoir fisheries. He drew a parallel between the yearly cycle in oxbow (cutoff) lakes and what might be accomplished with the same sort of "dry fallowing" operation in reservoirs. He reasoned that when the bottom is not aerated the availability of essential elements is reduced, and that these nutrients are essential to ultimate fish production. However, the 85 references Wood cited did not furnish quantitative data on how a drawdown actually affected individual components of a specific fish population.

Ten years earlier, Eschmeyer and Jones observed that permanent-level pools in TVA impoundments had provided poorer fishing than those with widely fluctuating levels. Several theories were advanced to explain this difference. Although the basic reasons have still not been adequately described, and represent a very fertile field for research, some states have employed water level fluctuation successfully in management. For example, Arkansas biologists combined extreme drawdown with intensive rough fish removal to improve sport fishing in flood control reservoirs. South Dakota biologists attempted control of carp reproduction experimentally through drawdown. Squawfish spawn was destroyed by lowering 3,200-acre Hayden Lake, Idaho, 2 inches per day for 30 days.

In summation, as concluded by Wood and Pfitzer, "available evidence supports the concept that water-level fluctuation employed without discretion may be deleterious to some desired fishes; on the other hand, with sound application it may be one of the most effective tools in fishery management."

Stocking as a Management Tool. The introduction of desirable species not present which contribute to the angler's catch or provide forage for sport species has proven to be one of the more successful tangible tools in reservoir management. The introduction of threadfin shad has been an amazing success in some southern and California reservoirs. Its superiority over gizzard shad as a manageable forage fish has been widely acclaimed, and offers great future promise due to its winter-kill proclimities, short life span, small maximum size, and prolificacy.

Introductions have been especially important in the West, where the native fish fauna lacks suitable reservoir fishes, and some introduced species have not proved ideal. The West also lacks the many species of undesirable rough fish common in the East, which should ultimately simplify management there.

Outstanding introduction success has been achieved in many instances with white bass, white crappie, rainbow, brook, and lake trout, threadfin and gizzard shad, smelt, and corvina. Very limited success has been experienced with walleye and muskellunge. The most promising sport species on the horizon is the striped bass, which has put South Carolina's Santee-Cooper Reservoir on the famous fishing-spot map, and is now established through stocking in Kerr Reservoir on the Virginia-North Carolina border.

Rough Fish Control. The trials and tribulations associated with the efforts to sell the public on the need for commercial fishing to control competing rough fishes in reservoirs, especially in the South, have discouraged enlightened management in many instances. Education of the public on the dynamics of reservoir populations has been, and continues to be, a vital need.

Efforts to control rough fish with conventional methods of commercial fishing have been little more than token. New, more efficient methods of much broader scope are needed. Recent new gear development involving large seines, trap nets, trawls and electrical devices shows real promise. New chemicals may provide selective control methods. Untried techniques, such as lethal ultrasonic sound production may pay off. Economic feasibility remains as a formidable bottleneck.

The principal problem fishes at present appear to be 1) the catostomids (buffalofishes, carpsuckers, Utah suckers, etc.) 2) carp and other cyprinids (squawfish, chub), and 3) freshwater drum. Much more knowledge about their life histories and habits is needed before control methods will be efficient. Some method of biological control which would limit reproduction would be much preferred to purely physical or chemical means.

Forage Fish Control. Gizzard shad have been alternately praised and maligned as a forage fish in most large impoundments. Population studies have indicated that shad often constitute 50 to 80 percent of the total standing crop, and many biologists believe that such overwhelming abundance acts to suppress abundance and growth of more desirable fishes.

Efforts to selectively kill shad on a large scale with various rotenone concentrations were first undertaken in Oklahoma and Texas in 1955, and have been recently climaxed by three successive annual treatments of 30,000-acre Lake Apopka in Florida. Many other states have tried it.

Thorough evaluations of this technique on large reservoirs have been lacking. A limited study of 5,700-acre Lake Murray, Oklahoma, following aerial treatment in 1955 with 0.35 gallons of emulsufiable rotenone per surface acre, suggested that about 65 percent of the adult shad had been killed, but the population quickly rebounded. No before and after measurements of sport fish yield were made. More careful evaluations of selective shad kills are needed to establish the value of this expensive tool.

Increasing Sport Fish Harvestability. The advent of the floating, heated fishing dock in the 1950's in the southwest has revolutionized winter fishing on many reservoirs. Their origin is generally attributed to 46,000-acre Grand Lake O'The Cherokees and 92,000-acre Lake Texoma in Oklahoma, where there are now more than 100 of these commercially-operated enterprises, plus many privately-owned boat house installations.

An estimated 60,000 fisherman-days were recorded in fishing docks on 19,000-acre Fort Gibson Reservoir, Oklahoma, in the period January through March, 1956. This represented 90 percent of the total fishing effort on the lake during the winter. Catches of crappie predominate. Dock fishing continues year-round, and accounted for 37 percent of the total man-days on Fort Gibson.

The "modus operandi" varies, generally including suspension of evergreen trees and bags of cottonseed cake under the dock to act as shelter attractant and plankton producer, respectively. Charges were usually $1 per day, with minnows, tackle, television and snacks available. The floating dock idea is spreading throughout the mid-south and is apparently one answer to the sedentary angler's dreams.

The establishment and annual refurbishing of brush shelters has been a fairly-valuable tool. Difficulties include placement to avoid exposure during drawdown, and periodic maintenance requirements. Such maintenance is often done by concessionaires, sportsmen's groups, or individuals. Few detailed evaluations have been made of reservoir brush shelters, but their use by anglers apparently justifies construction, principally to increase harvest of crappies.

Artificial means of establishing temperature gradients which attract fish in winter, based on a principle demonstrated by Hunter Hancock at Canton Reservoir, Oklahoma, may hold real possibilities for the future. Hancock introduced slightly-warmer water into headwaters of a cove, and it attracted crappies. Discharges from steam plants on reservoirs have also demonstrated the attracting power of temperature gradients.

The use of lights as attractants has been practiced by anglers at night (primarily as insect attractors) but their placement underwater has not been adequately tested, and represents needed experimentation. Sound and electrical discharges are also untapped concentrating device possibilities.

Public Information Services. In a paper given at the 1956 meeting of the Southern Division, American Fisheries Society, W. H. Irwin listed "advertisement of the impoundment" first in a list of methods to increase the harvest. He believed that more newspaper accounts of good catches would do much to increase fishing pressure on any reservoir. He stated: "It seems that no one need tell the complete truth. If one hundred parties go fishing and two of them return with good catches, publish accounts and pictures of the two good catches."

In this connection, management biologists could probably do more in conveying catch information to both departmental Information and Education sections and to newspapers by establishing liaison with concessionaires, resort owner associations, service station operators, and other convenient angler contacts around impoundments.

The depth distribution diagrams prepared on TVA reservoirs by Dendy for newspaper use in the 1940s were at least temporarily successful, and were surely more useful than most fishing calendars and tables published on sport pages today. Efforts similar to Dendy's could profitably be revived.

Employment of a skillful angler to determine, for public enlightenment, the best reservoir fishing methods from day to day, has proven successful in some states, notably South Dakota and Nebraska.

Present magnitude of management effort. What is the present level of management effort on 13 million acres of reservoirs nationally? Judging from state budget analyses submitted to Sport Fishing Institute for 1959, plus general knowledge of various state programs, Stroud and Jenkins estimated that about $2,100,000 were spent last year on stocking, population control, habitat improvement and other items of reservoir management. This comprised about 10 percent of the total management effort in these categories nationally. The proportionately low management effort (10 percent, compared to 20 percent of all *inland* fishing done on reservoirs) is probably a reflection of the scarcity of successful techniques to use on these big waters.

Fact-finding efforts are proportionately greater. Based on data provided by the Federal Aid Branch, USFWS, and on various state publications, Sport Fishing Institute estimates that about $1,400,000 were expended on reservoir studies in 1959. This equals about 20 percent of the total sport fishery fact-finding expenditure. In 1956, about $700,000 were spent on reservoir studies, so total effort has apparantly doubled in the past three years.

The great majority of states are now concerned with reservoir management, as 41 had one or more investigational projects of some kind going last year. Greatly-increased efforts are being made in the Western states, notably Arizona, California, Nevada, New Mexico, Oregon, and Utah. Stepped-up reservoir construction and fisherman-use has intensified the problem in these states. California has embarked on a bold management investigation plan to devise methods which will raise sport fish harvest by 5 pounds per acre in 82 reservoirs totalling 375,000 acres. Biologists calculate they might reasonably expect to increase state harvest by 2¾ million pounds within 20 years. The fact-finding effort would involve 14 men, and an annual cost of $225,000. The corresponding increase in recreational values would be immense. Twenty percent of all fact-finding in the Western states last year involved reservoirs ($350,000).

Reservoir studies in the southern states have increased gradually in the past decade, comprising about 35 percent of their fact-finding endeavors in 1959. Combined with TVA Fish and Game Branch efforts, about $700,000 were expended in attempts to unravel southern reservoir riddles. Texas led in total budgetary expenditures followed by Arkansas, Georgia, Kentucky, North Carolina, Oklahoma, and Tennessee.

A milestone in the field was marked by the establishment in 1958 of a Reservoir Committee within the Southern Division of the American Fisheries Society. It is composed of 17 members, including a representative from each southern Division state, the Fish and Wildlife Service, TVA and the Corps of Engineers. In its two years of existence, committee members have initiated the following: a Reservoir and Tailwater Bibliography; Standard Methods of Reporting Fish Population Data for Reservoirs; A Catalog of Reservoirs in the Southern Division States (including all available physical, chemical and biological data on impoundments over 5,000 acre-foot capacity); Standard Creel Census Methods; Model Commercial Fishing Regulations.

By these and similarly commendable efforts, the Committee hopes to encourage an increase in research and management, to coordinate presently disjointed individual work, and to serve as a sounding board for all reservoir management ideas. Much remains to be done to bring these ambitious programs to fruition.

About one-quarter of a million dollars were spent in the north-central states on reservoir studies last year. Leading states were Missouri and South Dakota. With more impoundment construction scheduled, investigations in that area are due to increase in tempo soon. Reservoir fact-finding equalled 15 per cent of overall research expenditures in the north-central area.

In the northeast, about $75,000 were invested in reservoir management studies in 1959.

Although a regional breakdown of management effort was not attempted, it probably paralleled that of fact-finding. Fifty percent of the total reservoir fact-finding expenditure was in Southern states, 27 percent in the Western states, 18 percent in the North-Central, and 5 percent in the Northeast.

Summing up—expenditures for reservoir management and fact-finding equalled about $3,500,000 in 1959 (not including development, or anadromous fishery research problems), which is equivalent to about 25 cents per acre. In comparison, intensive management of fertilized lakes in Alabama costs about $35 per acre. Complete rotenone rehabilitation averages about $25 per acre. It is apparent that expenditures are going to have to be increased many, many fold in the future if we are to intensively manage reservoirs with presently known techniques. If anglers were willing to pay $5 per reservoir fishing trip, about $30 would be available per acre for management. (National annual average equals six angler-days/acre.) As this is inconceivable at present, the need for new, economical methods of improving reservoir fisheries is acute.

Management study trends. Current attempts to improve sport fishing are being scrutinized more closely in many states. A cursory analysis of 55 D-J (federal aid) reservoir projects in 27 states suggests that more than one-third of them are concerned with evaluation of a management technique. Evaluations of the stocking of trout, catfishes, Japanese smelt, white and striped bass, threadfin shad, channel bass and redfish *(Scianops ocellata)* were underway. Also, gizzard shad reduction, population manipulation, regulation changes, rough fish control, and commercial fishing methods were being evaluated.

The two most prevalent activities, by far, are "population sampling," and "creel census," employed in conjunction with evaluations or as part of a general survey. Findings from these studies are extremely important in terms of defining the resource and measuring the extent of harvest. However, both methods still involve relatively crude estimates, and leave much to be desired in formulating future plans or predicting potential yields and optimum fisherman pressure.

Other D-J projects being undertaken by a number of states include general limnological observations, age and growth analyses, life history studies (including crappies, bullheads, paddlefish, walleye, white bass, river carpsucker, squawfish, Utah chub, buffalofishes, carp, gizzard shad, cut-throat trout), tagging, food habits studies, and pre-impoundment stream studies.

When the results of the current management evaluations are posted in the near future, there should be available a much better concept of the value of some currently favored projects and clues as to profitable new avenues of management experimentation.

Management investigation deficiencies. In spite of the impressive list of studies enumerated, some notable gaps are evident. They are to be expected in view of the fact that there are not more than 150 biologists working full-time on the many different types of reservoirs in the nation, in relatively isolated circumstances, with an average of less than $10,000 each for all operating expenses (including salary) per year. The short-term, practical aspects of most reservoir investigations also limit the scope and complexity of any study. It would appear that reservoir fishery workers are energetically treading water, with only an occasional effective stroke toward the shore.

Some of the more obvious deficiencies include: 1) our inability to estimate the size and composition of total fish populations, 2) the lack of knowledge concerning basic productivity as measured by refined limnological techniques, 3) scarcity of quantitative measures of the effect of shoreline length, area of shallow water, rate of water exchange, turbidity, and fertility of the watershed on fish production; with little real knowledge on: 4) the role of important trace elements, 5) species combinations and intra- and inter-specific competition, 6) the effects of standing timber on productivity and sport fish harvest, 7) the effect of water withdrawal at various depths, 8) some understanding of the reservoir as an identifiable ecosystem, 9) long-term trends in reservoir productivity and species composition, and 10) the many effects of water level fluctuation on reservoir ecology. This list could easily be expanded, but these topics are typical of those that urgently need concentrated study if there is to be more than hope of increasing sport fish harvest in the immediate future.

The challenge of the future. Most of our past management failures have been attributable to a lack of quantitative knowledge of fish populations, recruitment and survival, food chain relationships, and limnological factors. Armed with a chemical kit, some tattered gill nets, a measuring board, and scale envelopes, biologists have sallied forth (often-time singlehandedly) to solve the riddles of a reservoir. Recommendations have been too often based on skimpy limnological, catch per unit effort, and age and growth data.

We have spent more time and brain power on devising an efficient dispenser of rotenone for population sampling than on methods to accurately determine the number of fish we killed with rotenone. A hundred times more money has gone into repeated stocking of indigenous species than into studies which measure the value of such stocking.

Much of the past management effort has been of a stop-gap or trouble-shooting nature. Hurried answers had to be acquired utilizing largely untested techniques because of immediate pressure from the fishing public. Happily, this sort of pressure is diminishing as public enlightenment on reservoir problems increases through information dissemination. Reservoir managers are now able to take a more dispassionate look at reservoir problems, and to undertake evaluations of those procedures which they have been using.

The past 30 years of reservoir work represents, for the most part, the exploratory phase in the process of scientific inquiry. We have attempted to diagnose possible elements that are causing poor fishing, collect data and analyze it, and to identify the problems which may be involved.

We are now in the idea phase. An increasing number of schemes are being formulated to hypothetically explain existing facts and guide future investigations. At this stage we should be very careful in asking ourselves sensible questions about reservoirs. The questions should be open-minded and not designed to "prove" anything, because we can never ask of nature "Is this hypothesis true?" but only "Is this hypothesis capable of being defended?"

As reservoir investigations become more refined, available knowledge from related scientific disciplines will need to be brought into increased use. Data and methods from physical, chemical, and mathematical fields will become increasingly important. Limnological, physiological and ecological studies will be expanded greatly. The term "heat budget" will become as familiar to reservoir managers as "pounds per acre."

The question most likely to yield valuable results in the *immediate* future in reservoirs centers around "Is such-and-such a factor having a significant effect, either beneficial or harmful, on the fishery, and if it is, can we do anything effectively and economically to augment or reduce its effects?" This immediately brings to mind questions on factors such as relative abundance and competition of forage and rough fishes, water level fluctuations, turbidity, thermocline position, watershed fertility, standing timber, trace elements.

In view of the unorganized nature of reservoir investigations nationally, fastest progress could probably be made if individual studies concentrated on only one factor and followed its effects through to conclusive findings. In spite of the wide diversity of reservoir types, findings of a specific nature on isolated factors would do much to piece the whole puzzle together. The need for expanded, independent basic research becomes increasingly evident.

The large reservoirs which we have concerned ourselves with were built for purposes other than fishing. Their operation schedules were not designed to enhance fishery resources in most cases. Some block invaluable anadromous fish runs, and others are relatively unproductive. An international summary of both detrimental and beneficial effects of dams is contained in a 1958 symposium publication, "International Union for Conservation of Nature and Natural Resources, Seventh Technical Meeting, Athens, Greece, Sept. 1958, Vol. IV. Soil and Water Conservation. Natural Aquatic Resources."

Despite "other purpose" construction, most impoundments have greatly increased fish production and sport fish harvest over pre-impoundment conditions. As more is learned about reservoir ecology and population dynamics, various plans for operating reservoirs to enhance production will be developed. It is quite probable that reservoirs will be regulated more and more for greater sport fishing yields in coming years—especially those designed solely for flood control. The possibilities are exciting, and pose rare opportunities for the biologists involved.

New reservoirs are being created at a rapid pace. For example, 63 reservoirs are planned in California within 15 years, totalling 200,000 acres. Construction will nearly double the impounded water in Oklahoma within the next five years, From 230,000 to 450,000 acres at conservation pool level. The Corps of Engineers predicts that about 10 million acres of additional water area are a distinct possibility in the foreseeable future. A Hoover Commission Task Force report predicted that within a relatively few years we will see four dams for every one we have now!

With sport fishing pressure expected to increase at a rate even faster than reservoir construction, plus the fact that a disproportionately large amount of this increased pressure is expected to be absorbed by reservoirs, the challenge is squarely before fishery managers, researchers and administrators. What is done within the next five years will greatly influence reservoir fishing for the next twenty years, due to the lag time always occurring between research findings and actual development.

No doubt that the challenge will be met. It's going to take more trained men, more money, more thought, and more sweat. It will require fresh appraisals of present techniques and concepts, and preparedness to develop new tools as needed. It will necessitate a willingness to thoroughly evaluate each new technique which is advanced.

There is an innate appeal in reservoir management which is unique. Here the fishery biologist is dealing with animals in a *man-made* environment, and theoretically should be able to effectively manage them through *man-devised* manipulations. With an artificial environment under his partial control, the chances for human enhancement of the resource should be greatly increased.

SOME EFFECTS OF ENGINEERING DESIGN AT DAMS

To the dedicated preservationist, conservation means maintenance of natural resources in a completely undisturbed state. The preservationist point of view may be passive, even negative. Usually, it embraces a "hands off" policy. This may be a necessary last-ditch policy for remnant species like the whooping crane. Even for the whooper, however, it may be foredoomed to failure, involving too little and coming too late.

One big force of overriding influence often overlooked by preservationists is that of necessary *change*. On the part of water planners, for example, following some 20 years of dogged attempts to mitigate losses from river engineering works, this fact has become recognized and has brought about a dynamic change in philosophy. There's no denying the tremendous social and economic changes of the day, together with their profound impact on land and water use. As was true in the case of the recently extinct heath hen, this fact of environmental change no doubt controls the ultimate fate of all our fishing and hunting.

Recently, conservation has acquired a more vigorous meaning, injected by the growth of knowledge due to research in the past few decades. In the sport fishery field this has been stimulated largely by the advent of D-J funds derived from the 10 per cent manufacturers' excise tax on various items of fishing tackle. Conservation now includes the concept of *wise use* of resources and of their deliberate management to provide increased continuous yields to increasing numbers of people. Fishery research has shown, for example, that proper harvest usually benefits stocks of renewable fishery resources.

New conservation philosophies beneficial. This finding very nicely complements conservation's basic democratic philosophy that fish (and game) are the property of all the people, not of a privileged few. Thus, efforts to provide ample *quantity* as well as high quality of outdoor recreational opportunity for large masses of people must assume a primary role in resource management. At the same time unique high quality recreational values must not be sacrificed. Mere *mitigation* of losses due to change will not meet these needs adequately.

As a necessary corollary to this philosophical evolution, resulting from the force of change, the principle of *enhancement* has recently become applied to engineering works constructed on various river courses. This is a big step forward from the idea of mitigation of losses—which aimed to preserve former conditions, reduced in scope, as much like they were as possible. At best, the latter was passive in approach and seldom if ever fully attainable of its implied goals. The result was gradual retrogression—a shrinking resource base.

Enhancement, however, offers a positive approach. It recognizes that many engineering works may also provide vast potential for expanding the recreational resource base. Sport fishing on TVA storage reservoirs (on tributaries to the Tennessee River), for example, increased some 50-fold over original river fishing. This resulted from a great expansion of naturally present game fish populations and from greatly improved quality and quantity of sport fishing that accompanied impoundment. Fortunately, in the Tennessee River system there were no anadromous fisheries of consequence. The rivers affected were warmwater rivers. The situation is quite different where anadromous fish such as salmon, steelhead, shad, striped bass, and others are involved.

Impoundment is two-edged sword. Enhancement

is hardly possible where giant concrete blocks impede passage of invaluable anadromous species to their ancestral spawning grounds. On the contrary, impoundment in such situations often wreaks havoc. Unfavorable water temperatures, variable discharges, more or less inadequate fish passage devices, disturbed water currents, reduced or unfavorable areas for spawning, and increased hazards for downstream migrants, decimate populations at almost every turn as a result of construction.

Although it may seem well-nigh inevitable regarding anadromous fisheries that partial mitigation of losses is the most that can be attained where dams are built, in at least one instance—Shasta Dam on the Sacramento River—substantial enhancement resulted. In this case coldwater releases led to expansion of limited salmon and steelhead fisheries to abundance. In a few cases (the Salmon River, for example) the fishery resource is so valuable that interfering dams should not be built, regardless of other benefits.

While it is often argued by dam-builders that new fisheries of resident species could be developed to take the place of existing anadromous fisheries, this is fractional mitigation of a very low order—hardly enhancement in any sense. The anadromous fisheries, especially the salmon and steelhead of the Pacific Northwest, are uniquely valuable resources. Their value is well-nigh incalculable as they are perpetual resources, capable of yielding endless mental and physical nutrition and countless millions of dollars of revenues from recreational and commercial fisheries if perpetuated near present levels of abundance. Men of this or any single generation do not have the right to deprive all future generations of Americans of the fruits of these resources for a short-term economic advantage.

The overall benefits of large reservoirs in most older situations have been ably summarized in an article by Dr. Frank B. Cross of the University of Kansas:

"They provide badly-needed water areas for general recreation; the lakes behind the dams produce more fish than did the same stretch of river before impoundment; and they help to maintain permanent flows of cleaner water downstream from the dam, which is beneficial also. With proper management of areas surrounding the lakes, the reservoir sites can increase populations of upland game. The lakes serve as resting and hunting areas for waterfowl, accomplishing many of the same purposes as the Fish and Wildlife Service refuges."

An excellent illustration of this appears in the history of sport fishing provided by TVA storage reservoirs, dating back over 20 years. It was wholly unexpected that TVA fishing would continue to hold up reasonably well. Indeed, conservationists loudly predicted otherwise. Therefore, a team of fishery biologists was employed by TVA to find out why reservoirs "go to pot."

Surprisingly, the fishing failed to follow the expected pattern, and the biologists turned their talents to finding out all they could about the reservoirs and the fisheries in order to prolong this fortuitous development indefinitely. The research led to an unexpected result—year-round fishing. It also indicated one reason why TVA reservoir fishing failed to "go to pot."

"Biological deserts" avoidable. Predictions that TVA dams would hurt the fishing stemmed principally from earlier observations at 59,500-acre Lake-of-the-Ozarks—a storage type reservoir—in Missouri. That reservoir was for a long time labelled as a "biological desert" and held up as the horrible example of the results of impoundment. Early studies there indicated that aquatic vegetation and available game-fish populations had become sparse and slow-growing, and fishing poor, a few years following impoundment. It was also found that most of the water in the reservoir—below the top 20 feet or so—was stagnant. A major portion of the reservoir was depleted of oxygen and barren of fish life.

This situation was associated with the fact—largely overlooked at the time—that the water outlets on the upstream face of the dam were at shallow depths (less than 50 feet below maximum surface elevation). Consequently, there was a progressive accumulation of decomposition materials in the colder deep waters together with rapid depletion of oxygen that prevented use by fish life. More important, the warm, oxygenated surface water was drawn off the top and discharged downstream, substantially decreasing the fish-supporting habitat. Result was poor fishing in the reservoir and continued but limited river fishing below the dam.

By contrast, however, a recent review of the 20-year-long history of sport fishing at 34,200-acre Norris Reservoir, Tennessee—the oldest of the TVA storage reservoirs—has shown conclusively that Norris did not become another "biological desert" as forecast. It was shown, however, that the harvests of game fish populations have varied considerably over the years, with first one species than another dominating the catch at different times. The reasons have never been demonstrated.

Earlier research showed clearly, on the other hand, that game fish populations were extensive, varied, fast-growing, and underharvested. It indicated possible benefits to fish production from the long-term cycle of water-level fluctuations recorded for the reservoir. It was also found that game fish were widely distributed as to depth, correlated with temperature, in the presence of sufficient oxygen to sustain fish life.

This favorable situation was associated with the fact —rather quickly recognized in relation to novel limnological findings—that the water outlets on the upstream face of the dam were at relatively great depth (nearly 150 feet below maximum surface elevation). Thus, water was discharged from well below the warm, oxygenated upper layer. Consequently, there was a continuous discharge of oxygen-consuming decomposition materials with the colder, deep waters. This prevented stagnation and made maximum reservoir volume available for use by fish life. At the same time, the vital upper water was retained in the reservoir to promote fish production. The principal result was extensive good fishing in the reservoir. At the same time, the river below the reservoir was transformed from a warmwater fish habitat to a coldwater fish habitat.

Experience provides basis for planning. Proper application of this lesson from TVA storage-type reservoirs to comparable engineering structures on similar waters elsewhere would result in decided enhancement of warmwater fishing possibilities over original values in a large majority of cases. With suitable discharge features to guarantee maximum aeration of water releases below the dam, further benefits would usually follow from the creation of extensive tailwater trout fisheries where none occurred previously.

Original warmwater river populations are adversely affected by coldwater discharge in such situations. Recently, proposals have been made to mitigate limited losses below some such dams through discharge of warm surface layers from the reservoirs above the dams. The preservation of unique limited resources on this basis may well be justified in a few instances.

Most informed fishery workers will readily concede that we know all too little about reservoirs and the fishes that inhabit them. This is equally true of undisturbed warmwater river fish populations. Pending further research, it would seem rather unwise at this time—at the least, arbitrary—to recreate conditions likely to lead to poor reservoir fishing for the sake of preserving limited warmwater fishing downstream. At the same time, exceptions in the case of uniquely valuable fisheries may conceivably become involved on rare occasions.

Many dams of relatively low structural design fail to present a choice in the matter, being essentially run-of-the-river-type structures. Reservoirs behind such dams have proportionately less storage capacity. In effect, they are deeper, broader stretches of river through which the water continues to flow with a recognizable current much as before. They have essentially similar temperature characteristics from top to bottom.

Recreational fishing potentials substantial. Here, too, experience shows that impoundment benefits warmwater fishing. For example, a series of relatively low dams occur on the mainstem of the Tennessee River below Knoxville and its confluence with the Ohio River at Paducah. TVA studies have demonstrated a 10 to 15-fold increase in mainstream fishing as a result of impoundment. A considerable portion of it is concentrated on the tailwaters immediately below the dams. In 1957 an all-time high of 972,000-odd fishing trips were recorded below TVA's nine mainstream dams. The corresponding 1959 figure was 846,000-odd. Despite development of extensive rough fish populations in these mainstream reservoirs, a substantial net gain for recreational fishing is obvious.

Warm tailwater fisheries are concentrated in relatively short distances below dams. The tailwaters are intensively fished and may conceivably support 25,000 to over 250,000 fishing trips annually in some cases, under ideal conditions of access and safety. This is substantial. But tailwater trout fishing can also be substantial. A very important difference that must be given due consideration, of course, is that the latter will usually depend for maintenance upon artificial stocking with fingerlings. The warmwater fisheries, however, are invariably supported by natural reproduction.

Reservoir fisheries are typically far more substantial than tailwater fisheries. For example, 19,000-acre Fort Gibson Reservoir, near Tulsa, Oklahoma, supported 31 fishing trips per acre of reservoir surface in 1956—about 590,000 individual fishing trips annually. Norris Reservoir, Tennessee, probably supported upwards of 200,000 such trips the same year. Douglas Reservoir, Tennessee, sustained comparable fishing, and also supported over 7,500 tailwater fishing trips. Nearly 5.8 million angler-days were recorded in 1958 on nine Texas reservoirs totalling 88,560 acres, equivalent to 65 fisherman-days per acre.

At 75,000-acre Fort Randall Reservoir, South Dakota, tailwater fishing was extremely popular from the outset and about 26,000 fishing trips occurred below the dam there in 1957-1958. The huge reservoir above the dam, even though lightly fished, supported nearly twice as much fishing prior to 1957—estimated at about 50,000 fishing trips annually. Short-term studies showed that game fish were plentiful in the reservoir and that many more could be caught if proper angling methods were employed. The latter were demonstrated. An immediate result was that fishing pressure on the reservoir itself more than doubled in 1957—110,000 fishing trips estimated. Many-fold additional increases are possible.

Reservoir research badly needed. A possible excuse for ignoring or sacrificing reservoir potential in formulating engineering design recommendations affecting fishery resources may be the relative lack of knowledge to permit effective deliberate management of reservoir fish populations at the present time. It is true that shockingly little basic research into the detailed ecology and life histories of reservoir aquatic life, behavior of fishes, population dynamics, and the limnological characteristics of reservoir environments has occurred. But this is a wholly untenable basis for modifying engineering design in such a way to fix immutably unfavorable limnological characteristics of the impounded water and thereby deny future realization of vast reservoir fishery potentials.

SECTION V

WHERE TO FISH

Part 1. Fresh Water

Differences in character and quality of water as well as in the climate, especially in seasonal precipitation and runoff, produce a variety of fishing in North America that cannot be exceeded by that of any other continent. Such a vast area cannot be given intensive local coverage in one book, but the sketches of fresh waters for each state and province provide an outline of the best known waters. This information should be a useful guide to the great army of fishermen who travel the highways and byways of the continent to indulge in their favorite sport. Oceanic fishing is covered elsewhere.

Much useful information is given on baits, lures, and methods of fishing, but it is always wise to obtain local information from sporting goods stores, resorts, or local representatives of conservation departments. Such information is usually more exact and timely than general statements, no matter how accurate.

Nearly all states, as well as the U. S. Government, propagate and release fish for restocking public waters. The major emphasis has always been on Trout, although much effort has been devoted to a number of warm water fish as well. Bass, Crappies, and Sunfish have been the most widely used, but many others have been propagated to some extent.

The trend in recent years has been toward releasing fewer but larger fish. Many trout waters are frankly on a put-and-take basis. In these cases, legal-sized fish are released both before and during the season with the expectation that many will be caught immediately. Other waters, particularly newly-made ponds, are stocked with young fish which are permitted to grow for a season or more before fishing starts.

Trout fishing in most waters close to populations centers is dependent on stocking which takes a large part of available conservation funds.

Those who wish to enjoy fishing for "wild fish" must go to Canada, Alaska, or some of the relatively few wilderness areas remaining elsewhere in the United States or do their trout fishing in mountain brooks or zoned areas where killing is restricted. There are shy wild trout in the Fish-For-Fun areas, where there is no killing, but no closed season, and in the Fly-Fishing-Only areas where the size limit is high and the creel limit low. Because of the challenge of sophisticated fish of good size, some anglers prefer the zoned areas to primitive spots.

The conservation departments of the states and provinces of Canada have the responsibility of enforcement of fishing laws or regulations, including open seasons and bag limits. In Canada, the Dominion Government handles this and other enforcement in Northwest and Yukon Territories.

In most states, conservation departments have more or less authority to alter regulations to meet conditions. Therefore, any presentation of open season, bag limits, and other regulations would quickly become obsolete and such data has therefore been omitted. All persons planning to fish in any state or province are advised to write to the conservation department asking for information regarding open seasons, bag limits, and other regulations. Fishing license fees are still largely fixed by legislatures and therefore change more slowly.

It is, however, inadvisable to depend upon these fees remaining the same, and inquiries should also request information regarding non-resident license fees. Many states offer limited licenses, covering short periods, to tourists or visitors, but the conditions under which they are offered vary widely.

Addresses of conservation departments and amount of fees for fishing licenses at the time of publication are as follows:

Organization	Type of License	Fishing License Fees
STATES		
ALABAMA		
Department of Conservation, Montgomery, Alabama	Resident	$ 2.00
	Non-Resident	5.00
	7-day	2.00
ALASKA		
Alaska Game and Fish Department, Juneau, Alaska	Resident	5.00
	Non-Resident	10.00
	10-day	5.00
ARIZONA		
Game and Fish Commission, Arizona State Building, Phoenix, Arizona	Resident	3.00*
	Non-Resident	9.00**
	5-day	3.00***
	1-day res. or non-res.	2.00
	*plus $2 for trout	
	**plus $6 for trout	
	***plus $2 for trout	
ARKANSAS		
Game and Fish Commission, State Capitol, Little Rock, Arkansas	Resident	2.50
	Non-Resident	5.00
	14-day	2.50
CALIFORNIA		
Fish and Game Commission, Ferry Building, San Francisco 11, California	Resident	5.00
	Non-Resident	10.00
	10-day	3.00
	Alien	10.00
	Resident-Ocean	3.00
COLORADO		
Game and Fish Commission, 1530 Sherman Street, Denver 5, Colorado	Resident	4.00
	Non-Resident	10.00
	5-day	3.50
CONNECTICUT		
Board of Fisheries and Game, Hartford 1, Connecticut	Resident	4.35
	Non-Resident	6.35
	3-day	1.85
DELAWARE		
Board of Game and Fish Commissioners, Dover, Delaware	Resident	1.25
	Non-Resident	7.50
	Trout Stamp	2.10
FLORIDA		
Game and Fresh Water Fish Commission, Tallahassee, Florida	Resident	2.00
	Non-Resident	8.00
	14-day	3.25
	5-day	2.25
GEORGIA		
Game and Fish Commission, 412 State Capitol, Atlanta, Georgia	Resident	1.25
	Non-Resident	6.25
	3-day	1.25
HAWAII		
Division of Fish and Game, P. O. Box 3319, Honolulu 1, Hawaii	Resident	2.50
	Non-Resident	5.00
	30-day	2.50
IDAHO		
Department of Fish and Game, Boise, Idaho	Resident	3.00
	Non-Resident	12.00
	5-day	4.00
	1-day	2.00
ILLINOIS		
Department of Conservation, Springfield, Illinois	Resident	2.00
	Non-Resident	4.00
	10-day	2.00
INDIANA		
211 W. Washington St., Indianapolis, Indiana	Resident	2.50
	Non-Resident	3.50
	14-day	2.50
	Trout Stamp	2.00
IOWA		
State Conservation Commission, 914 Grand Avenue, Des Moines 8, Iowa	Resident	2.50
	Non-Resident Reciprocal Minimum	3.00
	6-day	3.00
KANSAS		
Forestry, Fish and Game Commission, Pratt, Kansas	Resident	3.00
	Non-Resident	5.00
	10-day	3.00
KENTUCKY		
Department of Conservation Division of Fish and Game, Frankfort, Kentucky	Resident	3.25
	Non-Resident	5.50
	10-day	2.25
LOUISIANA		
Department of Wildlife and Fisheries, 126 Civil Courts Building, New Orleans 16, Louisiana	Resident	1.00
	Non-Resident	5.00
	7-day	2.00
MAINE		
Department of Inland Fisheries and Game, State House, Augusta, Maine	Resident	2.75
	Non-Resident	8.75
	15-day	5.75
	3-day	3.75
MARYLAND		
Board of Natural Resources, Department of Game and Inland Fish, 514 Munsey Building, Baltimore 2, Maryland	Resident	3.00
	Non-Resident	10.00
	3-day	3.00
MASSACHUSETTS		
Department of Conservation, Ashburton Place, Boston 8, Massachusetts	Resident	4.25
	Non-Resident	8.75
	7-day	4.25
MICHIGAN		
Conservation Commission, Lansing 13, Michigan	Resident & wife	2.00
	Non-Resident	5.00
	15-day	4.00
	(Trout Fishing Stamp $2.00 additional on all licenses)	
MINNESOTA		
Department of Conservation Division of Game and Fish, State Office Building, St. Paul 1, Minnesota	Resident	2.25
	Resident & wife	2.75
	Non-Resident	5.25
	Non-Resident & wife	8.25
MISSISSIPPI		
Mississippi Game and Fish Commission, Pearl and South Congress Streets, Jackson, Mississippi	Resident	1.00
	Non-Resident	6.00
	3-day	1.00
MISSOURI		
Conservation Commission, Monroe Building, Jefferson City, Missouri	Resident	3.00
	Non-Resident	5.00
	14-day	3.00
	Trout Permit Additional	2.00
MONTANA		
State Fish and Game Commission, Helena, Montana	Resident	3.00
	Non-Resident	10.00
	6-day	3.00
NEBRASKA		
Game, Forestation and Parks Commission, Lincoln 9, Nebraska	Resident	2.00
	Non-Resident (Reciprocan minimum)	5.00
	5-day	2.00
NEVADA		
Fish and Game Commission, Box 678, Reno, Nevada	Resident	5.00
	Non-Resident	10.00
	5-day	3.50
NEW HAMPSHIRE		
Fish and Game Department, State House Annex, Concord, New Hampshire	Resident	3.50
	Non-Resident	8.25
	15-day	5.25
	3-day	3.75

Organization	Type of License	Fishing License Fees
NEW JERSEY Department of Conservation, Division of Fish and Game, State House, Trenton, New Jersey	Resident	4.15
	Non-Resident	7.15
	3-day	3.65
	Trout Stamp Res.	2.00
	Trout Stamp Non-Res.	5.00
NEW MEXICO Department of Game and Fish, Sante Fe, New Mexico	Resident	3.50
	Non-Resident	8.00
	5-day	3.00
NEW YORK Conservation Department, Division of Fish and Game, Albany, New York	Resident	3.25
	Non-Resident	5.50
	6-day	4.25
NORTH CAROLINA Wildlife Resources Commission, Raleigh, North Carolina	Resident	4.25
	Non-Resident	8.25
	1-day	1.65
	5-day	3.75
	Trout-Resident additional	1.25
	Trout-Non-Resident	3.25
NORTH DAKOTA Game and Fish Department, Bismarck, North Dakota	Resident	2.00
	Non-Resident	5.00
	7-day	1.00
OHIO Department of Natural Resources, Division of Wildlife, Columbus, Ohio	Resident	2.25
	Non-Resident	5.25
	10-day	3.25
OKLAHOMA Game and Fish Department, Room 118, State Capitol, Oklahoma City 5, Oklahoma	Resident	2.00
	Non-Resident	5.00
	10-day	2.25
OREGON Game Commission, P. O. Box 4136, Portland 8, Oregon	Resident	4.00
	Non-Resident	10.00
	7-day	5.00
	Trout and Salmon additional	1.00
PENNSYLVANIA Board of Fish Commissioners, Harrisburg, Pennsylvania	Resident	3.25
	Non-Resident	7.50
	5-day	3.25
RHODE ISLAND Division of Fish and Game, State House, Providence 2, Rhode Island	Resident	3.25
	Non-Resident	7.25
	3-day	3.25
SOUTH CAROLINA Game and Fish Department, Columbia, South Carolina	Resident	3.10
	Non-Resident	10.25
	10-day	3.10
SOUTH DAKOTA Department of Game, Fish and Parks, Pierre, South Dakota	Resident	2.00
	Non-Resident	5.00
	3-day	1.00
TENNESSEE Department of Conservation, Nashville, Tennessee	Resident	2.00
	Non-Resident	5.00
	3-day	1.50
	10-day	2.00
	Trout Stamp	2.00
TEXAS Game and Fish Commission, Austin, Texas	Resident	2.15
	Non-Resident	2.15
UTAH Fish and Game Commission, 500 Atlas Building, Salt Lake City 1, Utah	Resident	3.50
	Non-Resident	10.00
	5-day	4.00
	10-day	9.00
VERMONT Fish and Game Service, Montpelier, Vermont	Resident	1.75
	Non-Resident	6.25
	14-day	4.25
	3-day	2.25
VIRGINIA Commission of Game and Inland Fisheries, P. O. Box 1642, Richmond 13, Virginia	Resident	3.50
	Non-Resident	10.00
	3-day	1.50
	Trout, additional	5.00
WASHINGTON Game Commission, 509 Fairview North Seattle, Washington	Resident	4.50
	Non-Resident	15.00
	7-day	4.00
WEST VIRGINIA Conservation Commission, Charleston, West Virginia	Resident	3.00
	Non-Resident	10.00
	1-day	3.00
	Trout Stamp	5.00
WISCONSIN Conservation Department, Madison, Wisconsin	Resident	3.00
	Non-Resident	5.00
	15-day (husband & wife)	6.00
WYOMING Game and Fish Commission, Cheyenne, Wyoming	Resident	3.00
	Non-Resident	12.00
	5-day	4.00

CANADA

Organization	Type of License	Fishing License Fees
ALBERTA Department of Lands and Mines, Edmonton, Alberta	Resident	2.00
	Non-Resident	2.00
BRITISH COLUMBIA Department of Fisheries, Victoria, British Columbia	Resident	2.00
	Non-Resident	7.00
	Canadian Non-Res.	3.50
MANITOBA Department of Mines and Natural Resources, Winnipeg, Manitoba	Resident	1.00
	Non-Resident	6.50
NEW BRUNSWICK Fish & Wildlife Branch, Dept. of Lands and Mines, Fredericton, N. B.	Resident	2.50
	Non-Resident for Salmon and all sport fish	15.50
	Non-Resident all sport fish except Salmon	7.50
	Non-Resident 3-day tourist	5.50
NEWFOUNDLAND Department of Mines and Resources, St. John's, Newfoundland	Resident Salmon	5.00
	Non-Resident Salmon	30.00
	14-day	20.00
	1-day	5.00
	Non-Resident, Trout	5.00
NORTHWEST TERRITORIES Dominion Wildlife Service, Ottawa, Ontario	Resident	1.00
	Non-Resident	2.00

Organization	Type of License	Fishing License Fees
NOVA SCOTIA		
Department of Lands and Forests, Halifax, Nova Scotia	Non-Resident	13.50
	10-day	5.00
ONTARIO		
Department of Lands and Forests, Division of Fish and Wildlife, Toronto, Ontario	Resident	3.25
	Non-Resident	6.50
PRINCE EDWARD ISLAND		
Department of Fisheries, Charlottetown, P.E.I.	Resident	1.00
	Non-Resident	3.00
QUEBEC	Resident	1.10
Department of Game and Fisheries, Quebec, P. Q.	Non-Resident-salmon	15.50
	Non-Resident-other fish	5.25

Organization	Type of License	Fishing License Fees
SASKATCHEWAN		
Department of Natural Resources, Regina, Saskatchewan	Resident	2.00
	Non-Resident, Trout	10.00
	Non-Resident	5.00
YUKON		
Dominion Wildlife Service, Ottawa, Ontario	Resident	1.00
	Non-Resident	2.00

MEXICO

Mexican Consuls in the larger cities of the United States will furnish all information concerning fishing permits, or they may be obtained in Mexico City at the Marine Department of the Mexican Navy.

CANADA

Canada, including the newest province of Newfoundland, covers over 3,500,000 square miles. With the exception of the small maritime provinces of Prince Edward's Island, New Brunswick, and Nova Scotia, most provinces approach or exceed the size of Texas. The three prairie provinces of Alberta, Saskatchewan, and Manitoba all range just under the Lone Star State in area, while Quebec, Ontario, and British Columbia greatly exceed it.

All of these larger provinces still contain vast areas of inaccessible country filled with lakes and streams that are practically unfished. While the small float plane is making many formerly remote waters more accessible, the total amount of fishing area covered is yet relatively insignificant. Pack horses or canoe trips are still necessary to reach many areas that provide excellent fishing.

The following accounts cover only the more accessible waters that can be reached without too much difficulty.

Citizens of the United States traveling in Canada to fish should write to the provincial fish and game authorities listed in the introduction to this section regarding seasons, bag limits, license fees, and other regulations. No passport is required to travel into Canada, but it is well to carry proof of identification to show if it should be requested.

Wearing apparel, fishing tackle and equipment, guns, ammunition, portable boats and canoes, outboard motors, binocular, cameras, typewriters, and camping equipment for personal use may be taken into Canada but not for sale. Guns and some other valuable articles brought in by motorists are registered on the automobile entry form and must be taken out of the country within six months after the time of entry. Fifty cigars, 200 cigarettes, and 2 pounds of manufactured tobacco in open packages for personal use may be taken in without duty.

NEW BRUNSWICK NOVA SCOTIA NEWFOUNDLAND PRINCE EDWARD ISLAND

Any person thinking of angling in Newfoundland and the Maritime Provinces of New Brunswick, Nova Scotia and Prince Edward Island first visualizes Atlantic Salmon, judged by many to be the peer of all freshwater fish. New Brunswick, next door to Maine, is well endowed with salmon rivers. Some of the waters are privately owned, some leased by individuals or groups from the Provincial Government and others open to public fishing. Generally speaking, the leased or private waters offer the best fishing and on such waters fishing is by invitation or by arrangement with the owner or outfitter. The cost of fishing private water owned or controlled by an outfitter may not be much more expensive than fishing the open pools.

On the Restigouche, most famous of Canada's salmon rivers, there are 50 miles of private water, 45 miles of leased water, and 4 miles of public water. The public water is administered by the Province and bookings are available. The Kedgwick, a tributary of the Restigouche, is entirely owned or leased. The other New Brunswick rivers are divided between open and private water in varying degrees with the Miramichi and its tributaries, offering the visiting sportsman the greatest concentration of available fishing. Other well known salmon rivers of the Province are the Tobique, Dungarvon, Cains, Tabusintac, and their tributaries.

Nova Scotia's salmon waters are all open to public fishing, The Margaree, Medway and St.

Mary's are its best known waters, all carrying runs of good sized salmon. An average of more than 500 salmon a year have been taken from each of these three and also from the LeHave River. An average of over 100 per season were taken from the Mersey, Moser, Liscomb, North, Gold, Petite, Tusket, Wallace, and Philip Rivers. Nova Scotia's rivers are generally smaller than those of New Brunswick, since the province consists of a long, narrow peninsula and an island which make its watersheds, and consequently its rivers and their salmon runs, smaller in proportion. Almost all of Nova Scotia's many rivers contain some salmon and provide good fishing when conditions are right.

Newfoundland is a large island and her rivers, too, are smaller than New Brunswick's largest. A few Newfoundland rivers require canoes or boats for angling but most of them, like those of Nova Scotia can be fished by wading. The island has over 200 salmon rivers. The Humber, Portland Creek, River of Ponds, and the Serpentine are among the best. The salmon taken by angling on Portland Creek in some seasons average over 9 lbs. The largest runs of fish are found on the west coast; the south coast rivers offer good fishing but are difficult of access; the rivers of the north and eastern shore lines offer excellent fishing for salmon that average between four and five pounds. Newfoundland's salmon fishing is also open to the public and is best where it is hardest to reach.

Salmon fishing in Newfoundland's section of Labrador is as yet little developed because of the isolation of the rivers. Most fishing spots there can only be reached by chartered plane or cabin cruiser and advance arrangement for outfitting should be made. The Labrador runs of fish are plentiful, but the fish do not run as large as those in the rivers on Newfoundland's west coast.

Space limitations do not permit the listing of best seasons for each river or section for salmon fishing and this information is best obtained from innkeepers and outfitters, or from the information agencies of the various provinces. The quality and type of salmon fishing varies from season to season and from week to week. In planning a trip it is advisable to obtain as much information as possible in advance, seek the best possible advice, and bear in mind that weather and water conditions often upset normal fishing expectancy. Only specific local information can tell which rivers maintain their fishing in times of drought and which ones will fail completely.

Brook or squaretail Trout are plentiful in all the provinces covered in this résumé. Practically all salmon rivers also have a run of trout. In some rivers these fish arrive ahead of the salmon and in others later, in rare cases not entering the fresh water until September. The normal time of entry into the rivers is from May to early July. When they return to the rivers from the salt water, these trout, like the salmon, are bright and silvery. In this livery they are called sea-trout by local anglers. Sea-trout also enter many brooks that are too small or too shallow to attract a run of salmon. Fishing for them is carried on both in the streams and in the salt water bays and brackish waters around the river mouths.

Brook Trout of the non-migratory type are found in practically all the lakes. Excellent fishing for them is to be had in all the provinces covered by this review. The largest Brook Trout will probably be found in the salmon rivers. The size of trout in the lakes will depend upon a variety of factors such as the intensity of the fishing, the ratio of spawning area to available food supply, etc. In unfished lakes an angler may find great quantities of small fish and no large ones. In seeking big trout it is wise to select a lake with a reputation for large fish rather than seeking an inaccessible body of water with a dubious reputation . . . or none at all. Extended canoe trips through good trout water can be taken in both Nova Scotia and New Brunswick and such a journey gives a variety of fishing waters and fish sizes.

Both Brook Trout and Atlantic Salmon are native to this area. Other fish have been stocked and have gained a foothold. Rainbow Trout are found in some of the lakes of each of these provinces, and these newcomers seem to be gaining both in popularity and in range. As yet, these fish have not established themselves in the sea-going or Steelhead form.

The Brown Trout, imported to a few lakes in eastern Newfoundland have, however, established themselves primarily as sea-run fish, like the sea-trout of northern Europe. They are also established as a sea-running race in the Antigonish River of Nova Scotia. In Conception Bay, near St. John's, Newfoundland, sea-run Browns weighing over twenty pounds have been caught by anglers, and fish of from seven to ten pounds are not uncommon. Most of the sheltered bays or in the brackish water Barrachoix (lakes that connect with the salt water through small channels). Brown Trout that are restricted to fresh water seldom reach twelve inches in length in the same areas.

Another import to New Brunswick and Nova Scotia is the Smallmouth Bass. In the section near its northern Maine Border, New Brunswick offers some of the finest Smallmouth fishing to be found. The St. Croix, Magaguadavic, and Chiputneticook waters are among its best. Here the bass are plentiful and run to good size. Fishing for them is predominantly with the fly rod. Best fishing is in June and September, but it holds good through the summer in the deeper water.

Landlocked Salmon and Lake Trout are both found in the southwestern section of New Brunswick and in the larger and deeper lakes of Nova Scotia. Newfoundland has no Lake Trout or other game fish save her native salmon, the species of trout already mentioned and Landlocked Salmon in some of her interior waters.

Of interest to both fresh and salt water anglers is the Striped Bass, present in some of the lower rivers, brackish estuaries and bays of New Brunswick and Nova Scotia. These fish range as far north as Cape Breton in northern Nova Scotia, and catches have been made in the bay at Gabarus in the Shubenacadie and Annapolis Rivers, and at

G. E. Butler

Swift water in the Whiteshell—haunt of Smallmouth and Walleyes.

many other places. This sport has not yet attained full popularity in these northern waters but bids fair to command the interest of a growing number of anglers. There is plenty of pioneering work to be done in this field. The Shubenacadie River's run of Stripers comes in the fall, as does that of the Annapolis River. Stripers have been taken at Gabarus in mid-summer.

The big Bluefin Tuna are the most popular salt water prizes of the north Atlantic waters. Wedgeport, in southern Nova Scotia, is the most popular place for this fishing, and from this port the boats go out to the tide rip off the Outer Bald Tusket Island. It is here that the International Tuna Tournament was formerly held each September. Tuna are also fished for at Liverpool, Jordan Bay, and several other points between Wedgeport and St. Ann's Bay. Tuna have been caught on rod and line in Newfoundland, but their appearance in the coastal waters of that province is uncertain.

Broadbill Swordfish, most highly prized of all salt water fish, are to be found in the waters off the Nova Scotia and Newfoundland coasts in late summer. At Louisburg in Nova Scotia a fair number of Broadbills have been brought in by anglers. These great fish are harpooned and sold commercially by boats operating out of such centers as Louisburg, Sydney, Ingonish, and to a lesser degree on the southwest coast of Newfoundland.

Pollack, Mackerel and Cod round out the sport fishing picture, and these fish are found in the waters surrounding each of the provinces, except that Pollack are rare in Newfoundland waters.

Specific information on any type of fishing may be obtained directly, from The New Brunswick Travel Bureau, Fredericton, New Brunswick; Prince Edward Island Travel Bureau, Charlottetown, Prince Edward Island; Nova Scotia Bureau of Information, Halifax, Nova Scotia; and The Newfoundland Tourist Development Office St. John's Newfoundland.

QUEBEC

Quebec, with its great number of streams and lakes, offers to the fisherman a large variety of game fish, from the lordly salmon to the voracious pike. Due to the very extended area, the seasons vary to a certain extent, as well as the distribution of fish.

This province has vast areas of canoe waters

lying between the Canadian National Railway line and James Bay, and also the practically unexplored fishing territory in the Labrador Peninsula. Present fishing areas are in the southern part of the province, south of a line drawn from Lake St. John which lies almost directly north of the city of Quebec, west to Lake Abitibi. East of the Saguenay River, which drains Lake St. John, the river flowing into the St. Lawrence and the Gulf of St. Lawrence from the north, are all salmon and trout streams. The better ones are largely leased to groups or individuals and are therefore closed to public fishing.

The western part of Quebec offers mostly fishing for Lake Trout, Northern Pike, Walleye, and bass. It is not a country for Brook Trout fishing as this fish is only found in a few lakes.

The area north of Montreal and northeast of Ottawa, extending as far east as Quebec City, offers the same type of fishing as the western district, except that Brook Trout is much more abundant. Beginning fifty miles north of the St. Lawrence, Brook Trout are found in most waters.

The district immediately north of Quebec City as far as Lake St. John and Laurentide Park is Brook Trout country, and it is only occasionally that Northern Pike, Walleyes, and Lake Trout are found. Bass are unknown.

Farther east, the Lake St. John country is famous for its Ouananiche. It also offers very good fishing for Brook Trout, Lake Trout, Northern Pike, Pike, and Walleye. Brook Trout and salmon are the most important species here since others are not sought to any extent.

The country east of the Saguenay is a trout and salmon country, and other fish are practically unknown. Fishing begins when sea-run fish enter the streams. Trout and Salmon are also the major game fish south of the St. Lawrence from Quebec east to the Atlantic Ocean; Pike and Walleye are unknown, while Lake Trout are a limited distribution. The territory from the St. Lawrence to the United States boundary west of Quebec City offers a variety of species, including all the above named fish and the Muskellunge in certain parts of the St. Lawrence River, west of Montreal.

The fishing season usually starts the second week in May and extends until the first week in October. In certain areas over 2000 feet in altitude, the season may start later. The best months are May, June, early July, and September, although July and August sometimes produce good fishing.

SALMON

Fly fishing only. Most popular patterns of flies are Silver Doctor, Silver Grey, Black Dose, Thunder and Lightning, Jack Scott, Wilkinson, Durham Ranger, and also dry flies, such as the Rat Face, McDougall, the Grey Jackly, Brown Bivisible. The best time to fish varies with each stream according to the time of the run. It most streams Salmon start running in late May and continue into early July, although some rivers get their best run in August and September.

OUANANICHE

This land-locked salmon readily takes the fly when in streams. The most popular types are the bucktails and streamers of the following patterns: Grey Ghost, Black Ghost, and White Maribou, etc. Although formally reported only in the Lake St. John area, the Ouananiche is also present in most of the large lakes on the North Shore of the Gulf of St. Lawrence. They are often taken by trolling; wobbling spoons are the most popular lures.

Gilbert Parfitt

Taking a Walleye on the Winnipeg River.

BROOK TROUT

For fly fishing, the most popular patterns are the Parmachene Belle, the Montreal, the Mickey Finn, and other bright color flies. Those tied on No. 2 hooks are used for the large trout, although skillful fishermen use 6, 8, and 10 hooks. Sizes 6 and 8 are the most popular. Fly fishing is best from the time the ice leaves until late June or early July. It falls off then until late August, when it again becomes very good until the end of the season.

QUEBEC RED TROUT

This fish has a wide distribution covering the whole of the Province of Quebec but its true habitat is in large and deep lakes. The particular habits of the Quebec Red Trout make it a rather unknown species. It is a deep-water fish and is only found on the surface early in the spring and in September after the waters turn cold. It takes the fly readily and puts up a spectacular fight breaking water like a Brown Trout. The flies used for Brook Trout seem to interest it.

LAKE TROUT

This fish has the same habits as Lake Trout in other parts of Canada. It is a deep water fish, being on the surface or in shallow water only in the early spring immediately after the ice breaks up. At that time it takes bait made of chub, etc. Later on, when it moves to deep water, it will take spoons of the wobbly type trolled deep with a metal line.

SMALLMOUTH BASS

This fish is not widely distributed and is found most abundantly west of Three Rivers in streams and lakes not too remote from the St. Lawrence or Ottawa Rivers. It is not found in the lakes more than about 100 miles north of those two streams. It is also present in numerous streams and lakes south of the St. Lawrence River. Bait, usually worms or crawfish, small plugs, spinners, and streamer flies, are used successfully for these fish.

NORTHERN PIKE

This fish has a wide distribution over the northern part of the province and is also present south of the St. Lawrence. It is almost absent from the waters immediately north of Quebec City and east to the Saguenay River. It is entirely absent in eastern Quebec. Means of fishing are trolling and bait casting.

MUSKELLUNGE

This fish has a small range being found only in the St. Lawrence and Ottawa Rivers close to Montreal, most abundantly in the areas known as Lake St. Louis and Lake St. Francois. It is also known to be found in the St. Françis River which empties in the St. Lawrence River. Standard techniques of fishing are used.

WALLEYE

This fish is also well distributed and is found in all Pike waters and sometimes in Brook Trout waters. It has a general distribution in the province. Standard trolling techniques are suggested but in streams the Walleye will sometimes take a bucktail or streamer fly, fished deep.

ONTARIO

Ontario, like other Canadian provinces, has vast areas of practically virgin fishing water which can be explored only by extended canoe trips. A glance at the map of this huge province, which has 412,582 square miles, shows a tremendous area of lakes and streams suitable for fishing. The lakes vary individually in character, some being deep, cold lakes while others are relatively shallow. Distribution and abundance of water makes possible good angling within a small area for fish requiring remarkably varied conditions. The character of the fishing waters is similar to that in adjoining Quebec, but perhaps many of its areas have been more widely advertised and are better known to people south of the International Boundary.

The waters can be divided on a physical basis into two main sections: those in the Hudson Bay drainage, comprising an intricate system of rivers and tributaries of which the Moose, Albany, and the Severn are the largest. All other streams flow into the Great Lakes or the St. Lawrence River. The Ottawa, which forms part of the boundary between Ontario and Quebec, gathers its water well toward James Bay, but all other streams in the Great Lakes system are relatively short; and along the northern and eastern shores of Lake Superior, the headwaters of the Albany come close to that body of water.

Brook Trout, Northern Pike, and Walleye are widely distributed through much of the wilderness area. Most of the other sporting fish are more closely confined to the better known sections of the province. A line following the Canadian National Railway from the point where it crosses from Quebec into Ontario, just north of Lake Abitibi to the Manitoba boundary, froms for practical purposes the northern limit of areas accessible to fishermen. This line encloses more or less roughly the points that can be reached without too much difficulty by road or railroad. North of that line, travel is by canoe or aircraft.

TROUT

Brook Trout are widely distributed and are found in almost innumerable lakes and streams. In eastern Ontario numerous lakes lying south and southwest of Ottawa furnished good fishing for this species. Algonquin Park is famous for its Brook Trout fishing. There are many trout waters in the great peninsula that extends westward between Lake Huron and Lake Erie. Many of the lakes north of Lake Nipissing, particularly those close to the Quebec boundary, are also well known Brook Trout waters.

Further west, Sudbury, lying near the northeastern shore of Georgian Bay, is the center of an area known for its trout fishing. Lake Nipigon and the river of the same name are almost legendary among devotees of the squaretails.

In the Hudson Bay drainage, the headwaters of the Albany and the tributaries and main stream of Moose River, flowing into James Bay, also provide excellent Brook Trout fishing.

Good Lake Trout fishing is found over a vast part of the southern section of the province. A line drawn from Pembroke on the Ottawa River to Kingston on Lake Ontario roughly marks the eastern edge of Lake Trout fishing, which extends westward in suitable waters to a line drawn from the south end of Georgian Bay to Toronto. There is also a broad band of Lake Trout waters extending from Georgian Bay north and east toward North Bay, the fishing centering in Algonquin Park. Other well known waters include the shoreline of Georgian Bay and North Channel; the eastern shore of Lake Superior and the streams entering it; and a vast territory lying between Lake Timiskaming on the upper Ottawa, and the eastern shore of Lake Superior, including many waters in the Timagami and Mississagi provincial forests. Lake Nipigon and the territory to the east, the waters from the mouth of the Nipigon and west to Port Arthur, and a vast area extending north and east of Lake of the Woods and Rainy River, to the head of the Albany and the Severn Rivers are also good Lake Trout country. In such a vast aggregation of fishable water, it is impossible to list individual lakes and streams.

Rainbow Trout have been introduced and have become abundant enough to provide good fishing in somewhat limited territory. Principal areas are Nipigon River and the vicinity of Port Arthur, the territory around Sault Ste. Marie and east and south along North Channel, some lakes between Lake Huron and Georgian Bay, and along the shores of both including Lake Simcoe to the east of Georgian Bay, several small areas between Georgian Bay and Pembroke on the upper Ottawa, and waters along the north shore of Lake Ontario.

Brown Trout, also successfully introduced, are found chiefly on the big peninsula that separates Georgian Bay from Lake Huron; in an area between the city of Brantford and Lake Erie; a number of lakes and streams in the vicinity of Toronto and Belleville, both on the north shore of Lake Ontario; and scattered waters near Ottawa and Smiths Falls.

Splake, a cross between the Brook Trout and Lake Trout, has been introduced into several waters across Ontario. Algonquin Park is presently the best location to tie into one of these battlers. Splake up to 15 pounds in weight have been taken from some lakes in Ontario.

The Arctic Grayling has been recently introduced into Ontario and promises good fly-fishing for those using light tackle. At present, the grayling introduction is in the experimental stage, and no open season exists.

BASS

Bass waters lie largely in the southern part of the province with the Smallmouth occupying a much larger range than the Largemouth. Largemouth waters are largely confined to the lower Ottawa and the entire St. Lawrence River, together with some districts along the north shore of Lake Ontario. Eastern Lake Erie, Lake St. Clair, and a small area between Georgian Bay and Lake Erie, a district north of North Bay and a comparatively small area north and east of Lake of the Woods also provide Largemouth fishing.

Smallmouth Bass are more widely distributed and much more important from an angling standpoint. It occupies practically all of the territory of the Largemouth, although it may not always be in the same lakes and streams. All the territory from Lake Nipissing, French River, and the north end of Georgian Bay, south to Lake Erie, contains almost innumerable Smallmouth waters. This is a vast complex of lakes and streams. In addition, North Channel; the Sudbury district; an area north and west of Sudbury, extending to the Quebec-Ontario boundary at the north end of Lake Timiskaming; and international boundary waters from Lake of the Woods to Lake Superior and some distance northward are also good bass waters.

Ontario provides the cream of Smallmouth Bass fishing to be found in Canada and many American anglers visit the territory solely for the purpose of taking this excellent gamester.

MUSKELLUNGE

This province also contains the major part of the Muskellunge fishing to be found in Canada. Principal Muskie territory is the Ottawa and St. Lawrence Rivers from their junction westward; the north shore of Lake Ontario, including many waters in Prince Edward County; numerous waters in the Peterboro district; the north and west shores of Georgian Bay; French River up to and including Lake Nipissing; the north shore of North Channel between Manitoulin Island and the mainland; the Lake of the Woods, including a number of lakes to the north and east; Rainy Lake District; and comparatively small and isolated Muskie areas in Algonquin Park, Lake St. Clair at the western end of Lake Erie, and Niagara River.

NORTHERN PIKE

Northern Pike are not only found in abundance in accessible fishing water but in many canoe waters to the north as well. It is widely distributed through the unfished, practically virgin, waters in the Hudson Bay drainage. It is also found in many of the lakes and streams between the Canadian National and Lake Superior east to the southern end of Lake Nipigon. It is found east of Lake Superior, in almost all waters draining into North Channel, and Georgian Bay. Eastern shore of Georgian Bay and adjoining waters, Lake St. Clair, north shores of both Lake Erie and Lake Ontario, the territory south and west of Ottawa, the Ottawa River and the St. Lawrence River are also well known pike waters. A large part of the Peninsula lying between Lake Huron and the Georgian Bay are better for bass than for Northern Pike.

WALLEYE

Walleyes are also found over a wide territory in the generally fished area. They are found in almost endless waters south of the Canadian National Railway. There is good Walleye fishing at the extreme northern tip of Lake Superior on the headwaters of the Moose River, and also in the vicinity of Lake Nipissing and the big country to the north of Georgian Bay and North Channel. It is also found throughout the Ottawa River and St. Lawrence River areas. Niagara River, Lake St. Clair, west end of Lake Erie, and many waters south and west of the city of Ottawa also provide good angling, as well as the many waters between Georgian Bay and Lake Ontario. It is also generally distributed in the almost virgin waters north of this line.

MANITOBA

Manitoba offers a wide variety of angling and the enthusiastic fisherman is almost sure to find satisfaction if he explores the possibilities for good fishing. This variation is due in part to climatic conditions because the southern part of the province is in the temperate zone while the northern part approaches sub-Arctic conditions; and in part to the geological formations. In the southwestern section the lakes are generally shallow and the production of game fish is restricted to such warm water varieties as Walleyes, Pike, and Perch. The exception is provided by the lakes in the Riding, Duck and Porcupine Mountains which are quite deep and which, while not natural trout waters, have been successfully stocked with Lake Trout.

In the central district, a limestone belt extends in a north-westerly direction. This region contains the large lakes from which is harvested the greater part of Manitoba's commercial fish catch. The numerous rivers, tributary to these lakes, are now becoming famous for Walleye and Northern Pike fishing. The Whitemud River, flowing into the south end of Lake Manitoba, gives thrills aplenty to anglers when they hook one of its big Northern Pike. Casting and trolling are the usual methods of fishing. Further north, the rivers tributary to Lake Dauphin, and Lake Dauphin itself, are well known Walleye and Pike fishing grounds. The picturesque Mossy River, the connecting link between Lake Dauphin and Lake Winnipegosis, is also excellent Walleye water and anglers in its clear, swift-flowing waters find pleasure in the scenery and satisfaction in the catch.

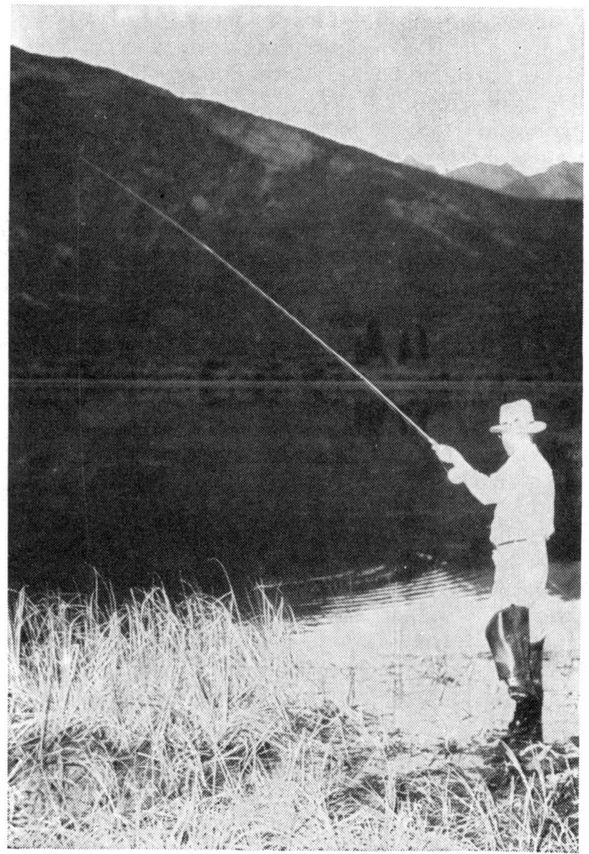

Trout fishing on Vermilion Lakes, Banff.

Many excellent fishing waters are situated along or within easy reach of No. 10 highway which extends from the U.S. Canadian border in the Turtle Mountains to the most northerly roads in Manitoba—those in The Pas district. The first important lake is Sandy Lake which has been extremely good Walleye water, the road to which is 120 miles or so north of the border. At a point 130 miles north of the border on No. 10 highway is situated Clear Lake in the Riding Mountain National Park. This deep and cold lake has been stocked with Lake Trout and which, when angling for the species is permitted, will provide excellent sport. Clear Lake now provides good Northern Pike fishing while the angler at the same time can enjoy delightful scenery. Three rivers, famous for large catches of Walleyes, are the Steep Rock, Red Deer, and Overflowing Rivers which are crossed by No. 10 highway at points approximately 200 miles north of Clear Lake. Each summer at the opening of the season large numbers of fishermen visit these rivers and obtain excellent fishing. The town of The Pas, 130 miles north of Swan River is the gateway to excellent fishing in northern waters. Lake Atikameg, 18 miles from the town of The Pas, is famous for Lake Trout. Once visited, Atikameg is never forgotten; it leaves a lasting memory; definitely the lake has personality—if such is possible.

Highway 10 extends from The Pas to the Cranberry Portage district, a center of excellent Lake Trout fishing in both the Cranberry Lakes and Lake Athapapuskow. Good cabins equipped with boats and outboard motors are available. The district is ideal for recreational boating, inasmuch as the wide sweeps of the lakes are broken by scores of rocky islands. More often than not these islands are clad with coniferous trees which blend most harmoniously with the colors of water and sky.

The world's record Lake Trout taken by an angler is a fish caught in Lake Athapapuskow by Miss Leona Hayes on October 22, 1930. Its weight was 63 pounds and its length 47½ inches. While fish approaching this size are now very rare, records of 20 to 30 pound fish are not uncommon. In mid-summer anglers use copper lines and fish with 200 feet or more when trolling. In the early summer Lake Trout are on the surface and may be caught with plugs, spinners, ruby-eyed wigglers, or other standard lures. When caught on the surface, this fish is an active fighter and provides a thrilling battle on light tackle. When caught in the deep water, it is not so satisfactory because it is somewhat distressed by being hauled suddenly from the greater pressure areas in deep water to the lighter atmospheric pressure near the surface.

In the southern part of the province and 90 miles east of Winnipeg is the Whiteshell Provincial Park, situated in the Pre-Cambrian or granite zone. This zone extends from the extreme southeastern portion of the province northerly and westerly along the eastern shore of Lake Winnipeg and then northwesterly to the northern boundary at the 60th parallel of North Latitude. In the Whiteshell Provincial Park, visitors can find good accommodations in numerous cabins. It is popular, however, and reservations for accommodations during July and August should be made in advance to avoid disappointment.

The popularity is well justified. Almost without exception the lakes are picturesque with beauty spots in any direction. In addition, the majority provide excellent catches of Walleyes, some good Pike, and in two lakes, West Hawk and High Lakes, anglers make good catches of Lake Trout throughout the summer months. In the early part of the season, as is the general rule, the Trout are on the surface and they provide excellent sport. In mid-summer, they can only be taken on a long deep line, usually copper line and heavy tackle. A spinner with triple hook and fresh minnow for bait usually brings results. A fairly heavy lead sinker is necessary when using a long copper line. The lakes referred to thus far in the Whiteshell Provincial Park are all adjacent to the highway or good gravel roads. There are, however, scores of inaccessible lakes within the park. Many of the more adventurous anglers follow the old water routes and portages to visit these remote waters where angling is almost sure to be excellent. Some of these lakes offer fair Lake Trout fishing such as Lake George, Forbes, and Mantario Lakes. One of the favorite canoe routes in the Park is north from Caddy Lake to South Cross Lake, then into North Cross, Sailing, and Mallard Lakes. Anglers making this trip usually find exceptionally good Walleye fishing in Sailing Lake.

In the wide expanse of more or less unsettled country between Lake Winnipeg and the Manitoba-Ontario boundary, there are hundreds of lakes, some of which may be 20 square miles or more in area and which contain highly desirable sport fish. Aikens Lake is worthy of mention. This is one of the deepest lakes in Manitoba with a known depth of 249 feet. It has excellent sandy beaches, and fine Lake Trout are taken by visiting fishermen.

A tourist lodge now is established at the lake, but the only means of communication in summer is the airplane. In winter an occasional tractor train may pass through, but the airplane is the most readily available means of transportation summer or winter. North of Aikens Lake, Sassaginnigak is interesting because it is a natural Walleye producer in its northern portion.

Although the vast expanse of rock, muskeg, lakes and rivers between the northern part of Lake Winnipeg and Hudson Bay is not well known, there are several lakes which are becoming known as transportation facilities improve. Gods Lake is perhaps the most important, and commercial fishermen and anglers take large quantities of Lake Trout from its waters. In the Gods River at the north end of Gods Lake native Speckled Trout are exceedingly plentiful and the fly fisherman excel in this area. There is a lodge at Gods Lake where tourists may obtain accommodation but all communication must be by airplane in summer, and by airplane, bombardier-snowmobile, or tractor train in winter.

From the town of The Pas in northern Manitoba the railway leads to Churchill, a distance of 512 miles. Good fishing is obtainable at various points along the railway. At Wabowden (Mile 137), there is a beautiful chain of lakes where the angler may take satisfactory catches of Walleyes and Northern Pike. Farther north, at Mile 327, in the vicinity of Gillam, Brook Trout fishing equal to the best may be found. There are limited accommodations for tourists, and the two trading companies operating at the town are equipped to provide guides, canoes, and outboard motors. Farther north, in the vicinity of the Weir River and Herchmer, the rivers are populated with Arctic Grayling, a most spectacular fighter. It is characterized by its large dorsal fin, spotted with purplish markings somewhat like the tail of a peacock and blending harmoniously with the body colors which shade to a light colored, nearly white belly. The anglers who have taken Arctic Grayling are few, but those who have are enthusiastic.

At the terminus of the Hudson Bay Railway, Arctic Charr are caught in the estuaries of rivers flowing into "The Bay." The Arctic Charr is a close relative of the Brook Trout and grows to 20 pound size or more, although the average will be 4 to 5 pounds. Eskimo take this fish with primitive hooks, but other than natives, the anglers are few in the remote areas where Arctic Charr are found.

In the inland northern areas of Manitoba the lakes are not well known, but at least one, Big Sand Lake (accessible only by airplane) Latitude 57° 50′ North and Longitude 99° 40′ West, supports an extremely large population of Lake Trout.

Probably the most satisfying fishing territory in the more settled part of Manitoba is to be found in the Winnipeg River. It provides Walleyes, Northern Pike, Goldeyes and Smallmouth Bass which may be taken with ease by the skilled angler. Fly fishing is productive, but trolling and casting are the more generally used methods.

This commentary on Manitoba angling would be incomplete without mention of its most popular angling spot. This is the Red River at St. Andrews Locks, 17 miles from Winnipeg. On the lower side, or the north side of the dam at the Locks, dozens of boats may be seen on week-ends or holidays, each carrying three or four ardent anglers. Scores of anglers line the shores and cast into the river. Cars are packed in parking places, and a festive atmosphere is apparent. Walleyes, Saugers, Perch, Freshwater Drum, Pike and even Suckers are taken in abundance.

Manitoba has some 27,000 square miles of lakes and streams, much of which is virgin fishing water. The more heavily fished streams and lakes receive annual allotments of hatchery-raised fish, and where considered advisable, desirable game fish are introduced into suitable waters.

SASKATCHEWAN

Saskatchewan is a wheat country—one of the great wheat producing areas of the world. Thirty-five million acres—forty percent of the entire cultivated acreage of Canada—is devoted primarily to grain farming. The top half of the province contains a large share of the Pre-Cambrian wilderness. This vast area of 80,000 square miles is covered by the lake-studded rocky terrain characteristic of the Laurentian Plateau. From the center of the province to the Northwest Territories are countless lakes containing Lake Trout, Walleye (Pike-perch), Northern Pike, and Arctic Grayling.

Southern Saskatchewan is not without its angling waters. Well spaced across the prairies and the rolling cattle land of the southwest are 8 provincial parks, each set in wooded lake country. A hundred miles north of the 49th parallel is the Qu'Appelle chain of lakes and Last Mountain Lake, favorites of anglers for fifty years. The south and north branches of the Saskatchewan River provide additional angling for a scattered farm population.

Of the thirty-eight native species of fish, those highly prized by anglers are Lake Trout, Walleye (Pike-perch), Northern Pike, Arctic Grayling, Goldeye and the Yellow Perch. While not indigenous, trout, Rainbow, Brown, and Brook, have been introduced into the Cypress Hills near the Montana border, and the Brook Trout has recently been established in the Fir River north of the 53rd parallel. The Smallmouth Bass has been introduced in the centrally located Prince Albert National Park, and although established, are by no means abundant. Walleye and Northern Pike are the most sought after fish. They are widely distributed and are abundant in most lakes of the province.

Spinners and spoons are used effectively for both species. Ruby Eyes No. 2½ and 3, Copper Devil 1, Wiggler 2½ blade and Water Witch silver and copper are lures most commonly used. Bait fishermen resort to frogs, grasshoppers, worms, and light steel casting rods are used extensively.

Those who like their sport with the added comfort of a summer resort may visit the Provincial Parks, Qu'Appelle chain and Long Lake within one hundred and fifty miles of the American border. Four hundred and seventy miles from North Portal, North Dakota, lies the beautiful Prince Albert National Park which has good angling and up-to-date accommodations.

In the Cypress Hills, forty miles from the Montana border, a more refined art is practiced. While the streams are not extensive, there is little difficulty in catching Rainbow, Brown, and Brook Trout. A 5-ounce, 7½-foot split can rod with tapered line and a 4-pound test gut or Nylon leader is recommended. No. 10 and 12 hooks are used, and preference given to the following fly patterns: Grey Gnat, Black Gnat, Grey Hackle, March Brown, and Royal Coachman.

Quite recently fly fishing for Goldeye in the Saskatchewan River has attracted an increasing number of anglers.

Virgin lakes in the northern half of the province are being made accessible to anglers by new roads

Perch and Jackfish fishing on Jackfish Lake near Edmondton.

and increased use of air transportation. Three years ago, a road was completed through difficult terrain into Lac La Ronge, 175 miles north of Prince Albert. Lac La Ronge contains 288,000 acres of water, and a thousand scenic islands. It has an abundant supply of Lake Trout, Walleye, Northern Pike, and Yellow Perch. It has approximately a dozen deep channels where the Lake Trout congregate during summer. As the more shallow areas become deficient in oxygen during the summer, the Lake Trout seek areas 100 to 125 feet deep. Anglers who know where these restricted channels are have excellent trout fishing during most of the summer. The numerous islands are so situated as to protect the fishermen against the prevailing winds, and makes it possible to fish even during rough weather.

From May 16th until the 10th of June (the last of June on the more northerly lakes), Lake Trout may be taken on light casting equipment. A light twenty pound test Nylon or cotton line is used and an assortment of lures: Copper Ruby Eye 2½", 3", 3½", near gold wobbler #3 Devil 1 Wobbler 3" blade and silver and copper Gibbs Stewart #6 and #7 and the Len Thompson spoon #2. As the surface water warms the lake, trout seek the deep holes. Anglers then resort to trolling on the bottom with heavy trolling rod, 300 or more feet of monel or copper line. The same type lure are effective with preference going to the large types. In September the trout again return to the shallow water and may be caught in three to ten feet of water on light casting equipment.

Scheduled or chartered airplane trips operate out of Prince Albert and the more inaccessible lakes are within two hours. Lake Trout and Arctic Grayling fishing are a big attraction on Reindeer, Wollaston, and Cree Lakes, and on the Fond du Lac River. The Arctic Grayling is an excellent game fish, and will satisfy the exacting fly enthusiast. Nine-foot split bamboo rods are used, but lighter equipment is recommended. A tapered line and six-pound test gut are preferred. The Grayling has a soft small mouth, and number 10 or 12 hooks are advisable. The March Brown, Brown Hackle, Mayfly, Stonefly, Grey Hackle, Royal Coachman, Black Gnat, and Blue Teal are among the flies used. When hooked, the Grayling heads for very fast water where it can use the huge dorsal fin to great advantage. Lake Trout are frequently found in the fast waters with the Grayling.

ALBERTA

There are two main types of angling in Alberta—cold-water angling for Trout and their allies, and warm-water angling for Pike, Walleye (Pickerel), Perch and Goldeyes.

The cold-water species are mostly confined to the eastern slopes of the Rocky Mountains and the river systems of these slopes provide thousands of miles of fair to excellent angling. The major fishing areas are as follows:

THE ATHABASCA RIVER AND TRIBUTARIES

This system is in the northern part of the province and is largely inaccessible except by pack-trip. It provides angling for Rainbow Trout, Arctic Grayling and Rocky Mountain Whitefish. Small Rainbow Trout are abundant in easily accessible parts of the system west of Edmonton. They may be taken readily on dry flies of almost any pattern. Larger Rainbow occur in one or two lakes and are taken mainly by trolling with spoons and wobblers. Fly fishing for large Rainbow is good in some of the more remote streams.

Arctic Grayling are native to the Athabasca system and provide an unusual fishing treat for visitors from the south. A number of streams accessible by good roads (notably the McLeod River and tributaries) provide excellent Arctic Grayling fishing. This species may be taken on dry flies, wet flies, nymphs, or with bait (maggots, worms, grasshoppers). The fish strike fairly well throughout the open season, and normally run from 8-16 ounces in size.

Rocky Mountain Whitefish are taken mainly in the fall. Wet Flies will take them at times, but bait is the method most generally used.

The Dolly Varden also occurs in this area. In deep holes, in the larger streams, this fish sometimes grows to ten pounds or more. Fishing is best in the late summer and fall; large hooks baited with fish, Salmon eggs, or raw beef provide the best lure.

THE NORTH SASKATCHEWAN RIVER SYSTEM

The waters of this system are accessible from Edmonton and Red Deer. The best angling is provided by small streams and beaver dams. The chief game fishes are the Brown Trout and Brook Trout, with the native Dolly Varden occurring frequently, and the Rainbow Trout occasionally. The average fish weighs less than one pound, although beaver dams often yield larger ones. Rocky Mountain Whitefish migrate to the upper reaches of many streams in large numbers each fall.

THE RED DEER RIVER SYSTEM

These waters lie to the west and southwest of the city of Red Deer, and include several streams which provide very good Brown Trout and Brook Trout fishing. The Raven River and Dogpound Creek are particularly good dry fly streams. Almost all streams provide limited numbers of Dolly Varden, and some of the smaller tributaries, though often inaccessible, contain some Rainbow Trout. Rocky Mountain Whitefish occur here also.

THE BOW RIVER AND TRIBUTARIES

This is an enormous drainage with hundreds of streams containing Trout, mostly Cutthroat. The area is accessible from Calgary. The larger rivers such as the Elbow, the Highwood, the Sheep, and the Jumping Pound provide angling for large Cutthroat, Rainbow, Dolly Varden and Rocky Mountain Whitefish. These rivers are swift and fishing them is no sinecure. Fly and bait fishermen are about equally divided. In the main Bow itself very large Trout are caught using bucktails or wobblers; below Calgary Rainbow and Cutthroats up to 8 pounds and commonly around 2 to 4 pounds are plentiful; above Calgary, and particularly in

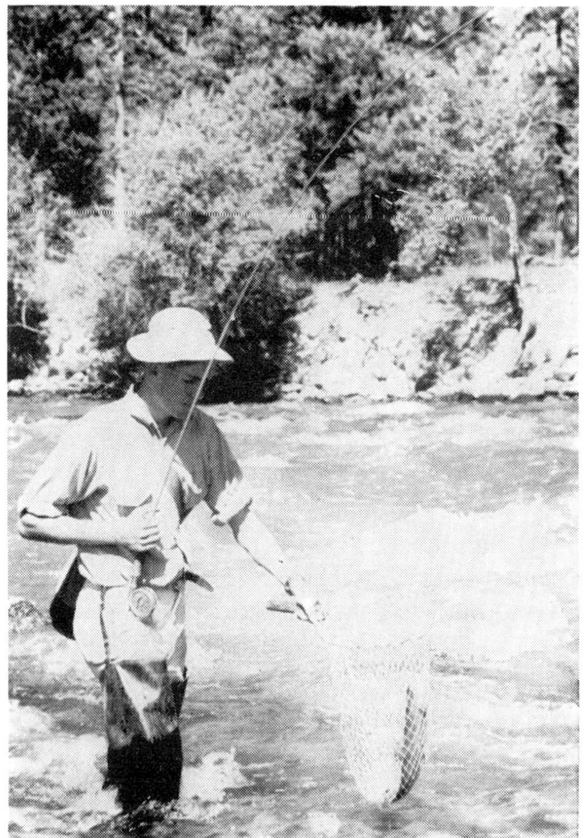

Trout fishing on Fiddle Creek, Jasper, Alberta.

the area known as Gap Lake, large Brown Trout are caught. In the smaller, upper tributaries there is excellent dry fly fishing for Cutthroat, mainly small fish of one pound and less.

Certain of the headwater lakes of the Bow system, notably the Spray lakes and the Kananaskis lakes, provide fishing for large trout, Cutthroat in the former and Rainbow and Cutthroat in the latter. These fish are taken by trolling with spoons, wobblers, flat fish, or minnows. They range up to twelve pounds in weight and are generally regarded as too large for successful fly fishing. Large Dolly Varden also occur in the lakes.

THE OLDMAN DRAINAGE

This system is in the southern part of Alberta and contains a number of locally famous trout streams. Among the best are the Racehorse, Dutch Creek, the Livingstone River, the Crowsnest River, the Castle River, the Belly River and Willow Creek. It is characterized by large, fast-growing trout, mainly Cutthroat, but Rainbows are numerous in the larger streams. Dry fly fishing is excellent, but many fishermen claim the larger trout are taken on salmon eggs. Most of the streams are easily accessible on all-weather roads.

WARM WATER FISHES

The sceond category of angling is for warm-water fishes such as Pike, Walleyes (Pickerel), Perch, and Goldeye. These fish may be taken anywhere in the province from May 16th to March 31st except in waters frequented by Trout, Grayling, and Rocky Mountain Whitefish. In the excepted areas they may be taken only during the open season for the cold-water species.

The Northern Pike is abundant in Alberta. It may be caught in the lower reaches of all the rivers and in hundreds of lakes throughout the province. Specimens up to twenty pounds are not uncommon and ten-pound fish are every-day occurrences. Pike are caught by casting with plugs, spinners, or wobblers, or by trolling, or by still-fishing, or casting with minnows.

Perch are also very abundant, being numerous in lakes throughout the province. They are mostly taken by still fishing with worms.

Walleyes are less abundant, although they are caught in the lower reaches of the main rivers and in some lakes, notably Lac Ste. Anne, Buck Lake, Lesser Slave, Lac La Biche, Baptiste, and numerous others. Fishing methods are the same as for Pike.

Goldeyes are not as frequently taken by anglers, although they are widespread in the lower reaches of the rivers of Alberta. They are particularly abundant in the lower Bow and Red Deer in the south and in the Pembina River and the main Athabasca River in the north. Goldeyes are taken on bait.

BRITISH COLUMBIA

British Columbia, a vast and generally well-watered province of some 350,000 square miles, has an enormous number of lakes and streams that provide good fishing. Much of the territory, particularly that north of the Skeena which empties into the Pacific at Prince Rupert as well as huge areas of mountain country adjacent to the coast north of Vancouver, are still relatively inaccessible and almost virgin country. To fish in most of the areas requires special pack or canoe trips of long duration, although roads and trails are continually opening new areas.

The fishing along the coast is largely for Salmon, and throughout the province for the various species of trout, although both Largemouth and Smallmouth Bass have been introduced in a few sections.

SALMON

Salmon fishing, with the exception of that for Landlocked Salmon (Kokanee), is confined to coastal waters and streams that flow directly into the salt water or are tributaries of such major streams. The sport fishing is in salt water or in the extreme lower end of major rivers. Of the five species of Pacific Salmon, only two, the King Salmon (Spring or Chinook) and the Silver Salmon (Coho) are regarded as having major sport qualities. These are found in all the coastal waters of British Columbia and may be located with some degree of success practically the year around.

April usually opens the fishing season. At this time the fishing is largely salt water trolling with lures of varying type. For the Chinooks or King Salmon, a 10-foot rod and reel holding five to six hundred feet of 15 to 20 pound test line are recommended. This is used with 6 feet of 10 or

12-pound test Nylon leader, although some anglers are inclined to use piano wire leaders. Tuna flies, as well as metal spoons and artificial plugs, are used. The No. 6 or 7 Martin plug is a favorite, although many Vancouver Island fishermen favor the metal lure known as Mahatma Ghandi, which has little resemblance to a fish but seems to attract. Herring strips are also trolled behind a metal flasher, and very little lead is normally used.

The world-famous salmon fishing at Campbell River on the east coast of Vancouver Island is at its height during August for King Salmon, with the Silver or Coho coming somewhat later since they spawn at a later period. These fish are largely taken at this time on trolled gear, although a number are caught on flies.

The Tyee Club of British Columbia has its headquarters at this place, and each year gives prizes to the largest fish caught in each class recognized under its rules. Length, character, weight of rod, and type of line are specified under these rules, and any angler wishing to compete should get in touch with the Tyee Club of British Columbia, P.O. Box 608, Victoria, B.C., or at the Tyee Point, Campbell River, B.C.

Fish weighing from 30 to 40 pounds are taken regularly while individuals over 50 pounds are not uncommon.

Silvers are somewhat smaller—the average being from 5 to 7 or 8 pounds, although fish up to 20 and 25 pounds are taken. Beginning in July, the Silvers commence to concentrate, and the tackle used for these fish is similar to that used for King Salmon, although somewhat lighter. Three or four hundred feet of standard lines testing 12 to 15 pounds are used. Leaders are from 6 to 10 pounds in weight. Although the Campbell River fishing grounds are the most famous, these fighting Salmon are taken also at many places along the coast with the same type of lures.

The Landlocked Salmon (Kokanee) is a Red Salmon (Sockeye) which has become locked in fresh water. While it varies somewhat in size, most of them do not run above a pound in weight. In British Columbia, they are found in Kootenay, Okanagan, Shuswap, Christina Woods, and Kalamalaka. This is a good fighting fish but is not much on taking flies. It is caught fairly regularly by trolling spinners baited with worms or salmon eggs. It is also caught still fishing with the same kind of bait.

TROUT

Steelhead which run in migration in most rivers spawn in the winter or spring between December and March. They take flies in both fresh and salt water, and in the streams will take wet as well as dry flies. They are most frequently taken by casting bait and allowing it to drift with the current, over riffles. Good tackle with at least 20 pounds test line is recommended for the big Steelheads that appear in these waters.

In the interior, trout fishing can be secured for all major species. Most common and widely distributed are the Rainbows, Cutthroat, and the Dolly Varden. The Rainbow, known as the Kamloops, is the commonest fish of the southern interior of British Columbia. It is found throughout the drainage of the Columbia River and has been introduced in many of the lakes on the lower mainland, as well as on Vancouver Island. It is also found north, to and including the Cariboo region and some of the more northern lakes.

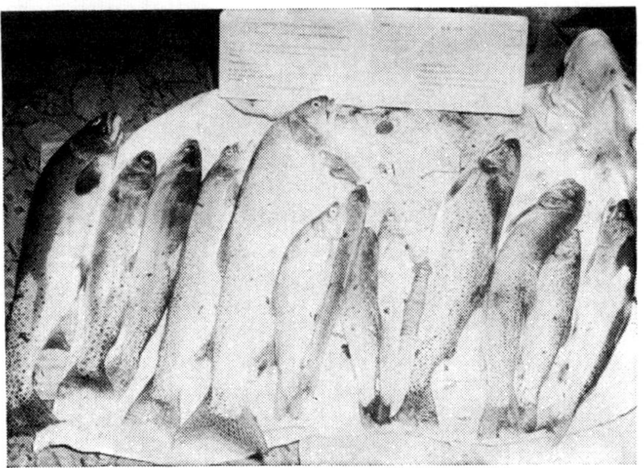

Native Trout taken in Boom Lake near Banff.

Best fishing is normally in the streams and northern lakes and at the mouths of streams flowing into larger bodies of water. During May and June, Nation's Special, Nation's Silvertip, and Carey's Special are very useful flies with the Black Gnat, Black O'Lindsay, and Alexander replacing them as the season advances. About mid-June, when the hatch of green and brown sedges occurs, dry flies are best.

No two lakes offer exactly the same seasonal opportunities to fish, but on most of the larger lakes, May, June, and September are the most favorable months for fly fishing. In July and August, trolling is usually recommended as more successful.

Cutthroats are divided into several local races. The coast Cutthroat is common in all coastal waters and may be either a resident or sea-run fish in the same stream. They are found in all streams and lakes of Vancouver Island and in all mainland coastal streams, including the Skeena River and its tributaries, and the smaller streams between the Skeena and Fraser. It is common in Harrison and Chilliwack Lakes and rivers, but does not appear in the Fraser above Hell's Gate. A form distinguished as the Yellowstone Cutthroat is found in the upper waters of the Kootenay River, including the basins of the Moyie and Elk Rivers, but it is not found in waters in which the Kamloop Trout abounds. Mountain Cutthroats occur in the high altitude lakes in the Revelstokes district, and to some extent in the Creston Fernie area. All will take almost any type of fly, but brighter patterns are usually more successful. Wet flies are also preferred to dry flies by most anglers who pursue these fish regularly.

Brown Trout are found only on Vancouver Island where it has been introduced and seems well established in the Cowichan and Little Qualicum Rivers.

The Dolly Varden, also known as Bull Trout, is fairly well distributed in all salt-water as well as fresh-water streams emptying into it. Many are sea-run specimens. They are normally quite voracious when found in fresh water and will take almost any type of bait or lure, although wet flies are usually more successful than dry flies. Despite their poor reputation among western anglers, in cold water they fight on light tackle as well as the Brook Trout. They are also successfully caught with casting rods and spinning tackle using most of the standard casting lures, although many who use these tackle types of rigs prefer Red Devils and similar wobblers.

Lake Trout are found in the interior, particularly in the Cariboo and north country. They are usually taken on deep trolls during the summer at which time the best lure is the large wobbler type of spoon trolled rather slowly. In both fall and spring, they are closer to the surface and may then be taken on lighter tackle with surface lures.

Brook Trout have been introduced into some of the lakes on the lower mainland and a few in the interior, but it is not widely distributed. It is not regarded there with as great favor as it is in eastern waters, and most western anglers prefer Cutthroats or Rainbows.

BASS

Smallmouth Bass have been introduced into several lakes on Vancouver Island and into Christina Lake in the southeastern part of the province. St. Mary Lake on Saltspring Island is also well stocked. Spider, Florence, and Langford Lakes also provide Smallmouth Bass fishing.

The Largemouth Bass has entered the southeastern portion of the province from the south and is now common in Kootenay, Osoyoos and Vaseaux Lakes where individuals weighing 5 to 6 pounds are regularly caught. Elk and Prospect Lakes, near Victoria on Vancouver Island, also contain goodly numbers of these fish. Bass are not widely sought by western anglers as long as they can find trout fishing of the quality that is available in British Columbia. Consequently, those interested in bass fishing find excellent sport in some of these waters.

UNITED STATES

ALASKA

Alaska has many remote waters which provide some of the most spectacular fishing to be found. As roads and trails make more waters accessible, they are rather quickly fished down to a less spectacular level, but excellent fish are still to be found close to the larger centers of population.

Where to cast a fishing lure in Alaska is no more important than *when* to do it; the two go hand in hand. For example, Sea Level River near Ketchikan is a happy spot for the Steelhead Trout fisherman, but only in late April through May. Spasskaia Creek which is just around a couple of bends from Hoonah produces large and abundant numbers of black-speckled Cutthroats, though not until the Salmon start spawning there in late July and August. The tremendous and brilliantly colored Arctic Char of Pilgrim River back of Nome are at their fightingest best only in August. So, *when* and *where* are a team.

Another point for the angler to remember about Alaska is that it is a vast country with weather, water and geographic conditions as varied as he will encounter in traveling from Yellowstone to the Florida Keys. Game fish species run all the way form a colorful six-inch Dolly Varden subspecies found only in high mountain torrents to the giant King Salmon of sixty or more pounds. Several of the sports-fishes will not be taken by the angler anywhere else than in Alaska.

Most accessible of fishing locations in the State, and also one of the most fruitful areas, is the region known as Southeastern Alaska extending from Ketchikan to north of Juneau. It is an area of salt water inlets, of densely wooded islands with short, fast streams pouring into the sea, of precipitous mainland mountains with hidden lakes, towering waterfalls and gravelly stretches where Salmon find ideal spawning conditions. Surrounding Ketchikan, Wrangell, Petersburg, Juneau, Sitka or any of the smaller towns of this section the angler will find good fishing.

In early season, late April to June, he will find Steelhead Trout in hundreds of streams. King Salmon fishing in the salt water is good. With the coming of July, just ahead of most Salmon migrations, the streams on mainland and islands alike fill with Dolly Varden, Cutthroat and Rainbow Trout. It is usually very good fishing, indeed, except in the vicinity of the towns where overfishing has been evident in the past few years. The best plan is to engage a boat, or fly with local airplane pilots to streams and lakes about which they will advise.

Across the Gulf of Alaska, northward to the wide stretches of interior Alaska, the angler leaves behind him most of the Dolly Vardens, Cutthroats and sea-run Steelheads. In their place he finds Grayling Stream Rainbows, Lake Trout and Northern Pike. He finds here, as elsewhere in Alaska, that streams and lakes adjacent to roadsides are heavily fished. He will do much better to penetrate to waterways off the beaten trail. In July and August he will find the Grayling rising beautifully to the dry fly. Below the Alaska Range in a stretch of country extending roughly from Cordova westward past Anchorage and to Bristol Bay, huge Rainbow Trout are found in many of the heavy, fast rivers. Noted are the waters of Russian River on the Kenai, Newhalen and Talarie Rivers flowing into Iliamna Lake, and Wood and Naknek Rivers of the Bristol Bay area.

North of the Alaska Range many of the deep lakes are well stocked, and naturally, with Mackinaw or Lake Trout. Shallow lakes, grass filled sloughs and sluggish rivers are likely to be teeming with Northern Pike some of which are truly enormous. On Seward Peninsula where the famed gold camp of Nome is located, the angling consists mostly of Grayling flyfishing, though in midsummer and later migrations of Arctic Char into the larger rivers to spawn provides spectacular fishing with spinner and streamer fly. These trout, a form of Dolly Varden, are like huge eastern Brook Trout in general appearance with their big, red spots and high coloration. While all these three species—Grayling, Lake Trout and Arctic Char extend their range far into the Arctic Ocean drainages, the waters near Alaska's Arctic Circle produce *yet another* game fish of extraordinary sporty qualities.

Mainly in the Kobuk River, though in scattering numbers as far south as the Kuskokwim, the Eskimo Sheefish hold great promise to the angler with adventurous ideas. Called Inconnu, the unknown, this silvery, scaled giant strikes with the fury of a tarpon. While the middle reaches of the Kobuk are its favorite waters it is known to range north and eastward to the MacKenzie River. It is best taken in midsummer.

LOCATION OF SPECIES

Brook Trout

An introduced species in Alaska. Confined to southeastern Alaska in lakes near Ketchikan, Juneau and Skagway.

Cutthroat Trout

In streams and lakes of southeastern Alaska mostly, but straying as far north as Prince William Sound. Often caught in salt and brackish water.

Dolly Varden Trout

Swims in practically every fresh-water stream in the Territory, as well as in neighboring salt water. Most abundant of all northern trout.

Grayling

Confined to clear, ice-cold streams from north of the Alaska Range to the Arctic Ocean. Occasionally in crystal, frigid lakes.

King Salmon

In all the salt waters of the Territory along the

coast line from Ketchikan to the Yukon River. Best sports fishing is found in the channels of Southeastern Archipelago.

Lake Trout

In deep lakes from the base of the Alaska Peninsula east and north to the Arctic Ocean. Lakes Iliamna, Clark, Becharof, Naknek, Wood, Summit and Norutak especially well known.

Northern Pike

In weed-grown ponds, lakes, sloughs and rivers from Bristol Bay drainage north to Arctic and east to Canadian border. Kuskokwim River, Innoko Valley, Lake Minchumina, Upper Tanana and Yukon, and drainages of Kotzebue Sound especially good.

Rainbow-Steelhead Trout

Sea-run Steelheads found from Ketchikan along coast to Bristol Bay. Freshwater Rainbows found in few places in southeast Alaska but Kenai Peninsula, and Anchorage-Bristol Bay are more productive of heavy fish.

Sheefish

Most abundant in waters of Kobuk River during summer season, dropping back to brackish Kotzebue Sound in winter. Scattering schools inhabit rivers from Kuskokwin north and east to MacKenzie.

Silver Salmon

July and August finds this jumping game fish along the coastline from Ketchikan to Kotzebue. First taken on trolled lures in salt water; later hits spinners, streamer flies and baited hooks in rivers en route to spawning grounds.

The great number of states makes it impossible to discuss in any detail the fishing to be found in each and, therefore, they have been grouped into sections to prevent repetition as far as possible. Each section has many types of water and fish, but the States do have major topographical and climatic features that create some likenesses among them.

NEW ENGLAND STATES

The six states of New England, with a water surface covering nearly 7 per cent of their 66,000 square miles, probably offer the angler more opportunities to catch a greater variety of game fish than many comparable areas.

Here in the three northern states dwells the Landlocked Salmon, native to three river basins of Maine and introduced successfully into New Hampshire and Vermont waters; here the native Brook Trout still abounds; here the introduced Brown and Rainbow Trouts have made their homes and endeared themselves to the angler; here the Black Bass lives and multiplies in almost every body of water except those in the very northernmost part of Maine; here are Pickerel, panfish of almost every variety and, in scattered locations, even Atlantic Salmon, Walleye, and the mighty Muskellunge may be found.

Connecticut

Connecticut, with less water area (only 145 square miles) than any other New England state, offers surprisingly good fishing due to an intelligent stocking program. It is blessed with two major trout rivers, the Farmington and Housatonic, and both hold Brown and Rainbow Trout, plus a scattering of Brooks, despite heavy fishing.

The Farmington is good, especially in the early season, in the New Hartford and Avon areas, while the West Branch at Colebrook and Hartland also rates high. Nearer the coast of Long Island Sound, the lower reaches of the Hammonassett River, which enters the Sound near Madison, contains both Brook and Brown Trout. It is here that George Heinold, well-known Madison angler, first discovered sea-run Brown Trout running up to 7½ pounds in weight. The Farm River at East Haven also produces sea-run Browns, the largest to date being a seven-pounder.

Much of the Connecticut fishing, however, is confined to the lakes and ponds. The most consistent producers include West Hill Pond at New Hartford for Brown Trout and Bass; Quassapaug Lake at Woodbury and Middlebury for Brown and Rainbow Trout, and Bass; East Twin Lake near Salisbury for Brown and Rainbow Trout; and Norwich and Uncas Lakes at Lyme for Brook, Brown and Rainbow Trout.

A relatively new, but interesting fishery in the state is the sport fishery for shad in the Connecticut River. From early May to mid-June, thousands of shad fresh from the sea are taken at such popular locations as the Enfield Rapids Dam, the Farmington River and the Windsor Locks Bridge. Popular lures include weighted jigs, small spoons and colored beads.

Maine

Maine, covering half of New England, offers the angler a truly delectable choice, with about 3,145 square miles of water surface. Here, and only here in the United States, can he cast a fly for Atlantic Salmon. Once virtually extinct south of the Canadian border, the sea-run Salmon has been re-established in the Dennys, Narraguagus, Machias, Pleasant, Sheepscot, and other rivers, which flow into the Atlantic north of Penobscot Bay.

The centers of sport fishing for Atlantic Salmon are at Machias, at Dennysville near the mouth of the Dennys, and at Cherryfield on the Narraguagus, 65 miles east of Bangor on U. S. Highway No. 1. In recent years no salmon have been taken from the famous Bangor Pool of the Penobscot, just outside the city of Bangor, and by custom the first fish caught there each season is sent to the President in Washington. But the Penobscot run has fallen off so alarmingly, due to inadequate fishways and pollution that this river can no longer be considered to have salmon.

The Landlocked Salmon, a close relative of the Atlantic Salmon and its twin in almost every respect except for its smaller size and non-migratory habits, has been stocked widely throughout its

Maine Dept. of Economic Development

Maine is the only state where sea-run Atlantic Salmon may still be taken. Here a group of Salmon fishermen compare notes before venturing out after that fighting game fish.

native state. Sebago Lake, which lies 15 miles northwest of Portland, once gave up the largest fish, including the present rod-and-reel world's record specimen of 22½ pounds. Sebago still offers excellent fishing for Landlocked Salmon, but other lakes, notably lakes in the Fish River chain of Aroostook County, now produce the trophy fish. Ten-pound Salmon have been taken frequently from Long Lake in recent years, whereas Sebago, one of the three original homes of the Salmon in Maine, today yields few fish heavier than 5 pounds.

Moosehead Lake, which lies in the great wilderness that reaches to Canada, at one time held no Landlocked Salmon at all, but the species is now firmly established there. This mighty body of water, largest in Maine, offers excellent fishing for Salmon in addition to native Brook and Lake Trout.

Other major fishing areas in Maine include the Rangeley section in the extreme western edge of the state, which provides dependable Brook Trout and Landlocked Salmon fishing in Rangeley, Mooselookmeguntic, and Upper and Lower Richardson Lakes. This area is reached by State Highway No. 4 out of Farmington. A few miles north of the Rangeleys lie Kennebago and Little Kennebago lakes and Kennebago Stream, which after exceptional fly fishing for native Brook Trout. The waters of Rangeley and Kennebago contain no Lake Trout or Bass.

There are other good waters in Jackman; Schoodic; and Sebec. The Fish River Chain of lakes in northern Aroostook County is the most remote of Maine's waters, and largely because of that fact offers superb Landlocked Salmon fishing at times. This includes Long, Fish, Portage, Eagle, Square, Cross, and Mud lakes; all furnish excellent angling during the spring and early summer months.

Another popular chain of lakes is that which leads into the St. Croix River near the lumber town of Princeton not far from the Maine-New Brunswick border. Starting in Penobscot County with Upper and Lower Sysladobsis lakes, the waters flow through Pocumpus into Grand Lake, down Grand Lake Stream into Big Lake, and thence into the St. Croix. Grand Lake originally contained the Canadian Landlocked Salmon *Salmo ouananiche.* Except for Grand and Pocumpus lakes, these waters now offer spectacular Smallmouth Bass fishing, the species having been recently introduced. Grand and Pocumpus, however, provide good fishing for Lake Trout, a species absent from the other lakes in the chain. All of them hold Salmon and a few Brook Trout.

The lakes of the Belgrade area, lying west of Waterville and north of the capital city of Augusta, are famous today chiefly for their Smallmouth Bass although one, Messalonskee, also contains large Brook Trout. Largemouth Bass and a few Landlocked Salmon are also taken in the Belgrades.

With the exception of the Kennebago area, the best of Maine's Brook Trout fishing is scattered throughout thousands of smaller lakes, ponds, and streams. The large rivers produce Trout, but almost all of the smaller ones provide fishing which rates from good to excellent. The native Brook Trout, more commonly known in Maine as "squaretails" or "red-spots," have found the Maine wilderness a stronghold from which they may never be driven by the Rainbow or Brown, for these waters, excepting the larger rivers along the more heavily-populated coast, remain pure and cold.

Maine has successfully introduced Brown Trout to a few areas. Branch Lake, east of Bangor, and Sabbathday Lake at New Gloucester, both produce mammoth Brown Trout.

Pickerel abound in all but the deepest and coldest lakes. The writer has seen them lying in serried ranks along the shores of Fourth Lake Machias in Washington County, and this is but one of the hundreds of ponds and lakes where the species is found. Few sportsmen fish for them preferring to take the tastier and more sporting Trout and Salmon, so except for limited market fishing, the Pickerel is left to flourish and multiply.

Since Maine has few warm-water ponds, the Largemouth Bass is rare, but the Smallmouth has taken a liking to the cold, clear waters of the state, and almost without exception has become firmly established wherever introduced. It is not uncommon for an angler to hook fifty Bass a day in some waters during the month of June when they are on their spawning beds, although the laws permits fly fishing only, with a three-fish daily limit and single-hook lures from June 1 to 21. Big Lake in Washington County, the Belgrades, Wayne Pond, west of Augusta, Unity Pond, between Augusta and Bangor, and Sebago are only a few of Maine's productive Bass waters.

Massachusetts

Moving south into industrial and densely populated Massachusetts, the angler finds less water per square mile. The intelligent stocking and management program of the Division of Fisheries and Game, however, provides Massachusetts anglers with better fishing than was ever experienced in the past.

The state has more than 1,600 lakes and ponds.

H. G. Tapply

Thomas Craven, Weston, Mass., landing a four-pound Largemouth Bass from the Sudbury River, Sudbury, Mass.

The largest of these, Quabbin Reservoir, 27,704 acres in extent, is a man-made water supply for metropolitan Boston. At Quabbin, 65 percent of the surface area and 47 miles of shoreline are open to fishing. The lake offers excellent fishing at times for Lake Trout and Brown Trout, in addition to Largemouth Bass, Chain Pickerel, and panfish.

There are 137 lakes and ponds scattered throughout the Commonwealth which qualify for trout management, and 44 of these have been reclaimed for trout. Excellent Largemouth Bass, Smallmouth Bass, and Chain Pickerel fishing may be found in the 87 reclaimed warm-water ponds subject to intensive management.

A continuing reclamation and intensive management program assures the angler of greater fishing opportunity year after year.

There are 4,230 miles of rivers within the state. The western portion of the state has several large streams which consistently produce good fishing. The best known are the Farmington, Westfield, Millers, and Deerfield, all with Brook, Brown, and Rainbow Trout. Reclamation to enhance the trout-carrying capacity and provide more sustained fishing in the Deerfield River was carried out in 1960. Similar treatment has been applied to the Tully River in the north central portion, and Squannocook River and Nashoba Brook in the northeastern portion of the state. Needed are some regulated trout stream areas, where killing is restricted, to produce quality fishing for those who prefer fishing for wild trout.

Two smaller rivers provide good fishing in eastern Massachusetts. The Shawsheen and Ipswich Rivers produce Browns and Rainbows, although they are heavily fished.

On Cape Cod, several streams yield an infrequent sea-run brook trout, or "salter."' The best known are Scorton Creek, and Santuit, Marstons' Mills, Mashpee, and Quashnet Rivers.

The mighty Connecticut River, New England's largest, rolling southward across the state, occasionally gives up a Walleye, but its fame stems from a Shad run each spring, when thousands of anglers try their luck below the dam at Holyoke. Parts of the river also hold Largemouth Bass, Smallmouth Bass, Chain Pickerel, Northern Pike, and Channel Catfish.

The Charles River, which enters the sea at Boston Harbor, and the Sudbury River, a tributary to the Merrimack, offer excellent fishing at times for Largemouth Bass, Chain Pickerel, and a variety of panfish. In the upper reaches of both rivers trout are encountered.

New Hampshire

New Hampshire, with a third of Maine's land area, has only a tenth of her larger neighbor's water surface—310 square miles. Nevertheless, fishing is a favorite sport of thousands who vacation there. One attraction is the rare Golden Trout of Sunapee Lake, a char of distinctive shape and coloration which has been recognized as a separate species *(Salvelinus aureolus)* since 1888. Sunapee Lake, a beautiful body of water lying northwest of Concord, still produces some Goldens in addition to introduced Landlocked Salmon, Rainbow Trout and Smallmouth Bass.

But Lake Winnepesaukee, the state's largest body of water, is the mecca for most visiting anglers. This great sprawling inland sea contains a bountiful supply of native Lake Trout, and is now well populated with Smallmouth Bass. Stocking

Albert Dixon Simmons

Smallmouth Bass fishing is becoming more popular every year in northern New England. This angler is fishing Sysladobsis Lake in Maine; the fish is a two-pound bass.

Manahan Studio, Hillsboro, N. H.

Second Connecticut Lake, in northern New Hampshire, produces excellent Lake Trout (togue) fishing. These fish were taken on deep-trolled bait—note rod with spoons in background.

experiments with Landlocked Salmon have proved moderately successful, and many are taken every year, especially in the area from Alton Bay to Long Island.

The northern tip of New Hampshire is similar in terrain to the wilderness of Maine. First and Second Connecticut Lakes, headwaters of the Connecticut River, offer excellent fishing at times, both for Landlocked Salmon and Lake Trout, with Brook Trout plentiful in nearby smaller waters. Other good fishing waters in the northern section of the state include the two diamond streams and the Androscoggin River.

New Hampshire has conducted an extensive Landlocked Salmon stocking program, and the species has become established successfully in Newfound Lake, west of Winnepesaukee; Squam Lake to the north, Merrymeeting to the south; and several others. However, continuous stocking is needed to maintain the supply. Many lakes have been reclaimed and stocked with Splake, Rainbows, or Brook Trout.

Although many of the smaller lakes and streams, particularly those of the White Mountain National Forest, provide excellent Brook Trout fishing, New Hampshire anglers are paying more attention to the Smallmouth Bass, now plentiful in nearly all of the larger lakes, Winnepesaukee, Winnisquam, Sunapee, and Squam Lakes all provide excellent bass fishing. Innumerable smaller ponds and lakes also contain Bass, while the warmer waters hold Pickerel, Perch, Sunfish, and Hornpout. Many of the small streams in the southern half of the state, now too warm to support native Brook Trout, have ben stocked with Browns and Rainbows and these species provide interesting fishing.

Rhode Island

Little Rhode Island, with only 1,248 square miles of land and 181 of fresh water, and all but bisected by Narragansett Bay, offers a greater attraction to the salt-water fisherman than to the fresh-water angler, but its limited inland waters provide surprisingly good fishing in the most densely populated state of the Union.

Seventy miles of trout streams depend, for the most part upon stocking to produce satisfactory fishing, but Wood River in Exeter carries Brook Trout, including a sizable spawning population. The Moosup River in Foster, and Abbots Run, in Cumberland, are excellent dry-fly streams.

Two border ponds, reclaimed in cooperation with neighboring states, provide excellent trout fishing; Wallum Lake, 320 acres, lies partly in Massachusetts, and Beach Pond, 340 acres, extends into Connecticut. Stafford Pond, in Tiverton, although considered the best Smallmouth Bass Lake in the state, also supports a thriving Rainbow and Brook Trout population. Largemouth Bass, the most popular warm-water game fish, are found in most of the state's larger lakes. Watchaug Pond, Charleston; Johnson's Pond, Coventry; Bowdish Reservoir, Gloucester; Waterman's Reservoir, Smithfield; Warwick Pond, Warwick; Brickyard Pond, Barrington; and Worden Pond, South Kingston, all have public boat launching sites and produce Bass up to eight pounds. Nearly all ponds in the state contain Yellow Perch, White Perch, Pickerel, and Bullheads.

Vermont

Vermont, with 440 square miles of water surface, is second only to Maine in water area. But much of her water is concentrated in two large bodies—Lake Champlain on the western border and Lake Memphremagog, which dips in from Quebec. Both offer excellent fishing, Champlain contains Smallmouth Bass, Walleye, Northern Pike, and Pickerel among the game fishes, the best areas being adjacent to the New Bridge, Vergennes, Shelburne Bay, Missisquoi Bay, and Grand Isle sections. Several tributaries to Lake Champlain also produce exciting Trout fishing at times, the better of these being the Missisquoi, Lamoille, and Winooski Rivers, and Otter Creek.

Lake Memphremagog is chiefly famous for the large Landlocked Salmon taken every spring from the bridge at Newport. But it also contains Brown and Rainbow Trout, Smallmouth Bass, and some Walleyes, with the best fishing in the Newport area, reached by U. S. Highway No. 5. The Clyde River, which flows into Memphremagog near Newport, offers good trout fishing in the upper stretches.

Among other large lakes in northern Vermont are Seymour, Echo, and Great and Little Averill Lakes, with Salmon, Lake Trout, Rainbow and Brook Trout; Willoughby Lake, Salmon, Brook, Lake, and Rainbow Trout; and somewhat to the south, Caspian lake, with similar fish. Most of these lakes also hold Smallmouth Bass.

The Rainbow and Brown Trout have both become better established in Vermont than in either New Hampshire or Maine, and several Vermont streams now provide fishing for these varieties. The Winooski above Plainfield offers exceptional fishing at times for both Browns and Rainbows, with an occasional Brook Trout in the early spring. Perhaps the most famous of Vermont's trout streams, however, is the Battenkill River between

Maine Dept. of Economic Development

Two heavy Brook Trout taken on Maine's Sandy River.

Manchester and the New York line. The clear waters of the 'Kill are noted for "fine and far off" fishing for Browns but Brook Trout are still plentiful. Other good trout streams include the White, Wells, and West, all of which are stocked regularly.

In mid-Vermont, several fair-sized lakes provide good fishing. Lake Dunmore, south of Middlebury, holds Landlocked Salmon, Lake Trout, Smallmouth Bass, and Northern Pike. Lake Bomoseen, west of Rutland, has Bass, Pike, and Yellow Perch while Lake St. Catherine, located near the New York line southwest of Rutland, produces Lake Trout, Bass, and Pike.

THE MIDDLE ATLANTIC STATES

These states, with the exception of New York have far fewer lakes than the New England area and, consequently are more dependent on streams for fresh water fishing.

Trout, including native Brooks and planted Rainbows and Browns provide the fishing in mountainous districts, while Smallmouth Bass are important in the clearer and cooler waters that are still too warm for Trout.

Further south, Smallmouth Bass decrease in importance, their place going more and more to their Largemouth cousins.

These states are heavily populated, but despite that fact, they furnish much good-to-excellent fishing in non-polluted waters.

Trout fishing is largely on a put-and-take basis since natural production is seldom able to meet present heavy fishing demands. The trend in planting operations is strongly toward planting only legal-sized Trout, despite the added expense.

Many waters furnishing warm-water fishing still produce abundantly by natural reproduction although some good fishing areas depend upon periodic restocking.

Delaware

Delaware enjoys a variety of fishing, ranging from worm fishing in fifty odd fresh water ponds, bay fishing in the Delaware estuary, to trolling for Tuna in the Atlantic. Depending upon an individual's taste, sport can be had throughout most of the year. Largemouth Bass, Crappie, Bluegills, Pickerel, Perch, Catfish, and Silver Chub are taken in many lakes, while tidal streams produce Shad, Herring, and Carp. In recent years more and more interest in surf casting has drawn hundreds to Delaware's beautiful public beaches bordering the Atlantic, but the biggest attraction of the year is the annual "Rock" or Striped Bass run through the Indian River Inlet between Rehoboth and Bethany Beach.

The state lists 34 fresh water ponds and lakes that are open to public fishing. These are all relatively small warm water areas, fertile, and as a rule good producers. In New Castle County, Lum's Pond near Kirkwood, and Silver and Noxentown Lakes near Middletown are the public waters. Boat liveries serve all three. Bass and Sunfish provide most of the sport with some Pickerel fishing being enjoyed. Further south in Kent County the

Maine Dev. Comm.

Mahlon Slipp, Princeton, Maine, with a two-pound Smallmouth Bass from Big Lake.

following lakes and ponds are heavily fished: Como, Massey, Silver, Wyoming, Voshell, Mud Mill, McGinnis, Andrews, Coursey, Killen, McCaulley, and Tub Mill. Wyoming, Voshell, and McGinnis Ponds are the most popular with those seeking Bass, Crappie, Sunfish, and Perch. Delaware's southern county, Sussex, has 19 impounded areas available for fishing. These lakes and ponds are similar to those already listed. They are as follows: Haven, Silver, Swiggett, Jensen, Waples, Diamond, Wagamon, Red Mills, Morris, Millsboro, Burton, Hearn, Concord, Chipman, Portsville, Records, Trap, Trussem, and Raccoon. In addition, good Bass fishing is provided by the Nanticoke River, Seaford.

It is interesting to note that about one-third of Delaware's angler licenses are sold to residents of Pennsylvania who apparently find Delaware a good place to fish.

Delaware Board, Game and Fish Comm.

A typical Delaware fresh water pond.

Maryland

Maryland's fresh water angling is not confined to any section and some fishing can be found in every part of the state. The principal cold water species are native Brook Trout, and introduced Brown and Rainbow Trout. The warm water fishes are Largemouth Bass, Smallmouth Bass, Crappie, Bluegill, Sunfish, Yellow Perch, Channel Catfish, Pickerel (locally called "Pike"), Walleyes, Shad, Striped Bass (locally called "Rock"), Silver Chub or Fallfish, and Rock Bass.

TROUT

The best trout waters are located in four western counties. Garrett County has Deep Creek Lake which supplies some deep water trout fishing. The tributaries of this lake and nearby waters are all trout streams, among which are Cherry Run (restricted to fly fishing), Bear Creek, Swallow Falls, Salt Block, Mill Creek, Wolf Run, Crabtree Run, and others. The best months for trout fishing in these and all other Maryland trout waters are May and June. Other good trout fishing waters are in Allegheny, Frederick, Howard, Montgomery, Baltimore, Harford, and Anne Arundel Counties. Many of the streams in these counties are stocked with legal size trout by the state both before and during the open season.

WARM WATER FISHES

Black Bass, Pickerel, Crappie, and Bluegills are found in almost every county. The upper Potomac River and its tributaries, which, when clear, supply some good Bass fishing, the majority being Smallmouths. Among the better tributaries are Town Creek, Wills Creek, Great Tonoloway, Conococheague, Antietam, Catoctin and Monocacy Rivers. Maryland controls the Potomac to the low water mark on the opposite shore; hence the Maryland angler's license is valid on the entire river. Good places to make headquarters on the upper river are Cumberland, Hancock, Williamsport, Frederick, Weverton, Harper's Ferry, Brunswick, and Point of Rocks.

Other good Bass waters are the Casselman at Grantsville, the Big and Little Gunpowder near Baltimore, the upper branches of the Patapsco River, Deer Creek, Octoraro River, and the Susquehanna River at Conowingo.

Deep Creek Lake in Garrett County is situated at an altitude of 3500 feet, has a shoreline of 64 miles, and supplies good angling for Bass, Crappie, Bluegills, and Yellow Perch. Good accommodations are found around and near the lake; boats and bait are available. Bait casting is popular with artificial and live bait, such as minnows, hellgrammites, and crawfish.

Triadelphia Lake in Montgomery County, controlled by the Washington, D. C., Suburban Sanitary Commission, is another popular lake. Fishing under permit is allowed in boats and from certain designated shores. Some good Bass and Crappie are taken from this body of water and below Brighton Dam.

Baltimore owns four reservoirs in Baltimore County on which fishing under restrictions is allowed. They are Prettyboy Lake, about 33 miles from the center of the city; Loch Raven, about nine miles from Baltimore; Lake Roland near the city limits; and Patapsco, on the Carroll County line. The first two mentioned produce some record Largemouth and Smallmouth Bass. No fishing is allowed from the shores, but permits and boats can be obtained at the lakes. Certain natural baits, such as large minnows, are preferred, although many fish are caught by plug fishing. Blue-

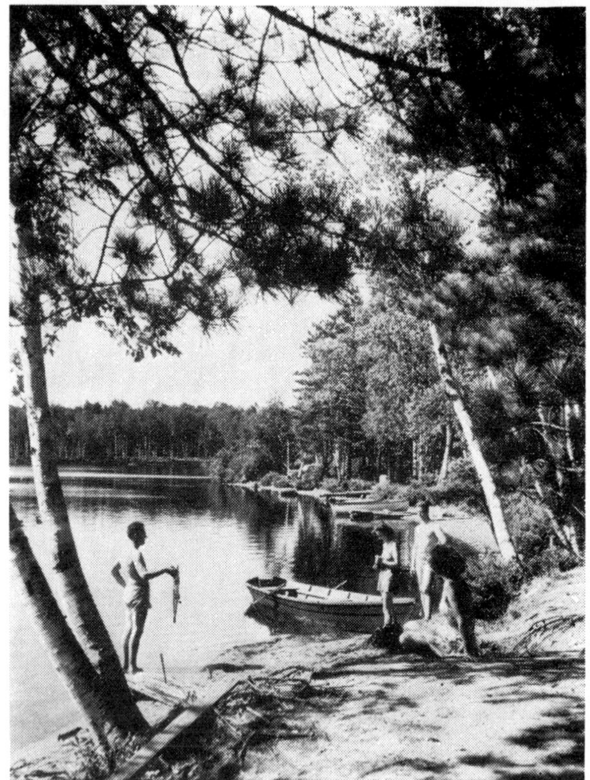

N. Y. State Conservation Dept.

Campers fishing at Fish Creek Pond camp site, Franklin County, New York.

gills and Crappie are taken on small dark colored flies, worms, or minnows. Fishing is best in June, September and October.

THE SUSQUEHANNA RIVER

There is excellent fishing at Conowingo Dam not far south of the Pennsylvania-Maryland line. Anglers are permitted on the bridge or dam, and on the shores between the dam and tidewater, a shoreline of about seven miles. There is also fishing in the lake above the dam. Striped Bass, Walleyes (locally called "Jack Salmon"), Channel Catfish, Perch, and Shad are the principal species. *Before the uninformed angler fishes the waters below the dam, he should obtain local advice regarding the currents, as the river rises rapidly when the turbines are placed in operation.*

The best time for Walleyes and Shad is May and the first part of June; the best time for Striped Bass is June, September, and October. Baits for Striped Bass are blood worms, shedder crabs, spoons, and spinners. Good Walleye bait is a June-bug spinner with blood worms and minnows.

PONDS AND FRESH TIDAL WATERS

Largemouth Bass and Pickerel are taken by the angler from nearly all fresh tidal waters of upper Chesapeake Bay. The best Pickerel fishing is found in such waters. Many of these estuaries have dams near their headwaters, and in such cases fishing is good both below and above the dams. Most of these ponds are on the Eastern Shore. At Frazer's Pond, near Chesapeake City, artificials, plugs, and bugs are best. Millington Pond, Unicorn Pond, one at Wye Mills, one at Still Pond, one at Smithsville, several near Pocomoke City, and also at Snow Hill are also open to fishing. Crappie grow unusually large in these ponds.

The rivers below these ponds offer excellent angling if boats are available. Artificial lures are mostly used. The Pickerel bite during the summer months in the ponds. However, they strike better in the rivers in early summer, late summer, and the fall. Good rivers are the Bohemia, Sassafras, Chester, Choptank, Transquaking, Black Water, Wicomico, and Pocomoke. Some of these rivers are almost virgin waters to the angler due to the lack of boats, and prospective fishermen should carry their own boats.

PIKE (PICKEREL)

Fishing for this species in fresh, tidal waters is worth special mention. The spring and fall, when the water is cool, are best times. Live minnows produce more fish but many are taken on artificials. Baits, using pork rind and spoons, are popular with both fishermen and fish. Among the best known among such waters are the Gunpowder River, Salt Petre, Dundee, Seneca, and the tributaries of Middle River, such as Sue's and Norman's Creeks, all in Baltimore County.

Anne Arundel County has the Magothy, Severn, South and West Rivers and tributaries. Near the head of the Chesapeake Bay are the North East and Elk Rivers, and the Susquehanna River at Havre de Grace. Pike also are found in most bass waters throughout the state.

STRIPED BASS (ROCK)

About the only place in Maryland, in non-tide waters, to take Stripers and Walleyes is the Susquehanna River from the dam to where Deer Creek enters it, which is the head of tidewaters. Best baits are shedder crabs, minnows, blood worms, and grass shrimp. Artificials are also good, red and white colors being preferable. There is no maximum limit on Striped Bass in non-tidal waters.

SHAD

The Susquehanna River below the Conowingo Dam is famous for its sport fishing for Shad. Shad are also taken from the upper Patuxent River in Anne Arundel County. The best lures are white and red streamer flies; bucktail flies are also good. Small spoons such as the 00 Drone, and smaller Nungesser, are extensively used, and the Trixoreno is very good. May 1 to June 20 is the best time to take both White and Hickory Shad.

New Jersey

The majority of New Jersey's inland waters are stocked or managed with those species best adapted to existing environment and lists of stocked lakes and streams can be secured from the Division of Fish and Game, State House, Trenton, New Jersey.

TROUT

Trout fishing is largely confined to the streams

N. Y. State Conservation Dept.

Trout fishing in the Adirondacks.

of the central and northern districts. Rainbow, Brook, and Brown Trout are available to the trout fisherman. The best known streams are Big Flat Brook, Little Flat Brook, Pequest, and Paulinskill (Sussex County); Musconetcong, Passaic, Rockaway, Black Brook, and Raritan (Morris County); the Hackensack, Saddle River, Ramapo, Pascack, Pequannock, Wanaque, High Mount, Preakness, Sproat, and Bear Brook (Bergen and Passaic Counties); the famed Gorge of the South Branch of the Raritan, Spruce Run, Mulhockaway (Hunterdon County), and shares with Warren County the opportunities offered by the Musconetcong; the South and North Branch of the Raritan River with the Indian Graves Brook and Middle Brook (Somerset County). In the south the Manalapan, Millstone, Wigwam, Shark, Topenemus, Hockhocksen, Manasquan, Stoney Brook, the Big and Little Lebanon, Trout, Beaver Brook, and Rowands Pond are the more important trout fishing spots.

Portions of Big Flat Brook, Paulinskill, Pequest River and that part of the South Branch of the Raritan known as The Gorge, have been set aside for fly fishing only after May 7. On other waters, the angler may chose any lure. There are fishermen using dry flies, wet flies, spinner and fly, spinner and worm, night crawlers, and variations of the above combinations on all trout streams. Dry fly enthusiasts find the larger streams, namely the Big Flat Brook, Paulinskill, Pequest, Musconetcong, Rockaway, and the South Branch of the Raritan best suited for his purpose, but this method of fishing is used on many other trout waters of the state.

WARM WATER SPECIES

Lakes also present an opportunity to angle for several species of fish. Pickerel and Largemouth Bass are the more prevalent but Yellow Perch, Smallmouth Bass, Bluegill Sunfish, Rock Bass, Crappie, and Catfish are also often present. The more important northern and central lakes are Lake Hopatcong, Greenwood Lake, Budd Lake, Lake Wawayanda, Cranberry Lake, Swartswood Lake, Mountain Lake, Pompton Lakes, Manalapan, Farrington Lake, Lake Solitude, Carnegie Lake, and several watershed reservoirs such as Clinton, Wanaque, Oak Ridge, Canistear, and Split Rock.

Further south are Union Lake, Lake Lenape, Rainbow Lake, Malaga Lake, Browns Mills Lake, Colliers Mills Lake, Medford Lake, Hammonton Lake, Atsion Lake, Sylvan Lake, Cooper Lake, Dennisville Lake, Cedarville Lake, Laurel Lake, Menantice Pond and Willow Grove Lake provide similar fishing. The Tuikahue Public Hunting and Fishing grounds are outstanding.

Many streams listed as trout waters become warmer in their lower reaches and support Bass and Pickerel, as well as other fishes. The Raritan, Ramapo, Rompton, Millstone, and Passaic, are good examples of such streams. The Mullica, Maurice, Egg Harbor, and Wading Rivers further south also provide fishing for warm-water fish especially pickerel.

The use of live bait is widely popular but bass bugs, plug casting, bucktails, and spinners are seemingly increasing in popularity. Trolling also produces results on the larger lakes.

The upper Delaware River is well known for

Walleyes and Smallmouth Bass, yearly offering sport to hundreds of fishermen. Trolling and drifting are favored methods of fishing this stream.

Inland tidal streams provide hours of fishing to those who desire to catch White Perch, catfish, and eels, Shad and herring are caught in good quantities in the Delaware River.

Ice fishing for Pickerel, Walleyes, Perch, Carp, and Suckers is permitted for a limited season.

New York

The Empire State, despite its millions of inhabitants, offers a wide range of fishing opportunities. The fishing waters consist of 2,300 lakes, ponds, and reservoirs, 65,000 miles of fishable streams and rivers, 600 miles of salt water coastline on Long Island, and great expanses of the adjacent Atlantic. To list all the places where each game fish species is taken is obviously impossible and only major angling spots are mentioned.

TROUT

The Adirondack region abounds with Brook Trout ponds and streams, but the upper Oswegatchie river system—Cranberry Lake and its tributary waters, particularly the Inlet River up to High Falls—is the largest and best known native Brook Trout area. Other outstanding Brook Trout waters are the Beaver River with its Stillwater reservoir in eastern Lewis and northwestern Herkimer counties; Cedar River and the remote West Canada Lakes, usually reached by seaplane, in Hamilton County.

As soon as the ice goes out in the Adirondacks, bait fishermen, using worms, go after the big Trout. Later, they seek them in the springholes created by tributary streams. Wet flies, particular Parmachene Belles and Montreals, streamer and small spinners, with or without bait, are used then.

The best Brown Trout waters are in the Catskills. They include the Beaverkill, East Branch of the Delaware, the Willowemoc, Neversink, Mongaup, Schoharie, and The Esopus. Fishermen on these streams have developed many outstanding dry fly patterns, most famous of which are the Fan-wing Royal Coachman, Henderickson, Beaverkill, Cahill, and Quill Gordon. Ashokan and Kensico reservoirs are also Catskill waters famed for the big Browns, and the state record Brown, 19 lb. 14 oz., came from Ashokan.

Other productive Brown Trout waters include the famous Ausable and Salmon River of the northern Adirondack region, the Battenkill and Kinderhook of the east central district, the Salmon River reservoirs of Oswego County, the Cohocton River in southern and the East Koy and Wiscoy in western New York.

Although the purists entice their Browns to rise and strike with dry flies of countless patterns, there are quite a few anglers who take substantial catches of big fish with minnow rigs.

Most famous Rainbow Trout water is Catherine Creek in the Finger Lakes region. That tributary of Seneca Lake, each year produces an exceptional poundage of big fish—some weighing over 15 pounds. Almost as well known are Naples Creek (tributary to Canandaigua Lake) and the Inlet to Keuka Lake. The state record Rainbow, 21 lbs., came from Keuka Lake.

Calvin E. Conklin

The north branch of the Susquehanna River between Mehoopany and Tunkhannock in Pennsylvania.

Fishing in the various tributaries of these lakes is best during the spring spawning run, and flies, lures, and baits of every kind are used. Natural baits make many catches, but use of fish eggs is now prohibited. Rainbows also are taken in the lakes by surface trolling with light spoons.

Ashokan Reservoir (Catskills) has a spring run of Rainbows that average four to five pounds. Schoharie Creek, lying north of Ashokan, also offers good Rainbow fishing. Although dry flies are used by a few anglers on the Schoharie with great success, most fishermen employ other lures.

Seneca Lake is outstanding Lake Trout water. Keuka and Cayuga, also of the Finger Lakes; a large group of Adirondack lakes, including Lake George, and Kensico Reservoir in the Catskills are other good Lake Trout waters. A copper line and spoon, fished deep, are most commonly used, but in the Finger Lakes, the Seth Green rig, a hand-line trolling outfit with leaders for spoons or live bait at different levels is popular.

MUSKELLUNGE

Chautauqua Lake's Tiger or Barred Musky fishing is widely known. The present record is 42 lbs. 8 oz. More Muskies are taken annually in Chautauqua than in other New York waters (8,540 in 1948), but the biggest fish (a different sub-species) came from the St. Lawrence River, another good Musky spot. It weighed 58 lbs. 5 oz. Muskies also are taken in the Chazy River. Trolling with spoons and jointed plugs is the usual technique. Best angling is in the late summer and fall.

WARM WATER SPECIES

The best known Smallmouth Bass area is the eastern Lake Ontario-St. Lawrence River region. Lake Champlain, particularly the northern half, is another productive Smallmouth water. Chautauqua Lake in western New York, Kensico Reservoir, and Friend's Lake outlet in Warren County are also good. The state record Smallmouth is a nine-pounder from Friend's Lake outlet. For Largemouths, Black Lake and the southern end of Chautauqua Lake and Kensico are good. Sacandaga Reservoir, in the southern Adirondacks, produced the state record fish, two weighing 10 lbs. 8 ozs. each.

Although probably most Smallmouth Bass are taken with live bait, small spoons, plugs, and big flies are used extensively. For Largemouths, it's bait casting and spinning with lures.

Sacandaga Reservoir produces the biggest Northern Pike; in fact, the world's record, 46 lbs. 2 ozs., but for fast fishing, Champlain is one of the best. Other good waters are the St. Lawrence River, Sandy Pond on Lake Ontario, Indian Lake, and Long Lake in the Adirondacks. Bait casting, trolling, and still fishing with minnows are employed.

Oneida Lake is famous for its Pike fishing. Lake Champlain also produces great quantities of Walleye with fish generally distributed over much of the lake during most of the year, and the Rouses Point area producing good catches in the spring. Pike also are abundant in Lake Erie and the Niagara River. Other good spots are Black Lake and Sacandaga Reservoir. The state record Walleye was a 14 lb. 7 oz. fish caught in Oak Orchard Creek. The most common practice for Walleye is trolling a June bug spinner, baited with worms. Catches are best in May and June and in the fall.

Calvin E. Conklin

A shady stretch along Standing Stone Creek in Huntingdon County, Pennsylvania.

Sunfish, Rock Bass, Yellow Perch, Crappies, and Bullheads abound in every region. An old pole, a hook-and-line, and a can of worms are enough, but there are many who use flies and light tackle for these fish.

Pennsylvania

Pennsylvania has more than 4,400 miles of streams and 63 lakes, which include 2,656 acres of water which are stocked with Trout. There are 2,000 miles of warm-water streams and rivers, and approximately 57,000 acres of ponds and lakes containing warm-water fish.

The Fish Commission annually stocks more than two and one-half million trout in its attempt to supplement the native population. The warm-water fisheries program is being expanded. The Muskellunge stocking program, which began in 1953 with the release of 840 fingerlings, had developed to include the distribution of more than 20,000 fingerlings annually by 1962. The range of the Muskellunge, which was originally confined to waters mostly in the northwestern region of the state, has been extended to include some 45 water areas in 32 counties, as a result of management work done by the Pennsylvania Fish Commission.

The Walleye is found in the large rivers, the Delaware, Juniata, Susquehanna and Allegheny.

McKeesport Daily News

Trout fishing in a typical Pennsylvania mountain stream.

It is also present in many lakes, and excellent fishing for this species is found in large lakes and reservoirs, such as Pymatuning, Conneaut and Wallenpaupack. Although Walleye fishing is best in the larger rivers and lakes, some small lakes provide good fishing.

Some good Northern Pike fishing can be enjoyed in Conneaut Lake, Conneaut Marsh, and Canadonta Lake in Crawford County. In Mercer County, Otter Creek, Sandy Creek, Nechannock Creek and Sandy Lake also provide Pike fishing, and some Northerns are caught in French Creek and the Allegheny River in Venango County. Presque Isle Bay on Lake Erie is another popular Pike water. In addition to these waters, Northerns were introduced in the Crooked Creek Flood Control Reservoir in Armstrong County; Glade Run Lake, Butler County; Sugar Lake, Crawford County; Eaton Reservoir, Erie County; Somerset Lake, Somerset County; and the Youghiogheny Flood Control Reservoir.

The Pickerel is a popular game fish of the northeastern portion of the Commonwealth, particularly in the Pocono region. An inhabitant of many of the lakes and streams which are tributaries of the Susquehanna and Delaware Rivers, this pike is not found in the western counties which lie in the Allegheny drainage.

Bass, Bluegills, Crappies and other species of warm-water fishes are found in most of the waters of the Commonwealth.

The Conservation Education Division of the Pennsylvania Fish Commission has published a complete guide to the fishing and boating waters of Pennsylvania. The booklet gives the name of the water area, the name of the nearest town, and the highway by which it is reached. Anyone planning to fish in Pennsylvania should acquire a copy.

The Spring Creek area, world-renowned as "Fisherman's Paradise," where prior to 1962 an angler was permitted to keep one trout per day, now is equally popular as a spot where the fly fisherman may still catch large trout, but is not permitted to keep any of the fish. A "fish for fun" area is open to fishing the year around.

For many years special fly-fishing-only areas have been extremely popular in Pennsylvania. Some 28 such areas, including 88 miles of the total 4,400 miles of streams, have been established. The Fish Commission annually publishes a listing of these areas along with the special regulations.

In addition to the many miles of streams open to public fishing within the boundaries of the millions of acres of land owned by the Pennsylvania Game Commission and the Pennsylvania Department of Forests and Waters, there also are 108 miles of major trout streams located within the Allegheny National Forest. The Forest comprises part of Elk, Forest, McKean and Warren Counties.

THE SOUTHEASTERN STATES

In this group of states, extending from the Potomac River to the Gulf of Mexico, Largemouth Bass, together with the associated species of Sunfish, Perch, and Crappies, furnish most of the fishing. Smallmouth Bass are found largely in the Piedmont section, decreasing in importance to the south.

Trout waters are limited to mountainous, western sèctions which are more extensive in Virginia and North Carolina than in those states to the south. The coastal plain offers the greatest quantity of sport fishing and the quality is high. In addition to Largemouth Bass, the Redbreast Sunfish attract many anglers, and Striped Bass are important in the lower reaches of most rivers. Crappies and many species of panfish are found in abundance, sustained largely, if not entirely, by natural reproduction.

Alabama

From the deep blue waters of the Guntersville Reservoir, to the reefs of Mobile Bay, anglers in Alabama find many excellent fishing waters.

The principal lakes in which the sport-fish are to be found are those impounded waters of the Tennessee Valley Authority, the many hidden swamp-lakes in the interior, and the multitude of farm-ponds that dot the entire state. The rivers that yield their annual crop of Catfish, Bream, Bass, and Pike are the Tombigbee, Alabama, Warrior, Coosa, and Tallapoosa.

Perhaps the most sought after fish, in the opinion of the "plugger" or "spinner" is the Bass, either the Large or Smallmouth. These are the men who support the sport-fishing industry. No artificial lure is too expensive; no rod is beyond Bass fisherman's pocketbook if he feels it will catch fish better than the one that he is using. The sputter of his outboard motor can be heard as he starts out for either a favorite or new hole in the body of water he is satisfied will yield the biggest Bass of the year. His fishing range extends the entire distance from Tennessee to the Gulf, and from Georgia to Mississippi. His favorite spots are likely to be the deep swamp lakes that are seldom fished, or the impounded waters of some power reservoir. When all of these fail he will try to get all the fish out of the nearest farm pond and, many owners of these ten- to fifty-acre ponds, have made a tidy sum from the bass-fisherman's pocketbook.

Near the end of the season such lures as a jointed minnow, a red-head, lucky thirteen, or a pumpkinseed are worth their weight in gold. There is some doubt as to which the fisherman values most; the lure that might catch fish or the fish itself.

The fly fisherman, either wet or dry, is just as enthusiastic about the Bass family, but their numbers are nowhere near as high as the rod and reel plugger. The two of them are usually after the same fish, the Basses, but they use slightly different spots and techniques. The fly fisherman, because of his lighter tackle will get a greater thrill out of a medium-sized "Bream" or Crappie than will the plug fisherman. This usually means that the fly-fisherman will catch more fish in a day's pleasure, but perhaps not the big ones that the plug-man is after. Either way is pleasant and it is entirely a personal choice.

There is another method of fishing that has created interest among fishermen. It is the system known as "jigger-fishing." A long bamboo pole with a very short line extending about sixteen inches from the end is used. The pole is bent at the end so that the tip will drag in the water. From the end of the short line an underwater plug is suspended. This plug trails behind the pole-tip about six inches beneath the surface. As the boat moves slowly along, the tip of the long pole just drags the surface of the water, and as it is moves along the weed margin, the butt of the pole is gently tapped with the anglers free hand. This causes the pole to riffle the water and to make a sound that is attractive to hungry fish. As a fish rises to investigate, the plug comes loafing by. Consistently the fish take the lure. Some states have already outlawed the system because it catches too many game fish, but it is legal in this state and promises to grow into an even greater system of catching fish.

Down in the deep swamps where the Bass fisherman loves to try his luck, there is one fish which is always ready to add sport but not fish to the day's enjoyment. This is the Bowfin, known by many names such as Mudfish, Blackfish, and in many cases as "tackle-buster." It is unexcelled as a fighting fish and with its sharp teeth it has severed many a leader. It has a very boney mouth

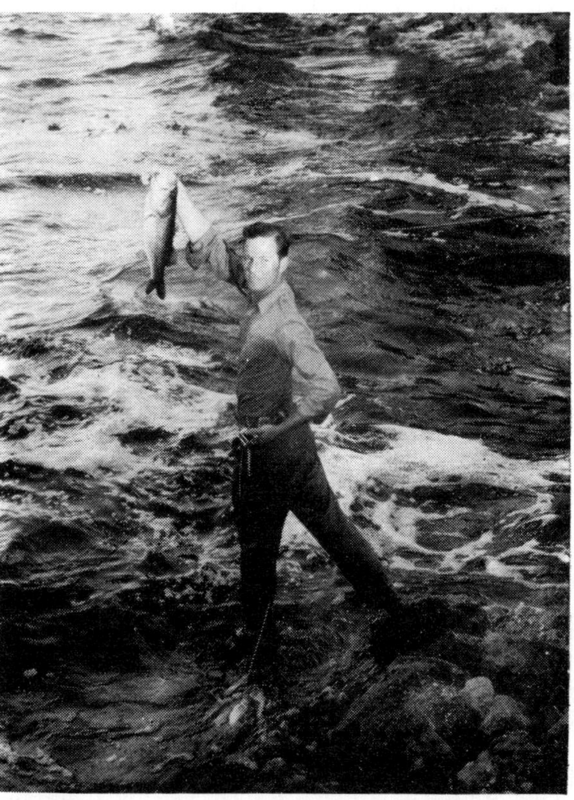

Florida Game & Fresh Water Fish Comm.

Fishing the roiled waters near one of Okeechobee's many spillways.

and the hook must be set firmly to bring the creature to the net, but when firmly hooked, it will put on a show that is well worth watching. Some of them reach very large size, and many are caught weighing over ten pounds. Unfortunately they are not very good eating, and their appearance is anything but appetizing. Once the fisherman gets used to seeing them, he will find greater and greater enjoyment in landing them.

The greatest number of fishermen are those men who go "fishin" for the relaxation and absence of action, or else for the sole purpose of getting something for the frying pan. These are the pole fishermen. No license is required in Alabama for this type of fishing and this further adds to the reasons for fishing in this manner. There are two types of fishermen using this system. One being the individual who is out for meat, and the other who hopes that if they are biting, they are not biting too fast. The first will be found busy with from one to five poles over the side of his boat, industriously working the likely looking spots. The other, of which there is an equal number, will be found in a shady spot under a tree, his line in the water, with or without a baited hook, sleeping the warm afternoon away. He, in his own opinion, is having just as good a time as the fly-fisherman, and that is what fishing is for, having a good time.

The pole fisherman is after any and all species of edible fish. Catfish, "Bream," Stumpknockers, Bass, Pike, and Warmouth Bass are all eligible for his fish-box. His favorite spot is where there are fish regardless of location or accessibility, and on week-ends lines of cars with poles attached are seen leaving the cities heading towards fishing sites through-out the entire state.

There are nearly 400,000 acres of large impoundments in Alabama, and they are made available to the angler by nearly 50 public access areas. These are 30,000 miles of public streams; plenty of water for all, and near all good fishing areas boats and guides are available at small cost. In addition there are more than enough areas that are open to the fisherman who either has his own boat, or has the determination to get to the more inaccessible spots, and public landings are everywhere.

There is another type of fishing in Alabama that, in the past, has been out of the reach of the average pocketbook, and that is salt-water fishing. The most common method is to use a small boat, a heavy rod and reel, a motor and a pail of fresh shrimp or mullet. By going upstream into the tidewater marshes there are to be found deep pockets in the tidal streams, and into these pockets are heaved a line with a hook with live bait. By watching the bobber which is attached to the line, the angler will soon know when to haul in on the line. What may be at the other end is a question. It may range from a big Striper weighing thirty pounds to a piece of driftwood going out with the tide, or it may be a Gar that is too big to land safely in a small boat. For excitement, this type of fishing can't be beat when they are striking, but many are the days that are spent getting a sunburn and nothing else.

However you fish, and whatever type of warm water fishing you prefer, Alabama can furnish it someplace within its extensive waters. The waters are available, and the amount of fish that one may catch depends entirely on skill and enthusiasm.

N. B. Webster and H. S. Caywood with a string of Florida Lightning—the St. Johns River Shad.

Florida

Florida has the largest inland water area of any state; its 4,298 square miles of lakes and rivers, ponds and streams top the 4,059 square miles of water in Minnesota. There are 30,000 lakes and 166 fresh water rivers in its 56,560 square miles.

It is possible to fish for a Bass from Pensacola to southwest of Homestead; a distance greater than that between Chicago and New York City. Conversely, there are focal points from which hundreds of lakes can be reached with but little driving.

Climate is dependent upon geography. During the winter months temperature tapers from the frosty northwest to the sub-tropical southeast. And the climate stamps its pattern on the fishing.

The Largemouth Bass is king in Florida's fresh waters. While found in many states, nowhere else does the effort to take Black Bass approach that of the Palm State. Few counties go for a year without a 10-pound Bass. A 10-pounder is considered large, but fish of from 15 to 19 pounds are required to better all-time records at the better lakes and rivers. So great is the interest in this species that a $50,0000 contest, based on tagged fish, was started at Lake Apopka.

State biologists point out that Bass spawn almost the year around; the supply is often so great it stunts average growth. Commercial netting, properly controlled, may be helpful to sports anglers. In applying this information, there is no closed season on Bass in nine-tenths of the state, no minimum length, and commercial fishing is permitted under close supervision.

Bass waters are eveywhere. The true addict will explore most of them over the years. Having decided on the section he likes, he will settle down, and the day he begins homesteading, news will reach him that "the big ones are biting" a few, or a few hundred, miles away.

Briefly, the best Bass months are the October-December and March-May periods. December is perhaps the finest month in south Florida. December-February are usually tops in mid-Florida. June is often a fine carry-over month in the northern part. October can be tricky in the southern portion. The Kissimmee water table can overflood river banks. Hurricanes frequently stimulate or retard Bass lakes, notable Okeechobee.

The paragraphs that follow are fraught with dynamite. Floridians take fierce pride in their favorite bodies of water. Each one listed below leaves dozens that go un-named. Space becomes a problem with 30,000 lakes to consider. Therefore, each body of water should be multiplied by at least ten.

For big Bass, the rivers present an easier target than the lakes. Two stand out. The St. Johns is thought to be the best in the state. Those intimate with the Kissimmee will argue the point. Fisheating Creek is a powerhouse when its table is normal. The Withlacoochee, Ochlockonee, and Ocklawaha Rivers are frequently discussed with doffed hats.

The St. Johns is unusual from many standpoints. For the lower 100 miles of its 250 mile length, the St. Johns is wider than the Mississippi. Its entire coursing is in a northerly direction; one of two such flows in the nation. More than 100 boat liveries and fishing camps dot the banks; a mute testimony to its appeal. The St. Johns even supports Noah's Ark, a luxurious house boat. However, skiffs and cane poles are a more common sight.

Numerous river widenings and lakes augment the St. Johns story. The lake George-Ocklawaha region is rated by many as the prime Bass sector; but that would be forgetting Lake Helen Blazes (Brevard County). Blazes is the headwater lake for the St. Johns. More than 40 Bronzebacks topping 10 pounds were caught there in one year.

The Lake county is properly named. Its 1400 lakes and ponds make it a true bass headquarters, with the Clermont chain being internationally famous. Yet, closeby is underpublicized Marion County. There one contacts a Cracker resident, picks up a car-top skiff, and ventures into unnamed ponds of from 5 to 25 or more acres. They are spring-fed, clear, deep sand-bottomed ponds that warrant further exploitation.

Lake Okeechobee is not only the largest lake in the state, it is the second largest wholly within continental United States. 'Chobee is also the best Florida lake for consistent bags of Bass from 2 to 8 pounds, and its ability to withstand terrible angling pressure is a present-day phenomenon.

Orange Lake (Alachua County), with its floating islands, connects to Lake Lochloosa by Cross Creek, a mile-long canal eulogized by Marjorie Kinnan Rawlins. Big Bass are found there. Lake Griffin (Lake County) is played by experienced hands for big Bass.

Brief biographies on other excellent lakes for large Bass are: Lake Marion (Osceola County) where Largemouths of 15 pounds, 5 ounces, and 13 pounds fell to one rod in a single day in 1948; the St. Johns River and its famous chain of lakes, not excluding Lakes Trestle, Sawgrass, Washing-

Florida Game & Fresh Water Fish Comm.

Bass fishing in the canal system leading into Floridas famed Lake Okeechobee.

Florida Game & Fresh Water Fish Comm.

Florida canal fishing is productive of good catches.

ton, Winder, Ponsett, Cone, Harney, Jessup, Monroe, Beresford, Dexter, and Doctors; the famed Tsala-Apopka group (Citrus-Sumter Counties) with emphasis on the outer, smaller ponds and backwaters; nearby Panasoffskee (Sumter County), for similar fare; the Clermont chain (Lake County) for more of the same; Istapoga (Highlands County) for a top south Florida spot; Lake Apopka (Orange-Lake Counties) because this lake is on its way back now that the sewage disposal plant at Winter Haven has removed a deadening algae bloom.

From there the list multipilies in geometric proportion, finally reaching the ultimate goal of 30,000. That's because one respected authority said every lake contains Bass, big or otherwise.

One of the smallest bodies of water, the drainage canals triangling out to Road 27 (Dade and Broward Counties), may have produced two of the greatest day's bags of small Bass. Three flycasters worked Road 27, in 1939, and got about 1,100 bass. In 1948, a pair of fly casters used a pocket adding machine (it actually happened) to tally 515 small Bronzebacks, to 5½ pounds. Only the limits were kept in either instance.

There are hundreds of miles of such ditches; big Bass dwell in some; small ones in others; and all play host to pan fish. Live bait fishermen catch the most big Bass. Best live bait is the Florida shiner, used in 4 to 6 inch sizes. Live catfish, frogs, small panfish, fresh and salt water shrimp, eels, and the seasonal "shadline" minnows are standard, too. Still others broadcast bits of bread, oatmeal, etc., to attract pan fish, then use live baits, plugs, or flies to take maurading Bass lured by the concentration of pannies.

Plugcasters now complain that things are not what they used to be. Maybe the constant parade of cast plugs has inbred caution into successive bass generations. Best tip, then, is to use 10 to 30 feet of monofilament Nylon leader ahead of regulation braided Nylon or silk bait casting lines. Nylon's lowered visibility would favor the plug caster.

Most commonly topped plugs are Dalton Specials, Johnson and Chum spoons (#2 size), and pet 15 spoon, all usually with pork rind; River Runt, River Runt Spook, Lucky 13; Creek Chub 2000 series, particularly 2019 and 2014; unjointed Pikie Minnow; Hawaiian Wiggler; Hula Popper; Florida Shiner; Eger Silver Flash; underwater Dillinger, with fore-and-aft spinner, in black-yellow and black-range colors; and 10,000 others, including many marvelous home-made plugs of local origin.

Fly fishermen split into two main groups—those favoring popping bugs and those who prefer streamer flies. Colors for the former run to solid yellow, black, white, orange, and frog-green. Combination colors almost always include white, red, and yellow. One standard streamer fly features white hackle, red and yellow wings.

Far more Floridians go after panfish than Bass. One reason is that canepolers can operate within the county of their legal residence without a license; another is that thousands of Floridians were born and raised in the noble Cracker tradition of fried fish and hushpuppies. A real Cracker is a fine hand at collecting the makin's for a fish fry.

Florida's panfishing is unequalled. Millions of pannies are caught each year. Exaggeration is almost impossible. The species represented are Bream (Bluegill, Copperhead, or Sunfish) which is more commonly taken than other species. It is almost everywhere, attains a size in excess of two pounds, and is a preferred good fish. Speckled Perch (Speeks, Crappie, or Calico Bass) run second in volume, first in size, among panfishes. A four-pound, nine-ounce Speck is a matter of record. The average weight is half a pound.

Prettiest of the inland midgets is the Redbreast (Redbelly), which is usually found in flowing waters. The Stumpknocker, a southern speciality, seems to prefer fast, small streams to the larger rivers, will take a fly and is much sought, especially in the panhandle counties. The Shellcracker is a good eating panster that approximates the Bream in size. It is generally found in sand-bottomed lakes.

The Warmouth (Warmouth Perch or Goggle-eye) can top a gross weight of one pound, likes mud-bottomed lakes and canals, and is a favorite with canepolers.

The catfish tribe—Channel, Yellow, and Speckled—is becoming more popular as food fish among some anglers. They are found in all types of waters. Set-line fishing for cats draws many Georgia and Alabama natives to north Florida.

A few renowned panfishing places are the same Orange-Cross Creek-Lochloosa triumvirate mentioned in connection with Bass (A Speck of more than four pounds was caught from Orange Lake in 1948); Dead Lakes (Gulf and Calhoun Counties) are a Bream heaven (Imagine an opening day with "half of Georgia and Alabama" filling over 1,000 skiffs and taking more than 20,000 bream); Ocheesee Pond (all 7,000 acres of it) and Blue Springs (Jackson County), where The Pond is shrouded in moss-decked trees, and where Bream chew catalpa worms for breakfast, lunch, and dinner.

With Withlacoochee River, home of big Bream, Shellcracker, and Redbreast, is also possessed of marvelous scenery and a 14,000 acre "backwater" area; the Wakulla River (Wakulla County); the Wacissa-Aucilla Rivers (Jefferson, Taylor, and Madison Counties); and the St. Johns River are famed Redbreast grounds; Lake Okeechobee, for Bream and Specks; the cut-off canal from Lake Istapoga to the Kissimmee River for Specks and Bream; the Wakulla and Wacissa, this time for Stumpknockers; the Suwannee (of Stephen Foster fame), for Redbellies, Stumpknockers, Shellcrackers, Bream and Warmouth, in addition to Bass, plus the controversial Smallmouth, a stunted localized species; Panasoffkee Lake and Shellcrackers go together like Lake Harris (Lake County) and Speckled Perch; and ad infinitum.

Live baits run the gamut of nature's providence. These include red worms, earthworms, various minnows, crickets, grasshoppers, bee-worms, roaches, catalpa worms, fresh water shrimp, pieces of white bacon, and bits of cloth.

Plugs, used with comparative sparingness, run to small spoons, spinners, and midget eagle claw lures. Trolling with plugs is often used to locate schools, at which point live bait, plug, spin, or fly casting takes over.

Flies are broken down into three classes: 1) Black and yellow popping bugs; 2) McGinty-type flies plus No. 3 Hildebrandt spinners for sinking flies: 3) Parmachene belles and like classicals for the dry fly fanatics.

Spinning, although not yet widely used, should come into its own. Some anglers already rotate spin and fly tackle. The fomer is used to reach past the natural range of light fly sticks. Clear lakes, too, would offer spinners an edge over plugging tackle, except where obstructions are prevalent, as at Lake Talquin.

A third general field of fishing exists. This is the catch-all or miscellaneous class. Thumbnail sketches cover a number of ways to bring home the bacon and please the inner and mental man. It is common practice, among many, to work the brackish areas of certain rivers. Salt water species are thus added to the legal inland bag.

Seatrout are taken in this fashion on the Steinhatches (Dixie County), Aucilla, and other west coast rivers; and Tarpon have upset the calculations of Bass fishermen on the Peace River (Charlotte and DeSoto Counties) and the Caloosahatchee River (Lee County). The famed North Fork of the St. Lucie River (Martin and St. Lucie Counties) offers a mixed bag of salt and fresh water species. The Caloosahatchee River between the locks at Alva and Artona can be a paradise for Snook, Bass, and Tarpon, though it is little publicized.

The Road 27 sector sports Tarpon to 50 pounds; the Tamiami Trail is frequently a fly and plugger's dream. No license is required to cast the stretch from west of the town of Ochoppee to Bridge 38 (Collier County). Here, Snook and Tarpon have combined to push Bass offstage.

Shad fishing sent out roots in 1942. Discovered at Deland (Volusia County), this St. Johns River pastime has created specialists from November to May. A derby is sponsored in March.

Deep trolling with fly rods, monofilament-type Nylon or plastic lines and small Reflecto or Drone spoons is a killing method. One angler took 34 Shad in one day.

Striped Bass are also known throughout the state. A 39-pounder rang a clarion note at the dam on the Ochlockonee River. The Escambia River (Escambia-Santa Rosa Counties), gives up Stripers, although the accent is on a salt water approach. The Striper is highly regarded at Jacksonville. During the summer months this sport is fairly well confined to Black Creek which flows into the St. Johns near Green Cove Springs. But the real emphasis takes place during the winter time. The Nassau River (Nassau County) and the St. Marys and little St. Marys Rivers (Florida-Georgia border) are concentration points. Plugs like River Runts, Pal-o-Mines, and Vamp Spooks are killers. Large streamer flies should work, though little has yet been done.

No world marks have been set, but six or seven fish is considered a good day's bag. After high water slack is the time to prepare for action.

Georgia

Abundant water and a zestful climate make Georgia a year-round fishing state. There are 15 major reservoirs in the state with a total with a total of 257,933 acres, in addition to 17 large rivers which flow some 2,818 miles across Georgia before entering the sea. Also, there are 700 miles of cold-water trout streams in north Georgia, and approximately 3,00 miles of smaller tributary warm-water streams. Small lakes and ponds number over 40,000, which adds to the fishing facilities for the state's legion of anglers and its visitors.

This vast water area teems with fish, and offers anglers a variety of challenges. There are 124

Florida Game & Fresh Water Fish Comm.

A Florida black beauty.

distinct species of game, pan, and forage fish in Georgia. Georgia fishing runs the gamut from Trout fishing in north Georgia to fishing for Spanish Mackerel on the coast. In north Georgia, the mountain streams are naturally populated with three species of Trout—Rainbow, Brown and Brook. Lakes Burton and Rabun in north Georgia are excellent Trout lakes as well as good spots for Bass, Crappie and Bream. Lake Blue Ridge, which is the southernmost point for good Muskellunge fishing, has much to offer anglers. Good fishing is found in Lake Blue Ridge for Bass, Crappie, Bream and Walleyes. Largemouth Bass, also known as "trout" or "green trout," are the prize game fish in most of the state. They are found in all backwater sloughs and slow-moving rivers as well as many of the mountain impoundments. Largemouth are the most widely distributed and abundant of the larger sport fish and provide more sport to anglers than any other game fish. The Kentucky Spotted Bass and Smallmouth Bass are found in the swifter streams of the central and northern parts of the state. Smallmouths are found, for the most part, in north Georgia.

Impoundments include Lakes Clark Hill, Allatoona, Jackson, Blue Ridge, Nottely, Chatuge, Burton, Rabun, Sinclair, Bartlett's Ferry, Goat Rock, Oliver, Blackshear, Worth, Seminole, and Lanier. These favored spots are frequently visited by anglers. Fishing from the mountains to the black-water swamp areas of south Georgia offers a striking contrast.

Southern Georgia is the area of lunker Bass and big Bream in waters shaded by Spanish moss. Adequate camping facilities are found on Georgia's lakes and landings are strategically located for launching your own boat. If you prefer to rent a boat, there are several rental places on lakes throughout the state. The Georgia Game and Fish Commission maintains 13 game management areas where excellent fishing and hunting are found.

Countless thousands of smaller lakes and ponds dot the countryside and blend into the cities. Georgia state lines are defined on the eastern and western borders by great river systems with other large streams in between. Thousands of smaller tributaries, some of them not even named, join the major river system. All of this vast water area is alive with fish . . . and fishermen are a natural by-product.

North Carolina

North Carolina is naturally divided into three sections; the Appalachian Mountain region, the Piedmont Plateau, and the Costal Plain. Each section has its own types of waters in which certain species of fish predominate.

TROUT

The best trout fishing is found in the cooperative wildlife management areas of the Pisgah and Nantahala National Forests and in the Great Smoky Mountains National Park. In the Nantahala Forest, the Nantahala River, Santeetlah Creek, and Fires Creek offer the best Rainbow Trout fishing. In the Pisgah National Forest important trout streams are found on four areas; the Pisgah National Game Preserve, where only artificial lures are permitted, Sherwood Management Area, and the Mt. Mitchell and Daniel Boone wildlife areas. Natural bait or artificial lures are allowed on the latter three areas, except for selected streams where only artificial lures are permitted. The streams in the Nantahala and Pisgah Forests are well stocked with catchable sized trout. In the management areas the streams are open to fishing over the weekends and holidays and on Wednesdays, from around April first to September first. Daily permits are sold by protectors at checking stations. In the Great Smoky Mountains National Park many fine Rainbow and Brook Trout streams are open for six days a week during fishing season. No special permit is required, and natural bait is permitted in most streams, although a few are restricted to fishing with artificial lures.

Hundreds of miles of trout streams are open to all anglers. Elk River and Upper Linville River in Avery County are famous Brown Trout streams; the head of the South Fork New River and upper Watauga River in Watauga County offer Rainbow Trout fishing. The Cullasaja in Macon County and other streams in Jackson, Wilkes, Haywood, and Madison counties also provide good trout fishing.

SPINY-RAYED FISH

Smallmouth Bass are found in the large rivers and foothill streams, including the lower Watauga River, parts of the Olichucky, the Oconalufty coming out of the Cherokee Indian Reservation, the Little Tennessee, the New River and its tributaries, and the north and south forks and Little River.

The Ohio Muskellunge is found in limited numbers in a few deep holes in the French Broad River and in Cheoha Reservoir.

Many impoundments also provide good fishing in the western district. Lake Fontana, Nantahala, Glenville Reservoir on the Tuckasegee River, Chatuge, Hiwassee and Appalachia Reservoirs on the Hiwassee River, Lake James on the Catawba and Lake Lure on Rocky Broad River all provide good fishing for spiny rayed fish such as Smallmouth and Largemouth Bass, Rock Bass, Bluegill Sunfish, and Channel Catfish. All of these impoundments provide year-round fishing which is best in May and June, and again in September and October.

The reservoirs on the Yadkin and Catawba Rivers offer fairly good fishing in April and May and again in October. The principal species are Largemouth Bass, White Bass, Catfish, Crappie, and assorted panfish. Private ponds and lakes take care of the bulk of the sport fishing in the Piedmont.

The Sandhills Wildlife Management Area lies between the Piedmont and Coastal Plain. About a dozen lakes on this area are open to the public during the summer season except when occupied by the Army on maneuvers, and daily permits are required. Largemouth Bass and Bluegills are the important species.

The Coastal Plain has both lakes and streams, many of them darkly stained due to humic and tannic acids. Lake Waccamaw, most productive of the group, White Lake, and Singletary Lake provide Largemouth Bass, Crappie, Bluegills, and other sunfishes.

Lake Mattamuskeet, which is a Federal migratory waterfowl refuge, offers fishing for Bass and Crappies in the canals in March and April and summer fishing for White Perch. Lake Phelps, the state's largest natural lake, provides good fishing in early summer for Bass, Crappie, and Bluegills. Large Black Crappie up to four pounds in weight are caught here.

Most anglers prefer the costal stream fishing to the lakes. The streams are lined with cypress hung with Spanish moss, and the water is clear but coffee colored. This country is not well settled, so a local guide is helpful in finding the best fishing holes. The Lumber and Waccamaw Rivers are fours for fishing for Redbreast Sunfish. This fish grows to weigh a pound or more, and provides the fly-rod angler with excellent sport. The Cape Fear River and its tributaries, the lower Neuse River and its tributaries, Tar and Pamlico Rivers, all offer good angling opportunities. Farther

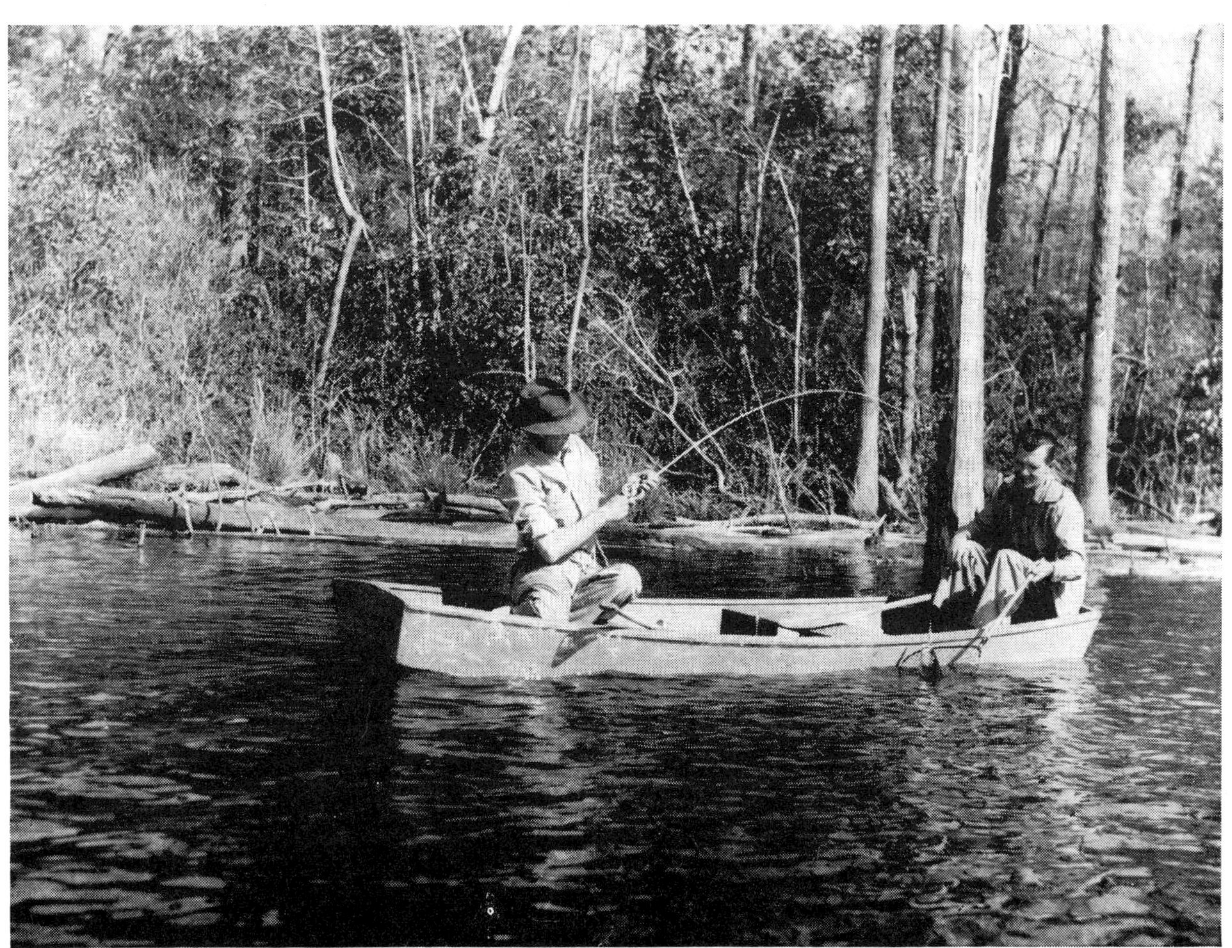

River fishing provides excellent sport for the fishermen of South Carolina.

north, fishing streams tributary to Albemarle Sound, include the Scuppernong River, Schlie River, Salmon Creek, Perquimmons, and Pasquotank Rivers, all contain a mixture of warm water fish.

The upper parts of the Sounds and their immediate tributaries in northeastern North Carolina afford the best bass fishing in the state.

In April and May the Striped Bass ascend the larger coastal rivers in search of spawning grounds. The spawning migrations occur in most of the coastwise streams, but the greatest numbers of fish are found in tributaries of the Albemarle Sound. The Roanoke River has long been famous as the principal migration stream of the Stripers. The Striped Bass, while in inland waters, may be taken by trolling or casting. During the summer and autumn months, the Stripers are in the bays and sounds and are fished for in the deep holes near the mouths of creeks and along bridges and causeways.

South Carolina

South Carolina enjoys some good trout fishing in the mountainous sections, but the vast majority of its waters are better for warm-water fishes.

TROUT

For a comparatively small state, South Carolina has a wide variety of fish, from the Trout in the northwestern mountains to the big Striped Bass of Santee-Cooper and the coastal rivers.

The mountain streams of Oconee, Pickens and Greenville counties are stocked with Brook, Brown and Rainbow Trout from the Federal and State hatcheries, with the area above Walhalla probably best for the visitor unfamiliar with the back-country streams. A new policy of stocking only catchable size trout in place of fingerlings has improved fishing.

There are no restrictions on the type of bait and most of the larger fish are taken on natural bait or spinning lures.

STRIPED BASS

When the Santee-Cooper reservoirs were impounded in 1942, some Striped Bass were trapped in the lakes but fisheries men expected them to disappear eventually, as the Striper had always been considered an anadromous fish. However, the catch kept increasing, and studies by the Wildlife Resources Department proved that the land-locked fish were successfully reproducing.

Starting in the early 1950's the population exploded, and the annual catch by 1957 was estimated at around 300,000 fish, averaging over five pounds. Since then the annual catch has declined, but the fishing is still exceptionally good, with the catch fairly constant through the year.

Stripers have been introduced into all other State reservoirs but, so far, there has been no evidence of reproduction.

Stripers are also found in the lower reaches of all the costal rivers, but not in salt water as in other states.

Favorite lures in Santee-Cooper are metal-nylon jigs, deep-running plugs and various types of cut bait.

From mid-summer to late fall the Stripers may be found schooling and will hit surface lures.

OTHER GAME FISH

Largemouth Bass are numerous in most waters—reservoirs, ponds and the low country rivers—but not common in the rather silted upstate rivers. In addition to live bait and the old standby plugs and spoons, the plastic worms are top lures.

Smallmouths are confined to a few foot-hill streams and are not found at all in the lower part of the State.

Bluegill are plentiful and their sporty cousin, the Redbreast, is common in the black-water streams of the coastal plain.

Crappie, Black and White, are found in all the reservoirs—Santee-Cooper, Lake Murray, Lake Greenwood, Catawba-Wateree, Clark Hill and recently impounded Hartwell Reservoir. A five-pound Black Crappie from Santee-Cooper is the recognized world record, and several White Crappie of five pounds have been caught.

White Bass, which were introduced into the Catawba River around 1950 have now spread and been introduced into all the reservoirs and many of the rivers.

Other common but less important game fish are the Pickerel, known locally as Jack, Warmouth, and Yellow Perch.

Exceptionally large Channel Catfish are found in Santee-Cooper's Lake Moultrie and the Cooper River, and the world record of 57 pounds came from the lake. Larger ones have been reported but not verified.

There is a good run of White and Hickory Shad in some of the rivers in early spring.

Spinning is now the most popular fishing method in South Carolina. The Mep and Shyster lures are among the most popular and are effective in fishing for nearly all species.

Virginia

Virginia's fresh-water fishing is essentially divided into three belts coinciding with the state's three clearly-defined topographical areas, the mountains, the Piedmont, and the Coastal Plain. These regions converge in the north and fan out to the southward, conforming rather closely to the triangular map of the Old Dominion.

Thus the trout fishing is confined to the great stretch of mountain country running northeast and southwest from Harper's Ferry to the Tennessee line. The typical Smallmouth Bass waters lie to the eastward of the mountain ranges and extend to the ridge which runs practically due north and south, through Washington and Richmond, where the tides cease to ebb and flow. East of the falls in the tidal rivers is the ideal country for Largemouth Bass and other warm water species.

For trout fishing it is only necessary to refer to a road map for access to the 37 counties in which the state annually stocks legal-size trout in 132 streams. Lists of these streams are available on request from the Commission of Game and Inland

Fisheries at Richmond. Only Brook and Rainbow Trout are released from Virginia's hatcheries, but 100 tons of these fish are planted each year.

As an example, a road map will show the counties in which are found the larger trout waters. These streams and their tributaries are heavily stocked, and provide a convenient index of the best places for the casual angler to go in Virginia. Some of these streams are Cedar Creek, Big Stoney, the Rapidan, Dry River, Big Piney, Tye River, Big Stoney, White Top Laurel, Wolf Creek, and Stoney Creek.

While Smallmouth Bass encroach to some extent into trout streams, just as their Largemouth cousins also are found in limited numbers in the colder Smallmouth waters, the principal areas for Smallmouth Bass and kindred species which prefer cooler temperatures are found from the upper Potomac, south and southwestward throughout a huge triangular territory. With the exception of a few streams in which pollution has gotten in its deadly work, Smallmouth Bass are to be found above tidewater in the Potomac, Rappahannock, James, Roanoke, Shenandoah, New River, and the Holston tributaries in the valley between the mountain ranges.

The state annually stocks such streams as the Shenandoah, Cowpasture, Rappahannock, Rapidan, Smith, Jackson, Clinch, and Maury. In recent years it has been the policy to release Longear Sunfish everywhere that Smallmouth Bass are stocked, for the dual purpose of furnishing added food supplies for the larger fish, and providing an excellent panfish for anglers. Large numbers of Rock Bass also are placed in these waters.

Smallmouth Bass and Trout are frequently found in the same waters. Trout work down from the smaller tributaries in quest of food and the angler for spiny-ray species is often surprised at landing a Brook or Rainbow.

The streams throughout the 1,500,000 acres of national forests are open to public fishing and comparatively few of the private streams are posted. Virtually all running water to the east of the mountains is open to the public, and a sport which is rapidly growing in popularity is wading these streams and casting for Bass, Longear Sunfish, Bream, Crappie, Silver Chub or Fallfish, Pickerel, and other game fish which raise readily to the fly.

While Largemouth Bass find their way into the upland regions, the coastal plain of Virginia provides habitat which is as nearly ideal as any in the East. Bottoms of the tidal streams and the clear

Richmond Times-Dispatch

Fishing in Curtis Pond, King William County, Virginia.

ponds are generally sand and gravel, providing ideal spawning grounds, and there is tremendous reproduction of the small fish on which Bass largely subsist.

While, unfortunately, large numbers of the best ponds in eastern Virginia are in the hands of fishing clubs, the Commission of Game and Inland Fisheries furnishes, upon request, a list of the 94 public ponds and 80 streams annually stocked from the hatcheries. Much of the best fishing is in the tidal streams and their tributaries which are so abundantly supplied with native brood stocks that it is unnecessary to stock them.

Natural baits are popular and are much the same as employed elsewhere in similar waters. Plugs and spoons are particularly adapted to the big tidal rivers and the larger lakes and ponds. Use of fly tackle is growing in popularity, not only for wadeable trout and smallmouth bass streams but for Bass and other species in the larger waters where boats are necessary. The popping bug is particularly effective.

LOWER MISSISSIPPI VALLEY

The lower Mississippi Valley is a well-watered land which provides an abundance of good fishing for warm water species. The warm climate, which provides both an abundance of food and a long growing season, is responsible for a truly huge production of fish. In recent years studies have shown that in many of these productive waters, unlimited hook-and-line fishing is unable to remove the fish as fast as they can be produced.

The result of these studies has been to shorten or remove closed periods entirely and to reduce other restrictions in many states. This procedure which seems entirely justified in these prolific waters may not be equally suited to more northern waters, and the tendency there has been more conservative.

The Largemouth Bass is king of fresh water sport fish in this area, but he has much competition for the honors by a great variety of pan fish which bring equal pleasure to many thousands of fishermen.

The catfishes are also highly regarded by contemplative anglers and furnish a fishing objective for a huge army of bait fishermen. The fact that fried catfish and catfish stew are delicious and traditional southern dishes does nothing to diminish the popularity of these toothsome creatures.

Moore-Tenn. Conservation Dept.

Fishing in the tailwaters of TVA dams is a year around sport in Tennessee and nearly always productive of good strings.

Arkansas

Arkansas, bisected in the center by the Arkansas River, covers some 53,000 square miles of which 800 are water. In the west section are found the Ozark and Ouachita Mountains which give the state its highest elevation of 3,000 feet. The eastern and southern portions are comparatively level, being comprised of the Mississippi Alluvial Plain and the West Gulf Coastal Plain. All of Arkansas drains southeast into the Mississippi River.

The principal game fish found are White Bass, Bass, Trout, Walleye, Bluegill, Crappie and Channel Catfish. Rough fish such as Catfish, Buffalo, Carp, and Gar are found everywhere.

The major rivers are the Mississippi, Arkansas, White, Ouachita, St. Francis and Red, but countless tributaries from each form a vast net-work of excellent fishing streams. The clear swift-flowing streams of the north and west with their Smallmouth Bass, Walleye, and Rock Bass afford excellent sport for the fly and bait caster. South and east Arkansas offer many natural lakes formed, for the most part, by changes in the courses of nearby rivers. In addition, there are artificial city reservoirs and hydro-electric lakes.

Because of the greatly increased fishing pressure in the last few years, the Game and Fish Commission has enlarged their hatchery and fish rearing facilities in order to stock regularly the streams of the state. The Lonoke is rated the largest fish hatchery in the United States.

FLOAT FISHING

The state is particularly famous for its float-fishing trips on the White, Buffalo, North Fork, Black, and Arkansas Rivers. This unusual method may be enjoyed in perfect comfort. A guide sits to the rear of the boat, paddling whenever necessary, while the fisherman, near the front, exercises his art from a low-back chair. The more ardent fisherman has his own boat but gregarious individuals can arrange a party for a larger boat on which the trip may last for several days. The boat drifts down stream with the current from one likely pool to another. Some of the more popular starting points are around Norfork, Henderson, Cotter, and Mountain Home. The guide points out the likely lurking spots for each particular species; in the brush piles for the Crappie, the lily pod or the overhanging banks for the Largemouth and Walleye; and the swifter water above or below riffles for the Smallmouth.

At night the party may camp ashore at some scenic spot or sleep on board, depending on the size of boat. The trip ends at some point where automobiles can be brought close by. Such trips may last from a day to more than a week.

FISHING NORTH OF THE ARKANSAS

The principal stream of this region is the White River, so named because it is the clearest of all tributaries of the Arkansas. Palisades and bluffs which rise above the river have been compared to those of the Hudson. Each particular bluff has an individuality of its own and were named when the settlers came into the areas. Probably the most picturesque point for the fisherman and the tourist alike is Penter's Bluff near Batesville.

Fishing for Smallmouth, Largemouth, Rock Bass, and Walleye is particularly good near Norfork, Sylamore, Batesville, Newport, and Augusta. On to the South, Crappie, Bluegill, as well as Bass, yield many fine strings. At the point where the North Fork of White River is crossed by U. S. 62, the stream is clear and cold and offers excellent Smallmouth Bass fishing.

Buffalo River is another cold clear stream which harbors an abundance of Bass, which are said to be gamier than those taken from the lakes and more sluggish streams. Buffalo State Park is located at the point of Highway 14 Crossing. Because of accessibility, it has become a popular starting point for float-fishing trips.

The Black River, which is one of the larger tributaries of the White, is famous for its Bass and float-fishing trips. Best fishing is to be had in the vicinity of Pocahontas and near Corning. In the lower section Crappie, Bluegill, and Catfish abound. Many eating places near the river advertise Catfish steaks which are said to be unexcelled.

Cache River, another tributary of the White, offers good fishing near its mouth. Catfish, Drum, Buffalo and Carp are the principal fishes taken throughout its entire length. The stream is lazy in nature and is hidden from view in many spots by willow thickets. In the vicinity of Grubbs and Beedeville fishing is to be had for Bass, Crappie and Bluegill.

The St. Francis River, rising in Missouri, flows directly south to its junction with the Mississippi River just north of Helena. The river throughout its length in Arkansas resembles somewhat a swampy lake. Fishing is best for Largemouth Bass, Bluegill, Crappie, and rough fish.

The L'Anguille River which is a tributary of the St. Francis was apparently named for its serpentine shape. During times of high water, the stream leaves its meandering bed to over-flow into the surrounding country. During such periods a new channel is often cut, thus leaving many oxbow lakes. These offer particularly good fishing for Crappie, Catfish, and rough fish.

Little River is another famous fishing stream. Including all loops, it furnishes some 60 miles of better-than-average fishing. Boats and guides may be obtained near Judsonia where fishing for Bass, Catfish and Crappie may be had. This stream can be reached from Herber Springs and Searcy.

Kings River near Fayetteville is noted for Smallmouth Bass fishing by way of float trips.

Big Lake is located in the Big Lake National Wildlife Refuge operated by the U. S. Fish and Wildlife Service. Good fishing for Bass, White Bass, Crappie, Bluegill, and Catfish may be enjoyed.

Black Fish Lake, so called because the water is coffee colored, is several miles in length. It has been developed as a recreational area and enjoys a reputation for Catfish, Crappie, and Bluegill fishing.

Lake Fort Smith, located just off U. S. 71, is a beautiful, clear body of water which has been offering excellent fishing. Boats are available.

SOUTHERN REGION

Near Hot Springs, Lake Catherine and Lake Hamilton offer very good fishing for Bass, Crappie, and Bluegill. These were impounded from the Ouachita River. Cabins, boats and some fishing equipment are available for rent. Lake Hamilton has 9,000 acres and was created in 1931. It is stocked regularly and is a recreational center for swimming and motor boat regattas as well as fishing.

Nimrod Lake, located just south of Highway 28, is a favorite spot of many who fish for Bass, Crappie, and Bluegill.

Lake Wallace, located in an abandoned bend of Bartholomew Bayou, is a relatively large lake bordered by a park belonging to the town of Dermott. Bass, Crappie, and Bluegill fishing is said to be good.

One of the better known fishing streams in the South is the Little Missouri River. It can be reached from Murfreesboro, where boats are rented near the bridge on U. S. 67.

Ouachita River near Camden, Arkadelphia and Oden, Arkansas, has fishing for Catfish, Bass, and Crappie.

Caddo River is a beautiful stream which can be located in the vicinity of Amity or Arkadelphia. This is a rather swift mountain stream offering fishing for Bass, Rock Bass, and Walleye.

The Saline River near Benton, Kingsland and Warren is noted for its Bass, Crappie, and Bluegill fishing. There are many cut-off lakes in the valley for the river wanders back and forth flooding alluvial bottom lands after each heavy rain. In these, in addition to the usual game species, Catfish, Buffalo, Carp, and Gar abound.

Cassatot, flowing through a gloomy valley, offers fishing for Crappie, Catfish, and rough species.

Kentucky

Kentucky has more miles of running water than any other state except Alaska. This, plus favorable climate and rich drainage basins, naturally makes it a good fishing ground. The state measures more than five hundred miles from east to west with a terrain that varies from the rugged mountains of the east to the flat alluvial plains of the west. With this diversity of lands is, of course, a diversity of waters. The mountain sections have cool, clear, rocky streams with long stretches of fast riffles that pour waters into deep holes, making this section ideal for Smallmouth Bass, Bream, and Rock Bass. The western rivers are large, slow-running streams,

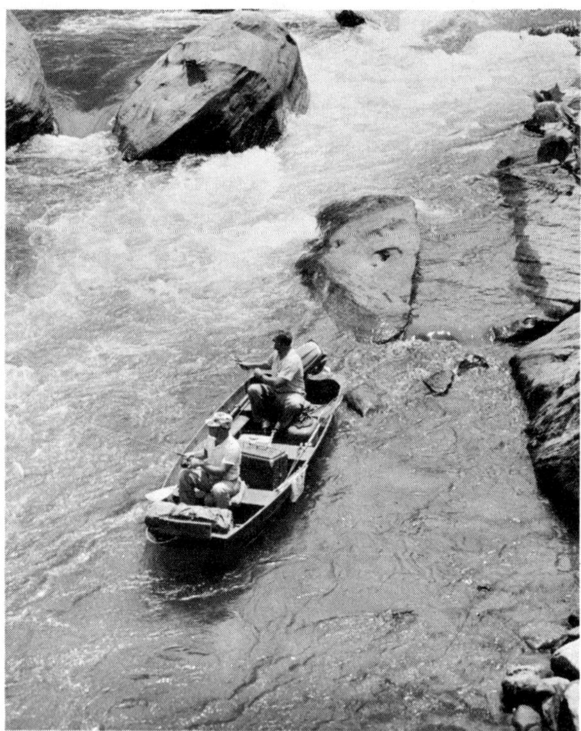

Kentucky Dept. of Fish and Wildlife Resources

Numerous streams in Kentucky offer float fishing. Fishermen shown above are anchored off a riffle of a mountain stream. Smallmouth bass offer excellent fishing for this type fisherman.

abundantly supplied with Largemouth Bass, White Perch, White Bass, Crappie, and various kinds of Catfish.

In addition to the hundreds of streams and rivers, Kentucky also has seven large man-made lakes that even outdo the running water in furnishing sport.

With a mild climate, bountiful waters, every type of natural scenic beauty, and a hospitable people, Kentucky offers much with its invitation to fish in its waters.

STREAMS

Excellent fishing can be found in the Kentucky, Ohio, Green, Cumberland, Licking, Big Sandy, Little Sandy, Rock Castle, Red, and Licking Rivers. These are the larger streams furnishing about the same species of fish.

The Ohio flows along the entire northern boundary and its waters are a part of Kentucky. At present, this large river yields tons of commercial fish such as Carp, Catfish, Buffalo, Drum, and some others. Most of these are taken by nets, trotlines, and seines; however, the same species furnish sport to the pole fisherman and small boats constantly ply these waters, seeking the fish that take live or cut bait.

The Kentucky River runs from the mountains through the central. part of the state. Many good catches of Bass, Sunfish, and Channel Cats are taken in its upper stretches and, as it nears its mouth, Bass, Buffalo, Crappie, and large cats of various types are caught on both artificial lures and baited lines.

Also rising in the mountains is the Cumberland which flows through the state into Tennessee and then back into Kentucky. Some of the best Smallmouth Bass fishing is found in this river. Near Cumberland Falls this fishing reaches its best. In addition to Bass, Walleye and many types of pan fish, plus the wondrous beauty of the surrounding hills and cliffs, make this an ideal spot. Throughout the length of this river, Bass and Walleye are taken during the fishing season.

The Licking furnishes about the same sport as the average Kentucky river with emphasis on Largemouth Bass and Muskellunge.

The Green River supplies fishing of almost any variety, form, or flavor. That stream, along with Triplett Creek, Kinniconick Creek, and the upper Kentucky, furnishes the only Muskellunge fishing in the state. Heading in Lincoln County, the Green flows in a westerly direction through deep gorges and fertile valleys. Large and Smallmouth Bass, Channel and Flat-head Catfish, Crappie, Bream, and White Perch are abundant throughout its course.

In the extreme east and forming part of the eastern boundary, are the Big and Little Sandy Rivers. These are famous fishing waters. While the basses are the outstanding species caught, Walleye, Catfish, and Sunfish are also taken.

The Rockcastle, Nolin, Chaplin, and Dix Rivers are the smaller streams of the river group that are considered some of the best Bass and pan fish waters.

Elkhorn Creek, in central Kentucky, was once considered one of the best Bass streams in the United States. Today, despite the heavy fishing pressure, Elkhorn is one of the best in central Kentucky. Along with Bass, this stream also yields Rock Bass, and various types of Catfish.

Every county in the state can boast of a good fishing stream or lake. Bass rank first in almost all of them. Bream, Crappie, White Perch, Catfish, and Rock Bass abound in almost all waters. During the spring, Suckers and Redhorse can be taken with pole and line in the smallest or largest stream.

LAKES

Kentucky Lake, in the western part of the state and created by a dam across the Tennessee River at Gilbertsville, is one of the largest man-made lakes in the world. This body of water is almost two hundred miles in length and has a shore line of 2,300 miles. It is comparatively shallow and floods the valleys of many small streams, creating bays and coves that are ideal places for Bass. All during the year at least one type of fishing is excellent.

From the first warm days of spring to midsummer, Bass can be taken by plug, flies, or minnows. July and August are slow months for Bass fishing, but the White Bass, Bream, and Catfish will take a deep bait in the morning or evening.

During most of the year, Crappie range from vicious to moderate biters.

Directly below the dam, the Tennessee River flows on to the Ohio and this twenty-two miles of water furnishes some of the best fishing in the South. Every type of fish indigenous to Kentucky Lake and the Ohio River are caught. Sauger catches are frequent below the dam. For camping, sightseeing, or just fishing, Kentucky Lake is numbered with the best.

Dale Hollow Lake, located in the extreme southern part of the state, is a recent impoundment of the Army Engineers. This lake is one of the finest Smallmouth Bass lakes in the mid-South. Along with these are Largemouth Bass, Rock Bass, and Crappie. Here, also, is an abundance of Bream and, in the quiet shadows of overhanging cliffs, these can be taken with worm or fly at any time of the year. This lake produced the world-record Smallmouth Bass.

Cumberland Lake, in South-central Kentucky, was completed in 1951, and lies wholly in Kentucky. It is 101 miles long with 1,255 miles of shoreline. The lake is fed by the North and South Forks of Cumberland River which originates in the mountains and offers cooler water, making Bass fishing excellent. In the spring, a fabulous Walleye run occurs in the headwaters of this lake, which also abounds in White Bass, which offer runs in the early spring months, and Crappie which are caught the year around. The lake is highly developed with excellent camps and docks and is accessible from a number of fine highways.

Dewey Lake is locted in the mountains of eastern Kentucky and is 17 miles long with a surface area of 860 acres at pool stage. A new lake, these waters offer excellent Black Bass and Crappie fishing with a sprinkling of White Bass. Large Bluegills are also harvested in the summer months. Rough River Reservoir, opened to fishing only in 1961, is located in north-central Kentucky, near Louisville, and is 35 miles long, with 4,860 surface acres. During the first year of fishing, excellent catches of Largemouth Bass were made, as well as good catches of crappie. The lake has been stocked with White Bass and Walleyes, and offers excellent fishing for catfish.

Buckhorn Reservoir, another Eastern Kentucky Lake, is located in Perry County, in the heart of the mountains, and is 21 miles long with a surface acreage of 1,200. An impoundment of the North Fork of the Kentucky River, home of the Muskellunge, it is, therefore, the only lake in Kentucky producing the musky. In addition it is a good Smallmouth and Largemouth lake and White Bass and Channel Catfish have been stocked there.

Barkley Lake was opened to fishing in 1961, and lies alongside famous Kentucky Lake, enclosing the Kentucky Woodlands National Wildlife Refuge with water. The lake is almost as large as Kentucky Lake and is joined to that lake by a canal. To form this body of water, Cumberland River is being impounded by a dam within three miles of Kentucky Dam on the Tennessee River. Other lakes under construction, all of which are scheduled to be completed by 1965, are: Nolin Reservoir and Barren No. 2, located in South-central Kentucky; Fishtrap in extreme Eastern Kentucky; Little Sandy near Greyson in Eastern Kentucky, and Green River, in Western Kentucky. Twenty-six state-owned lakes, containing 3,800 acres of water, are now in operation throughout the state, and a Chain-Of-Lakes program, in connection with highway construction, is now in effect. Kentucky has well over 50,000 farm ponds, scattered throughout the state, that have been stocked with fish.

Louisiana

Louisiana, a fisherman's deam, offers many types of fishing for, perhaps, more different kinds of fishes than other states in the Lower Mississippi River Valley. From the shady creeks of upland parishes to the pounding surf of the Gulf, game fishes wait to match the skill of the fisherman. Three distinct types of fishing are enjoyed: fresh-water bayous and upland streams for Black Bass, Crappie, Yellow Bass, various Sunfishes, and Catfishes; coastal lagoons for Redfish, Sea Trout, and Sheepshead; and Gulf of Mexico for deep sea species such as Tarpon, Jewfish, King Mackerel, and Sharks.

Fishermen who have never visited the state may conclude that Louisiana is entirely a low, wet, swampy region because it contains the delta of the greatest river on the continent. That is not a true picture for the state is intersected by numerous rivers and bayous and filled with lakes. All in all, there are 7,409 square miles of water in Louisiana.

The most important rivers are the Mississippi, Red, Atchafalaya, Ouachita, Sabine, and Pearl. A peculiar feature of many of these is that they run upon a higher elevation than their flood plains and are thus of little value as drainage channels. For instance, the only tributary of the Mississippi on the west is the Red River and on the east, Bayou Sara and Thompson's Creek.

This peculiar condition accounts for the numerous bayous which are in reality flood distributaries and drainage streams for swamps. Of these Macon, Teche, Lafourche, and Boeuf are the largest.

Lakes may be classified in three ways. Coastal lagoons, existing as arms of the sea behind barrier beaches or engulfed by deltaic ridges in the delta. The typical and better known ones are Barataria Bay, Lakes Pontchartrain, Maurepas, and Salvador. The Red River Valley Lakes such as Caddo, Bistineau, and Black, famous for their Bass, Bluegill, White Perch, and Catfish, were formed as a result of damming the Red River. Their level is dependent upon that of the river as high water results in a flooding of the lakes by backwater. In the alluvial plain which lies in a belt of some 50 miles along the Mississippi are lakes formed from cut-off meanders. These support fishing in Bass, Crappie, Buffalo, and Catfish. Examples of this type are Lakes St. John and Concordia, both noted for their fishing.

Because of the character of the streams and lakes, the heavy growth, trees and over-hanging shrubs, it is next to impossible to fish without using a boat. In order to aid fishermen unacquainted with the state, the parishes are divided into four general regions.

REGION I

The northern section including the parishes of Bienville, Jackson, Caldwell, Franklin, and Tensas offer some of the best fishing to be found. One of

Louisiana Dept. of Wildlife & Fisheries

A Louisiana fishing scene.

the outstanding spots in this area is Lake Bistineau, located west of Ringgold. This lake is stocked regularly, and contains a state game and fish preserve on its northwest boundary. Many camps as well as boats are available from which fishermen may try their skill on Largemouth and Spotted Bass, Bluegill, and Crappie.

Further to the east are located Caddo and Cross Lakes, both noted for their fishing. In these Bass are taken along with Bluegill and Crappie. In the eastern section of this northern region is found Lake Providence, just south of Highland, where good fishing for Bass and Perch is to be had. Boats and some camps are available.

To the south of Richland Parrish fishing may be had at Carpenter, Clear, Lafourche, Crew, St. John, or Louis Lakes.

The main fishing streams of the region are Ouachita, Boeuf, Tensas, and the Mississippi River. In these Bass, Bluegill, Catfish, Crappie, and Buffalo are the main species. The bayous such as Bodeau, Black, Sabine, D'Arbonne, Lafourche, and Tensas offer particularly good fishing. One of the better known spots on the Tensas is near its intersection with Highway 80.

Borrow pits along the Mississippi dikes offer fishing for the usual game species as well as rough fishes.

REGION II

Region II, called the central region immediately south of Region I, is bounded on the east by Mississippi River, on the West by the Sabine River, and on the South by the parishes Beauregard, Allen, Evangeline, St. Landry, and Pointe Coupee. This region contains many good fishing lakes, the larger of which are Larto, Catahoula, Latt, Sabine, Clear, Black, and the Cane River. Black, Clear, and Sabine Lakes are part of the O. K. Allen Fish and Game Preserve. Here, particularly good fishing may be enjoyed for Bass and the other species of small fish. These are stocked regularly and boats and camps are available at all times. Smaller lakes are Lakes St. John and Concordia in Concordia Parish; a second Clear Lake along with Smithport and Wallace Lakes in DeSoto Parish; Blue and Horse Shoe Lakes in Sabine Parish; Big Bend and Hamburg Lakes in Avoyelles Parish. All of these offer fishing for Bass, Crappie, Bluegill, and Catfish. Boats are available on all and cabins on some.

The outstanding fishing rivers of the region are the Red, Sabine, Black, Tensas, Old, and Calcasieu. These offer fishing for the usual species of game fish found in the state as well as Catfish and Buffalo. Along the Mississippi are found many borrow pits which offer fair fishing.

Bass, Crappie, and Bluegill are found in such creeks as Grand Cane, Trout, Clear, Flaggon, Fish, Little, Horse Pin, and Patricia.

The better known bayous are Boeuf, Rouge, Black, Dorcheat, Cocodrie, and Pierre. Because of the heavy growth of shrubs, it is necessary to use a boat in fishing for the Bass, Crappie, Bluegill, and Catfish found there.

Bayou Pierre offers excellent fishing near its mouth. There the Bayou is sluggish and choked with hyacinth. Many good catches of Bass and Crappie are made here.

REGION III

This region is that southern portion of the state south of Region II and west of the Mississippi River. Here, salt-water fishing is particularly famous along the coast. In the lakes such as Calcasieu, Grand, White, and Sabine, fishing for such salt water species as Speckled Trout, Croakers, and Redfish may be enjoyed. In Lake Charles there is an annual Tarpon rodeo attracting fishermen from all over the South.

One of the most famous fresh water lakes of the region is the Verret. This is a large lake in the Atchafalaya Basin. It is clear and deep and surrounded by large trees. Fishing supplies can be obtained and boats rented. Black and Striped Bass, Crappie, and Catfish are found here.

Stream fishing is particularly good in Calcasieu River near Kinder. There are many excellent picnic spots along with fine bass fishing. Other rivers which offer fishing are the Mermentau, Old, and Grand. From these are taken Striped Bass, Bluegill, and Perch.

The principal bayous are Grand, Nezpique, Corne, Cocodrie, Teche, Sorrel, Lacosine, and Choctaw. These contain Bass, Crappie, Catfish and Warmouth.

REGION IV

This southeastern region comprised of all parishes east of the Mississippi River has several good fishing spots. Of these Lakes Maurepas, Pontchartrain, and Borgne are the most notable. Good fishing is to be had for Speckled Trout, Croaker, Redfish, and Drum, with Tarpon fishing being good in Pontchartrain and Borgne. One of the better known fishing spots in this area is Lake Borgne, just out from Shell Beach on Highway 32. Bogue Falaya River near Covington is a favorite fishing place, and in spring and fall many Rock Bass are taken.

The Amite and Blood Rivers in the central section are the main fishing spots of that area. Near Port Vincent on the Amite River Catfish are caught which are said to be the finest in the country.

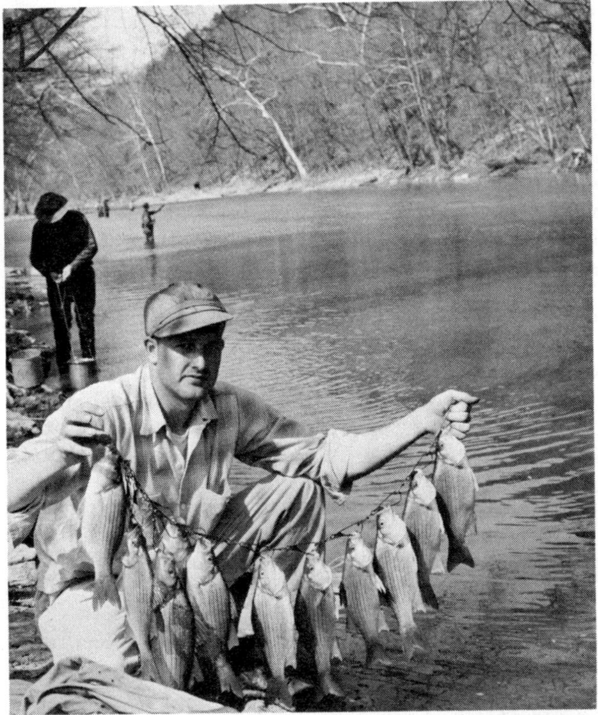

Kentucky Dept. of Fish and Wildlife Resources

Dix River, headwaters of Herrington Lake in Central Kentucky, is famous for the white bass run in the early spring months. The stripers move into the swift waters of this stream to deposit their eggs and when this occurs limits of two pounders may be caught.

In the western section, Thompson and Sandy Creeks offer Bass, Crappie, and Bluegill fishing. Of the bayous, Rapoma, Petite, Amite, Paul, Manchac, Colyell, Falaya River, Biloxi, and Chitto River are the spots chosen by the experienced fisherman. They furnish angling for Bass, Catfish, Bluegill, Crappie, and Warmouth.

Mississippi

In observing a map of Mississippi one may quickly see that this state probably has as many streams, lakes, and other waters as any other. On the west section the mighty Mississippi rushes its way to the Gulf, while on the south section the boundary is formed by the Gulf of Mexico. The interior is drained by a multitude of rivers, picturesque in name and setting, and great producers of both game and rough fish. All of this, plus the Southern climate, presents a perfect setting for a fisherman's paradise.

The most popular game fish is the Largemouth bass, which is found in almost every lake and stream. The Kentucky, or Spotted Bass, is also very prevalent and is found mainly in the smaller and clearer streams in the northern and central parts of the state. Crappie, Bluegill, Catfish, and other species abound in practically all the smaller streams, and also, in the hundreds of lakes.

LAKES

In the northern section of the state may be found four reservoirs. Sardis Lake, formed by the damming of the Tallahatchie and located in Panola and Lafayette Counties, consists of approximately 60,000 acres. Grenada Lake, formed by the damming of the Yalobusha River, is located in Grenada and Yalobusha Counties and also has about 60,000 acres. Enid Lake is located in Panola and Yalobusha Counties and was formed by the damming of the Yocona River. Arkabutla Reservoir, located in Tate County, has approximately 30,000 acres and was formed by damming the Coldwater River.

All of these are noted for their crappie fishing but also provide good Bass, Bluegill, and Catfish. Fishing in the outlet channels of these dams is excellent and provides an excellent place for bank fishing.

In the central part of the state, the newly-constructed Pearl River Reservoir, located in Hinds, Madison, and Rankin Counties, should furnish equally good fishing in the near future. This 36,000-acre lake was formed by the construction of a dam on the Pearl River just north of the capital city of Jackson.

The State Game and Fish Commission and the State Park Commission have constructed lakes ranging in size from 50 to 1200 acres in size throughout the state that offer excellent Bass and Bluegill fishing.

Down the western boundary of the state bordering the Mississippi River, large, overflow and borrowpit lakes are found, many of them impounding 1000 or more acres of water.

Moon Lake, located in Coahoma County, is the largest natural lake in northern Mississippi. It offers year-round fishing for Bass, Crappie, Bluegill, and Catfish and, in mid-summer, fine Crappie trolling.

Farther south, Lake Washington located in Washington County, also offers good Bass and Crappie fishing, together with rough fish.

Lake Albemarle, located in Issaquena County, Eagle Lake, and Yazoo Lake, both in Warren County, offer good fishing for Bass, Bluegill, and Crappie. Throughout other sections of the state may be found a multitude of lakes, ranging in size from 25 to 1000 acres of water. Many of these furnish excellent fishing for game fish, while others offer good fishing for rough species. Boats are available, and numerous camping sites, equipped with cabins, are also located in the areas.

Sunfish, of several varieties, abound also in these same waters, with the Bluegill and the Green Sunfish the most popular species.

Other varieties inhabiting these waters are the Warmouth Bass, Bowfin, Carp, and Buffalo. The Gar, which reaches an enormous size, affords an interesting sport to those who wish to get into the hundred-pound class. In fact, rodeos are staged on some of the delta lakes with prizes awarded for the largest Gar.

Space would not permit the mentioning of the many hundreds of smaller lakes scattered throughout the state. Practically every county is blessed with at least one or two. The majority offer good bass and sunfish fishing. Others bordering the Mississippi River excel in Buffalo, Carfish, and Crappie.

No picture of Mississippi fishing would be complete without mentioning the mighty river which

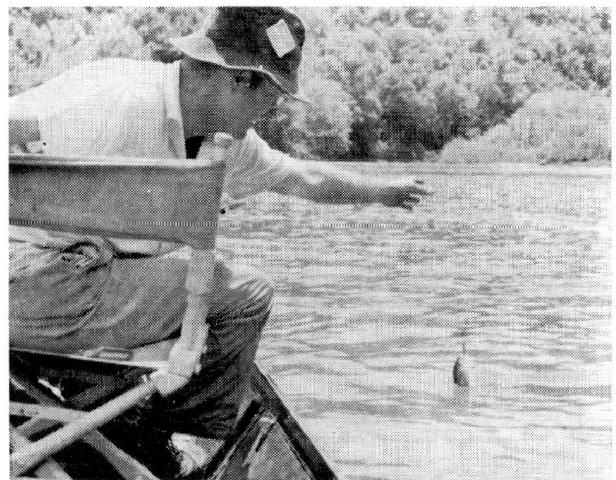

W. Va. Ind. & Pub. Comm.
"Fish" is the cry when a float fisherman hooks a Bass. The fisherman is reeling in a Small-mouth Bass.

flows down and forms the western boundary of the state, although in the eyes of the game fisherman, it does not rank nearly as high nor does it produce as many game fish as some of the smaller, clearer streams within the state. It is noted for its large commercial catches of Buffalo, Spoonbill Catfish, and the giant river Cats. Yearly, thousands of tons of these species are shipped to the New York markets.

Pearl River, which received its name because of the large pearl oysters once found on its banks, heads up in central Mississippi and winds its way into the Gulf Stream. It is one of the state's most famous streams for Bass, Crappie, and rough fish, not to mention the excellent salt-water catches at its mouth—Speckled Sea Trout, Redfish, and Sheepshead. Its many tributaries, such as the Yockanookany, the Strong and the Bogue Chitto also furnish good fishing in early spring and late fall.

The Yazoo, which flows into the Mississippi at Vicksburg, is a great producer of rough fish. Its tributaries, the Tallahatchie, Yalobusha, Yocona, Coldwater, Big Sunflower, and Little Sunflower are good producers of Bass, Crappie, Bluegill, and Catfish.

The Tennessee and Tombigbee, which drain the northeastern section of the state, are better than average as far as the game fisherman is concerned. However, the usual catch of Catfish and other rough fish is also taken.

In the southeast, the Leaf and Chickasawhay form the Pascagoula River. This stream and its tributaries offer from fair to good fishing for Bass, Crappie, Bluegill, Catfish, and rough fish.

In the southwest, the Big Black and the Homochitto run into the Mississippi. The Big Black, which heads up into Webster County in central Mississippi, is the more famous fishing stream. The Homochitto, in the southwest section, however, is considered by many to be one of the top fishing streams in that area.

When no other game fish are biting, streams produce excellent fishing for Channel Cat, Blue Cat, Yellow Cat, Buffalo, Drum, and Carp. Jug-fishing and trot lines are the most popular methods for taking these species.

Tennessee

Tennessee might well be called the lengthwise state since it is about four times as long as it is wide. The land slopes almost entirely from the east to the west, from the eastern boundary at an elevation of over 6,000 feet, there is a general westerly slope to the Mississippi where the height is only 300. Thus the state is diversified in nature—its soils, its waters and its fishes.

The eastern section has high mountains, deep valleys, and clear swift streams.

The great drainage basins are the Tennessee, Cumberland, and Mississippi Rivers. Of these the Tennessee is of most importance to the fisherman.

The Tennessee drains more than half the state. Seven streams, all originating in North Carolina transverse the mountains in a westerly direction and finally with the confluence of the Holston and French Broad Rivers near Knoxville the Tennessee is formed. Shortly thereafter the Clinch River joins it, later followed by the Elk and Duck Rivers of the central portion.

The Cumberland rising in eastern Kentucky enters central Tennessee in a loop to return northward to the Ohio River.

The Mississippi directly drains west Tennessee through a network of lazy streams, swamps and lakes.

As the state has three natural divisions, fishing over the state is so divided into eastern, central, and western.

EASTERN TENNESSEE

Fishing here may be brought to mind by simply thinking of three letters.—T.V.A. The Tennessee Valley Authority created in 1933 to develop the river in the interest of flood control, navigation and hydro electric power has provided much new water area.

Norris Dam, built in 1936, the first completed impounded waters of the Clinch and Powell Rivers, has a shore line of over 700 miles and covers 50 square miles. Few non-residents were familiar with the area prior to '36. Now the travelled fisherman can describe in detail the lake and the scenic sur-

Yellow Pike Perch and Smallmouth Bass taken from the New River, West Virginia.

W. Va. Ind. & Pub. Comm.

Small-mouth Bass fishing on the North Fork of the Potomac River in West Virginia.

rounding hills. For he came and often returned to match his skill with the Bass, Walleye, Bluegill, and Crappie which abound there. Norris is located some twenty-five miles north of Knoxville. Many docks, camps, boats, and motors are available.

Watts Bar Lake located in the southeastern section of the state is another TVA project offering some 39,000 acres of fishing water. Walleye, Bass, Crappie, White Bass, and Catfish are the principal game fish. Plenty of fishing docks with the best in facilities are available.

Cherokee Lake in the northeastern corner of the state is an impoundment of Holston River covering 30,000 acres. Excellent catches of large Crappie have resulted in much publicity for the lake. Additional species taken are Bass, Bluegill, and Catfish. Many camps and docks are available.

Douglas Lake located some 30 miles east of Knoxville on the French Broad River is about the same size as Cherokee Lake. It is easily accessible from Morristown and Jefferson City. Nice strings of Bass, Pike, and Crappie are obtained here in the spring and fall with fair fishing throughout the year. Camps, boats, and docks are available for the public.

Fort Loudon Lake, near Knoxville, is about half the size of Cherokee and Douglas Lakes. This reservoir offers good fishing for Bass and Walleye, and contains a good supply of rough fish. As on all TVA projects, boats, camps, and docks are available to the fisherman.

Chickamauga Lake, located just north of Chattanooga, is an impoundment of the Tennessee River covering some 35,000 acres. The species taken here are Largemouth Bass, Walleye, Sauger, White Bass, Bluegill, Catfish, and Carp. At the formation of the lake which reaches into the back yards of Dayton's residential section, the local business men declared a once-a-week holiday on which they all closed shop and went fishing. Many camps and docks are available for the fisherman.

This eastern mountainous section, filled with the swift clear spring-fed streams, offers fishing for Brown and Rainbow Trout in several localities. Of these Elk River near Elizabethton, Laurel Fork near Elizabethton, Little River near Knoxville, the Tellico Wildlife Management Area near Tellico Plains, and the Great Smoky Mountain National Park are the principal trout areas. The streams are stocked yearly from the hatcheries at Erwin and Morristown.

The region is also noted for its Muskellunge fishing in early spring and fall months. The better locations are Daddy's Creek near Crab Orchard, Emory River, near Oak Dale, Little Tennessee River near Loudon, and Obed River near Wartburg.

Smallmouth and Rock Bass fishing is best in Watauga River near Johnson City, in the Little Tennessee near Calderwood, Little Pigeon River near Gatlinburg, Holston River around Kingsport, and Hiwassee River above Charleston.

In addition to the larger lakes and streams several small lakes are found in the region that offer excellent fishing. Cove Lake located in Cove State Park near Caryville, offers 250 acres of good fishing. Reservations for cabins may be made by writing the Superintendent, Cove Lake State Park, Caryville, Tennessee. Bass, Crappie, and Bluegill fishing are very good.

David Crockett Lake located at Greeneville abounds in Bass, Crappie, and Bluegill. Several docks are available for the fisherman's use.

Laurel Lake near Maryville, operated by the Game and Fish Division, contains 59 acres and is reported to be an excellent fishing spot for Bass and Bluegill.

CENTRAL TENNESSEE

In the northern section of the region on the Kentucky boundary lies Dale Hollow Lake which was created by damming Obey River. Situated among the mountain peaks this lake is undoubtedly one of the most beautiful and picturesque in the state. One of the newer lakes, its fishing has been excellent and for this reason should be visited by all interested in that sport. Smallmouth, Largemouth, Crappie, and Bluegill are the outstanding species. Bluegill run exceedingly large and thus offer an excellent opportunity for the flyrod enthusiast as well as the cane pole fisherman. The lake contains some 40,000 acres and is well served with boat docks.

Great Falls Lake is one of the smaller bodies of water operated by the Tennessee Valley Authority and contains only 2300 acres of water. Although it is one of the oldest impoundments in the state, good fishing may still be enjoyed. Several fishing camps are available.

Hale's Bar is a TVA impoundment covering 6100 acres. It has been a favorite spot for the bass fisherman and many good strings have been taken. This was the first major hydroelectric development on the Tennessee River, being completed in 1913. Docks and camps are available.

Pickwick Lake located at Pickwick, Tennessee, is a 43,000 acre impoundment extending into Mississippi and Alabama. As is true below most dams, fishing is very good in the tail-water areas where Crappie, White Perch, and Catfish abound. In the main lake, in addition to these, Black Bass, Bluegill, and Walleye make up the main catch.

Center Hill Lake, an improvement opened to the public in June of 1949 is, at present, the fisherman's paradise of Tennessee. Many excellent catches of Large and Smallmouth Bass and Bluegill have been reported thus far. Several camps and docks are available with more to be built later.

Some of the more important small lakes are Brown's Lake near Nashville, Cumberland Park Lake near Crossville, Indian Lake near Hendersonville, Marrowbone Lake north of Nashville, Meadow Creek Lake near Crossville, Montgomery Bell State Park near White Bluff, Morton's Lake near Manchester, Napier Lake north of Hohenwald, Parksville Lake near Cleveland, Tullahoma Lake near Tullahoma, and Womack Lake near Manchester. All of these offer fishing for Bass, Bluegill, and Crappie and have boats available for rent. The majority have camps available on the lake.

A few of the better known streams of this section are listed below: Buffalo River in the vicinity of Napier and Lindon is well known to the fisherman for its production of Large and Smallmouth Bass, Rock Bass, and Walleye. Cumberland River in the upper section offers excellent fishing for Walleye in the early spring and fall and for Bass, Catfish and Crappie the year around.

Duck River in the vicinity of Shelbyville and Columbia is noted for the good catches of Small and Largemouth Bass. Harpeth River near Franklin and Nashville offers an excellent opportunity to fish for Bass, Crappie, and Catfish. Stone's River near Nashville and Red River near Clarksville offers fishing for Bass, Crappie, Bluegill, and Catfish.

WESTERN TENNESSEE

The two main fishing spots in Western Tennessee are Kentucky Lake and Reelfoot Lake.

Kentucky Lake is the greatest of the TVA lakes. Lying partly in Kentucky, its shore line extends more than 2300 miles around innumerable lagoons and harbors, making it the largest man-made lake in the United States. For 184 miles, the lake extends from Gilbertsville, Kentucky, to the base of Pickwick Dam near the Tennessee-Alabama state line. Fishing for Bass, Crappie, Bluegill, and Catfish has been excellent. Many docks and camps are available.

Reelfoot Lake, long widely known to anglers is a relatively shallow body of water, about 18 miles long and 2½ miles wide. Created by an earthquake in 1811, it has provided many excellent catches of Bass, Crappie, Bluegill, and Catfish. Numerous tourists and trailer camps are available at reasonable rates, as well as free picnic grounds and parking space.

Other important lakes are the Natchez, Trace Park Lakes near Camden, McCaskill Lake near Henderson, Chickasaw State Park Lake near Henderson, Twin Rivers Lake near Halls and Whiteville Lake near Whiteville. All of these offer fishing for Bass, Bluegill, Crappie, and Catfish. The river bottoms and cut off areas along the Mississippi, Big Sandy, Hatchie, Loosahatchie, and Obion conclude the better known fishing areas in the state. From these Bass, Crappie, and Bluegill are taken as well as many rough fish.

West Virginia Dept. of Nat. Resources

Little Falls at Bruce, West Virginia, on the Back Fork of the Elk, one of the state's popular Trout streams.

West Virginia

The 24,181 square miles of West Virginia offer a variety of good fishing. From the mountains of the East and South to the flood plains of the North and Central areas the taste and preference of freshwater fishermen can be satisfied. Swift, tumbling mountain streams, fast-flowing Smallmouth Bass streams; large reservoirs; artificial impoundments: placid, restful rivers with Largemouth and Smallmouth Bass, Muskies, Walleyes, Crappies, and Rock Bass. Ice fishing for the rugged outdoorsman and restful float trips fill the fishing menu.

Trout fishing is rising to an all time high due to the increased capacity of trout hatcheries. Stepped up enforcement of anti-pollution laws and the efforts of all divisions of the Department of Natural Resources has made West Virginia one of the fishing meccas of the East.

Trout are found on the eastern slopes of the Allegheníes in Grant and Pendleton Counties. The streams at the head of the Potomac, North Fork of the South Branch, South Fork of the South Branch, North Fork of Patterson Creek, Trout Run and Thorny Creek in this region are all good.

On the Western Slopes, streams flowing down to the Elk, Kanawha and Greenbrier offer excellent trout fishing. Cranberry, Williams, East and West Fork of Greenbrier, Gandy, Glady Fork, Shavers Fork, Back Fork of Elk, Black Water, Knapps Creek and Anthony are names well known to fishermen. Bass and Muskellunge addicts find good sport in the lower sections of the Elk, Greenbrier, New River, Upper Kanawha, Little Kanawha, Middle Island Creek and Hughes River. Muskies are numerous in most of these waters, and Bass are plentiful. The South Branch of the Potomac and the Cacapon should be included on any list of famous Smallmouth Bass streams.

Artificial impoundments are receiving a lot of attention from the Department of Natural Resources. Summit Lake, Spruce Knob Lake, Seneca Lake, Coopers Rock are stocked with Trout. Other warmer waters in Moncove, Teeters Creek Lake, Laurel Lake, Bear Rocks, Sherwood, Warden, Berwin, are filled with Bass, Bluegills, and Crappie.

A float trip on the Little Kanawha, the Greenbrier, or the South Branch of the Potomac through the "trough" makes an exciting fisherman's holiday.

The large reservoirs created by the Bluestone Dam and the Sutton Dams produce good catches of both Large and Smallmouth Bass, Crappie and Bluegills, and a planting of Muskies some time ago has produced some nice catches.

Lodging and other facilities are available within easy distance of practically all the mentioned streams and lakes. The Department maintains cabins and tenting areas at various parks and forests. A booklet is available that lists farm houses open to tourists. Maps, regulations, and guide books can be obtained on request to the Department of Natural Resources, State Capitol, Charleston.

NORTHERN MISSISSIPPI VALLEY

This area consists of all states north of the Ohio and north and east of the Missouri, plus the addition of Missouri which is partly south and west of that line. The Great Lakes area provides the major part of the sport fishing for Lake Trout and Muskellunge. The states in this unit, together with the province of Ontario, also include the most famous Smallmouth Bass waters. Trout fishing is also important both in the vicinity of the Great Lakes and in the Ozarks.

W. Va. Ind. & Pub. Comm.

At the end of a Greenbrier Float Party trip most guests can exhibit fish which tested their angling prowess.

In addition, there are thousands of miles of streams, almost innumerable natural ponds and lakes, and many artificial impoundments that provide an army of fishermen with angling opportunities. Northern Pike, Perch, Bass of several species, Bream, Crappies, Catfish, and Carp are the most widely utilized, but other species also contribute in a lesser degree.

Illinois

Even though Illinois is primarily an agricultural state, more than 100,000 acres of water distributed among 344 publicly-owned lakes are available to the angler. In addition there are about 7,000 miles of fishable streams, 1,100 club and association lakes, and 50,000 farm ponds. Because it is a rich agricultural state many of the waters are high in fertility and abound in fish worthy of any angler.

The Fish Division of the Illinois Department of Conservation with its staff of biologists has been given the job of managing the state's water resources for more and better fishing. A sound program has been set up which includes the construction of new impoundments, proper stocking, the elimination of undesirable fish in lakes that can be managed, and a manipulation of fish populations to increase the spawning of Bass and to speed the growth of panfish.

Tops on the game fish list on a state-wide basis is the Largemouth Bass; the state record for this species is 10 pounds 4 ounces. Some of the better Bass lakes are Little Grassy, Crab Orchard, and Devil's Kitchen, all federal lakes located near Carbondale; Lake Murphysboro, a state lake near Murphysboro; Lake Sara, near Effingham; New Lake Mattoon, about 10 miles south of Mattoon; Anderson Lake, a state owned backwater lake off the Illinois River near Havana; and Lincoln Trail, a state lake near Marshall. Good Bass fishing is also found in backwater lakes off the Mississippi River in Jo Davies and Calhoun Counties and in the Illinois River backwater lakes near Grafton.

Largemouth Bass are taken in a number of ways,

Jim Sherman

Fishing Iowa's Des Moines River

but the bait caster and spin fisherman probably account for most. In March and April underwater spinners and diving lures that simulate minnows are very effective. Some top bass fishermen prefer to scull along the shoreline, toss a spinner to the bank, and retrieve it to the boat. Another good underwater lure is the artificial nightcrawler. In May and June, a wide variety of surface plugs that make popping, gurgling, sputtering, and other odd noises produce exciting strikes. Early morning and late evening are preferred fishing times. In the hot months of July and August, the successful day-time angler often turns to a black or yellow jig with a black pork rind attached. During hot nights, fly rod experts take lunkers on cork-bodied popping bugs with hair wings. Not to be overlooked is the time-tested cane pole and live minnow. This is an effective method, particularly in back-water lakes or in other areas with brush and trees along the shoreline that make casting a lure difficult.

Excellent Smallmouth fishing is available in Central and Northern Illinois streams. The Salt, Middle, and North Forks of the Vermilion River and its tributaries between Champaign and Danville; Kickapoo Creek near Lawndale; Rock Creek in White Pines State Park near Oregon; Salt Creek in DeWitt and Logan Counties; the Kishwaukee River in the Kishwaukee Forest Preserve near New Milford in Winnebago County; and Bureau Creek near Princeton are but a few of the streams known for their Smallmouth fishing. The spin caster is usually at an advantage over the fly or bait caster since he can present a light bait without it becoming entangled too often in shoreline brush. Minnows, crayfish, and minnow-imitating lures and spinners are all good baits.

The Mississippi, in the upper part of the Illinois section, offers good Sauger fishing below the locks and dams, and some nice Walleyes are taken below the locks and dams on the Rock River in Northwestern Illinois. Walleyes are often mixed with Saugers in the Mississippi, but in the Rock, Saugers are rarely caught. Spring and fall are the best time to try for these good-eating members of the Perch Family. Minnow and various spinners top the "what to use" list.

The Northern Pike is not caught in great numbers in Illinois, but every year some nice ones are taken from the Fox Chain-O-Lakes area in northeastern Illinois. Grass Lake and Pistakee Lake have fair reputations as Northern Pike waters. The Golden Shiner, locally called golden roach, is the preferred bait.

Panfishermen in Illinois need take a back seat to no one. Choice Bluegill fishing is available at Horseshoe Lake, a state-owned oxbow lake near Cairo; many of the backwater lakes off the Illinois River near Frafton; Rice and Anderson Lakes, state owned backwaters near Havana; Lake Chautauqua, a federally owned backwater northeast of Havana; and in many of the artificial state lakes scattered throughout the state. The Fox Chain-O-Lakes region often produces good Bluegill fishing during the spawning season. The major waters in the "Chain" are Pistakee Lake, Mippersink Lake, Fox Lake, Petite Lake, Grass Lake, Lake Marie, Channel Lake and Lake Catherine.

The common earthworm and red wrigglers are especially good Bluegill baits and probably account for the majority of these scrappers caught. However, fly-rod anglers also have good luck with poppers and wet flies, especially when Bluegills are on the spawning beds. Crickets, insect larvae, catalpa worms, and other natural baits are also effective. Bluegills are caught in larger numbers than any other species and bite during the entire fishing season.

Illinois has a number of good Crappie lakes. Among the best are Horseshoe Lake, Crab Orchard, and Little Grassy, which yielded the state record 4¼ pounder; the Illinois River backwater lakes near Frafton; Lake Decatur at Decatur; Lake Chautauqua; Anderson Lake; Rice Lake; Spring Lake; a federally owned backwater off the Mississippi River near Savanna; and the channels connecting the lakes in the Fox Chain-O-Lakes.

Crappie fishing reaches its peak in the spring. The favorite method is minnow fishing around fallen trees and brush. In addition to minnows, small artificial lures and spinners produce good results.

Another popular panfish is the White Bass. Largest numbers of these fish are found in big rivers and river-connected lakes. It affords good fishing below the locks and dams on the upper half of the Mississippi River in Illinois, in Spring Lake near Savanna and in the Fox River immediately above Grass Lake in the "Chain" area. Minnows and bright spinners are the favorite of many anglers.

"Mr. Whiskers," the Channel Catfish, is a prized fish sought by anglers throughout the length and breadth of Illinois. Not only is it an excellent eating fish, but its sporting qualities are gaining attention. Trot lines, bank poles, jugs and cans baited with minnows, stink baits, blood baits, chicken entrails, cut fish and many other strange baits take large numbers of these scaleless fish each year. Lake fishermen take Catfish regularly by drifting in a boat with the current or wind and fishing on the bottom. Spinfishing with artificial lures is growing in popularity.

A relatively new fish to Illinois anglers is the Redear, a sunfish closely resembling the Bluegill. The Redear is a native of the southern states and was imported to Illinois in 1935. Good populations have been established in Lake Murphysboro; Lincoln Trail Lake, and Argyle Lake, a state park near

Macomb; Siloam Springs State Park near Quincy; and Lake Le-Aqua-Na, a state lake near Freeport. Angling methods are a bit different for Redear than for Bluegill. A spinner-worm combination fished deep has proven effective. Cricket fished deep are also good. These fish have been known to hit wet flies but not generally with the same regularity as bluegills.

Trout fishing is on a "put-and-take" basis, because Illinois streams and lakes do not have the natural requirements for trout survival and successful reproduction. Each spring Rainbow and Brown Trout are obtained from the U.S. Fish and Wildlife Service and stocked in a few areas. If they are not caught within a few weeks after release, they are usually lost due to flooding and warm water.

Species that make up most of the remaining sport fishing catch are the widely distributed Bullhead and Carp; Yellow Perch, which offer good fishing along the Lake Michigan shoreline in springtime; Blue and Flathead Catfish, popular with river fishermen; and Yellow Bass; Green Sunfish, Warmouth and Fresh-Water Sheepshead, which are found throughout the state.

About 60 percent of Illinois' ten million people live in the Chicago area, which makes the demand for fishing waters very heavy in the northeastern part of the state. But fishing opportunities are available within a radius of a few miles of Chicago, and there are 27 lakes with a combined total of 1,200 acres of water in the Cook County Forset Preserve. Many of these lakes are providing good Bass and Bluegill fishing as a result of rehabilitation and proper management. Wolf Lake, a 450-acre state lake in the southeast part of Cook County on the Illinois-Indiana boundary is a popular spot. And in Lake and McHenry Counties there are almost 12,000 acres of water spread over 42 public lakes.

In the mid-1960's such major projects as the Carlyle and Shelbyville Reservoirs on the Kaskaskia River are expected to be finished, also, Rend Lake in Southern Illinois will probably become a reality. With them, thousands of acres of fine fishing waters will be added to those now being enjoyed by Illinois anglers.

Indiana

"Land of the Indians" and birthplace of the Northwest Territory, Indiana has sparkling lakes and meandering streams, sweeping prairies, and rolling hills. Indiana state parks, forests, and sanctuaries, plus a thousand lakes and hundreds of miles of streams annually attract sportsmen from near and far. Hundreds of farm ponds offer additional fishing opportunities throughout the state.

North central Indiana is noted for its beautiful lakes, ranging in size from the larger lakes such as Wawasee in Kosciusko County and Maxinkuckee in Marshall County down to the smallest in size with about an acre of water.

These Hoosier lakes are filled with fish, and the fishermen crowd them in winter and in summer for the fish that can be had. Ice fishing in Indiana has reached a new high in recent years, but this is mostly in the northern and the central parts.

Bounded on the north in part by Lake Michigan and on the south by the Ohio River, Indiana has much to offer the anglers. The streams in the north have Trout, but as in so many other states, it's knowing where to go into the stream that gets the best results. Though the Trout are small in size there are Brooks, Rainbows, and Browns.

As one travels to the south, the fishing takes on a new complexion . . . mostly for Large and Smallmouth Bass, White or Spotted Bass, Walleye, Northern Pike, panfish such as Yellow Perch, Crappies, Bluegills, Rock Bass, Channel Cat, and now and then a Muskie. The Big and Little Blue Rivers have Muskies.

The best times of the year to fish are in the spring or early summer and in the fall because fish go deep during the heat of the summer and the lakes are crowded to capacity.

Bass is the important game fish in Indiana, and the lakes of northeastern Indiana boast good Bass fishing. Crooked Lake near Angola has good Smallmouth and Bluegill fishing. Nearby James and George Lakes are a part of a chain and are used often for canoe trips. They yield Walleyes, Bass, Northern Pike and panfish.

Oliver Lake in La Grange County has good Largemouth Bass fishing as well as Northern Pike and panfish. Cedar Lake and Shipshewana have Largemouth Bass, Perch, and Bluegills, and rival in a way the fishing in Adams and Third Lakes.

One of the best lakes for Largemouth and panfish is an artificial body called Sylvan Lake. The biggest lake is Wawasee with 21 miles of shoreline, and the state has planted this with Bass, Walleyes, and panfish. It's a summer resort lake, with all kinds of boating, but the fishing remains good.

The Tippecanoe River is famous for its canoe trips and a good fishing stream too. Other lakes in the area that are worth fishing include Barber, Chapman, Dewart, Webster, Winona, Pike, Silver, Manitou, Lake of the Woods, and Maxinkuckee, all of which boast fairly good Bass fishing.

Some of the finest fishing to be had in the state is in the many lakes around Columbia City. There are lakes like Big, Tri-Lakes, and Loon Lake where the Bluegills, Perch, Walleyes, and Bass are hefty.

Indiana streams run high and muddy in the spring, but they settle down in about June. The Wabash and its upper tributaries contain Bass, Walleyes, Sauger, panfish, and Channel Catfish. From Terre Haute to the Ohio River, the Wabash is a great river for Channel Cat fishing. There are Smallmouth Bass and Kentucky Bass in the lower portions of the Wabash.

In the southwestern corner of Indiana near Evansville, Hovey's Lake boasts wonderful scenery, cypress trees, draped with southern moss, and good Largemouth Bass fishing, panfish, and Channel Catfish.

Brown County in the south central part of the state is a wooded paradise. Flat Rock River near this area has good Smallmouth Bass fishing, and just south of Martinsville there is a 13,000-acre wilderness with six artificial lakes that are always good for a mess of panfish and some nice Bass fishing.

Brown County State Park is 251 miles from Chicago, and annually attracts tourists from many of the surrounding states. There are 3,822 acres of beautiful woodland set aside as a memorial to Kin Hubbard, creator of Abe Martin, the vagabond philosopher of the Brown County hills.

McCormick Creek State Park has 662 acres of wilderness scenery, with a picturesque waterfall, with fairly good fishing in the stream.

Turkey Run State Park of 1,301 acres has good fishing in Sugar Creek and also in Big Raccoon Creek. Fine Smallmouth Bass and Rock Bass fishing.

La Porte is known as the "city of lakes," which include Clear, Stone, Fish, Trap, Hudson, North Pine, and South Pine Lakes. Located between Chicago and Indianapolis, these lakes get a heavy play and are quite productive.

The best fishing near Fort Wayne is in the St. Mary's River for Largemouth Bass, White Perch, Walleye, and Catfish.

Freeman Lake, 1,800 acres of water, near Monticello has Largemouth and Smallmouth Bass, Rock Bass, Walleye, Perch, and other panfish.

Iowa

Sport fishing in Iowa is divided rather loosely by five geographic sections as follows:

1. Cold-water Trout streams in nine northeast Iowa counties.
2. Clear-water Smallmouth Bass streams of the northeast quarter of the state.
3. Turbid water Catfish streams extending from the center of the state to the south and west.
4. Artificial lakes and farm ponds located mostly in the southern half of the state.
5. Natural lakes of the northwest one-third of the state. The headwaters of the streams draining these areas also afford some fishing for Northern Pike, Walleye and Catfish.

These areas are loosely defined, there is much overlapping and many species are common to one or all of the regions.

Bullhead fishing is probably first in importance. Every section of the state has "bullheaders" from 8 to 80 to whom this fish ranks first in popularity. The Channel Catfish is widely distributed throughout the streams and lakes of Iowa and is the most sought-after species in Iowa streams.

Some of the best streams for Channel Catfish are

Iowa State Conservation Comm.

Lower French Creek.

the Des Moines, Little Sioux, Raccoon, Skunk, Cedar and Wapsipinicon. Flathead or Yellow Catfish are fished for chiefly below the dams on the larger rivers mentioned above. This is "sit and wait" fishing in its truest form. Common baits are large wads of night crawlers, large chubs, or other fish, either dead or alive. To the patient fisherman who knows the Flahead "holes," big fellows of 20 to 40 pounds are not uncommon.

Recently a technique of "jigging" has become popular for taking flatheads below the navigation dams on the Mississippi River. Heavy leadhead jigs are bounced along the bottom in the swift water below the roller dams in the main channel and when conditions are right are eagerly taken by Flaheads. Fish of over 50 pounds have been landed and terminal gear is often lost on large fish. Only about one of five of these large fish hooked are landed.

In northeast Iowa, fishing with blood for Channel Catfish is a common practice. Fishermen wading out into the current use several hundred feet of light line. Clotted blood that will not stay with the hook well enough to be cast is eased out into the current. A light sinker and a float are adjusted so the bait rides just off the bottom. When a fish strikes, it requires a vigorous heave of the long pole to take up the slack in the line and set the hook. This is a popular mid-summer sport on the Cedar River.

In some of the western streams, notably the lower reaches of the Sioux River, floating with grasshoppers is common. This is done by rigging the pole with a comparatively short line, and baiting the hook with grasshoppers so that it drifts just off the bottom. The boat is floated along with the current, and one man usually handles two poles. This method is exceedingly productive at times.

Wading the stream or following the bank and fishing with a casting rod is the most common successful method of taking Catfish. In this method the fisherman wades downstream, fishing in the thread of the current where it cuts under a bank, around a snag, or out past a submerged stump. Bait used is principally prepared Catfish bait, shrimp and chicken entrails. The prepared bait is fished with a treble hook. A comparatively heavy free running sinker is tied onto the line. About 18 inches above the hook and below the sinker a split shot is secured to the line to keep the sinker from coming up to the bait, yet leaving the sinker free running so a strike may be detected easily. At the first feel of a strike the hook is set. Chicken entrails are fished the same way except that a single hook is used. Commonly, a loop is tied in the line just above the shank of the hook, the chicken entrails threaded onto the hook up through the loop in the line and back under the hook so that the entire shank is covered. Preference is shown for the chicken entrails in early spring and fall fishing, and prepared bait works best during the heat of the summer. There has been a recent trend to spinning gear and the use of unweighted or light weighted natural baits for summer fishing in these streams. Minnows, crayfish and frogs are the most popular baits.

Smallmouth bass fishing is best in the Cedar River, the Wapsipinicon, Upper Iowa, Turkey, the Maquoketa, and tributaries. Fishing with live minnows and crayfish is common, but best success is had with the flyrod, using streamer flies and a variety of other small lures and spinners.

Jim Sherman

Summer on the Coon in Iowa.

Nearly all of Iowa's natural lakes as well as artificial lakes are productive of Largemouth Bass, and the favorite method of taking them is with a casting rod. A great variety of lures are used. In midsummer the most popular are surface baits such as poppers and wigglers.

Spirit Lake and Okoboji have good populations of White Bass, and at certain seasons these constitute an important part of the catch by fishermen casting underwater lures and spinners.

Spirit Lake, East and West Okoboji, Storm Lake, Clear Lake, and others, provide good walleye fishing. The most common fishing method is trolling at a depth of 12 to 15 feet with a live minnow and a spinner but many Walleyes are taken mornings and evenings casting off-shore with artificial lures. The new techniques of fishing leadhead jigs with and without a bobber have greatly increased the catch of Walleye for shore fishermen. Trolling at moderate speed and working a jig with a pumping motion has consistently provided limit catches of Walleye early in the season in rocky shoal areas. Later in the year a float and streamer-fly combination will take Walleyes in the same areas in and around the weed beds.

Bluegills are taken from all of Iowa lakes, either by still fishing or with the flyrod. The many artificial lakes and farm ponds in southern Iowa abound with Bluegills. Fishing for Bluegills from shore with a float and fly on spinning gear has become very popular in West Okoboji lake recently.

Crappies are found in most of the streams and lakes of Iowa. Bait fishing with small minnows hooked just back of the dorsal fin is the most popular method of taking crappies but they will readily take flies and small spinning lures on occasion.

Iowa has about 45 trout streams in nine northeastern counties. These are small spring-fed brooks in scenic valleys. The trout season is open year around with a good carry-over each year. Stocking is used to supplement the existing populations. Most of the Iowa trout fishermen fish with bait, particularly in the spring. Fly fishing is productive throughout the year. Wet flies are the bread and butter fare with occasional exceptionally good dry-fly fishing. Spinning lures are deadly on trout for those that have mastered their use.

The fall trout fishing is excellent and a trend to late fall and winter trout fishing by those addicted to trout fever has been noticed the past few years.

Northern Pike have been restored to importance as game fish in the northwestern Iowa lakes and in a few marshes. Clear Lake, West Okoboji and Spirit Lake are producing northern pike. Sweet Marsh and Bays Branch which were built as duck marshes have provided excellent Northern Pike fishing.

Suckers, Sturgeon and many more of Iowa's 140-odd species of fish are taken in various localities by a variety of methods.

Michigan

Michigan ranks third among the states in the number of fishing licenses sold, being passed only by Minnesota and California. Michigan offers excellent fishing the year around. Including ice-fishing during the winter months, Bluegills, Perch, and other pan fish may be taken in any month in the year. The opening for Trout, Pike, and Walleyes comes in late April, followed by a June opening for Large- and Smallmouth Black Bass.

Michigan is divided into two large peninsulas, connected by a bridge across the Straits of Mackinac. The Upper Peninsula is bounded on the north by Lake Superior, and on the south by Lakes Huron and Michigan; the Lower Peninsula is bounded on the east by Lake Huron and on the west by Lake Michigan. The Porcupine Mountains, facing Lake Superior on the Upper Peninsula, are the highest point in the state, being 2,023 feet above sea level. The eastern portion of the Upper Peninsula is lower, but is well known for its picturesque cliffs of the Lake Superior shoreline and its many scenic waterfalls.

The Great Lakes provide the greatest inland commercial fishery in the world, Michigan's share in it—over 25 million pounds a year—is exceeded only by that of the Province of Ontario. The most important species are Chubs, Lake Herring, Yellow Perch, Smelt, and Carp.

Summer fishing is a major tourist attraction to residents of Michigan and to out-of-state visitors. The fresh mid-summer climate is another major attraction as are the numerous scenic features. The result is that the tourist business ranks second only to the automotive industry in the state's total economy.

The state contains more than 11,000 lakes and 15,000 miles of good Trout streams. The waters produce excellent fishing for large Trout, Muskies, Northern Pike, Walleyes, Large- and Smallmouth Bass, and pan fish.

Michigan's 62 state parks and recreation areas, all of which furnish camping facilities close to fishing waters, are supplemented by 108 state forest campgrounds, each located either on a lake or a stream. The state has five national forests. Blaney Park in the Upper Peninsula northeast of Manistique is a private resort in the center of 22,000 acres of forest with its own fishing lakes and streams. Known as the "Playground of Paul Bunyan," it contains a museum of implements and machinery used in logging operations. Isle Royale National Park is an island just off the shores of Minnesota, but is adjacent to the Upper Peninsula and holds a wilderness area of 133,663 acres. Boat service can be obtained to the island from Copper Harbor, Michigan, as well as from Grand Marais, Minnesota. The island is 45 miles long and 9 miles across. The park forms a sanctuary for moose, lynx, beaver, and rabbits, and is one of the few places left south of Canada where the howl of the timber wolf may still be heard. Lake trout trolling was formerly an important sport around Isle Royale, but very few fish are taken in the waters of Lake Superior today.

Ice fishing is a popular sport in Michigan, and the catch may include Crappies, Perch, Bluegills, Pike, Sunfish, Smelt, and Walleye. In early winter the Bluegills will be deep, but they usually move up as the season progresses. To lure the fish, a spoon or jig is moved up and down in a rhythmic motion. Crystal Lake, Lake Charlevoix and other lakes in the western part of the state produce good catches of Smelt through the ice, using minnows as bait.

Lake trout trolling was all but eliminated in the Great Lakes by the invasion of the sea lamprey. Control of this predator and rehabilitation of the lake trout fishery are high priority projects in the region.

Some of the largest Muskellunge, Rainbow and Brown Trout taken in North America have been caught in Michigan. The biggest Muskies are taken from Lake St. Clair, mostly by trolling, and a few are taken each year from Lac Vieux Desert in the Upper Peninsula on the Wisconsin border. Other waters in which Muskies are found include many of the large inland lakes located close to the shore of Lake Michigan, bays along the Great Lakes, and Burt, Mullett, Black, and Thornapple Lakes.

The Rainbows, which were first planted in Michigan waters in 1876, hold a leading place in the hearts of fly fishermen. The largest are taken from the runs of fish which mature in the Great Lakes and enter the larger rivers during the spring to spawn. Most of the streams emptying into Lake Superior or into the northern half of Lake Michigan and Lake Huron have these spring Rainbow runs. Several hundred inland lakes also provide good fishing for Rainbow Trout planted from state hatcheries. Among the more famous streams are the St. Marys Rapids, the Ausable, Platte, Pere Marquette, the Manistee, Carp, Baldwin, the Boardman and the Jordan.

Brook Trout were first introduced to the southern peninsula when the Grayling began to decline. Since this popular Trout among fly fishing purists prefers pure, swift, cold waters with gravel or rocky bottoms, the Brookie did remarkably well after being planted in Michigan. Today Michigan boasts good Brook Trout fishing in several thousand miles of cold streams in the northern two-thirds of the state. The sad story in Michigan, of course, is that of the extermination of the Michigan Grayling, a sporty game fish that was wiped out by log-running in the big timber boom in the late 1800's. Michigan is famous for its float trips where fishermen drift down rivers while fishing. It is also a great state for canoeing, and a booklet entitled *Michigan Canoe Trails,* is available from the State Department of Conservation.

The Presque Isle Trip, Upper Peninsula, Gogebic County, offers the sportsman the wildest trip in the state because this stream is fast, flowing through rugged country, but it is a magnificent river and therefore worth the effort. One may put in at the bridge at Marenisco on US-2 and travel 100 miles to where the Presque Isle empties into Lake Michigan. It skirts the Porcupine mountains, and in many places the cliffs rise straight up. The fishing is for Bass, Northern Pike, and an occasional large Rainbow. The trip is over four waterfalls with good fishing in the pools below each of them.

Other famous Upper Peninsula trips are: Black River from the Michigan-Wisconsin border to Lake Superior with fishing for Rainbow and Brook Trout; the Ontonagon River from Crooked Lake to Lake Superior featuring wonderful Trout and some good Bass and Northern Pike fishing; the Paint River from Gibbs City of Crystal Falls. This stretch noted for its good Trout fishing. The fishing best for Bass and Northern Pike: the Net River, the Michigamme River, Menominee River, Escanaba River, Au Train Waters, the Tahquamenon River, and the St. Marys River.

Lower Peninsula trips are: Inland Lakes Route from Conway and East Jordan to Lake Huron, Ocqueoc River from Lake Emma to Hammond Bay in Lake Huron, Thunder Bay from McCormick Lake southwest of Atlanta to Alpena, Jordan River from Graves Crossing about 11 miles east of East Jordan down the river for some of the best Trout fishing in the state. Brook, Rainbows, and Browns: the Intermediate Chain of Lakes from Six Mile Lake near East Jordan to Elk River, Rainbows in the spring and with Walleyes and Bass in the summer, the Boardman River, the Au Sable River, the big Manistee River, the Pine River, the Little Manistee River, the Pere Marquette River, the Rifle River, the White River, the Muskegon River, the Grand River, the Thornapple River, the Kalamazoo River, the Brule River, the Black River, the Paw Paw River, the St. Joseph River, the Tittibawassee River, the Huron River, and the Saginaw Bay.

The Smallmouth and Largemouth Bass fishing in the state is excellent especially in the waters of the Great Lakes. Potaganissing Bay near the Lower St. Marys River is a good Smallmouth location; Lake St. Clair out of Detroit is another; Little Bay de Noc near Escanaba; Menominee and Michigamme Rivers near Iron Mountain; Hulbert Lake near Hulbert; Presque Isle River near Marenisco; Dinner Lake near Watersmeet; Lake Gogebic; Crystal Falls and the Paint River in Iron County; Gratiot Lake near Copper Harbor; Lake Bellaire at Bellaire; Thornapple Lake and River near Hastings; Crystal Lake near Beulah; Pentwater Lake;

Jim Sherman

Midsummer in Backbone State Park.

Lake Macatawa near Holland; Thunder Bay, Alpena; Au Gres River, Saginaw Bay; Harbor Beach, Lake Huron; Tawas Bay in Ionco County; and Houghton Lake near Prudenville . . . all are excellent Bass fishing waters.

Opening day for fishing in Houghton Lake is celebrated by sportsmen from all over America.

Minnesota

Minnesota, with its 11,000 lakes, has much to offer fishermen, both resident and non-resident. It is the mecca of many thousands of mid-western anglers who have favorite spots among the innumerable lakes.

These lakes furnish largely warm-water fish and offer a fine array of sport fishing species. There are considerable trout waters, although they comprise only a small portion of the available fishing. Some of the best are in the Walker-Park Rapids area, Brooks and Brown predominating. The Minnesota Department of Business Research and Development, Division of Publicity, State Capitol, St. Paul, issues a detailed pamphlet entitled "Free Fish Dope" which should be secured by anyone planning a fishing trip to the Gopher State. This pamphlet divides the state into districts, giving the names of principal lakes and streams, type of fish to be found, directions for reaching each one, and in many cases the type of lures most favored by anglers.

TROUT

Trout waters are largely but not entirely in the territory north and east of Duluth, lying north of Lake Superior. This includes the Quetico-Superior wilderness area as well as streams and lakes outside its boundaries. There are also scattered trout waters in other sections of northern Minnesota. Brook, Rainbow, and Brown Trout are all present. The streams and lakes are largely Trout waters, although intermingled with them are Northern Pike, Walleye, Bass, and Crappie lakes that are obviously warmer or otherwise more favorable for

Mo. Conservation Comm.

Man-made lakes with rugged, wooded shorelines offer a variety of fishing and a variety of fish. A nice Jack-Salmon (Walleye) is brought to boat in Lake Ozark.

these species. Lake Trout and Northern Pike are often found together in lakes predominately populated by these two fish.

In extreme southeastern Minnesota, in the unglaciated area about Wabasha and Winona, a number of small streams furnish Brook, Brown, and Rainbow Trout fishing. Most of these are in the vicinity of Red Wing, Lake City, Winona, and nearby towns. This district furnishes the same type of fishing as that found in the trout fishing section in the adjoining part of Iowa.

Baits most favored by Lake Trout in the northeastern section are June bug spinners with minnows, Jarvenen spoon hooks, K-B spoons, and Daredevil spoons; Rainbow Trout take small spinners either with or without minnows, grasshoppers, flies, and sometimes ordinary small plugs, particularly toward sunset. The same lures that succeed in taking Lake Trout are also useful for Northern Pike in the same waters, although they are fished somewhat shallower.

In the southwestern section, bait fishermen prefer worms, although the Trout here take standard types of flies.

Trolling for Lake Trout in Lake Superior during the summer months is becoming a popular sport. Large spoons trolled on copper wire are the preferred technique and anyone interested is advised to consult local guides at Duluth, Grand Marais, and other fishing centers along the lake shore. Most boat liveries furnish the special tackle required for this type of fishing. Another interesting feature here is the use of **trolling planes,** a devise hooked into the line ahead of the bait, which takes the bait down to 150-200 feet. When the fish strikes the plane is tripped and aids in bringing the fish to the surface.

MUSKELLUNGE

Muskellunge are scattered widely through suitable waters over the northern part of the state, but the greatest number of lakes in which they are found lie in the territory extending southward from Rainy Lake and Lake of the Woods.

Favorite lures used for these big fish are Jarvenen spoon, double Shannon spinner, large minnows used either with or without spinners, jointed pikie minnow, and large spoons of the K-B type. Again it is well to consult local guides or otherwise secure local information.

WARM WATER FISH

Northern Pike, Walleye, Largemouth and Smallmouth Bass, Crappies, Sunfish, Catfish, and Rock Bass are well scattered over the state. Many lakes contain a mixture of all species, while others are predominantly populated with some one variety. There are, however, few accessible lakes which do not offer a variety of fishing. If for any reason it is limited to one fish, it is usually so listed in the "Free Fish Dope." Many lakes are known as Walleye or Northern Pike lakes, while others are predominately Bass although nearly all offer opportunities to angle for other varieties.

Practically every known type of bait and lure is used at some time in these varied waters, but the following are widely favored.

Northern Pike at times take almost any spoon or plug although daredevils and jointed pikie minnow are widely used. They also take live minnows and frogs in many sections.

Walleyes are most commonly taken by trolling with such lures as Leech Lake spinners with minnows, Prescott spinners with minnows, June bug spinners with minnows, river-runt pikie minnows, redheaded bugs, daredevils, spoons with feathered hooks, Heddon river runts, and often equally well with live bait such as frogs and minnows.

Both Largemouth and Smallmouth Bass are regularly taken on live frogs and minnows. Bucktail and wet flies, red and white plugs, river runts, redhead plugs, basserinos, and artificial mice and frogs are the most popular artificial lures.

Crappies are taken largely with live minnows but they also respond to worms, small spoons, and small flies at certain seasons.

Perch and bluegills, as well as other varieties of sunfish, prefer worms to any other bait, although they will take flies or small spinners.

Silver Bass or White Bass are taken almost entirely with live minnows or with a minnow and spinner combination.

In general, it may be said that the warm water fish are found in the majority of the lakes. Northern Pike and Walleyes are major species in the north, becoming less important to the south, Pan fish, particularly Crappies and Bluegills, and to a less extent the bass, make a relatively more important contribution to angling in the southern part of the state. Catfish, Bullheads, and Silver Bass are also found in increasing abundance in the south, the Silver Bass being particularly abundant in some of the lakes in southern and southeastern Minnesota.

In addition to these major game fish, minor species of fish are present particularly to the south. Those that are most commonly found are Tullibees, Suckers, Buffalo, Sturgeon, and Whitefish. All of these are of minor fishing interest but are taken to some extent.

Visiting anglers desiring wilderness fishing conditions are advised to go to Grand Marais, Tofte, Hoveland, Ely, Tower or other outfitting points for canoe trips into the back country. This district offers opportunities for Trout, Pike, Walleye, and Bass, with major emphasis on the first species.

It is difficult to pick out any major area in a territory so abundantly blessed with fishing waters, but Detroit Lakes, Bemidji, Brainard, Grand Rapids, Walker Park Rapids, and Fergus Falls are centers of well known fishing areas each offering access to many waters and a variety of fishing opportunity.

Missouri

The fishing visitor to Missouri will find a variety of opportunities to indulge his favorite version of fishing sport. He can choose from four general types of water, according to his tastes. These types, and the section in which each predominates, are 1) the large impounded lakes; 2) the fast, clear-water streams of the Ozarks; 3) the semi-clear streams of the northwest. In addition, there are somewhat specialized fishing waters. These include the intensively managed trout streams, the Missouri and Mississippi Rivers, and numerous, scattered impoundments such as farm ponds and small city reservoirs which are found in every district.

The surroundings, methods of fishing, and the kinds of fish predominating in these areas are as different as the waters themselves. Each affords opportunities for excellent sport, and together they offer the fisherman a chance at almost every kind of fish, and every method of taking them, to be found in the Middle West.

Missouri seasons and limits are generous and the wildlife regulations are simple and easy to obey.

THE LARGE LAKES

There are eight major lakes, all south of the Missouri River and all created by dams for power or flood control. They are all located on well-known fishing streams. Boats, cabin, hotel and camping accommodations are available at or near each lake. A list of resorts on these and other waters is available from the Missouri Division of Commerce and Industrial Development, Jefferson City, Mo. There are no closed seasons on game fish in Missouri impoundments.

All these lakes afford good fishing, all are scenic. They differ considerably in size, extent of development, and kinds of game fish most requently encountered.

LAKE OF THE OZARKS

The largest Missouri impoundment, this lake in the Osage River sprawls its 1,300 miles of shoreline dragon-shaped across 61,000 acres in four counties. Innumerable bays and points deeply serrate and main body winding through the rock bluffs and forested slopes of the Ozark foothills. Especially well-known for its White Bass and Crappie fishing, it also yields catches of Walleyes, Channel Cat, Black Bass, and Sunfishes. The favorite area for White Bass fishing is the Niangua arm, near Camdenton; the Osage just below the dam yields some lunker Walleyes. Best catches are made during the first and last part of the open season.

Favorite lures for fly, spinning, or plug rods are the smaller, flashier plugs and spoons, or bucktail-spinner combinations imitating minnows, either cast or trolled. Bait fishermen lean to live minnows for White Bass, Crappie, and Channel Cat.

Boat and cabin accommodations are abundant, and the area contains a number of highly-developed resorts.

The character of the lake may be changed with the recent construction of the Pomme De Terre dam just upstream. Lake of the Ozarks is expected to become much clearer in years to come.

LAKE TANEYCOMO

This is the oldest of Missouri's large lakes, but in a sense it is also one of the newest. Lake Taneycomo is a 2,200 acre impoundment on the White River just north of the Arkansas line in Southwest Missouri. It was highly developed as a warm-water fishery with resorts, boating, swimming and water skiing offered in abundance. In 1953, however, Table Rock dam, at the upstream end of Taneycomo, was completed. The cold discharge from the new dam cooled Lake Taneycomo to temperatures in the lower 50's, even in mid-summer. Rainbow trout were stocked in the lake and it is fast becoming famous for the quality of its trout fishing. It is in an area now highly developed for tourism with particular emphasis on the angler's needs.

LAKE NORFORK

On the North Fork of the White River, in Arkansas, this lake extends into Missouri's Ozark County to cover some 900 acres. One of the newer impoundments, this lake is producing some high-class fishing. White bass and both Largemouth and Smallmouth Bass afford good catches; Crappie, Green Sunfish and Channel Cat are abundant and large. Some outstanding catches of Flathead Cat are made with set lines.

Both surface and deep-running plugs are used, and small plugs and bucktails in fly-rod size give good results. Trolling probably exceeds bank-casting in popularity. Boats and cabins are available and becoming more numerous.

Lake Norfolk is one of the four large lakes in the vast complex now known as the White River Lakes Country of Missouri.

BULL SHOALS LAKE

Filling a 23,000-acre gap between Lake Norfolk and Lake Taneycomo on the White River is Bull Shoals Lake, impounded in Arkansas and extending into Missouri as far as Taneycomo's Powersite dam. Bull Shoals has gained a nationwide reputation as the home of bull Black Bass and near-record Walleyes. It also contains a great abundance of White Bass, Sunfish, Catfish and the other species that thrive in a large warm-water lake.

A part of the White River Lakes area, Bull Shoals has its share of resorts and tourist attractions and boats and other fishing facilities are available.

TABLE ROCK LAKE

The bulk of Table Rock's 47,300 acres of water is in Missouri. Backed up by a dam near Branson, Missouri, completed in 1953, Table Rock is the

Mo. Conservation Comm.

"Juggin'." Jug (or block) fishing is one way to fish the Mighty Mississippi. Here fishermen follow a line of blocks down the current in hopes of picking up some of those big river Catfish.

newest of the White River lakes. Some of the finest scenery of the Ozarks is found here, and Table Rock is developing into one of the outstanding bass and walleye fisheries in the midwest. Table Rock is a deep, clearwater lake well adapted to the sport of underwater spearfishing and exploratory scuba diving.

Commercial development of the Table Rock area is proceeding rapidly and the facilities needed by anglers are available. A state park has been established at Table Rock dam.

LAKE WAPPAPELLO

This Missouri Lake covers 5,700 acres in Wayne County, impounding the St. Francis River just before it leaves the southeastern breaks of the Ozarks. Its "specialty" is large Crappies, which are taken on bait, flies, and small plugs early in the season. Accommodations are on the lake itself, in a number of resorts, but tourist camps are plentiful along U. S. 67, and in the nearby towns of Poplar Bluff and Greenville.

LAKE CLEARWATER

This smallest of the flood-control reservoirs dams, Black River in Reynolds County; it is just across the ridge from Lake Wappapello. The rugged setting makes this an especially attractive body of water, and every part of its 1,650 acres is fishing water. Excellent catches of Black Bass are taken early in the season, with plug fishermen, fly-casters, and bait users reporting equally good results.

The lake is extensively developed, inquiries regarding boats and accommodations should be directed to Chambers of Commerce in the nearby towns of Piedmont and Leeper.

POMME DE TERRE LAKE

This is Missouri's newest lake—so new, in fact, the fishery is not yet fully developed. The flood gates were closed late in 1961 to begin impounding the 7,280 acres of water which will provide West Central Missouri with another warm-water reservoir. The new lake is on the Pomme De Terre River, a tributary of the Osage and just upstream from the giant Lake of the Ozarks. Commercial and state park development already is planned for the area. The lake, built as a flood-control measure, can be reached on U. S. 54 and is near Hermitage, Mo.

THE CLEAR-WATER OZARK STREAMS

Most famous of Missouri fishing waters are the fast, spring-fed streams of the Ozarks. Names such as the Current, James, White, Niangua, Eleven Point, Gasconade, Piney, Jack's Fork, Black St. Francis, Kings, and Meramec with their many tributaries are familiar to Smallmouth Bass enthusiasts everywhere. It was on these streams that the unique method of "floating fishing" developed and became tradition. These streams are known for their clear waters and wild scenery as well as their fishing. Together, they cover the entire Ozark region in a network of water ways from east to west.

In addition to Smallmouth Bass, the clear-water streams yield Walleye, Largemouth and Kentucky Bass, Channel Cat, Goggle-eye, and the sunfishes. Occasionally large Rainbow Trout are taken near the trout management areas tributary to the Current, Niangua and Meramec.

Although the float trip is the most traditional and spectacular way of fishing these rivers, many fishermen bring their own boats or canoes, or rent these locally. Wading and fishing the smaller tributaries is also a popular and fruitful method. Bait fishermen frequently drive to accessible areas and still-fish the deep holes from the banks.

The variety of lures used is almost infinite. The river runt type of plug, and the bucktail-spinner type of fly are perhaps the most commonly used and the most consistent producers. Expert bug-casters find their art often pays off handsomely in the quieter waters. Though fishing is probably best everywhere early and late in the season, on these cold-water streams good actches are made during mid-summer as well.

All these streams yield fish; all are scenic. The visitor's choice might well be determined by chance, or convenience of location. Some visitors take a leisurely trip across the state, sampling several streams, before deciding on a favorite. All are accessible at some point by good highways, accommodations including boats are usually available at or near these points.

THE SEMI-CLEAR STREAMS

Not so well known, but equally good fish producers in their own way, are the streams tributary to the Mississippi River in the northeastern part of the state. Typical of these are the Salt, Fabius, Wyaconda, North Rivers, and their many tributaries. None of these are developed as resorts but accommodations can be found in highway tourist courts and nearby towns; boats are seldom available.

These streams are clear and relatively slow-moving during fair weather, turbid or murky during hard rains and for a period of from a few days to two weeks afterward. Artificial lures are good only during the clear periods; Largemouth Bass, Channel Cat, Crappie, and occasionally Walleyes are taken on either flies or plugs at such times. In murky water, bait fishing for Channel Cat, Drum, and the large river Catfish is customary. These rivers are rated among the best Channel Cat streams in the Midwest.

THE TURBID STREAMS

In the north-central and northwestern counties are the slow streams that drain the rich farmlands. Seldom clear, these yield mostly Channel Cat and non-game fish such as Catfish, Drum, and Carp. These are taken more consistently, however, and in larger sizes, than any other portion of the state.

Fishing is mostly by set lines, or by still fishing, with bait. Boats are used by residents on the larger streams, such as the Grand, Chariton, Platte, and Nodaway Rivers; bank fishing is the rule on their tributaries and on the smaller streams. Boats are seldom available for rent; accommodations are found in the towns and tourist courts. For bait fishermen—especially those who favor the Catfish and enjoy mixing with some really big ones. These streams are by no means to be overlooked.

TROUT WATERS

These are natural spring streams cold enough and extensive enough to support considerable trout fishing. The largest of these are in state parks; Roaring River, in Barry County; Bennett Springs, in Laclede and Dallas Counties; and Montauk in Dent County. These are regularly stocked with Rainbow Trout from the Commission's hatcheries.

A fourth managed trout park is not located in a state park. Maramec Spring Park is operated by the James Foundation under a grant of land which is the site of the first iron works west of the Mississippi. Like the others, the trout fishing is provided by the Conservation Commission and the stream is stocked from a commission hatchery. Maramec Spring is located near St. James.

Provision is made for both bait fishermen and fly fishermen, by marking off stretches of stream for these respective methods. Fly fishermen here, as elsewhere, indulge their fancies—but woolly worm flies, and others imitating insects or grubs, have long been stand-bys. Bait fishermen use minnows, worms, grasshoppers, hellgrammites, dough and meat baits.

Mo. Conservation Comm.

A string of Channel Cats taken from Lake Ozark. Channel Cat fishing is tops in Missouri either in lakes or in the streams.

Accommodations are available in or near the parks, and also in nearby towns. A daily fishing fee of $1.00 per person is charged, in addition to the regular state fishing permit.

OTHER WATERS

Scattered throughout the state are farm ponds, municipal reservoirs, and some shallow-water lakes, stocked by the Commission and operated under the regulations for impounded waters. Fishing is open to the public on Commission-stocked reservoirs, and on farm ponds subject to the landowner's permission.

The Conservation Commission's community lakes program, under which the commission builds a fishing lake on land supplied by the community had, as of 1962, added 573 acres of new fishing water in 14 community lakes. These lakes are built in cooperation with community leaders and funds for purchase of land are usually raised by public subscription. A community deprived by nature of fishing waters can thus help provide angling for its residents at a fraction of the cost of a lake built by the city or county.

The two big rivers—Missouri and Mississippi—offer a type of fishing that appeals to a large group, especially those interested in "big fish." These Catfish, Carp, Drum, and the like—are usually taken on baited trotlines or throw lines, set from the bank, or by the big-river kind of float fishing known as "jugging." In jug fishing short lines with big baited hooks are attached to the handles of corked jugs, cans, or blocks, sometimes secured at intervals to a line to keep them together. The flock of jugs is set adrift, and followed by boat as they ride the current downstream. Some very large Flathead Cats and Fulton Cats are taken by jugging.

The Mississippi also offers some very fine game

fishing, especially below the locks that are found at intervals along its course. Almost any kind of game fish known to the Middlewest can be taken at these locks, and sometimes the fishing is fast and furious. This is mostly the bait fisherman's stronghold; with minnows, worms, "stink-bait", or even hot-dogs, he may take Walleyes, Bass, both Black and White Crappie, Drum, Channel Cat, or any of the non-game fishes that take bait. Surprises are frequent, as when a man pulling out Crappie suddenly finds his bait taken by something big and powerful—most often, with results disastrous to the tackle.

Small streams anywhere in the state offer their own brand of fishing, from Bullheads and Sunfishes to Channel Cats and Smallmouth Bass. Although the visitor would advisedly select the larger, proved waters, many have found that it doesn't pay to pass up any stream.

Ohio

Under a liberalized fishing program the angler can catch any fish of any size, anytime, and keep any number caught. This complete fishing freedom has not proved detrimental to the fish population. Creel census reports taken by the Division of Wildlife's Game Protectors indicate that streams and lakes continue to produce good catches.

Ohio's 44,000 miles of streams are all fishable and provide some of the best fishing in the Midwest. Most contain the Smallmouth Bass, considered to be Ohio's prize game fish. Members of the Sunfish and Catfish families are also abundant in all streams, making a mixed bag possible for even the most leisurely fisherman. With the exception of navigable waters, permission is required of the land owner to fish in those waters flowing through private lands.

In addition to other impounded fishing waters, there are more than 20,000 farm and strip-mine ponds, many of which provide good fishing for Bass and Bluegills. Generally, these are privately owned and the owner's permission is required to fish. A fishing license, however, is not required, under the present law, to fish these private waters.

A single statewide boat license, including reciprocity for non-resident boat owners, permits the boat fisherman to sample any public waters within the state without the multiplicity of boat licenses once required. This, plus the fact that Ohio has acquired thousands of acres of public waters through new lake construction and lease or agreements, has resulted in unlimited fishing opportunities.

Close to a million persons fish in Ohio waters each year. The earliest fishermen out each spring are usually those seeking Muskellunge in one of several of Ohio's good Musky lakes. In March, soon after the ice is out, Musky fishermen head for Leesville Lake, which is one of the ten Muskingum Conservancy District flood-control reservoirs in Eastern Ohio. Leesville is only one of several good areas. Other productive Musky waters include: Rocky Fork Lake, Cowan Lake, Clendening Lake, Tappan Lake, Knox Lake, Deer Creek Reservoir, Scioto Brush Creek, Sunfish Creek, Wills Creek, Olive Green Creek, and Piedmont Lake. Any of these lakes or streams offer the opportunity to tangle with a Musky weighing 20 pounds or more.

The Mad River in the western part of the state offers the Trout fisherman his best opportunity. Fingerlings are stocked there annually by the Division of Wildlife. There are several private Trout clubs in Ohio; Rockwell Trout Club near Sandusky, Licking Springs near Newark, Castalia Club at Castalia, and Zanesfield Trout Club near Bellefontaine are some of the better known, providing Trout fishing for members and their guests.

Ohio's northern boundary includes Lake Erie and its Bass Islands, a recreational wonderland. This lake can be fished successfully almost any month of the year. Fishing is done in every conceivable manner—from shore or pier, from small boats, large boats, private ones or rentals, and through the ice. Catches are fabulous. Perch, Smallmouth Bass, White Bass, and Channel Catfish are predominant. The marshes between Vermillion and Port Clinton offer the archer top carp shooting opportunities in late spring. Ice fishing produces fabulous perch catches which often run up to 300 a day. Ice fishing is most popular around Sandusky and Port Clinton at Catawba Point, Marblehead, Cedar Point, Sandusky Bay, Bay Bridge, and East Harbor. Pier fishing on the Lake Erie shore is popular and productive; piers are located at Battery Park in Sandusky, Lorain, Huron, Port Clinton, Ashtabula, Conneaut, and Fairport Harbor.

NORTHWESTERN OHIO

In this area anglers should consider Maumee River, Indian Lake, Lake St. Marys, Lake Loramie, Oxbow Lake, Bucyrus, Lima, and Wauseon Reservoirs. The Miami River provides outstanding Smallmouth Bass fishing in the rapid areas between Maumee and Waterville. Northern Pike may be taken in Oxbow Lake with many being caught by ice fishermen. Very good fishing for Walleyes and White Bass may be found in the upground water supply reservoirs of Wauseon, Bucyrus, Lima, and Findlay. Channel Catfish and Crappies are abundant in Lake St. Marys, while Nettle Lake affords good Bass and Bluegill fishing. The Killdeer Plains Wildlife Area has several large ponds containing good populations of Bass and panfish.

NORTHEASTERN OHIO

This area contains a variety of fishing opportunities with an abundance of lakes and reservoirs from which to choose. The Division of Wildlife has been successful in establishing good populations of Chain Pickerel, Walleyes, Northern Pike, and Muskies in many waters in this area, in addition to the more common species present. Chain Pickerel are present in Long Lake, one of the Portage Lakes. Those seeking Muskies in this area should try Deer Creek Reservoir, Knox Lake, and Pymatuning Reservoir. Excellent Northern Pike fishing is present in early spring in Nimisila and Atwood reservoirs. Walleye fishermen will have a difficult time choosing between these excellent waters: Berlin Reservoir, Lake Milton, Pymatuning Reservoir, and Mosquito Reservoir. Bass and pan fishing are excellent in all lakes of this region. Mogadore Reservoir and Knox Lake are among the more popular waters with ice fishermen seeking pan fish.

SOUTHEASTERN OHIO

This area not only has some of the best fishing lakes and streams in the state, but includes the more rugged scenic areas of Ohio. Burr Oak Lake is considered by many as the best Bass and Bluegill producing lake in this part of the state. Many of the smaller lakes with scenic settings, such as Lake Hope, Dow Lakes, Tycoon Lake, Hocking Lake, Lake Alma, and Lake Vesuvius all offer Bass and pan fishing. Hocking Lake and Jackson Lake contain Muskies but they are better known for Bass, Catfishing is popular in this area with the larger ones being taken on trotlines. The Muskingum River and its tributaries, the Hocking River, and the lower reaches of the Scioto are considered best for large Cats.

CENTRAL OHIO

Fishermen living near the capital city are fortunate in having an abundance and variety of excellent lakes and streams nearby. Buckeye Lake contains good populations of all common species and provides a challenge to most fishermen. Hoover Reservoir is noted for Walleyes, while Delaware, Griggs, O'Shaughnessey reservoirs, and Clark, Madison, and Mt. Gilead lakes are considered better Bass and pan fishing waters. Rocky Fork is noted for its Muskies but also offers fair Bass and Crappie fishing, too. Smaller lakes such as Hargus Creek, Lake White, Roosevelt Lake, and Richwood Lake should not be overlooked for Bass and pan fishing. Many streams in this area are well known for Smallmouth Bass, Spotted Bass and good Catfishing. These are Blacklick Creek, Big Walnut, Olentangy River, Big and Little Darby Creeks, Paint Creek, Deer Creek, Ohio Brush Creek, Rattlesnake Creek, Clear Creek, Whetstone, and the smaller tributaries emptying into the lower Scioto River.

SOUTHWESTERN OHIO

Impounded waters in this portion of the state are fewer but provide a variety of good fishing opportunity. Indian Lake, an old canal reservoir, provides excellent Bass, Bluegill, Crappie, and Catfishing. Ice fishing there is highly productive for Bluegills, too. Cowan Lake is heavily fished and contains a Muskie population in addition to Bass and other pan fishes. Stonelick Lake is considered tops for Bass fishing, while Grant is noted for Bluegill and Bass fishing. Acton Lake, Winton Woods, and Kiser Lake provide good fishing for the persistent angler. The construction of three new large dams is under way on the Ohio River and will provide increased fishing opportunities in this portion of the state. Stream fishing for Smallmouth Bass is excellent here in many waters; Little and Big Miami, Todd's Fork, Massie's Creek, Stillwater River, and Caesar's Creek to name a few. In the absence of numerous public waters in this area of the state, a large number of privately-owned farm ponds and commercial pay fishing lakes provide additional opportunities for family fishing.

Information and lists of Ohio's public hunting and fishing areas which indicate special regulations and facilities may be secured by writing to the Ohio Department of Natural Resources, Publications Room, 1500 Dublin Road, Columbus 12, Ohio.

Wisconsin

Although its lakes are filled with Bass, Walleyes, Northern Pike, and panfish and its streams are well stocked with Trout, Wisconsin is still best known as the Muskie State.

There are more than 8,000 lakes and better than 10,000 miles of fast Trout waters in Wisconsin. This area is bounded in part by the Mississippi River on the west, Lake Michigan on the east, and Lake Superior on the north, thus giving this great state a wealth of recreational resources not enjoyed by many other states.

Wisconsin has an abundance of forest growth and fish life that annually attracts millions of tourists and sportsmen. The Conservation Department works steadily to keep the lakes and streams in proper balance, and it has made the most progress of all in the propagation and plantings of small Muskies in the northern lakes. Although some 'lunge plantings have been made in southern Wisconsin, Muskies are found mostly in the northernmost counties. The Muskie is the largest of the freshwater game fish taken with hook and line, and sportsmen have taken Muskies weighing around 70 pounds. A 102-pounder was caught in a net by conservation men many years ago.

Of all the Trout waters the Brule, in Douglas County is the best and is one of the famous streams in America. As in some of the streams in Michigan, big Rainbows from Lake Superior ascend the Brule in the spring to spawn, and many of these have weighed more than 15 pounds. Many six and seven pound Rainbows are caught annually, and the stream has an abundance of Brook Trout and Browns. The best time to fish the Brule is in the fall and spring after the usual Trout season or before it—when the big Trout migrate. A special season is provided on south shore streams. The town of Brule lies halfway between its mouth and headwaters, and there is a road that almost parallels this beautiful stream from its headwaters near Solon Springs to the mouth near Martinsen. One could fish this stream a life-time and never tire of its gorgeous scenery and its exciting fishing.

Rainbows, Brook, and Brown Trout are plentiful in the streams of northern and central Wisconsin, and Lake Trout fishing is rapidly becoming more popular among those who like to troll in Trout and Big Green Lakes during the summer months. A hundred lakes are managed for Rainbow Trout.

The Walleye and the Northern Pike are both important game fishes in Wisconsin. The best fishing for them is in the lakes of the northern part of the state. Panfish are plentiful everywhere.

The Large- and Smallmouth Bass are plentiful throughout the state, with Largemouth preferring weedy lakes and Smallmouth preferring rocky waters. Smallmouth and Perch in Door County's bays are famous. The White Bass is well known because annually in the spring of the year he puts on a show for the anglers in the form of spawning runs up the various rivers. There are several early fish runs that are well known . . . the Walleye run out of Lakes Winnebago, Winneconne, and Poygan and up the Wolf River in April, followed by the White Bass run in early May in the same waters. Best bet for taking them is still or drift fishing with minnows. Concentrations of gamefish occur seasonally below dams on the Mississippi, Chippewa, and Wisconsin.

The northern counties of the state are covered with lakes from the ice cap of bygone days. The country is hilly. Land O' Lakes is 1,700 feet above sea level. The streams that tumble from the northern plateau to the big lakes and rivers are fast, and in them is found good fishing. The woods are full of jack pine, spruce, white, and Norway pine, also hickory, oak, aspen, cottonwood, and tamarack.

The Chequamegon and Nicolet National Forests run to 1,300,000 acres, and the state owns several hundred thousand acres of forests and parks . . . all speckled with good fishing lakes and fishable streams. Two million acres of county forestland and 500,000 acres of stateland contribute to wilderness beauty and fishing opportunities.

Strangers to Wisconsin will be puzzled by the great duplication in the names of its lakes. In fact, there are two Brule Rivers—the famous Brule in the north and the one that follows the Michigan boundary to the northeast, and there are two Butternut Lakes.

While not a gamefish caught by hook and line, the Lake Sturgeon attracts the attention of many fishermen when the season is opened during a short space of time in February. Many of them are caught through the ice in Lake Winnebago. In fact, ice fishing has become a major sport during the winter months in Wisconsin. Their feet may get cold and their teeth may chatter, but these members of the earmuff clan are attracting the attention of more and more fishermen every year. They catch panfish, Northern Pike and some of the rough fish too.

The northern lakes country attracts the biggest numbers of summer tourists and fishermen. It is in these northern counties of Vilas, Oneida, Sawyer, Iron, and Ashland that we find the best fishing for Muskies, Walleyes, Northern Pike, and Trout.

There are those who have been Muskie fishing all their lives and who to-date have never caught

Missouri Conservation Comm.

The upper St. Francis River in Missouri provides excellent fly fishing.

one. This may be due to a number of incorrect practices. Poor choice of method and tackle may be in use or the bait offerings may be made at the wrong time. Many Muskie fishermen believe firmly in fishing when the barometer is high or rising, and there are many who will not cast a line before consulting their fishing calendar. The angler must remember that there are hundreds of lakes in Wisconsin that are loaded with Muskies, and the biggest of them are still to be caught.

Trolling takes the most Muskies, but the favorite method in Wisconsin is bait casting with artificial plugs, spoons, and spinners or with a sucker. The fishing calendar will tell you the best days. The best time of the day usually is between 10:00 a.m. and 4:00 p.m. as Muskies are not night feeders like the Walleye.

The best Muskie waters in Wisconsin are found in the northern four counties and include: Grindstone, Court O'Reilles, Chippewa Flowage, Spider, Teal, Chippewa River, Whitefish, Ghost, Twin, Stone, Lost Land, Moose, Pokegama, White Sand, Pelican, Crawling Stone, Lac Du Flambeau, Plum, Boulder, Trout, Gresham, Muskellunge, Gunlock, Sissabogama, Lost, Found, Squirrel, Sugarbush, Big and Little St. Germain, Big and Little Arbor Vitae, Lac Vieux Desert, Minocqua, Tomahawk, Manitowish Flowage, High Echo, Island, Turtle Flowage, Squaw, Star, Wild Cat, Buckatabon, Connors, Long, the Flambeau Flowage, Butternut, Fence, and Ike Walton. There are hundreds more.

The best Walleye fishing in the state is to be had in the northern counties from the Mississippi River to the Michigan Upper Peninsula boundary. In fact, some of the best Walleyes are taken from the good Muskie waters like Star, Chippewa Flowage, Flambeau Flowage, Manitowish Flowage, White Sand, Twin, Spider, Crooked, Crawling Stone, and Pelican. Other good Walleye lakes are Winnebago, Pepin, Namakagon, Webb, Devil, and in the Chippewa River. Now and then a Muskie is caught in Lake Winnebago.

The best Trout districts lie in the central part of the state around Waupaca, Oconto, Shawano, and Peshtigo. The most productive streams and their branches are the Pine, Peshtigo, Wolf, Oconto, Pembine, Pike, and the Evergreen.

Bass fishing can be had in almost every county in the state, with the best concentrations in the following counties: Barron, Bayfield, Brown, Burnett, Crawford, Dane, Dodge, Door, Douglas, Fond du Lac, Forest, Green Lake, Jefferson, Pepin, Pierce, Sawyer, Shawano, Sheboygan, Vilas, Walworth, Washburn, Washington, Waupaca, and Winnebago.

Lake Geneva in the southern part of the state is one of the best Large- and Smallmouth lakes. Door County in the northeastern section boasts excellent Smallmouth fishing along the shores of Washington Island in Lake Michigan, at Fish Creek, in Kangaroo Lake, in Sturgeon Bay, at Ephraim, Bailey's Harbor, and Whitefish Bay.

The best Bass area is around the towns of Spooner, Solon Springs, Danbury, Grantsburg, Siren, Webster, and Chilton. Another good area is in Winnebago, Walworth, and Waupaca Counties, in the waters of Lake Butte des Morts, Poygan, Winneconne, Delavan, and the Lauderdale Chain. Those lakes around Eagle River, Land o' Lakes, Three Lakes, and Crandon have wonderful Smallmouth Bass fishing in lakes like Butternut, Kentuck, Pine, Franklin, Arbor Vitae, St. Germain, Lost, Found, and White Sand. Lake Pepin, the widening of the Mississippi, is famous for its Black Bass and Walleye fishing.

In the south end of Lake Michigan fishing is limited to Lake Perch and Lake Herring, but thousands are attracted to the area during the summer months. The best of the fishing can be found from Door County and to the north.

Wisconsin is a great resort state. Some of the finest resorts on the North American continent operate in the state, mostly catering to the men and families who enjoy good fishing and other "north-country" recreational pleasures.

PLAINS STATES

In over-all perspective, the Plains States were discriminated against when fishing waters were being distributed. The abundantly watered lake area of Minnesota spills over slightly into the Dakotas, and the Ozark country of Missouri and Arkansas into Oklahoma. Aside from these intrusions, the Black Hills furnish the finest stream fishing to be found in the area.

Most streams have wide seasonal fluctuations in water levels and flow generally out of the high, dry plains east of the foothills of the Rockies and empty into the Missouri or other tributaries of the Mississippi. The Missouri itself is the most important single stream but does not furnish major fishing opportunities except in the impoundments along its course.

The most dependable fishing is generally in the natural and artificial lakes and impoundments. These vary from small ponds of a few acres to such huge impoundments as Lake Texoma and Lake Garrison.

These states have generally made the most of their opportunities and both citizens and visitors have enjoyable angling opportunities.

Kansas

Mention the word "fishing" to any Kansas angler and immediately he gets a vision of large lakes dotted with fishing boats, smaller lakes bordered by tree-covered hills, and meandering streams and rivers flowing over sandy bottoms or gurgling in riffles over rocky depths.

Kansas is rapidly becoming a state of vast opportunities for any angler who likes to flip a plug for Black Bass, troll a minnow for Walleyes or dunk a bait for Crappie or Channel Catfish. This statement by no means tells the story. Nearly all kinds of warm-water fish are to be found in abundance in Kansas waters.

Kansas has always had its stream and river fishing but it hasn't always been as good as it is now and the chances are that it will get better as time goes by. As in every other state, pollution and siltation were the limiting factors in such fishing

Cow pasture ponds in the Plains States supply local anglers with good sport fishing for Largemouth Bass, Crappie, Bluegill, Bullheads, and Channel Catfish.

and, fortunately, something is being done about it. Conservation and watershed districts are being formed to keep soil on the farms instead of channeling it into the watercourses. Industrial and city pollution are being combated with ever-increasing zeal. The result is clearer streams and better fishing.

Because of the nature of the terrain, the Sunflower state has no natural lakes of any magnitude. What nature did not supply, man is now making available. Prior to World War II, the Kansas Forestry, Fish and Game Commission had constructed 22 state lakes for the benefit of Fishermen. This was only a start. Kansas still lacked fishing lakes in many parts of the state and there were no lakes larger than about 300 acres in size.

While other states in the central part of the nation were receiving a great deal of attention from the Federal Government in the form of flood control and irrigation reservoirs, Kansas had been left high and dry. However, that situation began to change. In 1948 the first large reservoir in the state was completed by the U. S. Corps of Engineers on Fall River in east-central Kansas. The 2,600 acres of water impounded furnished the state with the first suitable water for the stocking of White Bass and Walleyes. In also provided outdoor enthusiasts with the first lake really large enough for all types of water sports.

Other large reservoirs in other sections of the state were soon completed and fishermen can now utilize eight of these impoundments. The largest of these is Tuttle Creek Reservoir with 15,700 acres followed by Cedar Bluff (6,600), Kirwin (5,000), Webster (4,000), Kanopolis (3,550), Lovewell (3,000), and Toronto (2,800). Several others are under construction at this time of publication and will soon provide several thousand more surface acres for fishing.

All reservoirs in Kansas are under intensive fishery management designed to produce maximum fishing potential. Each has been stocked with Walleyes, Black Bass, White Bass, Channel Catfish, Crappie and forage species. In addition Tuttle Creek Reservoir has received an initial experimental stock of 2¼ million Northern Pike. Additional stockings of Northerns are planned for this and some other reservoirs.

Growth rates of fish in some of the reservoirs have been outstanding and catches have, in some instances, exceeded expectations. Walleye fishing has been particularly good at Webster, Kanopolis and Kirwin, while excellent Black Bass fishing can be had at Toronto and Kirwin Reservoirs. The spring run of White Bass at Fall River Reservoir annually attracts thousands of fishermen; the Crappie run at Kanopolis can sometimes be labeled fabulous.

Even with the advent of the large lakes, there are those who prefer to do their fishing in smaller bodies of water. Since 1953, when the Fish and Game Commission reactivated its lake building program, 20 new fishing lakes have been built in all parts of the state. These range in size from 50 acres to nearly 200 acres. In addition, one new lake of 180 acres is now under construction.

While water sports of all kinds are permitted at the federal reservoirs, state lakes are reserved for fishing purposes only, with no water skiing or speed boating allowed. This feature makes these lakes attractive to the serious angler who likes to fish in relative peace and quiet. Nearly all state lakes contain fine populations of Largemouth Black Bass, Black and White Crappie, Channel Catfish and Bluegill.

Extreme southeast Kansas can boast a unique type of fishing water in its strip-mining pits. Large deposits of coal close to the surface have been mined out by removing the overlying soil and rock, thus forming deep water-filled pits. Most of these strip pits are capable of supporting a healthy fish population, and the Kansas Forestry, Fish and Game Commission has stocked and is managing many of these water areas. In fact, many fishermen claim that these pits furnish the best Bass fishing to be found anywhere. The pits are favorite waters for those who like to use light fly-fishing tackle or spinning gear, since there are few under-water snags and the waters are always crystal clear.

The spotted Smallmouth Bass is native to the Flint Hills streams of Kansas.

This Spotted Smallmouth Bass was in tight against the shore of this typical stream in the Flint Hills of Southeastern Kansas.

One of the best lakes in the state for spring Bass fishing is located on the state-owned and operated Marais Des Cygnes Waterfowl Management Area in eastern Kansas. Because it was designed primarily for waterfowl use, the lakes are relatively shallow, but they have produced some excellent growth in Largemouth Black Bass and Crappie. During the summer, the growth of aquatic vegetation causes difficulties for fishermen, but the water is relatively open during spring. Another waterfowl management unit, the Cheyenne Bottoms in central Kansas, is periodically a hotspot for Channel Catfish and large Bullheads.

Rounding out the angling picture in the Sunflower State are numerous city and county lakes of various sizes up to 980 acres. Some of these produce topnotch fishing such as Council Grove city lake which produced the state's biggest Largemouth Black Bass, a 9½ pounder. One of the newest city lakes is located north of Parsons; this 980-acre impoundment is already yielding large Bass, Crappie and Channel Cats.

Other angling opportunities are provided by the thousands of private ponds which dot the countryside and do double purpose of providing stock water as well as recreation for the farmer and his friends. Anglers should respect the property owners and fish only after obtaining permission.

If you are a Bass fisherman, you'll want to try Woodson County State Lake, Kirwin Reservoir, Crawford County State Lake #2, Webster Reservoir, Leavenworth County State Lake, Toronto and Fall River Reservoirs and Lovewell Reservoir in addition to the previously mentioned waters. White Bass should provide lots of action at Cedar Bluff, Fall River and Kanopolis Reservoirs and their feeder streams. Channel Catfish are found in nearly all waters of the state and to point to any one particular location would be a disservice. The top Channel so far recorded (26½ pounds) came from Shawnee County Lake near Topeka, but this lake is not especially noted for its Cat fishing. Almost all streams and rivers produce some fine Channel Catfish angling at various times. Veteran Channel fishermen insist that a rising river produces the best fishing.

There are no closed seasons or size limits on any species of fish in Kansas. Fish may be taken the year around and even through the ice on lakes and ponds. A copy of the fishing regulations plus a booklet entitled *Where to Fish in Kansas* is available to anyone who will write to the Kansas Forestry, Fish and Game Commission, Pratt, Kansas.

Nebraska

Nebraska, sprawling westward from the wooded bluffs of the wide Missouri to the buttes and foothills of the Rockies, unites the Middle West with the West.

This generous slice of the Great Plains was not originally blessed with fish producing waters. The Niobrara twists its way across the state's northern boundary to add its waters to the Missouri, and the Platte cuts a figure S across the southern third to make the wide Missouri wider below Plattesmouth. These are Nebraska's principle rivers, but streams and creeks thread the state.

However, with vision, planning, and work, the State Conservation Commission, in cooperation with the federal conservation agencies, has increased Nebraska's fish producing waters immeasurably. Along the western half of the Platte River is the rather extensive chain of the Tri-County Reservoir System where the State Conservation Department has leased and improved recreational areas open to the public.

These reservoirs are stocked with game fishes including Northern Pike, Walleye, Black Bass, Perch, Rock Bass, Crappie, Bluegill, and Catfishes. At Otter Creek Recreation Grounds, located in Keith County about 30 miles northwest of Ogallala, there is trout fishing, chiefly for Rainbows and Browns; the angler will also find the other species mentioned. Four miles north of Ogallala, the

A brace of Spotted Smallmouth Bass from a stream in the Flint Hills of Kansas.

Paul Threlfall, Staff Photographer Wichita Beacon

A tired Largemouth Bass "comes 'long side."

McConaughey Lake Area offers good Trout and White Bass fishing in addition to Walleye, Black Bass, Northern Pike, and the other warm water fishes native to the state. In fact, the entire Ogallala area is a fisherman's playground, and anglers visiting Nebraska should include this, one of the state's finest recreational areas, on their itinerary.

In Dawes and Sheridan Counties the angler may divide his attention between trout and warm water fishes: in the upper reaches of the White and Niobrara rivers there is good trout fishing, and Walgren Lake, just south of Hay Springs in Sheridan County, offers an excellent sample for the angler desiring Walleye, Crappie, Bluegill, Rock Bass, and Catfish.

In this district the fishing around Alliance, in Box Butte County should be investigated. Between Alliance and Hyannis in Grant County, stretches the Sand-Hill Country, an undulating sea of yellow sand splashed with lakes of ultremarine blue where ground water seeps into the "blowouts" between the dunes. Some of these lakes are stocked with warm water fishes, and at Hyannis there is good fishing.

The entire area running east and south from the Valentine district in Cherry County into the Ainsworth district has genuine angling possibilities. Thirty miles south of Valentine are Rat and Beaver Lakes which give good accounts of themselves with fine catches of Black Bass, Sunfish, Perch, and Bullheads. Twenty miles south of Ainsworth is Long Lake, a natural Sand Hill lake.

Dropping south to the state's southwest corner the visiting angler will find ample reward awaiting him. At Rock Creek Lake, five miles north of Parks in Dundy County, there is opportunity for real angling adventure. In addition to Black Bass, Crappie, Rock Bass, Bluegill, and Catfish the lake is well stocked with trout.

Directly north of Rock Creek Lake at Champion in Chase County is Champion Lake, and eastward, just north of Hayes Center in Hayes County, is the Duke Alexis Lake. Both lakes offer good Black Bass, Crappie, and Catfish fishing. Just northeast of the Duke Alexis Lake in southern Lincoln County, is Wellfleet Lake, and good Crappie, Bluegill, Black Bass, and Bullhead fishing.

The Loup River is the largest tributary of the Platte. The North, South, and Middle Loup have their origins in the Sand-Hill Country, and flow southeastward through the center of the state. Aside from the fishing in the Loup River and its tributaries, chiefly for Catfish, there are lakes and recreational areas scattered along its course where Black Bass, Crappie, Rock Bass, and other warm Water species may be had: a splendid example is the Ravenna County Lake, one mile east of the town on the Loup River in Buffalo County.

Along the Big and Little Blue Rivers in extreme southeastern Nebraska are numerous lakes and recreational areas which the angler should have on his agenda, especially the catfish angler, as these rivers afford excellent fishing for Blue, Channel, Goujon, or Yellow Catfish, and Bullheads.

From Verdon Lake, one mile west of the town of Verdon in the extreme southeasterly county of Richardson, to Dead Timber Lake in Dodge County and northward, there is good fishing.

From the southeastern corner of the state northward there are many abandoned sand and gravel pits which maintain constant levels with surface drainage and ground water seepage. These pits have been stocked with Black Bass, Crappie, Bluegill, and Catfish, and afford considerable recreation for local anglers.

Nebraska, lying as it does between the 40th and 43rd parallels of latitude, has a climate characteristic of the central Great Plains Region. The average range of temperature from summer to winter is perhaps 100 degrees. The principle migration of fishes native to the state occurs in the spring and again at the approach of winter. When the water warms up in the spring, fish move from the deep water into the shallows to spawn, and become more active in their feeding. The long, hot days of summer will send fish back to the deeper water for comfort ,and the angler who fishes early and again at twilight, or during the night, will be rewarded with better catches.

The fly and plug caster should employ wet flies and streamers and deep running plugs during early spring, but by June top-water lures will prove effective. The bait fisherman will find no appreciable difference between Nebraska fishing and that of Minnesota, Kansas, or other like areas. Fish will be in deep water during extreme high and low temperatures.

Anglers visiting Nebraska are certain to find a wide variety of game fishes, interesting water to fish, and a great deal of genuine angling pleasure.

North Dakota

North Dakota doesn't have the deep, rock-bottomed and tree-lined lakes of the Lakes States to the East nor the crystal-clear, tumbling mountain streams to the West. But North Dakota does have lakes and streams, and it does have some fine fishing.

Anglers will find fishing methods and scenery about as varied in the "Flickertail State" as in other parts of the nation. The Turtle Mountains, lodged against the Canadian border, are a bit of Minnesota transplanted to the plains. Lakes are numerous, and the rolling hills are covered with trees. Best fishing lakes are Lake Metigoshe, which contains Trout in the north half and Walleyes and Northern Pike in the south section; Gordon Lake, a Walleye spot; and Pelican Lake, which has Perch and Pike.

An ambitious program of dam construction, by federal agencies, has created huge reservoirs on the prairies where lakes did not exist a few years ago. These new reservoirs have provided good to excellent fishing for residents and visitors alike. A lake construction and rehabilitation program carried on by the State Game and Fish Department also has provided good fishing in areas where it was unknown ten years ago. Thus, artificial lakes have taken up the slack where natural lakes have failed to produce.

These new lakes in the fertile prairie country produce tremendous growth in the fish that inhabit them. By the same token, natural lakes and small areas in this region tend to winterkill easily. Where the new reservoirs and a few of the deeper lakes provide continuous fishing through the years, the marginal areas come and go. Growth rates are terrific and fabulous fishing flourishes for a few years, then a tough winter may set in and end it all. But, when water levels come back and the lakes are restocked, those same splendid growth rates put a lake back into production in short order.

Lake Garrison is the largest lake in North Dakota. It is formed along the winding Missouri River by huge Garrison Dam. Readily reached from all directions by hard-surfaced highways, Lake Garrison and the tailrace at the dam are popular fishing areas.

In recent years this man-made lake has given up the bulk of the lunkers caught in the state. Most popular species there are Northern Pike, Walleyes, Sauger, Ling, Rainbow Trout, Perch, Crappies and Channel Catfish. Many species of rough fish also abound in its waters.

In the eastern part of the state, Lake Ashtabula provides excellent angling for Northern Pike, Walleyes, Crappies, Perch, White Bass and Bullheads. This is another artificial lake, created by impounding the Cheyenne River about ten miles north of Valley City. Just to the West a few miles are Spiritwood Lake (a natural lake) and Jamestown Reservoir (formed by damming the James River). Both provide fair to good fishing for Walleyes, Northern Pike and Bluegills.

In southwestern counties another artificial lake holds the attention. This is Lake Tschida, on the Heart River south of Glen Ullin. This lake is the best Walleye, Crappie and White Bass lake in the state and gives up some occasional catches of Northern Pike and Channel Catfish of good sizes.

Tackle isn't important when the Crappie are biting at Lake Metigoshi, North Dakota.

Muskellunge were introduced into North Dakota in 1958 and are now providing a new thrill to anglers there. A few years ahead of the Muskies came White Bass and Trout. Two lakes provide very good White Bass fishing, and the State's accelerated Trout program really took hold in the late 1950's. Over a dozen special Trout lakes, mostly in the western half of the state, now provide good fishing for Rainbow Trout.

Although the Northern Pike is still the most popular and important game species in North Dakota, Walleyes, Perch and Trout are not far behind. And along the Missouri River the Sauger still attracts its share of ardent anglers. Best Sauger spots are the Missouri River, Garrison Tailrace, and Lake Garrison.

Best Walleye lakes are Lake Tschida, Lake Ashtabula, Jamestown Reservoir, Spiritwood Lake, Lake Garrison and Lake Darling. Best bets for Northern Pike are Lake Ashtabula, Lake Garrison, Jamestown Reservoir and Lake Tewaukon. Trout fishermen will find best results at North Lemmon Lake, Hamman Lake, Van Oosting Lake and the various small ponds in western counties.

Perch, Crappie and Bluegill fishermen have not been forgotten, either. Light tackle advocates will find plenty of action at Storm Creek Reservoir, Lake Tschida, Lake Ashtabula, Dickinson Reservoir, Jamestown Reservoir and Wood Lake.

When game fish season opens in May, Trout fishing provides the best results during the first two weeks. Pike, Walleye and Sauger angling picks up in late May and is tops through June. Panfish and Bass fishing is best in June and July. Warm weather and heavy natural food production slows catching results in July and August, but those who get out before daybreak will take plenty of fish. The coming of cooler weather again in September and October brings an increase in catches of Pike, Walleyes and Trout. Winter fishermen continue to catch Northern Pike and Perch through the ice until the spring break-up completes the yearly fishing cycle.

But the real attraction to North Dakota fishing

is the clear, clean air and the uncrowded lakes and camping areas. And a short-term visitors license make it possible for nonresidents to fish for a small fee, but to enjoy all the privileges of other fishermen.

Oklahoma

In the minds of many anglers Oklahoma is a state which must be crossed when going from the Black Bass fishing in the Ozarks of Missouri and Arkansas to the Trout fishing in New Mexico and Colorado, or vice versa. Such an idea warrants examination, for any fisherman seeking honest angling pleasure who finds himself in Oklahoma, should stop long enough to "wet a line" in one of the state's many lakes or streams.

Eastern Oklahoma is a network of excellent fishing streams and creeks. For the most part they are clear and moving, and the smaller creeks in the hill country cascade down their rockribbed, timber-fringed courses like hurried trout waters.

Western Oklahoma has but one major fishing stream, the Washita River, which enters the state from the Texas panhandle at the western edge of Roger Mills County and swings east and south across the state to empty into the Red River southwest of Durant.

Not every angler wants to go beyond the end of the road to fish the less visited waters of the back country, but there are many who do. It cannot be said that the Kiamichi and Winding Stair Mountain districts in the extreme southeastern corner of Oklahoma are trackless wilderness areas, but they are sufficiently remote and unspoiled as to invite the solitude-loving spirit of the hardy fisherman.

The Kiamichi River, rising just south of Talequah in Le Flore County, skirts the western edge of the Kiamichi Mountains and runs southward to empty into the Red River directly south of Fort Towson. The upper reaches of this stream afford most excellent fishing for Largemouth, Smallmouth, and Spotted Bass, which are native to the creeks and smaller streams of the region, Channel Catfish, Sunfish, and Rock Bass. Lower down on the Kiamichi and neighboring streams where the waters slow to large, deep pools, the crappie, and catfish anglers find real sports.

Oklahoma's Kiamichi Region has genuine and varied fishing possibilities. Cabin and lodge accommodations are lacking in much of the region,

Leo D. Harris

Bass are whimsical critters—maybe a change of lures is indicated.

Just fishin'.

but camping grounds are numerous. Visiting anglers, not wishing to establish a camp, should find accommodations in a village, or small town within the region, and sample the fishing from a central location. The fly, or plug caster preferring to wade the smaller creeks and streams casting for Black Bass, Sunfish, and Rock Bass, might locate in Wilburton, or Talihina in the northwestern corner of the Kiamichi Region, and the Catfish and Crappie fishermen, to be nearer the lower reaches of the stream, might locate in Antlers in the southwestern corner, or Broken Bow in the southeastern portion of the region.

While the Kiamichi Region is of primary interest to the stream fisherman, the area has many fine, though small lakes, some of which are natural, others artificial. In the Ouichita National Forest, between Talihina and Heavener, Cedar Lake offers a splendid example of the lake fishing. Other excellent streams and creeks in the Kiamichi area include the Black Fork, Glover, Little, Mountain Fork, Anderson, Bear, Big Beaver, Breakdown, Coal, and many others too numerous to mention.

Directly north of the Kiamichi Region, in the eastern counties of Sequoyah, Adair, Cherokee, and Delaware, is another area which offers much to the angler. The Cookson Hills have such fine streams as Barron Fork, Big Lee's, Sallisaw, and others. However, the Illinois River, which has its origin in the western edge of Arkansas, and flows southwest across this district, is one of the finest Oklahoma fishing streams. The water is clear and moving, and sufficiently heavy to permit float trips down most of its course.

Upstate from the Illinois River country is Lake Spavinaw, over 1,600 acres of clear water impounded by damming Spavinaw Creek. Fishing for Largemouth and Smallmouth Bass, Crappie, Rock Bass, Bluegill, and Channel Catfish is excellent.

A few miles north of Spavinaw is Grand Lake, a huge body of water spreading octapus-like over two counties. This artificial lake has 55,000 surface acres of water with a shore line of 1,300 miles. In every cove, and along the many arms the visiting angler will find excellent accommodations. Fishing possibilities for Black Bass, Crappie, Catfish, and all the native game fish are excellent.

In Northcentral Oklahoma, near the town of Cherokee, is the Great Salt Plains National Wildlife Refuge. Because of the high saline content in the water of this lake only Channel Catfish are found, but adjacent to the lake are sweet water creeks which offer good fishing for Bass, Bluegill, and Crappie.

The Wichita Mountains, located in the southwestern portion of the state, boast of a dozen fine lakes where there is good fishing for Black Bass, Crappie, Bluegill, Channel and Yellow or Goujon Catfish. East of this area, in southcentral Oklahoma, are the Arbuckle Mountains which should be included on the agenda of visiting anglers.

Perhaps the most notable fishing in the state is the Tevoma Lake Area. This large body of water, created by damming the Red River on the boundary between Oklahoma and Texas, is teeming with game fishes. With its 100,000 surface acres, far flung shorelines, and myriad arms and coves. Lake Texoma has almost limitless fishing possibilities. In addition to native game fishes the White Bass, an introduced species, abounds in these waters, and is exceedingly popular with local fishermen. It is so prolific that there is no creel or size limit, or closed season restrictions on White Bass.

Before the spawning season in April and May, the white bass fishing is at its best. Later the fish retreat to deep water where they may be taken with natural baits.

Fishing is best from early spring until the end of June, when the hot weather sends fish to the deeper water for comfort. However, for the most part, Oklahoma's winter is an excellent season. Autumn and the approach of winter brings fine weather and good conditions for the fly and plug casters. During July and August bait fishing is more successful except when the fly and plug casters get out at daybreak, and fish again during the twilight hours.

South Dakota

South Dakota is a rectangular slice of land which is about 375 miles from east to west and 220 from north to south. The state's geographical position is very near the center of the continent, and a brief glance at its topography suggests the idea that the Creator left His sample case there and it was called "Dakota," meaning "many in one."

Along its eastern portion are rich farm lands, wooded hills, broad meadows, and beautiful lakes. Flowing southeastward the Missouri River divides the state almost in half. West of the "Big Muddy" stretches the grass lands, the sage brush, the Badlands where the shallow rivers flow; then come the Black Hills.

South Dakota is divided into three fishing sections, and each section, to a great degree, possesses its own characteristics, and species of fish. A big handful of lakes, left over from Minnesota's stock pile, are generously scattered throughout the northeastern corner; all are well stocked with Largemouth Bass, Crappie, Rock Bass, Walleye, Yellow Perch, Northern Pike, White Bass, and Bullheads.

The Missouri River and its tributaries represents the mid-section of the fish producing waters; the principal fishes being several native catfishes. The old river has been virtually eliminated as the result of dam construction which has formed four large reservoirs. These reservoirs are: Lewis and Clark Lake (35,000 acres), Fort Randall Reservoir (81,000) acres), Oahe Reservoir (300,000 acres), and Big Bend Reservoir (55,000 acres, scheduled for completion in 1964.) These reservoirs have provided a unique and highly successful fishery for Paddlefish, Sauger, Northern Pike and Walleye.

Westward, beyond the Missouri, and through the Badlands are the Black Hills which represent the state's western angling territory. This up-ended, chaotic mass of limestone and granite has a unique flavor, scenic beauty, romantic history, and excellent trout fishing.

From White Rock, in the extreme northeastern corner, to Big Stone City, a distance of about 60 miles, stretch the narrow waters of the twin lakes Traverse and Big Stone. Big Stone Lake's setting is one of the most beautiful in the state. Angling interest is high, and justifiably so, for there is good Black Bass, Walleye, Perch, Crappie, North ern Pike, Rock Bass, and Bluegill fishing.

Several miles east of Browns Valley, (Traverse and Big Stone Lakes join here), the Sisseton area lies surrounded by good fishing waters. The lakes in this district are well stocked with Black Bass, Walleye, Northern Pike, Crappie, Bluegill, Rock Bass, and Bullheads.

Thirty-five miles northwest of Sisseton is Lake City, a village surrounded by Red Iron Lake, Cottonwood Lake, Clear and Long Lakes.

Southward the chain of lakes includes Enemy, Swim, and Pickerel. Pickerel Lake is a spring fed body of water about three miles long, stocked with Black Bass, Walleye, Crappie, Bluegill, Pickerel and Northern Pike, White Bass, Perch, and Trout. Excellent accommodations are available.

From Pickerel Lake south some 50 miles is Watertown, recreational headquarters for visiting anglers. Here, added to lakes scattered in every direction, is the Big Sioux River. In Lake Kampeska Walleye fishing is very good. Watertown expects visitors and is well prepared to accommodate them. Madison, 50 miles south of Watertown, was established 75 years ago because the settlers found the lakes teeming with fine food fish, and it is another area the angler should visit.

The Missouri River and its tributaries furnishes most of the Catfish angling, although some of the smaller creeks and streams also offer Crappie, Black Bass, and Sunfish. Numerous artificial ponds are also stocked with these fish, but are fished primarily by local fishermen.

Westward beyond the Missouri River stretches a region of buttes and badlands, semi-deserts and dry arroyos. Draining this vast area into the Missouri are the Moreau, Cheyenne, and White Rivers, and their hundreds of arroyo and creek tributaries. Because water levels are far from constant in these streams, fishing is not dependable; however, many artificial lakes and ponds, stocked with warm water fish, dot the region.

The Black Hills are almost sufficient unto them-

A typical North Dakota winter scene—Yellow Perch in the deep freeze.

selves, for geographically, socially, geologically, and economically they form a unit apart. The Black Hills area is largely contained within the boundaries of the Black Hills and Harney National Forests. While hundreds of thousands of people visit the Black Hills, to the credit of South Dakota and the U. S. Forest Service, the area is delightfully unspoiled. The roads twist through almost virgin forests, slip up quiet canyons, and along pine-clad ridges. Trout streams, pitching down timbered canyons, dash across the road and meander through high, peaceful meadows.

Although the Black Hills are fairly primitive, accommodations are not lacking, and it is possible to "rough it in comfort" almost anywhere. The Forest Service has provided camp sites located at appropriate spots near trout streams, and points of scenic interest, with many conveniences to make camping more enjoyable.

All through the Hills are footpaths leading to interesting spots, and horseback trails thread the more inaccessible areas. Some of these paths and trails lead to the less visited trout streams where solitude and high adventure are the angler's companions.

During early May and into June bait fishing and casting deep running lures will prove more effective on Walleye, Northern Pike, Perch, Carppie, and Bluegill in the eastern lake region. Later in June, when the Black Bass season is on, fish have become more active in the shallower water along weed lines and back in the bays; in these spots the plug and fly casters will raise their best fish.

By the end of June and during most of July, if the weather is not too warm, casters of artificials will find top water lures very effective on Black Bass, Crappie, Rock Bass, Bluegill, and occasionally on Walleye and Northern Pike. Late evening and the long twilight hours will be productive; during the day, especially if overcast, top water lures should be used.

Between the end of July and the last days of August, fishing is often not at its best because the warm days have raised the temperature of the shallow and top water, and fish are forced into the depths. At this time still fishing with natural baits and deep trolling produce better results.

If Blue Bird weather is encountered in September, the visiting angler will find this a most delightful season, both because of the weather and the fishing.

Catfish angling in the Missouri River and its tributaries runs fairly steady with the exception of the hot weeks from mid-July to the end of August, which is the low ebb. Natural baits prove best from spring through to the end of autumn, at which time "soft baits"—chicken, lamb, or rabbit liver, coagulated blood, and the other prepared "stink" baits, should be used.

The trout season in the Black Hills area is generous. From May until mid-June, when the streams have usually stablized their flow, the bait fisherman makes the best catches. But, from the end of June until snow flies is the fly caster's season. The fly fisherman visiting this area should be well supplied with all the standard patterns of nymphs, and wet and dry flies in sizes running from 10's to 16's.

With its scenic beauty, points of historical interest, and a variety of fishing, South Dakota has much to offer the visiting angler.

Texas

In the past two dozen years Texas has become fishing-conscious because of the creation of hundreds of thousands of acres of impounded waters and the removal of closed seasons through most of the state. Many of the lakes which contribute to this vast acreage offer excellent fishing. In some of them, fishing is no longer good. Some have been so recently impounded that there has been insufficient time to develop a fish population. Only a few of the larger lakes are being successfully fished at the present time. Nearly any chamber of commerce will provide a list of fishing places.

In addition to the lakes, several large streams and rivers offer good fishing, and the entire Gulf Coast of Texas offers almost any type of salt-water fishing that the sportsman may desire.

A few of the typical lakes and streams are listed.

Lake Texoma has an area of 95,000 acres and is located on the Red River between Texas and Oklahoma. 26,000 acres of the lake is in Texas and is accessible from U. S. Highways 75, 69, and 82. The dam is situated 6 miles from the city of Denison.

The fishes likely to be caught are Largemouth Bass, White Bass, Channel Catfish, Crappie, and many of the smaller sunfishes. Fishing is excellent at times, but the most consistently good fishing will be found in the Red River bend below the dam.

Miami Oklahoma News-Record

Catfish anglers are devoted to their sport.

Boats are usually available but cabins are still limited.

The monthly publication, *Texoma Holiday,* P. O. Box 700, Denison, Texas, carries an extensive listing of fishing camps, sporting goods dealers, and eating places along with latest news about Lake Texoma and other lakes in that area.

Possum Kingdom Dam is located on Texas Highway 16 and the Brazos River. It can be reached from Graford or from Graham. Built for hydro-electric power and flood control, Possum Kingdom Dam has an area of 26,000 acres. At no point is it more than 3 miles wide, and in many places it is considerably less. But what it lacks in width it makes up in length. On the map it looks like a long many-fingered snake.

Ice fishing in the Dakotas is a rugged sport, but it has many ardent followers.

A nice pair of Largemouth Black Bass.

This narrow lake has a very real advantage over a lake with open reaches of water, especially in a section where a brisk wind is common if not usual. Local fishermen have learned to appreciate its many bluff-sheltered coves while fishing on the windiest days.

Many varieties of fish may be taken, the most common of which are Black Bass, Crappie, Channel, Blue and Yellow Catfish, and Bluegill. This lake is one of the few artificial lakes in the state that has not been stocked with the prolific White Bass, and if local sportsmen have their way, the White Bass will never be introduced.

Very few large boats are present because almost everyone around the lake discourages it. The resort owners hope to keep it a mecca for the small boatman, the little guy who wants to spend a day or a week fishing the lake.

At the present time there are 32 resorts on the lake and with two exceptions cater exclusively to fishermen. Information on camping, fishing, and boating facilities can be secured by calling or writing the Graham Texas Chamber of Commerce.

The Colorado River Lakes with the headwaters of one reaching to the next upstream dam offers thousands of acres of fishing water. The lowest in this series is Lake Austin. The dam, located in Austin, forms a 3,000 acre lake. The next dam 15 miles northwest of Austin forms Lake Travis with an area of 11,000 acres. A small dam and lake at Marvel Falls, Texas, separates Lake Travis and Inks Lake of about 900 acres. The next and by far the largest is the 23,000-acre lake formed by Buchanan Dam.

Largemouth Bass, Crappie, various catfishes, and many species of smaller sunfishes are common through all the lakes.

Boats, camping sites and some cabins are available at all of the lakes.

Lake Bridgeport, located on the west fork of the Trinity River 3 miles west of Bridgeport, has a surface area of 9,600 acres. Fish most likely to be taken are Crappie, Channel Catfish, some Largemouth Bass, and many of the smaller sunfish. Boats and cabins are available at the lake.

The Lake Dallas dam is located near the town of Lake Dallas. It has an area of 8,400 acres. The fishes commonly taken are Crappie, White Bass, Channel and Yellow Catfish and many of the smaller sunfishes. The Largemouth Bass fishing is rather poor in this lake. Boats and cabins are available.

Eagle Mountain and Lake Worth. The dams for both of these lakes are located near Ft. Worth. Eagle Mountain Lake has an area of 9,600 acres, and Lake Worth has 5,400 acres. Fishes most likely to be taken are Largemouth Bass, White Bass, Crappie, Channel Catfish, and many of the smaller sunfishes. Boats and cabins are available at the lake and in the vicinity.

The dam which forms Lake Kemp is located near Mabelle and is also accessible from Seymore. This lake has an area of 22,000 acres and furnishes fishing for Largemouth Bass, Crappie, Channel Catfish, White Bass, and many of the smaller sunfishes. Lake Kemp is one of the older lakes with plenty of camps and boats available for the vacationing fisherman.

Fort Phantom Hill Lake is located about 14 miles north of Abilene. Three smaller lakes—Lake Abilene, Kirby, and Lytle—are also located near the same city. The best fishing and boating facilities are located at Phantom Hill Lake, but only a limited number are available at each lake.

Phantom Hill Lake offers good Crappie and Bass fishing, and many large Blue and Channel

Time out for food along an eastern Oklahoma Spotted Smallmouth Bass stream.

A fly caster rushing the season on an Eastern Oklahoma Bass stream.

Catfish are taken. Lake Abilene produces some excellent Bass fishing and also Crappie, White Bass, and Channel Catfish along with numerous sunfishes; Lytle Lake produces a few Bass, some Crappie, Catfish, and many sunfish.

Lake Brownwood. This lake furnishes water for the city of Brownwood and Bangs, and has an area of 8,000 acres and 95 miles of shoreline. The dam is about 12 miles northwest of Brownwood.

The fish usually caught are Black Bass, Crappie, Channel Catfish, some Drum, and various small sunfishes.

Large areas are available around the lake where camping can be done. Twelve fishing camps with cabins, boats, food and other facilities are located on the lake.

Lake Nasworth is located 7 miles southwest of San Angelo. It has an area of 2,000 acres and furnishes good Largemouth Bass, Crappie, Channel Catfish, and sunfishes with Crappie and Catfishes furnishing the most fishing success.

Red Bluff Lake. The dam is located northeast of Arla and has an area of 11,500 acres. Fishes most generally taken are Bass, Crappie, Channel Catfish, and many smaller sunfishes. Boats and cabins or lodge accommodations are available, but a special fee is charged for fishing.

Lake Cisco, located near Cisco, has an area of about 1,000 acres. Although this is an old lake, many nice strings of Bass, Crappie, Channel Catfish, and sunfishes are still taken. Boats and cabins are available.

Lake Walk and Devil's Lake are located on the Devil's River, north of Del Rio. Fishes most likely to be caught are Black Bass, Crappie, Channel Catfish, Rio Grande Perch, and many of the smaller sunfishes.

The Devil's River below these two lakes also offer good fishing, and many Rio Grande Blue Catfish are taken. Boats and cabins are available.

Lake Medena is located about 23 miles northwest of San Antonio. It is accessible by the Culebra Road from San Antonio. Near the lake the road forks and the right hand fork passes over a toll

Smallmouth Bass and Green Sunfish offer good sport for the fly caster in this typical Eastern Oklahoma stream.

road. There is a free road, but it is a little farther on.

The area of this lake is 5,575 acres. Fishes likely to be caught are Black Bass, White Bass, Crappie, Channel Catfish, and many of the smaller sunfishes. Largemouth Bass weighing up to 12 pounds are taken by trolling and White Bass are caught, by fishing deep, and using minnows for bait. Boats and cabins are available.

Lake Caddo lies in both Texas and Louisiana and has an area of about 35,000 acres. This lake is criss-crossed with cypress islands forming many small lakes and bayous. A guide is essential until one knows the lake. Largemouth Bass, White Bass, Pike, Pickerel, Bowfin, Crappie, Catfish, and many of the smaller sunfishes can be caught from this lake. Guides, boats, and cabins are available.

The following lakes are rather small and have only limited facilities available and usually require advance reservations: Buffalo Lake, near Amarillo; McClelland Lake, Gray County; Lake Blanco, Hartley County; Lake Marvin, Hemphill County; Buffalo Lake, near Lubbock; Lake Kick-a-poo, Archer County and Lake Sweetwater, near Sweetwater.

RIVERS

River and stream fishing in Texas is limited mostly to Catfish, Carp, Drum, and Sunfish. The exceptions are the waters flowing into larger lakes. The Red River, flowing into Texoma, provides some bass fishing for quite a few miles up the river and again for some distance below the dam. The same is true of the Colorado and Brazos Rivers. The Pecos River affords very little fishing, except at Red Bluff Dam.

The Rio Grande River between Texas and Mexico, provides good catfishing throughout its length and some Bass fishing where fresh streams from Mexico flow into the river.

Many of the small sluggish streams especially in the eastern half of the state, produce some Bass, more Catfish, and Crappie and sunfishes, but they are inconvenient for most fishermen.

A small section of Texas does offer clean, relatively swift, streams. The two principal rivers are the Guadalupe passing through Kerr County and the city of Kerrville and the Llano River, passing through Kimble County. Kimble County is said to have more miles of perennially flowing streams than any other county in the state. Many smaller crystal clear streams may be found through the Hill Country in Mason, Kerr, Llano and neighboring counties.

ROCKY MOUNTAIN STATES

This vast country lies roughly between the snow-clad peaks of the Continental Divide on the east where the Rockies cut like a sythe across Colorado to the equally high ramparts of the Sierra Nevadas on the west. From the Mexican line, it stretches northward across desert, prairie, and mountains—always there are mountains—to the Canadian border.

This is a big country and, to the fisherman, a challenging one. Within it are intriguing rod-and-reel adventures for the man who likes his fishing liberally spiced with camp life and seclusion.

This area includes most of the public lands states of the west, Idaho, Montana, Wyoming, Colorado, Utah, Nevada, New Mexico, and Arizona.

A typical stream in the Kiamichi Mountains of south-eastern Oklahoma.

Each would provide an angler with sport for the rest of his days if every lake and stream were to be sought out, tested, and tried.

Even in the west, one can fish in good-looking waters and fail to score, for industrial progress has encroached on the west as well as the east. True, invasion of virgin lands and waters has been slower, but it has come. Factories, steel mills, air bases, army camps, and new mining ventures have sprung up all over the intermountain west. Industrial progress has brought increased populations too. And yet there is good fishing to be had here . . . if one gets off the beaten path.

That boulder-filled creek with the riffles or that sparkling lake along a major highway looks enticing, but the chances are that it took a beating during the first week of trout season. Before you heed that urge to put your fly rod or casting outfit together, think of this: The residents get all the breaks on that kind of fishing. The easy places are hit hard during the first days when the back country is still inaccessible because of muck-filled roads. And in this region it must also be remembered that snow does not leave the roads and trails at the higher elevations until late June or early July.

If there is some particular area which it is desired to visit, chances are the conservation department will provide the address of a local deputy warden. The majority of these men are polite and helpful, know the limitations of their own waters, and desire to help visiting fishermen.

To enjoy intermountain fishing go prepared for drastic weather changes. Take along clothes for roughing it a bit. One needs more than a pair of boots, a fishing hat, and a jacket to hit any of those side trails that lead into the mountains—and to the best fishing.

The winter of 1948-49 was one of the most severe in history. For many days planes were used to drop feed to starving sheep flocks and hungry deer camped on the doorsteps of residents in Salt Lake City. The impact of that winter was felt well into the fishing season. Access into the high Uinta country of northeastern Utah, for example, was almost impossible until mid-July. Snowdrifts blocked the one major road leading in from the west. But the trails were open for those who were prepared to walk. And the fishing was excellent.

Not much additional gear is needed for this high country angling. A good woolen mackinaw, a suit of heavy underwear, heavy wool trousers, and by all means, a pair of comfortable walking shoes or boots. Nothing is quite so uncomfortable as rubber boots on a rough mountain trail. Hip boots are not of great importance on these high streams or lakes since plenty of good fishing can usually be obtained from the banks.

To really enjoy western fishing a tent and plenty of camping gear are necessary. While the U. S. Forest Service has begun charging a very small fee for maintenance costs on a few western forest campgrounds, most of them are free. If tent life does not appeal, at least include a small cooking unit in your gear, and prepare at least one meal a day along the road. If it is possible to cook along the way, pack in some of the staple groceries before you leave home. Shipping costs add surprisingly to grocery prices in western mountain towns.

And now, when should one go west with rod, reel, and high hopes? This is a big area and obviously there will be wide variations in temperature between spots in Arizona and Montana. Here, as a tip-off, are the official U. S. Weather Bureau recordings of high and low temperatures for the same dates in one summer in Albuquerque, New Mexico, and West Yellowstone, Montana.

	Albuquerque		West Yellowstone	
	High	Low	High	Low
June 15	90°	62°	70°	31°
July 15	90°	63°	83°	40°
August 15	89°	64°	80°	34°
September 15	76°	52°	65°	23°

Pay particular attention to those low temperatures, they are the ones for which visitors should be prepared.

By long odds, the best fishing month in the intermountain west is September. Note on the little weather chart how the high temperature down in the desert country at Albuquerque dropped off from 89 in August to 76 in September, and the low dropped from 64 to 52. Note how the high at West Yellowstone dropped from 80 in August to 65 in September.

September in the West is fishing weather. Insect life has decreased to a point where mosquitoes or deer flies cease to bother. There is a hint of fall in the air and those nippy nights will put new strength in your casting arm. Therefore, if at all possible, a western fishing vacation should be arranged for September. If that is impossible, try to

Texas Game, Fish and Oyster Comm.

"The Fishin's fine."

beat the mid-summer heat by heading for the highest fishing country available. No matter which one of these states is chosen for the vacation, high country will be available.

Here is another tip on western fishing which applies more or less to waters anywhere in the nation. During the hot days of summer, fish before 10 a. m. and after 5 p. m. The hours between are usually better for camp chores or just plain resting than for fishing.

Arizona

Arizona has been making rapid strides in recent years in the development of new fishing waters. The Arizona Game and Fish Department's Information and Education Division, points out that an even dozen lakes have been constructed or deepened to allow fishing over the last decade. In addition, five more are in various stages of planning and construction at press time.

Trout streams are few and mostly small, so they all get very heavy pressure during the summer months. All are stocked on a put-and-take basis from early May until mid-September. The new lakes, with but one exception, are all Trout lakes and have helped immeasurably to take the pressure off the streams and have aided considerably in economizing the Trout program.

The Colorado River and its impoundments are still the state's biggest attraction for anglers. Powell Lake, formed by the Glen Canyon Dam, Lake Mead behind Hoover Dam, Lake Mohave behind Davis Dam, Topock Marsh, Lake Havasu, Cibola Slough, Martinez Lake and Imperial are the major waters, but there are dozens of small, backwater lakes along the entire length of the stream. All of these are warm-water lakes, with Bass, Crappie and Channel Catfish as the most popular species.

Union Pacific Railroad

A lucky Idaho angler creels a whopping big Rainbow taken from Silver Creek near Sun Valley. Silver Creek is one of the west's most famous fly streams.

Best fishing for these lakes is usually in the spring and fall months, and waterdogs, artificial earthworms, doll flys and surface lures all work well at various times.

The waters below Hoover and Davis Dams abound with lunker Rainbow Trout, too. This water, being drawn off the bottom of the big lakes for power purposes, flows rapidly and at constant temperatures both winter and summer. Trout fishing is usually good all year long here, but for the really big ones—with poundages up in the mid-teens—night fishing during June and July is usually most productive. Most fishing here is done by trolling with deep flatfish and other bass rigs.

The warm-water irrigation lakes of the Phoenix area provide fine fishing also. Roosevelt, Apache, Canyon, Saguaro, Bartlett, Horseshoe and Pleasant are all popular with locals and produce some fine Bass, Crappie and Channel Catfish. Canyon and Saguaro are often used by water skiers and are not as popular with fishermen as in years past, but this doesn't always hold true on weekdays, and some real keepers are taken from both lakes.

Lower Oak Creek and West Clear Creek are the two waters in the state usually considered the best for the taking of Smallmouth Bass. To a lesser degree, Sycamore Creek and the Verde River also produce some Smallmouths.

Trout fishing in some 36 lakes scattered throughout the state in the higher elevations offer plenty of sports in addition to several other lakes on Indian Reservations where fishing is also allowed provided the angler purchases the proper Reservation permit. The state's trout lakes range in size from five acres to a potential 570 surface acres at Big Lake. Some of the more popular trout lakes, besides Big Lake, are Lee Valley, Luna, Show Low, Fool Hollow, Ashurst, Kinnikinick, Whitehorse, Woods Canyon and Lynx.

Live bait is not permitted in Trout waters in Arizona, and most anglers use salmon eggs or cheese when they are not experimenting with their usual assortment of artificial lures and flys.

Colorado

Colorful Colorado is a "have" state from the standpoint of fishing waters. A fishing inventory gives Colorado approximately 14,000 miles of Trout streams and approximately 2,500 trout and warm-water fishing lakes. Principal Trout are Rainbow, Black-spotted Cutthroats, Eastern Brooks, and Brown. A few lakes have Lake Trout. The principal warm-water species are Largemouth Bass, Crappie, Bluegills, Channel Catfish, and Perch. Walleye have also been introduced.

The best warm-water lakes are Jumbo and North Sterling Reservoirs near Sterling and Bonny Reservoir near Burlington. Large Crappie and Walleye are taken from all three lakes.

The principal Trout streams are the Arkansas and Poudre Rivers on the eastern slope; the Colorado and Gunnison Rivers on the western slope, and the Rio Grande and Conejos Rivers in the San Luis Valley.

Best Trout lakes are: Lake John and the Delaney Butte lakes near Walden; Williams Fork and Granby Reservoirs near Granby; Vega Reservoir near Colbran; and Williams Creek Lake near Pagosa Springs.

Approximately 2000 small high elevation trout lakes are present in the state. Many are remote and are reached only by hiking or horseback.

The warm-water fishing is found in the plains reservoirs in the eastern part of the state. There are few natural lakes in this section.

Colorado in 1962 changed to a year-round fishing season for all species including Trout. The winter bag limit is 6 trout and the summer limit 10 trout. Other new regulations include several fish-for-fun waters where only flies and single hook lures are allowed and minimum size for "keepers" is either 12 inches or 14 inches. Several sections of streams have also been designated as fly-fishing only areas.

In 1961, 414,000 fishing licenses were sold. Of this number 120,000 licenses were non-residents. The calculated catch in 1961 was 16,800,000 trout and 3,500,000 warm-water species. The catch per man hour on Trout waters was 0.68 and 1.39 on warm waters.

One program that is beginning to pay off is that of fishing lake construction. Since 1949, 34 fishing lakes totaling 3,800 acres have been constructed. An additional 37 lakes and reservoirs totaling 40,000 acres have been opened to public fishing through purchase, lease and management agreement.

This is believed to be the largest Rainbow ever taken. It weighed 52 lbs. 8 oz. and was caught in Jewell Lake in British Columbia in 1932. As no official record was kept of the catch, it has never been recognized as a record fish. Descendents of this beauty are now taken in Lake Pend Oreille in Idaho.

Idaho

Idaho, the Gem State, has varied and extensive water resources. Geographically, it is unique in that the southern section is a "world" apart from the northern or Panhandle end. Between the two lies a vast wilderness area adjacent to the "River of No Return" and the Salmon, major spawning area for Steelhead and Chinook Salmon. It is strange, but true, that many resident anglers at the opposite ends of Idaho never have fished the other section.

Rainbow and Cutthroat are the most popular species. However, in certain bodies of water, notably Spirit, Priest, Pend Oreille and Payette Lakes and Island Park Reservoir, the Kokanee, or Blueback Salmon, is rated as a top game fish.

When Idaho is mentioned, fishermen's thought immediately turn to the massive Kamloops Rainbow of Pend Oreille Lake which startled the angling world. All national Rainbow records are at present held by these giant imports from Canada.

It was mentioned previously that trips into the back country are necessary to find the best western fishing. This is particularly true of Idaho in which many small lakes and feeder streams afford extremely good fishing. Many of the best of these are in the vast wilderness area that lies in the headwaters of the Salmon and Clearwater Rivers. There are no highways here, and hiking or packing are necessary to reach good fishing.

The best fly fishing months are August and September. The large majority of resident and nonresident anglers fish their flies wet. A survey of sporting goods stores reveals that leading patterns purchased are Renegades, Gray and Brown Hackles, Royal Coachman, Silver Doctor, Mosquito, and Black Gnat. Trolling is the accepted method on most of the larger lakes.

The major productive lakes, species of game fish they contain, and most popular lures, include:

Henry's Lake, Cutthroats, Brook Trout streamer flies, bass plugs, daredevils, and Jack Lloyds.

Island Park Reservoir, Rainbow, streamer flies, and Jack Lloyds.

Mackay Reservoir, Rainbow, trolling gear.

Magic Reservoir, Rainbows, trolling gear.

Anderson Ranch Dam, Rainbow, trolling gear, salmon eggs, and flies.

Warm Lake, Rainbow and Kokanee, trolling gear, salmon eggs, and flies.

The famed North Fork of the Snake River in eastern Idaho yields many a fine Rainbow such as this angler is proudly displaying. The placid waters of the North Fork in Targhee National Forest on the road to Yellowstone Park draws thousands of anglers each year.

Payette Lake, Rainbow, Kokanee, and Brook Trout, trolling gear.
Pend Oreille Lake, Rainbow, Cutthroat, Dolly Varden Trout, and Kokanee, trolling gear (Jack Lloyds, daredevils, Colorado spinners and assorted plugs), and flies.
Preist Lake, Mackinaws in 30-40 lb. class. Cutthroats, kokanee Salmon.
Spirit Lake, Rainbow, Cutthroat, Kokanee, trolling gear, and flies.
Lost Valley Reservoir, Rainbows, trolling, Salmon eggs,
Palisades Reservoir, trolling, Salmon eggs.
Blackfoot Reservoir, trolling, Salmon eggs.

The principal streams, their game fish and most widely used lures are:

North Fork of Snake River, Rainbows, spoons, spinners, and wet flies.
The upper section in Island Park country is excellent dry fly fishing.
South Fork of Snake River, Cutthroat, spoons, spinners, dry and wet flies, and some bait fishing.
Snake River, American Falls to Burley, Rainbows, large spoons, and spinners.
Teton River, Rainbow and Cutthroat, principally wet and dry flies, some spinners, and salmon eggs.
Silver Creek, Rainbows, dry and wet flies, bait, and salmon eggs.
Lost River, Rainbows, spoons, spinners, dry and wet flies, salmon eggs, and garden hackles.
Wood River, Rainbows, spoons, spinners, flies, salmon eggs.
Boise River, Rainbow, spoons, spinners, flies, salmon eggs.
Salmon River and tributaries, Cutthroat, Rainbows, Dolly Varden Trout, Steelhead and Chinook Salmon, spoons, spinners, and salmon eggs.
Clearwater River and tributaries, Rainbows, Steelhead, Cutthroat, small spinners, spoons, flies, salmon eggs.
Coeur D'Alene River, Rainbows, small spinners, spoons, flies, salmon eggs, baits early in season.
Clark Fork River, Rainbows, Dolly Varden Trout, Cutthroat, small spinners, spoons, flies, salmon eggs, baits early in season.
Moyie River, Rainbow, small spinners, spoons, flies, and salmon eggs.

Salmon in Idaho must be taken by hook and line, and salmon eggs are the best bait, although attempts have been made to outlaw their use. The major argument against them is the use in "chumming" waters while Trout fishing. This is a serious offense.

Idaho provides some excellent wilderness fishing for Rainbow, Brook, Golden and Cutthroat Trout in its high mountain lakes. Among the best are the groups of lakes in the Bighorn Craigs, Sawtooth Wilderness Area, Seven Devils, McCall area, Selkirk Mountains, Buffalo Hump, and Burnt Knob areas. Groups of lakes in the Surveyor's Ridge, Gospel Hill, White Clous Mountains, and the Powell-Upper Clearwater River areas also provide superlative high-country fishing.

Idaho Game & Fish Commission

Chinook salmon fishermen find exciting sport angling for these big fish as they migrate into Idaho waters each summer. Edwin Vest of Morgan, Utah shows satisfaction with his 25 pound chinook caught on the main Salmon River last summer.

Very good Bass fishing may be enjoyed at lower elevations in the lower Snake River, Brownlee Dam Reservoir, Lake Powell, lower Clearwater River, Chat Colet Lake and several lakes in the North Idaho Panhandle.

Montana

Montana is a Trout state with some of the finest Trout fishing in the nation. Whether you prefer to dance flies upon a cool stream, cast into crystal snow-fed lakes of the high country, or just putt around a lake and troll, the big sky country of Montana has a lot to offer any fisherman.

Many Montana streams and lakes remain open to anglers the entire year, but the general fishing season opens in late May. About this time spring is really under way in the Treasure State and mountain snows are melting under persuasion of the warm sun. Dates of peak runoff vary from year to year, but it's a good bet that the first month of the general fishing season will find many streams high and roily.

Early in the year fly fishing in the smaller streams is productive, but in larger roily waters bait fishermen fill more creels. The spin and casting fishermen make out too by deploying a variety of spoons and lures.

In June while many waters are still swelled and colored by runoff, stoneflies creep from the streams, shed their juvenile skins and take wing. The stonefly hatch, sometimes called "salmon-fly hatch" is the signal for fishermen to take to the streams en-masse for some of the hottest fishing there is. Fly fishing improves as the season progresses into early summer. The bait fisherman does well too. Angle worms are a dependable bait year-round.

For fly fishing, some of the most commonly used lures are the thinly-dressed hair flies. All of the mite series and others of similar type, such as the fizzle are reliable. Conventional wet flies used in other western states are also successful here. The Gray Hackle with yellow body, Brown Hackle, Black Gnat, Professor, Royal Coachman, and similar flies will be found in the fly kits of most local fishermen. Larger streamer flies, tied with bucktail and squirreltail, are good at times, especially for large fish. Other popular fish-getters are the wooly worms tied in a variety of colors. The wooly worms are usually fished slow and nymph-like.

If the fish are interested in dries, almost any kind will turn the trick if properly presented. The whole bivisible series is worthwhile. Spiders are fine for late season water. In the conventional dry-fly patterns, those with brown hackles ranging from the very light to extremely dark are often more persistent fish takers than are the grays. The Cahill family and the Adams family are reliable.

For wet-fly work, resident fishermen are inclined to go for the larger sizes from four's on up to ten's. The usual dry-fly size, 16's on up to about 12's are about right. However, there are times when flies as large as number 6 or as small as 22 take good Trout. Big hopper flies are deadly during the summer as grasshoppers become common along stream banks.

During July and August, streams become lower as runoff subsides and irrigation waters are drawn from many streams and stream fishing becomes tougher. This is the time when fishermen enjoy the high cool country where lakes are still ice cold.

September comes to Montana and signals the retreat of summer. Nights begin to get crisp, the waters cool down, and the familiar green of summer is transformed to brilliant golds, reds and yellows. September brings some of the finest fishing of the season. Big Browns are active then and take to flashing spoons and big streamers.

Four major watersheds traverse Montana—the Yellowstone, Missouri, Kootenai and the Clark Fork of the Columbia. The Yellowstone River watershed is the most southerly and easterly. Upper headwaters of this system reach into Yellowstone Park and into the Beartooth Mountains. Scores of shimmering lakes dot the rugged Beartooth plateau.

In the upper reaches of the Yellowstone, one may expect to take Cutthroat, Rainbow, Brown Trout and Whitefish, while in the lowlands the main river becomes warmer, more turbid and supports a different variety of fish, including Sauger, Walleye Pike, Channel Catfish, fresh water Drum and Ling. Some of the more important tributaries for Trout fishing are the Stillwater River, Clark Fork of the Yellowstone, Sweetgrass, Shields River, Boulder River, Hellroaring Creek and Slough Creek. Cutthroat are most common in the headwaters of the tributaries with Rainbow and Brown Trout in the lower portions.

The Missouri River watershed drains all of Montana east of the Continental Divide not encompassed by the Yellowstone drainage. This is Mon-

Ross Hall

Two flying fishermen pose beside their plane with part of the catch they made at North Idaho's big Lake Pend Oreille. The pair took home a fine mess of Dolly Varden and Cutthroat Trout.

Ross Hall

A happy angler at North Idaho's big Lake Pend Oreille displays a 12-lb. Kamloops Rainbow Trout to an admiring little miss.

tana's largest watershed and boasts some of the most famous fishing streams in the United States, including the Madison, Gallatin, Jefferson, Big Hole and Beaverhead Rivers. The great diversity of game fish include Grayling, Cutthroat, Rainbow, Brown and Eastern Brook Trout, in the upper reaches, to Sturgeon, Sauger, Walleye, Northern Pike and Yellow Perch in the lower river and tributaries below Great Falls. Trout fishing for Rainbow and Browns is found also in some tributaries below Great Falls including the Musselshell, Judith, Marias and Milk rivers.

Moving west of the Continental Divide now we come to the Clark Fork of the Columbia River. Well-known tributaries include Flint Creek, Rock Creek, the Big and Little Blackfoot rivers, the Bitterroot, Flathead and Swan rivers. Most of the tributary streams as well as much of the main river offer excellent fishing for Cutthroat and Rainbow Trout, Dolly Varden (bull trout) and Sockeye Salmon.

The Kootenai drains big-timber country in the northwest corner of Montana. Some of the outstanding tributary streams are the Fisher, Tobacco and Yaak rivers. These streams offer Cutthroat, Eastern Brook and Rainbow Trout, while the main Kootenai offers Cutthroat, Whitefish, Rainbow and some big Bull Trout fishing.

You'll enjoy fishing in Montana. There's still lots of elbow room, beautiful country and streams full of wild Trout.

Nevada

Nevada is one of the "have not" states in water resources from a fisheries standpoint, and it is often overlooked by the visiting angler dazzled by the larger waters of states to the north. This is a mistake, because Nevada has good fishing.

A number of new reservoirs in the northeastern park of the state provide excellent fishing, especially in Elko County. Wilson and Wildhorse Reservoirs produce Trout of from 2 to 6 pounds.

Bass and Perch rank high on the list of game fishes, although trout fishing predominates as the major sport.

It is advisable to ask lots of questions about Nevada fishing, since the ordinary trip through the state on major highways will reveal little if any fishing water. Here, more than in most places, it is necessary to get off the beaten path.

The most famous fishing waters are undoubtedly Lake Mead, behind Hoover Dam, and the Colorado below that structure. The cold water discharged from this dam has turned 30 miles of the muddy Colorado into one of the west's finest trout streams. Four- or five-pound Rainbow Trout are common and much heavier fish are frequently taken. Boats and guides can be secured at access points to the river below the dam. Guides are recommended since the river is swift and filled with whirlpools and back eddies dangerous for small boats operated by those who do not know the stream. This fishing, plus that for Largemouth Bass in Lake Mead, attracts anglers from all over the nation to a state that has not been highly regarded as a fishing area.

Nevada merits serious consideration by the fisherman who must take his vacation early in the summer.

Principal waters, species they contain, best

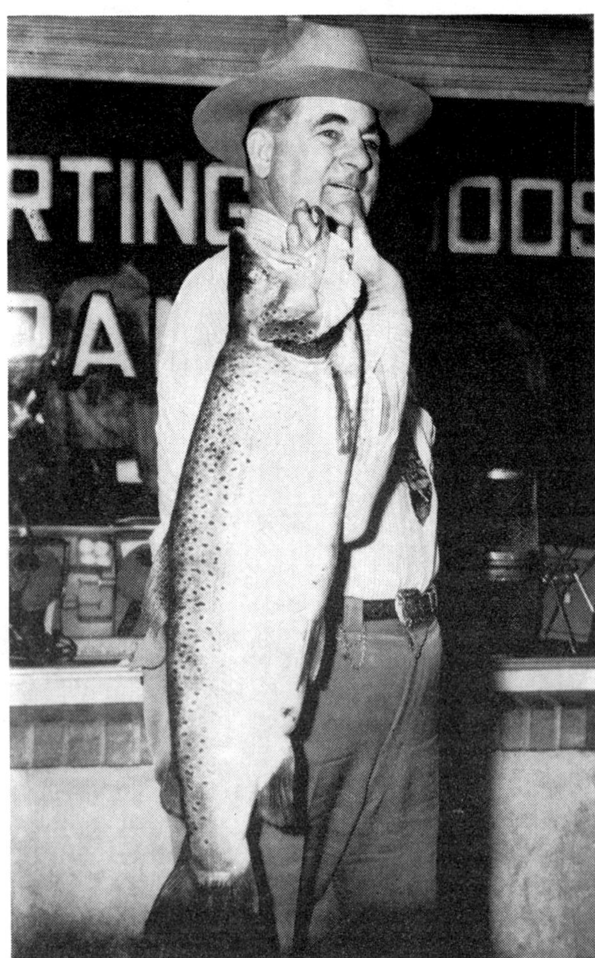

New Mexico could use more trout water, but it does boast some big ones in what water it has. Here is a 20½ pound Brown taken from the Chama River. The gentleman with it is Elliott Barker, New Mexico's veteran game warden.

months and most widely used lures, are:

TAHOE LAKE. Rainbow, Brooks, Browns, Cutthroat, and Mackinaws with the latter predominating, May, June and July, flatfish, spoons, and plugs.

WASHOE LAKE. Sacramento Perch and Catfish, May, June and July, small spoons.

WALKER LAKE. Sacramento Perch and Cutthroats, May, June and July, small spoons.

PYRAMID LAKE. Perch, June, spoons, Rainbow and Cutthroat Trout, 2 to 16 pounds, October through March, spinning lures and trolling. Special permit, $1 a day, $3 a season.

RUBY LAKE. Largemouth Bass, May, June, July and August, Hawaiian wiggler, and weedless plugs.

TRUCKEE RIVER. Browns, Rainbows, Cutthroats and Whitefish, May through September with fly fishing best in June, July and August, and spoon fishing most productive in September and October.

CARSON RIVER (both forks). Cutthroat, Rainbow and Browns, May to September, flies and spoons.

WALKER RIVER (both forks). Rainbow and Cutthroat, May to September with June, July and August best for flies, and spoons in May and September.

COLORADO RIVER (below Hoover Dam). Rainbow, all months except July and August, flatfish, Owyhee River, Rainbow, June through August, flies and spoons.

HUMBOLT RIVER. Rainbow and Cutthroat, May through July, flies, spoons, and fly combinations.

LAE MEAD. Largemouth Bass and Crappie, March, April, and May, plugs.

LAHONTAN RESERVOIR. Rainbows, Catfish and Yellow Perch, May and June, spoons.

RYE PATCH RESERVOIR. Largemouth Bass, May, June, and July, spoons, and plugs.

Majority of the better small trout fishing streams are in Elko, White Pine, Humbolt, and Nye counties. They contain Rainbow, Brooks, and Cutthroats which may be taken on flies, dry or wet, spoons and the popular Nevada spinner, and fly combination. All of the summer months, May through September, are productive.

New Mexico

If you are a dyed-in-the-wool fly fisherman and must take your vacation early, it is wise to investigate the possibilities in New Mexico. Due to its southern location, its spring runoff is usually over when the peak of the flow is reached further north.

Fly fishing starts to be good in southern New Mexico in May, but it will not be good in the northern mountains until early in July with a few isolated exceptions.

In New Mexico's best fishing areas the most consistent results will be obtained from the old standby fly patterns such as the Royal Coachman, the Rio Grande King, the Ginger Quill, and the Brown and Gray Hackles. Flies of most any pattern with a certain amount of white on them are used extensively by resident fishermen. On large bodies of water the wooly worm has come into considerable favor.

Small silver spinners are in wide use on smaller lakes and many streams, and good catches are made in the Rio Grande on spinners with attached flies or colored beads.

There are few plug fishermen in New Mexico, but good plug fishermen can and do take their toll of Bass. Principal bait used on all spiny ray fish is the minnow, although cut baits are used for taking Catfish.

With regard to spiny ray species, the most consistent producer of Bass and Crappie is Elephant Butte Lake and the river above. Conchas Lake was exceptionally good in 1948 for Crappie fishing, and Bass fishing is expected to be good in the same lake in the next few years. Catfish also are taken in quantity from Elephant Butte and Conchas.

The state has five major trout areas.

The first is the Sangre de Cristo Mountains, which include the Rio Grande and tributaries entering the Rio Grande from the east, such as the Canadian and the Pecos rivers. Species to be taken here are Rainbow, Brown, Cutthroat, and Brooks in order of their abundance.

The second major area includes the Chama River drainage from the Colorado line as far south as Abiquiu and affords Rainbow, Brown, Cutthroat, and Brook Trout fishing.

Rainbow, Cutthroat, and Browns can be taken from the third area, the Jemez Mountain region. This includes the entire headwater drainage of the Jemez River, as well as several small streams that flow east into the Rio Grande.

The fourth major area is the White Mountain region. Located in the vicinity of Ruidoso in Lincoln county. These streams are not large, but accommodate numbers of local fishermen. Major species in order of abundance are Rainbow and Browns. A few Eastern Brooks also are taken.

The last big fishing area is in the Gila Mountains, which include the headwaters of the Gila River and some of the San Francisco River. This section is very heavily fished and yields mostly Rainbows; however, a few Browns are taken.

Utah

Stick a pin in the exact center of a map showing all this desert, flowering cactus, sand, lava rock, mountains, forest, streams, and lakes and it will be in Utah.

Utah is a "have not" western state from the standpoint of available waters. The miles of productive streams are not nearly enough to take care of the pressure, yet national records for Brown Trout, caught by fly or by any lure, have been established on Utah waters.

But there is fishing in Utah if you will take the time to ferret it out.

The fisherman not too limited for time should, by all means, visit the high Uinta country. This unique mountain range which runs east and west is a primitive area, dotted with hundreds of lakes. They are so numerous that many do not have names.

Cutthroat and Brook Trout are the predominant game fish in these high waters, most of them above

Ross Hall

Lake Pend Oreille, the home of the Kamloops.

7,000 feet, but there are others. The Montana Grayling has been introduced successfully in lakes which have clear, cold feeder streams.

This is strictly country for hiking trips which can last for a week or three months without visiting all of the lakes. There are no cabins or modern conveniences.

Late August or September are the best times. Mosquitoes are bad earlier in the year and snow drifts are deep until early July.

Another fine area for the adventurous fisherman is the Boulder Mountain country in south central Utah. It is similar to the Uinta country, but not quite as rugged. Lake fishing predominates, although there are a few good streams. It has much warmer climate than the Uintas, and Rainbows are the major fish.

Both areas provide fine fly fishing and any of the less colorful patterns will take them. Gray Hackles, Ginger Quills, Black Gnats, and Red Ants are suggested.

These lakes are small and are usually fished with either fly rods or spinning outfits. Fish are not record-breakers, but 15 and 16-inch Trout are not uncommon.

Fish Lake is the most famous of the lakes. It is near Richfield in southern Utah. While it is fished very heavily, it still produces good catches of Rainbow. Mackinaw Trout, some of good size, have been taken here. Pop-gear trolling is the best method, but many catches are made with fly rod casting from the shores. Use the larger flies in Coachman and streamer patterns.

Utah has several major river drainages, notably the Provo, Weber, and Logan Rivers in the north, and the Sevier further south which are productive, but heavily fished. Brown Trout have gained a strong foothold in these streams and, although very few are now planted, they continue to make up a goodly share of the catches.

The Logan and Provo Rivers are noted for their Browns. A 29-pounder was taken from Blacksmith's Fork of the Logan in 1949 and 22-pounder from the Provo in 1947. Mostly these big ones fall to the resident fishermen. The visitors will take more Rainbows.

Utah's many reservoirs are productive with a few exceptions. However, the yearly water supply may often determine the quality of fishing in the irrigation reservoirs. Panguitch Reservoir in south-central Utah is one of the most productive.

There is some Bass fishing in the Cache Valley area in northern Utah. However, the major warm water fishery exists in 120 square mile Utah Lake which abounds with Channel Catfish and has a developing population of White Bass.

Lake and reservoir fishing is good in the early part of the season in June. However, good stream fishing usually may wait until after the spring "run-off" and the streams have had a chance to clear.

Wyoming

Wyoming, the Cowboy state, is one of the West's great fishing states. Wyoming estimates that the state's total mileage of fishable streams is considerably more than 19,000 and that the total acreage of productive lakes is more than 235,000. And that estimate does not include waters in Yellowstone or Grand Teton National Parks or the areas of any artificial reservoirs.

In addition, there are many miles of streams and vast acreages of lakes in wilderness areas, mostly in the western portion, which are barely known.

BROOK TROUT

The Brook Trout, while not indigenous to Wyoming waters, certainly has adopted the state. In larger streams and lakes, the fish taken average 10 to 12 inches, although lengths of 18 inches and weights of four pounds are not uncommon.

A national record fish of ten pounds was taken from Torrey Lake in the Wind River Mountains in the 30's. In Wyoming waters which are not heavily fished, such as Slide Lake in Bridger National Forest, Brook Trout of four pounds are frequently taken.

The lakes in the Snowy range sector of the Medicine Bow Forest provide Brook Trout that will average about 10 inches or slightly larger. They may be taken on almost any dry or wet fly in numbers. Four- and five-pounders are frequently taken from lakes in this region.

BROWN TROUT

Brown Trout are widely distributed on both slopes of the Divide. The largest recorded specimen was a 17½-pounder taken from a small reservoir in Johnson County. It shows a preference for dry flies here and is harder to catch than most other trouts.

The range of the Brown is being restricted wherever possible in Wyoming in favor of the native Cutthroat and Rainbow. If one likes this fish, however, the North Platte River in the Saratoga area is good water. Brown Trout also predominate in the lower Tongue River. An expert with dry flies has a better chance to catch large fish, and five-pounders are not uncommon.

Reservoirs provide a lot of the west's fishing. Here some young hopefuls try their luck in Deer Creek Reservoir of Utah. They probably took more Perch than Trout.

Extensive planting is necessary in the intermountain west to keep abreast of mounting fishing pressure. Here a bunch of legal Rainbows go into a northern Utah stream.

RAINBOW TROUT

Rainbows are widely distributed throughout the state and are the major product of the state's hatcheries. They will be found in Wyoming further downstream in high mountain streams than Brooks or Blackspotted Trout.

Early in the season, they bite best on spinners and worms. Later, from July 1 on, its's strictly dry or wet fly fishing. The best fishing for Rainbows is drainage of the Green River and its tributaries in the Pinedale area.

The average size here is about 14 inches, although five- and six-pounders are not uncommon. There is also good Rainbow fishing in the upper Platte River and in the Cody area.

GOLDEN TROUT

For a real trophy of your skill with a fly rod try your luck in Wyoming for that most beautiful of the trouts—the Golden. That bright-hued import from California has done better in high Wyoming lakes than any other area of the inter-mountain West.

The fishermen must climb for this fish because it likes the cold, clear waters of lakes above 10,000 feet. Here it grows to a length of 16 inches and a weight of two and a half pounds.

The best area is the high country on either the east or west slope of the Wind River Mountains where there are many lakes. The average fish taken is about 11 inches.

A world's record Golden was caught here in 1948. It weighed 11 pounds. Truly worth trying for, but it takes time and effort packing into the high waters. Once there, almost any standard fly will take them.

Mackinaw (Lake) Trout are present in many of the deeper, cold water lakes where forage fishes are present. Some of the best fishing is in Jackson, Fremont, Shoshone, Bull, Jenny, Phelps, Torry, Brooks, Dome, Deaver, Seven Brothers, and Middle Piney Lakes.

Jackson Lake, in the Jackson Hole country of Northwestern Wyoming, possesses the required Mackinaw assets of deep, cold water and plenty of forage fish almost to perfection. Deep trolling is necessary and fish up to 30 pounds are caught. The average will be about three pounds.

CUTTHROAT TROUT

For native Cutthroats, and many fishermen well acquainted with Brook, Rainbow, and Brown Trouts, prefer natives to all others, try the Snake River and its tributaries on the west slope of the Divide. Most of the fish taken will be 12 inches, or less, but three- and four-pound fish are common.

The native Blackspotted Trout seldom exceeds five pounds here, although there is record of a 14-pounder caught in 1932, and an 11-pounder and a 10-pounder, both caught in 1942. Cutthroat angling areas are being expanded in Wyoming.

You will find it a quiet fish, often loafing in pools and riffles. It does not often jump clear of the water when hooked as does the Rainbow. It can be taken on either wet or dry flies of almost any pattern after the spring runoff subsides.

It is wise to remember in this state that fly casting is best in all waters after high water subsides. On the Platte and Green Rivers that period comes about August 1 and on the Snake about September 1. Other than flies, the most popular artificial lures are the Flatfish and the Colorado Spinner.

There is some warm water fishing in Wyoming, but it gets little attention because of the fine trout fishing. Bass, averaging 12 inches, may be taken in large quantities from Ocean Lake near Riverton, and there are Walleyes and Catfish in the eastern and central portion of the state.

PACIFIC COAST STATES

The three Pacific Coast states are the original home of the Rainbow, Cutthroat, and Dolly Varden Trout, and of the Pacific Salmon. Any fishing enthusiast in any one of them is not apt to let visiting anglers forget that fact. Others, including Lake, Brown, and Brook Trout, have been introduced, but first loyalty is given by most coast anglers to the Rainbow.

Warm water fish of several species have also been successfully introduced into many of the warmer waters. Until comparatively recently, however, little effort was made to utilize these fish since everyone was primarily interested in Trout and Salmon.

A rapidly increasing army of fishermen has forced more interest in such species, and they are now sought out to a much greater degree than formerly. The fish and game commissions are also giving such fish increasing attention, and there is

Joe Mears, Pasadena

Hot Creek, named for the warm geysers that feed it, is a justly famous dry fly Creek in California's Owens Valley.

little question that the warm water fish will be rated higher in these states.

The successful introduction of Striped Bass in San Francisco Bay and their subsequent spread northward along the coast to Coos Bay has added another sport fish to the long list of superb natives that were already available.

California

California offers a wide variety and range of fishing. Bordered by the Pacific Ocean, and traversed by the Coast, Cascade, Sierra Nevada, and Sierra Madre mountains, much fishing for marine, brackish water and freshwater fishes is to be had. Mt. Whitney, 14,495 feet in elevation, and Death Valley, 250 feet below sea level, lie only 100 miles apart and the tremendous range in elevation, topography and character of its different areas easily account for the variety of fishing offered. The native Golden, Rainbow, and Cutthroat Trout with the introduced Brook and Brown Trout afford excellent sport in many high mountain lakes and streams. There are over 8,000 lakes of five acres or more in the Sierra Nevada alone, many of which can only be reached by trail or foot. Most of these lie in glacier-cut basins at elevations varying from 5,000 to 13,000 feet. Fed by melting snow or ice, these lakes afford magnificent mountain panoramas that well match the beauty of the trout dwelling there. In addition, California, like Washington, and Oregon has the incomparable King (Chinook) and Silver Salmon and Steelhead in its coastal streams. While indiscriminant dam construction has destroyed or greatly reduced the runs, the Sacramento, Klamath, Trinity, Eel, and other streams still offer sport fishing for such sea-run, migratory species. Lake Tahoe and Donner Lake also offer deep water trolling for Lake or Mackinaw Trout.

While California offers a tremendous variety of fishing in both salt and fresh water, it is beset at the same time by the critical stocking and management problems of heavily populated areas. With a rapid population increase after World War II, sales of fishing licenses have jumped to almost 1.5 million per year. The increased angling pressure has brought about serious depletion problems in many waters particularly those accessible by roads. As in any state, the angler who parks his car by any mainstem trout stream and expects to pick up a limit of fish in an hour's fishing may be sadly disappointed. On the other hand, if he is willing to do a bit of walking or horseback riding into less accessible waters, he will find both the fishing and the scenery better. Salt or brackish water fishing for Striped Bass or other fishes, on the other hand, is the most accessible of all fishing. Boat liveries are abundant and advice as to where, when, and how to fish is easily obtained. Good trout fishing on the other hand may be found in accessible areas, but it requires skill, luck, and knowledge of the waters to get results.

From the angler's standpoint, the state can be divided into four broad areas based on the types of fishing offered. These are: 1) Southern California waters south of the Tehachapi Mountains, 2) fresh waters of the Sacramento and San Joaquin Rivers in the great central valleys at low elevations including the brackish waters of San Francisco Bay, San Pablo and Suisun Bays and waters of the delta area generally in central California, 3) streams draining into the Pacific from the Coast range, and 4), mountain streams and lakes draining both the east and west of the Cascades, and Sierra Nevada mountain ranges. Each of these areas will be discussed separately.

SOUTHERN CALIFORNIA

California's climate is so dry from March to December of most years south of the Tehachapi Mountains that the freshwater fishing is largely restricted to man-made reservoirs and lakes. Stream fishing is mainly limited to permanent waters in the canyons of the Sierra Madre range. Legal-sized trout are stocked in most of these on a "put and take" basis to meet the extremely heavy angling demand. As one angler exaggerated: "In southern California, if a stream is stocked at 11:00 in the morning, the fish will all be caught by four, and the stream will be dry by six." So, in the area from Los Angeles to San Diego the visiting sportsman would do well to seek either salt water angling or the lakes or reservoirs which provide Bass, Crappie, Sunfish, and Catfish, A few of these near San Diego are Hodges, Murray, Otay, and Moreno. In 1942 a *Field and Stream* record Largemouth Bass, weighing 9 pounds 12 ounces, was taken from Lake Henshaw which lies only a few miles east of San Diego. The season is open the year-round in southern California.

Lake Arrowhead, and in Big Bear and other

Joe Mears, Pasadena

The south fork of the Kern River at Kennedy Meadows which is reached by a tough mountain road.

lakes in the mountains above San Benardino provide trout fishing. Big Bear Lake also offers Bass, Channel Catfish and panfish.

Corvina and Sargo may be taken all year in the Salton Sea and Bass, Channel Catfish, and other warm-water species are present in the Colorado River. Except in the winter, it is apt to be quite warm in this district, and for anglers who do not mind the heat in summer, much fishing is available under uncrowded conditions.

SACRAMENTO-SAN JOAQUIN AREA

The lower portions of the Sacramento-San Joaquin Rivers and their tributaries lying in the great central valleys comprise an area roughly 600 by 100 miles. This, with the irrigated portions of southern California comprises the "bread basket" of the state. Water utilization for stock and crops is so intense that the principal fishing areas are limited largely to San Francisco Bay, lower Delta area foothill reservoir and the main channels of the Sacramento River in the north and the San Joaquin in the south. Near the junction of these two streams in the Delta area and in San Pablo and Suisun Bays, Striped Bass fishing is centered and is excellent. These introduced fish provide fine sport when taken by casting, trolling, or bait fishing. According to the Department of Fish and Game, about two million of these fish are taken annually, ranging in size from around two to over forty pounds. The great bulk of Striped Bass are caught using small chunks of sardines for bait. These are usually placed on 4/0 to 7/0 hooks, two to a leader, with two to six ounces of lead fastened in a swivel-snap at the end of the 36 inch leader to hold the bait close to the bottom against tidal and river currents.

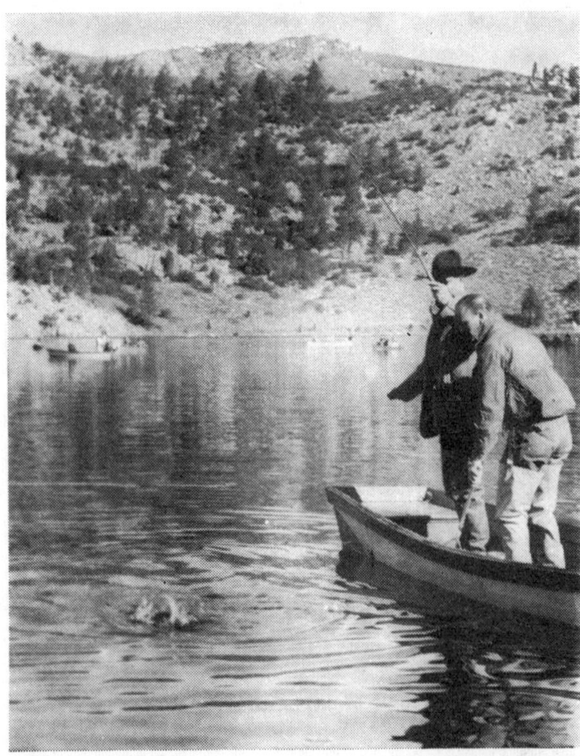

Joe Mears, Pasadena

Opening day on June Lake in California's Sierra. This lake is typical of the lakes that are stocked heavily and produce heavily for bait fishermen.

While bait fishing is the principal method used, trolling is increasing in importance. Trolling for Stripers is usually done in the summer and fall in the Bay area and in early spring in the Delta when the water is clearest. Trolling methods vary with the area and season. During the fall months adult King (Chinook) Salmon are on their spawning migrations upstream, and it is not uncommon to land a thirty or forty pound Chinook while trolling for Striped Bass.

Thousands participate in Striped Bass fishing, and there are numerous boat liveries in the Delta Area where one can obtain all necessary equipment. Quite a heavy poundage of fish, principally Starry and other flounders and Striped Bass are taken by anglers fishing off piers or docks using bait of various kinds. Aside from sardines, worms, grubs, bacon, potatoes, flour-dough balls, and fish offal used, one angler boasted that pieces of laundry soap made the best bait he knew of for Catfish. These fish are abundant in Delta waters near Antioch.

Shad fishing is carried on in the American, Feather, and Yaba Rivers. They may easily be taken on a small fly or spoon on their spawning migrations in May and June. Having delicate mouths, they must be handled carefully or the hook will tear loose. They are also taken by dipnet at night in the Sacramento River and upper Delta area in April and May.

Aside from Striped Bass and Shad, in the Delta Region near Rio Vista, Stockton, and Tracy, Largemouth Bass, Crappies, Sunfish, Catfish and Sturgeon may be caught. Except for Largemouth Bass, usually caught by casting, most of these fish are taken by bait fishing. Smallmouth Bass are found most commonly in the lower foothill areas of such Sierra streams as the Kings, Tuolumne, Consumnes, Stanislaus and American rivers, and in Folsom Lake and Lake Berryessa.

CLEAR LAKE

Clear Lake in Lake County, lying some 100 miles north of San Francisco between the Russian River drainage on the west and the Sacramento Valley on the east provides fine warm water fishing. Accessible by good roads, with many resorts, boat liveries and camps, it provides much fishing for Largemouth Bass, Catfish and panfish. Fishing is best from May to October. The nearby Blue Lakes afford the same type of fishing, and Upper Blue Lake is also stocked with trout.

COASTAL STREAM FISHING

It is fitting to begin discussion of coastal stream fishing by mentioning two of the outstanding west coast Salmon and Steelhead streams, the Rogue River in Oregon and the Klamath River in northern California. Lying only some fifty miles apart these two magnificent streams are famed the world over for the excellence of their fishing and the beauty of their settings. Both streams originate in the interior Cascade Mountain range and both break through the Coast Range to the sea in deep, rock-walled canyons.

KLAMATH RIVER

Starting in August, King (Chinook) Salmon begin to enter the estuary of the Klamath River and offer fishing which is heavily utilized. Boats are available near the mouth of the river, but many bring their own boat and trailer outfits. Silver Salmon and Steelhead follow the Kings so that in effect three separate waves of fish all of which afford good sport enter the Klamath each fall. While some of the river is closed by landowners, Steelhead and Salmon can be angled for over practically its entire 198 mile length which is accessible by a road which parallels the rivers from Weitchpec to Iron Gate Dam. Many prefer to fish mid-river areas near Orleans, Somesbar, Happy Camp or Seiad Valley while others may wait until the fish arrive in the vicinity of Yreka. The river at this point affords easier angling than the lower river, though the fish are in poorer condition. Iron Gate Dam is the end of the run so far as migratory fish in the Klamath are concerned.

The Trinity is the Klamath's main tributary. This is a beautiful stream except where it has been spoiled by hydraulic mining "doddlebugs" that have turned many of its lovely meadows into gravel pits. The best season for fishing in the upper Klamath and Trinity is from October through December. In the lower river August to October is the prime season. Silver and King Salmon are usually caught on large spoons or wobblers and while Steelhead may be taken on these too, fly fishing during periods of clear water affords better sport and often more fish.

Klamath River Steelheads usually average from three to five pounds though heavier fish are often taken. Silver Salmon usually average around ten pounds with Chinooks running anywhere from three- or four-pound grilse to fifty or sixty pounds though the average is around sixteen pounds.

Anglers frequently ask about "grilse" salmon. These are small, early-maturing male fish that mature and return after only one summer in the ocean. The larger Kings are mostly 3 or 4 years old at maturity. Many anglers believe that grilse salmon are spawn eaters and are not in the river to fulfill their function as males to fertilize eggs. This is a mistaken idea for as every fishery biologist knows, grilse are not interested in food and their stomachs are practically always empty; though as anglers well know, they will snap at spoons, plugs, salmon eggs, or other bait and can be caught on their spawning migrations.

OTHER COAST STREAMS

From Santa Cruz north to Oregon there are a host of other fine Steelhead and Salmon streams. Just north of the Klamath River, the Smith River affords fine sport in beautifully clear waters. This stream has excellent runs of Steelhead, Silver, and King (Chinook) Salmon. Some California coastal streams get midsummer runs of small Steelhead that are termed "half-pounders" by anglers. These fish at times, afford excellent fishing.

South of the Klamath about a dozen fine streams lie in the redwood belt north of San Francisco. These are Redwood Creek, the Mad, Eel, Mattole, Noyo, Little, Navarro, Ten Mile, Gualala, Garcia, and Russian River. The Eel and Russian rivers are the largest and all are readily accessible from good highways. Anglers going north will find the coast Cutthroat Trout in Redwood Creek near Orick. These beautifully streamlined fish are most abundant in Oregon coastal streams and are rare or absent from waters south of the Eel River.

South of San Francisco, the San Lorenzo River, Waddell, Pescadero and San Luis Obispo Creeks, and the Big Sur River have winter Steelhead runs. These streams get very low in summer.

MOUNTAIN WATERS

For the purposes of this encyclopedia, mountain waters of central California may be divided into two general groups: those flowing eastward from the escarpment of the Sierra Nevada and those draining west into the Sacramento-San Joaquin Valley. In these areas trout fishing is centered in hundreds of high lakes and streams. On the west side from south to north the principal fishing rivers are the Kern, Kaweah, Kings, San Joaquin, Merced, Tuolumne, Stanislaus, Mokelumne, American, Yuba, and Feather rivers. The colder headwaters and middle-river areas of these streams are rugged, but the fish are there for those who are willing to go after them. The Feather River in the vicinity of Lake Almanor is a popular area with anglers seeking heavy, tackle-smashing Rainbow and Brown Trout.

Between Chico and Redding, Deer, Mill, and Battle creeks, tributaries of the Sacramento, offer seasonal fishing for both resident Trout and Steelhead. The main Sacramento and its tributaries north and east of Redding supplies some of the best fishing in the state. A few of these are the Pit, and McCloud rivers, Squaw Creek, Burney Creek, Rising River, and Fall River.

Shasta Lake on the Sacramento River offers boat and bank fishing for Largemouth Bass, trolling for Kokance, and fishing for Trout near the points at which the main Sacramento, McCloud and Pit Rivers enter the reservoir. The McCloud and Pit Rivers are famous in California angling history. While long reaches of both are under control of private owners or power companies, the average angler can still find much open water in which to seek the deep, heavy-bodied Rainbow, characteristic of these streams.

Keswick Dam, a re-regulating dam, some six miles below Shasta Dam on the main Sacramento is the end of the run for Salmon and Steelhead. Between Redding and Tehama an intensive sport fishery is conducted for Kings, which are usually caught by trolling with spoons or plugs. Salmon caught this far up river are generally darker in color and less desirable for eating than fresh-run fish caught in the lower river. Governmental conservation agencies expended over $1,500,000 on saving the salmon runs blocked by Shasta Dam. A large hatchery was constructed on Battle Creek for artificial propagation. The Sacramento has become one of the top Salmon and Steelhead Rivers in America.

Three National Parks, Sequoia-King's Canyon in the southern Sierra, Yosemite in the north-cen-

Frank B. Wire

A 4 lb. Largemouth Bass taken in Upper Willamette, Oregon.

tral Sierra, and Lassen Volcanic National Park in the northern Cascade Range contain a fine combination of mountain fishing and scenery. Many lakes and streams reachable by road or trail are found in each, and newcomers should talk to park rangers, or anglers to locate the best spots. Fish are where you find them and finding them is sometimes a chore. In any case, even if the trout prove uncooperative, the scenery will more than counter balance the failure to catch fish. Yosemite Park has close to a million visitors a year, yet one well-known angler regularly gets his limit of Brown Trout in the late fall from the Merced River on the valley floor where thousands have fished before him.

About a dozen roads cross the backbone of the Sierra Nevada Range. Practically all of these highways lead from the valley across the summit to the high, arid, sagebrush plains lying east of the main escarpment. Anglers seeking trout fishing in the Sierra can take any one of these roads and on each, pack outfits will be found strategically located for trips into the high country where the fishing is best. Tioga Pass leading through Yosemite National Park is one of the most popular and many lakes can be reached by good trails a short distance from Tuolumne Meadows. Another popular area is Lake Tahoe, which is circled by an excellent highway.

EAST SLOPE STREAMS

These are all trout waters with four major river systems draining this region. These are the Owens River (water supply for Los Angeles) and the Walker, Carson, and Truckee Rivers. The last three originally only had the native, east slope Cutthroat Trout, but Brook, Brown, Rainbow, and Golden Trout have been introduced. The Owens River, originally barren of trout is now principally a Brown Trout stream, but it furnishes good Largemouth and Smallmouth Bass and Channel Catfish in Owens Valley below Pleasant Valley Dam.

Some of the best trout fishing to be found is in Owens Valley. The Owens River drains the Sierra east and south of Yosemite National Park. The fishing center is Bishop at an elevation of 4,450 feet where many streams, such as Bishop Creek, Rock Creek, Independence Creek, Convict Creek, Hot Creek, Mammoth Creek, Laurel Creek, and others provide excellent early May fishing. In midsummer, the fishing generally slows up, but it picks up again in September and October. The largest lake, Mono Lake, does not contain fish as it is extremely brackish. The Owens River from its source to Lake Crowley offers some of the finest dry fly water for Brown Trout in the west. It is spring fed and meanders through meadows for about 15 miles before flowing into Lake Crowley. Resorts close limited portions of this stream but the bulk is open to the public.

Lake Crowley, a Los Angeles water storage reservoir completed in the early forties, has been producing some mammoth Rainbow and Brown Trout. This lake is easily reached and lies approximately 35 miles north of Bishop. When the water warms up in the spring, these big trout move into shallow waters and for a short period, large, heavy fish can be taken on a fly. Later as the fish go deeper, trolling is the only possible method. Rainbow Trout up to 17 pounds and Browns up to 20 pounds have been reported. Boats can be obtained at a boat livery on the west side of the lake near the dam.

In addition to the stream fishing outlined, Golden Trout can be had in many high lakes above Owens Valley. Most can be reached only by trail. Side roads lead up many of the canyons to lakes on the east side of the escarpment, most of which are heavily stocked each year.

RESERVOIR FISHING

California was originally a land of rivers and streams with few lakes, and its fish were principally stream forms. A program of reservoir construction however, has resulted in the establishment of 82 major man-made lakes totaling more than 375,000 acres. Eventually through the construction of 63 additional reservoirs, 200,000 more surface acres will be added to this already impressive total.

Thirty-nine of the existing reservoirs are classified as warm-water lakes. Angling in these waters is supported by Black Bass, Crappie, and Catfish. Excellent growth is obtained on these species, and large catches of big fish are common.

The cold-water reservoirs are managed primarily for Trout and Kokanee Salmon, but they provide less intensive fishing because of their lower fertility.

Oregon

Oregon has many streams and lakes which can be divided into four general areas, the coastal region, the valley area (Willamette, Umpqua and Rogue River valleys), the central area, and the eastern area.

COASTAL AREA

The coastal area has King (Chinook) Salmon in two classes (spring run and late summer run), Silver Salmon which run in the fall, Steelhead

Trout (mostly a fall and winter-run fish but in a few instances in the summer), and the Cutthroat Trout. Anyone wishing to fish in the ocean can find boats available at Coos Bay, Newport, Depoe Bay, and Tillamook Bay, as well as at the mouth of the Columbia River. The Salmon are caught by trolling spinners and large salmon plugs. The Steelheads are caught by spinners and bait, mostly salmon eggs. Cutthroat Trout are caught by fly-spinner, single eggs, and cluster eggs.

There is a run of spring King Salmon in March, April, and May in the Columbia River. Many of these fish run into the Willamette River, which flows through Portland, and can be caught with a spinner. The larger streams and bays enumerated from north to south, where good fishing is to be had are Necanicum River (Trout, Silver Salmon, Steelhead); Nehalem Bay and River (Trout, Chinook Salmon, Silver Salmon, Steelhead); Tillamook Bay (King and Silver Salmon, Steelhead, Trout); Nestucca River closed to all commercial fishing; (Salmon, Steelheads, Cutthroat. Trout) Devils Lake (Spiny-rayfish, Bass predominating); Siletz Bay and River (all species of Salmon, Steelheads, Cutthroat Trout); Yaquina Bay (salmon); Alsea Bay and River (Salmon, Steelhead, Cutthroat Trout); Alsea River (Trout in May and June, winter run of Steelheads); Ten Mile Creek (Silver Salmon, spring Trout, winter Steelheads); Big Creek, Siuslaw Bay and River (Salmon in spring and fall, winter Steelheads, Cutthroat Trout in May and June).

There are a number of coastal lakes, most of which have outlets into the ocean, between the Siuslaw and Umpqua Rivers. The larger lakes, Mercer, Siltcoos, and Tahkenitch, have good spiny-ray fishing and in the fall have a run of Silver Salmon and Cutthroat Trout.

Umpqua River, the largest Oregon stream flowing into the ocean south of the Columbia offers spring and fall run salmon, including Silvers. It also has an added fishing attraction in the Striped Bass of which the larger are caught in May, June, and July. Smith River, flows into the same bay, has good Trout and Steelhead fishing. The Umpqua is one of two rivers that heads east of the coast Mountains, and offers excellent Trout and Steelhead fishing from May through the season. It also has a summer Steelhead run, and fly fishermen gather there during July, August, and September.

Just south of the Umpqua is Ten Mile Lake and several smaller lakes. Ten Mile Lake has a resident population of Cutthroat Trout and also a good fall run of Silver Salmon. Coos Bay and Coos River have runs of Trout in spring and fall, but the best fishing in this bay is for Striped Bass. Coquille River has runs of Salmon, Trout, and Steelheads in the spring and fall. South of the Coquille are a number of smaller streams that have Salmon, Trout, and Steelheads.

Next is the famous Rogue River which, like the Umpqua, heads in the high Cascades. It is world renowned for its Salmon and Steelhead fishing. This stream has regular Salmon runs starting in March or April, and carrying through until late fall. Many Salmon are caught at the mouth of the river as well as upstream. The summer run of Steelheads that strike a fly during the late summer and early fall months is the prized fishing of this stream.

WILLAMETTE VALLEY

Willamette River Salmon have already been mentioned. Most of its tributaries have a resident population of Rainbow and Cutthroat Trout. Fishing is good from May 1 to late September. The Santiam River one of the larger tributaries has a good run of winter Steelheads. The McKenzie, another tributary, is famous for Rainbow Trout. These are residential fish and are caught from May 1 to late September.

There are a few lakes which furnish good spiny-ray fishing, such as Horseshoe Lake in Marion County and Oak Ridge Reservoir in Lane County.

THE CENTRAL AREA

There are few streams in this area, but it includes many Cascade Mountain lakes. The Deschutes River, which heads in Little Lava Lake and flows north approximately 200 miles into the Columbia is the largest stream. It has a run of Salmon and Steelheads in the lower reaches, but is best known for its resident Rainbow Trout. The Deschutes one of the best fly fishing streams is good from May through September. The upper reaches also carry some Brown Trout, and some of the upper tributaries have populations of Brook Trout. The Metolius, a large tributary, has excellent Rainbow fishing. Crooked River is also good fishing.

The Williamson and Sprague Rivers flow into upper Klamath Lake, and in the early spring furnish fishing for large Rainbows that run out of the lake. A five- or ten-pound fish is not uncommon. The Klamath River, the outlet of upper and lower Klamath Lake, has good seasonal Rainbow Trout fishing. The lower Klamath River is also a fine summer and fall Steelhead stream. The upper reaches of the river are in Oregon, but it flows into California before reaching the ocean.

The lakes in this area accessible by road are Olallie Lake (Rainbow), Suttle Lake (Rainbow), Clear Lake (Cutthroat, Rainbow), East Lake (Rainbow, Brook and Brown Trout), Paulina Lake (Rainbow, Brook and Brown Trout), Sparks Lake (Rainbow and Brook Trout), Todd Lake (Rainbow), Devils Lake (Brook Trout), Elk Lake (Rainbow, Brook Trout), Big Lava Lake (Rainbow), Mud Lake (Brook Trout), Crane Prairie Reservoir (Rainbow, some Brook Trout), Big and Little Cultus Lakes (Rainbow), and Wickiup Reservoir (Rainbow, Brook Trout, Brown Trout). Other lakes are Odell Lake (Rainbow Trout, Brook and Lake Trout), Crescent Lake (Rainbow), Davis Lake (Rainbow), Fish Lake (Brook Trout), Lake of the Woods (Rainbow Trout, spiny-ray fish), Diamond Lake (Rainbow), and Crater Lake (Rainbow).

Many others can only be reached by pack trips. In all, there are about 800 fishable lakes. Space does not allow specific locations, but inquiry from the Oregon State Game Commission will bring definite directions. Most of the lakes are in the high mountains and because of snow cannot be reached until July, August being the best month.

THE EASTERN AREA

Throughout the eastern part of the state there are few lakes and streams of note. However, the Owyhee Reservoir is worth mentioning. This body of water is about forty miles long but not fishable except by boat. It contains Trout and spiny-rayed fish. The Owyhee River below the dam to the Snake River offers good Rainbow fishing.

The Wallowa Mountains contain a number of fine fishing lakes, all reached by pack train except Wallowa Lake. This lake has Rainbows and Silver Trout and can be reached by road.

Washington

Washington's 8,000 to 10,000 high and low lakes, and hundreds of mountain streams, and coastal rivers offer a choice of angling for a great number of both native and exotic game fish. Native game fish consist of Cutthroat, Rainbow, Steelhead, and the Dolly Varden Trout (char), the so-called Silver Trout, actually a landlocked, miniature Sockeye Salmon, and the Whitefish. The introduced or exotic species include Brook Trout (char), a few Brown Trout (Loch Levens), Largemouth and Smallmouth Bass, Crappies, Perch, Bluegills, and limited number of Channel Catfish.

As a general statement, it can be said that the trout inhabit both lake and stream, while the spiny-rayed varieties are confined principally to lakes. Some good Bass fishing both for the Large- and Smallmouths can be had in and adjacent to the Columbia, Snake and Yakima Rivers.

TROUT

Washington lakes produce excellent Rainbow Trout fishing. It is not uncommon for scores of lowland lakes of 50 to 100 acres to yield 5,000 trout each on opening day in April, from several hundred to a couple of thousand daily for the next month, and furnish many more days of good fishing during favorable weather throughout the remainder of the trout season which usually ends in late October. These lakes are heavily stocked with fish ranging up to 10 inches in size.

Courtesy of Ernie Hanson

King Salmon big enough for any angler.

Some lakes still have native Cutthroats, and others have been planted with Cutthroat originating from either native or searun stock.

Most of the fish caught in the Rainbow Trout lakes are taken with single salmon eggs and light test leaders, employing a No. 10 or 12 single egg hook, or gang trolls baited with worms, but a trolled artificial fly or nymph tied on a No. 10 or 12 hook and a 9-foot, 2-pound test leader is also becoming popular and productive. After the commotion of the early season wears off, there is usually some wonderful nymph fishing available

Hundreds of mountain gems like this lying off the beaten path await adventurous anglers.

Anglers hit the mountain lakes as soon as the snow begins to disappear.

from the opening day to mid-July on all of the Rainbow lakes, and again after September 15 with both nymphs and conventional fly patterns.

On waters still open fly fishing for Cutthroat Trout in the lowland lakes hits its peak at the outset of the season when the water is cold. It is virtually through by May 15, but improves again after September 15, when the water cools off. Any of the conventional flies and standard patterns will take Cutthroats.

High altitude lakes in western Washington are generally opened during the last week in May, but nature frequently keeps them under a lock and key of snow and ice until July 1, for Washington is an extremely mountainous state where snows at the 5,000 foot level often reach a depth of 20 feet. But most of these mountain gems ranging in size from a few acres to several thousand are well stocked with Rainbow, Cutthroat Trout, and Brook, and when they do shed their winter cloaks, open up some wonderful fishing for the hardy angler who enjoys his mountain hiking and incomparable scenery along with his angling sport. The best fishing to be found in the high country from the Canadian Border on the north to the Columbia River on the south in the Cascade Range, or in the Olympics on the coast, is in August and September. To plan a trip before July 15 or after October 1 in country lying above 5,000 feet elevation is inviting trouble with the elements, as most of these lakes are off the beaten paths.

RIVERS

The game fish in the rivers are principally Trout and Char. They are divided into two groups, resident fish (those which remain in the fresh water throughout their life) and anadromous fish (those which live part of their life in fresh water and the balance in salt). Rainbow, Cutthroat, and Brook are in the resident class, and Steelhead, Cutthroat,

British Columbia Government Travel Bureau

Searun Cutthroats to 4 pounds afford excellent fly fishing in both salt and fresh water in season.

and Dolly Varden in the anadromous or migratory group, although Dollies also frequently remain in fresh water throughout their life.

Resident fish are limited principally to those water courses which are inaccessible to the sea. The Western rivers which provide easy passage to fish from salt water carry virtually no resident stock but are populated by the anadromous species during such times as they are sojourning in fresh water, usually for the purpose of spawning, or during their babyhood days before they migrate seaward to more bountiful feed pastures where they attain their full growth.

Trout in the so-called resident or non-migratory streams attain length from 8 to 24 inches in a few venerable specimens in streams which have a high food content, but the vast majority will be of pan size of 8 to 10 inches. Most of the rivers in eastern Washington hold resident populations as do those in western Washington, which are above natural barriers.

The best Cutthroat fishing in western Washington occurs from mid-July until the end of October with various forms of bait, spinners, spinning lures, and flies all good. Between the opening of the stream season, usually late in May, until the middle of July, some of the snow-fed streams are too discolored with snow water to permit good fishing. Rain and spring-fed streams having their sources in the lowlands usually furnish good fishing throughout the season unless they become too low during dry weather.

Washington State Dept. of Game

A 17-pound Steelhead taken from the Freen River in Washington State on spinning tackle.

In streams that are easily accessible from the sea, mostly in western Washington, the fishing depends almost entirely upon the time of the various runs. At other times the rivers may be virtually barren of sizable game fish. Thus in planning a fishing trip here it is most important to know when these runs of adult fish occur.

All rivers flowing in the Pacific Ocean or its bays and inlets, and those flowing into the Lower Columbia River in western Washington, have runs of adult Steelheads some time between December 1 to April 30. The runs usually extend for a period of about 90 days in each river. About half of the rivers also have summer Steelhead runs between May 15 and October 1.

Especially good winter Steelhead streams are the Skagit, Cowlitz, Queets, Hoh, Quillayute, Satsop, Chehialis, Soleduck, Bogachiel, Quinault, Pyallup, Green, Snoqualmie, Skykomish, Snohomish, Stillaguamish, and Nooksack. The Skagit is especially famous for its marvelous boat trips in a scenic wonderland with fishing unsurpassed under the direction of expert, professional guides. Here, properly bundled with warm clothing, one can really enjoy a fishing vacation in the middle of winter.

Most noted summer Steelhead streams in Washington include the Snake, Columbia, Grand, Ronde, Quinault, Klickitat, Wind, Kalama, Tolt, North Fork of the Stillaguamish, and the North Fork of the Skykomish. The upper reaches of the Kalama and the North Fork of the Stillaguamish are restricted to fly fishing.

Sea-run Cutthroat Trout, which migrate to and from the sea into the coastal rivers, afford wonderful fly fishing in the lower reaches of the rivers from July 15 to the end of October. These fish average about one pound in weight, but range from a half-pound to 2 or 3 as adults. They can be taken on all forms of bait and lures and on any of the standard pattern flies, but for fly fishermen, the modified bright colored streamer fly, tied with buck hair in sizes from No. 10 to No. 4, is the most effective. They run upstream about the same time as the Salmon and for the same biological purpose, to spawn and not just to feed on salmon eggs as is popularly supposed. The peak of the run is in September and October in Puget Sound streams, August and September in tributaries of the lower Columbia River, and August and September in coastal streams.

Dolly Vardens ascend the streams in greatest numbers during the fall and winter months, but are resident in limited numbers in many waters. Brass wobblers and lures that represent minnows and the single salmon or cluster eggs for bait are most effective on Dollies, some of which occasionally reach a weight of 20 pounds.

Literally thousands of Washington's lakes and streams are accessible on good roads. Accommodations are available at or within a half-hour's drive of most fishing grounds, and there is no point in getting off the beaten path for sea-run fish. Boats and cabins are obtainable at or near most of the lowland lakes.

WARM WATER FISH

Lowland lakes are generally considered as those lying below 1,000 feet elevation in western Washington and below 2,000 feet in eastern Washington. It is mostly in these lakes in which the various kinds of spiny-ray fish, such as Bass, Crappies, Perch, etc. were liberated.

The outstanding Largemouth Bass lake in western Washington is Silver Lake in Cowlitz County, situated about 12 miles from the town of Kelso. It's best to fish it is in April and May in shallow water before the weed growth becomes too thick and matted, using surface lures in the shallows and underwater lures where the depth is 10 to 15 feet. September and October are also good after the weeds have died, and the bass haunts are once more accessible. There are many other lakes in which Largemouth are found. Smallmouths are found in a few lakes and in the Snake, Columbia and Lower Yakima River and adjacent sloughs and in some smaller streams.

Generally under-water lures of minnow and pork-rind types are most effective until the middle of May, surface lures and bugs are used until late June, and deeper lures again in fairly open water in mid-summer and fall. Eastern Washington lakes, especially in the Spokane area, which contain Black Bass and which are not over-run with carp, are considered better fishing than those in western Washington because of a greater abundance of natural food and higher water temperatures during the spring and summer months.

Crappie and Yellow Perch are by far the most popular pan fish. They abound in virtually all lowland lakes except in those restored as trout lakes. They usually begin to strike May 1 and furnish much sport for family parties and youngsters throughout the summer. Angle worms are the universal bait for Perch with a chamois spinner and streamer fly best for Crappie. Another good pan fish is the Silver Trout now stocked in many of the lakes which have depths greater than 50 feet. These fish attain a length from 8 to 14 inches and are inclined to school heavily and bite on salmon eggs or periwinkles. They can usually be located at a depth at which the water temperature is at 50° F. and furnish good fishing from May to mid-September, with the early part of the season generally better.

There is little fishing for warm water species in the streams. A few of the more sluggish rivers have small populations of Largemouth Bass and the lower 30 miles of the Yakima affords some fair summer fishing for Smallmouth Bass to the plug caster. The sluggish bayous along the lower Columbia also provide angling for Crappies, Bass, and Catfish.

FISHING IN NATIONAL PARKS

The national parks and monuments are sanctuaries for wildlife, and hunting is strictly prohibited. Fishing, however, is allowed. Protected creek, lake, and ocean waters are open to the angler under regulations designed to perpetuate the resource.

The National Park System comprises 186 areas, including national parks, monuments, historic sites, battlefield parks, and other categories. Twenty-two of these areas offer important fishing opportunities. They afford much more than opportunities to catch fish. In these highly scenic, unspoiled wonderlands, anglers may refresh their spirits and obtain new inspiration. Discriminating fishermen look to the national parks as places in which to enjoy a wilderness-type of sport.

Congress has set aside the wilderness parks as superlative examples of original America. It has charged the Park Service with the task of maintaining them unimpaired for the benefit and enjoyment of all the people. This applies equally to the waters and to the land.

Native species of fish are encouraged, while exotic fish are excluded. In areas where non-native species are already present, efforts are made to reduce their numbers and to check their further spread. Thus the use of live minnows and some other natural baits is prohibited to prevent undesirable intruders from becoming established. Artificial structures and stream improvements which would alter natural conditions are avoided.

Many of the scenic parks, especially those in the western United States, are high mountain areas. Their waters are not as fertile as those in the lowlands, and their capacity to maintain and produce fish is not as great. In the cold, rather barren waters, fish grow slowly and never become very large. Stocking is practiced, but the mileage of waters where fish populations can be maintained artificially is limited. These are the over-fished waters close to roads and living centers. The experienced angler who desires real sport with naturally reared wild fish will find it in the national parks, but he must hike away from the throngs to find satisfactory angling.

In several parks, some streams have been set aside for those who wish to catch fish only for sport. No restriction is placed on the number of fish that may be caught, but all must be returned to the water.

Regulations, based on research, endeavor to preserve and share the fish population. The rules vary, according to conditions. The dates of the fishing seasons of the different park areas are subject to change annually. The fisherman should consult the park superintendent's office for current regulations concerning length of season, hours of fishing, bait permitted, limit of size and catch, closed waters, and whether a state license is required or not.

ACADIA NATIONAL PARK
Bar Harbor, Maine

This park includes 44 square miles of scenic mountain and coast line on the eastern half of Mount Desert Island. It contains a number of comparatively short, swift-flowing brooks and beautiful cold lakes. Fish are stocked, and fishing is regulated by the Maine Commissioner of Inland Fisheries and Game.

Local residents consider that there are four kinds

of high-type game fish in the island waters: Brook Trout (which, in lakes, are termed "squaretails"), Landlocked Salmon, Brown Trout, and Smallmouth Bass. Pickerel and Perch are present also, but are placed in a lower category. Brown Trout, introduced long ago, have survived only in Eagle Lake. Bass are restricted to The Bowl, where they were stocked in 1891, but rarely exceed eight inches.

The island waters appear ideal, but angling generally does not result in large creels. Those with the best reputations are Aunt Betty's Pond, Richardson's Brook, Witch Hole Pond, Jordan Pond and Brook, Eagle Lake, Duck Brook, and Long Pond. Saltwater fishing is fine off shore.

Lodgings and meals are available near the park throughout the year. Campgrounds are located within the park. The inland fishing season generally begins when the ice goes out and ends in August or September, depending on the species and numbers.

BIG BEND NATIONAL PARK
Marathon, Texas

All fishing in this park is confined to the Rio Grande. The element of sport is not high, but many persons come to fish and to camp out for a few nights.

Catfish are most numerous. The average weight exceeds six pounds, but Yellow Cats fairly often attain thirty and sometimes as much as one hundred pounds. Other species are the Channel Cat and Blue Cat. Most anglers for Catfish use set lines baited with live minnows or small chunks of meat. When hungry, however, Cats may strike at any white or shining object such as a piece of soap or a safety pin.

Other fish sometimes caught are Gaspergon or Sheepshead which may weigh two or three pounds or more and are fairly good eating. Smallmouth Buffalo also are considered edible. Species which are so small, tasteless, or bony as to be considered usable only for bait are Carp, Carp Sucker, Bullhead or Pollywog Catfish, and Sunfish.

Some of the springs and their short tributary streams are inhabited by species of small fish which, through long centuries of isloations, have developed peculiar characteristics that distinguish them from all others. In order to protect and perpetuate them, fishing is not allowed in any spring or creek in the park, and live bait fish may not be brought in from outside.

There is fishing throughout the year, but only a few cabins are available.

CRATER LAKE NATIONAL PARK
Crater Lake, Oregon

The outstanding feature of this park, Crater Lake, is one of the rare fishing spots of the country. The hollowed-out base of an ancient volcano is now filled with a twenty-one square mile lake of magnificently blue, clear water. Lacking inlet or outlet, the lake can be reached by only one good trail which zigzags steeply down the precipitous crater wall for one and one-half miles. At the foot, rowboats are available for rent.

Two species have been stocked. Rainbow Trout and Silver Salmon, which average three quarters of a pound. Fishing from shore brings poor results. Trolling at depths of fifty to two hundred feet is excellent in some years, but poor in others. July is the best fishing month, but August is almost as favorable. Sudden storms are a hazard even in mid-summer. The lake is generally closed to angling from Labor Day to the Fourth of July. The park generally is open all year. A lodge, cabins, store, and campgrounds afford accommodations.

EVERGLADES NATIONAL PARK
Homestead, Florida

The only sub-tropical national park in the United States lies across the southern tip of Florida in a region famous for its salt-water fishing. The 1,875 square mile area includes the great shallow water expanse of Florida Bay and northward along the Gulf coast beyond Lostman's River. The latter area particularly, including a strip of the Gulf of Mexico, the southernmost of the Ten Thousand Islands, and such estuary rivers as the Shark, Harney, Broad, Rogers and Lostman's is a fisherman's paradise.

Tarpon and Snook or Robalo are two of the finest sport fish. They are found in shoal areas of the west coast of the park and (especially Snook) in rivers, estuaries, and canals. When small Tarpons run into Ingraham Canal, between Flamingo and Homestead, they furnish great excitement for fly fishermen. Bluefish and Spanish Mackerel move in and out of park waters on the Gulf coast and sometimes into Florida Bay.

Channel Bass or Redfish also are important sport fish along the Gulf coast, where they are captured by still-fishing, casting, or trolling. Sea trout, a shoal water species, is sought by still-fishing with shrimp as bait, or with plugs. Trout sometimes will strike at a streamer fly. Several other notable game fish, including Sailfish, Marlin, Bonito, Amberjack, Jewfish, and Shark, are found farther off shore in deep water.

Inland, fresh water anglers find several species of edible fish in canals and lagoons. Longnose Gars are abundant and put up a fight when hooked. Good fishing for fresh water species is accessible along or near the Ingraham Highway between Royal Palm Hammock and Cape Sable, and on the Tamiami Trail west of Miami.

Salt water fishermen hire boats and guides at Everglades, Coot Bay, Flamingo, and at Tavernier and other places along the Florida Keys. There are no lodges or cabins within the park.

FORT JEFFERSON NATIONAL MONUMENT
Key West, Florida

The Tortugas Islands, whose combined area is about eighty-seven acres, and several square miles of the surrounding Gulf of Mexico, comprises the Fort Jefferson National Monument. The area lies about sixty miles west of Key West, Florida. Being so far from any mainland source of contamination, the water is clear and pure. Aquatic conditions vary widely. Coral reefs, bare sand and growths of turtle grass and algae furnish habitats for a great variety of fish. Channels between the keys vary in depth from ten to twenty fathoms, but the

National Park Service

The Skipper gives a convincing talk on fishing by displaying a 7½ pound Cutthroat Trout which he has just caught from the dock on which he is standing.

water deepens to the southward where the Gulf Stream passes.

Among the many game fishes in the monument and adjacent waters are sharks, rays, Barracudas, little tunny (a tuna), Sailfish, Pompano, Amberjack, Grouper, and Jewfish. Others, like the Yellowtail, are small and poor fighters when hooked, but are delectable eating. The visitor who merely wishes to look at fishes through a glass-bottom box or diving helmet will be fascinated by bizarre animals such as the Sea Horse, Butterfly Fish, Angel Fish, Parrot Fish, Trigger Fish, Porcupine Fish, Frog Fish, Grunts, Scorpion Fish, Hog Fish, Sargassum Fish, and Trunk Fish.

Fort Jefferson can be reached only by chartered boat from Key West or more northern Florida ports. Living accommodations are not available at the monument.

GLACIER NATIONAL PARK
West Glacier, Montana

This park covering 1,558 square miles is one of the nation's most beautiful fishing areas. Towering mountains surround the long, deep lakes of cold, shining waters, and the swift, clear streams. Adjoining this park is the somewhat smaller but similar Canadian park, Waterton Lakes National Park. The two areas are called the Waterton-Glacier International Peace Park.

The outstanding game fish in Glacier is Blackspotted Cutthroat or "native" Trout. It is present in most streams and lakes but is most abundant on the western drainage of the park. East of the continental divide, its place is taken by the Rainbow. A subspecies, the coastal Cutthroat, is present in the streams of the Flathead drainage, but seems to be rare.

Rainbow Trout are caught readily in many waters east of the divide. They grow to fairly good size. Dolly Vardens are abundant in the larger lakes and streams of the Flathead drainage and in the tributaries of the Saskatchewan River. It is a native of the latter waters but was introduced to the western slope. Brook Trout, also an introduction, are popular in the park where they average about a pound but occasionally attain four pounds in the lakes.

Lake Trout weighing fifteen pounds or more are found in Lower Two Medicine Lake and in Waterton, St. Mary, and several other lakes in the Saskatchewan drainage. Landlocked Salmon or Little Redfish have been introduced into Swiftcurrent Lake, where they have been only fairly successful. Grayling have been stocked in many waters, but survival has been poor.

Three species of whitefish occur in Glacier Park. One of these, the Lake Whitefish of the Great Lakes, is not rated as a game species. The other two put up a fair fight when hooked. Of these, the Brownbacked Whitefish is rare, while the Rocky Mountain Whitefish is abundant in all lakes and larger streams at lower elevations.

Although accessible waters are heavily fished, good angling is available by trail. Bait is used early in the season, but fly fishing is excellent in July and the first weeks of August. Lake fishing is good during the fall. The fishing season generally extends from May 30 to October 15. Besides the campgrounds, there are several hotels, chalets and cabins which are available from June 15 to September 15.

GRAND CANYON NATIONAL PARK
Grand Canyon, Arizona

Being a desert area, Grand Canyon Park, with its 1,008 square miles, does not provide much fishing. However, two streams in the lower canyon are kept stocked with Rainbow Trout and provide some angling early in the season. Bright Angel Creek is easily accessible from the famous Phantom Ranch (for park hikers and riders, near Bright Angel Trail). The second fishing stream, Clear Creek, is nine miles east of Phantom Ranch and can also be reached only by trail. It is located in a very beautiful canyon on the north side of the Colorado River. Being a small stream that is subject to periodic and devastating floods, it affords little angling.

Hotels, lodges, cabins, and campgrounds are available. Those on the South Rim are open the year round. The fishing season is generally from May 30 to September 30.

GRAND TETON NATIONAL PARK
Moose, Wyoming

Few trout waters have a more magnificent backdrop of scenery than the streams that pour down the lower canyons of the Teton Mountains, and the cold sparkling lakes that lie at the bottom on the floor of Jackson Hole. The highest mountain peak, Grand Teton, is 13,766 feet high,—7,000 feet above the valley. The 150 square mile park adjoins the 269-square-mile Jackson Hole National Monument.

Dept. of Interior

Fishing at Crater Lake in the Rocky Mountain National Park.

The creeks and the series of six lakes at the foot of the mountains are stocked with Cutthroat or Blackspotted Trout. Brook Trout were introduced some twenty years ago, and small numbers are still taken, especially on the lower portions of the streams. They are not encouraged and eventually may disappear from these natural Cutthroat waters.

Mackinaw or Lake Trout also were stocked and are occasionally caught by trolling in Jenny and Phelps lakes. Being deep with steeply sloping sides, the food-producing capacity of the lakes at the foot of the Teton Range is comparatively low, so that even native Trout are not plentiful. The lakes, in order of preference are: Jenny Lake, Leigh Lake, String Lake, Phelps Lake, Taggart Lake, and Beaver Dick Lake.

Farther east on the floor of Jackson Hole, Snake River is an excellent fly-fishing stream. Cutthroat Trout are numerous and reach good size. Rainbows are taken occasionally.

Jackson Lake, a partially artificial reservoir, is noted for its fine Lake Trout. They are not numerous, but individuals weighing thirty-six pounds have been taken in recent years. Judging from sight observations, trout as large as seventy-five pounds may be present. Cutthroats also occur in Jackson Lake, but are not generally abundant.

Brook Trout have been introduced to a number of small ponds within two miles of park headquarters. Here they have been much more successful than in the larger lakes. They furnish excellent fly-fishing during the first month or six weeks of the season. The fishing season runs from about April 1 to October 31. The park is officially open from June 1 to October 15. There are only campgrounds within the park, but outside hotels, dude ranches, and cabins offer more complete accommodations.

GREAT SMOKY MOUNTAINS NATIONAL PARK
Gatlinburg, Tennessee

Part of this 720-square-mile area in the Southern Appalachians was first declared a national park in 1930. Although there were still extensive forests of virgin hardwoods, hemlock, and spruce, logging had destroyed thousands of acres of the original cover. Under protection, the cut-over lands have re-vegetated rapidly and the streams have grown colder. Accordingly, the single native trout (Brook) is now pushing down into waters from which high temperatures formerly excluded all but the larger individuals. This general limit varies between three thousand and four thousand feet elevation. Eventually it should stabilize a thousand feet lower. The angler who is willing to walk two miles or more from a road should find good fishing. Brook Trout maintain themselves in the Smokies without artificial stocking, except in waters near roads where fishermen sometimes line the banks.

Portions of the Bradley Fork, West Prong, Little Pigeon River, and Oconaluftee River are designated as "Fishing-for-Fun" waters.

The warmer waters below the Brook Trout range, down to fifteen hundred feet, are occupied by Rainbow Trout. This species was introduced about 1908. It has thrived and become a mainstay of sport fishing in the park. In accessible waters

Rinehart-National Park Service

Playing a Rainbow Trout in Thompson River, Moraine Park. The front range of the Rockies is in the background.

where pressure is heavy, Rainbow are stocked annually. Elsewhere they reproduced themselves. Rainbows as large as twenty five inches long, weighing five pounds or more, are taken at rare intervals.

On the fringes of the park, below two thousand feet elevation, the angler finds two native species of Bass,—the Smallmouth and the scarcer Rock Bass. Two- and three-pound Smallmouths are not exceptional, but the Rock Bass rarely attains one pound in weight. Both species maintain themselves without stocking.

A hotel, lodge, and campgrounds are within the park. The first two are closed during the winter, but accommodations are always available nearby. The park is open the year round. The fishing season runs from about May 16 to August 31.

ISLE ROYALE NATIONAL PARK
Houghton, Michigan

This forty-five-mile-long island is famous for its moose herd and pre-Columbian copper mines. Forty-nine kinds of fish have been found in the numerous lakes, small streams, and surrounding waters of Lake Superior. Although there is commercial fishing in Lake Superior near the shores of Isle Royale, the lake still rewards the sportsman with good catches.

Brook Trout occur in at least two lakes on the island, in several streams, and in Lake Superior around the island. It is most numerous in Little Siskiwit River, in Washington Creek, and in the upper end of Washington Harbor. Lake-run Brook Trout, called "coasters," are taken in Rock Harbor.

Lake Trout are numerous on the shoals and in deep water around the entire island. Deep-water trolling is a favorite sport of park visitors. Rainbow Trout from the West were stocked before this area became a national park and are numerous in streams and around the shore of Isle Royale. It is most successfully found in Washington Harbor and Washington Creek.

Northern Pike are in many inland lakes and around the shores of Isle Royale. There is one unconfirmed record of a Muskellunge being caught in Washington Harbor; but, if present, it must be extremely rare. Yellow Perch are scarce along the lake shore and in the mouths of streams, but are somewhat more abundant in the inland lakes.

Cisco (locally called "herring") and Whitefish are taken commercially in nearby Lake Superior waters and sometimes are caught by anglers.

The fisherman can reach Isle Royale by boat from Duluth, Grand Marais or Grand Portage, Minnesota, or from Houghton, Michigan. Most visitors camp out or stay at Rock Harbor Lodge, where boats and fishing guides are available. The park is open from June 15 to September 15. There is fishing of one kind or another throughout most of the year.

KATMAI NATIONAL MONUMENT
McKinley Park, Alaska

This is the largest unit in the National Park System. It covers 4,214 square miles. Located on the Alaska Peninsula, it embraces a long expanse of the Aleutian Range. One of these peaks, Mount Katmai, erupted in 1912 in one of the greatest volcanic explosions in recorded history. The monument includes the Valley of Ten Thousand Smokes.

Numerous Rainbow or Steelhead Trout are found in several beautiful lakes in the western portion of the monument. They grow to a large size. Until recent years, twenty-four-inch fish have been fairly common. Naknek Lake has excellent trolling possibilities. Brooks River, a stream about one mile long which drains the overflow of Brooks Lake into Naknek Lake, was formerly unrivaled for fly-fishing. Because of heavy angling pressure during World War II by military personnel, and subsequently by sportsmen who flew in by private and chartered aircraft, Rainbows over twenty inches in length are now seldom taken.

Brooks Lake and its tributary streams are an important spawning ground of the Bristol Bay Red Salmon. These great fish do not feed when they come into fresh water to spawn, but any real outdoorsman will be fascinated by the hordes of salmon as they ascend the rapids and leap over the seven-foot falls in Brooks River.

This superb wilderness, wildlife, and fishing area is reached by commercial plane from Anchorage to Naknek. Here small pontoon-equipped planes may be chartered for the ten-minute trip into the national monument. No tourist facilities have been provided within the area. The dates of the fishing season are determined by the current State law.

KINGS CANYON NATIONAL PARK
Three Rivers, California

Amateur fish culturists can be thanked for providing sport in most waters of Kings Canyon National Park where fish occur. Originally, all except the lower portions of the South and Middle Forks of the Kings River were barren. More than fifty years ago, cattlemen introduced various fish to lakes and streams near their summer grazing lands. Later, around 1910, the Sierra Club undertook stocking of Golden Trout in a number of streams. Subsequently, state-sponsored stocking was carried out by supplying fish to packers, trail parties, and stockmen. The result is a jumble of species, principally Golden, Rainbow, and Brook Trout. Cutthroat, Steelhead, and Lock Leven also have been planted. Several of these species hybridize readily, especially Golden, Rainbow, and Cutthroat Trout, so the angler may not be able to accurately identify some of his catch.

Since the swift, cold streams and the lakes of this lofty granite country are deficient in fish food, their capacity for growing trout is low. Accessible waters —those on popular park trail routes and those within an hour's hike of an automobile—afford sport only to the earliest arrivals each season. Most anglers who want to find reasonably good fishing must plan on a long walk or pack excursion.

The 710 square miles of this park adjoins the 604 square miles of Sequoia National Park. The two parks are known officially as the *Sequoia and Kings Canyon National Park.* (See Sequoia). Campgrounds and cabins are available. The fishing season is generally from May 1 to October 31. The Park is open the entire year.

LAKE MEAD NATIONAL RECREATIONAL AREA
Boulder City, Nevada

Lake Mead is the third largest artificial lake in the United States. The recreational area covers 2,344 square miles. Usually fine Rainbow Trout fishing can be found in the river below Hoover Dam. Fair to good Bass fishing is found in the lake, but boats are necessary. The angler may start out at Willow Beach, Arizona, or El Dorado Canyon, Nevada, in a rented boat. Boats are available here and at other landings on the lake. Salmon egg clusters are used for bait. The park is open the entire year. Lake Mead Lodge, cabins, tents and 38 camp sites offer accommodations.

National Park Service

Fishermen near the mouth of the Yellowstone River in Yellowstone National Park.

LASSEN VOLCANIC NATIONAL PARK
Mineral, California

Lassen Peak is the only recently active volcano in the United States proper. It erupted many times between 1914 and 1921. The most popular of the more than 50 lakes in this 163 square mile area are Manzanita, Butte, Twin, Snag, Rainbow, and Horseshoe. Lower Hat Creek is also a favorite fishing water. Less accessible waters which are reached only by hiking one to four miles are the finest and most beautiful fishing areas. May to June and September to October yield the best catches. Mid-summer is generally less productive because the larger fish retire to deep, cool water. Rainbow Trout and Salmon were the only game fish originally in Lassen. Loch Leven and Brook Trout were stocked and are now important catches.

A lodge, cabins, and campgrounds are open during the summer months. The park season is between approximately June 1 and September 30, depending upon the weather. The fishing season generally runs from May 30 to October 31.

MAMMOTH CAVE NATIONAL PARK
Mammoth Cave, Kentucky

One hundred and fifty miles of passages have been explored within the cave. No fishing is allowed in the subterranean lake and streams, but an eyeless fish is known to inhabit them.

The warm-water ponds and sections of rivers within the 78 square mile park, but outside the cave, are the habitat of Smallmouth Bass, Bluegills, Crappies, and Catfish. Several ponds which are intensively fished are stocked occasionally, chiefly with fish salvaged from overflow areas. Angling in Green and Nolin Rivers, which are under state regulation, is popular with local people. Fishing is usually open most of the year, from June 1 to April 30. The park is open all year.

MOUNT McKINLEY NATIONAL PARK
McKinley, Alaska

Most of the major streams of this 3,030-square-mile wilderness park are heavily laden with glacial silt and are not suitable for game fish. However, a number of smaller creeks which do not originate in the glaciers are beautifully clear and contain Grayling. Examples of such fishing streams are Riley Creek, near the administrative headquarters in the northeastern corner of the park, and the region of Clearwater Creek south of Wonder Lake. The latter area also contains numerous small lakes which are inhabited by Grayling and Dolly Varden Trout. The Clearwater Creek section can be reached only by pack trip.

Wonder Lake, on the park highway eighty-five miles west of the Alaska Railroad's McKinley Park station, is the most popular fishing lake. It

Waters of the Madison River which flows through the Yellowstone National Park. Visitors in the park are not required to have fishing licenses and each member of a party is entitled to 5 fish. Fishermen, however, should obtain a copy of the rules governing park fishing before indulging in this sport.

contains three species of fish: Lake Trout which average two pounds in weight, freshwater Ling Cod, and a Bullhead. Despite its accessibility by car, Wonder Lake has not been over-fished as few visitors are equipped with personally-owned boats. Craft are not available for rental, and shore fishing is not generally successful.

Named for its mountain peak, the highest in North America, Mt. McKinley is the only United States park which has caribou and wolves. A hotel and tent camp offer accommodations during the summer. The park is open from June 10 to September 15. The dates of the fishing season are determined by the current State law.

MOUNT RAINIER NATIONAL PARK
Longmire, Washington

The boundaries of Mount Rainer National Park were drawn tightly around the base or across the foothills of the spectacular 14,408-foot high ice-clad volcano. Most of the lakes in the park are so high that they are relatively infertile. Many of the streams within the boundaries are short, steep in gradient, and so laden with silt from the melting glaciers that what fish are present do not readily rise to lures. The scanty supply of game fish in all accessible lakes is held at a minimum by heavy fishing.

Fair to good angling may be obtained, however, by hiking to the more remote lakes or less accessible stretches of some of the clear streams. Results are best late in the season. The game species are Cutthroat, Rainbow, and Brook Trout. Anglers prefer them approximately in the order named. Ohanapecosh River, which is a beautiful, crystal clear stream, affords the best fly-fishing in the park. Deer Creek and Frying Pan Creek are rated fairly good.

The park of 377 square miles is open the year round. The approximate dates of the fishing season are June 1 to October 15. Hotels, lodges, cabins, and campgrounds offer accommodations.

OLYMPIC NATIONAL PARK
Port Angeles, Washington

There are few roads in this wilderness park covering more than 1,300 square miles. The finest sport fishing here is afforded by sea-run Rainbow Trout. Generally termed "Steelheads," these gamely fish come in numbers during the winter months into all of the large streams of the western slope and several of those on the eastern side of the park. Sometimes they weigh as much as 26 pounds. The rivers also contain fair numbers of Cutthroat Trout, King, Silver and Sockeye Salmon, as well as sea-run Dolly Vardens.

National Park Service

Fishing at the outlet of Yellowstone Lake near the fishing bridge.

In the high mountains lie many beautiful, small lakes. Originally most of these were barren of fish life since emigration was prevented by rocky barriers and cascades. Stocking, however, has established Brook Trout. Fish in these high cold lakes are small and generally not plentiful for plant foods grow slowly. Rainbow Trout predominate in the higher streams.

Lake Crescent, a large body of water on the north side of the park, is famous for its Beardslee and Crescenti Trout. For many years these trout were considered to be distinct and unique species. More recently, the Beardslee or Bluebacked Trout was recognized to be merely a Rainbow, while the speckled Crescenti is a Cutthroat. The former weigh ten to as much as twenty pounds. They are scare and can be caught only by trolling at least one hundred feet deep.

Many of the fishing waters of Olympic Park are accessible only by trail and do not offer great rewards in terms of fish. As a scenic wilderness, however, the area is unsurpassed.

Several hotels, cabins, campgrounds and trail shelters offer accommodations. The park is open all year. The approximate fishing dates are May 24 to November 1.

ROCKY MOUNTAIN NATIONAL PARK
Estes Park, Colorado

About twenty beautiful streams flow from this range of the Rockies. Sixty-five named peaks tower more than 10,000 feet above sea level. Food conditions for Trout are fair in the lower elevations and here the angler will find numbers of Cutthroats, Brooks, and Rainbows. Because most of the park streams are easily accessible from highways, fishing pressure is heavy, and the great majority of fish caught are undersize or, at best, small keepers. Natural reproduction, although good in terms of young fish, cannot possibly satisfy the demands for fairly large Trout because they grow too slowly.

As a rule, in this 394-square-mile area, fishing is more satisfactory in the sixty-five lakes which are five acres or larger. At a distance from highways, angling generally is fairly productive either from boats or on shore.

Within the park, boats must be provided by individual anglers as none are rented. On the western edge of the park, but outside the boundaries, Grand Lake and Shadow Mountain Reservoir usually offer good bait- and fly-fishing and trolling. Boats are available for rent there.

Hotels, lodges, inns, camps, and campgrounds are available during the summer. A few accommodations are open within the park the year around. The fishing season dates are approximately May 25 to October 31.

SEQUOIA NATIONAL PARK
Three Rivers, California

This park comprises six hundred square miles of superb scenery, chiefly on the western slope of the Sierra Nevada. The highest mountain in the United States proper, Mt. Whitney, is here. The park is named for its great groves of the largest and probably the oldest living things in the world—the Sequoias.

The 604-square-mile area adjoins the 710-square-mile Kings Canyon National Park forming the Sequoia and Kings Canyon National Parks. (See Kings Canyon).

Since waterfalls are impassable barriers to the natural passage of fish into most of the Kaweah drainage, many headwaters have been stocked with Rainbow, Brook, Brown, Golden, and Loch Leven Trout. Suckers are present, sometimes in large numbers, in the lower waters which are warmer and not too turbulent.

In most cases, the Sequoia waters are infertile and can support only limited numbers of slow-growing Trout. When waters are made accessible by roads or good trails, they are quickly fished out. Even Kern River, famous as a Rainbow and Golden Trout stream, is still good only because it is remote. During the first few weeks of the season, fishing in Sequoia Park is fairly good within an hour's walk from roads. In July and August, however, the ambitious angler must make a pack trip.

Various lodges and campgrounds offer shelter, a few of them the year around. The fishing season is generally from May 1 to October 31.

SHENANDOAH NATIONAL PARK
Luray, Virginia

While a number of streams originate in Shenandoah Park, the total mileage of fishing streams is not great because of the narrow width of the park. Forest protection since establishment of the park in 1935 has resulted in great improvement of fishing. Formerly, most streams dried up in summer, and trout were restricted (if they survived at all) to spring-fed pools at higher elevations. In recent years stream-flow has increased and water temperatures have become lower. In consequence, natural reproduction of native Brook Trout and introduced Rainbow Trout has been fairly good. Heavy stocking has been necessary wherever roads permit crowds of anglers to gather. The fisherman willing to hike two or three miles away from roads will find fairly good fishing, particularly for Brook Trout. A few Black Bass occur in the warmer water near the perimeter of the park.

The Rapidan and Staunton Rivers have been designated a "Fishing-for-Fun" waters.

Shenandoah Park covers 302 square miles in the heart of the Blue Ridge Mountains. The scenic Sky Line Drive extends along the entire ridge of the park. Lodges, cabins, and a campground are available from April to about the first of November. The fishing season is generally from April 20 to July 31.

YELLOWSTONE NATIONAL PARK
Yellowstone Park, Wyoming

This is one of the famous fishing areas of the United States. The foremost species is the Cutthroat Trout, highly prized for sport and food. While it may grow to eight pounds, it usually averages one to three pounds in the park. The best fishing waters are Yellowstone Lake and its tributaries, Yellowstone River above the Upper Falls, Lamar River, and Gallatin River and its tributaries. Yellowstone Lake and tributary streams are designated as "Fishing-for-Fun" waters.

Rainbow Trout were introduced from the west

coast in 1880. While more gamey than the Cutthroat, it hybridizes with the latter and destroys its identity. For this reason the Park Service attempts to limit the Rainbow to separate watersheds. The more famous Rainbow waters are Firehole and Little Firehole Rivers, Madison River, and Nez Perce Creek.

Montana Grayling originally were excluded from many Yellowstone Park waters by impassable falls. Since this fine game fish has become extirpated or scarce through much of its range, special measures are taken in the park to ensure its perpetuation. In small numbers, it is found in several streams and lakes of the western drainage. However, its real "stronghold" is Grebe and Wolf lakes.

Except by competing for food the introduced Brook Trout interfere little with native species. They average eight to twelve inches long, but occasionally grow to eighteen inches and a weight of four pounds.

Loch Leven Trout have hybridized with Brown Trout since their introduction many years ago. The resulting fish, which is termed a "Loch Leven," may become as heavy as twenty pounds in the lakes. Mackinaw or Lake Trout may attain thirty pounds. They are taken by trolling in Heart, Lewis, and Shoshone lakes.

July is the best fishing month in Yellowstone for most species, although Brook Trout usually bite readily throughout the season (approximately May 30 to October 15).

The 3,458 square miles of Yellowstone National Park are famous for the 3,000 geysers and hot springs (the world's greatest geyser area), canyons, waterfalls, enormous elk herds, moose, buffalo, bears, and other wildlife. Hotels, lodges, cabins, and campgrounds are open from June 20 to September 12.

YOSEMITE NATIONAL PARK
Yosemite National Park, California

The Rainbow is the only native trout in Yosemite Park. Originally, it did not occur above the waterfalls of Yosemite and Little Yosemite valleys. After years of stocking, it is now present from the Merced River in the main valley up to the alpine lakes. Although the Rainbow rarely exceeds three pounds, even in lakes, it is the angler's favorite.

The Sacramento Sucker and four kinds of small fish are the only other species that occurred in the park before the arrival of white men. Suckers were eaten by the Yosemite Indians who preferred them to Trout, but they are used by modern fishermen only for bait.

Four game fish have been introduced to Yosemite waters. Brook Trout are abundant and reproduce themselves in certain streams and lakes in the high country. They seldom thrive at elevations lower than seven thousand feet. Golden Trout were introduced in 1919-20 and are found in many lakes and streams at the headwaters of the Tuolumne and Merced rivers. They grow a foot long in lakes but seldom exceed seven or eight inches in streams. Tahoe Trout (Cutthroat) are established in a few waters but are not important as game fish. In lakes, they occasionally reach five to six pounds in weight. The final game species, a result of hybridizing between Loch Leven and Brown Trout, does well in the large rivers, such as the Merced, below seven thousand feet. It is a wary fish and furnishes some angling in summer in Yosemite Valley. The park record weight is twelve pounds, nine ounces.

Except early in the season, good fishing in Yosemite Park can be found only by packing into the wilderness high country. Crowds of fishermen soon deplete the "keeper" fish from all waters that are accessible by road or short hikes.

This superbly beautiful park extends 1,182 square miles. The Ahwahnee Hotel and Yosemite Lodge are open the year round. Other hotels are open in the summer. There are also four campgrounds and five hikers' camps within the park. The fishing season is generally from May 30 to October 15.

Part 2. Salt Water

With thousands of miles of coast line and vast areas of salt-water inland bays, sounds, and sloughs, salt-water fishing is readily accessible to a large number of anglers.

Thousands of boat liveries and more or less elaborate fishing camps and resorts offer their services to visiting fishermen. Salt-water fishing is more highly developed along the Atlantic and Gulf Coasts, and the California section of the Pacific Coast.

Interest is growing in other sections, but except for specialized types of fishing, such as Salmon on both coasts and Tuna in eastern Canada, relatively little attention has been given to salt-water angling in Canadian waters. The same is true of Alaska, the fishing being largely of local interest.

Mexican waters on both coasts have been increasingly explored in recent years, and a rapidly growing sports fishery is now organized. Thousands visit this country each year to indulge in some form of angling, and a section on this fishing is included. Mexico is largely a semi-arid country and does not supply a fresh-water fishery at all comparable in value and volume to that enjoyed in salt water.

While excellent Largemouth Bass fishing is available in some artificial reservoirs and natural waters, and a number of small Trout streams have been planted, the volume is so limited that it attracts relatively few visiting anglers. Those going to Mexico to fish, go primarily to participate in the exceptional fishing to be found in its bays and lagoons, and the waters of the Gulf of Mexico, the Gulf of California, and the Pacific Ocean.

ATLANTIC SALT WATER FISHING

It is well for any angler contemplating a salt-water fishing trip to consult local anglers, tackle dealers, and others on the spot, about the best places to fish, and the baits that are most successful at the time to be fished; for they are in close touch with the weather, water, tides, and other conditions affecting fish and fishing. They also can supply additional details that may have much to do with the success of the trip.

This section, will provide information regarding seasons and localities at which the most important species are normally found in the greatest numbers, the time when fishing for that species will likely be most successful, and the lures and baits that promise the most success. No one can make the fish bite if they refuse to cooperate; no information can guarantee to tell a veteran or a beginner just exactly where to go and take fish; but it can help shorten the time between bites, and add pleasure to the trip.

Every angler knows that fish are where one finds them; they are here today and somewhere else tomorrow. The successful lure today may be exactly the one that will be refused tomorrow. Generally the man who keeps his bait in the water the longest, takes the most fish. Nevertheless, knowledge will help. And if one believes in "Lady Luck," she also can be of some assistance. Even though the fishes refuse to cooperate, the angler who spends his day on the water in the great outdoors is well repaid, for the Atlantic Coast is noted for its beauty and its wildlife as well as its grand angling.

BAITS

Natural baits used generally from Maine to Florida are; squid (fresh and frozen), Louisiana shrimp (alive or frozen), small "grass shrimp" alive, bloodworms, sand worms, clam worms, shedder or peeler crabs, hard crabs, soft crabs, small crabs whole, and other crustaceans, clams and other shellfish, minnows, strips of fresh fish, flying fish, mullet, herring, etc.

Artificial baits are as numerous as the grains of sand on the beach, and increasing in styles daily. Every angler, every section, has his or its own best artificial lure. Different seasons, different tides, the weather, and the whims of the fish make it impossible to select from the vast number of popular spoons, plugs, feathers, bugs, jigs, spinners, flies, etc., any one, or even a dozen, that will work, any time any place; many hook the angler not the fish. Local authorities, familiar with local conditions, will gladly give advice on the right baits for any particular spot or time. All will take fish at times. Many anglers make their own artificials. Give heed to the advice of the local fisherman, and your tackle dealer if he is an angler.

Maine

The Bluefin Tuna is probably Maine's most important sport fish. Striped Bass angling has increased in popularity as the sportsmen have located waters heavily frequented by these gamesters at present. The Atlantic Salmon is coming back in some rivers. Bottom fishing for Pollock, Flounder, Cod, Haddock, etc., is good in many places off shore. There are many spots along the coast where there is excellent fishing from wharves and docks for those who do not care to venture out to sea, including those who do not have the stomach for that kind of fishing, and have not yet become acquainted with anti-seasick remedies.

Maine furnishes excellent angling for Tuna, the giant fighter of the deep. About the first of July schools of these fish arrive off the Maine coast; by the middle of the month they begin to feed extensively on Mackerel, Bluefish and others, and are taken in numbers by the angler and the commercial fisherman, along with Mackerel and Pollock. August is probably the best month, but from July to October hundreds of Tuna might be taken by sportsmen from an area between York Harbor and Muscongus Bay. Fish weighing over 700 pounds have been taken on hook and line, and

SALT WATER ANGLING CHART
(MAINE TO FLORIDA)

SPECIES	*TIME*	*WHERE*	*HOW*	*BAITS*
TUNA	July-October	Off shore	Trolling, chumming	Whole mackerel, chum
SWORDFISH	July-Sept.	Off N. Atlantic shore	Harpoon, trolling, by sight	Mackerel, bluefish, squid
MACKEREL (Common)	June & Sept.	Off shore, North Atlantic	Trolling, chumming still fishing	Spoons, feathers, cut bait
MACKEREL (Spanish)	April-July	Off shore, S. Atlantic, reefs, bays, inlets	Trolling	Herring, minnows, shrimp, spoons, feathers
POLLOCK	April-July	North Atlantic N. of New Jersey, Rocky bottom	Trolling, drifting, fly and casting rods	Spoons, feathers, cut bait, clams, squid
STRIPED BASS	May-Oct.	Surf, inshore waters, bays, hard bottom, swift waters	Trolling, surf casting, chumming, still fishing	Crabs, shrimp, eels, plugs, spoons, feathers
WEAKFISH	June-Nov.	Bays, surf, oysterbeds, roving	Still fishing, Trolling, chumming, surf casting	Crabs, shrimp, small plugs, spoons, feathers
BLUEFISH	June-Nov.	Roving, bays, surf, off shore	Trolling, chumming, still fishing	Spoons, feathers, cut bait, shrimp
TAUTOG	Summer & Sept.	Off rocks, wrecks, near shore & in bays & inlets	Bottom fishing	Small crabs, sea worms minnows
CROAKERS	May-Oct.	Bays, inlets, oyster bars, off shore	Still fishing	Crabs, squid, shrimp, bloodworms, cut bait
CHANNEL BASS	May-Nov.	Surf, mouth of bays, inlets	Trolling, surf casting, still fishing	Squid, cut bait, crabs, clams
BLACK DRUM	June-Nov.	Oyster bars; mouth of Chesapeake Bay	Still fishing	Squid, cut bait, crabs, clams
FLOUNDER (summer)	May-Oct.	Bays, inlets, off shore sandy bottoms	Still fishing on bottom	Crabs, squid, cut bait, sea worms, minnows
FLOUNDER (winter)	Spring & fall & early winter	Bays, inlets, off shore, sandy bottom	Bottom fishing	Crab, squid, cut bait, sea worms, blood worms
SEA BASS	May-Oct.	Off shore, rocks, jetties, piers, wrecks	Still fishing	Crabs, shrimp, squid, bloodworms, cut bait
PORGY—SCUP	June-Oct. (North Atlantic)	Sandy bottom, bays, wrecks, off shore	Bottom fishing	Clams, squid, crabs, cut bait, sea worms
SPOT	May-Oct. (South Atlantic)	Hard bottom any where in bays & inlets	Still fishing	Blood worm, shrimp, crabs, cut bait
KINGFISH (Whiting)	May-Oct.	Surf, inlets & bays near ocean	Surf casting, still fishing; sandy bottom	Cut bait, clams, squid, sand fleas, sea worms
SHEEPSHEAD	June-Oct.	Oyster beds, rocks, jetties	Still fishing	Crabs, cut bait, shrimp, squid
COBIA	Summer	Mouth of Cheasapeake Bay best	Chumming, still fishing, trolling	Crabs, spoons, small fish, cut bait

Note:—The time in this table may vary as much as two weeks either way, due to climatic conditions and water temperatures; and also the time will be slightly later or earlier according to the state the angler is fishing. Later in spring, earlier in fall towards Maine, and vice versa.

individuals of more than 900 with harpoon. Tuna are at times taken near shore. A good spot is Bailey Island area. Trolling with Mackerel, or feathers, or chumming with cut menhaden, are best methods.

Striped Bass angling was hardly known in Maine before the thirties; some years this fish seem to be absent; but new angling grounds for it have been located, and it can now be classed as one of Maine's major fishing sports. The lower or western end of the state is best. Striped Bass have been taken from Saco, Mousan, Kennebunk, Royal, Kennebeck, Penobscot, Union, Machias, and St. Croix Rivers, and numerous smaller streams. Surf casting has only recently become popular, but it is increasing as more good waters are discovered. A 49-pounder was taken off York Beach in 1948. Trolling is most popular method. Spoons, feathers and bucktails are popular lures. Swift tide waters are more productive. Natural baits include small eels, (a good bait for Striped Bass anywhere), bloodworms, sand worms, shedder crabs, and some places squids (artificial). July is probably the best month.

Schools of Atlantic Mackerel and Pollock range the Maine coast, and afford much sport. Pollock, not so well known as a game fish, will run as large as 30 pounds, and average about 10 pounds. They strike hard, and when a school is located bite fast. Most any spoon or bright spinner will take them; large pieces of herring with spinners will do the trick for either Mackerel or Pollock. Mackerel run smaller but are good fighters. Both afford sport with light gear. Some experts have been taking Mackerel with fly rods not far from shore. A popular Mackerel bait is known as mackerel jig, use with clams. Trolling is the best method. Boats often bring in several hundred from one day's angling. Chumming is good for both Mackerel and Pollock. Best time, July to September. Pollock appear off Cape Code early in May.

The Maine Department of Economic Development, State House, Augusta, publishes a folder including a map showing the best spots for Tuna,

SALT WATER ANGLING CHART
(FLORIDA)

SPECIES	TIME	WHERE	HOW	BAITS
SPOTTED WEAK-FISH	Spring & Winter	Bays, grass beds & inlets	Still fishing, casting	Shrimp, minnows, mullet, plugs
BLUEFISH	Jan.-March	Bays, off shore, inlets	Trolling, still fishing, surf casting	Spoons, feathers, cut bait, minnows
MARLIN	Jan.-May	Edge Gulf Stream	Trolling	Mullet, mackerel
SAILFISH	All year, best Jan.-May	Edge of Gulf Stream	Trolling, by sight	Mullet, bonito, baloa
TARPON	May-Sept.	Rivers, inlets, tide rips, trestles, bridges, canals	Trolling, casting, still fishing	Live & cut bait, spoons, jigs, plugs
KINGFISH (Cero)	Winter & Spring	Reefs, along shores & roving	Trolling, still fishing	Cut bait, spoons, feathers
DOLPHIN	Jan.-May	Gulf stream around drifting grass	Still fishing, trolling	Cut bait, squids, spoons, plugs, shrimp
BONEFISH	Summer best (Year round)	Shallow Flats, Keys	Casting with bait & fly rod	Hermit crabs, shrimp, bass bugs, conch—cut bait
WAHOO	Winter & Spring	Gulf Stream	Trolling	Mullet, bonito, cut bait
BONITO (common)	Jan.-April & summer	Gulf Stream	Trolling	Mullet, jigs, spoons
AMBERJACK	Winter-spring	Rocky reefs & coral bottoms	Trolling, still fishing, drifting	Cut bait, spoons, live bait, jigs
CREVALLE	Year round	Gulf Stream bays, coral reefs, piers, wrecks	Trolling, still fishing	Minnows, cut bait, artificials, crabs
BARRACUDA	All Year	Fla. E. coast, bays off shore, Keys.	Trolling, still fishing	Cut bait, jigs, spoons, minnows
JEWFISH		Reefs, wrecks, rocky bottoms	Still fishing	Live & cut bait
SNOOK	All year	Inlets, bays, passes on W. coast	Trolling, casting still fishing	Spoons, mullet, shrimp, crabs

Note:—Many other lesser species are found in Florida, off bridges, trestles, rock piles, reefs, etc., such as the snappers, groupers, yellow jack, and many others, affording good sport to many who use most any tackle and baits. Consult local authorities.

Mackerel, Striped Bass and ground or bottom fishing. A list of charter boats for salt-water angling, prices, etc., may be obtained from the Department of Sea and Shore Fisheries, Vickery-Hill Building, Augusta.

New Hampshire

This state has a short coastal line, but some good salt-water angling.

Tuna are found off shore. The most popular Tuna fishing spots are off the Isle of Shoals, and a mile or two off shore from Seabrook and Hampton Beaches, where boats, guides and bait may be obtained. Best natural bait is whole mackerel, either trolled or let down a chum line. The season starts about the middle of June and runs through September; some are taken in October. However, the sea gets rough in late fall and best months are July, August and early September.

Mackerel are found off shore in schools and also in the Piscataqua and Hampton Rivers. Sportsmen take Mackerel in this section with fly rod and streamer flies, most any pattern. Also taken with mackerel jigs, and small spoons with casting rods. Seasons and methods about the same as Tuna. Large Pollock are taken off the coast of New Hampshire up to 35 pounds, using double hooked metal squids which can be obtained locally, baited with sand eels. May to October, early morning and late afternoon best, however tides influence the fish also. Small Pollock are taken on light tackle (fly rod) in Piscataqua River, and in Newcastle, Rye, and Hampton Rivers; they will take a streamer cast into a school, most any pattern.

Striped Bass are also taken from Piscataqua River, and Great Bay near Dover Point Bridge; also off Seabrook Beach, and at the mouth of Hampton River. Many large fish, 15 to 40 pounds; seem to prefer large blue plugs, but also taken on squids, eel skins, and feathered jigs. A popular artificial for small Stripers is a spinner like the willow leaf with sea worms. Season starts about the middle of June and runs through October. September is probably best month, trolling most popular method, with a few surf casters.

New Hampshire prides itself on its smelt fishing in Great Bay, and also in Newcastle, Rye, and Hampton Harbors. July, and all winter through the ice. Universal bait seems to be a small piece of clam or blood worm. Taken still fishing with light tackle in summer. Fishing in winter is from shanties over holes cut through the ice; shanties can be rented. Tides are important, check locally.

Tautog or Blackfish are found around rocks, and jetties; off Hampton some good spots; small crabs for bait; still fishing. Best from June 15 to last of July. This information applies to Tautog wherever found, from New Hampshire to Chesapeake Bay.

Boats, bait, etc., may be obtained at all places named. For local information regarding boats, guides, best baits, etc. write to Fish and Game Department at Concord.

Massachusetts

The Massachusetts coast, with Cape Cod jutting out into the Atlantic, and the Islands of Martha's Vineyard and Nantucket, provides an ideal place for the summer angler and vacationist. Here the surf caster is in his glory. Its principal game fish are Striped Bass, Tuna, Mackerel, Pollock, Tautog, Flounders, Scup, Sea Bass, Shad, and Smelt.

Striped Bass are found along the entire coast, and in the bays and estuaries. Taken May through October; probably best months are May-June, and August and August-September. Lures include blood worms, eels, squid both natural and artificial, herring, all types of jigs, spoons, plugs and spinners, reds and whites preferred. Stripers are taken by surf casting, trolling and chumming; experts take them on fly rod and streamers; some are taken on blue plugs cast from boats near shore. Occasionally 60-pounders are taken.

Tuna are taken in Ipswich Bay, Cape Cod Bay, and off Provincetown, in July through September. Whole mackerel and feather jigs are popular lures for trolling. Mackerel are taken along the coast through September; July and August best time. Baits generally used are squid, crabs, worms, feathers, spoons, trolling and chumming. Also with fly rod and streamer flies. A few "hot spots" for Stripers are Martha's Vineyard, Nantucket, Cuttyhunk, Cape Cod Canal, Monomy Point, Outer Cape Cod Shore, Cape Ann, Plymouth Bay, and Orleans Bay. They run big in Massachusetts. For Pollock go to Provincetown, Mahomet, and from Plymouth north. Best runs in May and September; and any of the common already mentioned baits, casting from boats and still fishing, will take fish.

Women's World Record Striped Bass, weighing 64½ pounds, was taken on a plug at North Truro, Massachusetts.

Shad are taken from the brackish and fresh waters of numerous tidal rivers with fly rod, small spoons, streamers and spinning outfits. Best spot Connecticut River north from the state line to Holyoke Dam, May and June best. Massachusetts also boasts of some good bottom fishing for Flounders, Sea Bass, Scup, Cod, Haddock and Smelt; fishing good all summer; natural baits.

The Massachusetts Division of Fisheries and Game, 73 Tremont St., Boston 8, issues a free booklet on salt-water angling, that contains an excellent map of the coast, with the exact spots where best fishing is located. No one fishing the salt waters of the state should do so without this guide. It also contains a list of boats, guides, air fields, and even a list of shops where natural baits can be obtained.

Rhode Island

Commencing in late winter and early spring, Rhode Island's tidal and off-shore waters are a source of many species of sport fish. First to appear are the Winter Flounder and White Perch. Hardly a cove, bay or tidal pond does not yield substantial numbers. A little later, early in May, Tautog, locally known as "Blackfish," are found in upper Narragansett Bay, later and throughout the season, this species is found along the ocean front, especially rocky ledges. Blackfish are the most popular fish with the spear-fishermen. In rapid order, Striped Bass, Scup, Bluefish, Summer Flounder and Mackerel appear: all of which can be taken from shore or from a small boat anchored close to shore. Depending upon the skill of the angler, good numbers can be taken almost anywhere in Narragansett Bay, Sakonnet River, Point Judith, Charlestown Breachway, Newport Rocks, and Watch Hill Reef.

Recent catches include a 20-pound Tautog, a 19-pound, 2-ounce Bluefish, several 60-pound plus Stripers and a 16-pound Summer Flounder. With the catch of a 925-pound Bluefin Tuna taken within sight of shore and the largest such fish boated in American waters, it is little wonder that Rhode Island attracts the off-shore angler. The 17,854 pounds of Tuna taken during three days of the U. S. Atlantic Tuna Tournament made up of 34 fish with 20 of them over 500 pounds has set Little Rhody up as the Tuna capital of the world. It is not only the Tuna that attracts the off-shore fishermen, for White Marlin up to 90-pounds are fairly abundant and Swordfish taken by rod and reel in excess of 300-pounds have been landed with increasing frequency during the past few years. Although less spectacular than the famed sports fish listed above, the Cod provides good winter sport to the off-shore fisherman who can brave the wintery blasts of December and January.

Connecticut

As one would expect, angling along the Connecticut coast is similar in style, species, and seasons to those in Rhode Island and Massachusetts. Its proximity to New York City with its attendant pollutions is a disadvantage. However, Bluefish and Striped Bass are plentiful at times, and there is offshore angling from the ports of this state.

Fisher's Island is off the coast and a good spot. Catum Reef is a good place for large Stripers, between Fisher's Island and Watch Hill: also for Mackerel and Pollock. A plug known as the Atom Plug is popular with local anglers for Striped Bass. Trolling and plug casting are the best methods. Connecticut prides itself on its good Flounder (summer and winter) fishing in near-shore waters and bays and inlets; these tasty fish are taken still fishing with clams, shedder crabs, bloodworms and pieces of fish. Blackfish (Tautog) and Porgies also figure prominently in the total catch of Connecticut anglers.

New York

New York's coastal waters are confined to Long Island Sound and waters off the south shore of the Island. The best time for such species are Stripers will begin a little earlier than in New England and last a little longer as the fish travel north in spring, and south in fall. The best place to get first-hand information about angling on and off Long Island is from the Long Island Association, 273 Pennsylvania Station, New York City; their Fishing Information Bureau is at the service of the angler. Boats can be rented or chartered; guides, etc., can be obtained at a long list of such ports as Sheepshead Bay, Rockaway Beach, Point Lookout, Freeport, Amityville, Lindhurst, Babylon Bay Shore, Sayville, Center Moriches, Westhampton Beach, Shinnecock Canal, Sag Harbor, Montauk, Greenport, Shelter Island, Mill Creek, Riverhead, Mattituck Inlet, Port Jefferson, Northport, Cold Spring Harbor, Oyster Bay and Port Washington.

Most angling, except surf fishing, is done from party boats, which can be obtained at from $5.00 to $75.00 a day. Hook and line angling for Swordfish is at its best off shore from Montauk to Fire Island in summer months. Large Weakfish are taken in Peconic Bay and other salt-water bays by trolling with artificials and chumming with live shrimp, or with natural baits and light tackle mostly from anchored boats. The Shelter Island section is noted for its large Weakfish. Surf casting for Stripers and Weakfish is good along the ocean side of Long Island, and some of the Beaches reserve certain stretches for this sport, from which bathers are barred, and where Blues, Striped Bass, Weakfish, Kingfish and others are taken.

Weakfish show up the last of May and run until September, June good along the South Shore; natural baits are live shrimp, blood worms, sand worms, squid and shedder crab. Bluefish start in June; majority are taken by trolling either outside or in the Sound. Young Blues, or Snappers, come into the Sound, bays and around the docks in July and stay through September. Striped Bass start about first of June. September is also a good month for Stripers, and through October.

July is a vacation month and also a good angling month in New York salt waters. Fluke, Flounder, Pollock, Mackerel, Broadbill, Swordfish, Sea Bass, Weakfish, Stripers, Tautog, Bonito, Scup and others, all cooperate in this month. Big Blues, and large Weakfish are present in July. Some regard August as the best all-around month in these waters, particularly for still fishing.

Special fishermen's trains run from New York City to Montauk during the height of the angling season. The Long Island Railroad Fishing and Hunting Information Bureau, previously mentioned, issues a map showing exact fishing spots, best methods of angling, where the various species may be or should be found, how to fish for them, best seasons, proper sized hooks, and best baits. Party boats, holding as many as 50 anglers leave New York City daily, and fish successfully off Long Island and the New Jersey coast; two leave daily from the Battery.

New Jersey

New Jersey has a long coast and numerous large bays and inlets, all providing excellent angling at times when most people have leisure to fish. Extending from Sandy Hook to Cape May, with such inland bays as Barnegat, Great Bay, Absecon, Egg Harbor, and many others, it is impossible to name the best fishing area. It may be in one section today and in another next week, depending upon movements of the fish. Any city, town, or resort along the entire coast, also up the Delaware Bay, can furnish boats, guides, bait, and direct information as to the right spots, tides, and best time. Angling is "big business" in New Jersey. Surf fishing is good at times even in the great vacation cities such as Atlantic City, Long Branch, Island Beach, Cape May, Ocean City, Barnegat City, Beach Haven and others; favorite spots are at the inlets from the ocean such as Barnegat Inlet, Beach Haven Inlet, Absecon Inlet, and others. A few "hot spots" to fish from are Brielle, Barnegat City, Beach Haven, and Brigantine.

Anglers use from lightest to heaviest tackle according to taste and species sought. Surf casting is very popular, and the usual surf casting outfits are employed. Popular baits are squid, artificial and natural, shedder crabs, clams, bloodworms and eels. These baits also are good for still fishing in the bays. Boats leave from many ports for ocean fishing for Tuna, Bluefish, Weakfish and others. Striped Bass are taken by surf casting and trolling with spoons and feathers, in spring and fall on annual migrations. Best times are probably April and May and October through December. This also applies to Striped Bass, which run large on this coast. Summer Flounder fishing is popular with the summer vacationist; the winter flounder in late fall and winter. Many small Bluefish, or snappers, are taken in late August and September from piers, boats, jetties and shores and with light tackle this is real sport. Squid can be obtained at most angling centers either frozen or fresh; the fresh squid is preferable.

Artificial squids, such as the Belmont, Diamond, and others which originated in New Jersey, are popular and successful; eel skins also are used, as well as small eels. Stripers are taken trolling, casting and chumming. Best trolling is just outside the breakers. Many party boats from New York City and from local ports carrying as many as 50 anglers take Weakfish, Bluefish, Croakers, Spots, Dogfish, Tautog, Scup, Flounders, Blowfish and others on natural baits. This is an inexpensive and popular way to fish. Bonito are at times found off New York and New Jersey, but are not as popular, or as good eating as the more plentiful Bluefish.

Delaware Bay, between New Jersey and Delaware provides some fine angling for Weakfish, Blues, Croakers and others. Boats, bait and local information can be obtained at Bivalve, Fortesque, Greenwich, Norbury's Landing, Reed's Beach, and others. Best months are June and September. For angling information write the New Jersey Council, Department of Economic Development, State House, Trenton.

Delaware

This is a small state with only three counties but with a fine 25-mile coast line on the Atlantic Ocean, Delaware Bay, and Rehoboth Bay and Indian River, two salt water estuaries, Delaware provides good angling. Surf casting is popular along the entire ocean coast. The state has built roads from the main coastal highway to the beach, with parking spaces, for the convenience of the anglers and a check of auto licenses shows that anglers from all neighboring states avail themselves of these privileges. From Cape Henlopen up the Delaware Bay, good "spots" are Lewes, Cape Henlopen, Broadkill Beach, Slaughter Beach and Bowers Beach, where party boats are available. East of these points there is little difference between the Bay and the ocean. Fishing parties go out for Weakfish, Croakers, and Bluefish in season. June and September probably best, although some good angling is to be had all summer. Sea Bass, Tautog, Flounders and other bottom feeders are taken from the wharves and jetties on natural baits, such as squid, bloodworms, pieces of fish, clams, etc. Many party boats go out from Indian River Inlet where there also is good angling from the shore and jetties. It is said that party boats take out over 3,000 anglers from Delaware ports every day in season.

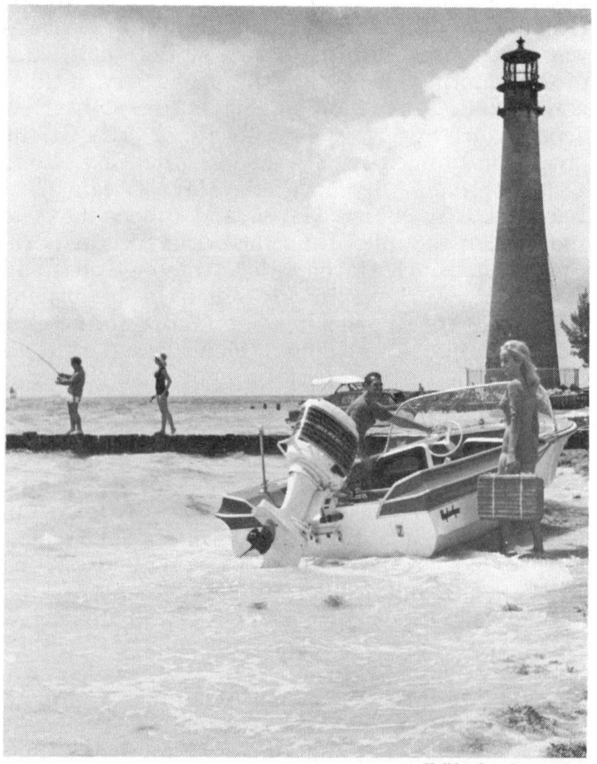

Keikhaefer Corporation

Lighthouses are the most prominent navigation aids. In conjunction with a chart of local waters, they are helpful in pinpointing the location of the boat in any coastal waters.

The best time along the Delaware side of the bay is September; after the first cold snap in this month there is a big run of large Weakfish, making for the sea, and everyone gets out any old boat, also from the shore, and with any tackle and the handiest bait, and catches Weakfish for about 10 days. Bottom fishing in the bay is good, during the summer.

Maryland

Here is a state with only 30 miles of coast, but with a good angling reputation. This is partly because of the discovery several years ago of Marlin, Dolphin, Sailfish, Mackerel and other southern species in an area known as the Jack Spot, some 40 miles off shore on the edge of the Gulf Stream. It is due to the fact that this state is split by Chesapeake Bay, the largest bay on the Atlantic Coast. Its waters provide angling for many salt-water species, such as Striped Bass, locally called "rock"; Weakfish, locally called "sea trout"; Spotted Weakfish, Sergeant Fish or Cobia, Bluefish, Croakers, Spot, Drum, and others. As the lower half of the Chesapeake Bay lies in the state of Virginia, much of that which is said here applies also to that state; the Jack Spot, of course, can be reached from Delaware and Virginia as well as from Maryland. There is little difference in baits and best times from those in the adjoining states. Surf casting for Channel Bass is good south of Ocean City, generally in June and September. Squid and shedder crab most popular baits, also strips of menhaden and herring. Not many Weakfish are caught surf fishing in Maryland, but Kingfish, Bluefish or Whiting, are taken by this method all summer.

Striped Bass fishing is best in the Chesapeake Bay; these fish move up towards the head of the bay by July, and few are located below Tilghman's Island after August and until fall; June is good month in lower bay. The best section during summer months is in the vicinity of Rock Hall, Swan Point, and off Hickory Thicket and the mouth of Chester River. As fall approaches, the Stripers start south and are taken at suitable grounds to the mouth of the Potomac, and up the Potomac River as far as Indian Head, Point Patience, near the mouth of the Patuxent River, is also good for Stripers in June, September and October.

Hardheads or Croakers start biting in the Maryland section of the bay about May 15, and run until July when they start back towards the sea. The Weakfish or Seatrout, come up the bay as the Croakers go down, and good fishing in Maryland waters for this species starts around July 1 and continues on through September. In good years many Bluefish are taken as far up the bay as Annapolis.

Stripers, Bluefish, and Weakfish are caught trolling with spoons, feathers and bucktails, and in some sections, small eels. They also are taken on light tackle chumming with live green or grass shrimp; this is a sporting way to capture them, for ordinary Black Bass tackle may be used, with plenty of line, however, for many large Rock are hooked by this method. Weakfish are taken on bottom with natural baits such as shedder crab, bloodworms, clams, and in the lower bay fresh squid is good; they are also caught trolling in the same manner as Stripers.

Good points to obtain boats, bait, and local information are: on the coast, Ocean City; on the eastern shore of the bay, Crisfield, Cambridge, Tilghmans, Claiborne, Love Point, Rock Hall, and others; on western side of the bay, Point Lookout at mouth of Potomac River (where is located the celebrated South West Middle Grounds, one of the best angling spots in the Bay); Solomons, Chesapeake Beach, Galesville, Herring Bay, Deale, Annapolis, and others.

Angling in the bay is mostly from chartered power boats, and the season runs from May to November with June and September probably the best months; but hardy fishermen troll for Striped Bass successfully even in November. A few choice Striper spots are: Eastern Bay, (June and September), Swan Point, (July and August), Herring Bay, Belvedere Shoals, Bloody Point, Thomas Point, the "Gooses" off Tilghmans, and Sharp's Island off the mouth of Choptank River. The boat captains know the exact spots where schools of Rock hang out, and take the angler where the fish are; the sea gulls help a lot also, as they do all along the coast.

For detailed information about boats, baits and where the fish are schooled, write the Commission of Tidewater Fisheries or Bureau of Information, State House, Annapolis. The Maryland Development Bureau of the Baltimore Chamber of Commerce issues a map entitled "Let's Go Fishing"; it contains a fishing map, cuts showing the various bay species, and a table of seasons, average weights, right tackle and baits; this can be obtained free upon request.

Shad have been taken on artificial baits and light tackle for a longer period in Maryland than elsewhere. Records of Hickory Shad taken on wet flies in the fresh waters of the Patapsco River, now polluted, go back for over 50 years. However, this form of angling came into its own some few years ago on the Susquehanna River from the Conowingo Dam to tidewater at the mouth of Deer Creek, Harford County. Shad are fast swimmers, hard fighters, and acrobatic. An angler is fortunate if he lands one out of every four hooked. Both the Shad, and Hickory Shad are taken from these waters, and also a few Herring, on flies and small spoons. The best baits are the Drone #00, the smallest sized Nungesser spoon, and the Trixoreno; streamer flies are excellent, containing whites, reds and yellows. The fly rod is preferable and the fly line should be backed with at least 50 yards of good level line, for Shad will run and jump like Tarpon; and when fishing for Shad the angler is likely to fasten into a good Striper, or Walleye. Spinning outfits are also popular. Best fly-rod angling is in May. Good points to fish from: Conowingo Dam, Shure's Landing, mouth of Deer Creek, and Octoraro Creek. Fishing is from boat and shores and many use spinning rods. An angler's license required in the waters named.

Virginia

This state has considerable coastal and tidal water angling territory, including the lower half of the Chesapeake Bay. Accomac County, known as the "Eastern Shore of Virginia," is a peninsula bounded on the east by the Atlantic Ocean and on the west by the Chesapeake Bay. There is good surf casting along the ocean front, and trolling and bottom fishing in the bay and estuaries. Cape Charles, at the southern end of the county, and at the mouth of the bay, provides some of the best Channel Bass and Cobia fishing along the Atlantic Coast, beginning in May and running through June; and again in September when the Channel Bass are returning southward. Franklin City, Wachapreague, Accomac, Smith's Island, Hog Island, and many others are good locations. Weakfish run large in these waters and are best in the last of May and the first of June and again in the fall. Croakers, Flounders and Spots, all summer. Virginia has the best waters for the Cobia (Sergeant Fish). Boats, bait and information about this large game fish can be obtained at Messick or Reedville. Bluefish are also taken from these ports; chumming with menhaden is best, although both species are caught trolling with spoons and feathers. Cobia are also taken at Cape Charles along with Channel Bass. Surf fishing from Cape Henry through False Cape; the usual species, as in New Jersey, Delaware and Maryland, are Channel Bass, few Stripers, Whiting, Seatrout, etc.

Write to the Commission of Fisheries, Newport News, Virginia, for additional information. The Virginia Travel Council, Hotel King Carter, Richmond, will furnish a list of fishing ports, fishing spots, and hotels. It will give the names and addresses, and in some instances telephone numbers of reliable boatmen, also prices. Ocean View, just outside Norfolk, is a good fishing port where hundreds of anglers embark daily during the summer season in row boats and power boats, after Spot, Trout, Flounders, Black Sea Bass, Virginia Perch, Croakers, and many others. Other good spots where there are boats, etc., are Chincoteague and Harborton in Accomac County; Glass in Gloucester County, the lower Rappahannock River; Colonial Beach in Westmoreland County.

North Carolina

This state is unrivalled for surf and bay angling. The "islands," mere strips of sand, form the sea coast, and enclose the great bays of Pamlico, Albermarle and Currituck Sounds; from Virginia Beach to Cape Lookout is an unbroken, surf-casting shore except for two inlets. The Sounds produce all the thrills of good bottom angling for salt-water species. Manteo and Wanchese on Roanoke Island, where Sir Walter Raleigh's first settlement was located, are two convenient places to reach via auto, where hotels, good boats, bait and local information can be obtained. Surf fishing from Nag's Head to Oregon Inlet is very good. Oregon Inlet is one of the best known fishing spots along the Atlantic Coast for Bluefish and Channel Bass; also New Inlet, north of Cape Hatteras and Ocracoke Inlet, and Drum Inlet south of the Cape. These islands, much of which are included in the Cape Hatteras National Seashore, are wild, lovely and well-worth the angler's time, and add to the enjoyment of the fishing. Blues and Channel Bass begin to bite about May 1, and continue through June. Good angling begins again around September 1 and continues through October. Whiting or Weakfish, Croakers, Black Drum, Sheepshead, Cabio, Kingfish, and others are taken by most every method during summer months. Anglers visiting these shores should obtain a copy of the Fishing Map of Eastern North Carolina from the State News Bureau, Raleigh.

Marlin, Tarpon, and Bonito are occasionally found off the coast, but better fishing for these species can be found further south. There is a bridge connecting the sand strip along the coast from Nag's Head to Roanoke Island, where some good Weakfish are taken when they are in the Sound, on "hairpin plugs" and spoons. The plug or lure is allowed to drift with the current (tide) and retrieved. Persons allergic to boats will find this whole section ideal.

South Carolina Wildlife Resources Comm.

There is plenty of elbowroom for the surf caster on the South Carolina Coast.

South Carolina

Salt water species found in the inlets and close to shore include Channel Bass, Cobia, Weakfish, Spot, Croaker, Flounder and Whiting, while farther offshore are Mackerel, Bluefish, Amberjack, Dolphin, Barracuda, Blackfish, Grouper, Snapper and some Sailfish and Marlin. Tarpon are found at several areas in July through September, although not numerous.

There has been much expansion in offshore fishing in recent years and charter boats go out to the edge of the Gulf Stream trolling for game fish and bottom fishing for Snapper and Grouper. Most of these are from Little River to Charleston.

There are several dozen fishing piers from North Carolina to below Charleston with the greatest number around Myrtle Beach.

Charter boats are available at Little River, Murrell's Inlet, the Myrtle Beach area, Georgetown and Charleston.

Georgia

Salt-water angling along the Georgia coast has been little publicized, or exploited; however, there are some good angling waters for those who wish to experiment. The usual species—some Stripers, Weakfish, and Blues are taken in the spring. The state published no circulars or bulletins on this form of recreation, but the following is a list of places along the coast where boats, bait, guides and local information can be obtained: Nick's Place, Shellman's Bluff, and Contentment Bluff Fishing Camp, all at Townsend.

Others are: Youman's Place, Midway; Sunberry Lodge Fishing Camp, Dorchester; Roscoe's Fishing Camp, Cresent; Doty's Fishing Camp, Eulonia; Taylor's Fishing Camp, St. Simon's Island; Crooked River State Park, Kingsland; Riverview Hotel, St. Mary's.

There is considerable angling along the Georgia coast during the winter for Black Bass and Weakfish; red and white plugs are good; also live shrimp; Tarpon are taken off shore during the summer months.

The State Game and Fish Commission, State Capitol, Atlanta, will supply a list of fishing spots by counties; however, most of these are for fresh-water angling. Other salt-water ports where boatmen, proper baits, and lodging can be had are: Sapeol River, and Shellman Bluff, east of Darian, both in McIntosh County; Hampton, Little and Turtle Rivers, northeast of Brunswick.

Florida

It is impossible to do justice to Florida angling in any short article; there are many books devoted to the subject, and it is not yet all written. The fishing may be divided into two classes, as in most other coastal states; 1) inland salt-water angling in the bays and estuaries, where Weakfish, Channel Bass, Mackerel, Tarpon, Sheepshead, Snook, Bluefish and many others are taken in some part of the year; and, 2) the deep-sea fishing in the Atlantic

Ocean for Sailfish, Marlin, Swordfish, Amberjack, the Snappers, Tuna, Dolphin, Barracuda, Bonito and countless other species. Almost every well-known saltwater game fish is taken some place in or near Florida. To mention a few: King Mackerel, Dolphin, Ladyfish, Bonefish, Amberjack, the Snappers, Wahoo, Crevalle, Permit, the Drums, Sea Bass, Groupers, etc. *A Guide to Florida Angling,* with map, list of game species, best baits, tackle, tides, and fishing locations for various species can be obtained from the Supervisor of Conservation, Tallahassee. The best known fishing ports are those towns along the coast such as Miami, Ft. Lauderdale, Palm Beach, Stuart, Flagler Beach, Daytona Beach, and scores of others. There are fishing piers at many of the coastal towns. Charter boats are available at most every point. Those interested in bonefishing, will find Rodriques Key and Long Key are good bets. The Mako Shark is sought in Florida waters. One of the best Tarpon waters is Shark River and the best month is June. Tarpon run from April to July; feather jigs and other artificials are good. The Tarpon are hard to hook, and many baits are lost. Lots of fun is had with fly rods and bass lures for small Tarpon in the canals.

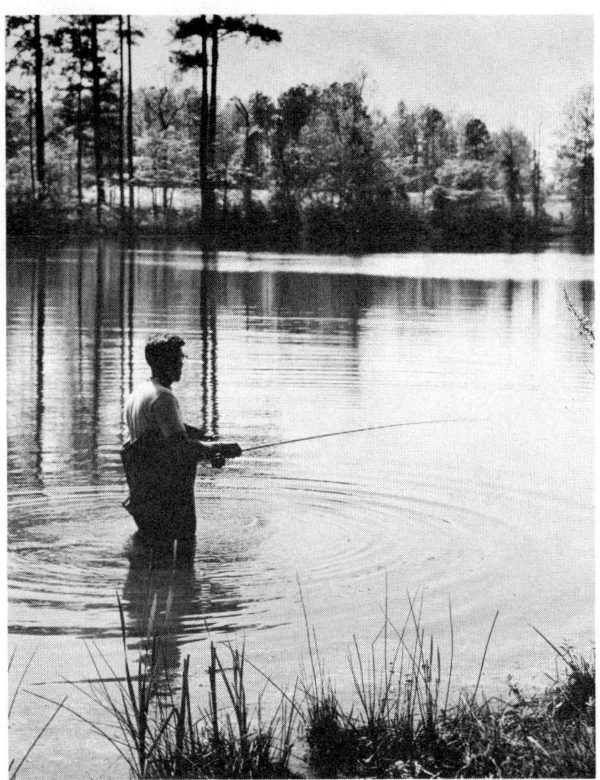

North Carolina Wildlife Resources Comm.

North Carolina has over 40,000 farm ponds, most of which provide good bass and panfishing.

GULF FISHING

The Gulf of Mexico sits like a gigantic fish bowl on the southeastern periphery of the North American continent.

Populated by a seemingly limitless quantity and variety of sea life, this vast fishery equals or exceeds practically any other area on earth of comparable size in the number and species of game fish which may be taken therein.

A careful glance at a map of the Gulf discloses how this wondrous situation came into being. From the southernmost tip of the Florida peninsula clear across the westward sweep of Alabama, Mississippi, Louisiana, Texas, and farther beyond into the Mexican states of Campeche, Yucatan and Quintana Roo, the coastline is broken by a continuous series of shallow, moderate or very deep indentations. Many of these inlets, lakes, bays and lagoons are fed both from the sea and from fresh-water sources, creating a highly fertile estuarine breeding and nursery ground for game fish and the smaller creatures on which they are dependent for survival.

For purposes of discussion, Gulf fishing can be categorized into three sub-topics including off-shore fishing in the open sea, angling along the beaches and other landward boundaries, and the sundry types of inside fishing in protected waters with which the Gulf connects. Each area offers its own peculiarities and fishing opportunities. Depending on geography, environment, ecology and season, the angler's choice may run the gamut from the smallest salt water fish almost to the very largest.

One of the most salutary features of Gulf fishing is that it can be enjoyed, in one form or another, for 12 months out of the year. To be sure, there will be some changes in types of fish to be caught from month to month but throughout the entire range of the Gulf of Mexico, it is possible to find considerable fishing variety in Summer, Fall, Winter or Spring.

Some species of fish encountered in the Gulf are widely migratory while others seem to travel only infrequently, and then not too far.

Among the most popular migrants are King Mackerel, which move northward along Florida's west coast in early Spring, following the coastline to the west and entering Mississippi, Louisiana and Texas waters in early to mid-summer. While many King Mackerel are caught trolling, they offer more enjoyment on spinning and casting tackle, baited with shrimp, Menhaden or cut Mullet which is allowed to drift in the current without a sinker. On the other hand, neophyte anglers who are not familiar with the intricacies of handling bigger fish on light tackle can obtain their early training with King Mackerel by trolling with a light monel metal wire line, and a heavy sinker. A Nylon or feather duster, weighing from two to four ounces, is an extremely effective King Mackerel bait when it is trolled on or near the bottom with the wire line and sinker. Some anglers add to the attractiveness of this rig by hooking a strip of Mullet or Bonito belly behind the duster. King Mackerel will average from 12 pounds up to 50 in Gulf waters. The fish are characterized by a hard, savage strike and an extremely fast initial run during which they might strip 200 to 300 yards from a reel. Occasionally, a hooked King Mackerel will jump straight out of the water, clearing the surface for 10 or 15 feet, and then plunging back in, like a champion diver, with scarcely a ripple.

Bringing in a trophy-sized Tarpon from Gulf waters.

Smaller Spanish Mackerel also abound in the Gulf but are not such notorious travellers as the Kings, which disappear completely from waters of the north Gulf coast at the approach of Winter. Spanish Mackerel can be found throughout the Gulf at all seasons of the year, even though they were once thought to be exclusively a summer fish. They will take a variety of artificial lures including small spoons, jigs, dusters and plugs, either trolled or cast.

One of the most popular and effective methods for fishing Spanish Mackerel is to run close to shore in an outboard speed boat. Rods are readied in advance as the fishermen cruise along looking for flocks of wheeling and diving seagulls. This is an almost certain sign that Mackerel are nearby because the birds like to feed on tiny fingerlings which the Mackerel have herded close to the surface. The technique is to run as close as possible to the fish without frightening them, cutting the motor, and casting into the school.

During the past decade, no single factor has made a more significant contribution toward the development of the Gulf sport fishery than has the petroleum industry which, through the construction of hundreds of offshore oil drilling structures and the dredging of many miles of access canals to oil well sites in the tidelands, has opened up countless new angling areas and opportunities that either did not exist in prior times or could not be properly exploited.

Curiously enough, this valuable by-product of offshore oil was roundly criticized in its early days by sportsmen's clubs and conservation agencies who felt that seismographic operations, involving the detonation of dynamite charges underwater, would damage the fishery resource. To be sure, the explosions did kill many thousands of game fish but whatever harm occurred was purely temporary. In the wake of the seismograph crews came oil exploration companies with their giant drilling "rigs" or structures. The first of these towering steel platforms was erected on the floor of the open Gulf some five miles from Grand Isle, Louisiana in November, 1947. The original platform had not even begun to produce oil before charter boats and privately owned fishing vessels began running out to watch the drilling crews at work. As a matter of experiment, some anglers began dropping lines overboard and found their efforts rewarded by immediate strikes from Pompano, Bluefish, Spanish and King Mackerel, giant Jewfish, Red Snappers and Cobia. It soon became apparent that these popular game fish were attracted to the platforms by the underwater forest of interlaced steel pilings and cross sections used to support the weighty drilling structure.

In the ensuing years, hundreds of additional drilling platforms have been erected all along the Louisiana coast and into Texas waters with as many as 75 new wells being drilled simultaneously every week. After they are submerged only a few days, the steel supports start gathering moss, barnacles and other marine growth on which tiny minnows and fingerlings come to feed. The bigger game fish, in turn, feed on these.

In the days prior to development of the offshore oil industry, Pompano were almost a rarity in Louisiana and Texas waters, being taken along the sandy beaches of offshore islands more through accident than design. "Rig fishing," as it has come to be called, produced drastic changes and in present times, the Pompano has become one of the Gulf Coast's most popular and plentiful game and food fish. Although scattered specimens are caught during the summer months, the Pompano season does not really begin until the onset of colder weather. Catches ranging from 50 to 250 fish per boat are quite common from November through March, when fishing starts tapering off. The proximity of the offshore structures to land attracts a large number of anglers fishing from outboard hulls, as well as a generous sprinkling of bigger private and charter fishing boats. The most effective system is to tie the boat as close as possible to the oil rig and cast beneath the rig where the Pompano congregate. Smaller outboards frequently run between the gigantic steel legs of the structures and moor directly beneath the drilling turntable. Light spinning tackle fitted with weighted bucktail or nylon jigs are cast in the direction from which the current is flowing, and allowed to sink. The angler, meanwhile, retrieves the line only fast enough to recover slack so as to feel the tender nudges of the Pompano when it bites. A tiny piece of shrimp impaled on the hook increases a jig's effectiveness. There is no need for a leader since Pompano have no teeth. On frequent occasions, a Spanish Mackerel or Bluefish will come along and slash through the thin monofilament. The angler should be prepared for this with an ample supply of extra jigs since Pompano strike much better without a steel leader.

The coastal tidelands at night are ablaze with the flickering yellow glare of waste gas being burned off in towering flares. This gas, which comes to the surface with petroleum, constitutes an explosive hazard unless it is properly disposed of. The flares are highly attractive to moths, mosquitoes and other forms of insect life, as well as to shrimp, fingerlings and minnows. Great schools of Bluefish and Spotted Weakfish congregate beneath the flares to feed on these winged and finned creatures. "Fishing the flares" has become a highly popular diversion along the Louisiana and Texas coasts and the catches made under such circumstances frequently stagger the imagination.

The general procedure is to set out for the flares in the late afternoon and wait for the approach of nightfall. Boats are anchored within casting distance of the steel flare pipes jutting straight up out of the water. Spinning tackle or casting rods are ideal for this type of fishing. Bluefish will take practically any type of artificial lure while the Spotted Weakfish are usually more particular, hitting a certain color of plug for awhile and then suddenly changing their temperament. It is virtually impossible to predict in advance what will be the most effective lure on a certain evening and experienced fishermen always carry an assortment of several styles, colors and sizes. Spotted Weakfish may run from one to four pounds, while Bluefish will average from two pounds to five. Flare fishing produces acceptable catches during the Winter but the warmer months are much more productive.

The oil rigs farther offshore attract numerous Cobia during the summer months and many of these fish are taken by fishing parties concentrating on Red Snappers. Cobia give the best account of themselves on light tackle, but heavier lines are recommended when fishing near the rigs because larger fish have the habit of running through the steel pilings and cutting themselves loose on the barnacles.

Bill Ackerman

Joe Brooks with a 7 lb. Bone Fish on Key Largo Flats.

Snappers are found in greatest abundance near the rigs situated in deeper water ranging from 50 to 120 feet. The same holds true for Pompano. The rigs closer inshore, in waters from 15 to 25 feet deep, provide excellent haven for Spotted Weakfish weighing from two to five pounds. These Weakfish prefer to feed on or near the bottom and will strike savagely at deep running plugs and spoons.

Spotted Weakfish are, by far, the most popular single species with Gulf Coast anglers. They are caught in quantity, both by sports and commercial fishermen, in every state bordering on the Gulf, and are present throughout the year.

During the Winter, Spotted Weakfish (commonly referred to in the Gulf states as "Speckled Trout" or merely "Trout" are most likely to be found in the deeper bayous, inlets, lakes or lagoons where they bite avidly on deep running artificials.

In the Spring when shrimp, small Croakers and baby Menhaden begin to appear in inside waters, Spotted Weakfish can be caught on or near the surface using artificial lures and fresh natural bait.

Channel Bass or Redfish also hold a fond spot in the hearts of many Gulf Coast anglers. Channel Bass of heroic proportions are taken occasionally from Gulf waters, but this species generally does not attain the size of Channel Bass caught along the Atlantic capes of Virginia, Delaware and the Carolinas. The largest Gulf fish, weighing from 35 to 50 pounds, are almost always encountered through accident by anglers working some distance offshore from the usual haunts of this species. These bigger Channel Bass run in large schools, and are apparently migrating. The fish swim just beneath the surface so that when the sun is shining, the water takes on a reddish bronze glow from the light reflecting off their burnished scales. At such times, the Bass will be extremely voracious, rushing to strike either natural or artificial baits.

In its more common environment along the sloughs and inlets of the Gulf beaches the Channel Bass' behavior is practically identical to that of his Atlantic Coast cousins. Notoriously nearsighted but fitted by nature with a highly developed sense of smell, the fish will quickly take a bright metal spoon, plug or weighted jig that is cast and retrieved right in front of him. With natural bait, he is particularly fond of chunks cut from fresh Mullet, or a whole shrimp. The only thing to be said against the latter bait is that Catfish also find it appealing and steal it off the hook much easier than they can the cut Mullet.

Johnson Motors

Fishing in open waters proves no chore at all for a 20-foot Cruisers, Inc., cruiser with a pair of Johnson 40-h.p. motors.

Game fish congregate along the tide rips where different densities of water meet but do not immediately mix.

Channel Bass from Gulf waters are locally defined as "rat reds" (weighing up to 5 pounds) and "bull reds" (weighing more than 5 pounds). Smaller fish predominate in the coastal bayous and lagoons where they are caught in abundance during Summer, Fall and Winter. While the water is still warm, they can be found feeding in the grassy shallows along the edges of salt and brackish water lagoons, stirring the bottom as they prod for tiny clams and shrimp and beating the round grass and rushes with their spotted tails. When the weather turns colder, they retreat to the sanctuary of deeper bayous where they remain through the Winter.

Every state bordering on the Gulf of Mexico has its own collection of popular sport fishing centers.

The west coast of Florida, for example, is liberally dotted with prime salt water angling areas. From Key West at the tip of the Florida Keys, ranging northward through the Everglades, around the bend of the state at Appalachicola, and on westward to the Alabama line, anglers have the choice of pitting their skill against dozens of varieties of fish ranging from the bottom-feeding Croaker up to the lordly Tarpon, Sailfish and Marlin. Much of the fishing in the Keys is concentrated in that vast, shallow arm of the Gulf referred to by geographers as the Bay of Florida. From such widely publicized resorts as Marathon, Key West, Islamorada, and Key Largo, light tackle specialists set forth aboard small, shallow draft skiffs in search of Bonefish, Tarpon, Permit, Barracuda and Channel Bass.

The accepted procedure in this style of angling is to stalk the fish and present the lure, either natural or artificial, before the prey can spot the hunter. This is considerably more difficult than it sounds because the extreme clarity of the water, coupled with the natural caution of the fish, requires utmost effort on the part of the fisherman and his boat handler. Outboard motors are used to propel the skiffs within a few hundred yards of where the fish may be expected to be feeding. In the case of Tarpon and Bonefish, the more ambitious guides will cut the motor while still a mile away from a proposed fishing area. Taking up a pole, they stand in the bow and push the skiff stern-first over the shallow flats while the angler prepares to cast at the first sign of a fish. Special

Polaroid eyeglasses and broad-brimmed hats increase the fisherman's chances of seeing the fish, which are extremely difficult to spot without such appurtenances. Special salt water fly, plug and spinning tackle is needed when tangling with the larger Tarpon, while medium weight fresh water rods and reels will suffice for Channel Bass and Barracuda. Bonefish and Permit do not require particularly stiff or heavy rods, but their extremely long runs necessitate using reels with considerable backing line (at least 200 yards).

Boca Grande, on the Northwest fringes of the Everglades, is one of the world's most famous Tarpon centers, with the fishing peak occurring during May and early June. Techniques employed for fishing Tarpon at Boca Grande have been highly refined by local native guides who worked out a system of drift fishing with live bait that produces more strikes than any known competitive method. The charter boats used in this style of fishing are simple, unadorned wooden hulls measuring from 25 to 35 feet, some with cabins but most without. The guides will accept several passengers per boat but prefer fishing not more than two lines at a time. Before leaving the dock, the angler's line is marked in two places, with a green thread woven through the line approximately 40 feet from the end, and a red thread tied at the 60 foot level. A snap swivel is tied to the end of the line. The remainder of the terminal tackle consists of a light six-foot piano wire leader and a sturdy 5/0 Swedish steel saltwater hook.

Fishing is done during daylight and after dark, with an attempt being made to drift from one hour before the tide changes to one hour after. The fish will strike other times, but not nearly as well as during tidal changes. As many as 100 boats may be drifting together through Boca Grande Pass when the Tarpon season is at its zenith. During the daylight hours, lines are baited with small live fish, the most popular being a species called Muttonfish. At dusk and after dark, small live hard blue crabs from which the pinchers have been removed are impaled on the hook to make a most tempting Tarpon bait. A heavy sinker weighing up to five ounces is attached to the top of the leader where it snaps into the swivel. Sinkers may be pinched on to the leader or fixed there with soft copper wire so they will break loose the first time a Tarpon jumps.

Boca Grande guides counsel the fishermen constantly, telling them to either let out or retrieve line so the baits will drift just a foot or so over the bottom. This is the purpose of the colored thread markers. By orienting himself with landmarks on the nearby shores of the pass, the guide can determine the varying water depths almost as accurately as if he were using an electronic depth finder.

It is quite common for a typical party of two anglers fishing at Boca Grande to experience several dozen strikes during the course of an average day. The proportion of fish struck to fish boated is unusually high, undoubtedly due to the use of live bait and the comparatively great depth of the water. Of the thousands of Tarpon brought to gaff at Boca Grande every season, only a few are actually killed and turned over to the taxidermist. The remainder are released after the guide has gaffed them carefully through the bony lower jaw and cut the leader. The errosive action of the briny Gulf water, combined with the natural body acids of the fish, serves to eliminate the hook in a short period of time.

Constant companions of the fishing boats are the graceful, fast swimming porpoises. They show little fear of fishing boats.

Tarpon frequent the entire coastline of the Gulf at some time or another during the year. Those who have observed this species at closest range believe they follow two separate and distinct migrational patterns, with one group of fish moving northward from the Florida Keys, past Boca Grande, Sarasota, and Tampa, and then swinging around westward toward the delta of the Mississippi River. Simultaneously, another migration starts up in Mexican waters, with some fish coming from the Laguna de Terminos at the southernmost end of the Gulf of Mexico, and others joining in from the estuarine waters of Tabasco, Vera Cruz and Tampico. These Tarpon also swim northward in early Spring and by May, they are encountered along the coast of Texas, finally meeting the Florida fish at the Mississippi Delta. Aransas Pass near Corpus Christi in Texas has long been one of the country's favorite Tarpon fishing centers.

During July, August and September, vast schools of Tarpon frequent the inshore waters of the Gulf near the mouths of the Mississippi, where they are found rolling and feeding in the murky waters where the river merges with the Gulf. A few of these fish are taken still fishing with live Mullet or by casting with artificial bait, but the most popular method is to troll with large spoons and salt water plugs.

A seemingly constant companion of the Tarpon is the Jack Crevalle, one of the biggest and hardest fighting members of the Jack family. Widely known for its slashing strike and bulldog-like tenacity, the Jack Crevalle gives an excellent account of itself on light to medium weight tackle.

The largest Jack Crevalle taken in Gulf waters weigh from 30 to 40 pounds. They are almost always encountered in large schools, feeding close in to the coastal beaches on Mullets and Menhaden. The Jack Crevalle is accepted as a food fish in certain rural areas of Central America, but it is too oily and coarse for more refined tastes and all fish should be returned to the water unharmed after they have furnished sport for the angler.

Still another of the popular Gulf fishes is the Snook which is taken in Florida waters as far north as Tampa, and along the Mexican coast as far north as Brownsville. Isolated specimens are caught infrequently at more northerly locations, but the places listed are the limits of their normal range. In addition to being a fine game fish on light tackle, the Snook has white, firm and flaky meat of excellent flavor. In Florida, the Snook became such a popular table delicacy that it was necessary to ban them from the list of salt waters fishes which could be taken commercially.

The greatest abundance of Snook in the United States is located in the Ten Thousand Islands section of the Everglades where the fish find an ideal environment in the brackish, coffee colored water and the maze of mangrove covered islets. During the day, they like to lie well back in the shade of overhanging mangrove branches, darting out to strike at schools of passing Mullets and fingerlings. A noisy surface plug or popping bass bug is needed to lure Snook into the open. When a fish is hooked, the angler has his hands full trying to keep the Snook from running back into the mangrove roots and cutting the line on the barnacles and oysters. At night, many Snook are caught in swift flowing tidal streams where they prefer to gather around the pilings of wharfs and bridges. Live shrimp, live Mullets, and weighted bucktail or Nylon jigs are all good baits for night fishing. Regular bass weight plug, spinning, or fly casting tackle is adaptable to Snook, although a heavier monofilament leader, up to 30 pounds breaking strength, is frequently helpful in withstanding the knife-sharp gill plates of these wonderful game fish.

Another fine light tackle fish found in Gulf waters is the Tripletail. This species is possessed of the curious habit of seeking out pilings, channel marker buoys, seaweed, or almost any type of floating debris which will cast a shadow. The Tripletail is almost always seen lying on its side in the shade of these obstacles, appearing to be asleep or dead. Weighing from just a few pounds to more than 30, the Tripletail receives its name from the greatly enlarged dorsal and ventral fins which extend almost as far back as the caudal, giving the fish the appearance of having three tails. Live or dead shrimp is the most widely used bait in fishing for this species, although Tripletails will take an artificial on occasion.

Along the Mississippi Gulf Coast in the vicinity of Waveland, Bay St. Louis, Gulfport and Biloxi, local fishermen have devised a unique method for fishing Tripletails. Aware of the fish's peculiar liking for untoward objects, these anglers create a small forest of pine saplings in the Mississippi Sound, an inshore body of water separated from the open Gulf by a long series of narrow islands lying from 8 to 15 miles offshore. Saplings are felled in the piney woods in the Spring and transported in skiffs to the proposed fishing grounds where they are thrust into the soft mud bottom so that only the upper branches protrude above the surface. In just a few days, the trunks begin gathering moss and barnacles. Tripletails start to appear around these "stakes," as they are called, anytime from mid-May on through the summer. Fishing the stakes involves a quick, cursory inspection of each tree, with most fishermen having from 50 to 100 of these as their own private domain. Serious arguments ensue if an outsider takes it upon himself to fish another person's stakes without prior permission.

The Tripletail will not always take a bait, even though it is dangled right in front of his nose. In such cases, the angler should leave that particular fish, examine the remainder of the stakes, and

Don Van Pelt

Cobias fight their hardest at boatside or on deck.

return some time later to see if the recalcitrant Tripletail has had a change of heart. Stubborn fish might remain by the same stake for several days without striking, and then suddenly decide to take a bait. Patience has its own reward in this kind of fishing because the Tripletail is one of the most delicious of all salt water fish.

Gulf Coast fishing resorts are well equipped to handle the demands of the simplest or most demanding fisherman. In addition to offering berthing facilities for larger vessels, most municipalities maintain launching ramps or hoists for outboard hulls, and fishing piers for those who prefer to pursue their sport from the sanctuary of terra firma.

Pier fishing is one of the least expensive ways of enjoying the pleasures of Gulf fishing. Access to these piers is either gratis or at nominal cost and the variety of fish that can be taken from them frequently surprises visitors from inland areas who are unfamiliar with the amazing productivity of Gulf waters. In an average day, it is quite common for pier fishermen to come up with a catch containing Spanish Mackerel, Spotted Weakfish, Pompano, Cobia, Sharks, Channel Bass, Groupers (several kinds), Croakers, Bluefish, King Mackerel and even an occasional Tarpon.

Since most fishing piers are built high above the water, there is the problem of how to land a fish that weighs more than the breaking strength of the angler's line. This predicament is solved through the use of a large wooden box which is lowered on a rope and allowed to sink. The fish is then maneuvered above the box, and the latter is hauled up with the fish inside. Another method involves the use of a grappling hook and a rope. It becomes an exciting game to see if the fish can be snagged with the grapple before he breaks the line.

Anglers desiring to venture offshore or into the coastal inlets of the Gulf have the choice of renting a standard charter boat or buying space on one of the commodious "head boats," so called because they accept large numbers of passengers on the basis of so much admittance charge per head.

These rates are comparatively reasonable and include not only transportation but bait and ice. The sportsman is expected to provide his own tackle, or he may rent rods, reels and handlines from the boat operators. Liquid refreshments, sandwiches, sun tan lotion, extra hooks and sinkers, and similar sundries are dispensed from a small commissary also operated by the vessel.

"Head boats" are particularly attractive to fishermen who are anxious to enjoy the pleasures of offshore fishing without going to the expense of hiring their own charter boat or making up a party to share this cost with them. The average trip aboard a "head boat" begins shortly after daylight and continues for approximately eight hours, including running time to and from the fishing grounds.

"Head boats" concentrate on the bottom feeding species including Red Snappers, Mangrove Snappers, and several types of Groupers. The boats are equipped with depth finding devices to facilitate locating the submerged reefs and other underwater obstructions where fish can be expected to congregate. The vessel may either be anchored or allowed to drift, depending on the mood of the fish and the wishes of the captain. It is not unusual for a "head boat" to produce several hundred pounds of edible fish in a normal day. The routine of hauling in smaller fish is frequently broken when someone ties into a Shark, King Mackerel, Tarpon or another of the larger species. Lines become tangled in a hopeless mess as excited fishermen attempt to clear the decks and make room for their fortunate companion to fight the monster he has hooked.

Naples, Sarasota, St. Petersburg, Tampa, Pensacola, Panama City and Destin are among the many Florida resorts offering "head boat" fishing. Still other "head boats" fish from Dauphin Island near Mobile, out of Gulfport-Biloxi in Mississippi, from Empire, La., and from several ports in Texas.

These boats range in size from 60 to 100 feet and are extremely wide in proportion to their length. Most of them are powered with two or three diesel engines and make up in stability and riding comfort what is lacking in speed.

In contrast to the "head boats" are the smaller charter boats which rent for one flat fee. Some of these vessels may be obtained for a half-day's fishing while others must be chartered for a full eight-hour day. The number of passengers which may be carried aboard "head boats" and charter boats is fixed by the Coast Guard and safety regulations are strictly adhered to.

During the summer months, the sport fishing docks along the Gulf Coast teem with activity every afternoon as the fishing fleets return home with large quantities of Cobia, King and Spanish Mackerel, Little Tuna (commonly called "Bonito"), Snappers, and numerous other fish.

The first Cobia are usually seen in these waters in early April, although a few early birds might show up even sooner if there is a mild Spring. The precise date of the Cobia's initial appearance is dependent almost entirely upon the vagaries of the weather. Within a week or two of the first Cobia, the Little Tuna can be expected to appear, followed a month or so later by the King Mackerel. There are definite indications that the migrations of all these species extend from east to west because they are encountered in such a directional pattern along the entire coast.

It has become increasingly popular among Cobia and King Mackerel fishermen to run their boats offshore until they locate a fleet of shrimp trawlers lying at anchor and working over their catch.

During the summer, most deep sea trawlers prefer to drag their nets at night and stop trawling at the first hint of daylight when the shrimp apparently burrow their way into the ooze of the Gulf bottom. Every shrimp caught in a trawl is accompanied by a weird collection of other sea creatures, including Jellyfish, Blowfish, Sea Robins, small to medium sized Croakers, Sand Trout, baby Flounders, Blue Crabs and hardhead Catfish. This conglomeration of fish life must be separated from the shrimp before the latter can be headed and iced for market.

The culls are shovelled overboard in a steady

stream. When several trawlers are anchored in close proximity to each other, game fish soon pick up the trail of this material and in minutes, they are concentrated in a feeding frenzy alongside the shrimp boats.

Charter boatmen and owners of private yachts make arrangements in advance with shrimp trawlers to save all or a portion of their refuse to be used as chum. The trawler will pinpoint the approximate location when he intends to anchor and a rendezvous is agreed upon. Upon meeting the trawler, the sport fishing boat will usually troll for at least an hour, circling around the shrimper and hooking Cobia, King Mackerel and Little Tuna almost as fast as lines can be placed in the water. Lures used for this type of fishing include feather and Nylon dusters, large spoons, and strips cut from the bellies of Little Tuna.

When the shrimp fishermen have completed the task of separating their catch, the sport fishing boats drop anchor a few hundred yards down current from the shrimpers and begin setting up their own "chum lines." One member of the crew on each boat is delegated to chop fish and crabs into small pieces and toss them overside at regular intervals. In the meantime, lines rigged with floats and wire leaders are baited with whole Trout, Croakers or Catfish. It is quite common to see six or eight fishermen on a single boat busily battling Cobia, Mackerel and Little Tuna simultaneously. The fun continues until the chum gives out, the fish become wise, or a big Shark moves in and frightens everything away.

Gulf Coast Cobia average from 20 to 50 pounds but still larger specimens are quite common. Every summer, Biloxi and Bayou LaBatre boats bring in Cobia from 70 to 90 pounds. Little Tuna taken in Alabama and Mississippi waters are almost always bigger than those found in other areas of the Gulf with fish weighing 15 to 20 pounds considered average. On the other hand, Little Tuna captured at Grand Isle, La., less than 150 miles westward, will average only 3-5 pounds.

The Gulf's reputation as a sport fisherman's paradise has been recognized for many years but it was not until fairly recent times that these same waters were known to harbor large quantities of the more exotic big game fishes including Blue Marlin, White Marlin, Sailfish, Wahoo, Barracuda, Blackfin Tuna, Allison or Yellowfin Tuna and Amberjacks. Prior to the early 1950s, an occasional Sailfish or small Blue Marlin was taken by adventurous anglers working far offshore from the Louisiana and Texas coastlines, or in the vicinity of offshore Tampa.

However, it remained for the U. S. Fish and Wildlife Service and its deep sea research vessel *Oregon* to really open the eyes of sportsmen to the pleasant fact that billfish and other fishes of the open sea could be taken virtually in their own back yards. The *Oregon's* assignment of determining the feasibility of fishing Tuna on a commercial basis in the Gulf involved the use of tackle known as the Japanese long line, in reality a very heavy and gigantic trot line measuring some 5000-7000 feet in length and baited with several hundred hooks ranging up to 250 feet.

The long lines brought up not only Allison (Yellowfin) Tuna, but Blue Marlin, White Marlin, Amberjacks, Mako Sharks, and even a few Broadbill Swordfish. The latter had been thought to be almost exclusively a fish of colder waters. These catches stimulated the appetites of several New Orleans sportsmen who organized a trip that produced the first White Marlin and Allison Tuna ever to be taken from Louisiana waters on rod and reel. This early experimental venture conducted off South Pass of the Mississippi River in 1955 was soon followed by many additional catches of White and Blue Marlin, Tuna, Amberjacks, Barracuda and other species.

In the meantime, the tempo of offshore fishing picked up with increasing speed along the Texas coast where Sailfish were found to congregate in great numbers during the summer months, particularly near Port Aransas.

The concentration of billfish and Tuna found near South Pass is believed to result from a combination of factors, chief among which is the proximity of the Continental Shelf to the vast out-pouring of fresh water from the Mississippi. Navigational charts show that the "Shelf," determined by the location at which water depths reach 100 fathoms, is closer to South Pass than to any other point in the entire northern Gulf of Mexico. From only 13 miles out from South Pass, the bottom drops away abruptly from 100 fathoms to 1000 fathoms at less than 24 miles. Violent current sets also occur in this area, sweeping back and forth at speeds ranging up to three and four knots.

PACIFIC SALT WATER FISHING

Approximately 2,000 miles of shore line on the Pacific Coast offer the angler as wide a variety of fish and fishing as is likely to be found anywhere in the world.

From the Mexican border (International Boundary Line) just below San Diego to Canada the shore line, roughly, extends a distance of 1,400 miles. Allowing for the numerous bays and sloughs, 1,800 to 2,000 miles is a safe estimate of the fishable water frontage on which the angler can catch anything from sand dabs to Swordfish. His choice is almost limitless. Surf fishing attracts anglers the year around, barges and piers dot the shore line, especially in southern California, and party boats, charter boats, all day and half-day boats are available to suit the taste, and purse, of all.

This shore line includes the fishable salt waters of Washington, Oregon, and California, most of it paralleled by an excellent highway. Nearby towns provide supplies, most have piers and some sort of boat service. The larger cities provide fishing facilities with interest in the piscatorial sport mounting as one proceeds southward until it becomes a highly specialized business in Southern California where the angler can rent a skiff or charter a de luxe cruiser for extended trips in quest of the big fish to be found in local and close-by Mexican waters. California is one of the few states that requires a license for saltwater angling.

Paul Kalman

Typical scene in the Louisiana and Texas offshore tide-lands. Oil drilling structures, erected in waters up to 200 feet deep, attract vast schools of Pompano, Snappers, Cobia, and other popular game fish.

Roughly, Pacific Coast fishing may be divided into two classes: off-shore fishing, into which falls practically all boat fishing, and in-shore fishing which takes in surf angling, fishing from piers and in bays, sloughs and at the entrance to the streams emptying into the ocean.

This division inevitably causes a certain duplication because many of the fish taken by angling from boats will also be taken by the in-shore anglers. Where such duplication occurs it will be noted, together with any variation of tackle, gear, or methods used in the different locations.

Offshore numerous islands lie within easy reach of the fishing boats which daily carry their quota of anglers who are usually rewarded with excellent fishing.

Tackle and gear is no problem as the piers and boats carry a complete stock of "rent tackle" which may be used for the day at a reasonable cost. Offshore boats have galleys where good food is prepared, and those specializing in the early trips for anglers who want the day-break fishing, have comfortable bunks. On many of these the angler can go aboard the evening before, get a good night's sleep, be awakened in time for breakfast, rig his gear and be ready to fish when the boat reaches the fishing grounds. As boats leave at one, two, three, and four A.M., this offers a decided inducement. Later boats leave on staggered schedules with eight A.M. being the latest. For the anglers pressed for time, there are the half-day or "two trip" boats which leave at six, six-thirty, and seven A.M., and again at twelve noon, twelve-thirty, and one P.M. These boats fish local waters, as do many of the all-day boats which usually leave around six, seven, or eight A.M. due to the short run to the nearer fishing grounds.

In season, barges provide day and night fishing. One can go abroad at any time, stay as long as desired and return as the spirit moves them. Shore boats usually run on an hourly schedule to these barges which are fitted up to accommodate anywhere from fifty to several hundred anglers. The barges have state rooms and bunks, galley, and space for sunbathing or just plain loafing as well as fishing facilities, and many families spend week-ends or even entire vacations aboard them.

Fishing from the barges is generally good but not as good as is to be found from the party and charter boats which can, and do, move about in search of the fish whereas the barges remain in one place. They are anchored on known fishing grounds and provide good fishing but, naturally, less variety than that to be had from the boats.

Piers are available in most waterfront cities and towns, and each has its bait and tackle stand and quota of anglers who get good fishing, with varieties and number slightly below that offered by the barges.

The beaches offer excellent surf fishing, and a sure sign of a good fishing spot is the bait and tackle stands along the highway. These little stands not only provide the right bait and tackle for the fish in that vicinity, but also prove a gold mine of information. Invariably the men and women operating these wayside stands are willing and eager to tell where the fish are biting best, whether to fish the incoming or outgoing tide, and what bait to use. Ask questions, take their advice, and you will not go wrong.

Many places along the coast, bays and sloughs also provide excellent fishing both from the shore and skiffs. In some of these, inland streams end their journey to the sea, and at such places, in season, there is good Steelhead fishing.

What fish will the angler find on his journey from Mexico to Canada?

Depending upon the season, he can catch, to take them in alphabetical order, Albacore, Bass (of many kinds), Barracuda, Bonito, Cabazone, Cod (including many varieties and countless species of the rockfish family), Corbina, Croaker, Dolphin, Grouper, Halibut, Cultus, Mackerel, Marlin, Mullet, Opaleye, Perch (many varieties), Pompano, Rays, Sailfish, Salmon (various species), Sand Dabs, Sharks, Sole, Sculpin, Sheepshead, Skipjack, Steelhead, Striped Bass, Swordfish (Broadbill), Tuna (Bluefin, Yellowfin), Turbot, Whitefish, and Yellowtail.

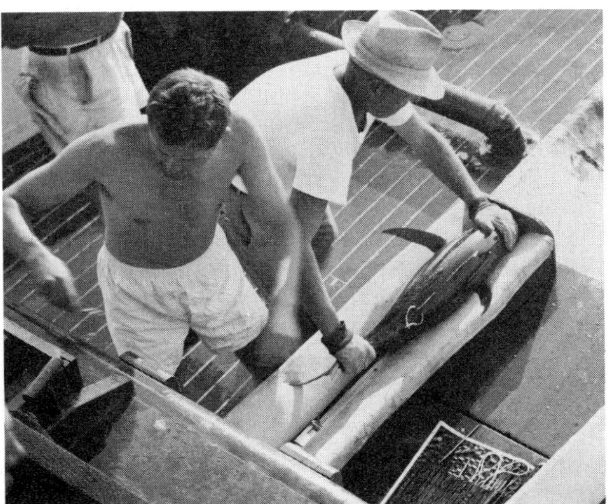

California Dept. of Fish and Game

This Yellowfin Tuna has been tagged off Acapulco by California state biologists and is ready for release. If recovered it will yield valuable information on its growth and migratory habits.

Off-Shore Fishing

ALBACORE

Common names: Longfinned Tuna, Pigs.

A strictly pelagic fish which is entirely unpredictable as to time of appearance and seasons. Ichthyologists admit a complete lack of knowledge of the migrations and habits of this fish; where, when, and how it breeds are as much of a mystery as are the similar facts of its cousins, the tunas. In recent months, some very small tuna, in early stages of development, were reportedly discovered by a scientific expedition in the South Pacific. This could be a hint as to their probable spawning grounds.

Albacore are taken commercially from Alaska to below central Lower California, but sport fishing for them is confined at present to the area between the Santa Barbara Islands on the north and Ensenada on the south. Principal concentrations of boats providing the angler with an opportunity to take these fish are out of San Diego (Point Loma), where party and charter boats are available, Oceanside, San Clemente (the town), Newport-Balboa, Long Beach, Wilmington, San Pedro, Redondo, Ocean Park, Santa Monica, Malibu, Hueneme, and Ventura. From the Channel Islands only Catalina provides boats for the anglers. These are strictly charter, trolling, no live bait.

Method of fishing: from the party boats and most charter boats, live bait fishing prevails. Boats troll feather jigs until the schools are located and thereafter they use live bait (anchovies) until the school is lost when they resume trolling in search of another school.

Most boats "run a chum line" in an effort to find the elusive Albacore. A chummer sits atop the live bait tank, throws over one anchovy at a time, intently watching astern the while. When fish are seen to break on the chum or fish are picked up on the jigs, several scoops of bait are dumped over at once, the boat is stopped and anglers start fishing with live bait.

It is of the utmost importance that the *first few fish hooked are not lost* as a lost fish usually means the departure of the entire school. As long as one or more Albacore remain hooked, the school will stay around. The name *pigs* is given them because they bleed so profusely. Blood in the water is bad, attracting sharks which scatter the fish and usually ending the fishing.

Equipment usually used is as follows: A live-bait boat rod or Calcutta is preferred—7½-to-8-foot tip of split bamboo, glass or metal, longer with the Calcuttas; A locking reel seat; 200- or 250-yard reel; 9- or 12-thread line (or equivalent in Nylon); wire leaders; hooks from No. 4 to 5/0 depending on the size and voracity of the fish. There are times when a very small hook and extremely light single strand leader are needed and times when the fish will take anything thrown at them.

This is a highly prized fish, terrific fighter, excellent eating, fresh or canned. Most anglers use pressure cookers to can their fish. The season is generally somewhere between June and October but they may show up at any time and may fail to appear at all. They have been taken in each month. Runs usually last several weeks, may last only a few days but may extend for months. This is a totally unpredictable fish.

A close-up of an Albacore as it is being lifted over the rail. Note long pectoral fin and large eye. Hook is visible in the mouth and part of the jig seen.

PACIFIC BARRACUDA

Common names: Scooter, Snake, Barrie.

Largest catches made from the live bait boats but plenty are taken from barges, piers, charter and trolling boats, and skiffs. A rugged customer, ready to meet all comers it will take live bait, plugs, spoons, feathers, bone jigs. It puts upa good scrap, especially on light tackle, is an excellent food fish. It is popular when smoked and anglers are starting to can them.

This is an all-season fish with best catches usually made from March through September.

RANGE: from Alaska south, well into Mexican waters, but seldom reported taken north of Point Conception. Heaviest landings from San Pedro south to San Diego; fair to good fishing out of Redondo, Ocean Park, Santa Monica, and Malibu. Plentiful for the boats fishing island waters. No season but sportsmen have limit and size restrictions rules which may be changed by the Fish and Game Commission at their discretion.

BASS

Under the general heading of *Bass* the angler will find several species, and while many of them are mainly inshore, bay and slough fish, some of them are taken from the party boats, charter boats, and those fishing offshore waters and therefore fall under both headings.

CALIFORNIA BLACK SEA BASS *is* a true bass, a game fighter and grows to enormous size; from 100 to 300 pounds is average and 500- and 600-pounders are recorded.

These fish are commonly, and incorrectly, called *Jewfish,* causing anglers to neglect them. The *Jewfish* is a grouper and rates very low both as a game and food fish. The Black Sea Bass, frequently called Giant Black Sea Bass, is a fine food fish, and is very game. It is found over a wide range,

Calif. Div. Fish & Game

Albacore. Note large eye, a feature of the tunas. The extremely long pectoral fin is the distinguishing mark of the albacore.

from below the Mexican Border (Cedros Island is famous for them) northward to the Farallon Islands, although reported not common above Point Conception. This is another fish which probably is to be found the entire length of the Pacific Coast, but lack of exploitation provides little knowledge of other areas.

They are fished for with heavy tackle by most anglers but have been taken on light tackle and even three-six.

They inhabit fairly deep water, usually 10 to 100 feet and are found around rocks, old wrecks, pilings, kelp beds, etc. Anacapa Island (of the Santa Barbara group) is famous for them. Numerous at the Coronado Islands, found at San Clemente Island and Catalina, as well as along the shore line from San Diego to Ventura. A bottom feeder generally taking dead bait because its huge bulk prevents its catching live fish, it prefers live bait if it can get it. A live whitefish is the best bait, but Mackerel, Barracuda, and Halibut are excellent. Two small Halibut, 2 to 5 pounds each, sewn back to back so that a white side is always visible are good.

The food value is high but the liver should not be eaten as it is highly toxic and will cause a breaking out of boils and may cause serious illness. This is believed due to its high vitamin content. The liver brings a high price because of this.

It is taken all year but best catches usually are made from March through September.

California Kelp Bass, with common names of Rock Bass, Sand Bass, and Cabrilla, are taken from the live-bait boats in large numbers; it will hit almost any fresh water plug, will take flies, and puts up an excellent fight on light tackle. It is found principally around the kelp beds, and the commercial cutting of kelp in California is a serious threat to this fish.

The islands provide better bass fishing than the mainland because heavy over-fishing by both commercial and sport fishermen, and the cutting of the kelp beds has depleted them shore-side. The Santa Barbara Islands, Catalina, San Clemente provide good bass fishing throughout the year with heaviest catches being made during the summer.

California Sand Bass is very similar to the Kelp Bass, found in the same area (both the Sand Bass and the Kelp Bass are taken from central California southward well into Mexican waters) and taken on the same kind of gear. They are frequently referred to as "rock bass". The Sand Bass, as its name indicates, will be found in greater numbers over a sandy bottom and not so numerous around kelp beds.

Red Spotted Rock Bass or Spotted Sand Bass is rarely taken by the live-bait boats but occurs frequently enough to be included in both classes. Found mostly from Southern California to Mazatlan, Mexico, it is a hook and line bait fish.

California White Sea Bass. Not a bass at all but a member of the croaker family, this fine fish is a close relative of the Atlantic Coast Weakfish. It is taken from Alaska to the Gulf of California, but is not numerous north of Point Conception. This is another fish furnishing sport all year, but best catches are made during the summer and fall months.

Most of these fish are taken by the live-bait boats in Southern California waters with all of the Islands being productive. The great submerged kelp beds of the mainland are also a favorite feeding ground of the big fish. Live bait is best with large sardines or small mackerel being favored; regular tackle is used, the only concession being the use of larger hooks, 3/0 up to 5/0 and even larger, and a heavy, twisted wire leader. A sinker is necessary at most times. White Sea Bass run

A 337 lb. Black Sea Bass. (Excellent example of giant Black Sea Bass, light tackle used. Caught by Gail Thompson at Malibu in 1941.)

large, 50- and even 60-pounders being taken and from 25 to 45 pounds a frequent occurrence.

The young of these fish are incorrectly called "sea trout," and are protected as to size and number which may be taken. Considered one of the best food fishes, it is also a fine fighter, can be taken from piers and even the shore. At Avalon, Catalina, they have an annual White Sea Bass Derby for fish taken both from the shore and by boats. Casting from Pebbly Beach proves very effective, with night being the best time. Large wooden plugs of red and white are killers. Trolling along the edge of kelp beds with a flying fish or large spoon is popular. The big fish lie in the kelp with their heads just protruding, awaiting the passing of some luckless fish. At times one can see large schools on or near the bottom. Experienced skippers watch for these and, when they locate them, "chum them up" around the boats; thus producing some sensational catches.

BONITO

Bonitos fall into several classes and are listed as Pacific Bonito, California Bonito, Mexican Bonito, and Chilean Bonito. All were formerly listed as members of the mackerel family, which includes the Tunas, Skipjack, and Albacore. No matter how the scientists classify these groups, sportsmen are going to consider them in the same group because they look alike, are found in the same areas and at the same time and, most important of all, are in the same behavior group.

The Bonito (California), commonly called *Striped Tuna,* is frequently mistaken for the Skipjack, and their appearance is remarkably alike. The novice can easily determine if he has taken Bonito or Skipjack—the Bonito has teeth, the Skipjack does not.

Bonitos are avid feeders, will readily hit feather lures, trolled or cast; cedar, bone, and metal jigs are effective for trolling and live bait is the most popular and deadly method of fishing for them, but the use of a "Bonito Splasher" is popular among sportsmen and commercial fishermen. This "splasher" consists of a length of leader wire of 3 or 4 feet with a round block of wood or a 3-inch cork used about 1 foot from the swivel and a feather lure attached to the other end of the leader. The wood or cork has a hole bored through it into which is inserted a lead sinker to give casting weight. This outfit is cast out and retrieved in violent jerks, the resultant splashing causing the Bonito to go wild and strike the feather, evidently under the impressions the splashing is caused by another fish after the lure. Frequently this splasher is attached to a cane pole and the angler flails the water with it. The Japanese use a cane pole which they split out, fan wise, much like a bamboo lawn rake; with this they beat the water to attract both Skipjack and Bonito. Frequently Bonito can be attracted by beating the water with the tip of the rod and then pulling a feather through the same area.

Bonito and Skipjack are both good food fish, more prized canned than eaten fresh, largely due to lack of knowledge of proper cooking methods. They are excellent smoked. They will hit a fly or spinner readily when chummed up. The White Miller, Scarlet Ibis, or Silver Doctor are all deadly flies and any bright colored one will take them. Small spinners are good and the fresh water bass fishermen will find they will hit his bass plugs savagely and fight hard; red and white, red and yellow are the best combinations. Be sure to have plently of line as these fish take long runs when hooked on this truly sporting tackle.

Island Photo Service

Alfred H. Bombard of Catalina Island with his 46 pound White Sea Bass taken on three-six tackle. This fish is within twelve ounces of the worlds record.

Bonito and Skipjack are reported from the Oregon Coast line to at least Magdalena Bay for the Bonito and to Chile for the Skipjack; they are rare above Point Conception. Season is throughout the year with late summer being the most productive. On rare occasions they are caught from piers but are generally taken from the party boats fishing for Tuna, Yellowtail or other "blue-water" fish. In weight they will average between 5 and 10 pounds but larger ones have been taken.

DOLPHIN

The Dolphin is found reportedly from the Columbia River to Peru (Walford), but it will be found generally, on the rare occasions when it makes an appearance, from the Coronado Islands just below San Diego to Catalina. It is a beau-

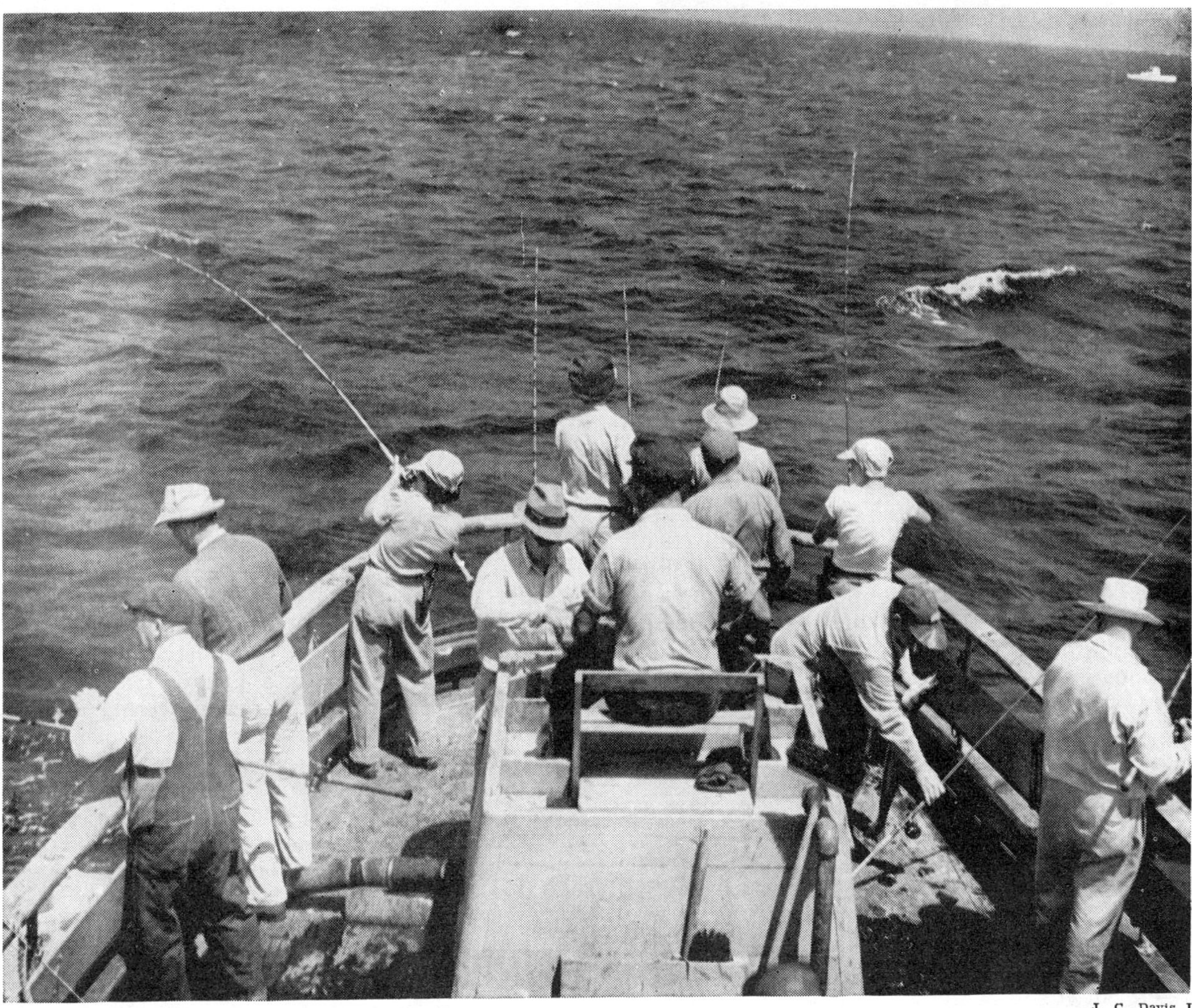

J. C. Davis II

Typical action scene on a live bait boat in Southern California waters. The chummer sits atop the bait tank where he throws live bait overhead to hold the fish around the boat. Pipe in rear of tank pumps steady flow of seawater into tank; pipe on deck carries off overflow.

tiful fish, extremely fast and always found in deep water, usually around beds of floating kelp. It will hit trolled feather lures and goes crazy when chummed up with live bait. They are great sport when taken on light tackle. It is a delicious food fish which, until recently, was considered poisonous. It is frequently taken by Marlin fishermen as the Dolphin likes flying fish. When hooked on heavy tackle, it affords no sport.

Mid-summer to early fall are the best times to look for the Dolphin.

PACIFIC MACKEREL

Listed as the only member of the mackerel family in California waters, the Pacific Mackerel, commonly called the Greenback Mackerel formerly despised by most sport fishermen, has become popular in proportion to its rapid decrease. Heavy commercial over-fishing has depleted it almost to the vanishing point.

An excellent game fish on light tackle, it will take feather lures, flies, spinners, and live or cut bait and put up a terrific fight; a great sport on a fly rod. It is good eating; excellent salted or smoked.

It is taken both from the live-bait boats and along the shore with piers, barges, and small boats providing plenty of action and is taken all year, but heaviest catches are reported from September through December. It is numerous all along the coast, but the heaviest fishing is probably done from San Diego to Ventura.

MARLIN, STRIPED

This is one of the greatest of the big game fish of the Pacific and is taken from Mexican waters to at least as far as Santa Barbara. In size, it ranges from slightly below 100 pounds up, mostly between 150 and 300, but they have been taken on rod and reel well above this. A 692-pounder taken by Alphonse Hamann of Balboa holds the record but even larger Marlin have been seen. From San Diego to Avalon, the main grounds for this fish, the season varies, but it is seldom taken before July. August, September, and October are the best months, and November frequently has furnished good fishing.

This fish taken entirely by trolling by charter boats which specialize in this sport, furnishing tackle and gear if needed. Heavy tackle, a 16-oz.

rod tip, 500 yards of 24 thread linen line, or its Nylon equivalent (72 lbs. test) on a 9/0 reel being best. Fighting chair and rod harness are needed. Flying fish is the preferred bait, but mackerel, mullet, small bonito, sardines, sauries, and strip or cout bait are used at times with good effect. They will frequently hit an albacore feather but are seldom landed on this gear. The leader should be of stainless steel twisted wire, 15 feet in length; and hooks should range from 5/0 up with an 8/0 about average.

Charter boats, manned by experienced Marlin fishermen are available from San Diego, Newport-Balboa, Avalon, Long Beach, Wilmington, and San Pedro. Fare ranges from $40.00 to $65.00 (in some few instances slightly higher).

Light and even 3/6 tackle is used by the experts but not advised for the beginner.

Black Marlin are relatively rare but have been taken at La Paz and some have been hooked off Balboa and Catalina, but few landed. It is a much thicker fish, distinguished by a short bill, and runs to good size. Apparently it is becoming increasingly numerous. The same method of fishing the same gear is used as with the Striped Marlin. It is not taken often enough to establish a season.

SAILFISH, PACIFIC

This fish is taken out of Guaymas and La Paz, Mexico, during the spring and summer months; there are no authentic records of it being taken off the coast of Southern California, although some ichthyologists list it as ranging north to Monterey.

It is strictly a light-tackle fish, and taken trolling using strip bait, feather lures, small mackerel, sardines, mullet, and squid, but most anglers prefer cut bait. A spectacular fighter, jumping repeatedly it is very tricky to hook. Many anglers release the fish after enjoying the battle as it is usually hooked in the jaw, and suffers no ill effects. Not especially good as a food fish but it is highly prized for its gameness.

SHARKS

The Mackerel Shark group includes the Mackerel Shark, Man-eater Shark (Great White Shark), and the Porbeagle. The Mackerel Shark, commonly called the Mako, is not too common. The Bonito Shark differs so slightly from the Mackerel Shark that only an expert can tell them apart. It ranges from below the Mexican border to an undetermined northerly point and is common in all Southern California waters. A vicious, hard fighter, taking almost anything for bait, it is a great nuisance when fishing Marlin. It jumps and fights hard. It is excellent eating and is preferred over Marlin by many.

The Porbeagle Shark is often called Mackerel or Bonito Shark, teeth are the best distinguishing characteristic of the sharks. Range appears to be northward from the northern portion of California.

The Hammerhead Shark, is easily distinguished by its odd, hammer-shaped head. It ranges from Mexico northward to at least Santa Barbara. Frequently encountered when fishing for Marlin or Broadbill Swordfish, it will take any bait readily and puts up an excellent fight. Zane Grey rated its fighting ability with that of the Broadbill.

The White or Man-eater Shark, is rare but encountered often enough to be included here. Attains a length of at least 40 feet. Less numerous than the Hammerhead, it is found in the same range, northward from Mexico to at least Monterey, California. It will take almost any trolled bait and is a hard fighter.

The Thresher Shark has a tail as long as or longer than the rest of the body. Fairly common from San Diego northward to Oregon but it is most numerous in Southern California waters. Grows to great size but most Threshers taken are medium size. Spectacular jumper, good fighter, it is excellent eating; feeds mostly on small school fish such as anchovies and sardines. They are frequently caught by anglers on live bait boats.

The Tiger Shark is extremely rare above the Mexican border, not likely to be encountered by the sport fisherman.

Heavy tackle essential to successful shark fishing. Use extra long leaders (30 feet), large hooks attached to the leader by a foot or two of shark chain as these fish have powerful teeth and jaws and can cut the ordinary leader easily. Unfortunately, most sharks will be hooked while fishing for other fish, and much gear will be ruined. Exercise extreme care when handling sharks; they are always dangerous and can inflict painful (and serious) wounds. Best method is to sever the vertebrae just back of the head immediately. Even so, watch out for the jaws which will continue to snap.

Two excellent specimens of Sailfish.

Mary C. Davis

An unusual picture of a Blue Shark biting his own tail. Sharks, when caught, snap at everything within reach which makes it dangerous to gaff them unless the angler knows how to handle them. Note the rows of teeth in the jaws.

SWORDFISH

The Swordfish is a world-wide species, the only member of the swordfish family. It follows the warm and temperate seas; on the Pacific Coast it is known to go as far north as Oregon, but heaviest fishing is done from San Diego to the Santa Barbara Islands.

In size, it is known to exceed 1000 pounds, although it is rare than one of above 500 pounds is landed by anglers. A heavy-tackle fish taken by anglers on charter boats or from private craft equipped for big game fishing, it puts up a terrific battle frequently escaping by wearing out the gear. An excellent food fish, it is also the most highly prized of the big game fishes.

The angler hunts this fish which is recognized by its fins as it cruises along the surface of the ocean. When located a bait is put over and fed to the fish, an extremely cautious and a fastidious feeder, it generally refuses the bait. The hooking of one is an occasion; the landing of one an event.

Commercial fishermen harpoon these fish and are rapidly exterminating them.

TUNA, BLUEFIN

While the usual season is listed as from May to December, this popular fish may be encountered any time between these months, or not at all! Its frequency, or infrequency, seems to be attributable to heavy commercial purse seining in the waters below San Diego, thus cutting off the schools before they reach our waters.

Some years see excellent fishing for the Bluefin, but of late the runs have been poor. Scientists lay this condition to cycles, but sportsmen insist it is over-fishing. Ranging in size from 10 or 15 pounds up to 35 pounds and, in rare instances larger, this fish has become very hook shy and anglers must resort to very light tackle; 18- to 30-pound test line, fine single-strand wire leaders and small hooks (as small as #6 or even #8 being needed). An extra long leader, frequently 6 feet or longer, is used. Sardines and anchovies appear to be the best bait. When they will take sardines, (infrequently in recent years), a larger hook may be used. A very long, light, and whippy rod is required, together with a free-spool reel with 300-yard capacity which must be very easy to cast.

Plastic spools are essential and a star drag is needed. These fish were formerly taken well above the 100-pound mark; the Tuna Club record is 251 pounds. Much larger fish have been seen, but all efforts to take them failed. Anglers claim this is due to the great depth of the ocean where the tuna are found. The big fish are taken by trolling a flying fish, and a kite is used to keep the bait skipping and off to one side away from the wake of the boat which appears to frighten them.

Small Bluefin (school) Tuna are taken from live bait and charter boats, generally close to the Coronado Islands or Catalina. Some years they have schooled close to the mainland side.

TUNA, YELLOWFIN

This is the rough and tough member of the Tuna family, not finicky about tackle, gear or bait, and a hard fighter. Caught from the live-bait boats and the charter boats it also takes a trolled lure, as does the Bluefin.

Discarding scientific data, the easy way to distinguish the tunas is by the pectoral fins. The Albacore has very long pectorals, extending beyond the front of anal fin. The Bluefin has short pectorals which extend only to the 11th or 12th spine of the dorsal. The Yellowfin has pectorals which reach just beyond the *front* of the second dorsal. Size averages from 25 pounds to above the 100-pound mark (450 pounds has been recorded but 50 or 60 pounds is large). Yellowfin are taken throughout the year but heaviest catches are made in summer and fall months; however, they have been very scarce in recent years. Both the Bluefin and Yellowfin are believed to be found as far north as Oregon and to occur throughout the year. Catches above Point Conception are rare.

Heavier gear is indicated for the Yellowfin, such as 36-pound test line, twisted wire leader, hooks to 5/0. Sardines and anchovies are best bait.

Spence D. Turner

Blackfish surfacing near boat.

WHITEFISH, OCEAN

The Ocean Whitefish is taken from the live-bait boats usually around the islands: the Coronados, San Clemente, Catalina, Santa Barbara, Anacapa (especially good place for them), and other of the Santa Barbara Islands. Its range probably extends still farther north. It is a bait fish taken at considerable depth by use of live or cut bait. As it has a small mouth and small hook is best. Be careful of the gill covers (opercle) which are razor sharp and will cut to the bone. A game fighter (called "bottom yellowtail" in the northern California area). It is excellent eating; while taken all year, winter is usually the best time to fish for them. They make excellent bait for big Black Sea Bass.

YELLOWTAIL, PACIFIC

Probably the most popular of the larger game fish taken from the live-bait boats, it is found from below the Mexican line to the Santa Barbara Islands, rarely much farther north. It is a school fish taken from live-bait boats which concentrate on this fishing. San Diego holds an Annual Yellowtail Derby with prizes bettering the $10,000 mark. A beautiful fish, wise and hard to entice to the bait, it puts up terrific fight when hooked. It ranges in size from 6 or 8 pounds (rarely taken much smaller) up to 50 and 60 pounds in southern California waters; grows much larger, probably approaches close to the 100-pound mark. But these big fish, although sometimes hooked, always seem to prove too much for the tackle, and the angler. Some remain in local waters all year and they have been caught in deep water (800 feet) in mid-January. The best season is from March through September. They may not be taken by purse seine and round haul nets and are restricted as to size on the commercial market in an effort to save them from depletion. A good fish food is very important to sport fishing in California.

The Yellowtail is definitely not a surf fish, as is sometimes erroneously reported.

Inshore, Bay, and Slough Fishing

A great many of the fish taken from the live-bait boats can be caught from piers, rowboats and even from the shore. Where this occurs and these fish have been listed in "Offshore Fishing," it is noted.

TACKLE AND GEAR

For real surf fishing one should use a salt-water spinning rod or surf rod, surf reel (free spool of about 250-yard capacity—line, star drag) and 18 to 30 pound test line. The surf rod as known to

Typical day's catch of White Marlin and Sailfish at South Pass of the Mississippi River.

Fishing with a fly rod is popular with some anglers on the live bait boats.

Eastern fishing is not suited to the West coast. It should be at least an 8-foot tip with double grip, having a butt of 30 inches. Large guides should be used for easy casting. A sand spike to hold the rod should have a hook for flashlight or lantern. Additional equipment should be included. Small gaff, a tackle box containing a knife to prepare bait (it should be strong enough to open clams and mussels), belt socket, extra reel or spools of additional line, leaders, sinkers, pliers, hooks, etc.

Excellent sinkers can be made from cigarette tobacco sacks or made of muslin. The amount of weight is regulating by the sand used, and the muslin is sand colored, rolls around with the washing waves, and does not scare the fish. If the gear hangs up on rocks, the sack tears, and the sinker only is lost. Use 3 hooks on a gut leader, bait each with a different bait: i.e. sand crab on one, mussel on another and rock worm on the third. When the bait the fish are feeding on, is determined, stick with that one.

Consult the little bait houses along the beach; whenever one is found it means there is good fishing nearby; the operators will be glad to tell *where* they are biting, on *which tide* and what *bait* to use and all important points. Buy a few hooks from them, make friends, they can help you a lot.

CORBINA, CALIFORNIA

This fish is a member of the croaker family, in which are found the Spotfin, Yellowfin Croakers, White Sea Bass, Queenfish, and Kingfish. It is one of the most highly prized of the surf fishes, protected by law with no sale permitted and may be taken in California only by angling. Fishing season: best in summer but is best taken throughout the year on sand crabs, mussels, clams and rock or pile worms. It is found on smooth sandy beaches with best catches on incoming tide, quite close in as they follow the incoming waves to pick up the food released by the breakers. Very game and excellent eating. Range: Point Conception south to Mexico.

CROAKER, YELLOWFIN

Belonging to the same family as the Corbina, it has about the same range. A highly prized sport fish, it is fully protected with no netting or sale. Late summer is the best season but can be taken all year. Frequently taken from live-bait boats, piers, barges and rowboats as well as by those fishing from the shore. Same bait, tackle, gear, tides and times as for the Corbina are used.

CROAKER, SPOTFIN

All data essentially the same as for the Yellowfin.

All three of these fish are excellent food fishes, very game, highly prized by sportsmen, they are among the very few salt water fishes protected in California. They are apparently unknown farther north but may be in more northern waters. Lack of fishing probably accounts for many fish being reported as unknown in these northern waters, although some of them undoubtedly exist there in good numbers. Some day some Columbus among fishermen will develop these great fishing waters.

STRIPED BASS

This fish, not indigenous to the Pacific Coast was introduced in 1879 with a small planting which was followed by another in 1882. Only 435 fish were planted, but this small beginning has grown into fabulous schools which have spread from San Francisco Bay, scene of the original planting, to southern California and the Columbia River. Coos Bay, Oregon, provides excellent fishing. It undoubtedly extends beyond this in a northerly direction as migrations are reported extending each year, but the southerly limits are rather definite, and it is not common below Monterey, although a few are occasionally taken as far south as Newport Bay. Efforts to introduce it in Southern California ocean waters and in the Salton Sea both failed, probably due to poor planning and handling in both instances.

Formerly a very important commercial fish, it was taken off the market in 1935 and is now an exclusive sport fish protected by size and catch limits.

Most important of the salt-water sport fish in the northern part of California, it is taken all year with regulation light tackle and the "live-bait-boat" type of rod being preferred. Chunks of sardine are the most popular bait, but it readily hits a trolled plug, the jointed red and white variety being best.

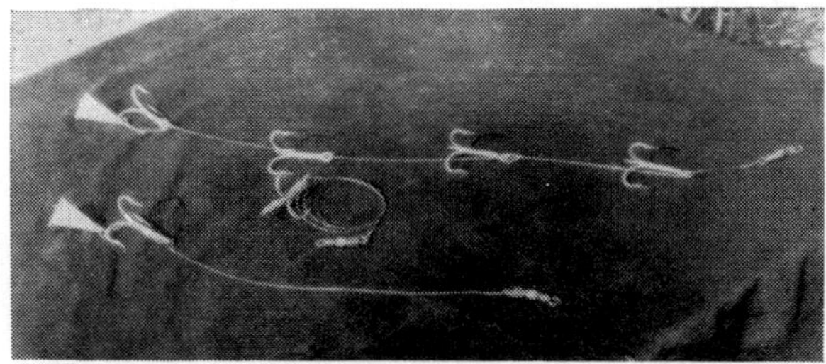

J. C. Davis II

Large triple hooks, barbs filed off, points needle sharp. Sinker is used below hooks which are attached to a wire leader and swivel. Most anglers prefer one (triple) hook, some use two or three as illustrated. (Mullet Rig Used at Salton Sea).

It is caught from charter boats, private cruisers, outboards and row-boats and, particularly along the rivers and in sloughs and backwaters, from the shore, jetties, and bridges. An excellent food and game fish, it deserves the attention of the angler.

PERCH

There are about 18 salt-water species found in California and farther north. Their distribution is from Alaska to Lower California (Mexico) with an all-year season. All are viviparous. Their general similarity makes it difficult to distinguish one from the other. They are commonly taken from piers, rock points along the shore, or boats fishing in very close to shore. Shrimps, mussels, clams, and cut bait are used. Some will readily hit a small spinner, the airplane being best, and put up an excellent fight on fly rod or similar light tackle, with gut leaders and very small hooks. They are excellent eating.

POMPANO, CALIFORNIA

This fish is a member of the butterfish family is not a true pompano. Frequently found in the live bait tanks, it is good bait for Yellowtail. It is also an excellent eating fish and can be caught from the piers quite close to shore. Very small hooks and cut bait are needed; the soft part taken from the nose of the shovel-nosed shark (guitar fish) being the best bait. Mussels and clams, small pieces of mackerel are also used. Fairly rare, they are most frequently taken during the summer months. Fairly rare, they are.

MACKEREL

See in "Offshore Section."

MULLET

An astounding game fish Mullet is found in California's Salton Sea, a fabulous body of water more than 200 feet below sea level. These fish are reportedly taken on bait and flies, but verification is missing except in one instance where a record of 17 were taken on ordinary garden worms by W. P. "Park" Burritt of Niland, California. They grow to a size of 25 pounds but 10 to 15 pounds is average and are taken by snagging, using a special heavy triple hook with barbs filed off and points ground to needle sharpness. It is necessary to carry a file and frequently sharpen the points as they are dulled by the heavy scales which form an almost impenetrable armor. Hooks made only by Earl Henking of Niland, are essential to this sport. The Mullet school at the mouths of the New and Alamo Rivers preparatory to going up stream to spawn. Heavy Calcutta rods, free-spool reels of 250- to 300-yards capacity needed, and 12- or 15-thread line work best. A very hard fighter causing plenty of broken tackle the Mullet is an excellent food fish. There is no season or size limit but there is a limit of 6 per day. They are taken commercially during certain seasons by netting. In late 1949 an effort was made to stop commercial fishing of Mullet due to depletion. Mullet Island, 6 miles out of Niland is the best place for these fish, where boats, cabins, and camp grounds are available. Mul-

J. C. Davis II

Boating Mullet at Alamo River, Salton Sea. Note heavy rods necessary in this unusual sport of "jigging" for these fish.

let fishing, a very rugged sport, attracts fishermen from hundreds of miles around. They are taken all year, but the best season is October through November.

Small Mullet are found in the bays and sloughs all along the coast from below the Mexican border northward to about Long Beach, perhaps farther north, but fishing is undeveloped. These fish are small and are used for bait in marlin fishing and are a popular food fish. They will take a hook baited with green moss and sometimes sweetened dough. They are excellent sport on a fly rod and they jump repeatedly. Extra light tackle is needed for these small mullet as is a fly rod, a gut leader, and a trout hook.

RAYS AND SHARKS

Sharks are treated of in "Offshore Section." They are also frequently taken from piers, in the surf, bays and sloughs. The rays, Sting-ray, (round sting ray) and Bat Sting Ray, have an unusually long spine or "stinger" on the tail, from which they derive their name. The sting is poisonous and very painful. Immediate application of spirits of ammonia, soaking the injured part in hot salt water is recommended: *See a doctor.* Fishermen wading the bays and sloughs sometimes are stung. There is little danger if care is exercised in handling them if taken incidentally when fishing for halibut and other bottom fish. The wings are good eating.

SKATES, GUITAR FISHES

Skates and Guitar fishes (shovel-nosed shark) belong to the same sub-class as the sharks, and are taken from piers, the surf, in bays and sloughs while fishing for other bottom fish. Skate wings are good to eat.

They are taken all year and all along the coast to Alaska although fairly rare above San Francisco. They are usually caught on regular surf tackle, but if fishing specially for them, heavier gear is recommended.

HALIBUT

The California Halibut is one of the most popular of ocean fishes being taken during every month of the year being caught from boats, barges,

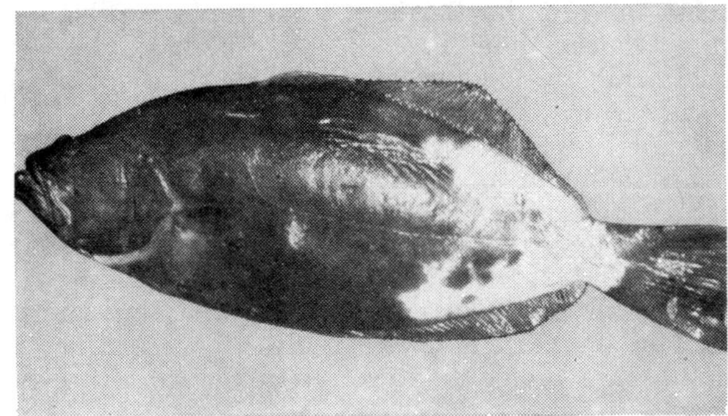

J. C. Davis II

Albino Halibut are sufficiently rare to be noteworthy. Usually brown on top and white underneath, this specimen, caught at Redondo Beach, California, has decided albino markings. Aside from the unusual coloring, it was in no way different from ordinary Halibut.

piers, rowboats, along the shore, in bays and sloughs. No special gear is needed, although proper tackle will improve the catches and the sport will be more enjoyable. A limber rod, 9-thread line, gut leader and Siwash hook is the best combination. The sinker should be *below* the leader which is attached to the line by a swivel at a height approximately the length of the leader. Anchovies, sardines, and herring are best baits. Halibut will hit a shiny, metal lure, and will take underwater plugs (especially in the bays and sloughs) with red and white deep diving plugs producing best results. The usual method employed in boat fishing is drifting over the Halibut grounds. The halibut is an inhabitant of sandy and mud bottom, and the sinker bumps along the bottom until the fish hits. It is a tricky fish to hook. They grow to above 60 pounds but 35 to 45 is good and the average will run from 5 to 25 pounds. They are taken from Mexican waters to Central California with best catches from San Diego to Ventura. They are good eating.

PACIFIC HALIBUT

This Halibut is found from central California north to the Bering Sea, rarely below central California although an occasional one is taken. They grow to 1,500 pounds but are rare above 500 pounds. No records of these larger fish being taken by angling, are available but they offer real opportunity to the ambitious big-game angler. Sportsmen take them the year around on live and dead bait, anchovies, herring, sardines, queenfish, and other fishes.

THE SOLES: FLOUNDER FAMILY

Some belong to the *Bothidae* group. Not true soles but this is the universal name. They resemble the halibut in appearance, habits, and habitat; taken throughout the year.

SAND DAB

Taken from Alaska to lower California throughout the year the Sand Dab is a deep water fish usually caught incidentally while fishing for other bottom fish. Cod fishermen sometimes attach small hooks below the sinker on regular gear and frequently pick up numerous Sand Dabs along with the Cod. They are delicious eating.

ROCK COD

There are about 60 species of these rockfish (which are not cod despite the common name) on the Pacific Coast, and at least 50 occur in California. It is taken throughout the year in deep water by anglers using special gear while not a game fish it is good eating and popular during the winter months when other fishing is slack. The Bocaccio, Chilipepper, Yellowtail Rockcod, Black Rock Cod, Priestfish, Red Rock Cod, Salmon grouper, Chucklehead, Chinafish, gopher, gefalutano, Striped Rockfin, Treefish, Widow, Channel Cod, are a few of the more frequently encountered varieties. Most of them are found from central through southern California, possible much farther north.

SCULPIN

Sculpin is also a member of this group, mentioned because it is frequently taken from live-bait boats, barges and piers and possesses a vicious stinger which inflicts very painful wounds. Handle with extreme care as a jab from the spines can be serious. Apply ammonia at once for relief. Do not eat the roe of this fish as *it is highly poisonous.* The flesh is excellent, and it it greatly prized as a food fish.

CULTUS

This fish is commonly called blue cod, green cod, or lingcod. It is an ugly fish with bright green or blue flesh which turns white when cooked but is delicious eating. Found from Alaska to Mexico, and taken throughout the year on cut bait; it will take live bait.

CABAZONE

Cabazone is also called blue cod. The lining of the mouth is a translucent turquoise green. Distributed from northern British Columbia through southern California, it is taken all year on hook and line with cut bait and jigs. Being very good eating, it is an important sports fish in central California.

KELPFISH

Common in tide pools, around kelp beds, and in all in-shore waters from British Columbia well into Lower California waters throughout the year, they are taken on live and cut bait.

SENORITA

The Senorita is a small fish taken incidentally by anglers from boats and piers and being generally found around kelp and is often called kelpfish. It is good eating.

SHEEPSHEAD

This in-shore fish is frequently taken from boats, piers, and at some places along the shore line from Monterey to the Gulf of California. It has spectacular coloring; the male is crimson and black, the female usually a rose color, sometimes black. Taken on cut mackerel, shrimps, razor clams, squid, the best fishing is during the winter but they are fairly numerous at all times. It is a bottom fish reaching a weight of 25 pounds, usually smaller with 5 to 10 pounds being a good average. Good eating, but must be skinned and when boiled in salted water with vinegar or lemon juice added and then allowed to cool, it is difficult to tell it from lobster.

GRUNION

This is the fabulous fish that "dances in the moonlight." It actually does just that when the male and female dash ashore at the peak of the highest tides, lay and fertilize the eggs before the next wave washes them back to sea. This marvelous sight, that attracts thousands of sightseers during the seasons is predicted to the hour and almost the second by the Division of Fish and Game experts. Dr. Frances Clark is considered the leading authority on this little fish. It is caught on the beach by anglers who may use only the bare hands. A member of the silversides family, it is considered a smelt and is highly prized by gourmets. Consult fish and tide tables for time of runs and open seasons on this fish. Found only from central California to lower California, it spawns on high tides during the full and dark of the moon from March through August.

SALMON, KING

King Salmon is also known as the Chinook Salmon, Quinnat, and Tyee. At sea it is taken from southern California to Alaska. It rarely enters streams south of San Francisco Bay. It is taken by trolling in the ocean and also with baits and lures.

SILVER SALMON

This fish in found from the Coronado Islands, Mexico, to Alaska and are taken by trolling, using baits and lures. Rare south of Monterey, it spawns in rivers and streams from Monterey Bay north but does not enter the Sacramento-San Joaquin system. It is a highly important sport fish.

STEELHEAD

The Steelhead is a sea-run Rainbow Trout and is found from Alaska south to at least the Mexican Border. It enters all streams which feed into the ocean. Steelhead are little sought by anglers in the ocean, but knowing fishermen have great sport at the mouths of streams when the run is on. Frequently good fishing can be had from the surf while the Steelhead are massing, waiting for the sand bars to be washed out so they can enter the streams. Fly rods and spinners are a good combination in the ocean. Steelhead will take live anchovies, and each year sees some taken from the pier at Malibu as the fish wait for Malibou Creek to open with the rains.

SALT WATER FISHING IN MEXICO

Mexico offers to the salt water angler any type of fishing desired, from trolling in the blue waters for the billed fish to fly casting along the shore for smaller varieties. The kinds of fish will depend to a great extent upon the time that can be devoted to seeking them. Mexico has 4,200 miles of coast line on the Pacific side and 1,600 miles on the Atlantic. The Pacific Ocean bathes the west coast and supplies the water for the Gulf of California which is bounded on the west by the Peninsula of Lower California and on the east by the mainland states of Sonora and Sinaloa. At the extreme southern end is found the Gulf of Tehuantepec. The Atlantic waters are made up of the Gulf of Mexico, the Bay of Campeche, and the Caribbean Sea. The Bay, or Gulf, of Campeche is part of the Gulf of Mexico, although its off-shore depths are much shallower than the gulf proper.

The Gulf of California has been called the greatest fish trap in the world, since the fish, in their migrations, move northward into the gulf only to find they must return south to get back into the Pacific Ocean. There are, of course, fish native to the waters of the gulf that are there in all months of the year. However, the Bay of Campeche, due to the shallow water and the large numbers of banks and reefs, also offers an abundance in marine life that is unexcelled in Mexican waters.

Mexico's salt waters have never been thoroughly explored by rod-and-reel anglers, although in every area nets, hand lines, and harpoons are used to capture members of the finny tribe for commercial purposes or for home consumption. Except in the better known localities, which are to be described, facilities for the angler are not available. This especially applies to boats for trolling, and hotel accommodations are not always good even when available in the smaller places. Possibly the airplane has stimulated salt-water angling more than any other thing in Mexico, since both coasts are served by dependable commercial airlines. It is now possible to leave almost any city in the United States one day and fish in Mexican waters the next. The Compania Mexicana de Aviacion (Mexican Aviation Company) and the Aeronaves de Mexico, both affiliated with Pan American World Airways, have landing fields on both coasts and have always given excellent service.

CLIMATE

The climate of Mexico is either temperate or tropical and during most of the year the coasts are more likely to be tropical than otherwise. However, during winter in the northern Pacific area, the weather is nearly the same as in southern California. When northers are blowing on the Gulf of Mexico, it is likely to be on the cold side, although snow and freezing temperatures are unknown. Mosquitos and sand flies are prevalent during the summer rainy season, so insect repellants and nets to sleep under should be carried as well as sunburn lotions or creams.

FISHING LICENSES

Fishing licenses can be obtained in Mexico City at the Marine Department of the Mexican Navy. They are good for a few days, a month or a year, and the charge is only a few pesos. Two front view passport photos are required. The address of the Tourist Department of the Mexican government in Mexico City is Calle Morelos No. 110. The Mexican Consul in the larger cities of the United

States will furnish all information the visitor needs concerning fishing permits. A three-day permit to fish can be obtained through fishing guides on the charter boats at Acapulco and the other ports catering to deep sea anglers. No pictures are needed for these temporary licenses.

THE PACIFIC COAST

Due to the extensive area and many unexplored waters, it is impossible to include all places of interest to the angler, but the principal fishing spots will be described.

ENSENADA, BAJA CALIFORNIA

Ensenada is located on the west coast of the peninsula of lower California, just below San Diego, California. Fishing is similar to that found off San Diego and anyone interested can secure all needed information from the Chamber of Commerce of that city.

LA PAZ, BAJA CALIFORNIA

La Paz, 34°10′ N., 110°19′ W., is a small city of fifteen thousand inhabitants, located on the east coast of Baja California, about ninety miles north of the southern tip. It was famous a few years ago for its pearl industry. La Paz is reached by boat or airplane, and there is an unpaved road to the American border which is only recommended to those seeking adventure. Three islands, Espiritu Santo, San Jose, and Cerralvo, lie a few miles off shore and the best fishing for Sailfish and Marlin as well as for smaller fishes is found around them. Espiritu Santo is in front of the Bay of La Paz, Cerralvo is to the south, and San Jose to the north.

Fishing at La Paz has become so popular with California anglers that the La Paz Sportsman Club, 9739 Cashio St., Los Angeles, California, has been organized. They make chartered flights usually for anglers interested in the Marlin fishing. Some go by way of Mazatlan and fly across the gulf on the Aeronaves plane, the service being twice weekly. Those desirous of trying La Paz waters should contact the club or write to the Hotel La Perla in La Paz to arrange for accommodations, boats, etc.

The series of off shore islands makes ideal trolling for Sailfish, Striped and Black Marlin, Tuna, Sierra Mackerel, Rooster Fish, Black Skipjacks, Dolphin, Ten-pounder or Chiro, Needle Fish, Albacore and Snappers; Broadbill Swordfish are also found at times. Bottom fishing yields Jewfish, Snappers, Groupers, and an infinite variety of small fish. Major Max C. Fleishman has caught Bonefish just north of La Paz at Puerto Escondita, fishing from a launch off his yacht *Haida*. The harbor at this latter place is perfectly landlocked and is a secure haven for small vessels in any weather.

The weather in the Gulf of California is best during April, May, and part of June. February is a windy month, and heavy blows are apt to come during July, August, and September.

Moving north along the west coast of the peninsula, numerous islands provide fishing similar to that at La Paz, but a yacht or a large boat is needed for this area.

PUNTA PENASCO, SONORA

Puerto Penasco, 31°20′ N., 113°40′ W., is at the upper end of the Gulf of California on the mainland side, sixty miles south of the United States border. During the past few years it has gained popularity with anglers from southern California and Arizona. There are two hotels, the Hotel Penasco and the Hotel Mexico. Shrimp fishing is the principal industry. The season begins in September and, until it is over, the people are very busy.

Excellent surf fishing is availale in Penasco for Weakfish, Sea Trout or Curbina, California Kelp Bass or Pinta, Pompano and an occasional Sierra Mackerel. Shrimp, clams, or pieces of cut fish are used for bait, but plugs and spoons will produce results when properly worked. A good surf beach lies just south of the town and can be reached by road.

If driving to Penasco by auto, take an outboard motor for trolling for Sierra Mackerel from a rented row boat. A small salt-water feather is better than larger lures, although at times they seem to take anything that moves. A bone jig, with a weight added at the swivel end of the leader to get it down, is another good lure for this fish. If a good spot is found, stop the motor and fish on the bottom for Trigger Fish, Grouper, Totuava (which is a white sea bass only found in the Gulf of California), and for any of the other fish found in the bay. Suitable boats for hire are available to troll for Sailfish and Dolphin in the blue water a few miles off shore. A strip from the belly of a Sierra or other fish makes an excellent bait, so it is not necessary to bring flying fish from California.

GUAYMAS, SONORA

Guaymas, 27°55′ N., 110°54′ W., was the first place in Mexico to become popular for bill fishing. It is an important port on the mainland side, commercial fishing being one of its principal industries. The oysters and shrimp from Guaymas are delicious. This popular spot can be reached by rail, auto, airplane, or boat. Numerous hotels and courts cater to the visiting angler of which the best is the Playa de Cortez. There are also the Miramar and Pacifico Hotels with moderate rates.

The bill fishing begins in April and extends into October, but June is the best month. Sailfish, Striped and Black Marlin, Tuna, Bonita, Dolphin, Jack Crevalle, Papagallo or Rooster Fish, are all present during the spring and summer months. Totuava is the most popular fish during the fall and winter months. While not so plentiful as in previous years, it is still to be found and makes excellent sport on light tackle. Sierra and Black Skipjacks are present all through the year in Guaymas, as well as most other Mexican waters on the Pacific.

The giant Mantarayas or Rayfish are common in the waters about Guaymas and are an interesting sight as one goes to the Marlin grounds. They appear as dark brown splotches under the surface and at times can be seen jumping clear of the water, making a characteristic splash entirely different from that made by a Sail or a Marlin. It is a bit frightening to hear this splash if one is nearby and does not see them jump. This is the fish for the rough and tumble harpooner, and it takes heavy rope to hold them. Steinbeck and Ricketts' "Sea of Cortez" is recommended reading for an excellent description of an experience in harpooning the mantaraya or devil fish.

Boats and hotel reservations are best made considerably in advance if one is going to Guaymas during the June tourist season. An annual fishing rodeo held each October is open to all, and it is becoming quite popular.

TOPOLOBAMPO, SINALOA

Topolobampo, 25°36′ N., 109°04′ W., is a small town overlooking the bay of the same name. It is located about midway between Guaymas and Mazatlan. It can be reached by plane or railway via Los Mochis which is about 17 miles distant. One can then drive by auto as a means of communication between the two cities. Accommodations for anglers have not been developed at Topolobampo, but Hart Stillwell visited the place and described it so well in his *Fishing in Mexico* that it should be included. Curbino, Weakfish or Sea Trout, can be caught by casting in nearby Lechuguilla Bay, as well as small snappers, called pargos by the Mexicans. One can catch Sierras and Black Skipjacks along the shore and, beyond a doubt, Sailfish and Marlin can be raised in the blue water around the adjoining islands. Unless one has friends or connections in Los Mochis or Topolobampo, it might be well to try one of the better known places, although everywhere in Mexico the inhabitants are kindly, and will take care of the visitor to the best of their ability and knowledge. It seems pertinent to mention that just because the native fisherman may not know much about a rod and reel, one should not presume they do not know how to catch fish. Their skillful use of the handline is often truly amazing.

MAZATLAN, SINALOA

Mazatlan, 23°12′ N., 109°25′ W., is a popular port located on the mainland about opposite the tip of Baja California. Fishing of some kind is available throughout the year, although the months of August and September are the poorest due largely to uncertain weather. If the water is not too rough, one can always catch fish at Mazatlan. The city can be reached by rail, airplane, or boat. Autos go by way of Durango or Guadalajara. It is an ideal location for those wishing to fly over weekends from California or from Arizona through Nogales. Anglers are now doing this, especially those seeking Sailfish and Marlin, from December to June. Compania Mexicana de Aviacion from Los Angeles or Oeronaves de Mexico from Nogales offer excellent service to Mazatlan and Mexico City.

All methods of salt-water fishing such as trolling or casting, etc., are enjoyed in Mazatlan waters for the usual species found in the Gulf of California. The Totuava is a rarity this far south but other fish taken are the same as those found in La Paz and Guaymas waters. Marlin fishing is best after January first and is very good in February and on through March, April, and May. For that matter, an occasional Marlin can be caught in almost any month. Mazatlan waters have produced the largest Marlin ever taken on Mexican fishing grounds. It was a Black Marlin weighing 662 pounds and was caught on June 4, 1948, about fifteen miles off shore. The majority of the Marlin taken are Striped and weigh from 120 to 250 pounds. The veteran angler can have good sport with light tackle since most of the guides are experienced in handling boats for this sport. Sailfish are also caught at all seasons, but the best months are June and July.

The brothers Luis and Victor Patron of Mazatlan can furnish any information desired about fishing. Both men are keenly interested in sportfishing and have a perfect command of English.

Three of the best hotels are the Bel-Mar, the Freeman, and the Central. Reservations should be made in advance.

MANZANILLO, COLIMA

Manzanillo, 19°03′ N., 104°20′ W., is the port of entry for the State of Colima. The city can be reached by boat or by railroad from Guadalajara.

The usual assortment of small fish can be caught in the waters along the shore. Sailfish and Marlin are present in all months, especially the Sail or Pez Vela as it is called in Spanish.

The weather from December to March is very pleasant. The temperature ranges 73° to 86° F. The prevailing wind blows from a direction between west and northwest. The rainy season begins in June and ends in November. The dry months from December to May are the most comfortable and safest to fish Manzanillo waters.

Sr. Alberto Caligaris at the Hotel Playa de Santiago can furnish fishing information for anglers desiring to go to Manzanillo.

ZIHUATENEJO, GUERRERO

Zihuatenejo, 17°37′ N., 101°33′ W., is a small village one hundred miles north of Acapulco and can be reached by plane or boat. It is possible to go by auto over a dirt road—but this is not recommended. The village is surrounded by mountains and has a beautiful setting. It has been called a miniature Acapulco with considerable reason. Nothing much has been done about developing the fishing possibilities for the visiting angler. Zane Gray had good luck in this area in the early days and wrote glowing accounts of the wonderful Sailfish and Marlin and smaller fish to be found here.

The beautiful tropical island of Ixtapa lies a few miles north of Zihuatenejo, about 400 yards off shore. A good anchorage is found on the mainland side of the island and, after going ashore, a path leads through the thick underbrush to the outside of the island, affording a magnificient view of the ocean. Native fishermen have lobster traps here and the lobsters are delicious. Fishing along the shores of the island and the mainland is excellent at times for Sierra, Rooster Fish, Black Skipjacks, Jack Crevalle, Snappers, and numerous smaller fishes. There are projecting rocks and

Dr. Roy Dean and the smallest Marlin caught in Acapulco. This fish is called Aguja de Paladar and has been classified as a young striped Marlin.

submerged reefs and care must be taken to avoid hitting them.

About a mile off the entrance to Zihuatenejo Bay, Black Rock, a 45-foot projection rises out of the ocean. Amberjacks and Pargo have a fondness for this area and best results will be secured by trolling around and around the rock using feathers and large No. 7 spoons. A cut bait that is weighted to take it down is also very good. Fifteen-thread should be used since the fish found here will dive for the rocks and cut the lines if they are not stopped.

Six or more miles to the south and east of Zihuatenejo is a series of large, pointed rocks called Los Frailles. Thousands of cormorants and other sea birds roost on the rocky craigs. At times it is difficult to troll a feather through here since the birds will dive for them in their clumsy, awkward manner and occasionally get caught. For a while it is fun to watch this show, but, after a time, it becomes a nuisance.

Unless the fisherman has his own craft, it might be best to charter a boat in Acapulco to fish Zihuatenejo. Along the sandy shores one can fish for the small stuff or stay out in the blue water and have Marlin and Sailfish to contend with and slow up the journey. A feather can be trolled at top speed and, if something seems to be pecking at it, merely lower the rod tip and strike hard. If lucky, you will snag a Sailfish or maybe a Marlin. No boat goes too fast to prevent fish from striking a bait in these waters. Mullet or strip bait is better, but the speed at which one makes the trip is hard on such lures and they are soon beaten to pieces and start spinning; which is fatal to lines.

ACAPULCO, GUERRERO

Acapulco, 16°51′ N., 99°56′ W., hardly needs introduction to most people interested in Mexico. It is a resort city of 35,000 inhabitants and is surrounded by mountains. The bay is said to be one of the most beautiful in the world. Acapulco has become the most popular resort in Mexico and there are hotels with modern conveniences to fit any pocketbook.

It can be reached by boat, auto, or airplane, but there is no railroad. A leisurely auto trip from Mexico City will allow a stop in Cuernavaca just over the mountains from the capital and an overnight stop at Taxco to enjoy that artists paradise. The next day's journey to Acapulco is an easy one. The auto trip from Mexico City to Acapulco takes about nine hours for the 450 kilometers and, the air trip is made in one hour and a quarter.

Many American and Canadian yachtsmen visit Acapulco in their boats to spend from weeks to several months on vacation in this lovely land. They usually come during the winter months, although Acapulco has a delightful all-year climate. The temperature varies but little during the year. Winter is the popular tourist season, but Acapulco is at its loveliest during the summer when the hills are green.

The most notable fishing at Acapulco is for Sailfish and, without a doubt, it is the most productive Sailfish ground in the world. There may be other places as good but they have not yet been developed. The angler can almost be sure of at least one strike each trip in a charter boat, and a catch of six sails is not unusual. Thirteen sails were caught, tagged, and released on one day in January by one party. There are twenty-five or more launches catering to deep sea anglers and on some the crews are extremely efficient. Acapulco is remarkably free of storms, the temperature of the water is usually around 80° F. and as a rule calm, although in September one is apt to have rainy weather.

Sailfish are so abundant in Acapulco waters that the Sailfish and Tarpon Club of Mexico started marking them with tags furnished by the U. S. Fish and Wildlife Service. They did this in the hope of learning something of the habits and migrations of these great game fish. Also, it was believed that conservation of resources would be helped, since the fish were usually caught, brought in on the boats, and carried out and dumped the following day. The supply of tags was limited, and since a monetary reward was offered for their return, it was decided to seek other sources for the supply. The Pan American World Airways furnishes not only tags but send a beautiful certificate and replica wallet card to those reporting the serial number of the tag placed on released fish.

An annual Sailfish rodeo, held each spring in Acapulco, has become very popular. Many novices learn for the first time the rules followed by skilled anglers, especially for club or world records. The now famous Light Tackle Sailfish Tournament for clubs affiliated with the International Game Fish Association has held three of its five annual tournaments in Acapulco. This meeting brings together some of the finest light tackle anglers in the world, and the tournaments are kept on a high sportsmanlike basis. It is team competition and points are allowed for sailfish caught. Since they do not have to be weighed, all are released unless one happens to be of record size. It is rather unique to have a fishing tournament without piles of dead fish as evidence when the boats return each afternoon. These tournaments have also been held in Florida and Panama, and the principal prize is an orante belt offered by the Sailfish and Tarpon Club of Mexico. The winning team keeps it for one year with an appropriate silver plate attached, containing the club's name and the names of anglers that comprised the team. It must be won three times for permanent possession.

Marlin seem to be present in Acapulco waters in all months, although there is rarely a run such as those at Mazatlan, La Paz, and Guaymas. The marlin as a rule are larger than those caught in the other places and are of three kinds, the Acapulco Black, the Striped, and the gamey Silver Marlin. An interesting fact has been discovered about the Acapulco Black Marlin. Its pectoral fin is movable and in life it folds back against his body and sometimes becomes rigid upon death. The Black Marlin reported from Panama and New Zealand are said to have the pectoral fins rigid at all times.

The marlin taken at Acapulco probably average two hundred and fifty pounds. Several in the six-hundred-pound class have been brought in and Dr. Roy B. Dean caught one of fifty-seven pounds which is the smallest brought in there to his knowledge.

Dolphin in the fifty-pound class are caught in Acapulco, but there is no particular season for them. When trash is in the water, they seem to be more abundant. Both Blue and Yellowfin Tuna are common. A two-hundred-pound tuna is a rarity and those taken are usually in the twenty- to thirty-pound group. The boats usually find them at least fifteen miles from shore, although at times they are to be seen in schools just outside the bay.

Trolling for the smaller varieties never seems to be as good as in places to the north. However, Sierras, Black Skipjack, Rooster Fish, Jack Crevalle, Pargo, not to mention the large variety of small bottom feeding fish caught in the bay and along the rocks, are all to be found.

Once a year, around Christmas, two or three whales show up and hang around the deep water adjacent to the cliffs of Acapulco. They are sometimes seen passing through the channel connecting Boca Chica with the bay. Out in the blue water when trolling for sails, one will sometimes meet thousands of porpoise in huge migrating schools. It is extremely interesting to watch them in their leaps and spins out of the water. Sometimes Tuna are found with them and it is exciting to have a Tuna on with these mammals all around while wondering just when the line will be cut by the sharp fin of a porpoise. The porpoise does not take a trolled bait or any other kind, but occasionally they are snagged while trolling feathers through a school. However, no one has landed one here. They simply go on about their business, paying no attention to the pricking of the hook, nor the frantic efforts of the angler. Usually the line is broken or the hook pulls out. Killer Whales or Orcas are sometimes encountered, but the boatmen give them a wide berth, claiming they are dangerous foes. Tremendous Whale Sharks are also found and some weighing several tons have been harpooned and brought into port.

Sharks are found in all Mexican waters. The Hammerhead, the Great Blue, and the Bonito are the most common. Now that shark's livers are sought for medicinal purposes, they do not seem so prevalent as formerly. Experienced anglers rarely fish for them when sportier fish are present.

Robalo or Snook fishing is to be had in the lagoons near Acapulco, and now that they have a good road, the fishing at nearby Playa Encantado for this sporty fish is producing catches of twenty to thirty pounds. Arrangements can be made at

Former world's record Black Marlin caught by Dr. Roy Dean at Acapulco.

Playa Encantada for boats to hire or information can be had at the Mexican Government Tourist Department office at the fiscal wharf at which the boats dock. Boat prices per hour or by the trip have been fixed by the government.

SALINA CRUZ, OAXACA

Salina Cruz, 16°10′ N., 95°12′ W., is the southern terminus of the railroad that crosses the Isthmus of Tehuantepec and is on the Gulf of Tehuantepec. Sport fishing has not been organized either there or at Puerto Angel to the north. Large Marlin and Sailfish are reported by shark fishermen to be present in the blue water and, of course, the usual smaller varieties of game fish are to be found along the coast.

SUMMARY—THE PACIFIC SIDE

With the possible exception of the Totuava, or White Sea Bass, one is apt to catch all varieties of fish at any place described in this article. Broad-billed Swordfish, for instance, are to be found around La Paz, but are hardly ever known in other parts. The fact remains, however, that one was caught in Acapulco some ten or fifteen years ago.

Probably the most popular fishes are the Sails and Marlin, with the Dolphin not far behind. Next are the mackerel tribe which includes the Blue and Yellowfin Tuna, Albacore, Oceanic Skipjack, Black Skipjack (called "barrilete" by Mexicans and very common in all Pacific waters on the Mexican Coast), Bonitos, Sierra, and finally the Wahoo or "Peto." The Tunas are usually found off shore in blue water along with the Marlin, Sails, and Dolphins. The other fish are likely to be found along sandy shores, especially the Sierras and the Rooster Fish.

The family of jacks is very large with the Amberjack the best of the lot. It is called "medregal" in Mexico. Apparently the Amberjack likes northern Mexican waters from Zihuatenejo up the line to Guaymas. It is not taken at Acapulco, but is common off Panama and the Perlas Islands. The Jack Crevalle is found wherever there is sandy bottom and it grows to thirty pounds or more. By some it is considered a nuisance, usually because it interferes with the catching of fish which are more desirable for the table. It is erroneously called "yellowtail" on both coasts of Mexico and is, therefore, confused with the great California Yellowtail, which is more of a streamlined fish and not so flat as the Jack Crevalle. The common Green-Jack is called "Cocinero" in Acapulco, and is caught by trolling near the shore. Fish such as Pompano, Goggle-eye, Moon-fish, Look-down, and Big-eyed Skad are all found in the bays. Many of these smaller fish will be desirable now that fly rods are becoming so popular with salt water anglers.

The Snapper's are usually found around banks and on rocky shores. They are called "pargos" in Mexico and there are various kinds such as Negro, Mullatto, and Colorado. There are other members of this family, and the delicious Red Snapper should not be confused with the Pargo, since it is usually caught in quite deep water and does not put up much of a fight. On the other hand, the Snapper caught in shallow water will give a good battle with every turn of the reel handle. Once he gets to his cave in the rocks, more than likely the line will be cut on its jagged edge.

There are about forty sea bass which occur in Mexican waters, many of them are negligible as sport fish, but the Black Sea Bass or "jewfish" weighs up to five or six hundred pounds. However, it is not much of a fighter for all its weight. It is caught for the table by fishing on the bottom with large pieces of fish or fish heads. The grouper is also included in this family, but it is not much sought after as a game fish. Still another common one is the Cabrillo, excellent for food but not considered much of a fighter.

Robalo or Snook are found all along the coast in the lagoons that parallel the ocean from Mazatlan south to the Guatemala border. The water in these lagoons is brackish and opens into the ocean at certain times. The "Robalo Blanco" is a better fighter than the "Robalo Negro" and due to a soft mouth great care must be exercised in its capture. The bait caster and the fly rod man could spend years exploring these lagoons, for many of them are practically inaccessible. Fishing for Robalo at the Papagayo lagoon near Acapulco has become popular and fish of thirty pounds have been caught there.

The croaker family includes about fifty which occur in Mexican waters. The most popular are the Corbinas, also called Weakfish or Sea Trout. They afford great sport with a casting rod. Mosquitoes and xexenes are pests along the shore when casting so insect repellents should be carried. The White Sea Bass of Mexico is the "totuava" of northern Gulf of Mexico fame. However, it is not a bass, but a croaker with a diamond-shaped tail. They like a slowly trolled spoon. Strip bait, with the use of a sinker to take it down, is an excellent lure for this fish as it is for pargo, groupers, and other fishes that feed mostly on the bottom.

The barracuda family: Barracuda are found in bays all along the coast. Sometimes they are found in large schools, and can be caught by any of the usual trolling methods. The school can be kept

Tarpon jumping near "La Roca" at Villa Rica.

for quite some time if one angler will always keep a hooked fish in the water until another bait is put over.

The herring-like fishes, the Tenpounder, "Chiro," Lady Fish or "piaguacho," as it is called in Acapulco, are interesting fish to catch on a plug. When hooked they jump all over the place and are hard to land for that reason. A tiny plug is ideal and the spinning outfit using a seven-pound-test line is excellent for this fish. The Bonefish or "macabi," is also in this family. It is found in bays and shoal water, but so far, angling for Bonefish has not become popular on the Pacific Coast, possibly because they are so difficult to find. Another herring-like fish is the Milk Fish or "chanos-chanos." It is called "sabalo" at Acapulco, and the only reason it is mentioned here is that it is not the "sabalo" of the Atlantic Coast, which is the Silver King or Tarpon. This fish is found in bays or near the shore in schools and will not normally take a lure.

THE ATLANTIC COAST

The coastline of Mexico, washed by the waters of the Atlantic, is sixteen hundred miles long. It extends in a southerly direction from the border of Texas at Brownsville to those wonderful fishing grounds in the Bay of Campeche, also called the Gulf of Campeche. Thence the Peninsula of Yucatan projects northeasterly, helping to form the Bay of Campeche on its western coast, then around to form the Canal of Yucatan on the east, with the Island of Cuba forming the other side of the canal. The eastern side of the Peninsula of Yucatan coast is bathed by the Caribbean Sea. The Island of Cozumel on which there is a good air strip, lies just off the east coast of northern Quintana Roo.

Excellent fishing is found all along this coast and in the offshore waters. Paved highways from Tampico, Tuxpan, Tecolutla, Nautla, and Veracruz, connect with Mexico City and with highways to the United States. Fishermen can travel by railway to Tampico and Veracruz. Best of all, on account of saving time, is the excellent airplane service on the entire east coast of Mexico, provided by the Compania Mexicana de Aviacion (Mexican Aviation Company), which is affiliated with the Pan American World Airways.

SOTO LA MARINA AREA

There is excellent Channel Bass or Redfish, Weakfish, Snook, and Tarpon fishing to be had at the mouth of the Soto la Marina River, which is about half way between Tampico and Brownsville. One can drive there via Ciudad Victoria or turn off the Brownsville-Victoria highway at Santander Jimenez. The road from this latter puebla is not paved although it is passable in the dry season. There is an air strip for those that fly their own planes but the commercial planes do not stop at Soto la Marina. For information write to Mr. G. R. Kennedy, Hacienda El Chamal, c/o Hotel Sierra Gorda, Ciudad Victoria, Tamps., Mexico.

Sr. Joaquin Cicero and Tarpon caught in Panuco River.

TAMPICO FISHING

The Gulf, the Lagoons and the Panuco River

Tampico, Tamaulipas, 22°16′ N., 97°50′ W., is a modern city, having all the conveniences needed by the anglers seeking the excellent fishing to be found in the Panuco River which flows along the edge of the city, or in the various lagoons surrounding the Tampico district. Tampico is more famous for Tarpon than for any other fish, but Snooks or Robalo, Perch, Sheepshead, Channel Bass or Red Fish, Jewfish or "mero," Jack Crevalle, Weakfish or Sea Trout, Pompano, the mackerals, catfish, pargo, and other bottom feeding fish are to be caught in nearby waters.

Information can be obtained from the hotels or from the sporting goods store, La Sonora, concerning boats, and the best places for the kind of fishing desired. Fishing can be done with good results all along the entire eastern coast of Mexico in all months. However, due to northers in the late fall and winter, fishing in the Gulf is at times not feasible. One can fish the Panuco River at any time although during the rainy season, after July, the water becomes muddy and the catch is prob-

Stillwell

Dr. Roy Dean tagging a Sailfish at Acapulco.

lematical. During the summer months one can fish the Gulf for Tarpon, Jacks, and Redfish. Sailfish and Marlin are said to be in the blue water some fifteen miles off shore although this type of fishing has never been developed.

Tampico has an annual Tarpon rodeo, usually during April, which is extremely popular among the Mexicans, as well as with visiting American tourists. The world's record Tarpon (247 pounds and 7′ 5½″ long) was caught in the Panuco River in March, 1938. The present world record on 30-pound-test line was a Tarpon weighing 191.8 pounds also caught in the Panuco River. Tarpon have always been released in the Tampico area when caught on hook and line by sports fishermen, although they are harpooned by natives for food there as well as at Tuxpan. Further south, in the Campeche area, the people do not eat Tarpon because other more edible fish can be caught with little effort. Tarpon flesh is coarse, but for those liking fish it is palatable, as is also Jack Crevalle, which is scorned by many as food.

Trips along the coast north of Tampico can be arranged by auto. Channel Bass, Weakfish, and Snook are the principal attraction, but Tarpon will be present to make it rough on the casting tackle generally used for such fishing, either with plugs or bait.

The Chijol Canal connects Tampico with Tamiahua Lagoon and thence by waterway to Tuxpan, a distance of 90 miles. Launches and barges make this trip, and the Tamiahua Lagoon provides excellent sea-trout or "curbina" fishing. Such trips can be arranged in Tampico and, if one is lucky in finding a run, a large catch can be made with bait casting rods, using plugs for lures.

LOBOS ISLAND

Lobos Island, 21°28′ N., 97°13′ W., is a beautiful spot a few miles off shore, lying about equidistant from Tampico and Tuxpan. It is composed of sand heaped up on a coral reef and covered with bushes and trees. There is a lighthouse on the island where accommodations for visiting anglers can usually be arranged. The island is small, being possibly a third of a mile in length, but the nearby reef provides excellent trolling for Pargo, Cubera, Barracuda, Jack-fish and Tarpon. If one wishes to fish on the bottom with bait, he can catch numerous tropical fishes of many colors, shapes, and sizes. Arrangements can be made in either Tampico or Tuxpan to fish the reefs off Lobos Island. June and July are the best months. Medio Reef is about three miles northwest of Lobos Island with Blanquillo three miles beyond Medio. Both are excellent fishing places and, sometimes by trolling between these banks, a Wahoo can be raised. Between Lobos Island and Tuxpan are the Tanguijo, En Medio, and Tuxpan Reefs, all capable of producing excellent fishing.

TUXPAN, VERACRUZ

Tuxpan, 20°59′ N., 97°19′ W., is located on the river of the same name, a few miles from its mouth. It can be reached by boat, highway, or airplane, but has no railway. Fishing is about the same as in the Panuco although the tarpon here are more temperamental. However, monsters are to be seen and caught. The Tuxpan is sluggish; so slow in fact that one night the boy running our outboard motor became lost, with the result that we traveled upstream instead of down, a fact that was not realized until arrival at a ferry landing far up river. Snook or Robalo fishing can be excellent a few miles above Tuxpan. One should look for grassy shorelines or submerged logs and trees when trolling for these fish. At the mouth of the river Jack Crevalle and sometimes Tarpon can be found.

Those driving from Mexico City to Tuxpan can leave the highway and pass through Poza Rica, of oil fame, to reach Guiterrez Zamora, on the banks of the Tecolutla River. Tecolutla is five miles away at the river mouth. Two new hotels have been built and Hotel Balneario de Tecolutla is used by Americans from Mexico City for week end trips. The usual types of fish are found both at the mouth of the river and in the gulf. A ferry transports autos and trucks across the Tecolutla River, about three hundred yards above the ferry and across the river from the town the entrance of the beautiful Estero Negro is found, a place of lush, tropical growth where Tarpon and Robalo are sometimes caught. However, Robalo fishing is best along the coast above Tecolutla during August.

After crossing the ferry at Tecolutla, one can

drive on to Nautla, in the State of Veracruz, where hotel accommodations are available both on the beach at the mouth of the Nautla River and in the town. The nearby lagoons, the river and the gulf provide angling similar to that at Tuxpan.

VERACRUZ, VERACRUZ

Veracruz, 18°12′ N., 96° 08′ W., is the capital of the state of the same name and is connected with Mexico City by railway, highway and air service. There are several first-class hotels and fishing is good for Tarpon, Wahoo, Mackerel, Jack Crevalle, Jewfish, the various Pargos, Sierra, members of the grouper family, and Barracuda. The best fishing is at the nearby reefs, namely Gallego, Blanquilla, Anegado de Dentro, and Pajaros. Verde Island is a small key about one and one-half miles southwest of Anegado de Dentro where it is possible to land. A lighthouse is on the key. On Isla en Medio, a few miles to the south, arrangements for meals and sleeping accommodations can be made. However, it is well to take a food supply, especially rice, beans, eggs, oil for cooking and plenty of drinking water.

Trolling provides the best sport although bottom fishing will yield excellent results, especially for large groupers and Jewfish, besides many varieties of bottom feeding battlers.

Tarpon fishing, using large number seven spoons, is at its best during May in the Veracruz reef area, and monsters are there to be caught. At least fifteen-thread is recommended since large Pargos are likely to take the lure and make for the coral bottom with disastrous results to the tackle.

Fishing launches can be secured at the hotels. Some of the boats are not too up-to-date but the guides are well acquainted with the area and will find fish any time weather permits gulf fishing

Villa Rica, located about thirty miles north of Veracruz, can be reached by boat. About half or three-quarters of a mile from shore, a large guano-covered rock affords lee anchorage in good weather. This particular rock seems to have a fascination for five- to seven-foot Tarpon. These fish will take anything trolled, including a handkerchief with a hook in it. They can be caught on light tackle, but fifteen-thread is indicated for the expert although twenty-four thread is used by most anglers. Barracuda are found as well as Ling, which is called "bacalao" by the natives. Jack Crevalle, as usual, will be striking when the Tarpon give them a chance, but the principal interest is the "silver king". One can follow the school of Tarpon as they make their journey around and around this rock on which roost hundreds of man-of-war birds. The months to fish Villa Rica are May, June and July. Later in the season northers whip up in the gulf suddenly and it would be hazardous to be caught so far from safe anchorage during these storms.

ALVARADO, VERACRUZ

Alvarado, 18°48′ N., 95°45′ W., is a fishing city of 10,000 people and is situated on the western shore of the harbor entrance. The lagoon of Alvarado is shallow but extends for twenty miles and receives small rivers, the principal one being the Papaloapan. The area can be reached from Veracruz by railroad or highway. Sport fishing has not been developed but the commercial fishing supplies the Mexico City market. Casting for robalo is excellent and the usual Tarpon and other fish are also found.

PUERTO MEXICO, VERACRUZ

Puerto Mexico, 18°09′ N., 94°25′ W., is located at the mouth of the Coatzacoalcos River, and Minatitlan, where there is a large oil refinery twenty miles up the river. Puerto Mexico is accessible by train from Veracruz or by boat; however, the best way to reach this area is by plane from Veracruz or Mexico City, landing at Minatitlan. The Tarpon fishing is as good as can be

Former women's world's record Pacific Sailfish on nine thread, caught by Mrs. Roy Dean at Acapulco.

Robalo caught at mouth of Papagallo River and lagoon near Acapulco.

found in any river in Mexico. However, one must be careful not to troll through the oil from the refinery since it is ruinous for tackle.

CIUDAD DEL CARMEN, ISLAND OF CARMEN, CAMPECHE

Ciudad del Carmen, 18°41′ N., 91°56′ W., is a clean little tropical city of 10,000 inhabitants, which the shrimp industry has converted into quite a busy place. The Island of Carmen is reached by boat or by planes of the Compania Mexicana de Aviacion. Due to the excellent airplane service, this area has become popular with anglers from Mexico City for it is possible to leave at five in the morning and arrive at Carmen at nine. While fishing is good near the town of Carmen, fishermen usually go by auto across the island to Puerto Real and thence across the channel, which affords one entrance into Laguna de Terminos. The little pueblo of Isla Aguada lies two miles across the channel. Isla Aguada, once an island, is now a peninsula about seven miles long and a mile wide. The village is on the lagoon side, a few hundred yards from the gulf. Just around the point, excellent casting for Robalo and Tarpon is to be found early in the morning and as the sun goes down. After dark the fishing reaches its peak. At this time a flashlight is needed for removing backlashes and for removing fish from the hooks.

Hotel accommodations are available at Ciudad del Carmen. April, May, and June are the best months since mosquitoes are bad during the rainy season, especially in August and September.

Trolling in the channel between Puerto Real and Aguada furnishes Tarpon fishing as good as any in Mexico. Off a rocky point on the Puerto Real side, Barracuda of around twenty pounds are regularly found. Six-thread line and a drone spoon is good tackle for these fish and possibly for the Tarpon, but in crosisng the channel one is likely to pick up large thirty-pound Pargo or snapper, as well as big, tough Jureles or Jackfish, as they are called in English. For these larger fish, it is better to use fifteen-thread. Chiro are usually found in schools and casting for them with small plugs or using spinner tackle provides excellent sport. Be prepared to rough it in this district and bring plenty of lures. Bonefish are reported to be found on the land side at the mouth of the Candelaria River and Sea Trout or "Curbina" are also native to this district.

CAMPECHE, CAMPECHE

Campeche, 18°51′ N., 90°33′ W., is the chief city and port of the State of Campeche. It has a population of some 40,000 inhabitants and can be reached by auto from Merida or by airline. Fishing similar to that at Carmen is available.

PROGRESO, YUCATAN

Progreso, 21°20′ N., 89°40′ W., a town of 12,000 is the principal port for Yucatan. The fishing is similar to that at Campeche. However, Sailfish have been reported in the channel between Yucatan and Cuba.

COZUMEL ISLAND

Cozumel Island, 20°16′ N., 87°00′ W., lies about nine miles off the mainland of the Territory of Quintana Roo. It is about twenty-four miles in length and eight miles in breadth and can be reached by boat and by plane. Arrangements for fishing should be made in advance. It is not recommended during the norther season, from October to February. Tarpon, Barracuda, Jack Crevalle, Snappers, and Groupers are all found in the surrounding waters. Sailfish and marlin are also reported in the swift current that flows by the island.

CHETUMAL, QUINTANA ROO

Chetumal was formerly known as Payo Obispo. It is located near the British Honduras border. Sport fishing is not developed in this area although one will find the usual fishes.

SUMMARY—THE ATLANTIC SIDE

The game fishes to be caught in the Gulf of Mexico and in the part of the Caribbean Sea that borders on the territory of Quintana Roo are about the same as those found in Texas and Florida waters. The most popular are listed but this is by no means a complete catalogue.

The most popular fish is the Tarpon. It is ready to do battle wherever found, although seem mighty more eager to take lures in the bays, in the gulf, and around the reefs than in the rivers. Trolling with spoons and large feathers and casting with plugs and flies for Tarpon are standard methods of angling; but Hart Stilwell and his angler friends at Brownsville have developed a comparatively new method for river fishing. They cast a sinking plug, letting it go to the bottom and then inch the lure along. When something is felt fumbling with the lure the strike is delayed for a second or two. This method will tempt Tarpon when they pay little attention to other lures.

The Robalo or Snook is a popular fish taken by casting along inlets and shorelines. They can also be taken by trolling and casting in rivers along submerged logs, grassy banks, and in shallow water. They take all types of lures and strike best at daybreak or sundown.

Redfish or Channel Bass are found in coves, inlets and in tide rips along the shore. They take artificial lures readily and also bait such as cut fish and shrimp.

The Weakfish or Sea Trout is called "Trucha" and "Corbina" in Mexico. This popular species is found in lagoons opening into the gulf. The passes connecting Laguna Madre with the gulf and the Tamiahua Lagoon, south of Tampico, are both well known to anglers using bait casting rods and plugs for this sporty jumper.

The Jack Cravelle known as "Jurel", "Toro" or "Gallego" in Mexico, and is found wherever there is salt or brackish water. It is a powerful, stubborn fighter, that never gives up until completely exhausted. If it were found in waters with poor fishing, it would be considered a trophy instead of a nuisance.

The Barracuda is found mostly from Lobos Island south wherever there are reefs and banks. It is a splendid fighter when caught on light tackle and experienced anglers usually use six-thread and a drone spoon. The average Barracuda weighs from ten to twenty-five pounds, although monsters of one hundred pounds have been taken. An interesting method of discovering the presence of these fish is to troll, as a teaser, an empty bottle, bottom foremost. If a lure with a hook is trolled nearby the angler can present it to any Barracuda that follows the teaser.

Amongst the many snappers are the School Master, the Lane Snapper, Dog Snapper, Cubera, and the Pargo Mulatto. The snappers or "pargos" provide good trolling sport when they weigh ten pounds or more; and the small ones found around stumps, rocky points, and the mangroves in the lagoons are fun on bait casting tackle. The Pargo dives for the bottom when hooked and, if the line is not of sufficient strength to stop it before reaching the bottom, it will likely be frayed and broken on the sharp rocks.

The groupers are not much sport. Their food value is high and they are sought more for the table than for sport. Native fishermen use pieces of fish or shrimp for bottom fishing. Some of those captured are the Spotted, Black, Red, Nassau, and the Rock Hind. They will take a trolled lure such as a large feather or spoon and can be cast for by slowly working heavy plugs, metal squids, or spoons near the bottom.

The Spotted Jewfish grows to as much as seven hundred or more pounds. It is caught by baiting with fish heads or large pieces of fish around rocky bottoms or in the Panuco River along the jetties and warfs. A large line or ¼ inch rope is necessary. Around Tampico and Veracruz the Jewfish is called "mero" but in Campeche it is called "cherna" and the mero down there is the Nassau Grouper.

The grunts such as Sheepshead and Bream are caught by bottom fishing with bait in the rivers and lagoons.

Pompano and Flounders occur in the Bay of Campeche. While not usually sought by sport fishermen in the presence of so many other game fish, they can be caught on sandy bottoms with cut fish bait. The Pompano is considered the best eating fish found in Mexican waters and is regularly netted for the market.

The bony fishes include the Tarpon, the Ten-

One of the largest Tuna ever caught at Acapulco.

pounder, and the Bonefish. The Tarpon has already been described. The Ten-Pounder or Chiro is called "macabi" in Mexico, a name also used for the Bonefish. Schools of Ten-Pounders will be found, usually when trolling in the gulf for Tarpon. They provide excellent sport on bait rods or spinner outfits, using small plugs or feathers. Small gang-hooks are better since, if one hook is used, these little jumping jacks will soon throw it.

Sawfish, Sharks, and Mantarayas (rayfish) are found all along the coast, but they are not sought by the angler. The rayfish is harpooned, dried and made into a local food known as "bacaloa." Dried shark meat is also used for "bacaloa."

MEXICAN EQUIVALENTS OF AMERICAN NAMED FISH
GLOSSARY

ENGLISH NAME	SPANISH NAME (In Mexico)
Albacore	Albacora
Amberjack	Medregal
Barracuda	Picuda
Bass, (largemouth)	Lobina
Bass, Channel (red fish)	Pez colorado
Bass, Giant Black Sea	Mero (Pacific coast)
Bass, Red-spotted Rock	Cabrilla
Bonefish	Macabi
Bonito	Bonita
Catfish	Bagre
Cobia or Ling	Bacaloa (Veracruz)
Dolphin	Dorado
Grouper, Black	Abadejo (Campeche)
Grouper, Nassau	Mero (Campeche) (Veracruz) Cherna
Jack, Common Green	Cocinero
Jack, Crevalle	Jurel, Toro, Gallego
Jewfish, Spotted	Mero (Veracruz)
Mackerel, King	Macerela
Mackerel, Sierra	Sierra
Marlin, Black	Merlin or marlin
Marlin, Blue	Merlin or marlin
Marlin, Silver	Merlin or marlin
Marlin, Striped	Marlin and aguja de paladar
Milkfish	Sabalo (Acapulco)
Mullet	Lisa
Needlefish	Agujon
Needlefish, Ribbon	Machete
Permit	Cojinuda
Pompano	Pampano
Roosterfish	Gallo
Shark, Hammerhead	Cornudo, tiburon
Sailfish, Pacific	Pez vela
Skipjack, Black	Barrilete
Skipjack, Oceanic	Tuna
Snook	Robalo
Swordfish	Pez espada
Tarpon	Sabalo
Ten pounder; Ladyfish	Piaguacho (Acapulco) Macabi (Aguada)
Totuava	Totuava
Triggerfish	Pez puerco
Tuna, Bluefin	Tuna or Atun
Tuna, Yellowfin	Tuna or Atun
Wahoo	Peto
Weakfish or Seatrout	Trucha or curbina

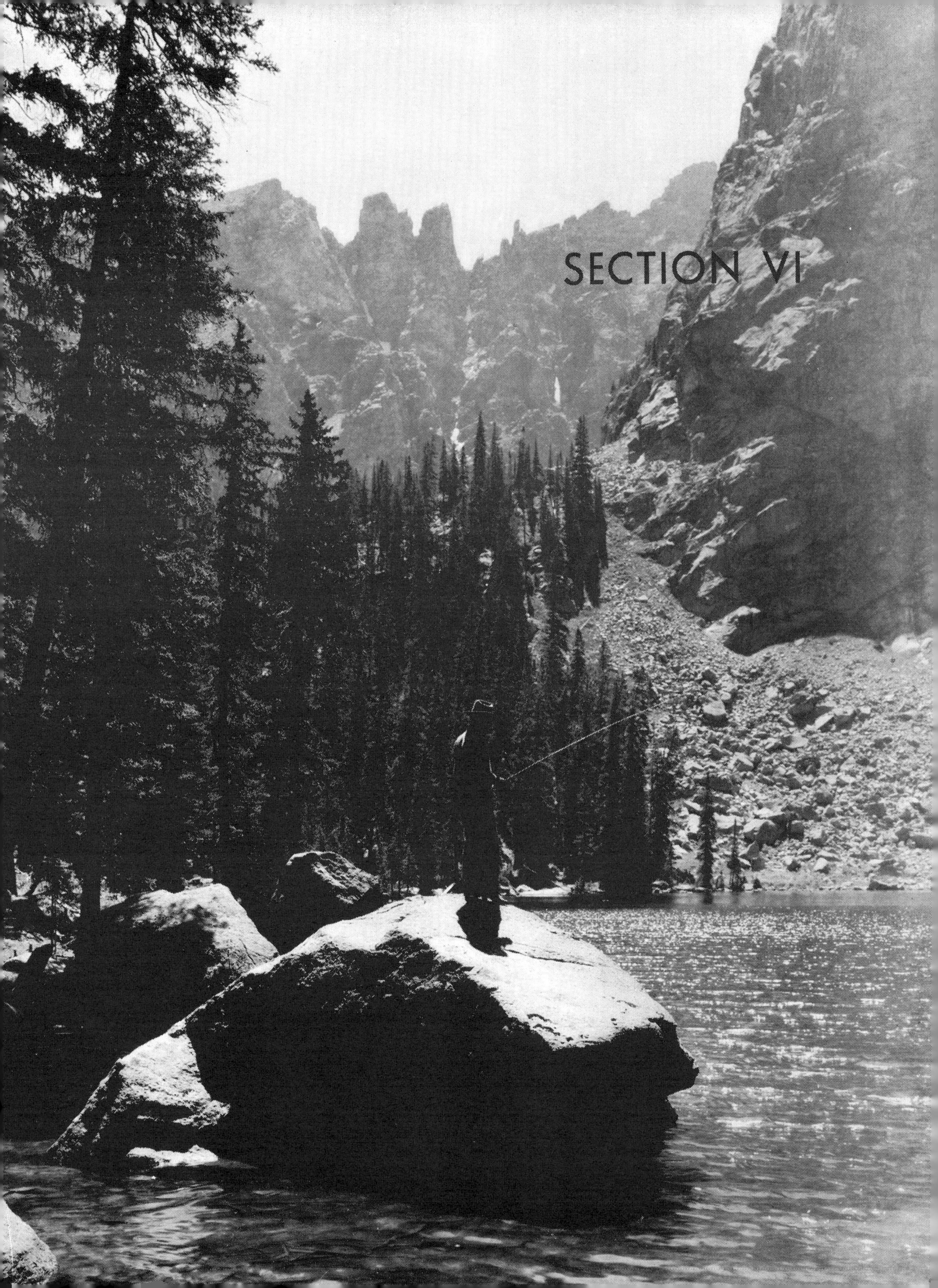

SECTION VI

WHEN AND HOW TO FISH

Part 1. Fresh Water Species

North American waters vary widely in temperature, chemical composition, fertility, and many other qualities that together determine the type and quantity of fish that can exist in them. The resulting wide variety of fishes has spurred ingenious anglers to develop special methods of fishing, sometimes special lures, and above all to acquire a detailed knowledge of the behavior and reactions of the fish sought. This latter knowledge called variously fish lore or water craft is essential to successful angling for many of the most highly prized game fish.

This section of the FISHERMAN'S ENCYCLOPEDIA has been developed to supply that knowledge. The information has been given by enthusiastic and successful anglers interested in each species. Not all species are presented in detail; rather those that can be taken by general types of fishing are either grouped or discussed very briefly. Those which have specialized habits or for which specific methods have been developed are the chief consideration. If a particular fish is not listed here, it will be found under the headings of trolling, fly casting, and similar techniques.

BASS

LARGEMOUTH BASS

The Largemouth Bass is one of the most sought after game fish. A native or introduced resident of nearly every state, and accessible for a great army of anglers it furnishes sport for countless Waltonites.

As a light tackle, fish it hits hard and fights hard enough to interest both the tyro and the veteran. Moody and unpredictable it offers enough test of angling skill to call forth the best efforts of the skilled fisherman; and often smashes viciously at the clumsy and ill-presented offerings of the beginner.

Largemouth Bass are found in ponds, lakes and rivers, and in brackish waters along the coastline. So widespread is their habitat that it is possible to find them somewhere throughout the year. They are within easy reach of any angler's lures and are usually ready to co-operate.

They make the best fight when taken on light tackle and reach their peak as scrappers when encountered in shallow water. The shallows are the place to look for them as that is where they feed. There they find minnows, crawfish, hellgrammites, frogs, bugs, moths, mice and other items of their varied menu. Brackish-water Largemouth like soft crabs and feed heavily on alewives and other salt-water minnows. Largemouth are voracious feeders —they have been known to eat small birds, small ducks, squirrels, snakes, and other small furred and feathered progeny. Bass will hit most any size lure and small ones will sometimes strike a lure larger than themselves. A big bass likes a big mouthful and with such monsters, big lures are needed for consistent results.

Largemouth are easily frightened and to get the best results one must exercise stealth and caution when nearing them. Do not scrape tackle boxes or feet across the bottom of the boat or knock an oar against it. Fish hear by vibrations through the water—their lateral lines picking them up and sending them along the numerous nerves leading to the ear stones.

They can be scared by the sight of an angler and by the movement of a casting arm. Stay low and cast at least forty feet and the catch will improve. Be quiet, careful and canny because Mr. Largemouth isn't just another fish. He deserves respect.

Largemouth Bass are found where there is cover and food. Fish for them in water from two to five feet in depth. When feeding in the shallows they usually strike the lures with force and abandon. When the fish are resting or in the shade under a log, dock or duck-blind, or in a hole in the underwater vegetation, they are harder to take. Then they are lazy and it requires coaxing to get action. Repeated casts to the same spot will often make the bass mad and he will finally come charging out after a lure.

In the heat of summer they usually loaf through the day, conducting their feeding for a short time following daybreak and again at dusk. During this

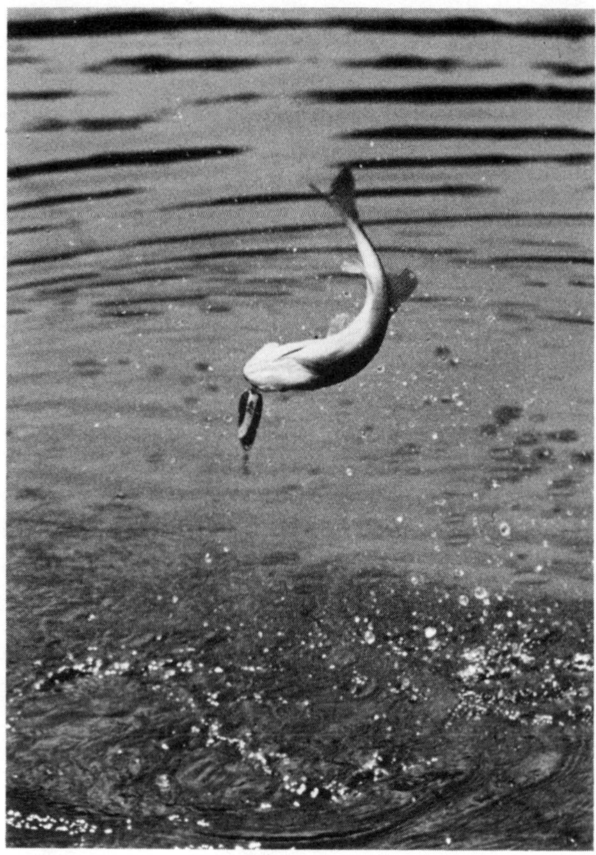

A real gamester, the most sought after fish in inland waters is the Largemouth Bass.

time they also feed at night and for those who like to fish then, the take should be very good.

Fly casting, plug casting, and spinning are the methods most used for Largemouth, each system offering the angler an opportunity to present his lures quietly and with effect.

In fly casting the rod should be at least nine feet long and be a slow stick with the action coming down into the grip. With large wind-resisting bugs, large streamers or bucktails, or the fly and spinner combinations, such a rod is needed to wait for the line to carry the lure back, and the rod's power is needed for the forward cast. When there is wind such a rod is invaluable. A nine and a half foot rod is even better than the shorter one.

A forward tapered line, usually a GAF, is needed to carry large lures along after it. The double tapered lines are almost impossible to use and the level lines while heavy enough, do not allow for "shooting" which makes for longer and easier casts. Nylon lines float better than silk, do not become as heavy when wet nor do they sink as fast. A heavy sinking line is very difficult to cast, takes away from the action of the lure and delays the strike impulse. It pays, if fishing all day long, to carry an extra line and when the one in use begins to sink, change it. Be sure to grease the line before starting to fish and rub the excess grease off with a clean cloth.

When using bass bugs play them slowly on the retrieve. During the summer, drop the bug on the surface, let it sit motionless a half-minute, give it a pop, another half minute rest, then bring it back in a series of pops until you pick it from the water for the next cast. In the fall they like a faster retrieve. A bit of experimentation on the speed of the retrieve will generally tell the tale for the particular day you are fishing.

When using streamers and bucktails or either of those lures in combination with a spinner, foot-long jerks on the bring-back seem best. The same holds true in summer as with bugs—play the lure slowly.

When the bass are deep a small fly rod spoon-type lure will bring strikes if allowed to sink before starting the retrieve. They are especially good in the spring and early summer before underwater vegetation has become thick.

Some of the best fly rod lures for bass are the Gerbubble Bug, Peck's Water Witch, Uppermans Popping Bugs, the Jaylures. Sporting-goods stores will usually have a good supply of fly rod lures all of which generally take bass.

The best color combinations in streamer flies and bucktails are red and white and yellow and white, and the spoon type lures that seem to stand out are the Metalure, the oo Huntington Drone and the Trix-orena.

More and more plug casters are using lighter equipment, longer and lighter rods and lighter lines and lures. Rods of six feet in length with lines testing as low as four pounds are used by many bass fishermen. They get more strikes and have more fun with light tackle.

Sports Afield

Largemouth Bass (Jason Lucas).

Surface plugs are effective specially if the anglers play them slowly. When the plug hits the surface, bass will quite often swim away five or six feet before turning and going back to investigate. If the lure is retrieved at once the fish will not have time to get back to strike. Wait for them and hits will increase.

Underwater lures are cast into the spot that looks like a fish hangout, and retrieved either in half-foot jerks or in a slow, steady manner. Be bold and try the hard spots as bass seek shade and shelter in out-of-the-way places. If the rig should hang up, it's only a matter of going in and freeing your lure.

The Crazy Crawler, and the plunger type lures are good surface lures. The Hawaiian Wiggler, the Johnson Silver Minnow, the Metalure, the Huntington Drone are all good underwater lures.

Spinning is gaining rapidly in popularity as a medium for catching Largemouth. Both surface and underwater lures can be used with this outfit; both types of fishing are effective and are fished the same as a plug.

Spinning tackle can now be purchased in most sporting-goods stores and a rod 7½ feet long and weighing about 5 ounces does very nicely for bass. The line can be of braided Nylon or monofilament and of whatever pound test is desired. Four- to seven-pound monofilament is used by most spinning enthusiasts. Almost any of the popular reels manufactured for spinning will do a workmanlike job.

SMALLMOUTH BASS

This splendid game fish can be taken by bait fishing, trolling, artificial bait, casting, and fly fishing. However, to be successful with any method the angler should have enough knowledge of the habits of the fish to indicate the time and places where they are likely to be found.

Why does any fish take either a bait or an artificial lure? It would be a wonderful thing for anglers to have a scientific answer to this question. Scientists have carried on research on populations of bass and conservation of bass, but they have concerned themselves with behavior and food habits only insofar as they affect conservation problems.

The most obvious fact is that to catch bass one must go to a place where there are bass. It is not simply a matter of a list of waters and the fish that they contain. If it can be assumed that bass are to be found in the lake or stream to be fished—what then? They are not uniformly distributed and one needs to know where they are most likely to be found. Here we are on a ground in which scientific data are available.

The bass is known to frequent well-defined types of habitat at certain seasons of the year. The Smallmouth Bass is a fish of clear, cool water, and only under severe conditions will it be found in weed beds and in muddy and stagnant water. The habits of the fish in large, open bodies of water differ markedly from those of the fish in inland lakes, and the angler must know of these habits if he is to be successful.

In the Great Lakes, where many excellent bass fishing grounds exist, the fish are gregarious in

Okla. Game and Fish News

A prize Largemouth Black Bass taken from an artificial lake in Oklahoma.

habit, and after spawning, which is usually completed about mid-June (in the southern lakes), they form into large schools which move haphazardly about, presumably in search of feeding grounds. At this time they are very susceptible to angling, and the party of anglers which finds itself over one of these groups will have good fishing. Experience indicates, however, that the bass caught from these schools are not the largest fish, although one or two fairly large ones may be taken. Many of the larger individuals appear to be solitary, in a more restricted feeding ground.

These schools of fish are easily located by guides and regular visitors who know the waters, for the feeding grounds are the same from year to year. Ledges of rock and gravel which rise from the lake bed to within five or ten feet of the surface provide the best feeding conditions, for it is on these that the nymphs and larvae of insects, and the crustaceans on which the fish feed are found.

In inland waters and smaller lakes, the bass are generally found in spots that are sheltered from the sun. This is noticed particularly in clear waters. High banks of rock dropping steeply into the water usually indicate deep water below, and the bass seem to move slowly along such banks from end to end. Very often a shoal or rock or rubble will be found at the end of such a bank, and the bass will be feeding there. If there is a strong stream flowing into the lake, or a current passing through it, angling is generally better at the upstream end than further down, and particularly where a rock shoal or outcrop creates an eddy.

In many northern lakes, drifting logs collect in bays and back-waters, creating a fairly large raft. Beneath such rafts the bass fishing is excellent, particularly if the water is fairly deep. The leeches and insect larvae which are found on the undersides of these logs offer excellent feeding, and the cool, dark pocket formed is apparently attractive to the fish.

In deep bays and along shorelines which are sheltered by overhanging trees, excellent fishing will be found, particularly for the fly fishermen, for the bass may be seen in the evenings feeding on the insects which drop into the water. The bass does not leap in the course of surface feeding, but seizes its prey in a flat swirl which frequently is quite silent.

It should be kept in mind that bass move about considerably in search of food, and, therefore, a location that provided a good catch one day may produce nothing the next. They also have a habit of moving in schools, and if one is fortunate in locating one of these schools, a day's limit may be taken in a short time.

In streams the angler will be most successful in bays and back-waters where an eddy is created, and where a sheltered pocket of relatively deep water exists. It must be remembered, however, that Smallmouth will be found only in clean, cool streams. In spots where a stretch of fast water flows abruptly into a deep pool, and slows down, the eddys and currents created seem to be particularly attractive to bass. Although the fish taken in such places are generally smaller than those found in clear cool lakes, they are generally gamier, will fight strongly, and will be of excellent eating quality.

Now that the most likely spots are outlined, bass still move around and may easily be at a spot other than the one chosen. But suppose the fish are where they were expected to be, what next? Everyone knows that there are times when one can see them plainly, and yet not catch one. The problem in simple terms is to induce the bass to seize a hook. There may be times at which bass will seize any object in the water, but this is certainly not the normal case. Why, then, do bass seize things?

Presumably most seizing of objects is related to feeding and in order to catch bass one should present with the hook either an article of food or a lure made to look or act like one. One would expect that a study of the food of bass would be the best guide in choosing the bait or lure, but this does not necessarily follow. Often the best baits appear seldom or never in the bass's stomach as natural food. The little frogs that are caught in wet grass and used at the summer's end with such deadly effect are normally inaccessible to the fish. They nevertheless release the much-desired seizing reaction. Crayfish are important natural food animals, but the moulting or soft-shelled animals hide themselves and are rarely found as food of bass. Nevertheless, the hard-shelled crayfish are a mediocre bass bait, and the soft-shelled animals are so good that the technique of changing water temperature to produce moulting is a stock in trade of a sizeable commercial bait industry. Among artificial lures, it is conceivable that a lure bearing no resemblance to any animal at rest or in action could take bass efficiently.

Quite evidently, then, the food of bass does not give an infallible clue to lures for any and all seasons. However, it is important enough that an angler cannot know too much about it. Again we find that the scientists have studied food with a view to estimating the productivity of lakes and streams, rather than with a view to catching bass. When their records are searched for the sort of information wanted, it is not there; all that can be given is a general statement.

Studies of the food habits of Smallmouth Bass reveal that the most important items are nymphs, hellgrammites, crayfish, and fish. This is not to say that the fish will not take, if available, such standbys as frogs, grasshoppers, and earthworms, but after making allowance for relative availability of food types, it appears that these are the most popular items of diet.

Any of these foods can be used as live bait. The greatest advantage to using a live bait is that it is alive; the longer it remains so, the greater its effectiveness in attracting fish. For this reason, it is wise to use care in placing the bait on the hook so that no vital organs are injured, and the natural movement of the bait is not impeded, for this will attract fish.

In streams the principal food items are crayfish and hellgrammites.

In lakes or very wide and sluggish streams, the crayfish is best fished on the bottom and the hellgrammites used in conjunction with a spinner for casting or trolling. There is no objection to still fishing, but it must be remembered that only a very small part of a lake or stream is inhabited by fish and a wide coverage is highly desirable in order to locate them.

A popular bait in Ontario lakes is the leach. This forms an important item of diet in some lakes, and may be placed on the hook like an earthworm, and trolled or cast with a No. 2 spinner, or on the popular June Bug lure. Leaches are easily caught in a minnow trap baited with a piece of raw liver or bacon, or a piece of canned meat. In most lakes, immersion of a bare foot in the water near the shore for a few minutes will bring these animals to the spot, when they may be thrown on shore with the hand or a canoe paddle.

The use of earthworms has long been a standby for fishermen both young and old, and they apparently continue to appeal to fish. The earthworm should be hooked through the thinner posterior and since no vital organs are found here and the worm has a greater chance of staying alive and active on the hook. The body is hooked in two or three places, having a good portion trailing in the water. A spinner added ahead of the hook makes this an excellent rig for bait.

Casting or slow-trolling live minnows is popularly overrated as bass bait. Not only do they yield limited success, but the unfortunate tendency of some fishermen to empty their minnow pail into the lake at the end of a day's fishing has lead to many introductions of non-native fish, and seriously damaged the fishing in many lakes.

Chub, dace, and shiners are the most popular minnows in use in Ontario and elsewhere, and are generally available at resorts, or they may be taken by a minnow trap. Minnows should always be hooked through both lips as hooking through only one quickly kills the fish by drowning. Once again, for casting or trolling, a spinner may be added ahead of the bait. It must be remembered that a minnow swims fairly slowly, and when casting or trolling a great deal of the natural action is lost due to the speed at which the bait is moved through the water. As in all fishing, take it easy.

A small frog makes a good bass bait, and once again, obey the cardinal rule of hooking it in such a way that it will stay alive, and fishing it in such a way that its natural movement is allowed full scope. Hook it through both lips, and if still fishing, give it several feet of free line. If casting or trolling, move it slowly through the water.

If bass are surface feeding in the evening, a grasshopper or cricket tied firmly to the shank of a small hook, and cast onto the surface of the water, in the manner of a dry fly, will usually give results, and if a fly rod is used, the ensuing battle will thrill the most seasonal fisherman. Crane flies and stone flies may also be used.

Artificial lures in their diversity of form, color, and action are surely equalled only in variety by fishermen themselves. Probably a wider selection is offered the Smallmouth Bass than any other game fish.

The most important group of lures are those designed in color, shape, and action to resemble various items of the fish's natural diet. The question of whether color actually has any influence on the efficacy of a lure is debatable, there being arguments on both sides. However, it is obviously necessary to attract a fish's attention before it will strike, and anything which contributes to this is highly desirable. Baits which have a brilliant shine are valuable for this reason. But it must be remembered that the bass will probably take most artificial baits from below, and looking up at the bait against the bright background of the surface of the water will probably distinguish little of the color. The glitter of a highly polished spoon or spinner will show, however, and plugs which incorporate such features are often very good.

The most important feature in artificial lures is the action and speed with which they are moved through the water. A frog swims with a thrust, slowing to a glide, followed by another thrust, and this action should be simulated in using such a lure. A minnow-like lure, on the other hand, should be moved in a slow and irregular manner similar to the questing path of a minnow in search of food. Above all else, a bait should be moved slowly, for the fish seems to require time to decide.

Another error which anglers frequently make is that of retrieving a cast bait immediately. The bait strikes the water with considerable force, and is certainly enough to startle any fish which may be in the vicinity. If a few moments are allowed to elapse before the plug is moved, the startled fish are given time to recover from the shock, and if interested, to investigate the plug. Many anglers also make the error of casting into likely-looking spots when they would be much wiser to cast beyond them, if this is possible, and retrieve the plug through the spot in which they believe there may be fish.

Plug baits and spoons are divided into types that move on the surface, below the surface, and at a considerable depth. Each of these have a particular function. Generally speaking, surface lures are best in the early part of the season, and deep running lures come into their own in the later part.

Bass fishing is at its best in the earlier part of the season. The bass at this time are feeding vigorously after the spawning and nesting periods, are aggressive and active, and will strike almost anything that is offered. Curiosity lures are very successful at this stage as are plugs which imitate minnows. Minnows themselves offer a better chance of success at this time, as well as do soft-shelled crayfish. The normal diet of the bass consists of the larger items such as these during the early part of July. Later in July, the bass will be seen surface feeding under the trees along rocky shores, and dry flies become attractive baits. Wet flies, trolled slowly, are also good, especially during the later part of the day.

After the first week in August, it becomes increasingly difficult to lure bass to the hook; not that the bass are not there, as often they can be plainly seen and will refuse to take bait even when dangled before their nose. At this season fly fishing has been found to be the most successful, using streamer flies tied on a No. 2 hook. The hair of the streamer should be of a kind that does not mat when in the water. The driftwood shores if well worked, will generally produce good results. The good dry-fly fisherman should try his luck, but will probably conclude that the streamer is the best all-round fly for Smallmouth Bass.

Trolling also has a fair chance of success by adding a small spinner and a few split shot above the streamer fly. Rocky shores with only a few feet of water may be trolled in this way. Although the persistent angler will take the Smallmouth during the early part of the day, it is the writer's experience, and that of most authorities consulted, that the late afternoon, especially just before sundown, is the time they bite most freely.

In bass fishing the paramount problem is always to get the fish to strike, and trial and error are the only means known as yet to find the right lure. Every angler knows that it is wise to take advantage of the other fellow's experience, but there should always be a willingness to experiment. Trial and error can be put on a reasonably sound scientific basis by keeping good records and critically evaluating each trial. Such an instance may be seen in a paper on angling in Lake Simcoe, Ontario, published by James R. Westman and Charlotte B. Westman. Lake Simcoe is a large lake, easily accessible to anglers and known to be full of Smallmouth Bass which were not being caught by anyone. As the authors said, "after a series of discouraging experiments" they succeeded in catching the bass by trolling a homemade bucktail streamer and spinner 35 to 60 feet astern in the wash of a power boat travelling two or three miles per hour.

The Pikie Minnow is one of the most popular lures. There are many color variations available, all of which are equally popular. Variations on the form are widely used, the jointed form being in demand, and a smaller variation, the River Runt. It is impossible to describe all variations, but generally speaking, these lures are below-surface running, heavy enough for bait casting, and are fairly conservative in shape. Colors vary widely from plain white with a red head, to the more recent plastic, semi-transparent models with an intricate simulated scale pattern. The other major choice in the plug field is the flat fish. The smaller sizes or fly-rod models are most popular.

Among the spoons, the most widely sought are the June Bug, for use in conjunction with a live bait, or with a feathered hook. Another combination which is coming into wide use is composed of a Yellow Sally fly with a No. 1 Indiana spinner, attached to a weighted gut lead, the whole being about nine inches long. Double or tandem spinners are also popular, and the so-called Viking spinner, combining a two bladed spinner with a red streamer fly, is also in demand.

WHITE BASS

It has only been within recent years that the White Bass has caught and held the interest of American sports fishermen. It is conceivable that an abundance of the better known game fishes caused anglers to overlook its sporting possibilities. Too, fishery commissions, in an effort to supply the great demand for game fishes, have planted the White Bass in districts far removed from its endemical range where it has prospered so well that some states, Oklahoma, for instance, has no restrictions on the taking of the fish. Certainly this has increased the popularity of the White Bass, which is destined to continue to fill an important niche in the fishery resources of the more arid states, especially where artificial lakes constitute the principal fish producing waters.

The White Bass as a game fish, when compared to either of the three species of black bass, leaves something to be desired, and as a food fish, it is also inferior. However, there is much to recommend it, either to the bait fisherman, or the angler using artificial lures, and, when taken on reasonably light tackle, it gives a credible account of itself before coming to net.

A careful study of the habits of the White Bass reveals a rather whimsical, unpredictable character. It is a fish of big, deep, open water in either lakes, or large streams, and in its spring migration it

The Photo Shop, Durant, Okla.

The White Bass is so abundant in some districts of Oklahoma that there is neither creel or size limits imposed.

rarely ascends the smaller streams, or creeks; preferring open water. It is not given to secretive habits of hiding among lily pads, weeds, log jams, or drowned tree tops.

The principal migration of the White Bass occurs prior to spawning in the spring. This period varies with the latitude, and often there are variations from season to season in areas at the same latitude. In its extreme southern range, which is perhaps east central Texas, spawning occurs in late April, or early May; northward as spring advances, the period is progressively later.

Not only the time, but the length of the migration varies from season to season. This has a direct bearing upon the spring fishing for White Bass. When there is an abundance of water in the spring of the year, and the flow is heavy in the streams, these fish will make extensive runs upstream, and fishing will be generally good along the entire length of the migration until the spawning season when it drops off sharply. After spawning there is a general movement back to deeper water, and the fishing is again good.

In the warm months of July and August trolling with deep running plugs, spinners, and other artificial lures, or still fishing, using live minnows, will prove most successful.

The White Bass is highly gregarious, and except during the spawning season, it may be found in large schools. When gathered in schools the fish has the interesting habit of surfacing in the deep bays of lakes, or off the sand bars in the quiet eddies of streams to feed avidly upon minnows. In the different areas where the White Bass is found this habit is referred to as "boiling," "surfacing", and "shoaling". These periods of feeding activity occur at different times of the day in different localities, but the hour will likely be the same, once it is established in a certain body of water.

When fishing for the White Bass the angler is certain to be harassed by its capricious, unpredictable character. Often, when schools of White Bass are "boiling" the surface while feeding on minnows, the fly fisherman's offering may go unnoticed for many casts, then suddenly, for no apparent reason, the fish begin taking the fly with a thrilling eagerness. They may continue to strike until the angler has taken a dozen, or more fish, or they may cease rising as suddenly as they began.

Save for the spawning season adult White Bass are not often found in shallow water. In lakes, the White Bass is "where you find him". This is disturbing to the angler who is fishing strange water, for he cannot so easily "mark his fish down" as when fishing for the black basses, for example.

The bait fisherman who is unfamiliar with a piece of water should troll, using a minnow with a June-Bug spinner ahead. When a bass is taken the spot may be fished either by casting over the area, or the boat may be anchored for still fishing. While the White Bass will take insects, grubs, and crustaceans, small to medium sized live minnows are generally preferred. The tackle may be a light bait, or plug rod, equipped with a dependable casting reel. The bobber may be omitted since the "tight line" method usually works best. It should be remembered that White Bass do not possess the casual temperament of such fish as Crappie, for example, and they will disperse quickly if frightened. For this reason, when a school has been located, fish quietly. If the fish disperse find the school again by casting in all directions around the boat, or lift anchor and troll in an ever widening circle.

The plug caster will get best results with such lures as the Dardevle, Flat Fish, Russellure, River Runt, Deep-R-Doodle, Johnson Silver Spoon, and many others, but all should be of small size.

The angler devoted to spinning will find the White Bass an excellent candidate for the many lures adapted to this method of fishing. These small, deep running spinning lures are particularly well suited for White Bass angling.

The fly caster will find the White Bass a most worthy gamester when conditions are favorable to the use of lures maneuvered on, or near the surface. In the spring, before the height of the spawning season, the fly rod and its lures are effective weapons for taking White Bass. Then again in early autumn, when the fish begin to feed actively on the surface, the fly fisherman may score heavily.

Fly rod lures should include streamers of Silver Doctor, Parmabelle, Jock Scott, Green Ghost, Mickey Finn, Aunt Ider, Grizzly King, Colonel Fuller, and other predominately light-colored patterns. These lures should be in streamers tied on slender, long-shank hooks. Some of the most effective top-water lures are bass bugs with white body, red head, and wings of the flank feathers of the mallard drake, feathered minnows with pearl bodies, and white streamers, gray bodies with gray streamers, and the yellow May. These lures are most effective when fished over schools of White Bass when they are "boiling", or feeding on the surface. However, trolling and bait fishing are probably the most productive of sustained results through the entire season.

In its southern range the White Bass offers excellent sport for the winter bait fisherman. November is usually a good month. December and January are not so good, but during February and March the fish again become active and bite well until the spawning season.

CARP

The question often debated but seldom settled is which is the most elusive, sagacious, and difficult fish to catch. Naturally only game fish are considered and the trout get the palm. Here, so the story goes, is a fish of discriminating tastes, that must be fished for with light tackle, small, lifelike lures, presented with flawless finesse and with a degree of caution that virtually hides the angler's presence.

Admitting that the trout has all these attributes, it still is not the most difficult fish to take on hook and line. That distinction is given by many anglers to a fish that is not a game fish at all. It is one of our most hated and also most common of fish. It is the Carp, detested, despised, and berated. Even

Okla. Game and Fish News

The Carp is gaining in favor among anglers living in districts where the more desirable species of game fish are scarce.

to fish for it is considered beneath one's dignity and is rarely deemed worthy even of passing mention. And yet no wiser fish ever swam than the Carp, and no harder fish to capture ever existed. The truth of the matter is that the best trout fisherman might prove a total flop in taking the Carp. If this happens to skilled fishermen, what chance do less skilled individuals have of hooking one of these keen-brained root-eaters?

First, the Carp is a vegetarian. It may not be a strict one, but vegetation provides the main items on its daily bill of fare. It does invade the beds of nest-making fishes, bass, sunfish, etc., and absorbs quantities of roe.

The vegetarian habits of the Carp are sharply defined. In Wisconsin and Minnesota Carp are netted by commercial fishermen by the thousands in summer when their flesh is soft and has the least food value. They are dumped into ponds and are fed on corn, potatoes, turnips, parsnips, carrots, rutabagas, etc., finely chopped. In the late autumn the fish, virtually rolling in fat, are shipped alive in tank cars to the large cities.

The best method for taking Carp starts by baiting with chopped vegetables a definite spot in a lake or stream. The vegetables are often placed in a pail with a raised rim around the bottom. A fine wire is twisted around the pail above this rim. Place a stone in the pail and let it down to the bottom by a cord on the pail. By upturning the bail with a pull on the wire, the bait is deposited in a small area on the bottom. When possible the bait should be placed on sand rather than on a mud bottom.

By baiting a spot by this method for a week, the Carp will be coming freely to it. The Carp is one of the most cautious of all fishes. They have been observed swimming around a baited place for an hour or more before venturing to take a bit of vegetable. Even then, the bait is tested by mouthing and dropping it before it is eaten. Gradually the fish comes freely and eats the bait.

In making Carp bait many fishermen use gloves covered with oil of anise. The doughball bait is made by digging out the interior of a half-baked loaf of bread. This can be worked into a semblance of dough, but unlike unbaked dough will "hang together." To aid in keeping it on the hook, finely shredded cotton is worked into it. The balls are usually the size of large peas, although larger ones sometimes work equally well. The cotton will hold the ball firm on the hook and will not break off. Oil of anise, red ink, carmine, honey or sugar are among the substances sometimes worked into the dough.

The use of raw vegetables on the hook is not recommended, but half-boiled vegetables are often used. They are trimmed into round bits and placed on the hook. A carrot or parsnip is most favored and anise is also frequently used on these baits.

Small pieces of fish, also anointed with anise oil and fished singly to cover the hook point, are useful. Grub worms, white tree borers, and round balls cut out of solid animal fat are also used successfully.

Carp fishermen, looking for real excitement, use the regulation fly rod outfit, preferably with a tapered line. Nine-foot leaders, tapered to .010 at the hook are best. The leader should be misthued, green or brown dyed or otherwise camouflaged.

Cast the lure to place it alongside or very near the baited spot. It will then lie directly in the path of the fish as it moves around the pile and he will discover it. In taking the lure, the Carp mouths it, a process which is indicated by the slight tug. A foot or so of slack line should be left beyond the end of the rod to insure that the fish will not feel resistance. As the fish backs up or moves away, set the hook.

In playing the fish, lead it away from the baited hole, but do this carefully so that it will not be alarmed. By carefully leading the fish away from the baited place, other Carp will not be frightened and as many as four or five Carp may be taken. Large Carp take the bait as well as smaller specimens. If possible, work the hooked fish into the shallows where it can be beached, but remember that the Carp uses its weight in fighting and that a 10 to 25-pound Carp can put up a real fight. Too, when landing the fish in shallow water, it should be remembered that it will put up a real struggle when shallow water is reached.

Remove the skin in preparing a Carp for the table. There is a red streak of flesh about one inch wide along its lateral line from gills to tail. Cut this entirely out on both sides. Removal of the skin and this strip greatly improves the fish for eating.

THE CATFISHES

Although they have individual characteristics, the habits of the numerous species of catfishes are essentially the same. Their seasonal movements are limited. From spring through to early autumn their feeding forays carry them into the shallower waters of lakes and streams. This is particularly true of the Channel Catfishes. During late autumn there is a general movement to deeper water where they remain for the winter, becoming much less active and more gregarious, particularly in their northern range.

The Catfish's wide range of foods includes insects, worms, frogs, toads, crayfish, mussels, snails, and fishes. To this array the Catfish angler has added the liver of chicken, beef, lamb, rabbit, coagulated chicken and beef blood, oviduct of fowls, beef milt, and a great variety of manufactured concoctions which may be grouped under the single heading "stink bait."

To say which of these baits is best would not only be presumptuous, but would certainly invite disagreement. However, as a rule, seasonal or natural baits are most effective during spring, summer, and early autumn, when such foods are present. For Channel Catfishes one of the best is the sand toad. Large catfish, especially the Flathead, or Goujon, which attains a weight of 100 pounds, prefer live fish, which many be a Gizzard Shad, Sucker, Bluegill, or a small specimen of his own kind.

Although the Catfishes are primarily nocturnal in habit, and are bottom feeders, this is not a hard and fast rule. They become active on dark, overcast days, or when the stream is turbid from a freshet; and often they feed on the surface when there is a hatch of mayflies, or when grasshoppers are abundant; or when accorns, elm seeds, and floating plankton are on the water.

A varied assortment of tackle is employed by Catfish anglers, but devotees of the sport lay considerable store in being equipped with the right tackle. A casting rod of plastic, steel, or split bamboo with ample "back bone" for striking a heavy fish on a long line is most essential. This rod is fitted with a reliable casting reel spooling 100 wards of 18 pound test braided silk, or Nylon line. If the water is quite clear a heavy three foot Nylon leader is best. Since night fishing is the general rule with anglers, the bobber is omitted and the bait is fished "tight line." Because the Catfish is a bottom feeder no weight is used, and the bait is rolled along the bottom down stream in the current, or dragged on the bottom in still water.

While every angler has his own theories regarding the influence upon feeding fish of the wind, moon, barometric pressure, and water conditions it is generally conceded that an east wind is an ill wind for Catfish angling. A full moon, other opinions notwithstanding, seems to have no influence on their feeding habits, but with a falling barometer, they definitely tend to cease feeding. Fluctuating water does not appear important; in fact, rising water often increases their feeding activities, provided it is not too heavy with mud. However, since observations on fish behavior are never infallible, there are exceptions to these rules.

The Catfish offer the angler a year round sporting proposition. When the water begins to warm up in the spring, the fish move out of their winter depths and range the shallows for food; and the angler fishes the deep runs and riffles of streams, the shallower bays of lakes and ponds, using frogs, crayfish, toads, or angle worms. During the day the fish may retreat to the deeper pools, where there is cover of overhanging banks, tree roots, and windfalls; here the still fisherman may arouse their appetites with a tempting offering.

When summer brings more stabilized water levels, and long, hot days, the Catfish waits until night has cooled the top water flowing into riffles and runs before setting out to feed. The angler finds gravel bars above deep runs at the upper end of large holes of water to be most productive. Using frogs, sand toads, minnows, or other natural baits, he lets the line run out with the current, thus allowing his bait to explore the bottom. Perhaps Catfish angling is at its lowest ebb at this season, particularly during the day in the fish's southern range, however, activity usually increases if rains bring high water. Yet, such species as the Bullheads seem obliging in spite of varying seasons and weather—which is a boon to the casual fisherman.

With autumn's approach bringing crisp days and cool nights, the Catfish become more active; and

Okla. Game and Fish News

The Catfish attains great size in the large, more sluggish streams of the Plains States.

the angler fishes riffles and runs of streams, the shallow water of lakes during the night, and the hollow banks, log jams, and windfalls in deeper pools during the day. Baits may be widely assorted, for cool weather stimulates an already voracious appetite.

While Catfish are extremely hardy they are not unlike other species in their preference for a narrow temperature range; in winter they retreat to deeper pools, where the temperature varies perhaps not more than 10° or 12° from mid-winter to mid-summer. Because of this characteristic, winter is generally considered the best season for the sport. Once the fish are located the angler has little difficulty in arousing their appetites with such "soft baits" as coagulated chicken, or beef blood, liver of beef, chicken, rabbit, and lamb (a prime favorite) or numerous commercial "stink baits."

From late summer until after the first hard freeze grasshoppers are usually abundant, and the angler who uses them for bait, and fly-rod equipment for tackle, attains the utmost in Catfish angling pleasure. A six-foot leader and a No. 2, or No. 4 hook, without weight, permits the grasshopper to float on, or near the surface. This type of angling is best done in streams that are small enough for wading. Let the current to take the grasshopper downstream, hugging the banks where there is overhanging grass, slipping into the deeper pockets and pools, or whirling into eddies below riffles.

The caster of artificials seldom concerns himself with the Catfishes. There are occasions, however, when these fish will strike his lures, especially fly-rod streamers and bass bugs, with all the gusto of a Black Bass. During late summer and well into autumn, twilight is the best time for taking Catfish with artificials. Were it not for the fact that they are nocturnal in feeding habits, and appear to have inferior eyesight, it is conceivable that fly fishermen would readily add the Catfishes to their roster of game fishes.

CRAPPIES

The Crappies, both the Black and the White species, are generally considered panfishes, however, they are quite capable of outgrowing the pan. Perhaps five pounds is near the maximum weight attained, but individuals weighing two pounds are not uncommon.

Because of their adaptability to pond culture, the Crappies, through the activities of both state and federal agencies, are now present in waters far beyond their endemic range. Today the Crappies thrive throughout the ponds, lakes, lagoons, bayous, and the more sluggish streams of the country.

The ranges of the two species are essentially the same—if there is much divergence it might be that the Black Crappie is more abundant northward, and the White Crappie southward.

There is no appreciable difference in the habits of the two species; both are fishes of quiet water, and seek the cover of weed beds, log jams, brush piles, and drowned tree tops when they are available. Their gregarious tendencies are more pronounced from late autumn until the approach of the spawning season in the spring. However, when the spawning has ended, Crappie will again school, and it is not uncommon to see great schools feeding upon the surface on a still evening.

The Crappie's food includes insects, larvae, crustacea, minnows, and small fishes. As a general rule the Crappies come to the surface and feed upon hatches of insects much in the manner of their distant relative, the Bluegill Sunfish. But, there seems to be a tendency, as the fish attain greater size, for them to become more piscivorous in their diet. The larger individuals are rather solitary fishes, ranging and feeding much as the Black Basses.

As to angling, the Crappies hold a widespread and genuine interest among fishermen. They take flies and spinners readily, as well as other artificials, but bait fishing, using natural baits, is the generally accepted practice among Crappie fishermen. In fact, because of their habit of congregating in some favorable spot, forming what fishermen call a "crappie bed," the Crappie is the especial delight of the sedentary angler. Establishing himself comfortably in a boat, or beneath the spreading branches of a friendly tree, the fisherman may pursue his sport in a leisurely manner.

The Crappies are greatly inferior to their relatives the Black Basses as fighters, but on light tackle, they resist sufficiently to sustain the interest of the sedentary angler at least.

There are occasions, however, when the Crappies afford more than casual angling pleasure; in early spring, when they have moved from the deep water into the shallower bays, the fly fisherman may experience lively, if not thrilling, sport, taking Crappie on wet flies, streamers, spinner lures, and other artificials. Such flies and streamers as Mickey Finn, Yellow May, Colonel Fuller, Canary, and Babcock are effective fly-rod lures for the early Crappie fisherman.

In early autumn the Crappie again become active, and the fly caster experiences little difficulty in taking his share of fish. At this season the angler should add dry flies and top-water lures to his assortment of wet flies and streamers. Dry fly patterns in Brown Bivisible, Brown Hackle, Ginger Quill, Evening Dun, Furnace Hackle, and Gray Hackle are all dependable dry fly patterns. These flies should be in sizes 8's and 10's. Large Dusky and White Millers, fished dry, are also most effective if used during late evening and twilight.

On dark, overcast days in mid-summer, especially in their northern range, the Crappies will feed actively during the day. Wet flies and streamers produce better results on these occasions; but, when evening shadows lengthen, and a hatch of insects is over the water, the observing fly fisherman, seeing rings on the surface of the quiet bay where Crappie are rising to insects, fishes the rise with a dry fly replica.

Recently there has been an upsurge of interest in spinning in this country, a method of angling which has found favor in England for more than a quarter of a century. The spinning rod and its lures is about mid-way between the casting and the fly rod, and their lures. Anglers devoted to spinning will find the Crappies willing takers, particularly during the warm months of summer, and again when cold weather sends the fish into deeper water for comfort.

As a general rule the casting-rod lures are a bit too large for the Crappie, but the spinning-rod lures may be as small as those used on the fly rod. When fish are down because of weather conditions the weighted lures of the spinning rod allow deep fishing, making them very effective for this fish. True, the fly fisherman may use unweighted spinner lures and by strip casting get down to the fish, but such tackle is not as well suited for this type of fishing as is the spinning rod.

Small minnows are considered standard bait when the bait fisherman angles for Crappies; however, the larger minnows, up to three and four inches long, will often attract the larger fish. For bait-fishing a light bait, or for casting rod, a multi-action reel, snelled hooks, light shot for sinker, and a very light bobber, preferably a quill bobber, are best. The live minnow should be hooked lightly under the dorsal fin so as to permit it to remain lively.

The mouth of the Crappie is very tender, giving rise to the name "papermouth," in some districts. The tender mouth makes it necessary for the angler to handle the hooked fish with great care lest the hook tear the thin membrane of the mouth and the fish pull free. (It is the steadfast conviction of many inveterate Crappie fishermen that the fish's lack of fighting spirit is more than compensated for because of the great skill required in landing the fish.) Be that as it may, the tender mouth does necessitate skillful handling of the fish on light tackle.

The still fisherman should locate a drowned tree top, or other like cover in fairly deep water, baiting with grasshoppers, worms, crayfish, or minnows which are generally preferable. The Crappie takes the bait rather gently and it should be given time to get the bait well in its mouth before the angler's strike, which should always be definite, but not too vigorous, for the hook will tear out. A light and very sensitive bobber is best because of the gentle manner in which the Crappie takes the hook. Larger bobbers resist the fish too strongly which causes it to release the bait.

As a food fish the crappies are held in high esteem by many who know them well. When taken from good water the flesh is firm, white, and flaky, with a rather neutral, but agreeable flavor.

GRAYLING

When Grayling are mentioned, three things come to the mind of anyone who has been associated with this beautiful fish: that long, flowing dorsal fin; an insatiable appetite for flies; and broiled, boiled, or fried—a delectable flavor. As if these were not enough superb qualities to wrap up in one irridescent package, there are still more. More often than not he will rise to a fly in the middle of the stream in mid-day, and if he misses the first time, it's still okay—he'll keep trying!

The writer's introduction to the Arctic Grayling occurred quite informally about ten o'clock one evening many years ago in northern Canada. Since then the acquaintance has been renewed whenever possible. It was early June just after breakup while trailing a 20-foot hunk of line on the end of which was a Dardevle spoon, a hook baited with rabbit meat, and a very bedraggled Black Gnat. This was just to be sure that no fish were passed up. At this point the Yukon River is crystal clear, and it isn't until the glacial silt of the White River enters it that it takes on the white complexion that turns into a muddy gray long before it empties into the Bering Sea 2,000 miles down stream. Just as we were engulfed by swarms of voracious mosquitoes, a leaping fish on the tow line, and splashing sound all around called attention to the Grayling. It was this first hatch of mosquitoes that created all this rumpus. Pulling ashore and setting up rods, Grayling struck on the first cast of a No. 12 Black Gnat and a Gray Hackle with a red tail. It was hard to see in the eleven o'clock twilight, but those Grayling came clear out of the water and tried to take the flies on a graceful, downward plunge. Every cast ended up with that solid feeling on the far end.

The fight usually started with a quick run downstream, trying to sound, followed by a cross current rush winding up with a short series of surface acrobatics, then three or four more attempts to take the fly to the bottom. This fight never lasted more than a few minutes, and it was no trick to land fish by the old western method of dragging them out on a little sand bar. This is characteristic of Grayling. He puts up a nice battle for a while, and then all of a sudden it's over. Whether he is just plain exhausted or suddenly decides that he can't live forever, the net result is an easy job of conversion to the creel.

The first few Grayling looked like twins. They were just an even 16 inches in length, weight about 1½ pounds, and had that kind of firmness found only in cold water fish.

Except for that occasional "grand-daddy," Grayling almost invariably run to even size; it seems to be true whether the fish are 8 inches or 20. This may be a case of adult fish having feeding habits different enough to segregate them from the immature, and that ordinarily one or the other is taken. There is also a possibility that the older fish beat the young ones to the punch and that normally the largest size that the water, feed, and environment can produce are taken.

Next to the Dolly Varden Trout, the Grayling is more widely distributed in Alaska than any other game fish. They occur in every major river drainage north of the Gulf of Alaska, and in adjoining British Columbia and Yukon Territory. They are apparently generally distributed over most of northern Canada. The larger rivers of Alaska are laden to varying degrees with glacial silt, and although the Grayling travel through these waters, they are found only in the clear tributary streams from the largest down to little streams that can be stepped across. There are none in the Aleutian Islands, but very large specimens can be taken at Becharof Lake on the Alaska Peninsula, and they are common in most of the Bristol Bay watershed, an area also famous for its big Rainbows.

Northward to the Goodnews River and Kuskokwim watershed they are found in all the clear tributaries, and in the streams of the Arctic coast from the mouth of the Yukon all the way to Demarcation Point. The Tanana, Koyukuk, Kantishna, and hundreds of small streams draining to the mighty Yukon River all support populations of Grayling with the best fishing usually found just below the outlet of lakes or at the confluences of the smaller clear streams with the parent drainage. His preference for crystal-clear water is demonstrated time and again. Where gold placer mining has riled the stream, or glacier water has cut through to despoil adjacent streams, he will invariably move on. Even a heavy rain will sometimes drive the Grayling into smaller, clearer, feeder streams until the river clears again. It could well be this trait is the result of his feeding habits—maybe he just doesn't want to miss any part of his summer meal which might otherwise be obscured by poor visibility.

The Grayling is a spring spawner, but spring in the Arctic might be any time from early May to the Fourth of July, depending on the area. Unlike the Brook Trout, Grayling will travel long distances to choose a spawning location which is usually in the headwaters of the stream, often in shallow depths. Along the Arctic Coast, the Grayling seldom occur on the muskeg flats close to the ocean but prefer the upper reaches of the stream beginning at the first rise of ground. They are sometimes seen finning on the spawning beds in less than a foot of water, alternately lowering and raising the big dorsal fin until it resembles a miniature schooner under a fresh breeze.

The size of the stream doesn't seem to have much relation to the size of the fish. On the Arctic coast near Teller, Alaska, Cobblestone Creek is only about twenty feet wide but produces some whopping Grayling—up to 22 inches and weighing four pounds. There are stories of even bigger ones running well over two feet in length.

It wouldn't be right to give the idea that Grayling will always rise to a fly. They occasionally get fed up, like any other fish, because there are times when they just aren't interested. At other times they sneak up and inhale the fly so quietly that it is spit out before the angler knows what happened. At times they are so distinterested that it is necessary to resort to all sorts of tricks including careful stalking and a No. 14 fly even to get a rise. Two days later on the same stream, they may hit anything—even the falling leaves from a willow bush. Just by way of experimentation, they have been taken on red and white river Runt Plugs, Dardevle spoons, chunks of caribou meat, and even salmon eggs; but it seems just a bit sacrilegious to take a Grayling any other way than with a light fly outfit.

PERCH, YELLOW

What the Black Bass is to the fly-rod and bait-rod addict, the Yellow Perch, in many respects, is to the fisherman who prefers a cane pole.

He does not quite rate as king of the panfishes, either on the basis of personality or fighting ability. Most unbiased still-fishermen reserve that place for a chubbier and gamer member, the Bluegill or Bream. Yet there are many waters in which Perch are the most important fish below game-fish size, and on those waters a host of ardent admirers stoutly proclaim that he is the best of all panfish, excelled by none either on the line or in the skillet. And certainly one who has eaten fried Perch will not dispute the latter claim.

Many traits combine to win this respect and affection of fishermen. His manners are good and his way of life is pleasing. Although he is no dainty aristocrat like the speckled trout, he is definitely a fish of clear water, avoiding mud and silt and other contamination. He comes from a clean habitat and his choice of home is reflected in his firm white flesh and excellent flavor. His appetite is vigorous and suffer no major seasonal slump. He bites as readily beneath the ice of a northern lake in February as off the weedy bars in June. Once hooked, he fights sturdily, giving a very decent account of himself if his weight is taken into consideration. And finally, his appearance is all in his favor. He is a slender, streamlined fish, but not too lean, carrying his weight forward where it belongs, well rounded and shapely. There is much about him to admire as he comes enraged and protesting from the water, mouth agape, spiny fins erect and bristling, greenish zebra stripes gleaming across his golden sides like burnished mail.

His range is wide, extending from the brackish waters and coastal streams of the Atlantic seaboard west to Kansas, south as far as the Carolinas, north to Lesser Slave lake and the Hudson Bay watershed. He reaches his greatest abundance through the central belt of this extensive range, and is probably nowhere more plentiful than in the Great Lakes and their drainage basin. In addition it has been successfully planted in many western waters. Wherever he is found, he is a dweller in lakes, ponds and the quiet pools of streams.

Like most panfish, and for that matter like most fish of currentless water, the Yellow Perch is prone to haunt the weed beds. He hides in them as a cottontail hides in a briar patch, and in the aisles of their underwater thickets an abundance of his favorite foods is his for the catching.

He is a lifelong carnivore. No vegetarian diet enters into his scheme of things. In the early period of his life he feeds on the microscopic living creatures that teem in his submarine world. With increasing size he turns to aquatic insects, the larvae of winged insects that mature under water, and other suitable fare. As soon as he is big enough he begins the cannibals' life to which he was born, feeding chiefly on fish smaller than himself.

With him, as with the Northern Pike and his own larger kinsman, the Walleye, this marked preference for little fish leads frequently to his downfall, since it makes him an easy victim to the wiles of a live minnow dangled on a hook.

He can be, and is, taken on other baits. Worms, crickets, grasshoppers, and the mayfly larvae known to ice fishermen as wigglers sometimes account for good catches of Perch. But none of them ranks in first place. Like most fish, the Yellow Perch is glutton enough to gobble down on occasion just about any edible morsel that is put before him, but his heart is not in such feeding. If one wants to tempt him beyond endurance, regardless of the water fished or the season of year, offer him a shiner, chub or other minnow not more than about two inches long.

The Perch of catchable size is a deep feeder, deeper than most other panfish, probably for the obvious and simple reason that there is nothing at the top to interest him. He cares not at all for flying insects, and not a great deal more for nymphs. It is small fish he wants and he seeks them down in the weed jungles. Perch rarely feed in less than ten feet of water, more often in twice that, and the fisherman who hopes to do business with them must send his offering down to their level.

For that reason the cane pole is the logical tool for Perch fishing and the one most commonly used. It can be done with flyrod, however, using live minnows for bait and sinking them with split shot pinched onto the leader two or three feet above the hook. The use of light tackle increases the fun, of course.

A few anglers take Perch now and then with wet flies by this same method, but the Perch is not a fly fish.

The user of live bait other than minnows must beware one pitfall in Perch fishing. The Perch does not take worms or crickets with the eagerness and reckless daring of the Bream or Rock Bass. He is a confirmed nibbler, cautious in his biting, and one of the most expert bait stealers that ever stripped a hook. The still fisherman in Bluegill water who suddenly starts losing bait may safely assume that he is dealing with a stray Perch.

Once he is hooked, however, all trace of caution disappears. He fights gamely, and on a slender cane-pole a big perch will provide first-class sport. But he rarely if ever grows into the heavy-weight class, and miracles cannot be expected of a fish of his size. Over most of his range eight to ten inches is an average size, and a perch weighing a pound is a rarity. In favorable habitat they grow larger. The world's record was a 4¼ pounder taken at Bordentown, New Jersey, back in 1865. That was a Perch most anglers would have liked to see! Other national records, include a 3-pound fish from Massachusetts and one of almost 2 pounds from Saginaw Bay, Michigan.

The Perch is a spring spawner, laying long, zigzag ribbons of eggs in moderately shallow water in March and April, and some of the best Perch fishing of the year gets under way with the onset of the spawning season. At that period heavy runs are likely to occur in streams emptying into lakes stocked with Perch. Especially is this true in certain tributaries of the Great Lakes, where Yellow Perch are plentiful and where they rate as an important commercial fish as well as a major sport species. News that the Perch are running, usually at about the end of March, ushers in one of the most spectacular outdoor events of the entire year for many a community along the shores of Lake Huron and Lake Michigan.

Anglers are weary of winter, eager for anything that will afford them an excuse to get outdoors for a few hours of sport. They troop north from the downstate industrial cities in a host that jams Perch-country roads with crawling ribbons of traffic. They stand literally elbow to elbow on the banks of rivers where the Perch runs are under way, and on the piers and breakwaters of Great Lakes harbors where the Perch are moving in. One of the heaviest of all these runs takes place in the Pine River, emptying into Saginaw Bay a short distance above Bay City. There are times in early April when it is difficult to find a place to put a line into the Pine, so densely packed are the anglers along both banks!

Although, in common with other fish, the Yellow Perch retires into the deeper and cooler areas of lakes in the hot weather of July and August, Perch fishing remains good throughout the summer if the angler will seek out the right spots and put his bait down where the fish are lurking.

This fish provides excellent sport, in the cool and windy days of October. Perch are never more active nor more hungry than at that charming season, when blue haze lies like smoke on the distant hills and birch and maple and aspen are arrayed in colors that make the rainbow a pale and insipid display.

There is a small deep bay on the east shore of Lake Michigan north of Traverse City, at the village of Omena, where the overgrown Perch of the big lake come schooling in a hungry horde each autumn. The right combination for sport then is a pitching, bobbing skiff anchored in the middle of the windswept bay, plenty of warm wool clothing, a casting rod and live minnows lowered down 50 to 70 feet to where the Perch are waiting. Hooked, they come battling to the top, twisting and corkscrewing, deep golden yellow from the depths where they dwell, heavy-bodied and fat, a foot or more long, fish to delight the eye and whet the appetite. October in that part of the country has little better to offer than a day on those waters when the Perch are running.

The freezing of the lakes in the north brings no period of inactivity for the Perch enthusiast. The Perch does not suffer any winter lull in appetite, and fishing for him is an around-the-calendar sport for those who like it.

Small, live minnows continue to be the most productive bait, and the bulk of winter Perch fishing is done with handlines, either on the open ice or from the cozy shelter of a heated shanty or darkhouse. In winter, as at other seasons, Perch are prone to school in fairly deep water. The ice fisherman should not look for them much less than 20 feet down.

A fish, then, of willing appetite, game in battle, abundant in many waters, and unsurpassed on the platter—that is the Yellow Perch. A midget fighter that plays a major role for a huge army of cane-pole anglers and would be sorely missed from our inland lakes and streams were disaster to overtake him. But in view of his prolific reproduction that, fortunately, is not likely ever to happen.

PIKE

NORTHERN PIKE

Some consider trolling for Northern Pike a rather dubious and profitless method. The fish is often difficult to reach because of its habits of seeking shelter in the lily pads, reeds, and weeds. Under such circumstances casting the lure instead of trolling it will reach many fish that would otherwise be missed.

Both spinning and wobbling spoons can be cast readily with ordinary casting equipment. Casting is a most successful method of taking Northern Pike and provides genuine sport and more action than trolling. Casting lures need to be selected with care. One of the best is the type known as a muskellunge spoon. This is oval in shape and of heavier metal than ordinary trolling spoons. It is from 3¼ to 3½ inches in length and instead of using a feather vane to mask the ganghook. It is decorated with a red bucktail. This type spoon is heavy enough to secure both distance and accuracy when cast. Lighter spoons are often caught by the wind in midair and blown out of a straight course. This trouble never happens with a spoon of fairly heavy metal. A heavy spoon finished in nickel on the convex and red on the concave side followed by a red or gray bucktail is a deadly lure in this class.

A spoon such as described above has a plain, smooth surface. Other types have ridgings or crimpings on the face, the object being to provide facets for flashing light rays as it revolves. The use of flutings or crimpings is not a new idea; indeed it is possible that it was used in the original Buel spoon. The crimped spoon ranks next to a smooth one as a pike lure. It is of somewhat lighter material but will cast well. These spoons are fitted with a vane of feathers over the ganghook to prevent the lure from turning.

Nickel finish on spoon blades is the most attractive and also the most natural. This holds true of all spinning lures, whether large or small. The flashing side of a minnow or small fish attracts the game fish. For this reason a Bass will seize upon a spinner-and-fly combination, and a Pike or Muskellunge will take a spoon. This does not mean that lures in finishes other than nickel will never take fish, but that a nickel finish will consistently produce results under varied fishing conditions. Unfortunately many spoons have a very poor nickel finish. When first used they have a real flash and gleam, but this soon fades and they become drab and discolored. Such spoons should be taken to a plating company and plated

Ben East

A Northern Pike as good as this would make any boy smile.

with the highest grade of nickel, or actual silver. The best nickel is superior to silver plating, since the latter needs to be polished continually to keep its shine, and is never as flashy as nickel.

Casting for Pike with large lures (3 to 3½ inch blades) requires at least a 24 pound test line. This does not mean that a large Pike cannot be taken on a lighter line, but that the line should have sufficient body to "carry through" with the lure. If the line is too light, it will belly in the air and not follow with the lure. This is not easily described, but can be better understood by casting a heavy lure first with a light line and then with a heavier one. If a medium-sized spoon (2 to 2½ inches in length) is used, a lighter line will carry through. With such a lure a fifteen or eighteen pound test, black, hard-braided line proves satisfactory. A rod with considerable backbone is needed in Pike fishing, since no one can predict the size of the fish that will strike. The better grades of solid steel rods, triangular or square, have sufficient backbone to handle the heaviest lures. Light seamless tubular steel rods and the average bamboo rods are rather light for the purpose.

Wobbling spoons are also good casting lures. In fact, the concentration of weight makes them even easier to cast. It is the action of the lure rather than the flash of the blades that intrigues the fish. This is demonstrated by the fact that one of the best wobbling spoons has a blade that has either black and white or red and white stripes.

Northern Pike are usually found along the edges of the pads and weeds that line the inshore waters.

Deep indentations into such vegetation often hold good fish and they are worth fishing carefully. There is a trick in operating a cast lure that often takes additional fish. This trick is to give the spoon a quick jerk as soon as it drops to water. The rod is held high, and quick reeling will cause the lure to boil up the surface water and resemble a small fish breaking on the surface. Any such movement often inspires a fish to strike quickly.

A variation of the same trick permits a wobbling spoon to sink a foot or more, after which, by holding the rod high and reeling fast, it is hurried to the surface to skitter or flutter along. It is then again permitted to sink by reeling more slowly and again rushed to the surface by fast reeling.

While Pike are sometimes taken in deep water (thirty or more feet in depth), this is rather an exception to the rule. Like the Muskellunge, the Northern Pike likes to cruise in inshore waters. Those small, tucked-in bays are sure to have some fine specimens to offer. The best time for taking the Pike is from daybreak to about six o'clock in summer. Few fishermen are abroad at this time, one reason why so few realize the potentialities of early morning shore fishing. At daybreak the large Pike come in to feed and they are really hungry. When they strike, they hit hard and with a viciousness reminiscent of the strike of a Barracuda.

Autumn is the best season for Pike fishing. From about September 10th, these fish are active through the autumn to the freeze-up, and the fishermen who fish at this season will have some of the finest sport of the year.

The Pike will often be found in fairly deep water (ten to fifteen feet) off mouths of streams flowing into lakes, in channels between islands, in deep water out from the mouths of narrow-throated bays, along the drop-offs out from points of land, etc. At such spots the use of a live lure, fished deep, is indicated. In such fishing, a good-sized minnow or a fish eight to ten inches in length should be used. The best bait is a Sucker of eight to ten inches. A bead chain six inches in length should have a ganghook on the snap at the end. (Note: these chains come with snaps at either end.) Apply a second ganghook by its eye to the snap at the other end of the chain, and to the eye of the snap, attach a snap which is on the end of the line. Now there are two ganghooks six inches apart and the rigging is securely attached to the line. The forward ganghook is attached to the lip of the Sucker or bait-fish, while the rear ganghook is inserted back of the dorsal (back) fin, under the skin and into some of the flesh. On seizing the lure, the fish invariably "runs" with it; that is, he holds the bait in his jaws and swims ten or fifteen feet preparatory to turning the bait and swallowing it head first. In doing so, the ganghook in the mouth of the bait will be headed down and an imbedding of the hook in the jaws or gullet of the pike is almost certain. Use a bobber on the line just buoyant enough that it will return to the surface if the bait-fish takes it under water. The presence of bobber resistance on the line does not make the Pike suspicious.

Other useful live fish lures are an eight- to ten-inch Bullhead with its spines clipped; large Yellow Perch, especially if they go eight or more inches in length; Mudfin or Dogfish of the same size; and buffalo minnows. Carp are not recommended. The Dogfish is the best lure because they remain alive for long periods. In fishing with such a rig, do not anchor the boat but let it drift.

Fishing for Pike with the fly-and-spinner combination, especially in the rivers, has much to commend it. A fly rod with generous backbone should be used with a C or D line and a level leader. A bass fly without wing feathers, with inch-long hackles at the head only and a No. 3 spinner (about 1¼ inches) makes a good combination. Casting with considerable ease, this light lure has possibilities. It can be placed in bays and openings in the lily pads and other vegetation with deadly effect. If the lure can be jerked or twitched along the surface occasionally, the possibility of taking Pike is greatly increased. Cast into a good spot several times before moving on as the sound of the lure may bring a fish to the spot.

MUSKELLUNGE

There is nothing tougher or meaner that swims than the mighty Muskie. He's the fightin'est fish that ever lunged at a Sucker, his favorite food. He is best known as "the tackle-buster of northern waters," and many fishermen claim him to be the best of all northern game fish.

Muskies are plentiful in many of the lakes and rivers of Ontario and northern Wisconsin and are also found in some of the waters of Minnesota, Michigan, New York, Pennsylvania, Manitoba, Vermont, Ohio, Quebec, West Virginia, Tennessee, Kentucky, Alabama, and North Carolina.

A Muskie is not shy like a Brown Trout. He does not flush like a Bonefish. He is cunning, malicious, and resourceful. He will follow the bait to the boat perhaps fifty times before striking. One tries all the tricks in the bag—fast retrieve, medium, slow—change of lures from plug to spoon to bucktail and to other favorite Muskie rigs. If patience holds out he will eventually strike.

When he strikes, anything can happen, and the worst break is to have him head straight for the boat full speed ahead. There isn't time to reel in; protection against invasion is what is most needed. Usually he goes under the boat or wraps the line twice around the outboard motor, but sometimes he leaps clear over the boat, and that is a real thrill. Toughest, is when he lands in the boat. Men have been known to jump overboard. Men with pistols handy have put several slugs into "Old Mose" and then have had to row or outboard for shore to save all.

Ichthiologists call him *Esox masquinongy;* fishermen often call him worse names. Colloquial names are: Great Pike, Lunge, Barred Muskellunge, Tiger Muskellunge, Ohio River Pike, Northern Muskellunge, Chautauqua Muskellunge, Mississippi Muskellunge, Spotted Muskellunge, Wisconsin Muskellunge, Allegheny River Pike, Great Lakes Muskellunge, Ohio Muskellunge, and True Tiger Muskie.

Except during the spring spawning period, the Muskie is a lone wolf. He has his place which he guards and which he uses as a point from which he attacks other fishes, small animals, and baby wildfowl. When he is caught, usually another Muskie moves in to take his place. Although he may be found in the weed beds, off sandy bars, alongside a big log and in medium to shallow water, the big ones are often lurking near the bottom of the lake.

Muskies are often mistaken for Northern Pike, especially in Minnesota where the conservation department has successfully crossed these two fish. These hybrids grow faster and are easier to handle.

There are at least forty ways to spell Muskellunge. The Indians called him Maskinonge, and this spelling is commonly used today in Canada. The French called him Masque-al-longe. A few of the most noted spellings are: Kinongé, Longe, Lunge, Mascallonge, Mascolonge, Mascalongé, Mascanongy, Maskalingé, Maskallonge, Maskalonge, Maskalongé, Maskanonge, Mas-ke-non-ge, Maskenonza, Maskenonzay, Maskenosha, Maskenonzha, Mas-Kinoje, Maskinonge, Maskinongé, Maskinongy, Maskinonje, Masquallonge, Masque-allongé, Masquenougé, Masquinongy, Muscalinga, Mascallonge, Muscallunge, Muscalonge, Muscalunge, Muskallonge, Muskallungé, Muskalonge, Muskellonge, Muskellunge, Muskinlongé, Muskinongé, Muskka-lone, Muskulunge, Musquallonge, Musquellunge, and Noscononge.

The best time to go Muskie fishing is whenever it is possible to get away during the open season. Since the seasons open in the late spring after spawning, most addicts of this form of fishing are out there pitching lures on opening day.

Any good guide will tell you to come back another time. He knows that the tiger of the north is unpredictable. At times he will strike at anything, but more often he will sulk and ignore most of the lures in the tackle box. A favorite guide's expression therefore is, "Not biting now; come back next month". In June he says, "Come back in July when the fish are located; now is too soon after spawning". In July he says, "Come back in September; too hot now; fish are down deep". In September he says, "Better to fish for Muskies in the spring; Muskies go mostly for live Suckers in the fall". Guides, you see, have their alibis too.

If an angler follows the fishing calendar for the best days to fish; the fishing tables for the best times of day to fish; watches the barometer and fishes on a rising or high barometer, he will catch Muskies in the lakes that are best known for them. Although many of the whoppers have been taken in the spring of the year, good proof that the biggest Muskies are caught in the fall can be found in the records and in studying the results of the annual *Field & Stream* Prize Fishing Contest.

Although hatcheries in many states are successfully propagating Muskies and planting them after they have grown to rather large sizes, they are not as plentiful today as they were ten or twenty years ago.

The Muskie is a great trophy and as a consequence too many fish are taken to the ice house. More Muskies should be released and resorts could encourage this by giving Muskie pin awards for released fish rather than for those brought to the dock. Only when the fish is a record or near-record should it be killed.

How big? The largest on record was taken in a net back in 1902 by the Wisconsin Conservation Department and weighed 102 pounds.

Big Muskies are not plentiful, but every year there are at least a dozen caught on sporting tackle that weigh in excess of 42 pounds. Back in 1935 Gust Peterson established a new world's record for Muskellunge with his 52-pounder taken from White Sand Lake, Lac du Flambeau, Wisconsin, and this same lake annually produces many big fish.

Then in June, 1938, Percy P. Haver of Detroit caught one that weighed 56 pounds, 7 ounces while trolling in the waters of Lake St. Clair, Michigan. Other world's records that followed were as follows: Aug. 27, 1939, 59 pounds, 8 ounces, Grindstone Lake, near Hayward, Wisconsin, by Louis Spray; October 3, 1939, 60 pounds, 8 ounces, Eagle Lake, Ontario, by John J. Coleman; August 19, 1940, 61 pounds, 13 ounces, Lac Court O'Reilles, near Hayward, Wisconsin, by Louis Spray; June 28, 1940, 62 pounds, 8 ounces, in Lake St. Clair, Michigan, by Percy P. Haver; May 17, 1947, 64 pounds, 8 ounces, Favil Lake, near Lac du Flambeau, Wisconsin; July 24, 1949, 67 pounds, 8 ounces, in Lac Court O'Reilles, near Hayward, Wisconsin, by Cal Johnson; and October 20, 1949, 69 pounds, 11 ounces, in Chippewa Flowage, near Hayward, Wisconsin, by Louis Spray. The Percy Haver Muskies are caught early in the season by trolling before the weeds get too tall. The biggest ones are caught while trolling method.

Big Muskies have been caught in the following lakes and rivers, and these waters still boast good fishing for them.

WISCONSIN—Grindstone Lake, Chippewa Flowage, Lac Court O'Reilles, White Sand Lake, Flambeau Flowage, Manitowish Waters, Turtle Lake Flowage, Lake Winnebago, Palmer Lake, Crane Lake, Big and Little St. Germaine Lakes, Minocqua Lake, Ghost Lake, Big and Little Spider Lakes, Teal Lake, Lost Land Lake, Lost and Found Lakes, Upper and Lower Gresham, Wildcat, Trout, Twin, Pokegama, Fence, Lac du Flambeau, Plum, Pelican, Boulder, Squirrel, Wolf, High, Fishtrap, Big and Little Arbor Vitae, Crawling Stone, Indian Wolf, and Chief Lakes, Allequash Lake.

ONTARIO—Lake of the Woods, Eagle Lake, Big and Little Vermilion, Musky Lake, Rowan, Lac Seul, Winnipeg River, Georgian Bay, Cliff and Cedar, Lake Simcoe, French and Pickerel Rivers, Nissinnabi, Perralt, Wabishgan, Lake Nipissing, Niagara River, Crow Lake, Lake Balsam, Seine River, Quill Lake, Pachwash, Lake Luzon, Manitou, Trent River.

MICHIGAN—Lac Vieux Desert, Lake St. Clair, Elk, Gun, Thornapple and Cheboygan Rivers, Lake Manistee and the Indian River.

OHIO—Muskingam River.

NEW YORK—Lake Chautauqua, St. Lawrence River.

TENNESSEE—Daddy's Creek.

KENTUCKY—The Forks of Sandy River, Upper Licking River.

MINNNESOTA—Big Fork River, Woman Lake Chain, Mantrap Lake, Bottle Lake.

PENNSYLVANIA—Conneaut Lake, Lake Le Boeuf, Edinboro Lake.

The secret of Muskie fishing is to select a good place, get a good guide, and use the best tackle possible.

Fishermen will get the most fun by casting; trolling catches the most fish; and there are other popular methods of catching this huge trophy. Because of the heavy drag of a Muskie, tackle must be stronger than bass-fishing equipment. The mouth of a Muskie is big and hard; it takes a flexible rod to get the most fun out of a Smallmouth Bass, but it takes a rod with a stiff backbone to set the hook in the mouth of a Muskellunge. Light tackle is recommended, of course, but not as light as bass tackle. Weight-test of the line (silk or Nylon) should be from 15- to 30-pound test, depending upon the kind of waters being fished. If there are lots of snags, use the 30-pound test line. Wire leaders 9-12 inches in length are necessary because a Muskie will cut a line close to the hook. Big plugs, spoons, bucktail spinners, and most other rigs are trolled or cast with a bait casting rod. In recent years there has been a trend to smaller lures, and many fine fish have been captured on runts, silver minnows, pikies, banana baits, and other smaller lures.

Trolling a live Sucker is the way to get a big one in Wisconsin waters, but most sportsmen prefer to troll big bucktail spinners, large-size plugs, big spoons, and the famous "Christmas-tree" type of trolling rig. Such fishing requires a rod with a stiff action. Now there are lures that resemble the natural food of the Muskie . . . duck plug, sucker plug, chipmunk plugs, and plugs that resemble minnows. The bucktail lures appear to be small animals swimming in the water—just what the Muskie likes the most. Trolling at slow speeds brings the best results. When fishing with artificial lures, set the hook hard several times with the strike, being careful not to break the line or the rod. When fishing with a live Sucker, the hook should not be set until the Muskie has taken the Sucker. Ofter this requires waiting five minutes or more. If during the waiting period the Muskie starts off with the line, set the hook. Rods of split bamboo, tubular and solid steel, and fiber glass are best.

Fly casting for Muskies is now very popular, and this requires a rod that has a stiff backbone and is about 6 ounces in weight. The best lures are bucktail dry and wet flies, wet streamer flies, bass bugs with or without spinners. The best colors are black and white, red and white, and the natural color of bucktail.

Skittering with a long bamboo or steel pole, touching the water every second with the swing of the body where ever a fish is known to be, is also growing in popularity. The lures can be the same as in fly fishing plus minnows, frogs, suckers, or bucktail spinners.

Spinning or slip casting with a spinning rod of bamboo, glass or tubular steel, and spinning reel is also a popular way of taking Muskies. The advantage of this method over fly casting is that the lures can be larger and the casts can be longer.

Still fishing or drift fishing with live bait (live sucker, crawfish, frogs, chipmunks, and minnows) in the current of a river, off the weed bed, alongside a sunken log, off rocky points, and in sheltered bays is one of the ways to get the big ones. While drifting with a live lure, many fishermen take this opportunity to tune up on bait casting with artificial lures.

A combination of casting and trolling is also a good way. The outboard motor is started after placing the boat proper distance from the shoreline (distance from the weeds is the important thing to know) the plug or spoon is cast in towards the weed beds. As the line is retrieved the lure swings and so half of the operation becomes trolling. In this way more Muskie grounds are covered.

SALMON

ATLANTIC SALMON

The Atlantic Salmon is a paradox among game fish. When it enters fresh water, it ceases to feed, yet for some strange reason, it still rises occasionally to a fly. They leave the rivers as fingerlings and return weighing from four to forty pounds. If they tried to maintain their strength by feeding, they would not only deprive the young salmon "parr" of their food supply but would probably clean out all of the parr in the process.

Why, then if a Salmon has no hunger does he rise to an artificial fly? There is no complete answer to that question. Salmon seem to rise out of annoyance and restlessness or as a result of a reflex action reminiscent of their early river days. Their stomachs are always empty and during their fresh water spawning period, they normally lose almost half their weight. The flies to which Salmon rise are very small in proportion to the size of the fish and the small hooks and fine leaders required to hook them make Atlantic Salmon fishing a most difficult form of angling.

Not only are Atlantic Salmon difficult to hold on the required tackle, but they are extremely difficult to bring to the hook. The annual run varies with the year and depends upon the temperature and character of the water. The time of entrance of the first bright Salmon into a river may vary a full month from one year to another. And two rivers with their mouths only a few miles apart (for example: the Grand Codroy and Little Codroy in Newfoundland), may get their first Salmon a month apart, one being consistently later than the other. How is the angler to plan his trip in advance to coincide with the peak of the run? If he gambles on an early run, he may find no fish in the river and, if he tries to play safe by setting a later date, he may find conditions very poor with the fish stale and the water low, for the longer the Salmon are in the rivers, the less likely they are to rise to a fly.

As their days in the river add up, Salmon lose some of their wild exuberance and eagerness to take a fly. As the water drops from spring run-

H. G. Tapply

Lenox Putnam of Everett, Mass. with four Landlocked Salmon from Sebago Lake, Maine. These fish were taken on streamer flies in the Dingley Island section near the town of South Casco.

off to summer level finer leaders, smaller flies, and more precise fishing are necessary for success. By August the early fish have changed their blue and silver coating for a darker, protective grey that blends more readily into the pattern of the stream bed. They have used up some of their great store of energy as well, which may account for their loss of interest in flies. Although the late fishing is more difficult, it may provide the best sport for the highly skilled angler.

Salmon enter the rivers in waves. The first run is composed mainly of fish having spent two straight years of feeding in the sea with an average weight of about thirteen pounds. Approximately ten days later the grilse (salmon of only one year's sea feeding) begin to arrive and their average weight is from four to five pounds in most rivers. Some of the largest Salmon, returning for a second, third, or fourth spawning arrive at this time. Throughout the summer and into early fall a new run of Salmon is likely to enter the rivers whenever a heavy rain raises the water. A few rivers like the Margaree in Nova Scotia get their main Salmon run in the fall.

The peak fishing usually lasts about two weeks and no one can be positive in advance when that period will be. One camp operator when chided by a doctor who had been advised to come at a time that, it developed, offered poor fishing, countered with, "Doc, when you accept maternity case you know the woman's going to have a baby and you can name the day and hour of its arrival six months in advance as well as I can predict the Salmon run."

The movements of Salmon in the rivers is a source of wonder to anglers. Many of the early fish rush right through to the headwaters and often the first fish to be caught are taken in the upper tributaries. The main run of fish tends to work its way slowly upstream, moving from pool to pool at night, but if low water and poor stream conditions hold the Salmon in the sea longer than usual they may streak straight through to the upper waters, giving the anglers at the lower pools only a few days fishing or none at all. Salmon lie in certain pools and at certain spots in a given level of flow. If the level drops three inches, the best Salmon pool in the river may become the poorest.

Salmon do not rise well when the water is low and warm. But when a heavy rain after a dry period raises the water and changes its character by revitalizing it with a fresh supply of air and oxygen, the Salmon are likely to go in a "taking" spree. Under such conditions fishing may suddenly change from very poor to excellent. The novice needs good fishing conditions to take fish. The expert fisherman or the skillful caster under the direction of a knowing guide, can take Salmon under almost any water conditions.

In practically all the Atlantic Salmon waters of this continent, Salmon must be fished for with an unweighted fly. Inasmuch as these magnificent game fish are decreasing in numbers rather than holding their own it is not likely that the rules will be liberalized to permit the use of other methods such as spinning or bait casting.

The wet fly is traditional with Atlantic Salmon and an overwhelming percentage of fish caught are taken in this way. The wet fly is cast across and somewhat down the stream and the flow of the current causes it to swing to a point directly down the flow. Starting at the head the fisherman moves slowly down the pool to the end that his fly will be fished across all the likely water. The wet fly travels just under the surface in normal fishing and the closer it is to the top the better the results seem to be. The rate of travel of the wet fly through the water depends upon the speed of the current and the action of the angler. There seems to be a certain "best" speed of travel and if the water moves the fly too slowly it can be speeded up by lifting the rod or taking in line. Conversely when the flow is too swift, the fly can be slowed down by lowering the rod or letting line out gradually as the cast is fished.

A second successful method of fishing a wet fly is called the "patent" method. Knowing the resting place of one or more Salmon a wet fly, preferably one of the hair or bucktail type, is cast well above the fish and allowed to drift slowly downstream with the current to pass over or near them. This approach is similar to fishing a nymph for wary Brown Trout and seems to derive its effectiveness from its accuracy in representing a submerged insect moving naturally in the stream flow.

A third and perhaps the most exciting method of fishing the wet fly originated at Portland Creek, Newfoundland, and is called the "riffling" fly. After the wet fly has been tied to the leader in the regular way, two hitches are taken around the shank of the hook just behind the fly head. This causes the fly to cock a little to one side and instead of travelling under the water it skims the surface leaving a small "v" wake behind it. In order to take this skimming fly, the Salmon must show himself. Even a "short" rise will be clearly visible to the angler although a similar movement on the part of the fish for a sunken fly might go unnoticed. All through the season on some rivers this recently discovered method is much more effective than conventional wet fly fishing.

Wet fly patterns are many and varied but some, with more than a century of fishing behind them, are favorites everywhere. Among these tried and true patterns are the Jock Scott, Silver Grey, Silver Doctor, Black Dose, Blue Charm, Thunder and Lightning, Dusty Miller, and Mar Lodge. None are true insect imitations but all have a quality about them that attract Salmon.

The dry or floating fly is a recent development in Salmon fishing. In imitation of a natural insect floating freely on the surface of the stream it is fished over the spot where Salmon are known or supposed to be lying.

The wet fly covers a considerable area of water on each cast and in a short time the wet fly fisherman can put his fly within reach of every Salmon in the pool but the dry fly moves much more slowly and to obtain a coverage equal to that of a wet fly much more time is required. However, the dry fly, drifting slowly with the current, covers the water much more completely. When the rivers are low and the angler knows just where the Salmon lie, he may concentrate his efforts on small areas and for this the dry fly is particularly good. When the rivers are high and the fish widely scattered the dry fly loses much of its effectiveness. Favored dry fly patterns are the bi-visibles, Spiders, White Wulff, Grey Wulff, Pink and Dark Cahill.

Since the Atlantic Salmon are not interested in food, they do not lie in the spots the Trout or other feeding fish would choose. Both, in the tackle employed and the type of water fished, Salmon fishing parallels Trout fishing, yet a well-qualified Trout fisherman turned loose on a Salmon river for the first time will spend about ninety per cent of his time fishing where there are no fish, while a good Salmon angler will have his fly passing over Salmon most of the time. It is for this reason that Salmon guides are so necessary. Until one has seen a river in both high and low water at all times of the season, he cannot accurately predict where the fish will be. Under the same conditions Salmon will be found lying in identical spots in a pattern, so much the same that it is hard to realize that each year's crop of Salmon is predominantly composed of new fish instead of the same ones returning year after year.

To learn where to look for Salmon it is necessary to understand their needs and desires. Salmon, returning to the rivers, have lost their hunger and as a result do not rest in the good "feeding" spots selected by normal river fish. They are interested in safety and comfort. A primary requirement for safety is deep or open water close at hand. Salmon occasionally choose shallow resting places, but when they do, it will be adjacent to open water, and while a Salmon can often be approached easily from the shallow side it is rarely possible to get between him and the open water he depends on for his escape. They naturally congregate in deep pools but except in very low water are found scattered through the steady runs at depths varying from eighteen inches to four or five feet. During his sea experience the Salmon has learned to depend upon speed for safety, and, having outsped every danger in the sea, counts on doing so the streams as well. Even when hooked a Salmon will stick to the open water and avoid tangles of brush and weeds were a Trout might try to foul a leader.

The Salmon is a restless fish. It has come back to the river to spawn but may enter the rivers a full six months before spawning takes place. Once in the river the fish has a great store of energy which must be conserved in order to make it last out the allotted period. It is healthy, strong, and super-charged with power but must wait patiently for the months to roll by. If it swims and leaps unduly it will be exhausted before spawning time in the late fall, yet there is a constant urge to keep moving. Therefore, the fish seeks an eddy where the flow of water will pass over its body in a soothing stream, yet where it need not waste strength by a constant battle with the current. Find such a spot where deep or open water is available and it is probably a good Salmon lie. A stone on the smooth stream bed near the tail of the pool is sufficient to form a satisfactory eddy. A sudden deepening of the stream generally forms a good resting place. The eddies behind a sunken ridge of rock near the center of a good pool should attract their share of Salmon. Inasmuch as a rise or fall of water level will change the stream currents materially the Salmon move frequently from eddies that are vanishing or growing too turbulent to others that have become preferable.

When low water forces the Salmon to seek safety in the motionless water of lakes or large, deep

H. G. Tapply

When Salmon are striking well, examination of their stomachs will almost invariably reveal a diet of smelt, the principal food of this species. These five Salmon, all of average size, came from the Songo River at Sebago Lake, Maine, during the spring spawning run of the smelt.

pools, they will be constantly on the move. Without the flow of the current over their bodies they swim endlessly and are much more difficult to take on the fly. This difficultly may arise from the angler's inability to time the cast perfectly for the fly's presentation to a moving target or it may be that due to constant swimming their tension is released and the fish are no longer keyed up to the "taking" point. The still waters, too, may have a lower air or oxygen content and consequently, exert a deadening effect on their impulse to rise.

Salmon take the fly most readily when they first arrive from the sea. As they re-adjust themselves to the fresh water and as the edge of their pent-up energy wears off, the impulse to rise is reduced. Freshly run fish take brighter, gaudier fly patterns than the Salmon which have been in the river for a few weeks. As the season progresses smaller fly sizes and more neutral patterns are in order. When the water drops to a low level the size of the fly must be further reduced and finer leader tippets used to achieve success. Fortunately, when the water is low, a Salmon is much more likely to stay in the pool where it is hooked, and an angler has a greater chance of holding a fish on a small fly than if it were played in high water in which it could easily travel the full width of the river at any point.

The flies in common use for Salmon range from 1/0 down to No. 12 on leaders ranging in diameter from .018 to 009 inches. This terminal tackle is lighter than that commonly used for Bass and not much heavier than is used to take Trout which are only a very small fraction of a Salmon's weight. Rods range in length from 7 to 12½ feet, averaging about 9½. A fly casting line to balance the rod with 100 yards or more of backing behind it and a suitable fly reel round out the tackle. Although a gaff is commonly used for landing Salmon there is an increasing use of tailers and nets which do not injure the fish and permit their release if desired.

Landing Salmon is a feat demanding top skill. A Salmon's sea experience gives it a sense of space, distance and speed, of long runs and high leaps, beyond the range of normal freshwater fish. A Salmon's great store of energy gives him a power not to be equalled by fish that can readily renew their strength from day to day. An Atlantic Salmon angler aims for a peak trophy and the satisfaction of achieving it is in proporation to the uncertainties encountered and the ability required.

LANDLOCKED SALMON

In shape and color, in habit and character, the Landlocked Salmon closely resembles its distinguished forebear, *Salmo salar.* It lives in a fresh water sea, ascends tributary streams to spawn, and returns to the lake to feed and fatten and spawn again. It wears an armor of shining silver flecked with X-shaped spots, and its body is lithe and powerful.

Place a five-pound Landlocked Salmon beside a grilse of equal size and only a practiced eye could detect differences between the two. The tail and fins of the landlocked fish are somewhat larger, as are the eyes, and the St. Andrew's crosses are perhaps a little more prominent. But examine the two fish separately and none but an expert could tell for certain which is the sea-going fish and which is its fresh water cousin.

Whether the Landlocked Salmon is a better fighter than the salmon from the sea is a matter of opinion. The writer has caught Landlocks that leaped as high and ran as fast and as far as any fresh-run grilse of comparable size. But in one respect the fresh water Salmon surpasses the Atlantic fish—it rises more readily to a fly.

Landlocked Salmon fishing begins in the early spring, immediately after the ice leaves the lakes. Then the fish move into the shallow waters close to shore, over the gravelled bars, and especially around the rocky points, and begin feeding upon smelt, without which no water can support salmon. In lakes where smelt run up the tributary streams to spawn immediately after the ice goes out, the Salmon follow them if they can, or gather at the mouths of the smaller rivers awaiting their return. In any event, Salmon follow the smelt, for that is their favorite food.

Until a few years ago standard tackle for Landlocked Salmon comprised a heavy trolling rod with reel to match, copper line and generous supply of live smelts or worms for bait. This tackle accounted for a lot of fish, and still does, but today more anglers are deriving greater pleasure from their hours of fishing with the more delicate, yet equally efficient, fly rod gear.

The troller usually fishes two depths, with one unweighted "top line" running close to the surface and the other ten or fifteen feet down. For shallow trolling the favorite bait is a smelt sewn on a short-shank gut hook in such a way that it revolves slowly, while the line is prevented from twisting by the use of swivels and at trolling rudder. On the deep line the same bait or a large gob of worms is used in conjunction with a flashing spoon or series of spoons such as the deadly "Dave Davis," comprising from three to five flashers of various sizes placed about four feet ahead of the bait. Hundreds of fish are taken by this method every year, but the sport of playing the salmon is partially lost by the weight of the spoons and the cumbersome tackle required for such heavy terminal gear.

During the first few weeks of spring, and lasting until warming surface waters drive the smelt and Salmon into the deeper parts of the lake, the fly fisherman enjoys the best sport of the year. He has his choice of two methods: trolling and casting, or a combination of both.

Trolling methods are simple. With two anglers in a boat, each strips off from 30 to 90 feet of line and with an unweighted streamer fly attached to the leader, allows his lure to trail along behind as the boat weaves in and out along the contours of the shore. Experienced fishermen vary the length of line, one angler trolling a short line of between 30 to 50 feet, sometimes with the fly in the very wash of the outboard motor, while his partner strips off nearly all the line in his reel so that his fly follows far behind the boat and, of course, somewhat deeper than the other. Except in calm water Salmon are not frightened either by splashing oars or the noise of an outboard motor, and will come to the short line readily. However, when there is little or no wind blowing, the longer line usually takes the most fish.

Although the fly caster probably does not hook so many Salmon as the troller, he enjoys the very quintessence of sport. He anchors his boat over an underwater bar or rocky ledge, or off a wind-beaten point, and covers the water thoroughly as he casts his fly into all the spots where Salmon might be expected to lie. Since his range is restricted, he exposes his lure to fewer fish than does the troller, but his chances of taking an individual fish are greater, and one or two Salmon a day will send him home as happy as the troller with his five or six.

Probably the deadliest method of taking Salmon in the early spring is the combination of trolling and casting. With two anglers in a boat, each trolls a fly, but a third rod is used to cast into the shore. The cast fly serves a dual purpose: it takes fish lying so close to the shore that the trolled flies would pass by unseen, and it also tolls fish out from the shallows and into the course of the trolled flies. It is common to see a fish follow the cast fly out from the shallow water without offering to take it, and then fall upon one of the trolled flies as it comes past a few moments later. The trolling-casting method obviously covers more water than any other, and its effectiveness is proven by the larger number of fish that will be taken on the trolled fly nearest shore.

Because Salmon feed largely upon smelt, flies which resemble this bait fish are the choice of most Landlocked Salmon fishermen. The smelt is a small, silvery fish with a bluish-green back, so the more popular fly patterns are those which contain those colors. Among the favorites are the Supervisor, Green Ghost, Green King and Nine-three, all with green the dominant color. However, there are others which many fishermen consider equally effective: the Black Ghost and Gray Ghost, Lady Doctor, Jane Craig, the Parmachene Belle streamer, and the Dark Edson Tiger. This latter pattern bears no resemblance to a smelt, but does suggest the fresh-water chub upon which Salmon often feed, and rates as one of the deadliest of them all.

H. G. Tapply

H. G. Tapply of Lexington, Mass. with a 4-pound Landlocked Salmon taken fly casting on Moosehead Lake, Maine.

Many fishermen use two flies when trolling. On a leader of from seven to nine feet in length, the second (dropper) fly is attached to a short strand of gut about midway down the leader. The dropper fly is usually of a different pattern, on the theory that if one fly does not appeal to the fish perhaps the other will. Since Landlocked Salmon seldom display so much selectiveness as, for example, Brown Trout, this theory may be accepted with caution. However, the angler derives some extra confidence in offering the fish a choice of lures, and occasionally he experiences the thrill of hooking two Salmon simultaneously.

At times salmon seem reluctant to take a fly, for no accountable reason, unless they are also offered something a bit more substantial. On such occasions, lip-hooking a small smelt or lake chub to the streamer fly may mean the difference between a blank day and a good catch. Trolling a lip-hooked bait fish on a bare hook is another method which at times takes fish, but the fly-and-bait combination is generally more productive.

Salmon and smelt remain in the shallow waters so long as surface temperatures remain at a comfortable level. But as the season advances and the waters become warm, the fish move out into the deeper parts of the lake and remain there until September frosts render the shoals habitable again. In lakes located in the southerly range of the Landlocked Salmon, such as Sebago in Maine, this movement into deeper water occurs usually between mid-June and the first of July depending, of course, upon the weather. Farther north surface fishing often remains good through the month of July, but seldom can Salmon be taken on a surface lure during August, although occasionally they move into the shallows for a brief period, either chasing vagrant schools of smelt or feeding upon a hatch of insects.

Obviously, fly fishing is rarely a productive method of catching Salmon during hot weather. But the deep-troller can and often does enjoy his best sport during mid-summer. Using wire line which will sink his smelt- or worm-baited hook down to between 50 and 100 feet of water, he can take fish consistently if he knows the deep, cool spots where the Salmon have taken refuge. This type of fishing, while often productive, does not afford the pleasure that the fly fisherman knows in the spring, however, for even a Salmon of five pounds, a large fish by present-day standards, cannot fight hard or long under the handicap of so much weight hanging from his jaw.

Still-fishing is another effective method of Salmon fishing during the mid-summer period. The secret of success, of course, lies in knowing where to find the fish. Every lake has its "deep

British Columbia Govt. Travel Bureau

A forty-two and one-half pound King from the Campbell River in British Columbia.

holes" where both Salmon and smelt seek refuge during hot weather, and if the angler should be so fortunate as to know the location of these areas, he can enjoy good fishing even during the August doldrums. Favorite baits for still-fishing are smelt, lake chubs and worms on a single hook, with enough sinkers to carry the line down to the necessary depth.

Soon after the first frosts have chilled the surface water, Salmon move back into the shallows for a brief period of feeding before spawning. This is September fishing, and while at times it is excellent, it is also unpredictable. But if the angler is fortunate enough to plan his trip to coincide with a period of feeding activity, he may find better fly fishing than he ever enjoyed in the spring.

During the spring and early fall when Salmon can be taken close to the surface with flies, the wind is probably the most important factor bearing upon the fisherman's success. Landlocked Salmon seem to have an affinity for wind, and the harder it blows the better the fish like it. Even the direction of the wind seems of little consequence, a strong northerly being better, in general, than only a gentle southerly. With a brisk wind piling waves on the shore, or causing them to roll and break over a sunken bar, Salmon feed more actively and closer to the surface than at any other time. Under such conditions points of land jutting out into the lake are especially productive—so much so that the fisherman will do well to troll back and forth across the tip of the point several times, always trying to bring his flies as close to shore as possible, or casting into the very smother of white water where the waves are breaking against the rocks.

The effect of the wind upon Landlocked Salmon fishing has been proven many times, but never so convincingly as upon one occasion near the mouth of Spencer Bay on Moosehead Lake, Maine. The day had been windless, the water lying like a glassy mirror under a hot June sun. Casting flies and trolling them over usually productive water had produced nothing, and by mid-afternoon prospects were too hopeless to continue fishing any longer. However, a bank of clouds had been building up in the west, and gradually the overcast approached, sending before it little cat's-paws of wind which became larger and more frequent as the overcast darkened. Soon a fresh breeze stirred the lake, then whitecaps showed their gleaming teeth, and less than twenty minutes after the first cat's-paw had broken the flat water surface, foaming waves were washing into the bay from the main body of the lake.

Under such circumstances a sixteen-foot smooth-bottomed canoe seems small and fragile, so rods were rested against the gunwales while paddling for camp. As the last rocky point before entering the mouth of the bay was passed, one reel screeched as a Salmon struck; a moment later the other rod bounced off the gunwale under the impact of a heavy fish. Handling two Salmon at one time under such conditions posed a problem, but somehow both were netted. Then stripping off a few feet of line, the flies were trailed behind as the canoe was again headed across the wind-swept bay to the sanctuary of the protected shore. But on three different occasions the journey through the whitecaps was interrupted by striking fish, and finally when calm water was reached four Salmon, plus a half-canoeful of water, had been taken within less than an hour.

The Landlocked Salmon fisherman prays for wind, as much wind as his boat can take, but he doesn't always get it. Glassy-calm days occur often in May and June, and then the angler faces the problem of finding a way to catch fish that do not want to be caught. If he belongs to the school which advocates a long line trolled far behind the boat, he strips out all his casting line, and perhaps much of his backing, and trolls very slowly a considerable distance from shore. Or he may resort to the opposite extreme, and troll a very short line with the fly in the wash of his outboard motor, on the theory that Salmon will be attracted by the turbulence of the propeller and move in to investigate the disturbance. On the other hand, he may anchor his boat on the edge of a steeply-shelving bar or point and cast his fly into deep water, allow it to sink close to bottom, and then retrieve it slowly imitating as best he can the darting action of a live smelt. All three methods sometimes take Salmon on windless days. More often, all three methods fail. That is why the Landlocked Salmon fisherman prays for wind—any wind, and the harder it blows the better he likes it.

The Salmon is an exciting fish to catch. He strikes a lure hard, even viciously, more often than not hooking himself before the angler has had time to make a motion toward driving the barb home. The following fight is a spectacular one. The fish usually leaps immediately upon feeling the prick of the hook, and then dashes off in a long run that may strip the angler's reel down to the backing line or even the bare arbor. An active fish will leap out of water repeatedly, four, five, six times—or even more. Upon one occasion at Sysladobsis Lake in Maine a three-pound Salmon leaped twelve times by careful count—and then gave up, utterly exhausted by his own prodigious efforts.

But seldom does a Salmon surrender without staging a battle that the angler will long remember. On light tackle—a fly rod weighing from five to six ounces, with reel, line and leader in proportion—the Landlocked Salmon will challenge the Smallmouth Bass as the fightin'est fish, inch for inch and pound for pound, that swims in fresh water.

PACIFIC SALMON

The most enjoyable period for salmon fishing from the viewpoint of weather is from May 1 to September 30, although excellent sport can be had almost anywhere in Puget Sound during a normal October with Silver Salmon, and throughout the late winter and spring months with grilse, or immature Kings and Silvers. In fact they can be found at one place or another in every month as they do not all migrate to the Pacific to attain their growth, some remaining and feeding in the Sound from the time they enter salt water on their seaward migration until the spawning urge sends them back to their parent river. Many hardy anglers follow the schools of feeding Blackmouth, or immature Kings, which are in their second, third, or fourth year of growth from November to March as they move from one feeding area to another.

There is a period during which adult Kings, or river-bound spawners, pass through the salt water fishing grounds for immature Salmon and these adults are most sought by anglers because of their great size and fighting qualities.

Adult Kings enter the sport fishing areas from May to the end of September at Neah Bay at the seaward entrance of Puget Sound, during the same period in the San Juan Islands which are on the migration routes to the Fraser River, from May to September 1 at Hope Island at the mouth of the Skagit River, from June 15 to September 15 at most other places on Puget Sound, and from April 15 to September 15 on the Lower Columbia River although the angling peak is definitely from August 15 to September 10 on the Columbia.

King Salmon are taken on a variety of lures and baits. Bait fishermen use whole herring, or spinners (fillets) cut from the side of a large herring, and candlefish or sand lance. No other bait for Kings is used enough to mention. Lures that are most attractive are salmon plugs, similar in appearance and action to the conventional bass plug but sturdier, various spinning lures, jigger spoons, and the popular flashing attractors known as herring dodgers, fished from 1½ to 3 feet ahead of the bait or lure. Salmon flies are occasionally used for Kings, not the gaudy flies used for Atlantic Salmon, but long streamer types which resemble candlefish or herring, both in color and size.

The methods employed are trolling, stripping, spinning, and mooching. Fly casting is rarely done except by the most expert because of the extreme difficulty in casting the large salmon flies and the constant fouling of the streamer hair around the bend of the hook. The fly is therefore usually trolled either as a bare fly or as a small spinner and fly combination.

Spinning, either with the newly introduced spinning reel or the old conventional revolving spool reel is also being widely used both with bait and artificial lures.

Silver Salmon grilse are caught extensively off the mainland shores between Seattle and Everett during February, March and April. In early February the small Silvers are barely of legal size (12 inches) and something less than a pound in weight, but they are caught by the tens of thousands by trolling, principally with gang-troll spinners and angle worms, or on small jigger spoons. By the end of May these fish have attained an average weight of 3 pounds. Fishing at this time is concentrated off the southwest shores of Whidbey Island where they feed in the tide rips throughout the summer, during which time they gain approximately 1½ pounds in weight per month until September and October, when as 3-year olds they return to the rivers to spawn.

Supplementing this population of Silver Salmon which are more or less resident in Puget Sound throughout their life cycle, a migration of larger Silvers come from the ocean each year. Known as Hooknose Silvers, they first enter the Straits of Juan de Fuca about mid-August and continuing to press inward toward the river mouths through September, and October to the middle of November. They are called "Hooknose" because of the pronounced hooked nose on the males. This variety attains a weight of from 8 to 16 pounds and is distributed throughout Puget Sound. A similar run enters the Columbia River in late August and through September of each year.

In addition to the gang trolls used on smaller Silvers, the larger fish are caught by methods similar to those employed for Kings. The Silver is also an excellent fly fish as it is a frequent surface feeder and will take a trolled or cast fly recklessly when in a feeding mood.

Humpback Salmon are caught in this locality only during the odd-numbered year. It is a 2-year old fish at maturity, and in Fraser River and streams to the south this variety appears in significant numbers only every other year. It is caught in the same manner during the early part of the Silver Salmon run.

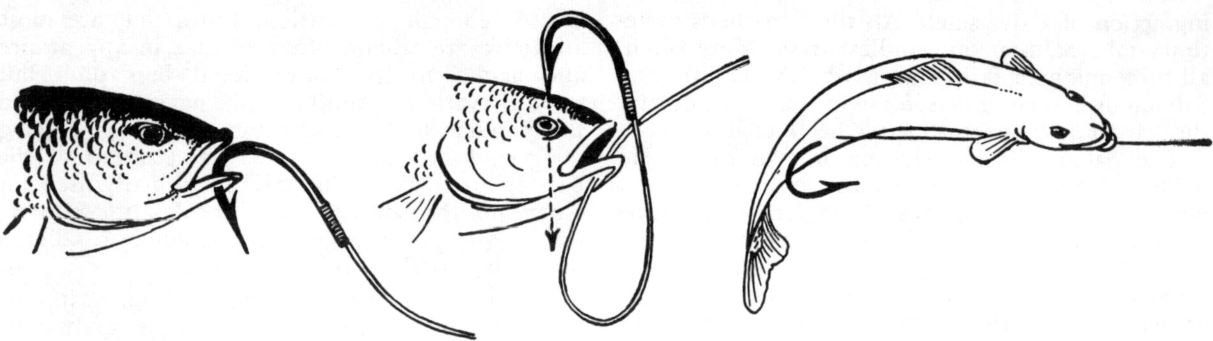

Jack Murray

This sketch illustrates the method of sewing a small bait-fish on a short-shank gut hook for trolling. Attached in this manner, the bait revolves slowly when trolled at a speed of from 2 to 3 miles per hour. It is a deadly lure for Land-locked Salmon as well as large Trout and Togue.

Dog or Chum Salmon actually do not rate as a sport fish. They are plenty game once they are hooked, but they are seldom caught by angling except at one place. They enter Puget Sound from the ocean in October and November of each year but are taken on hook and line with any success only at Gig Harbor, directly west of Tacoma. The best fishing is in December and early January when they are caught on cut-spinners from the side of a herring and by the stripping method, or by what is known as a dead spinner fished only by tidal action and slightly off the bottom. Occasionally they are also caught in Elliott Bay, Seattle's harbor, during the month of November on herring and dodger, or on a mooched herring.

Most of the salt water fly fishing for Salmon is by the trolling method already indicated. The flies most commonly used have an over-all length of 4 to 6 inches, using long strands of polar bear or other hair and are tied on either tandem or long shank single hooks in size 3/0 to 5/0. It is therefore obvious that such a big fly, particularly with the tendency of the hair to wrap around the bend of the hook would be extremely difficult to cast and fish properly.

Smaller flies on hook sizes of 1 to 3/0 are tied for casting, but because the larger flies are taken better, few fishermen will use the smaller flies when the fish are really striking. Popular patterns in Coho flies include Coronation (blue, red and white hair), Silver Killer (green, red and white), Green and White, Blue and White, Red and White and Green, Yellow and White, all with silver tinsel bodies to represent candlefish or herring.

Most of the fly fishing is done for Silvers, since this fish is a frequent surface feeder at any time of the day. Most of the Kings caught are taken incidentally when they happen to be near the surface. Kings are generally found deep in 50 to 150 feet of water, except near the hours of darkness. However, in the shallower waters of the Lower Columbia when it is running clear, Kings will take trolled Coho flies readily in late August and early September. Otherwise they are caught only occasionally in the salt water fishing grounds on flies.

On the other hand Silvers are ready fly takers, thousands of feeders from 2 to 6 pounds being caught off the southwest shores of Whidbey Island in Puget Sound each year from May to July. Following them come the larger Hooknose, from 8 to 18 pounds, and also an excellent fly fish that are caught in this manner whenever they run from August 15 to mid-November. While still prime, they are also a good riser in the lower rivers to a conventionally cast fly.

Cowichan Bay, Campbell River and other Vancouver Island salmon waters afford fine fly fishing in September and October. Clallam Bay, Sekiu, and the mouth of the Hoko River on the Washington side of the Straits give top sport in late September and through October. Bush Point, Mutiny Bay, and Double Bluff, all on the southwest side of Whidbey Island in Puget Sound, provide fine fly fishing until the commercial nets move in on October 5. Many are also caught in Elliott Bay and Shilshole Bay, both in the Seattle harbor, through October to Mid-November.

The best fishing is found when the schools of Silvers are feeding on the surface. This can be detected easily by the salmon rolling and swirling through the bait or from the action of gulls, chattering and diving into the feed as it is forced to the surface. Flies deftly cast ahead of the moving school, or trolled in the same manner will draw plenty of attention. Still another method is to keep the boat moving with outboard motor through feeding fish at about 4 miles an hour, casting at right angles to the boat and getting set for the strike when the fly enters the bow wave. Trolling without weight with about 40 to 50 feet of line out, and the fly bouncing in the wake of the motor, is also very effective.

Almost any 6 to 10-ounce single, or double grip fly rod designed for Salmon or Steelhead fly fishing is satisfactory. Reels should be capable of holding at least 200 yards of backing plus fly line if casting and more if trolling. Fifteen or 18 pound test flat-braided Nylon should be used for the backing on the fly line, or 6-pound single filament Nylons for ordinary fly trolling with no weight. A leader no longer than the rod and 6-pound test tippit for casting is ideal.

A No. 2 or 3 silver or brass spinner ahead of the fly when trolling will often attract deep feeding fish which otherwise refuse to rise.

However taken, a Pacific Salmon is a great sport fish and its future should be zealously guarded.

SHAD

Seined shad were a table delicacy before the Revolutionary War. But, until the early 1930's, these fish had eluded the hooks of sportsmen. Unlike Trout or Bass, Shad displayed no interest in such baits as the worm, minnow, and insect. Conventional bait and insect-imitating flies were also unsuccessful. The plugs and spoons whose gyrations arouse the predatory instincts of other fish only drove the skittish Shad out of casting range. Because fishermen had not discovered the fundamentals of this highly specialized form of angling, the Shad schools which ascended Connecticut River tidewater each spring to spawn were neither regarded nor accepted as game fish.

During the early 'thirties, in swift-flowing pools below a dam in the Salmon River, one of the Connecticut's tributaries, a few enterprizing anglers hit upon techniques which proved that Shad would strike at lures. Those early lures were tiny flashing spinners of the Junebug type and vivid flies made sparse with the aid of wear and moths. The observations of the fishermen also provided a clue to the water conditions under which Shad would strike; it was noted that these fish, when concentrated in water made swift by such obstructions as dams and boulders, would strike with fair consistency.

It was the manner in which the Shad performed after the hook was set, however, that charged the bloodstreams of anglers with high excitement. The Shad was bedlam on the end of a line. Few fish have done more to glamorize light-tackle. Given to aerial combat, swift, razoring runs, and bullish underwater capers, the Shad wasn't long in winning stardom in his new role of game fish.

The Eight-Mile River, a stream in the lower Connecticut River system, is ideally suited to fly-rodding for Shad. Gravel-bottomed, easy to wade, its short stretches of quick water form numerous pools. A short distance above the point where it empties into the Connecticut, there is an old mill dam, and in the mile-long section below the spillway some of the best Shad fishing can be found.

The methods employed are relatively simple. Until a Shad strikes, it is lazy man's fishing. Tinsel-wrapped Number 4 and 6 Sproat hooks are used, to which are attached on clear days, a wisp of red feather. (Rhode Island Red roosters are excellent suppliers). About four feet of six- or eight-pound-test leader is ample. The leader is threaded through two scarlet-red beads slightly larger than BB shots. The fishermen, making sure that their pockets hold a generous supply of split-shot sinkers, wade carefully as close as possible to the edge of the pool in which the Shad have been sighted and flip their flies into its waters. If the currents are too strong to hold the fly stationary about halfway to the bottom, enough split-shot is pinched on the leader to achieve the necessary weight. Seldom is it necessary to pay out more than ten or twelve feet of line, for the lure must be activated by the gentle undercurrents. In rivers as small as the Eight-Mile, a slow-flashing lure seems to be most appealing to the Shad.

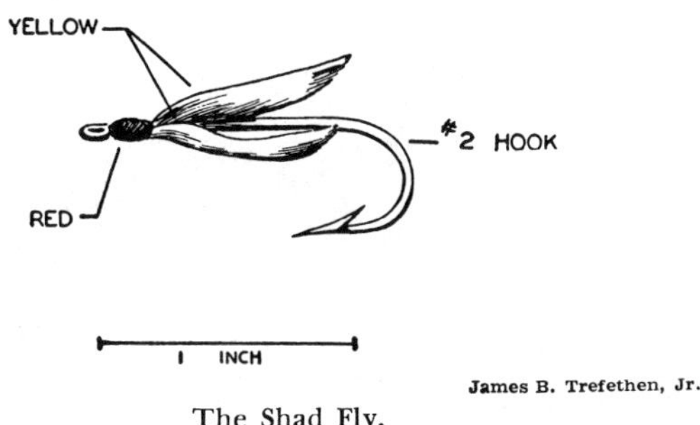

The Shad Fly.

Patience is the most valuable asset of one engaged in this type of Shad fishing. Although the system suggests monotony, one soon becomes fascinated by the fish that flash their silver sides around the lure. They will swim around, above, and underneath a dangling fly with aggravating aplomb. Seemingly ignoring the lure, they swarm back and forth from one end of the pool to the other. It is a sight which often causes the novice to lose control and rashly attempt to make the fish strike by casting or floating his fly into their wakes. This, however, is a grave mistake, for success or failure depends on keeping the fly fluttering in one spot, regardless of the direction in which the restless fish move. It may take five minutes, fifteen, or fifty, but sooner or later a husky Shad, fresh from the sea, will smash at the fly with tarpon-fury.

On rainy and overcast days yellowish and orange feathers, in combination with pinkish beads, work more effectively than the reds. Under gray skies hooks wrapped with gold, instead of silver, tinsel are more attractive to the Shad.

Rainy spells and flash floods create Shad fishing problems that call for different methods and, sometimes, different lures. Swollen stream beds make it impossible to wade close enough to pools so that the fly can be dangled in the manner just described. Although higher water sometimes tends to scatter the fish over wider areas, they will usually concentrate in the boiling currents around the inlets of the deepest pools. Because rain and seepage create roiled waters, flashier lures frequently work best; and many anglers, temporarily abandoning the bead-topped fly, now resort to such metallic fly rod devices as panfish-sized Trix-Orenos, crippled minnows, Colorado and Junebug spinners, yellow fluttering underwater darters with bangles at the ends to add flash, or duralumin wobblers with spinning tails. But many of the most successful Shad anglers remain loyal to the fly. Some of them add a haze of white feather to the red, yellow, or orange; others give the fly added flash by placing a tiny spinner before it.

One season of continuous high water in the Eight-Mile River prompted one ingenious Shad fisherman to try a series of intensive experiments. His efforts produced a flood water technique which has never since been excelled. Standing on a boulder at the foot of a Shad pool, he cast a weighted orange fly with a tiny gold spinner in front of it beyond the inlet of the pool. The weighted fly settled instantly, but the line quickly formed a bag that was soon sucked into an eddy

George Heinold

A nice catch made at the Shad fishing grounds at Enfield, Connecticut.

formed where the current dropped off into the pool's deep water. As the pressure increased on the line, the fly was dragged slowly into the pool. It rode deep, about halfway between surface and bottom, spinning crazily as cross-currents buffeted it among the Shad. The angler had just about recovered his slack line when a Shad struck savagely.

During many days of flood water which followed that angler skillfully employed his technique of utilizing the water's natural force to drag his weighted flies through Shad pools. Results were astonishing—further convincing proof that Shad are attracted to lure-action generated by currents.

While anglers of the lower valley were perfecting their shadcraft, their colleagues of the upper river were far from idle. Shad runs follow the Connecticut River and its tributary streams far beyond the city of Hartford. Despite dams, some of the fish manage to invade Massachusetts waters. Upstate anglers soon discovered at Enfield the fishing grounds that were destined to become the most productive of all. These waters are located below a power dam that spans the Connecticut River.

The Connecticut River flows swiftly below this dam. Milk-white waters hiss over jagged rocks, then divide into series of rivulets as they rush off to merge with rips, spinning eddies, and whirlpools—the pockets in which Shad, blocked by the dam, school. These grounds became so popular that the Board of Fisheries and Game took control and set it aside in 1941 as an area exclusively for Shad fishing. During each of several seasons it has produced nearly 10,000 Shad.

Fishing conditions at Enfield present unique problems. During low water many Shad anglers wade into the stream, seek out concentrations of fish in the fastest runs, and use the standard fly rod as it is used in the lower valley. But, under average springtime conditions, it is almost impossible to wade more than a few feet from shore

George Heinold

Hooking a nice one during the Shad run in the Connecticut River.

George Heinold

Shad runs attract anglers from far and wide. The stream shown here is the Connecticut River near Enfield, Connecticut.

because of powerful currents and abrupt depths. Alder-lined banks rule out the fly-rodder's backcasts.

Enfield's anglers have solved their problem by hybridizing tackle. Five-foot steel baitcasting rods and matching reels equipped with 12-pound-test casting line overcome the backcast difficulty. The sparse red, yellow, and orange flies are tied on to leaders of 10- or 12-pound test Nylon cut into 20-inch lengths, and as many lead sinkers are squeezed on to the leader as is necessary for the dual purpose of whipping out long casts and keeping the fly submerged as it drifts with the currents.

Shad at Enfield have shown a decided weakness for beads of several colors. Most fishermen string three or four (1/8 to 1/4-inch) on the leader. Three reds and a yellow are a popular combination. Blues, greens, ambers, and pinks are frequently used; and some fishermen even carry kits of quick-drying nail polish so that they can speedily transform their beads to the colors which appeal to Shad on a particular day.

The Enfield angler casts his terminal tackle across current, on a slight downstream angle. His cast is calculated to drift his fly into a boiling Shad pocket below. When casting skill and judgment synchronize, his line swings downriver in an arc until it straightens itself out when the fly rides into the swirling pocket. Strikes usually come when the fly glides into the boiling pocket, but it often pays to allow it to hang for a moment before retrieving. Shad concentrations vary with water depth, and astute anglers shift their locations until they have found a good spot.

In recent seasons many anglers have "prospected" successfully for Shad schools with the aid of boats. Anchored at both stern and bow, the boats are held in fast currents. Weighted, beadtopped flies are dropped overboard and held dangling until striking fish have been located.

Now one of Connecticut's leading angling sports, rod-and-line Shad fishing has an excellent future.

SHEE-FISH

The Shee-fish, called variously Chee, Shee, Shee-fish and Inconnu by the Eskimos, is one of Alaska's most exciting game fishes. It is also one of the largest. Less is known about it than any of the other species for the reason that its range is generally along the northern perimeter of the Territory in waters where few sportsmen ever penetrate. But to the handful of anglers who have battled it on rod and line, it is rated as one of the best sportsfishes on the continent.

The Shee-fish is different than most other northern game fishes. It is a long, big-scaled fish with underthrust jaw. Its build is somewhat along the lines of a Robalo, or Snook, of southern salt water. It is a voracious feeder, smashing into schools of smaller fish so forcefully as to foam the surface, and its leaps when hooked are likely to be prolonged and spectacular. Streamer flies will attract it, especially in the evening when it strikes most freely. The resulting fight is no short fray, but may last for as long as an hour. Shee-fish grow to respectable size, and while the average may not be more than from 10 to 20 pounds, there are records of it having exceeded 80 pounds in weight. Surely, then, it is a mighty fish to land with fly fishing equipment.

Small plugs, wobbling spoons, and other lures of the baitcaster with his multiplying reel are eagerly snapped up by the Shee-fish when conditions are right. For general purposes it may be said that equipment suitable for Pike, Muskellunge, Snook, and large Bass will do for this pinkish iridescent fish of boreal waters.

Time of year is important for the man who plans to catch a Shee-fish. Midsummer to early fall is best. At this season the Shee is likely to be well up the few big rivers in which it is found, descending at freeze-up to brackish waters of the bays where it spends the winters. In Kotzebue Sound, a noted place for Shee-fish, Eskimos take large numbers in winter by cutting a trench through the ice, then trolling an ivory lure along the narrow lane of exposed water. At this time the Shee-fish is feeding largely on a small smelt. The hook used by the native Eskimos is barbless, and the heavy fish is flung out on the ice with as little ceremony as commercial tuna fishermen yanking their catch over the bows of their ocean-going vessels. A lucky Eskimo may take two or three hundred pounds in a single day.

The flesh is delicious. Not only is it relished locally, but in recent times airplanes fly it from Arctic ice fields to many markets to the southward.

Center of abundance of the Shee-fish in Alaska is the Kobuk River flowing into Kotzebue Sound at the Arctic Circle. It is found in lesser numbers all the way south to the Kuskokwim River where it is called "Cony," and to the north and eastward as far as the Mackenzie River which is the type locality responsible for the latin name *Stenodus Mackenzii*. It is said that this great fish is extremely common in northern Siberian streams where it is called "Chi," and sometimes "Nelma," or White Salmon.

In the Yukon, largest of Alaska rivers, the Shee-fish has been caught in fishtraps as far up as Woodchopper, some 2,000 miles from the mouth. However, in that muddy water it is practically unknown as a game fish. Where fresh water rivers merge with the silt-laden waters of the larger river, Shee-fish occasionally congregate in the area where the waters blend. At the confluence of the Innoko and Iditarod Rivers in the lower Yukon Valley, Shee-fish sometimes school in large numbers, their presence often not suspected until they start flailing the surface during evening feeding periods. Several other lower Yukon River tributaries contain many more of these big fish than even local residents surmise. In sluggish waters its battle with the angler is considerably slower in tempo than when taken in fast current.

When taken from the water, the Shee-fish generally resembles a huge Whitefish. Its pearly scales, each as large as a dime, contain no spots from head to tail. The fish is colored much like the common great Lakes Whitefish, and except for that pugnacious jaw and rows of bristly teeth might be mistaken for one. But there is no question that the Shee-fish is a most capable predator. A prick of the fisherman's hook seems to set it off in the wildest jumps imaginable. Some day when the north is better explored, this truly wonderful fish will be better known to all anglers.

SUNFISH

Bluegill in the north, Roach in the east, Bream (or more familiarly Brim) in the south—by whatever name known this lusty, rotund, hard-fighting Sunfish is king of the panfishes, holding in the affections of a mighty host of fishermen a place unriveled by any other of his size and type.

He is found wherever there are weed-bottomed ponds and lakes not too cold, to furnish him food and cover, and in the quiet pools of streams as well, through a range that extends from Maine to Mississippi and from Florida to the Dakotas. It has been planted in western waters as well. And wherever he is found he holds an important place on the list of freshwater game fish, alike for flyrod fishermen and for those who prefer the cane pole.

In many respects Sunfish are to the sport of angling what the cottontail rabbit is to hunting, the darling of the common man. Neither costly tackle nor great skill is required to catch him. He is taken by small boys with dime-store equipment and by old men who like the tranquility of a blue lake under the summer sun, a boat, a long limber pole, and a bobber to tell when there is a fish to land. He is a prime favorite with women anglers, but he also yields abundant sport to men with custom-made flyrods and tapered lines.

Remove this versatile commoner from the lakes of America, and a major and irreparable gap would be left in the panfish ranks.

Two things chiefly endear him to fishermen. First is a vigorous appetite that remains active throughout the year. Second is his spirit and ability as a fighter.

He bites at all seasons and in all weathers, at all hours and on a wide variety of lures, both natural and artificial. And once hooked he battles with a stubborn tenacity and a strength far beyond anything that might be expected of a fish of his weight. He displays the strongest possible affinity for the weed beds that spawned and sheltered him, and he quits them with angry reluctance.

He is not a big fish. Throughout most of his range seven or eight inches must be considered an average length, with a corresponding weight of less than half a pound. Under favorable conditions he does better, of course. The big Bluegills of Indiana which the fishermen of that state call the "Hoosier Standard" must attain a weight of a full pound to qualify for that title, and standards are far from rare in Maxinkuckee, Wawasee, and various other Indiana lakes.

Existing records are too sketchy to indicate exactly how big Bluegills may grow to be. Wisconsin claims the world's record with a fish that weighed a little in excess of 3 pounds. Two of the largest authentic records were both Michigan fish. One, taken in 1948, measured 12½ inches in length and weighed 2 pounds 1 ounce. The other, caught three years earlier, was 12 inches long, 15 in girth and weighed 2 pounds 10 ounces. Such whoppers must be considered the very rare exception.

But even a Bluegill of seven or eight inches is capable of giving an extraordinarily good account of himself if taken on suitable tackle. No angler can land him, either on flyrod or slender cane pole, without being made to know that he has met a champion in the flyweight class.

Despite the ready appetite of this purse-mouthed bantam of the weed beds, there are of course days and periods when Bream fishing lapses into a slump. In the north this is most likely to occur in the extremely hot weather of midsummer, usually in August, and again in November and early December when the water is very cold shortly before freezeup. It is strongly suspected, however, that at the latter season the failure to catch them is largely due to the fact that unfavorable weather discourages fishing and the few anglers who do brave the late-autumn winds probably use neither the right baits nor methods. Certainly the Sunfish are as co-operative as anyone could ask and fishing for them is a highly successful sport once the northern lakes freeze over and ice fishing gets under way.

In the south the "Brim" is regarded as a year-long proposition. Many of the best lakes below the Mason-Dixon line are open to legal fishing throughout the year and yield consistently good catches.

The Bluegill is a spring spawner, nesting in late May or June across the northern half of the country, and in most of the northern states is protected by a closed season corresponding with the period when the males are on the reeds and protecting schools of very young fry. This necessary holiday eliminates what in all likelihood would otherwise be the most productive fishing period of the entire year.

For the confirmed fisherman in the north, unless the laws of his state prevent, the year's fishing gets into full swing in late March or early April, shortly after the ice has gone out and with the onset of the first warm, sunny days of spring.

The fish move into shoal water on bars and inside the dropoff at that time and are exceedingly vulnerable to wet flies or to natural bait spatted with a long slender pole that will reach far ahead of boat or wading fisherman. Dry flies also are sometimes very effective in early spring. Whichever method he uses, the angler needs to go about his fishing quietly and cautiously at this season, especially on windless days, since the Bluegills often lie in water only a foot or two deep and are wary and easily alarmed.

Early summer finds the big fellows of catchable size dug in along the weed beds, in moderately shallow water but not at the top, willing to feed through the day on any attractive offering that is put down to them. This period brings pan fishing to its peak of popularity in most sections of the country.

The bulk of this fishing, at least through the middle hours of the day, is done with cane pole tackle. The fish are too deep to be reached readily with flies. But about sundown they desert the lairs where they have lurked all day along bars and drop-off shelves and around the marginal weed thickets of the lake, and move up into shallow water to gorge themselves on aquatic insects.

That is the hour when the flyrod fisherman comes into his own on good water. He can wade or drift quietly along in a boat, depending on the depth and nature of the lake. He should stay close to weeds or work through sparse beds of rushes in water two to ten feet deep, and he can expect to do a brisk business on either wet or dry patterns.

As the air and water grow warmer with the advance of summer the Bream population retreats into the deeper, cooler areas of the lake. Late July and August are likely to find the bulk of the big fish too far down to be reached by the angler unless he uses special methods. Even then, however, the Bluegill does not sulk. He'll talk back to anyone willing to go where he has taken up temporary residence.

Fishermen often anchor their boats in 70 feet of water on the big Bluegill lakes of northern Indiana on a scorching July day, go down 30 to 40 feet with long lines on cane poles, reach the level at which hungry Bluegills are waiting, and catch fish at a rate to satisfy the most ardent angler.

And even in the hottest and dryest weather of August, the "dog days" period when all fishing is prone to slacken, the Bluegills still move into shoal water around the weedbeds each evening and spend the night and the daybreak hours feeding there, thus affording the flyrod addict his chance to establish contact.

The cooling of the waters in September brings some of the briskest fishing of the entire year. Autumn is not the best season for fly fishing, but it does find the Bream congregated once more in moderately deep water off bars and shelves, and they are never more ready to take natural bait put down to them than in the crisp cool days of September and October.

A little later the lakes freeze in the north and the ice fishing season gets under way. Up until about 1920 or 1925 the Bluegill was hardly recognized as a winter fish. He was not caught through the ice, even as a stray, for the simple reason that the ice fisherman did not use baits acceptable to his reduced winter appetite. In recent years, however, this panfish has become the backbone of ice fishing in many sections.

The list of natural baits that they will take through the year is longer than many fishermen realize, and unquestionably some excellent fishing is lost because anglers do not experiment with a sufficiently wide variety of lures.

Heading the list is worms, the ancient standby of cane-pole fishing the world over. In many waters red or manure worms are more tempting to Sunfish than the common variety, and save in the case of exceptionally large fish, night crawlers are normally not effective.

Next to worms crickets probably account for more Bluegills than any other live bait. Cricket season brings a spurt in fishing among the initiate all across the country. Not so widely recognized and used, but about equally effective, are grasshoppers. They have the added advantage of being easy to get and their season is a bit longer, too. Some fishermen use white grubs, but others have never found them successful.

Among the more uncommon baits that will take these small battlers readily are the small gray moths that congregate on the screens of lighted windows through the summer, the kind that are often called millers.

The least pleasant to use of any bait is the yellow-striped catalpa worm, as it is fished in Indiana. The angler grasps the worm between thumb and forefinger, places a blunt nail against the head and actually shoves the worm inside-out as you would turn a glove finger. Catalpa worms treated in that fashion are extremely messy, but they are killers in good Bluegill water in midsummer.

One of the most unorthodox and also one of the most deadly live lures used for this fish is the cockroach, a prime favorite on certain southern lakes. Veteran fishermen on Tennessee's Reelfoot, one of the best pieces of panfish water in the middle south, rely on nothing else the year around. They hold roaches far more effective than crickets.

Bluegill bait for ice fishing includes such oddities as corn borers, goldenrod grubs, wood grubs, the larva of the burrowing mayfly, meal worms and red worms. Tried at other seasons, some of these might well prove equally tempting to the fish.

FLY FISHING FOR SUNFISH

Few fishermen are aware of the excellent sport that can be found near almost any home, if one learns to use flies for Sunfish. Taking Sunfish thus is a very different matter from catching them on live bait; it is a true sport which any angler can enjoy.

In spite of a widely held idea, it is actually easier to learn to cast with flies than with plugs. The difficulties, so many beginners encounter, come from the fact that most Americans are plug casters before they are fly casters. Plugs can be thrown out awkwardly with almost any rod and reel, and with no knowledge of correct form. The result will not be true casting; it will be clumsy, laborious, and inaccurate. But many users of the casting rod manage to heave plugs out in the general direction desired, and at least think they are casting.

It is often taken for granted that flies too can be cast without troubling to make even a brief preliminary investigation of proper tackle or methods. Such people find fly casting difficult if not impossible. To cast a fly, one must have a reasonably good rod, and a line of suitable weight to bring out the action of that particular rod. The most skilful veteran cannot cast effectively with a badly mismatched rod and line, so it is futile for the beginner to attempt it.

Too, a fly cannot be heaved out a useful distance by incorrect methods or by awkward strength, as can a plug; there is a very definite series of movements which must be followed. But this "correct form" is so simple that a beginner by carefully following instructions (see page 200), can learn in one evening to cast a fly well enough to catch Sunfish successfully. After one month of careful practice for a short time each evening, ones fly casting should equal that of any but the most expert.

The term "easy to learn" being indefinite, it might be advisable to compare fishing with bowling, a sport which, with its twenty million participants, ranks second only to fishing in the United States, and which therefore should be familiar to many fishermen. Since the writer has been a league bowler for many years, he speaks from experience in stating that it is certainly five times, and probably ten times, as easy to become a moderately good fly caster as to become a moderately good bowler.

And, unless one wants to be a demonstration caster, there is little reason for spending long hours on the practice necessary for really, spectacular casting. The caster of moderate ability, with a fairly sound knowledge of fishing methods, will catch more fish than one who is mainly a showman. After all, fishing rods are made primarily to catch fish, not to be employed in skillful juggling tricks.

Sunfish are plentiful even in some of the most heavily populated states, in which other game fish are now so scarce that seeking them is almost a waste of time. In many places, this scarcity of larger fish, which formerly kept them thinned out, has permitted Sunfish to increase to such numbers that they are stunted from lack of sufficient food. Where such conditions prevail, the more who catch and take home daily limits, the larger the remaining individuals will become, to furnish increasingly good sport.

Since so little attention is usually given to Sunfish, casual inquiries are unlikely to disclose many good places for them. But some careful scouting, and a few chats with owners of small country stores—and with the local residents met in them—will often reveal some excellent spots, populated with surprisingly large Bluegills.

Some may consider Sunfish too small to furnish real sport. But they usually average larger than Trout caught in most popular waters, and sought with much gravity and formality. Furthermore, these diminutive Trout are often half tame stock, recently released from some hatchery. So one who prefers to offer his flies to Sunfish might be pardoned for smiling at the man who fishes so seriously for hand-fed Trout.

When it comes to game qualities, the Sunfish is among the best. He fights to the limit of his capabilities, is very fast, and should be rated among the most uniformly game of all fish.

True, to afford sport, he must be caught on suitably light tackle. So must any other fish. A Bass taken on line of Muskellunge strength, can be dragged in with little semblance of sport.

It is safe to say that no other North American game fish will take artificial bait so readily. Almost invariably, flies, properly used, will take more Sunfish than live bait, and especially more large ones. This is partly because Sunfish, all through life, feed on small creatures which flies and other diminutive fly-rod lures represent; other fresh water game fish, in the adult stage, feed on smaller fish.

Why flies are particularly effective for larger Sunfish is easily explained: Small Sunfish regularly gather in the shadow under a boat, to take live bait let down to them. The larger ones are generally too wary to do this, but will remain a good distance away, where they can be reached only by the fly caster.

Moreover, it seems that the larger a Sunfish becomes, the less able is he to resist the temptation to strike at an artificial fly presented with any skill.

Many anglers agree that the delicate flavor of the Sunfish can be equaled only by that of a Trout taken from the coldest mountain stream. Even in warm water he does not get that weedy, muddy taste and soft flesh so common among other fish during the hot months.

All fish are more or less susceptible to internal parasites, especially during hot weather; but the Sunfish is more resistant than many others. Incidentally, these parasites are practically all harmless to man and will not infect him, though they render the appearance of the fish unappetizing.

Here, it might be repeated that the sportsman usually need have little hesitation about taking home any legal number of Sunfish that he and his friends can eat, hesitant though he may be about killing many fish of other species.

Largemouth and Smallmouth Bass, Crappies, Rock Bass are all members of the family. A glance at all these fish will show their similarity.

There are many species of Sunfish proper, but the Bluegill and the Pumpkinseed, are of the most interest to sportsmen. The Bluegill, being somewhat the larger, is the one most frequently propagated and it has been introduced into most parts of the country in which it was not native.

Choosing a suitable rod is important, so it is best to go thoroughly into the matter.

Any reasonably good fly rod will do for Sunfish. Even a heavy bass-bug rod will serve, and there can be nothing unsportsmanlike about using it, since in fly fishing it is only the strength of the leader point that matters. The objections to using it for smaller fish are that it will be unnecessarily tiring and that they may be played better, and with more pleasure, on a lighter one.

On the other hand, few, even when purchasing a rod solely for Sunfish, care for the very short, ultra-light "fairy wand." This is partly because rather long casts are often most productive of large Sunfish, and only an expert can attain much distance with these small rods. Only a few veteran fly fishermen prefer these tiny rods; the rest are inclined to prefer, even for light fishing, about the heaviest that will not become tiring in long hours of steady casting.

That last point should always be remembered in purchasing a rod for Sunfish; fishing for them does entail steady casting. Usually there is no walking from pool to pool, as in Trout fishing, and no running around in a boat from spot to spot; when a good place for Sunfish is found, one stays there and keeps casting. Nor is there generally a current to "work" the flies; they are effective only when continuously cast and retrieved. Therefore it is better to err in getting a rod too light than to have one that is unduly tiring. The exact rod advisable will depend on one's strength, and upon how much one fishes, to keep arm muscles in training.

For that matter, the foregoing is equally true in other fly-rod fishing. One reason for the lack of popularity of the fly rod in many districts is that the average man is inclined to over-rod himself, thereby making fly fishing such tiring work that it cannot be enjoyed long at a time. The fact that one man can swing a 9½-foot bass rod all day without undue fatigue does not mean that another can; if he is to fish steadily, and to enjoy his fishing, he may need a rod of 8½ feet, or perhaps only 8 feet, even for Bass.

For the average person, except where, in fishing from shore, extreme distance is desirable, the most suitable rod is one of from 7½ to 8 feet. A man with a strong wrist and arm might prefer one longer, though rarely over 8 feet 6 inches.

It is not possible to recommend a rod for youngsters, since they are of all ages, sizes, and strengths. A well-grown boy is so adaptable, with muscles so quickly trained, that he can soon become accustomed to fishing with any but the heaviest rod.

For a woman of average strength, a rod of 7 feet or 7 feet 3 inches might be best.

However, it is a fact that only a rare woman will fish while catching nothing, as long as will any man worthy of the name of fisherman. Still more rare is the woman who will cheerfully suffer wet, cold, hunger, and almost any other hardship in the hope of catching a fish or two.

Thousands of women, however, would enjoy fishing if it did not entail long hours or hardship. For these, fly fishing for Sunfish is ideal. It can usually be practiced near home or within sight of the resort cabin. One can slip out for an hour or two and nearly always find good action; it is not comparable to traveling far, and working hard all day, in hope of one or two Bass or Trout. And while it sometimes seems that most fish prefer to be caught in the vilest possible weather, the Sunfish has a cheerful habit of taking flies avidly on a nice, sunny day during midsummer vacation, when fishing of other kinds is at its worst.

So it is suggested that the man who likes to have his wife as a fishing companion should get a light rod for her and teach her to use it.

As previously intimated, it is an error to purchase a poor rod, thinking it "good enough to learn with"; if an expert cannot cast well with it, how can a beginner? But there is no need for a novice to buy an expensive rod, that only a veteran could appreciate or fully utilize.

Too much emphasis is often given to the weight of a fly rod, in ounces; boasting of the lightness of a rod; merely shows ignorance of the basic principles of fly casting. To have correct action a rod must have a weight in proportion to its length, and this weight will vary according to the density of the bamboo and the type of reel seat. A heavy, locking reel seat does not detract from the sporting qualities of a rod; it merely helps balance it in the hand, and so renders it less tiring to use.

Correct action is a fly rod is important indeed, but the action that best suits one man may not be advisable for another. However, "wet-fly action," slow, weak, and spineless, is about obsolete; practically all experienced anglers now prefer dry-fly action, even for wet-fly fishing.

A rod is generally understood to have dry-fly action when it is quite stiff up to about the middle, the bend developing gradually from there, with the tip not too weak and powerless. Each good rod maker has his own idea of the exact taper, that will give best results; but these slight differences of opinion signify little to the practical angler who can obtain about equally good results with the best rods of any good manufacturer.

Rods having dry-fly action and of equal length can be roughly divided into three classes: those with Light, Medium, and Heavy Trout Action—some makers call the same actions Extra Light, Light and Medium Trout; but so long as these do not list a Heavy Trout, it will be known that they mean the same as the others. And exact weight for length is useful in comparing the rods of one maker, so long as they have reel seats of similar weight, though not in comparing one maker's rods with another's.

Light Trout action is probably best for the man who will not fish often nor go to the trouble of learning to cast well. This action verges toward the old "wet-fly," rather slow and weak. Its advantage is that it permits casting with very poor timing, and with the light line that so many use on a fly rod. A rod of this type will serve well wherever a fairly long cast is unnecessary; it is often liked by trout anglers whose fishing is confined to small streams.

For the man who practices enough to do better casting, and who needs to attain quite long distance, medium trout action is best. This seems to be the action preferred by most expert trout fishermen, since it will do good work and still is not tricky to use. It is capable of giving more distance than is ever needed for Sunfish, except in fishing from the shore.

Heavy trout action is needed only where real distance for rod length is desirable. A considerable amount of practice is necessary to do the accurate timing needed for such a rod; with it even the experienced fishermen, especially when tired from long hours of casting, may get "off timing" and find himself having trouble. Still, it will do beautiful work for the man who fishes enough to learn to use it.

There are fly rods with still more powerful action for their length, but they are of little interest to the man seeking Sunfish, and especially to the beginner, since he would find them too tricky to use.

Again let it be repeated—that if one expects to do anything remotely resembling real casting, one must use a line of the right size to bring out the action of a given rod; and the stiffer the rod, the more exact must line fit be.

Most fly rods now sold, are accompanied by recommendations for line size. But not infrequently it is easier to learn, and especially to achieve distance, by using a line one size larger than that specified. This is particularly true when a Nylon line is to be used, for it will be lighter than silk of equal size; it is the weight of a line that matters, not its exact diameter.

For the beginner, a level line is sufficient, and it is perhaps the easiest with which to learn. A level line of good grade is inexpensive and should last the average man for years; very cheap lines are to be avoided, for they are unsatisfactory in all respects and wear out rapidly. Later, an expensive three-diameter line will permit more distance, and will increase ease of casting beyond moderate ranges.

There are some poor lines, and poor rods, on the market, nor is the price by any means a safe determinant of quality; so the one protection for the beginner is to buy the product of a reliable company.

The beginner will undoubtedly confine himself to wet-fly fishing as easier than dry-fly to learn in fishing for Sunfish.

In wet-fly fishing, a six foot leader is sufficient. But it is best to use the tapered, dry-fly type, since the fine front end should result in more fish caught. Too, this fine leader point will afford more sport, by making it necessary to play a fish properly instead of merely hauling it in. A leader very small for its full length can not be cast well. A common rule states that the butt should be about two-thirds the diameter of the line that it joins, but, especially with level lines, considerably smaller sizes are often used. This same tapered leader will do very well in dry-fly fishing for Sunfish, but here one of 7½ feet might prove more satisfactory; it is rarely or never necessary to use longer for Sunfish.

Nylon leader material has almost completely replaced natural gut in fishing of this type. For

Sunfish, the finest leader point obtainable should be used; these will perhaps be of the size known as 5X, .006 inch in diameter, with a breaking strain of 1¼ pounds.

There is another advantage in using a light leader point. At least a few Bass are generally found where there are Sunfish, and at times even large Bass take tiny Sunfish flies quite readily; indeed, a Pike of ten pounds or more will occasionally be hooked on such a fly. The beginner using a strong leader point, and hooking such a large fish, might easily break his rod. Nothing short of a record fish is worth a broken rod; and, besides, the fish that breaks a rod is almost certain to escape. It is much better to let a big fish break a fine leader point than the more expensive rod. An expert can, of course, safely play surprisingly large fish on very light tackle; but it takes much practice, to become such an expert.

There are said to be thousands of patterns of artificial flies; probably no man could name even half of them. But the beginner need not worry over this diversity of patterns.

Most artificial flies are called "exact imitations," and named after natural insects which they resemble considerably less than a scarecrow resembles a man.

Even in trout fishing, some of the most noted authorities have questioned the utility of the exact-imitation theory, and have confined themselves strictly to "bivisibles," which are frankly supposed to look like nothing but a few wisps of feathers tied to a hook, the front being white, the rest of one color only. The Trout angler finds it necessary to carry these in many sizes, since the size most productive at one time might prove useless at others. Also, the fisherman will have them with bodies of various colors; scientists have exploded the theory, formerly held by some, that all fish are color blind.

So it is suggested that the beginner merely pick out a few flies of different colors, being sure to get some that are mainly black, white, brown, and gray. He should purchase eyed flies only, flies with gut attached being about obsolete for various sound reasons.

At any given time, there will be one color of fly that Sunfish will take more readily than any other; usually all the angler can do is to keep changing flies until he discovers the best one. On rather rare occasions, all the Sunfish will seem to insist on some one color and refuse all others; nearly always that will be because they are feeding upon natural flies of that color.

Sunfish are perhaps never so insistent as Trout frequently are upon exact size of the fly they will take. But it is in the matter of size that the beginner almost invariably makes his greatest mistake; he uses flies too large, forgetting that a Sunfish has a far smaller mouth than a Trout of equal weight. Sunfish strike his large flies readily, keeping him in excited suspense until he finds that he can hook few or none of them.

A fly larger than Number 10 is seldom advisable and there will be occasions when much smaller, even down to Number 18, will produce best. The size to use, naturally, depends to a great extent on the size Sunfish present.

Large, erect wings often keep Sunfish from taking flies well into their small mouths. And the beginner will get as many fish if he uses all hackle flies, which have no wings. Even these should not be too bulky; often the effectiveness of a fly can be greatly increased by trimming out half or more of the hackle with manicure scissors or a sharp knife; this trick is well known to veteran anglers. Less experienced fishermen cannot understand why some old, bedraggled fly is often much more effective than a pretty, new one; it is merely that fish have chewed away most of that superfluous dressing from the old one. Flies found in tackle stores are nearly always overdressed, since only a few anglers will choose those with the desirable scanty dressing.

Many who use the fly rod for Sunfish swear by various little imitation insects of rubber or plastic. There is no harm in trying such things, since half the fun of fishing comes from experimenting.

A metal spinner will rarely increase one's catch of Sunfish, so, since it will make casting somewhat more difficult and less pleasant, it is better not to use it; if one is used, it should be the tiniest obtainable. Since many who use the fly rod for Sunfish use it for Crappies too, it might be well to add that the exact opposite holds true in their case: a fairly large spinner will almost always greatly increase one's catch, except in surface fishing. The Crappie's liking for larger lures, more difficult to cast, makes him a less desirable fly-rod fish than the Sunfish; also, though much larger than the Sunfish, he is not nearly so game.

For the beginner who may wish a small list of patterns, here are a few, easy to obtain, that have proved effective for Sunfish almost everywhere.

Bee and McGinty (very similar); Coachman and Royal Coachman (quite different—it would be best to get both); Montreal; Alder; Silver Doctor; Black Gnat; Red Ant; Yellow Sally (better in some districts than in others); Red Tag Palmer; Black, White, Gray and Brown Hackle.

And, while bivisibles are intended for dry-fly fishing, they are excellent wet flies for Sunfish, by merely fishing them below the surface instead of on it. They can be found in nearly all colors.

A fly reel, unlike a casting reel, has nothing to do with the cast; it is present merely to keep line out of the way when it is not in use. And a Sunfish is played by stripping in line with the left hand; never, as are large fish, played from a reel with a drag or a heavy click.

Therefore the reel used is purely a matter of taste. Some like single-actions; some, automatics; some, those of the ratchet type, in which line is taken in by flipping a lever with the little finger of the hand holding the rod.

It is always well to get a fly reel quite large, and to fill the middle with a cork arbor. This prevents the line from getting set into tight little spirals that will not shoot through the guides. It also allows more line to be taken in at each turn of the spool.

Another reason for getting a large reel is that many anglers wrap sheet lead around the arbor, until rod-and-reel balance is brought back into or near the hand. The combination thus weighted feels heavy and clumsy when picked up, but it is much less tiring in a long period of steady casting, than a rod with unweighted reel; also, it permits faster movements of the rod tip.

A common complaint against the automatic reel is that it may jerk the hook into the top guide and break a rod tip. This shows ignorance of the proper use of an automatic, for only by misuse can it damage a rod. The spring tension should never be strong enough to pull the hook into the tip; it should be barely sufficient to draw the line straight with the hook in the fly ring by the grip, when the rod is not being used.

All through the season, Sunfish are inclined to remain in schools in favorite places. Many of these good spots are well known locally, so a few inquiries will often secure directions for reaching them. Sometimes, however, these places are fished so hard that the fly angler may wish to try elsewhere.

In the earlier part of the season, Sunfish will be found mainly in quite, shallow water, and close to weeds or brush. A fairly large open place far back in lily pads, near shore, is usually excellent for them at this time of year; so is a similar opening in floating water weeds. The early-season fishing in such places is often fast and furious, not demanding much skill or experience, though even here a moderately long cast usually produces more large Sunfish than short casts. Therefore it is well for the novice to begin fly fishing, if possible, in the early season and in such places. By the time the fish have moved to deeper water, his skill should be equal to catching them there.

In midseason, most of the larger Sunfish are found in deeper water. Usually, a depth of about six to ten feet is best for fly fishing though sometimes it is necessary to go still deeper allowing the fly to sink sufficiently to reach the fish.

In summer, the outer edge of a weed bed, where the water is quite deep or near the tip of a long point of weeds running out from shore are particularly likely spots. It is poor policy to spend much time in trying one place, no matter how promising it may look; if half a dozen casts do not produce a fish, or at least a strike, it is best to move on. Nor should time be wasted on a place that seems to hold only small Sunfish, if the water is known to contain larger; Sunfish are frequently found grouped roughly according to size.

A simple and rather lazy way to find a "bed" of Sunfish is to troll a fly, weighted to take it to proper depth; then, when a fish strikes, anchor and cast to see what the place will produce. This trolling should be done with oars, at speed slow enough to keep the fly barely moving. Thirty to fifty feet is enough line, and the deeper the fish, the more likely they are to strike near the boat.

In trolling, the reel should be laid on the rowing seat, with the tip of the rod on the boat transom, pointing directly back; otherwise a strike by a large fish might break the rod. The rod may also be broken if the arrangement is such that a fish cannot readily pull line out when he strikes. With a single-action reel, the click will usually give sufficient tension to permit a fish to partially hook himself, giving the fisherman time to reach for the rod and set the hook further. If the click spring is very weak, the reel may be laid on the seat with the handle down.

When a good spot has been found, it is likely to be productive for some days; therefore the fisherman should be able to return to it with certainty; fishing a very few feet off may be useless. Spots near shore are easy to remember. A few fishermen use a simple method of triangulation, which enables them to drop anchor at any time within a foot or two of a given spot perhaps half a mile or more from shore, but few beginners know or practice this trick.

A novice, can use a small buoy composed of a bottle or can, with some old fishing line (most twine will rapidly disintegrate in water) and a stone. He should not place this buoy immediately at his good spot; such a mark is an invitation to others to stop and find what makes the place worth marking, so that it will soon be fished out, or the discoverer crowded out. The buoy should be placed some distance away, and from it one must row toward some easily distinguished landmark on shore; a "sunfish bed," will nearly always have some tips of floating weeds that can be recognized when one gets close.

In fall, Sunfish show some tendency to return to shallower water, but rarely is it as shallow as that which they frequented in spring. Though Sunfish are, as a rule, readily caught in mid-summer when other fishing is poor, comparatively few have been taken in late fall, and it was long believed that they practically stopped feeding for the winter.

Recent investigations seem to indicate that Sunfish feed freely all winter, but change their diet to creatures far more minute that those commonly taken in summer. A few anglers, taking a hint from these findings, have been experimenting with some success, in the use of tiny Number 18 nymphs, fished deep, in this late fishing.

A dry fly is better during the early part of the season when the fish are in shallow water. In midsummer, it is often productive in the late evening and sometimes in the early morning, but rarely so good at other times of day. When a dry fly is good, a wet fly, fished very shallow, will usually catch as many Sunfish; and most anglers confine themselves to the wet fly.

Even when using flies sufficiently small, the angler often has difficulty in hooking Sunfish, since they are inclined to strike and let go in a flash. No matter how fast one's reflexes, it takes an instant to detect a strike, and swing the rod into action. Then, the quick backward movement of the rod causes the tip to dip forward, so that another appreciable loss of time ensues. Following this, the spring of the backward-flying tip added to the motion of the rest of the rod, often results in breaking the fine leader point.

Therefore it is suggested that in fishing for

Sunfish (often, indeed, in fishing for smaller Trout and for certain other fish) the usual method of setting the hook with the rod tip be abandoned, and the following method used.

After casting, point the rod toward the fly, its tip close to the water, keeping the line, from reel to fly, as straight as possible. Retrieve and work the fly entirely by stripping in line with the left hand, not moving the rod tip. For Sunfish, a very slow retrieve, with many pauses and short jerks, is usually the most productive.

When a Sunfish even touches the fly lightly, the slight tug is instantly felt by the fingers holding the line, and it is but a reflex action, to jerk the hand back and set the hook.

Since there is always a possibility that a large fish, may take the fly, the beginner should, in retrieving, hold the line lightly with the fingertips, so that it can slip easily between them. A solid grip on the line, with an unconsciously hard and quick backward movement, may break a light leader.

When the fish is hooked, the rod is immediately raised to the vertical, line being permitted to slip out through the guides to play him properly.

This method, unless too large flies are used, will result in hooking practically every Sunfish that strikes. And when a pluck is felt but the fish is not hooked, the fly is not snatched away from the fish; it is moved a short distance, so that he may follow and strike again.

In fishing the edge of a weed bed, best results will be obtained by anchoring well out and casting close to the weeds, either retrieving immediately or waiting for the fly to sink to proper depth. When only small Sunfish are caught near the surface, large ones may often be taken by permitting the fly to sink almost or quite to the bottom before retrieving.

In this deep fishing, a Sunfish will nearly always take most readily a fly that has been given time to sink by its own weight, since it will not have the quick, unnatural movements of a weighted one to render him suspicious. There are times when only an unweighted fly will get results.

However, few fishermen are patient enough to like this long wait after each cast. Also, the quicker sinking of a weighted fly permits more casts and the covering of more water; so, when Sunfish are striking freely, it may be more productive.

No more than a single grain of split BB shot should be used; or, by those who prefer it, an equivalent amount of thin strip lead. It is the line, not the fly, that is cast, the fly being really a hindrance rather than a help. The smaller and lighter the fly, the farther and more easily one can cast.

Most anglers clip the shot immediately above the first knot in the leader. A few prefer, in tying on a fly, to leave a short tag of gut, and attach the shot to this, making it easy to remove without damaging the leader. One objection to this method is that it gives the Sunfish a bulkier object to take into his small mouth, and so may reduce the chance of hooking him.

The man who has become fairly expert at catching Sunfish with wet flies should also learn to take them with dry flies; all he now has to learn is false casting, and perhaps to drop his fly more lightly, which merely means aiming it high over his mark on the water.

One who acquires the knack of hooking almost every Sunfish that strikes may often catch so many small fish that releasing them becomes annoying. One remedy is to try successively larger flies until one is found that is readily taken by the bigger fish but refused by the smaller; this is about the only case in which Number 8 flies, are useful for Sunfish.

Another good method, when Sunfish are not deep, is to draw the fly along the surface fast enough so that it makes a small V wake. Generally, many small Sunfish can be seen following a fly worked thus, but they seem afraid to take it. However, this movement often seems irresistible to a large one, who will charge through the small ones and take it instantly.

Barbless hooks make the release of smaller Sunfish a quick and simple matter. If the fish are skilfully played, the use of barbless hooks will decrease one's catch little or none; they may even increase the catch, since a slender, barbless point will penetrate more readily than a broad, barbed one. Any hook may quickly be rendered barbless by pressing down the barb with pliers.

The sportsman fishing for Sunfish should carry a small disgorger, to allow removal of hooks without injury to the fish. An effective disgorger can easily be made from a strip of sheet metal approximately 3½ in. long by about ¼ in. wide. A V notch can be filed in one end, and a short cut with a hacksaw in from that makes it somewhat easier to use. This notch is engaged in the bend of the hook, the leader held taut, and the hook easily pushed back and removed without damage to the fish.

This disgorger may be carried conveniently by drilling a hole in the handle end, from which a short piece of line, is looped over a button of the jacket or shirt. Thus the disgorger is always at hand, and it may be used without removal from the button.

TROUT

BROOK TROUT

Although angling literature has always described the native Brook Trout as a "shy" and "wily" fish, most veteran Trout fishermen agree that it is an easier fish to catch than either the Brown or Rainbow. In general, it feeds less selectively and displays less temperament in its feeding habits than either of the other species with which it now shares so much of its water. This trait has helped to endear our impetuous native Trout to all of anglerdom, but it is also responsible, along with pollution, heavy fishing pressure and the rape of our forests, for the gradual disappearance of this fine fish from much of the water it formerly occupied.

Brook Trout are denizens of the secluded, shady places. Look for them beneath undercut banks, among root tangles, in the depths of the shaded

Maine Development Commission

Kennebago Stream in northwestern Maine. This famous river produces excellent fishing for large Trout.

pools and in the deep feeding lanes that curl among the rocks. Seldom do they lie in "white water"; that is the lair of the Rainbow.

In the spring of the year, when melting snow and April rain flood the streams, the Speckled Trout seeks refuge in the deep holes, feeding upon nymphs and other aquatic foods washed down by the torrent. But even then it does not feed so avidly as when the floods subside and water temperatures arise above 50° F. As a rule of thumb, Brook Trout are lethargic in water colder than 50°, feed actively in water up to 70°, and cannot tolerate for long temperatures above 75°. Browns and Rainbows display more tolerance for warm water, the highest limiting temperature for the Brown being about 81° and for the Rainbow 83°.

Most early-season Trout fishermen use worms for bait, and their results generally vindicate their choice. It might surprise these same fishermen, however, to learn that worms comprise only a very small part of the trout's normal diet. * Insect life of various kinds constitutes approximately three-quarters of the Trout's year-around menu. But because worms are so easily obtained, and can be fished "slow and deep" with the addition of a few split shot to the leader, they probably account for more Trout in the early spring than any other bait or lure.

Minnows of various kinds also make an effective bait for early season Trout fishing. Shiners, lake chubs, and small dace all work equally well. The minnow may be fished in either of two ways: hooked lightly through the lips or under the dorsal fin and allowed to swim freely in the pools, or sewn on a short-shank gut hook in such a way that it revolves slowly while being drawn across the current or drifted through the pools. Any bait fished in high water must, of course, be weighted to carry it down close to the bottom where Trout usually lie under such conditions.

Although the fly fisherman generally prefers to wait for the spring floods to subside before he takes up the serious business of fishing, he needlessly denies himself, for it is not so much the choice of lure or bait that determines the angler's success in early-season Trout fishing as the manner in which it is presented. Nymphs, wet flies, and streamers can be used effectively if the angler sinks them and then fishes his lures *slowly* through the deep holes and runs. At this season of the year the larger flies generally prove more productive, for they must compete with flood-borne sticks and leaves for the Trout's attention. A small nickel or copper spinner flashing ahead of the lure helps to make it more attractive, in addition to adding weight for sinking the lure down to the necessary depth.

But when the streams drop to normal levels in May, and water temperatures rise above 60°, the fly fisherman then comes into his own. Insect life begins to stir, Trout come out of the deep holes and move into the rips and runs where they begin feeding actively. The angler then strips the split shot from his leader and casts his nymph or wet fly or streamer across the flow, letting it ride down with an occasional twitch imparted by the rod tip, and as it straightens out at the end of its journey he may be rewarded with the flash of a golden belly or the tug of a striking fish.

The Brook Trout, being somewhat more catholic in its taste than either the Brown or Rainbow, does not demand a lure that closely resembles its nor-

* Paul R. Needham in his book *Trout Streams* (Comstock Pub. Co., 1938) reports that 251 brook trout stomachs gathered over a 12-month period contained only 1.1% of earthworms, or 47 worms in a total of 4,078 items.—Ed.

mal food. It is more readily attracted to bright colors—the "fancy" flies which are so often disdained by other Trout. The red, white and yellow Parmachene Belle, originally tied to imitate the pectoral fin of a Brook Trout, is an old favorite among Trout fishermen in the northern states and Canada. The Royal Coachman, Montreal, and Silver Doctor are other effective Brook Trout patterns which have no resemblance to any form of aquatic life upon which Trout feed.

Among the streamers and bucktails, such gaudy flies as the Mickey Finn, the red and white bucktail, and the Light Edson Tiger all rate as deadly Trout lures, although none of them resembles any species of small bait fish which occur in Trout water.

The non-selective feeding habits of the Brook Trout become more evident during the dry fly season. The angler seeking Brown Trout or Rainbows must present a fly that rather closely imitates in color and size the living insect upon which his fish are feeding, and he must offer his fly carefully, without splash or drag. But the Brook Trout fishermen enjoys more latitude. Even when rising to a well-developed hatch, the native Brookie usually comes up eagerly to an artificial which may have no resemblance whatever to the "natural" on the water.

This happy trait of the Brook Trout's was apparent once on Kennebago Stream of northwestern Maine. Arriving at the Gravel Beds Pool in the upper reaches of this magnificent trout stream, fish were found rising freely to a heavy hatch of mayflies. After capturing one of the floating insects an effort was made to match it with an artificial fly. On finding nothing that even remotely resembled the living insect, a No. 8 Royal Coachman was tied on and cast. Instantly a Trout engulfed it. The fish was netted, a plump half-pounder, and the fly being too badly mangled to float again, was changed to a Gray Wulff. It, too, was taken almost instantly. So was a Quill Gordon and a Brown Bivisible. And while Trout continued rising to natural mayflies all around, fly patterns were changed after every fish without finding one that the trout would refuse.

Obviously, these were "wild" fish. Trout in heavily-fished waters are seldom so plentiful or so gullible. Even so, Brook Trout rarely display so much selectivity in their feeding habits as do Browns or Rainbows. And during periods when fish are not rising at all, Brook Trout can be teased into coming up for a floating artificial much more easily than can either of the other species.

As the season advances, water temperatures rise until they may reach the danger point of 75°, at which time Brook Trout desert the shallow runs and riffles and seek cooler, deeper water. Many of them drop back into the shaded pools and springholes; others leave the main stream altogether and seek refuge in the colder tributaries. During the critical period of summer heat Trout feed little during the day. However, in the evening after the water has been shaded for a few hours, the fish may begin to move about and feed. Late evening and early morning fishing is the Trout fisherman's general rule during July and August, although day fishing may again prove productive after heavy rains have cooled the water and filled the stream bed again.

But Trout do not live entirely in streams. They occur in many of the ponds and lakes throughout their range, particularly in the northern states. Lake fishing for Trout is somewhat different from stream fishing. True, the same fly patterns may be used and with equal success, but methods vary. The dry fly is not generally effective in lake fishing, except when fish are found in the shallow, weedy and spring-fed coves. Wet flies can be used effectively, but most present-day Trout fishermen agree that streamers and bucktails are superior to any other type of artificial lure.

Brook Trout in lakes feed upon aquatic insect life to a considerable extent, but small bait fish comprise a larger part of their diet. In the lakes of the northeastern United States, the dominant forage fish are smelt and chubs, and streamer flies which resemble either of these two small fish almost always prove attractive to Trout. The smelt-like flies include such popular patterns as the Supervisor, Green Ghost and Nine-three, while the Dark Edson Tiger offers an excellent imitation of the rusty-colored chub. But the non-imitative streamer patterns often prove just as effective. Among the favorites are the red and white bucktail, the Black Ghost, Gray Ghost, Mickey Finn and the Parmachene Belle streamer.

The lake fisherman may either cast his fly or troll it. The caster anchors his boat close to a rocky shore, jutting point or bar, drops his fly into the shallow water and retrieves it slowly, twitching the lure to give it the motion of a small bait fish darting through the water. When the surface of the lake is ruffled by the wind, the retrieve can be shallow and fast, but during periods of flat calm the angler improves his chances of success if he

H. G. Tapply

Thomas Craven of Weston, Massachusetts, with 2-pound Brook Trout taken on a trolled streamer fly from Moosehead lake, Maine.

H. G. Tapply

Three-and-a-quarter-pound Brook Trout from Moosehead Lake, Maine. This fish was taken fly casting with a nine-three streamer.

allows the lure to sink well down, ten, fifteen or twenty feet, and then twitches it in very slowly.

The word "trolling" usually suggests a short, heavy rod and a lure or bait dragging through deep water behind a spinner or two. To the Trout fisherman, however, trolling has a more sporting connotation. He used his stream tackle and trails his fly along behind his boat as he weaves along the lake shore, preferably the one upon which the wind is blowing, and pays particular attention to the rocky points and bars where trout love to lie. Twitching or "twiggling" the rod imparts additional motion to the fly, as does the rise and fall of the boat over the waves. It is axiomatic in Trout fishing that the more motion the angler gives his fly, the more attractive it looks to the fish.

Some lake fishermen combine fly casting and trolling with excellent results. With two men in the boat, both troll their flies, each on his own side, one line longer than the other. At the same time, the angler who is not rowing or running the outboard motor uses a third rod to cast a fly into the rocks along shore. This third rod not only takes an occasional fish, but also helps to lure Trout away from shore and into the path of the trolled flies. On many occasions Trout are seen to boil at the cast fly, miss it completely, and then fall upon the trolled lure as it passed by a few moments later. This combination of casting and trolling with flies is a deadly method of lake fishing not only for Trout but also for Landlocked Salmon and, in the early spring, Lake Trout.

Many Trout fishermen seem surprised when they learn that Brook Trout can be taken from salt water. Such opportunities are becoming more rare every year, but in some areas of coastal New England sea-run trout or "salters" can still be found in many streams which empty into the sea. These Trout feed principally upon mummychubs, a small forage fish, or shrimp, although when they ascend the stream beyond tidewater they assume the feeding characteristics of any Trout in fresh water. Salters can be identified as such even after they have entered fresh water by the silvery tone of their skins, but despite their anadrous habits they are blood brothers to the Squaretail of northern New England or the Coaster of Lake Superior.

As a fighter, the Brook Trout is strong, dogged, but unspectacular. Unlike the flashy Rainbow or the spirited Brown, it seldom leaps from the water when hooked. Rather, it tries to find refuge in the root tangles and among the rocks, and often succeeds in winning its freedom by entangling the leader and breaking it. In lakes and ponds, the Brook Trout seeks its fighting arena in deep water, where it lies shaking its head savagely, wrenching against the line and then starting off in long, fast runs which may tear as much as fifty or a hundred feet of line from the angler's screeching reel. On reasonably light tackle any Brook Trout of more than half a pound of weight will give an angler as many thrills as any other fish of comparable size.

BROWN TROUT

Although a rugged versatile creature, the Brown Trout must be said to be temperamental in that it feeds when the mood strikes it. Introduced from Europe, it has established itself widely and well in streams and lakes. Although not as gamey as other trouts and not as good as a food fish, it is still popular because of its wide range.

Because of its cautious feeding habits, it is more difficult to catch than possibly any other trout. It grows to sizeable proportions, being larger in average size than other members of the family, and is found in most waters inhabited by Rainbows.

However, it can tolerate higher temperatures than any other trout (as high as 76° to 80° F. if oxygen content is sufficient and pollution not too great). Because of this quality, the Brown has been considered the salvation of trout fishing in the warmer and slightly polluted streams.

The fish spawns in the fall in riffles above the larger holes of a stream. They do not migrate

A nice Brown Trout from Maine's Sandy River. The common and native species is the Brook Trout, "Squaretails" in Maine.

great distances, often spawning a few yards from their normal living quarters. They have a peculiar habit of establishing themselves in small areas over which they prowl for food. Because of this habit, they sometimes fall into disfavor with fishermen and are accused of taking great numbers of small game fish as food.

They will, however, take practically any species of insect, frogs, snails, slugs, worms, beetles and moth larvae, water spiders, and even mice and young birds, if they happen to fall into the water.

The Brown has few seasonal characteristics that can be taken advantage of by the fisherman. Early morning and late evening hours are more productive fishing times. The Brown feeds more regularly at the surface than do the Brook or Rainbow, and prefers the dry fly to wets.

However, the Brown, particularly at evening, will take spinners, spoons, wobblers, and minnows, and smaller fish will take worms on regular bait hooks. In the fall months, the larger fish are caught on bucktail flies which, in all probability, resemble minnows.

There is one pecularity which should be remembered. A large Brown will approach a bucktail or streamer fly cautiously and does not take the lure with the lusty jerk of other Trout. Rather it will pull it very gently and unless the angler is alert, he will not recognize this as a strike, and the fish will spit out the lure. Once this sensation has been recognized, the fisherman is able to set his hooks regularly.

Fall is most productive for Brown fishing in both streams and lakes. In lakes, the fish seek out the areas near tributary streams, congregating in considerable numbers at these points. During midday in bright sun, the Brown can be lured by a dry fly allowed to remain on the surface for a longer time than during an ordinary cast.

The Brown, being extremely cautious, will not usually strike wet or dry flies which are moved along the surface so as to leave a wake behind the fly. At times it takes a Brown as much as 15 minutes to decide to leave deep water and come to the surface to strike.

The smaller Brown, from eight to ten inches, can be taken in smaller streams, but as the fish grow larger, they prefer bigger waters than even the Rainbow or Cutthroat Trout.

Rivers and lakes in which there are submerged objects and overhanging banks are liked by the Brown. Fish of various sizes locate at the lower ends of large pools and like to lie behind or just ahead of rocks protruding from the current. They prefer flies and insects to greater extent than most other trout, but as they grow in size, this diet is augmented with snails, worms, and minnows.

CUTTHROAT TROUT

Much of the romance of the West, as far as fishermen are concerned, can be associated with the name, black-spotted or Cutthroat Trout.

There are several varieties of this Trout, all of which have more or less the same characteristics. They live in both lakes and streams, spawn early in the spring, have a good appetite most of the summer and respond well to the fisherman's lure. The different varieties are difficult to distinguish from each other, but can be readily separated from other Trouts by the bright red "trade mark" on the throat, the mark which gives the group its common name of Cutthroat.

Maine Development Commission

Look for Brook Trout in the shaded pools. This scene is a small stream near Stoneham, Maine.

The individual water in which Cutthroats are found determines how one should angle for them. They are extremely wary. The utmost stalking skill is necessary to get within casting distance as the slightest movements or ground noises will cause the fish to vanish into deeper waters of a lake or hide under rocks and brush in a stream.

In lakes, the Cutthroat can be taken by either surface or deep fishing methods. It takes a dry or wet fly very well in early morning or late evening, seems to prefer black or grey colors and is not too fussy as to the shape of the lure. However, the fly must resemble the trout's food in general size and color. A wide range in fly sizes is effective provided they are presented on a fine-tapered sunken leader.

In both streams and lakes, the Cutthroat, during their first two years feeds mostly on insects, both aquatic and terrestrial. Flying ants, midges, mayflies, caddis flies and the larvae of most aquatic insects makes up the bulk of the diet. After two years the fish becomes mature and the diet shows a marked change. It now prefers minnows or small fish to the insect diet, accounting for the unusually fine trolling this fish produces. Plugs, spoons, spinners and worm or minnow-baited lures work very well in most lakes. Small spinners, followed by large bucktail flies, will attract this fish.

To successfully troll for the Cutthroat, one must carefully observe conditions of the day and season. In the spring, trolling just below the surface will produce, while later in the season during hot weather the lure must be deep. During the hot August weeks this fish is less eager to take any lure. However, late in the fall they again come to the surface to produce excellent fly fishing.

In the small streams of the mountainous West the Cutthroat is more predictable. The younger fish feed largely on insects, is found on riffles both above and below large holes and takes very well to flies and small spinners. The latter may be fished baited or bare.

The species, being characteristically quiet, does not often jump clear of the water as does the Rainbow. The culinary quality of the fish is excellent. The meat is fine in texture and sweet to the taste.

DOLLY VARDEN TROUT

The Dolly Varden Trout, which received its name from the color of the dress worn by a character of the same name in Dickens' novel *Barnaby Rudge,* is a West Coast species naturally confined to streams emptying into the Pacific. It is one Trout which has never been widely distributed or propagated as have other species. It is largely looked down upon by western fishermen who condemn it for it spawn-eating habits, a rather unfair attitude since other Trout eat spawn almost as extensively as do the Dolly Varden. It does, however, have to compete in its native waters with both Cutthroats and Rainbow Trout, both of which are somewhat more spectacular fighters.

The Dolly Varden, in its habits and its behavior, is much like its eastern cousin the **Brook Trout.** As with other Chars, it has light spots on a dark background, but this one has fewer spots than the Brook. Its tail is somewhat more forked than its eastern relative, and otherwise it resembles it very much, except that it averages somewhat larger.

There are both migratory Dolly Vardens that run out to sea and back, and residents that remain in fresh water. The fish can be caught in either fresh or salt water. It takes flies, spinners, and other lures readily, and will strike at any lure that will take other Trout. It is somewhat less particular in its diet than others. When hooked, it usually puts up a good fight, but like the brook, fights under water rather than on the surface as the Rainbow often does.

Despite the prejudices against it, the flesh is as good as other fish; in fact, when cooked with Rainbows, it is almost impossible to select from a platter a piece of one fish or another, although the Dolly's flesh tends to be somewhat redder and more salmon-like than most other trout. However, this is a seasonal characteristic and cannot be depended upon to distinguish it, since the meat of the Dolly may range from white to a red, almost equivalent to that of the red salmon.

Anglers who have fished western waters have had the experience of taking this fish on many lures. Any standard pattern accepted by either Rainbows or Cutthroats may be taken as readily by the Dolly Varden. It also takes spinners of almost any type; and wobblers, such as the Red Devil, are taken avidly. It is most abundant in Alaska and in those waters it is not uncommon for fishermen to take Rainbows and Dollys alternately while standing on the spot. In Alaskan waters, Dollys of seven to ten pounds are not uncommon, particularly in the larger streams, although fish of this size are more rarely taken further south.

It is abundant in most Trout waters in Oregon, Washington, and British Columbia, and would unquestionably be more highly valued if it were not so closely associated with the more spectacular Rainbows.

GOLDEN TROUT

Golden Trout like other trout in high Sierra Lakes, are usually taken by still fishing with salmon eggs, worms, grubs, or other baits. But far greater sport is to be had if they are caught on dry or wet flies. Boats are seldom available on lakes containing Golden Trout and practically all fishing must be done from shorelines.

Because of the high elevation of these lakes, the ice seldom melts before the first of June so these fish are limited to an extremely short growing season of 60-70 days during which they must feed voraciously and store up sufficient food to pass the winter. Their natural aquatic food consists principally of midge larvae and pupae, shrimp (when present), alderfly larvae, and caddicefly larvae. Midges and caddiceflies usually form over 75 per cent of the underwater foods consumed. Much of their food consists of land insects that fall or are blown into the water from the land. Free-swimming, lake-dwelling copepods, and waterfleas (plankton) likewise furnish a portion of their diet. All of these organisms are small usually less than one-quarter of an inch in length, so the smaller flies or other lures are usually the most successful.

After the ice goes out in the spring, the surface waters warm up and Goldens are apparently attracted into shallow waters near the shore line to begin feeding. At such times, small dry flies tied on No. 12 or 14 hooks and fished dry will prove quite successful. Favorite patterns are the Midge, Captain, Blue-upright, Royal Coachman, Ginger Quill, and Hare's Ear. Bivisible flies are often successful if cast out and allowed to bob up and down on the surface of the water. They may float for as long as five minutes before a Golden takes it. Occasionally they can be taken on No. 8 or 10 bucktail Coachman flies worked in short jerks just below the water surface. Streamer flies of even larger size will take larger Goldens weighing up to three and four pounds. The best lures to take these fish, however, are small black Midges using light leaders. They will take small spinners at times but catching them this way does not afford the sport offered in fly fishing.

There are no more beautiful and gamey fish on the North American continent, and anglers should respect their relative scarcity. Out-of-state shipments of eyed eggs are now prohibited under California law to preserve the species. Any angler will earn every one he gets because Golden Trout can be obstinate. But if an angler has the patience and will try to learn, he can catch these "living flashes of light". They are as good to eat as they

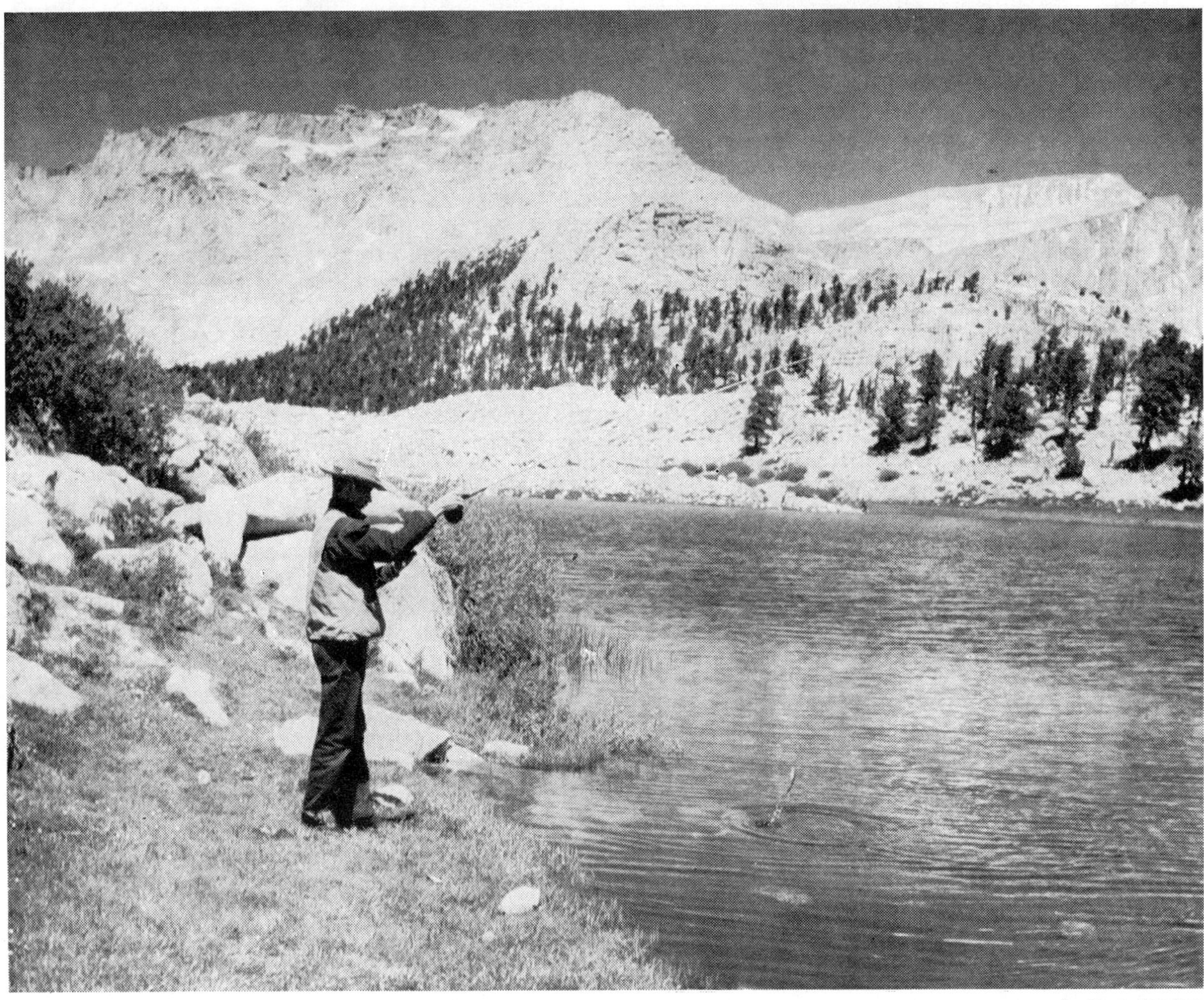

Joe Mears, Pasadena

Golden Trout are small, but game. Here a fisherman is playing one on South Fork Lake, one of the Cottonwood Lakes chain in the national forest of California's Sierra Nevadas.

are beautifully colored and represent the ultimate in the field of freshwater angling.

LAKE TROUT

The Lake Trout is the biggest of the trouts and is found in northern waters where the forests are forever green, rich in the fragrance of pine needles, and where the lakes are like jewels and gems . . . Anishinabi, Sea Gull, Saginaga, Crow, Reflection, Manitou, Atikameg, Mameigwess, Pytonga, the Vermilions, Superior, Huron, Michigan and Lake of the Woods.

It is one of the north country's most important fishes because it holds a prominent place in both sport and commercial fishing. The biggest and the most of the Lakers come out of Lake Superior, although some mighty big and powerful salmon trout have been taken out of Eagle Lake, Georgian Bay, Rowan Lake, Buzzard Lake, White Otter Lake, Harris Lake, Orangutang Lake and Big Cannon Lake in Ontario.

It takes a 40-pounder or better to win the annual magazine fishing contest which requires the fish to be taken on rod, reel, hook, and line. The world's record caught on sport fishing tackle weighed 63 pounds and came out of Lake Athapapuskow in Manitoba. It lacked half an inch of being four feet long and was caught by Miss L. L. Hayes. Lake Trout have been taken in nets that have weighed more than 100 pounds.

Common names of this much-respected battler are: Forked trout, Great Lakes trout, Mackinaw trout, salmon trout, landlocked salmon, longue, togue (Maine), namaycush (Canadian Indians), and gray trout (eastern Canada).

The Lake Trout demands waters that are cold and clear. In the summer Namaycush ("dweller of the deep") usually lives in deep waters. An exception to this is found in the waters off St. Ignace Island in Lake Superior where the waters are so cold Lake Trout are available close to shore nearly all summer. St. Ignace is an island at the mouth of the Nipigon River.

In the spring the Laker comes to the surface or near-surface for feeding in the shallow waters, and he often stays as long as three to four weeks. In the fall the Lake Trout comes to the surface near the rocky places for spawning. In Maine in the spring of the year, they are found along the shore lines, off rocky points and over reefs, and for the most part they will be in shallow water. Casting and trolling streamer flies catches the most togue. Best colors are the brighter colors for cold weather such as red, white, yellow, and shades of Gantron. When all other flies fail, sportsmen get them with the tandem streamer flies.

In the deep mountain lakes of the west the Laker is taken by sportsmen on a light spinner fly during the spring and fall seasons, but in the summer it can be handled on a deep-trolling rig. Western sportsmen do not want this species of fish as it is a menace to the other trouts.

The Lake Trout has an oyster-white body that is loaded with small black spots from snout to caudal tip, and the color varies slightly in different types of water. Now and then the spots are tinged with pink.

Having a delicious flavor, especially when the fish is not too fat, millions of sportsmen have fished for and caught Lake Trout. Lakers vary too in flesh color, being mostly white, but when the feed runs to fresh water shrimp you can expect the meat to be pink.

The Laker is not a true trout but a char and in this respect is closely related to the Dolly Varden Trout and the Brook Trout. It has a forked tail which gives this fish something extra in the way of speed and power. When a Laker hits, you know it. It gives you a hard jolt, which is followed by a depth dive towards the sheltered and sunken ledges. The Lake Trout has fine staying power, but it lacks the tail-walking or the aerial acrobatics of the Atlantic Salmon. It is said that the Laker likes in-fighting and slugging it out with the angler. The trout will run to the bottom and yank savagely against a tight line. Those who have taken Lake Trout on light weight tackle know that this fish is a real fighter.

Because the Laker has a ravenous appetite, find the school and then fire away at them. The best lures, everything from a live sucker to a wobbling spoon and from streamer flies to a large bucktail spinner, will attract the Lake Trout.

Salmon spoons make the best lures, but many are the sportsmen who use smelt, perch, suckers, and spinners with bucktail and feather finish, or a "Christmas tree" of spinners and beads tipped with a gob of worms, or with the tail of a sucker or the belly of a perch.

Indians and early pioneers were the first to discover that trolling or casting a glistening, flashing lure that wobbles will cause a Lake Trout to strike. In the beginning they used pearly shells, then the common spoon.

Now there is an amazing variety of spoons, spinners and wobblers. The most popular spoons are round, oval, and pear-shaped. Most fishermen prefer the spoon with a single hook. Many Lake Trout have been taken on the fluted spoon with trailer hooks dressed in feathers or bucktail. Best colors are: silver chrome, copper, gold, and pearl.

Salmon spoons that take the most lake trout are: McMahon, K-B Johnson, Gaper, Reflecto, Freak, Chum, C.&S. Jigger, Canadian spoon, Flash-eye, Dardevle, Bead-Eye, Williams Wobbler, Red-Eye Wiggler, L. G. Johnson, Al Wilson Spoon, L. G. Johnson, The Drone, The Doctor, Davis Dart, Buck-A-Roo, Pet Spoon, Pacific Arrow, Minnow Spoon, Silver Dart, Superior Spoon, Tear Drop, Martin Johnson, Trix Oreno. McMahon spoons are from 2/0 to 8½. Pflueger Record spoons are from 2/0 to 11/0.

Good Tip: As soon as you get a strike, jerk hard and start reeling in line. If using live bait, at the strike give out line and on the next strike set the hook. Lake Trout are found in schools, so the fisherman goes right back to the scene of the first strike for more fish.

Troll the lure near the bottom in summer fishing. If you feel the lure bounding against the bottom, reel in until you have cleared the floor of the lake.

In order to successfully catch the Lake Trout in the summer period, the fisherman should have an idea of what the floor of the lake is like. If the shore lines are rocky, the bottom is likely to be rough and perhaps carpeted with boulders. You can learn about this by taking soundings with a heavy lead sinker on a line that is marked for various depths. Remember the deepest stretches may not be in the middle of the lake or bay; the deepest is often in front of steep rocky shores of mainland or islands.

The coldest areas may be spring holes at 100 feet or half way down, so the fisherman is often forced to do some sleuthing to locate the Lake Trout. Taking thermometer readings at various depths will often aid in finding the cold spots. Wherever the water is cold, there you will find the trout . . . about 40 to 50 degrees.

The old-fashioned way to troll for Trout was to use a heavy dipsey lead and a silk or linen line using a lake trout triangle . . . one line leading to the dipsey and the other line leading to the hook; the popular way today is to troll with a Monel or some other metal line. The weight of the line will carry the lure to the bottom.

Some folks call this "deep sea" trolling for Lake Trout. The main line has a triangle about six to twelve feet from the bottom. From one point of the rig the metal line trails the trout spoon; from the other point of the rig there is extended on nylon, silk, or linen line the heavy dipsey. When the Lake Trout hits, he hits hard; often he hits hard enough to break loose the dipsey, so that the angler can play the fish from a single line.

A short stiff rod is preferred, although many sportsmen prefer the fun of taking Trout on light weight fishing rods of glass, tubular steel, and bamboo. The reel is a small deep sea reel, often with a star drag, with a capacity of about 300 yards of monel. Lines can be: (1) monel metal, (2) braided metal, (3) cuttyhunk, (4) 24- to 30-pound test nylon, or braided silk. The lure can be the twirling Ottertail that revolves around a shaft or the wobbling spoons so popular for salmon fishing in the northwest.

If the trolling is as deep as 300 feet the spoon must be of large size.

It is easiest to troll with an outboard motor or a boat with an inboard engine. A slow troll is best. Care must be taken in letting out line, always watching to see that the triangle rig works.

Another way to fish for Lakers is by letting a lure down to the depth desired and then jigging, which is bobbing a wobbling lure up and down. Many Lake Trout are hooked this way.

Fishermen who go in for Lake Trout fishing as a steady diet use a fishing thermometer to find the cold water level of 40 to 50 degrees.

Fishing through the ice in Lake Superior is fun, and here the Laker is taken by the bobbing method. The fisherman takes a sled, a canvas windbreak, a couple of poles, an ice spud, a heavy bobbing line, a half pound sinker, 8/0 or 10/0 hooks and use herring as bait. This fishing is usually done in 75 feet of water, and the Laker is attracted by jerking the herring up and down.

At the present time there is a considerable concern regarding the future of Lake Trout in the waters of the Great Lakes, especially in Lakes Superior and Michigan, because of the invasion of the sea lamprey which in the adult stage is parasitic on other fishes. The sea lamprey is a marine form that has adapted itself to the fresh waters of the Great Lakes. It has a sucker-type mouth and attaches itself to the Lake Trout; by means of rasp-like teeth it penetrates the outer skin of the Trout in order to feed upon the body juices.

The Lake Trout is particularly vulnerable because of the absence of a heavy scale armor which protects some fishes. Many feel that the sea lamprey is the primary factor in the decline of the Lake Trout in the Great Lakes, where the commercial yield has dropped to an all-time low. Although the sea lamprey is a factor, the taking of huge amounts by commercial fisheries also has a bearing upon the decline in the supply.

Anglers are asked to destroy all lampreys. Lampreys are destroying not only our Lakers, but also our Rainbows, Walleyes, Bass, and Panfish. No fresh water fish is immune to its attack.

There are two hopes for the future of fishing in the waters of the Great Lakes: (1) It has been proven to be a biological fact that sea lampreys will die without reproducing if prevented from reaching the spawning beds in the streams and rivers, and (2) The Fish and Wildlife Service and the Dominion of Canada plan to intercept the spawning migrants by means of traps.

Frank B. Wire

A Rainbow Trout weighing 22½ pounds taken in Diamond Lake, Oregon.

RAINBOW TROUT

Here is the bold adventurer of the Trout family. Here is no sluggard hugging the dark depths, but the fighter with a perpetual chip on the shoulder.

Originally, the Rainbow was a "west coaster" found only in streams flowing into the Pacific from California north. Man moved it east, and the Rainbow liked its new stamping grounds. Now it has been successfully propagated and introduced into many of the nation's streams and lakes with exception of the warm south.

Acclaimed by most Trout anglers as the greatest fighter of them all, the Rainbow possesses and displays more gamey qualities than any other member of its family. Robust of build, the fish combines great strength with a willingness to scrap.

And how it scraps! It doesn't just break water, it explodes! It strikes viciously and it doesn't give up as long as a fin functions. Many an angler has stood forlornly watching the trailing end of a broken leader, snapped off just as he made the error of thinking the Rainbow was played out and could be netted.

This fish likes swift water. It will be found in the fast currents under overhanging banks or willow clumps or out in a fast riffle. Seldom will it be taken in sluggish water. Work slowly along the edge of a strong current, or at the head of a riffle, not missing any of those undercut banks where the water runs swiftly, and the creel will be filled more easily.

It is well to know something about the Rainbow's spawning habits because it is possessed of a strong migration urge during spawning season. This varies from mid-October to mid-July. Some Rainbows are fall spawners in the East, but they are all spring spawners in the West.

A pair of fine Steelheads from the Sacramento River near Chico, California. The big run is in the fall but a few streams have summer-run fish.

It will move upstream from the larger river or lake where it has wintered to the small tributary streams to accomplish the spawning mission. In normal western conditions of high altitude and cold water the spawning season is usually a few weeks earlier than that of the native trout.

Thus, the angler will find them at the upper reaches of the particular drainage in the spring and farther downstream as the season advances into mid-summer and early fall.

The fish seems to find both warm and cold waters congenial with the upper limit of temperature in well-aereated waters about 80° F. They also are found further downstream than either the Brook or Blackspotted, in streams that have a wide range in altitude. In this respect they are much like the Brown Trout.

The feeding habits are quite uniform. They like insect larvae in mature stages, minnows and crustacea. So vicious are they in the strike for food that sometimes pieces of aquatic vegetation, pieces of wood or even small stones are found in their stomachs.

Fly fishermen find Rainbow yield to the temptation of both dry and wets in the smallest sizes. Western anglers prefer the medium range on both wets and dries and on heavy waters wet flies are most widely used.

The Rainbow likes streamers, bucktails, spoons and fly-spinner combinations. The plug caster will take them on smaller plugs or wobbler spoon with a conventional casting or spinning rod. The troller finds the Rainbow an easy mark in lakes where he can use large popgear type of lures baited with worms or dead minnows. Still fishermen, working from banks of lakes with baits, will take a fair share. For the real action of fast, powerful runs, interspersed with spectacular leaps, one should always attempt to take Rainbow on light tackle with small lures.

Sometimes the Rainbow's feeding activities are pepped up by the emergence of aquatic insects along with forest insects dropping into the waters. An example is the annual emergence of the salmon fly hatch in northern waters of the intermountain west, particularly Montana. The insects hatch out on the lower reaches of the rivers and move upstream. The observing angler takes advantage of this by using an artificial lure resembling the salmon fly and fishing just at the vanguard of the hatch or at its tapering off point:

In culinary quality, the Rainbow is equal to any trout if taken from high, cold water. However, when taken from warm waters at the high end of the tolerance range or just after release from a hatchery, it must be rated as only fair.

Rainbow taken from wilderness streams or lakes possess peculiar variations in flesh color. Some will be white and others pink. This is due to the type of food available. Diets consisting largely of crustacea usually produce the pink flesh.

STEELHEAD

Steelhead is a magic word to tens of thousands of West Coast anglers who annually pursue this majestic Trout of the coastal streams, this giant seagoing Rainbow of fast water that makes an angler's heart miss a beat at the mere mention

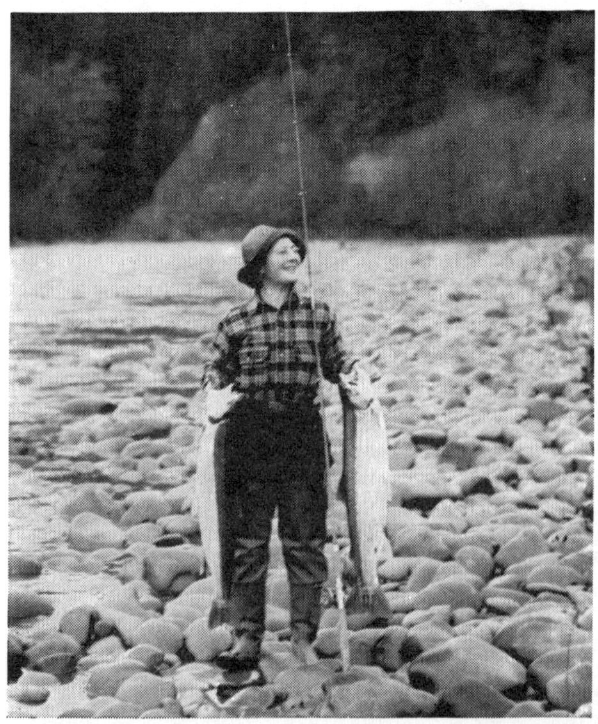

Ken McLeod

A fair angler with a pair of 16-pound winter-runs from the Queets River.

Ken McLeod

Summer-runs are a bit smaller, but a marvelous dry fly fish.

of its name. To tens of thousands of other fishermen who have never triumphed over such a Trout or come out second best in a tilt with one, it signifies a cherished dream. And well it may, for there is no fish on the continent that is more beautiful to gaze upon nor a more worthy antagonist for a man with rod and reel.

Steelheads enter the rivers of the North Pacific in every month, but there are two pronounced runs, the peak of one coming in the dead of winter and the other during early or mid-summer, depending on the individual river. Virtually all coastal streams carry runs of winter Steelheads, but only about 50 per cent of them support runs of summer fish.

The winter runs, heavy with spawn, usually make their first appearance about November 1, and dribble along until fairly sizable runs show up about the middle of December, the major run continuing into late March. These fish spawn principally in March, April, and May, or anywhere from a few weeks to months from the time they enter the river.

The summer runs start about mid-May and continue until the end of September. Their roe and milt is extremely undeveloped. They stay in the river, through the coming winter and spawn the following spring at approximately the same time as their winter-run cousins.

This is the general pattern of the migration of both winter and summer Steelheads but the peaks overlap in various rivers and there are actually stragglers coming into the streams that have both runs in every month.

The winter run of fish is larger and more abundant than the summer run in most rivers, the chief exception being the Columbia, where the peak of the migration occurs in August and September.

The various dates of migration are mentioned to demonstrate that anyone desiring to fish for Steelheads in the northwest can find Steelheads at almost any season. The best fishing periods are from December 15 to March 31 for winter runs and June 1 to August 31 for prime summer runs although the latter are also obtainable in holding pools far upstreams (if fishing is permitted) as long as water conditions are favorable. May and November are the two poorest months for Steelhead fishing.

Steelheads can be taken on a fly in both the winter and summer months. In fact there are anglers who have taken them on flies in every month. One may use the lightest of spinning tackle and spinning lures, but should be prepared for a long wearisome struggle which can easily become work instead of fun if an 18 or 20-pounder takes the lure. A bass casting outfit, with plenty of line, can be used, although most local anglers prefer the more conventional two-handed bait casting steelhead rod for flipping a half-ounce sinker and cluster of salmon roe 150 feet into the stream. Spinners, Devon minnows, jigger spoons, golf tee lures, flatfish, almost any conceivable contrivance designed to fool a fish will catch Steelheads in the hands of an expert or in those of a tyro, if the fish are really striking.

Salmon eggs are the almost universal lure used during winter in the northwest Steelhead streams. If a conventional casting reel is used, it should have capacity for at least 150 yards of 15-pound test braided casting line or 10-pound single filament Nylon. A leader two feet long of about two-thirds the strength of the line is ample and a size 1 to 3/0 S4320 Sealey hook is preferable. A cluster

Courtesy of A. N. Nickols

Tailing a 10-pounder to the beach. It's nice work if you can do it.

Courtesy of A. N. Nickols

Here's a 15-pound winter Steelhead taken on conventional bait outfit, 2-piece rod, free spool reel, pencil sinker attached by drop line, salmon egg cluster for bait, and 20-inch leader.

of salmon eggs about the size of a walnut is impaled in a loop thrust between the point of the leader tie and the hook eye and drawn tight. When a one-half ounce, or other suitable weight sinker is tied on with a 6-inch dropper thread to the line loop to which leader is attached, the outfit is ready for use.

The cast is made into smooth flowing water of 4 to 8 feet, slightly upstream and as far as desired. The purpose is to drift the bait as far as possible with the current, permitting the bait and sinker to drag slightly slower than the current speed along the bottom where the Steelheads lie. All possible slack line should be kept out of the drift in order to detect the gentle strike of a Steelhead, for he seldom strikes this type of bait viciously, merely stopping it in its drift and ejecting it rapidly if there is a suspicious drag to it. When recognized as a bite, the angler should strike sharply. An inexperienced steelheader may have a dozen strikes in a single day and yet never detect one. Contrary to uninformed opinion, this method of Steelhead fishing is the most difficult to master of any recognized means of taking this big winter Trout, but it is also the most deadly once a steelheader becomes expert at it. It's not uncommon, however, for a determined novice to make fifteen or twenty trips for Steelheads before he puts his first one on the beach, or even recognizes he has had one pick up his bait, yet the chances are excellent that he has actually had several strikes on each occasion. Others succeed on their first attempt when they know what to look for.

Other baits used more or less extensively and cast and fished in the same manner are night crawlers, crawfish tails and shrimp.

Many of the new devotees of spinning tackle use these same baits, but instead of the drop sinkers, they pinch two or three split buck shots directly onto the line or leader. Still others fish these baits with a fairly stiff fly rod, employing a 6-pound test single-filament Nylon line which they strip into loose coils in a "stripping basket," made out of canvas or wire, strapped around their waist, readying for the next cast. Others use a combination slip-cast and conventional reel, which permits the cast to be made on the slip-cast method, but makes the retrieve and plays the fish on a revolving spool. The belt reel is another innovation seen more and more frequently on Steelhead rivers.

Artificial lures such as those already mentioned are cast at right angles to the current, permitted to drift in a big arc and retrieved as closely to the bottom as possible. When a Steelhead strikes these lures, he usually is not fooling and there is no doubt whatever in the mind of the fisherman, for he hits savagely, while with a bait bobbing along the bottom he'll move only a couple of feet out of his way to intercept it leisurely. Still fishing with salmon eggs is also popular.

Although fly fishing for winter Steelheads was once looked upon as a figment of a purist's imagination, it is now recognized as a thrilling and productive winter sport when rivers are clear enough to permit a visibility of three feet or more, and it is not uncommon for a fly fisherman to take his seasonal quota of 24 Steelheads on flies during the winter months.

Conventional fly rods of 5½ to 6½-ounce weights are used with torpedo type line and a hundred or more yards of backing. A recent more satisfactory innovation in many ways to the expert fly caster is a 26- to 30-foot torpedo type casting line, backed up with 15- or 18-pound test surf-spin (flat braided) Nylon for shooting line. This, with the aid of a canvas stripping basket hung with a strap over the fisherman's neck in which to coil his shoot and drift line, will enable him to drift 75 or more yards of line with each cast, giving him unbelievable control of the drift and unheard distance. Steelheads prefer a fly that is drifting naturally.

The flies used are of the gaudy, streamer-type, principally with color combinations of red, yellow, white, orange, and tinsel ribbed or yarn bodies, in sizes of No. 4 to 2/0 during the winter months. There are many excellent patterns tied for local streams. There is no need to fish them weighted in any manner, but they should be fished wet at this season at depths of three to four feet, or as close to the bottom as safety will permit. Leaders should be 9 feet long with heavy enough tippits to stand the flexing in false casting with heavy flies. An 8- or 10- pound test tippit is quite advisable with a 2/0 fly.

The summer-run fish in many respects is finer than his winter counterpart although not as heavy and large. Occasionally, however, they'll better 12 pounds, but a good summer run is 8 pounds of greased lightning, a faster and much more spectacular fighter. He takes artificial flies readily and when water is low and clear, and conditions just right, he has no equal as a dry fly fish. Aristocrat of white water in the west, it's almost sacrilegious to tempt him with anything but a fairy offering.

Any of the baits and lures used on winter fish will take the summer run. Fly patterns of local design including Skykomish Sunrise, Yellow Hammer, Hoyt's Killer, Orange Shrimp, Purple Peril and conventional patterns such as Royal Coachman, Teal and Red, Governor, Professor, and Grizzly King are all successful. When fished wet, sizes 6 to 2/0 are most effective, if dry, 8's to 4's are best. Leaders should be 9 feet long with tippit sizes to fit the fly, but do not go smaller than 1X, for Steelheads hit with a shocking jolt.

Summer-runs also prefer a fly drifting naturally whether wet or dry and only on rare occasions will they hit a fly retrieved in the manner so effective on Cutthroats, and then usually in extremely deep and quiet pools where it is impossible to drift.

A good rule to follow in fly fishing for Summer-runs is to use bright flies on bright days and dark patterns when the sky is heavily overcast. Also when the water is excessively low and clear, go to a smaller fly, a 6 or 8, and on occasion even to a 10.

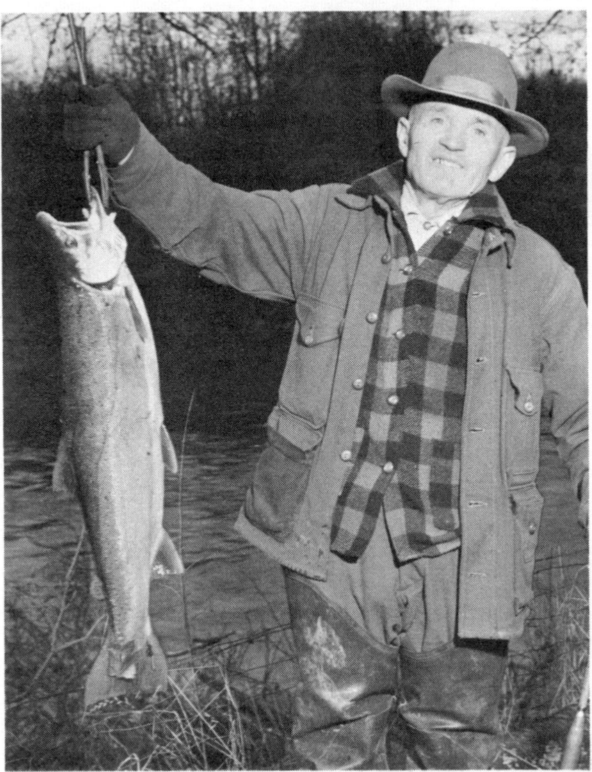

A nice winter-run Steelhead taken from the Samish River, Washington.

WALLEYE

The Walleye may not rate top-billing as a game fish, but it is sufficiently active to win its share of applause from the fishermen. Added to this, it is a fish famous for its delicious taste.

Successful Walleye fishing depends upon accurate knowledge of its habits and movement at all seasons. Generally it runs in fairly shallow water in the spring, from April to June. It spawns on the reefs and sand-bars during these months, making no nest but casting the spawn over the sands and rocks. Following the spawning period, the fish remain in the lesser depths and are often taken in numbers by trolling. A spinner on a shaft with a bare hook baited with a live minnow is the most widely used fishing method.

Many fishermen, aware that Walleyes may be taken in shallow water in the spring, do not know where to fish later in the season. Sometime after spawning, the Walleye goes into deep water, often to the deepest spots in a lake. At these times deep trolling is the only successful method for daylight

Courtesy of A. N. Nickols

The Skagit River is famous for its marvelous boat trips with professional guides.

fishing. But those who study this fish will discover that to a considerable extent it feeds at night.

With the coming of darkness on a summer night, the Walleyes rouse themselves from a day of inertia during which they have been hugging the bottom. These fish, in common with their close relatives, the saugers (from which they are not too greatly different) have the schooling instinct. These schools under cover of darkness move into the shallow bays, among the reefs and bars, crowding the minnows up ahead of them and hitting into them with great energy. Like the White Bass, they spread out seemingly in a semi-circle and move ahead in unison, pushing the food fish before them. Unlike the White Bass, they create no commotion in their feeding; in fact, there is little or no evidence of their presence because of any unusual sounds. The White Bass fairly churn up the water in their feeding operations, although they feed by day or in the early evening, whereas the Walleyes feed heavily at night.

This feeding period seems to be from ten in the evening to two o'clock in the morning, the best fishing usually being from ten to twelve. Night fishing can be said to be the simplest method of taking the fish. They are in shallow water and within range of the fisherman's lure at all times. As a rule plugs are not considered any too "taking," but this applies more to day-fishing than to night-fishing. While it is true that ordinary plugs, either poppers or wobblers made without luminous paint will take Walleyes, it has been found that a luminous lure increases the number of strikes. Both popping plugs and wobblers treated by this method are deadly night fishing lures. The new, so-called Gantron "fire-lacquer" which glows vividly has proven to be a killer for this type of fishing.

The luminous tandem spinner is also excellent for night fishing. These are propeller spinner blades revolving on a shaft. The inside of each blade is coated with luminous paint. At times it seems that these luminous tandems take Walleyes wherever the species is active at night. This is especially true in schools of considerable size, which naturally makes the competition for food greater.

Successful night fishing depends upon locating night feeding areas. If there are reefs and shallow water in the bays, and the bottom is sandy or gravelly the chance of finding the fish on the move is greatly increased. It is also well to examine the mouth of the stream flowing into a Walleye lake, especially if it has a rocky or gravel bed. The fish enter and ascend such streams for some distance at night if it is not muddy. Walleyes seem to abhor mud and marl.

After a night of heavy feeding, the Walleyes again move into the depths and spend much of the day in the deep holes. They move about very little, only changing position now and then. When filled with food, they pay little attention to a lure trolled a few feet above them. Under such conditions the trolled lure must scrape the bottom to get a response. Even if they are stuffed, they will strike—if they do not have to make too much effort to do so.

Day-trolling by normal method is often a profitless venture simply because of failure to contact the fish. The only logical method of day fishing at such times is still fishing deep enough to place

Sports Afield

Taking a Walleye.

the bait on the bottom. These deep places, best found by sounding, are often only pot-holes of greater or lesser diameter on a lake bottom, sometimes among tumbles of rocks and boulders. Such places are almost certain to hold Walleyes and once these spots are located, fish can be taken almost any time.

It is a fact that when Smallmouth Bass fail to strike artificial lures, they will still bite on night-crawlers, those large, super angleworms found on misty, warm nights on the lawns. But if Smallmouth Bass take night-crawlers with marked avidity, then the Walleye will go them one better for a super worm is even more desirable to this fish than a live minnow.

To rig these worms, tie one hook an inch or so from the end of the line, and one on the end. Either hook one night-crawler on each hook through the sexual band (the rim below the head), or in using one worm, the upper hook is through the band and the tail on the lower hook. In such fishing, fasten a dipsey type, pear-shaped sinker to the line about a foot from the tip, and let it down to lie flush on the bottom. Occasionally lift the lure and deposit it at another place.

A minnow hooked back of the dorsal fin, just under the skin, and also let down to the bottom will interest Walleyes if they are over-fed.

Medium-sized green frogs are also killers. This bait is rigged by soldering a fine wire across the shank of a hook and fastening the wire around the frog just above the crotch, just tight enough so that it cannot wriggle free. Let this down to the bottom and action is almost certain.

During the late summer and autumn when the frogs are migrating into the lakes to hibernate in the sunken inshore vegetation, these fish appear in numbers to hunt frogs. The lure can be cast either from a boat or from shore. It should be permitted to sink while slowly reeling it in. A hook rig for use with frogs includes a fine bead-chain which is soldered to the main hook shank. This chain should extend back to about the belly of the frog where it is joined by two short bead-chain bits to the end of each of which it is attached a small ganghook. Through a small ring at the jointing or meeting place of the two chain bits insert a strong thread, bring it over the frog above the crotch and tie it on. The reason for this extension rig to place hooks at the feet of the frog is to fool the short-strikers. The Walleye is a notorious short-striker. He will follow a lure and nip at its legs (of a frog) or at the tail if it is a minnow. The objective is to cripple the bait after which the fish can more readily seize it. With hooks at the feet of a frog, a short-striker is hooked almost instantly. A bead chain, soldered, or attached to the main hook shank, can be continued straight back with

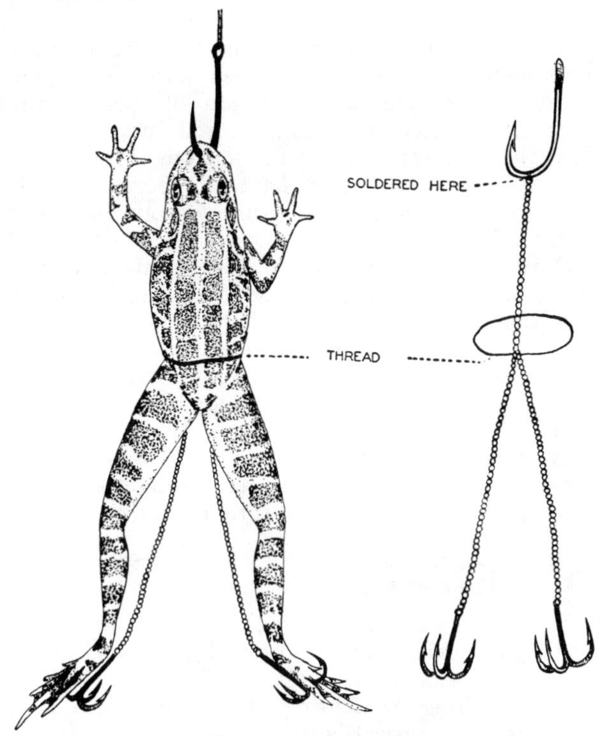

The green frog rig.

a small ganghook to be attached near the tail of a minnow to accomplish the same purpose.

Another interesting device is known as a tail-hook, pork-rind strip. These rinds come bottled and can be secured in most sporting goods stores. They have a hook crimped into the tail-end of the rind. Unless the fisherman is aware of these short-striking habits, he will not take one-third of the fish that follow his lure.

Jigging a spoon is also a good method of taking this species. Any small wobbling spoon, two to three inches in length, preferably with a nickel finish, can be used. To manage it, the lure is let down to the bottom, then lifted up a foot or so in a series of short jerks. The spoon darts about in erratic fashion and is often seized quickly by the fish. A lure such as this is desirable for fishing a pot-hole on the lake bottom. Sometimes if the use of this jigging spoon does not bring response, it is well to shift tactics and lower a live lure to the bottom. Use night-crawlers, crayfish, small lampreys, or green frogs and fish attracted by the jigged spoon may take these offerings.

River Walleyes are often taken on a fly rod by using a fly and spinner combination. However, the lure must be near the bottom. A few split shot on the leader about eighteen inches above the lure will get it down sufficiently in most water on a flyrod using night crawlers for bait, on a par with the best the angling pastime has to offer.

Part 2. Salt Water Species

Salt water game fish are taken by methods comparable with those used in fresh water. However, there is less definite segregation of species, and therefore particular techniques and lures, such as have been developed for the various Trout, Bass and Pike, and Sunfishes, have not been so finely distinguished and applied to the various salt water game fish.

The plugs, flies, or baits used will take a variety of forms in almost any water, and the fisherman is seldom entirely sure just what kind of a fish will strike next. Therefore, the necessary information that applies to many of these fish is covered in the section devoted to fishing methods and in "Where to Fish" section.

A few widely distributed and abundant species for which somewhat specific techniques have been developed are treated more fully in this section.

AMBERJACK

These are good game fish that furnish fine sport on light tackle. Taken largely by trolling either by live baits, spoons, plugs, or wobblers, but also by still fishing or drifting. They are found near rocky reefs and coral bottoms in Florida waters. (See Section V)

BARRACUDA

Barracuda are found on both coasts. The two are very similar although considered separate species. Both are fast, hard-hitting, predacious fish taken either by trolling or still fishing with bait. Probably the leading game fish in southern California waters; may often be taken while fishing for any fish in the bays and around the keys off the Florida Coast. (See Section V)

BASS

Many different salt water fish are known by the name of Bass. None are even closely related to the fresh water fish of the same name. The more important game species are included in those discussed here. It should be understood, however, that many others furnish sport in some localities.

CALIFORNIA KELP BASS

California Kelp Bass, also known as Rock Bass, Sand Bass, Cabrilla, is taken all year on live bait. It is most important as a game fish from central California southward into Mexican waters. (See Section V)

CALIFORNIA WHITE BASS

The California White Bass, found throughout the year, is taken most frequently from Monterey south. It is usually taken either by trolling or still fishing with bait or spinners. (See Section V)

CHANNEL BASS

Any angler who haunts the surf long enough, who keeps his tackle in tip-top condition, who learns as he goes along, and who keeps at it year after year is eventually going to tie into, and maybe land, a big fish. It may be a Striped Bass, a rip-snorting Bluefish which almost scares one with its savagery, or, if surf casting activities are concentrated from South Jersey to Panama, it will probably be that stalwart, popular citizen of the surf, the Channel Bass. He's also known as the Red Drum, Redfish, Reef Bass, Red Bass, Sea Bass (erroneously) or down in the Gulf of Mexico as the "Poisson Rouge" (see your French dictionary). If he's small, in his more southern range, he's a "Rat." Even by this latter name, he is worth the time and distance expended on him. The two fish that have made surf fishing popular on the Atlantic seaboard are probably the Channel and the Striped Bass.

While the Striped Bass all-tackle record has stood at seventy-three pounds since that lucky day of August 17, 1913 when C. B. Church took this sixty-inch-striper from the waters of Vineyard Sound, Massachusetts, the Channel Bass record (all-tackle) of seventy-five-and-a-half stood from November 29, 1941 (courtesy of the lucky and skillful angler, Capt. B. R. Ballance) and was taken off Cape Hatteras, North Carolina. This spot, by the way, is probably the best bet for big Red Drum, by and large, of the entire Atlantic coast. And yet one never knows. When young (fifteen years) Zack Waters went fishing with his father off Cape Charles, Virginia, on August 5, 1949, he hoped to catch some fish, maybe even a Channel Bass. But up until the instant when his father was hauling anchor with an eye over his shoulder at an approaching squall that threatened trouble and which had sent all other boats in the area scurrying for the safety of the harbor, they had caught only a few bottom fish. Typical of youth, Zack kept his "bunker" in the water until the anchor was actually on the way up, when he felt a heavy strike. Eight minutes later, his father gaffed a big Drum and headed the boat for shelter through the squall. At that moment safety was more important than the size of the Channel Bass, even though they realized that it was a bigger than average fish. Not until the Reliable Coal and Lumber Company's scales sagged down to the eighty-three-pound mark did any of them realize that they had set a new world's record for this species! Now there's a mark for the Striper anglers to shoot at—and a mark for the Red Drum fishermen to beat also.

There are other kinds of Drum but the Red Drum or Channel Bass is the only one with the distinguishing mark of a black spot about dime size at the base of the tail and showing clearly on both sides of the fish. While the big fellows are found in the outer ocean stretches of surf, don't for a minute think that the fish does not have other habitats. In the surf look for him in the inshore slues or holes, preferably where the incoming waves wash his natural foods over an offshore bar, at the entrance of inlets or even on the long inshore flats if the bait is there too. But he also frequents the bays and harbors, the protected waters of tidal rivers, bays, and lagoons. This latter fact is especially true in the more southern range of the Channel Bass. If there is a general rule for size it's as follows: the big "bull" Bass in the surf; the smaller Bass in the protected waters; bigger fish along the Atlantic range from Jersey to Florida with the smaller ones predominant in the Gulf waters. They seem to prefer sandy or muddy bottom, seldom being caught over rocky areas.

The season for Channel Bass along its range is fairly well established. Starting in the southern section, from the Indian River, Florida, past Key West and on down through the Gulf south to Panama they are an all-year biter and resident. North of Florida their first spring appearance is along South Carolina in March; then in North Carolina in April with Oregon Inlet as a hot-spot. In this latter state, the Channel Bass really hit in by May all along Oregon Inlet, Hatteras Inlet, Ocracoke, and the southeastern beaches. June in North Carolina means both inlet and surf fishing, and it continues from then on up to November, with the fall months showing some really big fish. From mid-June on, the Channel Bass is found in its more northern ranges until early October, barring unseasonable fall storms and cold weather.

Apparently no one knows the extent of migrations. There are definite movements of the fish: deeper waters in the fall with the coming of colder weather; inshore movement to the shallower surf and bay waters with the approach of spring and rising water temperatures. The young fish seem to spend their first year, at the end of which they are about twelve to thirteen inches long, in the shallower and sheltered waters. Incidentally, the fish up to about fifteen inches are nicknamed "Rats" in the Texas waters. Until they are about four or five years old, they return to the bays and inlets each with the general movement being inshore in the spring and offshore in the fall. After this, with their greater size, they are more apt to be found in the deeper waters and in the outer surf.

The Channel Bass is omnivorous in its eating habits. Even the most casual reader of any article about Channel Bass knows that cut pieces of "bunker" (menhaden) has been a favorite bait for many years. Other natural foods are mullet, crabs (sheddar or soft-shelled preferred), sand fleas, clams, silversides, shrimp, squid, and many other small fry. Both surface and sinking plugs can be used for surf casting. If fishing for smaller individuals with a fresh water bass bait casting outfit almost any surface, floating, diving or sinking plugs and spoons will produce. If trolling, almost any of the above will do the trick. Channel Bass also hit a fly; they provide good use for a salmon fly fishing outfit or a salt water fly rod outfit with streamers and bucktail flies. As one never knows just how big a fish may hit on fly fishing outfits, there should be plenty of backing (one hundred yards or more) behind the fly line. Surprisingly big fish can be worn down with a high rod tip, plenty of line, and careful handling.

The Channel Bass is a light biter on live or fresh bait. They have a habit of taking a bait in their mouth, apparently tasting or turning it for a moment before they really take off with it. This means that a slack line is necessary immediately after a fish picks up the bait. In surf fishing a pyramid sinker and fish finder combination helps prevent drag enough to cause the fish to drop the bait before the hook can be set. Actually enough slack can be put in the line by dropping the rod tip a foot or two and then lifting to set the hook; it should not be given the sharp jerk used in other kinds of fishing. As the fish turns to go away with the bait, he will exert enough pressure so that pulling back, and snubbing the line, will add enough pressure to drive the hook in over the barb. A too-sharp jerk can tear the hook out of any fish, including the Channel Bass. Be sure that the star drag is not set too tightly. While the Channel Bass is gentle when he picks up the bait and mouths it, he will quickly go into high gear when he feels the hook. That first run may be one hundred yards or more—and it's a fast powerful one too. One may think two or three times during the battle that the fish has given up, but keep that rod tip up during those lulls, as the Redfish fools many anglers with a sudden, unexpected rush.

This fish is not considered a great table delicacy unless in the so-called puppy class, which means a fish under six pounds; then properly prepared he is excellent. This means that there is no great point in killing all the Channel Bass hooked. Keep those needed for food and a big one for the picture-taking which is so much a part of fishing and return the remainder to the water unharmed. The days when it was good fishing etiquette to bring in all the boat could hold just to pile them up on the dock to rot is definitely of the past. This applies to other salt water sport fish too, of course.

In the case of Channel Bass there have been attempts to institute conservation laws which would include a minimum length, limit the number of fish per day per angler, for the netting of fish less than fourteen inches nor more than thirty-two inches in length, and prohibiting the use of Channel Bass for any purpose except human consumption. However, in spite of the activities of some wide-awake angling clubs, such regulations have not been adopted on the Atlantic Coast. There is a minimum length limit of not less than fourteen inches and a maximum of thirty-five inches in the Texas Gulf waters, designed to protect the large, breeding fish and thus preserve this brood stock.

GIANT BLACK SEA BASS

Giant Black Sea Bass, known only in southern California and Mexico, is a huge fish that is taken all year either by still fishing with bait or by trolling. For information as to tackle and baits (See Section V).

SEA BASS

Sea Bass on the Atlantic Coast are taken largely from May to October off rocky shores, jetties, piers, by still fishing with various types of bait, including crabs, shrimps, blood worms, and cut bait. (See Section V)

Albert Dixon Simmons

Ollie Rodman holds up a forty-pound Striped Bass taken at Cuttyhunk Island, Massachusetts, which is well known as Striper grounds.

STRIPED BASS

A fisherman anywhere along the sea coast from Nova Scotia to North Carolina, whether in the tidal waters far up into brackish water, in the bays and inlets, at the mouths of harbors, or along the rocky or sandy stretches where the Atlantic surf foams in, is in Striped Bass territory. The same applies on the Pacific Coast around San Francisco, California, and Coos Bay, Oregon. That means that each cast may connect with a line-sided, broad, square-tailed fish varying from two to sixty pounds —or more; called *Roccus saxatalis* but more commonly known to anglers as Striped Bass as far south as New Jersey, and as "Rock" or "Rockfish" farther south. No matter what the nomenclature, it's a fish that's tops for both tackle and table.

This fish is a real gamester; it may smash at anything offered on one day; on the next it may not move a fin to take the most tempting or skillfully offered lure or bait. When it's hungry, it will hit like a ton of dynamite; when not feeding the Striper's lack of interest can be maddening. Call him temperamental—most game fish of sweet or salt water are; surveys show that within its range it is the most sought-after inshore fish that bucks the tides and surging surf; that hides in the tidal streams or roams the flats of the bay, that is here today and gone tomorrow.

Any fish that's easy to catch holds little interest for the average angler. At times the Striper is easy to catch but those occasions are few as compared to the days when one can comb favorite waters and swear that there isn't a Striper within miles. They may be there but not be in the mood to cooperate. And that's what makes Striper fishing such a challenge, and accounts in great part for its popularity. Even the so-called experts can't know everything about Stripers. For example, the big Martha's Vineyard (Mass.) Derby of 1947 was won by an amateur fisherman who cast a seaworm bait out into the Island surf, let it roll around the bottom and connected, while the experts wore their arms and backs out with their long hundred-yard-or-better casts and didn't even come close to matching the weight of the beginner's big fish.

By and large the Striped Bass is an inshore feeder. It migrates in the spring from its winter home in the Chesapeake north, to an unknown point. Some authorities claim, and with good reasons, that the New Brunswick and Nova Scotia Stripers are resident local populations which become dormant in the winter. The main range is from Chesapeake Bay to the Maine Coast; they are found along Jersey and New York in May; in lower New England in late May; north of Cape Cod in June and then along this stretch of coast (Jersey to Maine) until the first frosts of fall start this schooling fish back toward their winter home in the Chesapeake.

One theory—a logical one—is that as the fish move northward, they move into a bay or inlet area, leaving some of the school there as summer residents while the main body moves on northward. It is even possible that Bass, like the Atlantic Salmon, return to their own particular spot on the coast year after year. This belief is prompted by the fact that after especially heavy seining in an area—now curbed by more stringent laws—that area is apt to have few Bass the following season. Be that as it may, the northward movement in the spring and the southward migration in the fall is a fact. In this way, the habits of the fish set the "open seasons" so to speak, so that no legal seasonal restrictions have been established except in New Jersey. There is a growing tendency to fix minimum-length limits of sixteen inches, so look up the laws before seeking this species. A license is unnecessary except above certain designated tidewater marks, as in the tidal rivers of Connecticut and in some other states.

Because of its habits, the Striper is every man's fish from May to November in most of his range. It can be taken from a bridge, tidal river bank, in the first breaking wave on the outside beaches, from an outboard or rowboat in the marshy creeks or from a luxurious cruiser down the bay. He'll hit flies, plugs, live bait, metal squids, feather jigs, little inch-long harbor shrimp, or a plain sea worm drifting in the tide on a plain hook. In short, it is one of the most accessible game fish as well as one of the best.

The Striper has another accommodating habit which helps the man who works five days a week: that is, it strikes at night as well as in the daytime. In fact, many claim that the best fishing for Stripers is at night, that this fish feeds more avariciously from dark to dawn than during the daytime. After fishing both night and day it's a toss-up which produces the greatest number of fish.

But for more fun in any kind of fishing, most anglers prefer the daylight hours. There's more to fishing—whether it's Stripers or Sailfish—than the taking and killing of fish: there's the flight of the birds; the shimmer of sun, sand and water; the passing ships; the comforting glow of the warm sun on exposed shoulder-blades and the relaxation of the summer heat. It is fun to see what goes on, whether it be the sudden rising of a school of bait fish, the clamor of the terns over feeding fish, or the soaring of the herring and black-backed gulls over the cliff where the wind gives them an updraft in which they can play.

In fairness it must be said that at night there's the added thrill of the booming unseen surf and the hissing of the foamy water as it surges up the beach; the blinking lights of a boat passing out to sea or down the bay; the extra handicap of not seeing where a hooked fish is going or knowing how close it is as it comes in fighting yard by yard.

Bass can be taken almost any time, so anyone primarily interested in taking Bass should try at all hours and regardless of tides—but more about tides later. In fact, if only one instruction could be given to the beginner, it would be that he fish every available moment. If there's one kind of fishing where patience counts, it's Striped Bass fishing. Sure, one wants the right tackle and wants it in good shape. It is well to know what live baits or artificial lures the fish have been taking—and polite, humble inquiry among the natives will help here. And one wants to know where to look for fish which may mean bay channels on the low tide, the flats and sand bars on the high tide. But most of all, "keep at it."

It has been stated that Striped Bass are an inshore fish and that is generally true. They can be taken trolling (slowly, just fast enough to keep the hooks off the bottom) along the edges of marshy creeks, bays and inlets; sometimes they are found behind the first breaker in the surf on sandy or rocky shorelines; when the tide is low they may be concentrated in the bay channels and most apt to strike on the last of the ebb or the first of the flood. In such an area as that on the inside of the hook of Cape Cod, they may be feeding two hundred yards offshore around the big weed beds. Or if a running tide makes a rip a hundred yards offshore, possibly around a sand bar or rocky reef, that rip is a good spot to place the lure. Sometime men who can cast even a few feet further can take fish while shorter casts fail. Speaking of distance, this is a good time to point out the paradox which exists between shore fishing and boat fishing for Stripers. Those in a boat cast into shore, getting as near the breakers as possible. The man on the beach, on the other hand, is forcing his cast far out to sea. So there you have it: by and large, it always appears that the "grass is greener in the other fellow's yard." But it is not always true.

The Striped Bass angler should keep his eyes open at all times. Bass may feed on the bottom; they may be taking bait six feet under the surface where the water is ten to twenty feet deep. But there are times when they will be chasing bait (sand-eels, herrings, minnows of one kind or another, small mackerel, menhaden, or squid) right on the surface. Watch the surface of the water in all directions—and keep watching. If a whirl, swirl or a sudden burst of white water appears, get over there fast and cast into the commotion. Another tip-off to the presence of Stripers is the action of gulls or terns. If they are dipping and diving and screaming, there's a chance that the Bass are driving the bait to the surface, and that a metal squid or plug will bring a quick response. Never run a boat into a school of breaking fish. Approach them slowly. Cast into their edge—and brace your feet. When Stripers are feeding on the surface one is pretty sure to get fast action. Remember that it may last only for a few minutes, a half hour, or an hour at best, so make the most of it. Watch the spooling of the line and the thumbing to prevent backlashes; a waste of time when fish are feeding is serious business. And one may get only one such period of minutes in a day's or even a week's fishing.

Before discussing the lures that will take Stripers, let's have a look at the ways to take them. Surf casting; fishing, from a bridge or a tidal river bank; trolling, from a row boat, outboard or inboard; still-fishing with live bait; fly casting from the shore or bank of a tidal stream (preferably when the tide is running hard either in or out) with bucktail flies; bait casting with regular fresh water bass tackle; and casting a live bait into the surf, bay or river, letting it drift in the tide or lying on the bottom.

Thousands of words could be written on baits and lures for Stripers, but it can be broken into several main categories.

A) For trolling:
   1) Eel skins on hollow-headed rigs, trolled fast and with constant jerking of the rod tip to give a diving, wounded, easy-to-catch action.
   2) Blood worms, hooked through the head on hooks behind smooth running spinners like the Northern—trolled slowly—are one of the best, consistent fish-takers.
   3) Feathers (feather jigs) tipped with narrow, two inch and three inch long strips of pork rind, fresh squid, or blood worms—trolled fast.
   4) Spoons such as the Drone, Record, Wilson, Rex, Pet, etc.
   5) Whole eels rigged with two hooks: one protruding at the vent; another protruding just under the throat; just fast enough to keep them from catching on bottom.
   6) Bug eye and Barracuda jigs, trolled fast.

B) For casting:
   1) Top water plugs such as the Atom, Sylvester Blue Mullet, Heddon Flaptail, Cap'n Bill's popper; etc.
   2) Metal jigs such as the Montauk, Sand Eel, Doc Johnston, Belmar and Butterfish; sometimes when you tip them with pork rind or with a feathered hook they'll be more effective.
   3) Underwater plugs such as the Creek Chub Striper, Husky Pikie, Silver Flash, the P & K, the Cap'n Bill Swimmer, the E & M.
   4) Weighted eel-skin rigs.

C) Live Bait:
   1) Whole squid (summer bettei than winter species) either floated in the surf or rolled around on the sandy bottom, weighted down with a sinker; or you can use just the head.
   2) Whole crabs of most any variety from the size of a quarter up to the palm-of-your-hand; floated out with the tide without a sinker or down near the bottom with a sinker.
   3) A blood or sea worm floated down-tide from a bridge or boat on a live line (without sinker); or still fished on the bottom.
   4) Shrimp (the inch-long harbor variety) on small hooks and using fly rods or light tackle; especially effective if you chum with the same bait.
   5) Small (six to eight inches) live eel hooked through the skin of the back, avoiding the backbone and fished on or near the bottom.
   6) Whole or cut pieces of herring.

D) Fly Fishing:
   1) In tidal rivers mainly but also effective if you can approach by boat to within casting distance of a surface-feeding school anywhere using what is commonly known as salmon fishing fly tackle (nine-foot rod, weight at least seven ounces, thirty yards

of level or tapered line plus a minimum of 150 yards of backing—silk braided or Nylon and latter preferred) using streamer or bucktail, or popping-bug lures tied on two-inch long-shank hooks.

2) Favorite flies are the Harold Gibbs, Fred Gibbs, Palmer Diller, Dean Bead Head, Quilby Minnow, red and white, and white bucktail or streamers.

3) Cast out across the running tide, let the fly sink about a foot, or even two; then retrieve with short flips of the rod tip and pull-in of the line in much the same manner as you would fish a streamer for square-tail trout or land-locked salmon. Even with the tidal current full of live bait, it is not unusual to see a striper disregard the real food and come right through it to take the fly with a smashing strike.

4) Other effective fly rod lures are the Magic Pearl, Dardevlette, or other small metal fly rod lures which simulate a small minnow.

E) Bait Casting:

1) Top-water popping lures, under-water swimming lures, wobbling spoons—all will take stripers.

2) Spinner, spoon and pork rind combinations such as the Al Foss, Rex, Record or other spoons.

3) Weighted feather or Nylon lures.

This outline gives some idea of the variety of baits (live or real, and dead or artificial) which will take Stripers. It seems that this fish will take most anything which moves which is smaller than it is. In fact, the food which the Striper absorbs is almost as varied as are the smaller varieties of fish or shellfish which inhabit his range. Let's just name the natural foods which have been taken from the stomachs of Stripers. Incidentally, that's a good thing to do, no matter what fish is caught. If the stomach pouches of all fish taken are opened and a record kept of the findings and checked against the season, it will be of invaluable assistance in taking heavier catches year after year. But to get back to the foods from Stripers stomachs: shrimp, sand fleas, whiting (up to a pound or more in weight), squid (up to seven in one fish); crabs (twenty in one fish); small mackerel; herring (up to a pound); sea worms; mussels; soft shell clams; eels; menhaden; and most all smaller fishes such as mummychaugs, sperling, billfish, tom-cod, flatfish, and small weakfish. In short, he's a voracious feeder who makes fair game of most anything smaller than he.

One of the most common beliefs is that there is a best time of the tide to fish for Striped Bass. Many fishermen believe this particularly in their earlier experience. But as knowledge widens there seems to be more and more exceptions to any established rule. Let's take Duxbury Bay, Mass., as an example. It is a good area to use as a sample as this section of coast is a mixture of bay, inlet, channel, marsh creek and off-shore weed-bed fishing. In 1948, nearly all the best fishing was during the last two hours of the ebb and the first two hours of the flood. No matter how hard they were fished, other tides just did not produce. But in 1949, just the opposite was true: the lower tides were no good; the best fishing invariably occurred, from June to October, on the top of the flood tides, or on the last two hours of the incoming or the first two hours of the outgoing.

But to get back to Duxbury as typical of the variety of Striper waters. At the very head of the Bay there is a sizeable marsh cut by two main creeks which have several smaller tributaries. In this area on the high tides, the creeks are trolled with smooth-running spinners and worms slowly, or eel-skin rigs fast. Best time is two hours before high tide to two hours after: there is plenty of water in the creeks and there is still a good tidal current. By zig-zagging from bank to bank fish are taken at the edge of the grass and sometimes in the middle of the stream.

Just below this marsh area there is the long, wooden Powder Point bridge which cuts across the narrow bay below the marsh and connects the mainland with the barrier beach which forms the outer side of Duxbury Bay (and cuts it off from Cape Cod or Massachusetts Bay). This bridge is a popular spot for Striper fishermen and those who fish it day and night take Bass fairly consistently, especially at night, drifting their worms or chubs out (or in) with the tide.

Below the bridge is the main Bay which has two main channels one to the East side near the barrier beach, the other well toward the mainland on the west. On the high tide trollers or plug casters work the inside shore of the barrier beach. But on the low tide this area is several feet above water forcing the fish to move down the Bay to the deeper water where Duxbury and Plymouth Bays join in the main ship channel. However, many fish move into the two main channels and tributary channels to the east of Clarks Island. On low tides one can fly fish these channels from a boat anchored at the edge; plug cast or troll slowly with spinners and worms. As the channels at this stage of the tide are fairly narrow and the water not too deep, nosing the boat along the very edge of the channels and making little disturbance and then casting is the most taking method. When the tide comes in and starts to cover the flats the bass often move in schools over the shallow waters, chasing bait. Incidentally in such shallow water, barely two or three feet deep, at this stage of the tide, Bass are very hard to approach or catch.

The north shore of Clarks Island is a jumble of big boulders with the channel skirting in close. This is good water for casting or trolling and at all tides.

Further down the Bay, at what might be called the convergence of the Duxbury and Plymouth Bay waters is a great mound of rocks at one end of a horseshoe-shaped shoal with a lighthouse (Bug Light) at the other end of the horseshoe and more rocks right under the light's platform. There is deep water at all tides around the edge of this shoal and it's a hot spot for Bass. Here again the Bass bite best in a running tide as then there are rips that really race and broil. Remember always that Stripers like active waters.

Across the channel from Bug Light is another area with great shoals extending out for over a mile, yet a pronounced channel near the sandy beach. On certain spots near the channel and offshore of the beach, as far out as four or five hundred yards, there are great weed beds. Here again is good Bass water, either for trolling or for top-water plug fishing. Occasionally there will be schools of menhaden moving along this bay area and with them come Bass. The menhaden are easy to spot as there will be a great mass of several thousand of them lying with their fins just out of the water. If they suddenly boil and make the water fly, it is certain that a Bass has moved into them, and that a plug or jig placed in there will probably bring a strike. It is an amazing sight to see the commotion which a few thousand fish a foot long can make when they are frightened.

Speaking of fishing the menhaden schools, there is a stunt which works. Cast into or on the far side of these fish which are massed as closely as the fingers on a hand, using a butterfish jig with a large treble hook swinging from the end. Jerk the lure as soon as it lands in the school and the chances are that a menhaden will be foul hooked. Then let the weight of the jig pull that fish down to the bottom of the school. If there are Bass underneath, they will see what to them is an easy meal in the wounded fish, and hit the hooked menhaden, jig, hook and all. This has worked time and again.

The Striper is a migratory fish, yet ichthyologists claim that only about ten per cent of the Chesapeake population migrate and it is generally conceded that this is the great parent population of Striped Bass for the Atlantic coast. Stripers undoubtedly spend the winters in more northern waters, from Jersey to Nova Scotia. Some years ago, Striped Bass were netted regularly through the ice in the Parker River in northern Massachusetts; this would mean January and February to get weather sufficiently cold to freeze the brackish headwaters of this river where there is quite a tide even though the current is sluggish.

Striped Bass will run into fresh water if no dams prevent, making them an anadramous fish. In fact, there is good authority for stating that Striped Bass have been caught in Grand Lake in New Brunswick and in a lake of the same name in Nova Scotia.

The big migration of Striped Bass northward in the spring rarely reaches Rhode Island before late May and northern Massachusetts in mid-June. Yet Striped Bass are taken in June in New Brunswick—one spot is the mouth of the Mirimichi River—by fly fishermen seeking the early salmon run. So it is most probable that these northern Stripers are local populations which winter in deeper water. Most all Striped Bass, even in the more southern part of their range are dormant in the cold winter months. They bite occasionally as one rabid Striper fisherman found when he took them through the ice in the dead of winter from a fresh water lake which formed the headwaters of a tidal stream in the southern part of Rhode Island. He used big (three and four inch) mummychaugs, alive, for bait and fished at night. Might be worth a try in one of the headwaters of a tidal way in the locality's off season for Striped Bass.

By and large, the approach of the Striped Bass should be on the theory that he is a wary citizen of the inshore waters. Like all fishing theories, this statement is definitely a generality but it *is* the proper approach most of the time.

On one trip four boats were trolling around a breaking school of Bass in fairly shallow water, probably not over six feet deep. No one even had a hit on the trolled eelskins, feathered lures, worms and spinners, and all the other combinations which had been previously producing. Each time a boat came near the breaking school they would go down and disappear for ten or fifteen minutes. Finally the motor was cut upwind and uptide of the school. By this time other boats had gone elsewhere. Two flyrods were rigged and the boat allowed to drift quietly up to within casting distance. On the first cast each man had a strike, followed by many others in which fish were either landed or lost before the activity was over. Those fish were wary.

On other days the fish hit avidly, even on fast-trolled lures within thirty feet of the boat. In fact, once when the eelskin was left hanging over the side, barely a foot under water, a Striper struck it within arms' length.

But as a rule it pays to approach a breaking school of Bass cautiously, stopping the motor well away and casting to the edge of the school. Many surf casters claim that if there are half-dozen men casting side by side from the beach, the constant landing of metal jigs or plugs will put the fish down. On the contrary, a bather who decided to plunge into the ocean, practically under the line, did not prevent a twenty-five pounder from striking.

Striped Bass are not native to the Pacific Coast but were introduced there in 1879 when one hundred and thirty-two fish were taken from the Navesink River, New Jersey, and released near Martinez in San Francisco Bay, California. Then three hundred more were released in lower Suisun Bay in 1882. By 1889 the commercial catch was averaging well over a million pounds per year and the Striper has been abundant ever since. This is probably the most outstanding example of a fish being successfully planted in another ocean. All commercial fishing for Stripers in California was stopped in 1935 and estimates are that over a million fish are taken by sportsmen each year. Full information on the San Francisco area can be secured from the California Division of Fish and Game which puts out an excellent pamphlet. The best Striper fishing season is from about mid-August to late October; the best areas are San Pablo Bay, the Carquinez Straits, Suisun Bay, and the Napa River.

Before coming back east to the Chesapeake Bay area, attention should be called to the Coos Bay area of Oregon. There are plenty of good fish there ranging up into the high twenty-pound class. In fact, it was here that Joe Brooks of Baltimore, Maryland, set a new world's fly rod record for Striped Bass with a twenty-nine pound, six-ounce fish on a popping bug of his own design. Best time of year is July and August.

No matter where one seeks or takes them, the Striper keeps pretty much to the same pattern in his feeding and striking habits. Each locality has its own favored methods, of course, and it is understood that Joe Brooks had a hard time persuading his charter boat captain that he could actually take a fish on a fly.

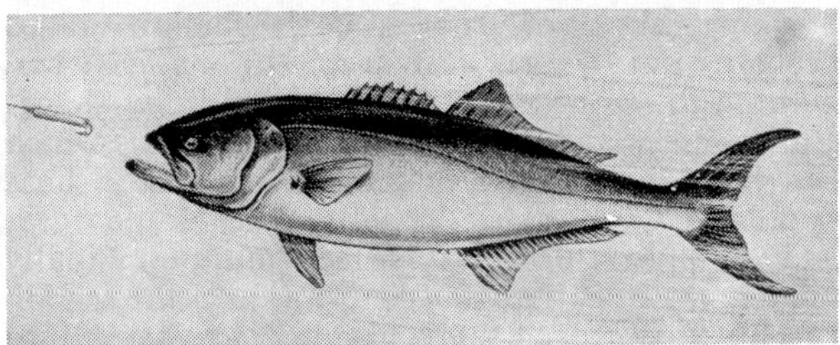

"The Saltwater Fisherman's Favorite Four"
By Wm. Morrow & Co.

Bluefish chasing a turkey-bone rig.

The Striped Bass, or Rockfish as it is known in the Chesapeake, has been pictured as a hard-hitting, tackle-smashing fish whether in the bays, inlets or tidal streams, or in the hard-pounding surf of the outer coastal beaches. But in April, in the main Atlantic spawning ground, the "Rock" becomes another character entirely. The urge of parenthood is rampant and heavy-bellied females full of ripe roe (a roe of a ten-pound fish will yield a million eggs!) and the males or bucks become sluggish and have no more fight than a limp mop at the end of a hard day. One of the centers of reproduction is the Roanoke River of North Carolina with the central spot at Weldon, which claims to be "The Rockfish Capital of the World." The fish are taken by fishing deep, and beginners never are sure whether they have a fish on their hook or some floating debris. Many are taken in great landing nets of Paul Bunyan size with fifteen foot handles and a net six feet across and three feet deep. In about a three-mile stretch it is not unusual to see three or four hundred boats trolling or netting. But this is not the great fish slaughter that it appears: the spawn is sold to the Rock Fish hatchery at five dollars per million eggs. This is a continuous carnival for the citizens for miles around for the six-week period of the Stripers' honeymoon. This fishing spree is pretty much a local event, although it has had nationwide publicity—and when it ends the residents have the freezers full of Bass (pardon us, we mean "Rock" steaks) against the many months to come when the fish have started down river and some of them on their northward migration.

Apparently the Striped Bass when they spawn give that duty the same full-time, absorbing energy which they use during the rest of the year to keep sport fishermen on their toes.

In conclusion, those who have never caught a Striped Bass, have missed something. If already Striper anglers, they need no urgin'.

BLACK DRUM

Black Drum, also called Drum, Sea Drum, Banded Drum, Gray Drum, and Striped Drum, is found on the Atlantic and Gulf Coasts from Long Island to Texas. During the summer months, it is largely taken by still fishing with squid, cut bait, crabs, or clams. It is not a major game fish. (See Section V)

BLUEFISH

There are many voracious game fish in the sea and most of them are mighty edible. There are salt water sport fishermen who insist that their favorite fish is the Tarpon, the Bonefish, the Striped Bass, the big Weaks, or the leaping Sailfish. But if there is a group of anglers who will stand together and make momentous claims about their favorite fish, it's the fraternity who prefer Bluefish. With teeth like a Barracuda; with the power of lightning in their lithe muscle-packed bodies; with an insatiable appetite when they are driving bait fish; with a trim, steel-blue, torpedo-like shape that slips through the water like a wraith, the Bluefish is ounce for ounce one of the best sport fishes of the ocean. And on the table, fresh from the shore, they make a meal about which one can justly exclaim! Incidentally, don't get fingers near their snapping mouths in landing them on the beach or in the boat; their mouth is like a steel trap and can give one a vicious bite.

Many fishermen from the Gulf of Mexico to Massachusetts think of the Bluefish as their own special super-fish. Actually this species is widely distributed, being found not only in the area mentioned but also in the Indian Oceans, off the coast of Africa, and in the Malay Archipelago among other distant places, including Madagascar. Primarily it is a warm water fish that looks for warmer climes when the temperature of the water gets down near forty degrees. In the "good old days," according to the authoritative Jordan and Evermann, their range extended north to Nova Scotia; but in more than thirty years of fishing remembrances, mid-Massachusetts has been about their recent northern limit of range on the Atlantic.

The piscatorial world is ordinarily an astoundingly well-ordered one; one can count on certain fish appearing at certain times of the year at certain spots along their coastal range be they migratory or resident. But that is not true of the Bluefish. He seems to be not only a nomad of the seas, both offshore and inshore, but to have no usual pattern to his appearance in any given area. One year he may be numerous in Jersey; the next year he may be numous in the Cape Cod waters and rare in Jersey. Then he may entirely disappear, as indeed he did from much of the north Atlantic for nearly ten years. Oddly, this disappearance started abruptly and completely the year after his greatest abundance in this latter area.

Many claim that his wanderings are not aimless but guided by hunger for his favorite food, the Menhaden; lots of Menhaden, lots of Blues and vice versa. That is true to a certain extent because the Blues do follow the schools of Menhaden northward in the spring as both fishes leave their southern winter quarters. Probably over-fishing of the Menhaden did influence the Bluefish population in our Atlantic waters. Some support of this theory is found in the fact that during the past three or four years, more and more Menhaden are appearing along the New England coast; and the Blues are coming back with them. Not yet the old eight to ten pounders, but increasing schools of two-, three- and four-pound fish with a number of the bigger Blues showing up in the early spring off the North Carolina coast.

Those living in Florida can catch Bluefish most of the year, and plenty of them in the winter months. In the great coastal and offshore shoal fishing grounds of North Carolina, May is the month when Blues are reported (excitedly) off Frying Pan, Hatteras, Oregon Inlet, Morehead City, and Wrightsville Beach with really good fishing for them breaking in June. By July, this species is not only in the Chesapeake and its bordering outside waters but is up off New Jersey too. From then on they seem to work northward until they become plentiful by early August in such well-known fishing spots as Buzzards Bay, Martha's Vineyard, Cape Cod's Monomoy Point, and Nantucket where they're taken from both boat and beach, trolling and casting respectively. That is, until the late October frosts start to cool the waters to send the Blues back to the south again. August, September, and early October seem to find the Blues pretty well distributed from North Carolina to Massachusetts, both inshore and off. It is in the fall period too that great schools of little Bluefish, called "Snappers," "Skip-jacks," and "Snapping Mackerel" appear in inner harbors, tidal rivers, bays, and inlets. Only eight to ten or eleven inches long, they are still as rapacious and vicious as their elders, chasing bait with a vengeance that is almost unseemly in so small a fish but portraying a characteristic which is a boon to the bridge, dock, small boat, and other inshore anglers who may not have the desire nor the means to get their bigger offshore relatives. All the equipment needed is fly rod tackle, a long shanked hook, some fresh sperling or mummies, and a running tide to have a chance to come home with a sagging creel filled with one of the best eating fishes that swims. And on light tackle they'll put a square-tail Trout of equal size to shame. Trout enthusiasts will raise cries of heresy at this statement but it's apt to come from those who have not caught the "Snappers" on trout tackle. These little Blues can be taken readily in the running tideways on flies, streamers, and bucktails; or by using spinning tackle.

As can easily be inferred, the Bluefish is a bit individual in that he not only roams the open oceans and outer bays but also ventures in close to the shore, well into such big bays as the Chesapeake and Narragansett, and is equally at home in the inshore tide rips and offshore shoals. Such distribution is no handicap to his popularity. But he is still unpredictable.

It's a pretty good plan to work on the theory that if Bluefish are in the locality, they'll be where the bait has concentrated. Remember that the Bluefish go in schools; if one strikes while trolling blindly (no fish showing), it's a good idea to circle that spot again, in widening circles. When they are feeding on the surface, there's no doubt of their whereabouts. A school of Blues will "herd" a school of bait into a thick, milling mass and then smash through them feeding like wolves until they are filled to overflowing. An angler hasn't seen savagery in the sea until he's seen a big school of Blues slashing, jumping, and thrashing into tightly packed bait. Add to the scene hundreds of screaming terns overhead, picking up the pieces; the pounding of blood in his ears as one of those Blues take a trolled or cast lure, and he's in the middle of a fisherman's heaven—and how!!! In the excitement of taking Blues on a trolled feather, metal jig, eelskin, or flashing spoon, be sure not to run the boat through the middle of the feeding fish. Skirt the outer edges of the school and handle the boat so that the trolled lures pass by the edges of the bunched fish. Hungry as they may be, they'll still sound and disappear if the boat is driven directly through them.

Time and tide seem to vary for the best Blue fishing. By and large, the incoming tide, or at least a running tide, whether fishing the surf, the bay or offshore is best. Watch the action of the gulls and terns; many a time they'll spot breaking fish long before a mans comparatively weak eyes can do so. Get there fast, as the fish may be on the "prod" for only a few minutes. If in a bay or inlet where there is a perceptible tide, it is better to troll across the tide rather than with or against it. This is especially true if it is possible to pass back and forth across the tide and fish behind (in the deep water) a series of bars or shoals. Bluefish are far from dumb and apparently know that by lying behind these shoals, the bait that comes washing over with the tide is easy prey. Early in the morning is another favorite time, especially if the right tide coincides with this early hour. Watch the local rod and gun columns; inquire politely among the native fishermen; keep eyes and ears open for gossip in the seacoast village. If there are Bluefish around and if there is an especially good spot, it can be found by following the local fishermen. Offshore calm weather will provide good fishing. In the surf, a bit of rough water seems to be best, probably because inshore winds create such a condition and at the same time drive the bait into the beach to be followed by the Blues.

Hungry as he is, the Bluefish has a bad (bad for the angler and probably for the Bluefish's teeth) habit of hitting at the swivel between the line and wire leader; if he does, he may bite the line off as neatly as if cut with a knife. Be sure to use a wire leader. As a rule Nylon leaders are best; but for Blues, it's wire, always.

It has already been stated that the favorite food of the Bluefish is menhaden. Other favorites are squid, mullet, herring, sand eels, small common eels, sperling, in fact, most any fish that is smaller than himself and is available in numbers. It is claimed, and there seems little cause to argue, that the Blue will eat twice his weight each day if he can get it. As in other kinds of fishing, the lures used to catch Blues should simulate in size and shape at least the food he is taking at that time. He'll take tin jigs, feather and Nylon jigs, spoons, spinners baited with a strip of squid or small bait fish. Also he'll hit, and with a vengeance, those big top-water Striped Bass plugs like the Sylvester Flaptail, Atom, Pikie-Minnow. He'll also take many of the good-producing top and under water fresh water bass plugs and spoons. Popular live baits are squid and eel-bobs, or eelskins on trolling rigs.

No matter what lure he takes, the Blue is one of the best fish into which any man can hope to set a hook; and one of the best into which he can set his teeth too.

The world's record Bluefish still stands at twenty-five pounds. This fish was taken by a Mr. L. Hathaway at Cohasset Narrows, Vineyard Sound, Mass. on June 16th, back in 1874.

BONEFISH

Known on the Atlantic Coast but most frequent in Florida waters. In recent years, Bonefish have become one of the most popular salt water game fish with those casting with bait or with fly rod. A special type of bait fishing has been developed to take them when foraging over the great, shallow flats that abound on the Florida coast. They are reputed to be one of the fastest of all game fish and are strikingly silvered when first taken from the water. (See Section V)

BONITO

There are several species of Bonito, some in the Atlantic and some in the Pacific. All are open water fish, taken by trolling with either cut bait, jigs, or spoons. They are sometimes found in large schools and often furnish the major part of the fishing for days at a time in some localities. They are not regarded with as high favor as some of their relatives, but put up a good fight when hooked. (See Section V)

CABEZONE

Cabezone is an important sport fish only on the West Coast where it is of particular importance in central California, although taken as far north as British Columbia. It is taken largely by still fishing with cut bait or with jigs. (See Section V)

CERO

Also called Kingfish

This huge mackerel is abundant in southern waters, particularly in and around Florida inshore of the gulf stream. It is taken either by trolling or still fishing, with the former method the most popular. It may be found along the reefs and shorelines, but also out in the deeper water. In Florida waters, it is much preferred over the Bonito, although both are often taken, fished in the same way and at the same time, either with cut bait, feathered jigs, or spinners. (See Section V)

CROAKERS

There are many different kinds of Croakers on both the Atlantic and Pacific Coasts. Most of them are taken by still fishing, although some of the California species are popular for surf casting, using natural baits, such as sand crabs, mussels, clams, or cut bait. They are popular with family parties and beginning fishermen on both coasts, and in salt water, together with the flounders, take the place of the pan fish, such as Bream and the Yellow Perch in fresh water. Most of them travel in schools and can be taken in numbers when a school is feeding.

Among their numbers are included the Corbino, which is one of the most popular surf fish in southern California waters. The most important sport fish are the Croaker, known as "Hardhead" on the Atlantic Coast, Yellowfin Croaker, Corbino, Spotfin Croaker, King Croaker. (See Section V)

COBIA

also known as SARGEANT FISH, CRABEATER, BLACK BONITO, COALFISH, LEMONFISH, etc.

Cobia is found most commonly from Chesapeake Bay south into the Gulf waters where it is taken during the summer months either by still fishing or by trolling with natural bait or spinners. It is most important as a sport fish off the coasts of Alabama, Mississippi, and Louisiana, and the Virginia capes. (See Section V)

DOLPHIN

The Dolphin is one of the most beautiful of all fish and gives a thrill to anyone who catches one. They shift rapidly from one color phase to another, with different combinations of green, yellow, and blue. They are, however, not an important game fish because they are usually widely scattered both in the waters of the Pacific and Atlantic Oceans. In the Atlantic area, they stay in or near the gulf stream, and in California and Mexican waters are most abundant in summer. Few anglers fish especially for them, and they are usually taken incidentally to other fishing by trolling or still fishing. (See Section V)

FLOUNDER

Usually called SOLE on the Pacific Coast

There are many different Flounders on both coasts. They go by a variety of names, but all are taken largely in shallow waters by still fishing with bait. They are one of the substitute among salt water for the panfish of fresh water. They can be taken in shallow bays and inlets, particularly on an incoming tide as they feed into the shallow water. Local fishermen on either coast can always tell those interested what particular bait is most useful at that season and where the fishing is apt to be good.

Considering the volume of fish caught, this is the most important of all salt water fish to the average angler. It can be taken either fishing from a boat or from piers that project far enough into the water to reach a feeding ground. They will take almost any type of bait, fished on or near the bottom. (See Section V)

THE GROUPERS

These are a group of tropical fish which are important only around the coast of Florida, and in a few cases, further north. They are taken largely by still fishing off trestles, piers, reefs, rock piles, etc. They are important locally and to those who visit southern waters. (See Section V)

GRUNTS

Grunts are another tropical group that are commonly found only in Florida waters, although a few of them are further north. They are taken in the same situations and by the same methods as Groupers. They furnish much sport to still fishermen and those fishing from trestles, bridges, etc., in their rather restricted range. (See Section V)

THE JACKS

Probably the strongest, meanest, orneriest fish that a man can get hold of on his bait casting rod is a Jack Crevalle. Most fishermen hate him with grudging admiration. He is not a good food fish, the meat being dark and oily, but he is a tackle wrecker. A 5-pound Jack feels like a 20-pound fish. His flat, powerful body is hard to turn, and he fights a fast, powerful underwater battle. Even after he is whipped, he will bark and curse the angler in fish language.

The other Jacks are small fish taken largely with cut bait or natural bait by still fishing around reefs, bays, piers, old wrecks, or similar locations, and less frequently by trolling with artificial lures, minnows, or cut bait.

MACKEREL

The Mackerel and the Spanish Mackerel are rather erratic fish which appear offshore in the north Atlantic during summer when they are taken by trolling or occasionally by still fishing, usually with bait or artificial jigs or spoons. When abundant, they furnish good sport for those who get into the schools. The Mackerel is more abundant further north, while the Spanish Mackerel is the more southern fish.

The Pacific Mackerel, found in the southern California waters from Monterey Bay south, is much like the east coast Mackerel. Like the others, it appears irregularly in large schools, but is most frequent in summer. In California it is one of the most popular game fish, as it will hit all kinds of lures and baits, and provides excellent sport when taken on light tackle. (See Section V)

MARLIN

Marlin are among the most prized of all the big game fishes of the sea, and must be sought out with special equipment and boats. They are most common from Martha's Vineyard south to Florida and Bahama waters. Blue Marlin is more abundant off Long Island than off Florida. Striped Marlin furnishes the major part of the marlin fishing in California. These great fish are found also in Mexican and South American waters. Few anglers have much chance to take these magnificent fighting fish. (See Section V)

MULLET

Mullet, widely known as a desirable and abundant food fish of southern waters, have never been considered as sport fish. However, with the application of fly fishing methods in salt water, fishermen on both coasts find that these small fish can furnish excellent sport on very light tackle. In addition to coastal waters, mullet also furnish much sport in the Salton Sea of southern California. (See Section V)

PERCH

Sea Perch, also called Surf Fish, all bear living young. There are many species found in Pacific Coast waters. They are important for surf fishermen and are usually taken on cut bait, fishing from the rocks or piers, or from boats. They furnish an important part of the sport for shore fishermen. (See Section V)

POLLACK

Pollack, also known as Coalfish, Boston Bluefish, is sought on the Atlantic Coast by trolling or by drifting while using casting rods. It is most abundant from Long Island north where it is taken on either cut bait, squid, clams, or with feathered lures or spoons. (See Section V)

POMPANO

Pompano, including the Permit, the African Pompano in Florida, and the quite different California Pompano, are all much prized food and game fish. Florida fishermen have developed quite a specialized form of angling for the Permit, or Great Pompano; and the smaller Pacific Pompano, which belongs to an entirely different family, is very highly prized by West Coast sportsmen. This latter is caught by still fishing with small hooks baited with cut bait. (See Section V)

PORGY

Porgy, or Scup, belong to another group that is somewhat erratic in their appearance, particularly the more northern species. It sometimes appears in enormous schools in summer. When it does, it is largely a small boy's fish in shallow water. The porgies are all bottom feeders and are taken in much the same way. They are not a first-class game fish, except that they do offer a lot of sport to bottom fishermen whenever they are present, and fill in many otherwise blank days.

ROCKFISH

Rockfish in a variety of species and under an endless variety of local names are found from Alaska to the Gulf of California and are present off rocky shores and reefs throughout the year. They form an important feature of the sport fishery in California and to a less extent on the Oregon Coast. They are taken largely by still fishing with cut or live bait, although at times they readily take spoons, plugs, and wobblers, either trolled or cast.

If judged by the volume of fish landed, they are probably one of the most important groups along the Pacific Coast. They offer an almost endless variation of color and form, and no one fishing these waters can be sure what the next fish landed will be. In fact, a good catch taken by still fishing is likely to contain a startling variety of these and other fish.

SAILFISH

Sailfish, both in the Atlantic and Pacific, are a highly valued game fish that are rather erratic in their appearance. They are found most frequently off Florida and off the coasts of Mexico. They occasionally appear farther north in California. These are usually taken by trolling; some fishermen locate them by sight before beginning to troll. They are taken by trolling with live bait or occasionally with artificial lures. (See Section V)

SHEEPSHEAD

The Sheepshead is usually found close to reefs, rocks, or jetties, taken by still fishing by crab, shrimp, cut bait, etc. In the north, it is a summer fish, but found the year around in Florida.

The Sheepshead in California, or California Redfish, belongs to an entirely different family. It is found from Monterey south, and is taken by bait fishermen using whole or cut bait. It is more frequently taken in winter in these waters, but in neither area are Sheepshead an important game fish. (See Section V)

SNAPPERS

Snappers are another group of tropical fish which are found in the Gulf of Mexico and in Florida waters. They furnish good still fishing with natural baits. Some occasionally take cast artificial lures. They are not generally important as game fish, although catching them is much enjoyed by those who have an opportunity to fish for them. (See Section V)

SHARKS

The big Sharks are most abundant outside of North American waters, although a few are taken. They are sought with special big game fish rigs, and especially equipped boats. Those taken include the Tiger, Thresher, Hammerhead, Mako, Maneater, and Porbeagle Sharks. Trollers or still fishermen also occasionally take the smaller sharks along both coasts, but they are not usually considered game fish. (See Section V)

SNOOK (or Robalo)

Snook, or Robalo as it is known in Mexico, is taken along bays and passes along the Florida Coast and along the Gulf Coast. It is a major sport fish in some Mexican rivers which it ascends for some distance.

The Snook is finally being recognized as one of the best game fish that swims. He will hit almost any kind of a lure—spoon, feather, or plug—and when he comes up for a surface lure, he really puts his heart into it. Once hooked, he puts up a great fight, leaping like a Smallmouth, boring down and away like a Walleye, and refusing to quit until he has exhausted every ounce of strength. And, as an old guide once said, "Most Snook are cross-eyed. They're watchin' that plug with one eye and pickin' out a mangrove root with the other!"

In the opinion of experienced fishermen, a Snook is far faster and stronger, pound for pound, than a Muskellunge. When a man whips a 25-pound Snook on orthodox fresh-water bait-casting tackle, he knows he has done something. And when the fish is skinned and the fillets come on the table, there's no better food.

Recommended Snook lures are Creek Chub Darter, South Bend Bass-Oreno, Pflueger Pal-O-Mine, Heddon River Runt. As is true with most salt-water fish, Snook seem to prefer silver-flash, red-and-white, or yellow-and-red combinations. The rainbow finish plugs are also good. A small Japanese feather lure is usually very effective on Snook, as is a drone spoon.

Snook are fond of lying under overhanging mangroves, around old pilings and bridges, and under submerged logs. As in Black Bass fishing, accuracy in presenting a lure is very important. A Snook lying under mangroves may refuse to hit a plug which falls a foot short of his shady lurking spot. This is not to say that he does not occasionally come out with a rush for a plug that strikes the water six feet short. The fact remains, however that a plug caster who can consistently drop his lure close to the bushes will take more of these fish than a less accurate fisherman.

Since Snook have razor-sharp edges on their cheeks and gill covers, a short wire leader is essential. This can be made of light piano wire and need not be over a foot in length. Heavy Nylon can be used, but will fray after repeated encounters with edged gill covers.

Unfortunately, this fine fish has been greatly reduced in numbers by commercial fishermen who operate specially designed power seines. Snook will cut right through a gill net of light twine, but are taken in small mesh nets, made of heavily tarred heavy twine. They are operated during May, June, and July when the fish are schooled up, spawning, and often ten thousand pounds are taken at a haul. Since the range of this fish is limited, it is obvious that some protection is needed to guarantee its future. It is to be hoped that both Florida and Texas will realize the value of the Snook as a sports attraction before it is too late.

On the Florida Gulf Coast, Snook are rarely caught north of New Port Richey, as they are strictly warm water fish. There are always a few individuals to be seen in Nature's Giant Fish Bowl, the natural aquarium at Homosassa Springs, but they are rarely caught in the Homosassa River, which flows out of the great spring to the Gulf. Their presence in the spring is undoubtedly due to the constant water temperature—seventy-four degrees.

On the east coast of Florida, Snook are caught as far north as Daytona Beach, but the best fishing is much farther south, in such spots as Banana River, Haulover Canal, Sebastian Inlet, and the canals behind Stuart, Palm Beach, and Miami.

SPOT

Spot, or Salt Water Bream, is a common Atlantic Coast fish in all bays and inlets, and is found largely around pilings, wharves, and rocky points. It is taken largely by still fishing with blood worms, shrimp, or cut bait. It is a small fish but does afford some sport to still fishermen. (See Section V)

SWORDFISH

Swordfish is another of the most highly rated big game fish. It is taken by trolling, using mackerel, bluefish, or squid for bait. It is also harpooned by some, although this practice is increasingly frowned upon by good sportsmen.

Boats specializing in Swordfishing often patrol the water until sighting a fish before putting out lines. This type of fishing requires special boats and special equipment for which the average fisherman is not prepared. (See Section V)

TARPON

Large Tarpon are taken by trolling with the usual feathered jigs, spoons, or plugs. Many consider them the greatest of all game fish. The smaller individuals are among the most spectacular fighters that American waters have to offer when taken on light casting equipment.

When using light casting rods in the creeks and bays of Florida's lower west coast, the angler never knows what will hit his plug. Mangrove Snappers, Schooner-rig Catfish, Pompano, Sharks, and small Jewfish are occasionally caught. As a matter of fact, *big* Jewfish will often hit the plug and occasionally will come up out of a deep hole to take a hooked, struggling Snook or Redfish. At such times the angler is helpless. A two or three hundred-pound Jewfish just inhales both fish and plug, then settles back under the snags.

It is not unusual to have Sharks and big Tarpon take smaller fish that have been hooked. This may happen far up one of the big rivers, such as Broad, Lostman's, or Shark, ten or fifteen miles from the salt water. If a big Shark is hooked, the angler simply points the rod tip at the fish, tightens his thumb on the spool, and lets the Shark cut off or break the line at once. But a Tarpon is a different story. It is possible to whip a "silver king" of over a hundred pounds on casting tackle, provided the angler has plenty of time, a good man at the oars, and is lucky.

There is probably no fishing on earth that is more hair-raising than tangling with big Tarpon on fresh water tackle, particularly in narrow creeks. When a 100-pound Tarpon comes up and smashes a surface plug 6 feet from the boat, the angler will never be the same again. It does something to everyone. It's exciting but it's scary business. And it's dangerous. For when these mighty fish feel those gang hooks, they go crazy, leaping 8 and 10 feet clear of the water in whatever direction they happen to be headed.

When a big Tarpon lands in a man's skiff, something or somebody is going to get hurt. The danger is not only from the power of the fish's tail, but from the ganghooks of the plug. It would not be fun to be hooked to the same plug with a 100-pound Tarpon—especially if the victim went overboard with him.

In casting for big Tarpon, the fisherman should never take his eyes off his plug until it is out of water, reeled up to the rod tip. Tarpon have a habit of following a lure, then smashing it as the fisherman starts to lift it from the water. This has caused many broken rods and weakened hearts! A man should choose the spot for his next cast *after* he has retrieved the plug, not *while* he is retrieving it.

Popping, darting surface lures are extremely effective, particularly in the calm inland waters. The plug should be played fairly fast and with plenty of action. Occasionally these great fish seem to prefer a deep-running lure and will hit red-and-white, silver-flash, yellow-and-red, or rainbow finish plugs best. They will also take a feather jig eagerly.

There is not much use in casting for Tarpon unless the fish or the tell-tale patches of bubbles which show where they have rolled can be seen. Generally a fast-running tide is better than slack water, although they often hit well at dead low water. High tide is rarely good, especially in the rivers.

Tarpon should be released, if possible, to fight again another day. This is, of course, difficult to do in the case of a big fish caught on a plug. The best method is to use a release hook instead of a gaff. This release hook is merely a gaff with a rope handle instead of a wooden one. Bring the fish alongside, slip the hook into his mouth and snatch it through his lower jaw. Then *cut* the hooks loose. It is extremely dangerous to try to grasp the plug.

Fortunately the plug caster rarely has to worry about releasing a Tarpon. The Tarpon usually attends to this on the first jump or two. Out of a hundred fish hooked, fifty will throw the plug on the first jump, twenty-five on the second or third jump, and fifteen more will be lost in some way or other. Any angler bringing to boat ten out of a hundred is good.

Innumerable devices have been tried to overcome the difficulty of hooking the "silver king"—single hook rigs, double hook rigs, and other kinds of rigs. But everything depends on the fish itself.

If the hooks happened to be turned right when a Tarpon grabs the plug and clamps down on it, the hook will be set. If the points of the hooks are against those bony plates, he couldn't be hooked with a trace chain; and certainly not with a fifteen or eighteen-pound silk or Nylon line.

Most anglers have little conception of the amount of pull they can exert with their little fresh water rods and lines. Try it sometime. Let a friend take out thirty yards of line and hold the plug between his thumb and forefinger. Then try to pull it away from him. It can't be done. It can't even be done with a surf rod and heavy line.

So when a big Tarpon hits, he'll either hook himself or he won't. It's more fun if he doesn't, for one can jump a dozen or two more in the two hours it would take to whip one big one. But if a fish is hooked solidly, don't try to fight him for the first few minutes. Let him furnish the fireworks, keeping just enough thumb pressure on the reel spool to keep it from backlashing. It is assumed, of course, that an orthodox, level-winding fresh water reel is being used. Star drag reels don't count with real dyed-in-the-wool plug casters.

And when the fish comes into the air, six feet of gleaming silver, don't gasp and tighten on him. Give to him. Lower the rod tip. "Bow to your fish," as the Canadian salmon guides say. Otherwise he'll snap that little line at the first shake of his massive head. If he throws the plug, don't worry. A good sportsman doesn't want to kill him anyway—and there are thousands more to give battle, such battle as one never forgets.

TAUTOG

Tautog is a well-known North Atlantic fish. It is taken off the rocky points, wrecks, piers, and similar locations by bottom fishing with small crabs, sea worms, or minnows. It is abundant in the summer up to September and goes offshore in the winter. It is not a great game fish, but does supply much sport to shore fishermen.

TENPOUNDER

Tenpounder, also called Bonyfish, Big-eyed Herring, and various other names, is most common in Florida. It is found in the coastal rivers and inlets, and is present the year around in southern Florida. It can be taken by still fishing or by casting.

It is not widely known as a game fish because of its limited distribution, but many anglers believe that the Tenpounder (Chiro) is the hardest-striking fish that swims—pound for pound. It hits with incredible speed, as many a fisherman who has had his knuckles barked by the reel handles can testify. For its size this slim, silvery little fish can make prodigious leaps, often traveling 10 or 15 feet laterally. It is an ideal fish for a fly rod man. It is not a good food fish, being very bony. As Uncle George Rawls once said, "I'd rather eat a paper of pins!"

TUNA

The Bluefin Tuna, one of the prized big game fishes of the world, is found in many waters. It, like other big game fish, must be taken with special tackle and specially equipped boats. It is, however, abundant enough to provide great tournaments. (See Section V)

This and all other Tunas are taken by trolling with feathered jigs or live bait. California has not only the Bluefin, but the Pacific Yellowtail, which is taken by the same methods.
(See Section V)

WAHOO

Wahoo are common only in south Florida. They are both strong and swift, and put up a wonderful battle when hooked. They are usually taken by trolling bait in or near the Gulf Stream and may be hooked during the time Bonito, Cero, and other fish are sought.

WEAKFISH

Weakfish, including the Spotted Weakfish of more southern waters, are one of the most popular salt-water sport fish. Their popularity is indicated by the great variety of common names applied to them. Squeteague is a common name in the north; Sea Trout, Gray Trout, and various other designations as trout, are also common appellations along the Atlantic Coast; with the word *spotted* or *speckled* before them, similar names are used for the Spotted Weakfish further to the south.

These are one of the most important of all salt water game fish within their range. Probably the greatest number of them are taken by still fishing and trolling, but they are favorites among surf casters and bait casters as well. They are abundant enough to offer sport to a great number of fishermen. In the total volume of fish landed, they are one of the more important salt-water sport fish of the inshore waters, and rank next to Striped Bass, Channel Bass, and Bluefish with surf casters and bait casters in northern waters. They have more competition in Florida and Mexico from other fish, but they are still important.

The Spotted Weakfish (Sea Trout) is more apt to be found on shallow, grassy flats than it is in the deep, swift channels. Where depth will permit, a red spotted clothespin-type plug will get excellent results and a Creek Chub Darter No. 2018 is a killer in shallow water. So is the red-and-white and red-and yellow South Bend Bass-Oreno.

Sea Trout are poor fighters, hitting hard but giving up easily. Their meat, however, is fine textured and sweet.

SECTION VII

MISCELLANEOUS TOPICS

SPORTSMANSHIP IN FISHING

Sportsmanship is that elusive quality that sets most fishermen apart from the fish killers and fish hogs. It is a quality that is much easier to recognize, or to find lacking, in a man after spending a few hours of fishing with him on ocean, lake, or stream than it is to define.

Many centuries ago man fished only for one reason—to catch fish to eat—and the means was secondary to the end. Traps, poisons, spears, nets, and any other devices that would put fish in the cooking pot were employed. Then, as the stratification of society evolved in the development of civilization, someone, somewhere along the line, discovered that fishing was a pleasant diversion for people who no longer had to fish to eat, and the world's first sport fisherman emerged on the scene. The event occurred before the time of Cleopatra, since Egyptian pictographs show nobles and royalty lounging on barges and angling in the waters of the Nile. To imagine that the demigods of the ancient world fished for any reason but recreation strains belief, since they were in a position to command the finest foods in the then known world without lifting a single finger.

As civilization spread across the Mediterranean and into Europe, much the same situation prevailed. The poor still fished for food, but many of the wealthy fished for pleasure. By the time of the Renaissance the noble land-owning "sportsmen" had reserved most of the better fishing streams for their personal use at the exclusion of the non-sporting and perennially hungry rabble. The Salmon, in particular, was considered a "noble" fish and in most countries only the aristocracy were permitted to kill it in inland waters. Poaching Salmon was a capital crime ranking only a little below high treason.

Sport fishing, therefore, began as a form of recreation for "gentlemen," in the then accepted sense of the term, since only the wealthy could afford the time for recreation. With the emergence of a middle class around the time of the Reformation, this distinction broke down considerably, and among the merchants, craftsmen, and professional men who constituted the new class there were still some who fished primarily to supplement their diets and men, like Izaak Walton, who fished primarily for pleasure. The latter group constituted the new sportsmen. Historically, at least the first qualification of a sportsman is that he fish for recreation rather than for food or profit.

Even at this point we run into some interesting ramifications. If a fisherman releases every fish that he brings to net, there can be no doubt that he is fishing only for sport. But is he lower in the scale of sportsmanship than the man who releases only half of the fish he catches and eats the remainder? The first man may release the fish because he dislikes the task of cleaning them or because he has not cultivated a taste for fish. Again, is the city angler, who may get two or three weekends of good fishing in the course of a season, a poorer sportsman if he brings home a legal limit of fish on each trip than the man who lives by a good fishing stream and takes only a third of his limit each time he goes out?

Most fishermen would consider that, under usual circumstances, there would be little difference in the degree of sportsmanship inherent in these individuals, provided all of the fish taken are put to use. The man who kills fish merely to satisfy his ego and who throws his catch in the garbage pail, on the other hand, even though he might take fewer fish, would rate far down on the scale.

Much too would depend upon the type of water in which the angler does his fishing. Suppose that these anglers were fishing on a small pond in which only a hundred or so trout or bass had been recently stocked and that all were aware of this fact. Under such conditions the degree of sportsmanship would be in opposite relationship to the number of fish that each man killed. The removal of two or three state-wide limits from such a pond would reduce the fishing opportunities for others close to zero.

In large waters, the state fish and game laws are a fair criterion of the limits of self-indulgence that may not be exceeded before a man can be called unsportsmanlike. Usually, although not always, special regulations protect the fish resources where special conditions apply. Anyone who knowingly violates the fish laws is a criminal and automatically sacrifices his right to the title of sportsman.

There are complications, however, even in the matter of self-indulgence. Up until a few years ago, youngsters who aspired to become sportsmen were taught that undersized fish—Perch, Bluegills, and other panfish as well as game species—should be carefully released to grow and reproduce their kind. Fishery biologists in recent years have proven that overpopulations of stunted panfish are a threat to future fishing and now encourage fishermen to take all of the rapidly reproducing warm-water species that they can catch. Creel limits and size limits have been removed entirely for panfish in most states and greatly liberalized in the remainder. The man leaving a lake with a string of two hundred 5-inch Bluegills, who a few years ago would have been branded a fish hog, emerges as the fair-haired hero of the biologists in the topsy-turvy world of today!

Most real sportsmen still find such spectacles distasteful and prefer to leave the control of undesirable fishes to more efficient and more mechanical means. If control is needed, the sportsman, with a clear conscience, can scuff through the redds of Bluegills or lend assistance to state biologists in fish poisoning and reclamation programs, but you will never find him laden with strings of undersized fish. Moderation in the personal take is one of the key signs of the sportsman.

Moving into salt water we find another set of circumstances. With a few exceptions, principally with species such as Striped Bass and Salmon and a few other game fishes in some states, there are no legal restrictions on the taking of marine fishes. The salt-water fisherman can take as many fish as opportunity presents as often as he wants, and his catch often will have high commercial value. The sale of fresh-water game fish, with few exceptions, is a serious violation of the law.

On salt water it is much easier to distinguish the sportsman from the fish hog, especially in dealing with species of little food value, such as the Tarpon and Bonefish. No one objects if the angler wants to bring back an especially large specimen for mounting, for measurement, for record, or for photographs, but killing whole strings of average and subaverage specimens and leaving them to rot is little short of criminal. Much more dramatic pictures can be taken while the fish is fighting and being released. The release of Bonefish, Tarpon, Marlin, and Sailfish is now being encouraged by most of the guide associations in waters where these fish are most prevalent, and the idea is one that deserves wider currency. Most of the associations and some chambers of commerce award attractive "release certificates" suitable for framing to sportsmen who free their catches. Many fishing clubs and guides now cooperate with scientific associations in tagging fish taken on sport tackle and released to fight again.

In dealing with more edible species of fish, especially those that may have high commercial value, the problem is often complicated by local custom. If the fisherman is on his own and fishing from his own boat or from shore, he is a real sportsman if he releases most of his catch except for trophy fish and those needed for home consumption. If he loads himself down with more fish than he can use at every opportunity, his sportsmanship is more than open to question.

In some coastal areas, however, it is customary for anglers to dispose of their catch by sale, even though the fish may be taken by accepted sportfishing methods. Here the dividing line between the sport fisherman and the commercial fisherman is thin. In favor of the practice is the fact that it helps anglers defray expenses during the sometimes long waits between schools of fish and that it permits the fisherman of modest means to engage more often in his favorite sport. Too, it is a logical means of disposing of extra fish, like Barracuda and large Bluefish, which are neither easy nor safe to remove from a hook with bare hands until they have been subdued by a blow on the head from a "priest" or billy, although these fish can be released by cutting the hook. The danger, from the ethical standpoint, when such customs prevail, is that the fisherman may become so engrossed in the profits that he ceases to fish for sport. Little more than a change in attitude is needed to move him over the line into the field of commercial fishing.

This is not to say that a commercial fisherman cannot be a sportfisherman, but it is difficult for him to be both at the same time. As a businessman, he must kill fish to make a living. Taking a busman's holiday with light tackle on a trout stream or even in pursuit of the same species for which he fishes for a living, the commercial fisherman might be a sportsman of the highest caliber.

Another complication arises in salt-water fishing when the angler hires a guide and charters a boat. In some waters it is the custom for the guide or boat operator to retain ownership of any fish caught, although he usually gives the angler a generous share of the catch. Any fisherman who tries to release fish under such circumstances is likely to have a cold, rough trip back to port. Misunderstanding can be avoided by determining beforehand exactly what the local custom is. If the sportsman wants to release fish and the guide is accustomed to keeping the lion's share of the catch for sale, the angler should be prepared to compensate him for the difference.

Still another complication arises in regard to participation in fishing contests and tournaments. These originated largely to add spice to the sport, but by the time the publicity agents of some local chambers of commerce had finished with them, many had degenerated into fish-killing contests.

Like many other new complicated things, the fishing competition had modest beginnings. Probably ever since two or three men first got together to fish for sport, small side wagers were made on who would catch the most fish or the largest. The winners usually had a free meal or drink at the local tavern at the expense of the losers. The fishing pool, a fund to which all fishermen on a party boat contribute small equal stipends, probably was the next development. Again, the man who caught the biggest fish or the greatest number of pounds collected the entire sum. There was, and is nothing wrong with these practices. Everyone in the party is fishing on equal terms, and little more than the element of luck dictates the winner.

Field and Stream Magazine started its fishing contest in 1910, making it the oldest continuous national contest of its kind in North America, if not in the world. The magazine offered relatively modest prizes in merchandise for the largest game fish of various species caught in American waters. Rules regulating the taking of the fish entered in the contest have always been rigid, and for many years only specimens of the Salmonids taken on artificial lures could be entered, although a separate class for those taken with live bait was originated later. For entering a trophy fish above a specified weight, the fisherman receives an attractive badge to wear on his fishing hat.

This contest, competitions operated under the rules of the International Game Fish Association, and others operated under similar rules, nationally or locally, are above reproach. The commercial incentive is either non-existent or insufficient to warrant a man fishing only for the prize. The catching of a prize-winning fish still is largely a matter of luck against fantastic odds. The *Field and Stream* contest and IGFA approved tournaments, also play an important scientific role in gathering data on fish growth and distribution and fishing methods and techniques.

Abuses, however, often can be found in some local fishing tournaments. The first of these probably originated with individual hotel or resort owners who offered cash or merchandise prizes to guests who caught the largest or most fish during the season. This was a useful advertising gimmick, since the publicity often made headlines in statewide newspapers and magazines. It was so good that publicity men with little interest in the fishing itself soon adopted it as their own.

They approached local chambers of commerce in well-known fishing areas and convinced them that the world of sport fishing would beat a path to their door if the prizes were made large enough and the contest were compressed within a few days. By soliciting local merchants and businessmen they were able to offer cash prizes up to thousands of dollars, new automobiles, and cabin cruisers.

As an advertising stunt, this often worked. It brought in hordes of fishermen, but most of them were not fishing for sport. They were gamblers avidly seeking a jackpot. This is the sort of fishing contest with which most sportsmen want nothing to do.

Similar abuses have marred the development of the once popular children's fishing derby. As originally conceived, this idea was good—to bring children, especially those in towns and cities, close to nature and to teach them the fundamentals of sportsmanship. Unfortunately, too often it had the opposite effect. For a while, state fishery administrators encouraged this idea, since it seemed to be a useful method of reducing overpopulations of stunted fish in a worthy cause. As the idea spread, however, the fish departments often found themselves under pressure to stock expensive hatchery fish expressly for the derbies, and their enthusiasm waned. A few states now prohibit the official fish agency from aiding such derbies or prohibit their staging completely, on the grounds that they encourage children to engage in unsportsmanlike fishing practices.

Competition, other than between man and fish, has no place in sport fishing except that entered into in a sense of cameraderie within a small homogeneous party of anglers. As soon as material gain becomes the primary motive, the fisherman is no longer fishing for sport and, by every definition, he is no longer a sportsman.

Motivation—that is, fishing for recreation rather than for meat or profit—was the first historic step in the development of sport fishing. The second step was method. As soon as man started to fish for pleasure, he soon discovered that some methods of fishing required greater skill and greater stealth than others. A single small hook, a light leader, and a wispy rod gave the fish a chance to break free and to fight longer than a heavy line armed with a large treble hook.

Judging the sportsmanship of an individual by the method of fishing or tackle that he uses, however, is a very touchy thing and not always entirely fair. The first objective of the fisherman, regardless of protestations to the contrary, is to catch fish. He may handicap himself by using ultra-light tackle. He may release every fish that he catches. But he expects or hopes to catch fish every time he goes out. Otherwise there would be little point in his traveling hundreds or thousands of miles to engage in the sport. He could exercise his casting arm in the backyard or on fishless waters nearer home and get close to nature on nearby nature walks. Obviously the sport fisherman wants to catch fish, expects to catch fish, and enjoys catching fish, or he would obtain his recreation in other ways.

As a sportsman travels from one part of the country to another, he is sometimes horrified at the methods employed by fishermen in other waters. His first inclination is to regard the local anglers who call themselves sportsmen as little better than fish hogs. But after trying his own methods a while, he finds that they fail to catch anything while the natives are taking all of the fish. The visitor has two choices. He can stop fishing, if he finds that the methods that produce fish are entirely distasteful to him, or he can adopt a method that is similar to that used locally.

Take the Striped Bass as an example. Along portions of the southern coast, they are taken regularly on light spinning outfits or fly tackle close to shore. A fisherman accustomed to taking these gamey fish in this manner moving north to Chesapeake Bay in the late fall would find the local fishermen dredging the bottom with 8-ounce sinkers to catch fish weighing from 2 to 3 pounds. Local fishermen have found that this is the only way to take fish lying in 30 to 70 feet of water at this time of year. The little spinning outfit of the visitor would not even place its half-ounce bucktail within sight of a fish.

If he traveled to the New England coast in early spring, the southern angler would find the local anglers using heavy surf rods and casting whole squids and eels up to three feet long. With his light rod, he might not be able to reach within 50 yards of the nearest fish. If he did, he would find that the small bait or lure that he must use is ignored by the Stripers.

On the other hand, if he traveled to the same waters at other times of the year, he might feel right at home with his light tackle. In May and June the stripers in Chesapeake Bay move in close to shore, and the same anglers who were using heavy sinkers will be using tackle not greatly dissimilar from his own. In the same month there is a large run of school Stripers in New England waters, well into the estuaries and tidal inlets where the light spinning rig is ideally suited for use.

On inland waters similar circumstances often prevail. There are many fishermen who regard the dry fly and the light fly rod as the only sporting way of catching fish. Nearly every fisherman who has developed skill with the fly rod will agree that taking fish on a dry fly is the most sporting type of fishing there is, but few except the most dedicated purist would agree that it is the *only* sporting method for all fishing. This attitude is snobbery, which itself is a violation of the rules of sportsmanship. The man who uses the dry fly exclusively will be able to fish only when conditions are suitable to the tackle that he uses. When conditions are not right for fly tackle other methods must be used. In early April when the weather is cold and most streams are roily and murky with the spring runoff, dry-fly fishing becomes a fruitless exercise. In such waters, a man uses worms or other live bait or spoons and plugs or he catches no fish at all. The real purist will not fish under such conditions, but if he is a sportsman, he will not criticize those who do. There can be very real degrees of skill even among bait fishermen.

Later in the season, when the Trout streams clear, the dry fly fisherman may outfish the worm-dunker by ten to one. The advantage is now all with the flyfisherman, but very few of them would consider changing to night-crawlers in the middle of a fly hatch to decrease their chances of hooking a fish.

There are, however, at least several very sound arguments in favor of fishing with artificial lures whenever possible. Greater skill is required to catch fish consistently on artificial lures. Not only must the artificial fly or plug be presented in a manner calculated to stimulate the striking response of a good game fish, but the angler, in most cases, must respond immediately to the strike or the fish is lost. With live bait, the fish often hooks itself. This makes fishing with artificial lures a much more rewarding experience since it increases the challenge to, and therefore the sport of, the angler. Secondly, fish taken on artificial lures usually fight harder and longer than those taken with live bait since they are almost always hooked in the lip. Many fish taken on live bait will have the hook imbedded in their gills or gullet. By the same token, it is much easier to release a fish taken on artificials, with some hope of its surviving.

The use of live baitfish has ruined many once-fine fishing waters by introducing undesirable competitors to the game fish. In many states and provinces the use of live fish for bait is prohibited by law for this reason rather than to impose a more sportsmanlike type of fishing on their anglers.

Several simple rules can be made for fishing in the most sportsmanlike manner:

1. *Use artificial lures, whenever they can be used to take fish consistently enough to maintain interest, and use the smallest lure that can be used practically on the fish you are seeking.*

A single-hook fly in the smaller sizes obviously provides much more sport than a heavy plug armed with three sets of treble hooks, but in some instances the heavy plug may be the only practical lure for taking fish consistently. At other times live bait may be the only practical lure.

2. *Use the lightest tackle that is practical under prevailing circumstances.*

Sport in fishing is almost directly proportionate to the lightness of the tackle, from the rod down to the leader, but featherweight tackle is not always practical for all types of fishing. The size of the local fish, the depth at which they customarily lie, the wind and weather, and the prevalence of obstructions and weeds are only a few factors that govern the practical limits of tackle weight in a given fishing ground.

3. *Take the fish as near the surface as possible.*

Nearly everyone agrees that fishing on the surface with floating flies, bass bugs and popping lures is more excting than bouncing a heavy sinker along the bottom of a deep lake. The fish can be seen as it strikes, adding to the excitement and the sport, but if the fish are hugging the bottom, the sportsman can use a weighted line with a clear conscience.

If anyone follows these rules, he can expect to catch fish and feel no qualms about the quality of his sportsmanship, regardless of what the dry-fly purist might think of it. The purist is a specialist and not a general fisherman, and he needs a special set of circumstances to enjoy his sport.

If a man is invited as the guest of a business associate or acquaintance to fish private waters and especially if he is the guest of a fishing club, he should familiarize himself beforehand of any restrictions that might be imposed by custom or rule on tackle. There are exclusive clubs where, if any uninitiated guest were to show up with live bait or the lightest of spinning tackle, he would be committing a serious social error. Many such clubs demand that their members use fly tackle only and some even specify that barbless hooks be employed. Knowledge of customs such as these beforehand can save a lot of embarrassment.

Consideration for Others. Beyond these considerations, sportsmanship is merely a matter of good manners and the application of the Golden Rule. Many men fish only for sport and use the most sporting tackle, but they still fall short of being entitled to the title of sportsman. They are deficient in the qualities that make the word "sportsman" synonymous with "gentleman."

Boisterousness, loud-mouthed talk, and excessive drinking may have their places in life, but not in fishing as most sportsmen think of it. Fishing is recreation, and men have a perfect right to interpret that word in any way they want and to find recreation as they see fit so long as they do not interfere with the rights of others. A homogeneous party of friends away from it all at an isolated wilderness camp can engage in all the horseplay they want, frighten the owls and loons with the caterwauling of transistor radios, and engage in practical jokes. If there are other parties camped close by, however, or if the party is made up of men of different temperament and background, the more exuberant members should make a point to check their own exhilaration. Many men, if not most of them, fish in such areas because they want to get peace and solitude, and there is little of either when camped with or near a group of noisy neighbors.

If a fly fisherman is cautiously stalking a rising fish, the sportsman will give him a wide berth. The non-sportsman will barge in beside him and cast to the same fish.

If a bank or boat fisherman is having good luck in a particular spot, the sportsman will congratulate him and keep his distance, the fish hog will crowd in and try to share in the bounty.

If another fisherman is in difficulty, the sportsman will do what he can to help him. The non-sportsman will welcome the reduced competition and go his own way.

Any of hundreds of similar hypothetical cases could be cited, but in every case the sportsman follows the dictum of the Golden Rule. The non-Sportsman is out for only one man—himself.

The same code of behavior should apply as well to the non-fishing public with whom the fisherman comes in contact. One of the worst nuisances on the fishing grounds is the litterbug who leaves trash around his campsite and who uses the lake or stream as a garbage disposal. Empty tin cans and bottles weigh much less on the way out than they did filled on the way in, and it is an easy matter to flatten tins with the flat of an axe or a stout rock for ease in carrying. Bottles should never be thrown in the water, since they are hazards to waders, swimmers, or other fishermen. If a convenient trash receptacle cannot be found, they should be packed out as they were brought in. If cans must be disposed of, they should be flattened, burned to hasten rusting, and buried. All papers should be burned, and garbage and fish entrails are best disposed of by burning and burial.

One of the marks of a sportsman is that he always leaves a campsite or picnic area a little neater than the way he found it. If every fisherman conducted himself in this way, fishing would be a much more enjoyable sport, and much more fishing territory would remain open. A number of state surveys have found that a major cause of posting of stream and lake banks is that the landowners dislike having their property littered by fishermen.

Caution with fire in the woods and fields is a necessity and, again, the mark of a sportsman. Smoking materials should be disposed of with care, and every precaution taken that cooking fires or campfires do not escape.

The sportsman conducts himself as a guest on private lands at all times and respects the rights and privileges of the owner. He is careful not to break down fences, not to leave open gates through which livestock may escape, and he asks permission before fishing private waters.

The Rewards of Sportsmanship. With populations building rapidly throughout America, the solitude that many fishermen seek in fishing is becoming an increasingly rare commodity, and pressures on fishery resources and fishing facilities are increasing.

Fishing, being one of the most cosmopolitan of sports, attracts people from every walk of life and from every stratum of society. There is no hope, therefore, that the unsportsmanlike element will be eliminated from it completely. Fish hogs, fish slaughterers, and even some hoodlums probably always will be present in the ranks of anglers. Because of its infinite variety, fishing attracts morons as well as geniuses, even some criminals as well as men of the highest moral and ethical standards. There is little than can be done to eliminate the unsavory minority elements completely, but the great mass of fishermen today, like those of any cross section of society, are decent, law-abiding people, and the majority are sportsmen.

Whatever shortcomings the average fisherman may have as a sportsman usually are the result of inexperience, local custom and misplaced values. In some communities, the size of the catch rather than the size of the individual fish brought in remains the mark of the "real fisherman." This has already changed in many places through the leadership and example of sportsmen themselves, and it has been abetted by guides who formerly encouraged their customers to kill every fish they could catch to give publicity to the local fishing. They have found that this enlightened attitude provided better publicity and attracted a more desirable clientele.

Sportsmen themselves have found that by refraining from killing fish they improve their own fishing opportunities. Legal limits apply only to fish killed, not to fish caught and released.

With Trout and other cold-water fishes, reproduction and rates of growth are both much lower than with the warm-water species. Although biologists have found that it is impossible to "fish out" a warm-water lake, as most fishermen believed a few years ago, the removal of too many large specimens of the predatory game fish can cause a population imbalance in favor of the prolific panfish. From the standpoint of the fisherman the result is the same as "fishing out" the lake.

Therefore when the fisherman releases a legal-sized Bass, Trout, or Pike, which preys upon the prolific panfish, he is helping to maintain the lake in balance. He is also sparing for future fishing pleasure a game fish that should be larger, heavier, and a better trophy the next time it takes a lure.

There are waters that, for practical purposes, can be fished out in the literal sense of the term. This is especially true of "put-and-take" Trout waters which are stocked by state agencies or individual landowners. In most of them a very limited number of fish can be stocked, and many streams and ponds that are stocked will not carry fish through the warmer months. From the pragmatical standpoint any fish that are not caught before the waters warm up are wasted. If a given stretch of water will support a hundred Trout during the spring and the legal limit is ten Trout, however, there are only ten legal limits in that stretch of water, and after three or four limits have been taken, the fishing becomes slow no matter what means are employed. It is usually a simple matter for a skilled fisherman to take ten Trout on live bait from a stocked stream during the first few days of the season. The stream, in other words can produce quality fishing for only four or five fishermen who measure fishing quality in terms of a limit creel.

Those same hundred Trout, however, can provide recreation for at least two months for as many as one hundred sportsmen fishing with flies and releasing all or the majority of their catch. This is the principle behind the "Fish for Fun" program that is now being used on many waters in the national parks and on designated streams in some states. Under this system, the fisherman may catch all the Trout he wants, but he can kill only one, or none at all. Usually the rules specify that barbless hooks and artificial flies only be used to minimize injury to the fish released.

A more general adoption of this principle is being advocated by Trout Unlimited, 900 Lapeer Ave., Saginaw, Michigan. Its objectives are to encourage the fishing for sport, and to retain and restore Trout habitat, especially that which can maintain Trout throughout the year in a wild state rather than depending on put-and-take stocking. Since fishing of this kind is non-depleting of the resource, it can maintain heavy fishing pressure without damage at minimum cost. This is exactly what is needed today and it is what will be needed more in future years.

The same principles that apply to fresh-water Trout apply equally to other species using a relatively limited habitat both in fresh water and salt. The release of Bonefish, Sailfish, Tarpon, Pike and Muskellunge can enhance local sport fishing as long as the habitat remains unimpaired. More prolific species that are found in a wider range of habitat can be taken more frequently and in greater numbers without injury to the fishery, and the removal of large numbers often is beneficial to the survivors by eliminating competition.

Since World War II there has been a marked trend toward the use of lighter tackle for all kinds of fishing. Fly rods have become shorter and lighter, leaders finer, and flies smaller. Bait casting rods have become longer and capable of casting quarter-ounce lures instead of the once standard five-eighths-ounce plug. Fly rods and light spinning rods have replaced the stiff five-foot salt-water boat rod in many types of salt-water fishing, and 20 to 30-pound-test line has replaced the once-standard 54 and 60-pound lines in many types of salt-water big-game fishing. This trend is all to the good since it demonstrates a broadening of interest in fishing for sport rather than merely for meat.

The following of a rigid code of behavior in his dealings with fellow fishermen, the non-fishing public, and the fish themselves will become more necessary as time goes on. For purely selfish reasons if for no other, the fisherman should adopt such a code. The object of sport fishing is sport and recreation. The sportsman can attain these ends simply by fishing where there is a chance to catch fish; the non-sportsman's day is ruined unless he brings in a long string of dead fish. When the sportsman hooks a good fish, his object is a long hard fight; the non-sportsman's objective is to get the fish into the net, to the beach or to gaff as soon as possible.

As fishing pressures build up in the future, there may not be enough fishing opportunities to assure all fishermen unlimited strings of fish, but there will be excellent fishing for those who conduct themselves as sportsmen, and the more rigid they make their standards of sportsmanship, the greater their own sport will be.

BOWFISHING

Catching fish with a bow and arrow is a method that antedates civilization and one that is still used by primitive peoples throughout the more remote portions of the globe. Bowfishing for sport, however, is a very recent development, but it has already been developed to a high degree of refinement, as an offshoot of the resurgence of interest in hunting with one of man's earliest weapons. More than 30 states recognize bowfishing as a legitimate method of taking designated species of fish in fresh water, and, in most instances, a regular anglers license is required. State laws always should be consulted, however, since a number of states bar the bowfisherman from certain waters and some restrict the type of tackle that may be used. No state or province permits bowfishing for game fish, such as Salmon, Trout, or Bass and only a few permit the taking of members of the Pike Family.

The majority of the states and provinces, however, permit the taking of Carp, Buffalo, Garfish, Suckers, and similar rough fish by means of the bow, and used against the larger specimens of these species it can provide exciting sport. Unless the arrow strikes the spine or brain of the fish, the quarry is rarely killed outright and will fight almost as vigorously as if hooked by more conventional angling methods. Fish have simple nervous systems and are little affected by shock or pain. Since the actual fighting of the fish usually is done by handlining, this phase of the sport cannot be classified with dry-fly fishing, but a Carp weighing 15 pounds or more can put up a strong fight.

Sharks, Rays and Skates are legitimate quarry of the bowfisherman in salt water in most coastal waters, although again the state laws should be consulted. Even where legal, the use of arrows against sport fish should be avoided except in waters where harpooning is an accepted local practice.

Any bow capable of throwing an arrow accurately in a relatively flat trajectory for short distances is suitable for bowfishing, and those designed primarily for hunting are ideal. The best bows are now made by laminating and bonding layers of wood and fiberglass or other plastic. They possess tremendous cast compared to the solid wooden bows of a generation ago, and they are all but impervious to damage by wetting; nor will they develop a "set" or warp under prolonged use. A modern laminated bow with a drawing weight of 40 pounds will throw an arrow as far as many solid lemonwood or hickory bows of 80 pounds. Many states, in setting legal minimums of bowhunting equipment use the distance a bow will throw an arrow rather than drawing weight as the criterion. All bowfishing is done at short ranges and most fish are taken by this method at ranges of little more than 10 yards. Unless the fish are rolling above the surface or the archer is shooting from a high vantagepoint, shots at distances greater than this are usually impractical because the surface of the water deflects the arrow.

Whatever bow is used, it must be equipped with a reel of some kind, and many commercial models are available. The simplest are 5- or 6-inch drums of sheet metal, usually and preferably brass or aluminum, equipped with "feet" which may be taped or otherwise mounted to the limbs of the bow on either side of the grip. The line is coiled around the drum and held in place with a rubber band or spring clip and the arrow is sighted and shot through the center of the drum. Working on the principle of the fixed-spool of the spinning reel, the line is released with little drag under the weight of the arrow, provided it is coiled carefully in the first place. Carelessness in coiling the line usually means a broken line. Heavy braided nylon lines testing between 40 and 70 pounds are used by most bowfishermen. Lighter lines usually snap as the arrow is released, and they may cut the hands severely in playing a heavy fish. Occasionally, too, the arrow is driven into submerged snags, stumps, or logs, and the heavier line permits the disengagement of the head, while the light line will break; and good commercial fish arrows cost more than good broadheads. Braided lines, because of their greater flexibility in the heavier breaking strengths, are preferred by most bowfishermen, although some use monofilament.

Reels similar to those described earlier can be fashioned by anyone handy with tools from coffee cans or comparable cylinders, a few inches of one-eighth by half-inch strap metal, a bit of flat brass spring, and a dozen rivets. The body of the can with the bottom cut out forms the basic cylinder; two "feet" are formed by bending strips of the metal strap at right angles and soldering or riveting them in place. The spring line-clip is held by a single rivet, which permits it to swing free when coiling the line. The entire rig is spray-painted with enamel for a finishing touch and to protect it from rust. Another simple home-made reel can be fashioned from a tapered bit of softwood, with the edges carefully rounded and sanded. The truncated triangle of wood, approximately 4 by 3 inches is backed on its broader edge by a strip of light wood or metal slightly longer than the base of the reel, and glued, screwed or nailed to it. The projecting ends form the feet for taping it to the face of the bow. A spring clip, similar to that used on the metal reel may be attached with a single roundheaded screw, or rubber bands may be used to hold the line. These flat-sided reels, mounted usually just below the grip are less bulky than the drum type, although they often do not release the line as smoothly.

A cylinder type plastic reel, available from Bear Archery Company, Grayling, Michigan, resembles a standard large-size spinning reel spool equipped with feet. The line is held by a small clip. This type of reel combines smoothness of release with compactness.

Some bowfishermen mount standard spinning reels on their rods, but the mounting usually is awkward, since the reel must be set upon a projecting angled foot to bring its axis in line with the arrow's flight. Even free-spool bait casting reels of conventional design cannot be used practically on bows because the inertia of the revolving spool usually snaps even the heaviest line when the arrow is released. Some closed-face spinning reels can be used, but care should be taken to be certain that the line release is disengaged since the snap of the released arrow can damage the mechanism of the reel severely. Actually, although the proponents claim that the mounting of such reels on bows provides greater sport by permitting them to play the fish as with a rod, the simpler and more fool-proof designs will provide more satisfactory results. The 50-pound bow is no substitute for a three-ounce spinning rod.

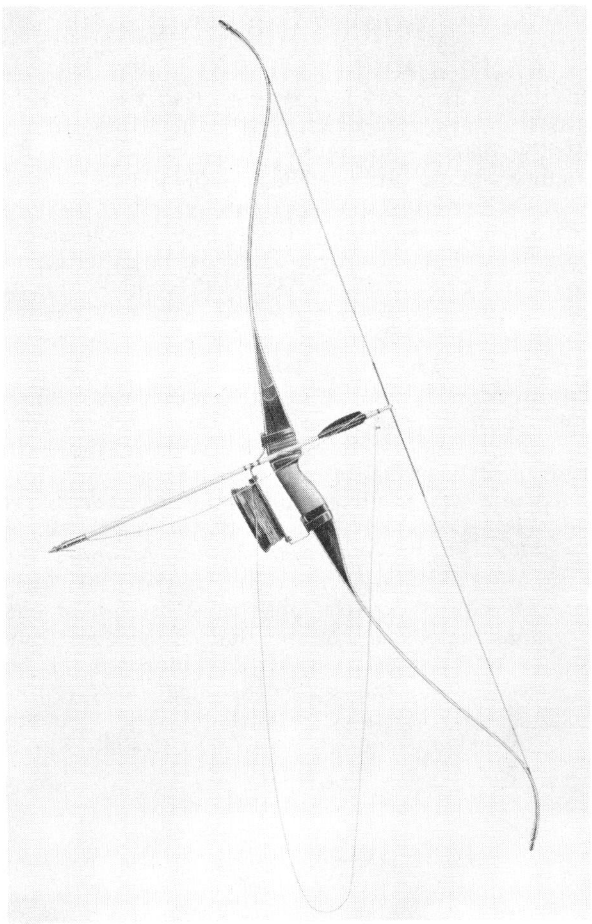

Bear Archery Co.

A modern bowfishing outfit made by Bear Archery Company.

Fishing arrows differ considerably from those used for other forms of archery. Field and target arrows are worthless since they will either pass completely through a fish or pull out. Old field arrows, however, can be converted for fishing by soldering one or two barbs of spring steel to the point. Usually after one or two shots, such makeshift fishing arrows will shed their fletching, but this is of small importance, since shots usually are made at very close range. The arrow must be drilled with a small hole, usually below the nock or above the point, for attaching the line.

Broadhead hunting arrows have little application in bowfishing, except possibly for finishing off large sharks, after they have been secured by the fish arrow.

Arrows designed primarily for fishing usually are from 6 to 10 inches longer than those used in field archery or hunting, and most of them have shafts of fiberglass or aluminum. Either material is satisfactory. Many are fletched with rubber vanes, usually mounted on a slip-on sleeve. Standard feather fletching cannot stand up under the rough treatment that a fishing arrow must be called upon to take. The heads come in a broad range of designs, but all are designed to permit the arrow to penetrate as deeply as possible but not to be withdrawn. The simplest is a sharp conical head equipped with one or more spring barbs, which fold against the shaft on their way in but prevent it from being withdrawn. Others have the barb hinged, like that of an old-fashioned whaling harpoon. One well-designed point has the barbs entirely recessed in the body of the point. When it strikes a fish, the points slide back under the activation of a plunger formed by the inner steel core, forcing the barbs outward. Most fish arrows are constructed so that the shaft disengages from the point upon entry. The slip-point remains in the fish, while the shaft, threaded on the line through a hole, slides up the line. The tendency of a fish when struck is to roll on the shaft, and a heavy specimen can snap a wooden or fiberglass shaft or bend an aluminum one into uselessness. Freeing the shaft not only prevents damage but permits the fish to fight more strongly.

Bowfishing can be done from boats, banks, or by wading. In some states the practice of bow-hunting fish at night by light is legal. Depending upon conditions, it can be sedentary or active.

Carp, which are the most nearly universal quarry of the bowfisherman, are most readily taken on their spring spawning beds, usually the mouths of streams entering lakes or broad rivers through marshy shallows. The fish are easily spotted since they roll near the surface, often with their backs out of water at such times. Standing in the middle of such a concentration of fish, the archer can get off many shots within a short space of time without changing his position. At other times of year, when the fish have moved into deeper water, other strategy will be needed. Shallow water can be prebaited to attract concentrations of fish, and such baited areas usually produce the best fishing in the early morning or evening. In ponds or streams where carp populations are high, the bowfisherman can often find productive shooting from boats drifted over the shallows or from wharfs, overhanging trees and windfalls, stumps, or other elevated vantage points. These permit the chancing of longer

Bear Archery Co.

Bowfishing for Sharks and Rays can provide novel sport in salt water.

shots than the wading fisherman will enjoy, since the arrow at any given practical range will enter the water at a wider angle. Deep-running fish also can be spotted more easily from above. Polaroid glasses, which eliminate much of the surface glare of the water are ideal accessories for bowfishermen.

Similar tackle and techniques are used in bowfishing for Gars, Buffalo, and other rough fish in fresh water and for the smaller salt-water species. For Sharks, especially the larger species, a modification is used. Large Sharks have exceedingly tough skins, and the arrow point must be very sharp to penetrate. A wire leader is useful in preventing the fish from cutting the line, but it is awkward to handle with a bow and is somewhat less necessary than when fishing with hook and line. A stricken shark usually will roll over and over against the line. If the arrow can be placed in or near the head, the chances of a kill are increased and the fish is less likely to get the line in his jaws.

Nurse Sharks, Dogfish, and other small species can be handlined in after placing the arrow, but the larger, more dangerous species usually are shot and permitted to fight a large float, which is attached to the end of the line and dropped overboard as soon as the arrow strikes home. Needless to say, no one should engage in this type of sport while wading. The struggles and blood of the wounded fish may attract dozens of others, and an aroused Shark will strike under such conditions at anything that moves.

Sharks have great vitality and primitive nervous systems; they can be shot through and through without showing much effect unless the tiny brain, the spine, or the gills receive a direct hit. The purpose of the fish arrow is not to kill but to fasten the float to the fish and tire it. A stricken fish usually will head for deep water, towing a float, usually an oil can, behind it. The next task of the bowfisherman is to follow in a boat and finish the quarry off. Regular hunting broadheads are excellent for this use, although rifle bullets will do the more efficiently if in a less exciting manner.

In shooting fish with the bow, refraction of light by the water plays havoc with marksmanship until the archer learns to compensate for this phenomenon. Any completely submerged object is never where it appears to be, except when viewed from a point directly above it.

Seen at an angle through clear water, a fish, or any other object, always appears much closer to the surface than it is. Seen at a sharp angle an object lying six feet below the surface appears to be only a few inches beneath it. Because of the reflections on the surface and the density of the water itself, fish will not be seen at such depths except under unusual conditions—extremely clear water, a dead calm, and over a white sand or marl bottom. Under such conditions it would be impractical to shoot, since the arrow would have too much water to penetrate.

A fish only two feet below the surface seen from an angle of 45 degrees, however, would be vulnerable, but it will appear to be just below the surface. The bowfisherman must compensate for this by holding his point of aim at least a foot below the apparent position of the fish. There are so many variables involved that the only way to attain proficiency in judging whether a shot is practical is to engage in target practice. White cloth sacks filled with sand and dropped in the water at various depths make good targets. A few hours of practice shooting at such targets will soon give the archer the skill to connect with fish when he tries his hand at the real thing.

Bear Archery Co.

Most shots in bowfishing are at close range and fletching is unnecessary on fishing arrows.

Bowfishing can be an exciting and fascinating sport. In fresh water it also serves a valuable purpose in thinning out Carp and other rough fish that compete with game fish and destroy waterfowl habitat.

FLY TYING

Too often when anglers gather to discuss fishing and fly patterns, too few know how their favorite flies are constructed, what materials were used, or how they were combined on a tiny hook to produce one of the most effective lures yet devised for the taking of fish. For years fly tiers have ingeniously combined bits of fur, tinsel, feathers, and thread to create delicately dressed hooks that resemble aquatic insects found in the fresh water streams. For many years comparatively few anglers tied their own flies, the by-standers feeling that it is actually a power invested in only a few.

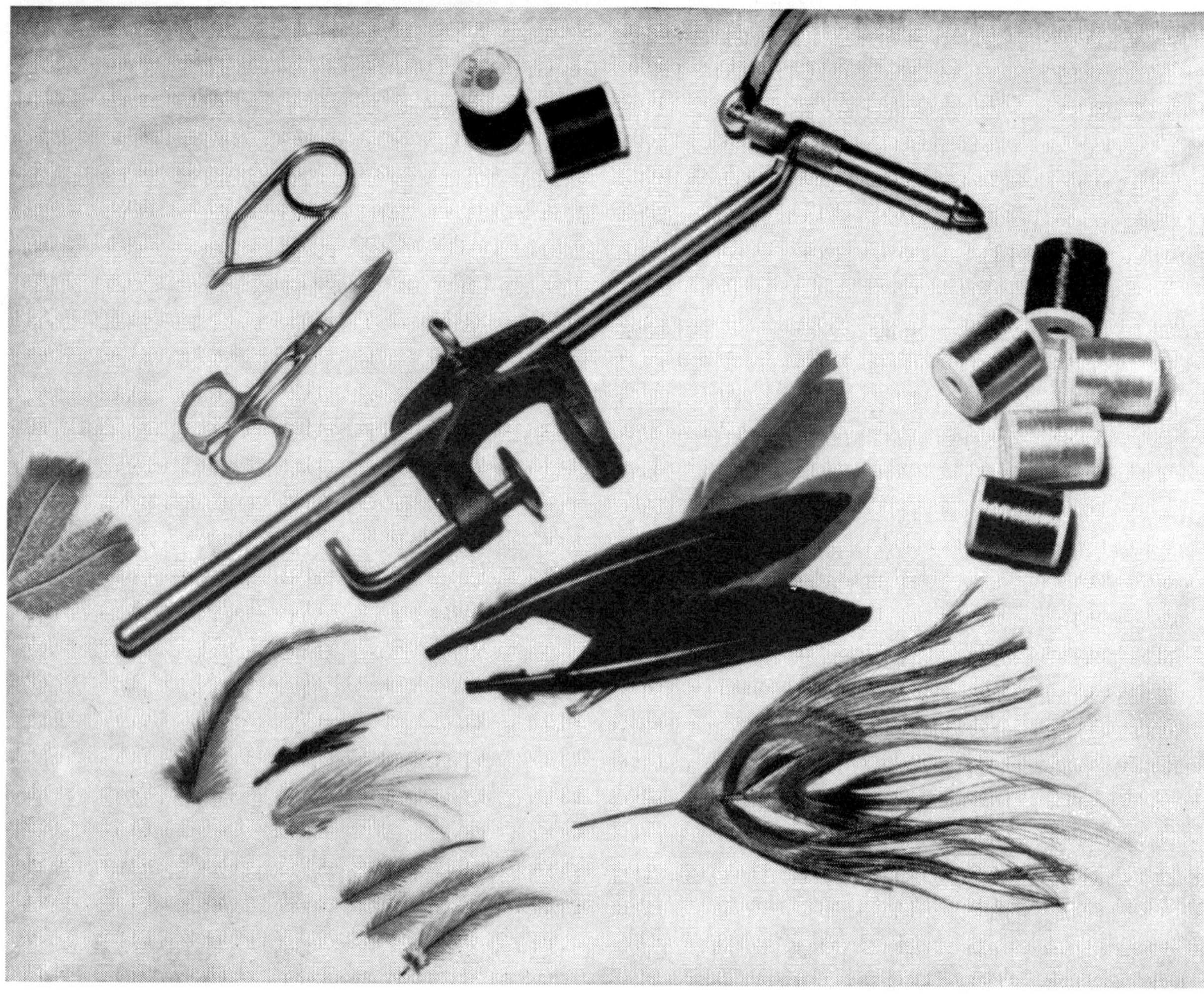

Only a handful of materials and tools are required to produce hundreds of feathered lures.

There is recorded in the *Book of St. Albans,* published in the year 1496 in England, the fact that fishermen went astream in quest of Trout, armed with a twenty foot rod and a dozen flies. Even at this early date bits of feathers were fastened to a hook to capture fish.

Long before Izaak Walton, men followed the sport of fly fishing. However, not until Alfred Ronalds (an Englishman) published a book in the year 1836, titled, *The Fly-Fisher's Entomology,* did fishing, particularly fly fishing, start to grow into the present-day popular sport. From all walks of life, from poverty to riches, men take their stand beside one another on a trout stream in an effort to outwit the finned creatures.

Tying flies has almost become an art of science, for many anglers, when not on a favorite stream, are engrossed in fly tying. Trying constantly to produce better flies from new materials and new color combinations that might yield more bountiful sport. Each year many new flies are created and added to the list of more than 30,000 recognized fly patterns, in contrast to the original twelve used in the year of 1496.

Tying even the tiniest trout fly is not a task performed by superman, for even the first fly tied by the novice may surprise him in its appearance, may surprise him still farther with its ability to lure fish into striking. These flies not only are the answer to a full day of sport, but catching educated Trout on flies constructed by the angler himself will add a charm to angling that is otherwise missed. It is one of the most pleasing pastimes yet found for the angler to pursue when not on a favorite stream.

Just how are flies constructed? Actually it is not complicated but comparatively simple. First a few materials and tools must be obtained. The basic and necessary tools are: a vise, hackle pliers, fine pointed scissors, and a pair of tweezers. These can be purchased for as little as $2.00 although, there are outfits offered that cost nearer $25.00. This high grade outfit merely has more refinements, that is, it will have a magnifying glass in front of the vise, a small fluorescent light, a bobbin for holding a spool of thread and a few other incidentals that can easily be omitted while still producing flies of good quality. For materials, a few quill feathers from a duck's wing, hackle feathers from a domestic rooster, a few spools of silk floss, chenille in various colors, a spool of thread, a cake of wax and perhaps some brightly colored feathers such as a peacock eye, tippets from a golden pheasant and breast feathers from a wood-duck will be

STEPS IN CONSTRUCTING A DRY FLY.

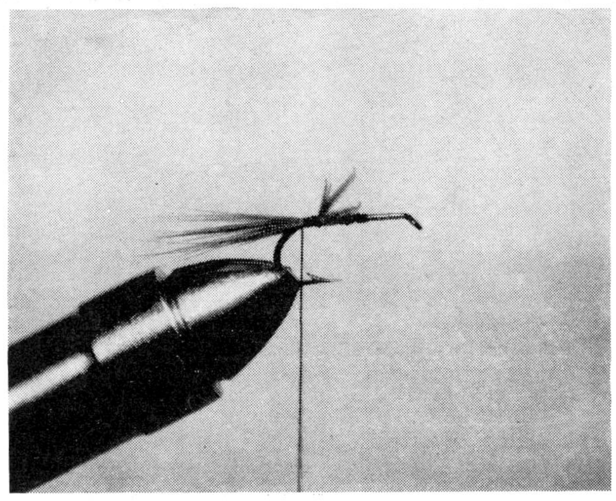

1) Tying in a few strands of hair or feathers to form the tail.

2) A piece of spun fur or yarn is tied in to form the body.

3) The breast feather of a wood duck is tied in to form the wings.

4) Body material wound around shank of hook.

5) Hackle feather tied into fly and wound around shank of hook in front of wings.

6) The Finished fly.

sufficient. With this material, the prospective tier can feel fairly well equipped and can produce flies in a few minutes!

Naturally the larger flies are somewhat more simple to tie than the tiny 18's and 20's, so the beginner should concentrate on the larger ones, those around 8 or 6, or even 4 sized hooks at first. A dozen flies of this size will train the fingers, the tier will also then be familiar with the steps and the procedure, and more speed can be accomplished on the tiny sizes.

Now that the necessary materials and tools are available it is possible to tie the first fly. Clamp the vise securely to a table or some other support at an appropriate height to facilitate easy working. Place a size 6 hook in the jaws of the vise and clamp it tightly. For dry flies, select a fine wire hook with either a turned up or down eye, for this insures a light weight fly for the finished product and one that will float better than would one with a heavier hook.

Cut a piece of tying silk about a yard long and run it over a cake of wax several times. This will water-proof the thread and the materials can be held more securely to the hook. Next, tie the thread fast to the shank. This is accomplished by wrapping various turns of thread around the hook and then going back over it again to bind the end fast. Then, allow the thread to hang down and fasten a weight to the line so that it is kept taut and not allowed to unravel. A snap clothes pin will work nicely for a weight.

The hook is now ready to have the tail tied in place. Select a half dozen fibers from a hackle feather (a long fine fibered feather found on the neck of roosters), tear them from the feather and hold them on top the hook near the bend, making a few turns of tying silk around them. Thus the tail of the fly is formed. The ends of the hackle fibers that extend towards the eye of the hook can be cut or allowed to remain and the body material wrapped over them.

For the body select a short piece of wool yarn, untwisted floss, or chenille about three inches long. Tie the end fast to the shank in the same manner as when tying on the tail. Only a few turns of silk are required to hold the body material securely to the shank. The illustration shows a Cahill Spider dry fly being tied and cream spun fur yarn is being used. Allow this material to hang down from the hook until the wings of the fly are tied on.

For wings, sections of a feather from a duck's wing, tips of hackle feathers, or breast feathers can be used. Whatever material you may choose, hold the material on the upper side so that a portion extends beyond the eye of the hook. Then, make a few turns of thread around the wing material and hook. Having fastened the wings securely, pull the ends of the wings back toward the bend of the hook and make a few turns of thread in front of them. This will cause them to stand erect. Next, wind the body material around the shank to the wings. Make a few turns of thread around the body material and hook directly behind the wings, binding the body securely.

The fly is now nearly complete, for the tail, wings and body have been formed. What remains yet is the tying of the hackle feather to the fly. These hackles are the fibers or finger like hairs that project outward from the fly and cause it to stand erect on the water. The hackle feather, as described previously, is the long fiber feather found on the neck of roosters. Hackles found on hens are rarely used when constructing dry flies, for these are of a short soft nature. However, they do make an ideal wet fly.

Stiff glossy hackles cause the fly to ride high on the water and thus is more appealing to the fish.

The hackle feather should have rather long fibers for such a large fly. Those 3/8 or 1/2 inch in length are about right. Tie this feather at the eye of the hook by means of wrapping the thread around the hook and end of the feather. Some prefer to tie in the tip of the feather, others to tie the butt end. The latter method works best. Grip the free end of the feather with the hackle pliers and slowly wind the feather around the hook, making one or two turns behind the wings and three or four in front of the wings next to the eye. As the feather is wound around the hook, the fibers stand erect and support the fly. Don't use hackle feathers that have too large hackles or fibers when tying the smaller size dry flies unless a "Spider" effect is desired.

The end of the tying thread must be knotted about the hook or the fly will not hold together. To prevent the fly coming apart, a good knot should be used. The one preferred by most tiers is called the 'whip' knot.

This knot is formed by holding a tooth pick or similar object slightly above the eye of the hook and wrapping the thread around the tooth pick and hook a number of times. The free end of the thread is then inserted through the loops and pulled tightly. It is a good idea to coat the head or whip knot with varnish or lacquer to further prevent the fly from unraveling. This knot if tied and properly coated with lacquer should hold the fly together even after a dozen fish have been caught on it.

Some pattern of flies call for a spun fur body. This is similar to wool yarn in appearance. To spin fur on a thread, wax the thread and rub this with a small bunch of fur between the palms of your hands. The fur will then cling to the thread and this can be used as body material on the fly.

Actually the tying of the fly described was far from being difficult. In only a short time you can produce a dozen or more flies an hour. What you may have believed to be tedious and complicated work turns out to be nothing more than about thirty turns of thread around the hook holding a few bits of material securely in place. Wet, streamer, nymph and spinner flies are all tied exactly the same way, although the materials may vary somewhat.

Streamer and spinner flies are tied with the wings streaming back over the shank of the hook and the hackle feather is generally eliminated. However, the steps to tie on the tail and body are exactly the same as that of a dry fly.

Constructing cork-bodied bugs is far from being difficult. Even though the finished bug is somewhat complicated in appearance, the novice can

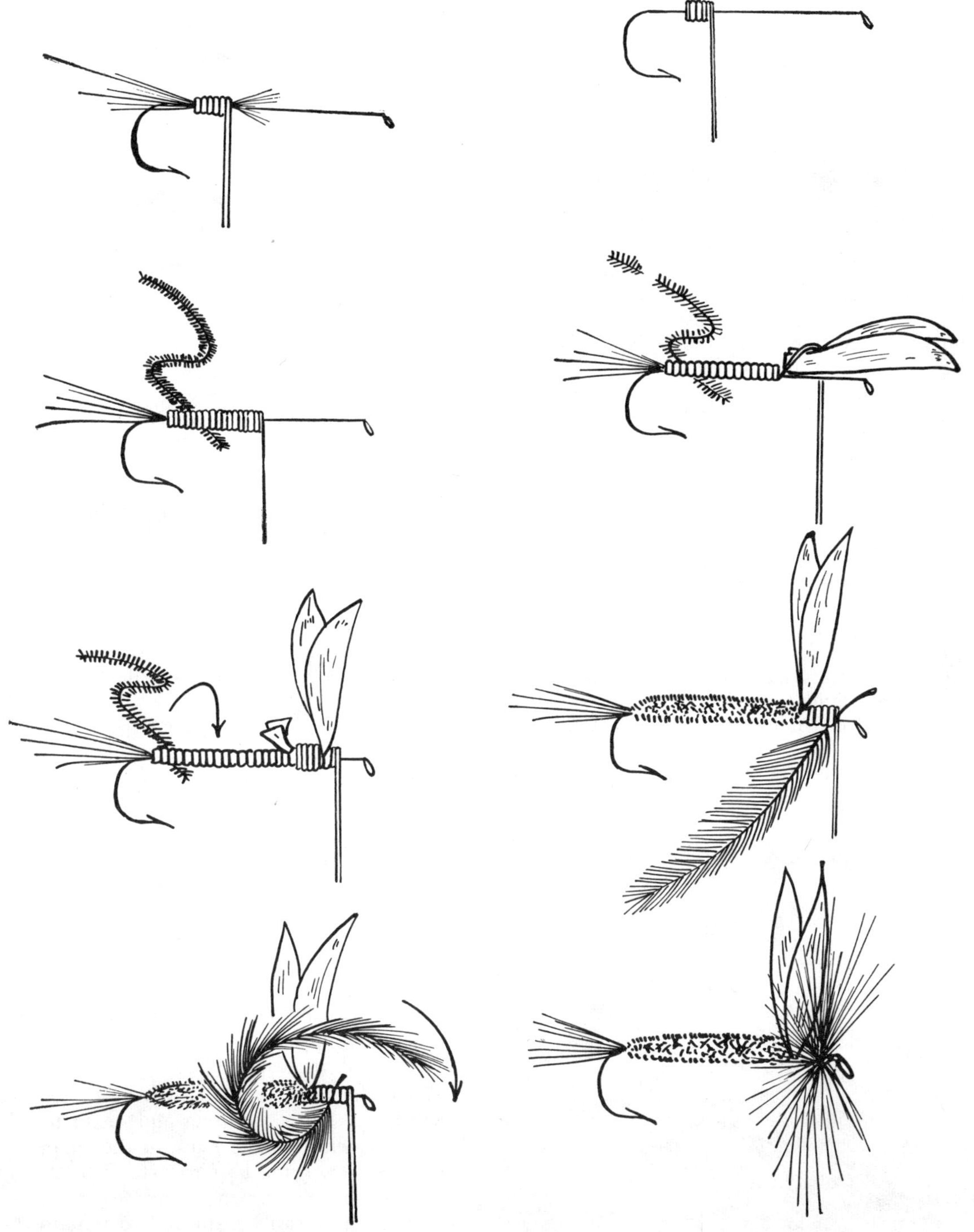

Steps in tying the popular dry fly. First, tie in the tail and body material. Second, fasten the wings by wrapping a few turns of thread around the wing material and shank of hook. Note that wings are forced to stand erect by adding a few windings in front of them. Third, wrap the material around the shank to form the body. Fourth, add a hackle feather, winding this around the hook both to the rear and front of the wings. The fly is then complete.

make good looking bug lures at his first attempt. The type hook used to construct hard bodied bugs on is somewhat different than the hooks used in streamer, wet and dry flies. These have a hump in the center of the shank, about half way between the bend of the hook and its eye. Then, when a cork or wood body is slotted and fitted over the shank of the hook, the hump prevents the body from twisting or turning on the hook. The shank may be coated with glue, thereby holding the body more firmly to the hook.

To construct a cork body bug, place a hump shank hook in the vise, tie on a small bunch of hair or feathers for the tail using the same method as when tying a dry or streamer fly. Then, continue to wind the tying silk around the shank of hook, over the hump, nearly to the eye. Coat this with a good grade of water proof glue.

For the first bug, an ordinary bottle cork can be used for a body. Cut a thin slot length wise through the cork to a point nearly half way through the diameter. Coat the slot with plenty of glue and place on the hook next to the tail. The wrapping of thread over the shank provides something for the cement to stick to. When the cement has dried thoroughly fill the slot with plastic wood.

After this operation, paint the body the color or colors you desire. Quick drying lacquers are ideal paints and two or three coats will cause the bug to have a glossy colored covering.

Hair or feather wings can be tied on the bug by simply wrapping tying silk around the body, covering the windings with the same colored lacquer or enamel.

You can make hard-bodied bugs to resemble crippled minnows, frogs, large moths, and a variety of other imitations of natural foods.

Making hair bodied bugs is somewhat different from the procedure for making cork-bodied lures. Here, hair of deer and caribou is used because the hair is hollow; thus causing it to flare out when tied on a hook and the tying silk pulled tightly. Good strong thread must be used when tying hair bugs.

To construct this lure, cut a small bunch of deer body hair from the hide. Hold the bunch of hair between the thumb and first finger on your left hand on top of the hook shank. Lay the hair parallel to the hook, not cross-wise. With your right hand, make three or four turns of tying silk over the shank of hook and hair. Pull the loops tightly. The pressure of the thread tightening on the hair will crush the hollow centers and the hair will flare upward. When the hair begins to flare, loosen your grip to allow the hair to creep or spin around the hook. Brush the erect hairs towards the bend of the hook and cut another bunch of hair following the same procedure.

When the hook is filled with hair, resembling a brush heap,' tie off the bug and begin to trim the hair rather close to the hook to the shape wanted. You can allow some hair to extend to the rear on each side of the bug thus representing legs; likewise some hair can be allowed to remain on each side of the hook near the eye to represent wings.

As can be seen, constructing feathered lures is not a difficult task, but on the contrary is a hobby

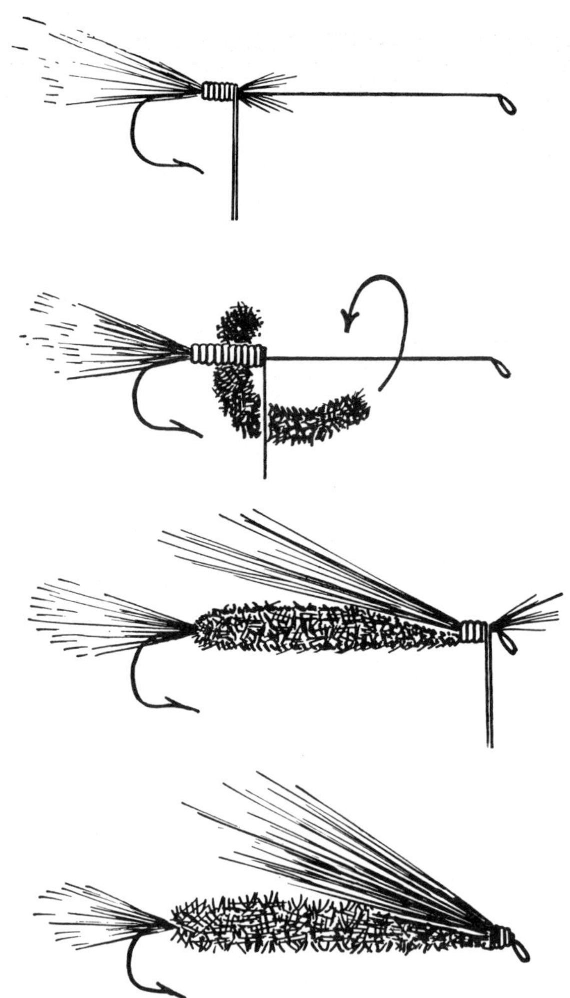

Steps in constructing a streamer fly. 1) Tie on a few feathers or fibers of hair for the tail. 2) Tie in a piece of chenille or wool yarn and wrap around shank of hook to form the body. 3) Tie on a small bunch of hair for the wings. Allow the wings to extend to the bend of the hook. 4) Tie off the head of the fly and the streamer is complete.

Bits of fur and feathers ingeniously combined on a tiny hook is one of the most effective lures yet invented by man for the capturing of game fish.

which every angler can practice. Tying flies, or dressing hooks with bits of feathers is indeed a delightful pastime.

Few fishermen should rely on others for their flies. They are so easily produced that there is no reason for this fascinating work to remain a mystery.

Hard on the eyes? Yes, if improper lighting is used or if too many tiny flies are tied during the course of a day; but for the average angler who needs only a hundred flies per season, it is far from detrimental to the eyes. Don't strain the eyes with bad lighting, instead suspend a 40 watt light with a reflector close to the vise and dozens of flies can be tied on rainy evenings. These same flies will bring added delight on those sunny days when fish are jumping at "home-made" lures!

TYING A SPINNER OR STREAMER FLY USING A LONG SHANK, STRAIGHT EYED HOOK.

1) Place hook in vise and tie on tail.

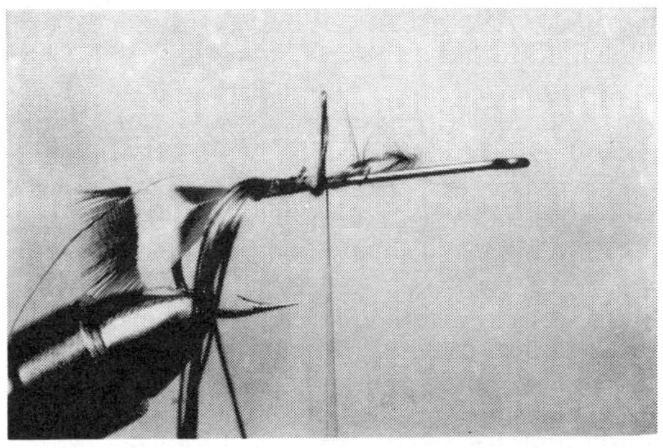

2) Tie on the body material and wrap towards the eye.

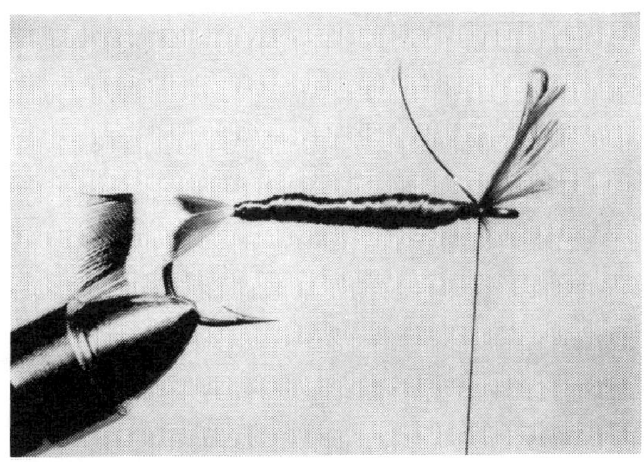

3) If the pattern calls for a ribbing, the ribbing material (generally tinsel) is tied in with the body material, however the ribbing is not wound with the body, but afterwards so that the tinsel is on the outer side of the body.

4) Next step to construct a spinner by is to tie on the wings. This may be hair or feathers.

5) Tie in some feathers for a chin (hairs beneath wings and shank of hook).

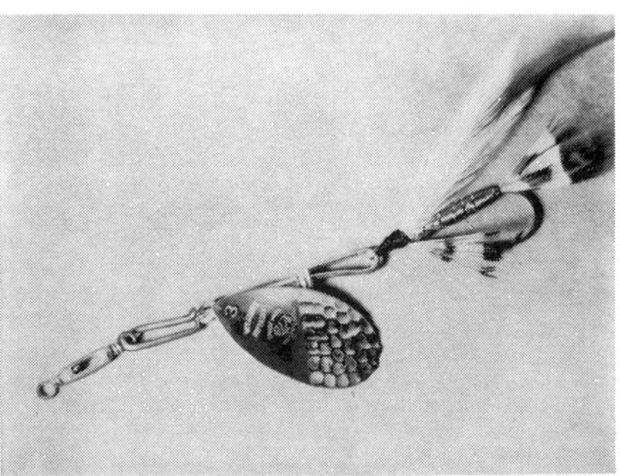

6) Tie the fly off forming the head and the fly is ready to be attached to a spinner.

MATERIAL NEEDED FOR POPULAR FLY PATTERNS

Dry Flies

ADAMS. Tail: Grizzly hackle. Body: Gray or Cream yarn or fur. Wings: Grizzly hackle tips. Hackle: Brown and Grizzly wound together.

CAHILL LIGHT. Tail: Brown hackle fibers. Body: Creamy white fur or yarn. Wings: Barred wood-duck breast feathers. Hackle: Ginger.

COACHMAN. Tail: Brown hackle fibers. Body: Peacock eyed tail fibers. Wings: White duck wing feather. Hackle: Brown.

PINK LADY. Tail: Ginger hackle fibers. Body: Pink silk floss, ribbed with fine gold wire. Wings: Gray duck. Hackle: Ginger.

QUILL GORDON. Tail: Dun gray hackle fibers. Body: Peacock eyed tail quill (herl removed from fiber). Wings: Woodduck. Hackle: Blue dun gray.

ROYAL COACHMAN. Tail Golden pheasant tippet fibers. Body: Peacock eyed tail fiber, center banded with red floss. Wings: White duck. Hackle: Brown.

WHIRLING DUN OR WHIRLING BLUE DUN. Tail: Brown hackle fibers. Body: Gray wool yarn or spun muskrat under fur. Wings: Slate duck wing feather. Hackle: Brown.

The hair bug may look like a complicated "brush heap" to construct, however it is as simple as tying a streamer fly.

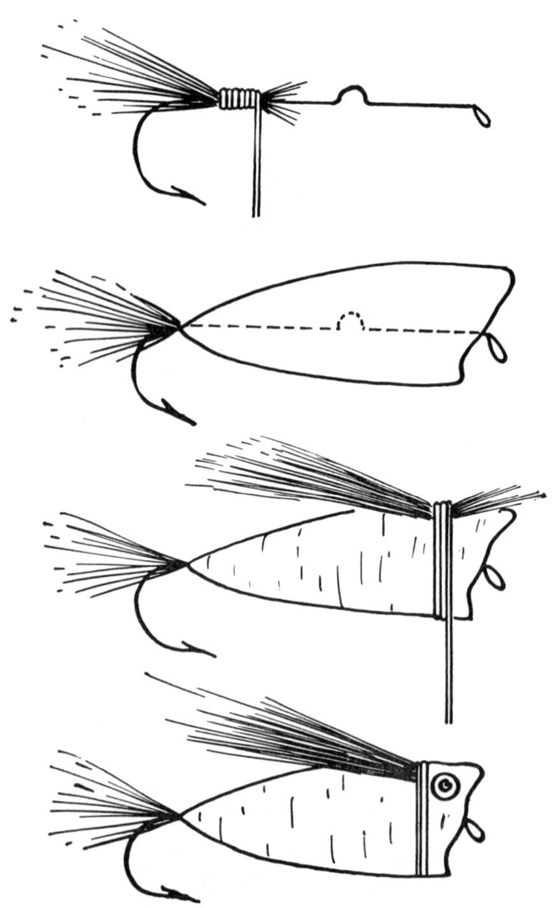

Steps in constructing a hard bodied bug. Reading top to bottom. 1) Tie on a few strands of hair on a hump shank hook to form the tail of the bug. 2) Cut a slot length-wise in a cork or wood body, fill with cement and insert over hook. 3) Paint the body the desired color and tie on hair or feathers for wings. 4) The finished lure.

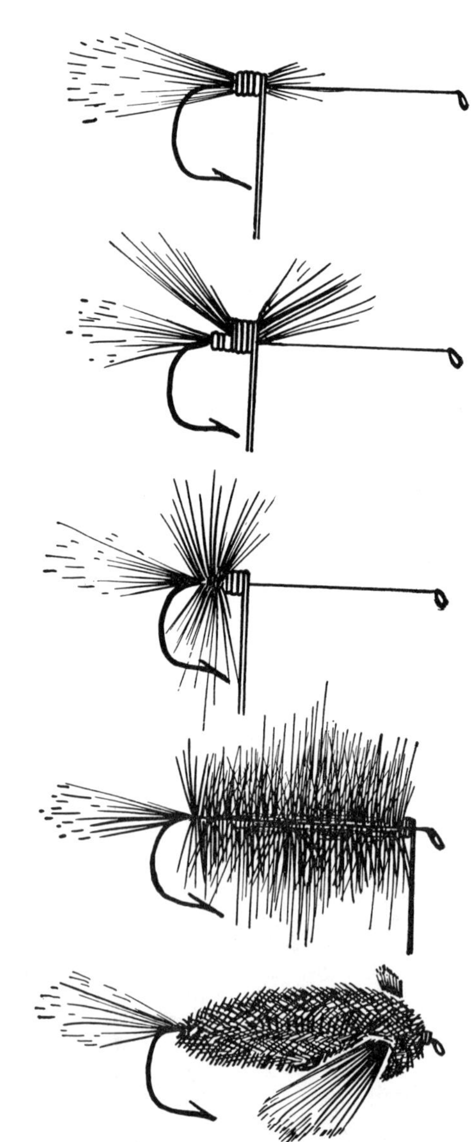

Steps in constructing a hair bug. 1) Tie on a few strands of hair to the hook to form the tail. 2) Lay small bunch of hair (deer) parallel to the hook, make a few turns of thread around it and pull tightly. 3) The ends of the hair will flare outward. 4) Continue this operation until the shank of hook is filled with hair. 5) The finished trimmed lure.

Wet Flies

BLACK GNAT. Tail: Usually none. Body: Black chenille. Wings: Black hen hackle. Hackle: Black hackle.

COLONEL FULLER. Tail: Black hackle fibers. Body: Yellow floss. Wings: Section of yellow and red duck quill feather (dyed). Hackle: Yellow.

DEER FLY. Body: Gray floss. Wings: Grey wild duck wing feathers. Hackle: Blue dun grey.

GRIZZLY KING. Tail: Red hackle fibers. Body: Green silk floss, ribbed with gold tinsel or wire. Wings: Gray mallard flank feathers. Hackle: Grizzly.

MCGINTY. Tail: Scarlet hackle fibers. Body: Alternate bands of yellow and black chenille. Wings: Bluish metallic black feather white tipped (taken from the wing of a mallard duck). Hackle: Brown.

RUBE WOOD. Tail: Fibers of a wood duck flank feathers. Body: White chenille, banded with red floss at rear next to tail. Wings: Gray mallard flank feather. Hackle: Dark brown.

Streamer Flies

BLACK GHOST. Tail: Golden pheasant crest or a number of strands of yellow hairs. Body: Black wool or floss, ribbed with silver tinsel. Wings: White neck hackles. Thoat: (Fibers placed under shank of hook near the eye, under the wings) Golden pheasant crest or some dyed yellow fur.

MICKEY FINN. Body: Silver tinsel. Wings: A small bunch of yellow buck tail or other hair, then a bunch of red fur and finally a small bunch of yellow hair tied over this.

PARMACHENE STREAMER. Tail: None. Body: Yellow chenille ribbed with silver tinsel. Wings: Two hackles (white) tied between two red ones.

SUPERVISOR. Body: Silver tinsel. Wing: Small bunch of buck tail (white) then two light olive green neck hackles, then two light blue neck hackles tied on, one on each side so that the olive hackle lies between the blue.

Spinner Flies. (These flies are all tied on straight ring-eyed hooks.)

FISH HAWK. Tail: Brown mottled turkey tail feather fibers. Body: Gold tinsel ribbed with brown thread. Wings: Brown mottled turkey. Hackle: Brown.

KING OF THE WATERS. Tail: Gray mallard flank feather fibers. Body: Crimson floss or wool, ribbed with silver or gold tinsel. Hackle: Brown.

MONTREAL. Tail: Scarlet hackle fibers. Body: Wine silk floss. Wings: Dark brown mottled turkey tail. Hackle: Dark wine.

SCARLET IBIS. Tail: Red duck or goose feather. Body: Red floss, ribbed with silver floss or tinsel. Wings: Red duck feather. Hackle: Red.

WHITE MILLER. Body: White chenille. Wings: White duck. Hackle: White.

SYNTHETIC FLIES & LURES

Modern synthetics have leaped into the production of many units of fishing equipment—glass rods, reels, rod grips and other ways. Lee Wulff has developed a process by which plastic material can be used, by anyone, to make most any type of fly and bug lure.

A bit of doughy plastic is molded onto a hook to make the fly body, dried out and hardened by warmth, painted the desired color with a special lacquer, or with several colors, and using this as the "stick-um" the feathers, hair, tinsel or other dressing is pasted in position. No wrapping, tying, fussing—just knead the fly together.

Bass bugs made with this process are constructed of a cork body, the hook being thrust through a hole in the cork which has been stuffed with the plastic material. The lacquer and other fittings then are applied.

Kits with all the necessary materials are available for making streamer flies bass bugs and nymphs. The adaptation of methods and materials to constructing dry flies allows the fitting of wing and leg material in a more natural manner than when they have to be tied; so they stick out parallel to the body and give a greater floating surface.

With this process developed by Wulff, an angler can stick a kit in his pocket, and without vise, thread, hackle forceps and other tools, merely with a bit of finger deftness, make practically every type of lure which falls in the fly or bug class.

ROD MAKING

A split bamboo or fiberglass fishing rod can be made by any man who has moderate skill with tools and who is willing to work carefully and accurately. Such a hand-made rod should be better than one made commercially for the same purpose.

Rod making, like fly tying, and the making of other fishing accessories, is one of the most satisfying hobbies associated with angling. The angler-craftsman is to be envied because he has a year-round recreation which employs his intellect and his skill, and which provides opportunity for experiment and invention.

There is no mystery about rod making. The tools and materials required are relatively inexpensive. The problem for those interested in making their own rods is the lack of information on the subject. There are no complete texts readily available, although *Idyll of the Split Bamboo* (2nd Edition, D. Appleton-Century Co., 1934) by George Parker Holden does explain the processes of rod making which the author has largely devised. Unfortunately the *Idyll* is out-of-print and copies are quite difficult to obtain.

There are many amateur rod makers throughout the country, most of whom will cheerfully give a new enthusiast a start and even share their supplies of bamboo and fittings. For example in the Pacific Northwest, in response to the demand for instruction, Edison Vocational School (Seattle, Washington) is giving night courses in rod making. The project both well received and popular, has about two hundred students, men and women, ranging in age from 18 to 70 years, many with no previous experience in the use of tools.

Fishing rods are made of other materials than split bamboo. They may be shaped from some suitable solid wood such as green hart, or made of steel; more recently rods are being made of glass or other fiber bound with plastic. But for a fly rod of pleasant action and long service no material has been found superior to split bamboo, usually of six splines glued and bound together to form the hexagonal rod sections.

The species of bamboo now used almost exclusively for rod making was formerly loosely referred to in the trade as "Tonkin Cane," but is now more correctly known as "Tsinglee Cane." Professor F. A. McClure, the botanist who established the identity of this plant, says that it is known to growers as "Tea-Stick Bamboo." It grows only in a small area about 25 miles in length, in Southern China. It has, above all other bamboos, the desired qualities of hardness and resiliency, uniform diameter, well-spaced nodes and easy clean splitting. Rod makers obtain supplies, under careful specifications, through the importers, and even then must carefully test and cull the stocks. The amateur may get his supply from the rod makers, or better yet, join up with some friends or with his dealer and import a supply of his own At this writing the Communists control the supply, and there is no trade with China.

It may be unnecessary to explain that a stem of bamboo (called a culm, because bamboo is a grass) in cross section shows a hollow interior and a relatively thin wall. The exterior is covered with a hard enamel, usually showing bruises and scars. Next to the enamel is a zone of very hard wood made of tough closely spaced longitudinal fibers and gradually becoming softer and pithier until the interior wall is reached. The six splines of which the rod is made are triangular in cross section, with angles of 60 degrees, one side of the triangle being the slightly curved original exterior of the culm. This curved side forms the outside of the finished rod. So a rod is much denser and stronger at the surface than at the center, and the tip, composed of very small triangles, is much denser than the butt. After the six splines have been glued together, the surface enamel is scraped off in dressing and finishing the rod.

Of course the first essential in building anything is a proper plan or design. Designing a rod is a fairly simple process once the essentials are understood. These principles, at least, can be outlined here. Assuming bamboo of uniform quality, the action of a fly rod, slow or fast, stiff or limber, top heavy or balanced, pleasant or unpleasant to cast, is largely determined by its design or "pattern."

Imagine a hexagonal cone of bamboo of the length and diameter of your rod; if this is too long and slender to cope with, plot it on a piece of paper, reducing the length to one-half inch to the foot and exaggerating the diameter to the scale of one-quarter inch to one-sixty fourth inch of actual diameter. This will produce a figure 4 or 5 inches long, about 1¼ inches wide at the top and perhaps six inches wide at the base. A rod of this design would not be pleasant to use, so let's experiment with it. Obviously, if the base is enlarged the rod will be correspondingly stiffened from end to end; reduce the base, and the rod will be more limber. The spring in a rod must be in the right place; by bulging the pattern about two-thirds of the way from butt to tip spring will be produced. If a stiff butt is desired; expand the butt on the pattern, but constrict it to a relatively weak zone ¼ to ⅓ of the distance from butt to tip and then start the spring, otherwise the rod as a whole will be too stiff.

That is the principle of rod design. Any type can be designed and built. It is true that some experience is desirable, but there is a way to meet this problem. Simply find a rod whose action it is desired to duplicate. Calibrate such a rod, plot its pattern and the design is ready for work to start. It is a good project to register the pattern of various rods. By this knowledge will be gained that will serve well, either in having broken sections replaced or in buying new rods. At the end of this article will be found a sample of the rod record sheets used for this purpose, with the design and tests of a 9-foot dry fly spiral rod shown on it. Remember, this will be reproduced on a reduced scale; the full sheet is letter size (8½ x 11 inches) ruled in quarter-inch squares.

The data on this rod record sheet is largely self explanatory, but there should be a brief explanation of some of the items: Item 5, "Rate of oscillation"; this is a simple but satisfactory test of resiliency, for comparison of one rod with another; have someone hold the handgrasp of the rod firmly on a table with the balance of the rod nearly horizontal and unsupported. With a finger put the rod in motion with a pendulum movement up and down; it will oscillate at its own natural rate of speed; with a watch, time the number of beats per minute and enter this on the rod record sheet as No. 5. Item 7, "Deflection"; this is a test of stiffness or backbone. Again have the handgrasp held on a table with the rod unsupported, but this time use a spirit level to be sure that the first two feet of the rod next to the table is level; then measure the distance from the rod to the floor next the table and at the tip; the difference is (a) free deflection. Repeat the measurements first with a one ounce weight hung on the tip and then with a two ounce weight, and enter as (b) and (c). Deflection factor is the difference between free deflection (a) and deflection with a one ounce weight (b), thus eliminating any sag due to a set in the rod itself. Item 9, "Calibrations"; use a pocket slide caliper rule divided in 64ths inches; measure and note both flat and corner diameter of the rod at each foot from the butt end. Pay no attention to column 3 "Rectified" (corner calibration) as this is to fill in from tables when ready to build a rod.

There are two more tests to be made and entered on the back of the rod record sheet as Items 10 and 11.

Item 10 is a record of a test that we call "Synchronization." Place the male ferrule of the middle section of the rod on a table and rest the other end on the hand with the section leaning at an angle of about 45 degrees. With the free hand, press downward on the middle of the section and roll it back and forth. It will be found that one of the flat faces always turns sharply upward. This is the soft or compression wood side of the rod; it is the side on which the guides should be

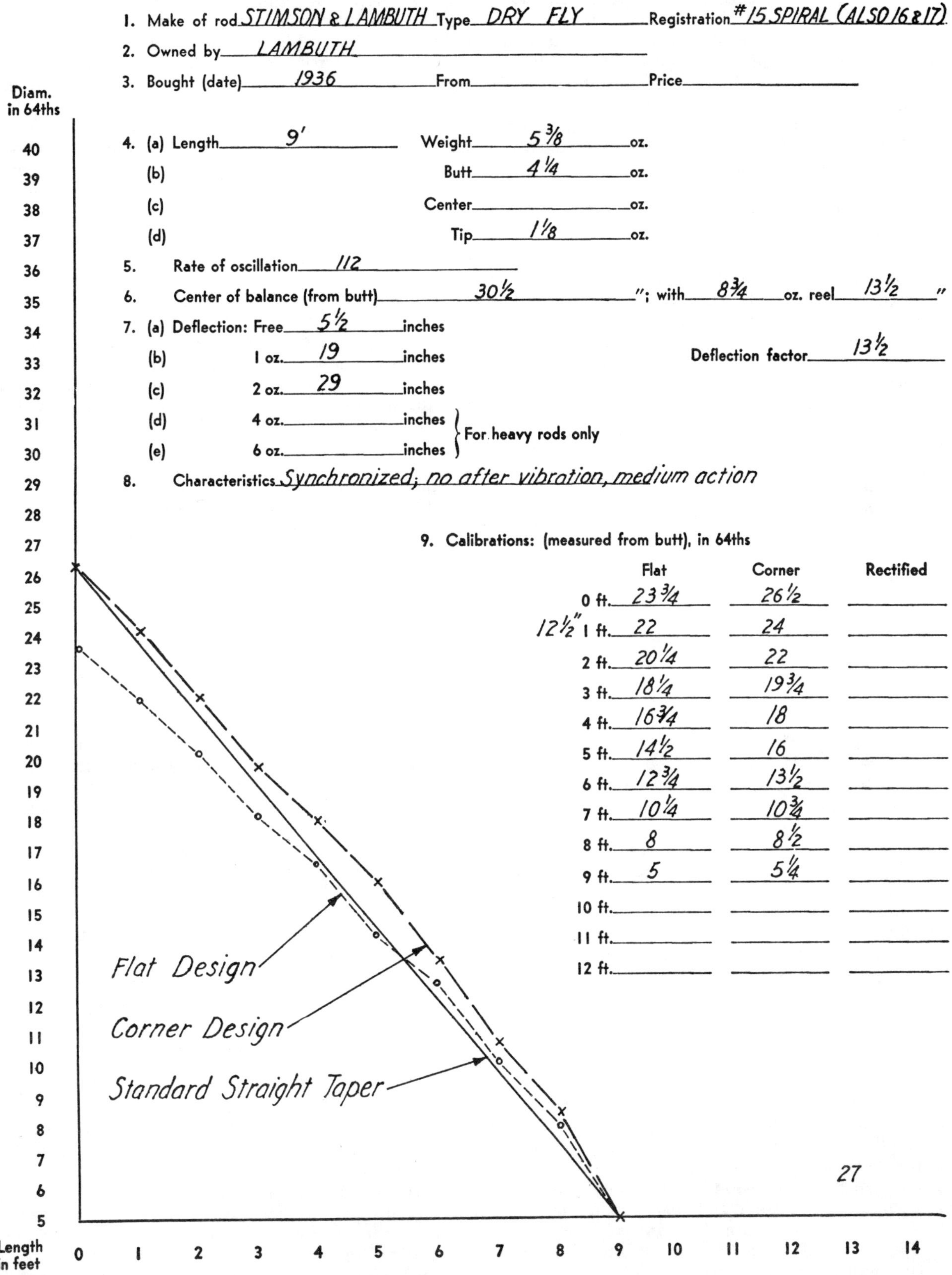

ROD RECORD

1. Make of rod *STIMSON & LAMBUTH* Type *DRY FLY* Registration *#15 SPIRAL (ALSO 16 & 17)*
2. Owned by *LAMBUTH*
3. Bought (date) *1936* From ____ Price ____
4. (a) Length *9'* Weight *5 3/8* oz.
   (b) Butt *4 1/4* oz.
   (c) Center ____ oz.
   (d) Tip *1 1/8* oz.
5. Rate of oscillation *112*
6. Center of balance (from butt) *30 1/2* "; with *8 3/4* oz. reel *13 1/2* "
7. (a) Deflection: Free *5 1/2* inches
   (b) 1 oz. *19* inches — Deflection factor *13 1/2*
   (c) 2 oz. *29* inches
   (d) 4 oz. ____ inches } For heavy rods only
   (e) 6 oz. ____ inches }
8. Characteristics *Synchronized; no after vibration, medium action*
9. Calibrations: (measured from butt), in 64ths

	Flat	Corner	Rectified
0 ft.	*23 3/4*	*26 1/2*	
12 1/2" 1 ft.	*22*	*24*	
2 ft.	*20 1/4*	*22*	
3 ft.	*18 1/4*	*19 3/4*	
4 ft.	*16 3/4*	*18*	
5 ft.	*14 1/2*	*16*	
6 ft.	*12 3/4*	*13 1/2*	
7 ft.	*10 1/4*	*10 3/4*	
8 ft.	*8*	*8 1/2*	
9 ft.	*5*	*5 1/4*	
10 ft.			
11 ft.			
12 ft.			

placed. They may not be so placed. Note as Item 10 about as follows:

"Center Section Synchronized" (or, *off 60 degrees clockwise,* or whatever the fact may be)

Repeat with butt and tip sections and make a note. Then assemble the rod with the butt on a smooth floor, hold it, as a whole, at an angle to the floor and roll it with the fingers. Pressure is not needed, as the weight of the rod will take care of this. Again one face will turn up sharply and this face should have the guides and reel lock. Enter as last note under Item 10:

"Rod Assembly Synchronized" (or whatever it may be)

The significance of this test is that a stem of wood, whether natural or artificial (such as a rod section) flexes most freely in one particular plane, that is to say, it acts as though rectangular in cross section like a lath, and unless all three rod sections are synchronized (guides on the same relative face) the rod will likely perform eccentrically and flutter. Also, to better understand why the guides should be on the "soft" or compression side of the rod, imagine the original growing stem of bamboo bowing before a prevailing wind; it is the tension wood that brings it back upright, and in the rod it is the tension wood that should pick up the line and hold the fish.

For Item 11, on the back of the sheet, make a half-scale drawing of the lower end of the rod showing the length and shape of the handgrasp, length of reel seat, position of the center of the reel and position of the center of balance with reel attached as shown in Item 6 on the front of your rod record sheet. The center of the handgrasp should be half-way between the center of the reel and the center of balance of the rod; thus the handgrasp will properly occupy the center of the "zone of comfort." If the handgrasp is not so centered, the rod is top heavy or otherwise out of balance.

Referring again to the plotted design on the sample illustrated, notice a straight line from 5/64 at the tip to 26½ sixty-fourths at the butt. This is the standard straight taper for a 9-foot rod, better described, perhaps, as the hexagonal cone of bamboo upon which the design of the rod is moulded. Here are the standard straight tapers for fly rods of different lengths in 64ths:

Rod Length (in feet)	*Butt*	*Tip*
8½	24	5
9	26½	5
9½	29	5
10	31½	5

For rods of intermediate length, use a corresponding intermediate figure. Always show the standard straight taper on the chart, because it operates as a "common denominator" for more convenient comparison of the design of one rod with another. Color red any portion of the rod design that lies above the standard straight taper. This is not done in the sample illustrated because of printer's limitations.

It will pay to experiment with this project. When a few rod record sheets are available, it is easy to see the designer's purpose and method of distributing his zones of relative strength and weakness to arrive at the rod action desired.

It should be pointed out that the plan that has been outlined to obtain the design for a rod, namely to find a desirable rod and reproduce it, eliminates all controversial problems. Anglers have preferences, and sometimes want to argue them endlessly. Follow a personal preference, whether it be a rod that is stiff or limber, designed for wet or dry fly fishing, hollow built, double built or conventional, parabolic or spiral, one, two- or three-jointed. If you want a five-sided rod or other abnormal arrangement, of course your jigs will be designed accordingly, but this is not recommended.

Basically, the construction processes are simple. Split the culm into quarters and use a gouge to remove the partitions and a rasp to level the exterior of the nodes. Then split the quarters into three splines each, so that each culm makes 12 splines. These are then straightened over the flame of an alcohol lamp; bamboo has the peculiar quality that it becomes plastic under dry heat. Next the splines are roughed out with a plane so that they are triangular in cross section and somewhat over size. They are then finished to their design dimensions with a fine plane, using a metal jig for close control. With proper care, an amateur can control his work within about two-one thousandth's of an inch. A finished tip spline for a two piece rod will be five feet long, with true 60 degree angles from end to end, a designed taper from end to end, and will weigh about one-sixth of an ounce. Nice work, but it can be done. The six splines are then trimmed so that the nodes are staggered spirally, glued together to form the rod section and firmly bound with strings wound spirally, straightened, and set aside to dry; when dry they are cleaned, the enamel is scraped off and the rod sections are ready to be assembled. Of course there are many secondary procedures in arriving at the glued-up rod sections. To illustrate only one, the splines are always kept in their numbered order as they were split out of the original culm; it will be remembered there were 12 splines; the odd numbers are used for one rod section and the even numbers for another, so that the tension and compression wood in the finished rod is in the same relative position it occupied in the original growing stem of bamboo.

Assembling the rod, means trimming the glued-up rod sections to length; fitting the ferrules; fastening on the winding check, hand grasp and reel seat and turning down the hand grasp; fastening on the guides, "wrapping" the rod, and varnishing. The hand grasp is made of cork discs with holes drilled through the center, which are tightly fitted and glued in place and then turned or sanded down to the desired shape. On a fly rod, use corks also for the reel seat, the reel being held by the butt cap and a movable band; but there are many forms of metal or composition reel seats that can be purchased at the stores. The guides are spaced carefully to take the strain off the ferrules, usually 12 to the rod including the stripping guide (a fixed ring) spaced at a comfortable distance from the reel, and the tip guide, usually a fixed loop. Guides should usually be made of Tungsten steel, chromium plated to prevent rust. Guides are placed on the compression wood side of the rod, as it is the tension wood that should pick up the line and hold the fish. Fit the ferrules to the corner diameter of the rod and pad the flat faces before placing the ferrules.

Most commercial rods are not bound with wrappings between the guides, on the theory that modern glues are so strong that these wrappings are unnecessary, and it is true that a good glued joint is stronger than the wood itself. However, I suggest that the amateur's hand-made rod should have wrappings spaced ⅝ to 1 inch apart, if only as a mark of the work of a craftsman. But there is also a practical reason for this. Good bamboo breaks with a long interlacing splintery fracture; if the rod is bound with wrappings, the rod is stronger and less likely to fracture, because the area that would otherwise have splintered is held together.

When the rod is finished, add two final touches. Coat the ferrules with a dark dull lacquer to kill the flash, and, with a small glass funnel, place three or four drops of warm raw linseed oil on the exposed wood in the female ferrule to protect the rod from moisture. There are no doubt other preparations that will serve the same purpose, but there should be some protection for this exposed wood if open female ferrules (not having a metal partition) are used.

BUYING A ROD

To most anglers, buying a good fishing rod represents a relatively heavy outlay for a luxury item. So efforts should be made to secure a rod that will be a pleasure and a satisfaction, as any fine tool or weapon should be.

It must be assumed that the angler has sufficient experience to know the type of water and kind of fish for which he is preparing. His casting outfit will consist of a fly or lure, leader, line and rod. The leader is probably the controlling factor; that is to say, the diameter or strength of the tippet of the leader required will indicate the length and weight of the rod, and the line will be carefully mated to the rod. It would be interesting to go into more detail on this subject, but the main problem is that of purchasing a rod.

Should an angler with a general idea of the length and weight of rod he wants, some money in his pocket and pleasant anticipation in his mind go into a sporting goods store and dicker for a rod? There are two good reasons against doing so. First, because in buying a rod, just as in building one, it is desirable that plans and specifications be as complete and definite as possible; and without such a specific plan, the result is more than likely to be disappointing. Even the most experienced and conscientious salesman cannot safely guide an incomplete or half-planned purchase.

The second reason is that, in the absence of a plan, the purchaser must ordinarily rely upon the "feel" of the rod when waved (or more often wiggled) in the hand. This is an unreliable test of excellence, if only for the reason that the angler has become so accustomed to the feel of his present rod (which he desires to replace) that a different rod, perhaps the correct one, will feel strange to him.

These are the negative aspects of the project. On the positive side, let us start with a plan. In the article on "Rod Making," it was suggested that a collection of Rod Record Sheets, in effect registration sheets, of friend's rods would be helpful. If among these is found the rod desired, the problem may be simple; go and buy one like it. If that pattern is not available in the stores, and is not obtainable through the manufacturer, then it may be custom built by a competent rod maker. If the rod maker is partly mechanized, chances are your rod will cost no more than it would in the store, and it might cost less; if he works entirely by hand, the rod may be somewhat more expensive than it would be in the store.

If a Rod Record Sheet can be made on the rod desired, it will provide a complete plan. The owner will no doubt permit a test on the lawn so that field tests as well as shop tests will be available to confirm the judgment.

Now assume that the rod can be obtained either from store or factory, or custom built. It should still be examined before acceptance to be sure of a few essential features, such as:

(a) Guides and fittings should be rust proof.
(b) The rod should be fairly well in balance, as outlined in Item 11 on the back of the rod record sheet,

Silhouette photographs like this are easy to take, and different. An exposure of three or four times the normal should be made to "burn in" the dark areas on the film. Still water is needed as a reflector of light against which the subject may be outlined.

and the handgrasp should be generous in length and diameter so it will not blister the hand.

(c) The rod should be synchronized as in Item 10 on the back of the rod record sheet. Some tolerance is allowable; if the rod assembled has the guides on the proper face, and if the rod does not flutter when put in motion and stopped suddenly, it is not essential that the guides be on the soft face of each section when tested separately.

(d) Examine the node spacing. On a hand-made rod, they should be staggered spirally, either singly or in opposing pairs. On a commercially manufactured rod, they may be staggered haphazardly. But view with disfavor the rod on which nodes are spaced with three together.

(e) The hand-made rod should have silk wrapping spaced one inch, or less, apart.

(f) There is one important feature that cannot be discovered by examination or tests. Most commercial rods are made of bamboo that have been heat treated. If heating has been too severe, the rod is somewhat fragile and if broken will shear instead of fracture.

These should be among your instructions to the rod maker if buying a custom-made rod.

PHOTOGRAPHY FOR FISHERMEN

Anglers who carry cameras seem united in one common desire: sparkling pictures which can be shown without need of a running commentary of explanations and excuses. When a picture requires its maker to say, "This is Joe doing so and so," it is a failure. As many such failures result when the wrong sort of camera is used for the job, let us first investigate the qualifications of the various types.

Of prime importance is a camera light enough and small enough so it can be carried comfortably. The instrument should be simple to operate so that it can be put into use quickly, and it should hold a large amount of film to eliminate the need for frequent loadings. The camera most likely to meet these specifications is the 35-mm. type.

There are several fine American makes on the market selling for from less than $100 to about $500; and excellent European and Japanese models which range through the same price field. Nearly all are small enough to carry in a pocket—even when contained in a plastic bag for safety's sake on hazardous water crossings—and light enough to carry from the shoulder in an ever-ready case. The camera can take 36 exposures at a loading; more if the user loads his own cartridges from bulk film stock, which also offers a considerable saving.

In addition, most 35-mm. cameras have a built-in range finder (if not, a pocket model can

This is a "framed" pictorial. The scene would have been worth only a passing glance but for the human element—the boatman. A yellow filter was used to help bring out the clouds.

Showing the effects of filters in "bringing out" cloud formations. At left, no filter; in the middle, a medium-yellow filter effect; at right, a red filter effect.

(All illustrations in this article, "Photography for Fishermen," are by Peter Barrett)

A wide-angle lense is most useful when taking pictures in a boat because the lens "takes in" so much more than the camera's standard focal-length lens. This is particularly valuable in cramped quarters, as here. In this case a 35-mm. lens was used in place of the camera's regular 50-mm. lens. Wide-angle lenses give great sharpness of detail in close, too.

In taking pictures with a camera having a top shutter speed of 1/200 of a second, action effects can be obtained by having an angler exaggerate his movements, though these may be slow movements. Here the feeling of action is obtained by having the fisherman stretch way out to net his fish. Shutter speed here was only 1/125 of a second.

be bought for about $5), a fairly fast "coated" lens of short focal length—most suitable because its great depth of focus makes for sharp pictures—and a shutter speed of at least 1/200 of a second, which will serve for all but jumping-fish shots and catching a man in the middle of a cast. The better miniatures, with shutter speeds of 1/500, 1/1000 and sometimes 1/1250 of a second, will "stop" this fast action.

A further refinement on some makes is a type of lens mount which permits lenses of different focal lengths to be interchanged rapidly, and be coupled automatically to the range finder. In boat fishing, for instance, a wide-angle lens is most useful because it "takes in" so much more than the camera's standard lens in these cramped quarters. Similarly, a telephoto lens secures close-ups of distant objects which the camerman may not care to approach, or cannot, such as an angler at work in the middle of a rough river, or a sailfish jumping 100 yards from the boat.

It should be mentioned that the 35-mm. has a small negative—about 1 x 1½ inches—which requires careful fine-grain developing if enlargements to 8 x 10 or 11 x 14 inches are to be made. In any event, smaller enlargements will have to be made, though the cost is low these days.

Roll-film models which fold compactly are often as small as 35-mm. miniatures, but they do not offer interchangeable lenses and their film capacity will be at least 50 per cent less. Those with a lens of longer focal length that is standard with 35-mm. models—50-mm. (2 inches)—will require more critical focusing in the close-ups. However, this deficiency may be compensated for when the camera takes a square picture; there will be no time lost in deciding whether to make a vertical or horizontal photograph. Also, the larger folding cameras have a negative size ample enough so that contact prints—never expensive—can be made for album and Christmas-card use.

The camera types just discussed usually come equipped with eye-level view finders which have the advantage of being easily handled fast. In operation, the camera is steadied by both hands and often the face serves as a sort of steadying backstop while one eye looks through the finder. But when picture taking is as simple as clapping the camera to the eye and shooting, usually from a standing position, a certain sameness in the photographs is apt to result because the viewpoint changes little. This is not the case with a reflex camera.

It is easy to make dramatic low-angle pictures

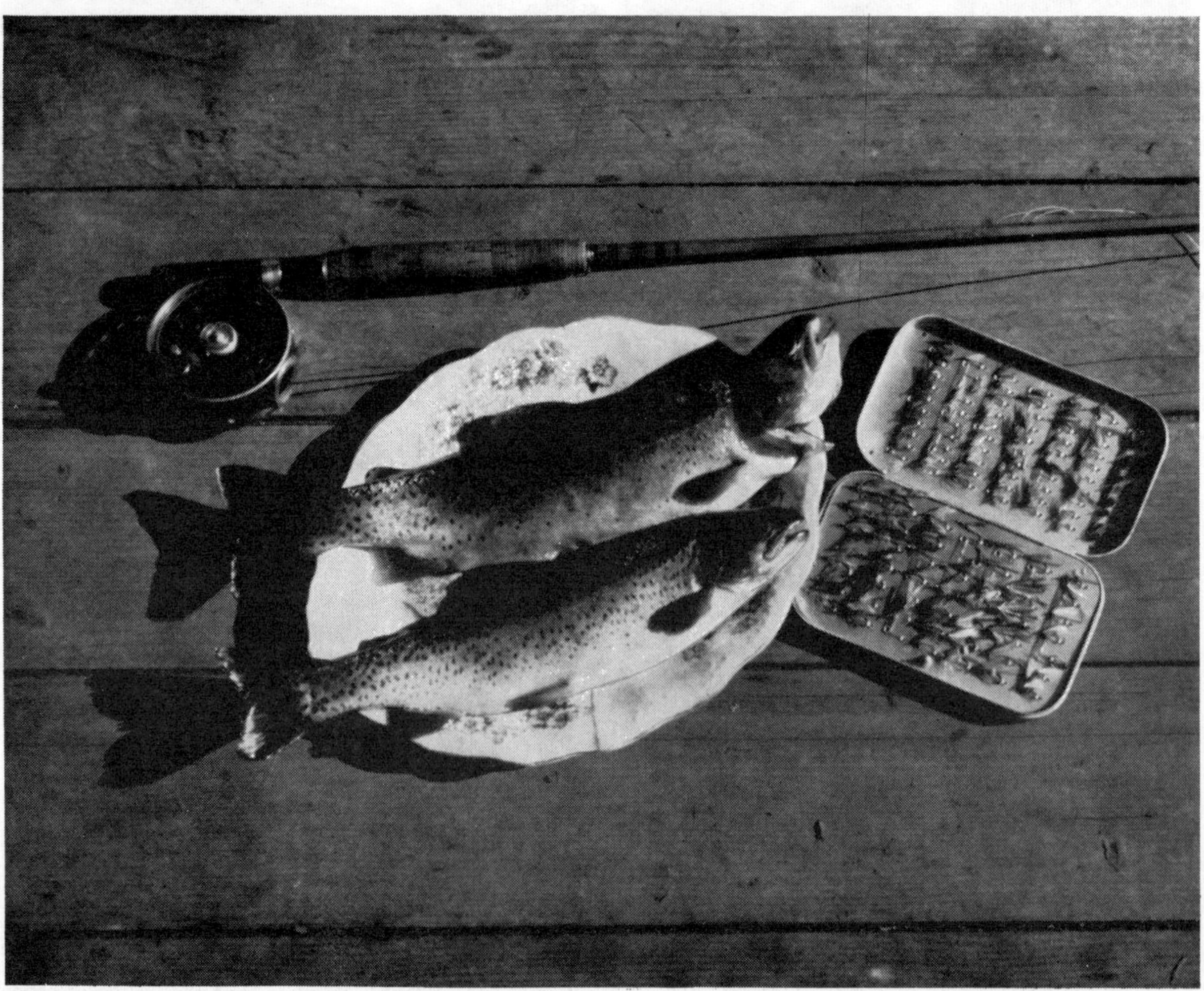

Close-ups of fish are most effective when angling equipment is included to show the size of the catch, as well as provide a record of the sort of tackle used. Anyone can tell these are eatin'-size rainbows. (A polaroid filter was not used in this picture because it would have been ineffective in this side lighting).

Though unhandy to carry because of its boxlike shape, the reflex-type camera makes it easy to get dramatic low angle shots like this. (And high-angle pictures, too.) Here a shutter speed of 1/500 was used, fast enough to freeze the rod but not the line. A yellow filter darkened the sky. Plain sky backgrounds are most effective in close-ups like this because they are not distracting and therefore tend to focus attention upon the angler.

with a reflex, and just as easy to hold the camera above the head and shoot downward. Also, the ground glass viewing screen is exceptionally good for taking sharp, well-composed close-ups. But this type has one serious disadvantage—its boxlike shape. It takes a very large pocket to accommodate a reflex, and the camera is not the most comfortable to carry in a case as it tends to roll against the body. But, fishing being a somewhat contemplative sport, many put up with the unhandiness of a reflex because of its versatile viewpoint.

There remains but one other type: the press camera. This is the least useful to fishermen because of its bulk and weight. Further, it is by far the most complicated to operate. But it does take excellent flash pictures and those who can afford to invest $150 or more in an extra camera keep this model in their car or fishing camp for flash shots in difficult light and at the end of a day, as well as for extra sharp close-ups of fish and people.

A few accessories will be needed. Thus if the camera does not have a "coated" lens, which is virtually unaffected by all kinds of glare, a sunshade will be necessary, otherwise strong reflections of the sun—and sunlight itself falling directly on the lens—will fog portions of the negative with flare "ghosts." These appear as irregular light-toned patches, or as circles, and ruin a negative for printing.

The use of a medium-yellow filter will cut haze and greatly enhance cloud effects which ordinarily would almost be lost, and a red filter will give even more dramatic results. Because a filter holds back some of the light which would ordinarily reach the film, this must be compensated for by opening the aperture of the lens to admit more light. Generally, a medium-yellow filter requires the lens to be opened one whole "stop" (or the shutter speed to be halved). As a convenience—because so many lenses are marked with both whole and intermediate stops—here is a list of whole stop numbers, ranging from small to large: F 32, 22, 16, 11, 8, 5.6, 4, 2.8 and 2. Precise information about exposures with common filter types, such as the Wratten series, is to be found on the wrapper that comes with every roll of film.

Most fishing photographers get along nicely with only a medium-yellow filter inserted in a sunshade —total cost, about $5. But it should be mentioned that a polaroid filter, which cuts surface glare from water, is wonderful for taking close-ups of fish that first have been wetted down. This way, the scales and markings will be clearly defined. This filter is also useful in pictures of fish being brought to the net and being netted because of the reduction of surface glare.

A compact, telescoping tripod with a tilting head is worth having but not carrying. It is useful for close-ups when the lens is stopped down for sharp-

A high shutter speed is needed to catch a high-jumping fish. This big rainbow, from Silver Creek, near Sun Valley, was caught in the middle of his third successive leap with a shutter speed of 1/1250.

In close-ups of people with fish, show them in a natural pose—looking at the fish, *not* into the camera. The use of flash here would have eliminated hat shadow, but in this case the shadow was left so that attention would be focused upon the fish.

ness, necessitating an exposure of, say, 1/5 or ½ a second (too long to hold a camera in the hands during exposure). The tripod also provides a dependable rest when a self-portrait is to be taken by using the delayed-action timer found on most shutters. After the shutter is cocked, the timer is cocked and set off, permitting the angler about 12 seconds to get in front of the camera and pose for the picture.

The one accessory that is a must is a dependable light meter. Photography near water is a tricky business, so that exposure guesswork is frequently unrewarding. Extinction-type meters, which nowadays sell for around $5, are a great help but are not entirely satisfactory because their readings are only approximate and depend upon the user's judgment. This type is too unreliable for color work. But a photoelectric meter is not; indeed, it will solve exposure problems for all types of film swiftly and with great accuracy. The cameraman has only to take a light reading, then transfer this to a dial arrangement which immediately indicates proper exposures for every possible combination of shutter speed and lens stop. The best meters of this type cost in the neighborhood of $30 and are worth it.

Flash equipment is strictly an optional accessory, as many do not care to invest from $10 to $60 in it, with the knowledge that every bulb used will cost about 12 cents at the least. Just the same, it should be mentioned that a flash is easy to use, and trustworthy. Understandable instructions about exposures are to be found on every bulb carton. And the small "midget" bulbs take up little space; several can easily be carried in a coat pocket. In terms of excellent pictures that could not have been made without it, flash equipment eventually pays for itself.

As to films, it has been found that one type is definitely unsuitable for all-around work—the so-called fine-grain panchromatic and orthochromatic emulsions. While this type yields excellent enlargements from a well-balanced negative, the film is so contrasty that many of the severe-light conditions found in fishing are beyond its range.

Most experienced angling photographers prefer a "pan" film of medium speed such as Ansco Supreme or Kodak Plus-X. The fastest pan films are occasionally used for fast-action shots of jumping fish or casting, but in good light medium-fast pan will suffice even for this.

There are two types of color film on the market at present. One, the positive type, yields transparencies which may be held up to the light and viewed, or, when in cardboard or glass mounts, may be shown on a home-movie-size screen by means of a projector made for the purpose. Color enlargements of these transparencies can also be made at quite moderate cost; however, the colors of these prints are not always as clear or true as those of their transparencies. The angler who has laid in a supply of color transparencies taken over the years will be richly rewarded.

The other type produces a color negative not suitable for viewing, from which color prints are made at the time the film is processed. Again, the print colors will not often satisfy the discriminating eye, but the pictures are certainly good enough for showing friends and for brightening up an album. Color photography demands accurate ex-

By taking advantage of the normal pauses that occur between most human actions, it is possible to show motion with only a slow shutter speed. Here an angler is caught at the top of sweeping a trout from the water—shutter: 1/200. Water streaming from the net heightens the effect.

In medium-distant shots of fishermen, it helps if they are shown in motion. If this fellow had merely stood beside the stream, the picture would have fallen flat.

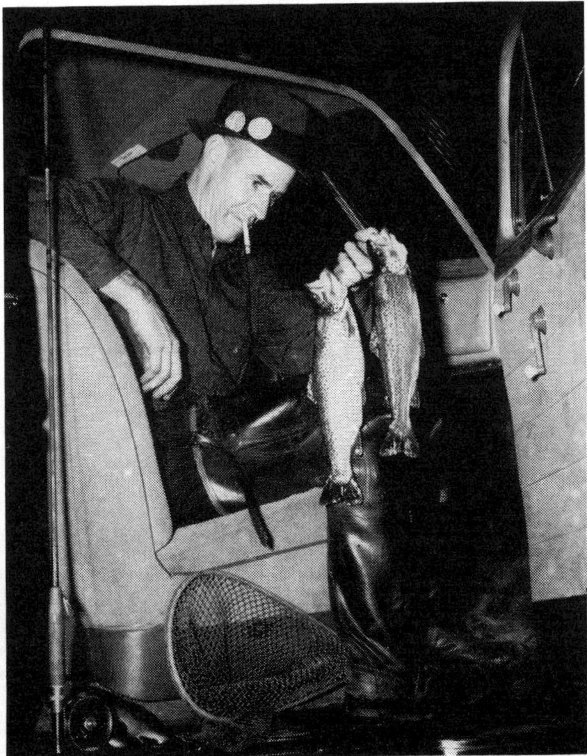

Flash equipment kept in the car or fishing camp can save the day when an angler returns with fish that would be faded out and stiff by morning.

posures and the use of morning and early-afternoon light for best results.

Few sports offer the opportunities for pictures that tell a story as does fishing, yet it is this very aspect of picture taking which so often defeats the amateur. This could be because the outcome of a day's fishing is frequently uncertain, so that it may seem pointless to record a trip from the beginning—with no fish, the lead-up pictures fall flat. But the solution is simple.

The cameraman who wants to chronicle a successful trip should refrain from shooting until a fair-sized fish is hooked. Then, with scenes of playing, landing and admiring the fish for a story mainstay, he can backtrack by taking pictures of casting, selecting the lure, rowing or wading out to the fishing grounds and so on. Later there will be dockside or streamside scenes to take of the catch being measured, cleaned, possibly even being cooked over an open fire.

Once the photographer begins thinking in terms of story continuity, he will find endless ways to show the interesting points of a trip. As an aid to this—and also to help those who simply want to take better fishing photographs as chances come along—several types of pictures, typical to all fishing, will be discussed.

Pictorials are the easiest to take. The idea, of course, is to portray an arresting piece of scenery. A most effective way of putting this over is to include a person doing something that will lead the eye into the picture. Thus a photo of a beautiful trout pool with an angler about to drop a fly upon it will rate a much longer appraisal than a picture of the pool by itself. The figure of the fisherman need not be large, just so long as it can serve as a focal point of interest. Tricks such as catching a sun glint on the rod or showing the angler in outline against white water add the professional touch.

Interest in the scene will be further heightened if weeds and grasses, a leafy branch, a tree trunk—anything of this nature—are permitted to edge into the picture and be shown a bit out of focus. In cases where this cannot be accomplished handily, and especially if the sky is cloudless, it will pay the photographer to break off a small branch and hold it above the camera so that part of the foliage can be included.

When "framing" a scene in this way, it is wise to focus the camera on infinity and use a small lens opening—two devices which will assure picture sharpness where it is needed. If clouds are present, a filter should be used, of course. In color photography, no filters are needed to bring out clouds, though a haze-cutting UV-16 filter is sometimes put over the lens. There is no change in exposure with a filter of this type.

When photographing people at recognizable distances and in close-ups, there are two important things to keep in mind: have them doing something

Another use for flash kept handy in the car—streamside pictures of night fishing. Flash is also excellent for needle-sharp close-ups of fish and people.

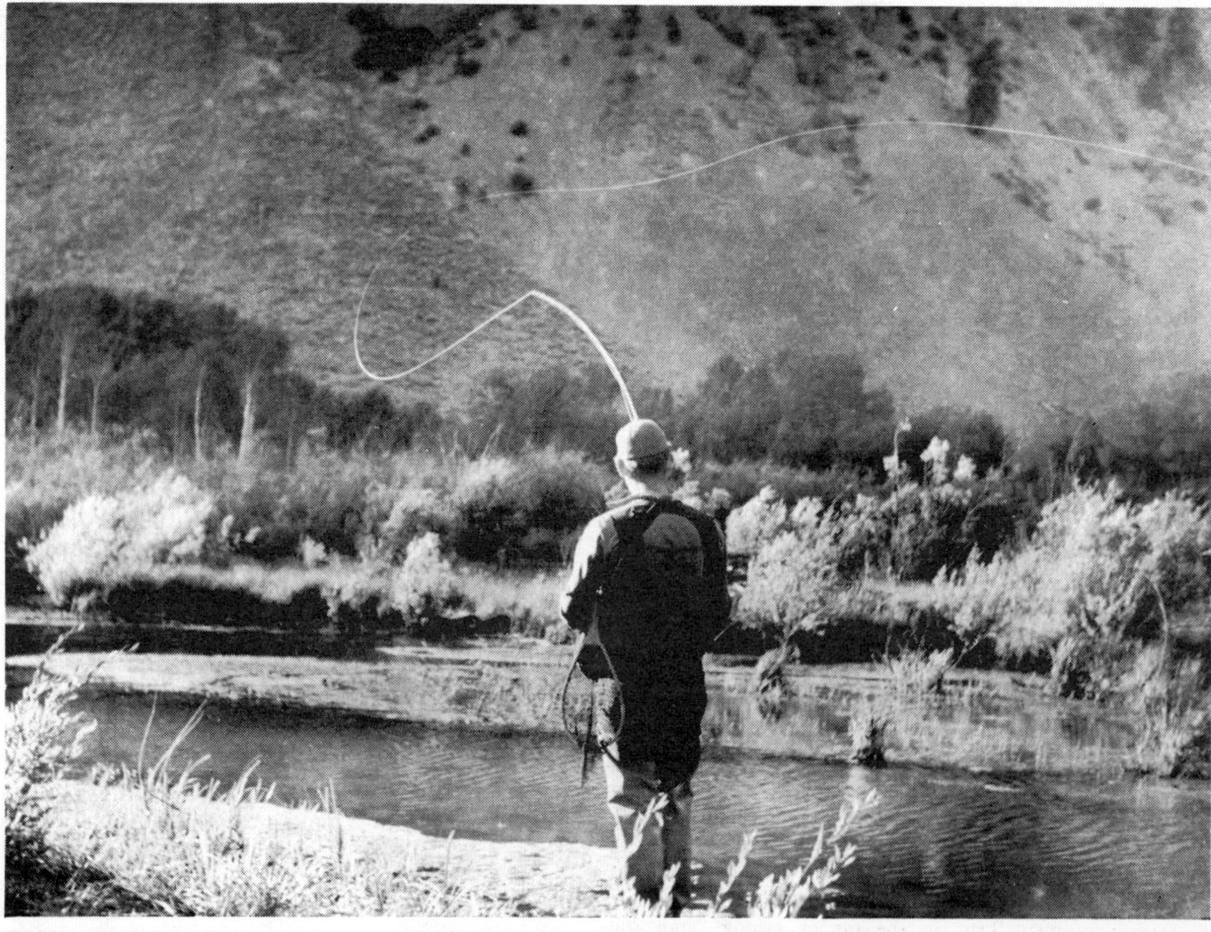

To show a line being cast, the sun should be shining through it and *toward* the cameraman. By waiting until the rod had completed its rapid forward whip, the rod was frozen at only 1/250 of a second.

The action of a rod can be stopped at relatively low speed if the shutter is snapped just as a cast is getting under way, or at the end of a forward or backcast. In this case 1/200 was used.

natural, and show them in motion if possible. Let us consider all but close-ups first. A shutter speed of 1/200 of a second, available to all but the cheapest cameras, will suffice to stop almost all action but a cast. And with co-operation from the angler, this can be caught at 1/200, too.

The trick is to suggest motion by slight exaggeration of movements—make your friend really stretch to land that trout, step high but slowly on the trail—and if the motion cannot be caught during its performance, snap the shutter during the natural pause between movements. Thus a fly caster's rod can easily be shown in a curving arc at 1/200 when it has just delivered a backcast or is just beginning a forward cast. Similarly, a man can be shown at the height of scooping a netted fish out above the surface; water streaming from the net will give the illusion of motion. The applications are endless.

A shutter speed of 1/500 is needed—and 1/1000 is better—to freeze a fast-moving rod. And the moving line, incidentally, will be difficult to show unless sunlight from a low angle is shining through it and toward the lens. Fly lines can usually be caught at 1/200, but faster-moving surf, bait-casting and spinning lines need 1/400 at least.

In medium-distant shots of fishermen, showing them in motion will help put life into pictures, but this isn't nearly so necessary in close-ups. Here the main idea is to catch the angler in a realistic, unaffected pose, which means looking at a fish just caught, unhooking it, tying on a lure, and so on. Don't let him look into the lens, this is the world's toughest pose to bring off well—even Hollywood rarely tries it.

To make a close-up effective, the background should not be "busy" or domineering and show such objects as part of a house, billboards, a jumble of dead trees and such. Instead, it should be kept simple by using the sky, a distant landscape that is plain, the broad trunk of a tree, a grassy hillside. The subject should not be facing into light that will cause a bad squint. Remember that morning and afternoon light do not cause severe hat shadow which, incidentally, can be banished any time by placing an opened newspaper near the angler's face and reflecting up at it. Flash will kill heavy hat shadow too.

A large lens opening is often used in close-ups of people because this blurs the background, making it less conspicuous. A shutter speed of 1/100 will catch all but brisk hand gestures, but a faster speed will probably be necessary if the lens is opened wide because of the background.

A little-used device for photographing a fisherman in or near water is the silhouette. A strong reflecting light source, such as a still pool or an unruffled stretch of lake water, is needed, with the sun shining toward the cameraman. The angler and his equipment will show up dead black, or nearly so, if an exposure of three or four times normal is made. Silhouettes require careful posing of the angler so that he will not appear stiff and unnatural. This type of picture is not well suited to color film because of the extremes of light contrasts.

Photographing jumping fish is both exciting and rewarding, once the technique is mastered. Because a rapid shutter speed must be used—1/500 of a second or faster—the lens has to be opened up. This in turn requires that it be accurately focused, particularly where the range is under 12 feet or so, since the depth of focus gets progressively shallower as the range decreases. As it is often impossible to tell just how far from the camera a fish will jump, it can be seen that focusing is no cut-and-dried affair.

Many solve the problem by estimating the range at which the fish will appear and focusing the lens by use of its distance scale—a fast, practical method provided the photographer is a good guesser. Another way is to toss out a stick near the action for a reference point upon which to focus with the range finder. A reflex camera, by the way, is too slow of operation for this work.

A leaping fish is usually at its dramatic best when snapped at the high point of its jump. Because the action occurs so fast, it is necessary to try to snap the shutter before the height of the jump is reached. That way, taking into allowance the normal delay in human reaction time, the cameraman will find himself actually snapping many a jumper at the height of its performance. This precaution is unnecessary with an expensive 35-mm. type—like the Foton, which takes bursts of 6 pictures a second at a top shutter speed of 1/1000 of a second or the Leica with its Leicavit attachment.

Most species of fresh-water fish, provided they are not too large, may be hurried into the boat or shore when spinning or bait-casting tackle is used—the idea being to get the fish coming, immediately upon hooking it, so fast that it cannot pause to fight or jump. Then, when the pressure is eased near the angler, the fish will still be lively and able to put on a good jumping display near the cameraman. The system has been used successfully with bass, members of the pike family, and various species of trout.

Good still lifes of fish, especially the big ones, are always desirable. The rules are few and simple.

Something should be included in the picture to indicate size—a landing net, a fly box, the butt section of the rod, and so on. The fish should be carefully arranged against a very plain background and wetted down just before the picture is made. Here a tripod will come in handy, though with most of the camera types which the fisherman finds light enough to carry all day, this won't be absolutely necessary. For sharpness, the lens should be stopped way down. And, as mentioned earlier, a polaroid filter should be used if it is desired to show the fish clearly and in the very minutest detail.

THE FISH AND WILDLIFE SERVICE

Public hunting and fishing, as we know it in the United States, is the envy of the entire world. In no other heavily populated country has public hunting and fishing been maintained as in the United States. On the British Isles, for instance, good hunting and fishing have been maintained for hundreds of years in the midst of dense populations. But there, game and fish belong to the landlords. As such, the owners have a personal interest, and they care for and protect wildlife as they do domestic stock. Fishing is never permitted to remove all the fish from the streams, and game is seldom over-shot, even though surpluses are sold in the public markets.

But there only the few may enjoy hunting and fishing. The United States attempts to manage the sport so that it will be available for all—rich and poor alike. In this country, where the bulk of the streams are over-run and crowded with fishermen who fight to see how many can surround a pool without their plugs becoming tangled with those of their elbowing neighbors, the governing agencies are supposed to supply fish so that each license buyer can have a chance to catch fish each day. In England on well-managed streams, two trout are often considered a reasonable limit. Few streams in the United States can now naturally produce the size and quantity of fish that the public expects.

A polaroid filter cuts surface glare from water, a great aid in taking revealing pictures of fish being played and landed. Here a trout has just risen to a dry fly. The bottom, which shows fairly clearly, is a good six feet down.

There is no other country in which so many people take part in this healthful and inspirational type of outdoor recreation. The number of fishermen (and their ladies) has constantly increased until now the licenses sold by the state fish and game departments have approached 20,000,000 in a single year. This does not include the youngsters and others who fish without licenses, some of these perfectly legal, as for example, those who may fish on their own lands, permitted in most states. In some years as many as 12,000,000 people have bought hunting licenses. Even though there are some who buy both hunting and fishing licenses, it is probably safe to estimate that at least 30,000,000 people annually take part in these, the greatest of all outdoor sports.

There are now no new frontiers insofar as hunting and fishing are concerned. Practically every stream and every lake has been fished by some hardy adventurer. In the past isolation prevented fishing in certain sections of streams, and in such places the fish could multiply and reproduce undisturbed. With the great extension of roads and trails during the past two decades, this situation has changed, and there are few places that are inaccessible to those willing to walk a few miles from the highway to reach the less crowded waters. Wilderness lakes are now accessible by float planes to those who can afford the price. With the exception of privately owned fishing streams and certain areas that are maintained in a wilderness status by Federal land management agencies, practically every body of water is accessible to this ever-growing army of anglers.

As the fish and wildlife resources, with all their inherent recreational, economic and social values, are the property of the people; the task of preserving, rebuilding and developing these resources is a public responsibility. With few exceptions the administration of these resources is carried out by the state fish and game departments. In some states the sport fishing and the commercial fishing are administered by the same department, while in others, the commercial fisheries are managed by separate agencies.

The Federal Government has a large responsibility in this effort to manage the fish and wildlife resources of the nation, and its efforts date back to 1871—prior to the organization of most state fish and game commissions. During the administration of President Ulysses S. Grant, action was initiated to protect and maintain the fishery resources to assure a supply of marine foods and to encourage sport angling. The preamble of the original authorizing legislation might have been written yesterday. The joint resolution of Congress, began "Whereas it is asserted that the most valuable food fishes of the coast and lakes of the United States are rapidly diminishing in numbers to the public injury and so as to materially affect the interests of trade and commerce; therefore, be it resolved . . . ." Thus a decrease of the food fishes back in 1871 led to the creation of the Fish Commission which later became the Bureau of Fisheries, now an integral part of the Fish and Wildlife Service.

A few years later those interested in the protection of birds and mammals also became alarmed at the rapid decimation of the passenger pigeons, and the virtual extermination of the buffalo. They saw other forms going the way of the dodo, and secured a small appropriation for economic investigations of birds in relation to agriculture. From this start in 1885, the Bureau of Biological Survey was organized in the Department of Agriculture. Through the ensuing years these two Bureaus were given new responsibilities, each springing from a new need brought on by the struggle of the wild things of the ocean, the forest, and the stream, against the growing human population. In 1940 these two scientific conservation bureaus were merged into the present Fish and Wildlife Service which is now the central organization of the Federal Government dealing with problems pertaining to fish and wildlife conservation.

In a complex civilization the needs of the fish and wildlife must be integrated with other forms of land and water use. With the growing demands for the products of our land and inland waters, and with the pressures of the fishing fleets for the products of the seas, the need for a strong federal agency to protect a resource of vast benefit and value becomes increasingly apparent.

Fish and wildlife must always be secondary in a civilization as dependent upon privately owned lands and waters as that in the United States. Wildlife needs must be integraded with all other forms of land and water use. But American traditions of hunting and fishing are so deeply ingrained that means of furnishing fish and game for an ever-increasing army of outdoorsmen must be provided. After all, there is more to life than the mere making of a living. To the 25 or more million people who buy licenses each year there is relaxation and contentment that can come only from the out-of-doors. In fact, it sometimes seems that trout and bass, ducks and geese and deer are more important than stocks and bonds or a stuffy old office.

SPENCER FULLERTON BAIRD

Old and mature scientific agencies of government, like old and successful business organizations, can usually trace their beginnings to outstanding individuals. In the field of natural science, Spencer Fullerton Baird's name is listed along with that of Audubon and Agassiz. To his great ability and to his untiring energy go much of the credit for the organization of not only the original Bureau of Fisheries, but also the Bureau of Biological Survey—which, some 70 years later were merged into the present Fish and Wildlife Service.

Baird was born on February 23, 1823, in Reading, Pennsylvania. His father died when he was ten years old, and his mother soon removed their family to Carlisle, Pennsylvania, the home of Dickinson College and a Government military post. Among its citizens were many people of culture and refinement.

He was a tireless worker from boyhood in the field of natural history. He was a famous walker, and on one of his excursions—although carrying a gun and knapsack weighing some 25 pounds—he is reputed to have walked 400 miles in 21 days, finishing with no less than 60 miles on the last day.

Birds were his first love, followed closely by reptiles, and in later life by mammals and fishes—all of which occupied his affections until the end of his life. It is a matter of record that when 27 years old, he had accumulated 3,500 bird skins, upwards of 500 glass jars, and numerous kegs and tin vessels of reptiles, 600 skulls and skeletons of North American vertebrates, and a number of fossil bones from the caves of Pennsylvania and Virginia. This collection, when shipped to the Smithsonian Institution in October, 1850, filled two railroad cars, and became the nucleus of the National Museum.

In July, 1850, he was elected Assistant Secretary of the Smithsonian Institution at a time when the Government was beginning its famous series of Pacific railway surveys planned to find a practical route from the Mississippi River to the Pacific. Baird, in his new position with the Smithsonian, organized several collecting expeditions, and secured the help of people in the Army and the Navy in bringing in materials for the Smithsonian. Baird's contributions to scientific knowledge, as a result of the vast collection that came in from these expeditions provide the basis for most of the early information obtained by that Institution.

It was Baird who originally encouraged and later employed in the Smithsonian, Dr. C. Hart Merriam who was to become the first chief of the Biological Survey when it was organized in 1885. After 25 years with the Biological Survey, Dr. Merriam returned to the Smithsonian to pursue other work, and was succeeded by Henry W. Henshaw—also a disciple of Baird's. Upon Henshaw's retirement, Dr. Edward W. Nelson, another naturalist, who was known to have received inspiration from Baird, became its chief. Dr. Nelson continued in that capacity until 1927. So for 42 years the chiefs of the Biological Survey were disciples of Spencer Fullerton Baird.

The resolution which established the Office of Commissioner of Fisheries required that the person appointed should be a civil officer of Government—of proved scientific and practical acquaintance with the fishes of the coast, and he was to serve without additional salary. The choice was thus practically limited to a single man, for whom in fact the office had been created—Professor Baird, then Assistant Secretary of the Smithsonian Institution.

As a preeminent scientist, who for 40 years had been in the front rank of biological investigations, and as the author of several hundred scientific memoirs, no one realized more thoroughly than he the importance of a scientific foundation for the new undertaking, and he immediately adopted the approach which had succeeded in other fields of natural history. The studies which he outlined were not investigations of single phases of the life history of the fish, but included also research of the most comprehensive type. They encompassed geographical range, migrations, movements, habits of life, phenomena of reproduction and growth, questions of food, enemies, temperature, and all the manifold relationships of each form to its environment. Then followed the relation of these fishes to man, the relative destructiveness of different methods of capture, and the effects of these methods on the fishery.

Baird's outstanding abilities have been recognized by scientists who have named more than 40 species of birds, animals and fishes in his honor. he received medals from many foreign countries, and built the Bureau of Fisheries into an organization that was recognized as a leader among the world's scientific fishery organizations.

Spencer Fullerton Baird died in August, 1887, at the age of 64 at the Woods Hole Laboratory in Massachusetts which, under his direction, had been developed into an outstanding marine biological laboratory. A memorial meeting was held by the scientific societies of Washington on January 11, 1888, in recognition of his distinguished services to his country. Among the addresses the following from that made by Major J. W. Powell characterized the large purpose and attainment of Baird's life.

> "Baird was one of the learned men of the world. He knew the birds of the air; he knew the beasts of the forests and the prairies; of the reptiles that crawled through the desert sands or slimy marshes. He knew the fishes that scaled mountain torrents—that bask in quiet lakes, or that journey from zone to zone through the deep waters of the sea. The treasures of land did not satisfy the desires of Baird. He must also have the treasures of the sea, and so he organized the Fish Commission with its great laboratories and vessels of research.
>
> "The Fish Commisison was an agency of research, but it was more. He made it an agency by which science is applied to the relief of the wants of mankind by which a cheap, nutritious, healthful and luxurious food is to be given to the millions of men.
>
> "In the research thus organized the materials for the work of other scientific men were gathered. He incited the men personally to undertake and continuously prosecute their investigations. He enlisted the men himself. He trained them himself. He himself furnished them with the materials and instruments of research, and, best of all, was their guide and great exemplar. Thus it was that the three institutions over which he presided, the Smithsonian Institution, the National Museum, and the Fish Commission, were woven into one great organization—a university of instruction in the methods of scientific research, including in its scope the entire field of biology and anthropology.
>
> "For many long months he contemplated the day of parting. Labor that knew no rest; responsibility that was never lifted from his shoulders, too soon brought his life to an end. In the summer of 1887 he returned to his work by the seaside—that he might die in its midst. There at Woods Hole he had created the greatest biological laboratory of the world, and in that laboratory with the best results of his life's work all about him, he kindly and philosophically waited for the time of times."

Davis Fishing Tackle Co.
51 lb. King Salmon caught in Puget Sound.

Though lesser leaders have carried the burden since the death of Spencer Fullerton Baird, the ideals and philosophies enunciated by him have remained the guiding principles of the former Bureaus of Fisheries and Biological Survey, now the Fish and Wildlife Service.

FISH CULTURAL ACTIVITIES

The early years of the Bureau of Fisheries were devoted to active investigations of the condition of the fisheries of the Atlantic Coast, the Great Lakes, and other sections, and to studies of the interior and coastal waters. Fish culture by artificial means was soon taken up and spread rapidly throughout the country. It was expanded from time to time by acts of Congress, and in a comparatively short period became an important part of the Bureau's operations.

The American Fish Cultural Association, organized in 1870 and the forerunner of the present American Fisheries Society, was active in promoting the philosophy of artificial propagation. It had previously taken part in the establishment of the Bureau. Attention was given first to the Shad, the Atlantic Salmon, and the Whitefish. This work proved so popular that it was extended annually and soon overshadowed all other branches of the operations. During the early years many hatcheries were built and the scheme of operations gradually extended as new kinds of fishes were added to the output of the hatcheries. At the end of the first 10 years the fishes that were being regularly cultivated were Shad, Carp, King or Chinook Salmon, Atlantic Salmon, Landlocked Salmon, Rainbow Trout, Brook Trout, and Whitefish. In addition, the propagation of several others had been undertaken experimentally. By 1908 the list included Catfish, Herring, Salmon and Trout of many different species, Grayling, Bass, Sunfish and Crappie, Perch, Seabass, Drum, Cod, Flounder, and Lobster. In addition, much salvage work along the overflows in the Mississippi Valley were being carried on and as a result Buffalofish, Pike, Pickerel, several Sunfishes, Blackbass, Crappies, Rock Bass, and Bluegills were being salvaged and planted in various adjacent waters.

Fish hatcheries to the average fishermen have always meant more fish for the creel, and as such they immediately elicit wide popular support. In more recent years there has been developing a philosophy that fish hatcheries are only a means to the end of producing good fishing. The early heavy reliance upon the hatcheries has been changed to a policy of increasing fishing by improving the native waters and the natural spawning conditions.

"Government fish culture is so popular and the demand for new hatcheries is so widespread that an extraordinary number of hatchery bills have been introduced and favorably considered in recent sessions of Congress. The Bureau advocates the building of new hatcheries, but it rarely has to take the initiative, and on several occasions the establishment of a hatchery has been proposed by Congress before the necessity for it has actually developed. If all the bills providing for new hatcheries in recent sessions of Congress become law the Bureau would have been seriously handicapped in designing and constructing the new buildings and ponds and in finding competent persons to operate them. In the first session of the 60th Congress, which began in December, 1907, and ended in May, 1908, 101 bills were introduced carrying an aggregate appropriation of $2,142,000, and providing for 74 hatcheries and 4 laboratories in 43 States and Territories."

The above was taken from a bulletin of the Bureau of Fisheries published in 1908, but the experiences of the Commissioners 40 years ago were little different than they are at present. The administrators in the Fish and Wildlife Service still have difficulty convincing well-meaning Congressmen and Senators that there is little need for new hatcheries in their particular districts. Officials of the Service have, on many occasions, testified in opposition to the construction of additional hatcheries, much to the surprise and oftentimes the resentment of the sponsors who naturally feel that additional hatcheries mean better fishing.

The Federal Government's share in the propagation and distribution of sport fishes from its various hatcheries is being covered in Section IV. Suffice to say that it is an important function which under existing policies and operations is, together with the state hatcheries, doing much to help the sport of fishing for 20 million licensed anglers.

To this program can be given much of the credit for many of the fish now taken on hook and line in different portions of the country. For example, the Rainbow Trout distribution has been greatly expanded through the use of hatcheries, and Brown Trout fishing is the result largely of early federal introductions. The Striped Bass fishing on the west coast, as well as the introduction of Shad in the Pacific Northwest, are due to Federal efforts. Many of the early experiments revolved about the attempt to transplant west coast Salmon to the east, an effort which was only temporarily successful.

In the minds of many the introduction and widespread abundance of the Carp was one of the early mistakes, although there are others who feel that bringing in Carp was a distinct benefit. Without engaging in the pros and cons of the subject, it may be said that they constitute a valuable commercial fishery in many waters. Elsewhere, in Colorado, for instance, the Carp provide a highly valuable source of fish food which the State Fish and Game Department uses in rearing legal sized Trout for planting.

FARM FISH PONDS

During recent years the building of farm ponds has been given great impetus, largely through the efforts of the Soil Conservation Service, the Agricultural Extension Service, and the Soil Conservation Districts. Farm ponds are exceedingly beneficial in conserving the soils by retarding waters and preventing floods and erosion. They are built, of course, primarily for agricultural purposes such as watering places for livestock. They are also beneficial in the conservation of wildlife, wood ducks in particular making splendid use of them.

While serving these other purposes excellent habitat is often created for fish, and farm ponds have become important to fresh water anglers in many states. In the last few years farmers in Texas have built 1,000,000. Missouri ponds have increased by 50,000 in 10 years, and Mississippi reports 22,000 new ones in the last five years. Oklahoma is another state where they are gaining in popularity, as many as 7,000 to 8,000 per year being built in that state.

Southern states have led in the introduction of farm fish ponds, but much interest is developing in the West as water tables fall and artificial impoundments are looked to with greater frequency for water supplies.

The Fish and Wildlife Service cooperates with the state fish and game departments in this very worth while endeavor by aiding in stocking with suitable types of fishes. Properly stocked in the right ratios between the sunfishes, usually Bluegills and Crappie, and Black Bass, the ponds can produce 50 to 100 pounds of fish per acre in a natural pond and will average 175 pounds or more if the waters are well managed and fertilized. This is a greater production of food per acre than could be realized from beef on adjacent land. Moreover, the production of fish for both food and recreation can be secured at a very small cost.

Ponds are stocked with fish that will maintain a natural balance between prey and predator species. Bluegills, which utilize the insect and small animal life of the ponds are the prey species and Largemouth Bass are the predators. In many western states where sunfish angling is not too popular, Northern Pike are introduced to keep down the fast developing sunfish. Fly casting for sunfish is becoming increasingly popular, however, and large fish of a quarter of a pound and up in weight are becoming recognized by westerners and northerners as good pan fish and excellent sport. In some northern waters which are cool enough and where other conditions are suitable, as in New England, ponds can be stocked with Trout.

In properly planned and developed farm ponds, the management need is usually for more intensive fishing rather than for less. In fact, ponds must be fished heavily to prevent overpopulation and stunted fish. Many ponds are not now producing properly because they are not fished heavily enough. Not every farm pond can be a fish pond, however. Ponds must be planned and built specifically for fish. Often they cannot be located on dammed streams where flood waters might wash away the fish stock or where there is too great a flow of water for the small plant and animal life to flourish. Silt from erosion can also make a pond unhabitable for fish. Ponds may be as shallow as three feet in the south but must be from 6 to 15 feet deep in the north to prevent winter killing of the fish.

The Fish and Wildlife Service, the state conservation agencies, and the federal agencies encouraging the construction of farm ponds are always glad to give advice on construction and management. The Service and the state fish and game departments cooperatively supply the fish for original stocking of new ponds.

THE ROLE OF RESEARCH

Even though assistance in the management of the sport fishes is one of the oldest activities of the Fish and Wildlife Service, there are still many unanswered questions. Wildlife conditions are never static. They alter and change with the changing requirements of an expanding human population. More and more the biologists working on fishery management problems are slanting their research to meet the conditions in the individual lakes, streams or other bodies of water. Much has been done in the past in the matter of fish diets, vitamin requirements and the control of diseases in hatcheries. These are essentials in fish hatchery management, but there is a much larger field that is now being studied intensely, both by federal and state research workers.

More and more it is realized that fishery research must include fisherman as well as the fish. Problems of fish and wildlife management are often concerned more with people than with Bass and Bluegills, Trout and ducks and deer. For this reason, the concept of fishery surveys has changed. The superficial type once conducted in many states is giving way to inventories of the fish available to the angler and what he takes out of the stream. These studies are both population analyses and extensive creel censuses. In some states much reliance is being placed upon continuing annual surveys in the streams to determine the total crop and the total harvest. Much is being learned about watershed fertility in relation to the fish producing capacity of waters. Many states are carrying on intensive investigations to determine whether or not the waters are fished heavily enough to support a good yield of larger fish instead of a poor yield of small ones.

Although Fish and Wildlife Service appropriations for fresh-water fishery research had never been adequate up to the close of World War II, cooperative state-federal funds became available after 1950 under terms of the Dingell-Johnson Federal Aid in Fish Restoration Act. Under its terms the federal excise tax on the manufacturers', producers', or importers' prices on fishing rods, creels, reels, artificial flies, lures, and baits was earmarked for allocation to the states for fishery research, development and management. The money is made available to the States and Territories in accordance with a formula based upon the number of the fishing license holders and the land and water areas of a State in relation to the total license holders and the land and water area of all States. Under the D-J Act, the Bureau of Sport Fisheries and Wildlife of the Fish and Wildlife Service reviews project proposals submitted by the States to determine if they are compatible with the terms of the Act. The Federal Government reimburses the State for up to 75 per cent of the approved cost.

There is a growing tendency towards closer collaboration between various governmental groups. In Oklahoma, for example, the Corps of Engineers, the University of Oklahoma, the Oklahoma Agricultural and Mechanical College, the Game and Fish Department, and the Fish and Wildlife Service, have pooled their resources to develop sound fish and wildlife management practices for impounded waters and their watersheds. The result of this coordinated and correlated study goes far toward answering problems revolving about the management of artificial reservoirs. The need is great. It is growing, particularly throughout the Plains States, and much needs to be done to make these waters fully productive.

THE COMMERCIAL FISHERY

From the beginning, the work of the Fish and Wildlife Service has been liberally slanted towards aiding the commercial fishing interests. As will be noted from the originally stated purposes of the organization of the Bureau of Fisheries, the Federal Government's entry into that field was to maintain the entire fishery resources of the country. Throughout the years the original concept of a federal organization, one of the scientific, statistical, and practical investigations of the fisheries, gradually expanded to other related fields. In 1905, the Bureau was charged with the administration and enforcement of the laws governing the salmon fisheries of Alaska, and in 1908 the control of the fur seals and foxes of the Pribilof Islands.

In 1906 it was charged with the duty of enforcing an act to regulate the taking of sponges in the waters of the Gulf of Mexico and the Straits of Florida outside of state jurisdiction. In 1920 it was given the supervision of the conservation of the sea otters, walruses, and other aquatic mammals in Alaska, and in 1922 it was authorized to conduct the rescue of fishes from flooded areas throughout the Mississippi Valley and to propagate mussels. Later laws have served to give protection to interstate shipments of Largemouth and Smallmouth Bass, to administer the Whaling Act, to study designs and construct experimental fish screens, ladders, and other protective devices in connection with western irrigation systems.

In recent years the Fish and Wildlife Service has had a large part in the formulation and enforcement of international treaties. Notable among these are the International Pacific Salmon Fisheries Commission for the protection of the valuable Sockeye Salmon runs of the Frazier River system; the International Halibut Commission for the regulation of the take of halibut off the coast of British Columbia, Alaska, and the States; the North Atlantic Fisheries Commission composed of ten northern European countries for the management of the fisheries of the Grand Banks and other areas in the north Atlantic; treaties with Mexico and Costa Rica for the protection of the Pacific tunas; and programs for the rehabilitation of the fisheries in the Philippine and Hawaiian waters.

At the present time, all of the states along the shores of the Atlantic, the Gulf, and the Pacific, have interstate fishery compacts looking toward better management and regulation of the fisheries in those waters. The Fish and Wildlife Service acts as a research agency and adviser in some of these interstate compacts.

Some very famous fishery research laboratories have been established and maintained by the Service. Woods Hole became the first of such stations, and attained international fame in the early days of the Bureau of Fisheries. Other laboratories have been established at Beaufort, N. C.; College Park, Md.; Pensacola, Fla.; Seattle, Wash.; and Ketchikan, Alaska. The Albatross III, a research and exploratory vessel berthed at Woods Hole, studies fishery problems along the banks of New England and works as far south as North Carolina. Two other vessels, one exploratory and one research, will soon be in operation in the Gulf of Mexico. One exploratory vessel has recently been plying the waters of the Bering Sea and the North Pacific attempting to find new fishing grounds. An expanded program of research and development is under way in the Great Lakes region where the predatory sea lamprey has for years devastated the fishes that are taken both by commercial interests and by sportsmen.

Aid to the industry is given by the Service in matters of technological improvements such as freezing, salting, drying and canning, packaging and shipping; statistical studies are carried on and reports are issued.

Assistance in the matter of fish cookery is rendered; aid in the school lunch program; and in general, matters pertaining to the fisheries are portions of the work of the Fish and Wildlife Service.

SPORT VERSUS COMMERCIAL FISHING

Because the Fish and Wildlife Service has the legal responsibility for aid to the entire fishery resources of the country, it finds itself involved frequently in the conflict between the sport fishermen and those who take fish for commerce. The Service is sometimes criticized by the game fish angler as being too "commercial fishery minded." On the other hand, executives of commercial fishing firms sometimes charge the Service with overemphasizing the recreational features of its work to the detriment of the conservation and utilization of the food fishes. The very fact that both charges are made at times seems to furnish good evidence that the Service divides its responsibilities quite equally between food and game fishes.

The Service strives to be not commercial-fish minded, nor to be game fish minded. Rather, it aims to be *conservation minded;* and the term conservation means *wise utilization* whether that be for recreation or for food purposes. That has been the Service policy since the beginning, and remains so at the present moment.

Almost without exception, Black Bass, Trout, and other fresh water species are not subject to commercial use and are reserved solely for game fishermen. Here, there is little conflict between the two interests. However, where the two groups come into competition for the Striped Bass, Salmon, Lake Trout, and Walleyes, there are some loud and vigorous public differences of opinion. The commercial interests in California, particularly, have been vigorously attacked by the sport fishermen, and in some instances laws have almost been enacted which would reserve the fishery of the inland waters to sport fishermen. This same conflict is found along the Columbia River and in the fishing waters of Washington as well as along the Atlantic Coast, particularly in some of the interior bays and sounds such as the Chesapeake.

The interests of both groups, in reality, are identical insofar as the conservation of the supply is concerned. If adequate management practices can be adopted to maintain the supply at a high enough level of abundance to afford profitable commercial fishing, there will be enough for the angler also. In cases where inadequate management is exercised and the supply allowed to diminish, there is controversy between the two groups.

Proper management does not necessarily mean the elimination of either type of fishing, but means the adoption of regulations that will permit the supply to be maintained at a stable level.

There are local cases where the protection of the supply solely for the use of anglers may yield the greatest revenue and the greatest benefit. Often the demands of anglers for the limitation or prohibition of commercial fishing may hide behind a smoke screen of conservation.

Four great northern pike weighing 80 pounds caught by Bob Lincoln.

On the other hand, there are local cases where the commercial fishermen abuse their privileges. In some areas, pound nets, trawl nets, and other forms of commercial gear take too great a toll of undersized fish, and the fishing interests oppose all attempts to correct the situation by the adoption of suitable regulations.

The fisheries of the United States play an important part in commerce and industry as well as furnishing sport to a large number of citizens. Commercial interests should recognize the very legitimate claim that the sport fishermen have to the joint resource, and sport fisherman should recognize legitimate commercial interests.

The Fish and Wildlife Service has no authority to regulate the fishery except in Alaska. It does, through its joint responsibilities to both the sport and commercial interests, attempt to gather information and to disseminate accurate knowledge so that all may receive their just share.

DAMS AND FISH

The development of rivers for power, irrigation, and navigation, poses endless problems in fishery conservation and management. To preserve even

Bob Lincoln's guide, Bill Glueheisen with a great northern pike and wall-eyes caught in Lake Kaierskone, Ontario.

the minimum requirements of fish populations in streams undergoing these vast modern engineering developments demands long study and careful planning by biologists and engineers.

Congress has recognized the need for biological studies in the development of river basins, and assurance that fish and wildlife requirements are given suitable consideration is contained in Public Law 732, passed by the second session of the 79th Congress. This important legislation not only authorizes the construction agencies to cooperate with the wildlife interests, but it also directs them to consider fish and wildlife problems in the construction programs. Much good has already come of this law, and it is confidently expected that greater benefits will accrue in the future as the demands for power, irrigation, and navigation make over the major river systems throughout the United States.

Such planning, of course, is only the initial step. In must be followed later by continuous management of the fisheries affected if the value of these resources is to be preserved for the public. Details of the management program must naturally vary from one situation to another, some requiring major salvage operations such as on the Columbia River. Many also embrace a program of artificial propagation.

Realizing that planning for the fish and wildlife resource must coincide with planning for other purposes, the Service has established field staffs of biologists and hydraulic engineers. These specialists, in close cooperation with the state fish and game departments, review the engineering plans for river development by the construction agencies, study the areas involved, evaluate the resources affected by the project, and suggest modifications necessary to mitigate losses and to derive maximum benefits for fish and wildlife. These studies give special consideration to the maintenance of proper water levels in reservoirs and flows in streams below the dams to preserve adequate spawning, nursery and rearing areas, to correct pollution, to develop areas for wildlife, and to develop practical means of protecting fish and wildlife from the hazards of such construction. Reports on projects are submitted by the Service to the Bureau of Reclamation and the Corps of Engineers for incorporation in their over-all reports.

The improvement of conditions for wildlife are not overlooked. Many of the contemplated projects will flood the habitat of important game species. The river bottom lands, generally speaking, are the areas most productive of wildlife. For example, ducks and geese and numerous upland species use the bottom lands, especially during the winter. It is conceivable that a series of reservoirs in a valley, for instance in the Missouri River development, might destroy the entire supply of winter cover on which deer and certain game birds depend. Where that occurs, the replacement of nesting habitat so eliminated is highly essential for the fulfilment of international treaties for the protection of migratory waterfowl and to avoid the loss of federal and state investments in existing wildlife projects.

In these developments, reservoirs are viewed from the standpoint of their future use for the production of sport and commercial fishing, as state or federal migratory waterfowl refuges, and as public fishing and shooting grounds. For the highest usefulness in the interest of conservation, the Service is attempting to devise means of increasing fish and wildlife habitat through reasonable and practical modifications in the structure and operation of the reservoirs. By such changes the project may be changed from the debit to the credit side of the evaluation ledger.

The classic conflict between fish and dams occurs in the Columbia River basin of Washington, Oregon, and Idaho. Here a fishery resource valued at between 17 and 20 million dollars a year for both sport and commerce is seriously jeopardized by the construction of hydro-electric dams to supply power for an ever-growing commercial need. Whether salmon and kilowatt hours can be made to get along peaceably in the same vast stretch of river system remains to be seen. Certainly it provides a challenge to both fishery experts and to the construction agencies.

Historically, the Salmon and the Steelhead migrated from the ocean to the upper reaches of the Columbia, far into Canada, and up the Snake into Idaho. The Grand Coulee Dam, construction of which began in 1933, completely eliminated 1140 miles of spawning grounds above that point. No fishery expert was willing to attempt to devise upstream ladders for the adult Chinooks, or downstream facilities for the fingerlings, for a structure that measures more than 500 feet from bedrock to cap.

So a monumental plan was conceived to trap the migrating adults in the spring and to transplant them to other streams below Grand Coulee, thus sacrificing the vast spawning beds above the dam. Through special trucks and an extensive development of artificial propagation, the program combined the transplanting of the runs to tributaries below the dam for natural spawning and a large expansion of artificial propagation. Four years after the original fingerlings were planted in the lower streams, the number of returning fish from that operation justified the original plans and expectations. The complete success of the program was indicated by the large runs of Salmon in 1947, these consisting especially of Bluebacks and fall Chinooks.

But this was not the end. Increasing demands for power again threaten the future of the Salmon because many other dams are now planned on the Columbia and Snake Rivers. Some of these will be almost as high as the Grand Coulee, and for that reason it seems imperative that all of the lower streams be developed and maintained for the fisheries while the upper portions of the Snake and Columbia are eventually to be devoted to the production of power and to navigation.

This later development in the power situation has called for a new plan to save the Columbia River fishery. This calls for the development of all of the streams below the site of the McNary Dam near Umatilla, Oregon, to be maintained and preserved as a fishery area. This is known as the "Lower River Plan." It includes the removal of obstructions in the lower Columbia tributaries to permit the free migration of fish, the abatement of pollution in tributary waters, the screening of water diversions, the transplanting of up-river salmon runs to suitable spawning areas on lower Columbia tributaries, the establishment of fish refuges where the needs of salmon conservation will have precedence over other uses, and the extension of artificial propagation. This plan has been worked out in close cooperation between the Federal Government and the fishery departments of the States of Washington and Oregon. Although promising the only practical means of maintaining the highly valuable Salmon and Steelhead runs in the Columbia River, it has been most difficult to secure adequate appropriations to provide the necessary facilities prior to the completion of the dams and the blocking of the streams.

But the problems of protecting the fish of the Pacific Coast are not confined alone to the Columbia Valley. Investigations of Salmon in streams of California's Central Valley continue to provide the basis for the effective maintenance of the fishery resources of that area. Studies in the Delta region of the Sacramento River have indicated the types of fish protective devices that are needed to see that Salmon, Trout, and other fishes do not find their way finally into irrigation systems to perish along the laterals which carry water to the rice and other agricultural fields. Although these Salmon and Steelhead are of great value in the commercial fishery, it is of interest to note that 3,000 Salmon and approximately 4,000 Steelhead have been taken in some years by sport fishermen.

This effort to protect and perpetuate the sport fishery in streams that are being impounded for hydro-electric power, for irrigation, and for navigation, will continue to loom large in the responsibilities of the Federal Fish and Wildlife Service and the state fish and game departments. As the needs of civilization expand and increase, the role of the protective agencies will become more and more difficult. In some areas an increase in both recreational and commercial fishing can be provided if there is proper planning in the first instance, and proper management after the dams have been completed. As an example, in the Tennessee Valley the impoundments created by the Tennessee Valley Authority have provided a great increase in the take of fish both by sport fishermen and by commercial interests. As will be noted elsewhere, these impoundments have created such good fishing that the entire philosophy of closed seasons during the spawning period has changed in this particular area. Through studies carried on by biologists of the Tennessee Valley Authority, it appears that closed seasons are unnecessary, and that there should be a greater intensity of fishing to keep the populations in proper balance.

Impoundments can be useful in providing more and better fishing. The secret lies in adequate research on each impoundment to determine the particular needs of the area coupled with a continuing program of proper management to see that these benefits are maintained. The angling public should demand that studies be made prior to the construction of the dams and reservoirs and that suitable policies and practices be continued to meet the needs of fishermen.

POLLUTION

Water transportation was the earliest form of moving both men and supplies from the coastal regions inland. The rivers became the common carriers of commerce and the bulk of the cities were built along the river banks. Likewise, a philosophy seems to have developed early in American history that another important value of a river was its use as a dumping ground for all of the waste and filth and unwanted things found in a community of humans.

Influenced by custom and implemented by law, the uses of waters now include those for domestic purposes and for irrigation and navigation, while the needs of the aquatic resources such as fish and wildlife have been given virtually no consideration whatsoever. The result has been, from colonial times to the present, that rivers and bays have been defiled with sewage and factory wastes. The effects upon animal resources have been so wastefully destructive that pollution is now one of the most serious and complex of conservation problems.

For many years the Service has carried on experiments to establish minimum standards of water

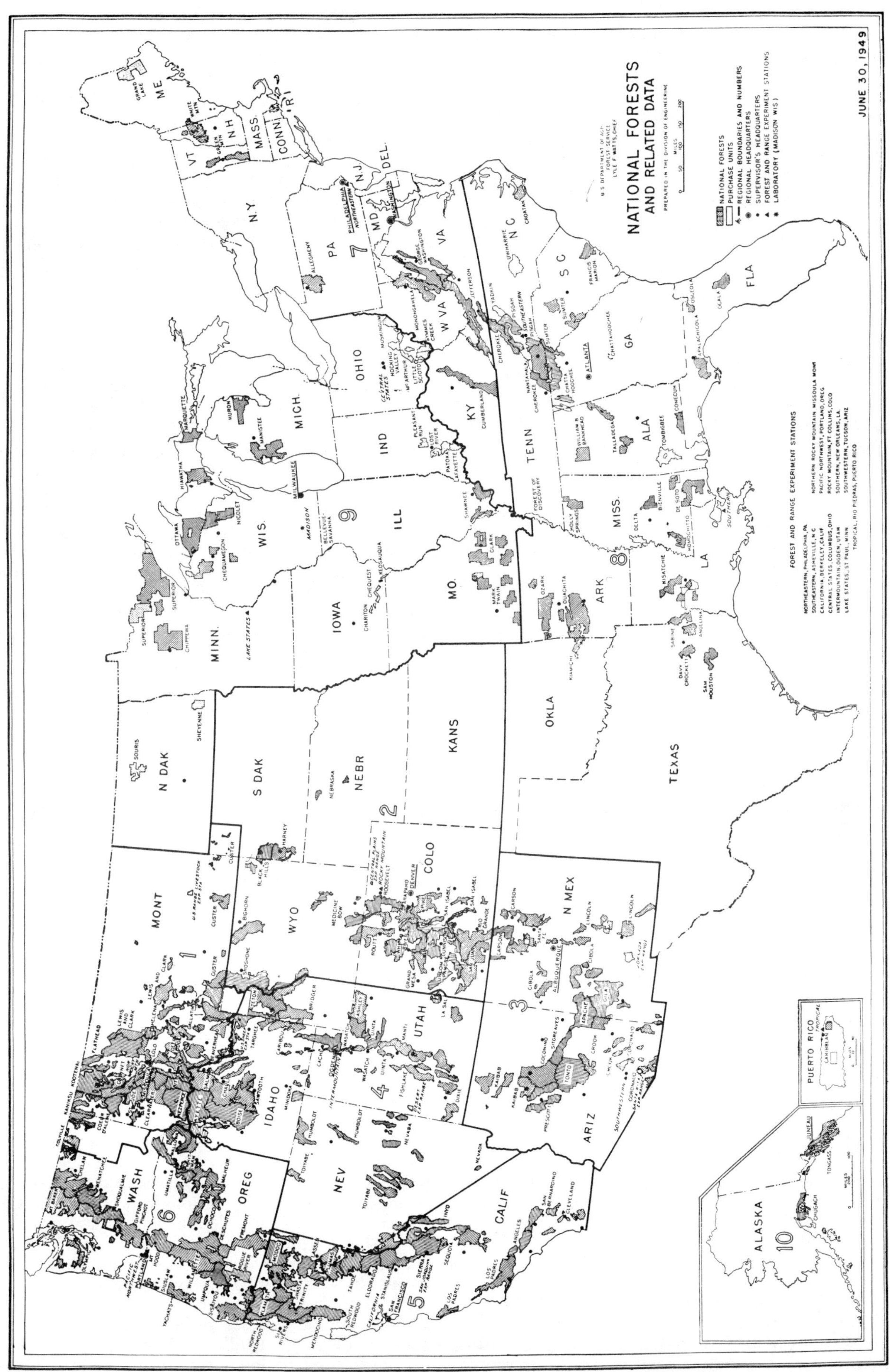
NATIONAL FORESTS
AND RELATED DATA
PREPARED IN THE DIVISION OF ENGINEERING
U.S. DEPARTMENT OF AGRICULTURE
FOREST SERVICE
LYLE F. WATTS, CHIEF
MILES
0 50 100 150 200
NATIONAL FORESTS
PURCHASE UNITS
REGIONAL BOUNDARIES AND NUMBERS
REGIONAL HEADQUARTERS
SUPERVISOR'S HEADQUARTERS
FOREST AND RANGE EXPERIMENT STATIONS
LABORATORY (MADISON WIS.)
JUNE 30, 1949
FOREST AND RANGE EXPERIMENT STATIONS
NORTHEASTERN, PHILADELPHIA, PA
SOUTHEASTERN, ASHEVILLE, N.C.
CALIFORNIA, BERKELEY, CALIF.
CENTRAL STATES, COLUMBUS, OHIO
INTERMOUNTAIN, OGDEN, UTAH
LAKE STATES, ST. PAUL, MINN.
NORTHERN ROCKY MOUNTAIN, MISSOULA, MONT.
PACIFIC NORTHWEST, PORTLAND, OREG.
ROCKY MOUNTAIN, FT. COLLINS, COLO.
SOUTHERN, NEW ORLEANS, LA.
SOUTHWESTERN, TUCSON, ARIZ.
TROPICAL, RIO PIEDRAS, PUERTO RICO
ALASKA
10
PUERTO RICO

purity necessary for the support of aquatic life. This information is required as a basis for effective pollution control measures. It has been established, for instance, that stream pollutants, regardless of their source, can be grouped into three classes: first, those which disturb the balance and general conditions of nature required to maintain aquatic life; second, those which have specific toxic action on fish or other aquatic forms; and third, those which combine both hazards.

The first group includes various effluents, both municipal and industrial, which reduce the dissolved oxygen, alter the acid and alkali balance of the water, increase turbidity and reduce light penetration, blanket the bottom with unproductive materials, and otherwise modify the general stream conditions. The second and third groups may be considered together because of the common hazard of toxicity to living things. In these groups are the various metallic poisons, acids, dyes, organic compounds and sulphur derivatives, noxious gases such as chlorine and methane and compounds like cyanides which enter the streams as byproducts or wastes from numerous types of industrial activities.

During recent years, effluents of these kinds have been increasing in quantity and have been introduced into new areas as a result of the expansion and dispersion of industry of all types. During the war, munition manufacturing plants created new and unknown hazards. To an already long list of industrial wastes known to be harmful to aquatic life, there were then added new kinds and additional quantities of harmful wastes from explosive plants, from rayon mills, and from the manufacture of synthetics. Not only has the quantity of waste materials increased from these processes, but under the pressure of war and with the shortage of materials for the construction of treatment and purification equipment, less attention was given to either the recovery of useful and valuable byproducts or to the treatment of harmful wastes for which no profitable market was found.

One of the fallacies of modern attempts to control pollution has been the use of standards for water quality which may be entirely erroneous so far as aquatic life is concerned. For example, humans may be able to drink with perfect safety water which would kill fish if they were exposed to it. Health standards as applied to Man do not signify equally good standards for Bass and Bluegills or even Catfish.

NATIONAL FORESTS AND THE FISHERMAN

The national forests are of particular importance and value to the sportsman. They include large areas of public land, distributed throughout the country. The national forests have many choice fishing and recreational areas, which annually absorb more than 100 million recreational visits, and one of each four visitors is a fisherman.

The popularity of fishing as compared with hunting is easily explained. Fishing is a recreation that can be enjoyed by the entire family. Moreover, fishing seasons generally are of long duration, and coincide with the school vacation period. Fishing licenses are normally considerably lower in price than hunting licenses, and one can fish with equipment that is inexpensive compared with that usually involved in hunting. These reasons, plus the attractive environment of the streams and lakes, and the inviting camping spots associated with fishing areas, combine to make fishing one of the most important public uses of national forest lands.

The exterior boundaries of the national forests embrace about 229 million acres of land. Excluding the interior private land holdings, there are 185 million acres of publicly owned land within their confines administered for the general welfare. National Forests and purchase units are located in 45 of the 50 states and Puerto Rico. Consequently it is generally possible to reach national forest areas in not more than one day's driving from any metropolitan center.

The national forest movement started in 1891 when Congress enacted a law giving the President authority to set aside forest reserves. Under this authority most of the present national forest areas were established. In 1905 the administration of the forest reserves was transferred from the Department of the Interior to the Department of Agriculture and the Forest Service established to manage these public lands. Up to that time the national forest areas were set aside from public domain lands and were primarily in the 11 western states. In 1911 Congress passed the Weeks Law which provided for building up national forest holdings in the eastern states through purchase of private lands. Consequently the national forests east of the Great Plains are primarily composed of lands acquired by purchase.

The national forests are administered under a program which aims to provide the greatest benefits to the general public. In working toward this end two principles apply; these are known as "multiple use" and "sustained yield." The multiple-use principle implies that the various resources and values of the national forest will be coordinated and managed so that each forest will provide for many needs. In this manner a national forest, yielding wood products, forage, water, and wildlife, can be extensively used for camping and other forms of recreation. In order to keep the lands permanently productive the second principle is applied, to maintain a sustained yield of the natural renewable resources. Thus the products of the forest are continually renewed and made available for the economic welfare, particularly that of nearby communities. Timber resources are managed and harvested on a basis of continuous productivity, as is the forage resource, and other economic uses of the national forest lands. Obviously, if the multiple-use and sustained-yield principles are followed, constant coordination with management practices and uses is required. This means that use may be curtailed somewhat, so that yield of timber, for example, may not be as great as it would be because certain areas are left unplanted to favor wildlife. However, the overall returns of the national forests in timber, forage,

U. S. Forest Service

Series of stream improvement dams built on North Creek, a tributary of James River, following plans advocated by U. S. Forest Service.

water, wildlife, and recreation are contributing more to the public welfare than would be possible if management were devoted exclusively to one of the forest resources.

The importance of good land management is readily understood by those who are interested in the fish resources of national forest waters. It is well known that land abuses are reflected in unsatisfactory stream and river conditions. Fires, overgrazing, destructive logging practices, and similar land abuses cause excessive run-off, which results in erosion, silt-laden waters, and destruction of good channel conditions. These effects are very harmful to fish life, for they destroy fish foods and change water temperatures as well as other habitat conditions.

The management of national forests is directed toward improving watershed conditions. This is accomplished through intensified fire control, regulated cutting of forest products, and the adjustment of livestock grazing to the capacity of the range. In addition, care is exercised in the location of roads so that they do not impinge on water courses or result in erosion which will be harmful to stream conditions.

The productive waters on the national forests are estimated at 90 thousand miles of streams and rivers and 1.5 million acres of lakes and ponds. These waters are primarily habitat for cold water fishes, but since they are distributed throughout the United States, some support warm water fishes as well. Therefore, the fish life varies in character, with the locality. The fish habitat varies from warm streams and ponds in the southern part of the United States to glacier-fed lakes and streams in the mountains and in Alaska. There may also be a sharp contrast on a single stream between placid sections flowing through a meadow and the precipitous, tumbling waters in rocky gorges above or below.

In common with the variable water conditions the fishing includes a great variety of species. Trout are the most common and the most important since the majority of the waters are mountain streams and lakes best suited for Trout. But the cold lake waters also include such fine game fish as the Walleye, Northern Pike, and the Muskellunge. In the warmer waters one finds the Common Sunfish and other kinds of pan fish along with the fighting Smallmouth Bass, and in the quieter waters the Largemouth Bass. Some of the streams also have important runs of Steelhead and Salmon which come in from the Pacific Ocean. Likewise in the Atlantic and Gulf Coast sections, some salt water species may be taken in forest waters during the migratory period. Thus local fishing conditions are typical of those in the adjacent areas, but provide over the country a great variety of fishing opportunities.

The variations can be best presented on a regional basis. National forest waters in the northeast are primarily headwater streams and occasionally ponds in the higher elevations. These are the native home of the Brook Trout but now also support Rainbow and other species of trout. By and large these streams are extremely attractive, being set in wooded terrain and flowing through rocky sections of the mountains. In general, the streams are popular, and the fishing resources are often supplemented through active stocking programs which are carried on in cooperation with the state game commissons and the Fish and Wildlife Service.

In the Lake States, particularly fine fishing conditions prevail. The national forests have large acreages of fishing water. In Minnesota alone the Superior and Chippewa National Forests have 1,170 lakes with an estimated acreage of 616,250. The Walleye and Northern Pike are common in these lakes, and in some there is also good fishing for Muskellunge and Black Bass. Trout are common, the Lake Trout in the larger and deeper lakes and the several other Trout in the lakes and streams. The Lake States, and particularly the national forests in Minnesota, are outstanding canoe-fishing country. Each year hundreds of canoeists invade the back-country to enjoy this fine form of outdoor recreation. Trips at any time during the summer are enjoyable, but nothing can compare with the extreme beauty of the area in the fall when the leaves are brilliant with autumnal colors.

Throughout the Rocky Mountains the national forests provide fine habitat for Trout. Originally these waters contained the native Cutthroat Trout of several varieties. As a result of stocking programs the streams now support a variety of Trout, and depending on conditions, Cutthroat, Brook, Rainbow, or Brown Trout may be most numerous. In the central and northern Rocky Mountains the Whitefish is associated with the Trout, and in the northern Rockies certain streams may also contain the Grayling. Although much of this national forest area is accessible by road, many of the more inviting areas are remote from highways and roads and are best reached by trail. For this reason these forests provide excellent opportunities for pack trips to such highly productive waters and delightful scenic settings as those found on the Middle Fork of the Salmon River in Idaho.

On the Pacific Coast the national forests in the Sierras, especially the southern section provide a rugged land of many lakes and picturesque streams including the native waters of the Golden Trout. It is pack-trip country and well worth visiting if one is properly prepared and has the time to go on a leisurely trip. In the Pacific Northwest is some of the finest fishing in the United States. Not only is there good fishing for resident Trout, but also for the sea-run Steelhead and Cutthroat, and the King and Silver Salmon. The headwaters of such world-famous rivers as the Rogue are on national forest land.

In Alaska the national forests encompass all of the island areas in the southeastern panhandle. The channels and bays throughout this section provide fishing for King and Silver Salmon that is excellent and is becoming more popular each year. The streams which flow from the islands are normally fairly short, but many of them start from or flow through lakes. Depending upon locality, these streams and lakes provide excellent fishing for Rainbow, Cutthroat, Lake Trout, and Dolly Varden. This is a land of great beauty, although the weather is often very trying, and one should be prepared to live comfortably in rain, fog, or wind.

The Southwest is normally considered a dry land. Despite this the mountainous sections, which include national forest areas, provide some very fine fishing. In addition to the native Cutthroat Trout, other species principally Rainbow and Brown Trout have been introduced. The warmer waters support Bass, Sunfish, and Catfish. All in all the fishing provided by the national forest areas in the Southwest is probably more important, mile for mile, than in any other section of the country.

In the Southeast and the South the national forests are located from the tops of the southern Appalachian Mountains to parcels of land at or near sea level. The mountain sections provide some fine Trout streams, which in beauty and productivity match streams elsewhere. They produce fine fighting fish and are extremely popular with the fishermen. In the warmer waters there is good fishing for both Large and Smallmouth Bass, pan

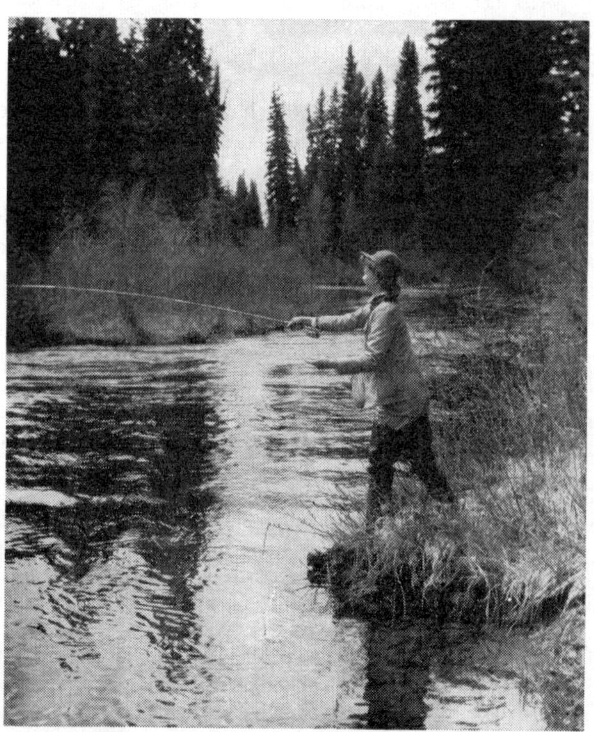

U. S. Forest Service

Mrs. Eileen Duncan fishing in Clearwater River, Lolc National Forest.

U. S. Forest Service

Fording outlet of small lake in Blue Paradise group, Gallatin National Forest.

fish, and in fact a great variety of warm water fishes.

The national forests are open to the public under the state fish and game laws. Normally the only requirement is that sportsmen obtain the proper state fishing license. In a few special management areas an additional permit is required. In Virginia, the state law requires that each person who hunts or fishes on the national forest must buy a one dollar State Stamp in addition to the regular license. On special management areas in other states in the southeast the states collect a special fee from each fisherman, normally a dollar a day. In all such cases the money collected by the state is shared with the Forest Service in furthering intensive fish management programs. These include careful surveys of the stream conditions to determine the carrying capacity, the maintenance of fish-rearing stations, and the planting of adult fish. Fishermen are checked in and out of the regulated fishing areas and a record is kept of the fish taken. These special areas have proved very popular, and, although they do not serve large numbers of fishermen, they provide high quality fishing for those who can take advantage of them.

Recreationists and sport fishermen are welcome to the national forests. All users of the national forests are expected to observe the prevailing state fish and game laws, and follow certain rules for the protection and maintenance of the forest. These include being careful with fire, maintaining a clean camp, and helping to keep the forest areas in an attractive and sanitary condition. On most national forests campfire permits are required of those camping at unimproved areas, and in some western national forests campfire permits are required even at improved campgrounds or picnic areas. These can be obtained from the local forest officers without charge.

The visiting and use of national forest areas is made more convenient for the public by a system of roads and trails. In addition to the roads maintained by other agencies, such as the states and counties, there are a little over 100,000 miles of forest development roads constructed by the Forest Service. To reach districts not accessible by roads, there is an interlocking trail system, which throughout the national forests amounts to some 120,000 miles. With few exceptions these roads and trails are open to the public. The public is occasionally excluded in periods of high fire hazard, or to provide protection of some rare or vanishing plant or animal species. The national forests contain approximately 40 airplane landing strips, open to the public, located outside designated wilderness areas. Most of these strips are not highly improved and, therefore, are not recommended to the general public, unless the aircraft pilot is experienced in mountain flying.

To further aid the public enjoyment of the national forests, the Forest Service maintains 4,500 camp and picnic areas. These developed areas are for public use and normally include a water supply, picnic tables, and sanitary facilities. Many of these are located near good fishing waters as well as providing very attractive spots for camping or picnicking. In fact, some of the areas are used almost entirely by people chiefly interested in fishing.

Some areas on the national forests have been set aside for summer home developments. These give an opportunity for a limited number of people to develop a summer home for the enjoyment of themselves and their friends. However, the setting aside of summer home areas is secondary to providing recreation areas needed for the general public. More than 500 privately owned hotels or resorts are located on national forest land. These facilities are made available under Forest Service permit and provide lodging, food, and other needs of the traveling public. Where situated on lakes, the resort operators or others frequently operate concessions to provide fishing tackle and boats. In addition to these facilities on national forest lands, there are also many resorts, hotels, and dude ranches located on private land within or adjacent to the national forests.

For those who desire to get away from the normal routes of travel, national forests offer many opportunities for wilderness trips. In fact, there are 77 special areas under the various classifications of roadless, wilderness, wild, and primitive areas, which together include nearly 14,000,000 acres of roadless back-country. For the most part this is high mountain country, especially attractive to fishermen because lakes and clear mountain streams and rivers abound. Under these classifications would fall much of the back-country in the Sierra Nevadas in California, the roadless sections of the Rocky Mountains, and the roadless area on the Superior National Forest in Minnesota. These are ideal sections of the national forests for pack trips, and there are outfitters near most of them who will make up parties and take them into these remote sections.

The fish management work of the Forest Service is related to land management and to cooperative wildlife management programs. As a basic approach the Forest Service is concerned first with carrying out a good program of wildlife management. This includes fire protection, regulated timber cutting, control of livestock use, proper location of roads and trails, and various other activities which if not controlled or coordinated would result in damage to the watersheds and injury to the fish habitat. Also, the Forest Service has carried out many projects designed to improve the fishing habitat. For example, many streams which have a constant gradient composed primarily of riffles have been converted into a mixture of pools and riffles by constructing simple barriers or dams at intervals along the stream's channel. A very important activity, especially in

U. S. Forest Service

Canoe party fishing on Caribou Lake, Quetico Prov. Park, Canada.

U. S. Forest Service

Snowmans' Peak and Lake, Holy Cross National Forest, Colorado.

sections where the land has been damaged severely by destructive logging and fire, has been to restore a forest cover on the watersheds and particularly along the stream banks. Where it has been possible to restore good cover conditions both on the watershed and along the streams, production of game fish in these waters has been reestablished. Throughout the forests additional fishing waters have been brought into production by building dams that impounded a few to several hundred acres. Not only have these impoundments produced new fishing water, but they have also been extremely valuable in providing other forms of recreation, such as swimming, boating, and picnicking. In a few areas where the headwaters of important streams flowed through granitic country with little soil, it is possible to keep the streams alive by impounding water to be released throughout the summer. In this way, particularly in the Sierra Nevada Mountains in California, many miles of stream which formerly became dry during the late summer and fall, have been kept flowing and have produced a surprising amount of fishing.

The stocking of national forest waters is now conducted primarily by state and Fish and Wildlife Service officials, although forest officers frequently cooperate. Over the years, however, the Forest Service has taken a leading part in the stocking of waters that were naturally barren of fish. This is particularly true of the high mountain lakes in the western section of the United States. It will probably surprise many people to learn that there are some waters in isolated sections of the national forests which have not yet been stocked. This is one indication of the remoteness of some of the roadless sections.

The Forest Service, as already mentioned, cooperates with the state fish and game commissions. This is because the wildlife resources on the national forest are available to the public under the prevailing state fish and game regulations, while the important work of managing the land and keeping the streams and lakes in a healthy condition is a responsibility of the Forest Service. To facilitate the cooperative work the Forest Service is guided by three regulations. The first, dating back to the early days of the Service, provides that forest officers will assist in enforcement of the state fish and game regulations. A second and very important regulation holds that the Forest Service, as the land manager, is responsible for determining the degree to which the lands will be devoted to wildlife production in combination with the other uses of the land. Plans are then developed in cooperation with the state for the protection, production, and utilization of the wildlife resources through application of the state fish and game regulations. A third regulation relates to the management of those Federal game refuges which are administered by the Forest Service. It provides for management by the Forest Service until cooperative programs can be worked out with a state for handling of the wildlife resources.

The wilderness and wild areas are set aside as portions of the national forests where motorized forms of travel are prohibited. To those who especially enjoy the back-country these territories will be of primary interest. An increasing type of travel is that of the "float trip" by boat or rubber raft. Parties are able to get into back-country of great national beauty and exceptionally fine fishing by merely floating down the streams. In recent years surprising success in navigating very rough waters has been attained by parties using the rubber-raft type of craft.

In all, then, the national forests offer to the fisherman a great variety of opportunities, both as to type of country and species of fish. There is opportunity for the beginner who wishes to use a short rod and a small amount of line to fish a small, brushy stream as well as for the expert fisherman who desires to fish in the big rivers or lakes and cast a long line. Thus the national forests invite any sort of fisherman, be he a user of angleworms or an expert with dry flies.

THE INTERNATIONAL GAME FISH ASSOCIATION

The International Game Fish Association was founded by a group of sportsmen and scientists for the purpose of gathering data relating to game fishes, promoting a friendly exchange of information among the world's anglers, and maintaining accurate records of marine game fishes taken on rod and reel.

It was the natural result of an increasing need among anglers for a central organization. During the 1939 Lerner Australia-New Zealand Expedition of the American Museum of Natural History, Dr. Gregory and Michael Lerner discussed the possibilities of such an Association with Clive Firth of Sydney who had long had a similar idea. As a result, on June 7, 1939, in New York, the IGFA was formerly organized.

The 1962 Officers and Committees were:

FOUNDER - CHAIRMAN

Michael Lerner

BOARD OF GOVERNORS

Dr. Albert E. Parr
Arthur Gray
Philip Wylie

OFFICERS

President

William K. Carpenter

Vice-Presidents

B. Davis Crowninshield
Van Campen Heilner
Francesca La Monte
Gene Tunney
Horace Witherspoon

EXECUTIVE COMMITTEE

George Collier
Michael Lerner
Erl Roman
Philip Wylie
The President

INTERNATIONAL COMMITTEE
1961

AFRICA
- Angola: Dr. Zeferino Cruz, Luanda
- Cape Province: A. R. Biggs, Simonstown
- Federation of Rhodesia & Nyasaland: G. Cartwright, Salisbury
- French North Africa: Tony Burnand, Paris
- French West Africa: A. P. Decantelle, Paris
- Gabon: Maurice Halley, Port-Gentil
- Ghana: H. E. Lironi, Accra
- Kenya, Tanganyika, Uganda: David Blunt, Mombasa
- Liberia: D. H. Peters, Cape Palmas
- Mozambique: Dr. Tomé Santos, Jr., Beira; Dr. A. E. deSousa, Lourenco Marques
- Natal and Zululand: A. R. Thorpe, Durban
- Nigeria: J. N. Zarpas, Lagos

AUSTRALIA: T. A. Bell, Victoria
AZORES: José Maria F. deSampaio, Ponta Delgada
BAHAMA ISLANDS
- Bimini: The Commissioner
- Cat Cay: L. R. Wasey
- Central Bahamas: R. H. Symonette, Nassau
- Walker Cay: S. Stanley Griffin

BARBADOS: D. W. Wiles
BERMUDA: L. S. Mowbray, Flatts
BRITISH HONDURAS: W. Ford Young, Belize
BRITISH ISLES: M. Wilcock-Holgate, Hale; J. A. L. Caunter, C. B. E., Looe; Maj. N. M. Bemister, London
CANADA
- Eastern: J. I. Pothier, Wedgeport, N.S.
- Newfoundland: Lee Wulff, Shushan, N. Y.

CANARY ISLANDS: A. Reyes-Parra, Las Palmas; G. Moreno B., San Sebastian
CAYMAN ISLANDS: E. S. Parsons, Georgetown
CEYLON: Rodney Jonklaas, Dehiwala
COSTA RICA: G. de la Peña, Puerto Limon; L. Beeche R., San Jose
CUBA: Thorvald Sanchez, Havana; G. K. Smith, Havana
DENMARK: Knud Kyvsgaard, Copenhagen
FIJI ISLANDS: E. H. Terry, Suva
FRANCE: Charles E. Ritz, Paris; Tony Burnand, Paris
GUATEMALA: R. Antonio Peyré, Guatemala City
HAWAIIAN ISLANDS
- Dudley Lewis, Honolulu; Charles Pietsch, Honolulu
- C. M. Cooke, III, Honolulu
- Mrs. Eastman Guild, Kona; R. L. Hind, Kona

ICELAND: Einar Pjetursson, Reykjavik
INDIA (South): Donald Ramble, Chirala
IRELAND: Michael Kennedy, Dublin
ITALY: Dr. A. Spartá, Messina; Dr. Geza Dell' Adami, Padova
JAMAICA: A. J. Thomas, Kingston; Denis Smith-Bingham, Port Antonio
JAPAN: Masaaki Hotta, Tokyo
JORDAN: Seth Thompson, Amman
LEEWARD ISLANDS: R. Camacho, Antigua
MADEIRA: Dr. Antonio Ribeiro, Funchal
FEDERATION OF MALAYA, SINGAPORE AND SARAWAK: Gordon D. Vinell, Pahang, Malaya
MARIANAS ISLANDS: Norman D. Flockman, Agana, Guam
MAURITIUS: René Rey, Port Louis
MEXICO
- South: Dr. Roy B. Dean, Mexico City
- North: Harold Steinfeld, Tucson, Arizona

NETHERLANDS WEST INDIES: W. F. Craane, Aruba
NEW ZEALAND: Dr. H. T. Pettit, Auckland
NICARAGUA: J. Nilo Román, Managua
NORWAY: Aage Rygh, Oslo
PAKISTAN: Seth Thompson, Amman, Jordan
PANAMA: Frank Violette, Balboa, C. Z.
PAPUA: W. E. Eginton, Port Moresby
PHILIPPINE ISLANDS: L. G. Wagner, Manila
PORTUGAL: Dr. A. Cordeiro, Lisbon

PUERTO RICO: Ralph G. Christiansen, San Juan; J. Adalberto Roig, Humacao
SAUDI ARABIA: Mr. and Mrs. C. F. Mead, Dhahran; B. F. Gates, Dhahran
SEYCHELLES ISLANDS: H. Savy, Mahé
SOUTH AMERICA
ARGENTINA: Pablo P. Bardin, Buenos Aires
BRAZIL: Dr. Raymundo O. de Castro Maya, Rio de Janeiro
CHILE: Federico Weisner, Santiago; M. F. de Peña, Jr., Valparaiso
COLOMBIA: Dr. J. Molano-Campuzzano, Bogotá
ECUADOR: Emilio Estrada, Guayaquil
PERU: Mgr. Cabo Blanco Club, Cabo Blanco; Enrique Pardo, Lima
URUGUAY: Ricardo Druillet, Montevideo
VENEZUELA: J. P. Phelps, Jr., Caracas
SPAIN: El Marques de Ciria, Guetaria; Max R. Borrell, Madrid
SWEDEN: Mogens Mogenson, Helsingborg
TAHITI: N. G. Rutgers, Papeete
TOBAGO AND TRINIDAD: Major Gerald Liddelow, Port-of-Spain
TURKEY: Avni Sasa, Istanbul
UNITED STATES OF AMERICA:
Anton Hulman, Jr., Terre Haute, Indiana
John Mahony, Miami, Fla.
Joseph D. Peeler, Los Angeles, California
WINDWARD ISLANDS: Claes Grubbe, St. George's, Grenada

MEMBER CLUBS

Member Clubs will be included in the list issued to Officers, Committees, and Member Organizations every year.

MEMBER SCIENTIFIC INSTITUTIONS

Academy of Natural Sciences of Philadelphia
American Museum of Natural History, *New York*
Asociacion Nacional de Piscicultura y Pesca de Colombia
Bermuda Government Aquarium and Museum
Bingham Oceanographic Laboratory, *Yale University, New Haven*
British Museum (Natural History)
Bureau of Marine Fishes, California Division of Fish and Game
California Academy of Sciences
Chicago Museum of Natural History
Fisheries Institute, Tokyo University
Instituto Forestal Invest. Exper. (Sec. Biol.), *Madrid*
Istituto Talassografico di Messina
Marine Laboratory, Texas Game and Fish Commission
Muséum National d'Histoire Naturelle, *Paris*
Oceanographic Research Institute, *Durban*
Quebec Biological Bureau
Smithsonian Institution, *Washington*
United States Fish and Wildlife Service, *Washington*
Woods Hole Oceanographic Institution

The Association is a non-profit organization, and its endowment is enough to make possible a stable and continuing operation. From the beginning until 1959 the Association was housed in the American Museum of Natural History, in New York City. This eminently suitable site was made possible by the interest of the Museum in the enterprise and through the interest of two ichthyologists originally associated with the organization: Dr. William King Gregory, the retired Chairman of the Museum's Department of Fishes, who was the first president, and Francesca LaMonte, the Museum's Associate Curator of Fishes, who has served as its Secretary. The headquarters were moved in 1959 to the DuPont Building in Miami, Florida.

Except for its committees, membership in the IGFA consists of angling clubs and sicentific institutions interested in marine game fishes. There are no individual members. At its inception, there were ten Member Clubs and the International Committee consisted of twelve representatives. At present there are one hundred and thirty Member Clubs, forty-five territorial representatives on the International Committee, and eleven Member Scientific Institutions. This tremendous growth attests the eagerness of anglers to share in the aims and purposes of the parent organization. The IGFA does not interfere with the rules of its Member Clubs. Its rules are, however, meticulously enforced in judging a claim for one of its world records.

The organization is internationally known as the keeper of the World Record catches of marine game fishes. At the time of its formation, records included only All-Tackle catches. In many cases, information concerning the tackle used and the method by which the fish was boated, etc. was lacking, and the claims were not checked as carefully as at present.

Concurrently there existed many standards for fishing methods and for tackle. Line made and used in England, for example, was differently appraised from line made and used in the United States. Certain old and meticulous fishing clubs had exact standards to which they rigidly adhered. Individuals, on the other hand, ignorant of the rules, often claimed world records for fish hooked, fought, and taken aboard boats by means which did not comply with existing club rules or with accepted sporting methods of the present. Since the International Game Fish Association standards for record catches were publicized, many of the older "records" have been deleted at the request of the anglers themselves. A better example of sportsmanship could hardly be cited.

The Association originally established seven categories in which fish could be entered as record claimants. These were based upon accepted means of classification: the number of "threads" in a given fifty thread linen line, each thread having a wet breaking point of not more than three pounds, the classes were 3-6-9-15-24- and 39-thread. Fifty-four thread and 72-thread catches were also acknowledged, although so few that they were not printed on the record charts unless they also proved to be All-Tackle catches. These classes represented breaking strains respectively of 9-18-27-45-72- and 117-pounds, with an additional All-Tackle class in which any strength of line was admissible.

Rules regarding maximum lengths of leaders or traces, numbers of hooks permissible, gaffing methods, and the like, were formed in accordance with practices generally accepted as proper and sportsmanlike. These rules were published and the press cooperated in giving them wide publicity.

About 15 years ago, it had been found necessary to change the classification system from the "thread" basis to classes based upon the breaking-strain in pounds. The widespread introduction of various synthetic lines which are braided rather than twisted and therefore are unlike linen lines, was a major factor in this decision. Two years of preliminary research by the Association preceded the adoption of the new system by the Member Clubs and the International Committee.

The World Record categories now consist of the following classes: 12 pound (all catches made on lines testing wet to and including 12 pounds), 20, 30, 50, 80, 130, 180 pounds, and All-Tackle. The slightly higher ratings primarily serve the purpose of resolving the new categories into easily remembered "round" numbers. All old records have been automatically moved into the proper new classes and will stand until and unless replaced by new and heavier entries. Each application must now be accompanied by a ten-yard sample of the line used in making the catch. This line is tested for the association by leading professional testing companies. The charts indicate clearly which records have been established by line test.

The World Records of marine game fishes include fish taken by trolling and still-fishing and such fish taken by casting as might be eligible under the rules. In the past decade, anglers everywhere have adapted various fresh-water fishing methods to ocean fishing. Among these are plug casting, fly casting, and spinning.

The need for several further World Record classes (two for fly casting, one for spinning, and one for heavy casting) to supplement the existing plug casting class then becomes apparent. Following standard practice, rules for the foregoing were formulated by the Executive Committee and forwarded for open discussion to the Tackle Committees of the Member Clubs. Although many anglers are enthusiastic about these forms of fishing, the response from our Member Clubs was too small to warrant the added labor and expense of setting up these classes at our headquarters.

The running record of all marine game fishes of World-record size taken by all sportsmanlike means everywhere in the world is now available annually.

RULES GOVERNING RECORD CATCHES

All IGFA angling rules are voted on by the Officers, Executive Committee, International Committee, and Member Clubs before being officially adopted.

All claims for an IGFA World Record catch must be approved by at least two Officers or members of the Executive Committee before being acknowledged as a World Record.

Questionable or protested applications for World Records will be referred to the Executive Committee. Such catches will be removed from the Chart until a decision is reached.

No claims without line sample will be considered.

In case of a disputed identification two competent ichthyologists will decide on the identification or discard the claim as not giving sufficient data for identification. In the latter event, the angler will be notified and given ample opportunity to send in further identification.

Scales

In areas where a government-tested scales is not available for weighing fish, a careful testing of the scales by the weighing of objects of known poundage is mandatory. The use of any standard steelyard is also recommended. The type of scales employed should be designated on the entry blank.

In circumstances where it is impossible to bring a fish before an accredited weighmaster, an affidavit of weight, together with exact measurements sworn to by the angler before a notary public and attested by at least two witnesses will receive consideration by the Association.

No fish weighed on yacht, charter boat or the like, and no fish weighed only at sea will be accepted as a claim for an IGFA record.

Fish must be weighed by an official weighmaster if one is available (see page 9 under Weighmaster); otherwise by a recognized local or IGFA official. All scales used in weighing by these weighmasters should be tested at least once each six months.

At the time of weighing, the actual tackle used must be exhibited to the weighmaster.

To replace a record for a fish weighing 100 pounds or more, the replacement must weigh at least one pound (16 ounces) more than the existing record. A catch exceeding the existing record by less than one pound will be considered a tie with the existing record. In case of a tie claim involving more than two catches, weight must be compared with the *lowest* weight involved in the existing records, but nothing *less* is a claim.

To replace a record for a fish weighing less than 100 pounds, the replacement must weigh at least one-half pound (8 ounces) more than the existing record. A catch exceeding the existing record by less than half a pound will be considered a tie with the existing record.

No estimated weights will be accepted.

Time Limit on Claims

Claims for fish caught in North American waters will not be accepted by the International Game Fish Association if the date of the catch is more than *60 days* before the date of receipt of the claim by the IGFA. Claims for fish caught in other waters will not be accepted if the date of the catch is more than *three months* before the date of receipt of the claim by the IGFA.

When a new fish is made eligible for record, an effort is made to establish the record without regard to the above ruling. After this fish is open to claimants, a time limit of *six months* from the date of publication of eligibility will be given for the establishment of back claims, no matter what the year of the catch if it complies with our rules and with the line test. After six months have expired, the regular time limit rules will apply. Appearance of the name of such a fish upon the Record Chart for the first time will be considered proper notification in lieu of previous notice.

Affidavits for Record Claims

The angler must appear in person to have his affidavit notarized. In territories where notarization is not possible or customary, the signature of a government Commissioner or Resident, a member of Embassy, Legation or Consular staff, or an Officer or member of the Executive or International committees of the IGFA may replace notarization.

The angler must fill in all items on the affidavit personally and the Association urges that the angler send in his own affidavit and line sample.

The angler is responsible for seeing that the

necessary signatures of boat captain, weighmaster and witnesses are on the claim. If an IGFA Officer, or member of the IGFA Executive or International Committee, or officer of a Member Club is available, he or she should be asked to witness the claim. The name of boatman, guide, or weighmaster repeated as witness will not be acceptable.

The claim form must be used in filing claims and must be accompanied by the mandatory yardage (see Tackle Rules) of actual line used, plus 2 feet of leader or trace. The claim form and line sample originally submitted will be the only one considered. Therefore it is of the utmost importance that claim forms be filled in carefully and correctly.

Photographs are mandatory in the case of the following fishes: Bonefish, Bonitos, Channel Bass, Drums, Jacks, Kingfish, Marlins, Permits, Sharks, Tunas, Wahoo and Yellowtails.

How to have your catch photographed: Do not stand in front of the fish. Do not hold the tip of the dorsal fin, thus concealing its height. All fins, and the tip of the jaws, sword or spear *must* show clearly. For identification purposes, a fish lying on its side is far preferable to one that is hanging or held. The surface beneath the fish should be smooth, and a ruler or marked tape should be placed beside the fish if possible. Shark photographs should show the full length of the fish and the nature of the front teeth.

TACKLE RULES

If a claim for a record is entered without full particulars, a period of two months is allowed during which the IGFA shall make an effort to complete the claim, and after which time, if the claim still remains incomplete, the catch shall be discarded as a claimant for a record.

Shore fishing: Any fish caught on regulation tackle from the shore is eligible to compete with the other catches in its line class.

Casting: The IGFA maintains no casting categories, but catches made by casting or with casting equipment are eligible for claims in our regular categories if they comply with our rules.

Any fish caught by any method of fishing in accordance with IGFA rules is eligible for a record claim if it outweighs the existing record in its line class.

The rod, reel and all other tackle must be in reasonable proportion, or "balance," to the line size. (See limits for Balanced Tackle.)

1. Record classes are based on the wet testing strength of the actual line used in making the catch, whether linen, or synthetic. Metal lines are prohibited.

All claims for records in line classes less than 50-lb. test must be accompanied by 2 feet of leader or trace and a 10-yard sample of the actual line used in making the catch. For line test classes of 50-lb. and more, 2 feet of leader or trace and 30 yards of line must be submitted. If a double line was used, 5 yards from the double line must be included with 5 yards of the line next to it. If less than 5 yards was doubled, the entire double line must be included in the yardage for catches in line classes less than 50-lb. test. Double this amount for catches in line classes 50-lb. test or more. The sample must be in one piece.

In light tackle claims, the entire double line taken from the end of the knot must be submitted.

Backing: If two lines of different test strength, *spliced or tied together* are used in taking a fish, that catch shall be classified under the heavier of the two lines and a sample of both lines must be submitted.

Lines will be tested by a professional testing company and claims will be judged on the result of the wet test.

NOTE: The IGFA tests lines only in connection with applications for records.

2. The leader and the double line on all weights of tackle up to and including the 50-pound line test class, shall be limited to 15 feet of double line and 15 feet of leader. For heavier tackle, the line shall not be doubled at the trace end for more than 30 feet and the trace shall not exceed 30 feet.

3. Rods must be in accordance with sporting ethics and customs. Tubular metal and glass rods are permitted. Considerable latitude is allowed, but rods giving the angler an unsporting advantage will be disqualified. This rule has been made broad enough so that an inch or so in the length of the tip will not affect the validity of a catch. However, the rule is intended to eliminate the use of freak rods, and to act as a means of protection to anglers. The tip length in use all over the world approximates a minimum of 5 feet.

4. No more than two single hooks may be attached to the leader or trace and then only if both hooks are imbedded in or attached to the bait. These must be attached or imbedded separately at least a hook's length apart and not more than 18 in. apart. The use of a dangling or swinging hook is prohibited. The use of double or triple gang hooks or clusters of hooks, being two or more fastened together, is prohibited. (The "dangling" or "swinging" hook is a second hook, attached to a separate leader so that it hangs far below the bait. Its purpose is to snag or foul hook a fish that does not swallow the bait.)

The IGFA will accept the type of bottom rig consisting of two hooks on two leaders, one set to rest on bottom, the other set some two or three feet above bottom, thus giving the angler a chance both to catch the bottom feeders and the fish passing his set above the bottom. This rig will only be permitted as long as the upper hook is far enough above the bottom to remain free and clear of fish taken on the bottom; the set must be such that a fish on one hook cannot be fouled by the other. All claims on two hook tackle must be accompanied by a photograph or sketch of the hook arrangement.

5. In a claim for an IGFA record, the use of a plug is permissible only if not more than two single hooks are attached to the plug. In this case, a photograph of the fish, plug, rod and reel must accompany the affidavit. The use of plugs carrying gang hooks is not permitted.

6. The use of any float is prohibited other than a small balloon, bladder, or cork, which may be attached to the line or leader for the sole purpose of regulating the depth of the bait or for drifting of the bait.

7. A detachable gaff not exceeding 8 feet in length may be used for boating a fish, but the length of rope or wire attached to the head of same must not exceed thirty feet and only a single, fixed prong or blade is permitted.

8. The angler must hook, fight and bring the fish to gaff unaided by any other person. (Note Item C, Rule 12 below.)

9. Resting the rod on the gunwale of a boat while playing a fish is prohibited. Harness may be attached to reel or rod; the use of a rod belt is permitted.

10. Changing of rod or reel, splicing the line, or removal or addition thereto during the playing of a fish is prohibited.

11. The use of the "double-handled" reel (a reel having handles on both sides) is prohibited.

12. The following acts or omissions will disqualify a catch:

A. Failure to comply with the rules or tackle specifications.

B. A broken rod.

C. Acts of persons other than the angler in adjusting reel drag or touching any part of the tackle during the playing of the fish, or giving aid other than taking the leader (or trace) for gaffing purposes, or in replacing or adjusting the harness (Only one person is permitted to hold the leader, but there is no restriction regarding the use of a gaffer in addition to the person holding the leader).

D. Handlining, or using a handline or rope attached in any manner to a line or leader for the purpose of holding or lifting a fish.

E. Shooting, harpooning or lancing any fish, including Sharks, at any stage of the catch.

F. *Injuries:* Small superficial cuts; scratches or small cuts made by leader wire or line; old healed scars and regeneration deformities shall not be considered disqualifying injuries.

G. Gimbals must be free-swinging. Any gimbal which allows the angler to reduce strain or to rest while fighting a fish is prohibited.

H. Chumming with flesh, blood, skin or guts of animals or mammals is prohibited. Chum must be consistent in size to that of the bait being used.

I. Beaching or driving into shallow water any fish hooked from a boat, in order to deprive said fish of its normal ability to swim, is prohibited.

Only fish caught in accordance with the above rules shall be accepted as record claims by the International Game Fish Association.

Tackle Classes

An All-Tackle record is the heaviest fish caught on any of the line strengths listed.

The IGFA record classes are: All-Tackle; 12-pound line test (line testing wet up to and including 12 pounds); 20-pound line test (line testing wet more than 12 pounds and up to and including 20 pounds); 30-pound line test; 50-pound line test; 80-pound line test; 130-pound line test; 180-pound line test (records in this class are not printed on the Charts unless they are All-Tackle records, but they are kept on file and credited to the angler.)

Limits for "Balanced Tackle"

Extra light tackle: Tip length not less than 5 feet. Butt length not more than 18 inches. Line 6-thread (20-lb. test).

Light tackle: Tip length not less than 5 feet. Butt length not more than 18 inches. Line 9-thread (30-lb. test).

Medium weight tackle: Tip length not less than 5 feet. Butt length not more than 22 inches. Line 15 thread (50-lb. test).

Heavy tackle: Tip length not less than 5 feet. Butt length not more than 22 inches. Line 24 thread (80-lb. test).

Extra heavy tackle: Tip length not less than 5 feet. Butt length not to exceed 27 inches. All butt lengths, including curved butts, to be measured in a straight line from the tip of the female ferrule to the end of the butt ferrule. This limitation does not apply to surfcasting rods used in surfcasting. Line 39 to 54 thread (130- to 180-lb. test).

From time to time, as new rules, and other material accumulates, the Association publishes a Yearbook. Each Yearbook includes the most recent rules, the current World Records, and reports from the International Committee and Member Clubs. These reports keep interested anglers appraised of the facilities and the fish available on almost every coast, and many have added valuable scientific information concerning the lesser known marine species.

The steady flow of information from anglers is exceedingly useful to scientists and other students of marine life. On numerous occasions, the Association has been able to obtain otherwise unavailable information for some scientists. The International Representatives constantly direct visiting anglers and visiting scientists to the Association headquarters, and they in turn have acted as hosts and guides to American anglers visiting their territories. In many cases, International Committee members are closely connected with one or more scientific institutions in their own countries, and thus the exchange of information and specimens has been greatly facilitated.

The Association is represented in all parts of the marine world. Member Clubs are spread from the Philippines and Australia across the United States and Canada, South and Central America, Europe, and Africa. The list of Member Scientific Institutions includes organizations in Bogota, London, Messina, and Paris. Tournaments insist on using Association rules; records are reprinted in hundreds of newspapers and sport publications,

RECORD CATCHES FOR BOTH MEN AND WOMEN—I. G. F. A.

FISH	*Scientific Name*	ALL-TACKLE RECORD						
		Weight	*Length*	*Girth*	*Place*	*Date*	*Angler*	*Line (pounds)*
ALBACORE	*Thunnus germo*	69 lbs.	3′ 6″	32½″	St. Helena, Atlantic Ocean	April 7 1956	P. Allen	130
AMBERJACK	*Seriola lalandi*	120 lbs. 8 oz.	5′ 2″	40″	Kona, T. H.	Oct. 25, 1955	C. W. McAlpin	130
BARRACUDA	*Sphyaena barracuda*	103 lbs. 4 oz.	5′ 6″	31¼″	West End, Bahamas	1932	C. E. Benet*	80
BASS (Calif. Black Sea)	*Stereolepis gigas*	514 lbs.	7′ 2″	82″	San Clemente, Calif.	Aug. 29 1955	J. Patterson	130
BASS (Calif. White Sea)	*Cynoscion nobilis*	83 lbs. 12 oz.	5′ 5½″	34″	San Felipe, Mexico	Mar. 31 1953	L. C. Baumgardner	30
BASS (Channel)	*Sciaenops ocellatus*	83 lbs.	4′ 4″	29″	Cape Charles, Va.	Aug. 5, 1949	Zack Waters, Jr.	50
BASS (Giant Sea)	*Promicrops itaiara*	551 lbs.	8′ 4″		Galveston Bay, Texas	June 29, 1937	G. Pangarakis*	80
BASS (Sea)	*Centropristes striatus*	8 lbs.	1′ 10″	19″	Nantucket Sound, Mass.	May 13, 1951	H. R. Rider	50
BASS (Striped)	*Roccus saxatilis*	73 lbs.	5′	30½″	Vineyard Sound, Mass.	Aug. 17, 1913	C. B. Church*	50
BLACKFISH or **TAUTOG**	*Tautoga onitis*	21 lbs. 6 oz.	2′ 7½″	23½″	Cape May, N.J.	June 12, 1954	R. N. Sheafer	30
BLUEFISH	*Pomatomus saltatrix*	24 lbs. 3 oz.	3′ 5″	22″	San Miguel, Azores	Aug. 27 1953	M. A. da Silva Veloso	12
BONEFISH	*Albula vulpes*	18 lbs. 2 oz.	3′ 5½″	17 15/16″	Mana, Kauai, T. H.	Oct. 14, 1954	Wm. Badua	80
BONITO (Oceanic)	*Katsuwonus pelamis*	39 lbs. 15 oz.	3′ 3″	28″	Walker Cay, Bahamas	Jan. 21, 1952	F. Drowley	50
COBIA	*Rachycentron canadus*	102 lbs.	5′ 10″	34″	Cape Charles, Va.	July 3, 1938	J. E. Stansbury*	130
COD	*Gadus callarias*	80 lbs. 4 oz.	5′ 6″	43″	Boothbay Harbor, Maine	June 2, 1960	James J. Duggan	50
DOLPHIN	*Coryphaena hippurus*	76 lbs.	5′ 3″		Acapulco, Mexico	Sept. 24, 1957	R. G. Stotsbery	50
DRUM (Black)	*Pogonias cromis*	94 lbs. 4 oz.	4′ 3½″	42″	Cape Charles, Virginia	April 28, 1957	James Lee Johnson	50
FLOUNDER	*Paralichthys*	21 lbs. 4 oz.	3′ ½″	35″	Maitencillo, Chile	Dec. 8, 1959	Daniel Varas Serrano	50
KINGFISH or **TANGUIGUE**	*S. Cavalla C. Commersonii*	81 lbs.	5′ 11½″	29¼″	Karachi, Pakistan	Aug. 27, 1960	George E. Rusinak	80
MARLIN (Black)	Name being revised	1560 lbs.	14′ 6″	81″	Cabo Blanco, Peru	Aug. 4, 1953	Alfred C. Glasseli, Jr.	130
MARLIN (Blue)	*Makaira ampla*	780 lbs. 8 oz.	13′ ¾″	66″	San Juan, P. R.	July 1, 1959	Eric Widdowson	80
MARLIN (Pacific Blue)	Name being revised	1003 lbs. 12 oz.	14′	80″	Kona, Hawaii	Mar. 25, 1960	Jim Schultz	130
MARLIN (Silver)	*Makaira mazara tahitiensis*	911 lbs.	13′ 4″	76″	Kona, T. H.	Nov. 16, 1957	Dale Scott	130
MARLIN (Striped)	*Makaira mitsukurii*	692 lbs.	13′ 5″		Balboa, Calif.	Aug. 18, 1931	A. Hamann	80
MARLIN (White)	*Makaira albida*	161 lbs.	8′ 8″	33″	Miami Beach, Fla.	Mar. 20, 1938	L. F. Hooper	80
PERMIT	*Trachinotus goodei*	47 lbs. 12 oz.	3′ 9″	32″	Boca Grande Pass, Fla.	May 5, 1960	Frank G. Burke, Jr.	50

*Line not tested.

RECORD CATCHES FOR BOTH MEN AND WOMEN — I. G. F. A.

FISH	*Scientific Name*	ALL-TACKLE RECORD						
		Weight	*Length*	*Girth*	*Place*	*Date*	*Angler*	*Line (pounds)*
POLLACK	*Pollachius virens*	42 lbs.	4′ 4″	39″	Scituate, Mass.	Aug. 13, 1960	Francis C. Ward	50
ROOSTERFISH	*Nematistius pectoralis*	114 lbs.	5′ 4″	33″	La Paz, Mexcio	June 1, 1960	Abe Sackheim	30
SAILFISH (Atlantic)	*Istiophorus americanus*	141 lbs. 1 oz.	8′ 5″		Ivory Coast, Africa	Jan. 26, 1961	Tony Burnand	130
SAILFISH (Pacific)	*Istiophorus greyi*	221 lbs.	10′ 9″		Santa Crus Is., Galapagos Is.	Feb. 12, 1947	C. W. Stewart	130
SAWFISH	*Pristis pectinatus*	890 lbs. 8 oz.	16′ 1″	92″	Fort Amador, Canal Zone	May 26, 1960	Jack Wagner	80
SHARK (Blue)	*Prionace glauca*	410 lbs.	11′ 6″	52″	Rockport, Mass.	Sept. 1, 1960	Richard C. Webster	80
SHARK (Mako)	*Isurus oxyrhynchus I. glaucus*	1000 lbs.	12′		Mayor Island, New Zealand	Mar. 14, 1943	B. D. H. Ross*	130
SHARK (Man-Eater or White)	*Carcharodon carcharias*	2664 lbs.	16′ 10″	9′ 6″	Ceduna, So. Australia	April 21, 1959	Alfred Dean	130
SHARK (Porbeagle)	*Lamna nasus*	366 lbs. 8 oz.	8′ 4″	46″	Montauk, N. Y.	June 5, 1960	D. P. Walker	50
SHARK (Thresher)	*Alopias vulpinus*	922 lbs.			Bay of Islands, New Zealand	Mar. 21, 1937	W. W. Dowding*	130
SHARK (Tiger)	*Galeocerdo cuvier*	1422 lbs.	13′ 7″	95″	Cape Moreton, Australia	July 20, 1958	J. H. Robinson	130
SNOOK or **ROBALO**	*Centropomus undecimalis*	50 lbs. 8 oz.	4′ 7″		Gatun Spill-way, Panama	Jan. 2, 1944	J. W. Anderson*	130
SWORDFISH	*Xiphias gladius*	1182 lbs.	14′ 11¼″	78″	Iquique, Chile	May 7, 1953	L. Marron	130
TARPON	*Tarpon atlanticus*	283 lbs.	7′ 2.6″		Lake Maracaibo, Venezuela	Mar. 19 1956	M. Salazar	30
TUNA (Allison or Yellowfin)	*Thunnus albacares*	266 lbs. 8 oz.	6′ 10½″	49½″	Kona, Hawaii	June 22, 1959	Brooks Kelley	130
TUNA (Atlantic Big-Eyed)	*Thunnus obesus*	295 lbs.	6′ 6½″	40″	San Miguel, Azores, Portugal	July 8, 1960	Dr. Arsenio Cordeiro	130
TUNA (Pacific Big-Eyed)	*Parathunnus sibi*	435 lbs.	7′ 9″	63½″	Cabo Blanco, Peru	April 17, 1957	Dr. Russel V. A. Lee	130
TUNA (Blackfin)	*Thunnus atlanticus*	44 lbs. 8 oz.	3′ 5½″	28½″	Capetown, South Africa	Jan. 27, 1957	G. B. Mercorio	130
TUNA (Bluefin)	*Thunnus thynnus*	977 lbs.	9′ 8″	94½″	St. Ann Bay, Nova Scotia	Sept. 4, 1950	D. Mcl. Hodgson	130
WAHOO	*Acanthocybium solandri*	139 lbs.	6′ 9″	33¾″	Marathon, Fla.	May 18, 1960	George Von Hoffmann	80
WEAKFISH	*Cynoscion regalis*	17 lbs. 8 oz.	3′ 10″	19″	Mullica River, N. J.	Sept. 30, 1944	A. Weisbecker Jr.*	50
WEAKFISH (Spotted)	*Cynoscion nebulosus*	15 lbs. 3 oz.	2′ 10½″	20½″	Ft. Pierce, Fla.	Jan. 13, 1949	C. W. Hubbard	50
YELLOWTAIL	*Seriola dorsalis or S. grandis*	105 lbs. 12½ oz.	5′ 5″	40″	Topolobampo, Mexico	April 30, 1955	M. A. Yant	50

*Line not tested.

FRESH-WATER RECORDS
ROD AND REEL CATCHES

SPECIES *Common Name*	*Lb. Oz.*	*Length*	*Girth*	*Where*	*When*	*Angler*	CAUGHT BY ANY METHOD
Bass, Largemouth	★ 22-4	32½″	28½″	Montgomery Lake, Ga.	6/2/32	George W. Perry	Same
Bass, Smallmouth	★ 11-15	27″	21 2/3″	Dale Hollow Lake, Ky.	7/9/55	David L. Hayes	Same
Bluegill	★ 4-12	15″	18¼″	Ketona Lake, Ala.	4/9/50	T. S. Hudson	Same
Bullhead, Black	8	24″	17¾″	Lake Waccabuc, N. Y.	8/1/51	Kani Evans	Same
Carp	55-5	42″	31″	Clearwater Lake, Minn.	7/10/52	Frank J. Ledwein	83-8 Pretoria, So. Africa
Catfish, Blue	97	57″	37″	Missouri River, S. D.	9/16/59	Edward B. Elliott	Same
Catfish, Channel	55	50″	27″	James River, S. D.	5/18/49	Roy A. Groves	Same
Char, Arctic	★ 19-15	33¾″	22″	Finger Lake, Que.	9/6/59	E. T. Asselin	Same
Crappie, Black	5	19¼″	18⅝″	Santee-Cooper L., S. C.	3/15/57	Paul E. Foust	Same
Crappie, White	★ 5-3	21″	19″	Enid Dam, Miss.	7/31/57	Fred L. Bright	Same
Dolly Varden	32	40½″	29¾″	L. Pend Oreille, Idaho	10/27/49	N. L. Higgins	Same
Gar, Alligator	179	93″		Rio Grande R., Texas	12/2/51	Bill Valverde	Same
Gar, Longnose	50-5	72¼″	22¼″	Trinity River, Texas	7/30/54	Townsend Miller	Same
Grayling, Arctic	4	19″	11½″	Clearwater R., Sask.	5/30/55	Dr. Van B. Weber	Same
Muskellunge	★ 69-15	64½″	31¾″	St. Lawrence R., N. Y.	9/22/57	Arthur Lawton	102 Minocqua Lake, Wis.
Perch, White	4-12	19½″	13″	Messalonskee Lake, Me.	6/4/49	Mrs. Earl Small	Same
Perch, Yellow	4-3½			Bordentown, N. J.	5/?/1865	Dr. C. C. Abbot	Same
Pickerel, Chain	9-3	27″		Medford Lakes, N. J.	7/6/57	Frank McGovern	9-5 Pontoosuc Lake, Mass.
Pike, Northern	★ 46-2	52½	25″	Sacandaga Res., N. Y.	9/15/40	Peter Dubuc	Same
Salmon, Atlantic	79-2			Tana River, Norway	1928	Henrik Henriksen	103-2 River Devon, Scotland
Salmon, Chinook	★ 92	58½″	36″	Skeena River, B. C.	7/19/59	Heinz Wichmann	126-8 Petersburg, Alaska
Salmon, Landlocked	22-8	36″		Sebago Lake, Maine	8/1/07	Edward Blakely	35 Crooked River, Maine
Salmon, Coho or Silver	31			Cowichan Bay, B. C.	10/11/47	Mrs. Lee Halberg	Same
Sauger	8-3	30″		Garrison Res., N. D.	10/16/57	Henry O. Anderson	Same
Sturgeon, White	360	111″	86″	Snake River, Idaho	4/24/56	Willard Cravens	Same
Trout, Brook	14-8	31½″	11½″	Nipigon River, Ontario	7/?/16	Dr. W. J. Cook	Same
Trout, Brown	39-8			Loch Awe, Scotland	1866	W. Muir	40 Great Lake, Tasmania
Trout, Cutthroat	41	39″		Pyramid Lake, Nev.	12/?/25	John Skimmerhorn	Same
Trout, Golden	11	28″	16″	Cook's Lake, Wyo.	8/5/48	Chas. S. Reed	Same
Trout, Lake	★ 63-2	51½″	32¾″	Lake Superior	5/25/52	Hubert Hammers	80-8 Lake Athabaska, Sask.
Trout, Rainbow, Stlhd. or Kamloops	★ 37	40½″	28″	L. Pend Oreille, Idaho	11/25/47	Wes Hamlet	42 Corbett, Oregon
Trout, Sunapee	11-8	33″	17¼″	Lake Sunapee, N. H.	8/1/54	Ernest Theoharis	Same
Walleye	★ 22-4	36¼″	21″	Fort Erie, Ontario	5/26/43	Patrick E. Noon	Same

and one may find an Association certificate anywhere from Montauk to Perak.

In short, in eleven years the organization has become recognized internationally as a clearing house for information on marine game fishes, whether this information concerns angling as a sport or whether it is scientific.

The organization's stated purposes are: to encourage the study of game fishes for the sake of whatever pleasure, information, or benefit it may provide; to keep the sport of game fishing ethical, and to make its rules acceptable to the majority of anglers; to encourage this sport both as a recreation and as a potential source of scientific data, and to place such data at the disposal of as many human beings as possible; to keep an attested and up to date chart of World Record Catches.

Communications may be addressed to: The Secretary, International Game Fish Association, Alfred II, duPont Building, Miami 32, Florida.

SPORT FISHING INSTITUTE

The Sport Fishing Institute was organized in 1949 by a group of farsighted fishing tackle manufacturers. The reason was rather clearly stated by one of the founders when he said: "We've milked the cow long enough. Now it's time to feed her." Its purpose, as expressed by the Institute's current President, is not so much to make fishing better today but "to make your children's fishing possible tomorrow." The Institute was set up as a professionally-staffed non-profit fish conservation organization and given a maximum degree of freedom in action—an important asset. Its purpose is to help fishing, and fishermen as a result. Over one hundred fifty manufacturers of fishing tackle, fishing accessories, outboard motors, boats, trailers, and sporting goods used directly or indirectly by anglers contribute funds to the Institute. Their contributions are the major source of income. In addition, however, many individuals contribute funds as well.

The over-all objective is to help improve sport fishing. With rapidly changing fish habitat due to man's activities, and with demand constantly increasing at the same time, good fishing can no longer be left to chance. It must be created—by professional fishery workers. Former "fish conservation" methods—more or less indiscriminate stocking with small fish and enforcement of arbitrarily-made regulations—did not prevent a gradual decline in the catch. Modern fish conservation methods must be employed to improve fishing. The immense progress evident in older fields, such as agriculture and medicine, has resulted mainly from fact-finding, education, and rising professional standards. Future progress in fish conservation is dependent upon these same factors. For this reason the SFI program is organized around three major functions: (1) *research* in fishery biology, (2) fish conservation *education,* and (3) professional *service* to official agencies and key citizen groups.

Institute headquarters are located in Washington, D. C., but SFI has no connection with the federal government. Moreover, it operates strictly as a fish conservation organization designed to help improve sport fishing. (The Institute does *not* give advice on where to go fishing in order to avoid possible charges of prejudice in favor of certain areas.) The organization has no "trade" functions of any kind, even though principally supported by industry, and does not serve as a lobbying agent or "Washington representative" for any group or groups with which it works. SFI represents only its own best judgement and policies, and has come to be regarded increasingly as the national "Voice and Conscience" of modern fish conservation.

Research. Sport Fishing Institute devotes about 25 per cent of its annual budget to research. It plans to increase both its staff and grant research efforts substantially in the next few years. Since 1950, in addition to continuing staff research studies, about $200,000 in the form of fellowships and cash or equipment grants have been made available to qualified sport fishery research workers in 43 colleges, universities, state and other agencies. This phase of SFI's research program has proved to be an effective "pump-primer" for important new research, generating an average of three dollars of supplemental expenditures for each SFI dollar invested. It has also helped provide new training opportunities for many vitally needed professional workers, with 55 researchers receiving SFI support.

The founders of SFI wisely recognized that maintenance and improvement of sport fishing is dependent upon a strong foundation of research-established facts, and that these facts must be published widely to establish public confidence in proper management. As a result, fishery research and its interpretation is a major part of the SFI program. Considerable research is done directly by the Institute staff. Recent examples include the publication of a bibliography of unpublished fishery theses at colleges and universities, a compilation of information on future needs of fishing for the Outdoor Recreation Resources Review Commission, and a detailed review of reservoir research findings and problems. SFI's research program is small in comparison with the total national effort. But it is clear that the public agencies need the understanding and support of informed organizations like SFI. The pump-priming efforts of the Institute are vital to demonstrate industry support for basic fishery research and to supply inspired direction and emphasis.

The research funds were awarded to these institutions, agencies, and organizations: University of Alaska, American Fisheries Society, University of Arkansas, Auburn University, Boy Scouts of America, Cornell University, University of Delaware, Illinois Natural History Survey, University of Indiana, Iowa State University, Izaak Walton League of America, Long Beach State College (Calif.), University of Louisville, University of Maine, Maryland Department of Research and Education, University of Massachusetts, University of Miami, University of Michigan, Michigan State University, University of Minnesota, University of Missouri, Montana State College, Murray State College (Ky.), National Academy of Sciences, Nebraska Game, Fish and Parks Department, North Carolina State College, Northeast Missouri State College, University of Oklahoma, Oklahoma Game and Fish Department, Pennsylvania State University, University of Rhode Island, St. Mary's College (Minn.), South Dakota Department of Game, Fish and Parks, University of South Florida, Southern Illinois University, Texas Agricultural and Mechanical College, Tulane University, Utah State Agricultural College, Virginia Institute of Marine Sciences, University of Washington, The Wildlife Society, Woods Hole Oceanographic Institution, and Yale University.

Education. About 50 per cent of the SFI program is devoted to fish conservation education. In addition to inadequate support for research, poor appreciation of modern fish management concepts by many key laymen and some career workers alike constitute a major bottleneck to progress. To help meet this critical need, SFI publishes an 8-page monthly fish conservation *Bulletin*—its chief education tool. Content of the SFI *Bulletin* is largely editorial comment on fish conservation activities, problems and needs, nationwide. Monthly circulation was about doubled several years ago bringing it to 23,000, in order to meet heavy demand from many fish-minded sportsmen's organizations.

This unique publication permits direct contact with a majority of the folk at all levels of conservation who exert significant influence over formulation of policies affecting fishery programs. These people include conservation administrators and commissioners, professional fish and game workers, conservation officers (rangers, wardens, etc.), outdoor writers and radio-TV sportscasters, legislative groups, outdoor recreation leaders and officials of sportsmen's organizations.

Feature and special interest items in the *Bulletin* are widely reprinted or used as source material for original articles in conservation magazines, sportsmen's publications, and a wide variety of other public news media. In this way, the Institute affects the thinking of many millions of sportsmen. Many important articles from the SFI *Bulletin* have been reprinted simultaneously in over fifty known outdoor publications having combined circulation amounting to many millions of copies.

Service. A variety of professional conservation services make up about 25 per cent of the SFI program. These are designed to facilitate the fishery research and management activities of key governmental agencies and certain other groups that play vital roles affecting action programs. Being located in Washington, D. C., as well as being the only national private fish conservation organization, SFI finds itself serving more and more as the natural clearing house for unbiased information about fish conservation.

The Institute publishes periodic reviews of fish conservation activities carried on by nearly seventy states, provinces, federal agencies, and private organizations in North America. Several reports, the only such summaries available to both professionals and non-professionals have been published, entitled *Fish Conservation Highlights.*

Occasional special reports on particular phases of fish conservation are issued. Recent examples (of significance chiefly to professional fishery workers) were a compilation of knowledge, philosophy and problems of fish management on reservoirs, and the 80-page *Bibliography of Theses on Fishery Biology*. This is a compilation of 1,743 previously unpublished (and largely unknown) theses—reporting results of important research by graduate students—currently on deposit in libraries at 58 colleges and universities.

The Sport Fishing Institute also operates an employment clearing house for professional fishery workers. It maintains a confidential employment register, periodically surveys employment needs, and notifies qualified fishery biologists of suitable openings. This service benefits both employer and employees.

State fishery agencies utilize SFI's technical consultation service. The SFI professional staff is available to official agencies for on-site review of fishery research and management projects and conservation programs.

The Institute collaborates closely in the conservation and jamboree programs of the Boy Scouts of America. Special events fish conservation materials are furnished. Publications like the merit badge book, *Fishing*, an *Outdoor Code*, and a feature *Conservation Kit* have been prepared and widely used. SFI cooperates in the annual summer program to train scout leaders in conservation principles. Current emphasis is on cooperative development of an instructional handbook of conservation activities for use in summer camps by scout counsellors and development of active fish conservation programs on scout properties. In all, about three million scouts, who constitute an important reservoir of potential future leaders, are influenced annually.

CASTING TOURNAMENTS

Practice casting either for fun or competition has long interested some anglers, and sporadic tournaments have long been a part of the scene. In recent years this type of casting has been standardized and provided with a set of rules. The game called Skish has grown rapidly in popularity, and there are now over 100 organized clubs. These have organized and promoted nearly four hundred Skish tournaments, and new Clubs are being started every month. Anyone desiring instructions and rules should write to the National Skish Board, Bond Building, Washington 5, D. C.

Clare Bryan, Chairman, National Skish Board, has summarized the objectives of the game of Skish in an article which is used through the courtesy of the *Industrial Sports Journal*. The article follows:

THE GAME IS SKISH

Skish, the Game which is to fishermen what skeet is to the hunter, is rapidly becoming a major American sport. While the game was originally developed as an aid to better fishing, it has been widely accepted, especially in congested areas, for its recreational values.

Among the twenty million or more fishermen in the United States, only a relative few can take time to fish when they choose. For this reason, an increasing number of sport-minded anglers have taken to Skish, as a competitive casting game. Another reason for the popularity of Skish is that it can be played with standard fishing tackle, and almost anywhere.

Many industrial Skish clubs have been organized with no other facilities than the lawn next to the office or administration building. A well-kept lawn serves as an ideal surface for either bait or fly casting. Management quite freely gives its support to this activity on the green because it does not mar the grounds and it has a lot of spectator appeal.

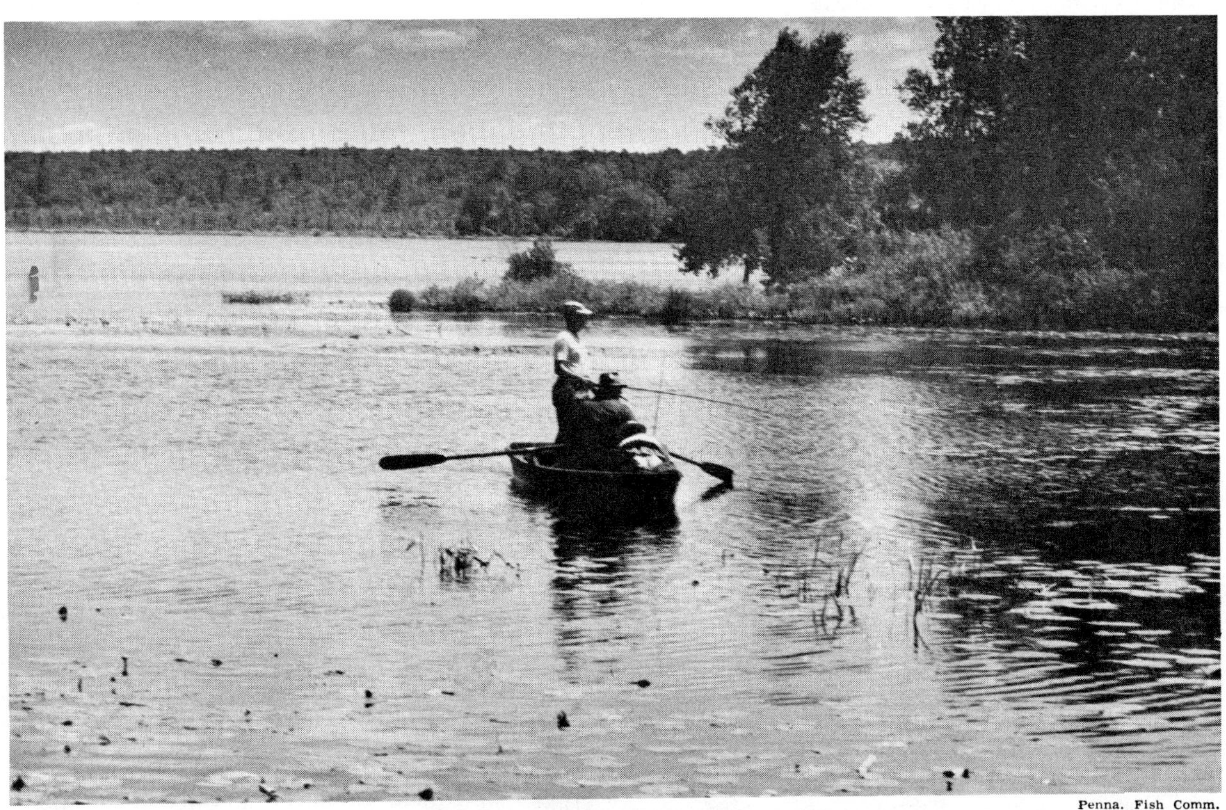

Penna. Fish Comm.

Peck's Pond, one of Pennsylvania's many Bass and Pickerel lakes.

Skish is not just a Summer activity. Confirmed Skishers take the game indoors during the long Winter months. Gymnasiums no smaller than 30 by 65 feet are ideal for casting.

Recreational directors are usually familiar with the hobbies of everyone in their organizations. By making a few inquiries, they can learn who are the most enthusiastic sport fishermen. These will be, most probably, the first to accept Skish. At first many anglers will consider the game dry land fishing, but this idea will vanish when the competitive aspect of the game becomes apparent.

Targets

The targets needed for Skish clubs are nothing more than five rings, 30 inches in outside diameter. While conventional rings are rolled from one and one-half inch diameter aluminum tubing, many clubs are using discs cut from one-quarter inch thick press wood. Others have cut costs still further by using five old bicycle tires painted five distinct colors, the usual colors being red, white, blue, green and yellow.

Targets for bait casting are normally placed at distances from 40 to 75 or 80 feet from the casting point. When indoor space does not permit 80 feet, targets should be spaced from 35 to 65 feet. A good spacing for outdoors is, 40, 50, 60, 70 and 80 feet. With this set-up the casters can get in form for official registered meets held anywhere in America.

Targets should not be bunched or put in line. The figures show standard layouts as used by many clubs. The layout for fly casting can be the same as for bait casting except the distances are from 20 to 40 feet from the casting box.

Scoring

When using regulation sheets, the scoring of games is a simple matter. Casters compete in turn from a casting box, each taking one cast at the first or 40-foot target, and then, in turn, repeating on the same target. After making a complete round of five targets clockwise, the procedure is repeated to make a full game of 20 casts. On the first cast a score of six points is given for a hit or perfect shot on or in the ring. For a perfect on the second cast at the same target a score of four is given, A perfect game of 100 in baitcasting consists of 20 perfect casts. While many casters have come very near a perfect Skish score, the very best have missed at least one cast of the 20.

Since it would take too much space to cover the complete rules on fly casting, the reader is referred to the National Skish Guide, a booklet which is available without cost through the National Skish Board.*

Handicapping

Not every caster taking part in competition will be able to make a high score; many clubs therefore, use a handicap system to build interest among their members. With the Skish handicap system, each caster gets a handicap of two-thirds the difference between his actual score and 100.

If the actual score of John Smith is 40, then his handicap would be two-thirds of 60 or 40; thus giving him 40 points at the start of the game.

Although the best caster will still have a slight lead over the beginner, handicapping does enable the beginner to score very near the best in the game. Monthly records should be kept and handicaps changed as scores improve.

Team Casting

Today, many sports are growing through team competition and Skish is no exception. As in most other sports, team competition stimulates interest. Team casting has also done much toward building good sportsmanship, and the subordination of individual struggles for top honors to team spirit.

Many industrial clubs now have inter-company matches as well as competitive games within their own club. A number of clubs have organized league competition.

Recreation directors are always looking for new activities for outings and picnics. Since a great number of their group will be fishermen, including a Skish game not only gives the crowd something new, but gives the fishermen an opportunity to prove their ability with rod and reel.

* The Board consists of a group of civic-minded sportsmen working voluntarily toward making better casters and better fishermen. Complete information on Skish will be sent in answer to inquiries addressed to the National Skish Board, 509 S. Wabash Ave., Chicago.

When conducting tournaments or games of this type, it is well to enlist in advance the aid of several anglers who will take an interest in promoting a strong turnout. Companies which do not have a regular casting club can use a cheap target set-up which can be made in a matter of minutes.

Tackle Needed

There is nothing special about the tackle used for Skish casting. Bait casters use their regular bass tackle. For the best results however, the line should not be heavier than nine or ten pounds test, as heavy lines make casting difficult. Small lines pay from the reel much faster and give less trouble. The average fly fishing outfit is ideal for Skish. Fly casters should be warned to break their hooks off back of the barb as a safety measure; bait casters should use regular practice plugs.

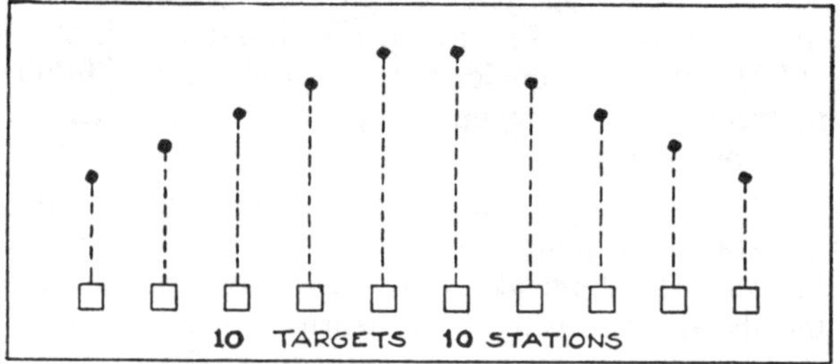

Ten targets and ten stations require ten clerks and ten judges. The first clerk starts all score sheets. After caster makes two casts at station one, he picks up score sheet and proceeds to next station, gives score sheet to clerk, makes two casts at that station and so on. Clerk at last station records score and holds all score sheets.

Diagram courtesy Industrial Sports Journal

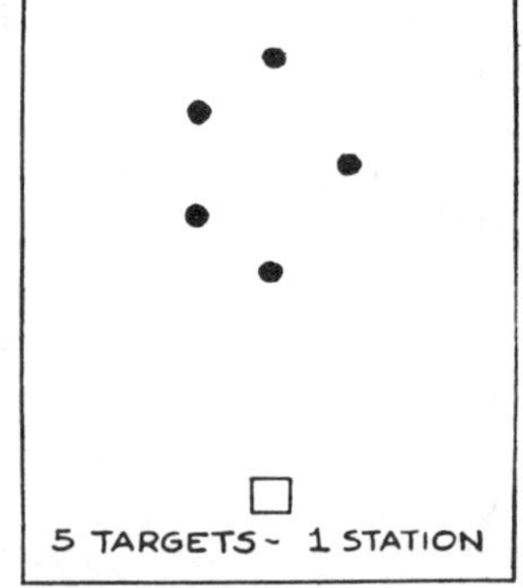

Five targets and one station require one clerk and one judge. All casters cast in turn, taking two casts at each of the five targets. After a round of five targets have been made this procedure is repeated.

FISH COOKERY

It would be next to impossible to present rules and principles for fish cookery which would meet with common agreement. Palates, like political and religious beliefs, are dogmatic and unyielding—if fish have customarily been rolled in cornmeal and fried then that is the way to cook fish, whether it be a bullhead, or a whitefish. However, stubborn, provincial palates notwithstanding, there is no universal method of fish cookery which is applicable to all species.

Some fish respond equally well to a variety of culinary treatments, while others are limited to two or three methods of preparation. For example, the Walleye is delicious when fried in deep fat, sautéed, a la Meuniere, poached, stuffed and baked, or broiled, while the Whitefish, or the Shad is limited to broiling, planking, or baking. Certainly a person may cook a fish any way he chooses, but there are "best" methods for cooking each of the several species, and these should be followed if the food is to arrive at the table at the peak of its goodness.

Other factors associated with fish cookery are the definite likes and dislikes of individuals. One person prefers a Bullhead to a Trout—a Crappie to a Whitefish. Another may want all fish fried, poached, broiled, etc. However, when passing judgment upon the savoriness of any particular fish several factors must be taken into consideration. First, the fish must be a prime specimen, that is it must be taken from water which in every respect contributes most to the fishes habitat requirements. Second, the fish must receive the proper care from the time it is removed from the water until it arrives in the kitchen; and finally, it must be properly prepared for the table and served with foods which complement its inherent goodness.

Since space will not permit detailed information on the cooking of each of many fish the grouping of those possessing similar characteristics and thus responding to like culinary treatment will suffice as a guide to general fish cookery.

Fatty, or oily fishes as a rule, are best when broiled, planked, or baked. This group includes the Herring, Shad, Whitefish, Pompano, Smelt, Trout, Salmon, the Mackerels, and their related species. However, small Herring, Pompano, Trout, and Salmon steaks may be prepared a la Meuniere, sautéed in clarified butter, or poached; the trout, if quite fresh, is most delicious when cooked au Bleu in court-bouillon.

For broiling, these fish should be split and preferably boned, leaving the skin intact, and where possible, broiled over glowing coals. Fish should be left whole if they are to be planked, or baked, unless they are too large.

It should be remembered that suggested methods for preparing these fish are merely basic and may be varied with the addition of any of the numerous fish sauces and garnishments.

The group of white-fleshed, drier fishes includes the Black Basses, Crappies, Sunfishes, White and Yellow Bass, Walleyes, and Yellow Perch, among the fresh-water species. To these should be added such marine fishes as the Flounders or Soles, and other flat fishes, the Sea Basses, Weakfishes, Croakers, Drums, Cods, Swordfishes, and other like fishes too numerou to mention.

The flesh of these fish lends itself well to such cookery as a la Meuniere, baking with the addition of wines and sauces, or bacon strips, frying in deep, hot fat, oven poaching in milk, au gratin, hot oven frying, sautéeing, and in some cases, grilling.

Such fishes as the Grunts, Snappers, Porgies, Groupers, and Whitings might also be included, but for the sake of variety it is suggested that they be prepared a la Creole, in gumbo, seasoned well with Filé powder, chowder, and other dishes where a firm, flaky fish is required.

The true pikes which include the Muskellunge, Northern Pike, and the Pickerels are fine flavored fishes, but they have a full quota of bones. These fish may be prepared by baking with stuffing, cooked au gratin, a la Meuniere, or fried in deep, hot fat. However, because the flesh of the Pikes is extremely firm, it is most excellent when made into forcemeat and quenelles.

Because of their wide distribution and abundance the catfishes have had general acceptance as food fishes. Their flesh is quite oily and when taken from warm, sluggish water is a bit too rank to be classified as delicious. Although the catfishes are prepared for the table in several ways, they are at their best when dipped in milk, rolled in corn meal, and fried in deep, very hot fat. Catfish cooked in this manner and served with hush puppies, molasses, turnip greens, and black coffee have a traditional standing in the South where they are extremely popular.

CARE OF FISH

Not every fisherman neglects to care for his catch, but because of carelessness, misinformation, or ignorance, much otherwise prime fish arrives in the kitchen either completely spoiled, or tainted, and unfit for food. This is unnecessary, for the observance of a few simple rules, and the practice of reasonable care will insure fish against spoilage.

The type of fish, district, weather, and altitude are all factors affecting keeping qualities. There is also considerable difference between the savoriness and keeping qualities of various species, and like other foods, the more delicately flavored are more susceptible to deterioration. For example, the flavor of the Trout suffers more from lack of care than that of the Carp. In short, some fish are more perishable than others, and the angler should know the carrying qualities of each so as to protect their goodness.

During rainy, humid weather at low altitudes, fish are highly perishable and it is not safe to hold them longer than a few hours without ice. At higher altitudes the cool, dry, rarefied air reduces humidity, and lessens and retards putrefaction. These are important facts to remember. If the weather is hot and dry fish keep longer if they are drawn, wiped dry, and hung in the shade where the wind keeps them dry. They must be protected from flies by screen wire, or cheese cloth. Dusting with ground black pepper aids in repelling flies.

Fish can be kept in a live box, and some species, the food value of catfishes for example, are not harmed, but the more excitable species, such as bass, suffer deterioration. The same may be said of holding fish on a stringer.

Kill fish immediately after they are caught, draw, remove the gills, and with the back of the thumb nail, strip out the kidney which lies along the spine at the back of the visceral cavity. Do not wash, but dry with paper, cloth, or grass; remember that bacteria develop more rapidly on a moist surface, so fish should be kept dry until ready for the fire, or refrigeration. The best way to dry their surface is to hang them in the shade where the breeze strikes them for a few minutes (fresh, dry air retards spoilage).

If you want to care for fish while fishing, kill, draw, remove the gills and kidney, wipe dry, and lay in the creel in dry grass. Do not permit the fish to touch when carrying them in the creel as this causes softening, which accelerates deterioration. Avoid using green grass, leaves, or ferns as they heat badly; dry grass, or hay allows the air to circulate freely around the fish, keeping them dry. This care should be practiced particularly with trout which "go soft" quickly when piled one on top of the other in a creel full of green, slimy vegetation.

Trout, if they weigh one-half pound, or more, can be held for a week, or longer at altitudes above 8,000 feet if cared for in the following manner: draw and wipe dry each fish as it is caught; wrap in brown paper and lay in the creel, but do not carry them too long in this way. When back in camp string the trout, well spaced, on a wire, or cord stretched between trees and in the shade; dip the index finger in a mixture of one part ground black pepper and two parts salt, and rub this along the back bone inside the viceral cavity. Hang the trout out at night, but take them in the tent, or cabin during the day and lay them in an abundance of dry grass, or hay. See that they do not touch, and avoid getting them wet when it rains. If this procedure is followed the trout will dry out almost like "jerky". When ready to cook soak them in cold water for 20 or 30 minutes. They will resume their natural appearance, and may be prepared as fresh trout.

Never put dead fish in water, regardless of how cold it is, with the idea of keeping them fresh. Kill, draw, and dry immediately.

The hot sun causes fish to soften rapidly and lose much of their original goodness. Keep them in the shade at all times.

An ice box which excludes air will taint fish, so avoid holding them in such a box for any length of time. Stale air contaminates fish almost as rapidly as it does butter and milk. Remember to clean and freshen your ice box occasionally by washing it in a boiling soda-water solution.

The practice of soaking dressed fish in brine on the theory that it improves the flavor, or extracts some objectionable taste is not only unnecessary, but altogether detrimental to the final results of good fish cookery. The "mossy" or "rotten log" taint often encountered in the flesh of fresh-water fishes is caused by mold-like, micro-organisms known as actinomyces, which exist in mud, decaying vegetation, and water. These micro-organisms are taken into the blood stream through the gills, thence into the tissues of the fish, producing an unsavory taint which prevails against all manner of soaking, seasoning, or other culinary treatment.

If fish are to be prepared by pickling, or smoking, it is necessary to soak them in brine for varying lengths of time, depending upon the method of processing desired.

It is important that fish be drawn immediately, since the stomach content starts putrefying shortly after the fish is taken, and the gastric juices quickly attacks the visceral cavity, often eating into the flesh, causing taint.

When fish are to be held for an indefinite period, they may be frozen; but this method should be used only as a last resort with some species. Freezing often results in an inferior dish, although modern deep freezing eliminates much of the early objections to this method of preservation. To eliminate the loss of natural juices in the freezing process fish should be "glazed" by building up a layer of ice around the flesh. Fish preserved by this process will keep for many months without loss of flavor.

CAMP FOODS AND COOKING UTENSILS

There is a saying that "What is one man's food is another man's poison." A man old enough to go on fishing trips that involve camping and outdoor cooking knows what foods he likes, and what foods agree with him, and give energy when working hard in the open air. Within certain limitations there is no reason why a camp food list should not be made from the things he prefers.

These limitations on camp food are about as follows: (1) The items must not spoil in hot or freezing weather. (2) They must be foods that the party knows how to prepare. (3) They must not be too heavy or bulky. (4) Under certain conditions ease of preparation may be important.

For example, canned goods are heavy in proportion to their food value, soups in particular. Where the fisherman cannot count on killing meat or catching fish, meat must be taken. Bacon and ham keep well and have the greatest nutriment for their weight and bulk, but one may tire of them as a steady diet, and some canned meats may be very desirable.

Bread is a little tedious and difficult to bake in camp. Cereals in the form of porridge are a good substitute for bread, contain even more food value, and are the lightest, quickest, and easiest of all foods to prepare. Dry breakfast foods are not appetizing unless one has fresh milk.

There is no reason why campers should deny themselves fresh vegetables. Potatoes and onions carried in a gunny sack keep well. Most other vegetables will keep fresh if wrapped first in waxed paper, and then in an outside wrapper of brown paper, both tied tight. Fresh butter keeps nice in brisk fall weather, or canned butter can be had. Fresh eggs will also keep for a month if wrapped in waxed paper, and then in crumpled newspapers to prevent breaking. Any of these foods can be prevented from freezing at night by placing them in a shallow pit within the tent and covering it with a tarp.

Except in warm and humid weather fresh meat can be kept for a time, by hanging in the shade and air in a meat safe. This is simply a large cheesecloth bag, suspended bottom up with a hook inside the bottom, and hoops like barrel hoops to extend it. The meat is inserted in the open under end and hung from the hook, the open end being then tied shut. The hoops keep the cheesecloth from touching the meat, and the safe is thoroughly flyproof. Free circulation of cool air keeps the meat fresh. Or meat may be cut up and placed in a covered pot in a cold spring. In canoe travel meat can be kept by placing it in the extreme bow or stern close to the keel.

Incidentally, it may be well to mention here that men, can live in excellent health, on a diet of meat alone, provided that some of it is eaten very rare, and that as much *fat* meat as the system craves is available. Fresh raw meat is a perfect cure for scurvy. In the absence of fresh meat, those obliged to subsist for long periods on dried and canned foods can now avoid scurvy by daily vitamin pills.

When fresh milk cannot be obtained, excellent substitutes are canned evaporated milk or powdered whole milk; the latter is considerably preferable. To prepare powdered milk, place a heaping tablespoonful in a cup of cold water and beat until dissolved.

Many canned food lists have been published, varying on components and amounts, with the preferences and experiences of the writers. These will seldom suit the tastes, appetites, and transportation facilities of any individual or party without considerable modification. Broadly speaking, when campers cannot rely on the country for meat or fish, 2 pounds per man per day of the fairly dry goods such as flour, cereals, beans, and bacon should be taken, or 3 pounds per day of the more liquid canned meats and vegetables. The amount of each article depends upon the number of portions one wishes to prepare, and the amount eaten at one meal; these data can be gained only by experience. For example, if rolled oats are used each morning, find out at home how many of the usual servings are contained in a 3-pound package.

The following is an old-fashioned list such as experienced wilderness campers preferred for trips on which they expected to catch at least some fish. It is based on canoe or pack-horse transportation. The amounts given are for one healthy, hard-working man for one month and should be used only as a general guide.

Flour	15 lbs.
Baking powder	1 can
Cereals (rolled oats, corn meal, hominy, rice)	6 lbs.
Salt	2 lbs.
Sugar, granulated	5 lbs.
Maple syrup	1 qt.
Black pepper	1 can
Butter, fresh or canned	3 lbs.
Powdered milk	3 lbs.
Eggs, fresh	2 doz.
Eggs, powdered	1 can
Bacon, breakfast	3 lbs.
Ham	2 lbs.
Salt pork (for beans)	2 lbs
Beans, white navy	5 lbs.
Lard or Crisco, 1 can	5 lbs.
Potatoes, fresh	15 lbs.
Onions, fresh	5 lbs.
Dried fruits (prunes, apricots, apples, figs dates)	5 lbs.
Tea	1 lb.
Coffee, powdered, instantaneous	2 lbs.
Sweet chocolate (for lunches)	20 cakes
Kitchen soap	4 cakes
Matches in cans—ample and then some more	
TOTAL WEIGHT, about	90 lbs.

Fill up to limit of transportation facilities with fresh fruit and fresh vegetables.

This list will not suffice unless at least a small amount of meat or fish can be counted on from the country. If not, add about five cans of meat or other foods according to preference. Always consult guides and cooks before finally completing the food list, and take foods they prefer. Unless they are well fed according to their tastes they cannot be expected to give their best and most enthusiastic services. There is no reason why some luxuries should not be taken. For example, a little fresh lettuce and celery, plus a can of mayonnaise dressing, plus canned lobster, plus hard-boiled eggs, spells lobster salad.

D. T. Abercrombie, N. Y.

A Reflector Oven, an Invaluable Aid.

Most of these articles had best be packed in waterproof cotton bags of 5 to 10 pounds' capacity. Bacon, ham, butter, etc., should be wrapped in waxed paper before placing in the bags. Lard, powdered coffee, milk, etc., go in pressed-top cans. Take an extra can into which to pour and salvage bacon grease. All the food can then be packed in panniers, packsacks, or duffle bags.

The place to learn to cook is over the kitchen range. There are a number of excellent camp cookery books which will help, but one planning to cook in camp *should not count on book knowledge alone.* Cooking in camp is no different from cooking over the home stove, as the campfire can be regulated to give any degree of heat desired. As a rule, however, home cooking utensils are extremely inconvenient for use over an open fire.

A camper planning to do his own cooking needs a carefully selected outfit of camp cooking utensils. He needs at least three kettles, as potatoes, boiled meat, and coffee may be desired at the same meal. Two frying pans permit bacon and flapjacks to be cooked simultaneously. There should be some sort of oven for baking, and a big pan that will do for both flour mixing and dishwashing. There should be a plate, bowl, cup, knife, fork, teaspoon, and tablespoon for each man, and one or two extras for serving, as well as the miscellaneous articles on the following list. The kettles should have covers and bails so they can be suspended over the fire, and they should also nest together. The smallest kettle will probably be used for tea and coffee, but *do not* get one with a spout; spouts are virtually impossible to clean, and unfit the kettles for other use. A spout with strainer is not needed if powdered coffee, which is preferable for camp is used. Frying pans are most conveniently packed if they have folding or detachable handles. Most of the utensils can be made of aluminum (but the cups should be of enamelware or tin, as aluminum burns the lips.

Excellent sets of aluminum cooking utensils, as

D. T. Abercrombie, N. Y.

A complete camp cooking outfit of aluminum which will nest in a small space.

shown above are on the market. All nest in a canvas bag about 12 by 12 inches, except the reflector baker which goes in a bag of its own. Thus the utensils for a party of three should consist approximately of the following:

3 Camp kettles, to nest.
2 Frying pans, 12", with folding handles.
1 Dishpan, large.
1 Folding aluminum reflector baker with pan.
4 each; plates, bowls, cups, forks, knives, teaspoons, tablespoons.
1 Large cooking spoon.
1 Large cooking fork.
1 Butcher knife with sheath.
1 Cake turner.
1 Can opener.
1 each; salt and pepper shakers.
2 Dish towels.
1 Dish mop.
1 Canvas water bucket.
1 Canvas bag to hold the outfit.

For four or five men, add one larger kettle, one more frying pan, and the necessary plates, cups, bowls, and cutlery.

COOKING FIRES

A word or two about fires may be helpful to those without experience. Place two 4-foot logs about 5 inches apart, raising them an inch or so off the ground with rocks at the ends. Build the fire between these logs, small dry pieces first, then long, split wood. While the small stuff is blazing up high, let the water in the kettles be heating. As the fire burns down, add the dry split wood; this will reduce the size of the blaze and soon the fine coals between the logs will be just right for frying and broiling.

The Best Arrangement for the Cooking Fire.

At each end of the logs drive a stout forked stake, with the forks about 4 feet above the ground. Lay a cross-pole of green wood in the forks. From this cross-pole suspend the kettles with reversed forked sticks with notches for the bails. These should be cut to hold the kettle bottoms the desired height above the fire. A kettle hung near the center of the fire boils hard; hung at the side close to the upright forked posts, it will keep the contained food warm. Frying pans can be balanced on the two logs. Regulate the fire by adding dry, split wood between the logs as needed. For baking, put on another backlog and pile split wood against it so as to make a high wall of flame, and stand the reflector baker in front of the blaze. Have a green-wood poker at hand, and a pair of cheap cotton work gloves to handle hot utensils. After the evening meal remove the cross-pole and pile 4-foot logs high for the friendship fire.

And before you leave camp put that fire DEAD OUT.

FISH TROPHIES

The first step in the preparation of a fish for mounting is to make measurements, color notes, and a traced outline of the fish on a sheet of paper.

Before skinning, wash the fish with a saturated solution of alum water to remove the slime. Select the best side for exposure and make a cut on the opposite side along the middle from head to the tail. The fish can be opened on the belly if both sides are to be shown.

When skinning, care must be taken not to cut the skin or injure the silver lining next to the skin.

After the body has been removed, clean out the inside of the skull, taking out the eyes and gills. Then immerse skin in a salt water bath to remove any blood. Drain well and salt both sides thoroughly leaving for a couple of days.

After this, remove the old salt and resalt. In order that the specimen reach the preparator in a good pliable condition, it should be well padded and securely wrapped in cloth, keeping the fish straightened out at all times.

If skinning is not possible, freeze the fish and ship in dry ice to its destination. Special care should be taken in the packing of a frozen specimen, padding well so as not to break the brittle fish.

HOW TO FILLET A FISH

Do you ever get tired of picking bones out of fish? Here is a method of filleting which will enable you to enjoy bone-free bass steaks.

Photos by Henry S. Mosby
From: Virginia Wildlife

1. With sharp knife slit skin from the head, along top of back, to the tail fin.

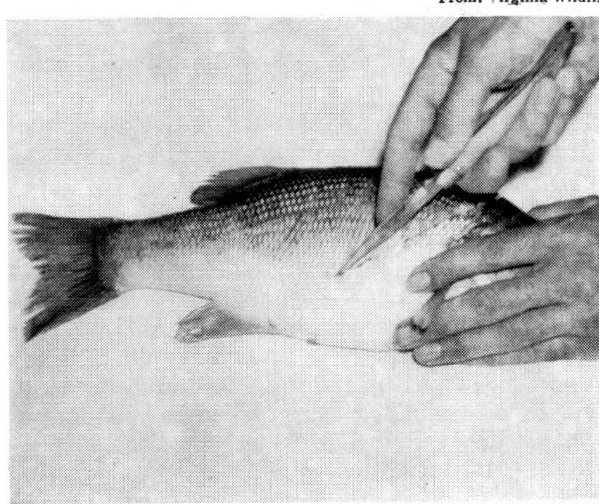

2. Extend cut in skin from head to lower fin and along bottom of fish to tail fin.

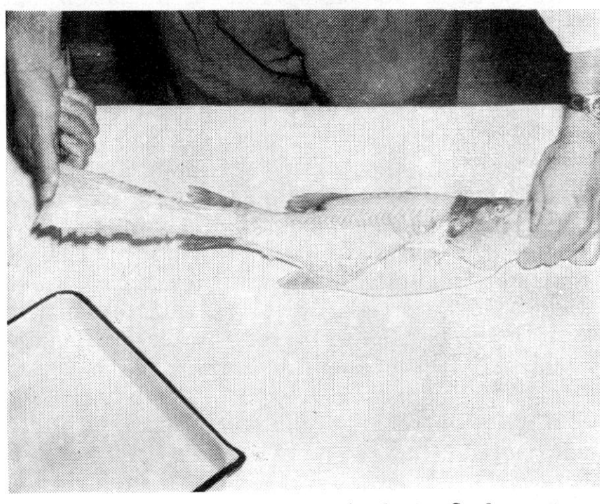

3. Being careful not to include flesh, pull skin off all the way back to tail fin.

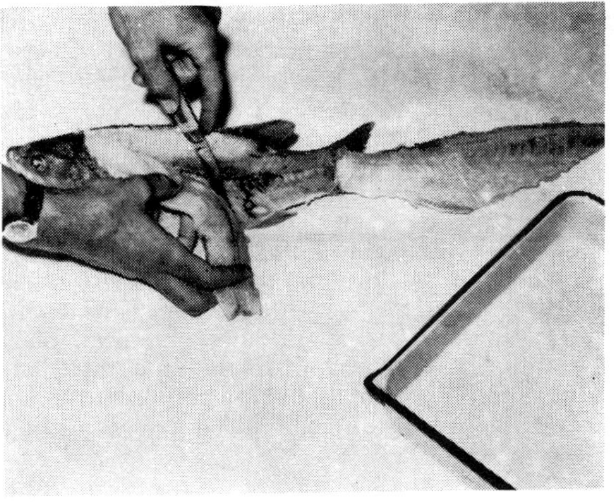

4. Run knife next to backbone from tail to head. Sever fillet close to the head.

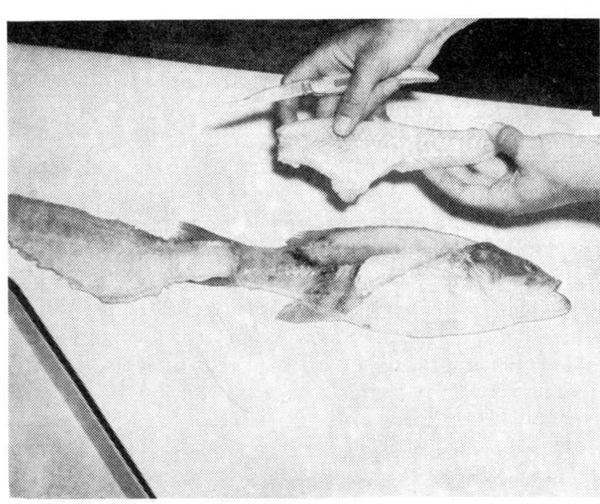

5. Use same procedure for both sides. Remove fillets and discard remainder of fish.

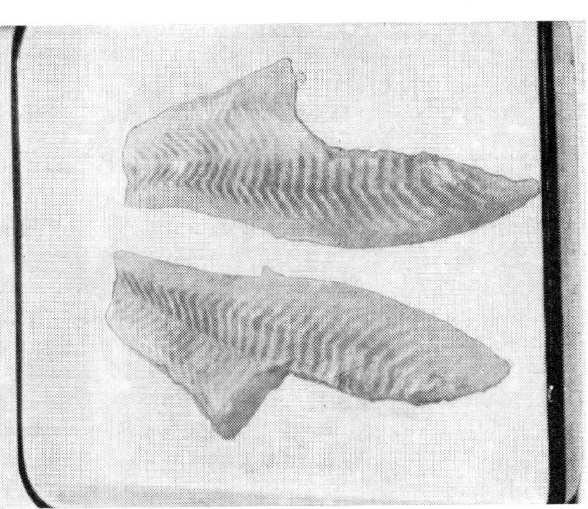

6. Fillets contain nearly all of edible part of fish. Salt, meal, and fry in deep fat.

FISH PREDATION

Fishermen are aware that beneath the placid waters of a lake, or under the ocean waves, or within the riffles of a stream, there exists an endless savagery of eat and be eaten that only civilized man can appreciate. This unceasing struggle is known as *predation,* the capturing and devouring of one living animal by another, and is essential for the wide variety and quantity of aquatic life that man himself captures or preys upon for one reason or another.

At the bottom of this struggle—or *food chain* as it is sometimes called—is the plant life upon which all animal life depends. This plant life occurs not only in the form of "weed beds" or rooted vegetation with which every fisherman is familiar, but also in the form of tiny, often one-celled, plants that are suspended in the water and are difficult to see with the naked eye except when so abundant as to make the water turbid. These minute plants, together with tiny, often microscopic, animals that are also suspended in the water and carried about by currents make up what is called *plankton.* Animal plankton feeds upon plant plankton (which manufactures its own food) and the two are fed upon by larger aquatic animals until the chain may end up with such large fishes as pike, pickerel, muskellunge, lake trout, bass, bonito, bluefish and tuna. Sometimes the food chains have only a few links, as when lake trout feed upon ciscos or alewives—both of which feed upon plankton—or when tuna or bonito feed upon menhaden or some other plankton-feeding member of the herring family. At other times the food chain may be so lengthy as to be reminiscent of the "dog that killed the cat that ate the rat, that ate the malt, etc." in "The House that Jack Built." In all instances, however, plant life is the foundation link in the food chain and makes possible the extensive predation and consequent wide variety of food and game fishes utilized by man.

It is questionable whether there is any such thing as a totally *non-predaceous* fish, in that most, if not all, species definitely include "a little meat in the diet." In fact, plankton-feeders such as herring and ciscos—which strain out plankton from the water—consume animal, as well as plant, plankton; and both the Atlantic herring and the cisco may seek out and devour various aquatic animals several inches in length. For example, adult Ciscos in Lake Simcoe, Ontario, feed almost exclusively on the Lake or Emerald Shiner during certain months of the year and can be readily taken on hook and line either by cut bait or with metal jigs and spoons. Similarly, the Alewife is often taken by anglers in the bays of our middle Atlantic coast while fishing with sea worms or blood worms. Again, such species of forage minnows as the Fathead Minnow, the Bluntnose Minnow, and the Silvery Minnow, which have specially elongated intestines for digesting plant material, feed upon small animal organisms to some extent.

On the other hand, it is highly doubtful whether many species of fish, e.g. members of the pike family, Largemouth Bass, Bluefish and tuna, ever devour plant material except by accident, although the voracious Atlantic Mackerel does feed extensively upon animal plankton.

The terms *predaceous* and *non-predaceous* therefore, when applied to fishes, often refer—and rather vaguely at that—to the *degree of predation* rather than to distinctly separate types of feeding behavior, and it is probably advisable to deal cautiously with the term *non-predaceous.*

Predation is essential to the food chains that provide the wide variety of fish highly valued by man, and it is easy to perceive that without the presence of highly predaceous species, not only would sport-fishing as we now know it cease to exist, but man's appetite for fish would have to be met by Herring, Pilchard, Sardines, Anchovies, Mullet, Menhaden, Ciscos, Paddlefish, Carp, Goldfish, Golden Shiners, and the like. Not an encouraging thought! Moreover, it should be noted that while man's tastes in food mammals and birds are for the herbivorous types, his appetite for fish tends toward highly predaceous species such as Halibut, Swordfish, Fluke, Salmon, Trout, Bluefish and Tuna.

Because these food chains and the predation that forms them are so important, it would seem advisable to illustrate in greater detail how they operate and how they may get upset or "out of line" to man's disadvantage. As may be suspected, the food chain for a particular species of fish in a particular body of water is often very complicated and may interlock with the food chains of several other species. For the sake of brevity and undersanding, therefore, the basic food chains of two species (Lake Trout and Smallmouth Bass) as they may occur in a large, deepwater lake have been diagrammed in Fig. 1. These happen to be very simple food chains in which only the essential links have been portrayed. A more complicated, yet still relatively simple, interlocking chain is illustrated in Fig. 2, which might portray the production of Pickerel or Pike together with Largemouth Bass in a warm water lake or pond.

It will be noted in Fig. 2 that game fish species may not only prey upon each other, but even upon members of their own kind. This may come about in two ways: one may prey upon another when the first is considerably larger than the second—as in the case of juveniles or adults vs. newly hatched young—or the first may prey upon the second when the former is only slightly larger than the latter. When members of a species prey extensively upon their own kind, the practice is known as *cannibalism,* and both Largemouth Bass and members of the pike family are noted for this behavior. In game fish hatcheries, for example, "sorting to size" is a common practice; and when a half dozen small Pickerel are placed in an aquarium, it is not unusual for one, or perhaps two, of the fish eventually to survive—bulging and victorious!

In ocean waters, with their wide variety and abundance of life, food chains and predation may be extremely complicated. Generally, however, ocean food and game fishes are grouped into two

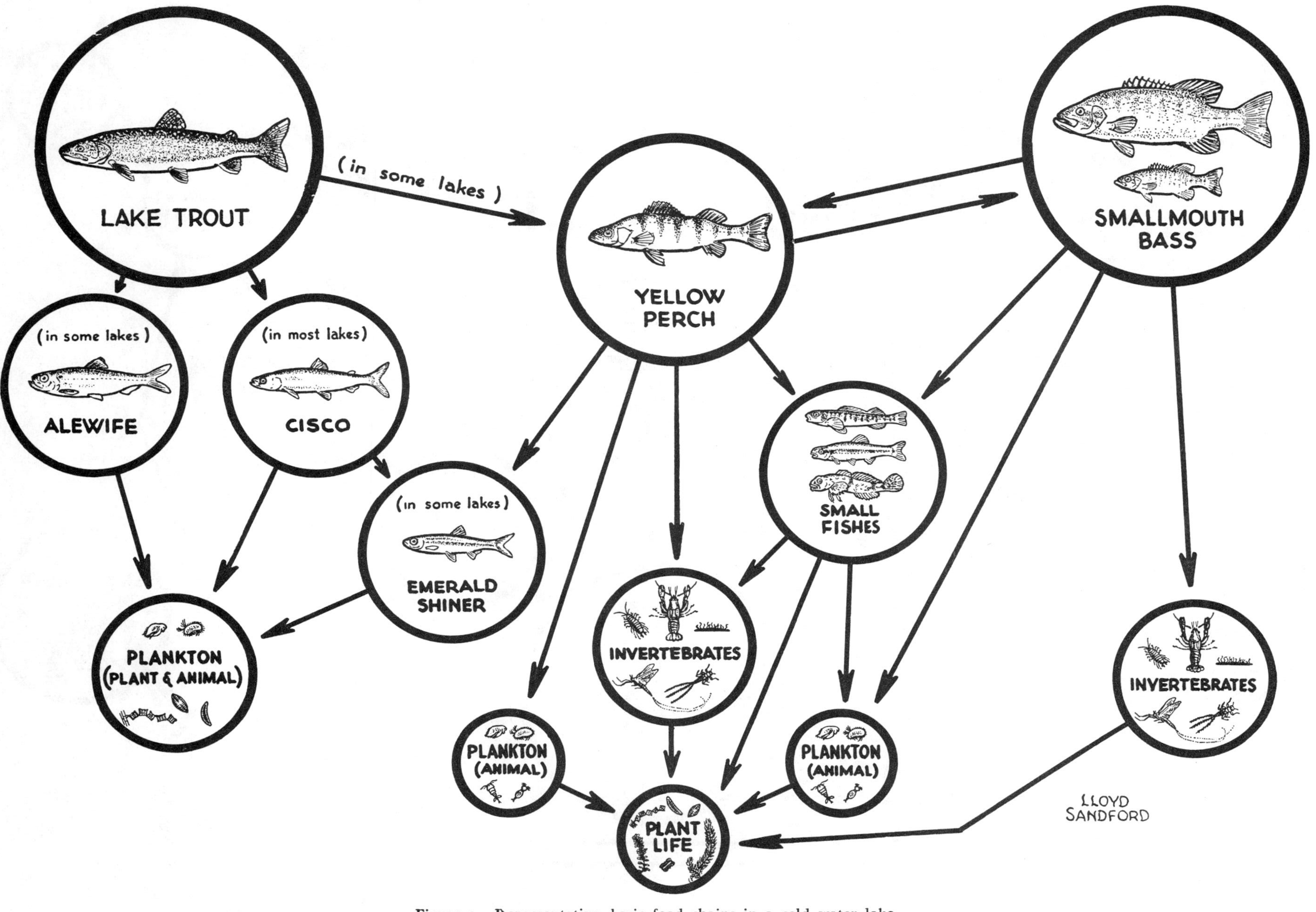

Figure 1. Representative, basic food chains in a cold water lake.

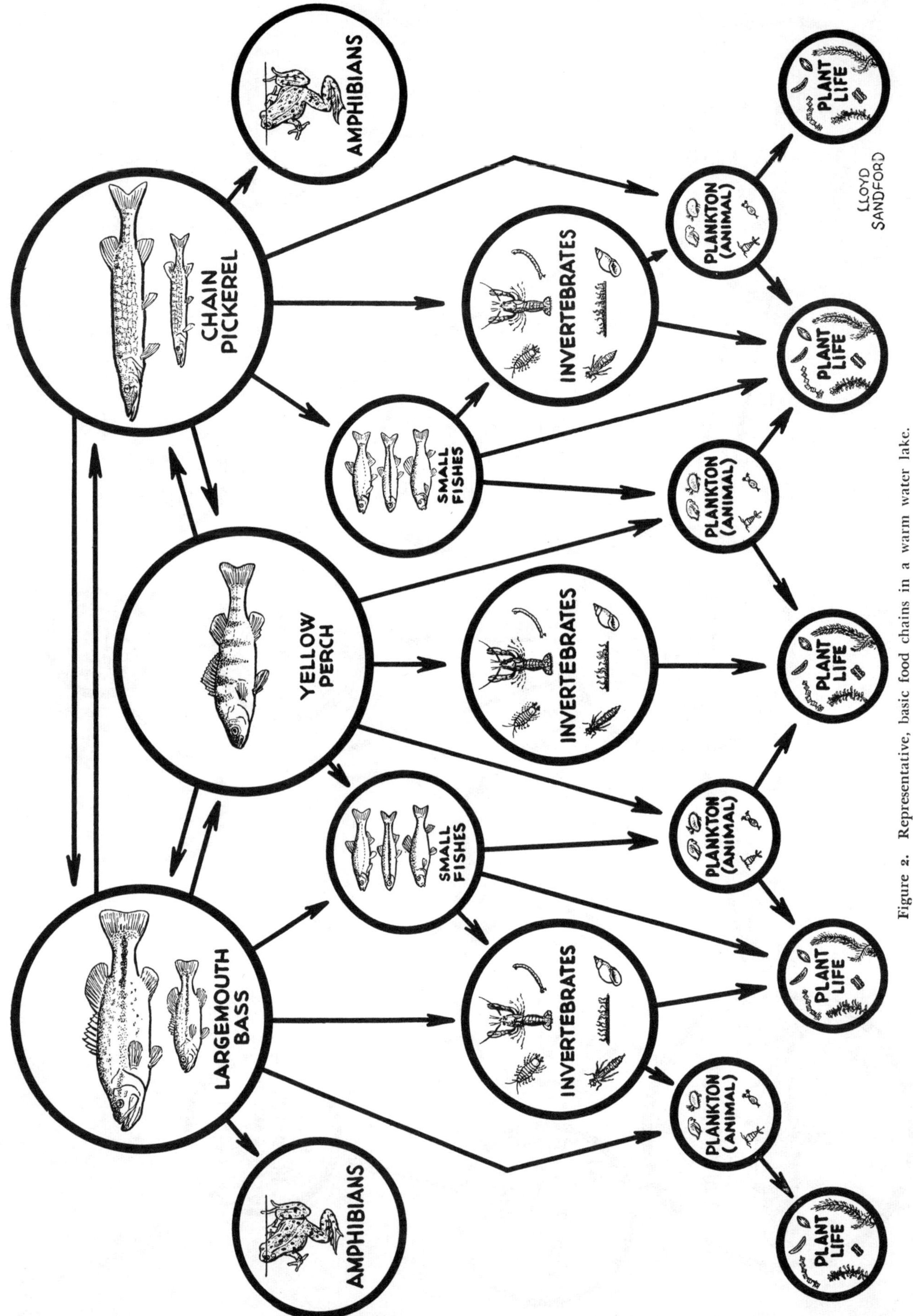

Figure 2. Representative, basic food chains in a warm water lake.

categories: *ground fishes* and *pelagic fishes.* The former, which include the flatfishes, cod, haddock, etc., live and feed for the most part at or near the bottom; while the latter, which include mackerel, tuna, bonito, and members of the herring family, live and feed largely near the surface. Ground fishes may feed heavily upon mollusks, including squid, and on crustaceans, fish and other bottom-dwelling animals. Pelagic species may feed upon plankton, squid, or other fishes that in turn feed upon plankton or plankton-eating fishes. (It should be noted that not all plankton-eating animals are pelagic, since many species of mollusks living on the bottom feed directly upon plankton by pumping water in and out of their shell chambers and straining out food. These mollusks are in turn preyed upon by starfish, certain crustaceans, and by other, predaceous, bottom-dwelling mollusks).

It has already been indicated that even some of the largest and most predaceous fishes may themselves be highly vulnerable to capture during their very early stages of life. The eggs and newly hatched young of such species, for example, may be semi-buoyant or buoyant and become a part of the plankton; or they may rest on the bottom or among vegetation and be subject to capture by a number of fishes including members of their own kind. Even White or Common Suckers, many catfishes, perch, darters, many species of minnows and other species will eat fish eggs *if and when they can find them,* and most fishermen know that salmon or trout eggs are a fine bait under some circumstances.

Nature, however, has developed a number of ways of absorbing the shock from this predation or of lessening vulnerability to it. First, there is the "numbers" or "shock absorber" method (the authors' terms here are their own) whereby survival is sought through sheer numbers of eggs laid. A three-foot codfish, for example, may lay between two and three million eggs. These eggs are simply broadcast by the female—the flanking male fertilizing them the meanwhile—and no more attention is paid them by either parent. With some species—as with Cod, Menhaden, California Sardine, Halibut, Mackerel, Black Sea Bass and Weakfish—the eggs are buoyant and become part of the plankton; with others, such as Whitefish, Cisco, Tarpon and Shad, the eggs are *demersal* and lie on the bottom or among vegetation; while with still others, such as Atlantic Sturgeon, Carp, members of the Pike family, Smelt, Winter Flounder and Atlantic Herring, the eggs are also demersal but adhere to stones, vegetation, etc. The "numbers" method appears to be by far the most prevalent one among salt water species, but less characteristic of freshwater fishes.

Second, there is the "hide and seek" method characteristic of the trout family but also used in modified form by the Common Shiner and several other freshwater species. In the case of most salmon and trout, a depression or *redd* is scooped out of gravel or small rubble, and the fertilized eggs fall into the cracks and crevices between the stones and are then covered up by the female. The male Common Shiner piles up small stones into a heap that serves the same purpose. The Grunion and Capelin lay their eggs in the sand of beaches. The quantity of eggs laid by the "hide and seek" species is far less than that broadcast by the "numbers" types, but the individual eggs are usually much larger in size.

A third method is the "homesteader" system in which not only is some kind of nest constructed by the parent fish, but the eggs, and sometimes the newly hatched young, are nurtured and guarded by the parent fish. Nearly always it is the male that does all this work, e.g. in Smallmouth and Largemouth Bass, Bluegills and Pumpkinseeds, Bluntnose and Fathead Minnows, various darters, Sticklebacks, Sculpins and others. In the Common or Brown Bullhead, however, these duties are sometimes shared by both parents, and in at least one North American fish, the little Mudminnow, the female fish takes over the nest immediately after spawning and keeps the male at a respectable distance thereafter. The behavior of "homesteading" fishes is often quite complicated. The Bullhead digs or takes over a hole or tunnel, and stands guard at the entrance, creating a current of water by moving the tail. Occasionally the eggs may be picked up into the mouth and "washed." The female Mudminnow keeps guard over the eggs, agitating the water from time to time, and occasionally picking up an egg and "cleaning" it in her mouth. The Bluntnose Minnow protects his "raft" of eggs which are usually stuck to the underside of a flat stone, and "fans" them almost constantly while waiting for night and the possibility of another visit from a female. Smallmouth and Largemouth Bass, Bluegills, and Pumpkinseeds employ a depression in the bottom that the male has prepared in advance of spawning. The male fish guards and "fans" the eggs, again while seeking to attract females to the nest. In the case of the Bullhead and Largemouth Bass, the parental care extends to "riding herd" on the young even after they have reached the free swimming stage.

A fourth method is the "case-hardened" system exemplified by the Common Skate. A rather stiff, leathery case encloses the eggs, thus affording them some degree of disguise and protection.

A fifth method is to "bring them forth alive," in which the young develop within the body of the female or, as in the case of the well known Sea Horses and Pipefishes, the eggs are incubated in a pouch possessed by the male. *Vivaparity,* or giving birth to living young, is characteristic of some species of Sharks, Rays, certain Topminnows and the Pacific Rockfishes and Sea-Perches.

The degrees of effectiveness for these various methods of protection and nurture are suggested by the numbers of eggs laid by the various species. In general, these numbers decrease as the amount of protection or nurture increases, until the number of eggs produced by a female fish may be in the dozens rather than the millions. The effects of egg predation, therefore, are not necessarily indicated by the numbers of eggs found in the stomachs of other fishes. Compared with birds and mammals, fishes have tremendous reproductive potentials, resulting from the relatively large number of eggs they produce, and this usually makes the problems of over-fishing somewhat different from those of over-hunting. It can be readily perceived that knowledge of the spawning habits of various species may be quite useful in evaluating these and other effects.

The observant fisherman recognizes that certain natural associations of fish species and other aquatic life exist in certain types of waters, that these associations relate to food chains and predation, and that they persist in the form of ever changing balances of interacting factors. We can recognize warm and cold water associations in ponds, lakes, streams and rivers, as well as deep and shallow water associations. Similarly, in marine waters, various associations exist in different types of environments. It is the interacting factors within these associations, together with other biological, physical and chemical factors, that in largest part determine the size and quantity of the fishes sought by man.

Sportsfishermen like their fish big: big bass, big trout, big pike. Commercial food fishermen, on the other hand, may sometimes prefer the smaller specimens. A surf fisherman, for example, would travel many miles to catch a 30 lb. Striped Bass, although this fish would bring much less money at the marketplace than a half-dozen five pounders. In general, however, large fish are preferred by both food and sport fishermen, and it is therefore to man's advantage to have natural conditions operating in such manner as to produce an abundance of fast-growing, large fish.

This desire for quantities of large food and game fishes leads fishermen to seek the enactment of measures they deem necessary for favorable conditions and rich harvests: stocking; control of competitors; protective regulations (control of predation by man); pollution abatement, etc. Unfortunately, however, this desire for abundance has been too frequently coupled with a blanket, or uncritical, faith in both the efficiency and the effects of these control measures; and this, in turn, has often resulted not only in prodigious waste of money and effort, but also in actually damaging some fishery situations rather than improving them. Because of the importance of these facts to future progress in management work, it would perhaps be helpful to explain and demonstrate how these control measures may operate in various situations.

STOCKING

The direct stocking of food and game fishes is an obvious attempt to replenish or build up a supply of fish where natural propagation and other control measures are deemed either inadequate or too slow. Aptly employed in certain correctly diagnosed situations, stocking can be a highly effective and indispensable means for gaining these ends. On the other hand, if ineptly employed, stocking can be not only wasteful but actually damaging.

In some instances, the survival of stocked fish may be very low as compared to the survival of naturally spawned stock. Studies on fingerling trout have revealed cases where survival of stocked fish was only about 6% as compared to around 24% for "natively spawned" fingerlings, and in at least one experiment on the stocking of Winter Flounder fry, no survival at all was noted.

In other cases, such as the largemouth bass, it has frequently been observed that there may be many thousands of young of the year present in a pond as late as August, with only a dozen or so one-year-olds. Whether or not this condition is due to cannibalism, or to predation by other species, e.g. yellow perch, it would appear obvious that any stocking of bass in these situations would be wasteful unless, perhaps, the size of fish stocked was sufficiently large to cut down on the indicated predation.

Again, there are environments wherein the growth rate of the desired species is inadequate, for one reason or another. Adding more fish to such situations could hardly be expected to improve matters.

In still other instances, certain species such as Smallmouth and Largemouth Bass and Pickerel have been introduced into trout waters with the result that the introduced species "took over" the body of water yet failed themselves to grow well and reach satisfactory sizes and numbers.

Finally, there is at least one case on record (in this instance a very large lake) wherein an abundance of smallmouth bass "masqueraded" under an appearance of scarcity simply because of the bass population's poor availability and susceptibility to the methods of angling being employed in the lake! In this case stocking measures were being used to remedy an incorrectly diagnosed situation.

To summarize, it may be readily perceived that a number of factors can govern the success of stocking, including such items as type and degree of predation, sizes of fish called for, time and technique of stocking, relative contribution to existing stock, carrying capacities of the environment, suitability of species, and many others. It may also be appreciated that fishery situations can differ widely and that uncritical faith in standardized methods of diagnosis, treatment and technology may lead not only to great waste of funds and effort but also to actual damage of the fishery resource.

CONTROL OF COMPETITORS

Another one of the obvious ways of increasing the number of desirable fish is by decreasing the number of their natural enemies. As in so many things, however, the gap between principle and practice is often a serious one. In theory, it would seem axiomatic that the elimination of those creatures preying upon a fish would lead to an increase in numbers of that species, but actually a number of difficulties arise that often make this logically sounding procedure an impossibility.

In the first place, we often do not know just what creatures are preying upon the desirable species *to a significant extent*. Every one knows that freshwater Gars prey on all kinds of fishes, but only in certain locales have they been proven to be significantly destructive to game fishes. It might be argued that Gars are never of any use whatsoever to man because they do not provide food for other fishes even when quite small and because at all sizes they compete with more valuable species for food even when not actually preying upon them. But if Gars are not really a limiting factor in the size of a game fish population, how can an expensive program of eradication directed against them (effective programs of this sort are costly) do anything for a fisherman except possibly raise his license fee? Moreover, it is entirely possible that the wholesale removal of Gars may allow certain coarse fish to become too abundant and so compete excessively with the game fish in question. The elimination of Gars may thus indirectly lead to a diminution rather than an increase of game fish. This is not to say that Gars should never be controlled. In Louisiana and in various places in other states, an increase in game fish caught has followed Gar eradication programs. In other places, however, no such result was at all apparent, although considerable money was spent. Only detailed study of each separate situation can give reasonable assurance as to the feasibility of predator control.

Very often the most conspicuous predator comes in for the most censure, while the real "villain" operates unseen. The depredations of kingfishers, water snakes and snapping turtles tend to be exaggerated for the very reason that they are so apparent. The attacks of many fishes, made under water, often go unnoticed, as in the case of young Largemouth Bass that was mentioned earlier.

Investigation may reveal that a supposed predator is scarcely one at all. The Red-breasted Merganser may feed almost exclusively on salmon eggs when living on certain fresh waters. Examination of eggs that have been consumed by these ducks revealed that they were chiefly opaque ones and probably dead or dying before they were eaten. There appears to be no evidence that the Red-breasted Merganser digs salmon eggs out of their covering gravel.

In one lake at least it has been shown, through carefully conducted analyses by Dr. W. F. Royce, that the attacks of the Sea Lamprey on Lake Trout are apparently without serious ill effects. Fish carrying up to 10 scars, resulting from previous attacks by these blood- and juice-sucking predators, and individuals with as many as 4 unhealed wounds, failed to show any emaciation whatever from these attacks. Lampreys have been present in this lake (Seneca) for more than 50 years, yet angling for Lake Trout continues to be good.

Sometimes the prey itself turns predator. Largemouth Bass, for instance, feed on Bluegills when the latter are available. If the Bluegills are too numerous, however, they may eat up practically all the spawn of the Largemouth, despite the parent fish's attempts to guard their nests. In this way bluegills can turn the tables on the largemouth so to speak, completely nullifying all its reproductive efforts.

When populations become "unbalanced", as in the case just mentioned, it is usually very difficult to get them back into the desired equilibria again. With a few notable exceptions, it has been found uneconomical to attempt to remove excess coarse fish or predators unless a complete "kill" of all of those fish in the body of water can be effected. Otherwise the undesirable species merely multiplies and grows at an excessive rate, quickly filling up the "space" that was left by the destruction of most of its fellows. This is simply another example of the tremendous reproductive potential of almost all fishes. So long as the environment remains suitable for large numbers of any particular species, only continuous and arduous efforts can keep its population below natural levels.

The complexities and difficulties indicated above may make it seem as if man were helpless to improve food and game fishing through predator control, but this is not so. Not all attempts have been costly failures, and it is worth noting that the outstanding successes have resulted from careful, considered investigations in which many factors were explored and carefully considered, before action was taken.

One of the most spectacular increases in food fishes, resulting from predator control, was obtained on Cape Breton Island. Painstaking study had revealed that the periodic scarcity of Atlantic Salmon was correlated with low water, that is, dry summers. It was also found that Belted Kingfishers and American Mergansers were preying on the young salmon, especially at this time, because the fish were more vulnerable to attack. Experimental elimination of these birds along a river more than doubled the number of salmon smolts going to the sea and resulted in a higher commercial catch and a larger return of mature fish for spawning. Although this experiment is not considered complete as yet, it is an excellent example of how practical research can be of great value in solving fishery problems. Another instance concerns Cultus Lake in British Columbia where the experimental, systematic reduction of Squawfish more then tripled the survival of young Sockeye Salmon. The value of this increase was far more than the cost of reducing the numbers of the predatory Squawfish.

In many other streams, lakes and ponds, efficiently conducted removal of undesirable species by means of electric shocking, netting and so forth, and the transplantation of the fish to more suitable waters has also proved profitable. Where salvage or transfer is employed, the primary body of water is, in effect, used as a natural fish hatchery. In other instances, the return of a lake to "trout water" has been successfully accomplished by chemically killing off all the fish, including predators and competitors of trout, and then restocking with the desired species of trout. To be successful, intentional poisoning apparently requires the complete elimination of trout competitors, and is therefore a program of action not to be undertaken lightly.

PROTECTIVE REGULATIONS

Control over the effects of man's own predatory activities is generally sought through such measures as catch limits, size limits, closed seasons and gear limitations. As in the case of stocking, however, it has been discovered that unless aptly tested in carefully diagnosed situations, protective regulations may not only be inefficient or wasteful, but actually damaging to a fishery.

Why is this so?

In the first place, there exist tremendous differences in the numbers of fish and in the "productiveness" of various fishery stocks. Most trout fishermen realize, for instance, that it is not difficult to "clean out" a Brook Trout stream—much easier than to "clean out" Brown Trout, for example. It may require a still greater amount of sustained fishing pressure to make even a "dent" in a population of Bluegills or Perch. And at the other extreme, we can observe that more than 3,000,000,000 pounds of herring are being removed annually from the north Atlantic Ocean without any preceptible depletion of supply. The observant fisherman is also quick to realize that not only may one trout stream, or pond, or lake, be much less productive than another, but also that there may be a difference in the productiveness of areas, or sections, of the same waters. If it is understood that *fishery stocks must be utilized, or harvested, for this productiveness to be realized,* then the major problem of *discovering the desirable degree of utilization for various waters and areas* can be appreciated. It is not sufficient merely to guess or theorize at a catch limit, and then apply it over wide geographical areas, and maintain it without checking.

One of the unsound assumptions that has figured largely in the maintenance of rigid catch limits over wide areas is a belief that the numbers of young produced by a stock of fish will always be correlated with the numbers of spawners present. While this may be true of certain stocks within certain situations, more and more instances are being brought to light wherein this condition does not hold. Indeed, the very reverse of this condition has been found to be true in some cases. The Striped Bass of our Atlantic coast showed one of the greatest additions of young fish to its population at a time when the number of spawners was so low that alarm was felt by many persons over the survival of the species. The number of young produced in this *dominant year class* was large enough to provide the foundation of a large fishery over a period of several years. In other species, such uncontrollable environmental factors as temperature, salinities, or the amount of phosphate in the water have been found to be highly important in the production and survival of eggs and young. In short, it has been discovered that differences in the survival of the eggs and young are often responsible for the wide fluctuations in the abundance of many species, being far more important than man's own predatory activities in such cases. Poor natural survival, and predation by man, may act together to our double detriment, so to speak, in cases where fishing pressure has created heavy dependence upon the annual addition of younger fish to the stock. Then, when "nature fails" for a year or more, the gap is reflected in the fishery. This may be particularly true with species that have natural, short life spans.

Another factor responsible for unsound catch limits is erroneous assumptions concerning "productivity" of fishery resources. This has been particularly true in the case of certain marine areas, and also of so called warm water, inland situations. In marine waters, with their great productivity and size, the annual catches of species are commonly measured in terms of millions, hundreds of millions, or billions of pounds. Yet in only a few instances has there been sound evidence of the serious depletion of stock, and in still fewer that any such depletions have resulted from over-fishing. Even with such species as Shad—which ascend rivers to spawn and which have been overfished—the greatest damage has come from pollution and other environmental changes. This is not to say that overfishing cannot be an important factor in maine areas. It definitely is a problem *with certain species in particular regions* and this problem is rendered more acute by the seasonal supplies of migratory species within particular localities. In a given locality, for instance, the "summer supply" of a species may be fished very heavily without the benefit of any significant replenishment until the following year, and this may lead to controversy over how this local seasonal supply should be utilized. In general, however, there has been a tendency greatly to exaggerate the possible effects of man's predatory activities on the overall supplies of marine species, and this exaggeration in turn has sometimes prompted stocking measures and catch regulations that are biologically unsound and mathematically absurd.

In inland waters, it is being discovered that while in general our guesses on catch limits for trout species may not have been very far out of line—in fact too high in some instances—our estimates on the so called warm water species, and particularly "pan fish," have been something else again! In some North American lakes, for example, there may be a creel limit of five Lake Trout and six Smallmouth Bass. Yet the productivity in numbers of the former may not only be far less—and its vulnerability to capture far greater—but Lake Trout may also attract many more anglers. Result: a "double whammy" on Lake Trout with bass going to waste. As for the "pan fishes" of our inland waters, e.g. perch, bluegill and other sunfish, it would appear that *more* predation by man, rather than less, is usually needed if favorable population "balances" are to be maintained. And it is significant to note not only that the trend of regulations today is in this direction, but also that "pan fishes" are beginning to be appreciated as having something to offer in the way of fighting spirit and excitement. Even the lowly Bullhead or "hawned paout," and the clownish puffer, or blowfish, of our Atlantic coast can provide much fishing pleasure and some mighty fine eating, if one will not be scared away by looks and will acquaint himself with the "ten second" method of cleaning them.

Size limits are even more tricky to apply effectively than catch or creel limits. One reason for this is that a species may have widely different rates of growth not only within different bodies of water, but also within different regions of the same body of water. Smallmouth Bass, for instance, may be very abundant and yet be so stunted in their growth as to be almost entirely protected from fishing by a 10-inch size limit and hence not subjected to any "thinning out." Moreover, in large bodies of water such as Lake Simcoe, Ontario, the Smallmouth may have a considerably more rapid rate of growth in one section than in another region only a few miles away, with the result that the legal size limit has a different effect within various areas of the same lake! Stunted populations of Brook Trout are also of common occurrence, and it is not unusual to catch old ones that are only five or six inches long, even though this size may be reached in a couple of years in other streams. Finally, size limits on many marine species are often entirely unfeasible because of the bulk, depth, or "mixed" nature of many fisheries. In other cases, however, size limits on marine species have been both practical and effective. In fishing for marine and some Great Lake species, the use of *savings gear,* which tends automatically to select fish of the desired size, has generally been far more effective than size limits. A great deal more research is needed along this line, however, if savings gear are to be made more practical and effective.

Protection of species during spawning seasons may or may not be desirable, depending largely upon the vulnerability of the species to capture at such times, and whether or not they can be taken in desired numbers on other occasions. River-ascending, or *anadromous,* species such as Shad or Atlantic Salmon, for example, are not yet taken in great numbers during their existence in the sea, and it is therefore desirable to harvest these species when they ascend rivers to spawn and can be readily put into creel or fish box. On the other hand, both Smallmouth and Largemouth Bass are extremely vulnerable to capture during their spawning season because a male guarding his nest will go after all sorts of things—from cigarette butts to water snakes—and this makes it desirable to protect the species against their own instinctive bravery during these periods. With species that do not have any greater vulnerability to capture during spawning seasons, it is a matter of simple mathematics that protection during this period is of no greater effectiveness than at other times of the year.

It may be perceived from the foregoing that ideal, protective regulation poses an administrative problem of huge proportions: the indicated, particular measures for particular situations cannot very well be administered when there are many bodies of water close together. Some sort of compromise is required. More and more successful attempts, however, are being made to adapt protective regulations to specific situations, even within geographic areas where it was not at first deemed possible.

What is perhaps most important is that an increasing number of fishermen are coming to realize that the analysis and control of predation—whether due to fish, reptile, bird, beast, or man—is not a simple matter, but rather a series of highly complex problems calling for much practical research, experiment, and patience.

Fish & Wildlife Service

Alaskan Graylings

CANOE TRIPS

Throughout North America there is a vast extent of wild country, plentifully supplied with fish, that can be reached only by canoe. Canada, east of the Rockies, and the plains is an intricate network of lakes and rivers, with virgin fishing everywhere. In the United States, Maine, Wisconsin, and Minnesota are famous for their canoeing waters leading into fine fish country, while the long rivers of the South, easily navigable by canoe have never been exploited.

THE CANOE

For such waters the canoe is the only practical craft. It can be easily portaged around rapids and falls, and between lakes, on one man's shoulders. It can be paddled, poled, steered, and swung by its occupants facing forward and is therefore the only satisfactory craft for running rapids and white water, or ascending swift streams.

The American Indian has given us three articles which have never been equalled for their particular use—the snowshoe, the tepee, and the canoe. For wilderness use the closer these approach the original Indian design the better.

The size of canoe to be chosen depends upon the weight to be carried, outfit and occupants, and on whether or not large lakes must be negotiated. The canoe must not be loaded so heavily that it will be loggy, hard to turn, and slow to paddle. It must ride large waves rather than plough through, and there must be sufficient freeboard so that the waves encountered on fairly windy days on large lakes will not swamp it. No canoe will weather a serious storm on a large lake—one simply goes ashore and waits for calmer weather—but the canoe should not be loaded so heavily that it will be unsafe in ordinary windy weather.

CANOE LOADING

A 10-foot canoe will carry two men for a day's fishing, and can be transported on the top of a car, but it is too small for cruising with an outfit. A 12-foot canoe will safely carry one man and his outfit, if the total loading is less than 400 pounds. A 14-footer will safely take two men and a light "week-end" outfit, its safe lading being about 500 pounds. All of the above lengths are easily portaged as they do not weigh over 60 pounds. The most practical length for two men, a camping outfit, and plenty of grub, is 16 to 18 feet, with a width of at least 36 inches, and depth amidships of at least 13 inches.

A canoe should always be loaded when it is afloat or nearly so, never when pulled high up on a beach. Place the heavier packs amidships and on the bottom. Allow space for the occupants' feet. Anything needed during the day, such as lunch, a kettle, or raincoat, can be tucked conveniently into a side space. The weight should be so distributed that when both men are aboard it will ride slightly deeper at stern than bow, and of course the side balance should be absolutely central. If rapids are expected during the day, crowd the weight as close to the center as possible; loaded thus, the canoe will turn much quicker. If rain or rough water is in prospect, place four light poles or spruce boughs in the bottom before loading to keep articles out of any water that might come aboard. Any water will then run back so that the stern paddler can bail it out and keep the outfit dry.

Gruman Aircraft Corp.
Fishing the weed beds in quiet water is easy from a canoe.

Old-timers usually have a light rucksack containing certain indispensables such as camera, matches *(in a waterproof container)*, fishline and hooks. This he stows under his seat, buckling one shoulder-strap fast. If sleeping bags are packed in waterproof duffle bags with sealer cloths at the opening, and if packsacks likewise have these sealer cloths, they will float in case of an upset.

For the novice it may be well to mention certain precautions and "don'ts" about canoes and canoe travel. (1) *Keep the center of gravity as low as possible* and the craft well balanced. Thus loaded a canoe is very steady and can hardly be upset except by gross carelessness or an extremely heavy curling wave taken side on. (2) *Never attempt to change places* with the other canoeist without going ashore. *Never stand up* in a canoe. This applies to everyone except the real expert using a pole, or rising to get a view of a rapid ahead (3) *In a landing, on a sand beach, just touch the bow to the beach.* The front paddler then gets out, *lifts* the bow and carries it up the beach a little, and steadies the canoe while the stern paddler climbs over the load and comes ashore dry-footed. *If it is a rocky shore, bring the side of the canoe to the shore.* One man then steadies it while the other throws out the outfit, and then gets out himself. (4) *Never pull a canoe over a beach or rocks; this will* wear, tear, and ruin the bottom. (5) When the canoe is empty, carry it up on the shore and turn it over; it will then keep dry inside, and articles not needed for that stop can be stored under it. (6) A dirty or sandy canoe can be cleaned by throwing a couple of buckets of water into it, rocking gently to stir and loosen the dirt, and then turning it over to drain.

Time out for a "breather" while on a combination fishing-hunting canoe trip.

TRAVEL AND PORTAGING

Two good men can average 3½ to 4 miles per hour paddling in quiet waters with no wind. Twenty miles a day is good going with paddles with a properly loaded canoe. In ascending, and sometimes in going down, swift rivers and rapids it may be necessary to pole the canoe, and sometimes in ascending swift rivers the canoe must be roped up, one or two men pulling with a long rope from the shore, while another in the canoe steers it just free from the bank. No progress can be made with paddles up a river that flows more than 4 miles per hour, nor with outboard motor over one flowing about 7 or 8 miles.

Canoes are now quite generally being used with light outboard motors. An outboard motor will get there and back faster, it does not tire, and when speed and time are considerations it is a great advantage. For many, the abominable noise, and smell of a motor and inconvenience at every portage ruins most of the pleasures in the silent places. Also, with a motor there is no healthy exercise, and one is cramped more or less in one position for long periods. Two men in a 17-foot canoe can normally carry about three months' food supply, and can paddle as long as the food lasts. With an outboard motor they can cover an equal distance in about one-fourth the time, but due to the weight of motor and gas only about three weeks' food can be carried, so that nothing is saved but time.

On a given water route there is seldom completely clear paddling or motoring. On most days there will be some rapids or carries between lakes that must be portaged. The length of a portage may vary from a mere lift around a falls to five miles or more. Here is one of the advantages of the light Indian canoe; it can be carried easily by one man. It is carried turned over, bottom up, resting on the man's shoulders For portaging, the paddles are tied to the bow and middle thwarts as shown in the illustration. When the canoe is inverted the carrier thrusts his head between the paddles where the junctions of the handles and blades rest naturally on the shoulders. The right spacing of the two paddles is soon learned by experience. To pad the shoulders the carrier usually drapes an extra shirt, shawl fashion, over his neck, or wears a mackinaw coat.

A canoe presses straight down on the shoulders, and therefore is easier, in a way, to carry than a back pack of equal weight. But one should never attempt to take a canoe on the first trip over a strange portage. The first man should carry a light pack and the ax to do any necessary clearing to allow the easy passage of the canoe. In portaging a canoe the view of the trail ahead is restricted to about 30 feet, so one should be familiar with the portage in advance. Some skill and strength are necessary to get a canoe on and off one's shoulders unaided. For the average sportsman, it is usually best first to turn the canoe over; then one man lifts the bow high, while the carrier gets under it, places his head and neck between the paddles, and stands erect. At the end of the portage it is taken off and lowered by reverse procedure.

Because of the portaging, all baggage, outfit, and foods should be packed in packsacks with shoulder straps, or in bundles, bed rolls, or duffle bags of such form that they can be conveniently carried with a tump line. These packs and bundles should not be too heavy to be carried by one man, for beginners not over 60 to 75 pounds each. If two men can get their outfit in two packsacks and one bed roll with tump line, then it means only two trips for each man across the portage. On the first trip the two packsacks are taken, and on the next trip one man carries the bed roll and the other the canoe.

Throughout northeastern United States and Canada, where canoeing with portaging has been done for many generations, the preferred type of packsack is that known as the Northwester, Duluth, Woods, or Porier. It consists of a waterproof canvas sack about 22 inches high, 16 inches wide, and 6 to 8 inches deep. Wide leather shoulder-straps are secured to the center of the top and the bottom corners. A tump line is also usually secured to the top of the sack. When the tump line is used in addition to the shoulder-traps it eases the pull on the shoulders, and also results in the top of the sack forming a sort of shelf on which additional articles such as duffle bags or even boxes can be perched and carried on top, the whole balancing so that these top loads do not fall off.

A tump line is a band of soft leather about 2½ inches by 18 inches to the ends of which are secured leather thongs or ropes about 9 feet long. The band goes over the forehead, centering about the hair line, and the thong or rope is so tied around the roll, bundle, or box to be carried that it rests on the middle of the back, rather sagging to the hips. The weight is thus borne by the head and muscles of the neck, the hips steadying it. The northern Indians and voyagers, "born to the tump line," can carry unbelievable weights with it. Loads of 400 to 500 pounds taken across several miles of portage without a rest have been recorded. The average sportsman will find the tump line an exquisite form of torture, and he had better confine his portaging to the packsack with a loading not to exceed 60 pounds at the start. Stand the packsack on the ground, sit down back to it, place the arms through the shoulder-straps and settle them on the shoulders; then turn over onto the knees and stand up. If the sleeping bag and air mattress in their duffle bag do not weigh over 30 pounds, then it is easy, when the lightest packsack with its tump line are in place on the shoulders, to lift up the roll, carry it over the head and settle it on top of the packsack, and take the two across together.

A regular routine makes everything go smoother, faster, and with less labor on a day's canoe journey and the attending camping. Arriving at the selected camp site for the night, both men unload the canoe, carry it up on the shore, and turn it over. The site for the tent and campfire are then selected, the ground cleared and smoothed, and the packs are carried up, both men working together. The cook then gathers wood, unpacks the cook packsack, gets water, and starts the fire and the cooking. The other man puts up the tent, makes the beds, and gets everything shipshape about camp. Then he gathers firewood for the evening and next morning. Kindling wood and shavings (or birch bark) for starting next morning's fire are always prepared the night before, and stowed in the tent where they will not get wet in case of rain. In the morning a reversal of the procedure and division of labor follows, and last thing of all a good look is taken all around to see that none of the outfit is being left behind, *and then the campfire is drenched, put absolutely out, so that not even a trace of smoke remains.* In packing in the morning a teakettle, a lunch, and the ax are tucked in conveniently, and a landing is made about noon, for lunch. In traversing a strange country it is best to stop at the first good camp site one sees after 3 P.M. to have time to make a comfortable camp and get supper before dark.

In Maine, the Adirondacks, Minnesota, and in portions of Canada adjacent to the roads there are many regularly established hunting camps where the sportsman has almost all the comforts and conveniences of a regular hotel. From these his guide takes him out every morning for fishing, either by canoe or afoot, and he returns every evening in time for supper. For such fishing, of course, no camping outfit is necessary.

Throughout wilder northeastern America it is customary for the sportsman to employ a guide who also acts as cook. The guide or outfitter supplies the canoe, tent, cooking utensils, and food, making a per-diem charge for the lot. The sportsman supplies bedding, personal effects, fishing tackle, and license. The guide paddles in the stern of the canoe, and the sportsman in the bow. The sportsman helps to carry the lighter packs across portages, and assists in all the other work according to his physical capability and skill. A good sport takes pride in doing his share of the work, and in doing it well. He is never ashamed to ask his guide to show him how. All financial and other arrangements are made in advance, and thereafter the relationship of sportsman and guide should be that of two good friends. There is no surer way to spoil a trip than for the sportsman to treat his guide as a servant.

On long expeditions, particularly into mountainous country, the sportsman will usually require two men, one as guide and one as cook, both to act also as packers. Usually a 20-foot canoe with outboard motor is taken as there are few portages, the trip being commonly ten days or more of motoring, poling, and tracking up swift rivers.

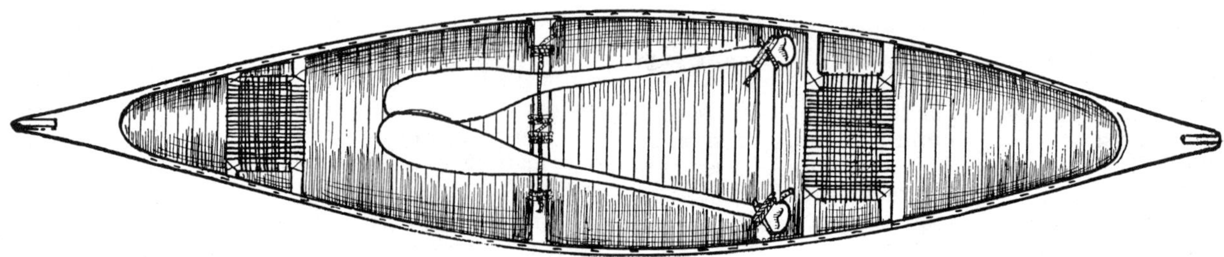

Method of Lashing Paddles for Carrying Canoe on Shoulders.

The End of the Portage—bed roll with tump line attached.

CHECK LISTS

The following lists of essential equipment and supplies are divided in two parts. The *personal list* includes the articles worn and taken by each member of the party. The guide also will usually require most of these articles. The *camp list* includes the outfit necessary for camping away from sources of supply. These articles are usually supplied by the guide or outfitter, but must be supplied by the sportsmen if going without a guide.

Superior figures (thus: [1]) refer to footnotes.

The lists have been formulated with a view to safety, comfort, and well-being in canoe and camp. Old-timers can dispense with many articles. Sportsmen should not overload with unnecessary and heavy equipment, but "the less a man carries on his back the more he must carry in his head."

Personal List

Worn: Felt hat, light wool underwear, blue denim pants,[2] belt, wool shirt, wool socks, leather-top rubbers or moosehide moccasins with moccasin rubbers, sun glasses,[3] binoculars.

Pockets: Jack knife, watch, compass, handkerchief, waterproof match box, pipe, tobacco.

Fishing Tackle: For type of fishing available.

Rucksack: Camera and films, exposure meter, knife, tape measure, matches in waterproof can, notebook, pencil, maps, warm gloves, fish line, hooks, sinkers, extra tobacco, hand ax .

Packsack: Containing personal effects as follows: Wool pants, wool shirt, wool undershirt, wool drawers, 3 pr. wool socks, light leather camp slippers, 2 handkerchiefs, small bath towel, toilet articles, toilet paper, repair kit, medicine kit, cleaning rod, oil, flannel cleaning patches, extra camera films, wool mitts, spectacles.[4]

Sleeping Bag: Air mattress, air pillow, pillow case.

Loose: Light water-repellent jacket or mackinaw coat, raincoat or poncho.[5]

Camp List

Canoe, of proper size and capacity.
- 2 paddles. (a third one, lashed to the canoe, is good insurance.)

Repair kit for type of canoe in use.
Tent, light weight, easily erected. (See under "Tents.")
Tarp, light, for floor cloth.
Cooking utensils, in packsack or fiber box.
- 3 kettles to nest.
- 2 frying pans, folding handles.
- 1 mixing pan.
- 1 folding aluminum baker.
- 1 plate, cup, bowl, knife, fork, teaspoon, and tablespoon for each man.
- 1 large spoon.
- 1 butcher knife.
- 1 set of salt and pepper shakers.
- 1 can opener.
- 2 dish cloths.
- 1 dish mop.
- 1 cake turner.
- 1 cake kitchen soap (per week).

Ax, 3 lb., 28" handle, with sheath.
Mill file, 8-inch, and carborundum stone.
Flashlight and candle lantern [1]
Wash basin.
Matches in friction-top cans (3 boxes per week).
DDT bombs.
Food in packsacks (about 20 lbs. per man per week).

---

[1] A 2-cell flashlight is suggested. Per hour of light its batteries do not bulk or weigh more than candles.

[2] Light pants on the assumption that weather will be warm at the start; the wool pants in packsack can be put on as it gets colder.

[3] If the sportsman requires spectacles to correct vision, at least two pair should be taken.

[4] Have small cotton bags to contain various kits, one for all underwear, one for toilet articles, slippers, repair kit, medicine kit, camera films, etc.

[5] These may be needed during the day, hence are carried loose in the canoe.

TENTS AND CAMP SHELTERS

At first tents were made of skins, then of heavy canvas, and now often of waterproof cotton or synthetic fabrics weighing scarcely five ounces per yard. The function of a tent, is to keep persons and equipment dry, warm, and protected from mosquitoes, flies, and other bugs.

Tents are not needed in all climates. In the Sierra Nevada mountains it does not rain in summer or early fall, and the only shelter needed is tarpaulin about 8 feet square. A bed is made on half of it, and the other half folds over to keep off the dew. This answers also for the deserts, although there another tarp may be useful as a windbreak. In wooded countries in fall and winter when there are no mosquitoes, a plain tarp makes a most convenient and comfortable shelter, pitched at an angle of 40 degrees. Beds are made and duffle stowed under it, and a fire in front thoroughly warms the interior. If winds blow or rain beats in the ends, this is easily cured by felling and placing a few small spruce in the openings. A tarp is also used for many purposes in camp; for example, it may be pitched as a dining or kitchen fly, or to cover stores. It is merely a rectangle of canvas or waterproof cotton, any size desired, usually with rings called "grommets" inserted every 2 feet or so around the edge for erecting or tying.

TYPES

Tents of many designs and sizes are made, from the diminutive mountaineers' tent designed to accommodate one man and weighing only three pounds, to enormous circus tents. There are, however, certain designs and sizes which have, as a rule, proved the best for the use of sportsmen. The oldest forms were the conical Indian teepee and the dome-shaped Tibetan yort which could be warmed by an open fire in the center. Both are practically obsolete today because of the difficulty of erecting. A teepee, for example, required at least 11 long, straight poles.

The most common small and medium tent is that known as the "A-Wall." If of suitable size it has plenty of headroom in the center with beds or cots at each side; it can be warmed with a tent stove. In hot weather the walls can be rolled up allowing free circulation of air, and it can be made mosquito-proof with a netting at the door. If it is furnished with an outside tape ridge it is comparatively easy to erect with shear poles at each end to support the ridge pole. Often one end of the ridge can be lashed to a tree, or poles can be dispensed with entirely and the tent be suspended from a rope stretched between two trees. The ordinary commercial "A-Wall" tent does not have the tape ridge, being arranged for commercial poles. To facilitate pitching in the woods, merely cut a 5-inch hole through the front and back walls at the peak of the tent; a ridge pole can then be stuck completely through the tent.

This tent has three slight disadvantages; it is tedious to erect; it can be warmed effectively only by a stove inside; and it is heavy for the amount of floor space.

To determine the practical capacity of a tent, draw a floor plan on a scale of one inch to one foot, and lay out on it what you propose to put in the tent. For each bed allow a space 3 x 7 feet, and remember that there must be 2 feet headroom at the head end to allow room to get into a sleeping bag. In locating a tent stove, remember that no canvas or bedding must come within 18 inches of it.

An "A-Wall" tent 9 feet square and 7 feet high at the ridge will accommodate two men, with cots or sleeping bags at each side, a headroom passage between the beds large enough to dress or work in, and a space for personal duffle at the foot of each bed. Such a tent of light waterproof cotton weighs about 16 pounds. If it is to be warmed by a wood-burning sheet-iron tent stove inside, it had better be 12 feet long, with the stove located about 2 feet inside the door, and a little to the right or left. An asbestos stovepipe hole is sewed in the tent roof at the proper location. The stovepipe must project a foot above the ridge so that wind will not blow sparks onto the roof. Sometimes tin stovepipe holes are sewed in, but they rattle abominably in the wind. Tops of stove pipes should be covered with a screen spark arrestor.

All tents should have a sod cloth, or else a sewed-in waterproof canvas floor. A sod cloth is a strip of canvas about 12 inches wide, sewed to the bottom of the tent all around. It is stretched on the ground inside as shown in the picture of the "A-Wall" tent, and then weighted down with poles, stones, logs, or tucked under the bedding. With it a tarp to make a floor cloth or carpet may be spread over as much of the dirt floor as desired. The sod cloth makes a wind- and bugproof seal at the junction of the walls and the ground.

A floor cloth of waterproof canvas, sewed to the side and back walls, is often incorporated in tents. This, with mosquito netting in front, makes the tent bug-, wind-, and waterproof, but it has certain disadvantages. It considerably increases the weight, a wood-burning stove or a balsam-bough bed cannot be used, mud and dirt tracked into the tent are continual problems, and there must be a smooth, level site on which to pitch the tent.

A tent that fastens close to the ground with sod cloth or ground cloth is made mosquito-proof by a curtain of mosquito netting or cheesecloth, cover-

D. T. Abercrombie, N. Y.

A-Wall Tent with Tape Ridge and Sod Cloth.

D. T. Abercrombie, N. Y.

Explorer's Tent

ing the entire front entrance to the tent, sewed fast at the junctions of the roof and walls, but loose at the bottom. It is made very full and long so that it can be weighted down with a pole, or tucked under the ground cloth. To enter, raise it and walk in. If made very full it can be tied up with tapes to the junction of roof and walls when not needed. This is a better opening than the mosquito fronts with zipper opening, or a hole in the netting with a puckering string, which are great nuisances in entering or leaving the tent, and in the way when there are no mosquitoes.

A tent about 9 x 12 feet can be made of one of the light waterproof cotton materials weighing about 5 to 6 ounces per square yard, thus economizing in weight and bulk when transportation is limited. But larger tents are best if made of 8- or 10-ounce canvas, as in high winds the lighter materials may rip. Very large tents should be of 12-ounce canvas. If the cotton or canvas is dyed light green or khaki color the tent will be cooler and the glare will not be objectionable in bright sunlight. There is, however, a very dark green canvas that is sometimes used, which makes the tent so dark inside that even in broad daylight lantern illumination is needed to work inside.

The advantage of an "A-Wall" tent with stove is that in inclement weather, even in Arctic cold, it makes an entirely habitable room. The stove must be kept going, however, as five minutes after it is out the tent is cold. Perhaps the only reasons for tents of other design than the "A-Wall" are the desirability of lighter weight for the space covered, greater ease and shorter time in pitching, and being able to warm the tent by a campfire in front.

One popular tent is the "Explorer's Tent," which has to some extent, all the above advantages over the "A-Wall." One of these tents 7 feet square and 7 feet high at the 18-inch ridge, will accommodate two sleeping bags with space to stow personal duffle, and in light waterproof cotton with sod cloth will weigh about 11 pounds. Only two long poles and one short one are needed to erect it. First, stake down the walls in rectangular form, then erect with the poles; drive the longer stakes for the rear wall, and then slightly move the butts of the long poles to make it taut and shipshape. A fire 4 feet before the entrance will warm the interior except in very cold, windy weather.

The "Lean-to Tent" is a type that can be warmed more effectively by a campfire. The sloping roof reflects the heat down on the campers' beds, and in rainy or very sunny weather the fly can be stretched out in front or it may be lowered completely to close the tent. In the rain, by stretching the front out just so it does not get overheated by the fire, the campers can cook over the fire without getting wet. It is, however, about as tedious to erect as the "A-Wall," and weighs almost as much.

The simple pyramidal tent is the easiest to pitch, and is popular with those who change camp each day and who do not need heat in the tent. Simply stake down the walls and erect with a center pole inside or two shear poles outside. Another form of this tent, about 14 feet square, and with 5-foot walls, is popular as a cook tent for pack-horse trips and can accommodate a cookstove inside. It has headroom for a standing man practically up to the walls, the peak being about 10 feet high. It is erected with a long center pole, and a 5-foot pole at each corner.

The "Forester's Tent" is about the lightest that

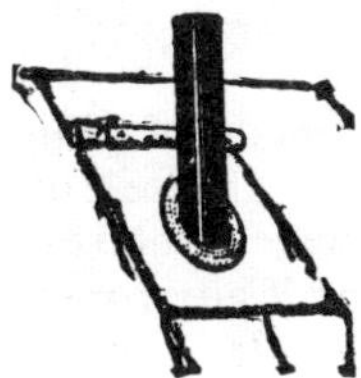

D. T. Abercrombie, N. Y.

Asbestos Stovepipe Hole in Tent Roof.

can be made, and it can be warmed effectively by a campfire in front. The fire can be built closer to the opening than with other tents, and it can be made comfortable even in extremely cold weather. It is easy to erect on a tripod of three poles. The back or ridge pole is longer than the others, and hence in the event of a beating rain it is possible to turn the tent toward the lee side quickly.

The "Mountaineers' Tent" is intended for mountain climbers who have to carry their entire outfit on their backs. It is 6½ by 4 feet on the

D. T. Abercrombie, N. Y.

Pyramidal Tent.

ground, 4 feet high, and rolls in a bundle 11 inches long by 4½ inches in diameter. With its sewed-in ground cloth it is entirely mosquito-tight, and weighs only 3 pounds 12 ounces. When one places his sleeping bag in it and crawls in there is only just room to go to bed. It would be stuffy inside in warm weather.

The best tent for the tropical jungle or for forests in extremely warm countries is an "A-Wall" tent with walls and ends entirely of mosquito netting and with a ground cloth. The roof extends 6 inches beyond the walls so the mosquito netting does not catch the drip.

In a tent that is not mosquito-proof it is always possible to place a common mosquito netting over a camp bed. Simply drive stakes at the corners of the bed to erect the net on, and tuck the bottom of the net under the mattress or sleeping bag. Outfitters sell nets of the correct size for cots and sleeping bags. A "bomb" of DDT or an atomizer with Flit or similar insecticide is desirable to eliminate the few mosquitoes that gain access to the tent when it is being erected, or when it is entered many times a day.

WATERPROOFING

Early tents were made of plain canvas. When it rained, if the inside of the roof were touched a drip started, and when wet the canvas and ropes shrank so much that if guy ropes were not loosened the tent pegs were pulled out. Also, a plain canvas tent increases greatly in weight when wet, and makes quite a load to pack when one has to break camp immediately after or during a rain. These troubles are avoided in the modern tent of waterproof material. Any closely woven cotton goods can be waterproofed by painting with a transparent waterproofing solution sold by tent and awning makers, or such a solution may be home made by dissolving paraffin in gasoline. After painting or soaking, hang the tent up until the gasoline evaporates. A spot that has lost its waterproofing can be "heated" by simply ironing it cold with a block of paraffin. A fire should not be built too near such tents. Tears in tents can be repaired with a small piece of the waterproof material cemented on with any cement recommended for

D. T. Abercrombie, N. Y.

Baker or Campfire Tent.

D. T. Abercrombie, N. Y.

Forester's Tent

cloth, or with canoe glue. With many forms of tents it is advisable to include several short pieces of rope to lash tent polies.

PACK-HORSE TRIPS

Throughout all the mountainous portions of western North America, from Mexico to the Arctic Circle, the best fishing country lies two or three days' travel from the railroad or the nearest auto or wagon road. Sportsmen must pack their outfit and supplies into these regions, and the most common method is with pack animals.

A large pack mule will carry 250 pounds, and a burro about half that amount, but the disadvantage of both mules and burros is that it is almost impossible to make them ford rivers or even fair-sized creeks, or to traverse boggy country, so that their use is confined largely to desert regions. For general work the pack horse is commonly used; a good horse will pack about 150 pounds. This limiting figure indicates the number pack animals needed for the outfit to be carried.

Pack horses and mules can travel from 5 to 25 miles a day, depending on the country, trails, and weather. On fairly good trails the pack train will average about 15 miles a day, starting about 10 A. M., and camping about 4 P. M. Burros are slower. However, the location of good horse pasture usually dictates the camp sites and the duration of each day's travel.

Most of the good mountain fishing in the United States is in the Forest Reserves, with good horse trails along almost every valley and across the passes. But even in wilder country it is possible to take a pack train through almost any country where steep cliffs, peaks, very heavy timber, and down timber do not prevent. Almost all the forests except on the northern slopes of mountains are open enough to ride. Also throughout most of this Western country good grass for horse feed occurs in many places. It is necessary that the camp sites be chosen where there is good horse feed, as otherwise the horses, when turned loose at night, will stray for miles in search of feed even though they are hobbled.

The typical pack train in this Western country carries a guide, a horse wrangler, and a cook. The sportsman usually arranges for his trip with an

The shape of wooden panniers is important.

"outfitter" who supplies these men, and also a riding horse for each member of the party including the man, the necessary number of pack horses to carry the outfit and supplies, all the saddles, pack saddles, horse blankets, panniers, tents, cooking and eating utensils, food, and other equipment. Each man supplies his own personal effects and bedding. The sportsmen supply their fishing equipment, clothing and personal effects, sleeping bag and air mattress, and purchase their fishing license. Such an outfit is necessarily expensive; on the basis described above, outfitters today commonly charge from $25 to $50 a day for one sportsman, with a slight reduction for two or more.

PACKING AND TRAVEL

One who has not previously traveled with a pack train should understand certain details about the pack horse and his load, and the procedures of traveling, and camping.

The horse is packed normally as follows: First the saddle blanket is laid smoothly across its back, and then the pack saddle is laid on this and cinched in place. The usual pack saddle is of the "sawbuck" type, with double cinches and breech and breast straps although improved military types of pack saddles are now coming into quite general use. Each horse also has a halter with neck rope, or neck rope alone, and a bell (cowbell) attached by a strap to its neck. The bell is stoppered except when the horse is turned loose to feed. The pay load usually consists of two side packs, usually panniers, weighing 50 to 60 pounds each, which are lashed on either side of the saddle, and a smaller top pack, usually bedding, a duffle or flour bag, box, or a nest of pans, laid on and also lashed on top and between the tops of two panniers. A heavy canvas pack cover, about 5 feet square, is then laid over all, and with a strong rope having a cinch at one end, a diamond hitch is thrown over the entire pack, binding the whole load tight to the horse.

An outfitter will usually assign one pack horse to each sportsman to carry his personal outfit, except rain or mackinaw coat, and camera. The camera is usually carried on the sportsman's saddle horse, a rifle, if carried, in a leather saddle scabbard. The sportsman will thus usually be furnished two panniers in which to pack all his personal effects except his bedding. The inside dimensions of a pannier are approximately 22 inches long, 8 or 9 inches wide, and 15 inches deep. They often taper to less width at the bottom so that this edge will not project beyond the horse and be continually crashing into trees and brush. These panniers are usually made of plywood, wood, canvas, rawhide, or fiber. They give excellent protection to the contents except that fragile articles and bottled liquids should be wrapped in clothing. They are usually quite rainproof, but if the horse falls in fording a river the contents will probably get wet. There should be waterproof cotton sacks for cameras, and films should be packed in pry-up tins. The weight in each pannier must not exceed 50 pounds, and should be the same in each so they will balance.

The sportsman's bedding—sleeping bag, air mattress, and pillow—are usually rolled in a tarpaulin about 8 feet square and tied with a rope, so that the bundle will measure about 3 feet by 18 inches, by 7 or 8 inches, flat rather than round. It can thus be conveniently laid on top of the saddle and panniers as a top pack. The pack cover of heavy canvas, laid over all before the diamond is thrown, protects the load from rain or snagging in the brush.

Outfitters usually furnish a tent for each one or two sportsmen, commonly a wall tent with a small heater stove. Another larger tent with cook-stove is also provided for cooking and eating, and probably a small portable table for this tent, panniers serving as seats. Occasionally one will find an outfitter who, for younger sportsmen, will furnish only a large canvas fly for shelter. This is pitched each night as a lean-to, all making their beds under it, and the fire in front serves for both warmth and cooking. Many prefer this arrangement, as it gives the pleasure and romance of a campfire, and a view from the shelter.

Assume now that a party already under canvas, are breaking camp to travel. At dawn the horse wrangler finds and drives in the saddle and pack horses which were turned out to feed. When the wrangler drives in the horses everyone but the cook turns out to catch, and saddle them.

In the meantime the cook, also arising at dawn, prepares breakfast. Immediately after breakfast each man packs his panniers, rolls his bedroll, sees that he has everything needed on his person for his day's travel.

It takes about three minutes to saddle a horse, and two men working together will pack one in about ten minutes. The actual packing is usually done by the horse wranglers and cook, working together. Every sportsman, however, should learn how to pack, as one can never tell when it may be necessary to lend a hand. Anyone can learn to throw the various lashes and hitches in two or three lessons.

CHECK LISTS

The following lists of equipment and supplies needed with a pack train are in two parts. The first, the *Camp and Horse Outfit,* which is usually furnished by the local outfitter or guide is included in his per-diem charge to the sportsman. Sportsmen going without a guide must provide most of this outfit. Some of it can be obtained from city outfitters, some only in small towns adjacent to wild mountain country where pack horses are commonly used, and some of it must be made.

The *Personal Outfit* includes those articles which it is suggested the sportsman needs, and which the outfitter or guide does not provide. These he can usually purchase from sporting-goods stores. Perhaps the most important single personal item is the mountaineering boots. They must afford secure footing on steep snow, ice, and rock slopes, and they must be comfortable and light. Success and safety depend more on them than on any other item. They cannot usually be bought, but must be made to order. For the necessary lightness they

Adjustment and balance are important.

should be only six inches high. *Remember* that the composition rubber soles seen on many sportsmen's boots will not hold hobnails; soles *must* be of oak-tanned leather.

The outfit for pack-horse trips may seem heavy and bulky to those used to lighter canoe outfits. There are several reasons for this. Unfortunately a horse cannot be educated to care for light and fragile articles, and the rough and tumble of pack-horse traveling both demand strong articles and make frequent repairs necessary. In high mountain country quick changes in weather from heat to blizzards are likely to occur. Trips of this kind often get far from sources of supply and replacement. (Question marks indicate items which are optional.)

CAMP AND HORSE OUTFIT

Tents with camp stoves, or large canvas fly.
Axes, 3-lb. head, with sheaths.
Bucksaw, with takedown frame (for stove wood).
Camp table and chairs (?).

For each saddle horse:
- Saddle blanket.
- Western stock saddle.
- Bridle, halter, and halter rope.
- Bell and strap, hobbles.
- Army saddlebags.

For each pack horse:
- Saddle blanket.
- Pack saddle with lash and hitch ropes.
- Halter and halter rope.
- Bell and strap, hobbles.
- Canvas pack cover.
- Panniers

Repair kit:
- Horse shoes and nails.
- Files, pliers, awls, rivets, sewing kit.
- Extra rope and leather.

Cooking utensils (for 4 men, packed in pannier)
- 4 kettles to nest.
- 2 frying pans, 12-inch.
- 1 folding baker (unless stove has oven.)
- 6 plates, 6 bowls, 6 enamel cups.
- 1 cream pitcher.
- 6 knives, forks, tea spoons, table spoons.
- 1 large cooking fork and spoon.
- 1 cake turner, butcher knife, can opener.
- 1 salt and pepper shakers.
- 1 large mixing pan (goes on as top pack).
- 1 tin wash basin " " " " "
- Water bucket (canvas).
- Flashlight or candle lantern.
- Alarm clock, carborundum stone, file.
- Dish cloths.
- Cans of matches, sugar, salt, pepper, lard, and soap for daily use.

Food. Most of it packed in small cotton bags and then in panniers. Sacks of potatoes, onions, and flour are usually carried as top packs.

PERSONAL OUTFIT

Worn: Wide-brimmed hat, wool shirt, light pants, light wool underwear, wool socks, mountaineer shoes, riding gloves, belt binoculars.

Pockets: Watch, compass, hunting knife, handkerchief, dark glasses, map, pipe, tobacco, matches, waterproof match-box.

On saddle horse: Rain or mackinaw coat on cantle (according to weather). Army saddlebags with lunch and camera.

On pack horse Top pack: Sleeping bag, air mattress, pillow, rucksack, rain or mackinaw coat and fishing equipment.

D. T. Abercrombie, N. Y.

An air mattress for campers' use.

In panniers:
- 1 wool short, 1 medium weight wool pants.
- 2 suits wool underwear.
- 4 pairs wool socks.
- 1 camp slippers or moccasins.
- 1 leather top rubbers (in wet country).
- 3 handkerchiefs.
- 1 pair warm gloves.
- 2 flannel pajamas.
- Toilet articles. Small bath towel.
- Medicine Kit.
- Flashlight, extra batteries and lamp.
- Films for camera (in pry-up tin).
- Tobacco and extra pipe.
- Boot grease.
- Notebook, pencil, fish license.

The guide, wranglers, and cook will require a similar personal outfit. They must be well shod, with plenty of dry, comfortable clothes to work efficiently and particularly if they smoke, they must have plenty of tobacco. If any of them are particularly fond of some food it is well to include it in the food list.

CAMP BEDDING

An angler in the wilderness spends one-third of the time in bed, and the energy enjoyed in waking hours depends on the quality of sleep—on the comfort and warmth of the bed. Perhaps it is incorrect to say that a bed should be warm. No bed is warm unless it is made so by an old-fashioned warming pan or the newer electric blanket. A camp bed can only retain the warmth that the body generates, by preventing it from being quickly dissipated. This is best accomplished by making the covering above and below so that it contains *dry, dead-air space,* which is the best non-conductor of heat. The body exudes much water vapor during sleep. Cotton retains this and makes the bed damp and cold. But even if the covering contained much dry air, a wind might dissipate that unless there is also a windbreak, which, however, should permit body vapor to escape. Thus we derive the principles on which a warm bed should be built.

The best bedding insulators are, in the order of their efficiency, feathers, Dacron, fur, and wool. They contain much dead air. An outside cover of shower-proof cotton will absorb the vapor which escapes, hold this moisture where it will be absorbed by the outside air, and at the same time protect the inner covering from wind.

Wool blankets are old-fashioned bedding so far as outdoor use is concerned. They are heavy in proportion to the warmth they retain. Two light blankets are warmer than one of the same weight because of the layer of dead air between them. Blankets can sometimes be taken from home without expense, and are thus not to be despised. They can be pinned into sleeping-bag form with horse blanket safety pins, and any sort of a tarp can be spread below and above them.

Next in order of low cost comes the wool comforter or quilt, which is warmer than a blanket because of the greater amount of dead air contained. These are best when used between two blankets, or lined on both sides with all-wool flannel. They can often be purchased cheaply from mail-order houses.

The warmest of all camp bedding for its weight is the modern down sleeping bag, composed of a comforter or quilt of goose feathers, often called eiderdown, lined with light all-wool flannel, and with an outer covering of cravenetted cotton. These are usually made in bag form by zipper or snap fasteners so they can be opened and spread flat for drying. Many weights and sizes are made, from the heaviest arctic robe or bag intended for temperatures down to 40° below zero, and weighing about 12 pounds, to very light ones of about 4 pounds intended for night temperatures down to freezing.

Commonly these bags are about 84 by 36 inches, about a correct size for small and medium-sized men but a large man would be uncomfortable in a bag less than 40 inches wide.

A sleeping bag should not be fastened or "zipped" more than halfway up the open side in the interest of safety, as it is sometimes necessary to get out of it quickly. The unfastened opening is kept closed and snug subconsciously, just as one keeps the edges of covers down in bed at home. When a bag is used in the open, without a tent, a duffle bag or pack should be placed at the head of the bed above the pillow to keep the covering snug around the neck. One cannot sleep warm in damp or wet underwear. Dry flannel pajamas, or underwear and, if necessary, dry socks should be put on before retiring.

Of course blankets or a sleeping bag are uncomfortable if laid on the bare ground, and also get dirty and damp. Some form of mattress is essential. The old-fashioned camp mattress often consisted of a bed-tick filled with grass or leaves gathered on the spot, or—much better—in the north, of the finer branches of balsam, hemlock, or spruce shingled thickly on the ground. Such a bed has a fine odor, and if laid at least 8 inches thick is comfortable the first night. It soon packs down and becomes hard. It takes half an hour to make a good bough bed, usually at the time when the camper is tired or busy with other camp chores. It does eliminate weight from the pack. Mattresses for camp usually made of kapok, are heavy and bulky.

Decidedly the best for camping is the air mattress, which need not weigh over 4½ pounds or occupy more space than a small blanket when deflated. It can be quickly blown up with a small pump, or by lung power. It makes a bed as comfortable and dry as the "four-poster" at home. Do not buy the big, full-sized mattress. One 48 inches by 26 inches, will provide all the cushioned surface the largest man needs. The overhang of the lower legs is never noticed—or if it is a small bundle of boughs, grass, or leaves will bring the bottom up even with the top. Further, a full-sized air mattress has a tendency to "bounce" the sleeper from side to side when he rolls over, and finally he rolls or bounces completely off the mattress. This is entirely avoided with the shorter 48-inch length, as the "drag" of the feet on the more stable bottom seems to keep one in control of one's position.

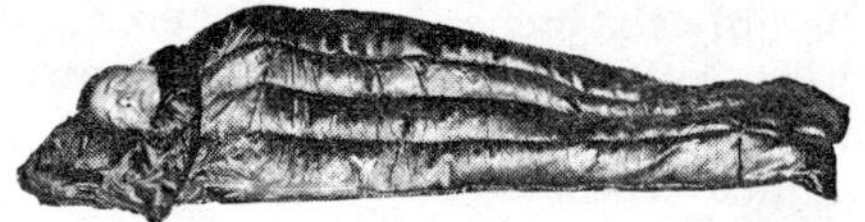

D. T. Abercrombie, N. Y.

A very light down sleeping bag for mountaineers and back packers, weighing only 3 pounds and satisfactory to freezing weather.

We now come to the best bed for cool weather camping. The arctic down sleeping bag is too warm when night temperature is over 40 degrees above zero. An air mattress is cold at temperatures below zero. So the experienced individual makes his camp bed approximately as follows, the whole process not taking more than five or six minutes:

Choose a level piece of ground for the bed, and clear and smooth it. On either side of this space about 3 feet apart, lay two small logs 6 feet long, and stake them down at the outside of each end or lay rocks there. These logs can usually be picked up on the forest floor, and do not often have to be cut. It makes no difference if they are rotten or wet, or if the ground is wet or partly snow covered. Over the cleared space between the logs lay a waterproof canvas or cotton tarp or rubber poncho. At the top of this bed lay the short air mattress and inflate it so that when kneeling on the ground along side it, and pressing down in its middle with the full weight on his hand, the ground underneath can be felt. On this lay the arctic down sleeping bag covered with the blanket. In extreme cold, the blanket, folded once, can be placed directly on the air mattress thus insulating one from cold below. Also do not neglect some kind of a pillow; an air pillow is the lightest and least bulky. To most people a comfortable pillow is as essential for a night's rest as a soft mattress.

Camp cots are also often used, and under certain

D. T. Abercrombie, N. Y.

An Arctic down sleeping bag with Hudson Bay blanket for cold weather in the fall and winter.

L. L. Bean

Clothes for the Fisherman.

Reading left to right and down. 1) Featherweight rain shirt. 2) Lightweight trolling shirt. 3) Ladies rubber fishing shirt. 4) Extra light waders. 5) Featherweight rain pants. 6) Fisherman's vest. 7) Standard type hip boots. 8) Wading shoes. 9) Rain hat, Sou'wester type.

conditions are essential, particularly in the tropics. The best and most convenient type, about 7 feet by 30 inches, folds into a bundle about 40 by 6 inches. A cot keeps the bedding clean and away from ants and other insects. It can be insulated from ants by placing the legs in cans filled with water covered with a film of kerosene. The canvas cot is the coolest bed known for hot nights in the South, but it will freeze its occupant out even at 45° above zero, unless a good, thick, and warm mattress is used on it. Any sleeping bag or blanket arrangement is cold in fall weather if used on a cot without a mattress.

In tropical jungle, hammocks tied between two trees are also commonly used. These are made of canvas, not netting, and are combined with a mosquito bar which stretches above. The top of the mosquito bar is sometimes made of waterproof cotton, or a waterproof tarp is thrown over all to protect from rain.

FISHING CLOTHES

There is no standard style of fishermen's clothes. Many prefer to wear old clothing that is loose-fitting and comfortable. This is one of the cardinal rules for fishing garments. The other is that clothing should be suitable for local climatic conditions.

This latter requirement might mean in southern waters, shorts or slacks, together with a sun hat and goggles. Before indulging in this abbreviated costume, however, northerners should gradually accustom themselves to the sun, or serious sunburn may follow. It is well when first going fishing to carry light clothing that can be put on if one is exposed to the weather too long.

At the other extreme, the ice fishing enthusiast with his fur-lined boots, heavy woolen underwear and socks, and sheepskin vest and coat, pullovers, parkas, heavy mittens, or other heavy clothing to serve both as a windbreaker and for warmth. In between are the great body of summer fishermen who use almost any available old clothing.

When fishing in clear waters, it is well to avoid white or bright colors. While the color may not frighten the fish, conspicuous clothing makes sudden movements more noticeable, and fishermen believe that movement does frighten fish when the visibility is good. Neutral shades of forest green or browns are preferred by those who have any choice in clothing color.

There are, however, certain types of clothing that add to the comfort and pleasure of a fishing trip, particularly under variable climatic conditions. Among the most useful are rain garments which may be found as thin plastic transparent garments, oilskins, or water-proofed cloth trousers and coats for both men and women. For colder weather, it is well to have such equipment for windbreaking, even though it may not be raining. The combination is very useful when fishing in northern districts or in offshore waters, except in the extreme south.

Commercial fishermen who are continually exposed to variable weather conditions prefer a sou'wester hat and slicker and oilskin trousers. The average angler will not need such heavy equipment, but their example is a good one to follow in fishing similar waters.

There are on the market light weight, waterproof jackets with parkas attached that are very useful for occasional wear. They also have the advantage of being less bulky than the heavier oilskins or slickers.

Those who do much stream wading for trout or bass or wading in the shallow waters for surf casting find that hip boots or, better still, waders which come up under the arms are necessary equipment. These come in a variety of styles that will suit almost any need. Hip boots, the most commonly used of all, are available in several styles. The common, heavy, pull-on ones, used where a person does not wear them for long periods, are the cheapest and are very satisfactory for occasional use. Just prior to World War II, ankle-fitting, lightweight, flexible boots were favored by many anglers. These are light to carry and prevent chafed heels because of the tight-fitting ankles. They are also so flexible that they are more comfortable around the knees. They have the disadvantage of being almost impossible to put on and take off unless the user is able to dry them out thoroughly between each trip. Even a slight amount of perspiration makes them almost impossible to remove.

In some of the later designs, this has been largely overcome by fitting on the outside of the boot a strap which can be used to gather it in to fit the ankle, but leaving the boot large enough to put it on and off easily. These have all the advantages of the ankle-fitting type without the more obvious disadvantages. However, those on the market are somewhat heavier and stiffer than the best of the flexible, light weight ones previously available.

There are also available waders so designed that wading shoes can be worn over them. These are perhaps the most comfortable outfits of all for those who are doing continuous wading. They can be purchased large enough to permit pulling up over heavy, warm clothing, so that they can be used even in cold weather with comfort.

Ankle-length, tennis-type wading shoes with non-skid bottoms, specially made to fit over these waders, are also available in a number of styles. This outfit is light, easily taken on and off, and allows variation in the amount of clothing and foot gear that is worn on different occasions.

In addition to the traditional Sou'wester, various types of fishermen's hats are on the market. These are selected according to personal preference and wishes. Many of those fishing in southern waters prefer a cap with a good visor for eye protection.

One other item of fishermen's clothing is quite commonly seen, a fishermen's vest made of light canvas or duck with almost innumerable pockets for carrying various items of gear. They resemble very much the shooting jackets worn by hunters except they are designed especially for fishermen's needs. They are light and comfortable; valuable for those who do much fly fishing or plug casting while wading since they eliminate the necessity of carrying a tackle box. The pockets are large enough to accommodate fly books or boxes or small boxes carrying plugs and similar lures. These are inexpensive and to many are worth their cost.

INSECT REPELLENTS

In many fine fishing districts, head nets or efficient insect repellents are necessities for comfort. Black flies, no-see-ums, and mosquitoes can, at times, become major nuisances anywhere from the Arctic to the tropics; they can greatly reduce or destroy entirely the pleasure of a fishing vacation.

Insect repellents of varying efficiency has been available for many years and can be purchased under a wide variety of trade names in almost any local drug store or sporting good center. If properly used, they reduce or eliminate biting for from one to several hours, and a good repellent should be a standard item in the tackle box.

War-time research developed several highly efficient repellents, the most widely known of which is 6-12. It was developed and patented by Rutgers University and is made and distributed for them by the National Carbide and Carbon Company. A less widely known but even more effective one is 6-2-2, made up, in part, of Rutgers 6-12 with the addition of dimethylpthalate and indolone. This contains elements which repel both sucking insects (*e. g.* mosquitoes) and those that bite (*e. g.* black flies). Repellents give effective protection for varying periods of time depending upon the concentration of active ingredients and the formula of the repellent. If light applications are renewed during the day, the annoyance from such pests is greatly reduced.

Some repellents are mildly toxic to some individuals and, in such cases, will cause skin irritations. For most people, however, they provide protection from insects with no unpleasant after effects, care always should be exercised to keep them out of the eyes and mouth.

COMPASS AND MAPS

Every sportsman visiting unfamiliar wilderness country should carry a compass and a map of the region. Properly used, they can keep him from being lost and thus avoid the privation or real disaster which is sometimes the penalty for getting confused over direction. Besides this important function, they will help keep appointments to meet companions at prearranged places. Under many circumstances these pathfinding tools are as necessary as fishing rods to enjoy successful fishing.

Many models of compasses are available and knowledge of their specifications is needed to help choose one suitable for the purpose. Size is an important distinction. Sizes vary from the small "pocket" instruments with one-inch dials to the large engineering types fitted with faces twice as wide and with special sighting devices which are valuable to lay off true courses and follow them precisely.

A small pocket compass can be selected if it is only necessary to know the general direction. Fine work, however, is difficult with them and they are not reliable for running long accurate lines, taking bearings from maps, or in making necessary allowance for the natural declination of the needle.

Pocket compasses use two devices to indicate direction, a revolving needle that swings above a printed stationary dial, and a revolving dial which replaces the needle and turns as the body of the compass is moved. The latter is fast to use because the instrument need not be adjusted to bring needle and "north" in line. No confusion can arise over which point of a movable dial indicates north, because it is plainly marked. Movable-dial models should be supplied with a sighting line if the user plans to take bearings or make declination allowances with them.

The bigger engineering-type compasses with wide dials and sights or sighting lines are recommended for exacting service and for working in conjunction with maps. Less skill is required to use large compasses and the results obtained are more accurate. The needle in some of these instruments is surrounded by a dampening fluid which blocks the fast oscillation present in dry-dial types. Liquid compasses are quickly put in use and their pivot bearing has long life. The liquid also acts to cushion needle and bearing against shock.

All compasses except the liquid-filled type need a brake to lock the needle when not in actual service. Otherwise the jeweled bearing wears loose.

A compass dial is divided into 360 degrees called "azimuth directions" and numbered consecutively in a clockwise direction. The letter *N* designating north is placed at numbers 0 and 360 ("0" is not shown) which occupy the same position. Thus the direction of south falls at 180 degrees, west at 270, and east at 90. A degree-numbered dial is necessary for safe, accurate pathfinding. Compasses with dials marked with just the eight main directions are practical for only the very roughest work.

Sportsmen use three main types of maps for finding their way through wilderness country; regular printed, homemade, and mental. Printed maps can be secured from the sources listed below. Homemade maps are drawn on the spot from data secured by observation and measurements or from the knowledge of companions or guides. Mental maps are merely memories of the direction and approximate distance of the turns made during the day's travel.

Woodsmen with extensive experience can keep these details orderly filed inside their minds and when it is necessary to backtrack, can call the turns with amazing accuracy. This ability forms what some call a "homing" or "direction" instinct, though it is actually nothing of the kind. Fishermen with less woods experience will be safer from getting lost if they rely on compass and printed or self-made maps instead of memory.

Among printed maps, the topographic sheets sold for about 15 cents each by the Geological Survey, Washington, D. C., are most popular with sportsmen. These maps are approximately 16½ by 20 inches and are drawn to scales varying from ½ to 2 inches to each mile, depending upon the character of the country charted. Topographic maps are very accurate and present a wealth of detail. Bodies of water are printed in blue, man-made works like towns, cities, roads, railroads, and boundaries in black, and features of relief (hills, mountains, and valleys) are indicated by brown contour lines. After some experience in reading contours, one can quickly determine from a map the height of elevated spots and the steepness of their slopes.

To order topographic maps first write for the free index of the state (including Alaska and Hawaii) in which you are interested. This index lists the quadrangles available. Canadian topographic maps are equally useful and can be obtained from Surveys and Engineering Branch, Department of Mines and Resources, Ottawa, Canada. Before ordering write for the key price list showing sections covered.

The U. S. Forest Service, Department of Agriculture, Washington 25, D. C., publishes maps of many lake and forest regions which may be obtained from the above address or from Regional Headquarters. With these, a key map is available which indicates areas covered and gives regional addresses. Some state conservation departments also issue maps, particularly of the canoe-cruising country inside their boundaries. It is wise to obtain as many different maps of the same region as possible. Prices are low, and one may show useful details not carried by the others.

The top of standard maps is usually north. When it is not, the map carries a compass rosette or arrow indicating that direction. Large maps are easier to handle in camp and on trails if cut into pocket-sized rectangles which are then pasted in proper order on muslin. Map sections should be spaced about one-eighth inch apart so the cloth between acts as a hinge and permits folding without creasing any of the print. Map faces can be protected from rain with a coat of transparent varnish. Note, however, that this prevents the hunter from marking his trail or making notes on them as he travels.

Maps should be carried and not left at camp, for they have many uses afield. For instance, bearings can be taken from a map which give the true course to reach any place listed upon it. A map shows the direction in which rivers and mountain ridges or valleys run, valuable help when one is lost. Contour lines of topographic sheets warn of steep hills or ravines ahead and also show how the sportsman can detour around them.

The first lesson in compass use is to know which end of its needle points north. This may sound unnecessary, but the fact remains that many have, in sudden panic, forgotten this important fact or have refused to trust their memory. The north end of most compass needles is colored red or blue or is shaped like an arrowhead to distinguish it from the other end that bears south. If a different marking exists to puzzle the sportsman, he can test the needle on objects about home whose true direction is known. Then the data can be scratched on the bottom of the instrument or, if it is the hunting-case watch type, written on paper pasted to the inside of the compass cover.

When using a compass its dial must be held horizontal or the needle may bind and register untrue. The instrument must be kept away from metal objects—several feet from an ax, or knife, much farther from metal bridge girders or railroad rails. Merely holding a compass against one's belt buckle

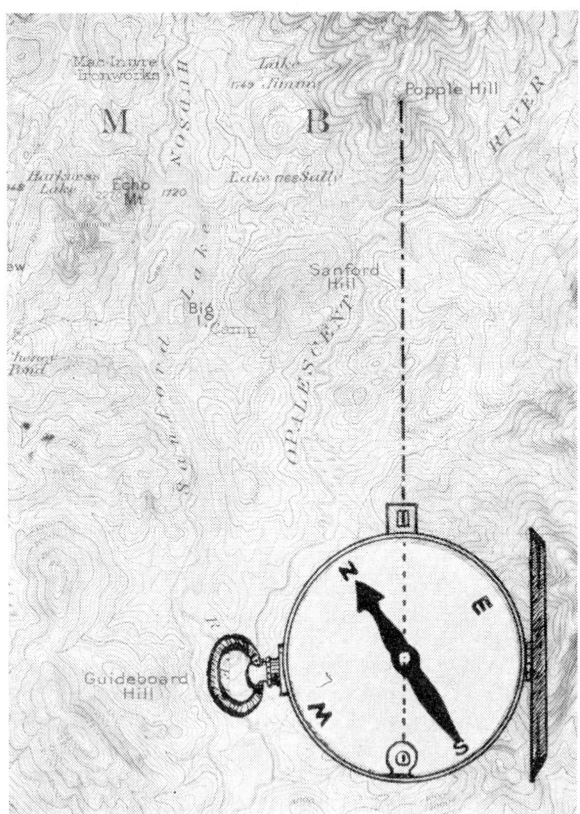

Taking a bearing on a prominent landmark.

can distort its action. Hidden bodies of certain ores act similarly, and when one of these is believed to lie close, the fisherman should move to a different position for his bearing.

A simple and common function of the compass occurs when it becomes desirable to fish in some general direction away from camp. For instance, he decides to try the lake some 2 miles distance. A sight over the compass shows that this direction is southwest. When he has finished fishing, he knows he must travel northeast to return. This direction is determined by compass and checked at intervals along the way.

In rugged wilderness country, or wherever one is apt to tramp more than 2 or 3 miles from camp, it is scarcely enough to know the general direction traveled. Now it is safer to record the directions of the main turns made and their approximate length. To do this, the compass must be freely consulted. For example, a camper strikes out north from his base. After a mile he swings northeast to follow a ravine. When the ravine ends, he turns east, climbs the right-hand ridge, and drops into a little valley below. Another turn is made farther ahead to miss the edge of a swamp.

If the fisherman notes the azimuth bearing of each turn with his compass and measures its approximate distance by consulting his watch (measuring distance in minutes is easier and just as practical as counting paces) he can always know his approximate position in relation to camp. And he will know how to proceed when he wants to return. As stated before, an experienced woodsman will often memorize these details, but one who visits wilderness country for only a few days each season should record them in a notebook or on a map.

A popular use of the compass consists of roughly surveying the ground about the fishing camp and making a map from the data. For instance, a flat-topped hill is visible some 2 miles away. The fisherman levels his compass (in some northern latitudes it may be necessary to tilt the dial slightly to prevent the needle from sticking on account of magnetic dip) and points its sighting line at the hill. The dial (if moveable) is turned until its letter *N* and the north end of the needle coincide. The fisherman notes that the sighting line falls across the azimuth degree figure 225. This means the hill lies at a bearing of 225 degrees, which is southwest.

This fact is recorded on the homemade map. Then the fisherman knows that should he ever become confused about direction when this hill is visible, a straight northeast course from it will take him home. If several visible landmarks lying in different directions can be charted on the home-prepared map, it will have real value as insurance against being lost in that region.

When taking bearings with compasses without sights or sighting line and which may also not possess a movable dial (meaning a dial which turns separately from the base), the fisherman sights across the face of the instrument through its center to check which degree figure points at the object being mapped. For extreme accuracy the compass should be laid on the level top of a stump, log, or rock. The user then steps 2 feet away, so that any small metal object in his pocket will not affect the needle, and reads the direction.

So far no mention has been made of the natural declination of compass needles because no allowance for this factor is necessary when fishermen draw their own maps or when they take bearings on natural objects like trees, hills, rocks, lakes, etc., and follow courses to or from them. But when printed maps are used, this allowance is important if it exists in any appreciable amount. Declination occurs because the compass needle points toward the magnetic pole instead of toward true north (the north pole). In only a few spots do these directions coincide.

Places where the needle points both magnetic and true north lie on a crooked line connecting a point above Lake Superior and running southeast near the southeast corner of Georgia. At points east of this line the compass needle bears west of true north, at points west of the line it bears east of true north. Because printed maps are drawn to conform with true north, declination must be compensated for to obtain absolute accuracy. Declination varies according to location from a fraction of a degree to as much as 22 degrees. Fractional amounts can often be overlooked in practical pathfinding, but one or more degrees should be compensated for to avoid following an inaccurate course.

Printed maps usually carry a note telling the amount of declination present in their area. The Government issues a chart periodically that shows these amounts in the different sections. A copy can be obtained by sending 20 cents (not postage stamps) to the Government Printing Office, Washington, D. C. Ask for latest "Map of the Compass Declination in the U. S."

A west declination requires correction toward the east, east declinations requires correction toward the west. Correction can be made by adding or subtracting the declination in degrees to the regular compass dial reading. If the bearing course reads 105 degrees and 5 more must be added to correct, the true line of travel will fall over the 110-degree figure. Correction can also be made by twisting the map underneath the compass without moving the latter. The map is first placed so that its meridians run north and south by compass. The compass is laid with the center covering the fisherman's position and the map is twisted clockwise to add declination, counterclockwise to subtract it. This puts the map in line with true north and accurate bearings can be taken from it in any direction.

The question of when to add and when to subtract declination depends on the problem at hand. When working from terrain to map, as when locating one's position on the map by sighting on physical objects actually visible to the eye and which are also shown on the map, then eastern declination is added and western subtracted. On the other hand, when the fisherman has picked out some spot on the map to which he will walk, he reverses the above, and subtracts eastern and adds western declination to the compass-dial reading.

Detailed instructions for handling this factor are sometimes provided with high-grade compasses. Sportsmen lacking them should write the rules as given on a margin of their maps.

WHAT TO DO WHEN LOST

PRECAUTIONS

Intelligent use of compass and map will normally prevent fishermen from becoming lost. But when unusual conditions exist, such as being caught in a sudden snowstorm or losing one's sense of direction, it is quite possible to get confused and forget the way back. Because there is no guarantee against the occurrence of such an emergency, every fisherman should know how to cope with it when it does occur.

EQUIPMENT

Everyone needs a compass and a map. Should some lack maps, sketches of the surrounding country can be made for them by someone familiar with the region. Or the individual can make his own map by taking exploring hikes in each of the main directions.

Beside compass and map, each person should carry a stout knife and a waterproof matchbox. The knife can be pocket or belt type. This will cut poles for emergency shelter and fuel for signal and warming fires. Four and one-half inches is a good length for sheath blades; one inch shorter will serve in pocket models. The knife should be sharp and so carried that it cannot be lost. A safety strap about the handle of the belt knife holds it securely in the sheath. Smaller models can be stored in a pocket with button-down flap or tied to the belt with a rawhide thong.

The matchbox must be genuinely waterproof to resist rain and perspiration. A good test is to submerge it in water overnight. If the matches inside strike readily next morning, the box is tight. It is vitally necessary to keep this box filled. To guarantee that it is, fishermen should carry an extra supply for smoking and other ordinary purposes.

These four articles comprise the very minimum of equipment one should carry in the wild country. Some add a light belt or pocket ax which speeds up the work of building shelters and cutting enough firewood to last an entire night. Several sandwiches or candy bars or both can be profitably added to these bare essentials. If the fisherman does not get lost he will eat and enjoy them. But if misfortune does come, the food will be a big morale builder.

SELF-CONTROL

A cool head is just as vital as these items to help a lost fisherman master his predicament. He must not submit to fear or panic when he realizes that he is lost. Fear and panic only make things worse. Unless a lost man forces himself to remain calm, he cannot think clearly and will certainly do something foolish.

Lost people who retain their self-possession are invariably found or find their way out. A night spent under the stars may bring small discomforts but nothing serious or fatal. One can easily survive a day or two without food. The worst thing is a blizzard or driving rain, and many times a lost man can build protection against weather.

The first move should be to climb a tree or hill and look for some familiar landmark. Many cases of being lost never go beyond this stage because the sportsman sights a recognizable landmark and from it orients his position and that of camp.

But if he does not he should sit down and, by thinking, try to recall incidents, facts, or objects encountered along the back trail that furnish clues to the direction of camp. Other lost cases end here when the sportsman succeeds in unraveling enough of his route to return along it. The importance of remaining calm and unworried can be realized now. Scared minds are incapable of logical, accurate thought.

Several actions can help induce calmness. Smoking is one. Drinking water and eating a sandwich (one only now) are others. A little vigorous exercise like climbing a tree and gathering wood for a fire also assist. If he is at all jittery—and a lost person has plenty of reason for feeling that way—he should briskly busy himself for a few minutes or until he has been able to conquer fear.

If a lost man decides with reasonable certainty that he is north of camp, he can produce his compass, take a southerly bearing across the country and follow it back. Should he through some dire misfortune have lost the compass or left it at camp, he can use the sun to determine direction roughly.

Even when covered by thin clouds the sun still casts a faint shadow and can be located by it. A match stick or knife blade placed erect on some bright surface like a thumbnail or scrap of paper will throw a dim shadow. The sun lies in front of the object and in line with this shadow.

Direction can also be determined with a watch. When the hour hand is pointed at the sun, the point halfway between that hand and the figure 12 is south. The accuracy of this stunt should also be checked the first day in camp.

If both compass and watch are lacking he can check with certain nature signs. They are not infalliable but usually prove fairly accurate when the evidence provided by two or more are averaged. Moss usually (but not always) grows thickest on the side of a tree that receives the least sun because more dampness exists there. Moss deposits are accordingly thicker on the north or nearly north sides of the trunk. Good test trees stand out by themselves where they are not heavily shaded by others. Moss can be thickest on the south face of a tree if that side is continually in deep shade.

The thickness of a tree's bark and the width of its growth rings will also help determine direction. Both are greater on the north and northeast sides of the trunk. Tests can be made with knife or ax; notches must be cut on opposite sides for comparison. The extreme top branches of pines and hemlocks sometimes point toward the rising sun or a little south of east. This sign is not as reliable as others and should be used only to supplement them.

When a lost man is unable to determine which way to move, he should stay wherever he is until his companions find him or until he can see or hear their signals when they realize his plight. To wait is safer than to struggle along an unknown course, because this blind travel might lead further from camp. Instead of attempting travel one should make himself as comfortable as possible for the coming night.

SHELTER

A shelter not too far from water is needed. It can be a big log, rock, cave, windfall, or thick clump of young trees, preferably evergreens. Sticks can be leaned against the log or rock or against a pole held by stakes driven in the ground and coniferous branches woven between them to thatch a roof. Or pieces of easily peeled bark like cedar and birch can be used in place of boughs. Sometimes a fallen log will yield large sheets of bark. Boughs are tight enough to shed snow, bark will often turn rain. Small hollows in the side of a bank or hill can be enlarged for shelter. They prove comfortable because they are easily heated with an open fire.

When dry foliage or grass is available, a quantity should be gathered for a bed. If nothing better is possible, the lost person can sit with his back against a tree and maintain fire several yards away. CAUTION: Extreme care must be exercised with fires kindled near thatched or dark shelters or browse beds. Their material is highly inflammable and if accidentally ignited could cause disaster. Especially beware of wood that tosses out live coals as it burns.

A Brush Lean-to.

FIRE

As soon as the shelter is ready the fuel should be gathered for an all-night fire. Much will be needed, and lacking an ax, he must rely on loose limbs lying on the ground. With an ax, sounder, easier-burning fuel can be chopped from deadfalls and lightning-killed trees. Hemlock and birch bark and rich pine make fine kindling. So do the small dead limbs projecting from the lower trunks of pines. If it has rained recently, the soaked exteriors of the limbs must be shaved off to expose their dry cores to the match.

The hunter's matchbox should be well filled because numerous trials may be necessary to ignite damp, stubborn kindling.

SIGNALS

With a shelter and a fire, the lost person can be comfortable. In the morning he should climb a tree or hill and look around for the signal fire his companions have kindled. Failing to discover it, he should make his own signal. The fire should be started on high ground if possible and its flames smothered with damp, sappy fuels that produce a thick smoke. Green pine branches are good. So is the damp sawdust found at abandoned logging camps. Fires started at sunrise are especially effective because early morning air is often still and the vapor rises in a tall column visible for miles.

Standard distress signals consist of three quick shots if a gun is available. Other signals that are used under varying circumstances include loud shouts, whistle blasts, flashes from mirror (daytime) or flashlight (night), and waves of shirt, coat, or blanket, all in series of three. The standard response is two of the same kind.

When one travels without companions upon whom he can depend for aid if lost, he will have to work his way out alone. His best help now is hard thinking about the back trail. Every effort should be made to recall details which help point the way home. Old trails in the forest lacking signs of recent use should be ignored. They are probably abandoned logging roads that lead nowhere. It is safer to follow a river, even a mountain range or ridge, walking downhill if possible. A map is invaluable now to show where these things lead.

RESCUE

A lost person knows that some recognizable landmark exists in *some* direction from him. The problem is to find it. When leaving an emergency overnight camp to search, he should walk in a straight line, using sun or compass as a guide to avoid circling to one side in a gradual curve as unobserving hikers sometimes do. It may be wise to blaze the trail as he goes. Then if he fails to sight a familiar object that shows his position, he can return to the starting point and try again in a different direction.

Persons traveling with pack horses have often found camp after being lost by merely giving their mount its head and permitting it to choose the trail. On the other hand, it is unwise to trust an ordinary dog's instinct, as his nose is likely to lead him anywhere. Trained animals, of course, are a different matter.

It is equally important that those back in camp remain cool and think clearly when a companion fails to appear at sundown. They should *not* light signal fires or fire signal shots if the hour is late, for that would encourage the lost man to struggle on in the darkness, which is dangerous because mishaps occur more easily and frequently at night.

But rescue work should start promptly in the morning. A signal fire should be kindled and when the early mist is gone, someone should climb a tree or high point to look for the lost person's rising column of smoke. One person should stay in camp to guard and feed the fire.

The rest of the party should begin a search as soon as the horizon has cleared. Some delay is usually necessary to obtain good visibility and to allow time for the lost man's signal smoke to show up conspicuously. If his general location is known, all can concentrate on that area. Otherwise every quarter must be combed. The most likely, of course, are covered first.

Searchers should proceed in a straight line, using a compass if necessary to prevent straying. If a crooked trail must be followed because of rough ground, rescuers can blaze their path to be sure of finding their own way home. They should also fire a gun or shout loudly at intervals and then stand still for a minute, listening for a reply. This may prevent them from passing the lost man unnoticed on his way in.

After each half-mile rescuers should climb a tree and look for smoke signals. NOTE: Before a lost man leaves his emergency camp to seek his way home, he should carefully extinguish both signal and warning fires to eliminate danger of their spreading through the timber and also to save his rescuers unnecessary steps in walking to the place he has quitted.

If a person has been missing overnight, rescuers can carry food and a thermos bottle of hot coffee for his refreshment.

Getting lost is a very unsatisfactory business for

all concerned and the sportsman should do everything in his power to avoid it. Caution, keen observation, and the judicious use of compass and map should be employed. As with other misfortunes, prevention is better than cure. But should a cure be required, he should remember that a cool head coupled with clear thinking is the best possible aid.

KNOTS FOR NYLON LEADERS

Nylon has for many reasons rapidly replaced gut as leader material. When this material was first introduced, fishermen had some difficulty in tying it so it would not slip, but experience and experimentation have shown how to tie knots that will stay in place. The DuPont Company has carried on many tests and recommends various knots as proper for use with Nylon.

In general knots in which the friction is against the turns of the material itself, there is little or no tendency to slip. The following are some of the knots which are now widely used in handling Nylon leaders.

THE "TURLE" KNOT
(for tying on wet or dry flies)

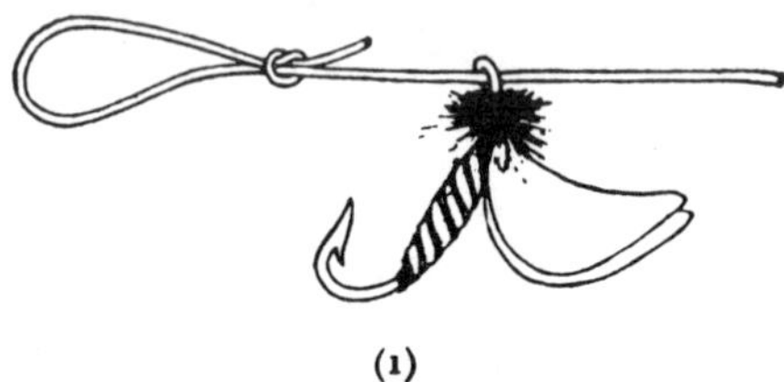

(1)
Run the end of the leader through the eye of the hook toward the bend. Make a "Single Running" knot in the end and pull the hook up tightly.

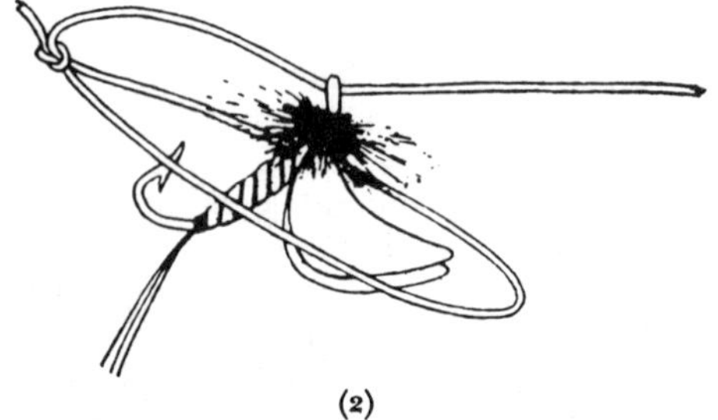

(2)
Open the loop large enough to permit the fly to pass through, and place the loop around the neck of the fly.

(3)
With the loop tight against the neck of the fly, pull the leader until the knot is tight against the neck of the fly.

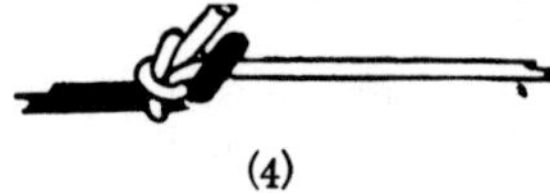

(4)
All that remains to be done is to draw the slack of the nylon through the eye and pull it tight.

THE "DOUBLE EYE" KNOT
(for bait hooks)

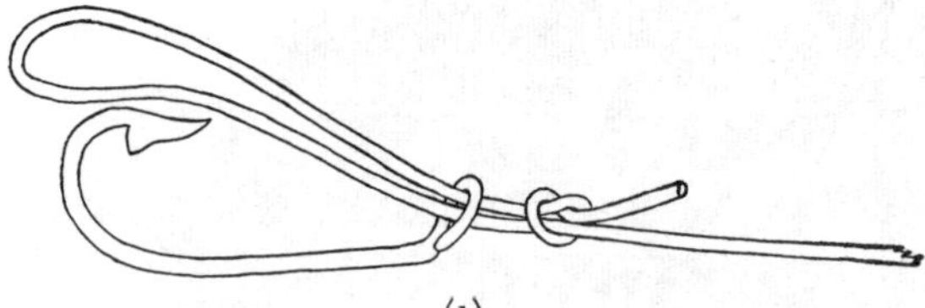

(1)
Tie a "Single Running" knot on the end of the leader and push it through the eye of the hook.

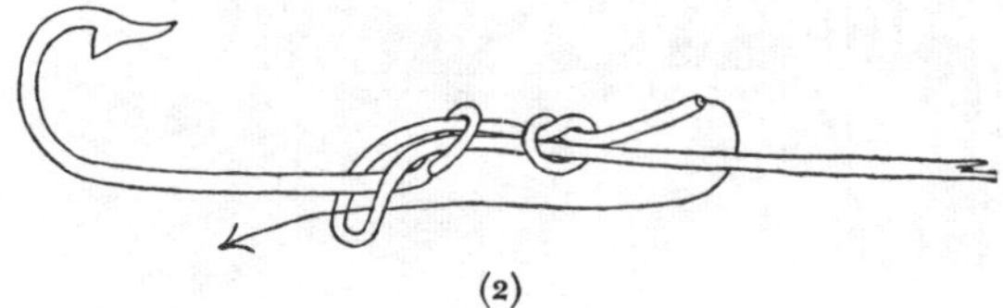

(2)
Pass this loop over the bend of the hook and draw up to the eye.

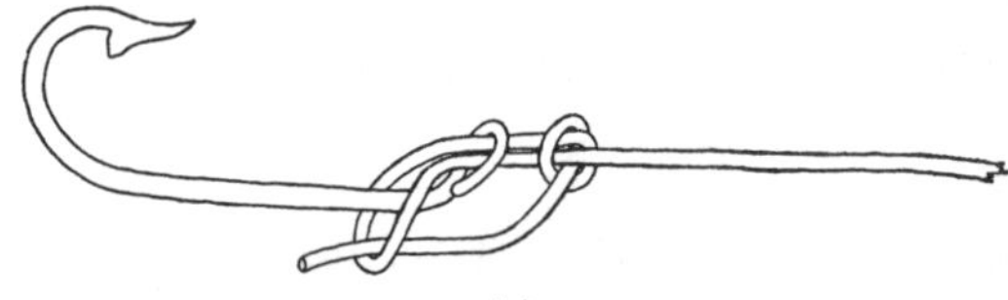

(3)
Take the short end of the "Single Running" knot, push it under the loop, against the shank, and draw up tight.

(4)
Appearance of finished knot.

TUCKED SHEET BEND
(for tying line to leader)

For this purpose the safest and easiest knot to tie is the "Tucked Sheet Bend." In this knot the end of the line is brought back and "tucked" through the loop on the end of the leader.

The method of tying this simple knot will be evident from the drawings without detailed instructions.

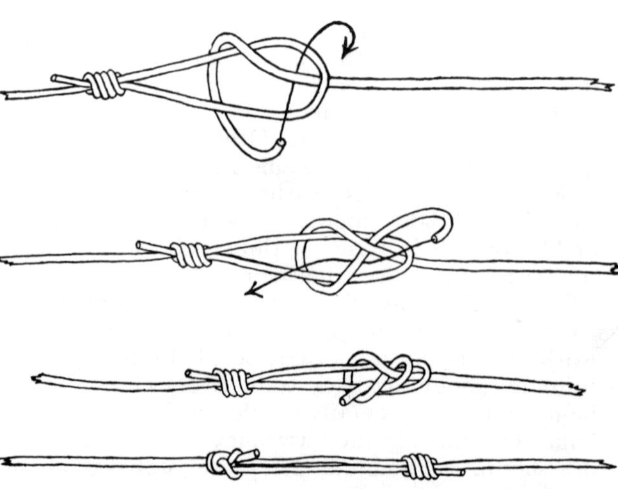

"BLOOD" OR BARREL KNOT
(for tying Nylon to Nylon)

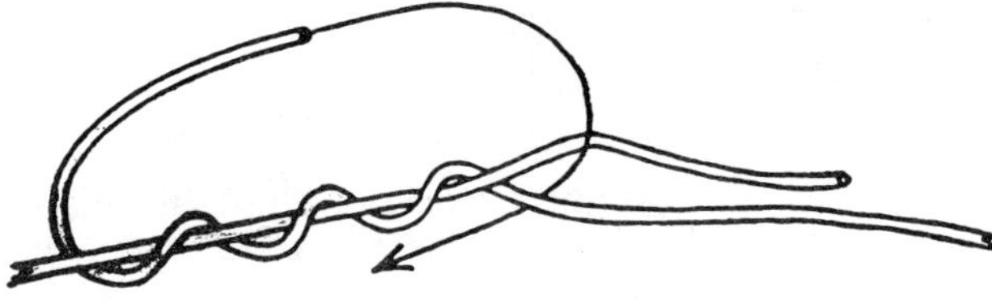

(1)

Lap the ends of the strands to be joined, and twist one around the other, making at least three turns. The drawing shows only three and a half turns, to avoid complexity. Count the turns made. Place the end between the strands, following the arrow.

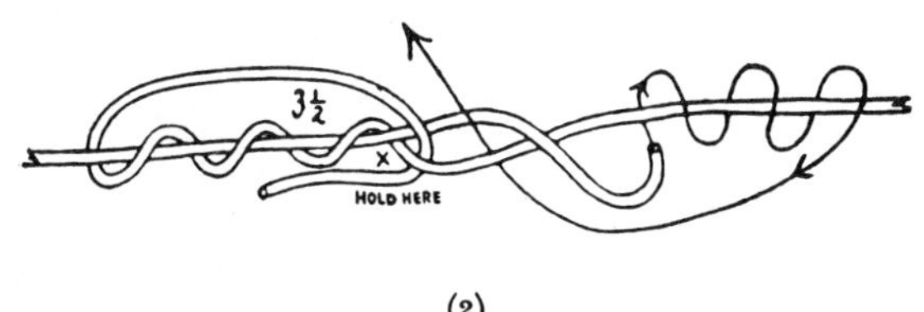

(2)

Hold the end against the turns already made, between the thumb and forefinger, at point marked "X", to keep from unwinding.

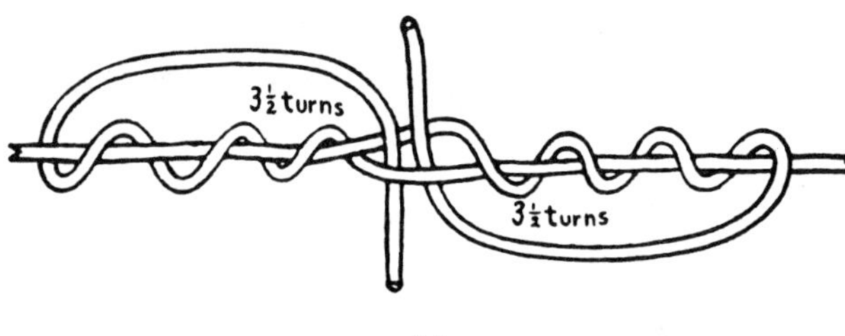

(3)

This shows how the knot would look if held firmly in place. Actually, as soon as released, the turns equalize.

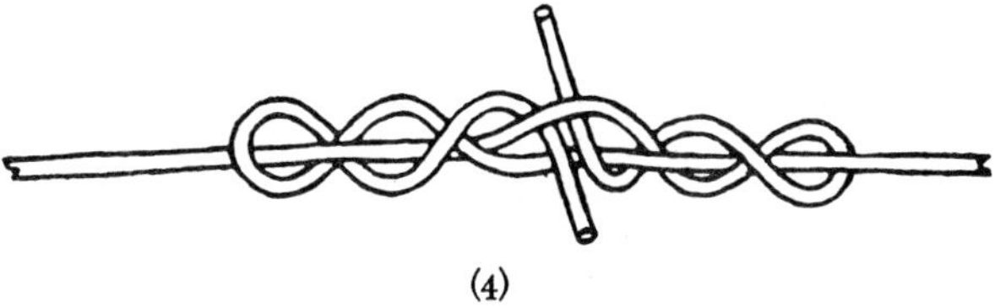

(4)

And the turns look like this. Now pull on both ends of the leader.

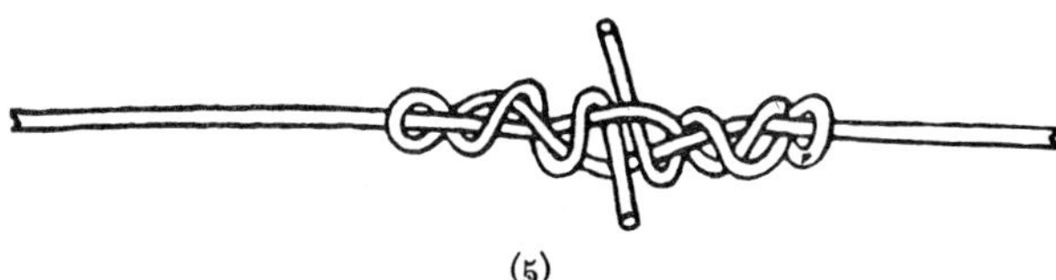

(5)

As pulling on the ends is continued, the turns gather as above, and draw closer together. (At this point, the short ends may be worked backward, if desired, to avoid cutting off too much material.)

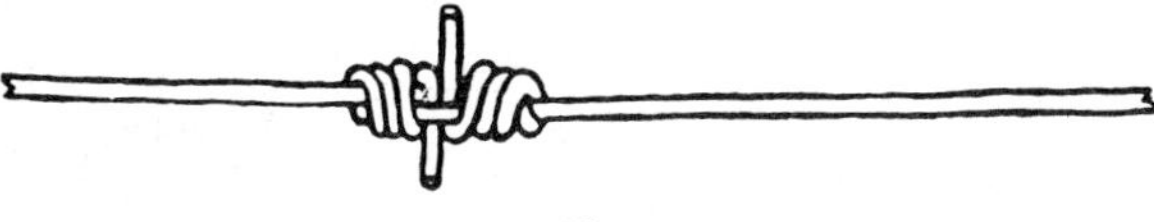

(6)

Appearance of the finished knot. All that remains to be done is to cut off the short ends, close to the knot.

LEADER KNOT
(for tying Nylon to Nylon)

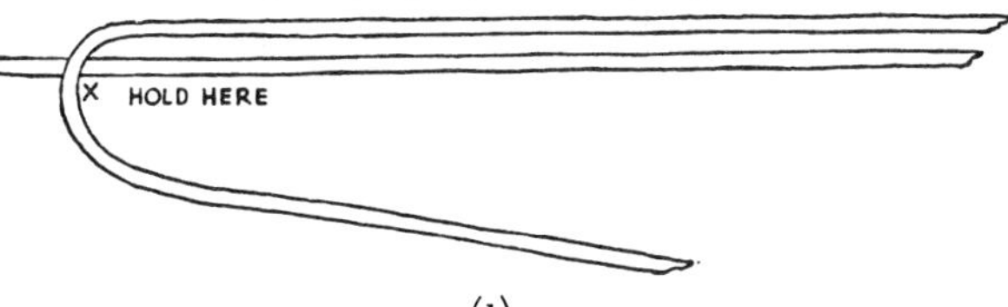

(1)

Lap the ends of the strands as shown, holding with thumb and forefinger where indicated,

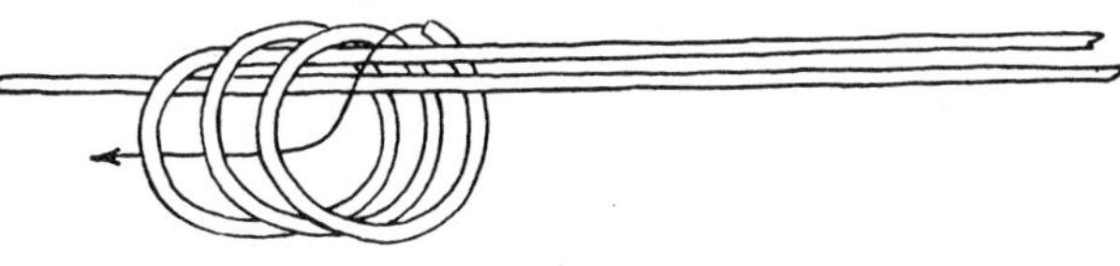

(2)

Loop end around both strands *three* times and pull end through all three loops as indicated by arrow. Then pull up slowly and evenly until this part of the knot takes the form of "A".

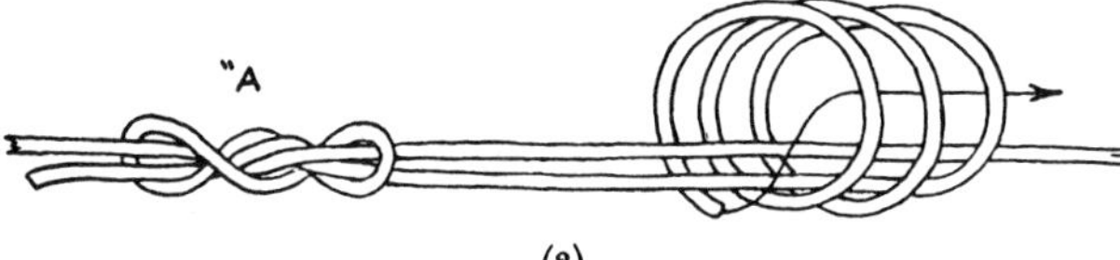

(3)

Now loop the other short end around the other strand similar to above,

(4)

When both sections of the knot have been pulled up to look like this, take the long ends and pull the two sections together slowly, then pull them up tight.

(5)

Appearance of the finished knot. All that remains to be done is to cut off the short ends close to the knot.

GLOSSARY

Algae. Simple plants most of which live submerged in water.

Anadromous. Referring to fish which spend part of their lives in salt and part in fresh water.

Anchor. A weight or hook used to hold a boat in a fixed position when not under way.

Anneal. The subjection of metal to intense heat and gradually cooling, in order to increase the strength and reduce the brittleness of metal.

Artifacts. Utensils used by early civilizations, relics.

Awl. A long needle-shaped instrument.

Backlash. A tangle of line caused by overrunning of the reel spool.

Bailer. A utensil for removing water from a boat manually.

Barbel. Whisker-like feelers about the heads of some fish.

Barbules. Tiny barbs which hold the rays of a feather together.

B. F. I. Better Fishing, Inc.

Bilge. The area along the keel inside a boat.

Bilge Pump. A pump for removing water from the hull of a boat.

Bloom. n. Microscopic organisms which are suspended in water.
v. To be discolored by microscopic or-organisms, pertaining to water in lakes.

Bobber. A small float used to hold bait off the bottom.

Brackish. Water that is partly salt and partly fresh.

Bricole. A metal gorge, forerunner of the fish-hook.

Bunker. Menhaden.

Cabin Cruiser. A large power boat with living facilities for the occupants.

Carrying Rack. A rack for carrying small boats on an automobile top.

Caudal Peduncle. Root of tail.

Chenille. Fluffy, silky material used for bodies of flies.

Chine Strips. Strips of wood at the base of the sides of a flat-bottomed boat to lend rigidity to the structure.

Chlorophyll. The green coloring matter of plants.

Chub. A bait fish.

Chumming. Throwing extra bait in the water to attract fish.

Claspers. Appendages on ventral side used to join fish during mating act, peculiar to sharks.

Clinker-built. See: *Lapstrake.*

Cloaca. A cavity in the body of vertebrates into which the intestine, urinary, and reproductive tubes open.

Clove Hitch. A knot made by making two half hitches around a post, useful for mooring boats.

Combing. An upright, water-tight rail around a boat's cockpit to prevent spray from washing aboard.

Cork Arbor. A cork filler to increase the diameter of reel spool.

Crane Fly. An aquatic insect.

Crayfish. A crustacean resembling a small lobster.

Crustaceans. Animals with hard exoskeletons.

Cuttyhunk. Linen line.

Dace. A bait fish.

Denticle. A small tooth or projection.

Devonian Age. That part of the Paleozoic which followed the Silurian Age, marked by rock forming.

Diatoms. Any of a class of microscopic algae.

Dinghy. Usually a short, broad-beamed, round-bottomed boat of light construction, usually used as a tender on yachts.

Dorsal. On or toward the back.

Dory. A rowboat with a high prow, flaring sides, and narrow bottom used chiefly for commercial fishing.

Drag. Unnatural motion of a lure in water.

Drop Line. A handline used without rod for still fishing.

Dry Fly. An artificial lure designed to imitate a floating insect.

Dugout. A canoe constructed from a single log.

Eagle Claw. A type of hook developed by Wright and McGill in which the point bends back toward the shank.

Eelskin. The skin of an eel used for bait.

Epilimnion. A thermal stratum in lakes above the thermocline.

Esophagus. The gullet.

Feathering. In rowing, bringing the blades of the oars back so that they are parallel with the surface of the water.

Feather Jig. A lure used in salt water having a metal head and a body of feathers to imitate a bait fish.

Female Ferrule. The socket part of a ferrule.

Ferrule. A friction joint in a rod to permit it to be disassembled for transportation or storage.

Fish Ladders. Structures to permit fish to climb over or around dams.

Flasher. A flashing spoon tied above the bait to attract fish to it.

Float Fishing. Angling while drifting down a stream.

Fluke. The point of an anchor.

Fulcrum. The point around which a lever turns.

Fusiform Fish. A round-bodied fish, tapering toward the ends.

Fyke Net. A bag net kept open by hoops.

Galley. A boat's kitchen.

Gang Hooks. Fish hooks fastened together in series so that they are effective from all directions.

Gills. Organs by which animals can breathe in water.

GORGE. A sliver of wood, metal, or bone hung by its center on a line, forerunner of the fish-hook.
GRAPNEL. A hook-shaped anchor with four or more tines.
GUIDES. Eyelets through which line is strung along a rod.
GUNWALE. The upper edge of a boat's side, or a wooden strip used to reinforce the upper side of a boat.
HABITAT. The environment in which fish find conditions satisfactory for existence.
HACKLE. Feather from the back or neck of a cock fowl. Used to simulate legs on flies for fishing.
HELLGRAMMITE. Larvae of the Dobson-fly.
HERL. Single ray of a feather, used in fly tying.
HORSE (A FISH). To pull in the fish by sheer strength.
HUSHPUPPIES. A southern dish consisting of batter with chopped onions, dropped in balls in hot deep fat.
HYPOLIMNION. A thermal stratum in lakes below the thermocline.
I. G. F. A. International Game Fish Association.
IMPOUNDMENT. An artificial body of water.
JAYCEES. Members of the Junior Chambers of Commerce.
JIG. An artificial bait for casting or trolling.
JOHN BOAT. A flat-bottomed, square-bowed boat developed for river fishing in the Ozarks.
JOLLY BOAT. A medium-sized boat used for rough work from a sailing vessel.
JUG FISHING. Fishing by tying baited lines to jugs which are allowed to drift on surface as floats.
JUG-CUT. Cut with grain.
KEELSON. A strip of wood fastened along the keel inside a boat.
KEELSTRIP. A plank fastened along the line of the keel in a flat-bottomed boat as reinforcement and protection.
KYAK. A long, low canoe-type one-man boat with a full deck, developed by the Eskimos.
LACUSTRINE. Pertaining to the Swiss lake dwellers.
LAMINATED ROD. Rod built by cementing several strips of wood together with grain parallel.
LAPSTRAKE. A type of construction in which the upper plank overlaps a proportion of the lower plank, like clapboards on a house.
LARVA. The early stage through which certain animals pass, usually referring to those that effect a complete change of habits and food in adult life.
LEA. A measure of linen line, usually 300 yards.
LEADER. A strand of gut or Nylon used between bait and line to minimize visibility. Also a strand of wire used to prevent fish with sharp teeth from cutting line.
LIMNOLOGY. The scientific study of fresh waters, especially ponds and lakes.
LONG BOAT. A large boat carried by a merchant vessel.
LUNATE TAIL. Moon-shaped tail.
LURE. A decoy or bait for fish.
MALE FERRULE. The insert part of a ferrule.
MAXILLARY. Pertaining to the upper jaw.
MEMBRANE. A thin sheet of tissue separating or supporting living organs.
MILT. In fish, the fluid bearing the sperm of the male.
MONOFILAMENT. Single-strand line.
MUMMIES. Mummichaugs, salt water bait fish.
NEOLITHIC. Pertaining to the last stage of the Stone Age.
NODE. A leaf scar or "joint" on a bamboo cane.
NOTOCHORD. An elastic chain of cells forming the supporting axis of the body.
NYMPHS. Any of certain insects in immature form.
OARS. Paddle-shaped levers for propelling a rowboat.
OMNIVOROUS. Having a universal diet.
OUTRIGGER. Long pole used in trolling for big-game fish to carry the line to one side of the boat.
OVIDUCT. A tube serving for the passage of the eggs out of the ovary.
PALEOLITHIC. Pertaining to the early Stone Age.
PAN FISH. A small fish which is more fun eating than catching.
PARR. A young salmon.
PHARNYX. The part of the alimentary canal between the cavity of the mouth and the esophagus.
PHOTOSYNTHESIS. The production of chlorphyll by plants.
PIROGUE. A small dugout canoe developed for swamp and marsh travel in Louisiana.
PLANKED. To cook and serve on a board.
PLANKTON. Minute plants and animals which live in the surface layers of salt or fresh water.
PLEISTOCENE. The epoch or age which followed the Tertiary Age; it preceded the present age.
PLUGS. Wooden or plastic lures designed in different shapes, colors, and sizes.
POACH. 1. To fish on land without the landowner's permission; to fish illegally.
2. To cook in boiling water.
PORTAGE. Carrying of a boat or canoe and its duffel by hand over or around a barrier in the water route.
PRAM. In the United States, usually a short boat with a square bow used as a tender for a larger boat.
PREDACIOUS. Killing other animals for food.
PROPAGATION. Breeding of fish to increase the species, usually but not necessarily under artificial conditions.
PULPIT. A protective railing around the bowsprit of a boat or a platform at the bow from which fish may be harpooned.
PUNT. A flat-bottomed boat with square bow and stern built for use on rivers.
PYLORIC CAECA. Finger-like outgrowths in the digestive tract.
QUADRATE. Pertaining to a bony element on each side of the skull of a fish to which the lower jaw is jointed.
QUENELLE. A fish ball, fish chopped fine and highly seasoned.
RIFFLE. A slight disturbance in the surface current of a stream caused by a subsurface obstruction.
RIG. Equipment.
ROILED (WATERS). Muddied or disturbed waters.
ROSTRUM. The front part of the skull.

ROWLOCKS OR OARLOCKS. Accessories fixed on the gunwale of a boat to serve as the fulcrum for an oar and to hold the oar in place.
SAUTÉ. Fry quickly in a little hot fat.
SCHOOLS (OF FISH). Concentrations of fish of the same species.
SCHUSSES. Runs down rapids in a canoe.
SCUTE. Extremely bony or horny plate on a fish.
SEA SKIFF. A rowboat with a narrow, flat bottom, high prow, and flaring sides.
SEINES. Nets.
SERRATED. Saw-toothed.
SKEG. A small V-shaped strip fixed toward the stern of a rowboat to serve in place of a keel.
SKIFF. A small or medium-sized rowboat.
SHINERS. Minnows, bait fishes.
SHOAL. A shallow area.
SILT. A fine earthy sediment carried and deposited by water.
SILURIAN AGE. Pertaining to that part of the Paleozoic period, marked by coral-reef building and the appearance of the great crustaceans.
SINKER. Weight for taking bait to deeper water.
SKITTERING. To draw the hook through or along the surface of the water with a quivering motion.
SNAGLINE. A line fitted with hooks for snagging fish.
SNELLED FLIES. Flies fastened to bits of gut.
SOLUNAR. A word coined by John Alden Knight to indicate his theory that living creatures have a tendency to become active during certain periods influenced by the sun and the moon.
SPAWN. The eggs of fish, oysters, or other acquatic animals.
SPERLING. A small salt water bait fish.
SPINNER. An artificial lure, blade of which whirls continuously in a circular fashion around the axis of the line of traction.
SPLINE. A thin wood strip.
SPONSON. A built-in flotation chamber along the gunwales of a canoe.
SPRAY RAILS. Strips along the side of a boat hull to repel spray.
STAR DRAG. A star-shaped adjustment on a reel to increase or decrease the rate at which fish may strip the line.
STEELYARD. A weighing device in which the fish is suspended from the shorter arm of a lever and its weight found by moving a counterweight along the longer arm.
STINK BAIT. A malodorous bait formed usually of overripe cheese, chicken viscera, and slaughterhouse wastes, used for catfishing.
STONE FLY. An aquatic insect.
STRIP PLANKED. A type of boat construction in which bottom and side planks are joined together smoothly and tightly. Patented joints usually are used and are sealed with marine glue.
TAGGING. Marking fish by affixing tags to them.
THERMOCLINE. A thermal stratum in a lake in which temperatures are static.
THOLE PINS. Hardwood pegs used in place of rowlocks.
THROW LINE. A line cast by hand for fishing without a rod.
THWART. Cross bracing between the gunwales of a boat; the seats in a rowboat.
TIPPET. A light extension of gut or Nylon between leader and fly.
TRAILER. A wheeled vehicle towed behind an automobile for transporting boats or dunnage.
TRANSOM. The board forming the end of a square-sterned boat.
TRASH FISH. Fish which have neither game nor high food value.
TROLLING. Fishing by trailing bait and line behind a moving boat.
TROLLING PLATE. Plate fixed to an outboard motor to decrease its speed for trolling.
TROTLINE. Line, stretched across a stream or between buoys, having many baited hooks.
TUMP LINE. A band of soft leather about 2½″ by 18″ to the ends of which are secured leather thongs or ropes about 9 feet long, used in portaging.
TYRO. A novice.
UMIAK. A large, skin-covered boat propelled by paddles, developed by the Eskimos.
VIVIPAROUS. Giving birth to fully developed young.
VOMER. A bone of the skull situated below the ethmoidal region.
WET FLY. An artificial lure tied to imitate a drowned insect or the larva of an aquatic insect.
WHALE BOAT. A round-bottomed, double-ended boat developed by the whalers of the 19th century for harpooning whales.
WOBBLER SPOON. An artificial lure attached to the leader at one end causing it to whip and wobble from side to side as it is drawn through the water.

SUPPLEMENT

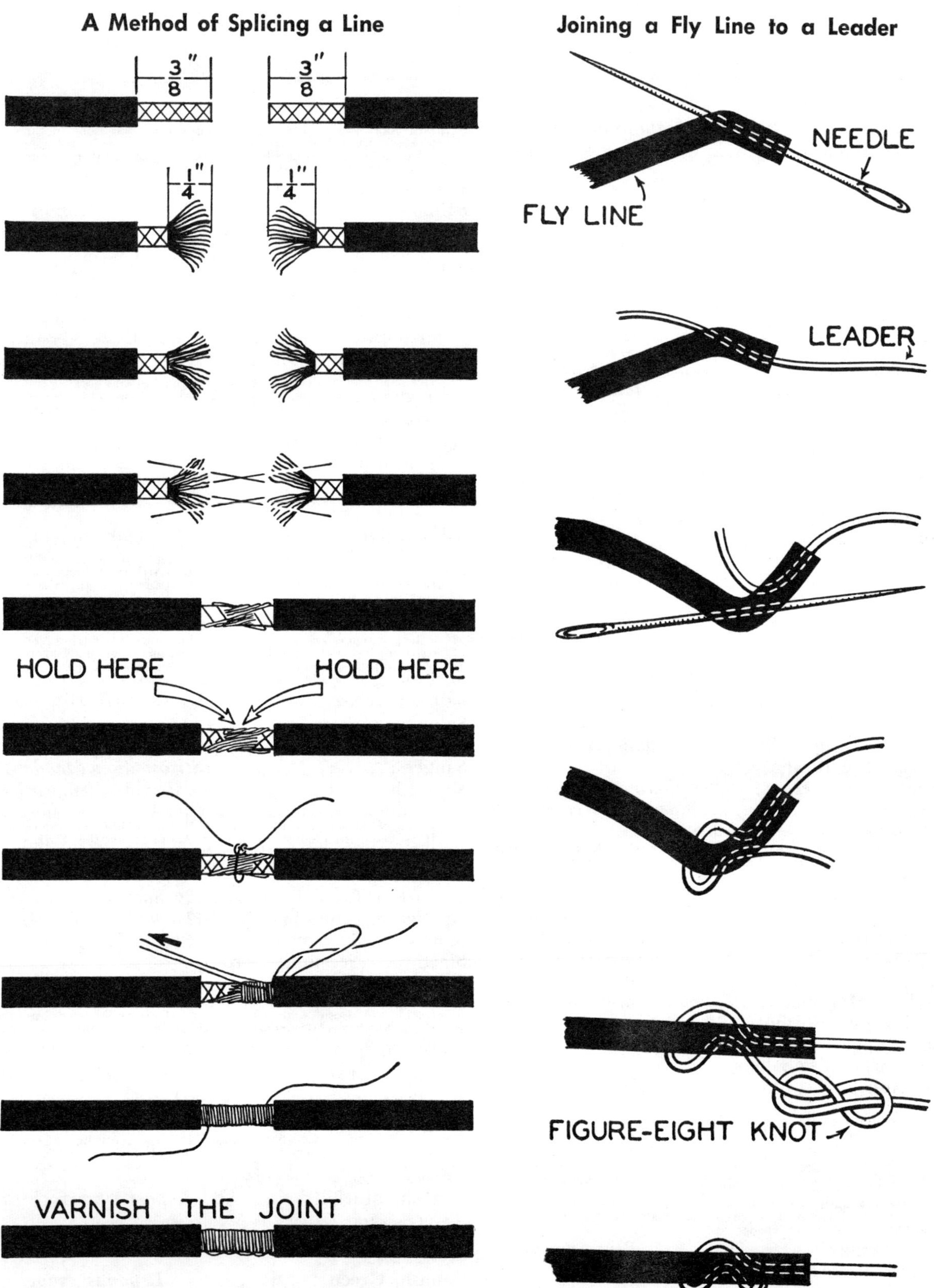
A Method of Splicing a Line
3/8"
3/8"
1/4"
1/4"
HOLD HERE
HOLD HERE
VARNISH THE JOINT
Joining a Fly Line to a Leader
NEEDLE
FLY LINE
LEADER
FIGURE-EIGHT KNOT

STANDARD CHECK LIST OF COMMON NAMES FOR PRINCIPAL AMERICAN SPORT FISHES

Compiled by Outdoor Writers Association of America

FRESH WATER FISHES

Common Name of Fish	Scientific Name of Fish
Bass, Largemouth	*Micropterus salmoides*
Bass, Rock	*Ambloplites rupestris*
Bass, Smallmouth	*Micropterus dolomieui*
Bass, Spotted	*Micropterus punctulatus*
(This is the game fish somewhat generally known as the Kentucky Bass, but as its range is far beyond that one state, the acceptable name is used in this list.)	
Bass, White	*Roccus chrysops*
Bass, Yellow	*Roccus interruptus*
Bowfin	*Amia calva*
(Also known as the Mudfish and the Dogfish.)	
Bluegill (See Sunfish)	
Bullhead, Black	*Ictalurus melas*
Bullhead, Brown	*Ictalurus nebulosus*
Bullhead, Yellow	*Ictalurus natalis*
Carp	*Cyprinus carpio*
Catfish, Blue	*Ictalurus furcatus*
Catfish, Channel	*Ictalurus punctatus*
Catfish, Flathead	*Pylodictis olivaris*
(Also known as Shovelhead Catfish.)	
Catfish, Spoonbill (See Paddlefish)	
Catfish, White	*Ictalurus catus*
Char, Arctic	*Salvelinus alpinus*
(Also known as Arctic Trout and Sunapee Trout. Is found all over Europe where it is known as the char.)	
Chub, Columbia	*Mylocheilus caurinus*
Chub, Creek	*Semotilus atromaculatus*
Chub, Silver (See Fallfish)	
Cisco	*Coregonus artedii*
Coaster (See Brook Trout)	
Crappie, Black	*Pomoxis nigromaculatus*
Crappie, White	*Pomoxis annularis*
Dogfish (See Bowfin)	
Drum, Freshwater	*Aplodinotus grunniens*
Fallfish	*Semotilus corporalis*
(Also known as Silver Chub in Northeast.)	
Note: There are four species of Gars now recognized by the American Fisheries Society, but the Alligator Gar is of chief interest to the sportsman-angler.	
Gar, Alligator	*Lepisosteus spatula*
Gar, Longnose	*Lepisosteus osseus*
Gar, Shortnose	*Lepisosteus platostomus*
Gar, Spotted	*Lepisosteus oculatus*
Grayling, Arctic	*Thymallus arcticus*
Grayling, Montana	*Thymallus arcticus tricolor*
Mudfish (See Bowfin)	
Muskellunge	*Esox masquinongy*
Ouananiche (See Salmon)	
Paddlefish	*Polyodon spathula*
(Last remnant in this country of a group of fossil fishes and confined to the Mississippi river system. Once abundant, but gradually disappearing. Taken chiefly in nets, but will take a hook. Also called Spoonbill Catfish, but is not a member of the Catfish family.)	
Perch, White	*Roccus americanus*
(This is a misnomer as this fish is a bass and not a perch, but this common name is so prevalent all over its range it would be unwise to change it.)	
Perch, Yellow	*Perca flavescens*
Pickerel, Barred (See Redfin Pickerel)	
Pickerel, Redfin	*Esox americanus*
(Sometimes known as the Barred Pickerel.)	
Pickerel, Chain	*Esox niger*
Pickerel, Grass	*Esox vermiculatus*
Pike, Northern	*Esox lucius*
(An effort was made to call it simply Pike, but some of the pickerel are called pike in many localities, so it was decided too much simplification would lead only to more instead of less confusion.)	
Pumpkinseed (See Sunfish)	
Salmon, Atlantic	*Salmo salar*
Salmon, Chum	*Oncorhynchus keta*
(Also referred to as Dog Salmon.)	
Salmon, Coho	*Oncorhynchus kisutch*
(This species is sometimes called the Silver Salmon.)	
Salmon, King	*Oncorhynchus tshawytscha*
(This species is sometimes called the Chinook Salmon.)	
Salmon, Kokanee	*Oncorhynchus nerka*
(This is the small Sockeye Salmon that is land-locked and is artificially propagated and planted in large numbers in the trout waters of the Northwest, especially the state of Washington.)	
Salmon, Landlocked	*Salmo salar*
(This is the game finny fighter so much sought after in Maine and parts of Canada and is being spread to other sections by artificial propagation. It is now landlocked by preference rather than by necessity. Sometimes referred to as the Sebago Salmon.)	
Salmon, Ouananiche	*Salmo salar ouananiche*
(The committee does not agree with those who hold that this fish is just a landlocked phase of the Atlantic Salmon, because in most of the area where they are taken they have easy access to the sea if they choose to take it.)	
Salmon, Pink	*Oncorhynchus gorbuscha*
(Most salmon are more or less humpbacked during the spawning season, but this odd deformation is more exaggerated in this species than all the rest. In fishing circles, this species is generally known as the Humpback Salmon.)	
Salmon, Sebago (See under Landlocked Salmon)	
Salmon, Sockeye	*Oncorhynchus nerka*
(Commercially referred to as the Red Salmon.)	
Sauger	*Stizostedion canadense*
Shee-fish	*Stenodus leucichthys*
(This is the mystery fish of the frigid waters of the Arctic Circle of Alaska. Mainly native to Northern Siberian waters, it is taken frequently enough in Alaska from the Kuskokwim river to Demarcation Point to be given a place in this listing. Sometimes called the Inconnu, which means "unknown".)	
Squawfish, Coastal	*Ptychocheilus umpqua*
Squawfish, Columbia	*Ptychocheilus oregonensis*
Squawfish, Sacramento	*Ptychocheilus grandis*
Steelhead (See under Trout)	
Stonecat	*Noturus flavus*
Note: While Sturgeon are taken in salty waters only by commercial fishermen, two fresh water species furnish splendid sport in the waters of Northern Minnesota and Wisconsin and Idaho.	
Sturgeon, Shovelnose	*Scaphirhynchus platyorynchus*
Sturgeon, Lake	*Acipenser fulvescens*
(Also known as the Rock Sturgeon.)	
Note: While the various species of sunfish continue to be the special joy of the small boy, present day artificial propagation and stocking of farm ponds has resulted in some crossing of species. There is also a tendency to drop some of the oldtime common names such as the Shellcracker, the Stumpknocker and the old-fashioned Pumpkinseed.	
Sunfish, Bluegill	*Lepomis macrochirus*
(This species has come to be "the sunfish" of the country through its tremendous propagation and stocking. Unfortunately sometimes it has crossed with other species of the family.)	
Sunfish, Green	*Lepomis cyanellus*
Sunfish, Longear	*Lepomis megalotis*
Sunfish, Pumpkinseed	*Lepomis gibbosus*
Sunfish, Redbreast	*Lepomis auritus*

Common Name of Fish — *Scientific Name of Fish*

Sunfish, Redear .... *Lepomis microlophus*

(In the South commonly known as the Shellcracker.)

Sunfish, Spotted .... *Lepomis punctatus*

Togue (See Lake Trout)

Trout, Arctic (See Arctic Char))

Trout, Blueback .... *Salvelinus oquassa*

Trout, Brook .... *Salvelinus fontinalis*

(This is the native Eastern Brook Trout, now found in many states thanks to artificial propagation. Known in localized areas as Squaretail and in some few areas they drop down to the mouths of tidal estuaries and are known as Coasters.)

Trout, Brown .... *Salmo trutta*

(This introduced species has come to be the salvation of trout fishing in worn out Eastern streams. Like many other fresh water game fish of the West, it has in some places become sea-run. Formerly the non-migratory Brownies were known as *S. fario* and the sea-run fish as *S. trutta,* but modern listing makes no difference between the two, both being known as *S. trutta.*)

Trout, Cutthroat .... *Salmo clarki*

(Some of this species have become sea-run, this tendency being manifested from Puget Sound northward through British Columbia to Southeastern Alaska.)

Trout, Dolly Varden .... *Salvelinus malma*

(This species reaches its greatest concentration in Southeastern Alaska, where most of them are sea-run. Actually it is the Western form of the Eastern Brook Trout. Over much of its habitat it is known as the Salmon Trout.)

Trout, Golden .... *Salmo aguabonita*

(Native only to the high Sierras at 10,000 feet or over. Several attempts have been made to reintroduce this species in California where it was once native.)

Trout, Kamloops .... *Salmo gairdneri*

(This is one of the many subspecies of the Rainbow Trout, whose differences from the parent stock are either imaginary or due entirely to environment. The Kamloops reached its highest concentration in Pend d'Orielle in Northern Idaho, although it has been introduced elsewhere.)

Trout, Lake .... *Salvelinus namaycush*

(This splendid game fish of northern waters is also known as the Togue in those parts of its habitat contiguous to Canada.)

Trout, Loch Leven (See under Brown Trout)

(Both the Loch Leven and the European Brown Trout were introduced into this country about the same time. In due course these two introduced species were crossbred until the present strain known as the Brown Trout resulted. It is doubtful if any true strain of Loch Leven Trout remain in this country.)

Trout, Rainbow .... *Salmo gairdneri*

(Originally native to Western America, it has been introduced widely wherever suitable habitat can be found. Because of its wide geographic range, it has developed many localized subspecies, of which the more important are included in this list. Its sea-going members of the species are called Steelheads, but ichthyologists refuse to differentiate between the two scientifically. Hence, both are known as *S. gairdneri*).

Trout, Steelhead .... *Salmo gairdneri*

(This is the accepted name of the sea-run branch of the Rainbow Trout, but is claimed by the experts to be the same fish in every other respect and so carries the same scientific name. In California the sea-run Cutthroat Trout is also called a Steelhead.)

Trout, Sunapee (See Arctic Char)

Walleye .... *Stizostedion vitreum*

Warmouth .... *Chaenobryttus gulosus*

Whitefish .... *Coregonus clupeaformis*

Whitefish, Rocky Mountain *Prosopium williamsoni*

(Sometimes erroneously referred to as a Grayling in some Western sections.)

Address all communications to
OWAA HEADQUARTERS
COMMITTEE ON NOMENCLATURE
10 EAST FAYETTE STREET
BALTIMORE (2), MD.

SALTWATER FISHES

Common Name of Fish — *Scientific Name of Fish*

Albacore .... *Thunnus alalunga*

Amberjack .... *Seriola dumerili*

Amberjack, Pacific .... *Seriola colburni*

Barracuda, Great .... *Sphyraena barracuda*

(This is the big fellow most abundant off the Florida coast and found ranging the seas alone or in groups of two or three.)

Barracuda, Pacific .... *Sphyraena argentea*

(This species is much smaller than the preceding and roams the seas in large schools. Sometimes called the California Barracuda.)

Bass, Channel .... *Sciaenops ocellata*

(This is the great battler of the Atlantic surf. A list of 22 common names have been collected, of which Red Drum in the Chesapeake Bay area and Redfish in Florida are the more generally used.)

Bass, Kelp .... *Paralabrax clathratus*

Bass, Sand .... *Paralabrax nebulifer*

Bass, White Sea .... *Cynoscion nobilis*

Bass, Black Sea, (See Sea Bass)

Bass, Giant Sea .... *Stereolepis gigas*

Bass, Spotted Sand ..*Paralabrax maculatofasciatus*

Bass, Sea .... *Centropristes striatus*

(The young of this popular sport and food fish come into tidal estuaries in great numbers and are called Black Wills. Also known as the Black Sea Bass along the upper Atlantic coast.)

Bass, Striped .... *Roccus saxatilis*

(This is the Rockfish of the Chesapeake Bay area, where it is claimed that about 90 per cent of all the Atlantic population of this species are spawned. Transplanted to the West Coast, it now flourishes all along the California and lower Oregon coast.)

Blackfish (See Tautog)

Black Bonito (See Cobia)

Bluefish .... *Pomatomus saltatrix*

(This species is an erratic wanderer. However, its young under the names of Snapper Blue and Tailor run into tidal estuaries along the Atlantic coast in great numbers, providing great sport on light tackle.)

Bonefish .... *Albula vulpes*

Bonito, Atlantic .... *Sarda sarda*

(Although distributed all along the West Coast is generally called the California Bonito.)

Bonito, Oceanic (See Tuna, Skipjack)

Bonito, Pacific .... *Sarda chiliensis*

Broadbill (See Swordfish)

Catfish, Gafftopsail .... *Bagre marinus*

Catfish, Sea .... *Galeichthys felis*

Cero (See King Mackerel)

Cobia .... *Rachycentron canadus*

(This great battler is known by many names in many places, among them being Cabio, Sergeant Fish, Black Bonito, Ling and Lemon Fish.)

Cod .... *Gadus morhua*

Cod, Pacific .... *Gadus macrocephalus*

Corbina, California ...... *Menticirrhus undulatus*

Crevalle (See Jack Crevalle)

Croaker, Atlantic .... *Micropogon undulatus*

Croaker, Black .... *Chileotrema saturnum*

Croaker, Spotfin .... *Roncador stearnsi*

Croaker, White .... *Genyonemus lineatus*

Croaker, Yellowfin .... *Umbrina roncador*

Cultus (See Lingcod)

Cunner .... *Tautogolabrus adspersus*

Cutlassfish .... *Trichiurus lepturus*

Devilfish (See Manta)

Dolphin .... *Coryphaena hippurus*

Drum, Black .... *Pogonias cromis*

Eel .... *Anguilla rostrata*

(A true fish and has a right to be included in this list.)

Flounder, Starry .... *Platichthys stellatus*

Common Name of Fish	*Scientific Name of Fish*
Flounder, Summer	*Paralichthys dentatus*

(This is the well-known Fluke of lower New England and upper Middle Atlantic waters and its newer name will be hard to make stick, but is used in this list for simplification. There is also a species *P. lethostigmus* commonly called Southern Fluke. Its range overlaps with *P. dentatus.)*

Flounder, Winter	*Pseudopleuronectes americanus*
Fluke (See under Summer Flounder)	
Fluke, Summer (See under Summer Flounder)	
Gag (See under Groupers)	
Graysby	*Petrometopon cruentatum*
Greenling	*Hexagrammos decagrammus*
Grouper, Black	*Mycteroperca bonaci*
Grouper, Coney	*Cephalopholis fulva*
Grouper, Gag	*Mycteroperca microlepis*
Grouper, Jewfish, Black	*Epinephelus nigritus*
Grouper, Jewfish, Spotted	*Epinephelus itajara*

(This is the largest of the Groupers.)

Grouper, Nassau	*Epinephelus striatus*
Grouper, Red	*Epinephelus morio*
Grouper, Rockhind	*Epinephelus adscenionis*
Grouper, Yellowfin	*Mycteroperca venenosa*

Note: The Grunts are a large family of tropical fishes. The following seven species are most familiar to anglers.

Grunt, Black Margate	*Anisotremus surinamensis*
Grunt, Bluestripe	*Haemulon sciurus*
Grunt, French	*Haemulon flavolineatum*

(Also called Yellow Grunt.)

Grunt, Pigfish	*Orthopristis chrysopterus*
Grunt, Gray	*Haemulon macrostomum*
Grunt, Margate	*Haemulon album*
Grunt, White	*Haemulon plumieri*
Haddock	*Melanogrammus aeglefinus*
Hake, Silver	*Merluccius bilinearis*
Halibut, Atlantic	*Hippoglossus hippoglossus*
Halibut, California	*Paralichthys californicus*
Halibut, Pacific	*Hippoglossus stenolepis*
Herring, Common	*Clupea harengus*

(Primarily a commercial species but used extensively for bait by anglers.)

Hind, Red	*Epinephelus guttatus*
Jack, Bigeye	*Caranx marginatus*
Jack, Crevalle	*Caranx hippos*

(Sometimes called simply Crevalle.)

Jack, Green	*Caranx caballus*
Jack, Horse-eye	*Caranx latus*
Jewfish, Black (See Groupers)	
Jewfish, Spotted (See Groupers)	
Ladyfish	*Elops saurus*

(This species is often confused with the Bonefish and is also called the Chiro and Tenpounder.)

Lemon Fish (See Cobia)	
Ling (See Cobia)	
Lingcod	*Ophiodon elongatus*

(Also called Cultus.)

Lookdown	*Selene vomer*
Mackerel, Atlantic	*Scomber colias*

(Also referred to as the Common Mackerel.)

Mackerel, Cero	*Scomberomorus regalis*

(Sometimes called the Painted Mackerel; also the King Mackerel is often miscalled the Cero in some Atlantic waters.)

Mackerel, Chub	*Scomber colias*
Mackerel, King	*Scomberomorus cavalla*
Mackerel, Pacific Chub	*Scomber japonicus*

called the Kingfish by commercial fishermen.)
(Called Cero in some Atlantic waters and sometimes

Mackerel, Spanish	*Scomberomorus maculatus*
Manta	*Manta birostris*

(This is not exactly a sport fish, but it furnishes fine sport with the harpoon. Also known as the Devilfish.)

Marlin, Black	*Makaira indica*

(The real range of this species is south of the border of the United States, but enough stragglers are taken or seen above the line to call for insertion in this list.)

Marlin, Blue	*Makaira nigricans*

(Occurs in the Atlantic and Tropical Pacific oceans. Also called Silver Marlin.)

Marlin, Striped	*Tetrapturus audax*
Marlin, White	*Tetrapturus albidus*
Menhaden	*Brevoortia tyrannus*

(An extensively used bait fish; also called the Fatback.)

Moonfish	*Vomer setapinnis*
Mullet, Striped	*Mugil cephalus*

(This is chiefly a food and bait fish, but in some sectors is taken also for sport as well as for bait.)

Muttonmouth (See Snapper)	
Palometa	*Trachinotus falcatus*

(This species of pompano is not too numerous anywhere, but is taken frequently in Florida waters.)

Permit	*Trachinotus goodei*

(The young of Permit are called Round Pompano.)

Pigfish	*Orthopristis chrysopterus*
Pollock, Atlantic	*Pollachius virens*
Pollock, Pacific	*Theragra chalcogramma*
Pompano	*Trachinotus carolinus*
Pompano, African	*Alectis crinitus*
Porgy, Grass	*Calamus arctifrons*
Porgy, Jolthead	*Calamus bajonado*
Porgy, Northern	*Stenotomus chrysops*

(Called Scup in some parts of its range.)

Porkfish	*Anisotremus virginicus*
Queenfish	*Seriphus politus*

Note: While the Rays cannot be classed as sport fishes exactly, they do furnish quite a bit of fun to the angler in some sections and so the more familiar species are presented to complete this check list.

Ray, Eagle	*Myliobatus freminvillei*
Ray, Northern Sting	*Dasyatis centroura*
Ray, Southern Sting	*Dasyatis americana*
Ray, Stingaree	*Dasyatis sabina*
Ray, Spotted Eagle	*Aetobatus narinari*

(Also known in some waters as the Spotted Whip Ray.)

Redfish (See Channel Bass)	
Robalo (See Snook)	
Rockfish (See Striped Bass)	
Rockhind (See Groupers)	
Runner, Blue	*Caranx crysos*
Runner, Rainbow	*Elagatis bipinnulatus*
Sablefish	*Anoplopoma fimbria*
Sandfish	*Diplectrum formosum*

(Also known as the Sand Perch.)

Note: Ichthyologists are at odds over several subspieces of Sailfish, but there is no need to recognize any of them for the purpose of this check list except the two following species. Even these two are believed to be the same fish, whatever difference there may be in size or action when hooked being environmental in origin.

Sailfish, Atlantic	*Istiophorus albicans*
Sailfish, Pacific	*Istiaphorus greyi*
Sailor's Choice	*Haemulon parrai*
Sawfish	*Pristis pectinatus*

(Hardly a sport fish, but it has been taken often enough with rod and reel in the Gulf of Mexico off the Texas coast to gain a place in this check list.)

Schoolmaster (See Snapper)

Note: The controversy continues between the use of Weakfish or Seatrout as the basic name for the four species following. As far as can be determined, adherents of each are about evenly divided. For the purposes of this check list, the four species will appear under both of these names.

Seatrout	*Cynoscion regalis*

Common Name of Fish	Scientific Name of Fish
Seatrout, Sand	*Cynoscion arenarius*
Seatrout, Silver	*Cynoscion nothus*
Seatrout, Spotted	*Cynoscion nebulosus*
Shad	*Alosa sapidissima*

(Formerly a strictly commercial fish, of late it has become a fine sport fish being taken on a fly, streamer or spoon on its way to the spawning grounds in the upper reaches of tidal estuaries. Sometimes referred to as the White Shad.)

Shad, Hickory .... *Alosa mediocris*

Note: Recreational angling for various species of sharks in the waters coming within the range of this check list is becoming more and more popular. Below you will find those species, and others, for which official records are kept by the International Game Fish Association.

Shark, Atlantic .... *Isurus oxyrinchus*

(This shark is also sometimes called the Mackerel Shark.)

Shark, Blacktip .... *Carcharhinus limbatus*
Shark, Hammerhead .... *Sphyrna zygaena*

(Generally found in the open ocean and near the surface and gives a good account of itself whenever hooked on rod and line.)

Shark, Mako .... *Isurus glaucus*

(This is the kingpin of all the sharks from the angler's viewpoint. Taken on rod and reel it gives the tops in sport. Also called Bonito Shark.)

Shark, Mackerel (See Atlantic Shark)
Shark, Porbeagle .... *Lamna nasus*
Shark, Spinner .... *Carcharhinus maculipinnis*

(This species is called the Spinner-Shark from its habit of shooting vertically out of the water and turning several times on its axis before falling back with a great splash.)

Shark, Thresher .... *Alopias vulpinus*
Shark, Tiger .... *Galeocerdo cuvieri*
Shark, White .... *Carcharodon carcharias*

(This is the species sometimes called the Man Eater Shark.)

Sheepshead .... *Archosargus probatocephalus*
Snapper Blue (See under Bluefish)

Note: The Snappers compose a large family, chiefly tropical. In the members of this family covered in this list there are two genera and seven species of interest to the recreational angler and four species that are important commercially.

Snapper, Dog .... *Lutjanus jocu*
Snapper, Lane .... *Lutjanus synagris*
Snapper, Mahogany .... *Lutjanus mahogoni*
Snapper, Mangrove .... *Lutjanus griseus*
Snapper, Mullet .... *Lutjanus aratus*
Snapper, Muttonfish .... *Lutjanus analis*
Snapper, Red .... *Lutjanus blackfordi*
Snapper, Schoolmaster .... *Lutjanus apodus*
Snapper, Silk .... *Lutjanus vivanus*
Snapper, Yellowtail .... *Ocyurus chrysurus*
Snook .... *Centropomus undecimalis*

(Called by many the Rabalo in parts of its habitat.)

Spot .... *Leiostomus xanthurus*
Surf Perch .... *Phanerodon furcatus*

(This is one of a number of similar small fish found in the Pacific surf, but of too little importance to be enumerated in full in this list.)

Swordfish .... *Xiphias gladius*

(The only representative of its family hence it becomes unnecessary to use the prefix Broadbill.)

Tailor (See Bluefish)
Tarpon .... *Megalops atlantica*
Tautog .... *Tautoga onitis*
Tomcod .... *Microgadus tomcod*
Toadfish .... *Opsanus tau*

(Given a place in this list because of its great nuisance value to all fishermen.)

Tripletail .... *Lobotes surinamensis*

Note: Following is the latest official listing of the Tuna family as published by the American Fisheries Society Committee. Authorities continue to differ over whether the Atlantic and the Pacific Yellowfin Tunas are the same fish. For the present at least, this list carries both.

Tuna, Allison (See Yellowfin Tuna)
Tuna, Blackfin .... *Thunnus atlanticus*
Tuna, Bluefin .... *Thunnus thynnus*

(The young of this species migrate closer to the shoreline and are commonly called School Tuna. The fully developed Bluefins are often called Giant Tuna. This is the principal tuna of the sportsman-angler and the commercial fisherman.)

Tuna, Giant (See Bluefin Tuna)
Tuna, Little .... *Euthynnus alletteratus*

(This is a species sometimes called False Albacore, but it is a true tuna and is now recognized as such.)

Tuna, Skipjack .... *Euthynnus pelamis*

(Found off both coasts. Known as Oceanic Bonito on the Atlantic Coast.)

Tuna, School (See Bluefin Tuna)
Tuna, Yellowfin .... *Thunnus albacares*

(It is now agreed by most of the authorities that the so called Allison Tuna is simply either an age or sex phase of the Yellowfin Tuna and so it has been dropped from the official check list.)

Wahoo .... *Acanthocybium solandi*

Note: See statement regarding interchanging names of Weakfish and Seatrout under the Seatrout listing.

Weakfish .... *Cynoscion regalis*

(In one sector of its range, this species is known as the Squeteague.)

Weakfish, Sand .... *Cynoscion arenarius*
Weakfish, Silver .... *Cynoscion nothus*
Weakfish, Spotted .... *Cynoscion nebulosus*
Whitefish, Ocean .... *Caulolatilus princeps*
Whiting, Gulf (See Silver Whiting)
Whiting, King (See Northern Whiting)
Whiting, Northern .... *Menticirrhus saxatilis*

(This frequenter of the surf along upper Atlantic shores is also known as both the Kingfish and the King Whiting.)

Whiting, Southern ...... *Menticirrhus americanus*
Whiting, Silver .... *Menticirrhus littoralis*

(Also known as the Gulf Whiting)

Yellowtail (See Snapper)
Yellowtail, Pacific .... *Seriola dorsalis*

TACKLE STANDARDS

In an attempt to achieve reasonable uniformity in tackle standards, the National Association of Angling and Casting Clubs adopted an official table of regular flyhook measurements with size designations and deviations, fly-line calibrations, leader material calibrations, etc.

This work has to a large degree standardized specifications and has been generally accepted by the industry and by anglers. In addition, the DuPont Company has set forth a scale for Nylon leader and spinning line material which to a large extent is the standard for plastic leaders and lines.

NAACC FLY-HOOK SIZES

Size Number	Length (inches)	Wire Diameter (inch)
2/0	1⅝	.045
1/0	1½	.043
1½	1⅜	.041
1	1¼	.039
2	1⅛	.037
4	15/16	.033
6	13/16	.030
8	11/16	.027
10	9/16	.024
12	7/16	.021
14	11/32	.018
16	9/32	.016
18	7/32	.014
20	5/32	.012

NOTES: The length is the over-all measurement of the shank, excluding eye.

Sizes No. 22 to 13 increase in size by 1/32 inch for each number.

Sizes No. 12 to 3 increase in size by 1/16 inch for each number.

Sizes No. 2 to 5/0 increase in size by ⅛ inch for each number.

The maximum permissible tolerances, plus or minus, shall be one-half of the difference between sizes.

The odd number sizes, in all respects, measure midway between the even number sizes.

In hooks used for flies and artificial lures, Mustad (of Norway) and the English manufacturers—and all of our good fly hooks come from these two countries—use chart sizes that conform roughly to this one. It would be ideal if the manufacturers all adopted it, but, of course, they won't. In fact, during the 1930's the British adopted a new chart of hook sizes. It is given here:

American Scale	New British Scale	American Scale	New British Scale
9	7	14	2
10	6	15	1
11	5	16	0
12	4	17	00
13	3	18	000

DUPONT'S TABLE OF NYLON LEADER MATERIAL CALIBRATIONS

	Diameter	Tolerance Plus or Minus	Pound Test
5X	006″	.0005″	1.25
4X	.007″	.0005″	1.75
3X	.008″	.0005″	2.25
2X	.009″	.0005″	2.9
1X	.010″	.0005″	3.5
0X	.011″	.0005″	4.3
9/5	.012″	.0005″	5.1
8/5	.013″	.001″	6.0
7/5	.014″	.001″	7.0
6/5	.015″	.001″	8.0
5/5	.016″	.001″	9.1
4/5	.017″	.001″	10.3
3/5	.018″	.0015″	11.5
2/5	.019″	.0015″	12.8
1/5	.021″	.0015″	15.6
	.023″	.0015″	20.0
	.028″	.002″	30.0
	.032″	.002″	40.0
	.040″	.002″	50.0
	.045″	.002″	60.0

NAACC OFFICIAL STANDARD TABLE OF SILKWORM GUT LEADER MATERIAL CALIBRATIONS

Gauge Designation of Size	Average (Nominal) Diameter (inch)	Minimum Permissible Breaking Test (pounds)
7X	0.004½	¼
6X	0.005	⅜
5X	0.005½	½
4X	0.006	⅝
3X	0.007	¾
2X	0.008	1
1X	0.009	1½
0X	0.010	2
10/5	0.011	2½
9/5	0.012	3
8/5	0.013	3½
7/5	0.014	4
6/5	0.015	4¾
5/5	0.016	5½
4/5	0.017	6¼
3/5	0.018	7½
2/5	0.019	8¾
1/5	0.020	10

NOTES: 1. From 7X to 4X the permissible variance in each gauge designation, or size, is ¼ thousandths, plus or minus. From 4X to 1/5 the permissible variance in each gauge designation, or size, is ½ thousandths, plus or minus.

2. Materials gauging over 20 thousandths shall be specified by diameter only, with a tolerance of ½ thousandths, plus or minus.

3. No minimum permissible breaking test above 10 pounds.

NAACC FLY-LINE CALIBRATIONS

Letter Size	Nominal Diameter (inch)	Letter Size	Nominal Diameter (inch)
I	0.022	B	0.055
H	0.025	A	0.060
G	0.030	AA	0.065
F	0.035	AAA	0.070
E	0.040	AAAA	0.075
D	0.045	AAAAA	0.080
C	0.050		

SUMMERKILL

Dead fish are often found floating on the surface during the summer months. On small bodies of water, this mortality can be attributed to a number of factors, one of the most common during the summer being waterweeds. During photosynthesis—the process by which plants produce their own food—living plants give off oxygen which is needed by the fish. But dead plants actually reduce the available oxygen by combining with it in the process of decay or oxidation. When the amount of dissolved oxygen drops to two or three parts per million parts of water, fish begin showing signs of distress and a further drop is likely to cause suffocation. Thick growths of algae—called "bloom" —are often the cause of such trouble. During hot, cloudy weather photosynthesis ceases. The algae die and begin to decay, as do the many rooted weeds from which the light has been blocked. In addition, warm water holds less dissolved oxygen than cool water. Before long, fish begin to suffocate. Decaying algae have been found to kill fish (and livestock) directly, too, by producing toxic substances. Treatment for summer kill consists of use of copper sulphate to kill algae and sodium arsenite to remove rooted water plants, but it must be used very carefully and preferably with supervision, since an overdosage will kill fish. Fertilizer is used at times, to create a bloom of algae to kill the underwater plants, but this must be used with caution, too, since fertilizer also uses oxygen.

Winterkill is similar to summer kill. Snow or ice cuts out light and prevents photosynthesis from taking place. Although rare, an entire fish population may be killed in this manner.

Shallow, fertile lakes, which are most susceptible to both summer kill and winterkill, also recover most rapidly, because there is plenty of fish food in the lake. Species balance may be disrupted in a lake suffering from kill and restocking will be necessary.

—*Wisconsin Conservation Department*

SUSCEPTIBILITY TO WINTERKILL

A severe winterkill on Lower Five Island Lake in Iowa worked to the benefit of sport fishing, according to biologist Earl Rose. Most of the fish killed were carp, which are highly vulnerable to this rather common wintertime depletion of oxygen in frozen-over lakes of the North. Carp are more susceptible, at least, than are yellow perch, northern pike, and bullheads. Many factors determine the degree of winterkill besides a lack of oxygen, Rose says, but test-net sampling of 566 fish in the spring yielded only one carp.

—*Iowa Conservationist Department*

SWIMMING SPEEDS OF FISH

Through various devices the swimming speed of various species has been clocked.

Species	*Miles Per Hour*
Swordfish	70
Broadbill	70
Blue Marlin	50
Bluefin Tuna	44
Wahoo	37
Tarpon	35
Blue Shark	35
Atlantic Salmon	23
Brown Trout	23
Bonefish	22
Pike	20
Striped Bass	12
Pacific Salmon	11
Yellow Perch	10
Perch	10.2
Dace	9.3
Mullet	8
Carp	7.6
Eel	7.5

GUIDE REQUIREMENT OF RODS

Type of Rod	*Length (ft.)*	*Guides Required*
Fly	9	13
Fly	8½	12
Fly	8	11
Fly	7½	10
Fly	7	9
Spinning	7½	6
Spinning	7	5
Spinning	6½	4
Spinning	6	4
Casting	6	5
Casting	5½	4
Casting	5	3
Casting	4½	2

HOW TO FIT LINE TO LENGTH AND WEIGHT OF ROD

Rod Length and Weight	*Double Taper*		*Triple Diameter*		*Level*	
7½ to 8 ft.—3½ to 4¼ oz.	Nylon H-D-H	Silk H-E-H	Nylon H-D-G	Silk H-E-G	Nylon E	Silk F
8½ to 9 ft.—4¾ to 5¼ oz.	Nylon H-C-H	Silk H-D-H	Nylon H-C-F	Silk H-D-G	Nylon D	Silk E
9 ft.—5½ to 6½ oz.	Nylon G-B-G	Silk H-C-H	Nylon G-B-F	Silk H-C-F	Nylon C	Silk D
9 to 9½ ft.—6½ to 7½ oz.	Nylon G-A-G	Silk G-B-G	Nylon G-A-F	Silk G-B-F	Nylon B	Silk C

STANDARD FLY PATTERNS

Key: (w) usually tied as a wet fly. (u) usually tied as a dry fly. (d) always tied as a dry fly.

Key	Name	Tag	Tail	Ribbing	Body	Wing	Hackle
w	Abbey	Gold Tinsel	Golden Pheasant Tippet	Gold Tinsel	Dark Red Floss		Light Ginger
w	Academy	Red Floss	Crimson		Peacock Herl	Claret	Ginger
u	Adams		Grizzly hackle fibers		Gray	Grizzly Hackle	Intermingled Grizzly and Ginger
w	Adder	Orange Floss		Orange Floss	Brown Floss	Brown Turkey	Ginger
w	Adirondack	Yellow Floss	Black Hackle Wisps		Gray Fur	White	Scarlet
w	Admiral	Gold Tinsel	Scarlet		Dark Red Floss	White	
w	Alder				Peacock Herl	Brown Turkey	Black or Ginger
w	Alexandria	Dark Red Floss (Optional)	Peacock Sword	Round Silver Tinsel (Optional)	Silver Tinsel, Flat	Peacock Sword (May have dash of scarlet on each side)	Deep Wine, Dark Claret or Black
w	Allerton	Gold Tinsel	Teal or Barred Wood Duck		Yellow Floss	Scarlet	Dark Blue Tied Palmer
u	Apple Green		Ginger	Yellow Floss	Highlander Green Floss	Slate	Ginger
w	Armstrong Fontinalis		White Hackle Fibers		Orange Wool	Orange edged with Gray and White	White
w	Arthur Hoyt	Yellow Silk	Dark Ginger	Yellow Silk	Bright Green Floss	Brown Turkey	Dark Ginger
w	Artful Dodger	Gold Tinsel		Gold Tinsel	Dark Claret Floss	Pheasant	Light Claret
u	August Dun	Yellow Floss	Dark Ginger	Yellow Silk	Light Brown Floss	Pheasant or Light Brown Turkey	Dark Ginger
u	Au-Sable		Light Blue-Gray Hackle Wisps		Blue-Gray Hard Body	Mandarin or White Tipped Starling	Light Blue-Gray
w	Babcock	Gold Tinsel	Black and Yellow	Gold Tinsel	Crimson Floss	Black Stripe over Yellow	Black
d	Badger Bi-visible		Badger Hackle Fibers				Badger Hackle Tied Palmer Faced with White Hackle
d	Badger Varient		Badger Hackle Wisps		Peacock Herl	Grizzly Hackle Tips	Badger
w	Baldwin		Teal		White Floss	Teal	Claret
w	Barrington	Gold Tinsel		Gold Tinsel	Peacock Herl	Grey Mallard	Ginger
w	Beamer	Silver Tinsel	Crimson and Dark Blue	Silver Tinsel	Dark Blue Dubbing	Brown Mallard	Mixed Crimson and Dark Blue
w	Beauty	Silver Tinsel	Guinea Fowl	Silver Tinsel	Dark Gray Floss	Guinea Fowl	Black
u	Beaverkill		Ginger Hackle Fibers		Gray Dubbing	Gray Mallard	Dark Ginger
u	Beaverkill, Female		Dark Ginger Hackle Wisps		Yellow Chenille Egg Sack and Gray Dubbing	Gray Mallard	Dark Ginger
w	Beatrice	Green Floss	Scarlet		Yellow Floss	Barren Mandarin	Yellow Tied Palmer, Gray or Crimson
u	Bee				Alternate Yellow and Black Chenille	Dark Slate	Dark Ginger
w	Beeman				Light Green Chenille	Gray Turkey	Ginger
w	Belgrade	Black Chenille	Crimson and White	Gold Tinsel	Yellow Wool or Dubbing	White Red Stripe, Jungle Eye	Claret Tied Palmer

w	Big Meadow	Gold Tinsel	Crimson		Peacock Herl	Gray Mallard	Ginger
w	Bishop				White Floss	Dark Red or Claret	Ginger
w	Bisset	Yellow Silk			Peacock Herl	Dark Slate	Guinea Fowl
u	Black Angel		Black Hackle Wisps		Black Floss, Fur or Wool	Black	Black
u	Black Ant				Black Floss or Dubbing		Black-Tied in Middle of Body
d	Black Bi-visible		Hackle Tips				Black Tied Palmer, Faced with White
u	Black Gnat				Black Chenille	Dark Slate	Black
w	Black June	Silver Tinsel		Silver Tinsel	Peacock Herl	Black	Black
u	Black Moose	Silver Tinsel	Green		Black Silk Floss	Guinea and Purple	
w	Black O'Lindsay		Ginger and Blue Jay Mixed	Gold Tinsel	Bright Yellow Wool or Fur	Under-Wing Peacock Sword. Over-Wing Mallard or Teal	Ginger and Blue Jay
w	Black and Orange			Gold Tinsel	Tail-Half Orange Dubbing Head-Half Black Dubbing	Brown Mallard	Black
u	Black Palmer Red Tag	Scarlet Wool			Peacock Herl		Black Tied Palmer
w	Bloa Poult				Yellow Floss		Grouse
w	Black Prince	Gold Tinsel	Crimson	Gold Tinsel	Black Silk Floss	Black	Black
u	Black Quill		Black Hackle Fibers		Black or Dark Gray Quill	Dark Slate	Black
d	Black Spider		Black Hackle Wisps		Gold Tinsel		Black (Large Diameter)
w	Block House	Gold Tinsel		Gold Tinsel	Yellow Silk Floss	Scarlet	Scarlet
u	Blondie		Pale Orange Barred (Baboon)		Cream Dubbing	Pale Orange Barred (As Tail)	Light Ginger
d	Blue Bi-visible		Blue-Gray Hackle Tips				Blue-Gray Hackle Faced with White
w	Blue Blow	Gold Tinsel			Blue Silk Floss	Slate	Black Tied Palmer
u	Blue Bottle		Black Hackle Fibers	Silver Tinsel (Optional)	Black or Dark Gray Quill	Very Dark Slate	Black
u	Blue Dun		Blue-Gray Hackle Fibers		Blue-Gray Fur Dubbing	Blue-Gray	Blue-Gray
w	Blue Jay	Gold Tinsel	Golden Pheasant Tippet	Gold Tinsel	Orange Floss Silk	Blue Gray	Orange
w	Blue Professor		Crimson	Gold Tinsel	Blue Silk Floss	Gray Mallard	Ginger
u	Blue Quill		Blue-Gray		Blue-Gray Quill	Light Slate	Blue-Gray
d	Blue Spider		Blue-Gray Hackle Wisps		Gold Tinsel		Blue-Gray
u	Blue Upright		Steel Blue Hackle Wisps		Stripped Peacock Quill		Steel Blue
w	Bob Lawrence	Silver Tinsel	Scarlet	Silver Tinsel	Cinnamon Dubbing	Scarlet Wing and Jungle Cock	Guinea Fowl
u	Bob Lincoln		Golden Pheasant Wisps		Grizzly Hackle	Gray Mottled Partridge Tied Spent	Ginger
w	Bog Pond		Golden Pheasant Tippet		Black Chenille	Brown Pheasant	Grizzly
w	Bonnie View	Gold Tinsel	Gray Mallard	Gold Tinsel	Brown Wool	Gray	Ginger
w	Bootes Black	Gold Tinsel	Black	Gold Tinsel	Maroon Wool or Fur	Very Dark Slate	Black

Key	Name	Tag	Tail	Ribbing	Body	Wing	Hackle
w	Bostwick		Barred Mandarin		Silver Tinsel		Mixed Ginger and Grizzly. Tied Palmer
w	Bottle Imp		Scarlet		Blue-Gray Wool or Fur		Black
w	Bouncer	Orange		Gold Tinsel	Black Floss	Yellow	Orange
u	Bradley		Ginger Hackle Wisps		Blue-Gray Fur	Gray Mallard	Ginger
w	Brandreth	Gold Tinsel	Scarlet	Gold Tinsel	Yellow Wool	Gray Mallard	Scarlet and Yellow
w	Bright Fox		Brown Hackle		Yellow Floss	White	Ginger
u	Bronze Quill		Dark Ginger Hackle Wisps		Dark Quill	Grey Speckled	Dark Ginger
w	Broughten Point				Light Blue Floss	Starling	Black and Ginger
u	Brown Ant				Brown Floss		Ginger-Tied in Middle of Body
d	Brown Bi-visible		Ginger				Ginger Faced with White
u	Brown Hackle			Gold Tinsel	Peacock Herl		Ginger
w	Brown Hen	Gold Tinsel			Peacock Herl	Brown Turkey	Ginger
u	Brown Mallard	Gold Tinsel	Brown Mallard	Gold Tinsel	Brown Wool	Brown Mallard	Ginger
u	Brown Olive		Brown Olive (Dyed)		Brown Olive Hard Body	Blue-Gray Hackle Tips	Brown Olive (Dyed)
u	Brown Sedge				Dun Fur	Light Slate	Ginger Tied Palmer
d	Brown Spider		Ginger Hackle Wisps				Ginger Hackle Tied Palmer, Faced with White
w	Brown Turkey		Brown Hackle		Brown Floss	Brown Turkey	Ginger Tied Palmer
d	Brown Varient		Brown Hackle Wisps		Gold Tinsel	Grizzly Hackle Tips	Ginger Hackle
u	Brown Wolf		Brown Impala		Yellow Wool or Fur	Brown Impala	Cream or Badger
w	Brunton's Fancy		Scarlet		Peacock Herl		Badger Tied Palmer
w	Bunting	Silver Tinsel			Black Floss	White	Black
w	Bustard and Orange		Golden Pheasant Wisps	Gold Tinsel	Orange Mohair	Bustard	Ginger
u	Caddis						
u	Cahill Dark		Dark Ginger Hackle Wisps		Dark Gray Dubbing	Mandarin or Wood Duck	Dark Ginger
u	Cahill Light		Light Ginger Hackle Wisps		Creamy Dubbing	Mandarin or Wood Duck	Light Ginger
u	Cahill Quill		Ginger Hackle Fibers		Gray Quill	Mandarin or Wood Duck	Ginger
w	Cairn's Fancy		Black Hackle Wisps	Silver Tinsel	Blue Floss	Slate (Starling)	Black
w	Calder	Peacock Herl	Barred Mandarin	Gold Tinsel	Orange Floss	Peacock Sword over Light Brown Turkey	Light Ginger
w	Caldwell		Brown Mallard	Yellow Silk	Brown Floss	Light Brown Turkey	Ginger
u	California Coachman		Golden Pheasant Tippet Fibers		Peacock Herl at each end, Yellow Floss in Middle		
u	Campbell's Fancy		Golden Pheasant Wisps		Gold Tinsel		Ginger Furnace
w	Canada	Scarlet		Gold Tinsel	Red Floss	Gray Turkey or Mottled Black and White	Red
w	Caperer				Red-Brown Wool	Copper Pheasant	Scarlet
w	Captain	Peacock	Scarlet and Yellow		White Floss	Slate	Brown
w	Cardinal				White Chenille	Cardinal	White
w	Carter Dixie Hair Wing		Yellow Hackle Wisps		Gold Tinsel	White Hair	Crimson

w	Carter Harrison[1]		Scarlet	Gold Tinsel	Black Seal Fur	Brown Mallard	Brown
w	Cassard		Scarlet, Yellow, Green and Barred Mandarin	Gold Tinsel	Scarlet Floss	Scarlet, Yellow, Green & Barred Mandarin	Yellow Tied Palmer
w	Cassin	Gold Tinsel	Peacock Tail and Scarlet	Gold Tinsel	Yellow Floss	Yellow	Ginger
u	Catskill		Mandarin or Dyed Mallard		Orange Floss	Mandarin or Dyed Mallard	Ginger Tied Palmer
w	Caughlan		Gray Turkey		Dark Claret Chenille or Wool	Gray Turkey	Dark Claret Tied Palmer
w	Challoner		Red Ibis	Gold Tinsel	Yellow Wool	Mottled Brown	Ginger
w	Chamberlain	Gold Tinsel	Golden Pheasant Crest	Gold Tinsel	Orange Wool	Gray Turkey	Ginger
w	Chantry	Gold Tinsel			Peacock Herl	Dark Slate	Black
w	Chateaugay		Brown Mallard		Pale Yellow Floss	Gray Mallard	Ginger
w	Cheney			Scarlet Silk	Yellow Floss	Slate	Yellow
w	Chenille Spider Green[2]				Green and Black Chenille		
u	Chocolate Dun[3]		Ginger Hackle Wisps	Gold Tinsel	Chocolate Brown Dubbing		Blue Grizzly and Light Ginger Intermingled
w	Cinnamon	Gold Tinsel		Gold Tinsel	Dark Brown Floss	Cinnamon	Ginger
w	Clare Flatte[4]	Black Chenille		Yellow Floss and Gold Tinsel together on rear two-thirds	Rear Two-Thirds Brown Floss; Front One-Third Red Floss		Ginger
w	Claret Gnat				Dark Claret Wool or Chenille	Slate	Dark Clarette
u	Coachman	Gold Tinsel if desired			Peacock Herl	White	Dark Ginger
w	Coachman Leadwing	Gold Tinsel if desired			Peacock Herl	Dark Slate	Dark Ginger
w	Cobler	Gold Tinsel	Mandarin	Gold Tinsel	Brown Wool	Barred Mandarin	Ginger
u	Cochy Bondhu Quill		Cochy Bondhu		Condor or Peacock Quill	Mandarin Speckled	Cochy Bondhu
w	Cole Fly		Mottled Brown	Peacock Herl	Yellow Quill	Gray Hair	Orange
w	Colonel Fullen	Gold Tinsel	Black	Gold Tinsel	Yellow Floss	Yellow with Scarlet Stripe	Yellow
w	Concher		Scarlet		Light Green Floss	Green Wing	Green
w	Cooper				Orange Floss	Brown Turkey	Black
w	Cornell		Black	Gold Tinsel	Black Floss	Black	Black
w	Cosseboom			Silver Tinsel	Dark Green Wool, Yellow Egg Sack	Gray Squirrel	Yellow
u	Coty, Dark		Dark Blue-Gray Hackle Wisps		Blue-Gray Dubbing	Dark Blue-Gray	Dark Blue-Gray
u	Coty, Light		Light Blue-Gray Hackle Wisps		Blue-Gray Dubbing	Light Blue-Gray Hackle Wisps	Light Blue-Gray
w	Cowdang				Olive Green Wool	Cinnamon	Brown
w	Critchley Fancy				Yellow Floss or Wool	Narrow Stripe of Scarlet over Gray Mallard	Yellow Tied Palmer and Faced with Gray Mallard

[1] Tip—Gold Tinsel [2] Legs—Fine Rubber [3] Shoulder—Yellow Chenille [4] Shoulder—Jungle Cock

Key	Name	Tag	Tail	Ribbing	Body	Wing	Hackle
w	Critchley Hackle	Gold Tinsel	Yellow	Gold Tinsel	Yellow		Pale Yellow Mixed with Grizzly
w	Cupsuptic		Yellow Hackle		Silver Tinsel	Narrow Guinea over Brown Turkey	Crimson Tied Palmer
u	Dark Spinner		Purple Hackle	Purple Silk	Dark Claret Floss	Dark Slate	Purple
u	Darling	Orange Floss	Golden Pheasant Crest		Black Dubbing	Brown Turkey	Ginger Furnace
w	Deacon				Yellow	Gray Mallard	Scarlet at Shoulder and Yellow Tied Palmer
u	Deer Fly				Blue-Gray Floss	Blue-Gray	Blue-Gray
w	Denison	Green Floss & Gold Tinsel	Barred Mandarin on Crimson, Yellow and Green		Orange Floss	Crimson, Yellow and Green, Topping Barred Mandarin	Yellow Tied Palmer
w	Dolly Varden	Gold Tinsel	Cinnamon	Gold Tinsel	White Floss	Cinnamon	Ginger
w	Dorset		Ginger Furnace Hackle Wisps		Green Floss	Teal	Light Ginger Furnace
w	Dotterel and Yellow				Yellow Floss		Small Gold Tipped Feather from Dotterel or small feather from under starling wing
w	Down Looker	Orange Floss	Brown Mallard		Brown Floss	Brown Mallard	Ginger Tied Palmer
w	Dr. Beck		Jungle Cock Eye		Silver Tinsel	White with Crimson Stripe	Crimson
w	Dr. Burke		Peacock Sword	Silver Tinsel	Flat Silver Tinsel	White with Jungle Cock Eyes	Yellow
w	Dugmore Fancy			Silver Tinsel	Black Floss	Bronze Black	Black
w	Dun Caddis		Golden Pheasant Wisps		Dark Straw Colored Chenille	Tuft of Male Deer Hair tied to flare at angle from hood.	Ginger
w	Dun Spider				Yellow Floss		Dun Feather from underside of Starling Wing
w	Dusty Miller (Trout)				Gray Wool	Blue-Gray	Blue-Gray
w	Early Brown Stone Fly				Ginger Hackle Stem	Two Dun Hackle Tips Tied Flat over Body	Blue Dun Hen's Hackle
w	Edrington			Black Floss	Orange Chenille	Black with White Tip Turkey	Ginger
w	Elliot		Pheasant and Scarlet		White Chenille	Gray Mallard, Scarlet Stripes	Green
w	Emerald		Light Brown	Gold Tinsel	Light Green	Pale Brown, Mottled	Light Ginger
w	Emma	Gold Tinsel	Light Claret	Gold Tinsel	Dark Red Floss	Jungle, Body Feather	Light Claret
u	Emu		White Hackle Wisps		White Emu Quill	Pale Starling	White

w	Epting	Red Floss	Orange		Yellow Floss	Gray Mallard	Black
w	Esmeralda		Brown Mallard	Yellow Silk	Light Green Floss	Light Slate	Ginger
w	Ferguson	Gold Tinsel	Yellow and Crimson	Gold Tinsel	Yellow Floss	Brown Turkey, Yellow Stripe	Green
w	Fern				Pale Pink Floss, Gold Tip	Light Slate	Ginger
w	Feted Green	Crimson Floss	Dark Green		Dark Green	Dark Green	Dark Green
w	Fiery Brown		Crimson		Fiery Brown Wool	Brown	Black
u	Fire Fly				Silver Tinsel Wound Over with Clear Plastic		Brown Deer Tail Hair
w	Fisher		Wood Duck or Mandarin	Gold Tinsel	Yellow Wool	Half White, Half Black, Married Jungle Eye	Claret
w	Fitzmaurice	Black Chenille	Peacock Sword		Crimson Chenille	Brown Mallard	Yellow
w	Flagger	Gold Tinsel		Gold Tinsel	Pale Yellow Floss	Slate	Blue-Gray
w	Flamer	Black Chenille	Crimson		Gold Tinsel	Crimson	Ginger
w	Fletcher	Silver Tinsel	Scarlet, Yellow, Guinea		Black Floss	Light Brown Turkey	Gray Tied Palmer
u	Flight's Fancy	Gold Tinsel	Brown	Gold Tinsel	Pale Yellow Floss	Light Slate	Ginger
w	Florence	Silver Tinsel	Brown Mallard		Pink Chenille	Brown Mallard	Black
u	Flying Caddis		Grizzly Hackle Wisps (optional)	Yellow Floss	Gray Deer Hair Clipped	Double Grizzly Hackle Wisps Tied Spent	Grizzly
w	Forsyth	Light Blue Floss			Yellow Wool	Yellow with Brown Stripe	Yellow Tied Palmer
w	Fosnot				Yellow Wool or Chenille	Light Slate	Light Blue
d	Fox Hendrickson		Bronze-Blue Hackle Wisps		Dubbin of Hare's Ear and Yellow Wool Mixed	Slate Duck Cut	Bronze-Blue
w	Francis Fly			Dark Red Floss	Peacock Herl	Jungle Body Feather	Dark Grizzly
w	General Hooker			Green Silk	Yellow Floss	Dark Slate	Brown
w	Getland	Gold Tinsel	Brown	Gold Tinsel	Green Floss	Gray Mallard	Brown
d	Ginger Bi-visible		Ginger Hackle Wisps				Ginger Hackle Tied Palmer. Faced with White Hackle
d	Ginger Furnace Spider		Ginger Furnace Hackle Wisps		Gold Tinsel		Ginger Furnace
u	Ginger Quill		Ginger Hackle Wisps		Brown Quill	Gray	Ginger
d	Ginger Varient		Ginger Hackle Wisps		Gold Tinsel	Grizzly Hackle Tips	Ginger
w	Gold Monkey	Gold Tinsel		Gold Tinsel	Pale Yellow	Slate	Guinea
d	Gold Ribbed Hare's Ear		Ginger	Gold Tinsel	Rabbit Fur not Plucked	Slate	
w	Gold Stork		Gray Mallard		Gold Tinsel	Brown Mallard	Ginger
w	Golden Doctor		Scarlet, Yellow, Green		Gold Tinsel	Gray Mallard, Blue and Red Edge	Claret
w	Golden Duke		Crimson		Back Third, Black Floss; Front Two Thirds, Gold Tinsel	Crimson	Black
u	Golden Dun		Gray		Orange Floss or Wool	Slate	Gray
w	Golden Ibis		Scarlet		Gold Tinsel	Scarlet	Scarlet

Key	Name	Tag	Tail	Ribbing	Body	Wing	Hackle
w	Golden Olive	Orange Floss	Golden Pheasant Crest	Gold Tinsel	Golden Olive Seal Fur	Tippet Fibers topped with Brown Mallard	Golden Olive
w	Golden Pheasant	Gold Tinsel	Black	Gold Tinsel	Orange Floss	Golden Pheasant Tippet	Orange
w	Golden Rod	Peacock	Crimson	Gold Tinsel	Orange Floss	Jungle Eye	Orange
w	Golden Spinner	Peacock			Pale Yellow Floss	Light Slate	Ginger
w	Good Evening		Golden Pheasant Tippet	Gold Tinsel	Scarlet Floss or Wool	Dark Blue, White Tip	Ginger
u	Gordon	Gold Tinsel	Brown Mandarin or Mallard	Gold Tinsel	Yellow Floss	Brown Mallard or Mandarin	Badger
w	Gosling		Gray		Green Floss	Slate	Gray
w	Governor	Scarlet Floss			Peacock Herl	Brown Turkey	Ginger
w	Grackle		Dark Scarlet		Peacock Herl	Dark Scarlet	Black
u	Grannom	Peacock		Gold Tinsel	Pale Yellow Wool	Light Brown Turkey	Ginger
d	Gray Bi-visible		Grizzly Hackle Tips				Grizzly Hackle Tied Palmer, Faced with White
u	Gray Drake		Teal	Black Silk	White Silk Floss	Teal	Light Grizzly
w	Gray Marlow	Gold Tinsel		Gold Tinsel	Red Floss or Wool		Grizzly
u	Gray Quill		Dark Grizzly Hackle Wisps		Peacock Quill	Gray Mallard or Teal	Dark Grizzly or Blue-Gray
d	Gray Wulff		Brown Bucktail		Blue-Gray Fur	Brown Bucktail	Blue-Gray
u	Gravel Bed	Gold Tinsel			Dark Slate Floss	Black	Black
u	Great Dun		Brown Mallard		Brown Cast Fur or Wool	Slate	Blue-Gray
u	Green Coachman	Gold Tinsel			Peacock Herl	Slate	Green
u	Green Drake		Green	Brown Silk	Pale Yellow Floss	Gray Mallard Dyed Yellow-Green	Green
u	Green Mag	Gold Tinsel	Dark Blue-Gray	Gold Tinsel	Cream-Cellophane, Composition or Silk Floss	Gray Mallard Dyed Pale Green	Grizzly Dyed Light Blue-Gray
w	Green Mantle	Gold Tinsel	Green	Gold Tinsel	Green Wool	Gray Mallard	Green
u	Greenwell's Glory	Gold Tinsel		Gold Tinsel	Olive Floss	Dark Slate	Ginger Furnace
u	Greig's Quill		Dark Badger		Peacock Quill	Wood Duck	Dark Badger
w	Grizzly King		Red Goose		Green Silk Floss	Gray Mallard or Gray Squirrel	Grizzly
d	Grizzly Varient		Grizzly Hackle Wisps		Light Claret Silk Floss	Ginger Hackle Tips	Grizzly
	Grizzly Wulff		Brown Bucktail		Pale Yellow Floss, Lacquered	Brown Bucktail	Mixed Grizzly and Ginger
w	Grouse and Peacock				Peacock Herl		Grouse Body Feather
w	Grouse Spider	Gold Tinsel	Scarlet	Gold Tinsel	Orange Floss		Grouse
w	Guinea Hen	Gold Tinsel	Scarlet Hackle Fibres	Gold Tinsel	Red Seal Fur	Guinea	Claret
w	Gunnison		Grey Mallard Fibres	White Silk	Green Floss	White Tipped Turkey	Ginger
w	Guzzler		Badger	Gold Tinsel	Yellow Floss		Badger
u	Half Stone		Blue Dunn Hackle		Rear, Yellow; front, mole fur		Blue Dun
w	Hardy's Favorite		Golden Pheasant	Red Floss	Peacock Herl	Woodcock	Ginger
w	Harlequin			Black Silk	Rear, Orange Floss; front, Blue Floss	Dark Slate	Black

w	Hawthorne				Black Floss	Black	Black mixed with Claret
w	Hemlock				Dark Grey Floss	Dark Brown Turkey	Ginger
w	Henshall	Gold Tinsel	Peacock Sword	White Silk	Peacock Herl	Light Grey Turkey	Grizzly
u	Hendrickson, Dark		Wood Duck		Fawn Fox Fur	Wood Duck	Bronze Blue Dun
u	Hendrickson, Light		Wood Duck		Cream Fur	Wood Duck	Light Blue Dun
w	Herman Fly			Gold	Crimson Floss	Slate	Ginger
w	Hofland's Fancy		Ginger Hackle Fibres		Red-brown Floss	Woodcock Tail	Ginger
d	Honey Dun	Grey Hackle Fibres	Grey Hackle Fibres		Muskrat Dubbing	Lemon Wood Duck	Honey Hackle
w	Hoskins				Yellow Floss	Light Slate	Blue Grey
d	Houghton Ruby		White Hackle Fibres		Red Quill	Blue Dun Spent	Ginger (dark)
u	Housatonic Quill		Speckled Mandarin		Quill	Speckled Mandarin	Grey Badger
w	Howell	Gold Tinsel	Light Claret	Gold Tinsel	Peacock Herl	White Tipped Turkey	Deep Wine
w	Hudson	Orange Floss	Green	Gold Tinsel	Brown-black	Light Brown Turkey	Orange
w	Hunt Fly			Yellow Silk	Green Floss	Cinnamon	Ginger Hackle
w	Ibis & White	Gold Tinsel	Red and White	Gold Tinsel	Crimson Floss	Red and White	Red and White mixed
w	Imbril	Black Chenille		Gold Tinsel	Yellow Floss	Slate	Ginger
w	Indian Yellow		Dark Honey	Pale Yellow Silk	Light Brown Floss	Grouse	Dark Honey
w	Invicta		Golden Pheasant	Gold Oval Tinsel	Yellow Mohair	Tan and Brown	Ginger Tied Palmer
w	Irish Grouse			Gold Tinsel	Orange Floss		Ginger furnace-palmer
w	Irish Turkey		Yellow	Yellow Silk	Green Floss	Light Brown Turkey	Ginger
u	Iron Blue Dun	Scarlet Floss	Furnace Hackle Wisps		Blue-Grey Fur	Dark Blue Slate	Ginger Furnace
u	Iron Blue Quill	Scarlet Floss	Furnace Hackle Wisps		Blue Quill	Dark Blue Slate	Ginger Furnace
d	Irrestible		Deer Hair		Clipped Deer Hair	Deer Hair	Ginger
w	James		Scarlet		Silver Tinsel	Brown Turkey	Light Claret
d	Jassid, Black				Black Floss	Jungle cock eye-flat	Black
d	Jassid, Green				Light Green Floss	Jungle cock eye-flat	Green
d	Jassid, Orange				Orange Floss	Jungle cock eye-flat	Ginger
w	Jay, Blue		Light Blue	Gold Tinsel	Light Blue Floss	Blue Jay	Light Blue
w	Jay, Silver		Golden Pheasant	Oval Silver Tinsel	Silver Tinsel	Blue Jay	Ginger
w	Jennie Lind		Light Purple	Gold Tinsel	Yellow Floss	Light Purple, Scarlet Stripe	Scarlet
w	Jock Scott		Golden Pheasant	Silver Tinsel	Black Floss at Head, Yellow Floss	Peacock, Blue, Scarlet & Jungle cock-eye	Guinea, Black and White
w	John Mann	Scarlet	Brown Turkey	Gold Tinsel	Yellow Floss	Dark Brown Turkey	Ginger, tied palmer
u	July Dun		Ginger Hackle Fibres	Gold Tinsel	Gold Floss	Blue Dun Hackle Tips, spent	Ginger
w	June				Alternate Scarlet and White	Light Brown Turkey	Black
w	Jungle Cock	Silver Tinsel	Wood Duck	Silver Tinsel	Red Floss	Jungle Cock	Ginger Furnace
w	Kate		Golden Pheasant		Rear, Yellow; Front Red Floss	Cinnamon	Black
w	Katydid		Green	Gold Tinsel	Green Floss	Green	Green
w	Kendal		Scarlet		Deep Wine Chenille	Brown Mallard	Scarlet

Key	Name	Tag	Tail	Ribbing	Body	Wing	Hackle
w	Killer Diller		Red Hackle Fibres	Gold Tinsel	Yellow Floss	Grey Squirrel	Ginger Hackle
w	Kimbridge			Silver Tinsel	White Condor	Woodcock	Ginger tied palmer
w	Kingfisher	Gold Tinsel	Golden Pheasant	Gold Tinsel	Scarlet Floss	Grey Mallard	Ginger
w	King of Waters		Grey Mallard		Crimson Floss or Wool	Grey Mallard	Ginger
w	Kitson	Gold Tinsel	Black	Gold Tinsel	Yellow Floss or Wool	Yellow-Black Cheeks	Light Claret
w	Knowles' Fancy			Silver Tinsel	Light Brown Wool	Black Cock's Tail Feather	Ginger
w	La Belle		Scarlet Wool Tab	Silver Tinsel	Light Blue Floss	White	Hackle Light Blue
w	Lachene		Dyed Yellow Mallard	Silver Tinsel	Rear, Silver Tinsel; Front, Black Chenille	Amherst Pheasant	Dark Claret
u	Lady Benson		Golden Pheasant	Black Silk	Pink Floss	Wood Duck	Mixed Ginger & Grizzly
w	Lady Gray		Barred Mandarin	Silver Tinsel	Blue Grey Rabbit Fur	Jungle Body Feather	Scarlet Tied Palmer
w	Lady Mite			Yellow Silk	White Horse Hair or Polar Bear		Deer Hair
w	Lady Mills		Golden Pheasant	Silver Tinsel and Black Ostrich	White Ostrich	Cinnamon with Black Tip	Blue-Grey
w	Lake Edward	Gold Tinsel	Yellow	Gold Tinsel	Light Brown Wool or Fur	Yellow, Dark Blue, Brown Turkey	Scarlet
w	Lake George	Gold Tinsel	Scarlet	Gold Tinsel	Scarlet Floss	White with Scarlet Stripe	White
w	Lake Green			Green Silk	Yellow	Teal	Light Ginger
w	Langiwin		Bright Yellow	Black Silk	Yellow Floss	Bright Yellow	Bright Yellow
w	Last Chance	Gold Tinsel	Crimson	Black Silk		Light Slate	Light Brown
w	Liberty		Dark Blue	Gold Tinsel	Pale Blue Floss	Scarlet	White
w	Light Blow		Light Brown Turkey		Striped Ginger Quill	Light Brown Turkey	Crimson
w	Light Fox	Gold Tinsel	Yellow Wool Tag	Gold Tinsel	White Wool	Slate	Yellow
w	Light Polka				White Chenille	Guinea	White
w	Lister's Gold		Yellow	Gold Tinsel	Rear, Gold Tinsel; Front, Claret	Guinea	Orange
w	Lord Baltimore		Black	Black Silk	Orange Floss	Black Jungle Eye	Black
w	Logan	Gold Tinsel	Crimson and Orange	Gold Tinsel	Black Floss	Orange and Crimson	Dark Ginger
w	Loyalsock				Pale Yellow Floss	Black	Black
d	Lunn's Yellow Boy		Honey Hackle Fibres		Yellow Quill	Honey Hackle Tips, Spent	Honey
w	Luzerne				Dark Claret Floss	Grey Mallard	Black
w	Magpie		Ginger	Gold Tinsel	Bross Floss	Magpie or Black Turkey with White Tip	Ginger
w	Major	Blue Floss	Golden Pheasant	Gold Tinsel	Purple Wool	Brown Turkey	Scarlet Hackle, Palmer
u	Mallard Quill		Ginger Fibres		Mallard Quill	Brown Mallard	Dark Ginger
u	March Brown, American	Gold Tinsel	Ginger Fibres	Gold Tinsel	Brown Body	Brown Turkey	Ginger
u	March Brown, English		Partridge	Yellow Silk	Medium Hare's Ear	Partridge	
u	March Dun	Gold Tinsel			Green Wool	Light Slate	Ginger
w	Marlow Buzz	Gold Tinsel			Peacock Herl		Ginger Furnace
w	Mascot	Yellow Floss	Scarlet		Peacock Herl	Slate	Black
w	Marsters	Gold Tinsel	Grey Mallard		White Floss or Wool	Widgeon or Grey Mallard	Scarlet
w	Martin		Yellow and Black	Gold Tinsel	Yellow Floss	Widgeon or Grey Mallard	Deep Yellow

w	Maxwell		Teal		Copper Tinsel	Wood Duck, Iridescent Green	Ginger Hackle
u	May Fly		3 Procupine Hairs	Peacock Quill	Pale Yellow Floss	Wood Duck	Ginger
u	May Fly, Green		Black Hackle Fibres	Gold Tinsel	Pale Green Floss	Mandarin Dyed Green	Cream & Blue-Grey
w	McGinty		Grey Mallard, Topping Scarlet		Black and Yellow Chenille	Black Turkey with White Tip	Ginger
w	McKenzie	Gold Tinsel	Ginger Hackle Fibres		Olive-Green Wool	Mottled Slate and Brown	Ginger
d	McQueen			Black Silk	Pale Olive Deer Hair		
d	McSneek		Black Hackle Fibres	Silver Tinsel	Black Dyed Peacock Quill	White Fan Wings	Black Hackle
w	Mealy Moth			Silver Tinsel	Lightest Grey Wool	White	White Hackle
w	Mershon		Black Hackle Fibres		Black Silk Floss	Dark Blue, White Tip	Black
d	Michigan Hopper	Loop of Yellow Wool	Red		Yellow Wool	Turkey	Ginger Tied Palmer
u	Mill's No. 1	Black with Gold Tip	Golden Pheasant	Gold Tinsel	Crimson Floss	Mallard Dyed Yellow	White
w	Mohawk		Brown		Light Claret Floss	Brown Turkey	Ginger Tied Palmer
w	Mole				Grey Wool	Brown Turkey	Ginger Tied Palmer
w	Montreal	Gold Tinsel	Scarlet	Gold Tinsel	Claret Floss	Brown Turkey	Claret
w	Moose	Gold Tinsel	Yellow	Gold Tinsel	Yellow Floss	Barred Wood Duck Golden Pheasant Tip Eye	Guinea and Yellow Intermingled
w	Mormon Girl	Scarlet Floss	Scarlet Hackle Fibres		Yellow Floss	Mottled Grey Mallard	Grizzly Tied Palmer
u	Moth, White	Silver Tinsel		Silver Tinsel	White Chenille	White	White
u	Mosquito		Grizzly Hackle Fibres		Peacock Quill	Grizzly Hackle Tips	Grizzly
w	Munro	Gold Tinsel	Scarlet & Yellow	Gold Tinsel	Green Floss	Scarlet with Brown Turkey Stripe	Yellow
w	Murray		Scarlet	Silver Tinsel	Black Floss	Brown Turkey	Orange Tied Palmer
w	Nameless		Mallard Dyed Yellow		Embossed Silver Tinsel	Light Brown Pheasant	Scarlet Tied Palmer half way
u	Neversink		Grey Mallard		Pale Yellow Floss	Grey Mallard	Yellow
w	Nonpareil	Gold Tinsel			Black Chenille		Black
w	Oak		Brown Turkey		Orange Floss	Brown Turkey	Ginger
u	Olive Dun		Olive Hackle Fibres		Olive Wool	Slate	Olive
u	Olive Quill		Olive Hackle Fibres		Quill Dyed Olive	Slate	Olive
d	Olive Spider		Olive Hackle Fibres		Olive Peacock Quill		Olive
w	Olive Wren	Silver Tinsel	Gray Mallard	Silver Tinsel	Olive-brown Wool Body	Light Brown Turkey	Ginger Furnace
w	Onondago	White Chenille	Black and White Tip Turkey		Black Floss	Black and White Tip Turkey	Black
w	Oquassac	Yellow Floss	Pheasant Tail	Pink Silk	Claret Wool	Pheasant Tail	Claret
w	Orange Cole		Golden Pheasant	Gold Tinsel	Yellow Floss	Woodchuck	Orange
w	Orange Fish Hawk			Gold Ribbing	Orange Floss		Badger
w	Orange Quill		Orange Hackle Fibres		Orange Condor Quill	Mallard	Orange
u	Orange Sedge			Gold Tinsel	Orange Floss	Land Rail	Ginger Tied Palmer
u	Orvis-Gray	Gold Tinsel	Blue-grey	Gold Tinsel	Olive Yellow Wool	Black Turkey with White Tip	Blue-grey
u	Pale Evening Dun		Blue-grey		Pale Yellow	Light Slate	Blue-grey
u	Pale Sulphur		Pale Yellow		Pale Yellow	Pale Yellow	Pale Yellow

Key	Name	Tag	Tail	Ribbing	Body	Wing	Hackle
u	Pale Watery Dun		Honey Hackle Fibres		Sulphur	Blue-grey	Honey
u	Pale Watery Quill		Greenish Yellow		Peacock Quill	Light Slate	Pale Greenish Yellow
w	Parmachene Belle	Black Ostrich	White and Scarlet	Silver Tinsel	Yellow Wool	White with Scarlet Stripe	Mixed Scarlet and White
u	Parson's Dun		Honey Grizzley		Brown-olive Wool	Grey Mallard	Honey Grizzly
d	Particular		Ginger Hackle Fibres		Ginger	Blue Dun Hackle, Spent	Medium Ginger
w	Partridge		Grey Partridge		Front, Pale Yellow; Rear, Silver Tinsel	Grey Partridge Tail	Honey
w	Passadunk		Peacock Sword	Green Silk Floss	Black Floss	Teal	Olive-yellow
w	Peacock				Peacock Herl Body	Slate	Black
w	Pellee Island	Black Chenille	Black	Gold Tinsel	Scarlet Floss	Scarlet	Black
w	Perkin's Idea	Black Ostrich Herl	Black	Gold Tinsel	Scarlet Floss	Grey Mallard	Black
w	Perkin's Pet				Silver Tinsel	Slate	Ginger Tied Palmer
w	Perry	Pink Chenille			Black Chenille	Black Turkey with White Tip	Black
w	Peter Ross	Gold Tinsel	Golden Pheasant	Gold Tinsel	Yellow Floss		Honey
u	Petries Egg Sack	Pale Green	Speckled Mandarin		Grey Wool or Fur	Speckled Mandarin	Blue-grey
d	Pheasant Tail		Purple Pheasant Tail	Gold Tinsel	Purple Pheasant Tail Wrapped		Blue Dun
u	Pink Lady		Golden Pheasant	Gold Tinsel	Pink Floss	Slate	Ginger
d	Pink Lady Bivisible		Ginger Hackle Fibres		Pink Floss		Ginger, Palmer White Face
w	Pink Wickham's Fancy		Light Brown		Pink Floss	Dark Slate	Light Ginger Tied Palmer
w	Plath	Gold Tinsel	Crimson		Light Green Wool	Grey Turkey with White Tip	Crimson
w	Plummer	Black Ostrich		Gold Tinsel	Front, Black Ostrich; Rear, Yellow Floss	Teal	Yellow
w	Poha	Gold Tinsel	Brown and White	Gold Tinsel	Scarlet Floss	Guinea	Scarlet
w	Pope	Gold Tinsel	Golden Pheasant		Pale Yellow Floss	Guinea	Green Shoulder and Yellow Tied Palmer
w	Potomac			Yellow Silk	Bright Green Floss	Cinnamon	Ginger
w	Potter	Black Silk		Black Silk	Blue-green Floss	Slate	Ginger
w	Preston's Fancy		Brown		Gold Tinsel	Guinea	Ginger
w	Priest		Scarlet		Silver Tinsel		Grey Badger
w	Prime Gnat	Orange	Black		Black Ostrich Herl	Black	Black
w	Professor	Gold Tinsel	Scarlet	Gold Tinsel	Yellow Floss	Grey Mallard or Teal	Ginger
w	Pronty	Orange Chenille	Blue and Gold Pheasant		Black Chenille	Married Slate, Scarlet and Yellow and Grey Mallard	Yellow Shoulder and Brown Tied Palmer
w	Pulasky	Gold Tinsel	Yellow and Red Hackle Fibres	Gold Tinsel	Red Floss	Fox Squirrel	Orange
w	Quack Doctor		Scarlet		Silver Tinsel	Light Brown Turkey	Scarlet
w	Quaker	Gold Tinsel	Grey Mallard	Gold Tinsel	Grey Floss	Grey Turkey	Grizzly
w	Queen of Waters				Orange Floss	Teal or Grey Mallard	Ginger Tied Palmer

u	Quill Gordon		Blue Dun Hackle Fibres	Gold Wire	Peacock Quill	Wood Duck	Blue Dun
w	Rainbow	White Floss	Scarlet	Gold Tinsel	Light Blue Floss	Cinnamon	Grizzly
	Ray Bergman		Brown Mallard		Rusty Orange Wool	Slate	Ginger
u	R. B. Fox		Honey Hackle Wisps		Grey Fox Fur	Grey Mallard	Mixed Honey and Ginger
u	Ramapo Special		Grey Mallard		Cream Fox Fur	Grey Mallard Clipped Short	Mixed Ginger and Blue-grey
w	Rangeley	Gold Tinsel	Orange	Gold Tinsel	Light Claret Dubbing	Grey Mallard and Jungle Eye	Orange Shoulder, Light Claret Tied Palmer
u	Red Ant				Cinnamon Nylon		Ginger Hackle Tied in Middle
u	Red Fox	Gold	Grey Mallard		Light Red Fox Under Fur	Slate	Ginger faced with Blue-grey
u	Red Fox Beaverkill	Gold Tinsel	Ginger	Gold Tinsel	Blue-grey Fox Fur		Ginger faced with Blue-grey
u	Red Quill		Ginger Hackle Fibres		Peacock Quill	Slate	Ginger
u	Red Spinner	Gold Tinsel	Ginger Hackle Fibres	Gold Tinsel	Dark Claret Wool	Dark Grey	Ginger
w	Red Tag		Scarlet Wool Tab		Peacock Herl		Ginger Tied Palmer
w	Rich Widow	Gold Tinsel	Yellow	Gold Tinsel	Light Blue Floss	Black	Yellow Tied Palmer
w	Riley	Black Floss and Gold			White Wool	Teal or Grey Mallard	Ginger
u	Rio Grand King	Gold Tinsel	Yellow		Black Chenille	White	Ginger
w	Romaine	Gold Tinsel	Guinea		Grey Wool Body	Guinea	Black
w	Roosevelt		Ginger		Front, Claret; Back, Yellow Wool	Slate	Dark Orange
d	Royal Coachman		Golden Pheasant		Peacock Herl with Scarlet Floss Center	White	Ginger
d	Royal Wulff		Brown Bucktail		Peacock Herl with Scarlet Floss Center	White Bucktail	Ginger
w	Rube Wood	Scarlet Floss	Teal		White Chenille	Grey Mallard	Ginger
w	Sage	Silver Tinsel	Scarlet, Green & Grey Pheasant	Black Silk	Yellow Wool	Dark Grey Mallard	Orange
w	Sallie Scott			Orange Floss	Pale Yellow Floss	Light Blue Parrot	Pale Yellow
w	Saltown	Gold Tinsel	Ginger Hackle Fibres	Gold Tinsel	Black Floss	Slate	Ginger
w	Sancutary	Gold Tinsel		Gold Tinsel	Dark Hare's Ear Fur		Ginger
w	Sand Fly		Blue-grey		Grey Fur	Light Brown Turkey	Ginger
w	Saranac	Gold Tinsel	Golden Pheasant	Gold Tinsel	Claret Floss	Golden Pheasant	Claret
w	Sassy Cat		Scarlet		Peacock Herl Body	Yellow with Scarlet Cheek	Yellow
w	Scarlet Ibis	Gold Tinsel	Scarlet	Gold Tinsel	Scarlet Floss	Scarlet	Scarlet
w	Schaffer	Gold Tinsel	Golden Pheasant	Gold Tinsel	Reddish Brown Wool	Scarlet, Blue and Green	Grizzly
w	Sheenan	Pinke Chenille	Golden Pheasant		Yellow Silk Floss	Grey Mallard	Black
w	Seth Green			Yellow Silk	Green Silk Floss	Light Brown Turkey	Ginger
w	Shad Fly				Peacock Herl, Gold Tinsel Center	Brown Turkey	Ginger
w	Shoemaker		Speckled Brown Mandarin		Grey Ostrich—White Silk Center	Speckled Brown Mandarin	Ginger
w	Shookum		Scarlet		Scarlet Chenille—Silver Center	Teal	Mixed Bright Green and Scarlet
w	Silver Doctor	Silver Tinsel	Golden Pheasant	Oval Silver Tinsel	Flat Silver Tinsel	Brown Turkey, Teal, Blue and Yellow	Blue and Guinea

Key	Name	Tag	Tail	Ribbing	Body	Wing	Hackle
w	Silver Fairy		Scarlet		Silver Tinsel	Jungle Cock Eye	Guinea
w	Silver Ghost		Barred Mandarin	Silver Tinsel	Peacock Herl	Silver Condor, Black Tip	Grizzly
w	Silver Stork		Grey Mallard		Silver Tinsel	Grey Mallard	Ginger
w	Silver Sedge	Silver Tinsel		Silver Tinsel	White Wool	Light Brown Turkey	Light Ginger Tied Palmer
w	Sir Sam Darling	Black Chenille	Brown Mallard		White Chenille	Grey Mallard	Ginger
u	Sky Blue		Yellow Hackle Fibres		Blue Rabbit's Fur	Starling	Yellow
w	Skinnum	Silver	Blue-grey Hackle Fibres		Peacock Quill	Woodcock	Blue-grey
w	Snipe and Yellow				Primose Silk		Snipe under Covert Feather
d	Snake River Varient	Black Floss	Grizzly Hackle Wisps		Orange Floss		Brown, Black and Grizzly
u	Soldier Palmer	Gold Tinsel		Gold Tinsel	Scarlet Wool		Ginger Tied Palmer
w	Something	Gold Tinsel	Golden Pheasant	Gold Tinsel	Black Floss	Green, Scarlet, Purple, Yellow—married	Black
w	Soo Nifri	Gold Tinsel	Barred Mandarin	Gold Tinsel	Black Silk Floss	White	Light Blue
w	Spencer	Yellow Wool		Gold Tinsel	Grey Fur		Light Badger Tied Palmer
d	Spent Gnat		Brown Mallard	Unstripped Peacock Herl	Cinnamon	Blue-grey Tied Spent	Grey Partridge and Badger
d	Spent Wing May Fly		Golden Pheasant	Gold Tinsel	Raffia	Black Hackle Tied Spent	Black
w	Spent Wing Wood Duck		Golden Pheasant		Clipped Grizzly Hackle	Wood Duck Tied Spent	Ginger
w	Squash Bub			Brown Quill	Orange Wool		Soft Badger
w	Split Ibis		Golden Pheasant		Silver Tinsel	White and Scarlet Married	Ginger
w	Stebbins	Gold Tinsel	Widgeon		Green Wool	Dark Grey Turkey	Ginger Furnace
w	St. Lawrence	Scarlet Chenille	Scarlet	Gold Tinsel	Yellow Floss	Light Grey Turkey, Top Brown Turkey	Scarlet
w	St. Patrick		Peacock Herl		Silver Tinsel	Peacock Herl	Light Blue-grey
w	St. Regis		Guinea & Golden Pheasant		Dark Grey Fur	Golden Pheasant over Brown Mallard	Ginger Tied Palmer
u	Stone Fly		Blue-grey	Yellow Silk	Blue-grey Fur	Light Grey Turkey	Blue-grey
w	Stranger	Gold Tinsel	Brown	Gold Tinsel	Dark Brown Wool	Brown Turkey and Golden Pheasant	Ginger
u	Sunset				Yellow Wool	White	Yellow
u	Swiftwater		Grey Mallard		Peacock Herl, Orange Center	White	Ginger
w	Teal		Teal	Black Silk	White Floss	Teal	Grizzly
w	Teton	Gold Tinsel	Brown	Gold Tinsel	Yellow Silk Floss	Slate, Jungle Eye	Ginger
w	Thistle	Gold Tinsel	Scarlet & Golden Pheasant	Gold Tinsel	Green Silk Floss	Jungle Cock Eye and Golden Pheasant	Yellow and Scarlet Tied Palmer
w	Thunder		Golden Pheasant	Orange Silk	Black Silk Floss	Guinea	Yellow
w	Tomah Joe	Peacock	Yellow		Gold Tinsel	Barred Wood Duck or Mandarin	Mixed Scarlet and Yellow
w	Toodle Bug	Gold Tinsel	Grey Mallard		Yellow Wool Front, Blue Silk Rear	Brown Turkey	Ginger
w	Telephone Box	Peacock Herl	Golden Pheasant	Black Silk	Orange Silk Floss or Wool	Brown Turkey, Jungle Eye	Ginger
u	Tup's Indispensable		Ginger Hackle Fibres		Rear, Yellow Floss; Front, Pink Wool		Ginger Faced with White

w	**Turkey**	Gold Tinsel	Scarlet	Gold Tinsel	Yellow Wool	Brown Turkey	Ginger
w	Tuthill		Golden Pheasant	Orange Silk	Purple Silk Floss	Light Brown Turkey	Ginger
w	Tycoon	Scarlet Floss	Scarlet & Yelow	Gold Tinsel	Orange Floss	Black White, Scarlet White, Married	Claret Shoulder
w	Undertaker		Black & White		White Wool	White and Black	Black
w	Union		Teal		Unstripped Brown Condor	Teal	Grizzly
w	Vance		Light Mottled Turkey		Gold Tinsel	Light Mottled Turkey	Yellow
w	Vanity			Gold Tinsel	Orange Floss	White—Jungle Body Feather	Ginger Tied Palmer
w	Victoria Green	Gold Tinsel	Golden Pheasant	Gold Tinsel	Green Silk Floss	Brown Turkey, Jungle Eye	Yellow
w	Volunteer	Gold Tinsel	Scarlet	Gold Tinsel	Yellow Silk Floss	Golden Pheasant	Green
w	Von Patton		Scarlet		Yellow Floss	Barred Mandarin	Ginger
w	Walker		Scarlet and White	Black Silk	White Floss	White with Grey Turkey Stripe	Yellow
w	Walker-Hays	Scarlet Silk		Scarlet Silk	Yellow Floss	Slate	Ginger
w	Walla-Walla	Gold Tinsel			Yellow Fur or Wool	Cinnamon	Ginger
w	Wanderer	Gold Tinsel	Barred Mandarin	Gold Tinsel	Amber Wool	Blue-grey with White Tip	Badger
w	Warden	Gold Tinsel	Guinea Dyed Yellow	Gold Tinsel	Tan Wool	Light Brown Turkey and Black	Ginger
w	Warwick		Orange	Gold Tinsel	Peacock Herl	Black	Orange
w	Wasp				Alternate Black and Brown Herl	Tan, Black and Tan	Ginger
w	Waters				Peacock Herl	Light Grey Turkey	Black
w	Watson's Fancy		Golden Pheasant	Gold Tinsel	Rear, Scarlet Floss; Front, Black Floss	Black	Black
w	Webbs	Gold Tinsel	Grouse	Gold Tinsel	Pale Green Wool	Green Parrot	Pale Yellow
d	Welshman's Button			Maroon Horse Hair	Peacock Quill Dyed Brown	Dark Brown	Ginger Furnace
u	Whirling Blue Dun	Gold Tinsel	Blue-grey	Gold Tinsel	Blue-grey Fur	Dark Slate	Blue-Grey
d	Whitchurch Dun		Honey Hackle Fibres		Primrose Floss	Pale Starling	Honey
w	White Hackle				White Silk Floss		White
w	White Jungle	Scarlet	Amherst Pheasant		White Wool	White Jungle	White
w	White King	Gold Tinsel	Orange	Gold Tinsel	White Silk Floss	White	Orange Face, White Tied Palmer
w	White Miller	Silver Tinsel		Silver Tinsel	White Silk Floss	White	White
d	White Wulff		White Deer Hair		Cream Wool or Fur	White Deer Tail	Light Badger
w	Whitney	Gold Tinsel	Yellow	Gold Tinsel	Tan Fur	Turkey-White Tip	Orange Face, Ginger Tied Palmer
w	Wickham's Fancy		Ginger Hackle Fibres		Gold Tinsel	Slate	Ginger Tied Palmer
w	Widow			White Silk	Black Silk Floss	Black with White Stripe	Black
w	Wilderness	Gold Tinsel		Gold Tinsel	Green Wool	Dark Red over Brown	Ginger Tied Palmer
d	Willow Fly		Olive Hackle Fibres		Olive Silk Floss	Slate	Ginger

Key	Name	Tag	Tail	Ribbing	Body	Wing	Hackle
w	Wilson	Gold Tinsel	Golden Pheasant		Orange Wool	Grey Mallard	Orange
	Winslow Midge		Brown Mallard	Light Grey Silk	Rear, Dark Grey Fur; Front, Light Grey	Brown-grey Mallard	Honey
w	Winters		Brown Mallard		Claret Floss	Brown Mallard	Ginger Furnace
w	Witcher	Yellow	Golden Pheasant	Gold Tinsel	Black Wool	Grey Mallard over Slate	Black Tied Palmer
w	Woodcock & Red		Ginger Hackle Fibres	Silver Tinsel	Red Floss	Woodcock	Ginger
w	Wood Duck	Gold Stinsel	Yellow	Gold Tinsel	Bright Green Wool	Barred Wood Duck	Bright Green
w	Wood Ibis		Orange-brown Mallard		Dark Claret Wool	Iridescent Black	Orange Tied Palmer
u	Woodruff		Grey Mallard		Green Wool	Grizzly Hackle Points, Spent	Ginger
w	Woolly Worm	Red Floss	Peacock Sword	Gold Tinsel	Black Chenille		Grizzly Tied Palmer
w	Woppinger		Blue-grey		Grey Silk Floss	Slate	Grizzly Tied Palmer
u	Wortendyke		Black Hackle Fibres		Grey-brown Fur	Speckled Mandarin	Black
w	Wren		Grey Mallard	Yellow Silk	Light Grey Floss	Brown Mallard	Ginger
w	Yankee	Gold Tinsel	White	Gold Tinsel	Light Blue Floss	White	Scarlet
w	Yellow Coachman	Gold Tinsel			Peacock Herl, Yellow Center	White	Ginger
u	Yellow Drake	Gold Tinsel	Black	Gold Tinsel	Yellow Floss Silk	Grey Mallard Dyed Yellow	Yellow
u	Yellow Dun			Yellow Silk	Grey Fur	Brown Mallard	Yellow
w	Yellow Sally	Gold Tinsel	Yellow	Gold Tinsel	Yellow Floss Silk	Yellow	Yellow
u	Yellow Spinner	Gold Tinsel	Yellow		Yellow Chenille	Black	Scarlet
w	Zulu	Scarlet Wool			Peacock Herl		Black Tied Palmer

DRAKES OR MAY FLIES—ORDER, *Ephemeroptera*

There are many sizes and colors of the Drake family with varying emergence dates, making it the most important of all aquatic insects to both game fish and anglers. The nymphs of some species live under rocks and in gravel, where as others bury in the silt. Fishermen call the sub imago, *duns,* and upon emergence they slowly fly from the surface of the water into convenient foliage, where they molt for several days. When the imago return to the water in nuptial flight and to deposit eggs, they are known as spinners. At rest the wings are in an upright position.

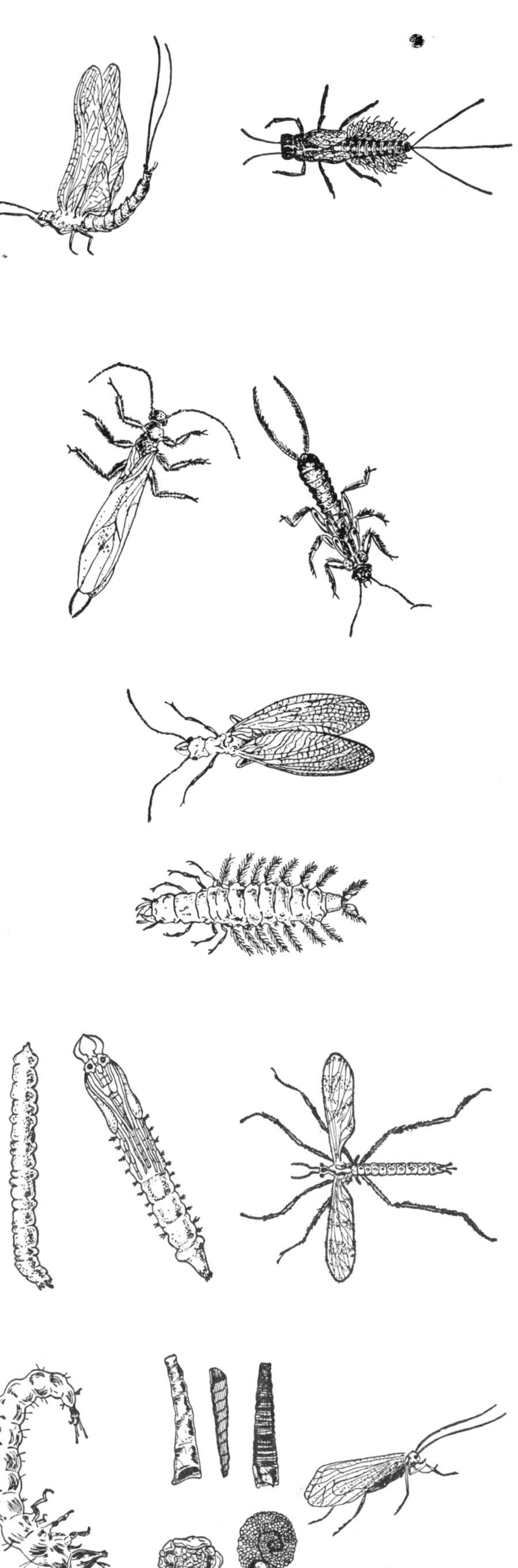

STONE FLY—ORDER, *Plecoptera*

The nymph, which is carnivorous, favors the sections of streams where there is a fast flow over a rocky bottom. Emergence is usually at night and the nymph leaves the water by crawling above the surface on limbs, rocks and weeds preceding pupation. When the adult is at rest, the four wings are folded flat on the top of the back. The two most common are the Large Stone Fly and the Yellow Sally, however they don't constitute great surface hatches and the common imitation of the angler is the artificial nymph.

HELLGRAMMITE AND DOBSON FLY—ORDER, *Corydalis*

The Hellgrammite is one of the most important forage foods in the warm-water bass streams. They live under the stones, particularly in shallow riffles. The black larva at the age of three years, when full grown, attains a length of three inches. The sharp mandibles are capable of inflicting injury. The Hellgrammite crawls from the water and pupates under a stone. The adult, the Dobson Fly, has four wings, is basically nocturnal and unlike most aquatic insects, the male is larger than the female.

CRANE FLY OR TRUE FLY—ORDER, *Diptera*

From the tiny, long-legged Midge to the large Whirling Crane Fly, there is great variation in size in this large family. They hatch from quiet waters particularly around swamps and mud shore lines. The tiny *Diptera* furnishes a most valuable food supply for young fish, particularly fingerling trout. Emergence frequently occurs in cold weather when the food supply is limited. The adult, which has two wings, is a delicate insect, and if handled, the legs break away from the body.

CADDIS—ORDER, *Trichoptera*

This class of flies when in the larval state make their own abode by cementing bits of sticks, stones and weeds with their own secretion, and they move, along with their cases, in the more quiet stream areas. Emergence generally occurs at night. The adult can be recognized by long antennae and by rough hairy wings which when at rest fold over the backs in a tent shape. Next to the Drakes, this large family is the most important to both fish and to anglers.

The emergence periods as designated by the numbers appearing in the emergence column are:

Period I. April 1 to May 10
Period II. May 11 to June 20
Period III. June 21 to August 1
Period IV. August 2 to September 10

ORDER: *Ephemeroptera*
Mayflies
Duns
Drakes
Lake Flies

General characters:

Nymph: Flattened in swift water forms, or elongate, or variable. Usually three tails, rarely two. Four to seven pairs of gills on back of abdomen. Three pairs of legs of moderate length. Usually small and delicate. Most abundant and typical of trout stream insects. Most often found in riffles although some are burrowing types. There is one claw on each foot.

Adults: Pale and translucent. Pale grey, brown, yellow, and reddish. Either two or three tail filaments (cerci). Wings are always held upright over the body when at rest, never held back over the body. Wings are roughly fan-shaped, delicate and membraneous. The fore wing is larger and the hind wing small or absent.

Genus and species	Form	Common names	Description of natural insect	Emergence	
Baetis sp. Leach	Nymph		Slender, stream-lined bodies. Body fish-like, 12-18mm. long.		One of the commonest nymphs.
	Adult	Little May Flies. Blue Quill. Black Quill.	Small mayflies, body length 2-8mm. and wings ranging from 2-8mm. Females rather unicolorous, usually reddish or brownish. Male imago usually pale but in others olivaceous to deep brown.	I, II, III	Wide distribution. Eastern and Western species.
Blasturus cupidus Say	Nymph	Dark March Brown.	Body length 10--1mm. General color is chestnut brown.		Commonest nymph in ponds through March and April.
	Adult	*Imago male:* Early Brown Spinner, Red Quill, Dark March Brown.	Body length 10-1mm. General color is chestnut species. Wings stained with brown. Antennae and legs brown (banded). Abdomen brown becoming blackish toward tails. Under parts fawn colored. Three tails, tan with central filament much shorter.	II	Variable species of wide distribution in eastern parts of United States.
Caenis sp. Stephens	Nymph	Square-Gilled Nymph.			Dwell in mud and silt, burrowing-type nymph.
	Adult	Caenis.	Small mayflies. Body length 2-4mm., wing length ranging from 2-5mm. Males and females very similar in coloration. Abdomen usually pale yellowish white. Tails three and usually very long.	II, III	Widely distributed.

Ephemera guttulata **Pictet**	Nymph	Green Drake Nymph.	Body length 20mm., tails 11mm. Gills on top of abdomen give nymph a purple grey color on top, lighter below.		Burrowing-type nymph.
	Adult	*Subimago:* Green Drake. *Imago male:* Green Drake. Coffin Fly, Spinner. *Imago female:* Grey Drake, Coffin Fly, Shad Fly, Grey Fox Variant.	Body length 13mm., wings 13-15mm. Abdomen largely creamy white, wings appear largely blackish. Tails olive to pale reddish brown.	II	
Ephemera varia Eaton	Nymph	Large Burrowing Nymph.	Body length 18mm., tails 8mm. Gills give nymph purple-grey color.		
	Adult	*Female imago:* Yellow Drake.	Body length 11mm., wings 12mm. Rather pale species. Abdomen purplish grey.	II	Eastern distribution.
Ephemerella Dorothea Needham	Nymph	Pale Evening Dun Nymph.	Body length 7mm. General color dark brown spotted with paler dots. Three tails, pale brown. Wing pads dark brown.		
(Invaria group)	Adult	Little Marryat. Pale Evening Dun. Small Cream Variant. Little Yellow Mayfly.	Body length 7-8mm., wings 8-10mm. A small species. Thorax and legs pale yellow. Abdomen pale yellowish. Three tails, whitish yellow. Wings hyaline and light gray.	II, III	Eastern distribution. Imago seldom reappears. The female spinner is glassy in appearance. The body is very light yellow and wings more yellow than the grey of the dun. Pale Evening and Pale Watery are English designations.
Ephemerella Fuscata Walker	Nymph	Olive Dun Nymph.	Body length 9mm. Head, legs, and body hairy. General color pale grayish to deep olive brown.		
(Fuscata group)	Adult	Olive Dun.	Body length 8mm., wing 8mm. Blackish yellow legged species. Abdomen deep smoky brown. Tails yellowish.	II (Sometimes earlier)	Eastern distribution.
Ephemerella subvaria McDonnough	Nymph	Prickle-Back.	Body legth 10mm. Reddish brown in color, sprinkled with numerous paler dots. Tails yellowish brown.		
(Invaria group)	Adult	*Female:* Hendrickson. *Male:* Red Quill (redder in color than female).	Body length 9mm., wings 10mm. Head deep brown. Thorax deep brown with reddish tinge. Abdomen light reddish brown dorsally, ventrally paler reddish brown. Lateral margins of segments yellowish. Wings hyaline. Tails pale with smoky joinings.	I	A species of the *invaria* group and close to *E. invaria.* Described sometimes as dark form of *E. invaria.*

Genus and species	Form	Common names	Description of natural insect	Emergence	Miscellaneous information
Hexagenia recurvata Morgan	Nymph	Dark Green Nymph.	Body length 20-30mm.		Burrowing nymph larger than *Ephemera*.
	Adult	*Subimago:* Dark Green Dun. *Imago:* Brown Drake or Brown Spinner.	Body length 18-20mm., wings 15-18mm. Wings heavily tinged with dark reddish brown. Abdomen yellowish brown. Tails light purplish brown.	II	Eastern distribution.
Iron fraudator sp. nov.	Nympth	Two-Tailed Nymph.	Body length 9-10mm. Color is usually greenish mottled with darker areas. Two tails, flattened bodies.		In swift cold water. Often more valuable than the adult.
	Adult	Quill Gordon.	Body length 9-10mm., wings 10-11mm. Dark reddish brown species. Male imago, head and thorax red brown. Abdominal segments dark red brown marked with *yellow*. Two tails dark brown. The female is slightly larger and lighter in color than the male.	I, II	Eastern distribution. Adults hatch underwater.
Iron humeralis Morgan	Nymph	Two-Tailed Nymph.	Body length 11mm. Two tails, flattened body.		
	Adult	Small Cream Variant.	Body length 10mm., wings 10-11mm. General color, yellow white. Thorax yellow white, legs whitish. Abdomen, semi-hyaline, whitish with slight brownish bands. Tails whitish. Variations are usually lighter.	II, III, IV	Eastern distribution.
Iron pleuralis Banks	Nymph	Two-Tailed or Red Quill Nymph.	Two tails, flattened body.		
	Adult	Red Quill.	Similar to *Iron fraudator*. Species often occur together and may be taken in same swarms.	I, II, III	
Isonychia albomanicata Needham	Nymph	Whie-Gloved Howdy. Howdy Nymph.	Body length 12-15mm. Rich chocolate brown color above and paler below. Front feet white. Gills dark purplish.		
	Adult	White-Gloved Howdy.	Body length 12mm., wings 11mm. Female imago. Head yellowish. Thorax tawny yellow brown. Abdomen brownish or dull red rose. Wings hyaline. Legs light in color. Tails white tinged with yellow.	I, II, III	Wide distribution, eastern United States. Female imago form is the form fished.
Isonychia bicolor Walker (suggested by some as a variable form equivalent of *I. albomanicata*).	Nymph				Nymphs crawl out on rocks previous to emergence of the adult.

	Adult	Leadwing Coachman.	Body length 11mm., wing 14mm. female subimago of species known with certainty. General color brownish, lighter beneath. Tails light yellowish brown. Legs of two colors, middle and hind legs yellowish, forelegs brownish (hence name bicolor).	II, III, IV	
Leptophlebia sp. *Paraleptophlebia* sp.	Nymph	Iron Blue. Fork-Gilled Nymph.	The nymph of *L. Johnsoni* is not known and *L. gracilis* agrees generally with the description of the gensu *Blasturus*. Nymphs are slender and body is usually compressed.		
	Adult		Body length 6-7mm., wings 6-7mm. Small flies. Wings dark blue. Tails three in number. Males are usually brownish or blackish. Females are typically reddish or reddish brown in color.	II, III	*Leptophlebia Westwood*. Type genus is poorly represented in North America but better known *(L. marginata)* in Europe. In America most species are included in the genus *Paraleptophlebia*. *L. Johnsoni* and *L. gracilis* are two American species placed in *Leptophlebia*.
Potomanthus distinctus sp. nov.					
	Adult	Golden Drake. Golden Spinner. Cream Variant.	Body length 11mm., wings 11mm. Pale yellowish. Tails yellowish. Conspicuous broad pure white wings. Appears more like a moth than mayfly.	III	Female imago fished.
Siphlonurus quebecensis Provancher	Nymph	Brown Quill.	Body length 12-15mm. Sternites yellowish.		
	Adult	*Subimago:* Little Brown Dun. *Imago:* Brown Quill or Brown Spinner.	Body length 11-13mm. Dark species. Head yellowish, thorax reddish brown. Wings hyaline. Abdomen dark reddish brown, lighter on the under surface.	II	Eastern distribution.
Stenonema fuscum Clemens	Nymph	Ginger Quill Nymph. Red-Tailed Nymph.	Body length 10-12mm. Flattened head and body. Tails long and often quite red in color.		
	Adult	*Subimago:* Ginger Quill. *Imago:* Ginger Quill, Grey Fox.	Body length 10mm., wings 13mm. General color normally brown, darker toward posterior bands of each segment. Wings hyaline.	II, III	Eastern.
Stenonema ithaca Clemens and Leonard	Nymph	Cahill.	Body length 11-12mm. Red brown.		
	Adult	Cahill.	Body length 9-10mm., wings 11-12mm. Reddish brown species. Head and thorax red brown. Legs yellowish. Abdomen banded yellow and reddish to purplish brown bands. Tails greyish or yellowish white.	II, III	

Genus and species	Form	Common names	Description of natural insect	Emergence	Miscellaneous information
Stenonema vicarium Walker	Nymph	March Brown Nymph.	Large species. Body length 18-20mm.		
	Adult	*Subimago:* March Brown male. *Imago:* Red Spinner.	Body length 12-14mm., wings 13-16mm. Large species allied with *S. fuscum.* General dark red brown. Head and thorax reddish brown. Tails usually rather deep olive brown.	II	Eastern distribution. Wings of adult slant back at about a 60 degree angle.

ORDER: *Plecoptera.*
Stone Flies
Yellow Sallys
Willow Flies
Creepers
Rock Rollers

General characters:

About two dozen genera in United States and Canada and at least 200 species. In some cases adults have been identified but not the nymphal stage.

Nymphs: Flattened bodies. Two segemented, filamentous tails. If gills are present, they are in tufts of thread-like gills on the thorax or base of legs and sometimes on sides and tip of abdomen. Gills always are on the underside of the body. There are two claws on each foot. With few exceptions they live in swift water. Form a major part of the trout's diet, especially in mountain streams. May be less important in lowland streams or more quiet water.

Adults: Vary from about 12-25mm. in length. Usually dull colored. Dark brown, yellow, and pale green are common colors. In general poor fliers. The two pairs of wings are held flat over the body when the fly is at rest.

Genus and species	Form	Common names	Description of natural insect	Emergence	Miscellaneous information
Acroneuria lycorias Newman	Nymph	Stone Fly Nymph. Water cricket.	Body length about 25mm. Antennae and tail about 20mm. Decorated with contrasting areas of brown and yellow on top of head and body. Antennae yellowish. Abdomen brown on top and yellowish underneath.		Large nymph similar to *Perla.*
Isoperla bilineata Say	Nymph	Yellow Sally Nymph.	Body length about 10-12mm. Antennae and tails 25mm. General color yellowsh with dark brown markings. Wing pads yellowish. Abdomen yellowish with three brown stripes on back.		
	Adult			III	Likes sunshine. Daytime fliers of wide distribution.
Isoperla signata Banks	Nymph	Light Stone Fly.	Body length about 10-12mm. Tails and antennae about 25mm. Yellow with brown markings. Abdomen yellow with brown bands on caudal half of each segment. Tails yellow. Wing pads yellow with		
	Adult		brown markings.	II	

Perla capitata Pictet	Nymph	Stone Fly Creeper.	Body length about 25mm. Tails and antennae about 50mm. Contrasting areas of black and yellow or brown and yellow on top of head and body. Adbomen yellow banded with black or brown. Tails reddish brown.		
	Adult			II	
Taeniopteryx fasciata *T. nivalis* Fitch	Nymph	Snowbank Nymph. Little Black Stone. Winter Stone Fly.	Body length 12-18mm. Slender, black, or brownish black. Usually a median dorsal yellow band. Wing pads diverge from body at angle of about 30 degrees. Abdomen nearly cylindrical.		
	Adult	Little Black Stone Fly. Early Brown Stone Fly. Early Brown.	Black or blackish brown. Body slender.	I	Common eastern form.

Order: *Trichoptera.*
Caddis
Sedge
Grannom
Shad Fly
Cinnamons
General characters:

Larvae: Body cylindric and elongate, arcuate in side view. No tails. Gills, if present, always on abdomen. Three pairs of long, dark colored legs. Living in cases of sand, leaves, wood, etc., or in fixed shelters on stones.

Pupae: Live in cases. Pupal cases are often fastened to a stone. All are more or less active with undulating motion. Pupae leave cases, swim to surface of water, and emerge as adult after shedding pupal skin. Pupae resemble adults. Pupal period is usually about two weeks but some spend the winter in this condition.

Adult: Looks like moths but bodies more slender and delicate. Soft brown or gray, sometimes black, very rarely bright colored. Thread-like antennae reach far out ahead of their bodies. Legs are generally long and slender. Both pairs of wings are membraneous but the front pair (anterior) is always heavier in texture. When at rest the wings are held roofed over the body.

Arctoecia consocia Walker	Larva	Leaf-Case Caddis.	Case triangular in cross section. 25-37mm. long.		Very common in quiet eastern trout waters. Case maker.
	Adult		Length to tip of wings 12mm. Rust colored. Feet and wings dull red or yellowish brown. Abdomen brownish yellow above and paler below.	III	
Brachycentrus fuliginosus Walker	Larva	Grannom.	Case of twigs. Tapers toward rear end and square in cross section. 12-18mm. long.		Common in headwaters of trout streams. Case maker.
	Adult	Grannom. Greentail.	Length to tip of wing 12mm. Black. Wings light brown, darker along front edge. Abdomen and legs black (Similar to the English Grannom). Green egg mass.	II	

Genus and species	Form	Common names	Description of natural insect	Emergence	Miscellaneous information
Chimarrha sp. Hagen	Larva		Many are bright orange and yellow. 12-18mm. long.		Net spinner. Nets are long and finger-like.
	Adult	Little Black Caddis.	Length to tip of wings 6mm. Deep black. Body, feet, and antennae black. Apparently a gray color phase for the species has been described.	I	
Hydrophysche alternans Walker	Larva	Caddis Worm. Green Caddis.	Bright green with black head and thorax. 12mm. long.		Very common, wide distribution. Net spinner. Nets are funnel-shaped. Live in rapidly moving water. Members (species) of *Hydrophysche* are among the commonest aquatic insect inhabitants of trout streams.
	Adult	Little Brown Sedge. Brown Sedge. Spotted Sedge.	Length about 18mm. Wings dusky, densely spotted with bright yellow or golden. Antennae dusky. Body dusky on top and yellowish beneath.	I, II	
Leptocella albida Walker	Larva	White Caddis.			
	Adult	White Caddis.	Length about 10mm. Wings with dense white pubescence. Legs yellow, antennae yellow. Abdomen yellow at base, darker posteriorly.	III	Nocturnal.
Psilotreta frontalis Banks *P. borealis* Prov.	Larva	Dark Blue Sedge.	Case 12mm. long. Case slightly curved.		Abundant in riffles of stony streams. Case maker at time of pupation. Range freely as larvae. Gregarious in habit at time of pupation, and large numbers may be found together.
	Adult	Dark Blue Sedge.	Wings gray hyaline. Head, thorax, and abdomen brownish. Antennae yellowish.	I	
Rhyacophila fuscula Walker	Larva	Green Caddis.			Abundant in swift water. Range freely as larvae, making cocoon at time of pupation.
	Adult		Body length to tip of wings 13mm. Iron rust in color. Partly covered with blackish hairs. Wings brown with lighter dots.	II	

Stenophylax sacbripennis Rambur	Larva	Large Red Brown. Caddis. Brown Sedge.	Large stick cases to 50mm. long.		Common in headwater trout streams.
	Adult	Brown Sedge.	Large brownish insect. Head, thorax, and antennae brownish yellow. Legs yellow. Wings brownish yellow, fore-wing speckled with brown raised dots.	III	

ORDER: *Diptera.*
True Flies
Two Winged Flies
Mosquito and Mosquito-like Flies
General characters:

Larvae: Slender, wormlike maggots. Tails lacking or very short, legs lacking. Diverse in form and size. White, yellow, red, or green in color. Vary in size from 12-50mm.

Adults: Only one pair of wings. This group contains most of the biting insects of the fisherman's pests. Many of them are mosquito-like. Mouthparts are formed for sucking.

Bibio femoratus Wied.	Adult	Red-Legged March Fly. March Fly.	Adult flies are generally black and red, sometimes yellow. The abdomen is robust and legs are shorter and stouter than in most other flies.	I, II, III	
Blepharocerca sp.	Larva and Pupa	Net Winged Midge Larva.	Body length about 6mm. Body darker above and lighter underneath. Deeply notched body and presence of sucking discs by means of which the larva moves about in swift water over the stones distinguish it.		
	Pupa		Pupae: A jet black pupa is produced. These can often be seen in large patches covering stones in shallow but swift water.		
Chironomus lobiferus Say	Larva and Pupa		Body length from 3-12mm. The larvae are very small and seldom observed. Larvae are blood red in color with fleshy prolegs at each end of the body. Larvae may be yellow and pupae are yellow, gray, or green.		Two broods of larvae usually maturing to adults in late May and late September. Blood larvae is one of the common midge pond larvae.
	Adult	Black Midge.	Body length about 6mm. Wings white, feet pale yellow and antennae yellow brown. Segments of the tergum with their bases black.	I, IV	

Genus and species	Form	Common names	Description of natural insect	Emergence	Miscellaneous information
Chironomus modestus Say	Larva and Pupa		Body length about 6mm. Larvae are buff colored or yellow with reddish tinge.		
	Adult	Pale Green Midge.	Imago male. Body length about 5mm. Abdomen pea green, feet greenish white.	I, II, III	
Chironomus plumosus L.	Larva and Pupa		Body length about 25mm. Larvae red in color.		
	Adult	Golden Dun Midge.	Body length about 12mm. Abdomen yellow, head yellowish or brownish yellow. Legs yellow, wings whitish with black spots.		
Chironomus sp.	Larva and Pupa	Midge Larva. Midge Pupa.	Larvae: Soft skinned and worm-like and the body segmented. Range in color, red, yellow, green, and white. Pupae: Some pupae are free swimmers and might be called "wigglers."		The family *Chironomidae* (midges) contains over 800 identified species. The three species listed above are given because they are common and to secure definite descriptions of several. Obviously many other species might be selected for description and imitation. Larvae and pupae of the midges are important as trout food. The general generic description given in the column opposite this is to aid in the tying of imitations which might be useful even though specific identification is absent.
	Adult	Midge Adult.	More or less mosquito-like. Usually less than 10mm. in body length. Appear humpbacked in side view. Abdomen long and slender. One pair of wings.		
Culicoides sp.	Larva		Less than 6mm. long. Needle shaped. No appendages.		
	Adult	Punkies. No-see-ums. Small Midges. Sandflies.			No doubt serve as food for trout but quite impossible to imitate with accuracy. These insects are commonly met with as pests along the stream.

Pedicia sp. *Tipula* sp. *Antocha* sp. *Eriocera* sp.	Larva	Crane Fly Larvae. Water Worms. Leather jackets. Pushring.	Larvae vary in length from about 12mm. to 50mm. Larvae leathery in appearance but thin skinned. Vary in color from pale gray to shades of light yellow and brown.		All larval forms may be called water worms. Widely distributed on trout streams.
	Adult	Giant Crane Fly. Typical Crane Fly. Yellow Crane Fly. Pushring Crane Fly.	Large, long legged insects. Look like giant mosquitoes.	II, III, IV	

ORDER: *Neuroptera.*

Fish Flies	Alder Flies	Humpbacks
Dobson Flies	Hellgrammites	Lace Wings

General characters:

Larvae: Long, slender, and flattened. One median tail, lond and tapering, or pair of double hooked prolegs. Three pairs of legs. One pair of lateral filaments on each segment of ab domen.

Adults: Called humpbacks. Poor fliers.

Chauliodes serricornis Say	Larva	Fish Fly Larva.	Pair of prolegs (see general description). Dark fuscous with black or dark colored head.		Hangs to underwater debris. Similar to but smaller than the hellgrammite.
	Adult	Fish Fly.	Body black, 25-37mm. Wings black or brown with white markings. An irregular band of white spots extending across middle of each front wing.	II	
Corydalis cornuta Latreille	Larva	Hellgrammite.	Specimens up to 100mm. long. Pair of prolegs. General dusky color.		Pupate in stream bank. Live in swift water.
	Adult	Dobson Fly.	Cinnamon brown bodies and gray white spotted wings. Wings fuscous with black and yellow veins. Wing-spread up to 100-125 mm.	II, III	
Sialis infumata Newman	Larva	Alder Fly Larva.	Body length less than 25mm. Brown and heavy skinned. Long slender tail filament on tip of abdomen.		Buried in sand. Larval period of at least two years.
	Adult	Humpbacks. American Alder Fly. Smoky Alder Fly.	Body length 25mm. Essentially black in color. Appear humpbacked in side view.	I	Seldom on surface of the water except when blown there or when female accidentally (or spent) falls when egg laying.

FACTS ABOUT FISH

SIGHT

Light travels in straight lines under the surface of the water in a manner similar to its passage through air, but it travels more slowly and not as far; therefore, the vision of a fish under water is reasonably good but by necessity distant view is limited. However, when the fish peers upward, the surface of the water is opaque except for a circular window surrounding the head. The effect is an impenetrable surface with a transparent window in the center. This is caused by the refraction of light. As the fish approaches the surface to view an object, the object appears larger as the fish approaches and at the same time the transparent window decreases in diameter. Waves or the riffles of flowing water cause many refracting units, all at different angles, continuously changing, thus making an object appear to be shifting in a dizzy fashion.

The left eye is connected to the right side of the brain and *vice versa,* therefore, a fish can see in two directions. Their judgment of distance is excellent, for certain species when traveling rapidly can catch a moving insect on flowing water. Vision is excellent at close range and they frequently inspect an object at a distance of several inches. Attention is readily attracted by quick movement.

ARE FISH COLOR BLIND?

This has been the subject of debate, but in the face of strong evidence produced in the laboratory in various types of experiments it must be concluded that fish can distinguish colors. It was found that bass respond in color vision very much like a human looking through a pair of yellow glasses. Brightness proved to play no part. Red could be distinguished from any other color except violet, and they were about equally sure of yellow. Greens and blues were the most difficult for them to distinguish from each other and from black.

HEARING

Water is a fine conductor of sound and the same is true of bone. There exists incontraversible proof that certain species of fish hear through bone. The air bladder and the lateral line are also sensitive to vibration and are, therefore, a type of hearing organ. Sounds can enter water but with difficulty, and sounds made under water travel far.

CAN FISH SMELL AND TASTE?

Fish have nostrils, but unlike mammals, they do not connect with the throat, but open into small blind sacs just under the skin and go no further. These sacs are lined with the organs of smell. All species possess a sense of smell but some have developed it to such a high degree that they depend on it. The sharks utilize the sense of smell to locate their food.

The tongue of a fish, although it is a gristly projection which cannot be moved, has taste-buds and most species have an acute sense of things sour, salty or bitter. The peculiar barbles of catfish are provided with taste buds and this species uses the sense of smell and the sense of taste rather than eyesight to locate its food.

DOES A FISH FEEL PAIN?

Pain can be felt, but it is modified and not keen as compared to a mammal, and either the mental impression is not keen or it is readily forgotten. Here again there is variation in the species, but the fact remains, a hooked fish would not pull hard in the opposite direction if it were greatly distracted by pain. It might be accurately expressed if it were said, they experience discomfort rather than pain.

WHY DOES A FISH JUMP?

There are various reasons for this spectacular showing: to capture food, to elude an enemy, to go over a barrier, to play, to wash off parasites and to break adhesions.

DO FISH SLEEP?

A mammal cannot close its ears but it can sleep; a fish cannot close its eyes but it can sleep. Some sleep suspended in the water, some erect on the bottom and others on their sides or against objects or even buried in the sand. Some of the schooling fish disperse at night to sleep, then reassemble by day.

WEIGHT OF SUBMERGED FISH

Submerged, most species weigh practically nothing, for the specific gravity is about the same as water, that is, the total volume of water occupied by the fish will weigh about the same as the fish. If this were not the case, there would be a constant struggle with environment. Species which dwell on the bottom in either salt or fresh water are heavier than water. When fish jump out of water, their weight corresponds to that indicated by the scales.

HOW DOES A FISH CHANGE COLOR?

Pigment cells located in one of the layers of skin determine color. Concentration or dispersement of pigment throughout the cells alter coloration.

CAN A FISH MAKE SOUNDS?

Some species can make a grunting noise by forcing air from the air bladder through the mouth, others gnash teeth or vibrate gill covers with the air bladder acting as a resonance box. During World War II it was necessary to screen out the sounds made by fish in the equipment utilized to hear approaching submarines.

SCALES

Fish do not shed their scales, but the scales continue to grow with the fish, the growth periods showing as rings on each scale. Thus it is possible to count the number of such periods to estimate age.

INDEX

D

E

F

M

N

O

P

Y